International Corporate Finance

Third Edition

International Corporate Finance

Third Edition

Laurent L Jacque
The Fletcher School, Tufts University, USA

World Scientific
NEW JERSEY • LONDON • SINGAPORE • BEIJING • SHANGHAI • HONG KONG • TAIPEI • CHENNAI • TOKYO

Published by

World Scientific Publishing Co. Pte. Ltd.
5 Toh Tuck Link, Singapore 596224
USA office: 27 Warren Street, Suite 401-402, Hackensack, NJ 07601
UK office: 57 Shelton Street, Covent Garden, London WC2H 9HE

Library of Congress Cataloging-in-Publication Data
Names: Jacque, Laurent L. author
Title: International corporate finance / Laurent L. Jacque,
Tufts University, USA & HEC School of Management, France.
Description: Third edition. | Singapore ; Hackensack, NJ : World Scientific Publishing Co. Pte. Ltd., [2025] |
Includes bibliographical references and index.
Identifiers: LCCN 2024044572 | ISBN 9789819802005 hardcover | ISBN 9789819806928 paperback |
ISBN 9789819802012 ebook | ISBN 9789819802029 ebook other
Subjects: LCSH: International business enterprises--Finance | Risk management | Foreign exchange futures
Classification: LCC HG4027.5 .J3193 2025 | DDC 658.15/99--dc23/eng/20250605
LC record available at https://lccn.loc.gov/2024044572

British Library Cataloguing-in-Publication Data
A catalogue record for this book is available from the British Library.

For any available supplementary material, please visit
https://www.worldscientific.com/worldscibooks/10.1142/14076#t=suppl

Desk Editors: Aanand Jayaraman/Yulin Jiang

Typeset by Stallion Press
Email: enquiries@stallionpress.com

In remembrance of **Philippe Louis Jacque** (1918–1972)

"My father, that hero with the sweetest smile,
followed by a single hussar whom he loved above all others
for his great bravery and his great height,
was riding, the evening after a battle,
across the field covered with the dead on whom night was falling.
He thought he heard a weak noise in the shadow.
It was a Spaniard from the routed army
who was bleeding, dragging himself by the road.
groaning, broken, ashen, and more than half dead,
and who said, "Drink! Drink, for pity's sake!"
My father, moved, handed to his faithful hussar
a canteen of rum that hung from his saddle,
and said, "Here, give the poor wounded man something to drink."
Suddenly, at the moment when the hussar bent
leaning over him, the man, a kind of Moor,
seized a pistol that he was still gripping,
and aimed at my father's forehead crying "Caramba!"
The bullet passed so near that his hat fell off
and his horse shied backwards.
"All the same give him something to drink," said my father".

"After the battle" in The Legend of Centuries by **Victor Hugo**

and in honor of his great grandchildren
Philippe, Adeline, Maia, Luca and Remi

Preface

As globalization is redefining the field of corporate finance, international finance is increasingly permeating most financial transactions, which in yesteryears were deemed to be strictly domestic transactions. In fact, it is very difficult to understand what is happening in capital markets without a firm grasp of currency markets, the investment strategies of sovereign wealth funds, carry trades, foreign exchange derivative products, and so forth. Similarly, project finance cannot be understood without a firm grasp of valuation concepts in a cross-border context. Indeed, international finance is now part and parcel of the basic literacy of any financial executive whether she or he is an investment banker, a treasurer, a CFO, a portfolio manager, or a loan officer. There is no hiding from international finance.

And yet the field of international finance textbooks is not terribly crowded, with the three or four leading titles showing signs of multiple-editions fatigue. What is needed is a book offering a fresh perspective on international finance that transcends the boundaries of *ethnocentric* thinking and an overly U.S.-centric approach — a book that brings the fascinating and rapidly unfolding story of emerging capital markets and their daring multinationals in the mainstream of international finance. *International Corporate Finance* is purporting to be such a book.

WHAT MAKES THIS BOOK UNIQUE

There are several features that will set *International Corporate Finance* apart from rival books:

1. Most chapters are developed around a real-life but simplified mini-case to anchor theoretical concepts to managerial situations. This allows the reader to grasp the practical relevance of the topic addressed before being introduced to the necessary theoretical frameworks.
2. Each chapter provides real-life illustrations. The purpose is to make international finance as alive as possible. Typically, this is done as feature inserts called "International Corporate Finance in Practice", written in a lighter style meant to wake up the reader by being reasonably provocative.
3. Most chapters provide simple decision rules and pragmatic "how-to" answers to key managerial issues — at least one in each chapter. Many texts often provide a narrative solution to managerial questions raised but fail to provide simple yet rigorous closure to the reader.
4. Several chapters, such as Islamic Banking and Finance, Asian Finance and Banking, Cross-Border Mergers and Acquisitions, and Project Finance, are completely new material that no other textbook currently covers. This book systematically incorporates the story of the BRIC countries (Brazil, Russia, India, and China) and their daring multinationals, thereby balancing out an overly U.S.-centric and Wall Street–anchored approach to international corporate finance.
5. Most chapters include separate case studies (also found on the website) that are real-life decision-making situations. Although much shorter than typical Harvard Business School case studies (the industry standard), they capture multifaceted financial management in an engaging manner and typically result in 30 to 45 minutes of lively class discussion.
6. When appropriate, historical perspective and landmark transactions are presented to put concepts in context. In-depth coverage of the subprime crisis (2008) and the euro crisis (2010–) is developed in the context of ill-functioning financial markets.
7. While primarily focused on international corporate finance, the book is structured in such a way that it could also be used for a course on global capital markets, as Parts One, Two, and Three provide comprehensive coverage of capital markets.

AUDIENCE FOR THIS BOOK

International Corporate Finance targets not only the business school market — primarily MBAs, undergraduate seniors, and executive MBAs — but also schools of international affairs and public administration. In draft form it has also been widely used in executive training programs at banks, multinationals, and increasingly government and regulatory agencies.

The book is intended for students taking an elective in international corporate finance that may be part of a finance major (but not necessarily). Although prior exposure to economics and corporate finance would be helpful, the book is self-contained and has no prerequisites.

International Corporate Finance should also appeal to a growing international/export market beyond the domestic university/college market. More generally, there is an explosion in the number of MBA programs offered in emerging market countries such as China, India, Brazil, Russia, and Mexico, where international finance is at the center in the curriculum simply because of the global orientation of these economies. For this rapidly growing market, it is imperative to approach international financial management from an emerging market perspective as well as a US or European perspective. Specific chapters on Asian and Islamic finance and banking as well as BRIC countries, along with illustrations and problems/exercises, should be strong elements of differentiation *vis-à-vis* existing texts.

THE CHALLENGE THIS TOPIC PRESENTS

International finance is one of the most topical and lively business topics making the front page of any business daily, but, perhaps because of the unique role played by financial derivatives, it is also a highly complex, arcane, technical, and mystifying subject for the average business student. Herein lies the challenge for the instructor and the student: how to capitalize on the star power and captivating nature of international finance without sacrificing the rigor of the explanation. Textbooks all too often err on the side of academic correctness and read like treatises written for other knowledgeable academics rather than fresh-faced students. My approach is to start (most) chapters with real-life decision — situations to hook the reader who presumably wants to know what possible answers struggling managers could implement — and then derive theory, rather than starting from a theoretical construct at the risk of losing the reader before turning to applications. For example, the chapter on trade financing starts with:

> *Tata Motors of India's export manager, Raju Aneja, has just signed an export order for 1,000 Nanos — its new revolutionary minicar — with Atlas Distributors, a Vespa scooter dealership based in Casablanca, Morocco. The export sale is denominated in euros (€) and calls for payment of €20 million on delivery, scheduled for approximately three months from time of shipment. Tata Motors has never had any commercial dealings with Atlas but was envisioning a long-term relationship with the Moroccan firm. However, it was concerned about the importer's solvency. The Moroccan dirham was pegged to the euro and partially convertible. How should Tata Motors finance its export trade? Raju knew that this would be the first of many similar deals that Tata Motors was hoping to forge with other emerging market countries where the Nano was expected to meet with much commercial success.*

Similarly, the chapter on debt financing starts with:

> *JetBlue Airlines was seeking to raise $250 million in a seven-year note to upgrade its aging fleet. Ms. Rousse — JetBlue's newly appointed CFO — was reviewing the different funding options offered by its investment bankers, which included a domestic dollar-denominated zero-coupon bond priced at 61 percent, a dollar-denominated Eurobond with a 7.25 percent annual coupon, and a samurai bond denominated in yen with a semiannual coupon of 4.00 percent. Last, a floating-rate note denominated in euros paying euro-LIBOR + 165 basis points was also being considered. Ms. Rousse was perplexed by the array of currency denominations and the significant differences in nominal interest rates, both of which complicated direct comparisons among the different funding options.*

Both chapters progressively build a more rigorous framework as they progress. In the same vein, a rich array of exercises and problems accompany each chapter; they are more than mechanical numerical applications of what is discussed in the chapter itself. Last but not least, most chapters offer a separate short case study (also found on the book's website) for fruitful discussion.

WHAT IS IN THE BOOK?

This book is divided into six parts:

Part 1: The International Monetary Environment

Part 2: The Foreign Exchange Market and Currency Derivatives

Part 3: International Financing

Part 4: Managing Foreign Exchange Risk

Part 5: Cross-Border Valuation and Foreign Investment Analysis

Part 6: Managing the Multinational Financial System

Part 1: The International Monetary Environment. Part 1 examines the monetary environment within which international financing decisions are made. How exchange rates are determined and the unique role played by central banks' intervention in setting currency values is the focus of Chapter 2, whereas Chapter 3 presents a brief history of the international monetary system. The architecture of the world economy is outlined in Chapter 4 through the lens of national balance of payments accounting, which records the key flows linking national economies.

Part 2: The Foreign Exchange Market and Currency Derivatives. After introducing the foreign exchange market and its inner workings (Chapter 5), Part 2 discusses the valuation of the mother of all currency derivatives — the forward contract — in the context of the theory of interest rate parity (Chapter 6). The international parity framework with *Purchasing Power Parity* and the Fischer Parity is completed in Chapter 7. Currency futures and options are detailed in Chapter 8, which shows how they can be harnessed for the purpose of risk management.

Part 3: International Financing. If globalization of financial markets has gone a long way toward eradicating differences in national cost of capital, they have not been entirely erased. This is why global financial markets are often characterized as mildly segmented rather than fully integrated (Chapter 9). Part 3 outlines funding as a global procurement decision from both equity markets (Chapter 10) and debt markets (Chapter 11). Risk(s) arising from investing in or financing via fixed-income securities can be managed with *Currency, Interest Rate and Credit Default Swaps* (Chapter 12). The idiosyncrasies of *International Trade Financing* are presented in Chapter 13.

The uniqueness of financing strategies and capital markets in two regions of the world that loom especially large on the global economy — namely East Asia and the Middle East — is addressed in separate chapters found at the end of the book. Chapter 26 profiles the idiosyncrasies of Asian finance and banking in the context of Japan, South Korea, and China, whereas Chapter 27 explores the mysteries of Islamic finance.

Part 4: Managing Foreign Exchange Risk. The exchange rate variable permeates all key financial management decisions and injects a considerable degree of variability in a firm's overall risk profile. Part 4 starts by asking whether hedging part or all of a firm's exposure to currency risk is indeed value creating for the firm's owners and therefore warranted (Chapter 14). To the extent that exchange rate forecasting (Chapter 15) is a treacherous activity in the context of clean floating exchange rates, we take a "total risk" view of risk management. Exporters and importers as well as multinational corporations and globally reaching financial institutions generally hedge both transaction and translation exposures by using forwards, futures, options or swaps. Measuring and managing transaction, translation, and economic exposures are discussed in Chapters 16, 17, and 18, respectively.

Part 5: Cross-Border Valuation and Foreign Investment Analysis. Part 5 develops a valuation framework for cross-border investments that uniquely incorporates the different variables such as foreign exchange risk, country risk, asymmetric tax treatment, and different inflation rates. Chapter 20 contrasts different metrics such as net present value of asset-based cash flows or equity-based cash flows versus adjusted present value metrics, and reviews the necessary adjustments to be made to the cost of capital used as the discount rate in international valuation. The framework is applied to cross-border mergers and acquisitions in Chapter 21 and large-scale infrastructural project finance in Chapter 22. Taking the perspective of asset managers manning the desks of mutual funds, pension funds, hedge funds, or sovereign wealth funds, global investing in stocks and bonds is addressed in Chapter 23, which gauges the limit of geographical diversification in the context of ever-increasingly integrated capital markets.

Part 6: Managing the Multinational Financial System. Chapter 24 shows how financial decisions should leverage the multinational enterprise system by deftly exploiting arbitrage opportunities arising from capital markets segmentation and heterogenous national tax systems. Finally, central to the successful implementation of a global strategy, multinational corporations need financial planning, budgeting, and control systems that incorporate the unique operating circumstances of each and every foreign subsidiary while ensuring that strategic goals are duly achieved (Chapter 25).

WHAT IS NEW IN THE THIRD EDITION OF INTERNATIONAL CORPORATE FINANCE

Chapter 1

- New section on globalization at the regional level with a discussion of United States–Mexico–Canada Agreement (formerly known as NAFTA) and the European Union.
- FinTech introduced as one of the key drivers of globalization in financial services.

Chapter 2

- Added a definition (in box format) of Special Drawing Rights (SDRs) used to show how to value Artificial Currency Units (ACUs).
- Graph of the dollar value of one SDR over time versus the dollar value of the yen.
- New appendix on valuing ACUs.

Chapter 3

- New section on dollarization.
- Major update of the euro crisis during the COVID pandemic and how the euro-zone is taking meaningful first steps towards building a fiscal union.

Chapter 4

- Updated discussion of remittances and how FinTech is reducing the cost of cross-border remittances.
- Revision and update of Brexit and how it is impacting the City of London and more generally the British economy and its Balance of Payments.

Chapter 5

- How cyber-attacks can disrupt the world payment system and the foreign exchange market including a new box on Bangladesh central bank heist.

Chapter 6

- New section on Non-Deliverable Forward (NDFs) contracts as found in emerging market countries such as India, Indonesia and others.
- New JAY/AUD graph illustrating how and when the currency carry trade was profitable over the last two decades between Japan and Australia.

Chapter 9

- Added a new section entitled "FinTech and Disintermediation 2.0" showing how FinTech lowers the cost of financial services in general and financial intermediation in particular; thus, countries which have embraced FinTech will benefit from a lower cost of capital thereby boosting their economic competitiveness and the standard of living of their households. FinTech-based financial services — because of their digital nature — are relatively easy to distribute and — as a result — are proving to be a formidable engine of financial inclusion as it reaches under-served and under-banked households and firms.

Chapter 10

- Added a new appendix on shareholders' wealth maximization and corporate governance systems around the world.
- Contrasted how Anglo-Saxon countries where capital markets and a dispersed shareholder base play the leading role in financing firms with other major capital exporting countries or emerging market countries, where banks, pyramidal family business groups, or even the state are the dominant owners and/or financiers.

Chapter 11

- Added a box on the LIBOR scandal. In June 2012, the LIBOR scandal exploded when the iconic Barclays bank admitted to repeated manipulation of its interest rate and agreed to paying $450 million in fine to the US department of Justice. ... The LIBOR scandal shortly thereafter engulfed several other leading banks — UBS, Deutsche Bank — with a total of $9 billion in fine as evidence of repeated intra-bank and inter-bank collusion became public. LIBOR ceased publication on June 30, 2023 and was replaced in the case of the US dollar by SOFR (Secured Overnight Financing Rate).
- Added a section on contingent convertible (CoCos) bonds.
- Added a box on the use by Credit Suisse of CoCos to meet capital adequacy ratios under Basel 3.0 and the death spiral that it unleashed when Credit Suisse faced a bank run.

Chapter 14

- Added "Hedging at Porsche" as International Corporate Finance in Practice 14.4 as an example of a pro-active foreign exchange risk management policy.

Chapter 19

- Added an in-depth discussion of *Bilateral Investment Treaties (BITs)* which provide a legal charter governing the relationship between foreign direct investors and their host governments. Most importantly, BITs establish a legal machinery to resolve disputes through *conciliation and arbitration* By formalizing the "rules of engagement" between investors and their host nation-states, BITs would lessen "political risk" by providing an international arbitration tribunal where investors could bring claims against their host for violating investment treaties standards and risk.

Chapter 20

- Added an appendix on capital budgeting for NGOs and showed how it should incorporate exchange rate risk in the decision metrics.

Chapter 21

- Updated data on cross-border Mergers & Acquisitions

Chapter 23

- New section on stakeholder capitalism and ESG Investing and how it is impacting the asset management industry.
- New box on Sustainability Linked bonds.
- New case study on Investing in sovereign sustainability-linked bonds issued by the Republic of Chile and Uruguay.

Chapter 24

- Updated the primer on international taxation with a discussion of how the US tax code was overhauled with the passing in 2017 of the *Tax Cuts and Job Acts (TCJA)* which impacts both domestic and international taxation of worldwide activities of US-domiciled multinational corporations as well US operations of foreign companies.
- Explained how the TCJA moved the US *worldwide* taxation regime closer to a *territorial* system and how two provisions in the new tax code — the *Global Intangible Low-Taxed Income* (GILTI) and the *Base Erosion and Anti-abuse Tax* (BEAT) practically amount to a form of a *global minimum tax.*

Chapter 27

- Updated current trends in Islamic banking and finance in the context of more deeply integrated national capital markets.
- Showed how ESG principles converge with well-established Islamic finance principles which called for the inclusion of moral and religious considerations in financial decisions. These are based on the Koranic concept of "vicegerency", known as "khilafah" in Arabic, which states that humans are appointed as stewards or trustees to manage and safeguard God's creation in a responsible fashion (Koran, 2:30).

WEBSITE AND ONLINE RESOURCES

Professors can readily download the following materials:

- **Instructor's Manual.** The Online Instructor's Manual offers detailed solutions for end-of-chapter discussion questions and problems. Elaborate solutions are also presented for each case with guidelines for facilitating a successful class discussion.
- **Multiple Choice Questions** to help students/readers to gauge their understanding of each chapter materials.
- **PowerPoint Presentation.** Professionally prepared slides provide detailed lecture outlines including selected graphs from the text of each chapters.

I would be grateful for *readers'* and *instructors'* constructive comments and suggestions for improvements and revisions. Please write directly to me at laurent.jacque@tufts.edu.

About the Author

Laurent L. Jacque is the Walter B. Wriston Professor of International Finance and Banking at the Fletcher School of Law and Diplomacy (Tufts University) and Academic Director of its International Business Studies Program. He previously served as Fletcher's Academic Dean and as such was responsible for the design and the establishment of the new Master of International Business degree and the Center for Emerging Market Enterprises. Since 1990 he has also held a secondary appointment at the HEC School of Management (France). Earlier, he served on the faculty of the Wharton School for 11 years with a joint appointment in the finance and management departments and taught at the Carlson School of Management (University of Minnesota). He also held visiting appointments at Instituto de Empresa (Spain), Indian School of Business (Hyderabad, India), Kiel Institute of World Economics (Germany), Pacific Asian Management Institute (University of Hawai), Institut Supérieur de Gestion (Tunisia), and Chulalongkorn University (Thailand) as the Sophonpanich Research Professor.

He is the author of an additional three books, *Global Derivative Debacles: From Theory to Malpractice* (World Scientific, 2015, 2nd edition), translated into French, Spanish, Russian, Chinese, and Korean; *Management and Control of Foreign Exchange Risk* (Kluwer Academic Publishers, 1996); and *Management of Foreign Exchange Risk: Theory and Praxis* (Lexington Books, 1978), as well as more than 25 articles on risk management and international corporate finance, which have appeared in leading academic and professional journals, including *Management Science, Journal of Risk and Insurance, Journal of Applied Corporate Finance, Journal of International Business Studies, Insurance: Mathematics and Economics, Journal of Operations Research Society, Columbia Journal of World Business,* and other publications. He served as an advisor and consultant to Wharton Econometrics Forecasting Associates, and as a member of Water Technologies Inc.'s board of directors. Since 2010 he has been a senior advisor to the director of the Bharti Institute of Public Policy at the Indian School of Business (Mohali, India) and a member of its advisory board.

A recipient of several teaching awards, Laurent Jacque also won the James L. Paddock award for teaching excellence at the Fletcher School and the Europe-wide HEC-CEMS award in 2008. He is a consultant to a number of firms and active in executive education around the world. Laurent Jacque is a graduate of HEC (Paris) and received his MA, MBA, and PhD from the Wharton School (University of Pennsylvania).

Acknowledgments

Over the years, research projects, consulting assignments, and discussions with many savvy executives and academics have helped me challenge received wisdom in the area of corporate finance, financial engineering, risk management, and derivatives; for their insight this book is a better one. Most notably I wish to thank Daniel Ades (Kawa Fund), Y. D. Ahn (Daewoo), Bruce Benson (Barings), Joel Bessis (HEC), Amar Bhide (Tufts University), Alex Bongrain (S.A. Bongrain), Charles N. Bralver (Oliver Wyman), James Breech (Cougar Investments), Eric Briys (Cyberlibris), Gaylen Byker (InterOil), Brian Casabianca (International Finance Corporation), Asavin Chintakananda (Stock Exchange of Thailand), Georg Ehrensperger (Garantia), Myron Glucksman (Citicorp), Anthony Gribe (J.P. Hottinguer & Cie), Gabriel Hawawini (INSEAD), Charamporn Jotishkatira (Stock Exchange of Thailand), Robert E. Kiernan (Advanced Portfolio Management), Oliver Kratz (Global Thematic Partners), Margaret Loebl (ADM), Rodney McLauchlan (Bankers Trust), Jacques Olivier (HEC), Craig Owens (Campbell Soup), Avinash Persaud (State Street), Guadalupe Philips (Televisa), Roland Portait (ESSEC), Jorge Ramirez (Aon Risk Solutions), Patrick J. Schena (Tufts University), Christoph Schmid (Bio-Oil), John Schwarz (Citicorp), Manoj Shahi (Shinsei Bank, Japan), Sung Cheng Chih (GIC, Singapore), Charles Tapiero (Polytechnic Institute at NYU), Adrian Tschoegl (Wharton), Seck Wai Kwong (State Street), and Lawrence Weiss (Tufts University).

I am indebted to several individuals who selflessly read and edited different versions of the manuscript, and I wish to express my appreciation to:

Blaise Allaz (HEC–Paris)
Patricia Bailin (Tufts University)
Rajesh Chakravarti (Indian School of Business)
Gunter Dufey (University of Michigan)
Shuvam Dutta (International Finance Corporation)
Gabriel Hawawini (INSEAD)
Lawrence Krohn (Tufts University)
Rishad Sadikot (Cambridge Associates)
Rajeev Sawant (Baruch College)
Patrick Schena (Tufts University)
Charles S. Tapiero (Polytechnic Institute-NYU)
Philip Ullmann (Bentley College and Tufts University)
Lawrence Weiss (Tufts University)

I owe a debt of gratitude to Patrick Schena and Ibrahim Warde, who contributed original chapters on Asian finance and Islamic finance, and to Martin Rietzel for writing the appendix on real options. Special thanks are owed to Olivier Jacque (Morgan Stanley) for building financial models used throughout the book and to Shuvan Dutta (International Finance Corporation) for developing several original case studies. Last but not least, I wish to thank my "editors in chief", Rishad Sadikot (first edition) and Kenichi Nozaki (second edition), who painstakingly reviewed the first two editions of this book and asked all the hard questions.

Special thanks are owed to the World Scientific editorial team for their professional guidance and enthusiasm for the project, which made the final stage of preparing the third edition of writing this book almost easy.

Yet with so much help from so many, I am still searching for the ultimate derivative that would hedge me from all remaining errors: but there is no escape — they are all mine.

Contents

CHAPTER 1

What Is International Corporate Finance?

The only trouble with going abroad is that you have to leave home to do it.
An English aristocrat when Britannia ruled the waves!

As we enter the third millennium, information technology — by crushing the cost of communications — is accelerating the globalization of manufacturing, commerce, and especially finance. News traveling at the speed of light through the Internet reaches an estimated 250,000 computer terminals in trading rooms around the world, morphing national financial markets into one huge, efficient global marketplace for capital. Indeed, the relentless rise of the digital cyber-economy is weakening the grip of the nation-state as government policies are subjected to a continuing referendum by financial markets. And yet die-hard sovereigns are holding firmly to their prerogatives of having a national *currency*, a national *regulatory framework*, and a national *tax code* of their own and much more. International business' vastly expanded global reach is redefining the risks and opportunities faced by financial executives, whether they are at the helms of international trading firms; old-fashioned brick-and-mortar multinational corporations (MNCs) such as Royal Dutch-Shell, IBM, Michelin, Nestlé, or Toyota; or "virtual" multinational enterprises such as Google, Facebook or eBay.

In this first chapter, we explain what is unique about international corporate finance. To do so, it is helpful to sketch how the process of globalization fueled by the relentless rise of the multinational enterprise is reshaping the global economy, thereby providing a backdrop against which to better identify the unique dimensions of international corporate finance. At the end of this chapter, the reader should have become convinced that the study of international corporate finance is a sine qua non-condition of success in tomorrow's business world. The old divide between domestic and international finance is blurring, so much so that our English aristocrat would no longer need to leave home to go abroad, because abroad has become home — at least in the world of finance.

In this introductory chapter, the reader will gain an understanding of:

- What globalization is and how the MNC is its handmaiden.
- What makes international corporate finance uniquely different from domestic corporate finance.
- How the exchange rate variable uniquely complicates financial decision-making.
- How the locus of decision-making in the finance function migrates as firms morph from strictly domestic entities to fully developed MNCs.
- What the international control conundrum is about.
- How MNCs can uniquely leverage their financial systems to minimize taxes and lower their cost of capital.

THE UNEVEN REACH OF GLOBALIZATION

Globalization is about the increasing integration of national economies as cross-border movements of labor, goods, and services, as well as money, continue at an unabated pace. In the words of Narayana Murthy, president and CEO of Infosys — an up-and-coming Indian multinational — "I define globalization as producing where it is most cost-effective, selling where it is most profitable, and sourcing capital where it is cheapest, without worrying about national boundaries." And in his best-selling book *The World Is Flat*, Thomas L. Friedman argues that the world economy has become a level playing field.

The reality is, however, somewhat more nuanced. Globalization is a multifaceted process that has evolved unevenly, with certain markets becoming dramatically more integrated than others. If one breaks down the world economy into three principal markets for (1) *labor*, (2) *goods and services*, and (3) *capital*, we immediately sense that globalization is an uneven three-speed process upholding major price differences across national markets. If the world were indeed a level playing field, there would be no price differences in the cost of labor, goods, services, or capital across nation-states, and what is known as the Law of One Price would hold true.

How global is the market for labor?

Globalization is at best sluggish in the labor markets where most international migration is still being curbed by severe national immigration quotas: we are generations away from a world of *Workers without Borders.*[1] Wages are lower in Vietnam than in China, China's wages are lower than Poland's, and Poland's wages are lower than Switzerland's. Convergence of national wages to a global wage standard — reversion to the mean — is light years away!

How global is the market for goods and services?

Globalization is healthy in the market for goods and services, but international trade is still regulated, with most countries maintaining tariff and nontariff barriers which impedes the free cross-border flows of goods and services. This process has been fueled by two forces among others:

(1) *Transportation technology aided by the marriage of computers and telecommunications*: As the cost of transportation, communications, and computing continues to decline exponentially, overcoming the natural barriers of spatial distance has become cheaper. The "death of distance" has enabled a nimbler division of labor among trading nations, allowing domestic and MNCs to leverage economies of scale better through outsourcing and offshoring.

(2) *Economic liberalization and deregulation*: The progressive dismantling of regulatory barriers — tariff and non-tariff as well as quotas is proving to be a powerful catalyst for increasing global integration in national markets for goods, services, and capital. Multiple rounds of multilateral negotiations within the framework of the General Agreement on Tariffs and Trade (GATT) and now the World Trade Organization (WTO) have resulted in the steady lowering of trade barriers as well as the reduction of trade subsidies. As a result, over the past 50 years, world trade in goods and services has grown more than three time as fast as world gross domestic product (GDP). For the last five years, however, the resurgence of protectionism, national industrial policies and economic sanctions is slowing down the globalization train!

At the regional level, Globalization scored two major resounding successes:

(1) The *North American Free Trade Association (NAFTA)* created in 1994 the largest free trading bloc in the world by binding the US, Canadian and Mexican economies with a total GDP of \$31 trillions and a combined population of 510 million far dwarfing the European Union (EU)–the second largest trading block. A free trade area dismantles tariff duties amongst its members but does not erect a common external tariff (unlike a custom union like the EU): for example, if a Korean exporter to the USA faces a 20% tariff whereas Mexico only imposes a 10% tariff it may be tempted to ship to Mexico first and benefit from a 0% tariff on Mexican exports to the US. The USA however would protect itself by requiring at the border transit points a certificate of origin on such imports from Mexico proving that such imports were indeed manufactured in Mexico — not outside NAFTA. Today Mexico and Canada are the two major trading partners of the US ahead of China, Japan or the EU.

(2) *European Union*: The dream of building a unified Europe traces its roots back to the signing of the Treaty of Rome in 1957. France, Germany, Italy, the Netherlands, Belgium, and Luxembourg established a common market (also known as the European Community or EC) among themselves, which meant abolition of intra-trade barriers and erection of common external tariff barriers. To facilitate the functioning of the common market and encourage intra-EC trade and investment, exchange rate stability was deemed an integral

1 "Workers without Borders" did find a home in the European Union (EU) when the Treaty of Rome (1958) mandated the freedom of movement for labor across its member states. Today the European Union encompasses 27 countries and allows its citizens to seek employment in any of the 27 EU member countries.

part of deeper economic, financial, and political integration among EC member states. The breakdown of the Bretton Woods system in 1971 and the subsequent chaotic experiment of generalized floating exchange rates revived the goal of a European Monetary Union which led to the launch of the single currency in 1999 (see next section). But a *unified* Europe called for a far deeper level of economic integration than a customs union by establishing Europe-wide freedom of movement for goods, services, labor and capital enshrined in the Maastricht treaty signed in 1992: the European Community became the EU in 2000. Today the EU is indeed a level playing field encompassing 27 European countries with a total population of 448 million. With a GDP of $17 trillion in 2022 it is the second largest economy only second to the United States. If the *World is not yet Flat* the *European Union is very close to being flat*. ... although the Mont Blanc in the French Alps does rise to an altitude of 4805 meters above sea level!

How global is the market for capital?

Globalization is unbridled and nearly all-encompassing in the market for capital. The deepening — but still incomplete — integration of national capital markets into a global "super-market" for capital is fueled among others by the following forces:

(1) *Currency convertibility*: With the breakdown of the Bretton Woods international monetary system of fixed exchange rates in the early 70s, countries have progressively dismantled exchange controls and restored currency convertibility, thereby fueling foreign direct investment and international portfolio investment.

(2) *European Monetary Union and the launch of the single currency*[2]: The hatching of the euro in 1999 created a single currency zone for most (not all) member nations of the EU. Twenty countries (out of 27) encompassing 344 million Europeans surrendered their national currency and adopted the euro as their legal tender. Displacing national central banks, a European Central Bank is now uniquely responsible for the formulation and implementation of the euro-zone common monetary and foreign exchange policy. Corporate and government bonds as well as stocks were re-denominated from now defunct national currencies into the euro thereby creating Europe-wide financial markets directly competing in depth and liquidity with US financial markets. The inception of the single currency has fueled further a EU-wide wave of cross-border mergers and acquisitions which in turn enhanced the efficiency of the EU economic fabric and its competitiveness in world markets. The euro is now the second largest reserve currency and the second most traded currency behind the US dollar. As a global currency the euro is increasingly challenging the dominance of the US dollar.

(3) *Privatization and emerging capital markets*: Privatization is the sale of state-owned enterprises to private investors. The transfer of ownership is akin to an initial public offering (IPO) whereby the state is offering for sale equity interest in the enterprise being privatized to domestic and/or foreign investors. The state may choose to divest itself partially or fully from the state-owned enterprise. Newly privatized firms in the hands of wealth maximizing investors are generally more efficient and better able to curb bureaucratic deadweight, waste and corruption. As major state-owned infra-structural, telecom companies, banks, and utilities became publicly listed, emerging capital markets largely benefited: indeed, newly listed blue-chips boosted emerging capital markets' daily trading volumes and market capitalization. Privatizations further encouraged large-scale international portfolio investment by institutional investors based in capital exporting countries to exploit the vastly expanded investment opportunity set created by the listing of previously state-owned enterprises. Privatization is often associated with the dislocation in 1989 of the Soviet empire but its scope in both time and space is far broader as it encompasses emerging market countries such as the Brazil, Russia, India, China, and South Africa (BRICS) but also many OECD countries such as The United Kingdom, France, Italy and many others. The world economy is free-er at last ... as the wave of privatization unleashed the "invisible hand" of free market forces where command economies in the Soviet Union, COMECON countries but also China, India and many others once struggled under the yoke of state bureaucracies.

2 See Chapter 3 for an in-depth discussion of the European monetary union and the single currency — the euro.

(4) *Market for financial derivatives*: The explosive growth of derivatives markets for currencies is generally associated with the break-down in 1971 of the Bretton Woods system of quasi-fixed exchange rates. Volatile exchange rates ushered the world financial system in a new era of deregulation and financial innovation with the introduction of currency futures, swaps, options and swaptions. When the world became a riskier place firms and financial institutions sought safe harbor by hedging with financial derivatives. Indeed, derivatives fundamentally facilitate efficient risk transfer from firms which are ill-equipped to bear risk, and which would rather not be exposed to risk to firms which have excess risk-bearing capacity, and which are willing to take on additional exposure to risk. Thanks to derivatives, risk transfer has become far more efficient and fairly priced as its cost plunged because of break-through in financial theory and computer technology.

(5) *Financial Technology (FinTech)* refers to the use of new technology — primarily the internet and the mobile phone — to deliver digital financial products and services. FinTech is disrupting traditional financial services and re-shaping its core financial intermediation function–that is the channeling of savings into productive investments. By combining technology break-throughs — exploding computational power, greatly enhanced data storage capacity, cloud computing and artificial intelligence — with faster internet connectivity FinTech is rapidly increasing the availability of financial services while reducing their cost. Payment systems, lending and credit granting, investing and asset management as well as insurance are the primary beneficiaries of the FinTech revolution. The reach of Fintech is magnified by the fact that as we enter the third decades of the 21st century it is generally estimated that up to one-third of the world population did not have a bank-account and that–similarly–small and medium-sized enterprises did not have access to financial services as basic as payment facilities and business loans. Indeed, FinTech services because of their digital nature, easier access and lower distribution costs are uniquely suited to serve under-banked individuals and firms.

THE RISE OF THE MULTINATIONAL CORPORATION

The growth of international trade, which now accounts for 30% of global Gross National Product (GNP) whereas it stood at only 11.6% in 1970,[3] is second only to the spectacular rise in foreign direct investment embodied in the MNC (see International Corporate Finance in Practice 1.1).

Integration of the world market for goods and services happens to a significant extent within the MNC itself, with as much as 40% of all cross-border trade in goods and services being of an *intra-corporate* nature (between sister affiliates of the same firm domiciled in different countries) rather than of an *arm's-length* nature (between independent firms). Supply chains now span the entire world. For example, consumer electronics may be designed in the United States, components manufactured in Japan and China and then assembled in Vietnam or the Philippines, and the finished product marketed around the world.

Lenin predicted that foreign direct investment would be the weapon of colonial imperialism and would signal the final stage of capitalism. By an ironic twist of history, foreign direct investment was growing about four times faster than the world GNP and at about three times the pace of world trade when the Soviet empire (the cradle of Marxism-Leninism) finally collapsed in 1989. Indeed, the torrential flow of foreign direct investment personified by huge, ubiquitous, and stateless MNCs has continued unabated and is no longer the prerogative of only old imperialist powers of the rich North. In fact, countries such as Brazil, Russia, India, China or Turkey, long shackled by communism, state socialism, or isolationist authoritarian governments, are not only playing host to foreign direct investors but are themselves becoming the proud homes of emerging-market multinationals: China-based Lenovo acquired IBM's PC business in 2005, and Indian Tata Motors took over the iconic British Jaguar and Land Rover in 2009, while China's Haier became one of the key global players in the white goods industry and Brazil-based Embraer competes head-on with Boeing and Airbus. But why do firms venture into distant and often unfriendly lands? There are at least three major motivations for doing so:

3 This is computed as global imports/global GNP, where global imports are the sum total of imports by each national economy. See *World Economic Outlook database* and *WEO aggregates* (International Monetary Fund, various years).

INTERNATIONAL CORPORATE FINANCE IN PRACTICE 1.1

What Are Multinational Corporations (MNCs)?

An MNC is a parent company that (1) engages in foreign production and other activities through its own operating subsidiaries, branches, and affiliates located in several different countries; (2) exercises direct control over the policies of those subsidiaries, branches, and affiliates; and (3) strives to design and implement business strategies in production, marketing, and finance that transcend national boundaries and allow them to capture economies of scale.

Many MNCs are owned by a mixture of domestic (the country in which the firm is headquartered) and foreign shareholders. Some of them are partially state-owned, such as China's CITIC or France's Electricité de France (EDF). Most large MNCs are headquartered in the United States, Western Europe, or Japan — for example, in 2017, Apple Inc. was the most valuable MNC with a market capitalization in excess of $3 trillion and employed 161,000 individuals worldwide. However, these are increasingly challenged by MNCs based in emerging-market countries — for example, India's Infosys (information technology) or China's Huawei (telecommunications).

MNCs are responsible for a sizable share of world trade and most foreign direct investment. As mammoth oligopolistic companies, MNCs possess market power that makes them global actors in their own right which loom large on the world economic stage. Unlike firms in purely competitive industries, MNCs enjoy managerial discretion in charting their strategic paths so much so that their actions may force nation-state changes in national policies.

(1) *Resource seekers*: From time immemorial, firms have sought access to natural resources that were either not available or only available in limited supply in their home countries. The French and the British East India companies and the Hudson Bay trading companies first chartered in the seventeenth century are the ancestors of modern multinationals; they were often established by their sovereign and closely aligned with colonization. It was not until the industrial revolution that oil and mining companies as well as agribusiness ventures emerged as powerful foreign direct investors that often grew under the mantle of the British, Dutch, and French colonial empires.

British Petroleum, Compagnie Francaise des Pétroles (Total), Union Minière du Katanga, Rio Tinto, Anaconda, Kennecott, and United Fruit trace their roots back to the nineteenth century and came to represent for many the evil of capitalism and imperialism. Because resource seekers have long been the villains of international business, they have been the prime targets of political risk, nationalization, and expropriation. More recently, the relentless drive by Chinese state-owned companies to secure access to foreign sources of energy, minerals, and other natural resources follows the same economic logic of their yesteryear Western counterparts.

(2) *Market seekers*: Access to foreign markets often initially achieved through exports is a primary driver of foreign direct investment by manufacturers of industrial products and consumer branded goods. Household names of long-established multinationals include US firms such as IBM, Ford Motor Company, and Procter & Gamble, but also European companies such as Unilever, Nestlé, Michelin, L.M. Ericsson, and many others. The ascent of the multinational enterprise really started after World War II and initially was a US phenomenon that primarily targeted Western Europe.

In the 1960s European firms jumped on the multinational bandwagon, investing heavily in the United States and the more dynamic economies of East Asia and Latin America. They were joined in the 1970s by Japanese firms such as Toyota, Hitachi, Komatsu, and Sony, and in the 1980s by South Korean firms such as Samsung and Hyundai. The past two decades have witnessed the onslaught of a new breed of multinationals domiciled in emerging market countries: Huawei, Wipro, Haier, Tata Motors, Lenovo, Cemex, and Petrobras are fast becoming household names.

Yet MNCs are hardly a new phenomenon and can trace their roots to the nineteenth-century industrial revolution: Early improvements in transportation and communications facilitated cross-border investments by American firms in Europe. Business historian Mira Wilkins recounts how in 1855 Singer licensed a French company to manufacture its new sewing machines and in 1867 set up the first plant overseas in Glasgow.[4] Similarly, in 1879, Westinghouse started to manufacture brakes in a Paris plant. In 1889 Eastman established a new company in London to manufacture films to be used by Kodak cameras imported from the United States. Noticeably, early foreign direct investments by US manufacturers were predicated on exploiting a competitive advantage due to new products, new manufacturing methods, and new marketing policies, rather than simple exporting of capital for acquisition.

(3) *Cost minimizers*: The search for lower labor costs and more generally efficient gains guide many market-seeking multinationals to establish assembly operations or call centers in low-wage countries such as Mexico, China, Vietnam, The Philippines or India. This is especially true of labor-intensive manufacturing processes characteristic of consumer electronics, garments, or footwear.

WHAT IS DIFFERENT ABOUT INTERNATIONAL CORPORATE FINANCE?

The reader will recall from his or her first corporate finance course that financial management is about *maximizing shareholder wealth* — that is, managers, on behalf of the firm's owners, should make all business decisions and manage the firm's resources with the objective of making its shareholders wealthier than before (see International Corporate Finance in Practice 1.2). More formally, shareholders' wealth maximization is all about increasing the firm's market value, defined as the present value of future net free cash flows (FCFs) discounted at the firm's weighted average cost of capital (WACC). This is typically achieved by making two types of decisions:

(1) *Value-creating investment decisions*, also known as capital budgeting, or the allocation of scarce resources (capital) among a company's present and potential activities/projects to uses that maximize shareholders' wealth. Such decisions run the gamut from modernization of plant and equipment to new product launches, entering new foreign markets, and acquisitions of new business firms, but also to wise credit granting to customers (accounts receivable), efficient management of inventory (raw materials, work in progress, or finished goods), and so forth. These are the decisions most closely linked to the asset side of the firm's balance sheet.

(2) *Cost-minimizing funding/financing decisions*, or the acquisition of funds — beyond internally generated financing — necessary to support investment. In effect, this is a quintessential procurement decision whereby the firm searches for the least costly sources of funds. Should the firm borrow short-term or long-term at a fixed or variable interest rate? Should it source debt (bank loans or bonds) or equity (straight or preferred) or lean on its suppliers (accounts or notes payable) for more favorable credit terms? What is the optimal mix of debt and equity financing that minimizes the firm's weighted average cost of capital? Such decisions are closely associated with the liabilities and owners' equity side of the balance sheet.

As firms expand beyond their own domestic borders, they are confronted with a myriad of new opportunities on both the investment and the

4 Mira Wilkins, *The Emergence of Multinational Enterprise* (Harvard University Press, 1970).

funding sides, thereby redefining the parameters and the scope of the corporate finance function. How financial managers should identify, gauge, and leverage these new opportunities to better achieve the firm's global strategic goals is the subject of this book. New decisions are now confronting the globally minded chief financial officer:

- How should foreign subsidiaries be financed?
- When and how should earnings be repatriated from foreign subsidiaries?
- How should similar investment opportunities in different countries be analyzed and compared?
- Where should financial decision making be located between the parent and its many far-flung foreign subsidiaries?
- How should managerial incentive and control systems be designed to be congruent with the firm's overall strategy but also account for foreign countries' idiosyncrasies?

Not only is the scope of international financial management far broader than it is for domestic financial management, but it is also compounded by a number of risk factors unique to international financial management as sovereign nations issue their own currencies, implement their own economic policies, and apply their own tax and regulatory rules. See Exhibit 1.1 for the different factors shaping FCFs and the weighted average cost of capital (WACC) at which they should be discounted.

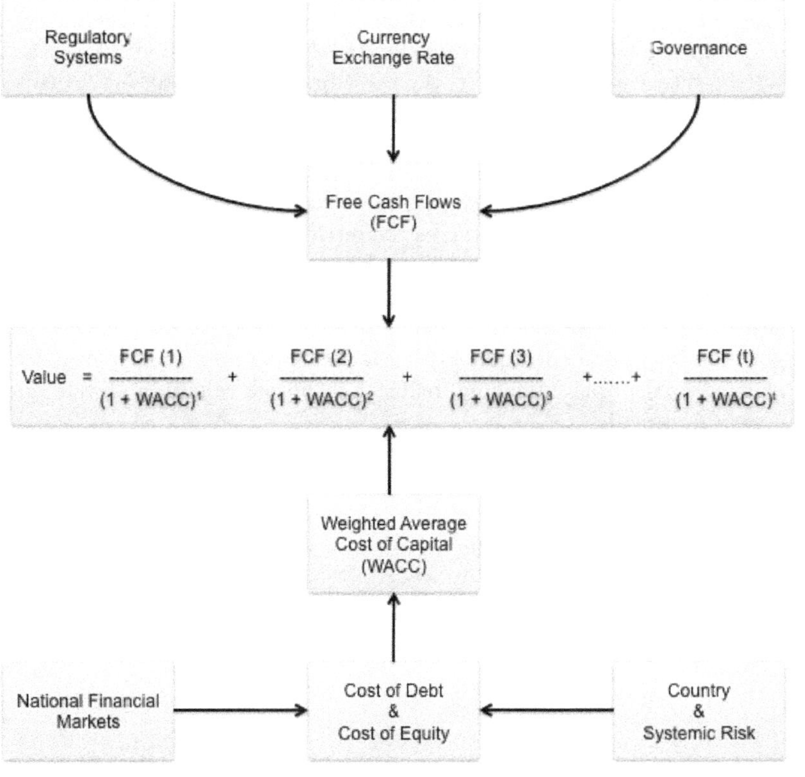

Exhibit 1.1. International valuation.

INTERNATIONAL CORPORATE FINANCE IN PRACTICE 1.2

Shareholders' Wealth Maximization and Corporate Governance Systems Around the World

If *shareholders' wealth maximization* is the dominant gospel of financial management in Anglo-Saxon countries where capital markets and a dispersed shareholder base play the leading role in financing firms, this is not necessarily the case in other major capital exporting countries, where banks, family groups, or even the state are the dominant owners.

In Japan, interlocking business groups formerly known as *keiretsu* focus on the health of the business group ahead of its individual firms and often emphasize market share more than share price maximization. *Chaebols* in South Korea mimic the Japanese model and may also maximize long-term growth more than short-term profits. *Family groups* in Southeast Asia, India, and Mexico often hold controlling interest in publicly listed firms and may expropriate minority shareholders by abusing their power and appropriating unfairly more than their share of the firm's profits. European firms often consider interests of stakeholders (primarily employees) on par with shareholders' interests. Many multinationals in countries like France, Russia, Brazil, and China are still partly *state-owned* and may put national interests ahead of shareholders' wealth.

Even in Anglo-Saxon countries, there is no guarantee that managers will indeed manage the firm in the best interests of its owners/shareholders. After all, managers are human beings whose personal goals may not be congruent with the firm's overarching goal of value creation. Thus, managers may act in their self-interest rather than pursue policies aligned with the best interests of the firm's shareholders. For example, managers may use company resources to benefit themselves rather than their shareholders by squandering money on lavish offices, large personal staff, corporate jets, country club memberships, and other wasteful perquisites.

Clearly, *corporate governance* — the charter that governs the relationship between the firm's owners and its managers — varies greatly across countries, reflecting legal, cultural, and sociopolitical national idiosyncrasies. The central problem, however, remains how to strengthen corporate governance to best protect outside investors (often minority shareholders) from expropriation by the controlling shareholders to ensure that the former are fairly rewarded for their investment. Indeed, resolving the governance conundrum equitably has far-reaching implications for efficient allocation of corporate resources, corporate financing, realistic corporate valuation, development of capital markets, and economic growth.

Needless to say, MNCs pursuing cross-border mergers and acquisitions or entering into joint-venture or licensing agreements with foreign firms should be well appraised of the nuances of national corporate governance systems.[5] Similarly, asset managers, whether they are pension funds or hedge funds, need a keen understanding of how idiosyncratic local corporate governance may bias valuation.

5 Chapters 26 and 27 are devoted to Asian and Islamic finance and banking.

RISKS IN THE WONDERLAND OF INTERNATIONAL FINANCE

As firms chart new territories by opening export markets or building plants in foreign countries, they expose themselves to a myriad of risk factors that need to be carefully calibrated and incorporated in financial decision-making.

Foreign exchange risk

For most firms, investment and funding decisions are carried out in the home currency context, which means there is only one currency to contend with. As soon as firms widen their market horizons and become active in international business, first by exporting some of their products or importing components or subassemblies and later by setting up operations in foreign countries, they expand their opportunity set. This brings with it new rewards and new risks.

Most obvious is the unique variable incorporated in most decisions that the firm tackles, namely the "fickle" and all too often "misbehaving" foreign exchange rate. Generally, foreign exchange risk can raise the cost of capital for the multinational firm, as international portfolio investors may require a risk premium in valuing debt and equity. Conversely, when foreign projects are analyzed — such as building a new plant to serve an emerging market or acquiring an existing business — a higher discount rate may be applied to capture the impact of volatile exchange rates on future cash flows. More specifically, consider the following transactions:

- **Imports and exports:** Foreign exchange risk is invariably associated with import and export transactions when future payment to or from a foreign firm is denominated in a foreign currency. Consider the case of US-domiciled Alaska Airlines purchasing five Airbus A320s at a cost of 100 million euros (€100 million) each, to be paid on delivery 24 months from the date of the purchase order. Such a transaction exposure (account payable is denominated in euros) may result in substantial cash-flow loss/gain depending upon the movement of the euro against the U.S. dollar over the next 24 months. For example, if, when the order was first booked, the exchange rate stood at €1 = $1.25, but on delivery day — 24 months later — the euro has appreciated to €1 = $1.50, Alaska Airlines would end up paying $25 million more per A320 than initially contemplated.
- **International financing:** Similarly, foreign exchange risk is at the core of the international financing decision. Consider the case of the US retailer JCPenney seeking to minimize the cost of financing its US$300 million working capital requirement. Should the US retailer source a short-term bank loan from a Japanese bank at 1.5% annually denominated in yen or stay home with a 6% loan from Bank of America denominated in US dollars? On the face of it, yen financing seems dirt cheap if we assume that the dollar price of 1 yen (the exchange rate) stays constant over the financing period. But what if the yen were to appreciate by more than 4.5% (6% – 1.5% = 4.5%) over the next year? The effective cost of yen financing would end up being more expensive than dollar financing.
- **Foreign direct investment:** An MNC such as General Motors, attempting to decide whether a car assembly operation in Malaysia should be expanded by 25% to capitalize on the rebound of the Malaysian economy in the aftermath of the 2008 sub-prime crisis, is confronted with a long-term foreign exchange risk exposure. The project returns an attractive 19% in Malaysian ringgit — but its return in dollar terms is clouded by the possible weakness of the Malaysian currency over the life of the project. Would the project in fact create value for GM-USA?
- **Lost in translation:** Another dimension of foreign exchange risk is the uncertainty that it creates in the financial reporting process. Exchange rates are used periodically (every quarter) in translating or consolidating the financial statements of foreign subsidiaries with the parent's to report an all-inclusive measure of global performance to financial markets — the much cherished earnings per share. Earnings per share are the tip of an informational iceberg (consolidated balance sheet, income statement, and cash-flow statement being the iceberg), which may show erratic movements from quarter to quarter as exchange rates fluctuate (sometimes wildly) over the reporting cycle, unless the MNC seeks to smooth its income stream by hedging selectively its translation exposure.

Country risk

A multinational firm is exposed to country risk — also known as political risk — when unforeseen events in the host country impair the firm's operations in that country. Indeed, international portfolio investors will require a country risk premium in evaluating such operations. That premium, in turn, will impact the value of the multinational firm's investment. Changes in the host country's political environment may result in reformed or new regulations as well as taxation or ownership guidelines that will impact the local subsidiary's performance. For example, the August 2009 nationalization of the Mexican firm Cemex's cement plants by the host government in Venezuela was an extreme form of country risk. The Chavez leftist government had announced its intention to nationalize the cement industry earlier in the spring of 2009 and had successfully forced both French Lafarge and Swiss Holcim cement multinationals to sell a majority stake in their local operations to the Venezuelan government.

Similarly, the January 2002 meltdown of the Argentine economy, with its abolition of the currency board that had constitutionally enshrined the Argentine peso 1 = US dollar 1 peg, led to the abrogation of the dollar-denominated tariff structure for foreign-owned telecommunications companies such as Telefonica S.A. of Spain. As a result, Telefonica S.A., which had been guaranteed a pricing schedule denominated in US dollars (since 1 dollar = 1 peso) and had heavily borrowed in US dollars, was now forced to price its services in a much-devalued peso and, facing price controls, had a much heavier debt burden.[6] In addition, scattered political violence and vandalism against brick-and-mortar facilities in Buenos Aires resulted in a major loss of income and damaged plant, property, and equipment.

In the same vein, Enron — better known for its ignominious collapse in 2001 — signed a contract in 1992 to build the largest power plant in India. After having spent more than $300 million in design and engineering costs, Enron abandoned the undertaking in 2001 when various political parties and environmental groups were able to kill the project in the local courts of the state of Maharashtra. Enron had discovered the importance of legal contract enforceability or lack thereof.

More generally, changes in the rules of the game that impact foreign direct investors' operations include:

- Imposition of exchange controls that restrict repatriation of dividends or payment of royalties by a foreign subsidiary to its parent.
- Restrictions on the availability of foreign exchange and discriminatory currency rates for importing parts or subassemblies.
- Imposition of price controls on local sales or local procurement requirements for parts, subassemblies, or raw materials.
- Expropriation and/or nationalization without adequate compensation in extreme cases.

Mildly segmented global financial markets

Closely related to the pervasive exchange risk conundrum is the notion that funding decisions are made in the context of national capital markets, with each offering a different cost of capital for both debt and equity financing. Such discrepancies are the result of national monetary policies creating different inflation expectations and therefore different yield curves, with central banks meddling in foreign exchange markets (resulting in currency overvaluation or undervaluation). They are also due to differences across countries in corporate governance systems (see International Corporate Finance in Practice 1.2) and various market imperfections such as asymmetries in tax regimes, disclosure, and reporting requirements, or other man-made distortions in money or capital markets. This is the notion of *capital market segmentation* that motivates the search for the lowest possible source of financing. In other words, national capital markets are less than fully integrated, and cross-currency cost of capital discrepancies warrant systematic scanning of funding options. Cross-listing of shares when issuing equity capital is a good illustration of the fact that the cost of equity capital is far from uniform across capital markets. Jazztel, an up-and-coming Spanish telecom company in the late 1990s challenging the monopolist Telefonica S.A., should have naturally scheduled its initial public offering on the Spanish Bolsa; instead, it decided to list on the New York NASDAQ in 1999, to lower its cost of equity capital.

With multiple *currency habitats* and their tax and regulatory systems to contend with or to choose from, the funding decision becomes far more complicated. A six-month working capital loan can be sourced domestically or from Japan, Switzerland, or any country or lending source offering a possibly lower interest rate. As we will discover in a subsequent chapter, lower interest rates are only half of the equation, since a lower interest rate is often an indicator of a currency likely to appreciate over time. It is difficult enough to decide on short-term financing, but long-term debt financing is even more perplexing because of the daunting task of forecasting exchange rates over the longer term. In all cases, borrowing firms will also compare domestic/onshore with international/offshore financial markets, as the cost of capital may be slightly different between each market's onshore and offshore tiers.[7]

6 Telefonica had a peso-denominated revenue stream with which it had to pay interest and principal on a much revalued dollar denominated debt. The currency mismatch between peso-denominated revenue and dollar-denominated cost that resulted from the abrupt devaluation of the peso was made worse by tight price controls on peso-denominated rates that Telefonica was charging its customers in Argentina.

7 Offshore markets (also known as euro-currency markets) are unregulated money markets that operate beyond the jurisdiction of their home currency's central bank. For example, the euro-dollar market functions anywhere but in the United States. See Chapter 6 for further discussion.

Equity financing is no easier. Firms can list their stock in different markets hoping to capture a cheaper cost of equity capital. The 1980s and 1990s witnessed a flurry of large Latin American firms deciding to list on the New York Stock Exchange by issuing American depositary receipts. Similarly, Russian, Chinese, and Indian firms have aggressively sought equity financing from Western capital markets by listing their shares on the Frankfurt, London, New York, and Hong Kong stock exchanges. Whether addressing a short-term or a long-term financing decision, the firm can choose from different financial markets and achieve a lower cost of capital.

INTERNATIONALIZATION AND THE LOCUS OF THE FINANCE FUNCTION

The finance function is managed by the chief financial officer, who directly reports to the firm's chief executive officer and its board of directors. He or she is usually seconded by a treasurer, risk manager, and comptroller. Depending on the size and the scope of the firm's domestic and international activities, each subfunction may develop its own staff.

The *treasurer* oversees short-term funding decisions, cash and near-cash management, and account receivables collection. The *risk manager* is responsible for purchasing insurance coverage as well as overseeing foreign exchange risk management, often coupled with hedging interest rate and commodity price risks. The *comptroller* orchestrates the consolidation of financial statements from both foreign and domestic operations for reporting the firm's aggregate results to its shareholders, debtors, and other stakeholders.

For firms that are primarily domestic in scope, the finance function is clearly anchored at headquarters. However, as firms begin to stumble into international business, whether by chance or by design, they will struggle with international financial management decisions whose scope becomes increasingly more complicated. The internationalization process is likely to be very incremental, with well-identifiable phases along the way and increasing allocation of responsibility in financial decision making between the parent and its foreign subsidiaries.

- **Stage I:** *Exporting and importing*: Most firms never venture beyond the confines of their domestic market but may experience imports competition from foreign-based firms. To overcome their cost handicap against lower priced imports, firms may source key inputs or subassemblies from the same foreign countries as their import-competitors. More likely than not, the management of foreign-currency-denominated payables will require foreign exchange risk management expertise to mitigate the risk of exchange losses associated with such imports. The treasury function will add a foreign exchange manager who will work closely with the procurement manager to factor in exchange risk in paying for and financing imports. The firm's market horizons may still be domestic, but its financial manager's mind-set is beginning to become more international.

  Whether the result of a random inquiry by a foreign distributor or the result of its own systematic effort, the firm may pursue international sales and progressively develop in-house exports-management capability. Pricing in the currency of the target market and decisions to grant credit to foreign distributors will require special expertise in analyzing *foreign credit risk*, managing *foreign exchange risk*, and exports financing. Here again the foreign exchange manager nested within the treasury function at headquarters will coordinate closely with the international sales department. Over time, as exports sales to a particular country reach a critical mass, a fully staffed foreign sales branch or subsidiary may be established in the target country, but treasury and foreign exchange risk management will remain housed at headquarters (see Exhibit 1.2, panel A).
- **Stage II:** *Foreign manufacturing*: As a foreign sales subsidiary matures, serious consideration may be given to establishing local manufacturing operations in the foreign country — perhaps in the form of local assembly — to reduce the impact of tariff barriers as is often the case in emerging markets. Now a more self-sufficient foreign subsidiary is constituted with its own financial function and a chief financial officer reporting to its own general manager but also coordinating more loosely with its parent chief financial officer. The locus of financial decision-making will migrate to the foreign subsidiary as it asserts its financial independence from headquarters (see Exhibit 1.2, panel B).
- **Stage III:** *Multinational enterprise stage*: As a firm repeats its successful market entry in different countries, a complex multinational enterprise is progressively evolving with distributed responsibility for financial decision-making. This gives the

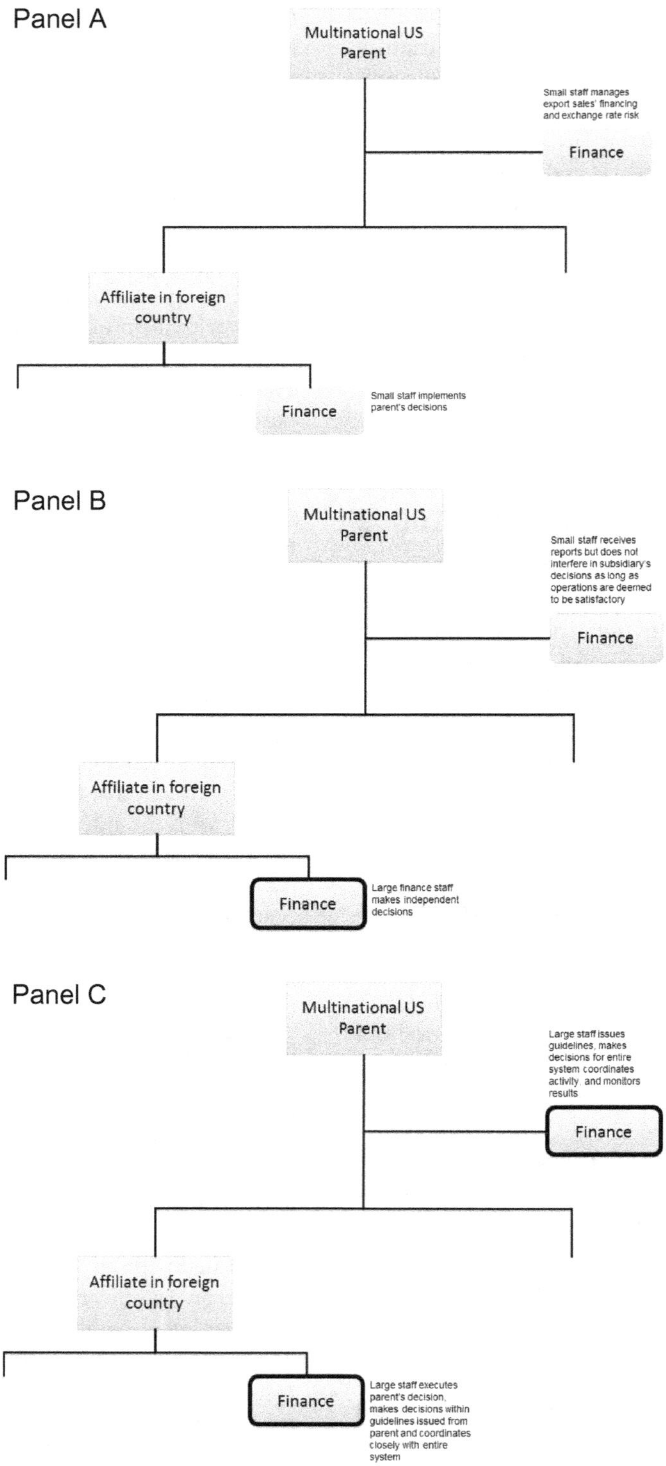

Exhibit 1.2. Locus of financial decision-making. (Panel A) Stage I of financial development of a multinational enterprise. (Panel B) Stage II of financial development of a multinational enterprise. (Panel C) Stage III of financial development of a multinational enterprise.

international financial management function its unique personality and complexity. As the locus of decision-making migrates from parent to foreign subsidiaries to regional centers, the mind-set of financial managers is correspondingly reshaped from a home-country bias characteristic of firms in the exporting stage to a more decentralized host-country approach in stage II and more global and systemic orientation in stage III (see Exhibit 1.2, panel C). More specifically, the center of gravity of financial decision-making will be equally distributed between parent and foreign subsidiaries, with close coordination between them and tight integration of all funding and investment decisions to best exploit the firm's multinational system potential.

The organizational dynamics of the global finance function is best understood in the strategic context adopted by the firm. As long as the multinational enterprise follows a *multidomestic* strategy, each foreign subsidiary will develop as a reasonably independent entity primarily responsive to the idiosyncrasies of its host market. Financial decision-making will be nested in the foreign subsidiary with relatively minor interference from the parent company, which at most will get involved in dividends repatriation decisions.

However, should the multinational enterprise adopt a more *global* strategy with strong production rationalization among its various subsidiaries, it will coordinate its financial decision-making more closely between the parent's finance function and its many foreign subsidiaries. Exploiting the multinational enterprise's potential (see next section) through skillful transfer prices1 of cross-border intra-corporate shipments of parts, subassemblies, or finished products requires strong financial decision-making capabilities both at the parent's and at the foreign subsidiaries' level, often reinforced by the establishment of *reinvoicing centers* that channel intra-corporate financial flows through low-tax jurisdictions. The danger, though, is that a skillful exploitation of the financial system may undermine the autonomy of each operating unit and disincentivize its management as performance measurement becomes murky. General Motors, for example, kept its currency risk management policies relatively decentralized at national operating levels even though that meant having redundant hedging policies that are clearly suboptimal from a system optimization perspective.

THE INTERNATIONAL CONTROL CONUNDRUM

At the core of a successful strategy are effective planning, budgeting, and control systems. For multinationals the challenge is to translate pro-forma financials, budgets, and performance measures first compiled in the currency of each foreign subsidiary into a common currency (numéraire) to allow for meaningful comparison and efficient resource allocation. The design of an effective management control system for MNCs is compounded by exchange rate fluctuations between the foreign subsidiary's local currency and the parent company's reference currency.[8] To be reliable, management control systems for MNCs must somehow incorporate a multiplicity of complicating factors such as exchange rates, differential rates of inflation, and byzantine national price and exchange controls.

MNCs tend simply to extend their domestic control systems to foreign operations. Indeed, performance relative to the operating budget continues to be the major evaluation and control system used. Simply put, budgetary *variance analysis* is based on the comparison of actual performance, whether it be measured by sales, operating expenses, accounting income, or FCFs as recorded *ex post*, and the corresponding budgeted amount as forecast *ex-ante* (at the outset of the budgetary cycle). Differences between actual and budgeted amounts are then explained in terms of *price and/or volume variance*, which can in turn be traced to *environmental variables* that are generally noncontrollable by the reporting subsidiary's managers. Clearly, operating managers should be held responsible only for budgetary variances that are deemed to have resulted from variables over which they do have control.

Unique to international control systems is the choice of exchange rates used for translating local currency budgets into reference currency terms. Technically, exchange rates enter the budgeting control process at two levels: in *drafting* the operating budget and in measuring or *tracking* results. Should the initial spot exchange rate be used in setting up the operating budget and the performance be tracked and gauged at the ending exchange rate? Under such circumstances, local managers will bear the full

8 The traditional dichotomy is made between the reporting subsidiary's foreign/local currency and the parent firm's reference currency, in which consolidated financial statements are prepared. See Chapter 25 for a full discussion of the international control conundrum.

responsibility for exchange rate changes during the period and, as a consequence, may be expected to behave in an overly risk-averse manner. A potentially harmful consequence of such a system may be the padding of budgets as well as decentralized hedging by local managers eager to reduce their perceived exposure to exchange risk (which is generally suboptimal from the parent's point of view).

Conversely, one may take the view that because foreign subsidiaries' operations are carried out in a foreign environment and are effected in the foreign currency, then a local currency perspective ought to prevail. However, when performance evaluation is based strictly on local currency, foreign currency translation gains and losses resulting from fluctuating exchange rates are generally dissociated from the subsidiary's performance, thereby transferring the responsibility of foreign exchange risk management to the treasury at headquarters. Specifically, initial spot exchange rates are used both to set budgets and to track performance, thus removing incentives for local managers to incorporate anticipated exchange rates into operating decisions or to react swiftly to unanticipated exchange rate changes during the life of the budget.

Alternatively, projected exchange rates could be incorporated in both the budgeting process and the tracking process. This approach allows the subsidiary to negotiate with its parent an *internal forward rate* that best reflects its anticipation of exchange rate changes. Such internal forward rates are deemed to foster goal congruence between home-country parent and foreign subsidiaries as well as fairness for operating managers, since they would receive neither blame nor credit for variance in performance attributed to exchange rate surprises. Local management is de facto shielded from unforeseen exchange rate changes, since the parent company acts as a banker, literally buying its foreign subsidiary's budget at a forward rate.

EXPLOITING THE MULTINATIONAL ENTERPRISE SYSTEM

Unique to the web of international business activities that firms weave around the globe is the making of a complex multinational enterprise system that gives the firm unique opportunities to move capital across borders from one subsidiary to the parent or to another subsidiary. For example, in the aftermath of the 1997 Asian financial crisis, countries such as Thailand and Indonesia imposed tight credit policies in the form of punishing interest rates. Foreign subsidiaries of many multinationals operating in these countries were able to bypass such restrictive policies by tapping into the internal financial market of their parent, in effect procuring low-interest-rate financing from other parts of the multinational financial system. This provided them with a significant competitive advantage over local firms and allowed them to capture market share. Let's consider first the architecture of the multinational enterprise's financial system before showing how its skillful optimization will create value in its own right (see Exhibit 1.3).

The architecture of the multinational financial system is anchored in the *equity and debt linkages* that tie foreign affiliates to their parent. Such linkages, typically established when the subsidiary is first set up, are likely to be upgraded over time as the parent provides additional capital to its subsidiary. They result in periodic *financial flows* such as dividends (on equity ownership) and interest payments on outstanding debt (see lower part of Exhibit 1.3).

Similarly, the parent company establishes *operational linkages* in the form of licensing contracts or management service agreements with its foreign subsidiaries, which also give rise to periodic royalty payments (on licensing agreements) and management know-how fees. Depending on the international division of labor that the MNC is implementing, intra-corporate trade in parts, subassemblies, and finished products among different national subsidiaries and its parent may be important and may generate a different kind of financial flows, namely payments for goods (see upper part of Exhibit 1.3).

Furthermore, MNCs have discretion to manipulate maturity structure of accounts and interest payables or receivables (leading or lagging) and adjust the magnitude of payment flow (over-invoicing or under-invoicing).

Constrained optimization and global tax minimization

In order to shift income out of high-tax-rate countries towards subsidiaries domiciled in low tax countries or tax havens, the multinational

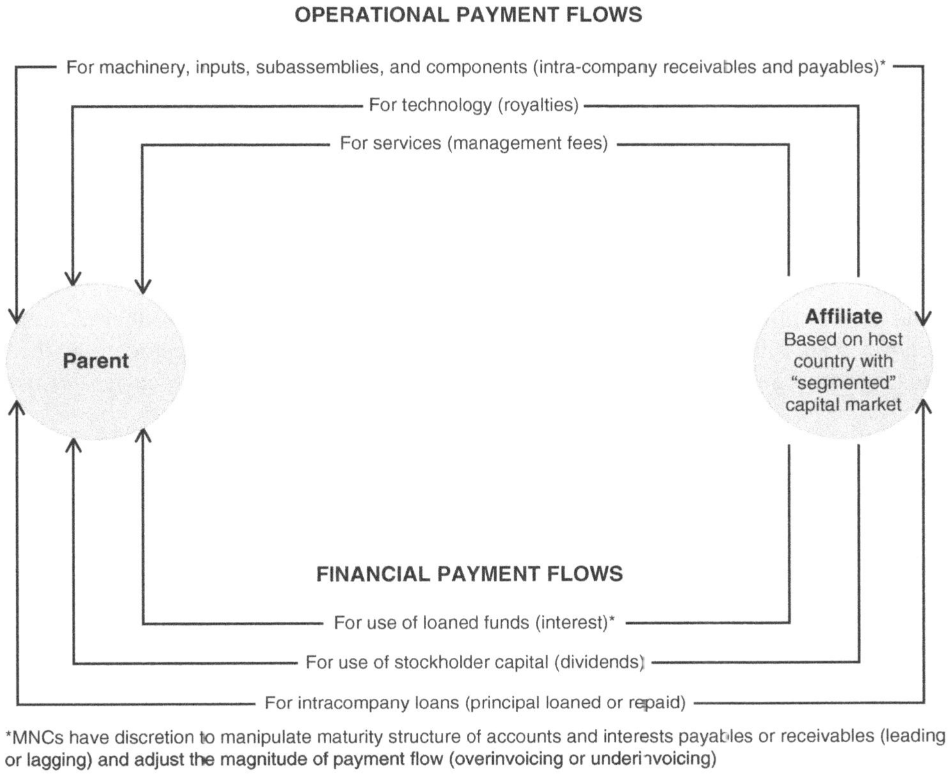

Exhibit 1.3. Exploiting the multinational financial system.

enterprise has several levers at its disposal to allow for skillful global tax minimization and therefore enhanced value creation: *transfer pricing*[9] in the form of *over-invoicing* of shipment to a foreign subsidiary domiciled in a high-tax country to reduce its taxable income or *leading payments/dividend remittances* ahead of a currency devaluation or *under-invoicing* in order to pay lower tariff duties on key imported subassemblies. Indeed, many US multinationals have established foreign subsidiaries in tax havens or simply low tax countries such as Ireland, Luxembourg, Switzerland, Bermuda etc ... for the express purpose of accumulating corporate earnings and deferring taxes while the money awaits reinvestment somewhere in the world or repatriation to the parent firm. *Tax haven subsidiaries* have much to do with the tax deferrals on foreign-source income that many countries such as the US allow. A tax haven subsidiary typically owns the equity of the MNC's foreign operating subsidiaries and is — in turn–100% owned by the parent multinational. Dividends would be remitted to and accumulated by the tax haven subsidiary instead of the parent. As long as the pool of corporate earnings is not remitted as dividends to the parent, it benefits from the tax-deferral treatment. These dividends may never in fact be taxed by the parent company's tax authorities as long as they are not repatriated. In the meantime, as the multinational expands its worldwide operations it can readily tap into the pool of funds parked tax free in the tax haven subsidiary (see International Corporate Finance in Practice 1.3)

9 By charging more (over-invoicing) for shipping parts or subassemblies to sister-affiliates domiciled in high-tax jurisdictions, the multinational corporations can shift income toward subsidiaries operating in low-tax countries while reducing taxable income in high-tax countries.

INTERNATIONAL CORPORATE FINANCE IN PRACTICE 1.3

How the Online Retail Giant Skirts Taxes in the European Union

Amazon holds its intellectual property such as software, trademarks and customer data into a Luxembourg-domiciled holding company which was granted a tax-exempt status. That holding company, in turn, collects royalties from Amazon's European national operating companies for using Amazon's intellectual property — so much so that between 2006 and 2014 it accumulated €4 billion which — as long as they were not repatriated to the US — escaped US corporate income tax and could therefore be deftly invested anywhere in the world (but in the US). These inflated royalties, in turn, completely drained profits and taxes from Amazon's European operations which reported a miserly profit of €10 million on a net turnover of €60 billion over that same period. In effect, this special tax arrangement with the Grand Duchy of Luxembourg allows Amazon to avoid taxes on three-quarters of all profits on its sales in the EU.

SUMMARY

1. Globalization is about the increasing integration of national economies as cross-border movements of labor, goods, and services, as well as money, continue at an unabated pace. It is fueled primarily by (1) technological breakthroughs aided by the marriage of computers with telecommunications, (2) the dismantling of tariff barriers and exchange controls that has returned many currencies to full convertibility, and (3) deregulation that has reasserted the rule of the "invisible hand".
2. Globalization is minimal in the international market for labor because of barriers to migration. It is significant in the market for goods and services, as multilateral rounds of negotiations have progressively lowered tariff and nontariff barriers. As more developed and emerging market countries return to full currency convertibility, financial globalization is almost — but not quite — a reality.
3. The scope of decisions confronting the global finance function is far broader than in the case of strictly domestic corporate finance: (1) How should foreign subsidiaries be financed? (2) When and how should earnings be repatriated from foreign subsidiaries? (3) How should similar investment opportunities in different countries be analyzed and compared? (4) Where should financial decision-making be located between parent and its many far-flung foreign subsidiaries? and (5) How should managerial incentives and control systems be designed congruent with the firm's overall strategy that can account for the idiosyncrasies of individual foreign countries?
4. International financial management is complicated by factors such as currency risk, country risk, and less than fully integrated national capital markets.
5. The challenge of designing an effective management control system for MNCs is compounded by exchange rate fluctuations between the foreign subsidiary's local currency and the parent company's reference currency.
6. By exploiting its system potential, the multinational enterprise has several levers at its disposal to shift income out of high-tax-rate countries toward lower-tax jurisdictions, thereby minimizing its global tax liabilities: *transfer pricing* in the form of *over-invoicing* of shipments to a foreign subsidiary domiciled in a high-tax country to reduce its taxable income; *leading payments/dividend remittances* ahead of a currency devaluation; *under-invoicing* in order to pay lower tariff duties on key imported subassemblies to allow for skillful global tax minimization and therefore enhanced value creation.
7. *Tax haven subsidiaries* are established in low tax countries to exploit the tax deferrals on foreign-source income that many countries such as the US allow. A tax haven subsidiary typically owns the equity of the MNC's foreign operating subsidiaries and is — in turn — 100% owned by its parent.

Thus, tax-deferred dividends would be remitted to and accumulated by the tax haven subsidiary instead of the parent before being re-deployed as needed anywhere in the world but the country of the parent.

QUESTIONS FOR DISCUSSION

1. Define in your own words what is meant by globalization.
2. Discuss the key drivers of globalization.
3. What is FinTech and how does it fuel globalization?
4. What is meant by "the world is flat"? (Was Galileo wrong?)
5. What are the key motivations for firms to expand abroad?
6. Is international financial management different from domestic corporate finance?
7. What is corporate governance, and how does it vary across countries?
8. What are the unique risks faced by multinationals?
9. Explain the international control conundrum faced by MNCs.
10. What are the organizational challenges of managing the finance function in a MNC? Where should the locus of financial decision-making be housed?
11. How can multinationals exploit their global financial systems to create value?
12. How do tax-haven domiciled subsidiaries of multinationals exploit the tax-deferral of foreign source income to minimize worldwide taxes?

REFERENCES

Desai, M. A. 2008. "The finance function in a global corporation". *Harvard Business Review*, July–August.

The Economist. 2008. A bigger world: A special report on globalization. September 20.

Friedman, T. 2005. *The World Is Flat*. New York: Farrar, Straus & Giroux.

Hawawini, G. and C. Viallet. 2022. *Finance for Executives Cengage*, 7th edition.

La Porta, R. Florencio Lopez-de-Silanes, and Andrei, S. 2002. "Investor protection and corporate valuation." *Journal of Finance* 57:1147–1170.

Organization for Economic Co-operation and Development (OECD) (www.oecd.org). The website provides comprehensive coverage of country members' corporate governance systems.

Sachs, J. 2020. *The Ages of Globalization: Geography, Technology and Institutions*. Columbia University Press.

Stiglitz, J. 2002. *Globalization and Its Discontents*. New York: W.W. Norton.

Stulz, R. M. 2007. "The limits of financial globalization". *Journal of Applied Corporate Finance* 19 (Winter): 8–15.

PART ONE

The International Monetary Environment

The first part of the book examines the monetary environment within which international corporate finance decisions are made. How exchange rates are determined and the unique role played by central banks' intervention in setting currency values is the focus of Chapter 2, whereas Chapter 3 presents a brief history of the international monetary system. The architecture of the world economy is outlined in Chapter 4 through the lens of national balance of payments accounting, which records the key flows linking national economies.

CHAPTER 2

Exchange Rates Regimes

So much of barbarism, however, still remains in the transactions of most civilized nations, that almost all independent countries choose to assert their nationality by having, to their inconvenience and that of their neighbors, a peculiar currency of their own.

— John Stuart Mill

The breakdown of the international monetary system of fixed exchange rates that had prevailed until March 1973 under the Bretton Woods (1944–1971) and the short-lived Smithsonian (1971–1973) agreements ushered the world economy into uncharted territory. The new international financial order that has emerged in its stead is commonly characterized as a system of floating exchange rates. Such a characterization, however, is misleading since it applies to only a handful of major currencies that float independently, such as the US dollar ($), the Japanese yen (¥), and the euro (€). Most other currencies are actually closely managed by their respective central banks when they are not pegged to or tightly controlled *vis-à-vis* the US dollar, the euro, or a basket of currencies.

This chapter develops a framework for understanding how exchange rates are determined and how different exchange rate regimes have developed in each country. It sheds light on the conceptual foundations of the three major systems of exchange rate determination within which actual exchange rate forecasts have to be made. In the companion Chapter 3, we illustrate how exchange rates regimes have been implemented over time by providing a brief history of the international monetary system.

After reading this chapter you will understand:

- How exchange rates are determined in a free market and what is the concept of an equilibrium exchange rate.
- How to calculate the percentage of currency appreciation or depreciation resulting from a given exchange rate change.
- The difference between floating, stabilized and controlled exchange rates and how central banks intervene in the foreign (FX, forex) market and what policy objectives do they pursue.
- What are artificial currency units (ACUs) also known as "basket of currencies" and how they are used in international finance.
- The difference between a "clean" float and a "dirty" float.
- The functioning of controlled exchange rates in emerging market economies.
- The choice of an appropriate exchange rate regime between *fixed exchange rates* and *floating exchange rates*.

SOME FIRST PRINCIPLES ABOUT EXCHANGE RATE DETERMINATION

A common element in international transactions that makes them uniquely different from domestic transactions is that one party deals in a foreign currency. When an American consumer — admittedly well-heeled — imports a British-made Aston-Martin, he or she pays in either dollars or British pounds. If the customer pays in dollars, the British manufacturer must convert the dollars into pounds. If Aston-Martin demands payment in pounds, the American buyer must first exchange his or her dollars for pounds. Thus, at some stage in the chain of transactions between the American buyer and the British seller, dollars must be converted into pounds. The medium through which this can be achieved is the foreign exchange market. The basic function of such a market is thus to transfer purchasing power from the US dollar into the British pound.

This is one of many transactions in which either the buyer or the seller must convert one currency into another. In general, the demand for pounds arises in the course of importing British goods and services (such as shipping or insurance), as well as making investments in pound-denominated stocks and bonds or extending loans to institutions domiciled in the United Kingdom. Conversely, the supply of pounds results from exporting US goods and services to the United Kingdom, as well as receiving investments and loans from British institutions. The interaction between supply of and demand for pounds thus sets the price at which dollars are going to be exchanged for pounds for immediate delivery (within one or two business days). This is called the *spot* exchange rate. Its determination is discussed in the next section.

Demand for foreign exchange

As is true of most goods, the amount of British pounds (£) demanded will tend to vary inversely with the price of British pounds. That is, at a high price (i.e., £ is expensive in $ terms) the amount of £ demanded by market participants will be less than the amount demanded at a low rate (£ is cheap in $ terms). Accordingly, an expensive pound makes imports of goods and services from the United Kingdom expensive to US residents in dollar terms, which should result in a reduced volume of imports as well as a lesser amount of pounds demanded by US residents. Conversely, a low exchange rate or a cheap pound will generally stimulate imports from the United Kingdom by US residents and thereby increase the amount of foreign exchange demanded. This demand relationship, $d(t)$, is portrayed graphically in Exhibit 2.1 as a downward-sloping schedule. The amount of British pounds demanded (measured on the horizontal axis) is a function of the exchange rate defined as the US$ price of one £ at time t (measured on the vertical axis) and denoted as $S(t)$. The more expensive the pound sterling is in dollar terms (moving higher on the vertical axis), the smaller the demand for pounds (resulting from a lower demand for more expensive British goods and services). It clearly indicates that the demand for foreign exchange is dependent on payments generating transactions in merchandise, services, and securities. It also suggests the influence that the exchange rate itself exerts over the volume of those same transactions.

Supply of foreign exchange

In our two-country world, the supply of pounds (measured on the horizontal axis) results from the sale of US goods and services to UK residents. When the pound is expensive and buys more US$ (higher US$ price of one £ measured on the vertical axis, which is tantamount to a cheap dollar in terms of British pounds), the amount of £ supplied will be large since US goods, services, and securities will appear cheap to UK residents who will supply £ to acquire the necessary US$. Conversely, a cheap pound in dollar terms (tantamount to an expensive US$ in £ terms) restrains exports of US goods,

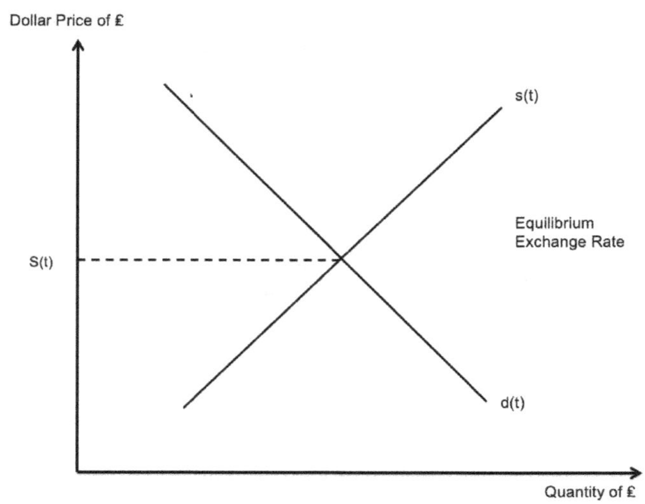

Exhibit 2.1. Equilibrium exchange rate.

services, and securities to the United Kingdom and lowers the amount of foreign exchange supplied to the market. In Exhibit 2.1, this supply relationship of pounds, *s*(*t*), is represented as upward-sloping for increasing dollar prices of pounds.

> ***Q:*** What are the key international transactions resulting in the supply of foreign exchange — £ in the case of our fictitious two-country world economy?
>
> ***A:*** Exports of US goods and services to UK residents result in the sale of £ (demand for US$). Similarly, repatriation of dividends earned by UK subsidiaries of US firms and payments of interest income on bonds or fixed income securities invested in the United Kingdom by US residents trigger £ sales. UK investors buying US stock and bonds or acquiring US assets such as timberland, mining operations, and companies also need to sell £ to acquire US$.

Equilibrium exchange rate

The free interplay of demand for and supply of pounds thus determines the equilibrium rate of exchange. At this rate of exchange and at no other rate, the market is cleared (as illustrated in Exhibit 2.1). Thus, the pound — like any other commodity — has an equilibrium market-clearing price at which it can be bought or sold. As an illustration, assume that on April 1, 2024, the dollar price of one pound is 1.31 for spot or immediate delivery (that is, within one or two business days). This means that an individual wishing to convert dollars into pounds would need to pay $1.31 for £1. Clearly, the United States deals with a multitude of countries besides the United Kingdom. Therefore for each conceivable pair of countries (United States and country *i*), there will exist a foreign exchange market allowing the purchasing power of the US dollar to be transferred into currency *i* and vice versa.

The equilibrium exchange rate, however, is unlikely to last for very long. The continuous *random* arrival of *news* such as information about the latest balance of payments' current account, inflation statistics, gross domestic product (GDP) growth, oil prices, and so on will result in a modification of supply and demand conditions as market participants readjust their current needs as well as expectations of what their future needs will be. Changing supply and demand conditions will, in turn, induce continuing shifts in supply and demand schedules until new equilibrium exchange rates are achieved.

Factors causing exchange rates to change

A myriad of factors drive continuous changes in exchange rates, but three factors stand out as the most significant in influencing international trade and investment decisions. The reader should keep in mind that this type of analysis is useful for pedagogical purposes as it allows for a better understanding of how a given factor drives exchange rate changes; however, it requires a "freezing of all other factors" (holding arbitrarily fixed all other factors) that also have an impact on exchange rate changes — this is what economists call partial equilibrium analysis:

- *Change in relative international price levels*: Suppose that US monetary policy causes a sharp and sudden growth in the US money supply, which in turn induces an increase in the prices of US goods and services relative to inflation in the United Kingdom. US consumers now find British imports cheaper and therefore switch away from US products toward British substitutes. Thus — at every exchange rate — US consumers will demand more pounds — see rightward shift in the demand curve for pounds in Exhibit 2.2. Meanwhile, British consumers will switch away from US goods and services that are now more expensive relative to British substitutes. As a result, for every exchange rate, British consumers now supply fewer pounds, resulting in a leftward shift in the supply curve of pounds for US dollars. On both accounts, the

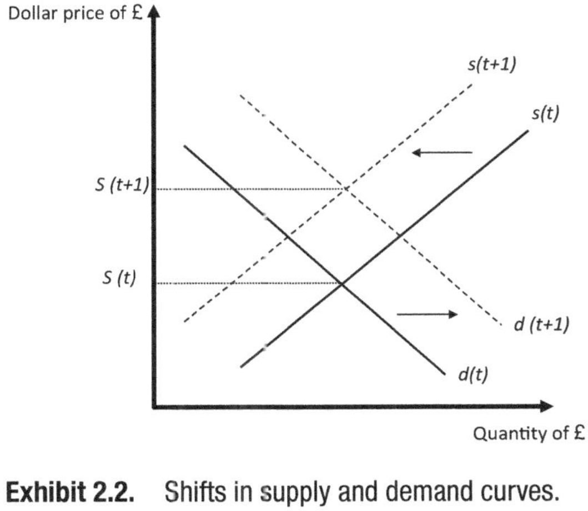

Exhibit 2.2. Shifts in supply and demand curves.

equilibrium exchange rate moves to a higher dollar price for each pound, which is tantamount to a depreciation of the US currency. Thus, higher US inflation relative to UK inflation results in a more expensive pound (cheaper dollar). This important relationship between inflation and exchange rate is known as purchasing power parity (PPP) and is discussed at great length in Chapter 7.

- *Change in relative national rate of GDP growth*: If the United States were to enjoy faster economic growth than the United Kingdom, foreign direct investment would seek to acquire US assets to partake in its faster economic growth. Similarly, a strong economy generally buoys its stock market, thereby encouraging portfolio investment by UK pension funds and other institutional investors on Wall Street. Both trends — ceteris paribus — would trigger an outward shift in the supply curve of pounds (demand for US dollars), thereby lowering the dollar price of pounds and leading to an appreciation of the US currency.
- *Change in relative interest rates*. Assume that the US Federal Reserve Bank, fearing a recession, decides to lower the US interest rate to stimulate the economy while the Bank of England leaves its interest rate unchanged. Short-term financial investments in the United States immediately become less attractive relative to British investments, which should encourage a capital outflow in search of a higher UK interest rate; meanwhile UK investment in the United States would be reversed. In both instances the demand for pounds increases at every level of exchange rate, resulting in a right and outward shift in the demand curve for pounds (Exhibit 2.2). Similarly, the supply of pounds (demand for dollars) contracts, resulting in an inward shift to the left in the supply curve. In sum, the equilibrium exchange rate will increase, which means a depreciation of the US currency. This important relationship between relative interest rates and changes in the exchange rate is discussed at great length in Chapter 6.

The importance of news and the role of expectations

With the nearly complete dismantling of foreign exchange controls in major countries, currency trading involving end users of foreign exchange (such as importers/exporters, multinational corporations, institutional investors, and others) accounts today for less than 10% of the currency market's daily turnover of 5 trillion US dollars! For that small market segment, the equilibrium exchange rate results from the interplay between supply and demand forces arising from currency flows, and consequently foreign exchange can be thought of as a medium of exchange for executing international transactions involving primarily trade in goods and services or capital flows.

This also means that the remaining 90% of daily transactions on the currency market is carried out between financial institutions that consider currencies as financial assets whose price — the exchange rate — is determined in very much the same manner as the prices of other financial assets such as stocks, bonds, and commodities. Thus, the question becomes whether such participants in the currency market want to hold that particular currency as a store of value — rather than whether they need to buy it to finalize international transactions (as in the case of end users of foreign currencies). These decisions, in turn, are based on the expectations that market participants hold about the factors that shape the currency's future value. What happens today is less important than what one expects will happen in the future or, more specifically, what one's expectation is of the future exchange rate. Thus, the spot exchange rate should adjust quasi-immediately to news — that is, everything that is known or expected to happen in the world economy. More formally, in this *stock view or asset approach* to exchange rate determination, the current spot exchange rate is valued as the present value of the expected future spot exchange rate discounted at the appropriately risk-adjusted rate of return for holding the foreign currency.

How to measure exchange rate appreciation or depreciation

A foreign currency is said to appreciate when its US dollar price increases. For example, if the dollar price of one pound sterling (£) increases from US\$1.55 to US\$1.63, one would measure its appreciation as

$$\frac{\text{New exchange rate} - \text{Old exchange rate}}{\text{Old exchange rate}}$$
$$= \text{Percentage £ appreciation}$$
$$= \frac{1.63 - 1.55}{1.55} = 0.0516 \text{ or } 5.16\% \qquad (2.1a)$$

Conversely, if the US dollar value of one pound were to decrease from 1.55 to 1.48, one would measure its depreciation as:

$$\text{Percentage £ depreciation} = \frac{1.48 - 1.55}{1.55} = -0.0452 = -4.52\% \qquad (2.1b)$$

However, if the same question were to be asked from the perspective of the pound sterling (rather than the US dollar), one would carry out the same calculation after restating the exchange rate as the £ price of one US$, which is simply the inverse of the US$ price of one £:

$$\text{Percentage US\$ depreciation} = \frac{1/1.63 - 1/1.55}{1/1.55} = -0.0491 = -4.91\% \qquad (2.2a)$$

$$\text{Percentage US\$ appreciation} = \frac{1/1.48 - 1/1.55}{1/1.55} = 0.0473 = 4.73\% \qquad (2.2b)$$

The reader will note that (1) depending on which currency is used as a reference, the same exchange rate changes will be in opposite directions — that is, if the £ appreciates *vis-à-vis* the US$ from a US$ perspective, the US$ will depreciate when the same exchange rate change is measured from the £ perspective, and (2) percentage appreciation from one currency perspective is not equal to the percentage depreciation from the other currency's perspective.

WORLD MAP OF EXCHANGE RATE REGIMES: THE FLEXIBILITY × CONVERTIBILITY SPACE

The concept of a foreign exchange market as presented in the previous section comes as close to the perfectly competitive model of economic theory as any market can. The product is clearly homogeneous in that foreign currency purchased from one seller is the same as foreign currency purchased from another. Furthermore, the market participants have nearly perfect knowledge, since it is easy to obtain exchange rate quotations from alternative sources within a reasonably short time. And there are indeed a large number of buyers and sellers.

Yet the actual exchange market deviates from the model of a perfect market because *central banks* act as a major agent of price distortion, either by directly intervening in the foreign exchange market and thereby impairing the flexibility of exchange rates or, indirectly, by limiting entry to the market (exchange controls) and thereby limiting the convertibility of the currency. In other words, the first source of price distortion is simply *limited flexibility* whereas the second is *limited convertibility*. In this vein it is helpful to think of a country's exchange rate regime along the two dimensions of (1) flexibility, ranging from 0% (controlled rate) to 100% ("clean" float), and (2) convertibility, ranging from 0% (tight controls on all current and capital/financial account transactions) to 100% (absence of controls on all balance of payments transactions).

In the chart in Exhibit 2.3, we portray the story of China, which in prior years moved cautiously toward higher convertibility and, since 2005, toward timid flexibility. The case of China is actually representative of many emerging market countries that are steadily moving toward more flexibility and more convertibility. Adam Smith's invisible hand is indeed reasserting itself, as many emerging market countries such as India, Turkey, and Brazil have recently moved toward freer foreign exchange markets.

Indeed, central banks are unlike any other participant in the forex market: they pursue objectives of national interest guided by their fiscal and monetary policies and they are not profit-maximizing entities the way private-sector banks are. Why, how, and to what extent central banks do actually limit fluctuations in market prices are major factors constraining exchange rate determination. Following ascending degrees of currency price manipulation by central banks, this chapter will discuss *floating*, *stabilized*, and *controlled* exchange rates.

Briefly, these three exchange rate determination systems can be defined as: (1) *floating* exchange rates in which the prices of currencies are largely the result of interacting supply and demand forces with varying degrees of stabilizing interference by central banks, (2) *stabilized* exchange rates — also referred to as "pegged yet adjustable" — whereby the market-determined price of currencies is constrained through central bank intervention to remain within a scheduled narrow band of price fluctuations, and (3) *controlled* exchange rates in which currency prices are set by bureaucratic decisions (see Exhibit 2.4)

Although exchange controls are most readily associated with controlled exchange rates, they are also found in most floating and stabilized exchange rate systems, albeit to a much lesser degree. The

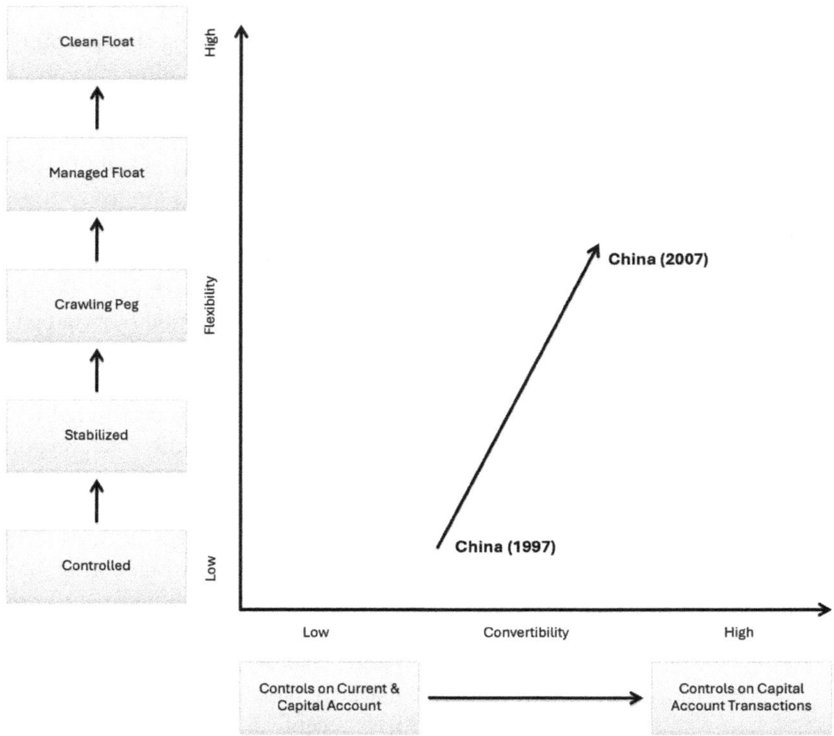

Exhibit 2.3. The convertibility × flexibility map.

sweeping deregulation that has engulfed financial systems around the world is certainly marching through the forex market but has not yet reached its final destination, as foreign exchange controls are still a way of life in many emerging market countries.

FLOATING EXCHANGE RATES

The free interplay of supply and demand for a given foreign currency was shown in the first section of this chapter to determine the rate of exchange at which the market is cleared. As pointed out earlier, however, this equilibrium exchange rate is unlikely to last for very long. The continuous random arrival of information such as news about the latest balance of payments' current account, inflation statistics, GDP growth, oil prices, and so on will result in a modification of supply and demand conditions as market participants readjust their current needs as well as their *expectations* of what their future needs will be. Changing supply and demand conditions will, in turn, induce continuing shifts in supply and demand schedules until new equilibrium exchange rates are achieved.

As an illustration, fictitious supply and demand curves for British pounds (£) at times (t), $(t+1)$, $(t+2)$, are depicted in Exhibit 2.5. Corresponding equilibrium exchange rates or dollar prices of one pound are denoted as $S(t)$, $S(t+1)$, $S(t+2)$, and are graphed in Exhibit 2.6. Over time, the exchange rate will fluctuate continuously or oscillate randomly around a longer-term trend, very much like the prices of securities traded on a stock exchange or the quotations of commodities traded on a commodity exchange.

In the real world, few countries have ever left the price of their currency free to fluctuate in the manner just described. For countries whose foreign sector (imports and exports) looms large on their domestic economic horizon, sharply fluctuating exchange rates could have devastating consequences for orderly economic development.[1] Picture, for instance, an industrialized country that imports nearly 100% of its energy whose price is denominated in US dollar: Abrupt fluctuations in the exchange rate between the country's currency and the US dollar would induce

1 This is particularly the case in smaller developed countries such as New Zealand, Taiwan, or Denmark, whose foreign sector often accounts for over 30% of GNP.

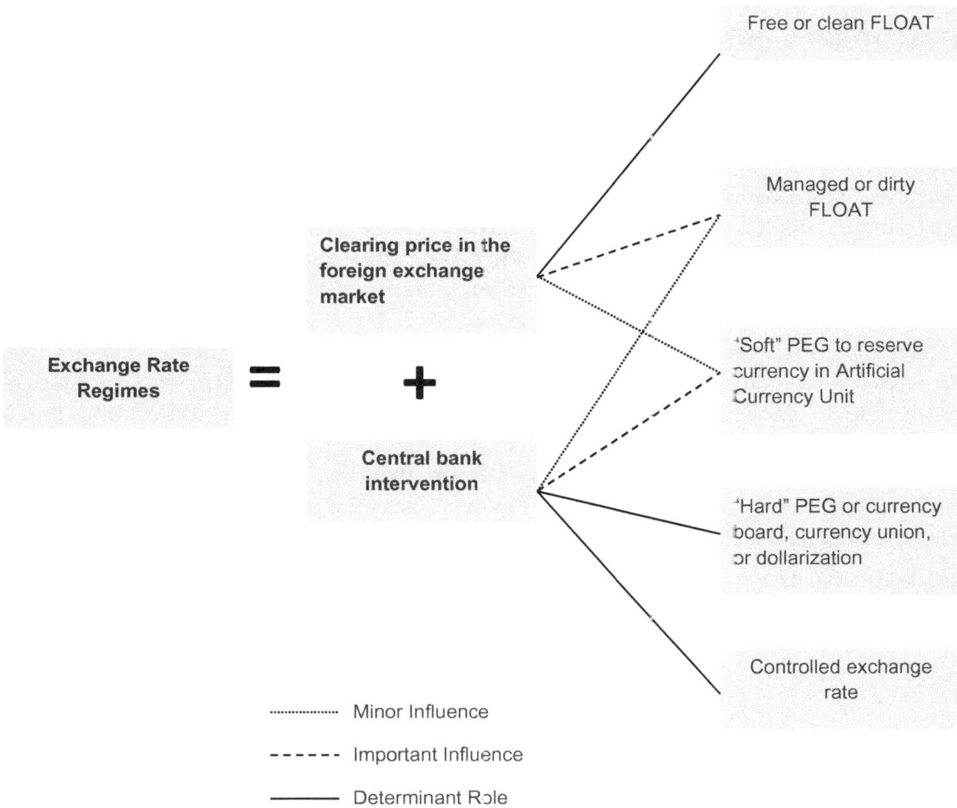

Exhibit 2.4. The role of central banks in exchange rate regimes.

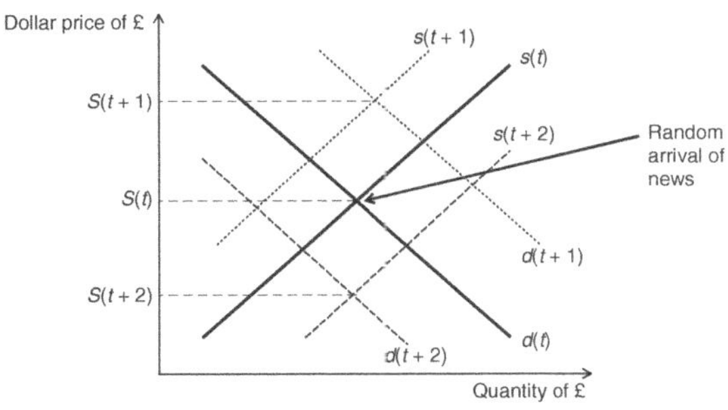

Exhibit 2.5. Shifts in supply and demand curves.

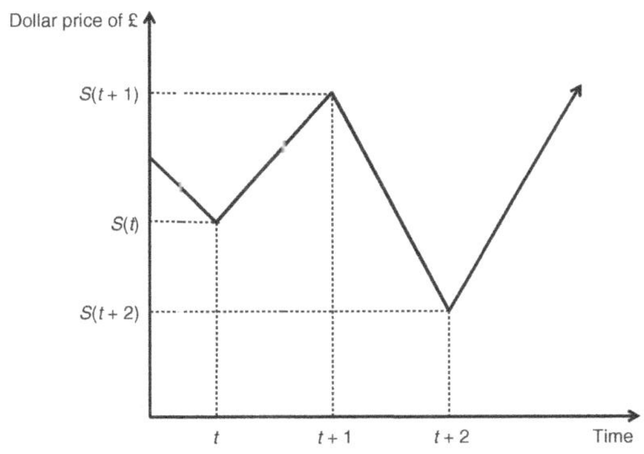

Exhibit 2.6. Oscillating exchange rates.

similarly abrupt fluctuations in the price of energy, and therefore affect the prices of nearly all finished products (since energy is a significant input in nearly all economic activities). This means that the cost of living index, the purchasing power of consumers, and the real wages of labor would be subjected to abrupt variations.

MANAGED FLOATING EXCHANGE RATES (DIRTY FLOAT)

It is not surprising, then, that a number of countries such as Japan have adopted a system of *dirty* or managed floating exchange rates in order to resist the economic uncertainty resulting from a *clean*

INTERNATIONAL CORPORATE FINANCE IN PRACTICE 2.1

Who Are the "Clean" and the "Not So Clean" Floaters?

Anglo-Saxon countries that have a long tradition of low regulation and reasonably unfettered markets would qualify as "clean" floaters; since the mid-1990s the United States, the United Kingdom, Canada, Australia, New Zealand and Switzerland have resisted intervening in the forex markets. Note that each of these countries with the exception of Switzerland is a common law country and maritime power and has a financial system that tends to be market rather than bank-centered.

Yet many central banks such as those of Korea, India, and Russia intervene in foreign exchange markets. But the dirtiest "dirty" floater of them all used to be Japan. Between April 1991 and December 2000, for example, the Bank of Japan (acting as the agent of the Ministry of Finance) bought US dollars on 168 occasions for a cumulative amount of $304 billion, and sold US dollars on 33 occasions for a cumulative amount of $38 billion. A typical case: On Monday, April 3, 2000, the Bank of Japan purchased $13.2 billion of US dollars in the foreign exchange market in an attempt to stop the more than 4% depreciation of the dollar against the yen that had occurred during the previous week. As a result of its aggressive interventions to stem too rapid a rise in the value of the yen, in 2007 Japan's foreign reserves exceeded a trillion dollars for the first time.

Source: Adapted from the Federal Reserve Bank of New York.

float (in which a central bank never intervenes) (see International Corporate Finance in Practice 2.1). By managing or *smoothing out* daily exchange rate fluctuations through timely central bank interventions, these countries have been able to achieve short-run exchange rate stability (but not fixity) without impairing longer-term flexibility. Most of the floating currencies discussed at the outset of this chapter are actually managed to a certain extent by their respective central banks. However, unlike central bank intervention in a stabilized exchange rate system,[2] neither the magnitude nor the timing of the monitoring agency's interference with the free interplay of supply and demand forces is known to private market participants. Furthermore, objectives pursued by central banks through their intervention in the foreign exchange market are not necessarily similar among countries.

Taxonomy of central bank intervention

Recent experiences with managed floats have unveiled three major classes of central bank intervention strategies. They can be described as follows:

- *Strategy 1*: At one end of the spectrum would fall countries concerned only with *smoothing out* daily fluctuations to promote an orderly pattern in exchange rate changes. Clearly, under such a scheme a central bank does not resist upward or downward longer-term trends brought about by the discipline of market forces.
- *Strategy 2*: An intermediate strategy would prevent or moderate sharp and disruptive short- and medium-term fluctuations prompted by exogenous factors recognized to be only temporary. The rationale for central bank intervention is to offset or dampen the effects of a random, nonrecurring event that is bound to have a serious but only temporary impact on the exchange rate level. The event could be the case of a natural disaster such as once-in-a-lifetime flood or tsunami, a prolonged strike, or a major crop failure, which would, in the absence of a timely intervention by the country's central bank, result in a sharp decline in the country's exchange rate level below what is believed to be consistent with long-run fundamental trends. Such a strategy is thus primarily geared to delaying rather than resisting longer term fundamental trends in the market, which is why this strategy is generally dubbed *leaning against the wind.*
- *Strategy 3*: At the other end of the spectrum, some countries have been known to resist fundamental upward or downward movements in their

2 Central bank intervention within the context of stabilized exchange rates is discussed at some length in the next section. It essentially results from a public commitment to maintain exchange rate variations within a narrow band of fluctuations whose ceiling and floor are unambiguously known to market participants.

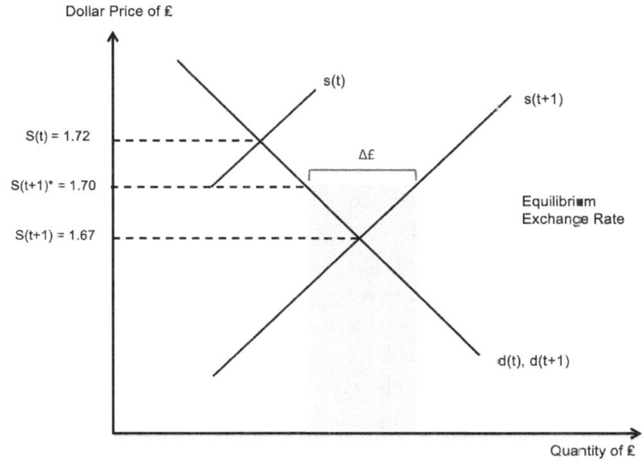

Exhibit 2.7. Modus operandi of central bank intervention.

exchange rate for reasons that clearly transcend the economics of the foreign exchange market. Thus, throughout the first quarter of 1976, the Bank of England prevented the pound from depreciating below the \$2 psychological level out of fear that a cheaper pound would mean a higher cost of imports and would thus fuel inflation. Similarly in 1994, the Federal Reserve Bank of New York resisted — if only briefly — the yen appreciation beyond the "traumatic" ¥100 = \$1 threshold. Such a strategy of *unofficial pegging* is, in effect, tantamount to a system of stabilized exchange rates that would not define an official par value. Similarly, in September 2011 the National Bank of Switzerland — a longtime clean floater — announced a dramatic policy reversal whereby it capped the exchange rate of the Swiss franc at CHF 1.20 = €1.

Modus operandi of central bank intervention under a managed float

The next question is how central banks actually intervene in the foreign exchange market. So far, we have been referring in a somewhat abstract sense to official intervention by responsible monetary authorities in their foreign exchange market. We will now describe the steps that central banks actually take to manipulate exchange rate levels.

Official intervention is primarily achieved through a central bank's spot purchases or sales of its own domestic currency in exchange for the foreign currency whose price it seeks to influence. Consider the following case: The Bank of England wants to moderate the depreciation of the pound (see Exhibit 2.7) from £1 = \$1.72 to £1 = \$1.67, which is expected to result from the free interplay of market forces (clean float) over the time interval $[t, t+1]$. Assume further that the (secret) target level — indicated by an asterisk — at which the central bank wants to maintain its exchange rate is $S(t+1)^* = 1.70$. From Exhibit 2.7, it can be readily seen that, at the target rate of \$1.70 to a pound, there is an excess supply of Δ£ or, equivalently, an excess demand of $[\Delta£ \times S(t+1)^*]_\$ = (\Delta£ \times 1.70)_\$$, which is the dollar cost of absorbing the £ excess supply (measured as the area of the shaded rectangle on the graph).

Purchasing Δ£ pound sterling for the equivalent dollar amount — that is, by supplying the foreign exchange market with $[\Delta£ \times S(t+1)^*]_\$ = [\Delta£ \times 1.70]_\$$ — the central bank will effectively stabilize its exchange rate at \$1.70 at time $(t+1)$ rather than letting it depreciate to \$1.67.[3] To do so it would have spent an amount of dollars (foreign exchange reserves) equal to $[\Delta£ \times 1.70]_\$$.

Moderation of the depreciation of the pound (strategy 2, the *leaning against the wind* type) will result in the Bank of England depleting its dollar reserves. Rigid pegging of the exchange rate at \$1.72 through large-scale central bank intervention (strategy 3, the *unofficial pegging* type) will result in an even steeper rate of depletion of the Bank of England's dollar reserves. In contrast, if the Bank

3 The reader will remember that the supply curve of £ is nothing other than the demand curve for \$. Similarly, the demand curve for £ is the supply curve of \$.

of England limits itself to *smoothing out* short-run fluctuations (strategy 1) in either direction, its stock of dollar reserves will hover around a constant trend.

Tracking central bank intervention

It is thus possible, on an *ex post* basis, to ascertain the type of objectives that the central bank is pursuing by tracking trends in its level of official foreign exchange reserves. Intervention should result in an increase or a decrease in the central bank's reserves, depending upon whether it is slowing down its currency's appreciation or depreciation. In a clean float, however, the central bank does not intervene and therefore the level of its official reserves should remain constant. It should be noted, though, that the resulting changes in reserves are often concealed by central banks and do not necessarily appear in official international reserve statistics. This may be due to central banks borrowing foreign currency but reporting only gross rather than net reserves. In addition, the profits and losses from intervention in the foreign exchange market are generally buried in the balance of payments accounts for interest earnings on assets. The various possible cases are recapitulated in Exhibit 2.8.

Strategy 0: ***Clean float.*** No intervention whatsoever by the central bank in its foreign exchange market. The level of the central bank's foreign reserves remains constant.

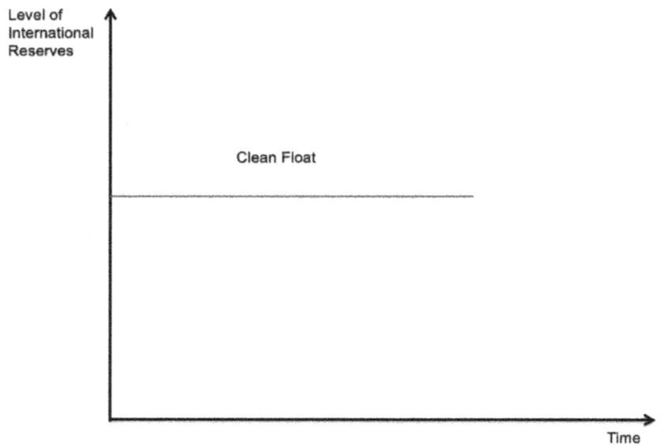

Strategy 1: ***Dirty float/intervention.*** Central bank intervenes only to mitigate short-run fluctuations without resisting longer-term upward or downward trends. The level of international reserves oscillates around a constant average level of central bank reserves.

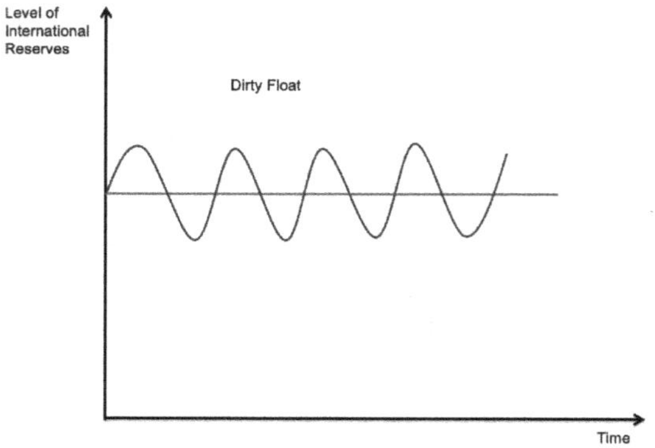

Strategy 2: ***Dirty float/leaning against the wind.*** Central bank purports to delay a downward trend in its exchange rate by leaning against the wind. The level of international reserves oscillates around a decreasing average level of reserves.

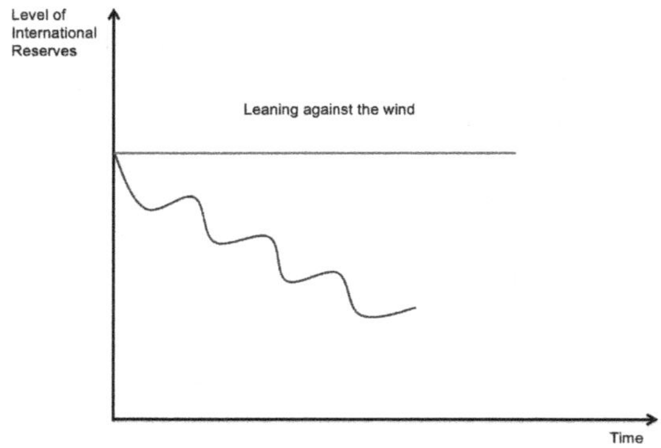

Strategy 3: ***Dirty float/unofficial pegging.*** Central bank resists depreciation through large-scale intervention. This is similar to unofficial pegging. A sharp depletion of reserves results.

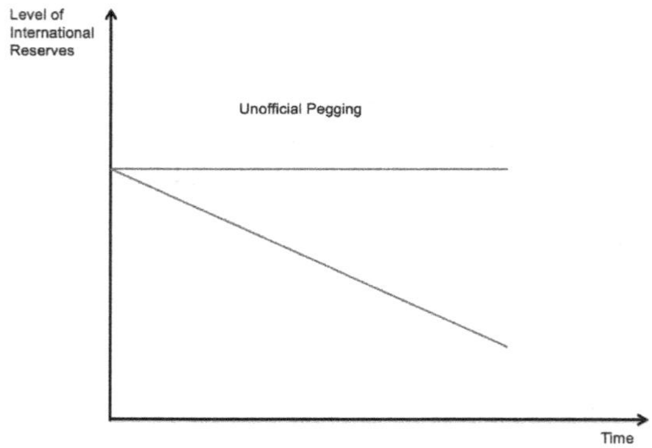

Exhibit 2.8. Taxonomy of central bank intervention strategies.

Central bank intervention and market expectations

Interventions in the forex market by central banks have — in addition to an obvious effect on supply and demand forces — a continuing impact on market *expectations*. Foreign exchange market participants will interpret the clues about central bankers' attitudes by carefully analyzing the magnitude, timing, and visibility of central bank intervention. Furthermore, actions to influence exchange rates are certainly not limited to direct intervention in the foreign exchange market. Equally and perhaps more important are domestic money market conditions, changes in monetary policy, and movements in short-term interest rates, which exercise a major influence on short-term capital flows that, in turn, will move the exchange rate.

STABILIZED OR PEGGED EXCHANGE RATES

Under a system of stabilized exchange rates, the fundamental economics of supply and demand remain as fully operative as they are under a system of floating exchange rates. The difference between the two systems lies in the fact that, under a system of stabilized exchange rates, central banks make a public commitment not to let deviations occur in their going exchange rate of more than an agreed percentage on either side of the so-called par value.[4] This result is achieved through official central bank intervention in the foreign exchange market. The definition of par values, as well as the width of the band of exchange rate fluctuations, have varied across countries and over

4 Par value is the official exchange rate prevailing between a given currency and the dollar. Par values are often defined in terms of a weight of gold, which amounts to the same thing because one ounce of gold was worth $35 throughout the Bretton Woods era (1944–1971).

INTERNATIONAL CORPORATE FINANCE IN PRACTICE 2.2

From Clean to Dirty Floats and Back — The Saga of the Swiss Franc

For the last century the Swiss franc (CHF) has been one of the most stable currencies and Switzerland has long been a safe harbor for foot loose capital in times of financial crisis. The fact that "neutral" Switzerland doubles up as a sophisticated tax haven which refined the art of bank secrecy only adds to its sex appeal in times of global political and financial turmoil. The Swiss franc is also the currency of a vibrant economy whose value over the last half-century has been steadily appreciating.

When the sub-prime crisis of 2008 and the euro crisis of 2010 shook the global financial system, foot loose capital sought refuge in Switzerland pushing up the value of the Swiss franc from CHF 1.60 to an all-time high of CHF 1.10 = € 1. Priced out of the world market, Swiss exports experienced a sharp decline due to lost competitiveness pushing Switzerland into recession; panicked business leaders called on the Swiss government to reign in the precipitous appreciation of the CHF. In late 2011 the Swiss National Bank obliged by establishing a floor of CHF 1.20 = € 1 and committing to intervene in the foreign exchange market for as much and as long as necessary to stem the CHF appreciation. De facto the Swiss franc had been unofficially pegged to the euro. Switzerland had switched from what had been historically one of the "cleanest" float to a very "dirty" float.

Exhibit 2.9 charts the precipitous appreciation of the CHF over the period 2003–2018 measured on the left axis as the CHF price of €1 (inverted scale which means that as the CHF appreciates the CHF price of one euro declines rather than increases). As the Swiss National Bank was attempting to curtail the Swiss franc appreciation it had to intervene heavily in the foreign exchange market by buying euros (selling Swiss franc) — see the rapidly growing level of foreign exchange reserves (measured along the right-hand side vertical axis) from less than $100 billion in 2009 to more than $800 billion in 2018. Please note that prior to 2009 Switzerland's foreign exchange reserves were stable — that is the Swiss National Bank was not intervening in the foreign exchange market and the Swiss franc was on a clean float.

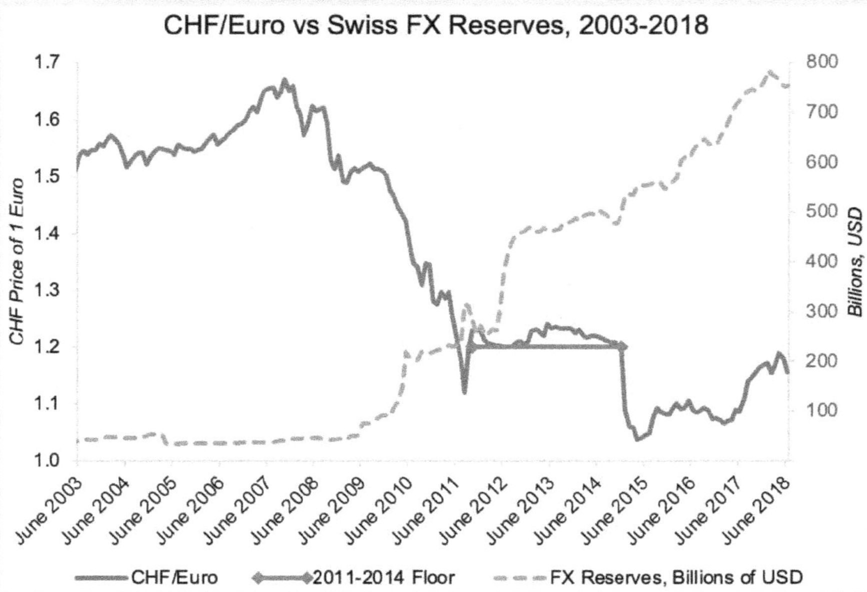

Exhibit 2.9. When a clean floater adopts an unofficial peg.

Q: Can you read from the graph when was the steepest rise in Switzerland's foreign exchange reserves?

A: When Switzerland first established the floor at CHF 1.20 = €1 in early 2012. Note that during the decade 2007-18 the Swiss National Bank's foreign exchange reserves were continuously climbing.
In early 2015, Switzerland abandoned it unofficial pegging policy: the Swiss franc immediately jumped reaching an intra-day high of CHF 0.82 = €1 before settling at 1.10. Heavy central bank intervention continued albeit at a less aggressive rate.

time. They are taken up in some detail in the balance of this section, which opens with an analytical review of the custodian role of central banks in a system of stabilized exchange rates.

Modus operandi of central bank intervention under a stabilized exchange rate system

A stabilized exchange rate system follows the same principles that guide intervention in the case of a managed float with one major difference: The central bank has a public commitment to maintaining the exchange rate within permissible floor and ceiling rates around the par value regardless of the amount of foreign exchange reserves necessary to do so. Consider the case of Malaysia, which pegged its currency, the Malaysian ringgit (MYR), to the US dollar at \$0.25 = MYR1.00 with a floor of US\$0.2440 = MYR1 and a ceiling of US\$0.2560 = MYR1. Whenever capital inflows or a strong balance of trade surplus pressure the ringgit to appreciate beyond US\$0.2560 = MYR1, the central bank intervenes by purchasing the excess dollars and flooding the market with ringgits at the fixed rate of US\$0.2560.

More specifically, it is the responsibility of the central bank to ensure that the exchange rate never escapes from the tunnel delineated by the lower and upper bounds. The band of fluctuations superimposed on a supply-and-demand diagram is shown in Exhibit 2.10 for the case of the MYR/US\$ exchange market. At time t, the dollar price of one MYR is "well behaved," since it falls within the allowed band of fluctuations. At time $(t + 1)$, however, news of a

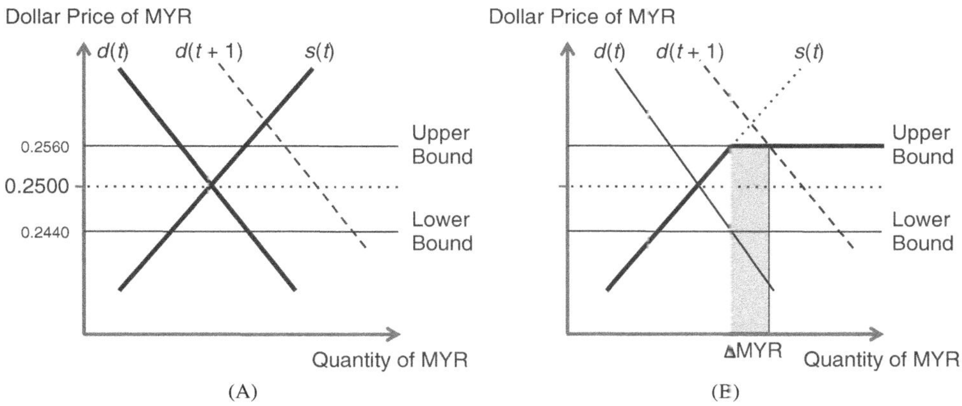

Exhibit 2.10. Central bank intervenes at the ceiling exchange rate.

buoyant Malaysian balance of trade, for example, causes an outward shift of the demand curve that pushes the equilibrium exchange rate well beyond the ceiling exchange rate (Exhibit 2.10, panel A). This high rate will not be permitted to prevail, because it does not fall within the prescribed band of fluctuations. The central bank will maintain the exchange rate at or below the ceiling of US$0.2560 per MYR by supplying the excess of (ΔMYR) demanded by the market at the ceiling exchange rate.[5] That is, the central bank sells Malaysian ringgits in the amount of (ΔMYR) or purchases US dollars in the amount of = $\{\Delta MYR \times 0.2560\}_{\$}$. It is sometimes said that because of official intervention, the supply curve of MYR becomes infinitely elastic at the ceiling exchange rate (central banks act as residual sellers of ΔMYR — Exhibit 2.10, panel B). If, on the other hand, exogenous factors were to induce a depreciation of the MYR below the floor exchange rate, the central banks would act as residual buyers of MYR (or, equivalently, as residual sellers of US$). This latter case is portrayed in Exhibit 2.11. The demand curve for MYR is said to become infinitely elastic at the floor exchange rate.

Once again, the mechanism of central bank intervention at either the floor or the ceiling exchange rate is identical to the one presented in our discussion of a managed float. However, in a stabilized exchange rate system, floor and ceiling exchange rates within which the going exchange rate is maintained through official intervention are known in advance. The uncertainty attached to future exchange rates, barring a change in par value, is clearly bounded, which definitely changes the rules of engagement for foreign risk management purposes (see Part Four of this book).

We now turn to a review of current institutional implementations and variants of this general scheme of stabilized exchange rates when currencies are pegged to a basket of currencies (rather than a single currency) or when they are traded in a two-tier market.

Pegging to an artificial currency unit (mid-1970s to the present)

When the world's major currencies began to float independently in early 1973, most small countries continued initially to peg their currency to the single reserve currency against which they had previously stabilized their exchange rate (mainly the US dollar, British pound, or French franc). However, the benefits of single-currency pegging were soon overshadowed by the costs of exchange rate fluctuations against other major currencies, especially as the currency to which they were pegging became prone to prolonged *over/undershooting*[6] against other major trading currencies. Consequently, a number of countries began to manage their exchange rates systematically against the currencies of their key

5 Theoretically, either the central bank of Malaysia (Bank Negara) or the US central bank (Federal Reserve), or both, in concert with other central banks, could intervene. In practice, such official intervention, in the context of stabilized exchange rates, has generally been the responsibility of foreign central banks; in this case, the central bank of Malaysia would prevent the exchange rate from going through the roof.

6 Over/undershooting refers to currencies appreciating or depreciating far away from their fair/intrinsic value. For example, in early 2000 the euro fell to $0.80, far undershooting its fair value, generally estimated at $1.20 to $1.25.

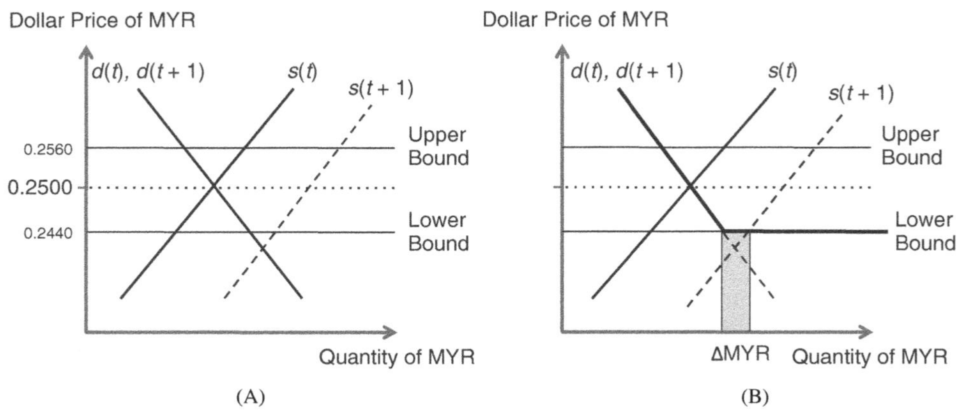

Exhibit 2.11. Central bank intervenes at the floor exchange rate.

trading partners. This could be greatly facilitated by pegging the home currency to a basket of currencies whose fixed composition would typically reflect the country's bilateral trade flow pattern (see International Corporate Finance in Practice 2.3). Indeed, a great many countries have abandoned a single-currency pegging in favor of pegging against a currency basket of their own choosing. These baskets of currencies are also called artificial currency units (ACUs) — for example, the special drawing rights (SDRs) issued by the International Monetary Fund and which is discussed in the next section.

Special drawing rights

As large trade deficits of the United States were underpinning the architecture of the Bretton Woods system and the credibility of the US dollar as a reserve currency, in 1969 the International Monetary Fund created the SDR. It was meant as an additional reserve asset to supplement gold and the US dollar which were then the principal reserve assets held by central banks but also to assist developing countries in coping with gapping balance of payment deficits. The SDR is used as a unit account against which many countries peg their exchange rates and as a currency of denomination in international trade and finance transactions. It is defined as a portfolio of five currencies — US\$0.7813, Euro 0.37379, Chinese renminbi 1.0993, Japanese yen 13.452 and Pound sterling 0.080870.[7] Its value is the sum of the values of each component currency. For example, on March 1, 2024 the SDR was worth:

$$\text{USD value of SDR } 1 = 0.7813 \times 1 + 0.37379 \times 1.0842 + 1.0993 \times 0.1389 + 13.452 \times 0.00666 + 0.08870 \times 1.2659 = 1.5408 \qquad (2.3)$$

The composition of the SDR basket is based on the relative GDP weight of each currency's issuing country. It is reviewed every 5 years and its composition is adjusted to reflect the changing relative economic weight of member countries. As the dollar value of member currencies fluctuates the dollar value of one SDR will also fluctuate but — because of the benefits of diversification — by less so than the value of any individual currency. Exhibit 2.13 illustrates the benefits of portfolio diversification: over the last 10 years the SDR dollar value index has fluctuated between +4% and −8% whereas the Japanese yen fluctuated considerably more depreciating as much as 26% over the same period. The same pattern would apply to the other four currencies in the basket. For a more formal discussion of ACUs see Appendix 2.A.

Two-tier exchange markets

The last institutional arrangement that falls under the general heading of stabilized exchange rates is the two-tier exchange market: It is a hybrid of a floating exchange rate system with a stabilized exchange rate system. This dual exchange market is characterized by the channeling of current and financial account transactions into separate exchange markets:

- An *official* exchange market constitutes the first tier. Only current account transactions (goods as

7 For most of its life the SDR was comprised of only four currencies — US dollar, Euro, Japanese Yen and Pound sterling. In 2014 the International Monetary Fund decided to add the Chinese renminbi to account with the rapidly increasing weight of China in the world economy.

INTERNATIONAL CORPORATE FINANCE IN PRACTICE 2.3

From Rigid Pegging to Dirty Crawling: China's Slow Quest for Convertibility

China's yuan (CNY) was tightly pegged to the US dollar at CNY 8.28 = $1 from 1997 to July 21, 2005 (see left-hand portion of Exhibit 2.12). Over the period, China sailed remarkably unscathed through the Asian financial crisis of July 1997 while growing at the astounding rate of better than 10% per year. How was China able to withstand the Asian financial crisis? To a large degree China, unlike its Asian neighbors, kept tight exchange controls on financial account transactions, which limited the mobility of short-term capital in and out of China. On July 21, 2005, the People's Bank of China (China's central bank) announced that it was "reforming the exchange rate system by moving to a managed floating exchange rate regime based on market supply and demand with reference to a basket of currencies." The yuan would no longer be pegged to the US dollar. The exchange rate of the US dollar against the yuan immediately adjusted to 8.11 yuan per US dollar and crawled up to CNY 6.82 while allowing a small band of +/−0.3% around the central parity published by the People's Bank of China. The yuan was repegged to the US dollar during the subprime crisis at CNY 6.82 = $1 for approximately 2 years before being allowed to crawl up again in late 2010. It now stands at CNY 6.14 = $1 for a total appreciation since 2005 of 25%. China is clearly relaxing exchange controls while nurturing a modicum of exchange rate flexibility — still a far cry from a floating — even "dirty" — exchange rate! Indeed the reader will note the meteoric rise in China's foreign exchange reserves which peaked at US$4 trillion in 2015 (measured on the right-hand side of Exhibit 2.12) which betrays the extent to which China was slowing down the appreciation of its currency.

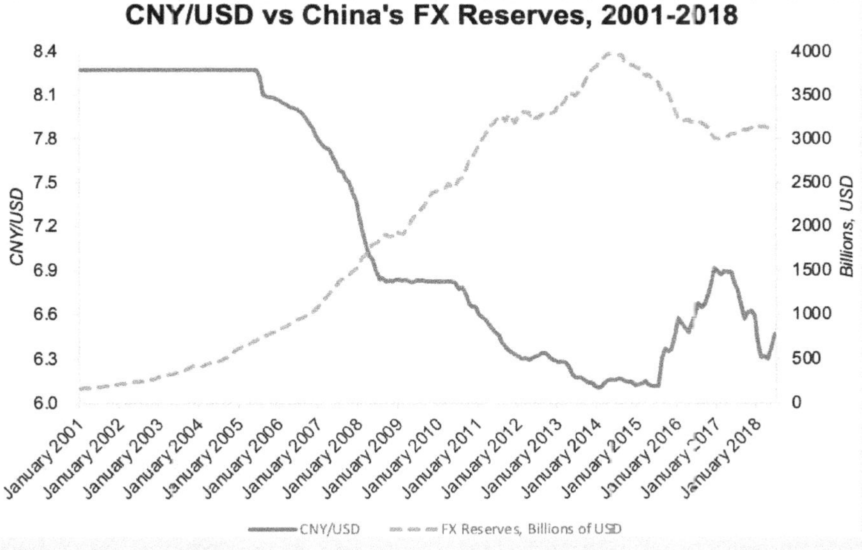

Exhibit 2.12. China's yuan over the period 2001–2018.

well as services trade transactions) are channeled through this market, in which the central bank intervenes to maintain the exchange rate within a band of permissible fluctuations around a par value. This is the stabilized exchange rate system segment of the dual exchange rate market, and it is meant to promote international trade by providing an environment that is free of currency risk.

- A *financial* exchange market makes up the second tier. Through this more or less freely floating exchange market, all financial account transactions are channeled. The central bank does not

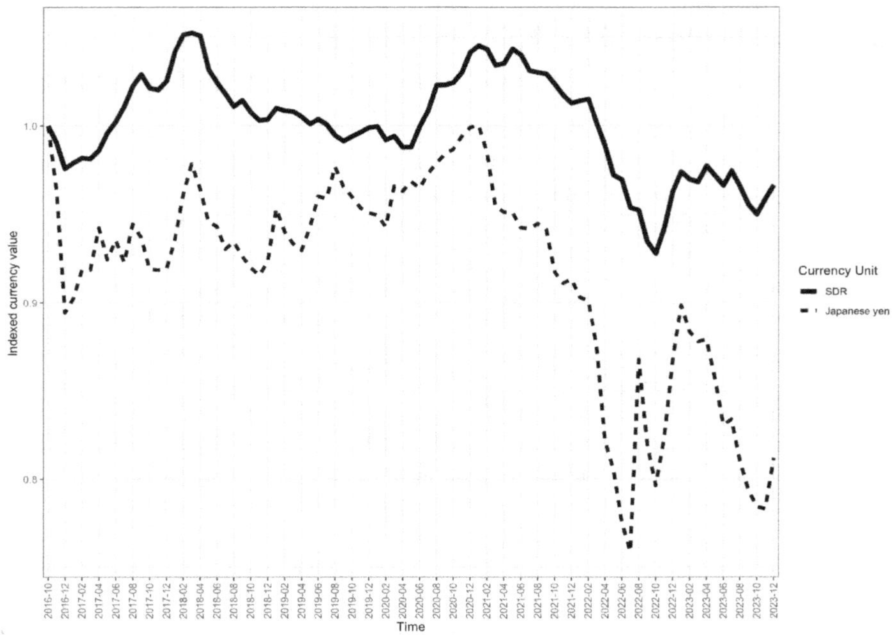

Exhibit 2.13. Tracking SDR and Japanese yen monthly fluctuations.

intervene in this market, but exchange controls may limit access to trading. Clearly, short- and long-term capital movements are believed to be less deserving than current account transactions and are fully exposed to currency risk.

Technically, the segmentation of the foreign exchange market into an official market and a free financial market may be achieved in a number of ways. For example, the banking system can be instructed to establish two types of foreign accounts, namely current accounts and financial accounts, and two similar categories of domestic currency accounts for non-residents. Administrative controls will then ensure that all payments and receipts, for instance, deriving from current transactions are correctly carried out through current accounts at the prevailing stabilized exchange rate. In practice, it will prove more difficult to control certain transactions such as tourism, commercial credits, or profits from foreign investment than it will be to control visible trade transactions (imports and exports of goods). It is therefore inevitable that this segmentation between the two markets will be imperfect, and the incentive for evasion will increase with any widening of the differential between the official rate and the free rate.

This system of a two-tier exchange market was actually implemented by the Belgium–Luxembourg Economic Union (1959–1974), France (1971–1973), Italy (1973–1974), and was used by South Africa and Mexico throughout the 1980s. A number of European countries have or have had separate exchange markets (closed-circuit markets) limited to portfolio investments (capital transactions) — for example, the investment currency market in the United Kingdom, the O-guilder in the Netherlands, and, until 1971, the security currency market in France.

CONTROLLED EXCHANGE RATES

Systems of floating and stabilized exchange rates allow for different degrees of interference (through central bank intervention) with the free interplay of supply and demand forces. This is not the case with controlled exchange rates found in many less developed countries and in centrally planned economies. Under such a system, the central bank supersedes the marketplace by becoming the sole buyer and seller of foreign exchange. There is no foreign exchange market per se. The exchange rate at which such transactions take place is no longer determined by the interaction of supply and demand forces. In other words, the controlled exchange rate does not directly respond to exogenously induced shifts in the supply and demand schedules (as it did in the case of both floating and stabilized exchange rates). Instead, the control authority — be it the central bank, a stabilization exchange fund, or any special agency — sets the price at which foreign exchange transactions will take place. The controlled exchange rate is thus the end product of bureaucratic decisions. Consequently, the control agency rationing supersedes the allocational function of the exchange market, and the currency is said to become inconvertible. This is the case of countries such as Belarus, Burma, Cuba, Bangladesh, and Iran.

In this type of institutional setting, all exchange earnings (e.g., from exports) must be sold to the control authority at its stipulated rate. Conversely, all foreign exchange expenses (e.g., from imports) must be bought from the same control authority at its prescribed rate. The rates for buying and selling foreign currencies are not necessarily identical, nor are they uniform across all foreign exchange earnings or payments generating transactions. In the next section, single-controlled exchange rate systems will be examined first. Multiple exchange rate systems that discriminate among different categories of transactions will be taken up second.

Single controlled exchange rate

The backdrop of controlled exchange rates is generally one of foreign exchange scarcity over which the control authority has limited influence. This is especially true of less developed countries whose export earnings are highly dependent on one staple commodity that faces a foreign demand characterized by low price elasticity. The control agency's main task is, therefore, the rational allocation of this more or less fixed supply of foreign exchange among the economic agents who demand it. The rationing function is generally achieved by an exchange control or a trade licensing system that forcibly chokes off all excess demand for foreign exchange at the controlled exchange rate. As an illustration, consider the controlled exchange rate system of Bangladesh in Exhibit 2.14.

At the controlled exchange rate of 69 taka (domestic price) for each US dollar (one unit of foreign exchange), the demand for dollars far exceeds its supply. At this controlled exchange rate, which clearly overvalues the taka, the control authority will choke off the excess demand of dollars by granting licenses for the purchase of only OA$ instead of the OB$ actually demanded by the market.

Why doesn't the control authority simply abrogate all exchange restrictions, thereby letting the taka find its true equilibrium level in a liberalized exchange market? Several reasons may be invoked:

- A devaluation of the taka would have to be very substantial for the new exchange rate to clear the market. The steep slope of the supply schedule

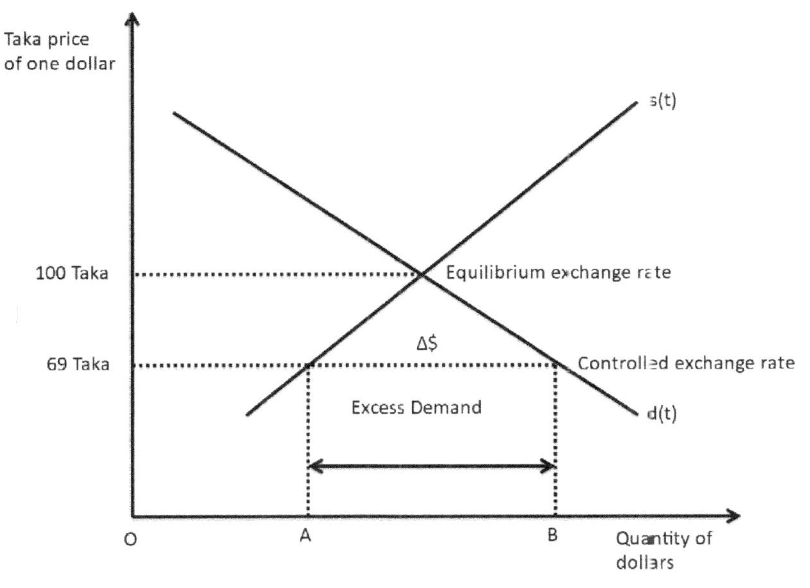

Exhibit 2.14. Bangladesh's controlled exchange rate.

of foreign exchange results from the fact that Bangladesh's exports earnings are primarily agricultural commodities such as cotton and jute, which face a relatively price-inelastic foreign demand.

- A large devaluation would breed inflation in Bangladesh. It would entail a hefty increase in the prices of key imports such as energy, which would feed into the basic cost of living commodities such as rice or cooking oil on which the lowest-income segment of the population is dependent for physical survival.
- A liberalization of exchange transactions would trigger a large-scale capital flight from taka-denominated assets into stronger, safer convertible currencies such as US dollars, Swiss francs, or Japanese yen. This would further compound the chronic situation of a foreign exchange shortage. Such an abrogation would be politically unacceptable.

By keeping its currency artificially overvalued, however, Bangladesh is denying its nonagricultural exports the price competitiveness in the world marketplace that a fairly priced exchange rate would give them. In addition, it is effectively subsidizing imports that may, in turn, exercise undue pressure on manufacturers competing with these imports. It is also discouraging foreign direct investment, because building a factory or acquiring a local firm is artificially expensive.

Furthermore, by combining tight quantitative controls on official foreign exchange transactions with an unrealistic (overvalued) exchange rate, the central bank is breeding a black market (sometimes called a parallel market) that accommodates transactors denied access to the controlled currency. Typically, the black market rate will understate the equilibrium exchange rate, with the latter being somewhere between the overvalued/official rate and the black market exchange rate. The existence of severe penalties associated with such illegal transactions (ranging from fines to incarceration) also explains the premium on the black market rate.

Multiple exchange rates

An alternative approach to allocating scarce foreign exchange resources is to rely on discriminatory pricing of foreign exchange rather than on arbitrary quantitative restrictions. The principle of this approach depends on the willingness of foreign exchange demanders to pay the price rather than on their ability to obtain a license. By discriminating among various types of import transactions, the central bank is thus able to alleviate the pressures on limited and scarce foreign exchange resources. This is achieved by charging increasingly higher exchange rates (defined as the domestic price of one unit of foreign exchange $S_{B,\$}(t)$) for imports of decreasing essentialness, thereby introducing a modicum of price signaling into the allocation process.

Consider the following illustration. Faced with a chronic shortage of foreign exchange resources, Venezuela, at different points in its economic history, has resorted to multiple exchange rates for channeling imports toward products deemed crucial to economic growth and to welfare in general. This was achieved by segmenting imports into several classes of decreasing essentialness, as perceived by Venezuelan exchange authorities. Thus, classes of less essential (or more luxurious) products were increasingly more expensive in bolivar terms as a result of correspondingly higher exchange rates. The fictitious correspondence between classes of import goods and exchange rates is represented in the following list.

Class	Import goods	Exchange rates
I	Preferential items: raw materials, spare parts, and so on	$[S_{B,\$}(t)]_{I} = 25$
II	Semi-preferential items: agricultural machinery, tools, pharmaceutical products, and so on	$[S_{B,\$}(t)]_{II} = 35$
III	Non-preferential items: consumer goods	$[S_{B,\$}(t)]_{III} = 50$
IV	Luxury goods: artwork, sports cars, and so on	$[S_{B,\$}(t)]_{IV} = 100$

Presumably, local demand for import goods is price-elastic enough to respond quantitatively to the price signals: The demand for imported luxury items, or so it is expected, should dry up because of the prohibitive exchange rate imposed on such transactions. Conversely, the importation of raw material inputs and spare parts for existing machinery is encouraged, if not subsidized, by the adoption of a low exchange rate.

TO FLOAT OR TO FIX: THE TRILEMNA OF INTERNATIONAL FINANCE

As this chapter illustrates, the choice of an appropriate exchange rate regime is between *fixed exchange rates* (or a variation thereof) and *floating exchange rates* (or a variation thereof). In a perfect world a country would adopt an exchange rate regime permitting:

- *Fixed exchange rates* which provides stability for its firms involved in international trade either as exporters or importers but also as foreign direct investors.
- *Independent monetary policy* which allows a country to adjust its money supply and interest rates to stabilize its economy and combat inflation. When facing slow economic growth or an outright recession the central bank would cut interest rates and boost the money supply. Conversely should the economy overheat the central bank would hike interest rates and constrict money supply growth.
- *Freedom of cross-border capital movements* which fosters better capital allocation and ultimately enable a country to access cheaper capital.

These three desirable attributes of an exchange rate regime are depicted in Exhibit 2.15 as the three vertices of a triangle. Each side of the triangle is labelled as the appropriate exchange rate regime consistent with two (but not three) attributes. Unfortunately, it is not possible to enact all three attributes at once and that is why this trilemma is often referred to as the *impossible trinity*. Let's be specific about what this impossible trinity means in practice:

- **Referring to side 1 of the triangle:** If the goals are an independent monetary policy and freedom of cross-border capital movement the exchange rate regime of choice is a "floating exchange rate" regime. The United States, the United Kingdom and Switzerland would – among many others – fall in this category having given up exchange rate stability.
- **Referring to side 2 of the triangle:** If the goals are exchange rate stability and freedom of cross-border capital movements the currency regime of choice is a "pegged exchange rate" with full currency convertibility. Member states of the Euro-zone such as France or Spain (by joining the euro), Hong-Kong or Saudi Arabia chose pegged exchange rate and freedom of cross-border capital flows but gave up their independent monetary policy (now in the hands of the European Central Bank in the case of euro-zone countries or the US Federal Reserve System in the case of Hong-Kong and Saudi Arabia whose currency is pegged to the US dollar.)
- **Referring to side 3 of the triangle:** If the goals are monetary policy independence and exchange rate stability the currency regime of choice is pegged exchange rates with exchange controls. China and most OECD countries under the now defunct Bretton Woods system achieve exchange rate stability and an independent monetary policy sacrificing freedom of cross-border capital flows by imposing exchange controls and keeping their currency relatively inconvertible.

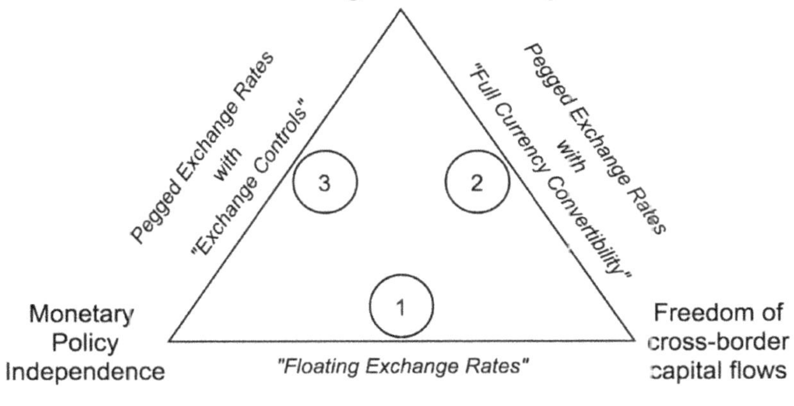

Exhibit 2.15. The trilemma of international finance.

SUMMARY

1. Floating exchange rates were defined as resulting from the interplay of supply of and demand for foreign exchange. If left to itself, however, such a system may lead to wide oscillations of exchange rates over relatively short periods ("clean" float).

2. To prevent such erratic trends in exchange rates from developing over time, the foreign exchange market is carefully monitored through the intervention of central banks ("dirty" float).

3. In a managed floating exchange rate system, the strategy of central banks may range from simply *smoothing out* short-run fluctuations without resisting the fundamental trend in the exchange rate to *leaning against the wind* (that is, delaying a given trend without actually resisting it) and to a strategy of *unofficial pegging* that consists of maintaining exchange rates at an artificial level through large-scale central bank intervention.

4. The currency forecaster needs to be well aware of the degree of distortion introduced in the interaction of market forces by central bank intervention. This information, however, is not generally publicly available to private foreign exchange market participants but can be traced on an *ex post* basis from variations in the level of central banks' foreign exchange reserves.

5. In a system of stabilized exchange rates, the central bank is contractually committed to maintaining the prevailing exchange rate within a narrow, publicly defined band of fluctuations. Clearly, uncertainty about future spot exchange rates is, barring a major devaluation or revaluation, the reason this system is often referred to as a system of "pegged yet adjustable" exchange rates, bounded from the standpoint of market participants.

6. Under a system of controlled exchange rates, the central bank supersedes the marketplace by becoming the sole buyer and seller of foreign exchange. The rate at which transactions take place is no longer determined by the interaction of supply and demand forces; rather, it is the end product of bureaucratic decisions. Furthermore, buying and selling rates are not necessarily identical, nor are selling and buying rates uniform across all foreign exchange earnings or payments-generating transactions.

QUESTIONS FOR DISCUSSION

1. What is the difference between a "clean" float and a "dirty" float?
2. Why do countries intervene in their foreign exchange markets?
3. What is the difference between currency convertibility and exchange rate flexibility?
4. Explain how central bank intervention allows a country to keep its forex rate at a certain level.
5. What is the difference between central bank intervention in the foreign exchange market in the context of floating versus stabilized exchange rates?
6. How would you contrast a controlled exchange rate with a stabilized exchange rate?
7. What does the explosive growth in China's reserves tell you about the nature of its exchange rate regime?
8. The last time the US Federal Reserve Bank intervened in the forex market was in 1995. Would you expect the US foreign exchange reserves to have increased or decreased over the past 18 years?
9. Why are ACUs such as the SDR often used for denominating international trade and finance contracts?
10. What is the difference between controlled exchange rates and stabilized exchange rates?
11. Why do many developing countries maintain controlled exchange rates at overvalued exchange rates?
12. What is the difference between a system of multiple exchange rates and the imposition of different tariff rates on imports?

PROBLEMS

1. **When the Swiss franc appreciates (beginner).** Over the past 5 years the Swiss franc (CHF) appreciated from CHF 1 = US\$0.8215 to peak at CHF 1 = US\$1.0697.
   a. Calculate the percentage appreciation of the Swiss franc at its peak (use a US dollar perspective).
   b. What is the percentage depreciation suffered by the US dollar over the same period? Is it simply minus (−) the rate of appreciation of the Swiss franc?

2. **When the Bangladeshi taka depreciates (beginner).** The central bank of Bangladesh is contemplating a devaluation of its currency — the taka (BDT) — from BDT 69 to BDT 100 = US$1:
   a. What would be the percentage depreciation of the taka? Is it the same as the percentage revaluation of the US dollar? Why or why not?
   b. The devaluation would be accompanied by a relaxation of exchange controls and a modicum of flexibility. The taka would be allowed to fluctuate as a result of limited forex trading within a band of +/−2.25% around the new par value of BDT 100 = US$1. What would be floor and ceiling exchange rates?

3. **The Malaysian ringgit peg to the US dollar (intermediate).** Malaysia pegs its currency, the Malaysian ringgit (MYR), to the US dollar. The par value is MYR 4 = US$1.
   a. What is the par value priced in US$ terms for MYR 1?
   b. Bank Negara decides to widen the tunnel of allowed fluctuations authorized to +/−7.50% around its par value. What are the new ceiling and floor exchange rates?
   c. Assume that the MYR revalues by 15% against the US$. What is the new par value? What are the new ceiling and floor exchange rates?

4. **The Hong Kong currency board in the shadow of the rising yuan (intermediate).** Since 1983, the Hong Kong dollar (HK$) is via a currency board pegged to the US dollar at the rate of HK$7.80 = US$1. Since 2005 the Chinese yuan (CNY) has appreciated from CNY 8.28 to CNY 6.23:
   a. What was the exchange rate between the Hong Kong dollar and the Chinese yuan in 2005? What is it today?
   b. Has the Hong Kong dollar appreciated/depreciated against the Chinese yuan over the period 2005–2012? Is this a favorable development for Hong Kong?

5. **Daily forex rates fixing by the Central Bank of South Korea (advanced).** The Central Bank of South Korea announces every business day at 9:00 A.M. a fixed rate at which it will buy or sell US dollars for won (KRW) throughout the trading day. No such commitments are made, however, against other major trading currencies.

   On August 9, 1990, the following rates were set at 9:00 A.M.: US$1 = KRW 715. Quotes for the cross-rate US$/¥ indicated 150. Thirty minutes later, the Japanese yen had appreciated to ¥148 for US$1.
   a. Explain how the treasurer of Samsung, one of the leading South Korean industrial conglomerates, could profit from the new situation at 9:30 A.M.
   b. As the central banker of South Korea, explain how you could prevent such arbitrage profits — short of imposing controls on foreign exchange dealings.
   c. Assuming that the central bank buying and selling rates are respectively 714 and 716 and that bid-ask rates on US$ versus ¥ are 148.20 and 147.30, what would be your answer to question 5a?

6. **Advance deposit schemes and effective exchange rates.** Over the years, a number of developing countries have maintained an advance deposit scheme for imports. Such systems typically require importers to deposit with the central bank a percentage of the face value, in local currency, of the contemplated import transaction, even though the foreign exchange has not been released, nor has the import been delivered. Characteristically, the percentage of the face value of the import will be linked to some import classification list established at the discretion of the central bank and should reflect the relative degree of essentialness of the product to be imported.

   Consider the case of Pakistan, whose currency, the Pakistani rupee (PKR), is pegged to the US dollar at PKR 95.16 = US$1. The Pakistan central bank defines an import classification list, to which it associates an advance deposit rate.

Import category	Advance deposit rate (%)
Preferential (food products and pharmaceuticals)	25
Semi-preferential (irrigation and agricultural implements)	50
Essential	75
Non-essential	100
Luxury	125

Assuming that the opportunity cost of funds for a Pakistani importer is 15% and that the average length of an advance deposit is

270 days, explain why our Pakistani importer is de facto transacting through a multiple exchange rate system, and compute the effective multiple exchange rates.

7. **SDRs (intermediate).** Referring to equation 2.3 in the chapter, what was on March 1 2024 the weight of the Pound sterling in the value of the SDR? Would you expect that it has changed since? How do you explain it?

8. **Telmex dual listing and the Mexican peso devaluation (intermediate).** Shares of Telefonos Mexicanos (Telmex) listed on the New York Stock Exchange fell from $60 to $48 when the Mexican peso (MXN) was devalued on December 19, 1994, from MXN 3.44 = US$1 to MXN 6.05 = US$1.
   a. Compute the percentage depreciation of the Mexican peso.
   b. As a trader for Barings Securities specializing in Mexican stocks, do you see profit opportunities? What are the risks involved?

9. **A single currency for a global economy (advanced).** The daily turnover in the foreign exchange market approaches $4 trillion or a yearly turnover of $1,000 trillion (with 252 working days in a given year). Assuming a bid-ask spread of 5 basis points (the difference at which currencies are bought or sold), what would be the annual savings of abolishing national currencies? What would be the costs of doing away with national currencies? Would you advocate a single world currency for an increasingly globalized world economy?

INTERNET EXERCISES

1. **Special Drawing Rights (SDRs) (elementary):** Visit the IMF website at www.imf.org and research the currency composition of the IMF's ACU. Explain the logic behind the currency composition of SDRs.

2. **Valuing Special Drawing Rights (SDRs) (intermediate):** Using the findings of the previous problem, visit the website of Yahoo! Finance at www.yahoofinance.com
   a. value in US dollar terms one SDR at today's exchange rate.
   b. What is the weight accounted by the Japanese yen in the total value of one SDR? Is this weight constant over time? Why or why not?

3. **Denmark's currency regime (intermediate):** Visit http://fx.sauder.ubc.ca/data.html to sketch the exchange rate of the Danish krone against the euro over the period 1999–2018. How would you characterize the exchange rate arrangement between Denmark and the euro-zone? What is Denmark's central bank foreign exchange policy?

4. **Special Drawing Rights (SDRs) and the Renminbi (advanced):** On October 1, 2016, the International Monetary Fund revised the composition of the SDRs by adding the Chinese Renminbi (RMB).
   a. Why did the IMF add the RMB to the SDR? How was the number of RMBs determined by the IMF?
   b. What is the weight of the RMB in the SDR today? Has it increased/decreased since October 1, 2016?
   c. What is today's weight of the euro in the SDR? What was it on July 1, 2016? Why has it decreased? Can you think of an exchange rate scenario for the Renminbi under which the euro would regain the same weight it had on July 1, 2016?

REFERENCES

Aliber, R.t Z. 2011. *The New International Money Game*. 7th edition. Palgrave-Macmillan.

Bhaghwati, J. N. 1978. *Anatomy and Consequences of Exchange Control Regimes*. New York: National Bureau of Economic Research, Ballinger.

Collins, S. M. 1988. "Multiple exchange rates, capital controls, and commercial policy. In *The Open Economy: Tools for Policy Makers in Developing Countries* (Chapter 7), edited by R. Dornbusch and F. L. Helmers. London: Oxford University Press and World Bank.

Copeland, L. S. 2005. *Exchange Rates and International Finance*, 4th edition. Upper Saddle River, NJ: Prentice Hall.

Dominguez, K. M. 2006. "Why do central bank interventions influence intra-daily and longer-term exchange rate movements?" *Journal of International Money and Finance* 25:1051–1071.

Dominguez, K. M. and Frankel, J. 1993. *Does Foreign Exchange Intervention Work?* Washington, DC: Institute for International Economics.

Lanyi, A. 1975. "Separate exchange markets of capital and current transactions." *International Monetary Fund Staff Papers* 22(November):714–750.

Mayer, H. W. 1974. The anatomy of official exchange rate intervention systems. *Essays in International Finance* (Vol. 104). Princeton, NJ: Princeton University, International Finance Section.

Obstfeld, M. and Taylor, A. M. 2017. "International monetary relations: Taking finance seriously." *Journal of Economic Perspectives*, 31(3):3–28.

Root, F. R. 1994. *International Trade and Investment*, 7th edition. Cincinnati, OH: South Western Publishing.

Taylor, A. and Taylor, M. 2004. The purchasing power parity debate. *Journal of Economic Perspectives* 18:135–158.

Taylor, D. 1982. "Official intervention in the foreign exchange market, or, bet against the central bank." *Journal of Political Economy* 90(April):356–368.

Tosini, P. A. 1977. Leaning against the wind: A standard for managed floating. *Essays in International Finance* (Vol. 126). Princeton, NJ: Princeton University, International Finance Section.

Walter, I. 1985. *Secret Money*. Lexington, MA: D.C. Heath.

APPENDIX 2A: VALUATION OF ARTIFICIAL CURRENCY UNITS

ACUs such as SDRs or ECUs are baskets or portfolios of currencies whose composition are fixed. Similarly to valuing a stock portfolio, *ACUs* are valued as the sum of the values of fixed amounts (a_i) of each component currency i in the portfolio. As an illustration, the Icelandic krona (ISK) — currency of Iceland — could hypothetically be defined as pegged one-to-one to a fictitious ACU called the Atlantica. Let's define one Atlantica as comprised of US$ (1.00), € (0.50), and £ (0.20). Assuming that the dollar price of one euro is $S_{\$,€}(t) = 1.40$ and the dollar price of one pound is $S_{\$,£}(t) = 1.50$, the dollar value of one Atlantica would be given by the simple summation:

Dollar value of one Atlantica:

$$\sum_i a_i S_{\$,i}(t) = a_\$ S_{\$,\$}(t) + a_€ S_{\$,€}(t) + a_£ S_{\$,£}(t) \quad (2.3a)$$

$$\sum_i a_i S_{\$,i}(t) = 1.00 \times 1 + 0.50 \times 1.40 + 0.20 \times 1.50 = 2$$

$$\sum_i a_i S_{\$,i}(t) = 2 \quad (2.3b)$$

where i denotes US$, €, or £ and $S_{\$,i}(t)$ is the dollar spot price of one unit of currency i at time t.

Alternatively, the Atlantica could be shown to be worth €1.43 or £1.33. Under such a valuation scheme, the weight $w_i(t)$ accounted for by each component currency in the total value[8] of the Atlantica will vary as the value of each component currency fluctuates:

$$w_i(t) = \frac{a_i S_{\$,i}(t)}{\sum_i a_i S_{\$,i}(t)} \quad (2.4)$$

8 The currency composition of the Atlantica though will remain unchanged.

For example, in formula (2.4), the respective weight of each component currency was, at time t,

$$w_\$(t) = 50\%;\ w_€(t) = 35\%;\ \text{and } w_£(t) = 15\%$$

If, at time t^*, the dollar were to depreciate by 100% to $S_{\$,€}(t^*) = 2.80$ and $S_{\$,£}(t^*) = 3.00$, the dollar value of one Atlantica would only appreciate by 50% to:

Dollar value of one Atlantica = (1.00)1.00 + (0.50)2.80 + (0.20)3.00 = 3.00

As a result, the Atlantica's value has moved in response to market events, but the movement is considerably less than that of any of the component currencies. Similarly, the respective weights of the component currencies will adjust to their respective values. Thus, the weight of the dollar will decline to 33% from 50%.

$$w_\$(t*) = \frac{1.00\times1.00}{1.00\times1.00+0.50\times2.80+0.20\times3.00}$$
$$w_\$(t*) = 33\% \quad (2.5)$$

Conversely, by applying formula (2.4), the respective weight of the euro and the pound sterling would increase to $w_€(t^*) = 47\%$ and $w_£(t^*) = 20\%$.

Currency portfolio diversification

The dollar value of one Atlantica is shown in Exhibit 2.16 to have been considerably more stable than any of the component currency values in dollar terms. Quite clearly, the portfolio diversification effect of the basket of currencies resulted

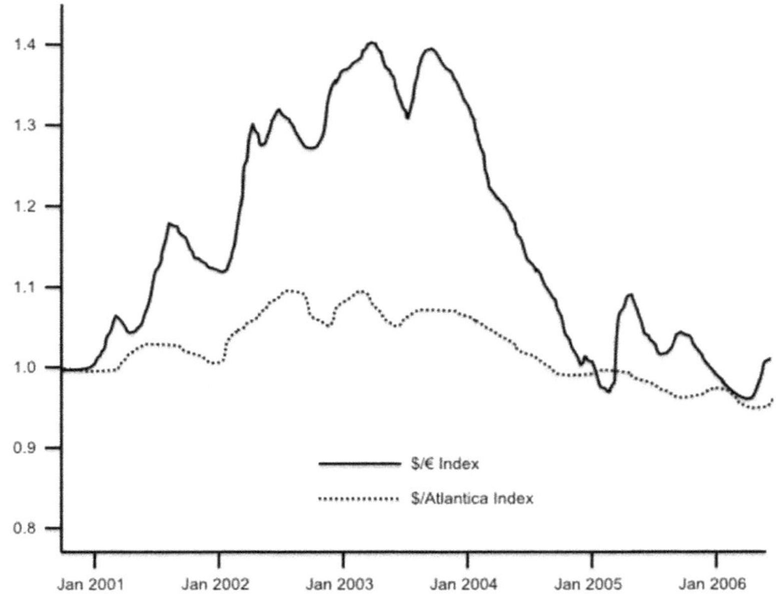

Exhibit 2.16. Artificial currency unit: Atlantica versus euro.

in a considerably more stable overall value of the Atlantica than any of the basket's component currencies. This is similar to what would be true of a portfolio of stocks held by a private investor. Exhibit 2.16 re-creates the path of the Atlantica over the period 2001–2006. Note the small range of 0.92–1.10 within which the Atlantica index moved, whereas the euro index fluctuated within a range of 0.95–1.40.

3

Yesterday and Yesteryear: A Brief History of the International Monetary System

The time has come,
The Walrus said,
To talk of all this ken:
Of pounds, and euros and dollar bills
Of renminbi and yen,
And how the winds have told me,
Let's all float, amen.
— Robert L. Bartley

On May 2, 2010, the euro-zone governments and the International Monetary Fund (IMF) announced a €110 billion rescue plan for beleaguered Greece. The country was mired in sluggish growth, a budget deficit at 13% of gross domestic product (GDP), and public debt-to-GDP ratio approaching 150%. The Greek government was forced to commit to drastic budget reductions in order to avoid bankruptcy. Would and could the Greek government impose so much pain on its citizens in order to remain in the euro-zone and keep the European Monetary Union intact? Would the austerity package only make matters worse and condemn Greece to endless recession? Theoretically, devaluation was not an option since Greece had been an integral part of the European Monetary Union since 2002! Or should Greece simply exit the euro and resurrect a devalued drachma in order to revive economic growth — ultimately perhaps the only (but painful) remedy to balance its budget by stimulating revenues? Crises such as the 2010 Greek near default are rooted in a long history of trial and error as countries attempt to adopt the optimal exchange rate regime. This chapter, by presenting a brief history of the international monetary system, will allow the reader to better understand the genesis of ongoing currency crises and therefore better anticipate changes in the rules of currency trading that are themselves so central to sound international financial management.

After reading this chapter you will understand:

- How the gold standard (1878–1914) was the first system of fixed exchange rates.
- How the Bretton Woods system (1944–1971) established "pegged yet adjustable" exchange rates enabling economies devastated by World War II to rebuild.
- How lax foreign exchange controls undermined the Bretton Woods system and eventually contributed to its collapse in 1971.
- The trials and tribulations of industrialized countries such as the United Kingdom, Japan, and Germany experiencing floating exchange rates in the aftermath of the Bretton Woods system's collapse.
- Why the Asian financial crisis of 1997 led to the dismantling of currency pegs against the US dollar.
- How the European Union in 1999 launched its single currency — the euro — and why its architecture is unstable.
- The roots of the euro crisis which lingers since 2010.
- What the current map of exchange rate arrangements looks like and how it is likely to evolve over time.

CHRONOLOGY OF THE INTERNATIONAL MONETARY SYSTEM

What began in the aftermath of World War II as an orderly international monetary system under the charter of the Bretton Woods system morphed into a complex and hybrid composite system continuously evolving with each country in constant search of the optimal currency regime in which to trade its currency.

As a guide to this brief history of the international monetary system, Exhibit 3.1 maps the path that the United States, Japan, India, and China each charted for trading their currency. The top row of Exhibit 3.1 is the time line of critical dates in the evolution of the international monetary system since World War II; the left column is organized according to declining degrees of exchange rate flexibility and increasing levels of exchange controls according to the general classification of the exchange rate system introduced in the previous chapter. Thus the matrix proposed in Exhibit 3.1 allows us to map the positioning of a given country's exchange rate regime according to time and the institutional arrangement it chose to trade its currency: For example, from 1945 to 1971 the Japanese yen (¥) was a stabilized exchange rate currency tightly pegged to the US dollar at ¥360 = $1; since the breakdown of the Bretton Woods system, the Japanese currency has been floating against all other currencies. The float, however, has been of the "dirty" kind for most of the past 50 years, with heavy bouts of intervention by the Bank of Japan to slow the relentless rise of the yen. We next highlight the chronology of the international monetary system:

1821: Great Britain is the first nation to formally declare full convertibility of its banknotes into gold at the *"mint" parity* of £4.2474 per troy ounce of gold.

1834: The United States formally defines the dollar as 480 fine grains per troy ounce, or US$20.67 per troy ounce, and preserves it until 1933. It formally adopts the gold standard in 1878.

1878–1914: Most industrial countries' currencies are on the *gold standard* — a de facto international monetary system of fixed exchange rates. The world economy experiences a period of unbridled prosperity — the first era of globalization.

1914: With the *outbreak of World War I*, belligerent countries suspend the gold standard. Governments print money to finance their war efforts.

1925–1931: Major industrial powers attempt to *reenact the gold standard* by repegging their currencies to gold.

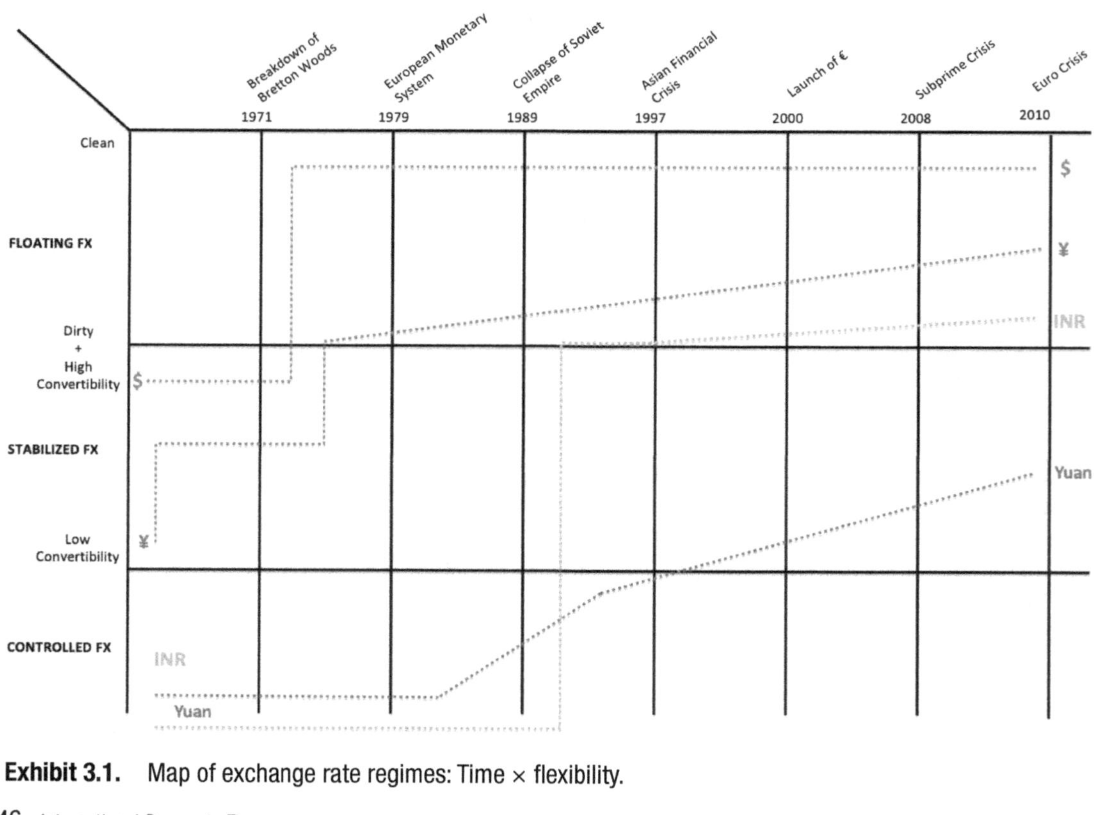

Exhibit 3.1. Map of exchange rate regimes: Time × flexibility.

1929–1938: The *Great Depression* plays havoc with the world economy, pushing most countries to protectionism and competitive devaluations.

1944: The *Bretton Woods Accord* establishes "pegged yet adjustable" exchange rates anchored around publicly defined par values, which are defined in terms of gold. The US dollar is convertible into gold at the par value of $35 = 1 ounce. A modicum of flexibility, however, is allowed as exchange rates are permitted to fluctuate within a narrow band of +/−0.75% around their par values. Central banks closely monitor exchange rate fluctuations and intervene when necessary to maintain exchange rates within these narrow bands.

1958: First-world countries start to dismantle exchange controls on current account transactions but continue to restrict financial account transactions. The foreign exchange market for the currencies of major industrialized nations takes off.

1971: The *Smithsonian Agreement* suspends the unconditional convertibility of US dollars into gold The US dollar is devalued against most Organization for Economic Co-operation and Development (OECD) currencies, and the permitted bands of exchange rate fluctuations are widened to +/−2.25% from +/−0.75% under Bretton Woods.

1973: The *Bretton Woods system* collapses because of much increased capital mobility and many countries abandon pegged exchange rates. Most of the first world's currencies trade within floating exchange rate regimes. The US Federal Reserve Bank adopts a passive policy, letting other central banks intervene in the foreign exchange market as they see fit.

1979: The European Community's 12 member countries launch the European Monetary System (EMS), anchored to a newly created European currency unit (ECU). De facto, a Europe-wide system of pegged exchange rates à la Bretton Woods is reenacted.

1982: During the *Latin American sovereign debt crisis*, Mexico, Brazil, and Argentina default on their sovereign debt obligations in excess of $100 billion.

1985–1987: *The Plaza and Louvre Accords* call for greater coordination among G-5 countries in intervening in the foreign exchange market. Responsibility for such intervention should be shared among the United States and other countries. Gross overvaluation of the US dollar is corrected.

1989: *Collapse of the Soviet Union.* Newly emancipated East European satellite countries scrap government-controlled inconvertible currency regimes and adopt market-based systems to trade their currencies.

1992: *EMS crisis.* The pound sterling and Italian lira are forced to devalue and exit the EMS. Remaining EMS currencies now float within a +/−15% band around their respective cross-par values (instead of +/−2.25%). EMS is shipwrecked!

1997: *Asian financial crisis.* East and Southeast Asian currencies are engulfed in a domino-like currency crisis. Thailand, Malaysia, Indonesia, the Philippines, and South Korea are forced to abandon overvalued exchange rates pegged to the US dollar and adopt a tightly managed float.

1999: *Launch of the euro* — the European Union single currency. Eleven countries join the euro-zone, adopting the euro as their official currency (and therefore burying their national currencies). Britain, Denmark, and Sweden opt out of the euro-zone and decide to retain their own currencies.

2002: *Argentina abandons its currency board.* Facing a deep economic recession on January 8, 2002, Argentina unpegs its currency from the US dollar; the peso, free to float, promptly loses more than 50% of its value.

2005: *China abandons a dollar peg for a tightly managed float.* The yuan revalues by 21% over 2005–2008 before being repegged to the US dollar in July 2008 to better weather the global subprime crisis.

2010–: Euro-land is shaken by speculative runs on the sovereign debt of Portugal, Ireland, Italy, Greece, and Spain (the PIIGS nations). Greece in particular seems to be on the verge of default before a €110 billion rescue package is engineered by the European Central Bank and the IMF. Yields on PIIGS's treasury bonds continue to escalate, compounding the difficulty of servicing their debt burdens. As of late fall 2011, core eurozone countries such as France and the Netherlands have become contaminated by the crisis. The *euro avoids break-up* but its future remains in doubt during the decade of the 2010s as the crisis lingers on against a backdrop of austerity-induced sluggish economic growth.

Before we embark on a more detailed discussion of each phase in the history of the international monetary system, let's propose a broad-brush generalization: The international monetary system is marching toward more exchange rate flexibility and laxer exchange controls.

The reader will notice in Exhibit 3.1 the crowding in the pegged/controlled exchange rates cell during the Bretton Woods period (1944–1971), whereas in the 2000s the managed floats cell seems to be the exchange rate regime of choice. The pace of this mostly irreversible process varies widely across countries due to their unique economic circumstances and certainly does not rule out some nations swimming across the current. Less developed countries are clearly the laggards in this process, as many are still mired in economic turmoil and latch onto tight exchange controls in an effort to mask their acute scarcity in convertible foreign exchange.

THE GOLD STANDARD (1878–1914, 1925–1931)

Since time immemorial, various physical commodities such as salt, bronze, silver, and gold have served as a means of exchange facilitating commerce beyond barter trade. Perhaps because of its magic glow and unique physical attributes,[1] gold progressively imposed itself as the store of wealth and the *numéraire* of choice.[2] In 1821, Great Britain was the first nation to formally declare full convertibility of its pound sterling (£) banknotes into gold at the "mint" parity of £4.2474 per troy ounce of gold, but it was not until 1878 that virtually all major industrialized countries adopted the gold standard by pegging their currency to gold. The gold standard was a system of de facto *fixed exchange rates* whereby monetary authorities stood ready at all times to buy or sell gold in unlimited quantities at the rate set by the mint parity to maintain that price (unlimited convertibility).[3] It also required monetary authorities to permit the free, unlimited export and import of gold at a rate fixed by the mint parity. The gold standard provided the world economy with a stable payments system, which fueled the first era of globalization with increasingly large flows of goods, capital, and people between countries.

The gold standard prevailed informally from 1878 to 1914 but was never officially sanctioned by an international treaty. Member countries unilaterally decided to follow the rules of the game. Gold standard currencies held a fixed relationship to each other because they all held a fixed relationship to gold. This meant that at any time one currency could be exchanged for another currency in exact proportion to its gold value. For example, if one ounce of gold was worth 4.2474 pounds in the United Kingdom and 20.67 dollars in the United States, the exchange rate was:

$$\frac{20.67}{4.2474} = \text{US\$}4.8665 / \pounds 1$$

Gold was used to settle international transactions, thereby keeping the international payments system in equilibrium. Under the gold standard, a country incurring a deficit in its balance of payments — that is, the net of all flows linked to either trade (payments of imports and exports) or capital flows (borrowing and lending abroad) — would experience an outflow of gold and a reduction in domestic reserves; this was equivalent to a reduction in the domestic money supply, since the gold stock of a country was in effect its real money supply. As a country's money supply shrank, prices of goods had to decline and interest rates had to rise. [4] In turn, this adjustment made domestic goods more competitive internationally. Similarly, higher interest rates attracted foreign capital. Both phenomena served to replenish the country's national gold reserves, thereby ensuring an automatic adjustment in the country's balance of payments. Inflation was basically absent, and indeed from 1878 to 1914 the world economy enjoyed a period of unprecedented growth, which left a number of nostalgic economists and policy makers with an idealized view of the gold standard as a smooth and automatic adjustment process to the world economy.

One problem, however, with this gold standard system was that the world money supply could grow only at the rate of new gold mining. Thus, the well-being of the world economy was held hostage to the discovery of new gold mines! In fact the idea of mining gold in countries such as faraway South Africa or Russia at great human cost, refining it before shipping

1 Gold is durable, it is homogenous, and it has a relatively high value compared to weight, which makes transportation economical.

2 Prior to the 1870s, many countries used both silver and gold concurrently, with coins minted in both metals — so-called bimetallism. Silver was, however, the dominant money through medieval times and well into the 19th century.

3 This required monetary authorities to hold reserves of gold to meet any fluctuations in demand. In practice, many countries also kept reserves in pound sterling because they knew that it was freely convertible into gold.

4 The important assumption of downwardly flexible prices and wages was more realistic in the pre-1914 period than it would be today with differentially branded products, unionized labor, or minimum wage laws.

it to the other side of the world to bury it again in the vault of Fort Knox under costly surveillance to deter the attacks of the likes of "Goldfinger" seems to be an economic aberration! Indeed, the economic growth rate in the early 1900s greatly outpaced the physical growth in gold reserves. Another major problem was that national economic policies were totally subordinated to the necessity of keeping the fixed exchange rate fixed. A country could not have its own independent monetary policy. As long as exchange rates remained fixed, any sudden disequilibrium in the balance of payments would lead to severe shocks in domestic economies.

With the 19th-century industrial revolution, the gold standard system became too rigid, and it was suspended during World War I when belligerent nations were forced to print massive amounts of money to bankroll their war efforts. The gold standard was revived briefly between 1925 and 1931 when major industrialized nations repegged their currencies to gold at par values that all too often overvalued their currencies. Faced with the ravages of the Great Depression, in 1931 the United Kingdom had to devalue its currency against gold and so did the United States in 1933. This ushered the world economy into an era of protectionism and competitive devaluations — so-called "beggar thy neighbor" devaluations — whereby countries desperately attempted to extricate themselves from the Great Depression by making their exports cheaper on world markets.

THE BRETTON WOODS SYSTEM (1944–1971)

As World War II was drawing to a close, the Allied powers met at Bretton Woods, New Hampshire (United States), in the summer of 1944 (July 1–22) to lay the groundwork for the reconstruction of the world economy. The overarching goal of the conference was to establish a global monetary and financial system that would guarantee the stability and ensure the orderly functioning of the world economy. The economic devastation of the Great Depression, which had played havoc with international trade and investment through competitive "beggar thy neighbor" devaluations and protectionism, was to be avoided at all costs.

The Bretton Woods conference established two new supranational agencies — the IMF and the International Bank for Reconstruction and Development (also known as the World Bank) — to implement its blueprint for the world economy. The IMF was charged with ensuring international monetary stability by overseeing its member countries' exchange rate policies. Today it advises its members on sound monetary and fiscal policies and often acts as a lender of last resort for members experiencing severe balance-of-payments difficulties (see International Corporate Finance in Practice 3.1). It is funded by taxpayers' money from each member country. The World Bank was to provide major funding to countries devastated by the war so that they

INTERNATIONAL CORPORATE FINANCE IN PRACTICE 3.1

Don't Cry for Me Argentina: The IMF Agrees to Beef up Argentina's Bail out

The Argentine economy is unravelling. Caving in under the weight of its twin deficits — on its government budget and balance-of-payments' current account — the peso lost more than half its value in the first nine months of 2018 pushing inflation to 34%. Its central bank raised interest rates to 60% to stem the capital flight. True to its mission the IMF agreed to come to the rescue of Argentina by committing to a jumbo bail-out plan of $ 57 billion — the largest ever in the Fund history. With $36 billion to be disbursed by the end of 2019 Argentina should be able to meet its external financial commitments estimated at $28 billion. In return Argentina has agreed to eliminate its primary budget deficit by the end of 2019 — a year earlier than initially pledged — by imposing a tax on exports and cutting subsidies on public transport and electricity. It also committed to a new exchange rate regime whereby the central bank would intervene in the forex market only when the peso escapes from a wider band of 34 to 44 peso to the US dollar, limiting intervention at no more than $150 million per day and allowing the band to depreciate by 3% per month. Under guidance (and pressure) from the IMF the center-right government of President Macri had chosen fiscal austerity and financial orthodoxy over spending profligacy. The verdict is still out as to whether this new lease on life will allow the Argentine economy to regain its footing before social mayhem is unleashed … Adapted from *The Economist* (2018, p. 71).

could rebuild their infrastructures. It now focuses primarily on less developed countries. Like any bank, it funds itself by issuing bonds on major capital markets.

Pegged exchange rates

Not surprisingly, the Bretton Woods Accord called for pegged or fixed exchange rates, with each national currency value defined in terms of gold, also known as *par value*. The US dollar was, in turn, the only currency convertible into gold at a fixed price of $35 per ounce. In effect, by defining its currency in terms of gold, each country was also defining the value of its national currency in terms of the US dollar. For example, West Germany defined the Deutsche mark (DM) as 1/140 ounce of gold, which amounted to $35 × 1/140 = $0.25. The Bretton Woods order became known as the *gold exchange standard*. As illustrated in Exhibit 3.2, the Bretton Woods system architecture was anchored to the dollar-gold convertible par value while allowing a modicum of flexibility, as all signatory countries would maintain their exchange rates within a ¾ of 1% margin on either side of their currency's par value against the US dollar. In theory, this provided the international economy with lasting stability. Nondollar currencies, of course, could always devalue their par values against the US dollar to restore their national economic competitiveness and resolve fundamental balance-of-payments disequilibrium (which could not otherwise be dealt with by domestic fiscal and monetary policy).

Such adjustments were not as few and far between as originally envisioned: Over the period 1946–1971 only the United States and Japan did not change the par value of their currencies. Out of the leading 21 industrialized countries, 12 of them experienced devaluations in excess of 30%, while four countries revalued their currencies and another four abandoned fixed par values to allow their currencies to float independently (see International Corporate Finance in Practice 3.2).

Exchange controls

To better comprehend how such a system of quasi-fixed exchanges rates could survive relatively unscathed for nearly a quarter century, it is important to remember that most countries throughout that period maintained very tight controls on all financial account transactions such as international short-term borrowing, foreign direct investment, or international portfolio investment. Meanwhile, current account transactions were being slowly decontrolled (see International Corporate Finance in Practice 3.3). It was thus relatively easy for each country's central bank to keep the price of its currency stable as long as it would disburse foreign exchange roughly in balance with its foreign exchange earnings. However, the foreign exchange market was slowly rising from the ashes of World

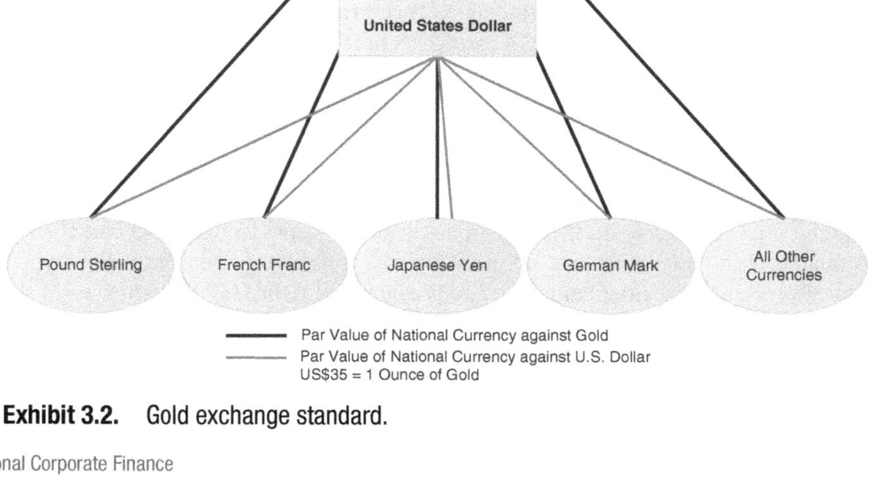

Exhibit 3.2. Gold exchange standard.

INTERNATIONAL CORPORATE FINANCE IN PRACTICE 3.2

How Did Central Banks Peg the Exchange Rate?

The Bretton Woods system was squarely associated with fixed exchange rates, but it did allow for a modicum of foreign exchange rate flexibility around each currency's par value. Referring to the dollar-sterling exchange rate relationship, this is how it worked: The Bank of England would set a floor for the price of its currency at −0.75% of the par value — that is, $2.80 × (1 − 0.0075) = $2.78. Whenever the spot price determined by the interplay between supply and demand forces would fall below 2.78, the Bank of England would immediately step into the market and buy as many pounds as necessary to bring it back above the floor rate; this is also known as central bank intervention, and it can be carried out as long as the central bank has sufficient foreign exchange reserves available. Conversely, the Bank of England would set a ceiling at +0.75% above the par value — or $2.80 × (1 + 0.0075) = $2.82 — at which it would sell sterling to bring its price back below the ceiling of $2.82 should market forces push the spot price above it.

Both floor and ceiling exchange rates were publicly defined, as was the par value of the currency: In effect the central bank would act as a guarantor of exchange rate stability. For all practical purposes, spot (currency purchase or sale for immediate delivery) forex transactions would be carried out between $2.78 and $2.82 — the Bank of England would make sure of it; in a way the Bank of England provided all participants in the foreign exchange market with insurance against price risk that was free of charge (Exhibit 3.3 illustrates the tunnel within which the exchange rate fluctuated over the period 1964–1965).

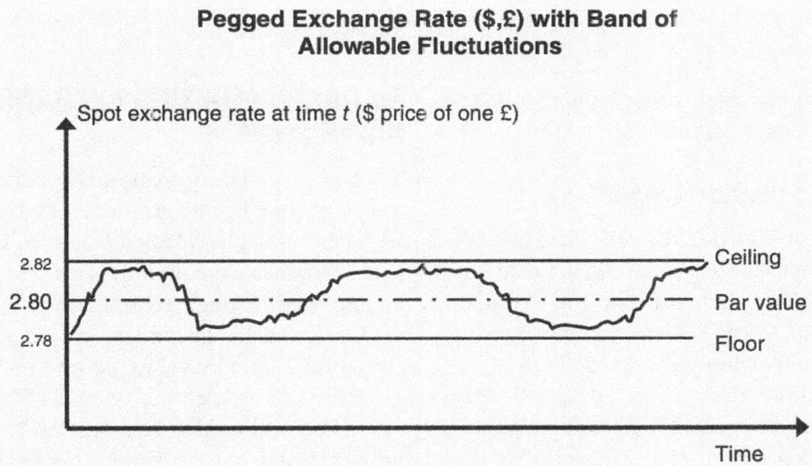

Exhibit 3.3. The gold exchange standard under the Bretton Woods System, 1944–1971.

War II but operated within the confines of tight controls — at least until 1958 when many industrialized countries freed up trade-related foreign exchange transactions.[5] As the foreign exchange market started to displace central banks as the principal conduit through which currency transactions were carried out, exchange rates would increasingly be determined as the result of the free interplay between supply and demand for dollars: There was no guarantee that the resulting equilibrium exchange rate would be close to the official par value. In response to this growing gap, central banks started to play a critical role in stabilizing exchange rates at

5 Even today China's tight pegging of its currency to the US dollar is secured by exchange controls. It largely explain why China sailed largely unscathed through the 1997 Asian financial crisis and the 2008 global subprime crisis.

INTERNATIONAL CORPORATE FINANCE IN PRACTICE 3.3

What Are Foreign Exchange Controls?

After World War II most countries' economies were devastated and needed to import food, machinery, and fuel to revive their fortunes. Most imports had to be procured from the USA and be paid in US dollars — the hard currency that every country needed and did not have. All countries enacted tight restrictions in order to allocate scarce dollars to the best of their ability. Under such circumstances, firms and individuals could not buy (or sell) foreign currencies freely. They were forced to apply formally to the central bank for whatever amount of foreign exchange they needed. Proper justification had to accompany the request — for example, a factory's assembly operation needs to import a conveyor belt to keep assembling irrigation pumps. A special department within the central bank would review the application and, depending on its merits, would authorize all or some of the required amount of foreign exchange to be released. All too often this administrative process turned into a political decision fraught with corruption. Authorization and actual availability of currency are two different things, and applicants may have to wait weeks or months before the foreign exchange is effectively released. Often the request has to be accompanied with a local currency deposit, which may not be remunerated. The exchange rate at which foreign currency is made available is determined by administrative fiat.

their prescribed par values through intervention in the foreign exchange market.

The demise of Bretton Woods

Unfortunately, continued US inflation and balance-of-payments deficits in the 1960s (due to the financing of the escalating Vietnam War and President Lyndon Johnson's Great Society social programs) resulted in an increasingly overvalued US dollar, which undermined the stability of the Bretton Woods system and eventually led to its demise in 1971. Confronted with a run on the dollar that was taking on crisis proportions, President Nixon suspended the convertibility of the US dollar into gold on August 15, 1971 — a decision that extended to all central banks. Briefly revived by the Smithsonian Agreement signed on December 17, 1971 — which established new par values and wider bands of 2.25% around them — the international monetary system of "pegged yet adjustable" exchange rates limped along until it was dealt a coup de grâce by the first oil shock in the fall of 1973. Indeed, the oil embargo and the quadrupling of the price of oil wreaked havoc on most OECD oil-importing countries which experienced severe balance-of-payments deficits that made pegged exchange rates regimes unsustainable. A new era of floating exchange rates began.

MANAGED FLOATING EXCHANGE RATES (1973–)

The new exchange rate regime allowed market forces to become the key determinant of currency values, with central banks taking a backseat. But now that exchange rates were no longer pegged, they had to be managed through central bank intervention in the foreign exchange market. Indeed, with so much riding on currency value, no one really expected governments to keep their hands off the exchange rate. If central banks' intervention could become heavy at times, it was no longer guided by an official obligation to defend a publicly known par value: The timing and magnitude of such interventions were now much more difficult to anticipate or gauge. Only *ex post* close monitoring of countries' foreign exchange reserves could reveal the extent of government intervention in the foreign exchange market. The IMF, which had played a central role in the orderly world of Bretton Woods, soon codified the new rules of the game by formulating guidelines in 1974 whereby central banks should:

- Intervene to avoid disorderly conditions in the foreign exchange market.
- Refrain from manipulating their exchange rates in order to gain an unfair advantage in international trade.

Although the US dollar was no longer convertible into gold at a fixed price, it remained the anchor currency of the new international monetary order and continued to be the preferred medium of exchange, store of value, and numéraire or currency of denomination for international trade, financing, and investment activities. Even so, the first decade of floating exchange rates proved somewhat chaotic, with the 1973 oil embargo and the quadrupling of oil prices in 1978 rocking the world economy. Considerable exchange rate volatility was marked by a sharp appreciation/overvaluation of the US dollar in the early 1980s, followed by a sharp drop after 1985. The Plaza Accord (1985) followed by the Louvre Accord (1987) among the Group of Five or G-5 (United States, Japan, United Kingdom, West Germany, and France) called for closer coordination among central banks to mitigate excessive volatility in the foreign exchange market. The United States, which had remained passive by not intervening in the foreign exchange market — a so-called policy of benign neglect — would now take a more active role by directly intervening in cooperation with foreign central banks to calm markets.

EUROPEAN MONETARY SYSTEM AND THE EUROPEAN CURRENCY UNIT (1979–1999)

The dream of building a unified Europe traces its roots back to the signing of the Treaty of Rome in 1958. France, Italy, Germany, Belgium, the Netherlands, and Luxembourg established a common market (also known as the European Community or EC) among themselves, which meant abolition of intra-EC trade barriers and erection of common external tariff barriers. To facilitate the functioning of the common market and encourage intra-EC trade and investment, exchange rate stability was deemed an integral part of deeper economic, financial, and political integration among EC member states. In the heyday of the Bretton Woods system (1944–1971), pegged exchange rates provided the necessary currency stability that made a monetary union a less urgent goal for the European project. The breakdown of the Bretton Woods system in 1971 and the subsequent chaotic experiment of generalized floating exchange rates revived the goal of an European Monetary Union (EMS). Launched on March 13, 1979, by the EC, the EMS aimed at reducing exchange rate variability and fostering monetary stability and economic convergence among its constituent members. In effect it resurrected on a Europe-wide basis the old Bretton Woods system of pegged exchange rates; the EMS called for closer monetary cooperation among EC countries, leading eventually to full monetary union — admittedly a lofty goal for Europe. A zone of European quasi-exchange rate fixity was to be achieved by establishing a two-pronged pegging system anchored to a newly created artificial currency unit called the European Currency Unit (ECU).

Grid of bilateral par values à la Bretton Woods

First, a parity grid, based initially on the definition of bilateral par values among the seven core EMS currencies, created a matrix of 21 tightly managed rates. Fluctuations were limited to +/−2.25% of central rates (Italy was allowed a wider band of +/−6%). Once a currency reached its bilateral limit against another member currency, the two national central banks involved were bound to intervene so as to prevent the exchange rate from escaping from the scheduled band of fluctuations. This was also known as the exchange rate mechanism (ERM).

The ECU and divergence indicators[6]

In addition to lower/upper intervention points, the EMS introduced an early warning system in the form of a divergence indicator for each currency from a fixed "central rate" against the European currency unit (ECU) (see International Corporate Finance in Practice 3.4 and Exhibit 3.4). The divergence indicator establishes a threshold for each EMS currency set at three-quarters of the maximum permissible difference between the currency's actual ECU rate and its central ECU rate. The maximum permissible rate will vary from currency to currency because of the relative weight accounted by each currency and will generally be within the +/−2.25% width of the parity grid. Thus, if the DM accounts for 40% of the value of the ECU at a given point in time, a 1% change in the value of the DM against ECU currencies will pull the ECU by 0.40%, whereas if the Greek drachma moves by 1%, it will barely affect the value of the ECU (it accounts for less than 2% of the value of the ECU). The divergence indicators are therefore adjusted so that each EMS currency reaches its threshold value after roughly the same degree of divergence from its central rate.

6 This section is technical and can be skipped without loss of continuity.

INTERNATIONAL CORPORATE FINANCE IN PRACTICE 3.4

What Is the ECU?

The ECU is an artificial currency unit or basket of currencies consisting of a fixed amount (number of units) of each of the 12 European community member currencies, as shown in column (1) of Exhibit 3.4; for example, in an ECU there were 1.332 French francs, 6.885 Spanish pesetas, and so forth. The ECU is named after a medieval French coin, the *écu*. The value of the ECU is computed by first determining the value of each component currency in the ECU — column (3) — and simply adding these values together — bottom of column (3). In the table, the ECU is valued in US dollars, but its valuation could be carried out in any currency, including the currencies that are part of the ECU. As of January 10, 1991, the ECU was worth US$1.3380. The weights accounted by each currency in the ECU reflected that country's relative importance in the EC and are computed by dividing the value of corresponding currency units — given in column (3) — by the total value of the ECU. The weights for any single currency should be fairly constant as long as each currency remains pegged to its par value and/or stays within its prescribed band of fluctuations. Should a given currency devalue or revalue *vis-à-vis* the other constituent currencies, its weight will decrease or increase. Interestingly, in addition to being used as a unit of account or numéraire for settling transactions among the EC's central banks, the ECU was used by private-sector firms for invoicing trade contracts or denominating bonds issues.

Exhibit 3.4. What is an ECU, and how much is it worth in dollars as of January 10, 1991?

Currency	Amount of each currency in one ECU (1)	Exchange rate of the currency in dollars (2)	Value of the currency *i*'s ECU component in dollars (3) = (1) × (2)	Weight of each currency in the ECU (4)
German mark (DM)	0.6242	0.6607	0.4127	30.8
French franc (FF)	1.332	0.1942	0.2587	19.3
British pound (£)	0.08784	1.90250	0.1671	12.5
Italian lira (IL)	151.8	0.000877	0.1331	9.9
Dutch guilder (DG)	0.2198	0.5848	0.1285	9.6
Belgian franc (BF)	3.301	0.032	0.1056	7.9
Luxembourg franc (LF)	0.130	0.0167	0.0021	0.2
Spanish peseta (Pta)	6.885	0.0104	0.0716	5.4
Danish krone (DK)	0.1976	0.1711	0.0338	2.5
Irish pound (I£)	0.008552	1.7415	0.0148	1.1
Greek drachma (GD)	1.440	0.00328	0.0047	0.4
Portuguese escudo (Esc)	1.393	0.00384	0.0053	0.4
			1.3380	100.0

Note: The currency composition of the ECU was valid from September 21, 1989, until the launch of the euro on January 1, 1999.

This system of divergence indicators acts as an *early warning* signal. Once a currency ECU rate diverges by three-quarters of its allowable band, there is a presumption that its government will take remedial action, such as raising interest rates and/or tightening fiscal policy if the currency is weak. Thus, divergence indicators establish which country is *at fault* when an exchange rate reaches its floor/ceiling against another currency, simply because the country at fault will reach its floor/ceiling against the ECU first. For example, if France pursues an inflationary monetary policy that forces its currency down *vis-à-vis* the DM, the French franc is also likely to be weak against other EC currencies and, consequently, against the ECU. In this example, France would be required to undertake corrective policies unilaterally or, as a very last resort, devalue its currency.

The *threshold of divergence* indicator simply eliminates the influence of a currency's own weight in the ECU given in the last column of Exhibit 3.4. Thus, if $w_i(0)$ measures the weight of currency i in the total value of the ECU, the band of fluctuation allowed to currency i *vis-à-vis* its central rate, given in Exhibit 3.4, column (1), is:

$$\text{Maximum divergence} = 0.0225 \times [1 - w_i(0)].$$

A good warning indicator should sound a warning signal before a currency reaches its maximum divergence: By setting arbitrary threshold divergence at 75% of maximum divergence, we can define the threshold divergence indicator effectively used by the EMS:

$$\text{Threshold divergence} = 0.075 \times 0.0225 \times [1 - w_i(0)].$$

Q: If, for example, the French franc (FF) accounts for 15% of the value of one ECU, what is its threshold divergence indicator?

A: Based on the threshold divergence equation, it will be less than the +/−2.25% mandated by the EMS grid of par values. It will also be less than the 75% of 2.25%. It will reflect the weight of the FF in the ECU of $w_i(0) = 0.15$ and is readily computed as:

$$(0.075) \times (0.0225) \times (1 - 0.15) = 0.0143 \text{ or } 1.43\%$$

which is considerably less than the +/−2.25% margin.

The EMS straitjacket comes unglued

In spite of the EMS's lofty ambition of providing a zone of monetary stability to the European Community, most member nations currencies' (with the exception of the Dutch guilder) devalued by at least 20% against the DM between 1979 and 1987. The French franc alone devalued by more than 50% against the DM, and the Italian lira did not fare any better. The severe currency crisis in the summer of 1992 hastened the demise of the EMS. The catalyst seemed to have been Germany's decision to tighten its monetary policy. Germany used higher interest rates to rein in inflationary pressures brought about by the massive expansionary fiscal policy that had been necessary to meet the cost of German reunification.[7] Higher German interest rates forced other EC countries to raise their interest rates dramatically to defend their currencies against the German mark. Britain and Italy hiked their interest rates to 15% and France to 13% at a time when these countries were combating sluggish economic growth and high unemployment. Speculators increasingly reckoned that exchange rate parities would become unsustainable and that weak economies would eventually turn to devaluation to prop up their economies.

On September 14, 1992, after having lost an estimated US$4 billion to US$6 billion in a futile intervention in the currency market, EC central banks finally surrendered to almighty market forces: Britain and Italy abandoned the ERM ship, whereas Ireland, Portugal, and Spain devalued their currencies. Indeed, in 1993, with most countries no longer willing or able to mimic Germany's high interest rates policy, the EMS widened its allowable band of fluctuations around cross values to +/−15%, in effect aborting its pegged exchange rates policy. The ill-fated ERM limped along until August 1993, when it finally came unglued. For all practical purposes the EMS morphed into a floating rate system.

Why did the EMS fail?

A short answer would point out that the EMS simply resurrected on a regional scale the architecture of the Bretton Woods system, which had been proven unstable and had collapsed 20 years earlier. The loosening of exchange rate controls in the 1980s as well and the pursuit of national policies — rather than a coordinated single European monetary and fiscal policy — largely explained the inherent instability of the EMS. No amount of central bank intervention in the currency markets could keep the edifice standing, as the punishing crisis of 1992–1993 painfully demonstrated. In spite of higher than anticipated exchange rate volatility, national interest rates and inflation rates did converge in the 1990s, paving the way to the launch of the euro in 1999. The lessons of the failed EMS were ignored!

---

7 The historic fall of the Berlin Wall in 1989 had led to a hasty monetary union between rich West Germany and not-so-rich ex-Communist East Germany. The newly formed monetary union had grossly overvalued the East German mark and made the cost of rebuilding the East German economy unnecessarily and exorbitantly high, not to mention that it condemned East German firms to be grossly under-competitive. To this day, unemployment in former East Germany continues to be significantly higher than in West Germany.

EMERGING MARKETS CURRENCY REGIMES AND CRISES

Developing countries and command economies of the Communist bloc were/are generally shackled with tightly controlled exchange rates whereby their currency trading is channeled through the central bank at an arbitrary rate set by administrative fiat. Referring to Exhibit 3.1, the reader will verify that developing countries were/are nested in the controlled exchange rates cell — at least during the Bretton Woods era. As many of these emerging economies — the Asian Tigers[8] come to mind — embarked on a fast-track development path often fueled by international trade and a tighter integration in the world economy, current account restrictions were progressively loosened and rapidly increasing currency trading migrated from the central bank to commercial banks in the framework of a budding foreign exchange market. By then, successfully emerging market economies increasingly adopted pegged exchange rate regimes, which were better suited to accommodate their greater integration with the global economy.

The reader will note in Exhibit 3.1 the steady migration of China and Russia over the period 1973–1997 — by now emerging market countries in the full sense of the term — to the middle row of "pegged yet adjustable" exchange rates. As globalization advanced, tight exchange controls on financial account transactions became increasingly difficult to enforce, especially as nascent local stock markets were becoming the darlings of international portfolio investors. Furthermore, greater openness to international trade and foreign direct investment made circumventing financial account restrictions increasingly possible, most notably through under-invoicing or over-invoicing of international trade transactions and intra-corporate transfer price manipulations. Indeed, it is generally believed that emerging market countries that have liberalized their financial accounts have achieved higher growth rates. The process, though, has not necessarily been a smooth or linear one, as currency crises punctuated their history.

Sovereign debt crisis (1982–1989)

High US interest rates and a sharply appreciating US dollar undermined the solvency of a number of rapidly emerging economies. Mexico, Brazil, and Argentina (MBA) had borrowed extensively from Western banks in the 1970s, which had naively lent under the false assumption that "countries never default, only firms do". Sovereign loans to MBA and other developing countries of South America, Eastern Europe, and Africa were all US dollar-denominated at floating interest rate = London Interbank Offered Rate (LIBOR) + country risk premium. Unfortunately, unsuspecting sovereign borrowers soon faced (1) a steady decline in raw materials prices due in part to slow growth in their exports markets, (2) an unprecedented rise in US short-term interest rates to 20% due to a staunchly anti-inflationary monetary policy under the new Paul Volcker–led US Federal Reserve Bank, and (3) a sharply appreciating US dollar, which conjointly made the servicing of sovereign loans, not to mention repayment of principal, unbearable for many debtor nations. Mexico defaulted in August 1982 on $100 billion of foreign debt, soon followed by Brazil, Argentina, and many others.

Collapse of the Soviet Empire (1989)

The fall of the Berlin Wall in October 1989 triggered the wholesale dismemberment of the Communist bloc. As former satellite economies of the Soviet Union started to fend for themselves — unshackling their economies from the command structure of central planning — the invisible hand of market forces started to reassert itself. Unconvertible currencies whose prices had been set by bureaucratic fiat were now determined by a nascent foreign exchange market. Eastern European countries — most notably Poland, Hungary, Czechoslovakia, and the Baltic republics — looked west toward the European Union (EU) and the EMS to anchor their currencies. None were quite ready to join the EU or to become a full-fledged member of the EMS, but pegged their currencies against the ECU and in certain cases (such as Bulgaria and Latvia) established currency boards and used the German mark as the anchor currency. East Germany established a monetary union with West Germany whereby East and West German marks fused at the parity of West German mark 1 = East German mark 1. Soviet republics such as Belarus, Ukraine, and Georgia that had seceded from the former Soviet Union (now reduced to Russia) kept their currencies pegged to the Russian ruble, which embarked on a volatile float.

Asian financial crisis (1997)

The Asian Tigers economic model built on high savings rates and frugal government finances, generally credited with a quarter century of breakneck

8 *Asian Tigers* generally refers to South Korea, Taiwan, Thailand, Malaysia, and Indonesia.

growth that had lifted impoverished countries to the enviable status of newly industrialized countries, came to a screeching halt with the abrupt and massive devaluation of the Thai baht on July 3, 1997. The devaluation had a domino effect, promptly engulfing Indonesia, Malaysia, the Philippines, and South Korea, all of which were forced into devaluing their currencies.

All victims of the Asian financial crisis had pegged their currencies to the US dollar, which had become grossly overvalued over time by as much as 35% to 50%. As the dollar strengthened in the latter part of the 1990s, Southeast Asian countries suffered from a loss of export competitiveness, which resulted in wider balance-of-trade deficits. Thailand, for example, ran a large current account deficit on its balance of payments of as much as 8% of its gross national product (GNP) in late 1996. In a pegged exchange rate system, such a current account deficit had to be financed by an equally large offsetting financial account surplus or by using up foreign exchange reserves.

Indeed — encouraged by a pegged exchange rate — companies started to raise significant amounts of debt in the euro-dollar and Eurobond markets in addition to massive dollar-denominated short-term borrowing from commercial banks, which were channeled into long-term domestic investments — often real estate projects.[9] When economic growth slackened, highly leveraged borrowers started to face debt-servicing difficulties. In some instances, borrowers faced outright default, as in the case of the South Korean *chaebol* Hanko Steel, which defaulted on $6 billion of debt, and the Thai construction company Somprasong on a $75 million Eurobond issue.

Very noticeably, Hong Kong and China escaped infamous devaluation of their currencies. The Chinese yuan had long been protected by tight controls on financial account transactions, and international speculators therefore were denied access to the Chinese currency. Meanwhile, the Hong Kong dollar anchored to the US dollar by a currency board barely survived the storm and defended its par value by large run-ups in interest rates and support from mainland China's central bank.

9 A fixed exchange rate made the cost of the dollar look deceptively cheap. When Asian currencies devalued massively against the US dollar, many firms found themselves unable to service dollar-denominated debt, whose cost had just increased by 30 to 50%.

Currency boards and the demise of the Argentine Peso (1991–2002)

Reminiscent of the gold standard, a currency board requires adopting countries to tie directly their money supply to the level of foreign exchange reserves. Thus, the establishment of a currency board freezes up a central bank's ability to follow an independent monetary policy and possibly monetize the nation's budget deficit. In effect, a currency board amounts to the hardest possible peg because it commits to exchanging the domestic currency for a specified "anchor" currency such as the US dollar or the euro at a fixed exchange rate enshrined in a law. Practically, the domestic money supply can only increase/decrease if the country runs a balance of payments surplus/deficit. In recent times, a number of countries have successfully implemented currency boards, with Hong Kong's quarter of a century peg to the US$ at the rate of HK$7.80 = $1 being the most vivid illustration.

Argentina — one of the richest countries in the world before the great crash of 1929 — became the basket case of Latin America. After enduring several decades of hyperinflation, Argentina embarked on a bold currency board experiment in 1991 by introducing a new currency set by law at Argentine peso 1 = US dollar 1. At first Argentina's inflation started to converge with the US rate of inflation, and so did interest rates. An ambitious privatization program of loss-making state-owned enterprises was geared toward restoring the health of Argentina's public finance, while a surge of foreign direct investment fueled the country's economic rebound. Unfortunately, Argentina's inflation never quite converged with US inflation; instead a slow but steady overvaluation of the peso started to undermine Argentina's price competitiveness as domestic inflation began to creep up. By the late 1990s Argentina was mired in a deep recession, with subsidized imports (due to the overvaluation of the peso) choking Argentina's manufacturing, and exports being priced out of the world market. In early 2002 Argentina abandoned the currency board and allowed the peso to float freely. The precipitous depreciation of the peso at first fueled inflation but very soon triggered an economic rebound: Argentina regained its competitiveness through more attractively priced exports and a reinvigorated domestic manufacturing sector, now better able to withstand more expensive imports.

The CFA franc zone (1945–present)

Part of the developing world enjoyed remarkable monetary stability over extended periods of time.

Fourteen African countries — former French colonies, for the most part[10] — are members of a monetary union known as the CFA franc zone whose common currency — the CFA franc — is fixed to the euro without any fluctuation margins. It is also freely convertible into the euro under a formal guarantee from the French treasury.

The CFA franc zone is actually comprised of two distinct regional groups: (1) the Western African Monetary Union (WAMU) is made up of eight western African countries — Benin, Burkina-Faso, Ivory Coast, Guinea Bissau, Mali, Niger, Senegal, and Togo — with a common currency known as *le franc de la Communauté Financière de l'Afrique* (CFA franc), and (2) the Economic and Monetary Community of Central Africa (EMCCA) is comprised of six central African countries — Cameroon, Central African Republic, Chad, the Republic of Congo, Equatorial Guinea, and Gabon — with a separate common currency also known as the CFA franc (but standing for *le franc de la Coopération Financière Africaine*).

Although the two CFA francs are administered by two different central banks headquartered in Dakar (West Africa) and Yaounde (Central Africa) and are legal tenders only in their respective regions, they are considered one single currency because both francs are freely convertible into euros at the same parity. The CFA franc has been remarkably stable since its creation in 1945: its parity was first set at CFA franc 50 = French franc 1 in October 1948 and was changed only once in 1994, to a new parity of 100 CFA franc = 1 former French franc. In 1999, when the French franc was fused into the newly hatched single currency at 1 € = 6.55957 French franc the CFA franc became formally pegged to the euro at 1 € = 655.957 CFA francs.

Beyond a hard currency peg: Dollarization in Panama (1903), Ecuador (2000), El Salvador (2001)

Dollarization means that a country abandons its own currency and adopts a more stable currency such as the US dollar as its legal tender. In effect the US currency is substituted for the local currency and becomes the country's new unit of account, medium of exchange and store of value. Panama legally adopted the US dollar as its currency in 1904, Ecuador in 2000 and El Salvador in 2002.

Dollarization is an extreme form of "hard" pegging to the US dollar since the peg — the US dollar — becomes the country's currency. For a country adopting a policy of dollarization the benefits are that it dispels forever the specter of devaluation, reduces the risk premium on foreign borrowing and more generally projects an enhanced economic profile of low volatility since it now imports stable prices and low interest rates from the United States. This comes at the cost of giving up two key (out of three) economic policy levers — namely, foreign exchange rate and monetary policies (it does retain control of its fiscal policy). Having dismantled its central bank, a dollarizing country can no longer perform as a lender of last resort should it face an acute banking crisis.

Panama adopted the US dollar as its legal tender as early as 1904. **Ecuador** ditched its national currency — the Ecuadorian sucre — in 2000 after failing to quell years of hyperinflation and recurring banking crisis and so did **El Salvador** in 2001.

EUROPEAN MONETARY UNION AND THE BIRTH OF THE EURO (1999–PRESENT)

The Maastricht treaty, signed in 1992, set the European Union on the path toward monetary union. On January 1, 1999, member countries would abandon their national currency and adopt a common currency dubbed the euro. On the launch day, each country locked in its exchange rate against the euro, which took over from the ECU. A European Central Bank (ECB) was established to issue the new currency, conduct the common monetary policy for the newly formed euro-zone, and set a common interest rate for all its members. Each member country retained its independent fiscal policy but surrendered its monetary autonomy. To join the euro club, countries would have to satisfy the Maastricht criteria, later codified into the Stability and Growth Pact. Specifically, applicant countries would have to meet tough requirements regarding their budget deficits (no more than 3% of GDP) and outstanding national debt (no more than 60% of GDP). The objective was to impose fiscal discipline on member countries, which would retain fiscal policy independence and might abuse it by running deficits, which would undermine the stability of the euro.

Officially approved by the European Parliament on May 2, 1998, the euro was formally launched on January 1, 1999, with 11 founding members: Austria, Belgium, Finland, France, Germany, Holland, Italy,

10 Guinea-Bissau is a former Portuguese colony, and Equatorial Guinea is a former Spanish colony.

Ireland, Luxembourg, Portugal, and Spain. Greece joined on January 1, 2001, Slovenia in 2007, Cyprus and Malta in 2008, Slovakia in 2009, Estonia in 2011, Latvia in 2014, Lithuania in 2015 and Croatia in 2023. The European Central Bank was formally established on January 1, 1999 and headquartered in Frankfurt (Germany); its prime mission is to conduct monetary policy with the overarching goal of keeping inflation at 2% or below. Three other countries known as the euro-skeptics — United Kingdom, Sweden, and Denmark — met the Maastricht criteria but decided to opt out. The remaining countries failed to meet admission criteria and were encouraged to put their financial houses in order before applying to become members of the euro club.

Is the euro-zone an optimum currency area?

The politically motivated launch of the euro in 1999 never met the acid test of what economists call an *optimal currency area*. The concept of optimum currency area is a helpful construct for answering the difficult question of when a group of geographically contiguous countries should adopt a single currency. Do the benefits of adopting a common currency resulting from enhanced economic integration and lower transaction costs (a single currency eliminates the cost of forex trading) exceed the costs of giving up the option of exercising monetary autonomy and an independent foreign exchange rate policy?

A group of countries (or regions) is deemed an optimal currency area when their economies are closely interwoven by trade in goods and services and characterized by mobility of capital and labor. The United States is the longest-surviving and most successful example of a well-functioning optimum currency area. Is the EU an optimal currency area? Intra-EU trade hovers around 15% of the eurozone's GNP, which is significant but considerably lower than in the United States. If footloose capital is increasingly the EU norm, labor mobility across Europe is only a small fraction of what it is in the United States and it remains very low within each of its national economies.

Ignoring these quintessential problems, the euro created a single monetary policy with the establishment of a European Central Bank, thereby depriving each country of two (out of the three) critical economic policy instruments: (1) an independent monetary policy to tame inflation or spur growth through interest rate adjustments and (2) a flexible exchange rate to keep its economy competitive. Furthermore, fiscal policy, the third critical instrument, is sharply constrained by the Stability and Growth Pact, which caps the budget deficit for each country at 3% of GDP. Furthermore, national debt should not exceed 60% of a country's GDP (with notable exceptions such as Italy and Greece, which breached the ceiling at 104% and 95% of their GDPs, respectively when they joined the euro). Given the obvious structural and cyclical differences between individual EU members, the much-reduced deftness of economic policy is of particular concern should a given member country suffer an economic shock that does not uniformly affect the rest of the euro-zone.

If the euro-zone were indeed an optimal currency area, an economically impaired country (high unemployment, no growth) would be able to adjust because of three factors: (1) mobility of its labor to the rest of the euro-zone as the unemployed move to high-employment countries, (2) downward flexibility of wages and prices to regain competitiveness, and (3) stabilizing transfer of fiscal resources from the European Commission in Brussels to assist the crisis country to finance its budget deficit. None of these conditions were met when the euro was first hatched in 1999, nor is there any sign that member countries are putting in motion structural reforms to bring the euro-zone any closer to being an optimal currency area. The third condition — which happens to be most difficult to meet — calls for a hefty dose of fiscal union and would transfer significant taxing and spending power away from national governments to the EU in Brussels. For fear of further diluting national sovereignty, this transfer remains as elusive as ever.

Indeed, the European Union — which itself has very limited taxing power (no more than 1.27% of the euro-zone GNP) — cannot make stabilizing fiscal transfers to smooth out national shocks. The brunt of the responsibility of fiscal policy remains in the hands of national governments, with Brussels accounting for less than 3% of euro-zone government expenditures. This stands in stark contrast to the United States, where more than 60% of government expenditures occur at the federal level. The United States also enjoys a significant degree of labor mobility and greater wage flexibility than Europe does. Even Germany's reunification, which fused the East and West German marks into one single German mark in 1991, hardly created an optimal D-mark zone. Instead, it faced a stubbornly high rate of unemployment (close to 20%) in East

Germany in spite of massive fiscal transfers in excess of €200 billion over a 10-year period and freedom of movement between East and West Germany!

Indeed, in its first decade the euro-zone has experienced at least two major asymmetrical shocks that did not impact all its members uniformly: the strong, overvalued US dollar over the 1999–2002 period and the oil shock of the 2005–2008 period. In the first case of the strong/overvalued dollar, euro-zone countries characterized by a large exposure and/or dependency on international trade (that is, trade not directed to fellow member countries of the euro-zone) have experienced faster imports-induced inflation than euro-zone trade-oriented countries. As expected, Ireland — more of an international trader than a European trader — experienced inflation at the rate of 4.1% over the 1999–2002 period, whereas Germany — more of a European trader than an international trader — remained in the slow inflation lane at 1.2% over that same period.

Similarly, the quadrupling of the price of a barrel of crude oil impacted national rates of economic growth and inflation more or less proportionally with a country's relative dependence on oil. For example, France, with its relatively lower dependence on oil (only 35% of its energy supply comes from oil because of its high dependence on nuclear power) was considerably less impacted than were Greece, Ireland, Italy, Portugal, or Spain, which depend on oil for more than 55% of their energy supplies.

How discrepant national rates of inflation undermine the stability of the euro

Unfortunately, the combination of centralized monetary policy and decentralized fiscal policy is resulting in localized differences in inflation, which in turn are leading to a national *over- or undervaluation* of the euro in terms of its purchasing power[11] in each euro-zone country. Under national exchange rate policy, this is easily corrected through monetary policy and competitive depreciation or appreciation of the national currency. However, such corrections are no longer possible since the straitjacket of the euro killed the exchange rate policy instrument and froze monetary policy at the national level. Because of this inability to respond flexibly to inflation, the purchasing power of the euro in several countries is rapidly eroding compared to the "German" and "euro-zone-wide" euros. Indeed, on the basis of labor cost indexes in Italy and Germany between January 1, 1999, and September 30, 2008, the euro in Italy was overvalued by 41% against the euro in Germany; Spain and Greece were not far behind.

Unless countries suffering from overvaluation can correct the problem through faster gains in productivity and/or wage and price downward flexibility, the problem is not reversible. More important, overvaluation is a cumulative process that becomes increasingly more difficult to correct over time. In this vein, the EU enlargement to Eastern European countries brought about a modicum of downward price and wage flexibility to the euro-zone; indeed, euro-zone–based firms can make increasingly credible threats to outsource to or relocate manufacturing operations to Eastern Europe (part of the EU but not of the euro-zone) in order to take advantage of the cheaper labor.

To make matters worse, the European electoral calendar continues to be asynchronous, with each country holding elections at the presidential, parliamentary, or municipal level on its own schedule. This, in turn, exacerbates cyclical discrepancies across the euro-zone because the run-up to an election is often accompanied by expansionary fiscal policy.

The euro crisis (2010)

In early 2010 the euro-zone was shaken by its most severe confidence crisis to date: Greece faced an exploding budget deficit and was close to defaulting on its national debt. The worldwide subprime crisis that had already resulted in negative growth was driving the Greek economy into an even deeper recession, undermining government tax revenues while fiscal expenditures remained more or less constant. Financial markets punished Greece: a massive sell-off of its sovereign bonds pushed up interest rates to an all-time high at which it needed to borrow to finance its budget deficit. Credit bureaus downgraded Greece's sovereign debt to "junk" status, pushing the price of its outstanding bonds to an all-time low, a yield to maturity close to 15% on 10-year bonds. The panic quickly spread to other peripheral countries — most notably Spain, Portugal and Ireland which had experienced massive housing booms fueled by very low nominal and even negative real interest rates.

In May 2010, the European Central Bank and the IMF hammered out a rescue package in the staggering amount of €115 billion, which gave Greece a stay of execution. Greece was forced into a drastic austerity budgetary plan whereby its budget deficit would be reined in from 13% of GDP to less than

11 See Chapter 7 for an in-depth discussion of Purchasing Power Parity and what it means for a currency to be over or under-valued.

8% of GDP over three years — still far exceeding the 3% of GDP guidelines of the Stability and Growth Pact. The European rescue plan — admittedly a grand display of European solidarity — failed to address the fundamental challenges faced by Greece: A sclerotic economy with a bloated public sector and shackled by a grossly overvalued "Greek euro" made Greece unable to compete in traditionally labor-intensive industries such as textiles, garments, agribusiness, shipbuilding/repairing, and tourism. Forcing down government expenditures when government revenues were decreasing even faster does not do much to remedy the national budget deficit: Greece needed to restore economic growth through expansionary policies and avoid a recessionary spiral that austerity will necessarily induce. The Stability and Growth Pact, for all its good intentions, is a straitjacket that kept the Greek patient in the sanatorium while its body was wilting away! As the Euro-zone was closing down on a full decade of crisis management its toll remains excruciatingly heavy with a rate of unemployment stubbornly high — 20.2% in Greece, 15.2% in Spain, 10.9% in Italy for the active population (EU average is at 6.9%) but significantly higher for 18–25 years old at 43.2% in Greece, 33.8% in Spain and 31.9% in Italy (EU average is at 15.1%). And yet, in spite of all the vicissitudes the single currency has endured it remains intact largely due to the deft tactical maneuvering of the European Central Bank which perfected the policy of "kicking the can down the street"!

Muddling through (2011–present)

By forcefully defying bond markets when he declared in August 2012 that *within our mandate, the ECB is willing to do whatever it takes to preserve the euro and, believe me it will be enough* the newly appointed president of the European Central Bank Mario Draghi defused the looming euro crisis. PIIGS' bond prices which had collapsed rebounded giving crisis countries a new lease on life as the cost of deficit financing returned to more manageable levels. Indeed, since 2012 the threat of massive bond purchase by the ECB has brought quiescence to the euro-denominated Treasury bond market.[12]

At the same time the euro-zone seems committed to continuing its policy of *muddling through* (see middle section of Exhibit 3.5) which, by enforcing a policy of austerity on the PIIGS, results in lower wages. Indeed, fiscal austerity by curbing government expenditures first induced deeper economic recession and higher unemployment which did bring about lower wages in the Mediterranean economies most affected by the euro crisis. Labor-intensive industries such as export-oriented tourism services clearly benefitted and rebounded. Unlike a classical or *external devaluation* which at once renders exports cheaper and imports more expensive such a policy is tantamount to a devaluation of its "national" euro which would apply only to the exports of goods and services but leave the price of imports unchanged. This is why it is often dubbed an *internal devaluation*. In the same vein quantitative easing ECB-style ushered in 2014 by Mario Draghi led to a significant depreciation of the euro which helped the export competitiveness of the entire euro-zone including member economies which did not need it such as Germany.[13] Will the euro-zone survive by *muddling through* without correcting its birth defects by building a *fiscal union* or teeter on the brink of partial *fragmentation* or even total *dislocation* (see Exhibit 3.5)?

The way forward toward fragmentation: The Euro-zone may splinter partially or fully. It may be a limited fragmentation whereby a small country such as Greece or Portugal exits the euro or it may be massive dislocation should Italy or Germany decide to break away from the single currency. Any talk of exiting the euro is vilipended as blasphemy of the European Union gospel and dismissed as the unbearable mother of all financial crises. It remains that an honest costs/benefits analysis of such a scenario remains to be carried out and would go a long way towards resolving the lingering euro crisis. Clearly depending upon national idiosyncrasies the drama of exiting the euro would unfold differently: let's consider the diametrically opposite cases of Greece versus Germany exiting the euro.

12 Higher bond prices mean lower yield to maturity and therefore a lower cost of deficit financing for euro-zone countries which need to bridge the gap between (insufficient) tax revenues and government expenditures. Stabilized bond prices also re-invigorated euro-zone banks whose asset portfolios are typically heavily invested in the treasury bonds of their country of domicile.

13 According to the IMF chief economist Olivier Blanchard "Without the power to devalue their currencies, peripheral economies would forever be forced to endure "tough adjustment", such as slashing their wages, to keep up with stronger member states. In this vein, Mr Blanchard dismissed any talk of a growth "miracle" in Spain — which has been hailed as a poster child for Brussels' austerity diktats. He added he was "surprised" that sluggish euro-zone economies were not doing better in the face of a cocktail of favorable economic conditions. "When people talk about the Spanish miracle, I react: when you have 23% unemployment and 3% growth, I don't call this a miracle yet".

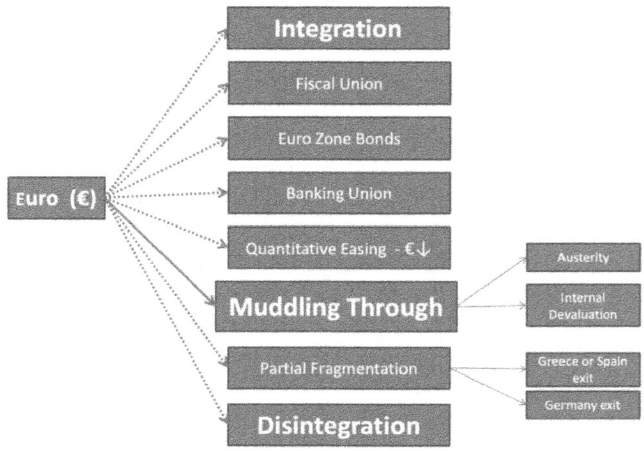

Exhibit 3.5. The Euro crisis policy continuum.

"Let my People Go": Would Greece exit the euro (Grexit)? Greece is facing a stark choice: it can continue to choose the agony of snail-pace growth, endless rounds of budget austerity mandated by the Troika, violent strikes and missed fiscal targets or it can "bite the bullet" and drop out of the euro-zone however traumatic an abrupt exit would undoubtedly be. The detractors of Grexit paint a grim picture of chaos engulfing Greece as it revives a national currency prone to inflation and devaluations. Let's not forget however that in the 20 years preceding its euro membership Greece enjoyed steadier growth and much lower unemployment. Unfortunately, the euro playbook does not include the possibility of members taking a leave — only new members joining!

Let's sketch what Grexit would entail. To be successful the divorce would have to be an amicable one with the ECB and European Commissions acting as good faith partners of the Greek government. Greece would have to resurrect the Drachma presumably imposing first exchange controls to prevent a capital flight and freezing all outstanding debt or bonds at the old exchange rate of Drachma 308 = €1 — at least initially.[14] Greece would also have to print new bank notes (unless the Bank of Greece was clairvoyant enough to have saved old Drachma bank notes in its vault when Greece joined the euro …). How would Greece weather this shock therapy? The Drachma would be allowed to float and presumably immediately lose a third or half of its value reaching perhaps the rate of Drachma 1000 = €1. The extent of the currency plunge would be dictated by the "Greek euro" overvaluation and the exchange rate should eventually settle at its Purchasing Power Parity value. The currency devaluation would restore the competitiveness of the Greek economy and Greek-manufactured products and services such as agri-business, mining, shipyards and tourism would no longer be priced out of the market. The Drachma price of imports would explode rapidly shrinking Greece imports bill while triggering imports substitution. The financial account of Greece's balance of payments would also benefit as devaluation powers inbound foreign direct investment. The Greek economy would rebound within 12 to 18 months, economic growth would return bringing about a steady decline in unemployment while tax revenues would surge and the budget deficit would be in check[15] …! Inflation would kick in and would have to be reined in.

Exiting the euro-zone is not necessarily limited to weak economies. How would Germany leaving the euro play out? If PIIGS' euros are "overvalued" the German euro is clearly *undervalued* which partly explains its mammoth current account surplus. By breaking away from the single currency, Germany would immediately see its re-kindled DM appreciate by 25–30% against the euro thereby curbing its current account surplus and allowing the *euro minus Germany* to depreciate. The debtor countries of the

14 Exchange controls imposed by the Central Bank of Greece should be short-lived allowing for an orderly transition to the new currency and be lifted as soon as the situation returns to normalcy. The risk of capital flight would likely happen in the days leading up to Grexit.

15 Some would argue that this virtuous spiral is already unfolding with "internal devaluation" of the "Greek euro". It is true that austerity has pushed wages down correcting some of the Greek euro overvaluation but has left the import side of the trade equation unchanged

euro-zone would regain at least partially their lost competitiveness and benefit from higher economic growth.[16]

The uneasy path toward fiscal union: Unlike the United States which has long functioned as a successful monetary union the euro-zone remains ill equipped to absorb asymmetric shocks. As a Monetary Union the euro-zone pursues a single monetary policy. Whenever a member country is hit by an asymmetric shock the ECB is unable to tailor-make its monetary policy to the idiosyncratic circumstances of the country under duress. The single monetary policy should be conducted in the interest of all euro-zone countries — not any euro-zone member in particular. By gearing its monetary policy to the average situation of the euro-zone the ECB's single interest policy may be too expansionary for some countries and too restrictive for others. The ECB's credo that "one size should fits all" ends up fitting none … unless fiscal policy can be appropriately leveraged to correct asymmetries exacerbated by a single monetary policy. Unfortunately, the single currency incomplete federal architecture lacking an adequate reactive stabilization apparatus is largely to blame. Hence the need for the euro-zone to equip itself with proper fiscal instruments to better channel the synchronization of business cycles and to be able to absorb asymmetric shocks. Deeper integration of the euro-zone would involve closer fiscal policies amongst its member states. At its basics fiscal policy is a three-pronged undertaking: (1) Fiscal expenditures — where should fiscal resources be spent, (2) Fiscal revenues — collecting taxes from households and corporations and (3) Financing — assuming a budget deficit — how to bridge the gap between expenditures and revenues. All three prongs are still very much under the control of each sovereign government and it is generally understood that full fiscal integration is politically unfeasible and that a more sensible goal would be to aim at fiscal coordination and harmonization.

Integration of fiscal policies still begs the question of what should be the allocation of fiscal revenues and expenditures between Brussels and national governments. Currently only 3% of total European budgets is controlled by the EU with 97% in the hands of sovereigns. By comparison the US federal budget accounts for 60% of the country total budget. A major re-allocation of fiscal resources on either the revenue or expenditure side would call for far-reaching amendment to current EU treaties and would ignite nationalistic reactions. A more modest initiative would be to work towards integrating deficit financing policies by issuing Eurobonds. Would such Eurobonds[17] issued collectively by the euro-zone rather than singularly by individual member countries remedy the euro-crisis impasse and prevent recurrent crises? In effect such Eurobonds — by replacing singular national issuance of bonds- would mutualize sovereign public debt. Such Eurobonds could be issued by a European Debt Agency backed by member countries or more simply by national government which would commit to guaranteeing not only their national debt but every other euro-zone sovereign bond issue. Thus, the Eurobond would be backed jointly and severally by the entire euro-zone rather than by single member countries[18] and should be rated as well as the strongest rated euro-zone issuer — namely Germany. For example, Spain instead of issuing its own sovereign bonds at an interest rate reflecting its country risk notation — say 4% for a 7-year bond — would now pay the same interest rate as Germany of 2% which would de facto become the euro-zone yield for sovereign Eurobonds. As long as the guarantee shouldered by the strongest sovereign does not damage its credit notation the Eurobond yield would remain at 2%. However, should this euro-zone wide guarantee weaken the strongest sovereign notation the Eurobond yield would progressively approach a weighted average[19] of yields facing each euro-zone member countries. This yield would be higher than what Germany — the strongest euro-zone borrower — pays and considerably lower than what Greece — the weakest borrower — pays. In effect Spain would piggy-back on the good

16 George Soros — one of the most savvy financier of our times — has been a strong proponent of this policy *if Germany left, the euro would depreciate. Debtor countries would regain their competitiveness; their debt would diminish in real terms.*

17 Euro-bonds should not be confused with Eurobonds. The former refers to bonds issued outside of the country of bond currency denomination — for example a euro-dollar bond is a bond denominated in USD but issued outside the USA. A Eurobond is simply a bond denominated in euros and issued by euro-zone sovereigns or any entity domiciled within or without the euro-area. Similarly a euro-eurobond would be a bond denominated in euros but issued outside the euro-zone.

18 According to Article 125 of the Lisbon Treaty European Union member countries are not liable for their fellow members' obligations — financial and otherwise. Eurobond issuance would therefore require that Article 125 be amended.

19 The weighting scheme would presumably reflect the market capitalization of outstanding euro-zone sovereign bond issues.

name of Germany and other strongly rated euro-zone members. Germany strongly resists this first step towards integration as it sees it as a disguised morphing of the euro-zone into a *transfer union*. Germany would now pay 3% instead of 2% before participating in this new scheme: in effect German taxpayers would provide a subsidy of 1% to any euro-zone country which would have otherwise borrowed independently at an interest rate higher than 3%.

Will the COVID-19 pandemic (2020–2022) prove to be a serendipitous gamechanger?

Hardly limping out of the euro-crisis of 2010, Mediterranean Europe finds itself in the path of hurricane COVID-19. Indeed, the geography of the corona virus pandemic mirrors the imprint of the euro-crisis of a decade ago. Here again, this asymmetric shock damages far more the highly indebted and infected "periphery" than the richer "core" countries not only because their weaker economies have far less fiscal space to respond to the sharp GDP contraction but because they are far more dependent on "contact" services such as tourism and hospitality — e.g., as much as 22% of Greece GDP is derived from tourism (mostly foreign) but as little as 7.5% of Germany GDP comes from tourism. Without fiscal aid the pandemic-induced deep recession would engulf the entire EU.

Rescue package dubbed Next Generation EU: Despite difficult and protracted negotiations pitting the "core" against the periphery, in July 2020 the EU Council hammered a jumbo recovery package of €750 billion amounting to 4.7% of the EU GDP[20] to counter the devastating economic toll triggered by the Coronavirus pandemic. When disbursed over the next three years "Next Generation EU" will add €250 billion to the annual EU budget of €166 billion or a mammoth increase of 150%. Most importantly more than half of the rescue package (€390 billion) will be provided as grants to sovereigns most in need rather than loans: grants add directly to budgetary revenues whereas loans finance budgetary deficits and compounds the sovereign's indebtedness. This landmark deal would have been unimaginable even six months earlier as it crosses two red lines in the EU treaties: first, it empowers the European Commission to borrow an unprecedented amount of money (€750 billion) riding on the good credit of member states and second, the majority of the rescue package (€390 billion) would be distributed as grants to mitigate the asymmetric shock devastating Mediterranean Europe (GIIPS) thereby amounting to intra-EU fiscal transfers.

How will the emergency rescue package be financed? The European Commission will issue long-duration bonds most likely to be AAA-rated and to be serviced by increased taxing power devolved by EU member states to Brussels. Presumably, this new collective European debt will enjoy joint-and-several guarantees but there is no plan to mutualize member states' legacy debt. It falls short of a "Hamiltonian" moment[21] when in 1790 the US Federal Union assumed all the debt incurred by US states during the war of independence thereby laying the foundation for a strong central government.

Governance: how will rescue funds be allocated? Each member state submitted their "National Recovery and Resilience Plan" to the European Commission along with their draft budget. The European Commission will then assess these plans against its own internally-generated country-specific recommendations. Unemployment and scale of COVID-19 induced GDP contraction in 2020 were the deciding allocative criteria with Italy and Spain expected to receive the lion's share (approximately 50%) of the €750 billion emergency fund. The European commission as the "central planner" may be politically challenged as the self-styled "frugals" — Netherlands, Austria, Denmark and Sweden — have reserved the right to apply an "emergency brake" on the final recovery fund disbursements should they disagree with the European Commission's technocrats distributive decisions. Indeed, the hammering of this mammoth fiscal rescue to a shared crisis demonstrates a rare moment of near-solidarity among member states and sets an interesting precedent. Will the EU embrace this opportunity to build more deliberately greater fiscal integration among its member states to complement its single monetary policy?

The euro @20: The Fathers of Europe had a grand vision: 'building peace through prosperity." The construction of a United Europe by creating a level

20 "Next Generation EU" is expected to be front-loaded and disbursed mostly in 2021–2022: it comes on top of national stimulus programs.

21 The first Treasury secretary Alexander Hamilton engineered this radically new centralized fiscal policy.

playing field unencumbered by tariff and non-tariff barriers would enable European firms to leverage economies of scale and scope thereby boosting growth and standards of living. The single market delivered on these promises — at least until the launch of the euro in 1999. The single currency by imposing a straight-jacket on the euro-area is denting if not reversing these cumulative gains. Today, close to half of the euro-area — the GIIPS mostly — is shackled to an "overvalued" euro and is struggling to fully recover from the euro crisis. The other half — Germany mostly — is super-charged by an implicit export subsidy courtesy of an "under-valued" euro. Short of seriously embarking on a common fiscal policy for the euro-zone, creeping pauperization will increasingly fuel Europhobia and could unleash political mayhem — peace through prosperity may be fading away! And yet, for all the havoc that the 2020 pandemic is unleashing on the euro-zone it may prove to be the *silver lining* of a renewed lease on life for the single currency: is the European Union finally embracing a fiscal union or is it a one-time response to a once in a lifetime mayhem?

TODAY AND TOMORROW: THE CURRENT MAP OF EXCHANGE RATES

Today's international monetary system is aptly characterized as a hybrid system of floating and pegged exchange rates. As we close this chapter, it is useful to take stock of the current international monetary system in terms of exchange rate regimes that major countries have adopted and to anticipate where it is heading. As globalization is relentlessly forging ahead, the international monetary system is no doubt marching toward *greater convertibility* (looser exchange controls) and *more flexibility* (cleaner floating exchange rates).

Few countries may be tempted by exchange rate fixity in the form of a currency board or even dollarization as Hong Kong or Panama have successfully done; this quasi-irreversible choice will presumably be limited to smaller economies that find that benefits of importing monetary policy discipline from an anchor country such as the United States are offsetting the loss of seigniorage. Exhibit 3.6 allows the positioning of any country's currency regime in a two-dimensional space measuring the degree of currency convertibility

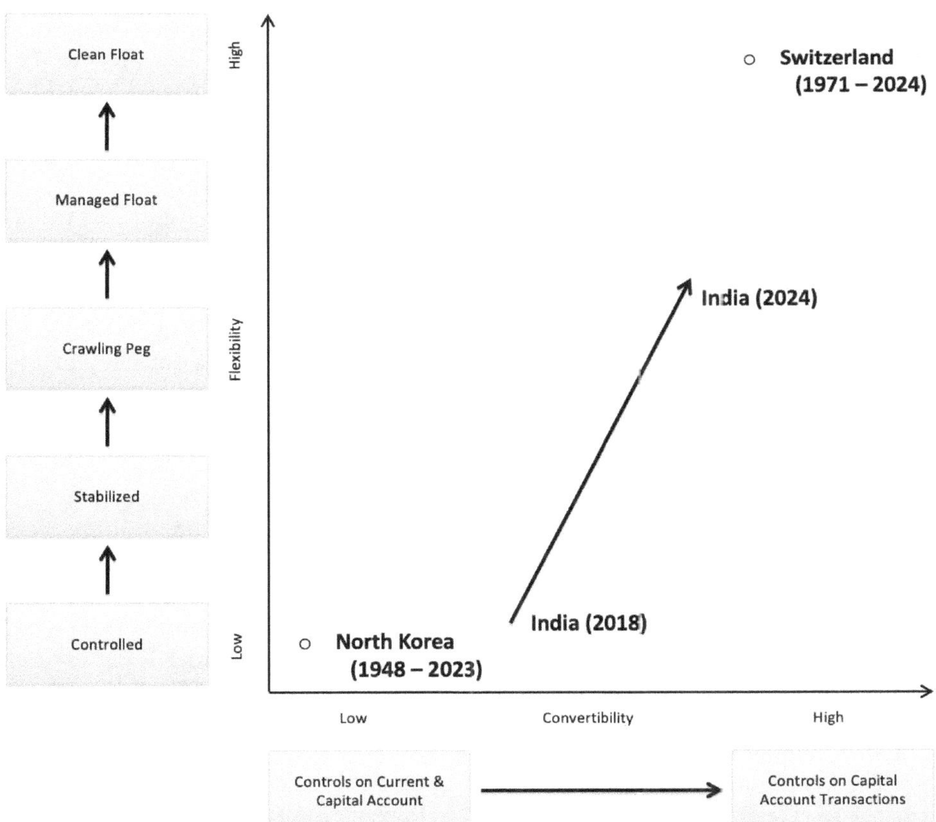

Exhibit 3.6. Flexibility × convertibility space with clusters of currencies.

(controls imposed on forex transactions) along the horizontal axis and the degree of price flexibility allowed to exchange rates on the vertical axis. India, for example, is shown to have relaxed exchange controls over the period 1993–2018 (increased convertibility along the horizontal axis) while allowing its currency to a managed float (increased flexibility along the vertical axis) over that same time period. Switzerland, on the other hand has enjoyed quasi-full convertibility of its currency and an almost clean float ever since the collapse of the Bretton-Woods system in 1971.

Floating currencies

A small core group of industrialized countries have maintained floating exchange rates ever since the Bretton Woods system and short-lived Smithsonian agreement collapsed in 1973. The United States, United Kingdom, Canada, Australia, Japan, and Switzerland have allowed their currencies to float independently with sporadic central bank intervention. Japan's heavy-handed intervention to control the ever-rising yen definitely qualifies the empire of the rising sun for the world title of "dirtiest floater." In 1999, hatching the euro meant fusing 11 currencies into one single currency that joined the club of independent floaters; it is today the second most widely traded currency.

A number of emerging countries also belong in the floating rates category but maintain significant exchange controls on their financial account transactions, thereby restricting their currency's full convertibility: Korea, Malaysia, Thailand, Taiwan, Mexico, Argentina, India, Turkey, and Russia would fall in this category. Central banks' intervention in these countries is persistent, and the "very dirty floater" label is appropriate.

"Pegged yet adjustable" currencies

A number of countries maintain official pegs against a major currency such as the US dollar or the euro. Saudi Arabia, Kuwait, United Arab Emirates, and Hong Kong have official pegs against the US dollar, while Denmark and the African CFA franc peg their currencies to the euro. China is publicly committed to letting its exchange rate crawl according to the value of a basket of currencies, but, for all practical purposes, it keeps the yuan tightly pegged to the US dollar. With more than $3.5 trillion in foreign exchange reserves, the yuan's peg to the US dollar appears unassailable!

Controlled exchange rates

Many African countries and some Asian or Latin American nations continue to be mired in a vicious cycle of underdevelopment and poverty. For this group of economic laggards, globalization is a fast-moving train that they have not been able to hitch to. For many of them, their limited integration in the global economy is restricted to earning foreign exchange from expatriate workers' remittances or from exporting staple commodities whose volatile prices are determined on a global commodity exchange. Typically, such countries, including Egypt, Iran, Syria, Pakistan, Bangladesh, Algeria, Uganda, Mauritania, Cuba, and Burma, will maintain tightly controlled exchange rates whereby the central bank is the sole buyer and seller of scarce foreign exchange. Scarcity will generally breed a black market where the exchange rate will fluctuate at a considerable premium from the official exchange rate. Lack of exchange rate flexibility is tightly paired with almost total lack of convertibility.

As we close this chapter, the reader should now be better equipped to understand the rationale (or lack thereof) for why countries adopt the exchange rate regimes that they do. The reader should also be better prepared to anticipate when those same countries may enact new exchange rate regimes and what that may entail for international financial decision making.

SUMMARY

1. The gold standard (1878–1914) required each country to define its currency in a weight of gold ("mint" parity), thereby guaranteeing fixed exchange rates.
2. The Bretton Woods conference of 1944 established a new world of pegged exchange rates designed to facilitate the reconstruction of the world economy after the devastation of World War II. Each country — in close consultation with the newly constituted IMF — defined an official par value, which is the value of its currency in terms of gold and therefore in terms of the US dollar. A narrow band of fluctuations of +/−0.75% around the par value would be enforced by the country's central bank through intervention in the foreign exchange market.

3. The Bretton Woods system (1944–1971) delivered rapid economic growth and even more rapid expansion in international trade and investment for more than a quarter century. Tight controls on financial account transactions until 1958 kept the international monetary system reasonably stable. Divergence in national monetary policies and fiscal policies resulted in significant exchange rate overvaluation or undervaluation, which had to be corrected by discrete one-time devaluations, as in the case of the French franc or British pound sterling, or revaluations, as in the case of the DM or Dutch guilder.

4. The lax fiscal policies of the United States in the 1960s resulting from President Lyndon Johnson's Great Society social programs and the war in Vietnam led to large balance-of-payments deficits that ultimately brought about the collapse of the Bretton Woods architecture of fixed exchange rates.

5. In 1973, major world currencies embarked on the uncharted path of floating exchange rates, although central banks continued to intervene — heavily at times — in their currency markets to avoid disorderly markets and to smooth excessive short-term volatility in exchange rates.

6. The collapse in 1989 of the Soviet empire unleashed market forces among the command economies of the former Communist bloc. Eastern European inconvertible currencies, long shackled by exchange controls, started to trade in newly established currency markets.

7. The 1997 Asian financial crisis engulfed most Tiger economies of East and Southeast Asia. The collapse of the Thai baht triggered a domino effect whereby the Malaysian ringgit, the Indonesian rupiah, the Philippine peso, and the South Korean won all experienced severe devaluations in short order. Grossly overvalued exchange rates that seemed securely pegged to the US dollar were abandoned for tightly managed floats. Meanwhile, the Hong Kong dollar and the People's Republic of China yuan sailed relatively unscathed through the Asian financial crisis.

8. On January 1, 1999, 11 EU member countries abandoned their national currencies and adopted a common currency called the euro. On the launch day, each country locked in its exchange rate against the euro, which took over from the ECU. The newly established European Central Bank became solely responsible for the euro-zone monetary policy. The politically motivated launch of the euro in 1999 never met the acid test of what economists call an *optimal currency area*, defined as a group of countries whose economies are closely interwoven by trade in goods and services and characterized by mobility of capital and labor. Lack of convergence in national fiscal policies resulted in discrepant national rates of inflation, with the PIIGS experiencing deep overvaluation in their "national" euros. The punishing sovereign debt crisis engulfing the PIIGS in 2010 shook the architecture of the euro-zone. The *euro avoided breaking up* but its future remains in doubt as the crisis lingers on against a backdrop of austerity-induced sluggish economic growth.

9. As globalization is relentlessly forging ahead, the international monetary system is marching no doubt towards greater currency convertibility (looser exchange controls) and more price flexibility (cleaner floating exchange rates).

QUESTIONS FOR DISCUSSION

1. Explain the role played by gold in the gold standard system of international payments. Why was the gold standard suspended during World War I?

2. Why did the major industrialized powers fail to reenact the gold standard after World War I? Why did they turn to a "beggar thy neighbor" policy in the 1930s?

3. What are the defining characteristics of the Bretton Woods international monetary system?

4. Why was the Bretton Woods system of "pegged yet adjustable" exchange rates reasonably successful until 1958 and increasingly unstable thereafter?

5. What are exchange controls on current account transactions? How do they differ from controls on financial account transactions? Which ones were the more important in ensuring the stability of the Bretton Woods system?

6. Why was China able to survive the 1997 Asian financial crisis without devaluing the yuan whereas most Asian countries had to massively devalue their currencies?

7. Why did the EMS fail? How does the euro differ from the EMS? Were the lessons from the EMS failure learned when the euro was designed?
8. What is the difference between a *currency board* and *dollarization*?
9. Would countries suffering from acute hyperinflation such as Argentina, Venezuela and Turkey benefit from dollarization?
10. Why did the Argentine currency board collapse whereas Hong Kong has been able to hold on to its fixed exchange rate against the US dollar?
11. What are the key macroeconomic variables that explained devaluation or revaluation under the Bretton Woods system?
12. Should Greece exit the euro-zone? What would be the implications for Greece versus the euro-zone and the European Union?
13. Would the euro-zone's economic problems be alleviated if the currency were to depreciate significantly against the US dollar and the Japanese yen? Which euro-zone country would benefit the most? Which one would benefit the least?
14. Why have England, Sweden, and Denmark refused to join the euro-zone?
15. The euro-zone is sometimes referred to as a DM-zone (the DM being the former currency of Germany); explain.
16. Why are member countries of the euro-zone experiencing different rates of inflation when the European Central Bank implements a single monetary policy with a single interest rate?
17. What are the defining characteristics of an optimum currency area? What are the main differences between the United States and the euro-zone in this respect?
18. Why is the euro-zone allowing "internal devaluation" but not "external devaluation".
19. What was the impact of the COVID pandemic on the euro-zone? Will it prove to have been a game-changer for the single currency?
20. Referring to the North American Free Trade Agreement (NAFTA), should the United States, Mexico, and Canada adopt a common currency?

PROBLEMS

1. **Brazilian real depreciates (beginner).** Wharton Econometrics Forecasting Associates expects the Brazilian real (BRL) to depreciate by 30% against the US dollar over the next 90 days from its current value of BRL 1.72 = $1.
   (a) What is the value of the predicted exchange rate?
   (b) Chase Econometrics expects the US dollar to appreciate by 22.5% against the real over the same period; what is the exchange rate forecast?
2. **The CFA franc devalues (beginner).** The CFA franc was defined in terms of the French franc (FF) as CFA 50 = FF 1 from 1947 until 1994, when its value changed to CFA 100 = FF 1. Was the CFA devalued or revalued against the FF? By what percentage?
3. **Calculating par values against the dollar and gold (beginner).** In 1958, the French franc (FF) was defined as worth $\frac{1}{175}$ ounce of gold. What was the FF's par value against the dollar? What were the floor and ceiling exchange rates within which the French franc was allowed to fluctuate?
4. **Asian financial crisis and the Thai baht (beginner).** On July 3, 1997, the Thai baht (THB) was unpegged from the US dollar and promptly depreciated from THB 25 = US$1 to THB 60 = US$1. What was the baht's percentage depreciation against the US dollar? Compute the percentage depreciation/appreciation of the baht from the US dollar perspective. Do you get the same result with a minus sign as you did from the baht's perspective? Explain.
5. **The ECU as a basket of currencies (intermediate).** What is the percentage/weight of the ECU's total value accounted by the Spanish peseta? Refer to Exhibit 3.4 in the text. Would you get a different result if you valued the ECU in Japanese yen instead of the US dollar? Would you expect this weight to change if the ECU depreciates by 10% against the US dollar?
6. **The CFA franc and the birth of the euro (intermediate).** In 1999, the launch of the euro buried the French franc to which the CFA franc was pegged: the CFA franc would now be convertible into euros (€) rather than French francs (FF). What is the new parity between the CFA franc and the euro if FF 6.55 = €1? Would you expect the African nations that make up the CFA franc zone to benefit from the change? Explain.

7. **Exchange controls for foreign portfolio investments (intermediate).** The Boston-based Flying Dragon emerging market fund (FDE) was planning to purchase 1 million shares of Bangkok Bank at the price of THB 129 when the Bank of Thailand introduced a 30% interest-rate-free deposit requirement for any new investment in the stock market. The Thai baht stood at THB 36 = US$1 on December 17, 2010. What is the effective exchange rate for FDE, assuming that it plans on holding the Bangkok Bank stocks for one year and that the opportunity cost of tying funds with the Bank of Thailand is 4% per annum? What is the likely impact of this new tax on foreign portfolio investment in Thailand?

8. **Hong Kong currency board and the Chinese yuan (intermediate).** For the last four decades Hong Kong has relied on a currency board to peg its currency against the US dollar at HK$7.80 = US$1. Since 2005, the Chinese yuan has steadily appreciated against the US dollar from Yuan 8.28 = US$1 to Yuan 6.14 = US$1:
   (a) What is the difference between a currency board and a pegged exchange rate system? Do you believe that a currency board is appropriate for a city-state such as Hong Kong?
   (b) Has the Hong Kong dollar appreciated or depreciated against the Chinese yuan since 2005? By how much?
   (c) As an increasing share of Hong Kong's international trade and finance is conducted with mainland China, do you believe that the Hong Kong currency regime should be reformed? Formulate alternatives that the government of Hong Kong should consider.

9. **Denmark pegs its currency to the euro (advanced).** Even though Denmark opted not to join the single currency in 1999, it has pegged its currency very tightly to the euro ever since and keeps the value of the krone within a +/−2% band. How do you explain that Denmark seems to be willing to bear the cost of a tight peg to the euro without fully enjoying the benefits of membership to the single currency?

10. **A single currency for the Gulf states (advanced).** Bahrain, Kuwait, Oman, Qatar, Saudi Arabia, and the United Arab Emirates have long been rumored to be seriously considering the adoption of a common currency. Research the current exchange rate system that each Gulf state currently implements. Would the Gulf states qualify as an optimal currency area? What would be the greatest potential costs and benefits of such a grand plan?

INTERNET EXERCISES

1. **Britain's love affair with the euro (intermediate).** Even though Britain was a member of the European Union, it opted not to join the euro-zone in 1999. Acrimonious debate within the British political sphere has raged ever since before leading eventually to Brexit. Using the IMF and World Bank Group websites www.imf.org and www.worldbank.org/:
   a. Compare Britain's macroeconomic performance with the euro-zone in terms of economic growth, unemployment, inflation, budget deficit/surplus, and balance of payments' current account over the period 1999–2018.
   b. Extend your comparison to Sweden and Denmark, which also refused to join the single currency.
   c. Compare interest rates in Britain versus the euro-zone. Would Britain have benefited from joining the euro-zone? How and why?

2. **Mapping central bank intervention strategies (intermediate).** Log on to http://fx.sauder.ubc.ca/data.html:
   a. Plot the Thai baht, Mexican peso, Indian rupee, and Egyptian pound against the US dollar over the period 1990–2015.
   b. Super-impose on previous graph the level of foreign exchange reserves held by each respective central banks (available from www.imf.org/).
   c. How would you characterize the exchange rate regimes implemented by each country over the 25-year period?

3. **When Switzerland becomes a dirty floater (intermediate).** Log on to http://fx.sauder.ubc.ca/data.html and chart the Swiss franc price of one euro over period 2008–2018. Explain the National Swiss Bank foreign exchange policy over that period. Would a partial fragmentation of the euro change it? How?

4. Special Drawing Rights (advanced). Access the IMF website www.imf.org/external/np/tre/sdr/sdrbasket.htm and to http://fx.sauder.ubc.ca/data.html to compute the dollar value of one Special

Drawing Right. What is the weight of the Japanese yen in the value of one SDR? Has it changed since the Renminbi was added to the SDR?

REFERENCES

Aliber, R. Z. 2011. *The New International Money Game*, 7th edition. New York: Palgrave Macmillan.

Alogoskoufis, G. and L. Jacque. 2020. "The Euro@20: How Economic and Financial Asymmetries Marred the Promise of the Single Currency." *Journal of Applied Corporate Finance* (Fall 2020).

De Grauwe, P. 2014. *Economics of Monetary Union*, 10th edition. Oxford, UK: Oxford University Press.

Eichengreen, B. J. 2008. *Globalizing Capital: A History of the International Monetary System*. Princeton, NJ: Princeton University Press.

Lane, P. R. 2012. The European sovereign debt crisis. *Journal of Economic Perspectives*, 26(3):49–68.

Lane, P. R. 2021. "The Resilience of the Euro." *Journal of Economic Perspectives*, 35(2): 3–22.

Mundell, Robert. 1961. "A Theory of Optimum Currency Area." *American Economic Review*, 657–665.

O'Rourke, Kevin H., and Alan M. Taylor. 2013. "Cross of Euros." *Journal of Economic Perspectives*, 27(3): 167–192.

Prasad, Eswar S., and Rajan G. Raghuran. 2008. "A Pragmatic Approach to Capital Account Liberalization." *Journal of Economic Perspectives* 22(3): 149–172.

Prasad, Eswar S., Kenneth Rogoff, Wei Shang-Jin Wei, and M. Ayhan Kose. 2003. *Effects of Financial Globalization on Developing Countries: Some Empirical Evidence*. IMF Occasional Paper 220. Washington, DC: International Monetary Fund.

Reinhart, Carmen M., and Christoph Trebesch. 2016. "The International Monetary Fund: 70 Years of Reinvention." *Journal of Economic Perspectives*, 30 (1): 3–28.

CASE STUDY 3.1. WILL THE EURO-ZONE SHUTTER? PLANT LOCATION AND EXCHANGE RATES FOR HYUNDAI

Within our mandate, the ECB is willing to do whatever it takes to preserve the euro and, believe me, it will be enough.

Mario Draghi,
President of the European Central Bank

Min-Soo — senior analyst at Hyundai, the South Korean automotive company — was reviewing the country reports prepared by Hyundai's economic research department and putting finishing touches to a strategic review of where the South Korean multinational should locate its power-train factory within the European Union. The factory planned to export to sister affiliates that assembled the Hyundai Sonata. Labor costs (as much as 25 to 30% of the total cost of manufacturing a car) played a critical role in the location decision. Should Hyundai favor one of the lower-cost Eastern European countries such as Poland or Hungary, or should it locate within the euro-zone itself where regional governments in France and Spain offered significant incentives in terms of tax holidays and concessionary financing?

The municipality of Tarragona in the Spanish province of Catalonia had vigorously lobbied Hyundai, promising a five-year corporate tax exemption on profits. Concessionary financing was guaranteed at an annual rate of 2% for up to 40% of capital expenditures for the first three years. With a rate of unemployment exceeding 25%, Spain offered a productive and skilled labor force whose wages were increasingly downwardly flexible. Spain was mired in a deep recession and a banking crisis; it was expecting a lifeline from the European Central Bank to tame its bond market, which was pushing interest rates on Spanish government treasuries ever higher. Last but not least, Catalonia was in a protracted battle with the central Spanish government and was threatening to become politically autonomous if not politically independent from Spain.

The city of Gdansk in Poland had an industrial park that would readily accommodate Hyundai's power-train factory but it offered no municipal or national tax incentives. Financing would have to be procured at market rates hovering around 6.5% for a three-year note. The workforce was generally 20% cheaper than its counterpart in Spain, but it was also less productive, with estimates ranging from a 5 to 10% handicap. Absenteeism, however, was below 2%, with no work stoppage to be concerned about, whereas similar estimates put Catalonian rates of absenteeism and lost days to strikes at approximately 5%.

Spain

In early 2012 the Spanish economy had fallen back into recession as the euro-zone's growth turned negative. As a result, recession in Spain was expected to deepen throughout 2012 and into 2013, with output forecasted to contract by 2.2% in 2012 and by 0.7% the next year, before recovering very slowly from 2014 onward. Spain faced a protracted adjustment as it underwent a correction of the major imbalances accumulated during its decade-long boom up to 2008, including a burst house price and construction bubble, overindebted consumers, a fragile banking sector, and a still significant balance-of-payments current-account deficit.

The government sought to implement far-reaching economic reforms to improve competitiveness as part of a long-term program to revive the Spanish economy. The goal was through an "internal devaluation" to erase 40% to 50% of the Spanish euro overvaluation accumulated by Spain since joining the euro-zone in 1999. This was to be achieved through deep reduction in wages and social cost overheads. In the same vein, significant labor market reforms, aiming at overhauling and decentralizing collective wage-setting procedures, were already under way, although their overall impact will be modest or negative in the short term.

Fiscal policy: The Public finances would remain largely in deficit and would continue to constitute a major concern for investors, who feared the country could be forced into a full-fledged bailout. For 2011, the budget deficit turned out to be far higher than previously expected, at around 8.9% of gross domestic product (GDP). Under intense pressure from the EU and financial markets to restore fiscal order, the government had passed as many as four successive austerity packages since taking office in late 2011. It expected the latest package to save about €65 billion in net spending by end of 2014. Unfortunately, austerity on such a scale at a time of recession might prove self-defeating, as spending-side cuts hardly compensated for the deeper fall in tax revenue. Budgets would remain restrictive in later years, and the general government budget was expected to improve only gradually: New and relaxed deficit targets of 6.3% in 2012 and 3% in 2014 set in accordance with the European Commission were likely to be missed by a wide margin. Public debt, estimated at just under 70% of GDP in 2011, was expected to jump to over 80% in 2012, reflecting weak economic growth and therefore weak tax revenue, and to stabilize in 2013 as a result of European Stability Mechanism (ESM) intervention.

Economic growth: Even then, the economy and consumer demand will grow significantly more slowly than in the decade up to 2008, and unemployment will remain at depression levels. Annual real GDP growth is expected to average about 1.2% during 2014–2016. Private consumption was forecasted to fall during 2012 and 2013 as highly indebted households would hold back on purchases because of high unemployment and restricted access to credit. Public consumption is expected to contract until 2015, when it will rise only marginally, as the government cuts its spending to improve the public finances. Gross fixed investment will fall in 2012 and 2013, held down by the overhang in construction, and will return to modest growth thereafter.

Inflation: Despite inflation pressures from still-high global commodity prices and a rise in the value-added tax (VAT) rate, consumer price growth should be restrained by spare capacity in the economy and by the fact that wages will be held back by high unemployment and the need to regain competitiveness. Inflation is forecast to fall back in 2012 to an average of 2% as a result of weak demand, from 3.1% in 2011. Inflation should then stabilize at about 1.8% on average in 2013–2016.

Exchange rates: Although not central to Hyundai's economic forecast, there is a high risk that several countries, including Spain, will be forced to leave the euro-zone during the next two years. Even assuming that it survives in its present form, the euro would remain volatile in response to the region's debt and banking crises. The euro weakened from above US$1.40 = €1 in July 2011 to US$1.28 = €1 in mid-July 2012, as fears over the possible breakup of the single currency caused a flight from euro assets. Given persistent uncertainty over sovereign debt sustainability and banking solvency, the euro is expected to remain under pressure, averaging US$1.28 = €1 in 2012 and US$1.25 = €1 over 2013–2016, with significant risks of sharp movements in either direction.

Poland

The Polish economy grew by 4.3% in 2011, bolstered by strong domestic demand and robust export growth, but was expected to slow in 2012 to 2.6%, in line with a forecast of mild recession in the euro-zone (−0.6%). External demand would be much weaker in 2012, but a weaker zloty should help keep exports competitive. Exports, however, form a relatively small percentage of GDP, with around 27% of Polish exports going to Germany, a country expected to avoid recession in 2012. Of concern to Min-Soo, however, was the deterioration in Poland's industrial output due largely to the performance of its car industry. Car production decreased by an estimated 28% year-on-year in May 2012. Despite low labor and other costs, leading car manufacturers are giving preference to other destinations in central Europe for expanding their production bases — most notably the Czech Republic and Slovakia — which have managed to diversify their exports to markets outside the EU.

Fiscal policy: On the public finance front, the government's target was to narrow the consolidated budget deficit to 5.6% of GDP in 2011, from 7.8% in 2010. Under EU rules on the excessive-deficit procedure, Poland has until the end of 2012 to narrow the general government deficit to less than 3% of GDP. The government beat its 2011 target, recording a deficit of 5.1% of GDP, but it does not expect the deficit to narrow to 3% of GDP until 2013.

Monetary policy: The National Bank of Poland (NBP) was expected to continue its efforts to meet the official inflation target of 2.5% (±1%) over the medium term, despite fluctuations in the short term owing to currency volatility and high commodity prices. Tension between maintaining exchange-rate stability and setting monetary policy to meet the inflation target would become more acute when Poland joined the EU's ERM II, a two-year membership to which is a requirement for admission to the euro-zone. The current government was in no rush to join the euro-zone with a likely entry date set no earlier than 2016. In 2011 inflation averaged 4.2% (up from 2.7% in 2010) and outside the target range of 1.5 to 3.5% set by the NBP, owing to a rise of 1% in VAT, and the zloty depreciation against the euro. Inflation is forecast to average 3.6% in 2012, and ongoing inflation targeting by the NBP is expected to cap inflation below 3% in 2014–2016.

Exchange rate policy: Amid volatility in the international currency markets, the zloty was hit especially hard in the second half of 2011 and the first half of 2012, depreciating sharply against both the US dollar and the euro (see Case Exhibit 3.1A) In a rare digression from long-established policy practice, the NBP intervened several times to support the zloty in September–December 2011. The zloty regained some ground against the euro in the first and second quarters of 2012, before stabilizing at the start of the third quarter. If the zloty were to depreciate further as a result of a deepening euro-zone crisis, the NBP would most likely intervene simply because a weaker zloty lifts the foreign-currency component of public debt toward the constitutional limit of 55% of GDP.

External sector: The current-account deficit reached 4.3% of GDP in 2011. The winding down of large infrastructure projects related to the European soccer cup — Euro 2012 — combined with less robust consumption growth in 2012 should allow the trade deficit to moderate to a smaller current-account deficit of 4% of GDP in 2012 and average around 3.4% of GDP annually in 2013–2016. On average, net inflows of foreign direct investment (FDI) are forecast to cover around 50% of the current-account

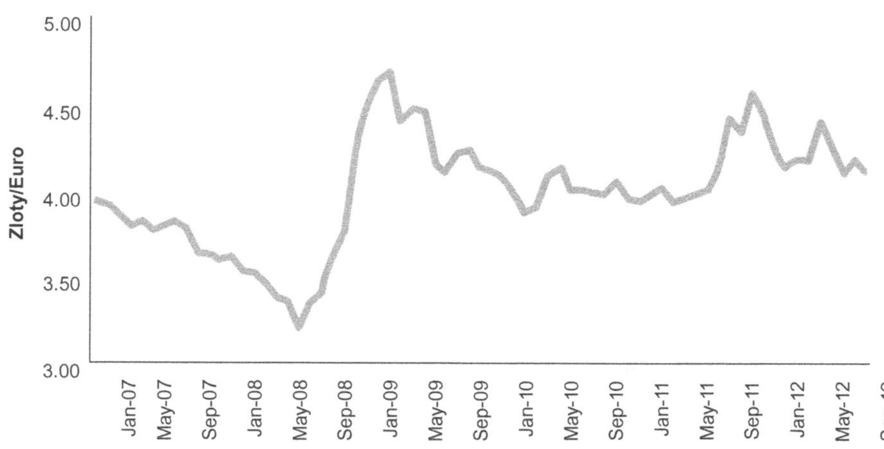

Case Exhibit 3.1A. Zloty/euro exchange rate.

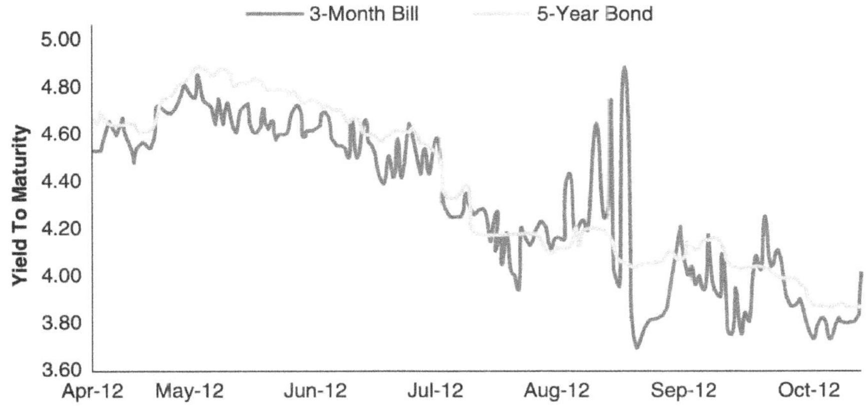

Case Exhibit 3.1B. Zloty-denominated bond yields.

deficit in 2013–2016, with the balance met mainly through a combination of new debt issuance and rollover of existing debt.

Overall, Poland's success in avoiding recession during the first phase of the sovereign debt crisis in Europe and its relatively good fiscal position enhanced by declining interest rates (see Case Exhibit 3.1B) have strengthened market confidence in its creditworthiness, with public debt at 56.1% of GDP at the end of the first quarter of 2012 — far below 88.2% for the euro-zone. The relative strength of the banking system, which is mostly foreign-owned, and Poland's freedom to pursue its own monetary policy have made local assets more attractive to a wide group of investors who wish to reduce their exposure to riskier investments elsewhere.

Questions for Discussion

Refer to Case Exhibit 3.2 to answer questions 1–4 (see the following pages).

1. What is the current exchange rate regime used by Poland?
2. Would you expect Poland to join the euro-zone in the short term?
3. What is your outlook for Spain as a member of the euro-zone?
4. Considering all-inclusive labor costs to be a primary determinant in locating its plant, where should Min-Soo recommend that Hyundai locate its power-train plant?

Case Exhibit 3.2. Summary of macroeconomic statistics for Poland and Spain (2007–2013).

Poland	**2007**[a]	**2008**[a]	**2009**[a]	**2010**[a]	**2011**[b]	**2012**[c]	**2013**[c]
Fiscal indicators (% of GDP)							
Central government debt	44.6	46.7	49.4	52.8	53.4	54.7	54.2
General government balance (ESA)	-1.9	-3.7	-7.3	-7.8	-5.1	-4.0	-3.0
Prices and financial indicators							
Exchange rate PLN/US$ (av.)	2.77	2.41	3.12	3.02	2.96[a]	3.25	3.17
Exchange rate PLN/€ (av.)	3.78	3.52	4.33	3.99	4.12	4.17	4.00
Consumer prices (av., %)	2.4	4.3	3.8	2.7	4.2[a]	3.6	2.8
Money market interest rate (av., %)	4.7	6.4	4.7	3.9	4.7	4.5	4.2
Current account (US$ m)							
Trade balance	-19,111	-30,729	-7,642	-11,782	-14,178[a]	-11,833	-15,299
Goods: exports FOB	145,300	178,701	142,071	165,901	193,908[a]	197,529	213,282
Goods: imports FOB	-164,411	-209,430	-149,713	-177,683	-208,086[a]	-209,362	228,581
Services balance	4,765	5,010	4,784	3,103	6,081[a]	5,694	6,326
Income balance	-16,381	-12,842	-16,568	-16,953	-20,183[a]	-17,418	-15,311
Current transfers balance	4,220	3,647	2,148	3,735	6,113[a]	5,250	5,548
Current-account balance	-26,507	-34,914	-17,278	-21,897	-22,167[a]	-18,308	-18,735
Debt stock	195,376	218,022	250,878[b]	297,028[b]	318,366	311,660	315,209
External debt (US$ mn)							
Debt service paid	47,969	57,188	50,307[b]	52,849[b]	66,253	68,965	72,379
Principal repayments	41,439	47,732	43,878[b]	46,354[b]	57,689	61,032	64,403
	6,530	9,456	6,429[b]	6,496[b]	8,564	7,933	7,976
Total international reserves	65,734	62,168	79,576	93,488	97,856[a]	97,399	102,279
Spain	**2007**[a]	**2008**[a]	**2009**[a]	**2010**[a]	**2011**[b]	**2012**[c]	**2013**[c]
Nominal GDP (US$ bn)	1,443.5	1,599.6	1,459.9	1,394.9	1,493.8	1,359.1	1,353.7
Nominal GDP (€ bn)	1,053	1,088	1,048	1,051	1,073	1,063	1,072
Real GDP growth (%)	3.5	0.9	-3.7	-0.1	0.7	-2.2	-0.7

Population and income							
Population (mn)	45.2	45.5	45.8[c]	45.9[c]	46.1[c]	46.3	46.5
GDP per head (US$ at PPP)	32,008	33,208	32,179[c]	31,842[c]	32,603[c]	32,277	32,645
Recorded unemployment (av., %)	8.3	11.4	18.0	20.1	21.7	22.7	23.0
Fiscals indicators (% of GDP)							
General government budget revenue	41.1	37.0	35.1	36.3	35.1[c]	36.0	36.3
General government budget expenditure	39.2	41.5	46.3	45.6	43.9[c]	42.6	42.4
General government budget balance	1.9	–4.5	–11.2	–9.3	–8.9[c]	–6.6	–6.1
Public debt % GDP	36.2	40.2	53.9	61.2	68.5[c]	83.7	83.6
Prices and financial indicators							
Exchange rate US$/€ (end-period)	1.47	1.39	1.44	1.34	1.29	1.28	1.26
Exchange rate ¥/€ (end-period)	164.45	126.35	134.09	110.33	101.33	104.96	107.05
Consumer prices (av., % change; EU harmonized measure)	2.8	4.1	–0.2	2.0	3.1	2.0	2.2
Producer prices (av., %)	3.6	6.5	–3.4	3.2	6.9	4.6	2.7
Lending interest rate (av., %)	6.6	7.4	7.0	7.2	8.1	7.4	7.4
Current account (US$ bn)							
Trade balance	–125.2	–126.6	–58.2	–63.3	–55.2	–38.4	–37.1
Goods: exports FOB	264.1	284.7	228.8	256.8	309.6	305.4	314.6
Goods: imports FOB	–389.3	–411.3	–287.0	–320.1	–364.9	–343.8	–351.7
Services balance	31.7	38.2	35.0	36.1	47.6	50.7	55.1
Income balance	–41.4	–52.1	–35.7	–26.2	–36.3	–40.0	–39.7
Current transfers balance	–9.6	–14.0	–10.9	–9.8	–8.3	–7.5	–7.4
Current-account balance	–144.5	–154.5	–63.8	–63.1	–52.3	–35.3	–29.1

Notes: [a]Actual.

[b]Economist Intelligence Unit estimates.

[c]Economist Intelligence Unit forecasts.

Source: International Monetary Fund, *International Financial Statistics.*

CHAPTER 4

The Balance of Payments

Money is sent from one country to another for various purposes: such as the payment of tribute or subsidies; remittances of revenue to or from dependencies, or of rents or other incomes to their absent owners; emigration of capital, or transmission of it for foreign investment. The most usual purpose, however, is that of payment for goods. To show in what circumstances money actually passes from country to country for this or any other purposes mentioned, it is necessary briefly to state the nature of the mechanism by which international trade is carried on, when it takes place not by barter but through the medium of money.

— John Stuart Mill, 1848

The dollar is looking vulnerable. It is propped up not by the strength of America's exports, but by the vast imports of capital. America, a country already rich in capital, has to borrow almost $2 billion net every working day to cover a current account deficit forecast to reach $500 billion this year. To most economists, this deficit represents an unsustainable drain on world savings. If the capital inflows were to dry up, some reckon that the dollar could lose a quarter of its value. Only Paul O'Neill, America's former treasury secretary, appears unruffled. The current account deficit, he declares, is a "meaningless concept" which he talks about only because others insist on doing so.

— *The Economist*, September 14, 2002

Globalization is reshaping the world economy by deepening the web of international trade in goods and services and integrating ever more tightly national capital markets. But we are not quite living in a *borderless* world, and globalization has not yet washed away the need for a national scorecard of individual countries' performance on the world economic stage. Former Treasury secretary O'Neill, as quoted in the opening paragraph, may be ahead of his times, but he would still be today a lonely voice of an inconsequential minority! Indeed, we still live in a *mercantilist*[1] world that demands national statistical measures and recordings of all economic transactions between domestic and foreign residents over a given period (usually a quarter or a year); as such, a nation's balance of payments provides a summary account of its international economic position and a gauge of its currency strength, which is critical information to government authorities charged with making orderly international payments and managing the nation's exchange rate and fiscal and monetary policies.

Exporters, treasurers of multinational corporations, international bankers, and asset managers of globally reaching funds pay close attention to balance of payments statistics because they are known

1 Mercantilism is an economic doctrine first formulated in the 17th century that equated a nation's wealth with the accumulation of precious metals — gold and silver. It advocates a strong balance of trade surplus as a key policy goal, as excess exports over imports are paid for in precious metals. First articulated by Colbert — Louis XIV of France's finance minister — mercantilism guided most of Europe's economics in the 17th and 18th centuries until challenged by Adam Smith and David Ricardo. More recently, colonial empires and protectionism are also rooted in mercantilism, which dies hard in today's world of globalization as we witness the continued accumulation of trade surpluses by Japan, China, and others that results in massive hoarding of international reserves — today's equivalent of yesteryear's gold and silver.

to have a direct bearing on the nation's foreign exchange (forex) market and the value of its currency and to influence the course of government policy. This is especially true of countries that maintained quasi-fixed exchange rates or are known as very dirty floaters. A country experiencing a widening balance of payments deficit should expect to see its currency depreciating or even have to impose exchange controls; this is, for instance, the case of Argentina, whose weak balance of payments may signal reduced convertibility of the peso. This would result in delayed payments of export receivables to Argentina or suspended payments of royalties and dividends by foreign-owned Argentinian subsidiaries of multinational corporations. Conversely, a strong balance of payments surplus as experienced by Japan may signal a more aggressive intervention policy in the foreign exchange market by the central bank buying the foreign currency (by selling its own currency) to slow down its currency appreciation.

In this chapter, the reader will gain an understanding of:

- How to read the principal accounts of a balance of payments.
- The difference between current and financial account transactions.
- The relationship between balance of payments transactions and the foreign exchange market.
- The relationship between a country's national income account and its balance of payments.
- How a country's budget deficit is directly equal to its current account (CA) deficit and, therefore, has to be financed by an equivalent surplus in its financial account.

FUNDAMENTALS OF BALANCE OF INTERNATIONAL PAYMENTS ACCOUNTING

A country's balance of payments is a statistical record of its international transactions and summarizes all economic transactions between its residents (individuals, corporations, and various branches of government[2]) and the rest of the world. The information is typically reported on a quarterly or yearly basis. Unfortunately, different monetary authorities — national central banks, the International Monetary Fund (IMF), the Bank for International Settlements, and other international organizations — use somewhat different nomenclatures and formats in reporting balance of payment statistics. However labeled, the reader should focus on the following four key principal accounts that comprise the balance of international payments (BOP):

1. **Current account (CA)**, which records payments associated with the international flow of goods, services, factor income, and transfers to and from foreign residents.
2. **Financial account (FA)**, which records payments corresponding to cross-border direct investment, international portfolio investment, and lending/borrowing activities to and from the rest of the world.
3. **Errors and omissions (E&O)** or statistical discrepancy. Because recording of payments and receipts arising from international transactions is often estimated independently of one another and at different times, they often fail to balance out. Recording may also be simply omitted. Hence there is a need for a "plug" account to correct for the statistical discrepancy.
4. **Official reserve account (ORA)**, which measures changes in foreign currencies, gold, and special drawing rights (so-called reserve assets) held by a country's central bank.

Misconceptions about the balance of payments

We often make reference to a *deficit* or a *disequilibrium* in the balance of payments. By definition, the balance of payments must balance; if it doesn't balance, then something has been left out or miscounted, and that is why we need the E&O account to ensure that the balance of payments does balance. Thus, it is conceptually flawed to talk about a balance of payments deficit or disequilibrium: Only subaccounts such as the balance of trade can be in disequilibrium; indeed, when all subaccounts are summed up the balance of payments will be balanced.

The second misconception is the parallel often made between the *balance of payments* of a country and the *balance sheet* of a firm: The balance of payments is an accounting statement that resembles a

2 Foreign affiliates of multinational corporations are generally incorporated as *foreign subsidiaries* in their country of operations and are therefore self-standing legal entities. *Foreign branches*, on the other hand, are legal extensions of their parent and for tax purposes are treated as residents of their parent company's country of domicile. For balance of payments purposes, though, both foreign subsidiaries and foreign branches are considered as residents of their country of operations.

firm's *sources or uses of funds statement* known to students of corporate finance; it doesn't take stock of a country's assets or liabilities position as a balance sheet of a firm does.

Balance of payments accounting

In their simplest form, international transactions represent a two-way exchange of assets between domestic and foreign residents. Recalling that assets can be defined as *real* (goods or services) or *financial* (monetary claims of various maturities including money, which is the shortest-term claim), we can classify international transactions as either of these two types:

(1) The exchange of goods and services for money or other financial claims; in this case one side of the transaction is *real* and the other is *financial*.

(2) The exchange of financial claims such as stocks and bonds for other financial claims such as money, in which case both sides of the transaction are *financial*.

Therefore, an international transaction involves two opposing transfers of assets: one resulting in a payment from foreigners (recorded as a *credit* +) and the other resulting in a payment to foreigners (recorded as a *debit* –). Indeed, balance of payments accounting uses a double-entry bookkeeping system analogous to financial accounting used by corporations. Every international transaction enters the balance of payments twice because every transaction brings about a credit entry offsetting an equal debit entry. Hence, total debits and credits are always equal in a balance of payments. Thus each transaction can be viewed as the combination of a *source of funds* matched with an equal *use of funds*.

A source of funds is entered as a credit — it corresponds to (1) a decrease in the country's assets or (2) an increase in its liabilities; a use of funds is entered as debit — it corresponds to (1) an increase in the country's assets or (2) a decrease in its liabilities. For example, when Fluor Corporation (a US firm) exports an offshore oil drilling platform to Pemex (the Mexican oil company) for US$500 million, the transaction combines a *source of funds* as an export credit (a decrease in US assets — in this case a merchandise good) with the export's proceeds being added to Fluor's bank account with Citibank or a *use of funds* entered as debit. Thus, by definition, the sum of all credits will be balanced by the sum of all debits.

However, as mentioned earlier in our definition of the E&O account, there may be statistical discrepancies (E&O) between debits and credits that need to be corrected by a separate entry (plug) because sources and uses of funds are reported or estimated independently. This ensures that the balance of payments does balance. In the next section we illustrate how double-entry bookkeeping works with different kinds of transactions.

Reading a balance of payments

The US balance of payments statistics for 2023 are presented using the IMF financial statistics format in Exhibit 4.1. The CA shows a deficit of US$819 billion (line 1). This is explained by a large balance of trade deficit amounting to US$1059 billion (lines 1.1a and 1.1b), which is somewhat reduced by both a surplus of US$280 billion on the balance of services (lines 1.2a and 1.2b) and on the balance of net income in the amount of US$137 billion (lines 1.3a and 1.3b) from foreign factors of production (dividends and interest income). Note the significant deficit of US$176 billion on unilateral transfers due to large international remittances by US workers (including undocumented aliens) — see International Corporate Finance in Practice 4.1.

The capital and FAs show a large surplus of US$895 billion (line 2), explained in part by a net inflow of portfolio investments in the amount of US$1,157 billion (lines 2.3a and 2.3b). The ORA shows a minuscule decrease of US$6 billion (line 4) over that time period, indicating that the Federal Reserve Bank has not intervened in the foreign exchange market. To make the balance of payments balance, the E&O account (line 3) needs to plug a hole of US$70 billion — a number that has become significantly larger in recent years.

China's balance of payments, shown in Exhibit 4.2, is radically different: China enjoys a large CA surplus of US$253 billion (line 1), resulting primarily from a healthy balance of trade surplus of US$594 billion (line 1.1) partly offset by a substantial deficit of US$ 208 billion on its balance of services (line 1.2). This CA surplus is partly compensated by a large deficit in its FA in the amount of US$210 billion (line 2) due to a sizable net outflow of foreign direct investment of US$142 billion (lines 2.2a and 2.2b).

China's very modest change in official reserves indicates that its intervention in the foreign exchange market has aimed primarily at smoothing daily fluctuations rather than resisting upward or downward trends.

Exhibit 4.1. United States balance of payments, 2023 (billions of US dollars).

	Debit	Credit	Net
1. CURRENT ACCOUNT			(819)
1.1a Goods: Exports f.o.b.		2,053	
1.1b Goods: Imports	(3,112)		
1.1 Trade balance			(1,059)
1.2a Services: Credit		999	
1.2b Services: Debit	(719)		
1.2 Balance on Services			280
1.3a Income: Credit		1,416	
1.3b Income: Debit	(1,279)		
1.3 Balance on Income			137
1.4 Current transfers: Net			(176)
2. FINANCIAL ACCOUNT			895
2.1 Capital Account: Net	(13)		
2.2a Direct investment abroad	(494)		
2.2b Direct investment from abroad		394	
2.3a Portfolio investment assets	(56)		
2.3b Portfolio investment liabilities		1,213	
2.4 Financial derivatives: Debit		16	
2.5a Other investment assets		(416)	
2.5b Other investment liabilities		251	
3. NET ERRORS AND OMISSIONS			(70)
4. CHANGE IN ORA			(6)
Total			0

Exhibit 4.2. China balance of payments, 2023 (billions of US dollars).

	Debit	Credit	Net
1. CURRENT ACCOUNT			**253**
1.1a Goods: Exports f.o.b.		3,179	
1.1b Goods: Imports f.o.b.	(2,585)		
1.1 Trade Balance			594
1.2a Services: Credit		332	
1.2b Services: Debit	(540)		
1.2 Balance on Services			(208)
1.3a Income: Credit		240	
1.3b Income: Debit	(388)		
1.3 Balance on Income			(148)
1.4a Current transfers: Net			15
2. FINANCIAL ACCOUNT			(210)
2.1 Capital Account: Net		0	
2.2a Direct Investment abroad	(185)		

	Debit	Credit	Net
2.2b Direct Investment from abroad		43	
2.3a Portfolio investment assets	(77)		
2.3b Portfolio investment liabilities		14	
2.4 Financial Derivatives		(8)	
2.5a Other investment assets	44		
2.5b Other investment liabilities		(41)	
3. NET ERRORS AND OMISSIONS			(38)
4. CHANGE IN ORA			(5)
Total			0

INTERNATIONAL CORPORATE FINANCE IN PRACTICE 4.1

International Remittances

International remittances are unilateral transfers — gifts of a sort — made by expatriate migrants from the host country in which they work to their family living in the country from which they emigrated. Indeed, more than 250 million migrant workers (more than 3% of the world population) work abroad and help their homeland family relatives by remitting cash — $794 billion in 2022 — on a larger scale than the $120 billion in official aid from Organization for Economic Co-operation and Development (OECD) countries. In 2022 — according to the World Bank — the five largest recipient countries were India ($100 billions), Mexico ($60 billions), China ($51 billions), The Philippines ($38 billions) and Egypt ($32 billions). This is the partial labor market globalization dimension, which, as pointed out earlier, is the most constrained vector of the globalization process. India alone received from its diaspora far more than it received in foreign direct investment. In Mexico, remittances primarily from the United States, exceeded foreign direct investment capital inflows and were only second to oil exports revenues. In the same vein, foreign remittances surpassed Morocco's tourism income, Egypt's receipts from the Suez Canal, and Sri Lanka's export revenues from tea. For more than 23 countries such as the Philippines and Bangladesh, foreign remittances amounted to more than 10% of gross domestic product (GDP), and they reached 50% in the cases of Tajikistan and Haiti.

Unfortunately, the percentage cost of cross-border remittances remains, however, inordinately high at an average of 6.93%. According to the World Bank, commercial banks are the most expensive channels for cross-border remittances charging 11.84% of the amount being remitted followed by Post Offices at 8%, Money Transfer Operators (such as Western Union and MoneyGram) charging 5.38% and mobile operators 4.53%. In the latter case the mobile phone is the conduit through which the remittance is channeled from the sender to the recipient and — needless to say — it is increasingly popular.

Indeed, digitalization of remittances through online payments, mobile apps, payment cards and digital wallets is cheaper and increasingly displacing Money Transfer Operators. To wit, *WorldRemit* — established in 2010 — is a digital cross-border remittance firm that provides services in 70 currencies from 50 countries to 130 countries. "*WorldRemit* is 100% cashless. Money is sent from a WorldRemit account on the sender's mobile phone to a recipient's mobile phone. The recipient can then choose to deposit the money in a bank account, pick up cash, deposit mobile money in a digital wallet, or top up airtime on a mobile phone. The transfer can be tracked, with both the sender and recipient notified when the transfer is initiated and received. The transfer fees vary depending on where the money is sent, but the fee for most country is $3.99, with a currency conversion rate of only 1%".[3] FinTech is clearly disrupting the money transfer industry and it explains the lofty ambition of The United Nations Sustainable Development Goals (SDGs) which has set a target for reducing the cost of cross-border remittances at 3% or less by 2030.

3 King, Michael R. *FinTech explained* (University of Toronto Press, 2023), p.261

As we will explain later in this chapter, China's pegged exchange rate policy prevents the current and financial accounts from adjusting through an appreciation of its currency and therefore requires large-scale intervention by its central bank. This is the opposite case of the United States' policy, which allows the value of the dollar to adjust so that its balance of payments would balance without the intervention of the Federal Reserve Bank. Let's now consider each major account in some detail.

CURRENT ACCOUNT

The **current account** records all payments resulting from the international transfer of merchandise trade, services, factor income, and unilateral transfers between a country's residents and the rest of the world. As its name implies, the CA covers transactions "here and now" that create no future claims in either direction. The CA is subdivided into four accounts.

The *goods or visible merchandise trade account* summarizes the imports/exports of physical products such as raw materials, agricultural products, subassemblies, or manufactured products. For example, when Boeing Corporation (a US resident entity) sells 10 Boeing 737-900s to Singapore Airlines (a non-US or foreign entity) for $1 billion, the US balance of payments will record a credit (+) on its merchandise trade account (a source of funds that reduces the US stock of merchandise); but where is the offsetting transaction? Singapore Airlines may remit to Boeing a check drawn on its US$ account with Bank of America: In effect, Singapore Airlines sells a US asset — a bank deposit worth $1 billion — which will appear as a debit (−) or use of funds (a reduction in foreigners' short-term financial claims on the US economy).

Conversely, when Nestlé-USA (a US resident entity even though it is owned by a Swiss multinational corporation) imports $500 million of arabica coffee beans from Colombia, the US balance of payments will record a debit (−) on its merchandise trade account (a use of funds adding to the US stock of merchandise). This is matched by an offsetting credit (+) or increase in foreigners' short-term financial claims on the US economy reflecting payment to the Colombian exporter (source of funds). In effect Nestlé would deposit $500 million in the Citibank account of the Colombian exporter — thus selling a bank deposit in the amount of $500 million to the Colombian exporter. Countries such as Japan, China, and Germany have traditionally enjoyed sizable surpluses on their balance of trade, whereas the United States is known for its colossal chronic deficit (see Exhibit 4.3).

The *services (invisible trade) account* summarizes payments made or received for *intangible* products such as transportation, tourism, travel,

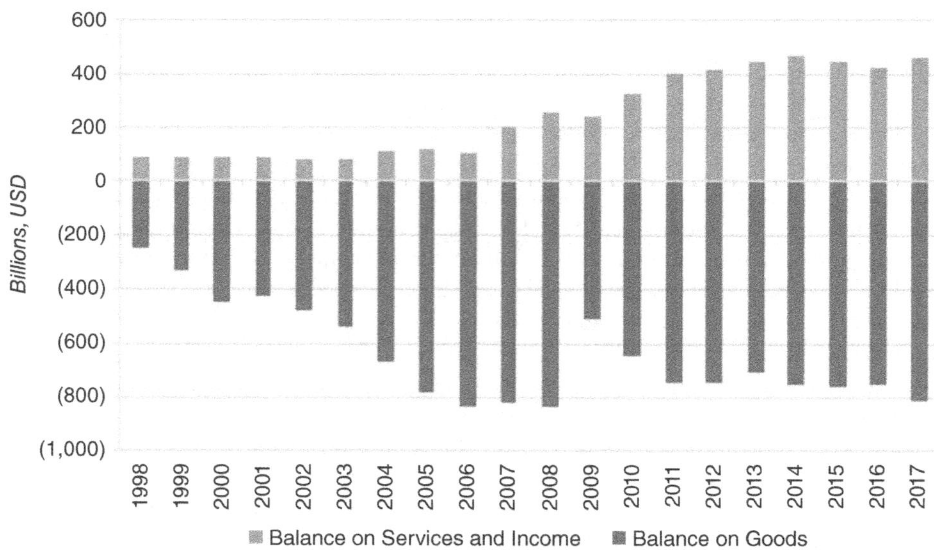

Exhibit 4.3. US trade balance and balance on service and income, 2001–2023.
Source: International Financial Statistics, IMF.

communications, insurance protection, banking services, business services, technical assistance, and royalties for licensing and franchising (use of intellectual property rights measured as income from patents, trademarks, and copyrights). Referring back to Nestlé-USA's imports of coffee, if delivery is carried out by the French shipping company Chargeurs Réunis (a nonresident entity) at a cost of $5 million and insured by Lloyds of London (a nonresident entity) for an insurance premium of $1.5 million, the US balance of payments will further record two debits under its service account that correspond to the importation of a transportation service (from the French shipping company) and an insurance service (from the British marine insurance market). Payment by Nestlé-USA would show as a credit to its bank account as it depletes its financial claim (drawing down its cash balance) and transferring cash to Chargeurs Réunis ($5 million) and Lloyds of London ($1.5 million). Countries such as France and Spain enjoy sizable surpluses in this account due to a large net export of tourism services. The United Kingdom, through the City of London, similarly runs a large surplus due to net exports of insurance, shipping, and financial services.

The use of information technology and the Internet makes outsourcing of a number of services increasingly compelling: A Canadian accounting firm may e-mail tax returns for preparation to a subcontractor in the Philippines, and an Australian hospital may have X-rays read by an Indian radiologist. Exhibit 4.3 further illustrates how the US balance of trade deficit has deepened steadily since 2000 while the surplus on the balance of services has grown over the same period yet failed to fully compensate for the trade deficit.

Factor income consists of payments resulting from past investments and is typically made in the form of interest payments on foreign loans, dividends on foreign stock, rents on foreign property, and so on. Japan is the largest creditor investor nation, consistently investing its visible trade surplus of the past 40 years in foreign stocks, bonds, and factories. Consequently, it collects large dividends from its multinationals' foreign subsidiaries and interest income from its large holdings of US Treasury bonds.

The *unilateral transfer account* records payments corresponding to institutional gifts for missionary and charitable purposes, personal gifts, and grants to foreign countries to help in their economic development. Such unilateral transfers would also include earnings remittances by expatriate workers to relatives who stayed back home. For countries such as the Philippines, India, or Mexico, these payments are a major source of foreign exchange revenues (see International Corporate Finance in Practice 4.1). These transfers are called "unilateral" simply because unlike other transactions considered so far there is flow in only one direction — the direction of payment. As a way of keeping the spirit of double-entry accounting, aid grants are considered as a purchase or import of "goodwill."

The next question to address is how the persistent deficit on the US balance of payments' CA can be financed: The United States can either borrow from the rest of the world or sell off some of its foreign investments. In other words, the United States has to run a surplus on its FA and/or draw down its foreign exchange reserves.

FINANCIAL ACCOUNT

The **financial account**[4] measures the difference between sales and purchases of financial assets by a country's residents to or from foreigners. Such transactions are typically associated with long-term foreign direct investment, portfolio investments in stocks or bonds, and short-term financial investments. US sales of assets to foreigners result in a capital inflow whereas US purchases of foreign assets lead to a capital outflow. Unlike imports/exports of goods and services, transactions in financial assets directly impact future payments and receipts of factor income such as interest and dividends (recorded in the invisible trade section of the CA).

Foreign direct investment represents the acquisition of fixed assets in a foreign country to conduct manufacturing and/or service activities. If Cisco Systems builds a hard drive production facility in Malaysia at a cost of $75 million, it would be considered a capital outflow for the United States. Conversely, when Vivendi — the French media giant — purchased Universal Studios for $1 billion, the United States recorded a capital inflow.

4 Note that the IMF balance of payments classification makes an awkward distinction between financial and capital account transactions, with the latter referring to certain transfers of wealth between residents and nonresidents resulting from nonmarket activities such as debt forgiveness. These transactions are generally very small and for the purpose of this book we have lumped financial and capital account transactions into one category — the FA to conform to traditional use of the term.

Such long-term capital movements are not easily reversible. In 2017 the United States sizably invested slightly more abroad than foreigners invested in the United States, and consequently ran a small deficit on its foreign direct investment balance of US$355 billion – US$379 billion = –US$24 billion.

Portfolio investments correspond to the purchase by US residents of stocks and bonds owned by foreigners and the sale to foreigners of stocks and bonds owned by US residents. The investor should limit its stake to less than 10% of the company; otherwise it would be viewed as exercising managerial control and therefore fall into the category of foreign direct investment. For example, a US pension fund, TIAA-CREF, invests in Alstom — the French manufacturer of Trains à Grande Vitesse (TGV) and rolling stocks by purchasing common stock in the amount of €100 million. This corresponds to a capital outflow: It would be recorded as a debit/increase in foreign portfolio investment (use of funds) and a credit/decrease in foreigners' short-term financial claims on the US economy (source of funds) since TIAA-CREF draws down its € financial assets held on deposit in its bank account and transfers €100 million to the bank account of the foreign seller of Alstom shares. Note that the motivation of the US pension fund is strictly greed in the old-fashioned sense. TIAA-CREF is interested in capital gains resulting from Alstom's stock price appreciation and periodic dividend payments; it is not interested in managing or controlling Alstom.

Conversely, if a Japanese life insurance company such as Fuji Life were to purchase $25 million of 30-year US Treasury bonds issued by the US government, the purchase would correspond to a capital inflow. Cross-border portfolio investments have grown exponentially in the past decade, fueled in part by the emergence of capital markets and the desire of investors to reap the benefits of international diversification.

Short-term financial investment includes international bank loans or money market investments that are typically motivated by short-term interest differentials as well as expectations of exchange rate movements. They can be extremely volatile. If Fuji Life, the Japanese insurance company, buys 180-day Treasury notes from the US government, the purchase would result in a short-term capital inflow or a supply of foreign exchange for the United States (and a capital outflow for Japan): Fuji Life is effectively extending a short-term loan to the US government. Conversely, when JPMorgan Chase extends a 180-day loan to Nortel — the Canadian telecom company — this leads to a capital outflow or a demand for foreign currency for the United States (and a capital inflow for Canada).

Exhibit 4.4 illustrates the massive net capital inflows in the United States due to foreign investors

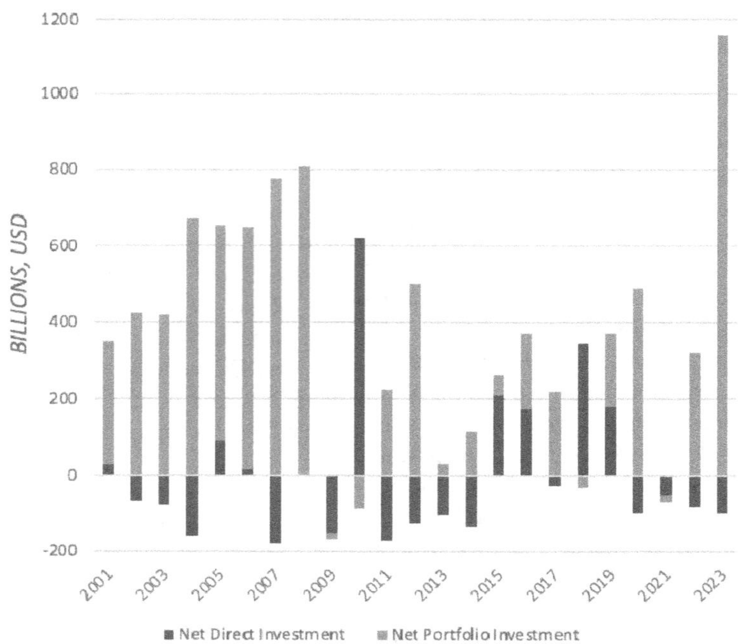

Exhibit 4.4. The United States financial account, 2001–2023 (billions of US$).
Source: International Financial Statistics, IMF.

purchasing US stocks and bonds. Recall the massive US CA deficit. Clearly, the latter would not be possible without the former.

Returning to the US balance of payments capital account in 2023 (Exhibit 4.1), we note a very large surplus of US$1,157 billion on the portfolio investment subaccount (lines 2.3a and 2.3b), whereas the subaccount on foreign direct investment shows a more modest deficit of US$100 billion (lines 2.2a and 2.2b).

OFFICIAL RESERVE ACCOUNT

A nation's central bank ORA measures the changes in both owned reserve assets (gold, foreign currencies, and special drawing rights) and liabilities owed to foreign official agencies such as other countries' central banks or the International Monetary Fund. Changes in the reserve account will simply offset the net of the current and FAs, providing the "balance for the balance of payments to balance." In other words, if the US economy buys more from or sells more to the rest of the world than it borrows from or lends to the rest of the world, then the US Federal Reserve Bank will either pay the difference (by drawing down its assets or adding to its liabilities) or accumulate (by adding to its assets or drawing down its liabilities). If we denote the current account balance by CA and the financial account balance by FA, the net change Δ in the central bank's ORA (ΔORA) over a given period is equal to[5]:

Change in official reserves = Current account balance + Financial account balance

$$\Delta ORA = CA + FA$$

STATISTICAL DISCREPANCIES: ERRORS AND OMISSIONS

Given the scope of the measurement effort and the millions of transactions to be measured and recorded, it is highly unlikely that the sources and uses of foreign exchange will balance. This is due in part to two factors: (1) large smuggling and illegal operations that escape the official recording apparatus and (2) discrepancies in timing and measurement. Essentially, the E&O account is simply a *plug* that enables the balance of payments to balance.

5 In this simplified formulation, capital and financial accounts are lumped into one FA to follow common terminology. E&O are assumed away entirely.

INTERNATIONAL CORPORATE FINANCE IN PRACTICE 4.2

Brexit and the United Kingdom's Balance of Payments

On June 23, 2016 Britain voted on the quintessential question *"Should the United Kingdom (UK) remain a member of the European Union or leave the European Union?"*. Surprisingly 52% of voters opted in favor of leaving the European Union (EU) — also referred to as Brexit. What led to this shocking divorce between the UK and the EU? It seems that the UK could live within the confines of the EU customs union allowing free movement of goods, services and capital as enshrined in the Treaty of Rome (1957) — but increasingly balked at inward migration of eastern European nationals seeking a better life in the UK — the fourth freedom of movement for EU nationals. Brexit would severely impact Britain's relationship with the world economy. Britain's balance of payments traditionally shows a CA deficit largely financed by an equally large CA/FA surplus (see Exhibit 4.5). The CA suffers from an overwhelmingly large ***visible trade*** deficit (goods) — partly compensated by a surplus on the ***invisible trade*** surplus (services) with three key sub-accounts — namely tourism, higher education and financial services — accounting for most of the surplus. Of special note is the stellar surplus in financial services of $83 billion.[6] Most importantly the CA deficit is largely financed by a surplus on the FA; indeed, the UK is the leading recipient of Foreign Direct Investment among the 28 EU members as foreign multinational corporations privilege the UK as a manufacturing platform to serve the EU. How would Brexit impact the United Kingdom's balance of payments?

6 The City of London — the hub of UK-based financial services — is a significant contributor to the UK economy with top line revenue of approximately $270 billion, employs 1.1 million and contribute to the UK balance of payments a surplus of $83 billion.

Exhibit 4.5. United Kingdom balance of payments, 2023 (billions of US dollars).

1.	**CURRENT ACCOUNT**	**(110)**
1.1	Trade balance	(42)
1.2	Balance on Services	190
1.3	Balance on Income	(69)
1.4	Current transfers: Net	(30)
2.	**FINANCIAL ACCOUNT**	**154**
2.1	Capital Account: Net	(2)
2.2	Direct investment abroad	214
2.3	Portfolio investment	348
2.4	Financial derivatives: Net	40
2.5	Other investment assets	(222)
3.	**NET E&O**	**25**
4.	**CHANGE IN ORA**	**(23)**

The United Kingdom could have chosen a ***soft* Brexit** which would have meant that it remained a quasi-member of the EU single market, continue to pay into the EU budget albeit at a reduced level; it would have lost its seat at the EU governance table but would partially have extricated itself from the EU administrative and legal framework. This amicable arrangement of parting of the ways would have been similar to Norway's agreement with the EU and would have required the UK to allow freedom of movement for EU workers.[7] A soft Brexit would have had a minor impact on the United Kingdom's balance of payments. Instead the United Kingdom decided on a ***hard Brexit*** which entail that it completely disengage from the EU and renounce access to the Single Market. Consequently, the UK is required to renegotiate not only its trade relationships with the remaining 27 EU members but also with the rest of the world. It is now forced to trade with the EU like most other non-EU members and face tariff and non-tariff barriers admittedly much lower than they were when Britain first joined the EU in 1973 but still detrimental to its economy.

As a result it was widely expected that the United Kingdom's **visible** trade account with the EU would suffer greatly as EU-bound exports would now face the external tariff barrier imposed on any imports from non-EU member countries. The **invisible** trade balance would experience a reduced financial services surplus currently standing at £18 billion with the EU as UK-domiciled financial institutions — commercial banks and insurance companies mostly — would lose their ***passporting***[8] privileges in cross-selling their products in the EU and therefore reduce their activities in the City of London to re-locate their European headquarters to Paris, Amsterdam or Frankfurt. Not only would Foreign Direct Investment by both manufacturing and service firms into the UK sharply contract as multinationals Europe-wide supply chains and logistics network are reconfigured but divestment — exodus of MNCs relocating to the EU — would also takes its toll on the UK **FA.** If the CA gap is no longer easily financed by a FA surplus the UK balance of payments could only stay in balance if the pound sterling continues to depreciate against the euro.

7 Norway never joined the EU but signed in 1973 a treaty of association with the EU: it has access to the Single Market, pays an annual contribution of €735 million and adheres to all four freedoms including the freedom of movement for EU nationals. About 1/3 of the EU legislative body including directives are abided by Norway. If scaled up to a population of 65 million the UK would pay an annual contribution of €9.55 billion.

8 A ***banking passport*** gives the right to sell financial services throughout the EU without establishing a branch or a subsidiary. EU member states are restricted in their ability to impose additional regulation.

But Brexit's doomsday never arrived: 8 years after Brexit the pound sterling trades against the euro at about the same rate that it did in 2016 and the United Kingdom's CA deficit hovers around 3.5% of GDP and is slightly higher that it was when Brexit was first voted in. The exodus of international bankers to rival financial centers such as Paris, Frankfurt and Amsterdam happened on a limited scale and the United Kingdom's balance of invisible has actually increased by approximately 25%.

BALANCE OF PAYMENTS AND THE FOREIGN EXCHANGE MARKET

The different transactions making up a country's balance of payments will have a defining impact on its exchange rate, and vice versa. In fact, most but not all transactions resulting from an inflow of foreign exchange (such as exports, repatriation of dividends, or a loan from a foreign bank) make up the supply curve of foreign exchange. Transactions resulting in an outflow of foreign exchange such as imports or foreign direct investment make up the demand for foreign exchange. At its simplest, the foreign exchange market is built on the interplay between the supply curve $s(t)$ of foreign exchange (demand for the domestic currency) and the demand curve $d(t)$ for foreign exchange (supply of the domestic currency). The clearing price is the equilibrium exchange rate (cf. Exhibit 4.6 for the case of the US dollar–Chinese yuan foreign exchange market).

> ***Q:*** Referring to Exhibit 4.6, what are the transactions between the United States and China that give rise to the supply of foreign exchange — yuan in this case?
>
> ***A:*** Exports to China of goods and services, China's investments in US factories, stocks and bonds, as well as loans by China to US resident entities.

Depending upon how much the central bank interferes with this price-clearing mechanism, the balance of payments' ORA will show no, some, or significant activity.

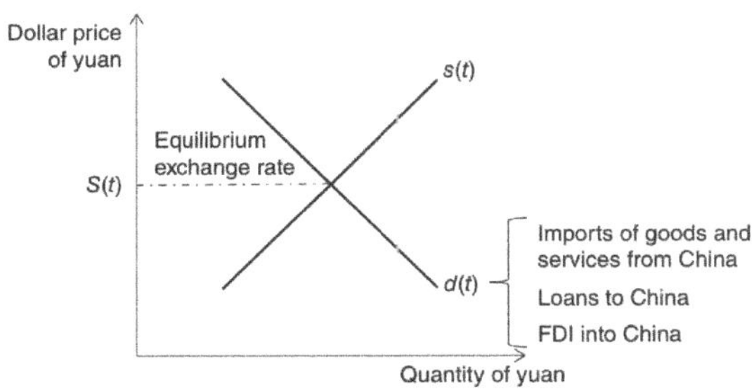

Exhibit 4.6. Equilibrium exchange rate.

- *Clean float.* If the central bank leaves market forces to solely determine the equilibrium exchange rate (clean float), there will be no change in the ORA (ΔORA = 0) and the balance of payments will simply balance as:

$$\text{CA} + \text{FA} = 0 = \Delta\text{ORA}$$

Thus, a CA deficit will be financed by a net capital inflow, as has been the situation of the US economy for the past two decades. It should be emphasized that the US Federal Reserve Bank almost never intervenes in the foreign exchange market. This allows the exchange rate to find its equilibrium level at which all transactions leading to the purchase or the sale of US dollars will clear the market (cf. Exhibit 4.7, which shows how the current account deficit closely mirrors the financial account surplus).

- *Managed float.* Should the central bank intervene in the foreign exchange market to slow down its currency appreciation (dirty float) due to a large surplus in its CA, its ORA will grow over time:

$$\text{CA} + \text{FA} = \Delta\text{ORA}$$

  This is the case for a number of East Asian countries such as Japan, China, and Taiwan, whose ORAs are reaching stratospheric levels (see Exhibit 4.8 and International Corporate Finance in Practice 4.2 for East Asian central bank foreign exchange reserves).

- *Pegged exchange rates.* When the central bank is committed to keeping the exchange rate fixed or quasi-fixed, it has to intervene heavily in the foreign exchange market to do so. When a country experiences a deficit in its current account and the deficit is combined with a massive capital outflow, the central bank will have to sell a large amount of foreign currency (to buy its own currency) in order to stave off a devaluation. When the 1997 Asian financial crisis first hit Thailand, its central bank used up more than US\$50 billion in reserve to keep the baht (THB) fixed at THB 25 = \$1.

A more recent case is China, which has often been accused of keeping its currency undervalued

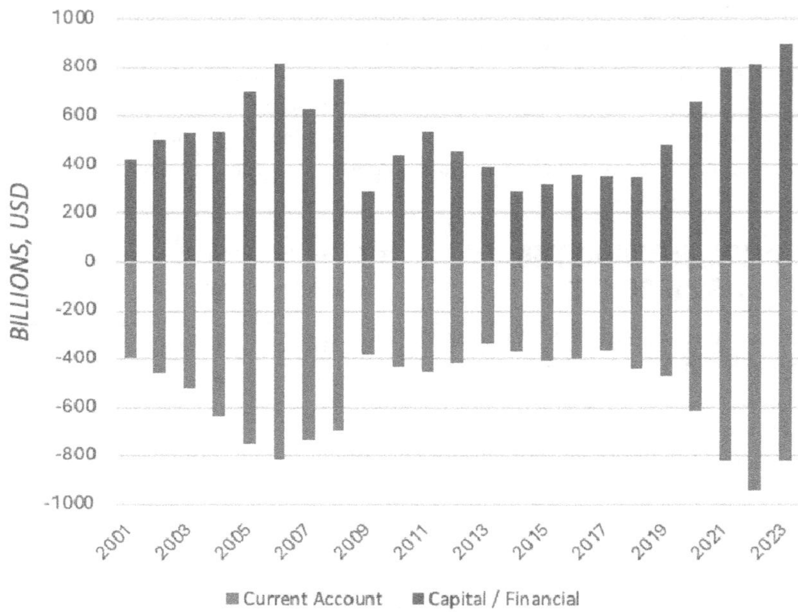

Exhibit 4.7. Current and financial account balances for the United States, 2001–2023 (billions of dollars).
Source: International Financial Statistics, IMF.

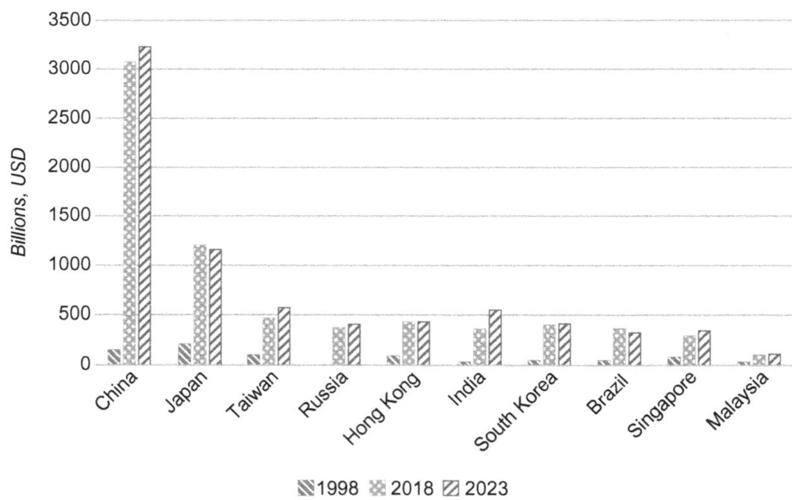

Exhibit 4.8. Rising reserves in Asia (billions of US$).
Source: International Financial Statistics, IMF.

vis-à-vis the US dollar or other major currencies. China's exports are very price sensitive, and the country has accumulated a staggering balance of trade and current account surplus over the past decade (see Exhibit 4.9). Until 2013, China was also experiencing a large surplus on its financial account due to massive foreign direct investment by foreign multinational corporations and portfolio investments in Chinese stocks. Until then its central bank was intervening heavily in its foreign exchange market by mopping up excess foreign exchange inflow in order to keep its currency quasi-pegged to the dollar (or allowing it to appreciate very slowly). This is no longer the case as in the last decade China has started to experience a sizeable financial account deficit reflecting large scale foreign direct investment by Chinese firms.

INTERNATIONAL CORPORATE FINANCE IN PRACTICE 4.3

Asian Central Banks' Forex Reserves and The US Government Budget Deficit

Over the past decade, the seven biggest Asian central banks — China, Japan, India, Taiwan, South Korea, Hong Kong, and Malaysia — have accumulated more than $5 trillion in foreign exchange reserves, with the majority of it held in US dollars (US national debt currently stands at $17 trillion). These staggering quasi-cash hoards are the result of large balance of trade surpluses with the United States combined with either quasi-fixed exchange rates such as in the case of China or Hong Kong, or very managed floats for all other currencies. Instead of allowing their exchange rates to appreciate to dampen their strong surplus on their visible trade, central banks have to purchase dollars to slow down their currency appreciation. Rather than simply hoarding their dollar reserves, central banks will typically purchase dollar-denominated US government debt, which keeps the yields on Treasury bills low. Should Asian central banks decide to stop investing dutifully in US Treasuries, it is generally estimated that Treasuries' yields would have to increase by 1.5% from their current level of 0.25% and the dollar to depreciate by 30% to attract enough private investors to offset what would be lost in central banks' purchases. With the establishment of sovereign wealth funds taking a more aggressive approach to global investment, it is widely expected that Asian countries will quietly start to diversify away from US Treasury bonds and dollar-denominated investments.

Source: Adapted from "How One Word Haunts the Dollar: Investors Tremble as Foreign Central Banks Speak of Diversification," *Wall Street Journal*, March 17, 2005.

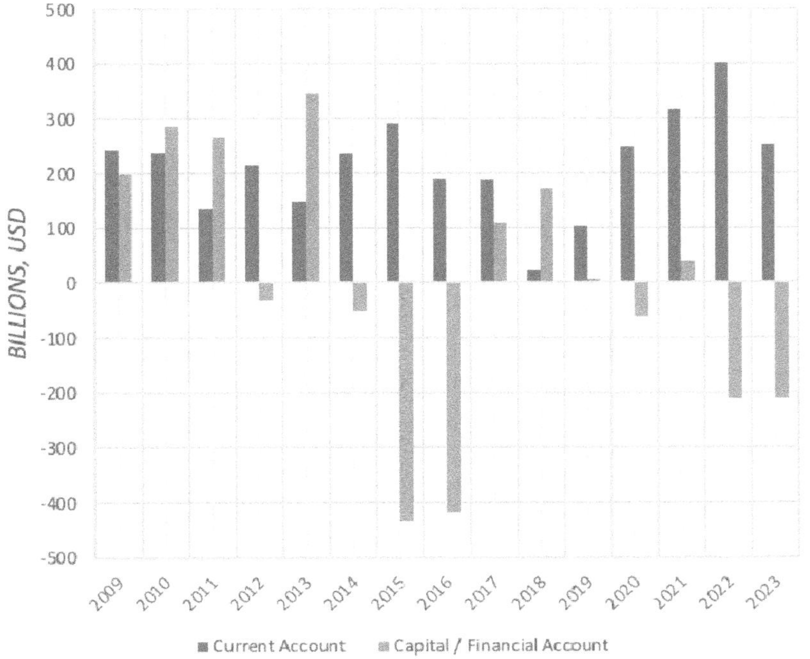

Exhibit 4.9. Current and capital account balances for China, 2009–2023 (billions of dollars).

Source: International Financial Statistics, IMF.

> ***Q:*** What would happen to China's foreign exchange reserves if it allowed the yuan to float freely without central bank interference?
>
> ***A:*** China's foreign exchange reserves would stop growing since its central bank would no longer be buying dollars to keep its currency quasi-pegged. In all likelihood, the yuan would appreciate substantially by as much as 25 to 30%, slowing down exports and encouraging imports while discouraging capital inflows.

DEBTOR VERSUS CREDITOR NATIONS

Balance of payments accounting takes a cash-flow view of a country's dealings with the rest of the world. The cumulative result of ongoing transactions between a country and the rest of the world is captured by the country's net investment position or its net foreign wealth — a "stock" rather than a "flow" concept more akin to a firm's balance sheet than its cash-flow statement. For example, the Bureau of Economic Analysis of the US Department of Commerce reported that the United States has a negative net foreign wealth far greater than that of any other country. As the United States has experienced massive current account deficits over the past quarter century, the rest of the world has steadily built up a massive creditor position as a lender to the US government by purchasing Treasury bonds and holding equity positions by buying US companies, real estate, and land. Indeed, the United States has become the *world's biggest debtor* nation (cf. Exhibit 4.10). It is keeping good company with major emerging market countries such as Argentina, Mexico, and Brazil, which also shoulder massive international debt burdens. It should be noted, however, that in relative terms the US international indebtedness is only 25% of its GDP whereas foreign indebtedness reaches 50–100% for Argentina and other countries.

For every debtor nation we expect to find creditor nations that have accumulated large claims on foreign economies through virtuous current account surpluses. This is the case for Japan, which has emerged as a major creditor nation as illustrated by Exhibit 4.11. Similarly, the gargantuan foreign exchange reserves amassed by China are largely invested in US government bonds (see Exhibit 4.12).

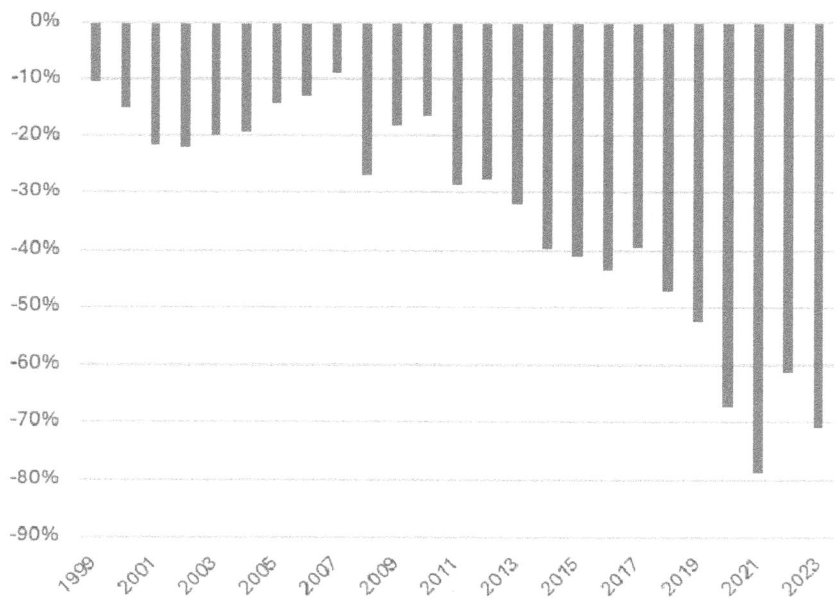

Exhibit 4.10. US net international investment position as a percentage of its GDP.
Source: International Financial Statistics, IMF.

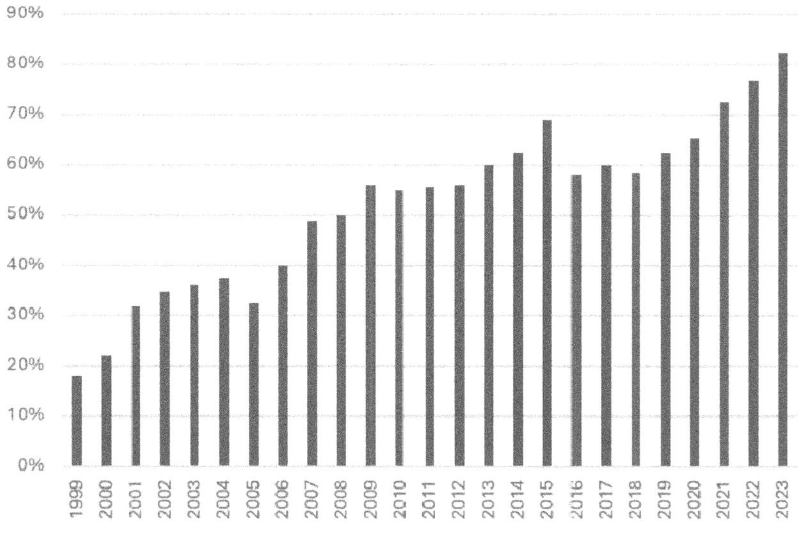

Exhibit 4.11. Japan's net international investment position as a percentage of GDP.

Source: International Financial Statistics, IMF.

Exhibit 4.12. US treasury holdings by foreign central banks (US$ billion).

Source: Bloomberg.

LINKING THE BALANCE OF PAYMENTS TO NATIONAL INCOME

The *gross national product* (GNP) of a country is the sum total of all final goods and services produced by the national economy over a given period — usually a quarter or a year. Thus, the GNP can be readily estimated by aggregating what households, business firms, all branches of government (federal, state, and local), and foreigners spend on goods and services.

In a *closed* economy with no foreign trade, GNP is the sum of all expenditures on goods and services consumed by private-sector residents (C);

the amount invested[9] by private-sector firms to build new plants, acquire new equipment, or build inventory (I); and government purchases for both consumption and investment purposes (G). It can be readily written as:

$$\text{GNP} = C + I + G$$

In an *open* economy things become slightly more complicated because foreign entities will purchase some of the nation's goods and services — also known as exports (X), whereas domestic entities may purchase foreign goods and services — imports (M). Thus, the GNP equation should be adjusted by additional expenditures (X) carried out by foreigners whereas expenditures on foreign goods and services (M) should be subtracted:

$$\text{GNP} = C + I + G + (X - M)$$

The last term (X – M) is nothing more than the current account (CA) balance[10] and offers a simple link between the GNP and the balance of payments.

The production of goods and services measured by the GNP generates an equal flow of gross national income (GNI) to the different factors of production (labor and capital) responsible for the production of those same goods and services. This national income may be partly spent by households (H) on consumption (C) or saved (S_H); similarly, business firms will save the income they generate (S_B) by reinvesting in their firms — so-called retained earnings — while the rest is paid to various branches of government in the form of taxes (T). Gross national income (GNI) can thus be expressed as

$$\text{GNI} = C + S_H + S_B + T$$

Since by definition GNP has to equal gross national income, we can write the important identity:

$$C + I + G + (X - M) = C + S_H + S_B + T$$

which can be re-arranged as

$$X - M = S_H + S_B - I + T - G$$

where aggregate savings by the private sector S is equal to S_H plus S_B. Since tax revenues (T) minus government expenditures (G) are simply the net government budget deficit or surplus, the CA balance is equal to the private-sector net savings ($S - I$) plus the government net budgetary deficit or surplus ($T - G$).

or

This is a powerful relationship that gives us a framework to better understand how domestic macroeconomics tie up with a nation's economic relationship with the rest of the world economy. Consider the case of China, which saves approximately 30% of its GNP — a third of which (10% of GNP) is invested in the private sector in the form of infrastructure, new capital equipment, and/or accumulation of inventory. If the Chinese government runs a deficit of approximately 5% of its GNP, this means that China's net national savings — the private-sector surplus (30 – 10% of GNP) minus the government deficit (5% of GDP) — would be 15% of GDP. What is not used in China must be sold abroad, which means that China would run a CA surplus of 15% of GNP!

> ***Q:*** The US private sector saves 6% of GDP and invests approximately 4% of GDP. The US government runs a mammoth budgetary deficit of 10% of GDP. Is the United States running a surplus or a deficit on the CA of its balance of payments?
>
> ***A:*** The US private sector saves 2% of GDP — which, subtracted from the US government dis-saving of 10%, amounts to a CA deficit of 8% of GDP.

Thus, there is a simple relationship between GNP, GNI, and the balance of payments' CA. If a country generates a surplus on its balance of payments' CA, this means that it is saving, in the aggregate, more than it is investing. Conversely, a country running a persistent deficit on its CA is spending more on investment than it is saving or dis-saving.

Since in a "clean" float the CA surplus or deficit is directly financed by a surplus or deficit on the FA, we can readily infer that a nation's aggregate (private-sector and government-sector) saving or dis-saving is matched by an equal capital outflow or inflow. For example, Japan runs a government deficit of 10% of GNP but enjoys a net private-sector savings of 15%, which should translate into a CA surplus of 5% of GNP and a capital outflow of 5% of GNP. However, Japan's central bank intervenes in the foreign exchange market to prevent the Yen from appreciating — so-called dirty float — such

9 This investment should not be confused with the purchase of stocks or bonds, also known as investments, which are not part of GNP.

10 For ease of exposition, we are assuming away unilateral transfers and net income from foreign factors of production and thereby approximating the current account balance by the balance on visible and invisible trade.

that capital outflow is only 4% of GNP and 1% accumulates into the ORA.

SUMMARY

1. A balance of payments is a statistical and accounting record of all the payments between the residents of one country and the rest of the world during a given period — usually a quarter or year. It is analogous to a firm's cash-flow statement.
2. A balance of payments is comprised of three principal accounts: (1) a current account, which nets all transactions of goods and services as well as investment income, remittances, and unilateral transfers; (2) a financial account, which records the net of all financial asset-based transactions such as loans, equity portfolio investments, and foreign direct investment; and (3) the official reserves account, which tracks the country's central bank transactions with the outside world.
3. The balance of payments is based on double-entry bookkeeping whereby every transaction recorded as a credit is matched by an offsetting debit entry, and vice versa. A credit entry records the sale of domestic goods, services, and assets or an increase in liabilities to foreigners. Conversely, purchases of foreign goods, services, and assets or a decrease in liabilities to foreigners are recorded as debits. By design, double-entry bookkeeping ensures that the sum of all credits equals the sum of all debits and that the balance of payments balances.
4. For a country whose exchange rate is truly floating, the surplus/deficit on its current account will be exactly compensated by a deficit/surplus on its financial account.
5. Changes in a country's official reserves account will occur when its government's central bank intervenes in the foreign exchange market. If intervention aims at slowing its currency appreciation, the official reserves account will show an increase in foreign reserves. Conversely, intervention to resist its currency depreciation will result in a decline in foreign reserves. If the exchange rate floats freely with no central bank intervention ("clean float"), the official reserves account will remain unchanged.
6. Countries that consistently finance a current account deficit by borrowing from the rest of the world accumulate debt obligations that will have to be serviced by paying interest or dividends to their creditors. The United States is the largest debtor nation; Japan and China are the largest creditor nations.
7. A country's aggregate savings deficit or surplus (from both the private sector and government) is equal to its current account deficit or surplus; it is financed by its financial account surplus/deficit and a decrease/increase in its official foreign exchange reserves.

QUESTIONS FOR DISCUSSION

1. Why should a balance of payments always balance?
2. If the balance of payments always balances, how can a nation have a balance of payments surplus or deficit?
3. What are the major transaction categories making up the current account?
4. What is the difference between international portfolio investment and foreign direct investment? Where do they appear on the balance of payments?
5. What are the major differences between the United States' and China's balance of payments?
6. Why is China accumulating forex reserves so rapidly? Is its balance of payments indeed balancing?
7. What are the key transactions making up the balance of invisible trade? Where does it appear on the balance of payments?
8. What are international remittances? Where do they appear on the balance of payments?
9. Where are illicit activities such as drug trafficking and international terrorism recorded on the balance of payments?
10. What is the cash-flow relationship between the net international indebtedness of a country and its balance of payments?
11. What major differences would you expect between the balance of payments of a country that operates under a system of fixed exchange rates versus floating exchange rates?
12. Does it make sense for France or any other member country of the euro-zone to keep a national balance of payments? Given the single currency, do you believe that the euro-zone balance of payments is really what matters?

PROBLEMS

1. **Balance of payments accounting (beginner).** For the following international transactions, identify the balance of payments accounts and whether the transaction would generate an inflow or an outflow of foreign exchange for the two countries involved.
   - US-based General Electric (GE) sells 25 air turbines to Airbus-France for the total sum of $500 million.
   - US-based Goldman Sachs advises the French government for the partial privatization of state-owned utility Gaz de France for a lump sum of $10 million.
   - American Airlines purchases five propeller aircrafts from Canada-based Bombardier for the total amount of $75 million.
   - TIAA-CREF — the pension fund of American college professors — purchases 1 million shares of South Africa's Standard Bank for $16 million.
   - Air France purchases $2.5 million of jet fuel at Boston's Logan Airport. Payment is made directly from Air France's bank account with State Street in Boston.
   - Hong Kong-based Cathay Pacific pays a $25 million annual lease on two Boeing 777s to US-based lessor GE Capital.
   - The University of Minnesota enrolls 600 Chinese students, who each pay $15,000 in annual tuition. Each Chinese student spends $7,500 a year for lodging and food; 300 students take loans in the amount of $5,000 each from the Hong Kong branch of Citigroup; 300 students receive full scholarships for their tuition from the US-based Fulbright Association.
   - A group of 25 US tourists visit the Greek islands aboard a Norwegian cruise ship for the total cost of $125,000. The cruise ship is insured with American International Group (AIG), the US insurance carrier, for $10,000.
   - Ten US students from Pennsylvania State University spend their junior year spring semester at the University of Geneva. They pay $2,500 each in tuition to the Swiss university, and each spends $3,000 for lodging, food, and books while in Geneva.
   - The Colombian drug cartel delivers 100 kg of heroin to its distributor in Miami, who pays $25 million in cash.

2. **Balance-of-payments double-entry bookkeeping (beginner).** Show how the following transactions should be recorded in the US balance of payments using a double-entry accounting system:
   - Newmont Mining — a US mining concern — exports $400 million worth of copper to China and is paid in the form of a payment drawn on a US bank.
   - DuPont expands its plastics manufacturing capacity in its Polish plant by investing $250 million financed by a dollar bond issue in London.
   - The central bank of the People's Bank of China purchases $2.5 billion in the foreign exchange market to slow down the appreciation of the renminbi. The dollars are invested in five-year US Treasury bonds.
   - The US government provides food assistance to Sudanese refugees in the amount of $25 million worth of flour.

3. **Boeing's big-ticket exports (beginner).** Cathay Pacific, the Hong Kong-based airline, purchases five Boeing Dreamliners for $750 million. The US Export-Import Bank provides a seven-year loan for the full amount of the purchase with no interest or principal payments due in the first year. Explain how the transaction would be recorded by the US balance of payments.

4. **Taiwan's official reserves account (beginner).** Assume that in 2018 Taiwan ran a surplus on its current account of US$125 billion and a financial account deficit of US$25 billion. What would be the net impact on Taiwan's official reserves account? Spell out your assumptions.

5. **International debt forgiveness (intermediate).** Assume that France decides to write off €10 billion of debt to Morocco. What would be the impact of debt forgiveness on (1) France's balance of payments and (2) Morocco's balance of payments?

6. **Bank of China's international reserves management (intermediate).** How would China's balance of payments be affected should its central bank decide to sell one billion of dollar-denominated US Treasury bonds and immediately invest the proceeds into euro-denominated five-year notes newly issued by Portugal? How would the US balance of payments be impacted by China's decision?

7. **Accounting for natural disasters (intermediate).** The earthquake-cum-tsunami that devastated part of Japan on March 11, 2011, is estimated to be a loss of US$250 billion. What is its likely impact on the Japanese balance of payments?

8. **The world's largest creditor nation (intermediate).** How is Japan's annual balance of payments impacted by the country's dominant international creditor position? Which accounts are directly affected? Is Japan still the largest creditor nation?

INTERNET EXERCISES

9. **Grexit (beginner).** Access the IMF Balance of Payments query tool at https://data.imf.org/bop:
   a. Prepare a bar graph showing Greece' current account deficit since 2001 to present,
   b. How does it compare to Greece's budget deficit over the same period?
   c. How was Greece's current account deficit financed?
   d. How would Greece's exit from the euro (i.e., the reenactment and subsequent float of the drachma) impact Greece's current account and financial accounts?
10. **Comparing the downfall of the Turkish lira and Argentine peso (intermediate).** Access exchange rate data at http://fx.sauder.ubc.ca/data.html and the IMF Balance of Payments query tool at https://data.imf.org/bop:
    a. Map the Turkish lira price of one US dollar from January 1, 2016 to the present. Superimpose on the same graph Turkey current account during the same period
    b. Repeat the same exercise for Argentina over the same period
    c. Track the level of foreign exchange reserves held by Turkey and Argentina over the same period. Were either central bank attempting to stem the precipitous decline of their currency
    d. Comment on the similarities and differences between the two crises.
11. **Tequila Crisis (A — intermediate).** Access exchange rate data at http://fx.sauder.ubc.ca/data.html to graph the Mexican peso price of one US dollar over the period 1992–1996. Can you characterize the exchange rate regime(s) implemented by Mexico over the same period? What was the role played by the central bank of Mexico over the same period?
12. **Tequila Crisis (B — intermediate).** Access the IMF Balance of Payments query tool at https://data.imf.org/bop to present and analyze Mexico's current account over the period 1992–1996. Break down your analysis among merchandise trade, services, net income, and transfers. Link your interpretation to the discussion of problem #11.
13. **Tequila Crisis (C — intermediate).** Access the IMF Balance of Payments query tool at https://data.imf.org/bop to present and analyze Mexico's Financial account over the period 1992–1996. How can you reconcile your findings with the discussion of problems #11 and #12?
14. **Tequila Crisis (D — intermediate).** Access the IMF Balance of Payments query tool at https://data.imf.org/bop to present and analyze Mexico's official reserves account over the period 1992–1996. What can you infer about Mexico's central bank activities during that period? Was Mexico's balance of payments indeed balancing over the 1992–1996 period? How can you reconcile your findings with the discussion of problems #11, #12, and #13?
15. **Foreign remittances and the subprime crisis (A — advanced).** Access the IMF Balance of Payments query tool at https://data.imf.org/bop and track the flows of expatriates' remittances to Mexico before, during, and after the subprime crisis of 2008. What is your interpretation?
16. **Foreign remittances and the subprime crisis (B — advanced).** Access the IMF Balance of Payments query tool at https://data.imf.org/bop and track the flows of expatriates' remittances to the Philippines before, during, and after the subprime crisis of 2008. What is your interpretation? How do they compare to Mexico's flows? How do you account for the difference?
17. **Trials and tribulations of Argentina's Peso (advanced).** Access the IMF Balance of Payments query tool at https://data.imf.org/bop and the Bank for International Settlements statistics explorer at https://stats.bis.org/statx/toc/LBS.html, and chart the current account (balance of both visible and invisible trade) and financial accounts of Argentina over the period 1997–2017 against the peso/dollar exchange rate. *Hint:* The peso was pegged to the US dollar through a currency board until January 2002 when it collapsed and started to float more or less freely against the US dollar.
    a. Comment on how the balance of merchandise trade behaves over that period. What is your interpretation?
    b. Did the Bank of Argentina intervene heavily during that period? Can you detect a change in policy after the currency board was abandoned in 2002?
    c. Assuming that the peso was fairly valued in Purchasing Power Parity terms when the

currency board was first established in 1991, is the Peso over-valued or over-valued on December 31, 2017?

REFERENCES

International Monetary Fund. Latest edition. *Balance of Payments Manual*. Washington, DC: International Monetary Fund.

International Monetary Fund. Latest edition. *Balance of Payments Yearbook*. Washington, DC: International Monetary Fund.

Kemp, Donald S. 1975. "Balance-of-Payments Concepts — What Do They Really Mean?" *Federal Reserve Bank of St. Louis Review* (July): 14–23.

Ohmae, Kenichi. 1991. "Lies, Damned Lies and Statistics: Why the Trade Deficit Does Not Matter in a Borderless World." *Journal of Applied Corporate Finance* (Winter): 98–106.

CASE STUDY 4.1. WHEN ONE OF THE BRIC(K)S FALLS: TRIALS AND TRIBULATIONS OF THE INDIAN RUPEE

The chapter on the Fall of the Rupee you may omit. It is somewhat too sensational.

Miss Prism, in Oscar Wilde's
The Importance of Being Earnest, 1895

Narendra Aneja is the chief investment strategist at the Flying Dragon Fund — an India country fund domiciled in Boston — that has close to $1 billion under management in Indian stocks. The first semester of 2012 had been an utter disaster, with the Bombay Stock Exchange down more than 18%, further compounded by a steep depreciation of the rupee. Narendra was reviewing the latest balance of payments statistics and short-term projections (see the case exhibits) in preparation for the board quarterly meeting, when he would have to map out the rupee's likely course. Somehow he would have to make amends for failing to anticipate the reversal in the rupee's fortunes, which only a year ago had seemed so much more auspicious.

Economic Growth and Fiscal Deficits

In spite of its economy expanding at the rate of 6% in the first two quarters of 2012, India's currency was now down 20% on the year, while its budget deficit at 5.9% of GDP (March 2011 to March 2012) grossly overshot its target of 4.6%. Structural economic reforms are hindered by the government's lack of a reliable parliamentary majority, and it is likely to focus on the more pressing concerns of high inflation, slower economic growth, and a falling rupee. For almost a year, India's central bank — the Reserve Bank of India (RBI) — has spent billions of dollars to support the beleaguered rupee but still seems powerless in bucking the downward trend. Some analysts see the exchange rate weakening further toward 60 rupees per US dollar by year-end, versus its closing rate of 54.48 rupees.

Current Account

Because of subdued global demand and sustained import growth, the deficit on the current account will widen from 2.2% of GDP in 2011 to 3.7% in 2012. This would primarily result from a widening trade deficit, expected to reach US$182 billion in 2012. Services exports such as information technology and business process outsourcing continue to attract Western firms to India. The rupee has been declining partly because of a flight of capital from emerging markets, but also because of concerns over India's deteriorating financial health. Unsurprisingly, the country's current account deficit recently hit its highest level ever, as the federal government's heavy spending widened its budget deficit. India's government failed to raise fuel prices to reduce demand for costly imported oil, while government spending on massive fuel subsidies kept inflation high (see Case Exhibit 4.1).

Financial Account

Historically, capital inflows have been financing India's structural current account deficit; however, the deepening of the euro-zone crisis is triggering a new increase in investors' risk aversion. The central bank also has made it easier for foreigners to invest in rupee-denominated assets. And more drastically, it recently ordered Indian exporters to convert foreign-currency earnings into rupees. By mid-December, the rupee hit a then-record intraday low of 54.29 to the dollar, and the bank took actions aimed at increasing capital inflows and curbing speculative activity. For example, it restricted banks' ability to cancel and rebook forward contracts, thereby taking bets on the currency's movement. The RBI also tried to lure Indians living abroad to move more money back onshore, by allowing banks to offer higher interest rates on deposits held by nonresident Indians.

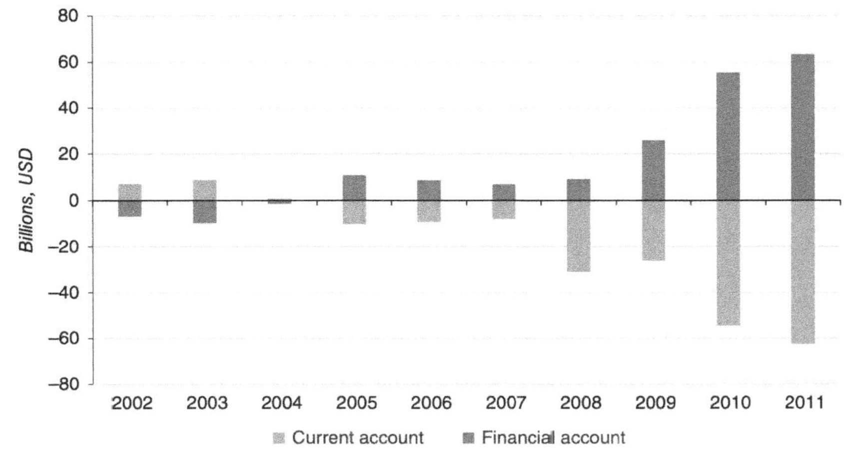

Case Exhibit 4.1. India's CA and FA.

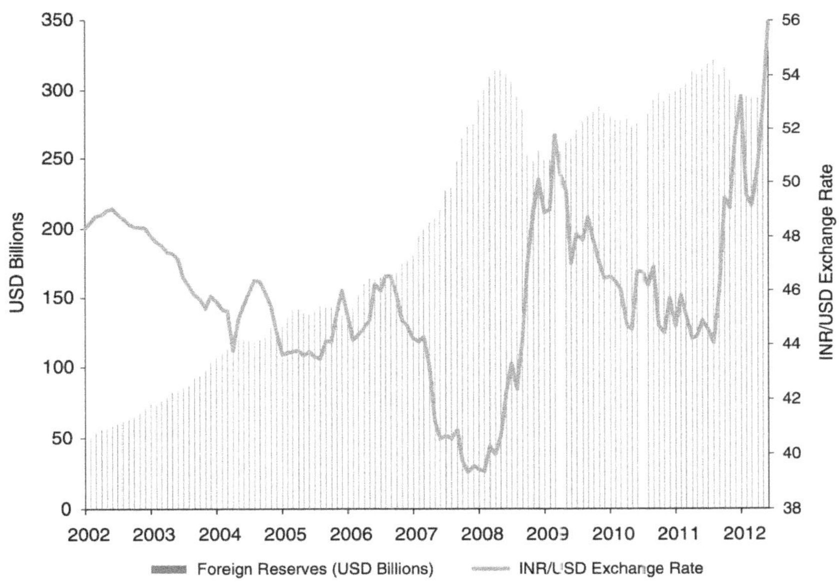

Case Exhibit 4.2. India's foreign exchange reserves.

Unfortunately, controversial new proposals to retroactively tax foreign investors have scared capital away. Between April and June 2012, for instance, foreign institutional investors pulled out $350 million from Indian stocks versus net inflows of $1.15 billion in the same period a year earlier (see Case Exhibit 4.1).

Reserve Bank of India's Intervention Policy

It appears that the central bank's principal objective is to tamp down day-to-day volatility rather than draw a line in the sand. India's central bank has foreign reserves of $286 billion or equal to 6 months of imports, compared to China's $3.3 trillion. Shortly after the rupee's descent started in August 2011, the central bank began to intervene by selling dollars to steady the decline. It spent $22 billion in foreign reserves between September and April, according to data from the bank (see Case Exhibit 4.2).

Narendra Aneja was finding it difficult to reconcile a wealth of statistics which were not particularly auspicious for the Indian economy with his deep belief that somehow India would regain its footing and financial health. Admonishing and convincing investors to be patient may be a tall order.

Case Exhibit 4.3. Summary of macroeconomic statistics for India (2007–2013).

Prices and Financial Indicators	2007	2008	2009	2010	2011	2012	2013
Exchange rate Rs: US$ (av.)	41.35	43.51	48.41	45.73	46.67	52.94	52.59
Consumer prices (end-period, %)	6.4	8.3	10.8	12.0	8.9	8.4	7.6
Producer prices (av., %)	4.9	8.7	2.4	9.6	9.5	7.7	6.2
Stock of money M1 (% change)	15.0	11.5	17.8	17.3	6.8	11.2	13.6
Stock of money M2 (% change)	22.3	20.518	17.8	16.1	12.3	15.2	
Lending interest rate (av., %)	13.1	13.3	12.2	10.2	10.2	9.2	8.3
Current account (US$ mn)							
Trade balance	−77,845	−124,452	−106,348	−132,183	−162,010	−182,193	−198,308
Goods: exports FOB	153,784	198,599	168,218	225,314	299,386	339,667	401,293
Goods: imports FOB	−231,629	−323,051	−274,566	−357,497	−461,396	−521,860	−599,601
Services balance	39,370	47,436	37,193	42,426	58,792	65,470	81,500
Income balance	−6,135	−3,539	−6,850	−13,141	−15,906	−18,133	−23,468
Current transfers balance	37,144	48,753	49,292	52,093	61,817	66,231	78,426
Current account balance[a]	−7,466	−31,802	−26,713	−50,805	−41,401	−68,625	−61,850
External debt (US$ mn)							
Debt stock	202,929	225,994	249,993	290,282	288,082[b]	302,588	310,718
Debt service paid	39,367	30,964	16,503	20,081	55,737	36,198	44,714
Principal repayments	32,097	23,685	10,985	14,708	47,413	28,244	36,417
Interest	7,270	7,279	5,518	5,373	8,324	7,954	8,297
International reserves (US$ mn)							
Total international reserves	273,859	254,024	274,668	297,747	297,905	302,202	315,244

Notes: [a]Includes statistical discrepancy.
[b]Economist Intelligence Unit estimates.
Source: International Monetary Fund, *International Financial Statistics*.

Questions for Discussion

1. Analyze India's current account performance over the period 2007 to 2012.
2. What is the relationship between India's fiscal policies and its current account?
3. Does it explain the recent rupee's steep depreciation?
4. How would you characterize RBI's forex policy?
5. What is the outlook for the rupee over the next 6–18 months?

PART TWO

The Foreign Exchange Market and Currency Derivatives

After introducing the foreign exchange market and its inner workings (Chapter 5) Part 2 discusses the valuation of the "mother" of all currency derivatives – the forward contract – in the context of the theory of interest rate parity (Chapter 6). The international parity framework with purchasing power parity and the Fisher parity is completed in Chapter 7. Currency futures and options are detailed in Chapter 8, which shows how they can be harnessed for the purpose of risk management.

CHAPTER 5

The Foreign Exchange Market

The price of an article is charged according to difference in location, time, or risk to which one is exposed in carrying it from one place to another or in causing it to be carried. Neither purchase nor sale according to this principle is unjust.
— Saint Thomas Aquinas, ca. 1264

If there were a single world currency, there would be no need for a foreign exchange market. At its simplest, the raison d'être of the foreign exchange market is to enable the transfer of purchasing power from one currency into another, thereby facilitating the international exchange of goods, services, and financial securities. Trade carried over great distances is probably as old as humankind and has long been a source of economic power for the nations that embraced it. Indeed, international trade seems to have been at the vanguard of human progress and civilization: The Phoenicians, Greeks, and Romans were all great traders whose activities were facilitated by *marketplaces and money changers*, both of which set fixed places and fixed times for exchanging goods. From time immemorial traders have been faced with several problems: how to pay for and finance the physical transportation of merchandise from point A to point B, which could be several hundreds or thousands of miles away and weeks or months away; how to insure the cargo (from the risk of being lost at sea or to pirates or bandits); and last, how to protect against price fluctuations in the value of the cargo across space (from point A to point B) and over time (between shipping and delivery time). In many ways, the history of foreign exchange and its derivative contracts parallel the increasingly innovative remedies that traders devised to cope with their predicaments.

Long confined to enabling international trade, foreign direct investment, and their financing, foreign exchange has recently emerged as an *asset class* in its own right. This largely explains the recent surge of money flowing through the foreign exchange (FX or forex) market. Catalyzed by improved technology, the unrelenting dismantling of foreign exchange controls, the accelerating pace of economic globalization, and the design of powerful algorithmic trading models, the daily turnover in the forex market now exceeds US$5 trillion, thus dwarfing equities and fixed income securities markets. Surprisingly, though, only 10% of trading is motivated by international trade of goods and services.

This chapter first describes the institutional framework within which forex transactions are carried out, emphasizing how Internet-based electronic automation has overhauled the market microstructure. Second, it catalogs the different foreign exchange products currently traded on the foreign exchange market. Last, it details the mechanics of exchange rate quotations and explains how the foreign exchange market, even though it is geographically dispersed, is very much one global market: spatial arbitrage — also known as the Law of One Price — makes sure of it.

After reading this chapter you will understand:

- How the *interbank* foreign exchange market is organized.
- How the Internet is steadily displacing the "visible human hand" in currency trading.
- What the different forex products are.
- What the mechanics of exchange rates quotations are and the meaning of *bid-ask spreads*.
- How spatial arbitrage transforms a geographically dispersed foreign exchange market into one globally integrated marketplace.

HOW FOREX IS TRADED: THE INSTITUTIONAL FRAMEWORK

The FX market is by far the oldest and largest market in the world. It is the medium through which end users of foreign exchange — exporters, importers, multinational corporations, institutional investors, hedge funds, and central banks — are able to buy or sell currencies as needed. Unlike the New York Stock Exchange, the Paris Bourse, or the Chicago Board of Trade, which are physically organized and centralized exchanges for trading stocks, bonds, commodities, and their derivatives, the foreign exchange market consists of a network of trading rooms found mostly in commercial banks, foreign exchange dealers, and brokerage firms — hence its name of an *interbank market*. It is largely dominated by approximately 20 major banks that trade via their network of branches, which are physically dispersed throughout the major financial centers of the world — London, New York, Tokyo, Singapore, Zurich, Frankfurt, Hong Kong, Paris, and Shanghai.

Thus, the interbank market consists of large multinational commercial banks whose *dealers* trade either directly among themselves or with the help of *brokers*. In this sense the interbank market is very much an *interdealer market*. Banks' FX dealers act as principals in transactions with customers and may commit the bank's capital to one side of the transaction. Very often, however, they will turn to another bank to close the transaction. In doing so they may find it beneficial to enlist the help of a FX broker, whose principal function is to match a buyer with a seller in exchange for a commission but without taking positions or holding an inventory of currency. Brokers were formerly humans known as *voice brokers*, but today they are predominantly *electronic brokers* (automated order-matching systems). It is generally estimated that approximately one-third of all interbank FX trading is still in the form of direct dealing between banks' FX dealers while two-thirds are guided by either voice or electronic brokers.

The FX trading room

The key building blocks of the FX market are the trading rooms found at most banks around the world. In appearance they look quite similar, with their rows of computer screens, fancy telephones, dedicated lines to customers and voice brokers, and direct links to electronic broking systems and newsfeeds. In the 1960s, when FX started to take off, foreign exchange trading rooms were linked simply by telephones (and later telexes), which allowed for fast communication (but not quasi-instantaneous as it is today with computer terminals and the Internet). Each currency trader would have "before him a special telephone that links the trading room by direct wire to the foreign exchange brokers, and the most important commercial customers. The connections were so arranged that several of the bank's traders could 'listen in' on the same call".[1] Today telephone, telex, and facsimile machines play a secondary role as computer terminals have established themselves as the undisputed medium of transaction allowing for instantaneous communication in this *over-the-counter*[2] market. FX traders with display monitors on their desks are able to execute trades at prices they see on their screens by punching in their orders on a keyboard.

FX trading, however, is not a stand-alone activity: Because exchange rates are continuously fluctuating in response to news — whether that be developments in interest rates, commodity prices, inflation, and other macroeconomic variables — FX trading is an integral part of banks' trading activities in other financial products, including financial derivatives.

How is the FX trading room organized?

Most trading rooms — also known as the "front office" — would implement some degree of division of labor within the staff, with various traders specializing in individual currencies or different products such as spot versus forwards or FX swaps (see the next section for definitions of these different products). Most FX trading is carried out on behalf of customers — so-called *agency* trading — but banks may also trade for their own accounts using their own capital — *proprietary* trading[3] — handled by a separate group of traders. To manage the hectic

1 A. R. Holmes and F. H. Scott, "The New York Foreign Exchange Market." Federal Reserve Bank of New York, 1965.

2 *Over-the-counter* means that FX brokers/dealers negotiate directly with one another. There is no central physical exchange or clearinghouse.

3 Agency trading is consistent with the primary function of banks to act as financial intermediaries and is a relatively low-risk activity. Proprietary trading, on the other hand, is akin to hedge funds' speculative trading and generates hefty (usually) but volatile profits for the bank. Both activities should be kept separate with their own reporting and risk control systems. Recent banking reforms in the United States severely curb FX proprietary trading.

flow of FX deals, trading rooms are supported by "back offices" whose staff is responsible for clearing and settling transactions, executing their payments, and managing risk.

How to control FX trading

Foreign exchange trading is a very lucrative business, and for many large commercial banks it may account for as much as 10%–20% of net profits. It is also a fast-paced and hectic activity with billions of dollars flowing through trading rooms. Currency traders are required to observe trading limits applied to a single transaction; for example, the bank may mandate that no single FX trade be in excess of $100 million and that the aggregate limit of a trader's net position be no more than $25 million during the day, to be reduced to very close to zero by the end of the business day to avoid unwelcome price surprises overnight. Without these rules, the bank CEO would lose sleep at night because of a few unauthorized trades gambling away the bank's capital. Indeed banks, for the most part, earn a living by buying and selling foreign currencies at slightly different rates — also known as the *bid-ask spread* — for their corporate customers. The idea is that the bank buys currencies at a slightly lower FX rate than the rate at which it is selling, thereby generating slim but positive profit margins. This is indeed a relatively safe way to make a living, as it does not entail outright speculative positions on currencies. In fact, most banks have established control systems aimed at keeping traders honest by implementing the *square position* requirement; this is nothing more than requiring that each trader keep his or her trades in balance and that for each currency the amount sold forward[4] in a given currency (or a liability position in that currency) equals the amount purchased forward in that same currency (asset position).

Indeed, the computerized systems offer currency traders the opportunity to enter orders that are then automatically matched with other outstanding orders already in the system. This globally reaching and linking trading system substantially reduces the time and cost of matching and settling trades and, more important, provides the foreign exchange market with the ticker tape to record the actual prices at which foreign exchange transactions are executed. However, it should be emphasized that the specifics of the actual transaction (price and volume) have, so far, never been made public, as foreign exchange markets' biggest traders have profitably kept this secret to themselves.

"The market that never sleeps"

This ethereal, ubiquitous, electronic foreign exchange market is literally trading around the clock. At any time during a 24-hour cycle, FX traders are buying and selling one currency for another somewhere in the world. By the time the New York FX dealers start trading at 8:00 A.M. EST, major European financial centers have been in full swing for four or five hours. San Francisco and Los Angeles extend US FX trading activities by three hours, and by dinnertime on the West Coast, Far Eastern markets, principally Tokyo, Hong Kong, and Singapore, will begin trading. As their trading activities draw to a close, Mumbai (Bombay) and Bahrain will have been open for a couple of hours, and Western European markets will be about to start trading, beginning the cycle all over again.

One major implication of a 24-hour currency market is that exchange rates do provide a continuous real-time market assessment of new developments and therefore will change quasi-instantaneously in response to any new information. Thus, FX traders must be light sleepers ready to work the night shift if necessary, since they may need to act on news resulting in a very sharp exchange rate movement that occurs on another continent in the middle of the night. However, over the course of the day the volume of foreign exchange trading does not flow evenly, as illustrated by Exhibit 5.1. A good portion of foreign exchange trading activity will happen when most market participants are accessible and may become counterparties: This happens when European and North American trading overlaps, which — given the six-hour difference — is in the late afternoon in Europe and the morning in North America, when trading becomes very hectic. FX trading will usually subside in the mid and late North American afternoon.

4 Forward contracts are defined and further discussed in the next section. Note that the square positions requirement still allows for the mismatching of forward contracts' maturities in a given currency.

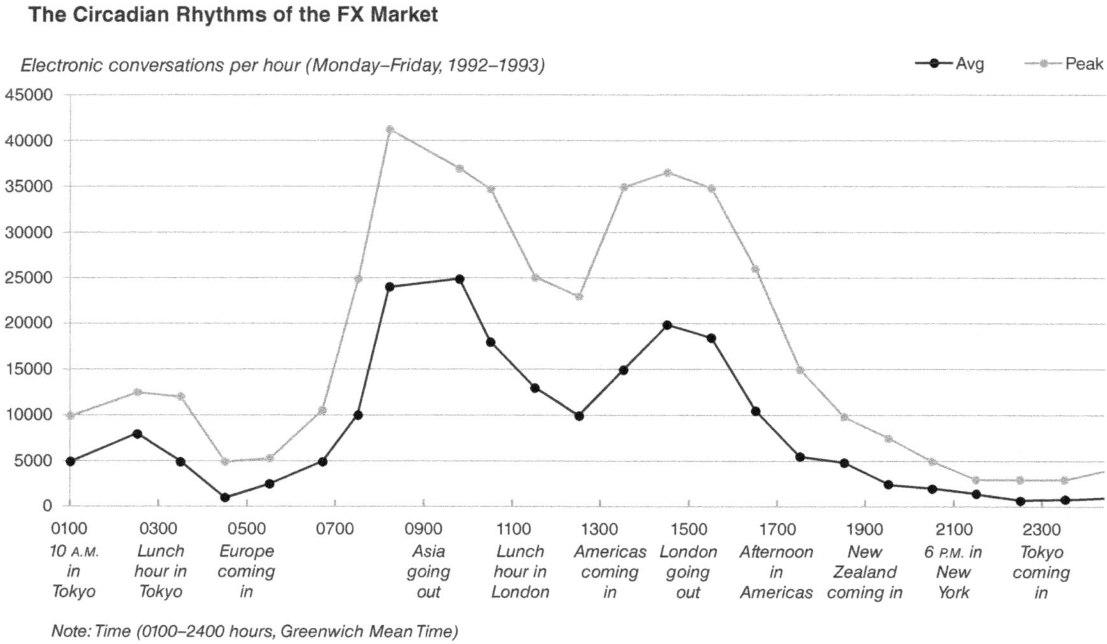

Exhibit 5.1. The 24-hour forex market.

Source: Reuters; Sam Y. Cross, *All about the Foreign Exchange Market in the United States*, Federal Reserve Bank of New York, www.newyorkfed.org.

Buy side meets sell side in the FX market[5]

The buy side or customer market refers to the market for end users of foreign exchange. Customers include importers and exporters settling foreign currency accounts, multinational corporations repatriating dividends or extending an intra-corporate loan to one of their foreign affiliates or concluding a cross-border acquisition, central banks intervening in the FX market or simply managing their currency reserves, commercial banks extending a loan to a foreign client, insurance companies adjusting a foreign claim, investment banks' proprietary trading, and hedge funds involved in carry trades or other forms of high-frequency algorithmic trading (see left side of Exhibit 5.2). However, such FX transactions account for less than 15% of the daily FX market turnover, and this percentage has actually declined over the years; the other 85% of daily FX trading occurs within the interbank market as FX dealers/brokers continuously adjust their inventories of currencies.

Because it would be difficult for customers to find another customer directly as a counterparty to their trade, they typically turn to their bank and declare their intention to trade by asking for a two-way quote[6] (thereby not revealing if they intend to buy or to sell the given currency). In fact, some of the largest market makers in FX trading, such as Deutsche Bank, Barclays, and UBS, have developed their own electronic trading platforms to better accommodate FX end users' needs and to improve bank-customer relationships.

5 *Buy side* refers to consumers and *sell side* to merchants. The buy side would, for example, purchase euros (selling dollars) while the sell side is selling euros (buying dollars). Because of the nature of forex trading, both buy and sell sides are buying one currency and selling the other.

6 A two-way quote means that the bank would quote the price at which the bank would be buying (bid) or selling (ask) the currency.

INTERNATIONAL FINANCE IN PRACTICE 5.1[7]

The Bangladesh Central Bank Heist (2016)

It remains one the most brazen cyber attack in history and resulted in the theft of $81 million. The attack began on February 4, 2016, when hackers managed to infiltrate the Bangladesh Bank's computer systems. Using a malware called "SWIFT Client", the attackers were able to gain access to the bank's SWIFT credentials, which enabled them to communicate with other banks and financial institutions around the world to transfer funds internationally.

Like most countries' central banks, Bangladesh central bank maintains an account with the Federal Reserve Bank of New York to deposit, maintain and transfer foreign currency reserves to Bangladesh. The Society for Worldwide Interbank Financial Telecommunications (SWIFT) plays a pivotal role in international financial transactions, serving as a secure and standardized messaging network. It enables financial institutions worldwide to exchange financial information, including payment instructions, securely and reliably. Once the hackers had obtained the SWIFT credentials, they began to send a series of transfer requests to the Federal Reserve Bank of New York to have close to $1 billion wired from the Bangladesh Bank's account to various accounts in the Philippines and Sri Lanka though only $81 million was ever actually transferred, as many of the requests were rejected by the New York Fed. The hackers disguised the transfers by using the names of fake charities and non-profit organizations, making it difficult for authorities to trace the funds.

The Bangladesh Bank Heist could have been even more catastrophic if not for a typo made by the hackers, which raised suspicion among the staff at the Federal Reserve Bank of New York. The hackers had requested a transfer to a non-existent entity called "Shalika Foundation", which prompted the bank to investigate the transfer. The attack resulted in the loss of $81 million, which is a significant amount for a country like Bangladesh. The stolen funds were transferred to the Philippines, where they were laundered through the country's casinos. Although some of the funds were eventually recovered, the incident had a significant impact on the country's economy and the reputation of its banking system.

The plan was extremely complex, and took advantage of the different time zones involved in international banking. Transferring money from the New York account of the Bangladesh Bank into bank accounts in the Philippines meant the involvement of three time zones. The timing was expertly planned, meaning that when the New York Fed began receiving fraudulent payment orders on Thursday afternoon, the Bangladesh Bank was closed (their weekend begins on Friday). Then, when the Bangladesh bank reopened on the Sunday, the New York Fed was of course closed for the weekend. At this realization, the Bangladesh Bank tried to contact the banks in the Philippines, which was closed for Chinese New Year. The attack came at a time when banks were unable to communicate effectively, increasing their chance of success. By the time the banks in their respective countries were able to contact each other, it was too late. The SWIFT system, once thought to be impenetrable, underwent a significant overhaul in response to the attack. This incident served as a wake-up call to banks worldwide, prompting them to reevaluate their cybersecurity measures and the adequacy of their SWIFT-related security protocols.

---

7 Abridged from https://cyber.uk/areas-of-cyber-security/cyber-security-threat-groups-2/nation-state-hackers-case-study-bangladesh-bank-heist/, https://www.linkedin.com/pulse/case-study-bangladesh-banking-heist-digialert and https://www.linkedin.com/pulse/2016-bangladesh-bank-heist-lesson-cyber-espionage-digialert-9b1gc.x.

Buy side meets sell side through a bank FX dealer

The bank FX dealer provides quotes directly to inquiring customers, thereby acting as a market maker[8] (see arrow 1 in Exhibit 5.2). The bank would hope to use its existing inventory of foreign exchange to meet its customers' needs but is often unable to do so. The bank's dealer/trader will then turn to the *interbank* market to cover the customer's trade. He will ask for a quote from another bank (bilateral trade) without revealing his real intentions to buy or to sell (but revealing his identity) or how much of the currency he is interested in trading (see arrow 2 in Exhibit 5.2).

---

8 Market makers are dealers — generally based at a bank trading desk — ready to quote buy and sell prices upon request. The market maker provides liquidity to the market and is compensated by the spread between buy and sell rates.

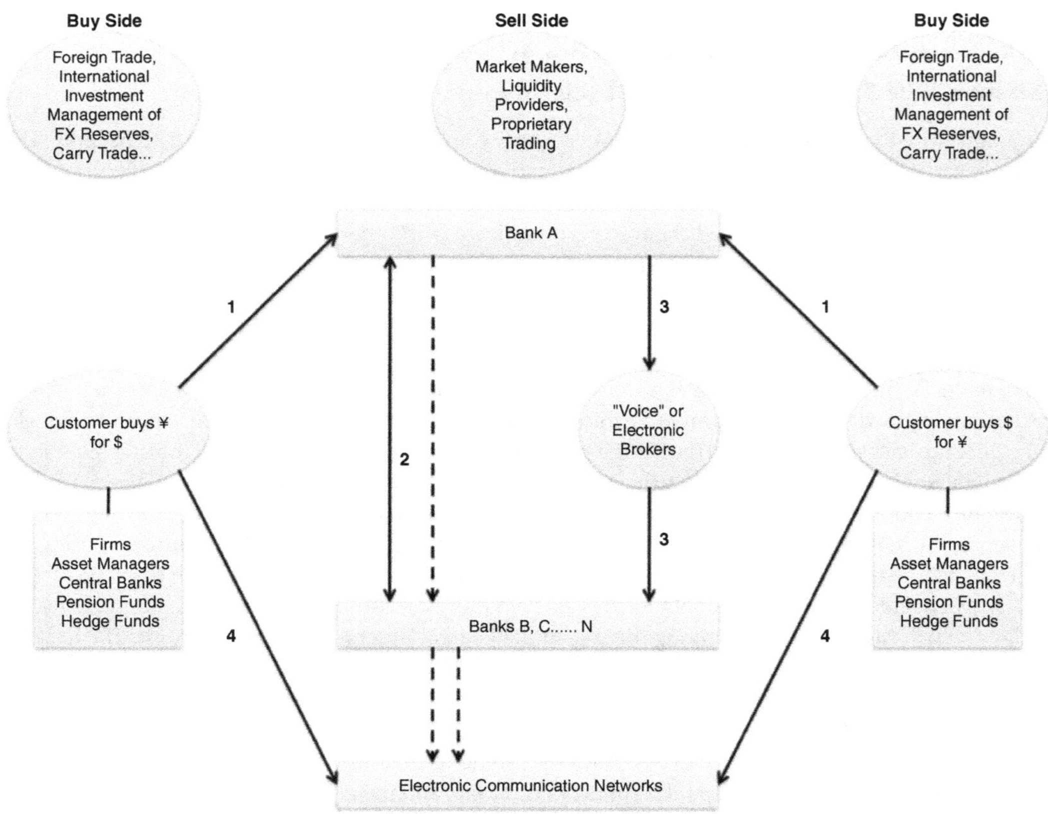

Exhibit 5.2. "Buy side" meets "sell side" in the FX market.

The advantage of direct trading is that no commission has to be paid; there is, however, no guarantee that the trader has secured the best bargain. Indeed, there are more than 1,000 banks trading foreign exchange and probably more than 10,000 FX traders. Direct trading is thus decentralized and fragmented, since transactions amount to bilateral deals between two dealers and cannot be observed by other market participants. However, it should be noted that approximately 10 banks account for a disproportionate 50% share of FX trading in each currency pair, with heaviest volumes found in $/€, $/£, and €/¥ transactions. Specialization in terms of currency pairs traded is widely known among market participants, which facilitates bilateral direct trading. However, it is next to impossible to know if, in such a physically dispersed market, the best possible deal has been secured.

When FX trading is mediated by electronic brokers

The second approach is for the bank FX trader to contact a broker (formerly referred to as a voice broker, but more likely to be today an electronic broker); this is known as indirect trading[9] (see arrow 3 in Exhibit 5.2). Brokers are sometimes referred to as bulletin boards. "Brokers do not make prices themselves. They gather firm prices from dealers, and then communicate those prices back to dealers".[10] Such broker-intermediated trading used to be conducted over the phone, but today FX brokering is channeled through two dominant computer systems — Reuters D3000[11] and Electronic Broking Services (EBS).[12]

9 Voice brokers used to work through closed telephone networks, whereas electronic brokers today use Reuters D3000 or Electronic Broking Services (EBS).

10 R. K. Lyons, *The Micro-Structure Approach to the Foreign Exchange Market* (Cambridge, MA: MIT Press, 2001), p. 40.

11 Reuters introduced the Reuters Market Data Service (RMDS) as early as 1981, which allowed for the exchange of information over computer screens but without actual trading. In 1989 Reuters Dealing 2000-1 replaced RMDS and allowed computer-based forex trading, displacing telephone (and human) trading. The platform was updated in 1992 with Reuters D2000-2 and again in 2006 with Reuters D3000.

12 To counter the dominance of Reuters, Electronic Broking Services (EBS) was created in 1990 by a consortium of large banks — ABN-AMRO, Bank of America, Barclays, Chemical Bank, Citibank,

EBS dominates trading in the three major currency pairs — \$/€, \$/¥, and €/¥ — whereas Reuters leads in £ trading and other lesser or emerging market currencies. Both electronic platforms are effectively electronic limit order books akin to the electronic trading systems used by stock exchanges. A limit order book aggregates buy and sell orders for a given currency by order of priority. Dealers when entering their orders will also specify the volume they intend to buy/bid or sell/ask as well as the price at which to buy or sell. The order is kept in the system until a corresponding order with matching volume and price is entered or the order is revoked/withdrawn by the original bidder. Posting limit orders through brokers will also serve to protect the dealer's identity. Brokers act as matchmakers and do not put their own money at risk. Through computerized quotation systems such as Reuters D3000 or EBS, electronic brokers monitor the quotes offered by the forex trading desks of major international banks. By continuously scanning the universe of forex traders, brokers perform a very useful searching function and provide the bank's forex trader with the best possible price. Such service is provided at a cost to its users, as dealers will pay commissions to brokers with the hope of having accessed the best possible deal.

Buy side meets sell side directly through electronic communication networks (ECNs)

Increasingly, the buy side would rather access a multiple-dealer portal that functions as a price aggregator or bulletin board, streaming quotes from key dealer banks that are active and routing buy-side orders to the most cost-effective sell-side providers (arrow 4 in Exhibit 5.2). Today this consumer segment has direct access to electronic communication networks (ECNs) such as FXall, FXconnect, or Currenex. ECNs are electronic trading systems that automatically match buy and sell orders placed by various customers and directly bypass (disintermediate) banks' FX dealers. Access to ECNs, however, is limited to subscribers who have an account with a broker-dealer before their orders can be routed for execution. ECNs post orders on their systems for other subscribers to view and then automatically match orders for execution.

Has the human trader at major FX dealer banks been completely disintermediated as a result of electronic automation of FX trading? Not quite. According to several industry reports, approximately one-third of all FX transactions continue to be intermediated by traditional traders. The buy side of the market channels a significant proportion of its business to FX dealers in order to keep the relationship alive since it values the advisory content of human contact with traders. This is particularly true in times of market turbulence and high price volatility, when FX traders prove to be especially useful as algorithmic pricing tends to err or fail outright. Similarly, for currencies that are more lightly traded and for more idiosyncratic tailor-made FX products, the buy side will benefit from the human touch.

Further strengthening the functioning of the interbank market is the settlement service offered by CLS Bank (standing for continuous linked settlements), which began operating on September 9, 2002, and links all participating countries' payment systems for real-time settlement. This eliminates or greatly reduces counterparty or default risk in the settlement of spot transactions.[13]

Algorithmic FX trading

With foreign exchange widely considered an asset class, hedge funds and other institutional investors are increasingly relying on automated trading models that seek and act instantly on market opportunities. As new FX quotes and news items arrive on the newsfeed, they are instantly incorporated into pricing and trading algorithms, which will trigger a buy or sell order on a particular currency. Banks in turn have built pricing algorithms to handle this new high-speed flow of FX trading and to better accommodate the needs of their customers. Ironically, such algorithms make life tougher for banks, as they help to squeeze the already thin gap between the prices at which banks buy and sell currencies, where most of them make their profits; meanwhile, well-heeled corporate customers have followed suit by engineering their own hedging algorithms.

Market efficiency

As emphasized previously, the FX market is best described "as a multiple-dealer market. There is no

Commerzbank, Credit Suisse, Lehman Brothers, Midland, JPMorgan, Nat-West, Swiss Bancorp, and Union Bank of Switzerland.

13 On January 26, 1974, the liquidation of Bankhaus Herstatt sent shock waves through the foreign exchange market, giving new meaning to counterparty and settlement risk. On that day several banks had released payment of Deutsche marks in Frankfurt in fulfillment of FX transactions; in exchange Herstatt was supposed to deliver US dollars in New York later that day but failed to do so because it had ceased operations between the times of respective payments (time zone difference). This type of settlement risk — a form of very short-term counterparty risk — is often referred to as Herstatt risk.

physical location — or exchange — where dealers meet with customers, nor is there a screen that consolidates all dealer quotes in the market".[14] Because of its idiosyncratic microstructure, the order flow of foreign exchange transactions is not nearly as transparent as it would be in other multiple-dealer markets. There are no disclosure requirements for forex trading as there are for most bond and equity markets, where trades are disclosed within minutes by law. Because the volume of currency trades or order flow is generally not observable immediately, the critical information about fundamentals that would have otherwise been made available to all market participants is released more slowly, thereby impairing the efficiency of the forex market.

Electronic trading, however, is metamorphosing the price discovery process and speeding up price dissemination to the point of becoming quasi-instantaneous. Indeed, with dealers and most customers now able to access current prices in real time, the over-the-counter forex market is becoming increasingly transparent. With price discovery quasi-automated and increasingly centralized, this over-the-counter market is taking on some of the characteristics of centralized exchanges. However, even if increased transparency and speedy, widespread price dissemination are bolstering the informational efficiency of the forex market, secretive central banks' intervention in the spot market remains a major impediment.

FOREIGN EXCHANGE PRODUCTS

There are three major types of products traded in the forex market: spot, forward, and swap. In all cases contracts are tailor-made.[15] They are negotiated by the two counterparties in amounts of no less than $1 million; worth noting is that the two parties to the contract are left to assess and monitor the credit risk of their counterparty.

- *Spot* contracts are transactions for the purchase or sale of currency for currency at today's price for settlement within two business days (one day if both parties are domiciled in the same time zone, such as US dollar for Canadian dollar or Mexican peso).
- *Outright forward* contracts are agreements to purchase or sell one currency for another currency whose terms are set *today* — in terms of delivery date, price, and amount — for delivery at some *future* date. Delivery date is set for some time in the future (any time usually between one week and 12 months) at a price agreed upon today and known as the forward rate. No money changes hands when the contract is agreed, although dealers may require their customers to provide collateral in advance to minimize counterparty risk. At maturity of the contract, physical delivery of the currencies will occur according to the terms agreed when the forward contract was first entered into and regardless of the spot price prevailing on the due date. If the forward contract is not matched with a spot transaction, it is known as an outright forward.

For example, a forward contract entered today to purchase £100 million for delivery in 90 days at the forward rate of $1.31 = £1 would require the buyer to deliver $131 million in 90 days and receive £100 million. Should the £ spot rate have depreciated to $1.28 = £1 on delivery day, the transaction will still be executed at the less favorable rate for the purchaser of forward pounds.

- *FX swaps*. If a forward contract is combined with a spot transaction, it is referred to as an FX swap. More specifically, foreign exchange swaps combine two simultaneous transactions of equal amount, mismatched maturity, and opposite direction with the same counterparty. For example, the bundling of the *spot purchase* of €10 million for dollar at today's price of $1.30 = €1 with the 60-day *forward sale* of the same amount of €10 million at the forward rate[16] of $1.28 = €1 would constitute a foreign exchange swap.

More complicated FX swaps would combine two forward contracts instead of a spot and a forward transaction. For example, a *forward-forward* swap could consist of a forward purchase of €10 million for delivery in 30 days at the forward

14 Lyons, *Micro-Structure Approach*, 39.

15 Foreign exchange derivative products in the form of currency futures and options are also traded as standardized products on organized exchanges such as the International Monetary Market (IMM) in Chicago. See Chapter 7 for further discussion.

16 The forward rate is agreed upon today and binding 60 days later when the sale is consummated regardless of what the spot rate may be on that day. The forward rate is set according to the interest rate parity formula discussed in Chapter 6. Examples of transactions necessitating such contracts are provided in Chapter 6.

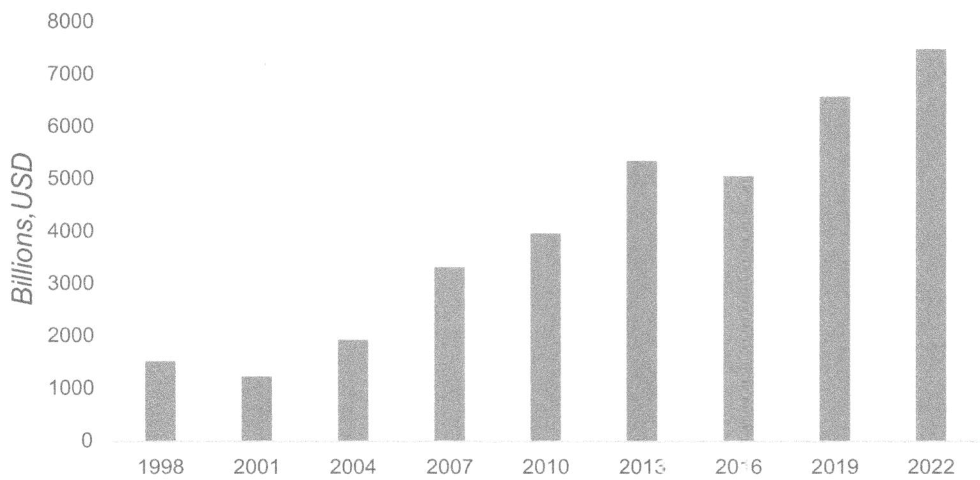

Exhibit 5.3. Global foreign exchange market turnover daily averages (1995–2022).
Source: Bank for International Settlements Triennial Survey of the FX market.

rate of $1.28 = €1 combined with the simultaneous (reverse) sale of €10 million at the rate of $1.29 = €1 for delivery in 60 days.

- *Non-deliverable forwards (NDFs)* are similar to regular forward exchange contracts but do not require physical delivery of currencies. At maturity, settlement is made in US dollars for the difference between the NDF rate and the prevailing spot rate, as the other currency is non-deliverable. This non-deliverability feature is typically due to the fact that the other currency is the currency of an emerging market country that maintains exchange controls and thereby limits the convertibility of its currency. NDFs are second-best to forward contracts and are therefore actively traded for currencies of countries such as China or India that restrict an unfettered forward market.
- *Cross-currency swaps* combine two bonds of equal value and maturity but denominated in different currencies. They commit the two bondholders to (1) exchanging principal amounts at the then initial prevailing exchange rate, (2) swapping a stream of interest payments denominated in two different currencies also at the initial exchange rate, and (3) re-exchanging the principal amount also at the initial exchange rate.

In effect, currency swaps amount to a series of long-dated forward contracts bundled into one. They should not be confused with FX swaps and are similar in structure to interest rate swaps. As a practical matter, it is often only the difference in interest between the two bonds that is actually paid between the counterparties. These sorts of swap contracts do not necessarily require the actual exchange of currencies at either the beginning or the end of the contract's life.

According to the most recent triennial survey by the Bank for International Settlements (see Exhibit 5.3), the FX market averaged $4 trillion of daily trading in April 2018, with one-third accounted for by spot transactions (Wall Street has a daily turnover of approximately $75 billion). A breakdown of the relative importance of each FX product is provided in Exhibit 5.4. The US dollar was involved in 86% of all FX transactions, while the euro was a distant second at 37%. London is the undisputed hub of FX trading with a daily volume of $1.359 trillion, followed by New York City with $661 billion during the same month of April 2018.

EXCHANGE RATE QUOTATIONS

It is relatively easy to find currency prices: Most financial newspapers such as the *Financial Times* and the *Wall Street Journal* publish detailed quotes at the close of the trading day, which means that by the time you read your paper the quotes are obsolete. Of course, you can turn to various websites that

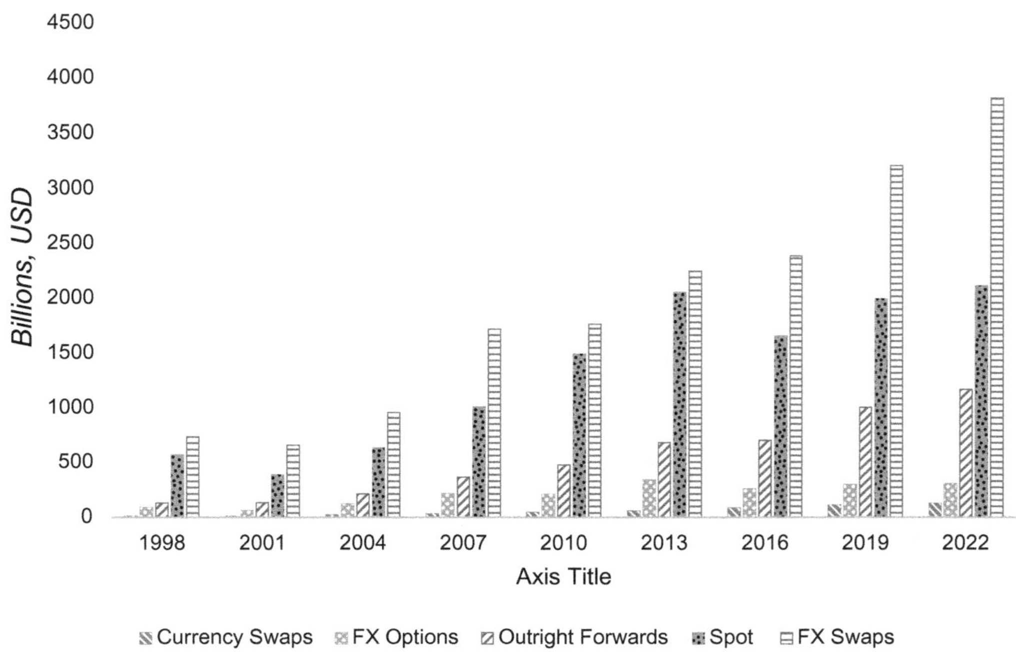

Exhibit 5.4. Foreign exchange market turnover by instrument.
Source: Bank for International Settlements Triennial Survey of the FX market (2019).

will provide quotes in real time — Bloomberg and Reuters being the best known and used widely by professionals in trading rooms of multinationals and financial institutions. Yahoo! Finance and other Internet sites are accessible free of charge to retail consumers.

Exchange rates — because they are relative prices — can be quoted in two ways:

- The *direct way* (American terms[17]) will price one unit of foreign currency in terms of the domestic currency. For example, a currency trader at the New York City desk of Citibank will quote the US dollar (\$)/euro (€) as \$1.3100 = €1 or \$1.3100/€. We denote the exchange rate as $S_{\$,€}(t) = 1.3100$ where S is the spot price at time t of one € (second subscript) priced in \$ (first subscript).
- The *indirect way* (European terms) will price one unit of domestic currency in terms of the foreign currency. Thus the euro (€)/US dollar exchange rate would be quoted as €0.7600 = \$1 or €0.7600/\$ or, to use our notation, $S_{€,\$}(t) = 0.7600$.

17 Strictly speaking, American and European terms quotations refer to currency pairs including the U.S. dollar. Since the US dollar is still by far the world reserve and vehicle currency, it is the case of 75% of all forex transactions.

Most interbank quotations around the world are stated in indirect or European terms. For example, the Swedish krona/US dollar pair would be quoted as SEK 7.8100/\$. Similarly, the Indian rupee/US dollar pair would be stated as INR 52.0000/\$ (note that the European terms characterization of an exchange rate quotation applies to Asian or other non-European currencies). There are two important exceptions to this rule: Both the pound sterling and the euro are routinely quoted in American terms — that is, as the US dollar price of one pound or one euro. In the case of the pound sterling this is due to historical reasons dating back to the nineteenth century when the City of London was the undisputed hub of international commerce, finance, and insurance. The euro of course is still relatively young, as the single currency was launched in 1999, and one may surmise that, by imposing indirect quotations against the rest of the world, euro-land (the countries making up the euro-zone) would immediately achieve the status of reserve currency. Exchange-traded currency futures and options, which are discussed in some depth in Chapter 7, are also generally quoted in American terms.

Referring to published quotes in the *Wall Street Journal* of August 21, 2018 (see Exhibit 5.5), the reader will note that for each currency (column 1) exchange rates are provided for the prior day — August 20. For each day, exchange rates are provided as both direct and indirect quotes against the US dollar.

Q: Referring to currency quotations for August 20, 2018, in the *Wall Street Journal* (Exhibit 5.5), what is the direct and indirect quote for the Turkish lira (TRY) against the US dollar? What is the relationship between the two quotes?

A: It takes \$0.1644 to buy one Turkish lira (direct or American quote) and 6.0818 Turkish lira will buy one US\$ (indirect quote or European quote). One rate is the reciprocal of the other: \$0.1644/TRY = 1/(TRY 6.0818/\$).

Exhibit 5.5. US Dollar Foreign Exchange Rates in Late New York Trading for August 20, 2018.

Country/Currency	ISO Currency Code	In US$	Per US$	US$ vs. YTD % CHG
Americas				
Argentina peso*	ARS	0.0335	29.8555	60.5
Brazil real	BRL	0.2519	3.9702	19.9
Canada dollar	CAD	0.7666	1.3045	3.8
1-mos forward		0.7665	1.3046	4.3
3-mos forward		0.7674	1.3031	4.3
6-mos forward		0.7688	1.3007	4.2
Chile peso	CLP	0.001496	668.5	8.6
Mexico peso*	MXN	0.0526	18.9952	−3.4
Uruguay peso‡	EYU	0.03179	31.46	9.2
Venezuela bolivar	VEB	0.00000403	248409	2401878
Asia-Pacific				
Australian dollar	AUD	0.7338	1.3628	6.4
China yuan	CNY	0.1458	6.8534	5.5
Hong Kong dollar	HKD	0.1274	7.8494	0.5
India rupee	INR	0.01434	69.7585	9.2
Indonesia rupiah	IDR	0.0000686	14573	8.1
Japan yen	JPY (¥)	0.00909	110.07	−2.3
1-mos forward		0.00909	110.01	−1.9
3-mos forward		0.00913	109.52	−2.1
6-mos forward				
Kazakhstan tenge	KZT	0.00277	361.08	8.5
Macau pataca	MOP	0.123736	8.082	0.4
Malaysia ringgit	MYR	0.2437	4.1035	1
New Zealand dollar	NZD	0.6643	1.5053	6.8
Pakistan rupee	PKR	0.00817	122.46	10.7
Philippines peso	PHP	0.0188	53.333	6.7
Singapore dollar	SGD	0.7303	1.3693	2.4
South Korea won	KRW	0.000894	1118.17	4.8
Sri Lanka rupee	LKR	0.00623	160.51	4.6
Taiwan dollar	TWD	0.03255	30.72	3.6
Thailand baht	THB	0.03036	32.94	1.1
Vietnam dong	VND	0.00004297	23273	2.5

(Continued)

Exhibit 5.5. (*Continued*).

Country/Currency	ISO Currency Code	In US$	Per US$	US$ vs. YTD % CHG
Europe				
Bulgaria lev	BGN	0.58713	1.703	4.5
Croatia kuna	HRK	0.1548	6.4607	4.3
Czech Rep. koruna	CZK	0.0446	22.42	5.4
Denmark krone	DKK	0.154	6.4956	4.7
Euro area euro	EUR (€)	1.1484	0.8708	4.5
Hungary forint	HUF	0.00354484	282.1	8.9
Iceland krona	ISK	0.009244	108.18	4.5
Norway krone	NOK	0.1184	8.4456	2.9
Poland zloty	PLN	0.2665	3.7525	7.9
Romania leu	RON	0.2471	4.0473	4.1
Russia ruble‡	RUB	0.01494	66.946	16.1
Sweden krona	SEK	0.1092	9.1543	11.8
Switzerland franc	CHF	1.0086	0.9915	1.8
1-mos forward		1.0103	0.9898	
3-mos forward		1.0185	0.9818	1.5
6-mos forward				
Turkey lira**	TRL	0.1644	6.0818	60.3
Ukraine hryvnia	UAH	0.0361	27.678	−1.7
UK pound	GBP (£)	1.2795	0.7816	5.6
1-mos forward		1.2797	0.7814	6.3
3-mos forward		1.2833	0.7792	6.2
6-mos forward		1.2910	0.7746	5.9
Middle East/Africa				
Bahrain dinar	BHD	2.6515	0.3772	0.01
Egypt pound*	EGP	0.0558	17.913	0.8
Israel shekel	ILS	0.2737	3.6542	5
Kuwait dinar	KWD	3.297	0.3033	0.6
Oman sul rial	OMR	2.59703	0.39	0.03
Qatar rial	QAR	0.2753	3.633	−0.4
Saudi Arabia riyal	SAR	0.2666	3.7509	0.01
South Africa rand	ZAR	0.0688	14.5261	17.5
SDR††		1.389220	0.719830	0.03

Notes: *Floating rate; †Financial government rate; ‡Russian central bank rate; **Rebased as of January 1, 2005; ††Special drawing rights (SDRs) from the International Monetary Fund based on exchange rates for US, British, and Japanese currencies.
Based on trading among banks of $1 million and more, as quoted at 4 P.M. EST by Reuters.
Source: Wall Street Journal, August 20, 2018.

Nicknames in the FX market

Currency traders often refer to currency pairs by their nickname rather than their formal name. The US dollar and pound sterling pairing is known as the *cable* (from the days when exchange rates between London and New York were communicated by transatlantic cables). The Canadian dollar as the *Loonie*, the Swiss franc as the *Swissie*, the Australian dollar as the *Aussie*, and the New Zealand dollar as the *Kiwi*. More recently, the pound sterling paired with the euro is referred to as the *Chunnel* and as the *Geppie* when the pound is paired with the Japanese yen.

It is important to remember that the direct and indirect quotes are exactly the same thing since one is the reciprocal of the other. For example, the relationship between the direct and indirect €/$ exchange rate quotations is simply:

$$€0.76/\$ = \frac{1}{\$1.31/€} \text{ or } S_{€,\$}(t) = \frac{1}{S_{€,\$}(t)}$$

For most heavily traded currencies such as the pound sterling or the Japanese yen, 1-month, 3-month, and 6-month forward dollar rates are also provided — a topic to which we will return later in this chapter.

Currency symbols

Rather than writing the full name of each currency, parties entering into foreign exchange contracts use abbreviations that should be easily understood. The International Organization for Standardization (its acronym ISO is the classical Greek word for *equal*) established currency abbreviations now widely used in both trading rooms and commercial transactions. ISO currency symbols are the two-letter country code and a third letter from the name of the currency. For example, the Canadian (CA) dollar (D) is denoted as CAD. Similarly, the Thai (TH) baht (B) is abbreviated as THB. Exhibit 5.6 provides a comprehensive list of such symbols. For the widely traded currencies, the time-honored symbols for the US dollar ($), pound sterling (£), Japanese yen (¥), and euro (€) are used in this book; all other currencies are denoted by their ISO symbols.

Cross-rates

As indicated earlier, most FX trading involves the US dollar on one side of the transaction, and as a result currencies tend to be quoted either *directly* or *indirectly* in terms of the dollar price of one unit of foreign currency *i*: $S_{\$,i}(t) = 1/S_{i,\$}(t)$. But suppose a bank customer wants to sell yen (¥) for Australian dollars (AUD). How should the bank quote a cross-rate $S_{¥,AUD}(t)$ (which is not readily available) when available rates are yen against US dollars $S_{¥,\$}(t) = 76$ and US dollars against Australian dollars $S_{\$,AUD}(t) = 1.12$? Believe it or not, the bank will first buy US dollars with yen and then purchase Australian dollars with the US dollar proceeds. It will therefore quote a cross-rate based on the respective rates of both currencies against the US dollar:

$$¥76 \rightarrow \$1 \rightarrow \text{AUD } 1/1.12 = \text{AUD } 0.89$$

or it will cost[18]:

$$¥85 = \text{AUD1}$$

or, to use our notation: $S_{¥,AUD}(t) = S_{¥,\$}(t) \times S_{\$,AUD}(t)$.

The reader should note how easy it is to express the cross-rate in the first and last subscript currencies by simply adding the US dollar as the middle subscript/currency. The reader may still wonder why the bank is taking this detour via the US dollar rather than directly trading yen for Australian dollars. The reason has to do with how banks organize their forex trading activities. They would typically have a trader or trading desk dedicated to a given currency against the US dollar, reflecting a heavy trading traffic in that currency pair. Let's say 10 currencies are heavily traded against the US dollar. That means the bank must have a minimum staff of 10 currency traders — and probably more. Ten currencies also correspond to 45 cross-rates (exclusive of said currency vs. the US dollar). It would indeed be unprofitable to make a market in so many cross-rates, and that's why banks

18 Since it costs ¥76 to buy AUD 0.89, it will cost ¥(76/0.89) = 85 to buy AUD 1.

Exhibit 5.6. Currency symbols.

Country	Currency	ISO Currency Code	Country	Currency	ISO Currency Code
Argentina	New peso	ARS	Malaysia	Ringgit	MYR
Australia	Dollar	AUD	Mexico	Nuevo peso	MXN
Bahrain	Dinar	BHD	New Zealand	Dollar	NZD
Brazil	Real	BRL	Norway	Krone	NOK
Canada	Dollar	CAD	Pakistan	Rupee	PKR
Chile	Peso	CLP	Peru	New sol	PEN
China	Renminbi	CNY	Philippines	Peso	PHP
Colombia	Peso	COP	Poland	New zloty	PLN
Czech Republic	Koruna	CZK	Russia	Ruble	RUB
Denmark	Krone	DKK	Saudi Arabia	Riyal	SAR
Ecuador	US dollar	USD	Singapore	Dollar	SGD
Euro-zone*	Euro (€)	EUR	South Africa	Rand	ZAR
Hong Kong	Dollar	HKD	Sweden	Krona	SEK
Hungary	Forint	HUF	Switzerland	Franc	CHF
India	Rupee	INR	Taiwan	Dollar	TWD
Indonesia	Rupiah	IDR	Thailand	Baht	THB
Israel	Shekel	ILS	Turkey	Lira	TRL
Japan	Yen (¥)	JPY	United Arab Emirates	Dirham	AED
Jordan	Dinar	JOD	United Kingdom	Pound (£)	GBP
Korea, South	Won	KRW	United States	Dollar ($)	USD
Kuwait	Dinar	KWD	Uruguay	New peso	EYU
Lebanon	Pound	LBP	Venezuela	Bolivar	VEB

Note: *The euro-zone includes Austria, Belgium, Cyprus, Estonia, France, Germany, Greece, Ireland, Italy, Luxembourg, Malta, Netherlands, Portugal, Slovakia, Slovenia, and Spain.

concentrate for the most part on trading currencies against the US dollar.

Bid-ask spreads

To complicate matters somewhat, a typical foreign exchange quotation gives two rates rather than one. The *bid price* is the price at which an FX trader in the market is willing to buy (remember *b* for *buy*) and it is quoted first. The *ask* or *offer price*, is the price at which a trader is willing to sell. For example, suppose the euro is quoted in US dollar terms as 1.2504-54. This means that our FX trader is willing to buy euros at $1.2504 (the *bid* price) and sell them at $1.2554 (the *ask* price). Usually, the FX trader gives the quote as 04-54, assuming that the counterparty knows the "big" figure — in this case 1.25. As one would expect, the bid price is lower than the ask price; the difference is known as the *bid-ask spread*. Thus, the cost of transacting in the foreign exchange market can be expressed in percentage terms as:

$$\text{Spread\%} = \frac{\text{Ask price} - \text{Bid price}}{\text{Bid price}} \times 100$$

$$= \frac{1.2554 - 1.2504}{1.2504} = 0.40\%$$

The difference between the bid price and the ask price is the bank's compensation for making the trade, which is the reason why banks do not charge commission fees. The FX trader is in effect a *market maker* in the currency he or she trades, who will keep an inventory of said currency. In this sense the spread is the cost of being in business, tying up capital in order to maintain an inventory and being compensated for bearing the risk of holding in inventory an asset whose value is volatile. For widely traded currencies such as the euro, the Japanese yen, or the pound sterling and trades of at least $1 million, the size of the bid-ask spread is approximately 0.2–0.5%. Its size varies from one currency to another. For a given currency, the spread depends on the level of competition among FX traders for that currency, the currency's volatility, and the average volume of daily trading. Less heavily traded currencies from emerging market countries such as the Russian ruble, the Turkish lira, the South African rand, and many others will exhibit wider spreads that reflect in part their volatility and the thinness of their currency market.

Direct versus indirect quotation of the bid-ask spread

Bid-ask exchange rates can also be expressed as the euro price of one US dollar: The reciprocal of the bid price becomes 1/1.2504 = €0.7997/$ and, similarly, 1/1.2554 = €0.7966/$ for the ask price. The reader may wonder why the reciprocal of the bid price is now more expensive than the reciprocal of the ask price when quoted in euro terms per one US dollar. In effect, when the bank is offering to buy euros for $1.2504 (the bid price for euros) it is also offering to sell US dollars for €0.7997 (the ask price for US dollars). In other words, the reciprocal of the bid price for euros has become the ask price for US dollars.

> ***Q:*** Explain why the reciprocal of the ask price is cheaper than the reciprocal of the bid price when quoted in euro terms per one US dollar.
>
> ***A:*** When the bank is offering to sell euros for $1.2554 (the ask price for euros), it is also offering to buy US dollars for €0.7966 (the bid price for US dollars): The reciprocal of the ask price for euros has become the bid price for US dollars.

Cross-rates with bid-ask spreads

Assume that the Thai baht (THB) is quoted as THB 30.2511-3987 per $1 and that the Japanese yen (¥) as 76.2518–7985 per $1. What is the cross ¥ price for buying one Thai baht that the bank would quote? The cross-rate $S_{¥,B}(t)$ combines two transactions: purchase of US dollars (selling yen) at the asking price of $S_{¥,\$}(t) = 76.7985$ and buying Thai baht (selling US dollars) at the asking price of $S_{\$,B}(t) = 1/30.2511$ (which is the reciprocal of the bid baht price for US dollars):

$$¥76.7985 \rightarrow \$1 \rightarrow \text{THB } 30.2511 \text{ or}$$

$$¥\frac{76.7985}{30.2511} = ¥2.24/\text{THB}$$

Or in terms of our notation, the yen bid price for baht is:

$$S_{¥,\text{THB}}(t) = S_{¥,\$}(t) \times S_{\$,\text{THB}}(t)$$
$$= 76.7985 \times \frac{1}{30.2511} = 2.24$$

Spatial arbitrage and the law of one price

Our discussion in Chapter 2 of the equilibrium exchange rate set in a two-currency world made no mention of the geographical origin of the quotation. Because FX traders are part of a worldwide network of trading desks at banks, brokerage firms, hedge funds, or multinational corporations rather than being housed together in a centralized market, it is most unlikely that they will quote identical exchange rates at a given point in time. These price discrepancies are inevitable in a geographically dispersed market such as the foreign exchange market and are generally referred to as price dispersion. For example, is 1.31 the dollar price of one pound prevailing in New York City, London, or in some other distant foreign exchange market such as Singapore? As it turns out, the matter is irrelevant because of the integrative role played by arbitrageurs.

Suppose, for instance, the price of one pound is 1.32 in London but only 1.30 in New York City.[19] Exchange arbitrageurs (that is, currency traders manning the foreign exchange desks of large banks and assisted by computer models) will correct the discrepancy in prices quoted for the same currency (pounds) in two distinct geographical locations (London and New York City) by buying pounds in New York City at $1.30 and selling them in London at $1.32.[20] Increased demand for pounds will push up

19 This assumes that both markets are trading simultaneously. Because of different time zones, overlapping trading hours are relatively limited.

20 Arbitrageurs would thus net 2 cents for each pound bought in New York City and sold in London. Transaction costs incurred in such arbitrage operations will reduce the profit of 2 cents per pound. However, such transaction costs are generally very small in relation to the amount that may be transacted.

the price of pounds in New York City while, at the same time, increased supply of pounds in London will push down the rate until one single price prevails in both locations. As a result, foreign exchange arbitrageurs provide the mechanism whereby geographically distinct exchange markets are integrated in an economic sense. This equilibrium condition can be expressed as:

$ price of one £ in New York = $ price of one in London = $ price of one £ in Singapore

or formally,

$$[S_{\$,£}(t)]_{\text{New York}} = [S_{\$,£}(t)]_{\text{London}} = [S_{\$,£}(t)]_{\text{Singapore}}$$

where $S_{\$,£}(t)$ denotes the spot dollar price of one pound for immediate delivery prevailing at time t.

Trilateral arbitrage

The preceding condition of bilateral equilibrium can be easily generalized by relaxing the restrictive assumption of a two-currency world. Let us consider first, as an intermediate step, a three-currency world (US dollar, British pound, and euro). Arbitrageurs' operations will ensure that purchasing pounds directly with dollars at the unit price of $S_{\$,£}(t)$ or through the intermediary of a third currency — for example, the euro (€) — should be equivalent alternatives. That is,

$ price of one £ = $ price of one € × € price of one £

$$S_{\$,£}(t) = S_{\$,€}(t) \times S_{€,£}(t)$$

where $S_{\$,€}(t)$ denotes the dollar price ($) of one euro (€) for spot delivery prevailing at time t, and $S_{€,£}(t)$ denotes the € price of one pound (£) for spot delivery also prevailing at time t. The trilateral equilibrium condition simply expresses that whether dollars are used to purchase one pound or to purchase the amount of euros necessary to acquire one pound, the costs incurred should be identical. Suppose, for instance, arbitrageurs were confronted with the following configuration of exchange rates:

$$S_{\$,£}(t) = 1.72,\ S_{\$,€}(t) = 1.41,\ S_{€,£}(t) = 1.20$$

Here, indirect purchase of pounds — that is, purchasing euros first and using the resulting proceeds to purchase pounds — would cost them only 1.69 US dollars as opposed to a direct purchase of pounds at a cost of 1.72 US dollars. Arbitrageurs would thus net a profit of 3 cents per pound transacted by buying pounds indirectly at \$1.69/£ and selling immediately at \$1.72/£. Each € costs \$1.41, and each £ costs €1.20. Indirect purchase of £ via € thus costs (\$1.41/€) × (€1.20/£) = \$1.69/£:

$$\text{Indirect £ purchase costs: } £1 \rightarrow \text{‹}\,1.20/£ = €1.20/£ \times \$1.41/€ = \$1.69/£$$

This is cheaper than direct £ purchase at the cost of \$1.72, or, using our notations:

$$S_{\$,£}(t) = S_{\$,€}(t) \times S_{€,£}(t) = 1.41 \times 1.20 = 1.69$$

In doing so, however, both the dollar price of euros and the euro price of pounds should be driven up as a result of stepped-up purchases, whereas the dollar price of pounds should be driven down because of the additional sales of pounds, since arbitrageurs are buying pounds indirectly at \$1.69/£ and selling at the higher direct rate of \$1.72/£ until the trilateral equilibrium condition is obtained. Thus, regardless of where dollars are traded for pounds, spatial arbitrage ensures that the foreign exchange rate will be the same. This is what is generally known as the *Law of One Price*.

Forward exchange contracts

We defined earlier a forward exchange contract as a commitment to buy or sell a certain quantity of foreign exchange on a certain date in the future (the maturity of the contract) at a price (the forward exchange rate) agreed upon when the contract is signed (the present).

Consider, for example, the case of a 90-day forward sale contract of 100 million pounds sterling (£) for US dollars (\$) at the forward rate of \$1.5135 per £1, denoted as $F(90) = 1.5135$.[21] At delivery time, 90 days later, fulfillment of the sale contract calls for the delivery of 100 million pounds sterling in exchange for taking delivery of 151.350 million US dollars.

More generally, the forward exchange rate itself is defined as the domestic currency price (\$) of one unit of foreign currency i for delivery at a stipulated future date; the symbol used is $F(d)$, where d is the time interval between the day the contract is signed

---

21 The definition of a forward *purchase* contract would be symmetrical. A forward *option* contract would allow the transaction to leave the maturity of its commitment open within a given time period. Characteristically, *option* forward contracts provide for the delivery of foreign exchange to be made within the first, middle, or last 10 days of the month (option period) rather than on a specific date.

and the day the actual transaction takes place. In this example, we would simply write:

$$F(90) = 1.5135$$

Forward discount and premium

A foreign currency is said to be at a *forward discount* when the domestic currency forward price of one unit of foreign currency i is less than its spot price:

$$F(d) < S(0)$$

Conversely, a foreign currency is said to be at a *forward premium* whenever the domestic currency forward price of one unit of foreign currency i is more than its spot price:

$$F(d) > S(0)$$

As an illustration assume that the following exchange rates were prevailing for one pound sterling as expressed in US dollars:

Spot exchange rate (today):	$S(0) = 1.5255$
Forward exchange rate (30 days):	$F(30) = 1.5201$
Forward exchange rate (90 days):	$F(90) = 1.5135$

The forward discount for the pound sterling $F(d) - S(0)$ is seen widening over the next 3 months:

$$F(30) - S(0) = 1.5201 - 1.5255 = -0.0054$$
$$F(90) - S(0) = 1.5135 - 1.5255 = -0.0120$$

Implicit interest rate

Premiums and discounts over a d-day period are generally expressed as percentage earnings per year. This *annualized* earnings rate is called the *implicit interest rate* and lends itself directly to comparison with interest rate differentials. It is defined as:

$$\text{Implicit interest rate} = \frac{F(d) - S(0)}{S(0)} \times \frac{360}{d}$$

In the previous example, the annualized implicit interest rate corresponding to the different maturities would be computed as:

$$\frac{F(30) - S(0)}{S(0)} \times \frac{360}{30} = \frac{-0.0054}{1.5255} \times \frac{360}{30} = -0.432$$

or a 4.32% per annum discount and

$$\frac{F(90) - S(0)}{S(0)} \times \frac{360}{90} = \frac{-0.0120}{1.5255} \times \frac{360}{90} = -0.315$$

or a 3.15% per annum discount.

The practical usefulness of the implicit interest rate will become clear in the context of the interest rate parity theory discussed in the next chapter, when it is compared to interest rate differentials. More specifically, according to the interest rate parity theory, when interest rates and exchange rates are free to adjust (no central bank intervention), the forward premium or discount on a foreign currency is equal to the difference in interest rates between the domestic currency and the foreign currency. A foreign currency commanding a higher interest rate than the domestic currency is at a forward discount; conversely, a foreign currency commanding a lower interest rate is at a forward premium.

Q: It is May 11, 2015, and Crédit Suisse's head currency strategist has just learned from her chief economist that there is an 80% chance that Greece will leave the euro-zone by year-end. By then, because of footloose capital abandoning the euro to seek shelter into the Swiss franc seen as a refuge currency the Swiss National Bank would abandon its unofficial peg to the euro at CHF 1.20 = €1 with an immediate appreciation of the Swiss franc of 12 to 15% against the euro. Current 3- and 6-month forwards are quoted at CHF 1.1900 and CHF 1.1750 = €1. How should she speculate?

A: The currency trader would sell 6-month euro forward at CHF 1.1750 hoping that the euro would indeed devalue by 12 to 15% to CHF 1.0800 or 1.0500. At maturity of the contract, our trader would purchase euros at their depreciated value of CHF 1.0500 and immediately deliver each euro, receiving the forward rate of CHF 1.1750 for a profit of CHF 1.1750 –CHF 1.0500 = CHF 0.1250 per euro sold forward.

Bid and offer/asked quotations

As pointed out earlier, spot and forward interbank quotations are announced as two prices rather than one: a bid price at which the dealer is willing to buy another currency and an offer/asked price at which he or she is willing to sell the currency. Dealers will bid (buy) at a somewhat lower rate than they ask (sell), with the spread between both rates constituting their profit.

INTERNATIONAL CORPORATE FINANCE IN PRACTICE 5.2

Citibank's Forex Losses[22]

On June 19, 1965, in the heydays of the Bretton-Woods system of fixed exchange rates, the First National City Bank — the second largest American commercial bank with 177 offices in 58 countries — announced a loss of $8 million.[23] The loss was attributed to unauthorized forward speculation on the pound sterling by a Belgian trader in the bank's Brussels branch who was betting that the pound sterling pegged then at $2.80 would not devalue. The amount of the underlying transactions was rumored to be close to $800 million.

How could a single employee fool one of the largest and most sophisticated commercial bank? How could such a large speculative bet go undetected by the firm's back office and lose so much money for the bank when — for all practical purposes — currency prices were quasi-fixed? Indeed banks, for the most part, earn a living by buying and selling foreign currencies at slightly different rates — also known as the *bid/ask spread* — mostly on a spot basis and to a lesser extent on a forward basis for corporate customers (and more recently on options, swaps and other derivative products); this is indeed a relatively safe way to make a living as it does not entail outright speculative positions on currencies. This is known as *agency trading* whereby the bank acts as a forex broker on behalf of its client and unlike speculative *proprietary trading* as practiced by hedge funds. In fact, most banks have set in place control systems aimed at keeping traders honest by implementing the *square position* requirement: this is nothing more than requiring that each trader keep his trades in balance and that for each currency the amount sold forward would equal the amount purchased forward. For example, our Belgian trader could sell 1 month short £10 million at $2.77 = £1 and buy 6 month long £10 million at $2.75 = £1. Should sterling devalue to $2.40 after 15 days the trader would generate a gain on the forward sale contract maturing on day 30 in the amount of £10,000,000 (2.77 – 2.40) = $370,000 but incur a loss on the 6-month forward purchase contract to the tune of £ 10,000,000 (2.40 – 2.75) = $350,000.

Our Belgian trader made a simple bet that the pound sterling would survive the speculative pressure and would not devalue in the following 12–18 months. Turning this bet into a profitable trade involved buying pound sterling forward (going long pound sterling) at rates as low as $2.69 = £1 for maturities ranging from 9 to 18 months. The reader may wonder how could the forward rate fall below the floor spot rate and trade at a discount when the spot exchange rate was limited to fluctuating within a tunnel closely monitored by the Bank of England? It has to do with the interest rate differential between dollar and sterling and the theory of Interest Rate Parity (discussed in Chapter 6); as the Bank of England defended the $2.80 = £1 parity, it increased interest rates from 4.50 to 7.50% to encourage short term capital inflow which in turn pushes up the spot dollar price of sterling while driving down its forward rate.

Here is the loophole exploited by our Belgian trader which allowed him to conceal his speculative bet that the pound sterling would not devalue. Recall that our trader had purchased 360 days forward pound sterling at $2.69 thereby creating a pound sterling long/asset position, which had to be neutralized by a short/liability position of matching amount (but of mismatching maturity). Otherwise, his large pound sterling asset position would have undoubtedly attracted Citibank comptroller's attention. To balance his long and long-dated pound sterling position our trader had — to satisfy the square position requirement — to sell pound sterling (short) to create an offsetting liability position. Of course, the *amounts* had to be matching but forward contract *maturities* would be mismatched as our trader sold sterling 30 and 60 days forward (while buying 270 and 360 days forward) thereby reporting a *square* position at all times. However, as long as the pound did not devalue he would stand to benefit

22 Adapted from Jacque, L. 2014. *"Global Derivative Debacles; From Theory to Malpractice,"* 2nd edition (World Scientific: Singapore and London), pp. 29–40.

23 Approximately $120 million in 2018 dollar.

handsomely from his long asset position as long as the losses incurred on the short positions were kept small. More formally our Belgian trader was hoping that *Losses on sterling short sales < Gains on sterling long purchases.*

Our trader never got a chance to bring to closure his creative speculative scheme. Indeed, the pound sterling did not devalue and at least his sterling long position would have paid off in due time but he was never allowed to find out. Sometimes in the spring of 1965, Walter Wriston — then head of Citibank's foreign operations — was alerted by *a friend of his, Paul Jeantly, who mentioned that his firm, Montague, had a $100 million contract coming due the following week with Citibank's Belgian branch. "I almost dropped my teeth", Wriston said, "because that was ten times the contract a branch that size could possibly have"* (Zweig, p. 175). Shortly thereafter the comptroller's department exposed the Belgian trader and unwound the outstanding positions at unfavorable current spot and forward rates as it is often the case with forced liquidation of large scale speculative position resulting in a loss of $8 million. Indeed, losing close to 10% of Citibank's entire annual worldwide consolidated profits because of a rogue trader's ineptitude in the Belgian branch was a humbling experience — especially at a time when the bank was readying itself to issue $250 million of subordinated convertible debt.

Suppose the pound sterling is quoted at $1.5250–1.5260. This means that banks are willing to buy/bid pounds at $1.5250 and to sell/ask at $1.5260. In practice, dealers will not quote the full rate to each other but instead quote the last two digits of each currency price — in this case, 50–60. Assuming that the leading digits are displayed on a video screen, which is the primary medium for communicating exchange rates, the bid and offer spot rate for pound sterling would appear as 1.5250–60. Similarly, suppose a 1-month forward rate is quoted as 53–56 discount (premium?) and a 3-month forward rate as 182–187 discount. Such quotes should be directly subtracted from the spot bid/offer outright quotation, in this case: (explain outright and point)

Outright quotations:	Spot exchange rate	1.5250–60
	1-month forward rate	1.5197–1.5204
	3-month forward rate	1.5068–73
Point quotations:	Spot exchange rate	50–60
	1-month forward rate	53–56
	3-month forward rate	182–187

As in the case of spot foreign exchange rates, the spread between bid and offer rates for a forward currency is based on the breadth and depth of the market for that currency, as well as on the currency's volatility. In the case of a widely traded currency, the spread will range from 0.2 to 0.6%, and a higher spread will occur for less heavily traded currencies.

SUMMARY

1. The foreign exchange market is the oldest and largest financial market. It trades around the clock — 24/7. The trading volume is at its highest when both Western Europe and the Eastern United States are trading.
2. One major implication of a 24-hour currency market is that exchange rates do provide a continuous real-time market assessment of new developments and therefore will change quasi-instantly in response to any new information. Furthermore, electronic trading is metamorphosing the price discovery process and speeding up price dissemination to the point of it becoming quasi-instantaneous. With price discovery quasi-automated and increasingly centralized, this over-the-counter market is taking on some of the characteristics of centralized exchanges. However, even with increased transparency and speedy widespread price dissemination bolstering the informational efficiency of the forex market, secretive central banks' intervention in the spot market remains a major impediment to full market efficiency.
3. The forex market is made up of two distinct but closely connected tiers: the customer market (buy side) and the interbank market (sell side). The interbank market consists of large multinational commercial banks whose dealers trade either directly among themselves or with the help of brokers. In this sense the interbank market is very much an interdealer market.

4. Banks' FX dealers act as principals in transactions with customers and may take one side of the transaction, thereby committing the bank's capital. Very often, however, they will turn to another bank to close the transaction. In so doing they may find it beneficial to enlist the help of an FX broker, whose principal function is to match a buyer with a seller in exchange for a commission but without taking positions or holding an inventory of currencies. Brokers were formerly humans known as voice brokers, but today they are predominantly electronic brokers (automated order-matching systems).
5. Foreign exchange products are traded on a spot basis (for immediate delivery) and a forward basis (for delivery at future dates, usually one, three, or six months ahead). Forward products include outright forwards, forex swaps, and non-deliverable forward contracts.
6. Foreign exchange rates are quoted on a bid/ask basis depending upon whether the bank is buying/bidding or selling/asking. The bid price is slightly lower than the ask price, reflecting the profit that the bank is realizing in trading currencies. The difference between the bid price and ask price is called the spread.
7. Spatial arbitrage ensures that exchange rates prevailing in different market locations are quasi-identical. Price discrepancies are indeed corrected by arbitrageurs (primarily forex traders at large banks) through their swift (if not quasi-instantaneous) purchase of the currency where it is a little cheaper for immediate sale where it is slightly more expensive until exchange rates are equal. This is the Law of One Price.
8. Forward exchange contracts are defined as a commitment to buy or sell a certain quantity of foreign exchange on a certain date in the future (the maturity of the contract) at a price (the forward exchange rate) agreed upon when the contract is signed (the present).
9. A foreign currency is said to be at a forward discount when the domestic currency forward price of one unit of foreign currency is less than its spot price. Conversely, a foreign currency is said to be at a forward premium whenever the domestic currency forward price of one unit of foreign currency is more than its spot price.

QUESTIONS FOR DISCUSSION

1. What is the basic function performed by the foreign exchange market?
2. What are the differences between a FX trader/dealer and a FX broker?
3. Contrast a voice broker with electronic broking systems.
4. What are the activities performed by the front office and back office of a trading room?
5. What is algorithmic trading?
6. Do you believe that currency traders are a dying species?
7. Why is foreign exchange trading directly linked to trade in goods and services accounting for only 15% of the foreign exchange market turnover?
8. Why is the foreign exchange market often referred to as "the market that never sleeps"?
9. Why is foreign exchange considered an asset class?
10. Why is the price of Swiss franc for US dollar in Zurich and New York City almost — but not quite — the same? What do you think explains the small difference in rates?
11. What is meant by bilateral arbitrage in the foreign exchange market?
12. What is meant by trilateral arbitrage in the foreign exchange market?
13. What is the bid-ask spread in foreign exchange?
14. State the Law of One Price. Why does it hold in the foreign exchange market?
15. Would you expect the bid-ask percentage spread to be different for the Indonesian rupiah versus the US dollar than for the Japanese yen?
16. What is the meaning of a forward premium or discount?
17. What is the difference between a forward and a non-deliverable forward contract? For which currencies are non-deliverable forward contracts usually traded?
18. What is the implicit interest rate for a given currency?

PROBLEMS

1. **Currency quotations (beginner).** Ford Motor Company has successfully negotiated the sale of Volvo Car Corporation for the cash amount of SEK 10 billion. Svenska Handelbank quotes the Swedish krona at SEK 6.7100-37 = US$1. What is the dollar amount that Ford Motor Company will receive?

2. **Bid-ask prices (beginner).** A currency trader at UBS in New York City quotes to a customer the Swissie-dollar as CHF 1.1975-85 = US$1. What is the bid price for the US dollar? What is the bid price for the Swiss franc? At what price is UBS willing to sell Swiss francs to its customer? What is the percentage spread of the bid-ask quote?

3. **Currency quotations (beginner).** Weyerhaeuser Inc. — the US lumber multinational — is importing a shipment of pine trees from Canada. The invoice is for CAD 250 million. Wells Fargo's currency trader quotes the Canadian dollar at CAD 0.9802-47 = US$1. What is the US dollar cost of this import transaction for Weyerhaeuser Inc.?

4. **Bilateral currency arbitrage (intermediate).** If the dollar price of one Russian ruble (RUB) is US$0.03282 = RUB 1 in New York City and at the same time the Russian ruble price of one dollar is 31.469 in Moscow, show how arbitrageurs could take advantage of the situation.
   - **a.** What would be the dollar profit per Russian ruble transacted accruing to US-based arbitrageurs?
   - **b.** What would be the Russian ruble profit per US dollar transacted accruing to Russia-based arbitrageurs?
   - **c.** Explain what the eventual outcome would be on exchange rates, as quoted in New York City and Moscow, resulting from arbitrageurs' operations.

5. **Cross-rates (intermediate).** Siam Commercial Bank in Bangkok (Thailand) quotes the US dollar at THB 31.25/US$ whereas Standard Chartered Bank of Singapore quotes the US dollar at SGD1.31/US$. What is the cross-rate THB/SGD?

6. **Cross-rates (intermediate).** Referring to exchange rate quotations provided in the *Wall Street Journal* (Exhibit 5.5) for the Brazilian real and the Thai baht, compute the cross-rate price of one Brazilian real in Thai baht terms.

7. **Forward premiums/discounts (intermediate).** Referring to the forward quotes in the *Wall Street Journal* (Exhibit 5.5) for the Japanese yen, determine whether the yen is at a premium or discount against the US dollar. What is the percentage premium/discount for maturities of one, three, and six months?

8. **Forward premiums/discounts with bids/asks (intermediate).** Referring to the following spot and forward bid-ask rates for the US$/€ exchange rate, answer the questions that follows:

Maturity	$/€ Bid Rate	$/€ Ask Rate
Spot	1.2389	1.2401
1 month	1.2396	1.2408
3 months	1.2403	1.2415
6 months	1.2407	1.2418
12 months	1.2408	1.2420

   - **a.** Is the euro at a premium or discount *vis-à-vis* the US dollar?
   - **b.** What is the annualized forward premium or discount for each maturity?
   - **c.** Restate the bid-ask quotations as a euro price of one dollar. Is the dollar at a premium or discount *vis-à-vis* the euro? What is the annualized premium/discount for each maturity? Are they different from the results you obtained in part b? Why?

9. **Forward speculation (intermediate).** The chief currency strategist at the Copenhagen-based Viking hedge fund was reviewing the forecast that the fund's chief economist had just released. Within 6–9 months Greece would exit the eurozone, and fears of contagion to other PIIGS countries would result in a 12–15% depreciation of the euro. The Danish krone is currently pegged to the euro at DKR 6.71 = €1 and three, six, and 12 months forward krone against the euro are at an annualized discount of 1.5, 2.25, and 3.50%. Show how our currency trader could speculate to capitalize on the in-house prognosis of a euro partial fragmentation. Explain which forwards are best suited for this speculative scheme. Show the cash flows and their timing.

10. **Transaction costs (advanced).** Assuming that transaction costs represent 1/16 of 1% of the amount transacted, what is the maximum/minimum dollar price of one Japanese yen that

you would expect to prevail in New York, given that the dollar is quoted at 79 yen in Tokyo?

Hint: Transaction costs simply reduce the amount of the currency purchased by 1/16 of 1%.

11. **Transaction costs (advanced).** Geneviève received as a graduation present a one-week cruise on the Baltic Sea that will take her from Kiel (Germany) to Copenhagen (Denmark), Stockholm (Sweden), and Saint Petersburg (Russia) before returning to Kiel. She embarks on the M/S *Sibelius* in Kiel. She decides to exchange her €2,500 savings in the currency of the next port of call (Copenhagen) and will exchange what she does not spend in Copenhagen in the currency of the next port of call. To her disappointment, she does not find any souvenirs to buy that she likes at any port of call and returns to Kiel without having spent a single cent. How many euros is she left with? €1 = DKK 9.3847-82 = SEK 10.4717-57 = RUB 51.2108-98.

12. **Cross-rates with bid-ask spreads (advanced).** Assume that the Thai baht (THB) is quoted as THB 30.2511-3987 per US$1 and that the Japanese yen (¥) is quoted as 76.2518-7985 per US$1. What is the cross ¥/THB bid-ask price that the bank would quote to its customers?

13. **Trilateral arbitrage (advanced).** Assuming that the pound is worth 1.1567 euros in Paris and 1.4393 Swiss francs in Zurich, can Britain-based arbitrageurs make profits, given that the Swiss franc is worth 0.8102 euros in Paris?
    a. Work out the solution first by disregarding transaction costs.
    b. Assuming that transaction costs amount to 1/16 of 1% of the amount transacted, are there still exploitable arbitrage opportunities?

14. **Band of fluctuations (advanced).** Show that if two currencies i and j independently maintain their exchange rate within a band of fluctuations defined as +/−1% around a par value $S_{\$,i}(t)_{\text{PAR}}$ or $S_{\$,j}(t)_{\text{PAR}}$ *vis-à-vis* the US dollar, the currencies i and j will automatically maintain their cross exchange rate within a band of fluctuations +/−2% around their cross par value $S_{i,j}(t)_{\text{PAR}}$.

    Hint: Cross exchange rate $S_{i,j}(t)$ is simply defined as $S_{\$,j}(t)/S_{\$,i}(t)$. Similarly, a cross par value is defined as:

$$\left[S_{i,j}(0)\right]_{\text{PAR}} = \left[S_{\$,j}(0)\right]_{\text{PAR}} / \left[S_{\$,i}(0)\right]_{\text{PAR}}$$

15. **Law of One Price (advanced).** Shares of Yacimientos Petroliferos Fiscales (YPF) – Argentina's integrated energy conglomerate listed on the New York Stock Exchange and the Argentine Bolsa fell from US$20.76 to US$19.21 when the Argentine Peso (ARS) depreciated from ARS 1/.040 to ARS 1/0.036 = $1.
    a. At what ARS price should YPF shares be trading at in Buenos Aires before the ARS depreciated? Right after the ARS depreciated?
    b. YPF is actually trading at ARS 521 right after the 10% abrupt depreciation of the Argentine peso. As a trader for Banco Santander specializing in Argentine stocks, do you see profit opportunities? Show through a simple numerical example how the trader could take advantage of the peso devaluation.
    c. What are the risks involved? YPF stock is traded simultaneously on both the New York Stock Exchange in US dollars and on the Buenos Aires Bolsa in pesos.

INTERNET EXERCISES

16. **Trilateral arbitrage (advanced).** Log in to www.oanda.com and select three currencies: using the bilateral exchange rates between the three currencies can you identify arbitrage opportunities. Which currency pair have the largest absolute and relative spreads?

17. **Forward premium/discount (intermediate).** Log in to FXStreet exchange services www.fxstreet.com/rates-charts/forward-rates and identify the three currency which are at the deepest discount *vis-à-vis* the US dollar. How do you explain them?

REFERENCES

Attfield, Chris, and Mel Mayne. 2011. "Systematic Trading in Foreign Exchange." Chapter 16 in *Financial Engineering*, edited by Tanya S. Beder and Cara M. Marshall. Hoboken, NJ: John Wiley & Sons.

Bank for International Settlements. 2001. "The Implications of Electronic Trading in Financial Markets." (January).

Bank for International Settlements. 2016. *Triennial Central Bank Survey of Foreign Exchange and Derivatives Market Activity in 2010.* Basel, Switzerland: BIS.

Jacque, Laurent L. 2011. "The Foreign Exchange Market." Chapter 7 in *Financial Engineering*, edited by Tanya S. Beder and Cara M. Marshall. Hoboken, NJ: John Wiley & Sons.

Kubarych, Roger M. 1983. *Foreign Exchange Markets in the United States*, 2nd edition. New York: Federal Reserve Bank.

Lyons, R. K. 2001. *The Micro-Structure Approach to the Foreign Exchange Market*. Cambridge, MA: MIT Press.

Rime, Dagfinn. 2003. "New Electronic Trading Systems in Foreign Exchange Markets." Chapter 21 in *New Economy Handbook*, edited by Derek C. Jones. New York: Elsevier Science.

CASE STUDY 5.1. BANCO MERCANTIL INTERNACIONAL'S FOREX LOSSES

A speculator is a man who observes the future and acts before it occurs.

— Bernard Baruch

Rogue Trader

On March 19, 2001, in the heyday of the Argentine currency board of fixed exchange rates, Banco Mercantil Internacional (BMI) — the second-largest Mexican commercial bank with 177 offices in 11 Latin American countries — announced a loss of US$80 million. The loss was attributed to unauthorized forward speculation on the Argentine peso (ARS) by a Chilean trader in the bank's Buenos Aires branch. The amount of the underlying transactions was rumored to be close to US$1.8 billion, and initial reports indicated that the losses could be traced to short sales of the US dollar for the Argentine peso.

Preliminary accounts indicated that the trader was betting the Argentine peso would not devalue and that the fiscal situation would stabilize. Accordingly, the trader had purchased Argentine pesos for six and nine months' delivery at respective forward rates of ARS 1.15 and ARS 1.25 = US$1, fully expecting that as Argentina restored economic growth, the forward discounts on the peso would narrow.[24] Banco Mercantil's officials stated that the trader involved had violated corporate guidelines when he persisted in maintaining an uncovered position in his trading accounts. For Banco Mercantil the year 2001 had commenced with a two-for-one stock split and ended with record operating profit of $94 million in spite of this one-time loss of US$80 million.

How could a single employee fool one of the largest and most sophisticated Latin American commercial banks? How could such a large speculative bet go undetected by the firm's back office and lose so much money for the bank when — for all practical purposes — the Argentine peso peg to the US dollar had been enacted into a law?

Trials and Tribulations of the Argentine Economy After a Decade-Long Hard Peg

In 1991, Argentina ended decades of hyperinflation by instituting a rigid one-to-one peg of the peso to the US dollar known as the Convertibility Plan. In effect, Argentina adopted a currency board whereby its central bank committed itself to tying the money supply to its holding of foreign exchange (forex) reserves — primarily US dollars. More specifically, Argentina's money supply could grow only if the country accumulated additional foreign exchange reserves. Monetary policy had become an automatic and unbending rule (reminiscent of the gold standard), and politicians or bureaucrats were no longer in charge.

As inflation abated and the Peronist Menem government pushed through ambitious privatizations, the Argentine economy grew rapidly until 1997 — growth that was fueled in part by large borrowing in world capital markets at low interest rates. The 1997 Asian financial crisis, followed by the 1998 debacles of the Russian and Brazilian economies, resulted in emerging market risk premiums,[25] which burdened the Argentine budget deficit. The sharp devaluation of the Brazilian real in 1999 and the appreciation of the US dollar against the euro

24 Forward rates are linked to interest rate differentials between the US dollar and Argentine peso through the theorem of interest rate parity. The higher the interest rates in Argentina, the deeper the discount on the peso. Tighter fiscal policy in Argentina meant higher interest rates. An IMF-led rescue package would allow the Argentine government to relax its high interest rate policy, which would in turn narrow the discount on the ARS. One-month and three-month forward contracts were available at ARS 1.05 and ARS 1.08.

25 The emerging market risk premium refers to the high interest rate at which the Argentine government could borrow on international capital markets to finance its budget deficit. The benchmark against which the market risk premium is calculated is the interest rate on US Treasury bonds at which the US government finances its budget deficit.

dragged along[26] the Argentine peso, which had become increasingly overvalued *vis-à-vis* its major trading partners.

Argentina's economic situation began to unravel as the recession worsened an already bad public deficit and deepened the balance-of-payments current-account deficit. National debt, which had stood at 41% of gross domestic product (GDP) in 1997, reached 64% of GDP in 2001, while risk premiums on long-term Argentine government debt more than doubled from 3% or 4% in 1997 to 7% or 8% in late 2000 as compared with US Treasury bonds of similar maturities. With monetary policy and foreign exchange rate policy off the table, Argentina was left with fiscal and wage policy as the only active policy instruments. Unfortunately, with tepid or mildly negative economic growth, tax revenues increasingly lagged projections. Attempts to tighten fiscal policy further by increasing taxes and slashing expenditures merely postponed economic recovery. Thus the burden of restoring growth fell squarely on wage policy — a form of internal devaluation: Workers had to accept lower wages to enable Argentina to compete in international markets. Indeed, the consumer price index started to fall in 1998 but not enough or soon enough to restore Argentina's exports' competitiveness.

In spite of a new International Monetary Fund (IMF) financing package and a stabilizing balance of trade deficit, rumors of a peso devaluation were increasingly circulating in banking circles. The cost of unpegging the Argentine peso from the US dollar, however, was considered exorbitant and dimmed the probability of such an occurrence. Forward rates, however, reflected a tightening of the monetary situation (see Case Exhibit 5.1).

Currency Trading in the Tranquil Days Of Argentina's Currency Board

Although forex trading is often shrouded in secrecy, there is a widespread consensus that forex trading profits at commercial banks come primarily from trades carried out on behalf of corporate customers (so-called agency trading); for example, when IBM-USA repatriates ARS 50 million of dividends from its Argentine subsidiary, it purchases the amount on the spot market through the Buenos Aires branch of Banco Mercantil. Indeed, banks' currency trading desks, for the most part, earn a living by buying and selling foreign currencies to customers such as IBM at slightly different rates — also known as the bid/ask spread — primarily on a spot basis and to a lesser extent on a forward basis for corporate customers (and more recently on options, swaps, and other derivative products). This is indeed a relatively safe way to make a living, as it does not entail outright speculative positions on currencies coming from speculative *directional trades* through the spot or forward currency market based on forecasting of exchange rates (so-called *proprietary trading* as practiced by hedge funds). In 2001 the Argentine peso had been pegged (tied) to the US dollar by its par value at the price of US\$1.00 = ARS 1.00 and backed by a currency board since 1991.

How Banks Keep a Lid on Their Foreign Exchange Trading Operations

Banco Mercantil puts overnight limits on its currency traders, though the actual amount varies from branch to branch depending upon the volume of business transacted. Traders are required to observe trading limits for a single transaction; for example, the bank may mandate that no single forex trade be in excess of \$10 million and that the aggregate limit of a trader's net position be no more than \$25 million during the day and very close to zero by the end of the business day in order to avoid unwelcome overnight surprises.

Banco Mercantil, however, kept track of its foreign exchange transactions only on a net basis. For example, overall US dollar sales and purchases of either a spot or a forward nature would be toted up and only the balance — plus or minus — would be shown. Thus, Banco Mercantil, like most banks, had set in place control systems aimed at keeping its traders honest by implementing the *square position requirement*, which is nothing more than requiring that each trader keep his or her trades in balance and that for each currency the amount sold forward would equal the amount purchased forward. Thus, in all likelihood, the Chilean trader must have entered into shorter-term speculative positions to offset and mask his speculative gamble.

Hasty Conclusion

According to Mr. Santiago Munoz, the manager of the Buenos Aires branch, he didn't become aware of the trader's positions until September, at which point

---

26 Twenty-five percent of Argentina's exports are destined to the euro-zone.

Case Exhibit 5.1 Selected macroeconomic statistics for Argentina (1996–2000).

	Argentina				
Annual Indicators	**1996**	**1997**	**1998**	**1999**	**2000**[a]
GDP at market prices (ARS bn)	272.2	292.9	298.9	283.3	282.3
GDP (US$ bn)	272.2	293	299.1	283.4	282.5
Real GDP growth (%)	5.5	8.1	3.9	-3.4	-0.3
Consumer price inflation (av, %)	0.2	0.5	0.9	-1.2	-0.9
Population (mn)	35.2	35.7	36.1	36.1	37
Exports of goods FOB (US$ mn)	24,043	26,430	26,441	23,333	26.251
Imports of goods FOB (US$ mn)	22,283	28,554	29,558	24,103	24,002.9
Current-account balance (US$ mn)	-6,842	-12,498	-14,602	-12,312	-11,121
Foreign-exchange reserves gold (US$ mn)	18,104	22,320	24,752	26,252	25,147
Total external debt (US$ bn)	111.4	128.4	141.5	147.9	156.3
Debt-service ratio, paid (%)	39.4	50.0	57.5	75.8	76.2
Exchange rate (ARS per US$)	1.00	1.00	1.00	1.00	1.00

Note: [a]March 2, 2001: ARS 1.00 = US$1.
US interest rate = 3.00% for three-month deposit, 3.25% for six-month bank deposit, and 3.60% for nine-month deposit.
Argentine interest rate = 12.00% for three-month deposit, 13.25% for six-month bank deposit, and 13.60% for nine-month deposit.

he moved to have the trader close his position expeditiously. The losses thus had come in two ways — from the trading itself that had accumulated since March and from liquidating the large outstanding positions. The bulk of the losses apparently had come from trading itself. The trader was betting that the large forward premium on the US dollar would shrink as Argentina won a reprieve on its international debt burden and was able to stave off a devaluation of the peso. But as Argentina's international debt position continued to deteriorate, the premium on the US dollar only increased across all maturities. Banco Mercantil also took a loss in closing the position, as it had to purchase forward dollars that had previously been sold forward — just the reverse of what the trader had done to build his position. And yet the Argentine peso still had not devalued!

Questions for Discussion

1. How would the Chilean trader speculate on the Argentine peso? Spell out his exchange rate forecast and how and when he would earn a profit.
2. Why would an outright speculative position be easily found out and exposed by the BMI's branch back office? How was the currency trader able to hide his trades?
3. Given that the Argentine peso did not devalue until January 2002, explain what would have been the end result of the Chilean trader's speculative scheme if the bank had let it ride until maturity. Detail timing and amount of cash flows.
4. Why were forward exchange rates trading at significant discounts or premiums from the spot price when the latter was fixed at ARS 1 = US$1 and backed by a currency board?
5. What are the control systems that Banco Mercantil should institute to prevent the recurrence of such a speculative scheme?
6. Do you believe that trading rooms within large commercial banks should be forbidden to engage in directional trades? Under what conditions would you allow trading rooms to engage in directional trades?

CHAPTER 6

Interest Rate Arbitrage and Parity

Theory takes for granted, that whenever enormous profits can be made in any particular trade, a sufficient number of capitalists will be induced to engage in it, who will, by their competition, reduce the profits to the general rate of mercantile gains. It assumes that in the trade of exchange does this principle more especially operate, it not being confined to English merchants alone; but being perfectly understood, and profitably followed, by the exchange and bullion merchants of Holland, France, and Hamburgh; and competition in this trade being well known to be carried to its greatest height.

—David Ricardo's reply to Mr. Bosanquet

Akiko Isobe is the money market fund manager at Fuji Life — the life insurance company headquartered in Tokyo. Frustrated by the paltry 0.25% return per annum offered by short-term deposits in yen (¥), Akiko has been tempted by the significantly higher yields offered in Australian dollar (AUD) at 6.25%, South African rand at 12%, and Turkish lira at 17.5%. Would abandoning the almighty yen for a few months or even a year be a chance worth taking? Can these more exotic currencies be trusted? What are the risks involved? Can these risks be hedged?

This chapter explores the relationships known as *interest rate arbitrage* (IRA) and *interest rate parity* (IRP), which bind interest rates in two different currencies with their spot and forward exchange (FX or forex) rates. The theory of *IRA* and parity is the bedrock concept for international finance. It is at once a macroeconomic equilibrium relationship — the notion of interest rate parity — that explains remarkably well how forward rates are determined by interest rates, and a powerful microeconomic decision model — the notion of interest rate arbitrage — that guides both short-term investment and short-term financing decisions. This chapter introduces the theory by first formulating simple *IRA* interest rate arbitrage decision rules for short-term investing or short-term funding before providing a macroeconomic generalization *interest rate parity.*

After reading this chapter you will understand:

- *Interest rate arbitrage* or how money managers can compare the yields on short-term investments of the same credit risk class but denominated in different currencies such as the US dollar, the Japanese yen, the Swiss franc, and the euro.
- How corporate treasurers can compare the cost of financing sourced from different currencies.
- How forward exchange rates are determined by interest rate differentials.
- *Interest rate parity* or how interest rate arbitrage keeps nominal interest rates at par when they are corrected for the cost of hedging exchange rate risk.
- Why interest rate parity may not hold exactly and what sources of friction may account for small deviations from parity.
- What the *carry trade* is and when it can be profitable.

INTEREST RATE ARBITRAGE THEOREM

To introduce the concept of *IRA*, we consider first the *short-term investment* (or *multicurrency cash management*) problem faced by pension funds, multinational corporations, banks, and institutional investors. These entities often accumulate liquid funds earmarked for expenditures at some future point — for example, dividends to be distributed by quarter or year-end to shareholders, interest payments and principal repayments due on long-term bonds, and tax liabilities due to the government or pension checks due to retirees. Such idle funds will be invested in low-risk and very liquid securities such as domestic Treasury bills, time deposits, certificates of deposit, or commercial paper.[1] The guiding principle here is that there should be no risk whatsoever that less than 100% of the principal will be recovered on the maturity date. In selecting the optimal investment alternative, money managers will include foreign securities in similar very low-risk classes that may offer higher nominal returns than their domestic counterparts.

Arbitraging short-term investment opportunities: The international cash management/investment decision

Interest rate differentials among equivalent risk-class securities should prompt risk-averse investors (interest rate arbitrageurs) to shift funds from one money market to another until interest rates are brought back into equilibrium. This process of arbitrage of interest rates is complicated when such interest-bearing securities are denominated in different currencies and the risk-averse investor is faced with a foreign exchange risk that may wipe out the differential in interest rates that initially prompted the investor's move.

An example will help clarify the idea. Let's return to the predicament faced by Akiko Isobe — our Japanese fund manager who is responsible for optimizing the yield on a ¥25 billion cash balance idle for the next year. On December 15, 2018, one-year Japanese yen–denominated certificates of deposit were yielding a paltry 0.25% annually, whereas similar risk class one-year Australian dollar certificates of deposit were yielding a much more attractive 6.25% annually. Clearly, such a *nominal* difference in interest rates (6.25% – 0.25% = 6% p.a.) should entice our friend Akiko to invest her ¥25 billion in Australian dollar certificates of deposit.

Here is how the comparison would be constructed[2]:

- *Option 1: Domestic investment ("Stay home").* Akiko would compute the total return on a domestic ¥-denominated 1-year investment:

  ¥25 billion × (1 + 0.0025) = ¥25.0625 billion. (See arrow 1 in Exhibit 6.1.)

- *Option 2: Foreign investment.*

  Step 1 ("Passage to Australia"). Akiko would convert ¥25 billion into AUD at the spot rate of ¥100 = AUD 1 prevailing on December 15, 2018, receiving ¥25bn/100 = AUD 250 million. (See arrow 2 in Exhibit 6.1.)

  Step 2 ("Discover Australia"). With the AUD 250 million proceeds, Akiko would then buy 1-year AUD-denominated certificates of deposit yielding 6.25% annually for a total return of: AUD 250 million × (1 + 0.0625) = AUD 265.625 million available on December 15, 2019. (See arrow 3 in Exhibit 6.1.)

  Step 3A ("Purchase travel insurance"). However, Akiko is concerned with her return in yen rather than in Australian dollars; hence, the profitability of this arbitrage of interest rates would depend on the spot exchange rate prevailing 1 year from now, when Akiko will convert principal and interest earnings AUD 250 million × (1 + 0.0625) = AUD 265.625 million back into yen on December 15, 2019.[3] Clearly, on December 15, 2018, Akiko does not know what the spot exchange rate will be 1 year hence. However, this risk can be readily avoided by selling forward on December 15, 2018, AUD for yen at the forward exchange rate of $F(365) = 96$ that prevailed on December 15, 2018, guaranteeing that she will receive AUD 250 million × (1 + 0.0625) × 96 = ¥25.50 billion on December 15, 2019.

  Step 3B ("Fly home"). The actual delivery of AUD 265.625 million in exchange for AUD 265.625 million × 96 = ¥25.50 billion will take place on December 15, 2019, even though everything else (amount of contract, delivery date, exchange

1 These are short-term debt instruments (one year or less) issued by highly rated institutions such as the US Treasury, large financial institutions, or multinational corporations with very strong credit ratings. Their purpose is to finance the government budget deficit (in the case of Treasury bills) or working capital for firms. The securities themselves have very low credit risk — if any — and are issued in large quantities that guarantee a very liquid secondary market where the instruments are easily negotiable.

2 A folksy metaphor is used here whereby Akiko is taking a vacation in faraway but possibly more exciting Australia rather than settling for a somewhat sedate, cheaper, but boring vacation at home. She compares costs and wants to avoid surprises while maximizing fun and excitement.

3 (Principal in AUD) × (1 + AUD interest rate) × $S(365)$ = (AUD 250 million) × (1.0625) × $S(365)$ = AUD 265.625 million × $S(365)$.

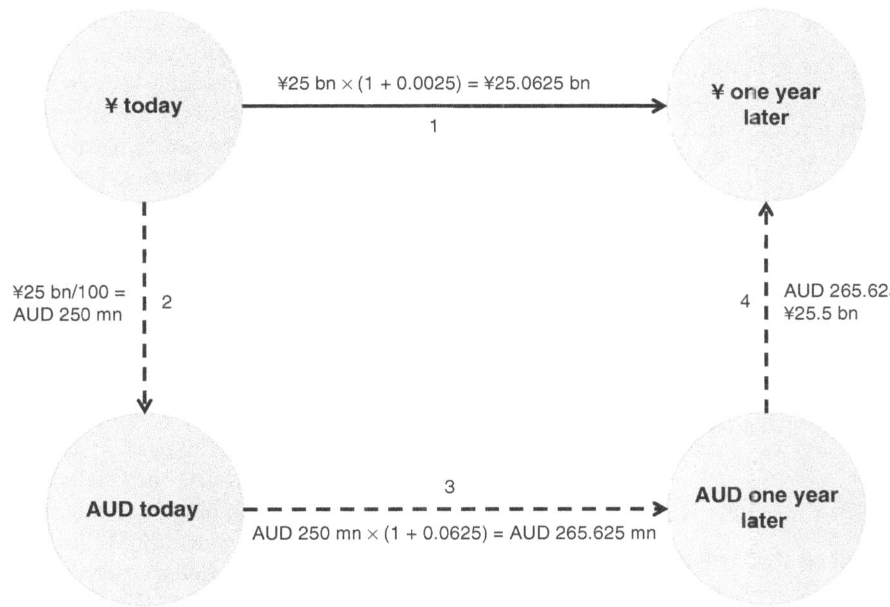

Yield on Japanese yen one-year investment:	$i_{¥} = 0.25\%$
Yield on Australian dollar one-year investment:	$i_{AUD} = 6.25\%$
Spot exchange rate defined as ¥ price of one AUD:	$S(0) = 100$
Forward rate for one-year delivery as ¥ price of one AUD:	$F(365) = 96$
Unknown spot exchange rate one year hence as ¥ price of one AUD:	$S(365) = ?$

Exhibit 6.1. Interest rate arbitrage.

rate) is agreed upon on December 15, 2018.[4] (See arrow 4 on Exhibit 6.1.)

Let us consider further what risks Akiko faces and revisit why the forward cover is so critical to this transaction. In the absence of a forward cover, should the Australian dollar depreciate *vis-à-vis* the yen during the investment period (that is, the AUD buys fewer yen than on December 15, 2018, one year hence), the real or effective rate of interest from Akiko's point of view will be less than the nominal rate of 6.25%. It may even drop below the 0.25% earned on one-year yen-denominated certificates of deposit were the AUD to depreciate dramatically enough over the one-year period.

Such an eventuality would deter our Japanese investor, who is by definition risk-averse, from undertaking the investment if it were not for a perfect way of protecting herself from the uncertainty of the future spot exchange rate between the AUD and the ¥ — a form of travel insurance against trip cancellation, health hazards, or any unsavory, costly surprises occasioned by Akiko's venture into treacherous foreign short-term investing!

Such a protective device is provided by a forward contract. In the example, Akiko would simply sell forward both AUD principal and interest income back into ¥. The price of the transaction would be set on December 15, 2018, but would not be carried out until December 15, 2019. In so doing, our risk-averse Japanese fund manager knows for certain how many yen her investment in AUD certificates of deposit versus yen-denominated certificates of deposit will return, and she will act accordingly; that is, she will invest in AUD certificates of deposit, since the yen investment would return only ¥25.06 billion.[5]

4 (Principal in AUD) × (1 + AUD interest rate) × $F(365)$ = (AUD 250 million) × (1.0625) × 96 = AUD 265.625 million × 96 = ¥25,500 billion.

5 (Principal in ¥) × (1 + ¥ interest rate) = ¥25 billion × (1 + 0.0025) = ¥25.0625 billion.

Algebraic formulation of the interest rate parity theorem

A generalization of the previous example is now provided, denoting by $S(0)$ the spot exchange rate expressed as the yen price of one Australian dollar prevailing at time $t = 0$, $F(365)$ as the forward exchange rate for delivery in 365 days, and $i_{¥}$, i_{AUD} as interest rates on one-year ¥ and AUD certificates of deposit, respectively:

1. *Domestic investment at no currency risk.* A Japanese investor with a yen amount of $\{a\}_{¥}$ to be invested over a one-year period should consider investing them in ¥ certificates of deposit yielding $i_{¥}$. Thus $\{a\}_{¥}$ invested at such a rate would return, in 365 days,

$$a \times [1 + i_{¥}] \tag{6.1}$$

2. *Foreign investment covered against exchange rate risk.* Alternatively, she could consider a *covered/hedged* investment in AUD-denominated certificates of deposit. To do so, she would convert, at time $t = 0$,

$$[a]_{¥} \text{ into AUD}: \left[\frac{a}{S(0)}\right]_{AUD} \tag{6.2a}$$

and simultaneously (still at time $t = 0$) contract to sell forward both principal and interest earnings denominated in Australian dollars,

$$\left[\frac{a}{S(0)}\right]_{AUD} \times \{1 + i_{AUD}\} \tag{6.2b}$$

for yen at the prevailing forward exchange rate of $F(365)$. The covered investment in the AUD money market would thus return, in yen terms:

$$\left[\frac{a}{S(0)}\right]_{AUD} \times \{1 + i_{AUD}\} \times F(365) \tag{6.2c}$$

Again, it should be emphasized that the yen return on the AUD investment has zero foreign exchange risk because it is entirely a function of known quantities at time $t = 0$.

3. *Foreign investment without cover against exchange rate risk.* Finally, our investor could invest in AUD-denominated certificates of deposit without covering either the principal or interest earnings against a risk of depreciation of the Australian dollar against the yen. She would wait for her certificates of deposit to mature (at time $t = 365$) and then convert the AUD-denominated principal and interest earnings (expression (6.2b)) back into yen at the then-prevailing spot exchange rate of $S(365)$. At the outset of the investment horizon (at time $t = 0$), the future spot exchange rate $S(365)$ is clearly an unknown quantity. The yen return on this uncovered investment in the AUD money market is also an unknown quantity at time $t = 0$:

$$\left[\frac{a}{S(0)}\right]_{AUD} \times \{1 + i_{AUD}\} \times S(365) \tag{6.2d}$$

This simple international cash management decision is portrayed in Exhibit 6.2, using the numerical illustration of Akiko's short-term investment predicament. It charts the total yen return (principal and interest earnings) as a function of the end-of-period exchange rate $S(365)$. Yen domestic investment and Australian dollar covered investment are sketched as horizontal lines (1) and (2) — that is, independent of $S(365)$. Uncovered AUD investment, from a Japanese investor point of view, is an increasing function of $S(365)$, as shown on line (3).

Clearly, our risk-averse Japanese investor is only able to compare yen amounts (expressions (6.1) and (6.2c)) at time $t = 0$ for both domestic and covered foreign investment:

$$a \times [1 + i_{¥}] \gtreqless \left[\frac{a}{S(0)}\right]_{AUD} \times \{1 + i_{AUD}\} \times F(365) \tag{6.2}$$

Depending on which inequality holds, our Japanese investor will decide to invest in ¥ securities (expression (6.1)) or in AUD securities (expression (6.2c)). In so doing, she will set into motion supply and demand forces in both the Japanese and the Australian money and foreign exchange markets that will tend to move toward parity the values in expressions (6.1) and (6.2c). Accordingly, lines (1) and (2) in Exhibit 6.2 will tend to merge. We will return to this process in greater detail (see next section) when we consider *interest rate arbitrage* from a macroeconomic perspective. For the time being, suffice it to say that *interest rate arbitrage* results from the fact that lines (1) and (2) are different, which indicates a small difference in risk-adjusted yields — also known as a mild degree of *money market segmentation*. Arbitrage should bring about parity by erasing the gap between lines (1) and (2) as money markets become fully integrated.

Of note are the intersection points between lines (1) and (3) and between lines (2) and (3).

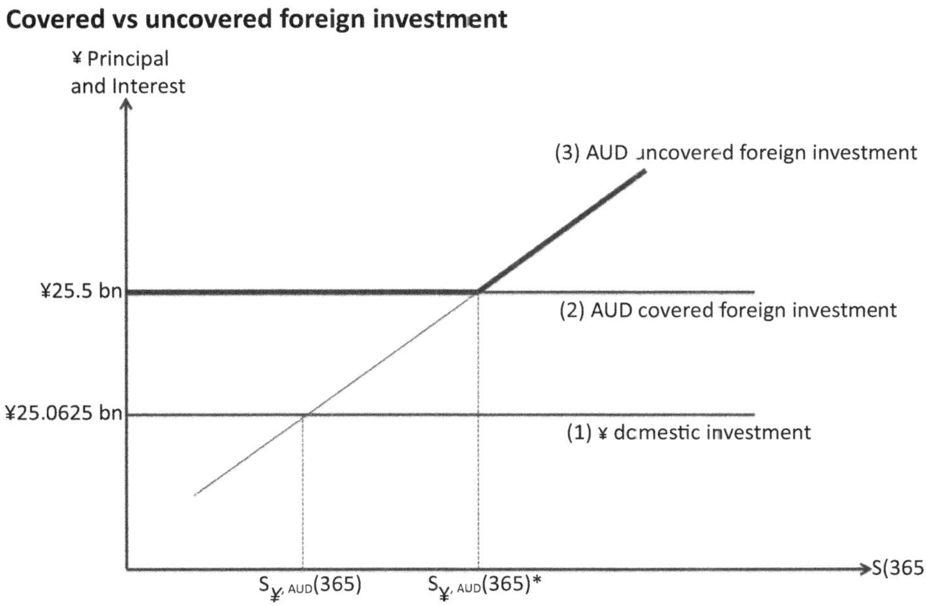

Exhibit 6.2. Covered versus uncovered foreign investment.

The break-even exchange rates are given by setting equation (6.2d) equal to equation (6.1) or (6.2c). In plain English, we are searching for the unknown spot exchange rate one year hence $S(365)$ at which uncovered foreign investment is equal to domestic investment or equal to foreign covered investment:

$$\left[\frac{a}{S(0)}\right]_{\text{AUD}} \times \{1+i_{\text{AUD}}\} \times S(365) = a \times [1+i_{¥}] \quad (6.3a)$$

or

$$S(365) = S(0) \times \frac{[1+i_{¥}]}{[1+i_{\text{AUD}}]} \quad (6.3b)$$

In this first instance, the break-even exchange rate is simply the "no-profit" forward rate 1 year hence that ought to prevail in an *interest rate parity* world without arbitrage opportunities (see next section for a discussion of the no-profit forward rate). Similarly, the second break-even spot rate is found by solving:

$$\left[\frac{a}{S(0)}\right]_{\text{AUD}} \times \{1+i_{\text{AUD}}\} \times S(365) = \left[\frac{a}{S(0)}\right]_{\text{AUD}} \times [1+i_{\text{AUD}}] \times F(365) \quad (6.3c)$$

or

$$S(365) = F(365) \quad (6.3d)$$

In this second case, the break-even exchange rate is simply the market's forward rate that prevailed one year earlier. The fact that the *first and second* break-even spot rates are different illustrates a case of mild money market segmentation. In a perfectly integrated *interest rate parity* world the two rates would be equal!

Arbi-loan and the financing decision

We continue our exploration of *interest rate arbitrage* by considering the symmetrical decision on how best to procure a loan (minimizing liabilities) as opposed to how best to maximize return on a short-term investment (maximizing assets). Let's now consider the following example Suppose China Airlines, the Beijing-based air carrier, is in need of 1 billion yuan (CNY) to finance its working capital requirement for 1 year. A yuan-denominated loan from the Industrial and Commercial Bank of China (ICBC) is available at 9%, while a yen-denominated loan from Mitsubishi-Tokyo Bank costs only 1%. The deputy treasurer of China Airlines is tempted by the low cost of the yen loan, but concerned — as she should be — that the Japanese yen may appreciate over the course of the loan, making it more expensive in yuan terms. In fact, appreciation in excess of 9% – 1% = 8% would negate the advantage of the yen loan, costing China Airlines more than the 9% it would pay on the domestic currency loan. The effective (rather than nominal) cost of yen financing can be established at the inception of the loan by locking in the yuan cost of buying yen forward for delivery one year out to pay back interest and principal. The following rates are available:

Spot rate: CNY 1 = ¥13.5 or CNY 0.074 = ¥1	$S(0)=\frac{1}{13.5}=0.074$
Forward rate: CNY 1 = ¥13	$F(365)=\frac{1}{13}=0.077$
Chinese interest rate: 9%	$i_{CNY}=0.09$
Japanese interest rate: 1%	$i_{¥}=0.01$

Here is how it works:

- *Domestic financing.* Borrow domestic yuan at the financing cost of:

  CNY1 × (1 + 0.09)bn = CNY 1.09 bn due in 365 days

  Yuan are borrowed and yuan are repaid: no surprise here!
- *Foreign financing.* The alternative to domestic financing is the seemingly cheaper yen short-term loan — but is it really cheaper when the cost of eliminating foreign exchange risk is taken into account?

  Step 1. Borrow the ¥ equivalent of CNY 1 billion (1 bn/0.074 = ¥13.5 bn) and convert the proceeds into yuan to finance working capital. Repay both principal and interest expenses:

  $$¥13.5 \times (1 + 0.01)\text{ bn} = ¥13.635\text{ bn}$$

  in 365 days. The principal borrowed is the yen equivalent of CNY 1 billion or ¥13.5 billion when the spot yen price of one CNY is ¥13.5 or CNY 0.074 = ¥1.

  Step 2. Cover ¥ principal and interest payment liability. One year from now, the yen principal and interest due to Mitsubishi Bank will be worth more yuan should the yen appreciate over the next 365 days. By purchasing yen forward at the rate of ¥13 = CNY 1, China Airlines locks in the total cost of its loan in yuan terms:

  $$\frac{¥13.365}{13}\text{bn} = \text{CNY } 1.05\text{ bn}$$

Yen financing is cheaper than yuan financing.

The reader will note the symmetry between a covered short-term investment (an asset story) and an arbi-loan (a liability story). In the case of Fuji Life Insurance, an asset position is created in the foreign currency into which the short-term investment is carried out. Hedging the AUD asset position requires the creation of a liability AUD position in matching amount and maturity to neutralize the AUD asset position, which is readily achieved by a forward AUD sale. Symmetrically, an arbi-loan in the case of China Airlines will create a short-term liability denominated in ¥ that can be hedged by purchasing an amount of ¥ forward, thus creating a ¥ asset position matching the principal and interest owed to Mitsubishi-Tokyo Bank. In effect, forward contracts are instruments that permit Fuji Life Insurance to transform an AUD-denominated cash flow into a ¥-denominated cash flow. Similarly, China Airlines would use a forward ¥ contract to transform a ¥-denominated cash outflow into a CNY-denominated cash outflow.

Pure interest rate arbitrage

A third form of covered interest arbitrage, often undertaken by currency traders, consists of borrowing in the lower-yielding domestic money market and investing in the higher-yielding foreign money market — in a way a hybrid of the first two interest rate arbitrage scenarios introduced previously. Consider the case of Mr. Yamamoto — Akiko's godfather, a senior currency trader at Mitsubishi-Tokyo Bank — who is exploring the opportunity of a riskless profit from a round-trip investment in AUD by borrowing at 0.75%: At first sight the higher yield in AUD at 6.25% should be very enticing since the cost of the funds is only 0.75%.[6] However, since Mr. Yamamoto has to fully protect his trade from exchange rate risk, the outcome will depend entirely on the forward discount on the AUD and how much it eats away at the favorable interest rate differential. To gauge the opportunity for arbitrage profit, follow his round-trip as we did earlier for Akiko's.

Step 1. Borrow *a* yen at the interest rate of $i_{¥} = 0.75\%$, incurring an obligation to repay one year later for each yen borrowed:

$$a \times (1 + i_{¥}) = a \times (1 + 0.0075) = a \times (1.0075) \quad (6.4a)$$

Step 2. Invest in Australian dollars at the rate of i_{AUD} = 6.25%, after spot conversion at the rate of $S(0) = 100$.

6 Note that the borrowing interest rate in Japan at 0.75% is higher than the yield on short-term investment of 0.25%.

One year later, this yields the following Australian dollar amount:

$$\left[\frac{a}{S(0)}\right]_{AUD} \times (1+i_{AUD}) = \frac{a}{100} \times (1+0.0625)$$
$$= \frac{a \times (1.0625)}{100} \quad (6.4b)$$

Step 3A. Cover against the risk of Australian dollar depreciation by selling forward both principal and interest income at the rate of $F(365) = 95$, which should return more than the yen initially borrowed for the round-trip covered *IRA* to be profitable:

$$\left[\frac{a}{S(0)}\right]_{AUD} \times (1+i_{AUD}) \times F(365)$$
$$= \frac{1}{100}(1+0.0625) \times (95) = 1.0094 \quad (6.4c)$$

Step 3B. This returns more than the yen initially borrowed, so the round-trip covered interest rate arbitrage is profitable. Algebraically:

$$\left[\frac{a}{S(0)}\right]_{AUD} \times (1+i_{AUD}) \times F(365) > a \times (1+i_{¥}) \quad (6.5)$$

By isolating the break-even forward rate $F(365)$ in equation (6.5), the condition for a profitable round-trip can be expressed as the forward rate being larger than the no-profit forward exchange rate:

$$F(365) > S(0) \times \left[\frac{1+i_{¥}}{1+i_{AUD}}\right] \quad (6.6)$$

> ***Q:*** Alternatively, the currency trader could borrow AUD and invest in ¥ with forward protection: Would the round-trip covered interest rate arbitrage be profitable?
>
> ***A:*** Compare the cost of borrowing AUD 1 at 7%, buying ¥100, earning 0.25% for total ¥ proceeds 1 year later of 100 × (1 + 0.0025) to be sold forward for AUD in the amount of $\frac{100 \times (1+0.0025)}{96} = 1.04$, which is clearly less than AUD 1.07.

INTEREST RATE PARITY

As participants in the money market continuously arbitrage short-lived interest rate differentials adjusted for the cost of forward cover, they collectively push money markets toward interest rate parity — a state at which arbitrage opportunities illustrated in the previous section have vanished. We now revisit the dynamics of the interest rate arbitrage process and how it brings about an equilibrium state of interest rate parity.

Equilibrium in the forward exchange market and the no-profit or synthetic forward exchange rate

Returning to expression (6.2a), let us consider the following disequilibrium situation whereby at a given point in time the yield on the domestic ¥ short-term investment is somewhat lower than the covered yield on the AUD investment:

$$a \times (1+i_{¥}) < \left[\frac{a}{S(0)}\right]_{AUD} \times (1+i_{AUD}) \times F(365) \quad (6.7)$$

¥ return on Japanese investment < ¥ return on covered Australian investment.

Interest rate arbitrageurs funds will flow out of the Japanese money market (putting upward pressure on the Japanese interest rate $i_{¥}$) to the Australian money market (putting downward pressure on i_{AUD}). The added demand for spot AUD will trigger an appreciation of the AUD *vis-à-vis* the ¥ (higher ¥ price of AUD denoted as $S(0)$), and the added supply for forward sales contracts will depress the forward rate of exchange (lower forward ¥ price of AUD denoted as $F(365)$). Overall, the left-hand side of equation (6.7) will increase, while the right-hand side will decrease, until both sides of equation (6.7) become equal and interest rate parity is restored:

$$a \times (1+i_{¥}) = \left[\frac{a}{S(0)}\right]_{AUD} \times (1+i_{AUD}) \times F(365) \quad (6.8)$$

When interest rates, spot, and forward exchange markets are at parity, simple algebraic manipulation will allow us to isolate the forward rate of exchange $F(365)$ on one side of equation (6.8) so that the "no-profit" or "synthetic" forward rate of exchange $F(365)^*$ can be derived as a function of $i_{¥}$, i_{AUD}, and $S(0)$:

$$F^*(365) = S(0) \times \left[\frac{1+i_{¥}}{1+i_{AUD}}\right] \quad (6.9)$$

Equation (6.9) provides a simple model for valuing forward contracts. Indeed, when forward contracts are not actively traded, as is the case in many emerging capital markets, this is precisely how banks will offer quotes.

Q: Honda Motors is seeking one-year forward quotes on the yen-rupee (INR). The contract is not actively traded, but interest rates are 1% in Japan and 9% in India. If the spot yen-rupee rate is ¥2 = INR 1, what would the forward rate be?

A: In the absence of actively traded forward contracts, the interest rate parity formula (6.9) allows for the computation of an equilibrium or "no-profit" forward rate:

$$F(365)^* = 2 \times \frac{1+0.01}{1+0.09} = 1.85$$

Whenever the prevailing forward rate coincides with its equilibrium value (as provided by the interest rate parity theorem in equation (6.9)), arbitrageurs will have no incentive to shift their funds from one money market to the other. Hence, this equilibrium exchange rate is dubbed the "no-profit" forward rate of exchange. Let's illustrate this process further by reformulating the interest rate parity equation.

Interest rate differential and the implicit interest rate as an approximation of the interest rate parity theorem

Rewriting expression (6.8) as

$$\frac{1+i_{¥}}{1+i_{AUD}} = \frac{F(365)}{S(0)} \tag{6.10a}$$

and further subtracting 1 from both members of expression (6.10a), we have:

$$\begin{aligned} \frac{1+i_{¥}}{1+i_{AUD}} - \frac{1+i_{AUD}}{1+i_{AUD}} &= \frac{F(365)}{S(0)} - \frac{S(0)}{S(0)} \\ \frac{i_{¥}-i_{AUD}}{1+i_{AUD}} &= \frac{F(365)-S(0)}{S(0)} \end{aligned} \tag{6.10b}$$

which is the exact formulation of interest rate parity. It can be further approximated as expression (6.11) if the term $1 + i_{AUD}$ is omitted.

This is a reasonable approximation as long as the interest rate differential is very small compared to $1 + i_{AUD}$, which is currently the case of many short-term interest rates being in very low single-digit numbers. It is not a good approximation if one of the interest rates is in the high single digits or in the double digits. Obviously, no economic meaning should be attached to these purely algebraic manipulations.

$$i_{¥} - i_{AUD} \approx \frac{F(365)-S(0)}{S(0)} \tag{6.11}$$

% interest rate differential
≈ % forward premium/discount.

The reader will recognize the second member of equation (6.11) as the forward premium or discount on the foreign currency, also known as the implicit interest rate. Recall that if $F(365) > S(0)$ the AUD is said to be at a premium and conversely at a discount when $F(365) < S(0)$. Equation (6.11) is a good approximation of the more cumbersome (6.10a). In practice, equation (6.11) is often used by arbitrageurs instead of the exact decision rule provided by equation (6.10a) because it allows for a direct comparison between the *interest rate differential* — what prompts arbitrageurs' interest in foreign money markets in the first place — and the forward premium/discount. Akiko, in our earlier example, could readily tell that the interest rate differential 0.25% – 6.25% = –6% was more than the discount on the Australian dollar of (96 – 100)/100 = –4%, and therefore that she should invest in AUD.

Graphical illustration

The interest rate parity theory (*IRPT*), as approximated by equation (6.11), lends itself readily to graphical illustration. In Exhibit 6.3, the interest rate differential, $i_{¥} - i_{AUD}$, is measured on the vertical axis. The positive portion of the vertical axis corresponds to an interest rate differential favoring the Japanese money market *vis-à-vis* the Australian money market with $i_{¥} > i_{AUD}$. The horizontal axis measures the forward premium/discount of the Australian dollar or implicit interest rate. Specifically, the positive portion of the horizontal axis corresponds to the Australian dollar being at a premium *vis-à-vis* the Japanese yen when:

$$\frac{F(365)-S(0)}{S(0)} > 0$$

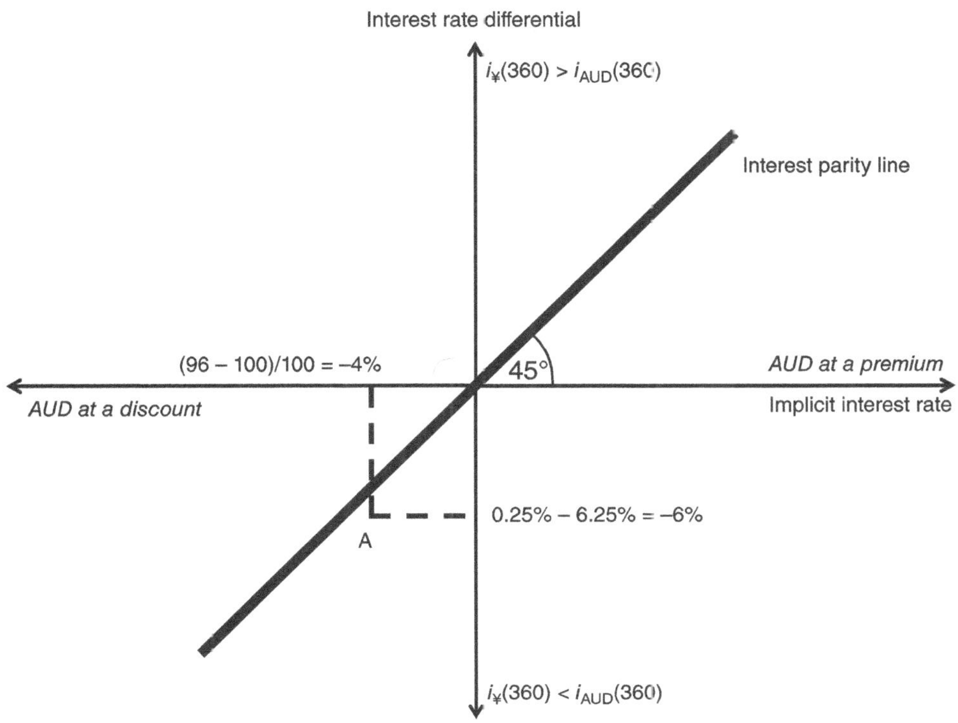

Exhibit 6.3. Interest rate parity theory.

or, more simply, when $F(365) > S(0)$. The negative quadrants of the graph reflect the opposite situation: $i_¥ < i_{AUD}$ and $F(365) < S(0)$.

Equilibrium situations (equation (6.11) holding as an equality) are depicted as a 45-degree line, sometimes referred to as the interest rate parity line. In such cases, the interest rate differential is fully offset by the implicit forward rate, and there are no incentives for arbitrageurs to shift their funds from one money market to the other.

A disequilibrium situation is illustrated by the numerical example presented at the beginning of the last section. The numerical information is recapitulated here:

Interest rate differential:
$i_¥ - i_{AUD} = 0.0025 - 0.0625 = -6\%$

$$\text{Implicit interest rate: } \frac{F(365) - S(0)}{S(0)} = \frac{96 - 100}{100} = -4\%$$

In this example, arbitrageurs' funds are expected to move from Japan to Australia, reducing the interest rate differential (a smaller supply of short-term funds increases the Japanese interest rate, whereas a larger supply of short-term funds on the Australian money market drives down the interest rate) and increasing the implicit interest rate (an increased demand for spot Australian dollars pushing up the spot rate whereas a greater supply of forward Australian dollars drives down the forward exchange rate). As can be readily seen from Exhibit 6.3,[7] the movement of arbitrageurs' funds set into motion forces (whose directions are portrayed by arrows) that progressively tend to replace the disequilibrium situation (as with point A on the graph) with a state of equilibrium (a point on the interest parity line). See International Corporate Finance in Practice 6.1 for forward contracts without free market forces.

7 Adapted from Grubel, H. G. 1966. *Forward Exchange, Speculation and the International Flow of Capital.* Palo Alto, CA: Stanford University Press, p. 18.

INTERNATIONAL CORPORATE FINANCE IN PRACTICE 6.1

Non-Deliverable Forward Contracts in Emerging Market Countries

Forward exchange markets are the hallmark of industrialized countries with well-developed money markets and fully convertible currencies. By contrast, many emerging market countries still have embryonic capital markets and controlled foreign exchange markets. In such an environment, standard forward exchange contracts are not readily traded, and when they are, they tend to be forward cover insurance schemes — often subsidized by the central bank — rather than financial derivatives whose prices are freely determined by market forces. Instead — starting in the 1990s — so-called *non-deliverable forward* (NDF) contracts have become available for many emerging market countries whose currencies are not fully convertible such as the Indian rupee, Chinese renminbi, Philippine peso, Thai Bhat or Brazilian reals.

Like traditional forward contracts, NDFs lock in a forward exchange rate for future delivery when the contract is first signed. Unlike traditional forward contracts, however, there is no physical delivery of the foreign currency bought or sold forward — instead the NDF is cash-settled most likely in US dollar in New York City, London or Singapore. Indeed NDFs are *off-shore* contracts which escape the regulatory reach of the country whose currency is traded. Since NDFs are cash-settled and therefore notional amounts are never exchanged NDFs are far less exposed to counter-party risk. Lastly, NDFs are negotiated in an over-the-counter market and follow guidelines mandated by the International Swaps and Derivatives Association (ISDA).

The amount to be cash settled is the product of the *notional amount* times the difference between the *forward rate* agreed upon at inception of the contract and the prevailing *spot exchange rate* at delivery (*fixing rate*). As an illustration consider a Thailand-based exporter entering into a NDF contract to sell US$ 100 million for Thai Baht for delivery in 90 days at the rate of $NDF_{THB,\$}(90) = 35$. If the spot \$/Baht exchange rate on delivery date turns out to depreciate to $S_{THB,\$}(90) = 38$ the exporter will cash out — that is pay \$100 million × (38 – 35) = THB 300 million or THB 300 million/38 = \$7.89 million to the NDF counter-party. In effect our Thai exporter nets \$100 million x 38 = THB 3.8 billion – THB 300 million = THB 3.5 billion which corresponds to the forward rate of $NDF_{THB,\$}(90) = 35$. The reader will note that had our exporter been able to contract a deliverable forward sale contract he would have delivered \$100 million on maturity date and directly received from the counterparty THB 3.5 billion.

Typically, the NDF exchange rate will approximate the *no-profit* forward rate as determined by the interest rate parity formula (see equation (6.9)). A basic difficulty, however, with this quasi-market valuation approach is that it applies well only when both the domestic and the foreign financial markets are free from controls, taxes, or subsidies — which is the exception rather than the rule in emerging market countries. In practice, interest rates tend to be manipulated by monetary authorities, resulting in synthetic forward rates that are not always realistic. However, as these countries experiment with greater financial deregulation, their money markets should become more liquid, and deliverable forward contracts should become more easily available. When the currency becomes fully convertible though, deliverable forward contracts will progressively elbow out NDFs which will become extinct.

Critical assessment of the interest rate parity theory

What is the explanatory power of the interest rate parity model? How accurately is the relationship between real-world interest rates, the spot exchange rate, and the forward exchange rate accounted for by the interest rate parity theorem (*IRPT*)? For fully convertible currencies the interest rate parity theorem is very "robust": Deviations from interest rate parity theorem tend to be short-lived and lasting only a few minutes, as informed traders step in with the speed of the Internet and arbitrage them away. In practice, deviations from interest rate parity theorem are found when there is a risk of counterparty default (as evidenced during the subprime crisis), risk of exchange controls, or country risk (present

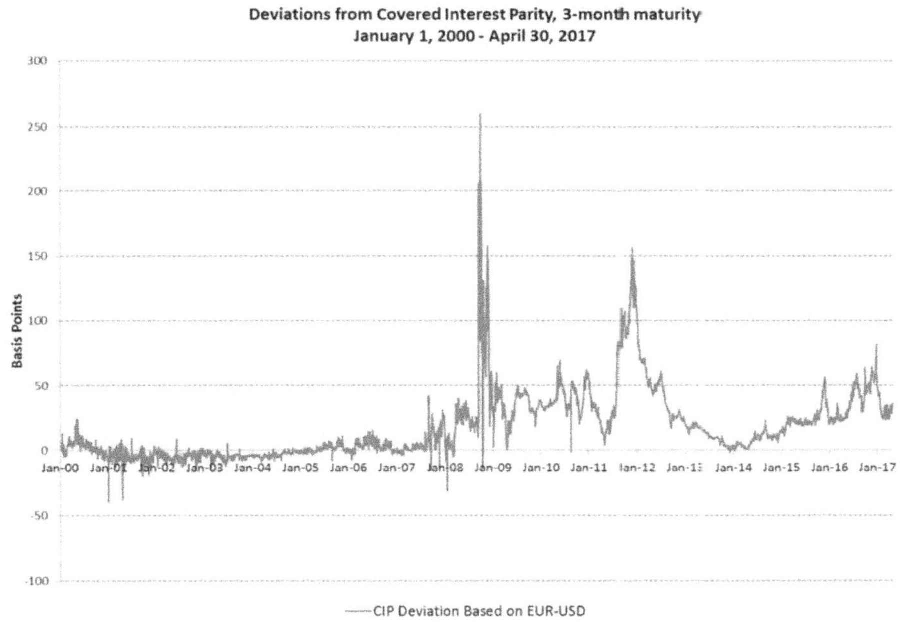

Exhibit 6.4. Deviations from interest rate parity during the subprime crisis.

The covered interest rate parity is estimated using daily euro-dollar exchange rate and the US dollar–LIBOR versus euro-LIBOR.

Source: Richard M. Levich. "CIP Then and Now: a Brief Survey of Measuring and Exploiting Deviations from Covered Interest Rate Parity," unpublished working paper (Stern School of Business: New York University, May 29, 2017).

in emerging markets) and results from transaction costs. Under such circumstances, however, deviations from interest rate parity theorem are not necessarily easy to arbitrage away.[8]

Counterparty risk

For foreign short-term investment or borrowing to be perfectly substitutable with domestic investment or borrowing, the forward contract has to be truly riskless. What this means is that on delivery day the other side of the contract — the counterparty — will execute in full the terms of the contract. If the counterparty is for some reason financially impaired, it may have to delay or forfeit the execution of the contract. Counterparty risk on short-term forward contracts has historically been quasi-nonexistent in Organization for Economic Cooperation and Development (OECD) countries as long as the bank or financial institution bound by the contract is strongly rated. However, a AAA-rated bank at the inception of the forward contract may be subsequently downgraded before its maturity. If arbitrageurs perceive *ex ante* that such a risk exists, they will demand to be compensated for this additional risk, and interest rate parity will not hold. Indeed, during the subprime crisis when most financial institutions were under a cloud of doubtful creditworthiness, significant deviations from interest rate parity could be observed with some of the most widely traded currency pairs such as the $/€ or the $/¥. (See Exhibit 6.4 for an illustration.)

Country risk

Under otherwise perfect conditions there is always a small chance that central banks may impose

8 This has been a well-researched empirical question that documents slimming deviations from *IRPT* over the years. See Aliber, Robert Z. 1973. "The Interest Rate Parity Theory: A Reinterpretation." *Journal of Political Economy* 81(6): 1451–1459; Frenkel, Jacob A. and Richard M. Levich, 1975. "Covered Interest Arbitrage: Unexploited Profits?" *Journal of Political Economy* 83(2): 325–338; Moshen Bahmani-Oskooe and Satya P. Das. 1985. "Transactions Costs and the Interest Parity Theorem." *Journal of Political Economy* 93(4): 793–799; and Akram, Farooq, Dagfinn Rime, and Lucio Sarno. 2008. "Arbitrage in the Foreign Exchange Market: Turning on the Microscope." *Journal of Financial Economics* 76: 237–253.

exchange controls on short-term capital movements. The reasons could be a balance of payments emergency and the urge to stem a capital flight. Conversely, emerging market countries that are the target of speculative capital inflows, such as Brazil and Chile, may impose surprise punitive withholding taxes on short-term capital inflows.

Indeed, analogous tests conducted with the Eurodollar and Eurocurrency markets (rather than the domestic US dollar money market and national foreign currency money markets) show the interest rate parity theorem to hold with much greater accuracy. Two lines of reasoning can be invoked to account for the greater explanatory power of the interest rate parity model in Eurocurrency markets (see International Corporate Finance in Practice 6.2).

1. Eurocurrency markets[9] have exhibited complete freedom from capital controls and other restrictions throughout their existence, and therefore a country risk premium, however small, is not necessary.
2. All Eurocurrency markets are equally exposed to future capital controls, and thus expectations of future controls do not inhibit interest rate arbitrage between Eurocurrencies. This is because it is unlikely that capital controls could be applied to assets denominated in one Eurocurrency and not to others. In other words, it is possible that capital controls could block Eurocurrency assets, but such controls are not expected to discriminate among assets denominated in different Eurocurrencies and hence should not influence the movement of funds between the Eurocurrency markets.

9 See Chapter 9 for further discussion.

UNCOVERED INTEREST RATE ARBITRAGE AND THE CARRY TRADE

Hiko, Akiko's first cousin, is a currency trader for Apex, a hedge fund based in Melbourne (Australia). He has been eyeing the wide interest differential between the near-zero yen interest rate and high single-digit yield in the Australian dollar, South African rand, and a few other emerging market currencies. He is unencumbered by the tight risk control guidelines under which his cousin Akiko could invest in foreign currency-denominated investments and can place an aggressive bet on uncovered interest rate arbitrage. He decides to borrow ¥10 billion at 0.75% and immediately invest in a one-year AUD-denominated certificate of deposit yielding 6.25%. His trade — unlike Akiko's fully hedged interest rate

INTERNATIONAL CORPORATE FINANCE IN PRACTICE 6.2

What Are Euro-Currency Markets?

Eurocurrency markets are *offshore* unregulated money markets that operate beyond the jurisdiction of their home currency's central bank. For example, the Eurodollar market functions anywhere but in the United States. A bank in London can borrow US dollars and extend a US dollar or Eurodollar loan: such a bank would be referred as a Eurobank. Thus Eurocurrency markets are banking systems that run parallel to the domestic banking system of the country that issued the currency and are therefore also known as *external* or *off-shore* markets.

Because the intermediary Eurobank is not subject to reserve requirements or insurance costs as its domestic counterpart would typically be, its cost of doing business is somewhat lower. For example, in the case of the United States domestic banks are subject to Regulation D that mandates reserve requirements on bank deposits, and must pay to the Federal Deposit Insurance Corporations insurance premia on deposits.

Eurocurrency markets are *wholesale interbank* markets where the minimum transaction is $1,0000,000 or equivalent. They are dominated by the Eurodollar market which is primarily domiciled in London. Eurocurrency loans are made on a floating-rate basis with interest rates set at a fixed margin above LIBOR — The London Interbank Offering Rate- for the given maturity and currency chosen. The Eurocurrency markets have no material relationship to the euro as a currency nor to the European continent as a Eurodollar loan can be intermediated in Hong-Kong or a Euro-sterling loan in Dubai.

arbitrage — is uncovered. In other words, there is no guarantee as to the actual exchange rate at which he will purchase back ¥ with AUD principal and interest available one year hence. For the trade to be successful, Hiko must be able to repay the ¥10 billion loan (left-hand side of equation (6.15)) with the proceeds of his AUD investment (right-hand side of equation (6.15)) and still be left with a profit:

$$¥10\,\text{bn} \times (1+0.0075) < \frac{¥10\,\text{bn}}{100} \times (1+0.0625) \times S(365) \tag{6.12}$$

As long as:

$$S(365) > 100 \times \frac{1+0.0075}{1+0.0625} = 95$$

the trade will be profitable; $S(365)$ denotes the ¥ price of AUD1 in one year or 365 days. Indeed, the reader will recognize the break-even exchange rate $S(365)^* = 95$ as none other than the no-profit forward exchange rate as defined by interest rate parity in expression (6.6).

Thus Hiko's bet is that AUD will depreciate by less than the interest rate differential between the AUD and the ¥. This clearly goes against the notion that market forward rates (quasi-equal to no-profit forward rates) are the best predictor of future exchange rates. If Hiko had indeed believed that $S(365)$ was going to be precisely equal to the market forward rate $F(365)$ prevailing at the outset of his trade, the most he could have hoped for was to break even and simply be able to repay his yen loan without making any profit. Hedge fund managers are risk takers of the greedy kind! We will have a chance to return to the important role that forward rates play in currency forecasting in Chapter 15. The mammoth volume of carry trade activities during the recent decade indicates that forward rates are useless when it comes to forecasting future spot exchange rates.

Exhibit 6.5 shows the profit/loss profile of the trade (in ¥ on the vertical axis) as a function of the unknown exchange rate at maturity $S(365)$ defined as ¥ price of 1AUD (at the close of the trade) along the horizontal axis. Line 1 shows the total ¥ cost of the ¥ loan (see left-hand side of equation (6.12)) — it is depicted as a horizontal line since it is not impacted by the exchange rate. The total ¥ return of the AUD investment (see right-hand side of equation (6.12)) is an upward-sloping line (line 2); as the AUD appreciates with higher $S(365)$ or ¥ cost of AUD1 increases beyond the break-even exchange rate $S(365)^* = 95$, the ¥ profit from the carry trade increases. Should the AUD depreciate — to the left of $S(365)^*$ — the carry trade becomes unprofitable. See International Corporate Finance in Practice 6.3 for a folksy account of how the carry trade went "retail" in Japan. Exhibit 6.6 depicts the actual ¥/AUD exchange rate over the last twenty years and illustrates the sub-periods when the carry-trade was profitable.

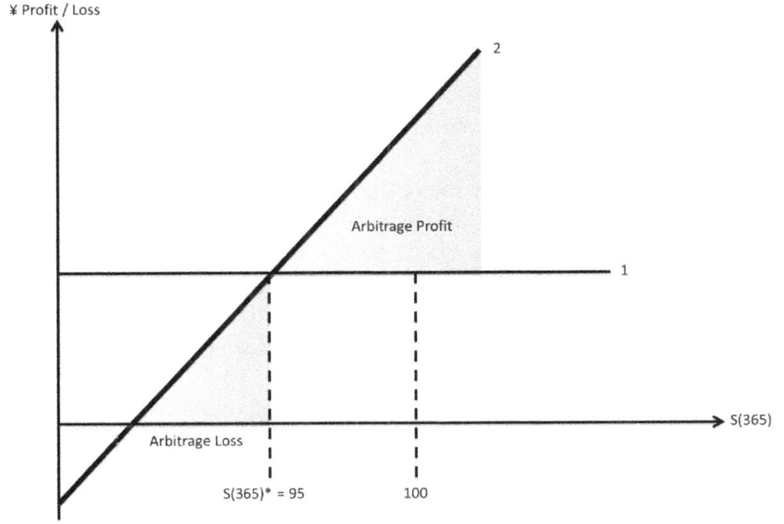

Exhibit 6.5. Profit/loss in carry trade.

Exhibit 6.6. JPY/AUD spot exchange rate 2000–2023 Japanese yen per Australian dollar (monthly).

INTERNATIONAL CORPORATE FINANCE IN PRACTICE 6.3

Shopping, Cooking, Cleaning ... Playing the Yen Carry Trade

Nakako Ishiyama sits quietly in the living room of her apartment in the old Nihonbashi quarter of Tokyo, not far from its famous stone bridge — the point from which in Edo times all distances in Japan were measured. She has been telling me about her investment history since around 2000 — the time, not coincidentally, when the Bank of Japan first pushed interest rates down to within a hairbreadth of zero. Largely without the knowledge of her husband, Ishiyama began investing the couple's money, mainly in lots of $50,000, in funds such as the "Emergency Currency Something-or-Other Fund" or "The Australian Fixed-Term Whatever-You-Call-It Fund." Shy and anxious 66-year-old Ishiyama does not look like someone who has played a role — however modest — in the drama that has engulfed the global financial system. Yet she and many others have done exactly that. Japan's housewives have acted as the guardians of the country's vast household savings built up since its rise to prosperity after the devastation of war. At more than ¥1,500,000 billion (some $16,800 billion), these savings are considered the world's biggest pool of investable wealth. Most of it is stashed in ordinary bank accounts; but from the early 2000s, the housewives, often referred to collectively as "Mrs. Watanabe," a common Japanese surname, began to hunt for higher returns.

Many were dissatisfied with the paltry interest rates banks were offering. The 0.02% return on a typical fixed-term deposit was so negligible that the annual payment on even substantial lifetime savings might come to a mere few hundred yen. "If you got a puncture on the way to the bank, you'd be out of pocket," scoffs Ishiyama. She, like hundreds of thousands of others, found more appealing returns in foreign bonds and other overseas investments. "I was walking in the street and I saw a poster advertising a 5% interest rate. I got quite giddy with the idea," she says. "I saw TV advertisements with everyone grinning and I thought: I suppose it should be okay."

It wasn't long before the markets began to notice something was stirring. In the first half of 2003, individual Japanese investors bought ¥2,700 billion of foreign bonds — easily a record. Brokers were delighted, partly because they made a killing on fees. But there was nervous chatter, too: If Japanese housewives opened the floodgates and sluiced money abroad, there could be a collapse in Japan's enormous bond market. Up to this time, the large sums of money trapped inside the country in savings had allowed the government to negotiate remarkably low interest rates on the country's massive public debt.

Professional traders began to study Mrs. Watanabe's every move. She impressed them by holding her nerve whenever the yen temporarily strengthened, using each occasion as an opportunity to buy more foreign assets at knockdown prices. The lines of Mrs. Watanabes outside banks and brokerages became a barometer of what might happen to the yen. While highly paid foreign exchange traders dithered, Mrs. Watanabe cashed in and began to acquire the reputation of an investment genius. Some professionals quietly began to do whatever Mrs. Watanabe was doing.

Source: Adapted from David Piling. 2009. "Shopping, Cooking, Cleaning ... Playing the Yen Carry Trade: Why Japanese Housewives Added International Finance to Their List of Daily Chores." *Financial Times*, February 21, 2009, p. 30. Reprinted with permission.

SUMMARY

1. This chapter has explored the relationship between domestic and foreign interest rates and the spot and forward exchange rates of the corresponding currencies. The exploration proceeded at two levels: (1) from the firm's perspective, when portfolio managers compare the yields of domestic and foreign investments, or treasurers compare the cost of short-term financing from domestic and foreign sources, and (2) from a macroeconomic perspective that considers the equilibrium relationship that ties national interest rates to the forward premium or discount, also known as covered *interest rate parity*.

2. Interest rate arbitrage requires comparison of the yield on two similarly risky securities denominated in different currencies — for example, the yield on 90-day US Treasury notes (US$ denominated) versus the yield on 90-day British gilt or treasury notes (sterling denominated). Clearly the two treasury notes are perfectly substitutable securities except for their currency of denomination.

3. Interest rate arbitrage combines interest rate arbitrage with a forward cover against exchange risk. Indeed, if money markets are well integrated, the yield on US Treasury notes will be equal to the yield on British treasury notes adjusted for the cost of eliminating exchange rate risk through a forward contract. Thus interest rate parity does not mean equality of nominal interest rates — it means equality of interest rates in different currencies adjusted for the cost of a forward cover against exchange rate risk.

4. According to the interest rate parity theory, the forward exchange rate — in a two-currency model — should stabilize at a level that would leave arbitrageurs indifferent between domestic and foreign covered investment opportunities. This equilibrium forward exchange rate is dubbed the "no-profit" or "synthetic" forward exchange rate.

5. Various empirical tests, however, have shown the explanatory power of the interest rate parity hypothesis to be far from perfect when applied to national markets; a better fit can be obtained with Eurocurrency or offshore markets, which are not subject to the same level of exposure to exchange controls.

6. At the height of the subprime crisis, interest rate parity showed significant deviations from equilibrium. Presumably, counterparty risk — the risk that the other party in the forward contract may default — became very significant. The risky counterparties were generally banks believed to be at risk of bankruptcy or highly illiquid.

7. The currency carry trade consists of borrowing in low-interest currencies to fund investments in high-yielding currencies. Uncovered interest rate arbitrage means that the risk that the high-yielding target currency will depreciate against the low-yielding currency if left unhedged. Clearly, for the carry trade to be profitable, the interest rate differential has to exceed the percentage devaluation of the high-yielding currency. The US dollar, Japanese yen and Swiss franc are the most popular low-yielding funding currencies. The Australian dollar, South African rand, Norwegian crown, Brazilian real, and Turkish lira are the most widely used high-yielding investment currencies.

QUESTIONS FOR DISCUSSION

1. What is interest rate arbitrage?
2. What is covered interest rate parity?
3. What are the risks involved in covered interest arbitrage? Can they be eliminated?
4. Why do currencies yielding low interest rates tend to sell at a forward premium?
5. What are the main reasons accounting for the fact that covered *IRP* may not hold as perfect equality?
6. Why were large deviations from covered interest rate parity observed during the subprime crisis?
7. What are non-deliverable forward contracts? How do they differ from deliverable forwards?
8. How are NDFs priced? What does it mean for NDFs to be cash-settled?
9. What is the carry trade?
10. What are the risks involved in the carry trade?
11. Is the carry trade consistent with covered interest rate parity?
12. What is the difference between the carry trade and speculation through forward contracts?

PROBLEMS

1. **DuPont's cash balance (foundational).** The treasurer of E.I. DuPont de Nemours has a \$500 million cash balance to invest over the next six months. She has been instructed to play it safe and to avoid unduly speculative risks. She has narrowed her options to dollar-denominated P-1 commercial paper yielding 4% annually or Mexican peso–denominated certificates of deposit yielding 12% annually issued by AAA-rated Banco Mercantil of Mexico. The spot dollar price of one Mexican peso is US\$0.080 and a six-month forward peso costs US\$0.075. Where should the funds be invested? Is *IRP* holding?
2. **Indian rupee forward contracts (foundational).** The Indian rupee (INR) is currently trading at INR 50 = US\$1. With 90-day Indian-rupee and US dollar treasury bills currently yielding 10% and 2% per annum, respectively, what would be the forward INR price of US\$1? What assumptions are you making with respect to the credit rating of either government securities?
3. **Interest rate parity for asset managers and hedge fund arbitrageurs (foundational).** You have been given the following information:

$i_\$$	$i_£$	S(0)	F(90)
3%	6%	2.0000	1.9815

where $i_\$$ = Annual interest rate on three-month US dollar commercial paper

$i_£$ = Annual interest on three-month British-pound commercial paper
$S(0)$ = Spot dollar price of one pound sterling
$F(90)$ = Forward dollar price of one pound sterling for delivery in 90 days

Taking the perspective from a US-based asset manager or hedge fund arbitrageur:

a. In which commercial paper would you invest?
b. In which currency would you borrow?
c. How would you arbitrage interest rates between the dollar and sterling denominated commercial paper?
d. What is the profit from interest arbitrage per dollar borrowed?

4. **Covered interest rate arbitrage with withholding tax (intermediate).** On September 1, 2018, the treasurer of Volvo, the Swedish automotive manufacturer, is faced with the following investment dilemma: he could invest the 500 million Swedish crowns (SEK) that will be available for the next 180 days in the Swedish money market and earn a return of 6.25% on an annual basis, or he could invest his funds in the euro (€) money market and earn a much lower return of 3.75%.

a. Do you have sufficient information to reach a decision as to selecting the optimal investment opportunity? What are the additional pieces of information needed to reach a meaningful decision?
b. On September 1, 2018, the following information concerning the relationship between the Swedish crown and the euro (€) was made available: SEK 7.84 = €1 on a spot basis; the € was at a 3.00% premium (annual basis). Where should the funds be invested?
c. Does the interest rate parity theory hold in the previous case? Why or why not?
d. How would a 10% withholding tax imposed by euro-zone governments on interest earnings accruing to nonresident foreign entities affect your decision in part b?

e. What is the maximum rate of withholding tax that would leave your decision to invest your funds in the euro money market unchanged?

5. **Covered interest rate arbitrage (intermediate).** As a trader for the London-based money market Commonwealth Fund, you see the following quotes:
   a. From Barclays Bank, one-year sterling deposits/loans at 6.0% to 6.125%.
   b. From Bangkok Bank, one-year Thai baht (THB) deposits/loans at 12.50% to 12.75%. Spot exchange rate is THB 45 = £1, and 1-year forward Thai baht is at a 6.00% annual discount *vis-à-vis* the pound sterling.

   Do you see profitable opportunities for interest rate arbitrage? What are the risks, if any, involved in these transactions?

6. **Carry trade (intermediate).** Felipe Lemos is a currency strategist with the Miami-based hedge fund Kawa. With the annual interest rate at 8.5% for real-denominated deposits with AAA-rated Brazilian banks, Felipe is considering taking $10 million from Kawa money market mutual funds currently yielding a paltry annual 0.75% to invest in real (BRL). The current spot exchange rate between the US and Brazilian currency currently stands at BRL 1.82 = $1.
   a. Under what exchange rate scenario would the carry trade be profitable?
   b. What are the risks involved in the carry trade? How can they be hedged?
   c. To discourage speculative short-term capital inflows, the central bank of Brazil is imposing a 10% withholding tax on interest earnings by foreign investors. Will Felipe's decision be changed?

7. **Selecting a construction loan (intermediate).** Italthai, the Bangkok-based construction company, has recently been awarded a baht (THB) 2,500 million contract for the renovation of Phuket International Airport. The project is to be completed six months hence on October 1, 1996, with payment in full due upon completion and guaranteed by the Thailand Airport Authority. Italthai is seeking to raise a construction loan collateralized by the contract and is considering two alternative short-term financing options:
   i. A 180-day commercial paper issue at an annual rate of 9% denominated in baht with a letter of credit guarantee opened by Siam Commercial Bank at the cost of ½ of 1%.
   ii. A euro-dollar loan sourced from Standard Chartered Bank's Singapore branch carrying a semiannual rate of 3.25%.
   a. Which financing option do you recommend to Italthai? The spot exchange rate is THB 25 = $1. The US dollar is at a 1.75% annual premium *vis-à-vis* the baht, which is otherwise pegged to a basket of currencies, primarily US dollars. The baht has been stable against the US dollar, trading within a narrow range of THB 24–26 to US$1.
   b. What are the risks involved in borrowing euro-dollars? What are the risks involved in lending to Italthai from Standard Chartered Bank's point of view?

   Hint: The THB 2,500 million contract award is the revenue that Italthai will collect in six months.

8. **Speculating on the collapse of Argentina's currency board (intermediate).** Dr. Lawrence Krohn is the New York–based lead currency strategist for Latin American currencies at Standard Bank. On the eve of its long-overdue devaluation (January 10, 2002), the Argentine peso (ARS) could be purchased or sold 90 days forward at ARS 1.35 for $1. On January 10, 2002, $1 = ARS 1.
   a. Is the Argentine peso at a discount or premium to the US dollar? What was the forward premium/discount on Argentine peso forward contracts? Compute the yearly implicit rate of interest on 90 days forward pesos.
   b. Assuming that on January 10, 2002, you expected the peso to devalue by 50% within days, explain how you could speculate through the forward exchange market. What would be your expected profit? Show how your expected profits would be affected should you be required to put up a margin of 20% on your forward purchase (sale) contract (the opportunity cost of speculators' funds are supposed to be 12.5% annually).
   c. Would you speculate differently (from the answer to part b) if you expected the post-devaluation exchange rate to be ARS 1.25 to $1? Explain.

9. **Non-deliverable forwards (NDFs).** Garuda Indonesia (GI) — the national flag carrier — just booked the purchase of five Boeing 737-200 for the total amount of US$500 million to be paid one year from now. The Indonesian rupiah (IDR)

stands at IDR 15,407 = USD1 and GI is concerned about the potential appreciation of the US currency. It decides to hedge its dollar position by entering into a NDF contract. One year money market rates stand at 6% in Indonesia and 4.5% in the United States

a. What is the one-year NDF rate at which Garuda Indonesia could hedge its dollar exposure?

b. Detail the cash-flows paid and received at both the inception and the delivery dates assuming that the IDR depreciated by 2.2%.

c. Would these cash-flows be different if Garuda Indonesia had used a Deliverable Forward contract? Explain why only NDFs are available in Indonesia.

10. Fuji Life Insurance Co. global money management (intermediate/advanced). Hiko Yamamoto, the deputy treasurer of Fuji Life Insurance Co. (FLI), was reviewing 1-year investment opportunities for the 100 billion yen of cash balances. As interest rates were becoming negligible in Japan at 0.50% on one-year yen-denominated treasury bills, Hiko was seriously considering euro notes issued by the Dutch government and offering a yield of 3.25% when the attractive yield on zero Uridashi one-year zero-coupon bonds (UAZ) denominated in Australian dollars (AUD) caught his eye.

a. Assuming that UAZ are currently priced at 95%, what is the forward yen (¥) price of one Australian dollar for 1-year maturity? Be explicit about your assumptions; ¥100 = AUD 1.

Hint: Compute the 1-year interest rate on UAZ first.

b. Assuming the forward rate is ¥97 = AUD 1 and 1-year borrowing cost in Japan for FLI is 65 basis points, show how Hiko could set profitable arbitrage opportunities between the ¥ and the AUD. Would your answer be different if the tax rate (40%) on interest income is twice the tax rate (20%) on forex gains?

c. Hiro, Hiko's first cousin, is the procurement manager for the specialty steel division of Mitsubishi Heavy Industries (MHI). Having just contracted for the imports of iron ore from Australia in the amount of AUD 100 million payable in 360 days, Hiro is advised by his cousin Hiko to consider using UAZ for hedging currency risk on behalf of MHI. What is your advice to Hiro?

d. Would you classify UAZ as samurai bonds or euro-yen bonds? Should Japan's Ministry of Finance ban them?

Note: Samurai bonds are yen-denominated bonds issued in Japan by firms domiciled abroad. UAZ are foreign currency bonds for sale in Japan. According to the *Wall Street Journal* (March 7, 2003), Japanese investors were gobbling up Australian dollar–denominated offerings, purchasing a total amount of AUD 8 billion in 2002 and close to AUD 5 billion in the first two months of 2003.

11. Yen carry trade at the Conan Doyle Galaxy Fund (intermediate). Dr. Watson is the chief trader at the currency arbitrage desk of the US-based Conan Doyle Galaxy Fund. He is considering arbitrage opportunities between the Japanese yen (borrow at 60 basis points/lend at 40 basis points) and the Eurodollar (borrow at 2.15%/lend at 2.06%).

a. Under what exchange rate scenario does interest rate arbitrage make sense? The current spot exchange rate stands at ¥100 = $1.

b. The market forward rate quotes at ¥98 = $1. Show how covered arbitrage could be profitably exploited.

c. Revisit questions a and b with the corporate income tax rate in the United States at 30% and the capital gains rate at 15%.

d. The carry trade refers to uncovered interest rate arbitrage; is it consistent with efficient foreign exchange markets?

e. Dollar-denominated one-year US Treasury Inflation-Protected Securities (TIPS) pay 1% plus consumer price index (CPI) inflation. Under what exchange rate/inflation scenario does uncovered interest rate arbitrage between yen-denominated loans/deposits and dollar-denominated TIPS make sense? TIPS are not available in yen.

12. Carry trade at a macro hedge fund (intermediate). Ms. Ivanhoe is the chief strategist of Caran d'Ache — the Fribourg-based (Switzerland) macro hedge fund. Newly issued 1-year Greek government zero-coupon (Z) bonds rekindled Ms. Ivanhoe's interest in the carry trade.

a. What is the currency carry trade all about? Caran d'Ache can borrow 100 million Swiss francs (CHF) at an annual cost of 115 basis points and invest in Greek Z bonds currently trading at 89% and to be redeemed at par in

360 days. Zs are denominated in euros (€). The spot rate for euros is CHF 1.25 = €1.

b. What are the risks involved in this carry trade? Under what exchange rate scenario(s) is the carry trade profitable?

c. Would you advise Ms. Ivanhoe to hedge her investments in Greek Z bonds? Current one-year government bond yields are 95 basis points for AAA-rated one-year Swiss government bonds, 330 bp for AAA-rated German one-year government bonds, 360 bp for one-year AA-rated French government bonds, and 1,125 bp for BBB-rated Greek one-year government bonds. Illustrate graphically both hedged and unhedged investment policy. Discuss the significance of the intersection point. (What forwards are available?)

13. Yen carry trade with investment in US dollars/ Icelandic króna (advanced). Louise is an associate with Charlemagne, a hedge fund domiciled in Luxembourg, who is considering the following arbitrages:

Amount of transaction:	US$200 million
Start date of transaction:	January 1, 2008
End date of transaction:	November 30, 2008
Term of the transaction:	330 days

Two funding alternatives from banks with loanable funds:

i. Deutsche Bank, Tokyo — Current interest rate on yen loans: 1.875% per annum.

ii. JPMorgan Chase Bank NA, New York — Current US$ prime interest rate: 7.25% per annum.

January 1, 2008, spot exchange rate: US$1 = ¥107.74.

Trader's view of expected US$ versus yen spot exchange rate in 330 days: US$1 = ¥107.74.

Two investing alternatives:

i. Citibank N.A., London, England, branch — Certificate of deposit, 330 days: 3.56% per annum on Eurodollar deposits at LIBOR rate.

ii. Kaupthing Bank, Reykjavík, Iceland head office — Certificate of deposit: 14.5% per annum.

January 1, 2008, US$ versus króna spot exchange rate: 64.3 króna per US$.

Trader's view of expected US$ versus króna spot exchange rate in 330 days: 64.3 króna per US$. (again, no change in the exchange rate?)

Answer the following questions:

a. Draw two arbitrage diagrams — one for funding and one for investing — to engineer a yen carry trade transaction (only a yen carry?); show the transaction that maximizes the profit opportunity (or the one with minimum loss if you do not see a profitable opportunity), and clearly state the profit or loss on the engineered transaction.

b. If the yen exchange rate on November 30 is 96.89 instead of 107.74, how does that change the cost of the yen loan?

c. If the króna exchange rate on November 30 is 135 instead of 64.3, how does that change the revenue of the króna investment?

d. What is the difference between a covered and an uncovered interest arbitrage transaction?

e. Summarize in bullet form five risks in this transaction — be as specific as you can be.

f. In 2008, how might an interest arbitrage trader's worst nightmare have been realized?

(Prepared by Dr. Phil Ulhmann.)

14. Covered interest rate arbitrage with transaction costs (advanced). Assume that US-based potential arbitrageurs do not hold cash, but hold dollar-denominated securities. Covered investment in sterling-denominated securities then requires the execution of four transactions: (1) sale of domestic securities with transaction costs of τ_d%, (2) spot purchase of pounds sterling with costs of τ_s%, (3) purchase of sterling-denominated securities with transaction costs of τ_f, and (4) forward sale of pounds sterling with transaction costs of τ_F.

a. Reformulate the *IRP* theorem taking into account these transaction costs.

b. What are the upper and lower limits on the implicit interest rate?

c. What do your conclusions reached in parts a and b imply in terms of the interest parity line as drawn in Exhibit 6.3?

15. Covered interest rate arbitrage with a two-tier exchange market (advanced). Monsieur Dassault, the treasurer of Renault-Finance S.A. — the Geneva-based international finance subsidiary of the French automobile manufacturer — was intrigued by the apparently high yield offered by South African government bonds. Specifically, he could purchase rand-denominated ESCOM bonds (issued by the South African government-owned Electricity Supply Commission) at par that pay an 11% coupon in two equal half-yearly installments. The transaction would have to be channeled through South Africa's two-tier exchange market: nonresident investors in South African bonds have to contend with a system of two different exchange rates that allows for investment (and divestment) to be made through the financial tier, whereas interest payments are repatriated through the commercial tier. On July 19, 1989, the commercial rand was worth \$0.38 while the financial rand traded at \$0.24. The central bank traditionally stabilizes the commercial rand while it allows the financial rand to fluctuate.

a. What is the effective rate of return on a rand (ZAR) 25 million uncovered investment, assuming that the investment is liquidated after one year?
b. Assuming a 6% discount on the financial rand, compute the effective yield on an uncovered investment of ZAR 25 million, assuming that the investment is liquidated after one year.
c. Discuss credit risk, exchange risk, interest rate risk, and country risk faced by nonresident investors in ESCOM bonds.
d. Compute the break-even exchange rate on the financial rand if Renault-Finance is comparing its ESCOM investment with similarly risky dollar-denominated high-yield bonds offering a coupon of 12⅞%. Sketch graphically your analysis.

(Adapted from "Of High-Yield Bondage," *The Economist*, August 5, 1989, p. 65.)

16. **Interest rate arbitrage with bid-ask spreads (advanced).** Consider the configuration of bid-ask spot and 90-day forward US\$/£ exchange rate on June 12, 2013, keeping in mind that the lower rate is the selling/lending rate and conversely the higher rate is the buying/borrowing rate:

$$S(0) = 1.5250 - 1.5260$$
$$F(90) = 1.5068 - 1.5073$$

with 12- and 3-month Eurocurrency interest rates, respectively, at

$$i_{US}(90) = 2.27\% - 2.30\%$$

$$\text{or} \quad i_{UK}(90) = 3.50\% - 3.63\%$$

a. Compute the no-profit bid-ask 90-day forward rates.
b. Show how interest rate arbitrageurs can take advantage of the gap between no-profit and market bid-ask forward rates.
c. Explain how such arbitrage transactions should narrow the gap.

INTERNET EXERCISES

17. **Forward speculation (intermediate).** Log in to www.oanda.com: are the Swiss franc and Japanese yen at a 90 day premium or discount to the US dollar? Are these currencies forecast to appreciate or depreciate *vis-à-vis* the US dollar over the next 90 days? Explain how you could use these forecasts to speculate through forward contracts.

18. **Forward premium/discount (advanced).** Log in to FX Street exchange services www.fxstreet.com/rates-charts/forward-rates and identify the currency which is at the deepest 180 day discount *vis-à-vis* the US dollar. How do you explain it? Show how you could mount a carry trade transaction between the US dollar and said currency. Under what exchange rate scenario would the carry trade be profitable?

REFERENCES

Accominotti Olivier, Jason Cen, David Chambers and Ian W. Marsh. 2019. "Currency Regimes and the Carry Trade." *Journal of Financial and Quantitative Analysis* 45: 2233–2260.

Baba, Naohiko, and Frank Packer. 2009. "Interpreting Deviations from Covered Interest Parity during the Financial Market Turmoil of 2007–08." *Journal of Finance and Banking* 33: 1953–1962.

Billingsley, Randall S. 2006. *Understanding Arbitrage: An Intuitive Approach to Financial Analysis.* Philadelphia: Wharton School Publishing.

Coffey, N., Warren B. Hrung, and A. Sarkar. 2009. "Capital Constraints, Counterparty Risk, and Deviations from Covered Interest Rate Parity." Federal Reserve Bank of New York: Staff Report no. 393, September.

Dufey, Gunter, and Ian H. Giddy. 1994. *The International Money Market.* Englewood Cliffs, NJ: Prentice Hall.

Frenkel, Jacob A., and Richard M. Levich. 1976. "Transaction Costs and Interest Arbitrage: Tranquil versus Turbulent Periods." *Journal of Political Economy* 85(6): 1209–1226.

Jacque, Laurent L. 2014. *Global Derivative Debacles: From Theory to Malpractice*, 2nd edition. Singapore and London: World Scientific.

Quick, Peter J., Graham Hacche, and Viktor Schoofs. 1988. "Policies for Developing Forward Foreign Exchange Markets." *International Monetary Fund Occasional Papers* no. 60. A comprehensive study of how forward exchange facilities can be developed in LDCs.

APPENDIX 6A: TRANSACTION COSTS AND INTEREST RATE ARBITRAGE WITH BID-ASK SPREADS (ADVANCED)

One additional reason for deviation from *interest rate parity* can be traced to the frictions associated with borrowing or lending, buying, and selling currencies on a spot or forward basis. Indeed transaction costs reflected in bid-ask spreads can be shown to be a significant source of disequilibrium from an interest rate parity world. Let's return to the pure interest rate arbitrage problem from a market equilibrium point of view (macroscopic perspective) and explicitly incorporate transaction costs in its formulation as bid-ask spreads. Using slightly different notations and considering interest rate arbitrage between the United States (US) and the United Kingdom (UK), the interest rate arbitrageurs would be confronted with the following configuration of exchange rates and interest rates:

Spot exchange rate = $S(0)^b > S(0)^a$
Forward exchange rate = $F(t)^b > F(t)^a$
Domestic (US) interest rate = $i_{US}{}^b > i_{US}{}^a$
Foreign (UK) interest rate = $i_{UK}{}^b > i_{UK}{}^a$

where "b" and "a" superscripts stand for *bid* (buying/borrowing) and *ask* (selling/lending) prices.

The reader will note that the arbitrageur always faces higher buying rates than selling rates due to the fact that the bank earns a living by pocketing the spread between the two rates. Similarly, arbitrageurs borrow at a higher interest rate than the rate at which they can invest.

For pure interest arbitrage to be profitable, the interbank trader in the above example must follow either of two strategies: (1) borrowing dollars and investing in sterling with covered or forward protection or (2) borrowing sterling and investing in dollars with covered or forward protection. For arbitrage to be warranted, both strategies should yield a profit that is free of exchange rate risk and that exceeds the present value of the amount borrowed.

Strategy I: Borrow in the domestic money market and invest in the foreign money market

1. Borrow dollars at the interest rate of i^b_{US} and thus incur an obligation to repay 90 days later for each dollar borrowed: $1 + i^b_{US}$.
2. Invest in sterling at the rate of i^a_{UK}, after spot conversion at the rate of $S(0)^b$, which 90 days later yields the following sterling amount:

$$\left[\frac{1}{S(0)^b}\right]\times\left(1+i^a_{Uk}\right) \tag{6.12a}$$

3. Cover against the risk of a sterling depreciation by selling forward both principal and interest income at the rate of $F(90)^a$, which should return more than the dollars initially borrowed:

$$\left[\frac{1}{S(0)^b}\right]\times\left[1+i^a_{Uk}\right]\times F(t)^a > 1+i^b_{US} \tag{6.13a}$$

or

$$F(t)^a > S(0)^b \times\left[\frac{1+i^b_{US}}{1+i^a_{Uk}}\right] \tag{6.13b}$$

Alternatively, the interbank trader could borrow sterling and invest in dollars with forward protection.

Strategy II: Borrow in the foreign money market and invest in the domestic money market

1. Borrow sterling at the interest rate of i^b_{UK} and thus incur an obligation to repay 90 days later for each pound borrowed: $1 + i^b_{UK}$.
2. Convert sterling loan proceeds at the spot rate of $S(0)^a$ and invest in dollars at the rate of i^a_{US},

which 90 days later yields the following dollar amount:

$$S(0)^{a} \times (1+i_{US}^{a})$$

3. Cover against the risk of a dollar depreciation by selling forward both principal and interest income at the rate of $F(t)^{b}$, which should return more than the pounds initially borrowed:

$$\left[S(0)^{a}\right]\times\left[1+i_{US}^{a}\right] > \left(1+i_{UK}^{b}\right)\times F(t)^{b} \quad (6.14a)$$

or

$$F(t)^{b} \leq S(t)^{a} \times \left[\frac{1+i_{US}^{a}}{1+i_{UK}^{b}}\right] \quad (6.14b)$$

Thus a neutral band (see expressions (6.13a) and (6.14a)) resulting from transaction costs between $F(t)^{a}$ and $F(t)^{b}$ will deny interest rate arbitrageurs any opportunity for profit. Conversely, whenever the no-profit forward rate as defined by expressions (6.13a) and (6.14a) falls outside the neutral band, covered *IRA* is profitable.

APPENDIX 6B: INTEREST RATE PARITY AND ASYMMETRIC TAXATION[10]

Pension funds, banks, and multinational corporations actively involved in optimizing short-term investments are all subject to taxes. The covered interest rate arbitrage game that they so relentlessly play makes sense only if effective yields are computed on an after-tax basis. The discussion in this chapter, by ignoring the tax variable, assumed implicitly identical tax treatment for domestic and foreign-based investors. It also assumed similar tax rates on interest income (normal corporate income tax) and foreign exchange gains/losses (capital gains tax). This appendix reformulates the interest rate parity theory between the United States (US) and the United Kingdom (UK) under the general condition of asymmetry in taxation between income and capital gains rates ($t^{I} \neq t^{K}$). Although each country has its own set of tax rules, corporate income tax rates are generally higher than capital gains tax rates, hence the importance of breaking down the yield from covered foreign investment between the interest income and the foreign exchange gain/loss embedded in the forward premium/discount.

Equation (6.8) can be rewritten to isolate the yield on domestic investment (left-hand side of equation) and to compare it with covered foreign investment in a pound sterling–denominated security:

$$i_{US} = i_{UK} + \frac{F(365)-S(0)}{S(0)} \times \left(1+i_{UK}\right) \quad (6.15)$$

10 This section is adapted from Maurice D. Levi, "Taxation and Abnormal Capital Flows," *Journal of Political Economy* (June 1977), 635–646.

Thus the covered foreign investment yield is made up of two components: (1) the interest income on the sterling-denominated security and (2) the exchange gain/loss on principal and interest income. After tax, from the perspective of a US investor, equation (6.15) becomes:

$$i_{US}\left(1-t_{US}^{I}\right) = i_{UK} \times \left(1-t_{US}^{I}\right) + \frac{F(90)-S(0)}{S(0)} \times \left(1+i_{UK}\right) \times \left(1-t_{US}^{K}\right) \quad (6.16)$$

where t_{US}^{I} and t_{US}^{K} are, respectively, the US corporate *income* tax and the *capital* gains tax for US resident investors. Nominal interest income in either dollar or sterling is adjusted by the corporate income tax rate t_{US}^{I} applicable on interest income. The foreign exchange gain on both principal and interest income is adjusted by the capital gain tax rate t_{US}^{K}.

Isolating the forward premium/discount, equation (6.16) is rewritten as

$$\frac{F(365)-S(0)}{S(0)} = \frac{i_{US}-i_{UK}}{1+i_{UK}} \times \frac{1-t_{US}^{I}}{1-t_{US}^{K}}$$

which is clearly different from the pretax, no-profit forward premium/discount equation referred to earlier.

Thus the *IRP* line — depicted as a 45° line in Exhibit 6.2 — will rotate depending upon the ratio $\left(1-t_{US}^{I}\right)/\left(1-t_{US}^{K}\right)$. If $t_{US}^{I} > t_{US}^{K}$, the interest rate parity line will rotate downward. Conversely, if $t_{US}^{I} < t_{US}^{K}$, it will rotate upward.

CASE STUDY 6.1. BRAZIL REDE GLOBO'S SHORT-TERM FUNDING

On an early Monday morning, Dr. Guadalupe Philips was reviewing pro forma cash-flow statements in preparation for an upcoming staff meeting of the treasury department. Guadalupe would first consider various proposals before deciding on how to fund the firm's working capital.

Dr. Philips was the newly appointed treasurer of Rede Globo Ltd., the Brazilian media conglomerate headquartered in Rio de Janeiro. Rede Globo was a producer of TV programs (mostly *telenovelas*) and operated several cable television channels, primarily in Portuguese and catering almost exclusively to the Brazilian market. In this cash-flow budget, Guadalupe and her staff had estimated a net short-term funding need in the amount of 250 million reals (BRL) for the next 6 months. Guadalupe Philips' easy solution would be to take out a BRL 250 million, six-month loan from Banco Pactual in Rio. Rede Globo had done business for years with Banco Pactual, and a six-month loan from the bank seemed to be a natural way to proceed. However, with the real's newfound strength and its near-full convertibility, Dr. Philips intended to consider all options, including international ones.

First, should Rede Globo borrow reals in Brazil, as in the past, or should it borrow in the somewhat cheaper off-shore euro-real money market? Should the offshore market for real be considered along with the onshore real money market as a funding option? What was the risk of the latter? Guadalupe had been able to obtain the following information about six-month real interest rates:

Deposit Rates (per annum)		Loan Rates (per annum)	
Domestic real bank deposits	10.56%	Domestic real bank loan	13.00%
Euro-real deposits	11.06%	Euro-real loan	11.92%

Second was the crucial question of which currency to borrow in. Dr. Philips knew that the short-term dollar financing was plentiful and that both onshore and offshore dollar money markets offered considerably lower interest rates than the real market (see Case Exhibit 6.1). However, she feared the exchange rate risk involved in borrowing in dollars, as the Brazilian currency had reached an all-time high against the dollar at BRL 1.61 = US$1 only a little over a month ago (see Case Exhibit 6.2). According to Bloomberg consensus forecasts, the real could continue to appreciate as the US Federal Reserve Bank's quantitative easing (QE2) fueled a large-scale carry trade whereby higher-yielding real-denominated short-term marketable securities were financed in dollars at very low US interest rates. Guadalupe had a vivid recollection of her graduate school lectures on the theory of interest rate parity and was determined to put them to good use.

Questions for Discussion

1. What would be the rationale for Rede Globo to consider dollar financing? What are the risks involved?

Case Exhibit 6.1. Interest rates for different funding options.

Instrument	Annual Interest Rate (%)
Eurodollar loan rate	2.50
Euro-real loan rate	11.92

Case Exhibit 6.2. Spot, forward, and forecast exchange rates.

Exchange Rates	Reals per Dollar	Dollars per Real
Spot rate today	BRL 1.7100	US$0.585
Six-month forward rate	BRL 1.8032	US$0.554
Six-month forecast for spot rate	BRL 1.6200	US$0.617

2. Why are borrowing rates slightly lower in offshore money markets for dollars or reals? What is/are the risk(s) involved for Rede Globo to raise short-term financing from these markets?
3. How could the different funding options be structured? Can all risks be hedged?

   How?
4. What are the real costs of six-month financing in either currency?
5. Portray in a simple diagram the different funding options as a function of the six-month BRL/US$ spot rate. Comment on the significance of different intersection points. Is interest rate parity holding?

CHAPTER 7

Purchasing Power Parity and the Fisher Parity

Our willingness to pay a certain price for foreign money must ultimately and essentially be due to the fact that this money possesses a purchasing power as against commodities and services in that foreign country.
—Gustav Cassel, 1922

In its heydays GE Capital — the finance arm of General Electric — was constantly on the prowl for foreign investment opportunities and — in the early 1990s — it had been eying Thailand for its auto-leasing business. As a South-East Asian dragon economy with one of the most vibrant automotive industry Thailand was one of the missing pieces on GE Capital global chessboard. There was certainly no lack of candidates for acquisition and yet GE Capital had been procrastinating throughout most of the 1990s. What was holding back GE Capital from establishing a solid foothold in the Thai automotive leasing business? GE capital believed that the Thai Baht-firmly anchored to the US dollar at THB 25 = US$1 since 1984 — was grossly *overvalued*. Overvaluation is a relative concept and begs a benchmark against which to establish whether a currency is indeed *overvalued or undervalued*. It was not until the Asian financial crisis when the Thai Baht was in 1997 the first domino to fall — precipitating a 100% devaluation — that GE Capital made its move: it acquired several automobile leasing companies — "cheap buys" by any standards as the Thai Baht had collapsed from THB 25 = US$1 to less than THB 50 = US$1 and the Asian financial crisis had sunk the market value of auto-leases (and most other financial securities).

Of the many factors shaping currency movements over the long term, one stands out: that factor is inflation. In the first part of this chapter, we examine the theory and evidence of the long-term relationship between inflation and exchange rates. More specifically, given the existence of such a link, how should a country's currency value respond to monetary disturbances that raise the country's price level relative to foreign nations' price levels? One answer to this question, is the so-called purchasing power parity (PPP) theory which allows managers to establish benchmark exchange rates against which to gauge whether a currency is *over or under-valued.*

The second half of this chapter develops an integrated *International Parities* framework showing how interest rates — either directly (*Uncovered Interest Rate Parity* discussed in Chapter 6) or indirectly through the intermediation of inflation (PPP) or forward exchange rates (*Covered Interest Rate Parity* also discussed in Chapter 6) — shape future spot exchange rates. To complete the loop this will require the introduction of two additional parity conditions — the *Fisher effect* which ties interest rates to inflation — and the unbiasedness of forward rates as predictors of future exchange rates.

In this chapter you should understand:

- The meaning of the "Law of One Price" and its importance as a lynchpin of international finance.
- Why — over the longer term - inflation rate differentials between two countries explain the change in the exchange rate between these two countries' currencies.
- How PPP exchange rates can be used as benchmark equilibrium exchange rates against which to gauge whether nominal exchange rates are *under or over-valued.*

- Why PPP explanatory power is greatest when one of the countries involved suffers from a high rate of inflation.
- How nominal interest rates are equal to a real interest rate (assuming no inflation) + inflation rate expectation.
- How differentials of nominal interest rates are good predictors of expected inflation rates differentials.
- How forward rates can be used as unbiased forecasts of future spot exchange rate.

PURCHASING POWER PARITY

The Law of One Price

The concept of PPP arises from the simple observation that identical products should cost the same in two countries when their prices are stated in the same currency. This is known as the Law of One Price. For example, if a bottle of Hennessy Cognac costs €40 in Paris, it should cost in Boston €40 × (US$ price of one €) = €40 × 1.30 = US$52. If the price of our bottle of Cognac were to cost US$60 in Boston, importers (also known as arbitrageurs) would step up purchases of Cognac in Paris (stronger demand pushing up its price) and sell them in Boston (increased supply pushing down its price), thereby initially netting a profit of US$8, which would progressively diminish until parity (equality of prices) were to prevail.[1]

Absolute purchasing power parity

To formalize the concept of the parity between the purchasing powers of two currencies, consider a simplistic two-country world (the United States and the Philippines) producing and trading only one commodity (wheat). If at a certain time ($t = 0$) one bushel of wheat is worth 100 dollars ($) in the United States and 1,000 pesos (PHP) in the Philippines, the exchange rate $S_{\$,PHP}(0)$ (defined as the dollar price of one peso prevailing at time $t = 0$) that establishes parity between the purchasing power of the dollar and peso has to be $S_{\$,PHP}(0) = 0.10$, because one needs $100 to buy PHP 1,000.[2] The reader is referred to the Big Mac index presented in International Corporate Finance in Practice 7.1 for a powerful generalization of the absolute version of PPP.

Relative purchasing power parity

Now assume that during the following year the rate of inflation affecting the US economy is 5%, so that one bushel of wheat will be worth $100(1 + 0.05) = $105 one year later; similarly, the rate of inflation affecting the Philippines' economy during the same period is 50%, so that the price of one bushel of wheat in the Philippines will be PHP 1,000(1 + 0.50) = PHP 1,500 at the end of the period.

> ***Q:*** If a Big Mac costs 161 pesos (PHP) in the Philippines and US$5.69 in the United States, is the Philippina currency properly valued, overvalued, or undervalued when the market rate is PHP56.30 = US$1?
>
> ***A:*** The equilibrium PPP exchange rate by the Big Mac index is given by the exchange rate at which the price of a Big Mac in the Philippines is equal to the price of a Big Mac in the United States (see columns 2, 3, and 4 respectively in International Corporate Finance in Practice 7.1):
>
> PHP 161 = US$5.69 × PPP PHP price of one US$
>
> PPP PHP price of one US$ = 161/5.69 = 28.29
>
> By comparing the Big Mac PPP implied exchange rate PHP 28.30/US$1 to the actual market exchange rate PHP 56.30/US$1, it is possible to measure the degree to which the peso is over- or undervalued:
>
> (PPP implied FX rate – Actual FX rate)/ Actual FX rate
>
> (28.30 – 56.30)/56.30 = –0.50 or an under valuation of 50%

For the parity between the purchasing power of the dollar and peso to continue, an adjustment in the exchange rate between the two currencies is needed: Equilibrium will be restored if at the end of the period (360 days later), the new prevailing exchange rate $S_{\$,PHP}(360)$ becomes:

$$105 = 1500 \times S_{\$,PHP}(360)$$
$$S_{\$,PHP}(360) = 105/1500 = 0{,}07$$

1 Assuming away transportation and other transaction costs.

2 Here again, this assumes a frictionless world characterized by the absence of transaction costs, transportation costs, and tariff barriers between the Philippines and the United States so that wheat arbitrageurs will be able to correct discrepancies in the price of one bushel of wheat between the Philippines and the United States.

INTERNATIONAL CORPORATE FINANCE IN PRACTICE 7.1

McCurrencies

The London magazine *The Economist* has yet to win the Nobel Prize in economics, but it certainly made a lasting contribution to the "dismal science" when its economics editor invented the Big Mac index in 1986 as a light-hearted introduction to exchange-rate theory. As *burgernomics* is closing on its fourth decade, the Big Mac index is widely used and abused around the globe. It is time to take stock of what burgers do and do not tell us about exchange rates.

The Economist's Big Mac index is based on one of the oldest concepts in international economics: the theory of PPP, which argues that in the long run, exchange rates should move toward levels that would equalize the prices of an identical basket of goods and services in any two countries. Our "basket" is a McDonald's Big Mac, produced in around 120 countries. The Big Mac is indeed a representative basket since it includes a reasonable mix of widely consumed goods and services such as meat products, flour, vegetables, wages, rent, mortgage costs, and energy. The Big Mac PPP is the exchange rate that would leave burgers costing the same in the United States as elsewhere. For example, a Big Mac in China costs CNY 25 in 2023, against an average price in four American cities of $5.69 (see Exhibit 7.1). To make the two prices equal would require an exchange rate of CNY 4.39 to the dollar, compared with a market rate of 7.20. In other words, the CNY is (4.39 – 7.20)/7.20 = –39% undervalued against the dollar.

Exhibit 7.1. Exchange rates according to the big Mac Index in 2023.

	Big Mac Prices				
	In Local Currency	In Dollars	Implied PPP[a] of the Dollar	Actual Dollar Exchange Rate December 2023	Under (–) / Over (+) Valuation against the Dollar (%)
United States[b]	$5.69	5.69	—	—	—
Argentina	Peso 3150	3.83	553.60	821.44	–33
Australia	A$7.7	5.07	1.35	1.52	–11
Brazil	Real 23.90	4.81	4.20	4.97	–15
Britain	£4.49	5.71	0.79	0.79	0
Canada	C$7.47	5.56	1.31	1.34	–2
Chile	Peso 4050	4.46	711.78	908.85	–22
China	Yuan 25	3.47	4.39	7.20	–39
Czech Republic	Koruna 105	4.61	18.45	22.77	–19
Denmark	DKr 39.00	5.69	6.85	6.85	0
Egypt	E£85.00	2.75	14.94	30.90	–52
Euro area[c]	€ 5.39	5.87	0.95	0.92	3
Hong Kong	HK$23.00	2.94	4.04	7.82	–48
Hungary	Forint 1,400	3.98	246.05	352.05	–30
Indonesia	Rupiah 38,000	2.43	6678.38	15635.00	–57
Japan	¥450	3.04	79.09	147.86	–47
Malaysia	Ringgit 13.15	2.78	2.31	4.73	–51
Mexico	Peso 89	5.19	15.64	17.14	–9
New Zealand	NZ$8.2	5.01	1.44	1.64	–12
Peru	Sol 15.9	4.25	2.79	3.74	–25

(Continued)

Exhibit 7.1. *(Continued)*

	Big Mac Prices				
	In Local Currency	In Dollars	Implied PPP[a] of the Dollar	Actual Dollar Exchange Rate December 2023	Under (−) / Over (+) Valuation against the Dollar (%)
Philippines	Peso 161	2.86	28.30	56.30	−50
Poland	Zloty 19.09	4.97	3.50	4.01	−13
Singapore	S$6.65	4.96	1.17	1.34	−13
South Africa	Rand 51.09	2.71	9.12	19.19	−52
South Korea	Won 5,500	4.11	966.61	1338.90	−28
Sweden	SKr 61.29	5.87	10.77	10.45	3
Switzerland	SFr 7.1	8.17	1.25	0.87	44
Taiwan	NT$75	2.39	13.18	31.3475	−58
Thailand	Baht 135	3.78	23.73	35.6775	−33
Turkey	Lira 120	3.97	21.09	30.25475	−30

Notes: [a] Purchasing Power Parity: Local price divided by price in the United States.
[b] Average of New York, Chicago, Atlanta, and San Francisco.
[c] Weighted average of prices in Euro area.

In contrast, using the same method, the Swiss and Swedish currencies are overvalued, by 44% and 3%, respectively. Note that most emerging-market currencies also look too cheap. The index was never intended to be a precise predictor of currency movements, simply a take-away guide to whether currencies are at their correct long-run levels. Curiously, however, burgernomics has had an impressive record in predicting exchange rates: Currencies that show up as overvalued often tend to weaken in later years. But you must always remember the Big Mac's limitations. Burgers cannot sensibly be traded across borders, and prices are distorted by differences in taxes and the cost of non-tradable inputs, such as rents.

Source: Adapted from "Burgernomics," *The Economist*, 2018.

because $105 is now needed to buy one bushel of wheat worth PHP 1,500. In other words, where previously (at time $t = 0$) $0.10 was needed to buy PHP 1 only $0.07 is now needed (at time $t = 360$) to acquire PHP 1. Obviously, inflation has bitten much more voraciously into the purchasing power of the Philippines peso than into the US dollar — and hence the steep rate of depreciation of the Philippines currency *vis-à-vis* the US currency induced by the differential of national rates of inflation over the period of time considered (relative version of PPP).

Generalization

The previous discussion can be generalized to real-life multiproduct economies. All that is needed is to substitute for a bushel of wheat a representative basket of goods and services that can be priced in both countries and that accurately represents the type and relative quantities of various goods and services produced and consumed in each country.[3] We now proceed with the algebraic formulation of the PPP theorem.

First, denote $P_{US}(0)$ and $P_{US}(360)$ as the dollar prices of the representative basket of goods in the United States at time $t = 0$ and $t = 360$, $P_{PH}(0)$ and $P_{PH}(360)$ as the peso prices of an equivalently representative basket of goods in the Philippines at time $t = 0$ and $t = 360$, respectively, and r_{US} and r_{PH} as the rates of inflation in the US and the Philippines economy over the forecasting horizon [0, 360].

If at time $t = 0$ the purchasing powers of the dollar and peso are at parity, the prices of equivalent

3 Price indexes, because of their very nature, are used as a measure of the price of a representative basket of goods and services in empirical tests of the purchasing power parity hypothesis (see the following numerical illustration in the text).

representative baskets of goods as expressed in terms of either currency should be the same. In dollar terms, at time $t = 0$, the parity between the purchasing power of the dollar and the peso can be expressed as follows:

$$P_{US}(0) = P_{PH}(0) \times S_{\$,PHP}(0) \tag{7.1}$$

Similarly, one year later at time $t = 360$, taking into account the differing rate of price increases (r_{US} and r_{PH}) as reflected in the new price of each representative basket of goods $P_{US}(360)$ and $P_{PH}(360)$ in the United States and the Philippines, respectively, a new exchange rate $S_{\$,PHP}(360)$ must be obtained in order for the purchasing powers of both currencies to remain at parity. Algebraically, in dollar terms, we have the new expression:

$$P_{US}(360) = P_{PH}(360) \times S_{\$,PHP}(360) \tag{7.2}$$

Expressing prices at time $t = 360$ as a function of prices at time $t = 0$ and rates of inflation over the 360-day period, we write:

$$P_{US}(360) = P_{US}(0) \times (1 + r_{US}) \tag{7.3a}$$

$$P_{PH}(360) = P_{PH}(0) \times (1 + r_{PH}) \tag{7.3b}$$

Or restating expression (7.2) as expression (7.4):

$$P_{US}(0) \times (1 + r_{US}) = P_{PH}(0) \times (1 + r_{PH}) \times S_{\$,PHP}(360)$$

Using expression (7.1), expression (7.4) thus becomes:

$$\frac{1+r_{US}}{1+r_{PH}} = \frac{S_{\$,PHP}(360)}{S_{\$,PHP}(0)} \tag{7.5}$$

By subtracting 1 from both members of equation (7.5) and further assuming that both rates of inflation r_{US} and r_{PH} are very small percentages, the PPP theorem can be rewritten as the following approximation:

$$r_{US} - r_{PH} = \frac{S_{\$,PHP}(360) - S_{\$,PHP}(0)}{S_{\$,PHP}(0)} \tag{7.6}$$

In other words, equation (7.6) expresses that the differential in rates of inflation between the United States and the Philippines equals the percentage change in the exchange rate over the same period.[4]

4 The reader will notice that the theory of purchasing power parity follows a similar formulation to that of interest rate parity presented in Chapter 6. Indeed, if one substitutes inflation rates for interest rates in the interest rate parity formula, the no-profit forward rate, $F_{\$,PHP}(360)$, becomes the end-of-the-period exchange rate, $S_{\$,PHP}(360)$.

INTERNATIONAL CORPORATE FINANCE IN PRACTICE 7.2

Crawling Peg or System of Mini-Devaluations

The system of "pegged yet adjustable" exchange rates, characteristic of the Bretton Woods and Smithsonian agreements and more recently of the European Monetary System, meant that par value changes (adjustments in the peg) were carried out infrequently as an overdue response to a significant balance-of-payments disequilibrium and therefore in a sizable discrete step. By contrast, under a *crawling peg* system, par-value changes of very small magnitude will be implemented very often, which makes the process of exchange rate adjustment continuous for all practical purposes. The peg (par value) would thus crawl from one level to another.

This system of *mini-devaluations* has been consistently implemented over the past three decades by Argentina, Brazil, Colombia, Indonesia, Israel, Mexico, Turkey, Ukraine, Venezuela and many other countries. Plagued by runaway inflation (an annual rate often in excess of 100%), Brazil, for example, devalued its currency almost weekly by small increments, reflecting a trade-weighted differential between its rate of inflation and its major commercial partners. In so doing, Brazil ensured that the purchasing power of its currency would remain in line with that of its major trading partners. The underlying economic hypothesis on which these mini-devaluations were predicated was PPP.

For example, if in a given year Brazil experienced an inflation rate of 90% while the US inflation rate was only 4%, PPP would predict that the Brazilian currency would lose 86% (90% – 4% = 86%) of its value to compensate for the relative loss of its currency's purchasing power *vis-à-vis* the US dollar. However, to better capture the multilateral nature of Brazil international economic relationships PPP can be re-formulated as a relationship between the size of a small devaluation and the trade-weighted differential of inflation rates between Brazil and its major trading partners.

Denoting by $S_{Cr,\$}(0)$ and $S_{Cr,\$}(t)$ the cruzeiro price of one US dollar before (time 0) and after devaluation (time t), the percentage change in the par value of the cruzeiro (Cr) can be expressed as:

$$\frac{S_{Cr,\$}(t) - S_{Cr,\$}(0)}{S_{Cr,\$}} = \sum_{i=1}^{n} w^i_{BR} \times \left[r_{BR}(0,t) - r_i(0,t) \right] \quad (7.6A)$$

where w^i_{BR} is the percentage of its foreign trade that Brazil conducts with country i, and $r_{BR}(0,t)$ and $r_i(0,t)$ are the rates of inflation experienced respectively by Brazil and country i over the time interval $(0,t)$ when Brazil trades with n countries.

Again, Brazil carries out small incremental changes in the par value of the cruzeiro to maintain the purchasing power of its currency and therefore the competitiveness of its exports. This step function, like the pattern of a crawling peg, is depicted in Exhibit 7.2. The reader will notice the bulging overvaluation gap (the hash-marked part of the graph) that the central bank of Brazil allowed to develop. In effect, each mini-devaluation understates the extent of the realistic devaluation called for by the systematic application of the PPP theorem. As the overvaluation gap deepens, the pressure for a maxi-devaluation increases, as evidenced by the large devaluations carried out by Brazil in 1980 and 1983.

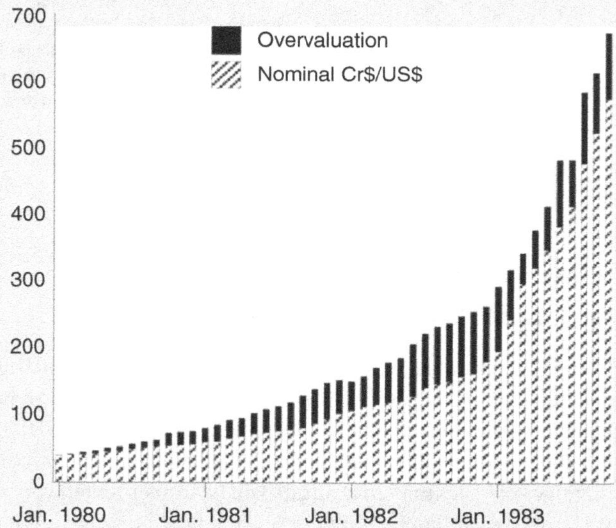

Exhibit 7.2. Brazil's mini-devaluations, 1980–1983.

Equivalent formulation

Instead of introducing rates of inflation, the PPP theorem can be equivalently expressed in terms of price levels prevailing at the beginning and end of the period considered. Equations (7.1) and (7.2) can be written respectively as

$$\frac{P_{US}(0)}{P_{PH}(0)} = S_{\$,PHP}(0) \quad (7.7)$$

Exhibit 7.3. PPP exchange rates for the ARS/$ (2015–2017).

Year	United States Consumer Price Index (2015 = 100)	Argentina Consumer Price Index (2015 = 100)	Exchange Rate	
			$/ARS	ARS/$
2015	100	100	0.0773	12.9425
2016	101.26	140.17	0.0558	17.9076
2017	103.42	170.41	0.0469	21.3162

Source: International Financial Statistics, International Monetary Fund (IMF), various issues.

and

$$\frac{P_{US}(360)}{P_{PH}(360)} = S_{\$,PHP}(360) \qquad (7.8)$$

or dividing equations (7.2) and (7.1) member by member,

$$\frac{P_{US}(360)\,/\,P_{PH}(360)}{P_{US}(0)\,/\,P_{PH}(0)} = \frac{S_{\$,PHP}(360)}{S_{\$,PHP}(0)} \qquad (7.9)$$

which is clearly equivalent to expression (7.5) if r_{US} is written as

$$\frac{P_{US}(360) - P_{US}(0)}{P_{US}(0)} \qquad (7.10)$$

and r_{PH} is written as

$$\frac{P_{PH}(360) - P_{PH}(0)}{P_{PH}(0)} \qquad (7.11)$$

Subtracting 1 from each member of equation (7.9), we have:

$$\frac{P_{US}(360)\,/\,P_{PH}(360) - P_{US}(0)\,/\,P_{PH}(0)}{P_{US}(0)\,/\,P_{PH}(0)} = \frac{S_{\$,PHP}(360) - S_{\$,PHP}(0)}{S_{\$,PHP}(0)} \qquad (7.12)$$

which signifies that for the parity of the purchasing power of two currencies to prevail over a period of time, the rate of change of the exchange rate has to equal the rate of change in relative prices.

Numerical illustration

Consider the case of the United States and Argentina over the 2015–2017 period. The value taken on by the price indexes in the United States, $P_{US}(t)$, and the Argentina, $P_{ARS}(t)$, are recorded in the second and third columns of Exhibit 7.3 (year-end values only). The actual exchange rate $S_{\$,ARS}(t)$ — the dollar price of one peso (ARS) at time t — that prevailed throughout the period (again, year-end values only) is recorded in the fourth column of the same table.

Using expression (7.9), it is now possible to determine the PPP exchange rate $S_{\$,PHP}(t)^*$ prevailing at the end of 2015, 2016, and 2017. Rewriting expression (7.9) as

$$S_{\$,P}(360)^* = S_{\$,P}(0) \times \frac{P_{US}(360)\,/\,P_{ARS}(360)}{P_{US}(0)\,/\,P_{ARS}(0)}$$

where $P_{US}(0) = 100$ is the US price index in the base period on the first day of 2015, $P_{ARS}(0) = 100$ is the Argentine price index in the base period (2015), and $S_{\$,ARS}(0) = 0.0773$ is the exchange rate expressed as the dollar price of one peso in 2015. We then find the equilibrium PPP exchange rates on the first day of 2016 and 2017 to be:

$$S_{\$,ARS}(2016) = 0.0773 \times 101.26/140.17 = 0.0558$$

Critical evaluation of the purchasing power parity hypothesis

Various objections of both a theoretical and a practical nature have been leveled at the PPP theorem[5]:

- Equilibrium exchange rates are the results not only of transactions of goods and services but also of other financial transactions that are not responsive to relative price levels, such as loans, loan repayments, unilateral transfers of gifts, and

5 For a critical evaluation of the purchasing power parity hypothesis, see Alan M. Taylor and Mark P. Taylor. 2004. "The Purchasing Power Parity Debate." *Journal of Economic Perspectives* 18(Fall): 135–158.

royalties. These latter transactions also give rise to supply and demand of foreign exchange and thereby contribute to the determination of the equilibrium exchange rate.

- Transportation costs, tariffs, quotas, exchange controls, and other obstacles to trade are lasting characteristics of the real world and may allow an existing exchange rate to overvalue or undervalue a currency in relation to a PPP exchange rate without corrective trade flows being fully operative. If restrictive enough, tariff quotas, exchange controls, and other man-made trade barriers could ruin the responsiveness of trade to prices and so make the hypothesis irrelevant.
- Government measures of inflation naturally differ from one country to the next as they are based on different consumption baskets. The price of such representative baskets of goods and services is measured in practice by price indexes that will vary substantially among countries in terms of both the assortment of goods and services included and the weighting formula.[6] Furthermore, price indexes, especially cost of living indexes, by weighting heavily non-tradable goods and services, will offer little guide to developments of prices for exportable goods and for domestically produced import-competing goods, which are, after all, the most significant ones for exchange rates equilibrium. Another problem is the choice of an appropriate base period during which prevailing exchange rates can be presumed as equilibrium exchange rates.

The purchasing power parity hypothesis as a predictive tool

Despite its theoretical and empirical shortcomings, what can be said about the explanatory and predictive power of the PPP theory? In other words, is there strong empirical evidence lending support to the hypothesis of PPP? Is such a model of any use in predicting actual exchange rates?

The answer to the first question is that the theory does badly in explaining the relationship between exchange rates and national price levels except under either of the following circumstances: (1) The theory is tested over the long run, or (2) one of the countries suffers from a high rate of inflation, as is often the case in emerging market countries. In the latter case, the PPP theory offers a good fit, even over the short run. The answer to the second question is that, to the extent that we are able to forecast successfully the rates of inflation in the two countries over the longer term, yes, the model may be used in a predictive capacity. This is a question to which we will return at some length in Chapter 15.

The purchasing power parity hypothesis as a gauge of currency over/undervaluation

If PPP is a poor exchange rate forecasting model it nevertheless offers reliable benchmarks for gauging the *real* value of currencies — often referred as *real exchange rates* — as opposed to *nominal* value of currencies. Short of a precise forecast, a gauge of over/undervaluation is still a useful managerial guide to time major forex transactions such as repatriation of dividends, foreign acquisition or divestment. We know that as an over/undervaluation gap develop, arbitrage forces will force in time a reversal in exchange rates which will eventually close a gap — the difficulty is, that of course, precise timing is not part of the user's manual.

We now turn to real life illustration of the long-term explanatory power of the PPP hypothesis and how it can be used to measure over/under-valuation of foreign exchange rates by considering the case of the Japanese yen, Argentine Peso, Thai Baht and Chinese renminbi. If exchange rates are measured as the foreign currency price of one US dollar the percentage of over/under-valuation is computed as

% over/undervaluation =
(PPP rate – Nominal Rate)/Nominal Rate

> ***Q:*** In 2005 the Chinese controlled nominal exchange rate stood at RMB 8.5 = US$ 1 when the PPP rate consensus was 7. Was the RMB over or undervalued and by how much
>
> ***A:*** The RMB was undervalued by (7 – 8.5)/8.5 = –17.64%

Dollar-Yen. Exhibit 7.4 shows the nominal and PPP ¥/US$ exchange rate over the period 1970–2018 and confirms the PPP hypothesis' explanatory power over the very long haul — in this case half-a-century. However, the reader will note significant deviations over the short and medium term. Reminding ourselves that the dollar is overvalued when the actual/nominal $S_{¥,\$}(t)$ — full line on the graph — is above the PPP prediction — dotted line — we observed

6 This is to be expected, since the price indexes are meant to reflect national patterns of production and consumption.

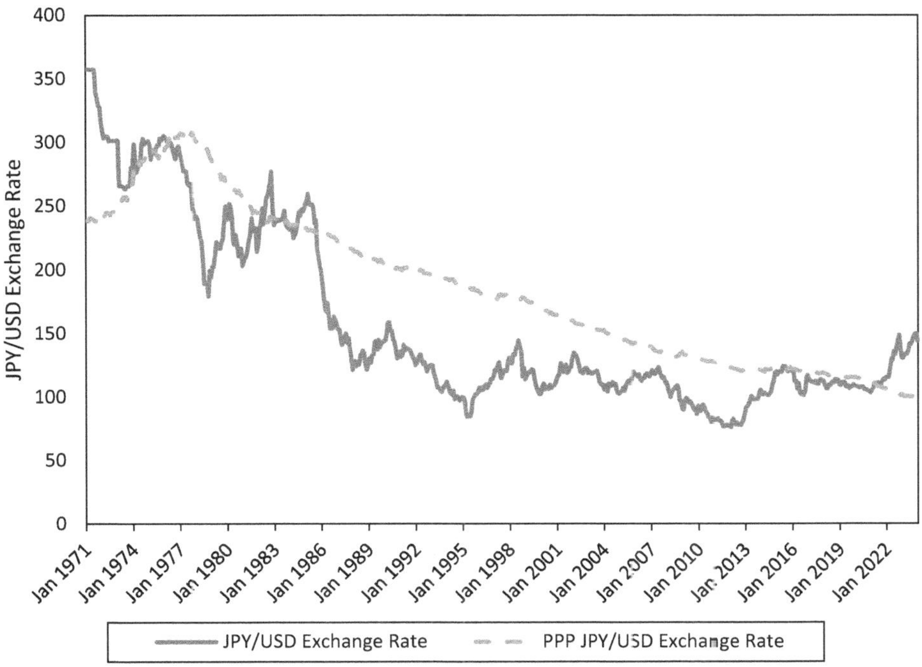

Exhibit 7.4. Yen/dollar exchange rate and PPP trend (1971–2022).

that the PPP rate is actually increasing from 1971 to 1977: this positive slope simply reflects that inflation in Japan was higher than inflation in the United States. Thereafter — from 1978 to 2018, the PPP rate is steadily declining indicating that inflation in Japan is continuously lower than in the United States. The 1980–85 period show significant overvaluation of the US dollar *vis-à-vis* the Japanese yen largely due to double-digit US interest rates aimed at curbing US inflation. It peaked in February 1985 the nominal exchange stood at 260 versus a PPP rate of 199 when the yen undervaluation/dollar overvaluation reached (191 – 260)/260 = –27%. From 1986 onwards — after its sharp appreciation in the early 1986 from 260 to 185 — the yen remains steadily overvalued for nearly 20 years; in October 2011 the nominal rate peaked at JPY76 = $1 when the PPP rate stood at 102 or Yen overvaluation of (76 – 102)/76 = –34% until Prime minister Abe embarks on an aggressive depreciation of the Japanese currency: By June 2015 the yen had depreciated back to 123 when the PPP rate stood at 99 or a yen undervaluation of (99 – 123/123 = –19.5%.

Thai Baht–US dollar. From first being pegged to the US dollar at the rate of THB 25 = US$ in 1984 until the onslaught of the Asian financial crisis in 1997 the Thai baht became progressively overvalued when the gap between the nominal rate of 25 against the PPP rate of 34 peaked at a maximum overvaluation of (34 – 25/25) = 36% (see Exhibit 7.5). As the first Asian financial crisis domino to fall in July 1997 the baht entered a period of significant undervaluation peaking in January of 1998 at (34 – 53)/34 = –56% which lasted until December 2006. This chapter opened by relating the story of a savvy foreign direct investor being mindful of not investing in Thailand when the THB was significantly overvalued. GE Capital patiently awaited for the THB to correct its overvaluation during the summer of 1997 before making a timely acquisition of approximately US$1 billion of automobile-leases.

Q: Since December 2006 the Thai baht nominal exchange rates has hovered between 36 and 28 when the PPP rate held steady at 34. Has the THB been over or under-valued during the last decade?

A: Over the period of January 2007 to December 2018 the THB has been mildly overvalued with peak overvaluation reached in April 2013 at (36 – 28)/28 = 21%.

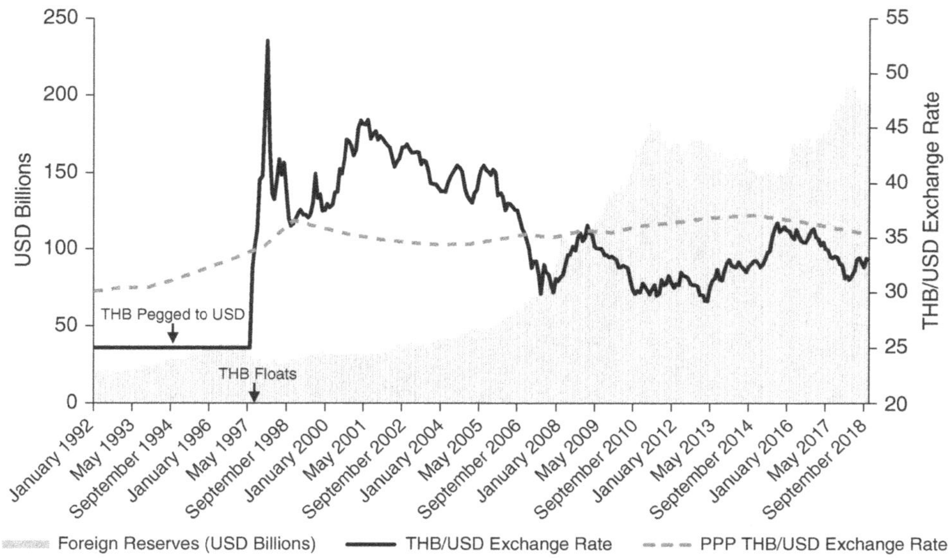

Exhibit 7.5. Thai Baht/dollar exchange rate and PPP trend (1992–2018).

Argentine Peso–US dollar. The currency board established in 1991 enshrined the ARS1 = US$1 exchange rate and the parity held firm for a decade. However, as Argentina suffered from higher inflation than the United States the peso became progressively overvalued as shown in Exhibit 7.6. The overvaluation peaked in January 2002 at 34% which precipitated a financial crisis and forced Argentina to let its currency float and to declare bankruptcy on its international debt. In 2002 the Peso plunged from ARS 1 to ARS 3 = US$1 and remained consistently undervalued to this day when the nominal rate reached a low of ARS38 = US$1 versus a PPP rate of 13 for an undervaluation of (13 – 38)/38 = –66%.

Renminbi–US dollar. During the first half of the decade 2001–2005, the renminbi (CNY) was pegged to the US dollar at CNY 8.5 = US$1 and showed significant and steadily increasing under-valuation which stood at 20% in 2005. China was lambasted by the West — the United States in particular — for providing its industrial firms with an unfair subsidy which fueled Chinese exports and resulted in large account surpluses (and rapidly accumulating foreign exchange reserves). Under pressure by its commercial partners, China allowed its currency to appreciate to CNY6.1 = US$1 by 2015 — thereby doing more than closing the undervaluation gap. Interestingly — faced with China's unrelenting current account surpluses the West continued to demand further appreciation of the renminbi. And yet, as the diagram in Exhibit 7.7 indicates the PPP rate reversed direction in 2007 as inflation in China became higher than in the United States due in large part to higher labor costs. If anything, the renminbi is now over-valued forcing China to lessen its reliance on labor-intensive exports as Japan did more than 40 years ago.

THE LINKAGES BETWEEN INTEREST, INFLATION, AND EXCHANGE RATES

This section recaps and integrates the key parity relationships that we already encountered and discussed at great length:

- *PPP* which links inflation rates with the expected future spot exchange rate.
- *Covered interest rate parity* (see Chapter 6), which links interest rates with the forward exchange rate.
- *Uncovered interest rate parity* (see Chapter 6), which links interest rates with the expected future spot exchange rate.

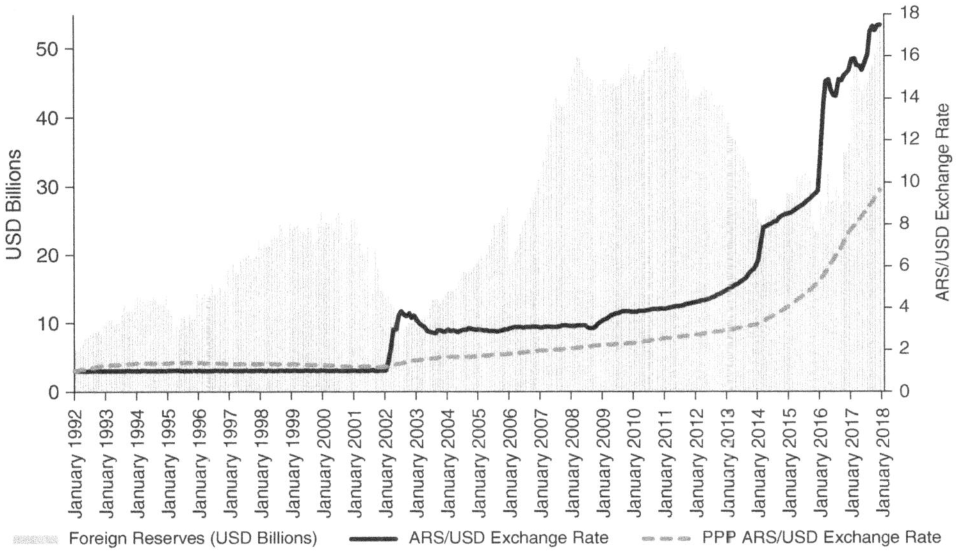

Exhibit 7.6. Argentine peso/dollar exchange rate and PPP trend (1992–2018).

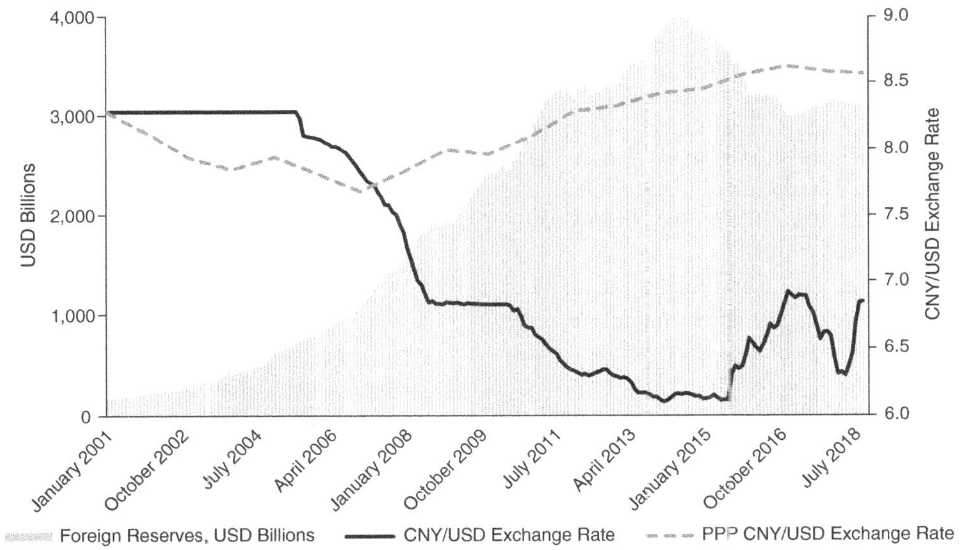

Exhibit 7.7. Chinese renminbi/dollar exchange rate and PPP trend (2001–2018).

It completes the international parity framework by introducing two additional relationships:

- *Fisher hypothesis*, which links interest rate differentials to expected inflation rate differentials, and the
- *Forward Un-biasness hypothesis*, according to which forward exchange rates can be construed as unbiased predictors of future spot exchange rates.

While reviewing the international parity relationships, this section maps sequentially and illustrates numerically the alternative paths linking interest rate differentials to expected exchange rate changes. Specifically, the reader should follow the three alternative paths in Exhibit 7.8 which show how interest rates determine future exchange rates via the Fisher effect + PPP **(path 1A and 1B)**, directly

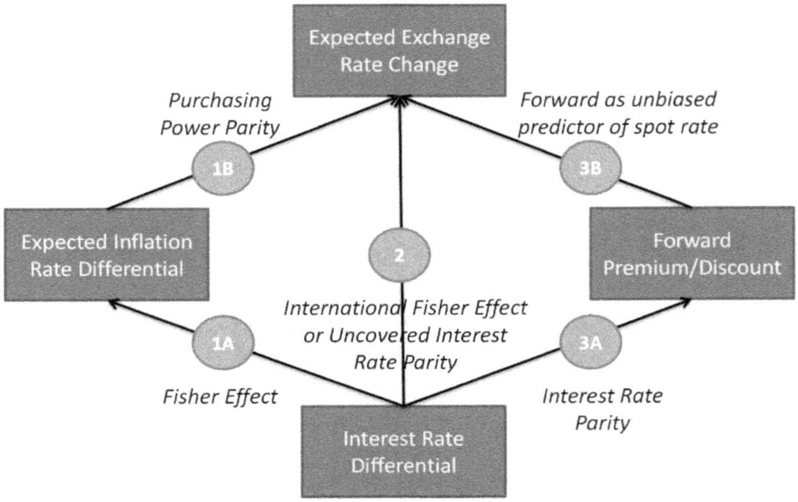

Exhibit 7.8. International parity linkages.

through Uncovered Interest Rate Parity **(path 2)** or through Covered Interest Rate Parity + Forward rates Unbiasedness **(path 3A and 3B)**.

The reader should be cautioned that, although international parity relationships can be configured into a powerful conceptual framework for understanding exchange rate determination, it is a greatly simplified view of reality that is controversial because it assumes perfect markets for goods, capital, and currencies with minimal interference from government regulation and controls.

> **Path 1:** *From interest rate differential to expected inflation rate differential to expected change in the exchange rate (see links 1A and 1B in Exhibit 7.8).*
>
> *This first path links — via the Fisher effect — interest rate differentials to inflation rate differential (1A) which are then showed — via PPP — to determine exchange rate change (1B).*

Fisher hypothesis

Irving Fisher's insight was that the nominal interest rate i is equal to the required real rate of return i^* plus compensation for the expected rate of inflation $E(\tilde{r})$[7]:

$$1 + \text{Nominal interest} = (1 + \text{Real interest}) \times (1 + \text{Expected inflation})$$

$$1+i=\left(1+i^*\right)\left(1+E(\tilde{r})\right)=1+i^*+E(\tilde{r})+i^*\times E(\tilde{r})$$

which is often approximated as

$$\text{Nominal interest} = \text{Real interest} + \text{Expected inflation}$$

$$i = i^* + E(r)$$

as long as both real interest and expected inflation are low single-digit numbers making the last compound term of relatively minor value which can be dropped.[8]

> **Q:** If the nominal annual interest rate is 40% in Argentina and the expected rate of inflation is 36% for the coming year what is the real interest rate?
>
> **A:** According to the Fisher hypothesis the *expected real interest rate* is equal to the nominal interest rate minus the expected rate of inflation or 40% – 36% = 4%. The actual inflation in Argentina turned out to be 38% — higher than the expected 36% — resulting into an *actual real interest rate* of 40% – 38% = 2%.

7 Expected rate of inflation formally means the expected (mean) value of the random variable $\tilde{r}$, which models the future rate of inflation.

8 Denoting interest rate as i and expected inflation as $E(r)$, the Fisher theorem is formulated as:

$$1+i=\left(1+i^*\right)\times\left[1+E(\tilde{r})\right]=1+i^*+E(\tilde{r})+i^*\times E(\tilde{r})$$

and approximated as $1+i^*+E(\tilde{r})$ if the term $i^*\times E(\tilde{r})$ is small enough to be assumed away.

Another way to consider the notion of real interest rate is to imagine a world without inflation: the real interest rate in the net increase in wealth that investors expect to enjoy when they save and invest their current income. Because financial contracts are drawn on the basis of *nominal* — not *real* — interest rates a forecast of inflation has to be added to the real interest rate to compensate for the expected loss in purchasing power of the money invested. However, inflation is difficult to forecast and the parties to a financial contract may want to protect themselves against surprises in the form of a forecasting error by adding a risk premium to the expected rate of inflation.

The generalized international version of the Fisher effect postulates that real interest rates between the domestic country (*d*) and foreign country (*f*) should equalize through arbitrage — that is $i_d^* = i_f^*$. Thus, the nominal interest rate differential $i_d - i_f$ should equal the expected inflation rate differential between those same two countries. If real interest rates i_d^* and i_f^* are equal and constant over time, fluctuations in nominal interest rates simply anticipates continuously changing expectations of inflation rates.

$$E(\tilde{r}_d) = i_d - i_d^* \quad \text{and} \quad E(\tilde{r}_f) = i_f - i_f^*$$

Thus, the differential in expected rates of inflation between the domestic and foreign countries can be expressed as:

$$E(\tilde{r}_d) - E(\tilde{r}_f) = i_d - i_f \text{ since } i_d^* = i_f^*$$

Purchasing power parity

The theory of PPP introduced earlier in this chapter argues that in the long run, exchange rates should move toward levels that would equalize the prices of an identical basket of goods and services in any two countries. In its *absolute* version, PPP states simply that the prices of identical baskets of goods, when expressed in the same currency, cannot differ between two countries because arbitrageurs will take advantage of such situations until price differences are eliminated. This is nothing other than the *Law of One Price*, which can be readily extended from representative baskets of goods to the price level of an economy at large, thereby directly linking price indexes in two countries with their exchange rates. Denoting by P_d and P_f the price level in the domestic country *d* and the foreign country *f*, the Law of One Price is expressed as:

$$P_d = P_f \times S(0)$$

where $S(0)$ is the domestic currency price of one unit of foreign currency.

By taking a *dynamic* view of the absolute (and *static*) version of PPP, the more commonly used *relative* version of PPP contends that the exchange rate between the domestic and foreign currencies $S(t)$ will adjust to reflect domestic inflation $\tilde{r}_d$ and foreign inflation $\tilde{r}_f$ (or the change in the price levels of the domestic and foreign countries). By taking into account the rate of inflation at which domestic and foreign price levels should be adjusted, the Law of One Price shown before is reformulated as:

$$P_d \times (1 + r_d) = P_f \times (1 + r_f) \times S(t)$$

Recalling that $P_d = P_f \times S(0)$, the relative version of PPP simplifies to:

$$1 + r_d = \left(\frac{1}{S(0)}\right) \times \left(1 + r_f\right) \times S(t)$$

This relationship was shown to be approximated as

Percentage change in the exchange rate
= Inflation rate differential

$$\frac{S(t) - S(0)}{S(0)} = r_d - r_f$$

Numerical illustration: Assume that the United States and Brazil one year interest rates on government treasury bills are 2% and 8%, respectively. What is the expected exchange rate change between the Brazilian real (BRL) and the 1-year future US dollar price of one BRL or S(365) if today's exchange rate is US\$0.50 = BRL1 or S(0) = 0.50?

According to the Fisher effect (path 1A), the expected differential in inflation rates between the two countries is approximated by the interest rate differential 0.02 – 0.08 = –0.06. According to PPP (path 1B), this is the extent to which the BRL should depreciate. Numerically:

$$\frac{S(365) - 0.50}{0.50} = 0.02 - 0.08 = -0.06$$

$$\Leftrightarrow S(365) - 0.50 = -0.06 \times 0.50$$

$$\Leftrightarrow S(365) = 0.50(1 - 0.06) = 0.47$$

where S(365) is the US\$ price of one BRL 365 days later.

Path 2: *From interest rate differential directly to expected change in the exchange rate (see link 2 in Exhibit 7.8).*

This second path links — via the Uncovered Interest Rate Parity — interest rate differential to exchange rate changes. Uncovered interest rate parity — discussed in some depth in the previous chapter — is recapped next.

Uncovered interest rate parity

As participants in the money market continuously arbitrage short-lived interest rate differentials they borrow in low interest countries and convert the proceed into currencies that offer a much higher yield. This type of arbitrage is deemed *uncovered* because the investor does not hedge the exchange rate risk — that is, he does not use a forward contract to protect the value of his investment in the higher yielding currency and accept the uncertainty of repatriating his investment at whatever exchange rate will prevail at maturity. Thus, arbitrageurs collectively push money markets toward interest rate parity — a state at which the expected future spot exchange rate equalizes the return on a domestic investment with the return on an uncovered foreign investment. If indeed Uncovered Interest Rate Parity prevailed the carry trade discussed at length in the previous chapter would have never seen the light of day! Formally, one currency unit invested in the domestic currency at the interest rate i_d is compared with the uncovered yield in the foreign currency at the interest rate of i_f:

$$1+i_d=\frac{1}{S(0)}\times\left(1+i_f\right)\times E\left[\tilde{S}(365)\right]$$

where both spot $S(0)$ and expected future spot exchange rate $E\left[\tilde{S}(365)\right]$[9] are denoted as the domestic currency price of one unit of the foreign currency. This equation can be further approximated as:

$$i_d-i_f=\frac{E\left[\tilde{S}(365)\right]-S(0)}{S(0)}$$

Numerical illustration: assume again that the United States and Brazil one-year interest rate on government treasury bills are 2 and 8%, respectively. What is the expected rate of exchange rate change between the Brazilian real (BRL) and the US dollar assuming that US$0.5 = BRL1 or S(0) = 0.50? According to the uncovered interest rate parity hypothesis, the expected change in the future spot exchange rate is equal to the differential in interest rates:

$$\frac{E\left[\tilde{S}(365)\right]-0.50}{0.50}=0.02-0.08=-0.06$$
$$\Leftrightarrow E\left[\tilde{S}(365)\right]-0.50=0.06-0.50$$
$$\Leftrightarrow E\left[\tilde{S}(365)\right]=0.50(1-0.06)=0.47$$

Path 3: *From interest rate differentials to the forward premium/discount as an unbiased predictor of the expected change in the future spot exchange rate (see links 3A and 3B in Exhibit 7.8).*

This path first links — via the Covered Interest Rate Parity — interest rate differential to the forward rate (3A) which are then showed — via the Forward Unbiasedness hypothesis — to predict the future spot exchange rate (3B).

Interest rate parity

This relationship was discussed at length in Chapter 6. It establishes a strong arbitrage relationship between the interest rate differential on the one hand and the forward premium or discount on the currency. In essence, nominal interest rate differentials among equivalent risk-class securities should prompt risk-averse investors (interest rate arbitrageurs) to shift funds from one money market to another until interest rates are brought back into equilibrium. This process of arbitrage of interest rates is complicated when risk-averse investors are faced with a foreign exchange risk that may wipe out the differential in interest rates that initially prompted their moves. Exchange rate risk, however, is hedged with the use of a forward contract, whereby principal and interest earnings in the foreign currency are protected by a forward sale of the currency of exposure. Formally, this relationship was expressed as comparing the yield on a domestic investment at the domestic interest rate of i_d (left-hand side of equation) with the covered investment in the foreign currency purchased at the current spot rate $S(0)$, invested at the foreign interest rate of i_f and hedged through a forward sale at the rate of $F(d)$[10] if the

9 The expected future spot exchange rate formally designates the expected mean 0 value of the random variable $\tilde{S}(365)$, which models the future spot exchange rate in 365 days.

10 Both spot rate $S(0)$ and forward $F(d)$ exchange rates as the domestic currency price of one unit of the foreign currency.

investment matures in d days (right-hand side of equation):

$$1 + i_d = \frac{1}{S(0)} \times \left(1 + i_f\right) \times F(d) \qquad \text{(6.8, repeated)}$$

This equation was shown to be approximated as

Interest rate differential =
Forward premium/Discount

$$i_d - i_f = \frac{F(d) - S(0)}{S(0)} \qquad \text{(6.11, repeated)}$$

whereby the interest rate differential between the domestic currency i_d and the foreign currency i_f is quasi-equal to the forward premium/discount on the foreign currency. The next step is to connect the forward rate $F(d)$ with the future spot exchange rate $E[S(t)]$.

Forward rates as unbiased forecasters of future spot rates

Simply put, this theory postulates that the forward rate is the best, unbiased (in the statistical sense) predictor of the future spot exchange rate.[11] Formally that means that the probability distribution of the future exchange rates $S(t)$ is centered on the forward rate — or that the forward rate is the mean value of all possible values that the future spot exchange rate may take. Most importantly, that does not mean that the future spot exchange rate will actually be equal to the forward exchange used as a predictor. Another rationale for this hypothesis is to consider how speculators who think that the forward rate is above their expectation of the future spot exchange rate will sell the foreign currency forward, thus bidding down the forward rate until it equals the expected future spot rate.[12] Conversely, speculators who see the forward rate undervaluing the expected future spot rate will buy foreign currency forward, thus bidding the forward rate up until both forward and expected future spot exchange rates becomes equal. If speculative demand for forward contracts were infinitely responsive and all speculators held homogeneous expectations with respect to the future spot exchange rate, the current forward exchange rate would be equal to the expected future spot rate. Formally, in statistical terms, the current forward rate is an unbiased predictor of the future spot exchange rate if it is equal to the mathematical expectation $E\left[\tilde{S}(t)\right]$ of the random variable $\tilde{S}(t)$ modeling the future spot exchange rate defined as the domestic currency price of one unit of foreign currency to prevail at time t:

$$F(d) = E\left[\tilde{S}(t)\right] \qquad \text{(15.1, repeated)}$$

where $F(d)$ is the dollar price of one unit of foreign currency for delivery d days forward as quoted at time 0. This relationship can be equivalently formulated as the forward premium/discount being equal to the expected change in the future exchange rate:

Forward premium/discount
= Expected percentage change in spot rate

$$\frac{F(d) - S(0)}{S(0)} = E\left\{\frac{\tilde{S}(t) - S(0)}{S(0)}\right\}$$

Numerical illustration: Assuming again that the United States and Brazil one-year interest rates on government treasury bills are, respectively, 2 and 8%, what is the expected rate of exchange rate change between the Brazilian real (BRL) and the US dollar given that today's spot exchange rate is US\$0.50 = BRL 1 or S(0) = 0.50? According to interest rate parity, the forward discount on the BRL is equal to the interest rate differential of:

$$\frac{F(365) - S(0)}{S(0)} = 0.02 - 0.08 = -0.06$$
$$\Leftrightarrow \frac{F(365) - 0.50}{0.50} = -0.06$$
$$\Leftrightarrow F(365) = 0.50 \times (1 - 0.06) = 0.47$$

Assuming further that the forward rate is equal to the mean (mathematical expectation) of the future spot exchange rate:

$$F(365) = 0.47 = E\left[\tilde{S}(365)\right]$$

We readily conclude that the expected devaluation of the spot exchange rate change one year hence is therefore 6%:

$$\frac{F(365) - S(0)}{S(0)} = \frac{E\left[\tilde{S}(365)\right] - S(0)}{S(0)} = -0.06$$

11 In Chapter 15 on forecasting foreign exchange rates, this theory will be revisited and shown to be tantamount to asking the question: Is the FX market efficient?

12 For a detailed explanation and illustration of speculation through the forward market, see Chapter 7.

To conclude, the reader should be cautioned that in spite of its intellectual elegance and analytical simplicity, the international parity framework suffers from poor empirical validation: PPP is weak in the short term but holds better over the (very) long term, while Uncovered Interest Rate Parity is seldom verified *ex post* and is certainly difficult to reconcile with the booming currency carry trade. Forward rates seem to be consistently biased (rather than unbiased) predictors of future spot exchange rates. Only the Covered Interest Rate Parity — unlike other parity relationships about expectations — holds tightly as an arbitrage relationship.

SUMMARY

1. **How parity relationships link interest rates and inflation rates with spot, future and forward exchange rates.**
   - *PPP* links inflation rates with the expected future spot exchange rate.
   - *Covered interest rate parity* links interest rates with the forward exchange rate.
   - *Uncovered interest rate parity* links interest rates with the expected future spot exchange rate.
   - *Fisher hypothesis* links interest rate differentials to expected inflation rate differentials, and the
   - *Forward Un-biasness hypothesis*, according to which forward exchange rates can be construed as unbiased predictors of future spot exchange rates.
2. This international parity framework maps out the alternative paths linking interest rate differentials to expected exchange rate changes. Specifically, the reader should follow the three alternative paths in Exhibit 7.8 which show how interest rates determine future exchange rates via the Fisher effect + PPP **(path 1A and 1B)**, directly through Uncovered Interest Rate Parity **(path 2)** or through Covered Interest Rate Parity + Forward rates Unbiasedness **(path 3A and 3B)**.
3. **Purchasing Power Parity (A).** According to theory of Purchasing Power Parity (PPP) in the long run, exchange rates should move toward levels that would equalize the prices of an identical basket of goods and services in any two countries. In its *absolute* version, PPP states simply that the prices of identical baskets of goods, when expressed in the same currency, cannot differ between two countries because arbitrageurs will take advantage of such situations until price differences are eliminated.
4. **Purchasing Power Parity (B).** A *dynamic* view of the absolute (and *static*) version of PPP, the more commonly used *relative* version of PPP contends that the exchange rate between the domestic and foreign currencies $S(t)$ will adjust to reflect domestic inflation $\tilde{r}_d$ and foreign inflation $\tilde{r}_f$ (or the change in the price levels of the domestic and foreign countries). By taking into account the rate of inflation at which domestic and foreign price levels should be adjusted, the Law of One Price shown before is reformulated as

   $$1+r_d=\left(\frac{1}{S(0)}\right)\times\left(1+r_f\right)\times S(t):$$

   Percentage change in the exchange rate
   = Inflation rate differential

   $$\frac{S(t)-S(0)}{S(0)}=r_d-r_f$$

5. **Purchasing Power Parity (C).** Is there strong empirical evidence lending support to the hypothesis of PPP? The answer is that the theory does badly in explaining the relationship between exchange rates and national price levels except under either of the following circumstances: (1) The theory is tested over the long run, or (2) one of the countries suffers from a high rate of inflation, as is often the case in emerging market countries.
6. **Purchasing Power Parity (D).** If PPP is a poor exchange rate forecasting model it nevertheless offers reliable benchmarks for gauging the *real* value of currencies — often referred as *real exchange rates* — as opposed to *nominal* value of currencies. Short of a precise forecast, a gauge of over/undervaluation is still a useful managerial guide to time major forex transactions such as repatriation of dividends, foreign acquisition or divestment.
7. **Covered Interest Rate Parity.** It establishes a strong arbitrage relationship between the interest rate differential on the one hand and the forward premium or discount on the currency. In essence, nominal interest rate differentials among equivalent risk-class securities should prompt risk-averse investors (interest rate arbitrageurs) to shift funds from one money market to another until interest rates are brought back into equilibrium. Exchange rate risk, however, is hedged with the use of a forward contract, whereby principal and interest earnings in the foreign currency are protected by a forward sale of

the currency of exposure. Formally, this relationship was expressed as comparing the yield on a domestic investment at the domestic interest rate of i_d (left-hand side of equation) with the covered investment in the foreign currency purchased at the current spot rate $S(0)$, invested at the foreign interest rate of i_f and hedged through a forward sale at the rate of $F(d)$[13] if the investment matures in d days (right-hand side of equation):

$$1+i_d = \frac{1}{S(0)} \times \left(1+i_f\right) \times F(d)$$

Interest rate differential
= Forward premium/Discount

$$i_d - i_f = \frac{f(d) - S(0)}{S(0)}$$

8. **Uncovered Interest Rate Parity.** As participants in the money market continuously arbitrage short-lived interest rate differentials they borrow in low interest country and accept the uncertainty of repatriating their investment at whatever exchange rate will prevail at maturity. Thus, arbitrageurs collectively push money markets toward interest rate parity — a state at which the expected future spot exchange rate equalizes the return on a domestic investment with the return on an uncovered foreign investment. If indeed Uncovered Interest Rate Parity prevailed the carry trade discussed at length in the previous chapter would have never seen the light of day!

9. **Fisher effect.** Irving Fisher's insight was that the nominal interest rate i is equal to the required real rate of return i^* plus compensation for the expected rate of inflation $E(\tilde{r})$[14]:

1 + Nominal interest = (1 + Real interest)
× (1 + Expected inflation)

$$1+i = \left(1+i^*\right)\left(1+E(\tilde{r})\right) = 1+i^* + E(\tilde{r}) + i^* \times E(\tilde{r})$$

which is often approximated as

Nominal interest = Real interest
+ Expected inflation

10. **Forward rates as unbiased predictors of future spot exchange rates.** The forward exchange rate is the best, unbiased (in the statistical sense) predictor of the future spot exchange rate.[15] Intuitively that means that the probability distribution of the future exchange rates $S(t)$ is centered on the forward rate — or that the forward rate is the mean value of all possible values that the future spot exchange rate may take. Most importantly, that does not mean that the future spot exchange rate will actually be equal to the forward exchange used as a predictor.

11. Although international parity relationships can be configured into a powerful conceptual framework for understanding exchange rate determination, it is a greatly simplified view of reality that is controversial because it assumes perfect markets for goods, capital, and currencies with minimal interference from government regulation and controls.

QUESTIONS FOR DISCUSSION

1. What are the alternative paths linking interest rate differentials to expected exchange rate changes?
2. What is the "Law of One Price"?
3. What is the meaning of PPP?
4. How do you gauge whether a currency is under or over-valued?
5. Under what circumstances would you expect PPP to be a reliable explanation of exchange rate changes.
6. What is the difference between covered and uncovered interest rate parity?
7. Under what conditions would you expect PPP to be a reliable model for forecasting future spot exchange rates?
8. What is the relationship between interest rates and inflation.
9. What are the risks involved in uncovered interest arbitrage? Can they be eliminated?
10. Why do currencies yielding low interest rates tend to sell at a forward premium?

13 Both spot rate $S(0)$ and forward $F(d)$ exchange rate as the domestic currency price of one unit of the foreign currency.

14 Expected rate of inflation formally means the expected (mean) value of the random variable $\tilde{r}$, which models the future rate of inflation.

15 In Chapter 15 on forecasting foreign exchange rates, this theory will be revisited and shown to be tantamount to asking the question: Is the FX market efficient?

11. What are the main reasons accounting for the fact that covered interest rate parity may not hold as a perfect equality?

12. Why were large deviations from covered interest rate parity observed during the subprime crisis?

13. What is the carry trade?

14. What are the risks involved in the carry trade?

15. Is the carry trade consistent with uncovered or covered interest rate parity?

16. What does it mean for forward rates to be "unbiased" predictor of future spot exchange rates?

PROBLEMS

1. **Hyperinflation in Turkey.** Turkey experienced hyperinflation in the late1990s and early 2000s. The exchange rate stood at Turkish lira (TRY) 650,000 = US$1 on January 1, 2000. With actual quarterly rates of inflation in 2000 and 2001 at 35%, the central bank of Turkey implemented a policy of mini-devaluation at the rate of 7.5% monthly devaluation.
   a. What would be the official exchange rate on February 1, 2001?
   b. What would be the official exchange rate on December 31, 2001? (Use monthly compounding.)
   c. Was the Turkish lira properly valued?

2. **PPP and the Argentine currency board (A — elementary).** In April 1991, Argentina established a currency board whereby for all practical purposes the Argentine peso was pegged to the US dollar at parity US$1 = ARS 1 during the entire decade of the 1990s. Ten years later, as result of a deep economic crisis, the peso was unpegged and promptly collapsed to US$1 = ARS 2.20.
   a. During the first year of operating its currency board, Argentina experienced inflation at the rate of 11% whereas the US rate of inflation was 3%. What was the real exchange rate US$/ARS at the end of the first year?
   b. Was the peso overvalued or undervalued?

3. **PPP and the Argentine currency board (B — intermediate).** Assume over the 10-year period 1991–2001 the US economy experienced an annualized inflation rate of 1.5%. While the currency board was in place, Argentina experienced annual rates of inflation of 172% in 1991, 24.6% in 1992, 10.7% in 1993, 4.3% in 1994, 3.3% in 1995, 0.2% in 1996, 0.5% in 1997, 0.9% in 1998, −1.2% in 1999, 0.9% in 2000 and 0.7% in 2001.
   a. What was the annualized inflation rate in Argentina over that same period (use annual compounding)?
   b. What was the real/PPP exchange rate at the very end of the 10-year currency board before the peso was allowed to float? Was the peso then undervalued or overvalued?

4. **PPP and the Argentine currency board (C — intermediate).** In 2002, Argentina suffered from inflation at the rate of 25% (still 1.5% in the United States):
   a. What should be the equilibrium exchange rate at the end of the year?
   b. At the end of 2002 the floating exchange rate stood at US$1 = ARS 3.20. Was the peso then overvalued or undervalued?

5. **Big Mac currencies (intermediate).** In 2006 a Big Mac cost ARS 7.00 in Argentina and US$3.10 in the United States. Four years later, in 2010, the same Big Mac cost ARS 14.00 in Argentina and US$3.73 in the United States.
   a. What is the implied exchange rate according to the Big Mac currency parity in 2006 and 2010?
   b. Knowing that the actual exchange rates in both years was ARS 3.06 = US$1 and ARS 3.93 = US$1, was the peso under- or overvalued in each year?
   c. Assuming that the increase in the cost of the Big Mac is a reliable measure of price inflation in both countries, what should the PPP implied exchange rate be in 2010, assuming that the Big Mac exchange rate in 2006 was fairly overvalued?

INTERNET EXERCISES

6. **Big Mac Currencies.** Search *The Economist* website www.economist.com/market-data to access the latest version of the Big Mac of currency over/undervaluation. Compare how the valuation of the Indian Rupee, Argentine Peso, Japanese yen and Canadian dollar have changed since 2018 (see Exhibit 7.1 in this chapter).

7. **Interest Rate Parity.** Access the Financial Times website markets.ft.com/RESEARCH/Markets/

Interest-Rates to download 3 month LIBOR and CD rates for US dollar and the pound sterling, the Euro and the Australian dollar. Compute the no-profit forward rate between the US dollar and pound sterling, euro and Australian dollar. How do they compare with the market forward rates? Is Interest Rate Parity holding?

8. **Hyperinflation in Turkey (intermediate).** Visit www.imf.org to sketch the nominal lira price of one US dollar over the period 1994–2001. Contrast it with the real/PPP rate over the same period. Was the lira over- or undervalued *vis-à-vis* the US dollar? Use monthly data and log scale to contain exchange rates on one page.

REFERENCES

Baba, Naohiko, and Frank Packer. 2009. "Interpreting Deviations from Covered Interest Parity during the Financial Market Turmoil of 2007–08." *Journal of Finance and Banking*, Vol. 33: 1953–1962.

Billingsley, Randall S. 2006. *Understanding Arbitrage: An Intuitive Approach to Financial Analysis*. Philadelphia: Wharton School Publishing.

Coffey, N., Warren B. Hrung, and A. Sarkar. 2009. "Capital Constraints, Counterparty Risk, and Deviations from Covered Interest Rate Parity." Federal Reserve Bank of New York: Staff Report no. 393, September.

Du, Wenxin, Alexander Tepper and Adrian Verdhalen. 2018. "Deviations from Covered Interest Rate Parity." *Journal of Finance* 915–957.

Dufey, Gunter, and Ian H. Giddy. 1994. *The International Money Market*. Englewood Cliffs, NJ: Prentice Hall.

Frenkel, Jacob A., and Richard M. Levich. 1976. "Transaction Costs and Interest Arbitrage: Tranquil versus Turbulent Periods." *Journal of Political Economy* 85(6): 1209–1226.

Giddy, Ian H. 1976. "An Integrated Theory of Exchange Rate Equilibrium." *Journal of Financial and Quantitative Analysis*, Vol. 11(5): 883–892.

Jacque, Laurent L. 2015. *Global Derivative Debacles: From Theory to Malpractice*, 2nd edition. Singapore and London: World Scientific.

Parsley, David C. and Shang-Jin Wei, 2007. "A Prism into the PPP Puzzle: the Micro-Foundation of Big Mac real Exchange Rates." *The Economic Journal* 117:1336–1356.

Quick, Peter J., Graham Hacche, and Viktor Schoofs. 1988. "Policies for Developing Forward Foreign Exchange Markets." *International Monetary Fund Occasional Papers* no. 60. A comprehensive study of how forward exchange facilities can be developed in LDCs.

Shapiro, Alan C., 1983. "What Does Purchasing Power Parity mean." *Journal of International Money and Finance*, Vol. 2(3): 295–318.

Taylor, Alan, and Mark Taylor. 2004. "The Purchasing Power Parity Debate." *Journal of Economic Perspectives* 18: 135–158.

CHAPTER 8

Currency Futures and Options

A dog, used to eating eggs, saw an oyster; and opening his mouth to its widest extent, swallowed it down with the utmost relish, supposing it to be an egg. Soon afterward suffering great pain in his stomach, he said "I deserve all this torment, for my folly in thinking that everything round must be an egg."

— The Fables of Aesop

Forward exchange contracts had been available for decades, but it was not until the breakdown of the Bretton Woods system of fixed exchange rates and the resulting heightened volatility in currency prices that new foreign exchange (FX or forex) risk management products started to appear. Futures contracts on foreign exchange were first introduced in May 1972, when the International Monetary Market (IMM) of the Chicago Mercantile Exchange (CME) began trading contracts on the British pound, Canadian dollar, Deutsche mark, Japanese yen, and Swiss franc. Currency options started to trade in the over-the-counter market in the early 1970s, but standardized contracts were not introduced until 1982 on the Philadelphia Stock Exchange Market.

By reading this chapter you will understand:

- How financial derivatives came into being.
- What currency futures contracts are and how they differ from currency forward contracts.
- How counterparty risk in futures contracts is mitigated.
- What currency options are and how they differ from futures and forwards.
- How currency options are priced.
- How the put-call parity binds the option market to the forward market.
- What the different option strategies are.

A BRIEF HISTORY OF DERIVATIVES

From time immemorial traders have been faced with three problems: how to finance the physical transportation of merchandise from point A to point B (perhaps several hundred or thousands of miles away and weeks or months away), how to insure the cargo (risk of being lost at sea or to pirates), and last, how to protect against price fluctuations in the value of the cargo across space (from point A to point B) and over time (between shipping and delivery time). In many ways the history of derivatives contracts parallels the increasingly innovative remedies that traders devised in coping with their predicament.

Ancient times

Trade carried over great distances is probably as old as mankind and has long been a source of economic power for the nations that embraced it. Indeed, international trade seems to have been at the vanguard of human progress and civilization: Phoenicians, Greeks, and Romans were all great traders whose activities were facilitated by marketplaces and money changers that set fixed places and fixed times for exchanging goods. Some historians even claim that some form of contracting with future delivery appeared as early as several centuries B.C. At about the same time, in Babylonia — the cradle of civilization — commerce was primarily effected by means of caravans. Traders bought goods to be delivered in some distant location and sought financing. A risk-sharing agreement was designed whereby merchant-financiers provided loans to traders whose repayment was contingent upon safe delivery of the goods. The trader borrowed at a higher cost than an ordinary loan would have cost, the difference being the cost of purchasing an *option to default* on the loan contingent upon loss of the cargo. As lenders were offering similar options to many traders and thereby pooling their risks, they were able to keep its cost affordable.[1]

Middle ages

Other forms of early derivatives contracts can be traced to medieval European commerce. After the long decline in commerce following the demise of the Roman Empire, medieval Europe experienced an economic revival in the twelfth century around two major trading hubs: in northern Italy the city-states of Venice and Genoa controlled the trade of silk, spices, and rare metals with the Orient; in northern Europe the Flanders (Holland and Belgium) had long been known for their fine cloth, lumber, salt fish, and metalware. It was only natural that trade would flourish between these two complementary economic regions. Somehow, as early as the 1100s, Reims and Troyes in Champagne (eastern France) held trade fairs that facilitated mercantile activity; there, traders would find money changers, storage facilities, and (most important) protection provided by the counts of Champagne. Soon rules of commercial engagement started to emerge as disputes between traders hailing from as far away as Scandinavia or Russia had to be settled: A code of commercial law — known as "law merchant" — enforceable by the "courts of the fair" was progressively developed. Although most transactions were completed on a spot basis, "an innovation of the medieval fairs was the use of a document called the *lettre de faire* as a forward contract which specified the delivery of goods at a later date".[2]

In 1298 a Genoese merchant by the name of Benedetto Zaccharia was selling 30 tons of alum[3] for delivery from Aigues Mortes (Provence, France) to Bruges (Flanders, Belgium).[4] Maritime voyages around Spain and the Atlantic coast of France were then hazardous and fraught with dangers — the cargo could be lost at sea or to pirates. Zaccharia found two compatriot financiers, Enrico Zuppa and Baliano Grilli, who were willing to assume the risk. Here is how it worked: Zaccharia sold "spot"[5] the alum to Zuppa and Grilli and entered into a *forward* repurchase contract contingent upon physical delivery. The repurchase price in Bruges was significantly higher than the spot price in Aigues Mortes. It reflected the cost of physical carry from Aigues Mortes to Bruges (several months at sea), insurance against loss of cargo, and the *option to default* granted to Zaccharia in the case of non-delivery. The merchant Zaccharia had secured financing and insurance in the form of a forward contingent contract.

Renaissance

If medieval fairs had gone a long way in establishing standards for specifying the grading and inspection process of commodities being traded as well as date and location for delivery of goods, it fell short of the modern concept of futures traded on centralized exchanges. The first organized futures exchange was the Dojima rice market in Osaka (Japan), which flourished from the early 1700s to World War II. It grew out of the need of feudal landlords, whose income was primarily based on unsteady rice crops, to hedge and monetize their revenue. By shipping surplus rice to Osaka and Edo, landlords were able to raise cash by selling warehouse receipts of their rice inventory in exchange for other goods on sale in other cities.

Merchants who purchased these warehouse receipts soon found themselves lending to cash-short landlords against future rice crops. In 1730, an edict by Yoshimune — also known as the "rice Shogun" — established futures trading in rice at the Dojima market apparently in an effort to stem the secular decline in rice prices. It certainly allowed

1 This "option to default" gave the trader the right to default on the loan in case the cargo never reached its destination. To benefit from this right, the trader paid an option premium in addition to normal interest on the loan. Jorion, Philippe. 1995. *Big Bets Gone Bad.* San Diego, CA: Academic Press, p. 138.

2 Richard J. Teweles and Frank J. Jones. 1999. edited by Ben Warwick, *The Futures Game: Who Wins, Who Loses, and Why*, 3rd edition. New York: McGraw-Hill, p. 8.

3 White mineral salt.

4 Jean Favier. 1991. *Les Grandes Découvertes.* Paris: Le Livre de Poche, cited in Briys, Eric, and François de Varenne. 1999. *The Fisherman and the Rhinoceros: How International Finance Shapes Everyday Life.* New York: John Wiley & Sons.

5 Spot sale is for immediate delivery and cash payment.

rice farmers to hedge against price fluctuations between harvests. Interestingly, all the hallmarks of the modern standardized futures contract were found in the Dojima rice futures market.[6] Each contract was set at 100 *koku*,[7] and contract duration was set according to a trimester trading calendar, which consisted of a spring semester (January 8–April 28), a summer term (May 7–October 9), and a winter term (October 17–December 24). All trades were entered in the "book" transaction system, where the names of the contracting parties, amount of rice exchanged, future price, and terms of delivery were recorded. Transactions were cash-settled (delivery of physical rice was not necessary) at the close of the trading term. Money changers soon functioned as de facto clearinghouses, eliminating counterparty risk by forcing margin requirements on individual rice traders, whose contracts were marked to current market prices every 10 days.[8]

Industrial revolution

Forward contracts progressively evolved from the need to hedge price risk associated with international trade. Consider the case of a mining firm in California shipping copper to London and wanting to lock in the value of its merchandise by selling its cargo forward (known then as "on a to-arrive basis") — possibly at a lower price that it would expect to receive several months later. A copper-processing firm in London might want to lock in the value of its core raw material input so that, in turn, it could bid on construction projects at fixed prices. Neither firm would know of the other, being domiciled far apart. A middleman would act as a matchmaker. Merchant banks (or their predecessors) having representation in the two distinct physical locations would be able to arrange the trade: They would receive a handsome fee for bringing the two parties together and acting as a guarantor of the good execution of the transaction.

In the early 1800s, grain commerce in the United States was vulnerable to large swings in prices; farmers would flood the market with their crop at harvest time and grain prices would collapse. Shortages would develop within a few months and prices would rebound. Instead of shipping their crop all at once and facing inadequate storage facilities, farmers (sellers) and millers (buyers) increasingly turned to forward contracting as a way to cope with price volatility while staggering grain delivery over time. During this time, Chicago was rapidly emerging as a hub for grain storage, trading, and subsequent distribution eastward — along rail lines or through the Great Lakes. In 1848, organized futures trading made its debut with the Chicago Board of Trade: Forward contracts morphed into futures through standardization of contracts, which allowed trading that was easier (uniform grading of commodities) and safer (margin requirement eliminating counterparty risk). Physical commodities — both hard (minerals) and soft (agricultural) — became the objects of futures trading.

Information age

More than a century later, the breakdown in 1971 of the Bretton Woods system of fixed exchange rates heralded the burst of innovation in financial derivatives (as opposed to commodity-linked derivatives). Volatile exchange rates ushered the world financial system into a new era of deregulation and financial innovation with the introduction of currency futures, options, swaps, and swaptions, as illustrated in Exhibit 8.1. As early as 1972, currency futures started to trade at the newly established IMM (a subsidiary of the CME). Rumor has it that Milton Friedman, anticipating in the late 1960s the demise of the Bretton Woods system of fixed exchange rates, wanted to speculate on the impending devaluation of the dollar by purchasing Deutsche marks forward. The forward exchange market was then (and still is) an over-the-counter wholesale market open to corporations and banks but not to retail investors. No bank was willing to enter his trade for lack of an underlying business transaction. Milton Friedman thus championed to the Chicago Board of Trade the concept of currency futures open for trading to individual speculators like himself. Unfortunately, the first currency futures contracts did not become available for trading until 1972.

The deregulation of interest rates in the United States soon set in motion the introduction of interest rate derivatives, which eventually would dwarf currency and commodity derivatives. In 1977 the Chicago Board of Trade introduced what was soon to become the most successful contract of all time — U.S. Treasury bond futures. As illustrated in Exhibit 8.1, the financial services industry continued

6 West, Mark D. 2000. "Private Ordering at the World's First Futures Exchange." *Michigan Law Review* 98(8).

7 *Koku* is a unit of measurement used in medieval Japan that corresponds to the amount of rice consumed by a person in one year. It is equal to 180 liters.

8 West, "Private Ordering," 2588.

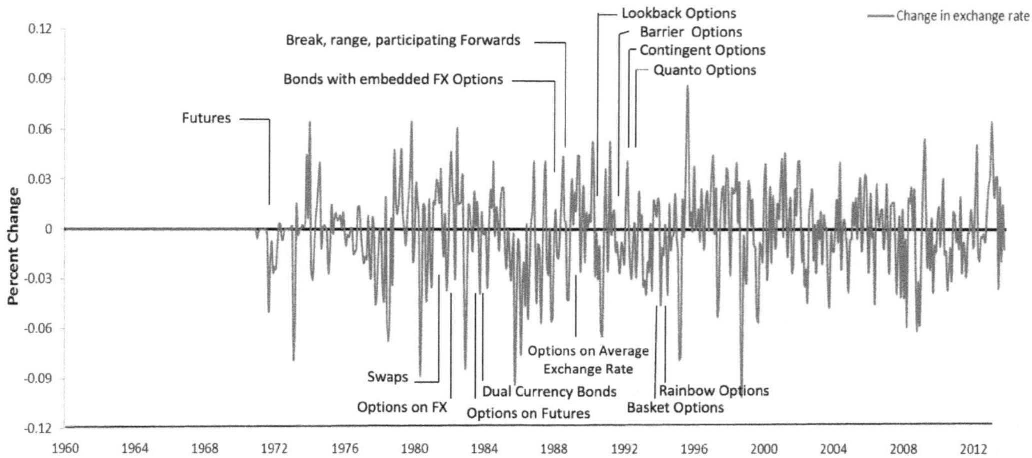

Exhibit 8.1. Financial innovations in the FX market as a function of time.

Source: Updated and adapted from Charles W. Smithson and Clifford W. Smith Jr., with D. Sykes Wilford. 1995. *Managing Financial Risk*. Chicago: Irwin, p. 22.

to respond to the need for currency products more versatile than forwards and futures. Cross-currency swaps — akin to bundles of long-dated forwards — were next to emerge as a natural evolution to "back-to-back loans", with the World Bank–IBM cross-currency swap marking in 1981 the first public transaction. In 1982, the Philadelphia Stock Exchange introduced a standardized option contract on the pound sterling, which was soon followed by similar contracts on the Canadian dollar, Deutsche mark, Japanese yen, and Swiss franc. Slightly different option contracts on currency futures (rather than the currency itself) were introduced by the CME in 1984, and they traded the same currencies as the Philadelphia Stock Exchange. Commercial banks, refusing to be sidelined, responded by offering tailor-made over-the-counter option contracts as well as more innovative optionlike products such as range forwards and forward participation contracts. When the world became a riskier place, firms and financial institutions naturally sought safe harbor by hedging with financial derivatives.

CURRENCY FUTURES

A currency futures contract is defined as a legally binding agreement with an organized exchange to buy (or sell) today a set amount of foreign currency for delivery at a specified date and place in the future. As such, a currency future does not appear terribly different from the old-fashioned forward contract discussed at great length in Chapters 5 and 6, except perhaps for the fact that such contracts are entered into with organized (and generally regulated) exchanges — a fact that has far-reaching implications for counterparty risk. There are, however, a number of additional differences between futures and forwards, which we address next.

Contract standardization

To promote accessibility and foster trading and liquidity, futures contracts specify a standardized face value, maturity date, and daily price movement limits.

Standardized amounts. Futures exchanges standardize the face value or amount of foreign currencies traded in each contract. This means that futures contracts, unlike forwards, cannot be customized to the exact needs of corporations when they hedge currency risks. In fact, standardized contracts are for relatively small amounts, thereby encouraging retail clients to trade futures contracts. For example, the face value of currently traded futures contracts on the IMM — a division of the CME — against the US dollar are €125,000, CAD 100,000, £62,500, ¥12,500,000, CHF 125,000, MXN 500,000, and AUD 100,000.

Standardized maturity. Currency futures are available for the months of March, June, September, and December. The settlement date for each contract month is the third Wednesday of the month, but the contract expiration date (last trading day) is two business days before Wednesday — which means they expire on the preceding Monday assuming that there are no holidays in between.

Standardized dates for currency futures greatly facilitate their trading, which in turn makes them liquid — that is, easy to buy or sell at any time during the life of the contract. This is an important difference from forward contracts, which generally are drawn for 30, 60, or 90 days' maturity from the signing date in amounts that are directly negotiated between the parties; as such, forwards are difficult to trade and are very illiquid. This means that if you signed a forward contract for delivery in 90 days hence and you want to liquidate your position on the 52nd day, it is unlikely that you will find another party willing to take your position for a customized amount maturing in 90 – 52 = 38 days.

Daily price movement limits are specified by the exchange. They set an upper or lower bound within which the futures price can move during a given day. Normally, trading ceases for the day if the futures price reaches its upper bound/ceiling or the lower bound/floor. Daily price limits aim at curbing speculative excesses.

Reading futures quotations

The prices of exchange-traded futures contracts appear daily in the financial press. Exhibit 8.2 shows futures quotations for August 31, 2018, as published by the *Wall Street Journal*. Seven currencies are quoted against the US dollar. For each currency the size of the contract is indicated as well as the unit in which it is priced; for example, in the case of the Japanese yen, the size of the contract is ¥12,500,000 and it is quoted in dollar terms per ¥100. For most currencies at least two contract months are listed — September 2018 and December 2018.

The Swiss franc September contract opened at \$1.0330/CHF, traded as high as \$1.0373/CHF, as low as \$1.0318/CHF, and settled at \$1.0327/CHF. The number of outstanding contracts — so-called *open interest* — stood at 81,031. Very few futures contracts are ever delivered; instead contract holders will progressively cash-settle their positions by entering into an offsetting contract. As a result open interest will gradually diminish as we approach the maturity date.

Q: Referring to Exhibit 8.2, what is the closing rate for a Mexican peso (MXN) September futures contract? How many contracts are outstanding? Can you quote the contract in Mexican peso per US dollar?

A: On August 31, 2018, the Mexican peso futures contract closed/settled at US\$0.05227 per MXN. There were 216,674 outstanding contracts. It could be quoted as MXN 1/0.05227/US\$ = MXN 19.13/US\$1.

Marking to market and the elimination of counterparty risk

In order to minimize the risk of *default* (*counterparty risk*), a futures exchange such as the CME takes at least two precautionary measures for every contract it enters into: (1) It requires the buyer to set up an *initial margin* similar to a performance bond and generally consisting of cash, Treasury bills, or a letter of credit from a bank that at a minimum should be equal to the maximum allowed daily price fluctuation; and (2) it forces the contract holder to settle immediately any daily losses resulting from adverse movement in the value of the futures contract. This is the practice of forcing the contract holder to a daily *marking to market*, which effectively reduces counterparty risk to a daily performance period with daily gains/losses added/subtracted to/from the margin account. To avoid a depleted margin account, the futures trader is obligated to replenish his or her margin account (so-called *margin call*) when it falls below a preset threshold known as the *maintenance margin*. (See International Corporate Finance in Practice 8.1.)

One practical question is, of course, how the initial margin and maintenance margin are determined. The initial margin should protect the clearinghouse against default of the futures contract holder and will therefore well exceed the maximum daily allowance; ultimately, however, it will be determined on a case-by-case basis reflecting in part historical volatility of the currency price — let's say 5% of the face value of the € futures contract or 0.05 × €100,000 = €5,000 or \$7,000 (assuming that the spot rate is at \$1.40/€). The maintenance margin typically would be set as a percentage of the initial margin — let's say 75% of €5,000 = €3,750 or \$5,250.

Quite clearly, the marking to market of futures contracts differentiates them significantly from

Exhibit 8.2. Currency futures.

	Open	High	Low	Settle	Change	Open Interest
Japanese Yen (CME) ¥12,500,000; $ per 100¥						
Sep. '18	0.9018	0.9044	0.9006	0.9017	0.0002	177,382
Oct. '18	0.9036	0.9057	0.9034	0.9036	0.0002	867
Nov. '18	0.9079	0.9079	0.9060	0.9058	0.0003	1,190
Dec. '18	0.9076	0.9103	0.9067	0.9077	0.0002	6,615
Canadian Dollar (CME) CAD 100,000; $ per CAD						
Sep. '18	0.7709	0.7709	0.7642	0.7665	–0.0037	137,560
Oct. '18	0.7713	0.7713	0.7653	0.7669	–0.0037	396
Nov. '18	0.7708	0.7757	0.7705	0.7674	–0.0037	328
Dec. '18	0.7717	0.7720	0.7656	0.7678	–0.0036	6,410
Mar. '19	0.7694	0.7695	0.7668	0.7690	–0.0036	919
Jun. '19	0.7724	0.7724	0.7695	0.7700	–0.0036	224
British Pound (CME) £62,500; $ per £						
Sep. '18	1.3016	1.3036	1.2951	1.2964	–0.0057	243,525
Oct. '18	1.3031	1.3041	1.2992	1.2980	–0.0058	603
Nov. '18	1.2915	1.3042	1.2913	1.2999	–0.0058	1,033
Dec. '18	1.3069	1.3084	1.3006	1.3016	–0.0057	12,600
Mar. '19	1.3146	1.3146	1.3146	1.3076	–0.0058	1,172
Swiss Franc (CME) CHF 125,000; $ per CHF						
Sep. '18	1.0330	1.0373	1.0318	1.0327	...	81,031
Dec. '18	1.0414	1.0456	1.0403	1.0411	...	642
Australian Dollar (CME) AUD 100,000; $ per AUD						
Sep. '18	0.7264	0.7267	0.7176	0.7180	–0.0077	139,255
Oct. '18	0.7264	0.7265	0.7183	0.7181	–0.0076	255
Dec. '18	0.7262	0.7268	0.7179	0.7182	–0.0077	5,040
Mar. '19	0.7240	0.7240	0.7195	0.7189	–0.0077	177
Mexican Peso (CME) MXN 500,000; $ per MXN						
Sep. '18	0.05218	0.05238	0.05174	0.05227	...	216,674
Dec. '18	0.05139	0.05164	0.05104	0.05155	0.00001	1,977
Euro (CME) €125,000; $ per €						
Sep. '18	1.1678	1.1703	1.1597	1.1609	–0.0068	499,612
Oct. '18	1.1704	1.1723	1.1627	1.1635	–0.0068	2,233
Nov. '18	1.1754	1.1754	1.1663	1.1666	–0.0068	1,346
Dec. '18	1.1763	1.1785	1.1680	1.1692	–0.0069	25,783
Mar. '19	1.1854	1.1869	1.1780	1.1786	–0.0069	1,723
Jun. '19	1.1893	1.1964	1.1877	1.1880	–0.0071	896
Sep. '19	1.2023	1.2028	1.1974	1.1977	–0.0072	786
Dec. '19	1.2075	1.2075	1.2075	1.2075	–0.0074	237

Source: Adapted from the *Wall Street Journal*, August 31, 2018.

INTERNATIONAL CORPORATE FINANCE IN PRACTICE 8.1

The Mechanics of Futures Trading: A Week in the Life of a Currency Speculator

Assume that on June 1, 2024, a currency speculator is bullish on the future value of the euro and believes that the market consensus embedded in the current March 2025 futures price of $1.12/€ understates its likely value on the expiration day of the March 2025 futures contract.

June 1, 2024. Our currency speculator purchases a March 2025 €100,000 futures contract at the price of US$1.1200/€. The contract is secured by a $7,000 deposit in the margin account. The maintenance margin is set at $5,250.

Close of June 2, 2024. € futures contract closes/settles down at US$1.1050/€. Our contract holder — who is long euros — is forced to settle his loss in the amount of $(1.1050 – 1.1200) × 100,000 = –$1,500. The initial margin account is now reduced to $5,500 ($7,000 – $1,500 = $5,500), which is well above the maintenance margin of $5,250.

Close of June 3, 2024. € futures contract weakens further and settles at $1.1000. Marking to market further depletes the initial margin account by $(1.1000 – 1.1050) × 100,000 = -$500, bringing the margin account down to $5,000, which is below the maintenance account by $250 and will trigger a margin call requiring the futures holder to add back $250 to his account.

Close of June 4, 2024. € futures contract rebounds to $1.1225/€. The contract holder receives €100,000 (1.1225 – 1.1000) = $2,250, which is added to his margin account that now stands at $5,250 + $1,250 = $6,500.

June 5, 2024. € continues to appreciate, and the currency speculator sells € futures contract at $1.1315/€ for a profit of ($1.1315 – $1.1200) × 100,000 = $1,150. However, the currency speculator held on deposit an average of ($7,000 + $5,500 + $5,250 + $6,500)/4 = $5,312 for four days and incurred an opportunity cost of 10% or approximately $7.00. Net profit is $1,143 per contract for an investment of $7,000 or 1,143/7,000 or 16.4% for four days or an annualized profit of 16.4% × 365/4 or 1,496%. So much for the power of leverage — the notion that $7,000 allowed our currency speculator to purchase a currency futures contract with a face value of €100,000.

forwards, whose performance period is the contract maturity rather than a single trading day. Thus trading currency futures with a well-capitalized exchange that happens to implement conservative, prudential trading guidelines is considerably less risky than trading forward contracts, which requires the risk evaluation of one's counterparty on a case-by-case basis (see Exhibit 8.3 for a comparison of the two instruments).

Hedgers and speculators

The futures market price setting process results from the ongoing interfaces between *hedgers*, *speculators*, and *arbitrageurs*.

Speculators aim to profit from the change in futures prices (or the future spot price if the contract were to be held to maturity). For example, if a speculator expects the euro-zone to fragment and one of the PIIGS nations (Portugal, Ireland, Italy, Greece, Spain) to drop out of the euro in the next few weeks, the speculator will sell the June euro futures contract at $1.36 = €1. The expectation is that upon breakup the euro futures price will fall to, say, $1.21, at which point our speculator will simply close the position by buying an offsetting futures contract (same month and same amount). This should generate a profit of $1.36/€ – $1.21/€ = $0.15/€ per euro transacted minus the cost of maintaining an adequate margin with the futures exchange.

Hedgers seek to avoid the impact of price uncertainty on the future value of a *long/asset* position or *short/liability* position in a given currency by locking in its price. This is readily achieved by entering into an offsetting futures position — selling a currency

Exhibit 8.3. Futures versus forward contracts.

Characteristics	Forward	Futures
Size and delivery date	Tailored to individual needs	Standardized
Marketplace and method of transaction	Established by the bank or broker via telephone contact or computer/Internet links worldwide with a limited number of buyers and sellers	Determined by open auction among many buyers and sellers on a central exchange floor with worldwide communications
Participants	Banks, brokers, and multinational companies. Public speculation not encouraged	Open to anyone who needs hedge facilities or has risk capital with which to speculate
Commissions	Set by spread between bank's buy and sell price. Not easily determined by the customer	Published small brokerage fee and negotiated rates on block trades
Margin/collateral account	None as such, but compensating bank balances are required	Initial margin that is marked to market daily
Clearing operation and counterparty risk	Handling contingent on individual banks and brokers with significant counterparty risk. No separate clearinghouse function	Handled by exchange clearinghouse Daily settlements to the market Counterparty risk quasi-eliminated
Frequency of delivery	More than 90% settled by actual delivery	Less than 1% settled by actual delivery

futures contract in the currency in which you hold an asset (long) position or buying a currency futures contract in a currency in which you hold a liability (short) position. For example, an importer owes its Japanese suppliers ¥1 billion in 90 days with a due date of April 1, 2013; hedging or locking in the value of its ¥ short/liability position requires the purchase of ¥1 billion/¥12,500,000 = 80 contracts for the nearest month (which would be March 2013).

Arbitrageurs are exploiting profit opportunities between *traded* futures and *synthetic* futures engineered as a combination of asset/liability positions in the domestic and foreign currency money markets (as explained in Chapter 6 in the case of forwards).

Pricing currency futures

We have argued how similar currency futures are to currency forwards. The question then is: can we apply the valuation model of currency forwards to currency futures? In other words, is *interest rate parity* the appropriate valuation model for currency futures? For all practical purposes it is if we keep in mind a subtle difference: Since futures are marked to market on a daily basis over their lives, interest costs on additional margin when the contract is *out-of-the-money* or interest savings on reduced margin due to exchange gain when the contract is *in-the-money* should be taken into account. Needless to say, it is difficult to forecast precisely future interest rates to properly take into account the slight difference in cash payoffs associated with futures but not with forwards. Practically speaking, these are minor differences that can be safely assumed away — in other words, interest rate parity applies to currency futures.

CURRENCY OPTIONS

Forwards and futures afford hedgers protection against adverse exchange rate movements, but they have one common major disadvantage: They prevent users from partaking in any windfall profits in the case of favorable exchange rate movements. This led commercial banks to offer the first customized over-the-counter currency options in the early 1970s, which combined downside protection with upside potential. Exchange-traded standardized option contracts appeared relatively late in 1982 on the Philadelphia Stock Exchange, where they now trade on the United Currency Options Market. As we will discover in this section, currency options singlehandedly revolutionized the praxis of foreign exchange *financial engineering*. This section first reviews basic definitions before considering options trading strategies; the equilibrium (parity)

INTERNATIONAL CORPORATE FINANCE IN PRACTICE 8.2

Enterprise Oil's $26 Million for a Dollar Call Option

UK company Enterprise Oil in 1989 paid more than $26 million for a 90-day currency option to protect against exchange rate fluctuations on $1.03 billion of the $1.45 billion that it had agreed to pay for the oil exploration and production assets of US-based transportation company Texas Eastern. This is one of the largest currency options ever undertaken by any company. While acquisition financings have boosted the size of individual option contracts over recent years, the average size of most options bought by corporates is still between $100 million and $200 million.

The option — a dollar call option — gave Enterprise Oil the right to buy dollars at a dollar/sterling rate of $1.70. The dollar/sterling exchange rate was $1.73 when Enterprise Oil bought the option on March 1. "We are bearish on sterling", said group treasurer, Justin Welby. "And we did a very careful calculation between the price of the option premium (which is cheaper the further out-of-the-money) and how much we could afford the dollar to strengthen. We decided that this was the best mix between the amount of protection we could forgo and the amount of up-front cash we were prepared to pay out for the option". Welby believed that the additional cost would be £4.5 million ($7.7 million) for every cent the dollar strengthened against sterling.

Postscript: On April 17, 1989, the pound stood at $1.7050, which made the call option just about needless at the modest cost of $26 million for Enterprise Oil.

Source: Adapted from *Corporate Finance*, April 1989.

relationship between the option and forward markets as well as the pricing of currency options are discussed last.

Currency option contracts

A currency option gives the buyer the right (without the obligation) to buy (*call* contract) or to sell (*put* contract) a specified amount of foreign currency at an agreed price (*strike* or *exercise* price) for exercise on (*European* option) or on or before (*American* option) the expiration date.[9] For such a right, the option buyer/holder pays to the option seller/writer a cash premium at the inception of the contract.

A European option whose exercise price is the forward rate is said to be *at-the-money*[10]; if it is profitable to exercise the option immediately (disregarding the cash premium), the option is said to be *in-the-money*. Conversely, if it is not profitable to exercise the option immediately, the option is said to be *out-of-the-money*. As expected, in-the-money options command a higher premium than out-of-the-money options. When held to maturity, the option will be exercised if it expires in-the-money and abandoned when it expires out-of-the-money. (See International Corporate Finance in Practice 8.2.)

Option markets

Over-the-counter currency options can be negotiated with commercial banks with features (face value, strike price, and maturity date) tailor-made to the special needs of the buyer, who is responsible for evaluating the counterparty risk (that is, the likelihood that the option writer — in this case the commercial bank — will deliver if the option is exercised at maturity).

Alternatively, standardized currency options can be traded on organized exchanges in much the same way as futures contracts. Such option contracts are standardized instruments in terms of both amount and maturity, with the underlying product being either the currency itself, as in the case of the Philadelphia Stock Exchange (PHLX), or a currency futures contract as traded on the Chicago Mercantile Exchange (CME). Standardized option contracts are available from organized exchanges and are practically devoid of counterparty risk, since

9 The terminology of American or European option does not refer to the location where the option contract is traded. Both American and European option contracts are traded on both continents as well as in the Far East. (so what is the origin?)

10 American options' exercise prices are generally compared to the spot rate (rather than forward), with similar definitions of at-, in-, or out-of-the-money applicable since they can be exercised immediately.

Exhibit 8.4. Quotations for €10,000 option contracts from CME.

Strike Price	Maturity	Calls	Puts	Spot 1.1607
1.1550	Sep. 2018	0.82	0.24	—
1.1600	Sep. 2018	0.60	0.40	—
1.1650	Sep. 2018	0.32	0.64	—
1.1700	Sep. 2018	0.16	1.12	—
1.1550	Dec. 2018	2.97	—	—
1.1600	Dec. 2018	2.54	1.50	—
1.1650	Dec. 2018	2.11	1.43	—
1.1700	Dec. 2018	1.96	1.69	—

the appropriately capitalized exchange stands as the contract's guarantor of last resort. The option buyer, however, is limited to a relatively small set of ready-made products directly available off the shelf.

Q: What is the nature of credit risk to which the buyer and the writer of currency options are exposed?

A: The buyer of a currency option faces the risk that when exercising the option the counterparty may fail to fulfill its obligation — counterparty risk is thus similar to the risk faced by the buyer of a futures contract. The seller of a currency option is not facing any counterparty risk since he or she receives the option premium up front.

Premium/strike price trade-offs

Of practical interest is the trade-off between strike price and premium: The further in-the-money the strike price, the more expensive (i.e., the higher premium) the option becomes, and conversely. Consider, for example, the quotes for June and September call and put options shown in Exhibit 8.4. The left-hand column shows the different strike prices ranging from \$1.1550/€ to \$1.1700/€. The second column indicates the maturity of the contracts — September 2018 and December 2018. Next — in the third column — are the call premiums for September and December delivery in ¢/€ shown to decline from 0.82¢ to 0.16¢ (September contract) and from 2.97¢ to 1.96¢ (December contract) as the strike price increases from 1.1550 to 1.1700 (for both September and December contracts). The fourth and last column indicates that the put option premiums increase as the strike prices increase.

Q: Referring to Exhibit 8.4, why is the premium increasing for increasing strike prices in the case of € put options but decreasing in the case of call options?

A: A put option gives the buyer/holder the right to sell euros at a given strike price. The higher the price at which the option holder can indeed sell the euros, the more valuable it becomes and therefore the more expensive it is to buy.

RISK PROFILE OF CURRENCY OPTIONS

This section considers the value at expiration of European call and put options from the perspective of the buyer as well as the writer before exploring in the next section some often-used option strategies.

Buyer of a call option

Consider the purchase on June 1, 2013, of a 90-day call option on pound sterling with strike price $E(90) =$ \$1.57 per pound and premium $p(0) =$ \$0.05. The holder of such a sterling call contract has the option to purchase sterling on August 31 at the strike price of \$1.57 if it is advantageous to do so. Specifically, if the spot exchange rate $S(90)$ turns out to be less than 1.57 on August 31, the option holder would either purchase sterling on the spot market if he or she were indeed in need of sterling or else simply abandon the call option with a total loss no larger than the future value of the premium paid 90 days earlier; in Exhibit 8.5, see the horizontal portion to the left of 1.57 on line (1), which sketches the terminal value of the call option as a function of $S(90)$. For an exchange rate in excess of 1.57, the option holder will exercise the call option so as to profit from the difference between the spot

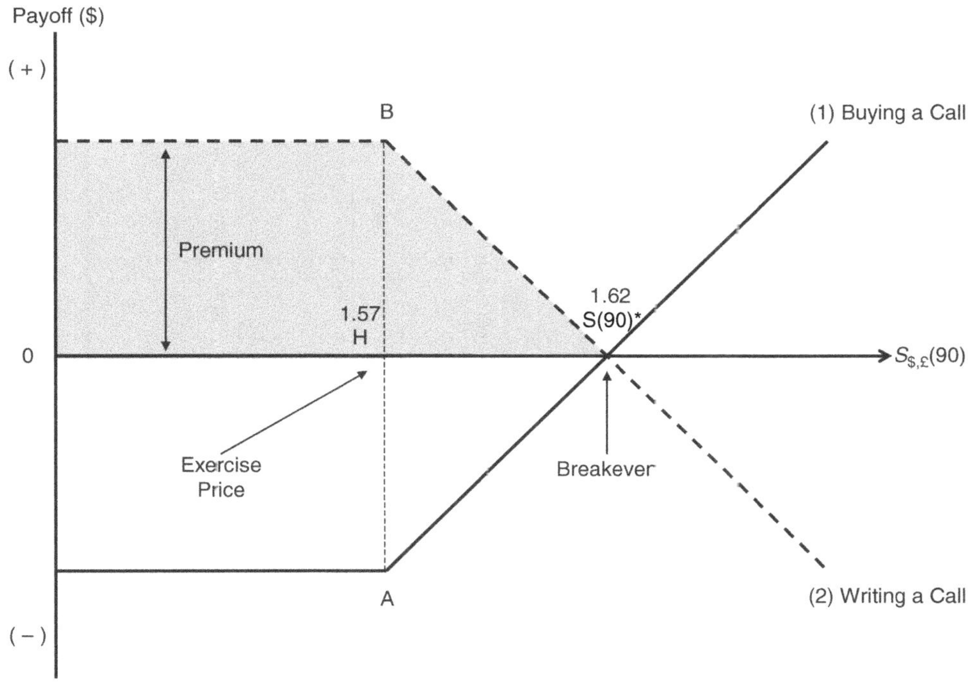

Exhibit 8.5. Call option.

rate and the strike price. Thus the payoff to the option holder can be summarized as follows:

For $S(90) \le E(90)$: Payoff $= -p(0) \times (1 + i_{US})$

For $S(90) > E(90)$:

Payoff $= S(90) - E(90) - p(0) \times (1+i_{US})$

where $i_{US} = 0.06/4$ is the quarterly opportunity cost to the option buyer of tying up the cash premium for the life of the option. The intersection point $S(90)^*$ at which the option holder is starting to make a profit in excess of the up-front premium (breakeven) can be readily found to be:

$$S(90)^* = E(90) + p(0) \times (1 + i_{US})$$

$$S(90)^* = 1.57 + 0.05 \times \left(1 + \frac{0.06}{4}\right) = 1.62 \quad (8.1a)$$

In Exhibit 8.5, the reader will note that the option premium (shown as the distance of the horizontal portion of the call option profile to the horizontal axis along the abscissa, AH or BH) is equal to the distance HS between the exercise price and the break-even rate (disregarding interest costs).

Writer of a call option

The call option writer's payoff — the broken line (2) in Exhibit 8.5 — is symmetrical to the option buyer's payoff since, combined, they have a zero-sum gain (disregarding transaction costs). In other words, what the option holder loses, the option writer keeps — option premium for $S(90) \le 1.57$ shown as AH = BH in Exhibit 8.5 — and what the option holder gains, the option writer loses — for $S(90) > 1.57$.[11] The reader will also note that the option writer may face potentially large losses when the option is exercised, whereas the writer's gains are limited to the option premium.

Put options

Consider the purchase on September 1, 2013, of a 90-day European sterling put option maturing on November 30, 2013, with strike price $E(90) = \$1.48$ and premium $p(0) = \$0.02$. The holder of such a sterling contract has the option (the right without the obligation) of selling sterling on November 30 at the strike price of 1.48 if the spot rate $S(90)$ on November 30 makes it advantageous to do so. Referring to line (1) in Exhibit 8.6, the reader can readily see that only if the spot rate at the expiration of the option is below 1.48 will the option holder actually *put/sell* the sterling, which can be acquired on the spot market at a lower price. For example, if at expiration the spot price had fallen to 1.40, the

11 Indeed, the "graphical" sum of line (1) and line (2) is the horizontal axis (i.e., it is a zero-sum game).

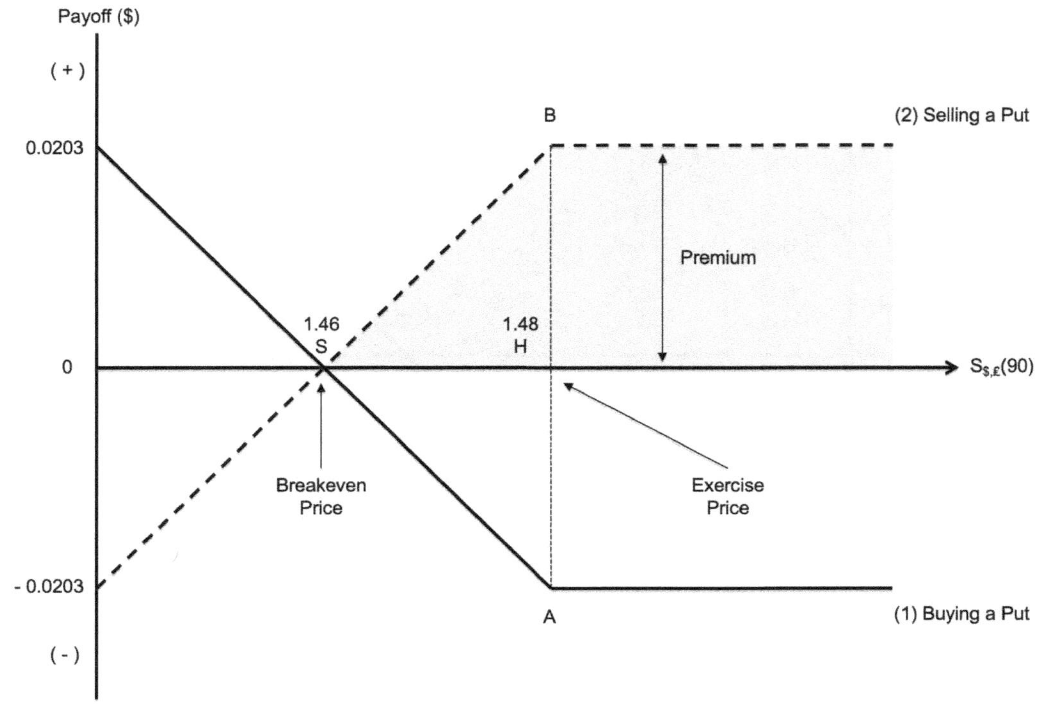

Exhibit 8.6. Put option.

option buyer would buy spot pounds at \$1.40 and put/sell them at \$1.48 for a profit of \$1.48 – \$1.40 – \$0.02 = \$0.06 or a profit of 6 cents per pound. Above 1.48, the option holder is better off abandoning the option, which expires worthless with the resulting loss limited to the premium.

Meanwhile, the writer of the put option stands to earn a maximum profit of 2 cents per pound if the option expires unexercised (spot rate at maturity stands above 1.48), whereas the writer's exposure to losses is virtually unlimited; see line (2) in Exhibit 8.6. It is also equal (but of opposite sign) to the option buyer's gain. The break-even exchange rate $S(90)^*$ can be readily found as:

$$S(90)^* = E(90) - p(0) \times (1 + i_{US})$$

$$S(90)^* = 1.48 - 0.02 \times \left(1 + \frac{0.06}{4}\right) \cong 1.46 \qquad (8.1b)$$

OPTION STRATEGIES

There are many options combinations or strategies, ranging from the simple (e.g., writing covered options) to more complex ones known under such colorful names as *straddle*, *strangle*, *butterfly*, *condor*, and *bull price spread*, to name a few. After reviewing the mechanics of simple option combinations such as *writing covered options*, this section considers the *straddle* strategy which depends on the volatility rather than on the absolute level of the exchange rate.

Option combinations

Currency options are often bundled with long/asset or short/liability positions in the underlying currency — presumably to construct a hedge. These simple combinations are the basis for financial engineering and are helpful foundations for more complex financial architectures. Generally, combining an option that is an asymmetrical position with a matching amount of forwards (a symmetrical position) amounts to creating another asymmetrical position but does not eliminate risk. All it does is change the risk profile of the original option to create that of another option. For example, writing a call option and combining it with buying the underlying currency forward amounts to writing a put option, as we explain further next.

Writing covered call options

This option strategy combines the writing of a call option on sterling (see line 1) with the buying of a sterling forward contract. Exhibit 8.7 sketches the payoff of both positions at maturity as a function of

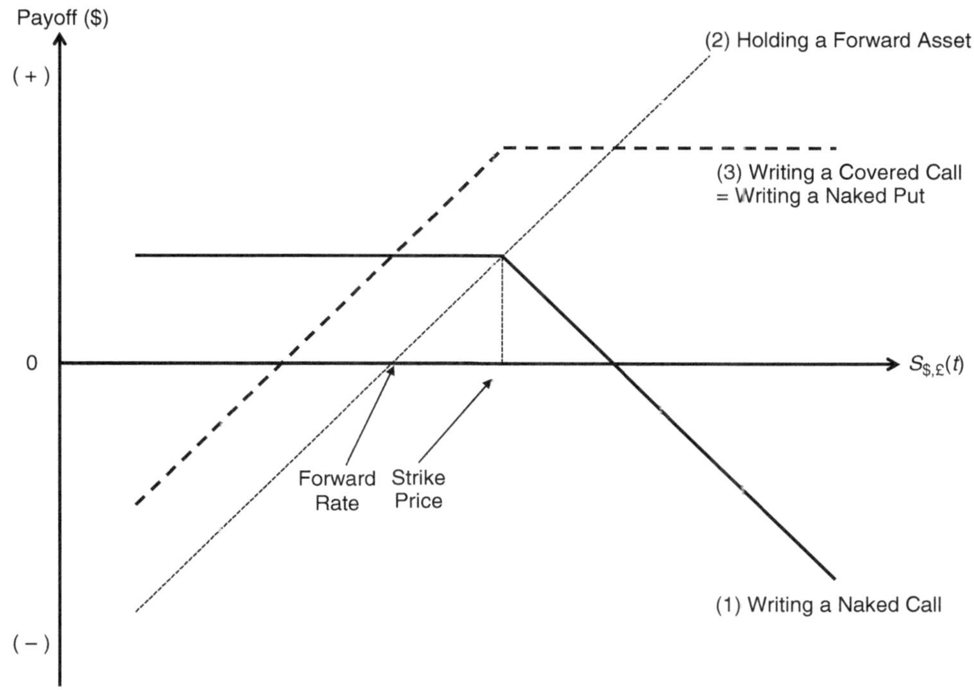

Exhibit 8.7. Writing a covered call option.

the then-prevailing spot dollar price of pound sterling $S(90)$. The sterling long position — line (2) — is in-the-money if $S(90)$ exceeds the forward purchase price $F(90)$. The writer of a *naked* (uncovered) call option on sterling speculates by accepting an up-front payment (premium) in exchange for a possibly large loss if sterling were to appreciate against the dollar. Conversely, should the pound depreciate — $S(90)$ is below the strike price — the option writer keeps the option premium; see line (1) in Exhibit 8.7.

It would stand to reason that the call option writer who holds a forward asset position in sterling — line (2) — has effectively covered the selling of a naked call option — hence the reference to writing a covered call option. In fact, this is misleading, since a *covered call option* is nothing more than writing a *naked put* option on sterling, as illustrated in Exhibit 8.7 by line (3), which is constructed as the graphical sum of lines (1) and (2). Indeed, writing a naked put option is no less risky than writing a naked call option. (Because the risk profile has simply been swapped.)

Straddle

Buying a *straddle* is the simultaneous purchase of one put and one call option at the same exercise price and maturity. This strategy is especially attractive when one anticipates high exchange rate volatility but is hard-pressed to forecast the direction of the future spot exchange rate. Let's consider the case of Allied-Lyons, the British manufacturer of teabags, which experimented with this option strategy at the outset of the Gulf War in 1991 and lost big (see International Corporate Finance in Practice 8.3). Allied-Lyons actually sold straddles on the premise that exchange rate volatility was going to subside as soon as the Allies launched their air offensive against Iraq and would stabilize at a low rate. Consider the market situation faced by Allied-Lyons on January 15, 1991, and how it constructed the writing/sale of a straddle.

Written:	1/15/91		
Assume:	90-day maturity		
Call strike:	$1.95/£	Put strike:	$1.95/£
Call premium:	$0.027/£	Put premium:	$0.0313/£

Let's now sketch with precision the building blocks of a straddle strategy — that is, the writing of call and put options on the pound at the same strike price of $1.95 = £1.

INTERNATIONAL CORPORATE FINANCE IN PRACTICE 8.3

Allied-Lyons's Deadly Game

Allied-Lyons — better known for its teabags than for its forays into the currency market — announced a stunning $269 million FX loss (approximately 20% of its projected profits for 1991). Facing a sluggish economy, its treasury had elaborated a sophisticated scheme that gambled not so much on the absolute level of the dollar/sterling exchange rate as on its volatility. This gamble was achieved through combinations of currency options known as straddles and strangles that, in this particular case, would have produced profits had the exchange rate turned out to be less volatile than the option premium implied.

This ingenious scheme was elaborated at the beginning of the Gulf War when the relatively high price of option premiums (due to heavy buying from hedgers) convinced Allied-Lyons that it was propitious to place an attractive short-term bet that volatilities would decrease as soon as hostilities started. Thus Allied-Lyons wrote deep-in-the-money options in straddle/strangle combinations, thereby netting hefty cash premiums. However, when the Coalition launched their air offensive, the initial uncertainty as to the outcome did not reduce the option volatility — at least not soon enough for Allied-Lyons to see its speculation gambit succeed. Indeed, it took another month for the ground offensive to appease the forex market, by which time it was already too late for Allied-Lyons, which had been forced by its bankers to liquidate its options position at a great loss.

Source: Adapted from Jacque, Laurent L. 2010. *Global Derivative Debacles: From Theory to Malpractice*. Singapore and London: World Scientific, pp. 105–124.

Writing of a call

For a cash premium of $0.027 collected on January 15, 1991, Allied-Lyons would commit to delivering one pound sterling at the strike price of $1.95 = £1. If the spot price were to remain below the strike price of 1.95, the option would not be exercised and Allied-Lyons would keep the option premium. Should the pound appreciate above the strike price of $1.95, Allied-Lyons would have to deliver pounds at the cost of $1.95. These pounds would have to be purchased at a higher spot rate. Thus, the more expensive the pound would get, the higher the losses incurred by Allied-Lyons.

Line (1) in Exhibit 8.8 sketches the payoff profile from the writing of a call option. Allied-Lyons makes a profit equal to the premium ($0.027) at any spot rate up to the strike price of $1.95, since the call option would not be exercised. Beyond $1.95 the profit line is downward sloping. Between $1.95 and $1.977 (strike price + premium) the premium is at least partially covering losses due to the adverse movement of the exchange rate. At $1.977 the loss due to spot price movement is exactly equal to the premium. This is the break-even point. Beyond $1.977 Allied-Lyons incurs an ever-increasing loss.

Writing of a put

For a cash premium of $0.0313 Allied-Lyons would commit to buying pounds at the strike price of $1.95. Line (2) in Exhibit 8.8 sketches the payoff profile from writing a put. Up to the strike price of $1.95, the buyer would exercise the option to sell pounds at $1.95. Allied-Lyons would incur a cash-flow loss in this range due to the fact that it must buy pounds at $1.95 and can resell them only at the lower spot price. Losses will be incurred up until $1.9187 (strike price – premium) where the loss due to spot rate movements equals the profit from the premium. Beyond the strike price of $1.95 the option will not be exercised and Allied-Lyons retains the full premium of $.0313 per pound transacted.

Plotting the straddle

Writing the straddle is the bundling of a put and a call shown in Exhibit 8.8 as the graphical sum[12] [line (3)] of a call [line (1)] and a put [line (2)]. Note the pyramid top (heavy line) of a straddle is

12 Referring to Exhibit 8.8, the graphical sum of lines (1) and (2) shows for each exchange rate (horizontal axis) the algebraic sum of gains/losses for lines (1) and (2) on the vertical axis.

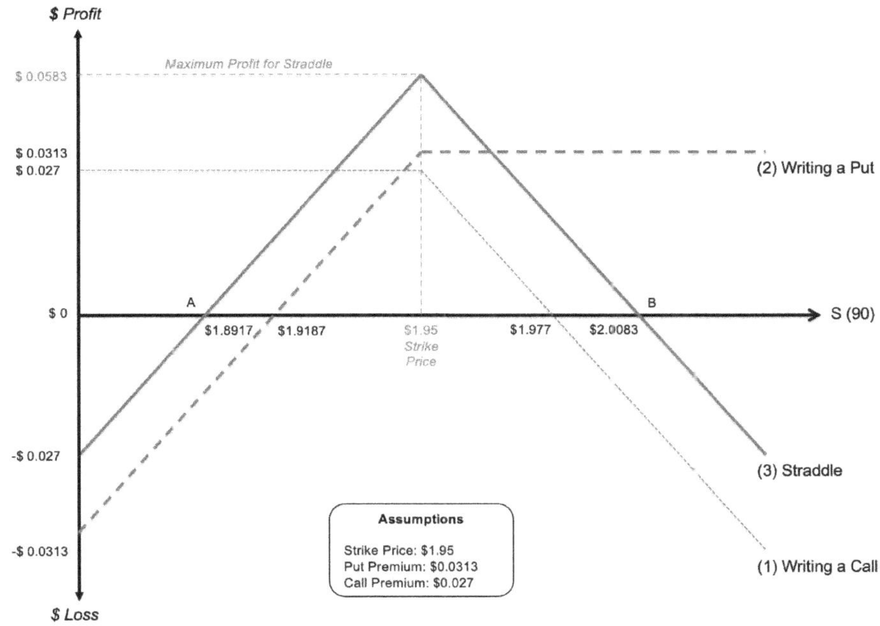

Exhibit 8.8. Writing a straddle.

where Allied-Lyons nets a profit. Of interest are the break-even exchange rates A and B within which Allied-Lyons makes money because of very low volatility and outside of which it incurs deepening losses because of increased volatility.

To figure out the spot rates at which the straddle will cross the x-axis (the break-even points), we simply subtract the sum of the call and put premiums from the strike price (for A) and add the sum of the call and put premiums to the strike price (for B).

$$\text{Break-even A}: S(90)^{\text{A}} = \text{Strike price}$$
$$- (\text{Call premium} + \text{Put premium})$$
$$S(90)^{\text{A}} = 1.95 - (0.027 + 0.0313) = 1.8917$$
$$\text{Break-even B}: S(90)^{\text{B}} = \text{Strike price}$$
$$- (\text{Call premium} + \text{Put premium})$$
$$S(90)^{\text{B}} = 1.95 - (0.027 + 0.0313) = 2.0083$$

Therefore, when the spot rate is below $1.8917 or above $2.0083, Allied-Lyons will lose money, and the loss is literally unlimited if the spot exchange rate falls far below $1.8917 or appreciates well above $2.0083. Conversely, within the same range, when volatility is low, Allied-Lyons stands to gain. Its maximum profit comes when the spot rate is exactly equal to the strike price of $1.95. At that point neither option will be exercised. Therefore Allied-Lyons would suffer no loss due to currency movement, and it retains the full amount of both premiums — equal to $0.0583 per £ transacted.

In this case, Allied-Lyons decided to write straddles because it believed that once hostilities began in the Persian Gulf, the current volatility of the US dollar *vis-à-vis* the British pound would subside. If this were the case, Allied-Lyons would keep most of the substantial premiums since they were writing deep-in-the-money options. This meant that it would have been favorable for the option buyer to exercise those options immediately. However, the buyers could not do so because these were European options, which could be exercised only on the expiration date. The risk for Allied-Lyons was that if volatility remained high, it would be exposed to unlimited losses, and this is indeed what happened. The pound was high when the options were written, but most importantly, the high volatility due to the uncertain outcome of the Persian Gulf War made the options expensive.[13] By writing call and put options, Allied-Lyons was able to collect rich premiums. Clearly, Allied-Lyons thought that the expected decrease in volatility would result in cheaper option premiums, which would allow Allied-Lyons to buy back the same options it had sold at a high price much more cheaply, thereby locking in profits once and for all.

13 One of the key determinants of an option value/premium is the volatility of the underlying currency. See next section for a discussion of option valuation.

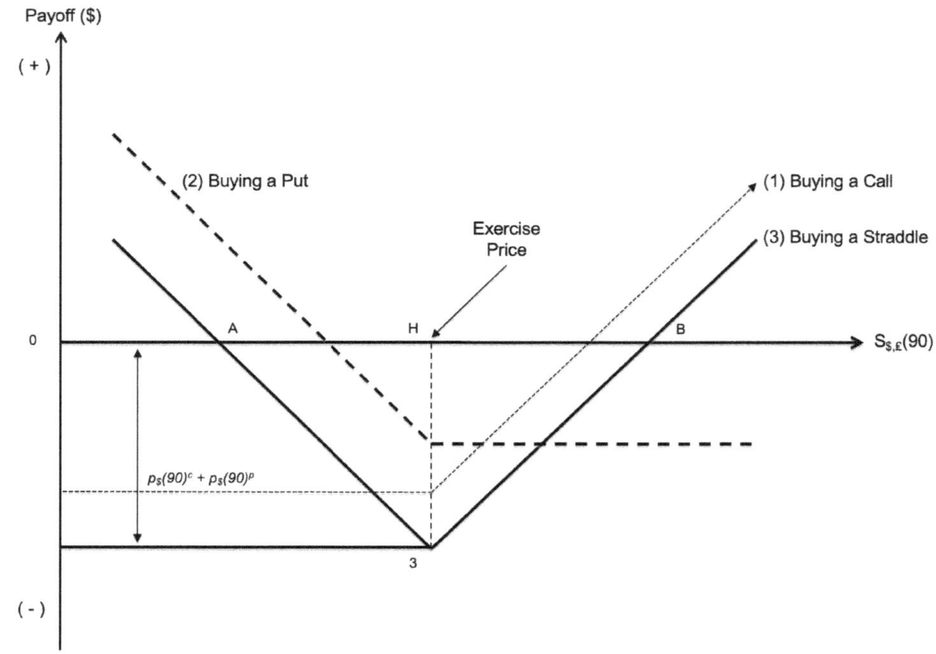

Exhibit 8.9. Buying a straddle.

Buying options straddles

Let's now consider the symmetrical strategy of buying rather than selling an option straddle. Buying an option straddle is defined as the simultaneous purchase of put and call options of the same strike price and maturity. This strategy is especially attractive when one anticipates high exchange rate volatility but is hard-pressed to forecast the direction of the future spot exchange rate. Most important and unlike selling an option straddle, this is a low-risk strategy since options are bought, not sold/written. Exhibit 8.9 superimposes the purchase of a call option (1) on the purchase of a put option (2) at the same strike price $E(90)$ to create a straddle; see line (3), which appears as a V in the graph of the graphical sum of lines (1) and (2). Of interest are the break-even exchange rates (labeled A and B in Exhibit 8.9), which are symmetrical *vis-à-vis* the exercise price, with

$$S(90)^A = E(90) - [p(0)^c + p(0)^p] \quad (8.2a)$$

and

$$S(90)^B = E(90) + [p(0)^c + p(0)^p] \quad (8.2b)$$

where $p(0)^c$ and $p(0)^p$ are the premium paid on the call and put options, respectively.

If the future spot rate $S(90)$ turns out to be very volatile and escapes the AB band, the straddle will be profitable, as shown by the positive portion of line (3) depicted in Exhibit 8.9 as left of A and right of B. Conversely, if the exchange rate were to move within the narrow AB range, the buyer of the straddle may lose as much as the sum ($H\Sigma = AB/2$) of the two options premiums but no more. Inversely, as pointed out earlier, the writer (seller) of a straddle bets on low volatility of the end exchange rate by writing both put and call options with the same exercise price. However, should this bet be wrong, the loss would be potentially very large. The most that the writer would stand to gain is the sum of the two options sold.

PUT-CALL PARITY THEOREM

We now turn to the powerful arbitrage relationship that binds the options market to the forward exchange market. For example, a 90-day forward sale contract can always be replicated by simultaneously selling a 90-day call and buying a 90-day European put option at the same strike price $E(90)$. The price of such a synthetic forward contract created by combining options can be readily compared to the prevailing rate in the forward market.

This fundamental equivalence between the option and forward markets drives the constant arbitrage activity between the two markets and is known as the *put-call forward exchange parity*. To understand this arbitrage relationship, consider how a 90-day forward yen sale/dollar purchase contract can always be replicated by simultaneously buying a 90-day European yen put option and selling a 90-day European yen call option at the same strike price, assumed to be $E(90) = ¥117$ per dollar. By combining the purchase of a yen put option, portrayed as line (1) in Exhibit 8.10A, with the writing of a yen call option — line (2) in Exhibit 8.10A — at the same exercise price $E(90)$, one effectively (or synthetically) sells forward yen at the options' premium-adjusted exercise price — line (3) in Exhibit 8.10A, which is the graphical sum of lines (1) and (2). Indeed, the same amount of yen can be immediately purchased on the forward market at the prevailing market forward rate of $¥120 = \$1$ or $F(90) = 120$; see line (4) in Exhibit 8.10B.

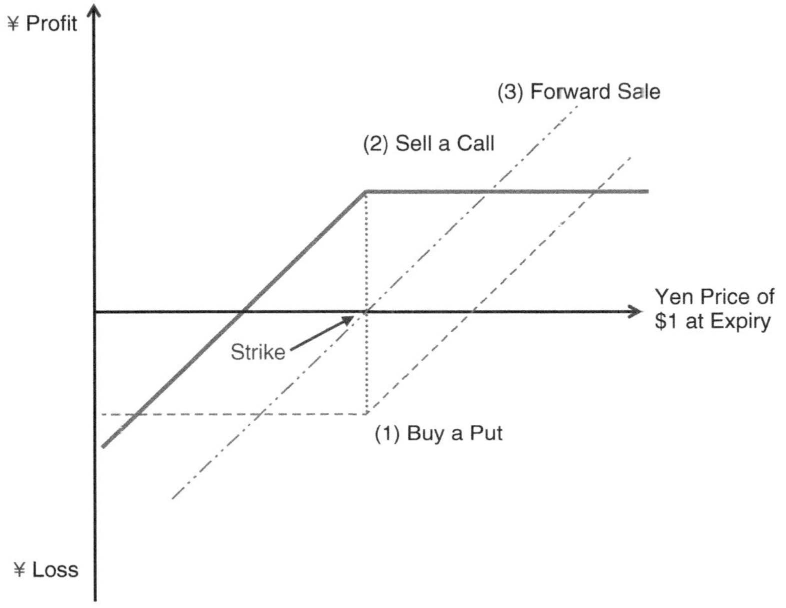

Exhibit 8.10A. Arbitrage through international put-call parity — I.

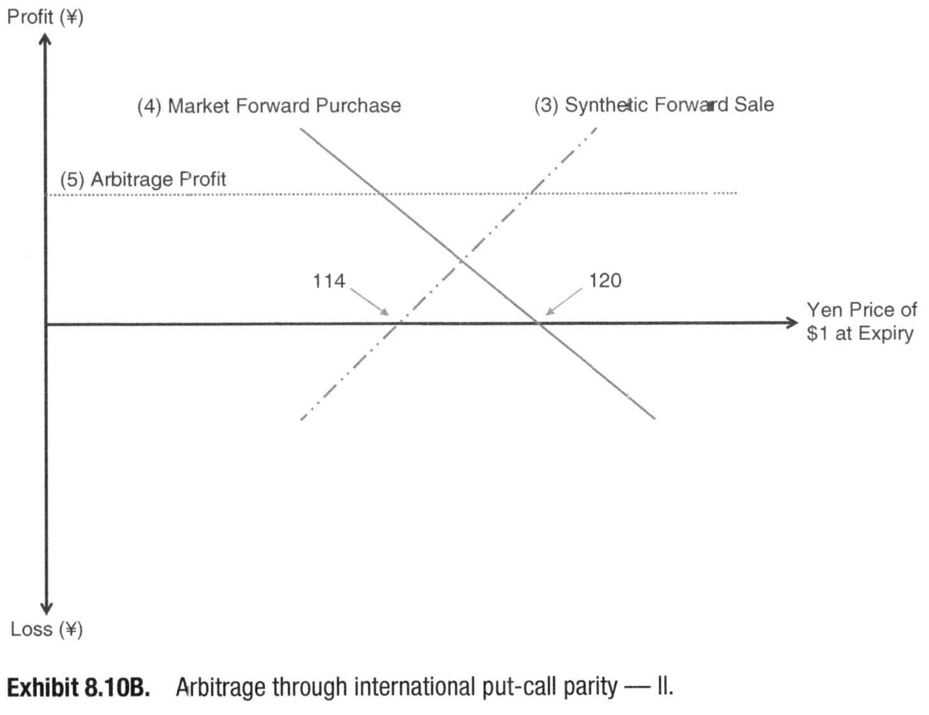

Exhibit 8.10B. Arbitrage through international put-call parity — II.

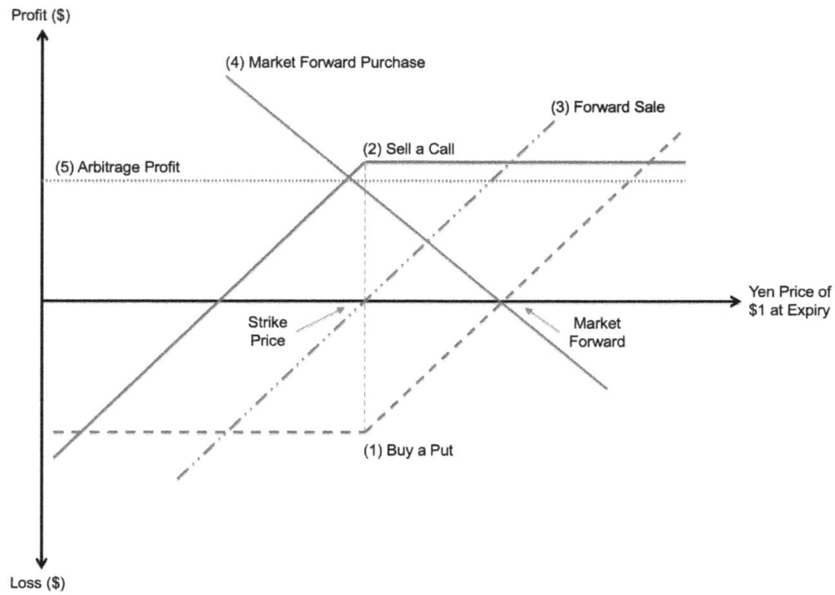

Exhibit 8.10C. Arbitrage through international put-call parity — III.

However, it should be noted that the rate of the synthetic forward contract created by selling a call and buying a put at the same strike price will be slightly different from the strike price.[14] It will reflect the cost due to the difference between the premium $p(0)^{p} = 8$ paid for buying the put and the income generated from writing the call, $p(0)^{c} = 5$. Accounting for the fact that this difference is paid (received) when the option contract is entered into rather than exercised, the total yen cost of selling synthetically yen forward:

$$F(90)^{*} = E(90) - [p(0)^{p} - p(0)^{c}](1 + i_{US}) \\ = 117 - (8 - 5)\ 0.015 = 114 \quad (8.3a)$$

where $i_{US} = \frac{6\%}{4} = 1.5\%$ is the interest rate over the 90-day period (or $\frac{90}{360} = \frac{1}{4}$ year). Thus, by buying forward yen at the cheaper market rate of $F(90) = 120$ and selling them (buying back dollars) at the higher synthetic price $F(90)^{*}$ given by the equation (8.3a) of ¥114 = $1, the arbitrageur is generating a risk-free profit of ¥6,[15] shown as line (5) in Exhibit 8.10C — line (3) plus line (4).

$$F(90) - \{E(90) - [p(0)^{p} - p(0)^{c}]\} \times (1 + i_{US}) \\ = 120 - 114 = 6 > 0 \quad (8.3b)$$

This disequilibrium will set equilibrating forces into motion as arbitrageurs are eagerly selling yen/buying dollar synthetically at the higher rate of ¥114 = $1 while buying it back at the lower price of ¥120 = $1 in the forward market. As a result, the price of the put option is bid up and the price of the call option is bid down, thereby depressing the synthetic forward rate. As arbitrageurs purchase yen at the market forward rate of $F(90)$, its rate will be driven up. Simultaneously, by selling at the higher synthetic forward rate $F(90)^{*}$, arbitrageurs will depress its level, thereby forcing equation (8.3b) toward zero.[16] Arbitrage therefore will relentlessly erase such risk-free profits until the put-call parity prevails. Such discrepancies tend to be small and short-lived, as trading desks equipped with powerful computer software are continuously monitoring rates. But while discrepancies will be arbitraged away in a few seconds and quasi-parity between the option and forward markets will soon prevail, small profits can still be steadily accumulated at almost zero risk.

14 Exhibit 8.10A shows the strike price of both options equal to the synthetic forward rate. This is a simplification due to the fact that the graph assumes both put and call premiums to be identical — which would not necessarily be the case.

15 $1 buys ¥120 but it takes only ¥114 to buy back the initial $1, leaving a profit of ¥6 per $ transacted.

16 The reader is reminded that when the yen price of one dollar increases, the yen is depreciating, and conversely, when it decreases the yen is appreciating. Before arbitrage forces are set into motion, the synthetic forward rate is $F(90)^{*} = 114$: It will steadily depreciate as $F(90)^{*}$ goes up to 115, 116, and so on.

THE VALUATION OF CURRENCY OPTIONS

The value of a European option at expiration is simply the absolute amount by which the option strike price is more beneficial than the spot exchange rate. Pricing an option *before* its expiration is far more complicated. Indeed, option premiums fluctuate very rapidly as a response to price movements of underlying assets and are valued by sophisticated computer models that build on the famous stock option formula first introduced by Fischer Black and Myron Scholes in 1973. Generally, the option premium paid by the buyer to the writer can be broken down into two basic components: *intrinsic* value and *time* value.

Intrinsic value

Most currency options traded today are American options, which — unlike European options — can be exercised before maturity. This simply means that their premiums must be at least equal to the profit that the option holder would earn from immediately exercising the option; it is generally referred to as the option's intrinsic value, defined as the difference between the exercise price of, say, a 90-day option $E(90)$ and the spot exchange rate $S(t)$ with $0 < t < 90$. Whenever the spot price of the underlying currency exceeds the exercise price of a call option, it stands to reason that the call option holder can make a profit by buying the currency at the exercise price and selling it at the prevailing spot price. Conversely, the option writer will seek fair compensation by charging a premium that is at least equal to the difference between the spot price and the exercise price:

$$\text{Intrinsic value of a call option} = S(t) - E(90) \quad (8.4)$$

Time value

Time value is the component of the option premium referring to whatever amount option buyers are willing to pay above and beyond the option's intrinsic value. Since options are in a sense a bet on the volatility of the underlying currency, the longer the time remaining until expiration of the option $(90 - t)$, the more likely it is that at some point the spot price will exceed the exercise price. Conversely, as the option expiration date draws closer, the option's time value will decline very sharply.

In Exhibit 8.11 the value of the premium of a pound sterling call option prior to maturity is shown as a function of the prevailing spot exchange rate. The option's *intrinsic* value, line (1), is zero when the option is out-of-the-money, to the left of the exercise price $E(90)$, or equal to the difference between the spot rate and the exercise price when the option is in-the-money (to the right of the exercise price). In other words, the intrinsic value equals the immediate exercise price of the option. The *time* value is shown as the difference between the total value, line (2), and the intrinsic value, line (1). It demonstrates that the

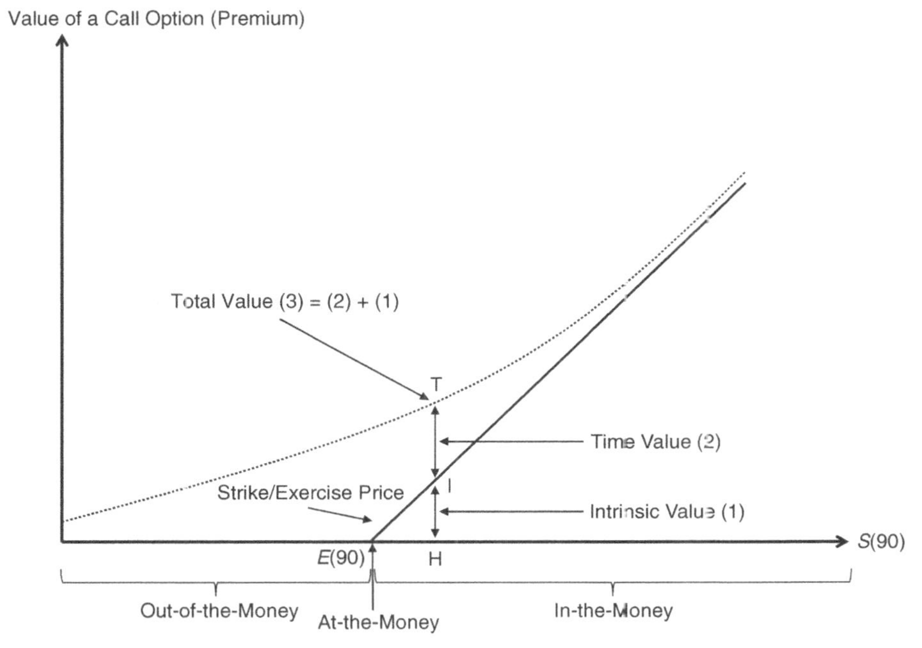

Exhibit 8.11. Value of a pound sterling call option prior to maturity.

value of an option is always larger than its intrinsic value provided that there is time left until expiration ($t < 90$). Clearly, at expiration ($t = 90$), the value of an option is its intrinsic value, since there is no time value left. More specifically:

- For *deep out-of-the-money* call options (left-hand side of Exhibit 8.11), which have a very low probability of being exercised, the intrinsic value is zero and the time value is negligible because the upside potential is trivial.
- For *slightly out-of-the-money* call options (left of center in Exhibit 8.11), the option's intrinsic value remains zero, but the time value becomes very significant as there is now substantial upside potential.
- *At-the-money* (center of Exhibit 8.11), when the market rate is equal to the strike price, the call option's intrinsic value is still zero but its time value is at its maximum because of both the greatest downside protection and upside potential.
- For *slightly in-the-money* call options (right of center on Exhibit 8.11), the value comes from the increasing difference between spot price and strike price (intrinsic value) and considerable time value because of great upside potential and significant downside protection.
- *Deep in-the-money* call options (right-hand side of Exhibit 8.11) have a high likelihood if not near certainty of being exercised, and their prices reflect this. In fact, because such options look like a forward contract — the ultimate sure thing — their value is almost equal to the difference between the spot price and the strike price (intrinsic value), with a negligible time value because of trivial downside protection.

Key parameters in pricing currency options

Black and Scholes showed that option values — that is, put or call option premiums — depend primarily on the following three key parameters:

1. *Volatility.* Put or call option premiums increase with the volatility of the underlying exchange rate on which the option is based. Thus the more volatile the exchange rate, the greater the potential gains that the option buyer may realize and thus the more expensive the premium. Of course, the reader should keep in mind that the option buyer cannot lose more than the option premium (see *vega* coefficient in International Corporate Finance in Practice 8.4).
2. *Time to expiration.* Option premiums are an increasing function of the time to expiration. Consider the case of a call option: It stands to reason that the opportunity for the exchange rate to far exceed the strike price simply increases with how much time is left before the option expires (see *theta* coefficient in International Corporate Finance in Practice 8.4).
3. *Asset price compared to strike price.* The higher the exchange rate relative to the option strike price, the more expensive the put option premium becomes. Conversely, the lower the exchange rate relative to the strike price, the cheaper a call option becomes (see *delta* coefficient in International Corporate Finance in Practice 8.4).

Volatility is the only parameter used in pricing options that is not known in advance; it is crucially important and yet difficult to measure. Volatility may be *historical* (backward-looking), *expected* (forward-looking), or *implied* by current option prices. Clearly for valuation purposes, option traders should use expected/implied volatility, which, very unfortunately, is impossible to measure directly — hence their reliance on historical volatility at least as a starting point for predicting volatility:

- *Historical volatility* is usually approximated by the standard deviation of past exchange rate fluctuations. This approximation, in turn, assumes that exchange rates are well enough behaved to follow a normal probability distribution. One practical problem about which option pricing models offer no guidance is how far back historical data should be used to construct the estimate: 30 days, or 260 days (number of trading days in a year), or 365 days. Furthermore, *historical* (*ex post*) volatility is not necessarily a reliable predictor of *future* (*ex ante*) volatility unless the immediate future will be the same as the recent past.
- *Implied* volatility (derived from the options market price) captures the market consensus. It is determined by equating the "model" price of the currency option (expressed as a function of unknown volatility) to its "market price" and solving for volatility. Because there are different option prices corresponding to different strike prices for puts or calls, implementing this approach would typically lead to different estimates of volatility for the same maturity, which contradicts the assumption of constant volatility (regardless of strike prices) implicit in option valuation models such as Black-Scholes. As a practical matter, as volatility rises, option premiums should increase, and vice versa.

INTERNATIONAL CORPORATE FINANCE IN PRACTICE 8.4

Currency Options Price Sensitivity

To use currency options effectively for hedging or speculation, the trader needs to understand how their value responds to key defining parameters. The *Greeks* are those elasticity coefficients measuring an option premium's sensitivity to such parameters.

Delta. Delta measures the expected change in a currency premium induced by a 1% change in the exchange rate. The higher an option's delta, the more likely it will expire in-the-money. The extent to which the delta changes with a 1% change in the spot exchange rate is called **gamma**. Delta is the first derivative and gamma the second derivative of the value of the option with respect to the underlying spot exchange rate.

Vega. For an option buyer, higher volatility means the possibility for a bigger favorable move in the underlying currency and therefore an increased profit potential. Big unfavorable moves do not matter since at worst the option will expire without having been exercised. **Vega** measures the expected change in an option premium for a 1% change in volatility. The higher an option's vega, the more expensive it becomes with an increase in exchange rate volatility.

Theta. Option values increase with the length of time to maturity. However, as an option's expiration date approaches, its value declines faster and faster and it becomes more sensitive to a small change in time to expiration. **Theta** is calculated as the change in the option premium over the change in time to expiration; it measures the rate of time decay as market participants are interested in option values' sensitivity to the passage of time: It is the expected change in an option premium as the time remaining until maturity decays. As an option's expiration draws closer, its theta increases. All things being equal, currency options lose most of their value in the last couple of weeks before expiring.

Delta and delta hedge

For both the option writer and the buyer, it is important to understand how the value of the option responds to the spot exchange rate. The delta coefficient (or hedge ratio) is defined as the percentage change in the price of the option premium for a 1% change in the value of the exchange rate. This is indicated in Exhibit 8.11 by the slope of the tangent to the premium curve shown as line (2). When the spot exchange rate is at-the-money, the delta coefficient is equal to 0.50. As the spot exchange rate grows larger than the exercise price (i.e., the option becomes in-the-money), its delta increases asymptotically toward 1. Conversely, when the spot exchange rate falls below the exercise price (i.e., the option becomes out-of-the-money), its delta tends asymptotically toward zero.

Making a market in options without losing a lot of money requires the writer of such options to track continuously his/her exposure to losses resulting from exchange rate changes. This is why most option writers routinely "delta hedge" their positions by taking an offsetting position in the spot or forward market. For example, if a trader writes a £10 million call option at-the-money (delta = 0.50), the trader would neutralize the position by owning (or buying forward) £10 million × 0.50 = £5 million, since a 1% change in the underlying spot price triggers only a 0.50% change in the value of the option now compensated by an offsetting change in the long £ position. However, since an option's delta is continuously changing as the underlying spot exchange rate fluctuates, the hedge will have to be rebalanced to reflect a changed delta.

Q: You observed that the premium for buying a £ call option at-the-money \$1.52 = £1 has increased from 3¢ to 4¢ as the spot exchange rate changed from \$1.52/£ to \$1.54/£. What is the sensitivity of the option premium to the spot exchange rate, also known as its delta?

A: The change in premium induced by an incremental 2¢ change in the exchange rate amounts to:

$$\frac{\Delta \text{Premium}}{\Delta \text{Spot rate}} = \frac{4¢ - 3¢}{\$1.54/£ - \$1.52/£} = 0.50$$

INTERNATIONAL CORPORATE FINANCE IN PRACTICE 8.5

Lexicon for Nonstandard Hedging Instruments

The **average spot rate option** (also known as an Asian or path-dependent option) is an option whose payoff is determined by comparing its strike price with the average of the spot rates over its lifetime. The average reference rate is defined by taking spot readings daily, weekly, or monthly. The cost of an average spot rate option is generally lower than that of a standard Black-Scholes option due partly to the dampened volatility of the average rate as time passes.

A **basket option** is an option whose strike price is defined against the total value of a specific basket of currencies (rather than against the price of a single currency). Since the prices of the different currencies making up the basket are generally less than perfectly correlated, the value of the basket tends to be less volatile than the value of a single component currency. Thus, buying an option on a basket of currencies is cheaper than buying options on each currency individually.

Barrier options specify a trigger price in addition to the regular strike price. When the spot exchange rate hits the trigger price, the option is activated ("knocked in") or terminated ("knocked out"). More specifically:

A **knock-in option** differs from a standard option in that an "in-strike" level must be selected in addition to the regular strike price. The in-strike represents the level at which the option will come into existence if that level is reached or crossed by the spot exchange rate at any time before expiration. The in-strike level is set such that the option is out-of-the-money when it comes into existence. The option does not exist until the in-strike level is hit. As a result, the price of a knock-in option is less than or equal to that of a standard option.

A **knock-out option** differs from a standard option in that an "out-strike" level must be selected in addition to the regular strike price. The out-strike represents the level at which the option will cease to exist if that level is reached or crossed by the spot exchange rate at any time during the life of the option. The out-strike is set such that the option is out-of-the-money when it ceases to exist. The knock-out option performs exactly like a standard option unless the out-strike level is hit. The price of a knock-out option will be less than or equal to that of a standard option.

A **kick-in option** differs from a standard option in that an "in-strike" level must be selected in addition to the regular strike price. A kick-in option is a knock-in option with the in-strike placed in-the-money. The in-strike represents the level at which the option will come into existence if that level is reached or crossed by the spot exchange rate at any time before expiration. The option does not exist until the in-strike level is hit. The price of the kick-in option will be less than or equal to that of a standard option.

A **kick-out option** differs from a standard option in that an "out-strike" level must be selected in addition to the regular strike price. A kick-out option is a knock-out option with the out-strike placed in-the-money. The out-strike represents the level at which the option will cease to exist if that level is reached or crossed by the spot exchange rate at any time during the life of the option. The kick-out option performs exactly like a standard option unless the out-strike level is hit. The price of a kick-out option will be less than or equal to that of a standard option.

DERIVATIVES AND ZERO-PREMIUM OPTIONS

The limitation of the forward contract is that while it gives hedgers 100% protection against an adverse movement in the future exchange rate, it also eliminates any opportunity for gain from a subsequent favorable movement in the exchange rate; such a potential missed gain is generally referred to as an opportunity cost. Currency options, in contrast, allow full participation in this upside potential at a substantial up-front cash-flow cost that discourages many would-be users. Of the many FX derivative products to have appeared recently, two products that allow participation in those potential gains — without incurring the up-front cash expenses — are of particular interest to corporate treasurers: (1) *forward range agreement* and (2) *forward participation agreement*. Both products are based on the simple idea of writing an option whose premium finances the purchase of another option. This creates, when superimposed on the underlying naked exposure, the desired risk profile.

Forward range agreement and currency collars

Like forwards, forward range agreements will lock in a worst-case rate with a floor. Unlike forwards, though, they allow the hedger the opportunity to benefit from an upside market up to a best-case rate; they are also known as cylinder options, or zero-cost tunnels. Assuming an underlying pound sterling asset position $a(90)$, shown as line (4) in Exhibit 8.12, the hedger would structure a pound sterling forward range agreement by:

- *Buying a pound sterling put option* at a strike price of $E(90) = 1.8450$ below the forward rate of $F(90) = 1.8750$ and paying an up-front put premium of $p(0)$. The defensive option is represented by line (1) in Exhibit 8.12.
- *Selling a pound sterling call option* at a strike price of $E(90)^* = 1.9000$ above the forward rate and earning a call premium $p(0)^*$, which finances the put option. The financing option is represented by line (2) in Exhibit 8.12 with line (3) being the graphical sum of line (1) and line (2). (By necessity, such products require European options.)

By entering into such a contract, the user would lock in the worst-case exchange rate with a put option floor at a strike price of $E(90) = 1.8450$, while retaining the opportunity to benefit from a pound sterling appreciation favorable to the underlying sterling asset position up to the ceiling strike price of the call option with strike price of $E(90)^* = 1.9000$. Thus the risks of an open foreign exchange position are limited to the range between the floor and ceiling strike prices. Typically, the hedger would choose the floor rate, which would then dictate the strike price at which the call option would be sold. The resulting risk profile is represented by line (5) in Exhibit 8.12, which is the graphical sum of lines (1) + (2) + (4) = (5). In sum:

- If the actual end of the period exchange rate falls below the floor protection level, the user will exercise the put option and sell sterling at $E(90) = 1.8450$.
- If the actual end-of-the-period exchange rate falls within the protection range bounded by the floor put option and the ceiling call option strike prices, the hedger will benefit from the actual spot exchange rate $S(90)$ and receive $a(90) \times S(90)$ with $1.8450 < S(90) < 1.9000$.

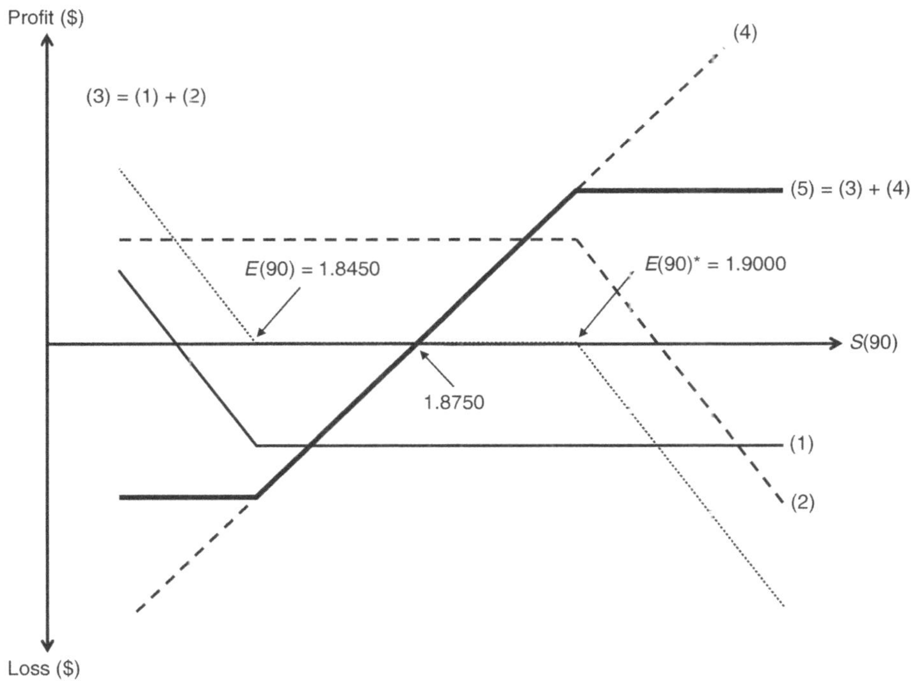

Exhibit 8.12. Forward range agreement.

- If the actual end-of-the-period exchange rate exceeds the ceiling rate set by the call option strike price, the hedger is obligated to sell the sterling proceeds $a(90)$ at the rate of $E(90)^* = 1.9000$ as the call option is exercised by the bank that sold the forward range contract to the hedger in the first place.

In a *currency collar*, the hedger is willing to pay a *reduced* premium (as opposed to a *zero* premium in the case of a forward range agreement) to enjoy a wider range between the floor put option and ceiling call option strike prices and therefore a greater profit potential. This is achieved by writing a defensive call option at a higher strike price, which generates less premium income that is necessary to fully finance the purchase of the put option. The hedger thus contributes the missing difference between the put option premium paid and the call option premium earned by paying an additional "reduced" premium.

Forward participation agreements

This type of protection contract shares certain characteristics with the forward range agreement in that there is no up-front fee and the user has the flexibility to set the downside protection level. Unlike the forward range agreement, however, where the maximum opportunity gain is capped at a prearranged level, the forward participation agreement allows its user to share in the upside potential by receiving a fixed percentage (the participation rate) of any favorable currency move irrespective of magnitude. Specifically, the downside protection level is tied to the participation rate, to be negotiated with the bank — the lower the floor rate, the higher the participation rate, and vice versa.

Consider again the example of holding a sterling asset position maturing in 90 days, $a(90)$ — see line (3) in Exhibit 8.13. The user will purchase a put option, line (1) in Exhibit 8.13, whose premium $p(0)^p$ is more than fully financed by writing a call option, line (2) in Exhibit 8.13, generating a net revenue of $p(0)^c - p(0)^p$. Instead of restituting the difference, $p(0)^c - p(0)^p$, to the user, the bank allows the user instead to partake in the upside potential to the tune of α percent regardless of the extent of pound sterling appreciation above the floor put option strike price.

- If the actual exchange rate falls below the protection level $E(90)$, the user will exercise the put option, line (4) in Exhibit 8.13.
- If the actual exchange rate exceeds the protection level, $S(90) > E(90)$, the user will participate — participation rate α is a function of $E(90)$ — and receive a rate of $E(90) + \alpha[S(90) - E(90)]$, shown as line (4) in Exhibit 8.13.

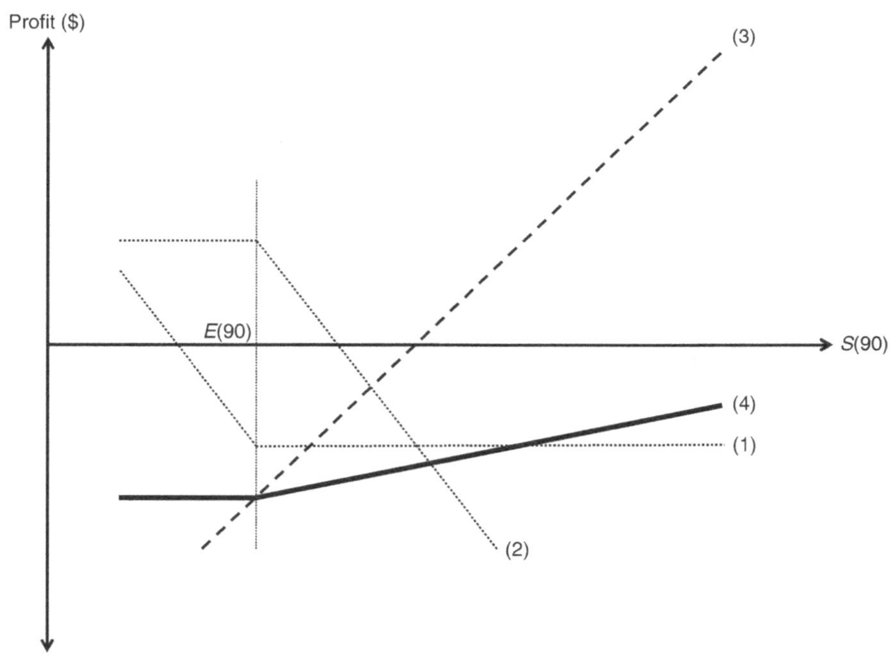

Exhibit 8.13. Payoff profile of a forward participation agreement.

INTERNATIONAL CORPORATE FINANCE IN PRACTICE 8.6

When Hedging with Exotic Options can be Lethal

The South-Korean firm Kumkang Mfg. manufactures ball valves that open and close oil and gas pipelines for global energy companies such as Royal Dutch Shell and Total. In the 2000s it won accolade from the South Korean authorities for its stellar exports performance. And yet, in spite of booming export activities, in September 2008 Kumkang filed for bankruptcy. Its founder and CEO Choi Kyung Shik claimed that his company demise came from exotic options meant to protect its exports competitiveness revenues against the won appreciation but which, instead, turned sour and triggered losses of $15 million (half Kumkang's gross revenue). Choi's involvement with soured currency transactions started in 2007, when he worried that the rising won would make his ball valves too expensive for overseas customers. He bought from Standard Chartered Plc and three other banks a complex option-like derivative known as *knock-in/knock-out*, or KIKO, which combine barrier options with leverage. Choi admitted that he really did not understand the currency contracts he had signed with the banks.

The design of KIKO options started by bundling won call options (bought by Kumkang) and won put options (sold by Kumkang) at the same strike price of KRW 1200 per one US dollar; the premium paid for purchasing the call option was financed by the premium earned by writing the put option so that the hedging product was seemingly costless to Kumkang — at least at inception (assuming the put-call parity holds). Should the won appreciate beyond 1200 the call option generated a cash profit while the put option remain unexercised. The cash-flow gain would allow Kumkang to hold back price increases (otherwise induced by the won appreciation) and remain competitive on export markets. Conversely, if the won depreciated — Choi had been advised by his bankers that this was an unlikely scenario — the call option would be worthless (unexercised) but the put option would be exercised and Kumkang would incur a loss. But gearing complicates the architecture of KIKOs as the amount of puts sold is twice the amount of call purchased or — in other words — losses arising from puts being exercised would be twice as large as profit earned if calls are in the money and exercised. Last but not least, is the role of barrier rates that caused the gains to be knocked out and determine when the losses begin to be knocked in. The knock out rate was set at KRW 990 (a substantial won appreciation against the USD) and once the spot exchange reached it the call option would be terminated — that is exchange gains would no longer accrue. In the opposite direction the put option becomes exercisable at the strike price of KRW 1200 only when the spot exchange rate passes the knock in rate of KWR1300 — that is the losses do not start to accumulate until that second barrier is reached and exceeded.

Choi had purchased a strip of eighteen $500,000 won call options with notional value of $9,000,000 while selling eighteen $1,000,000 won put options with a notional value of $18,000,000. Each strip consisted of European-style currency options with maturities staggered over an eighteen month period. Choi ran into trouble when the won plummeted against the dollar in early 2008, as US investors started repatriating funds from overseas assets amid the sub-prime credit crisis at home. That triggered the "knock-in" provision that forced him to settle the large losses on the put options that he had sold and pushed his firm into bankruptcy.

Had Choi — a small business owner — been played, manipulated and deceived by its bankers? Indeed, as a zero-cost seemingly innocuous hedge product, KIKOs could readily mislead an entrepreneur whose expertise and business savvy does not necessarily lie in the dark alleys of financial engineering. Or, was Choi not the naïve and gullible entrepreneur he claimed to be but simply a risk taker if not an outright speculator? But Choi was hardly an isolated case and Kumkang misfortunes reached epidemic proportions amongst emerging market exporters during the 2007–2010 period. According to Dodd (2009) an estimated 50,000 firms were affected by the misuse of exotic financial derivatives such as KIKOs with 571 small and mid-sized exporters in Korea and 10% of all Indonesian exporters. Losses amounted to $28 billion in Brazil, $5 billion in Mexico and Poland and $3 billion in Indonesia. Even government-owned firms were engulfed by these losses with Ceylon Petroleum Company in Sri-Lanka incurring a loss of $600 million and China's Citic a loss of $2.4 billion. Should exotic financial derivatives be tightly regulated and their sale to non-financial firms restricted? How can exporters' understand when a hedge is truly a hedge and not a bet? Or is it Caveat Emptor — buyer beware!

Abridged from Randall, Dodd. 2009. "Playing with Fire." *Finance & Development* 46(2).

SUMMARY

1. Futures contracts are forward contracts that are standardized in terms of nominal amounts and delivery dates. As such, they are liquid (there is an active secondary market), which makes it easy to exit from a futures contract at any time before expiration. They are valued according to the interest rate parity theorem.
2. Futures contracts are traded on organized exchanges such as the International Monetary Market (IMM) of the Chicago Mercantile Exchange (CME). The exchange's clearinghouse is thus the counterparty to all futures contracts. Counterparty risk — unlike the case of over-the-counter forwards — is easy to gauge and very low because futures buyers and sellers are required to maintain margin accounts. Furthermore, the exchange will force *marking to market* on a daily basis and — if necessary — will make *margin calls* to avoid defaulting by futures contract holders.
3. Currency options give the right without the obligation to buy (call) or sell (put) a set amount of foreign currency at a predetermined price — the strike price. For the privilege of doing so, the option buyer will pay an up-front cash premium. Currency options are primarily traded in the over-the-counter market, as are currency forwards.
4. The put-call parity binds European put and call options to the forward and the domestic money markets. It is a no-arbitrage relationship between a put option and a call option with the same strike price, forward rate, and domestic interest rates.
5. The option premium paid by the buyer to the writer can be broken down into two basic components: *intrinsic* value and *time* value. The *intrinsic* value refers to the difference between the exercise price of the option and the spot exchange rate. The *time* value component of the option premium refers to whatever amount option buyers are willing to pay above and beyond the option's intrinsic value. Since options are in a sense a bet on the volatility of the underlying currency, the longer the time remaining until expiration of the option, the more likely it is that the spot price at that time will exceed the exercise price.
6. Option strategies such as the *straddle* and the *strangle* allow option traders to speculate not only on the absolute level of exchange rates but also on their changing volatility.
7. Options contracts are used for speculating, but they are especially suited to hedging currency exposures that arise from bidding situations when there is uncertainty as to whether the contract will be signed.

QUESTIONS FOR DISCUSSION

1. What are the key differences between currency forwards and futures contracts?
2. How is counterparty risk mitigated in a currency futures contract? Explain how the daily marking to market of currency futures reduces the risk of trading this derivative.
3. Compare counterparty risk for over-the-counter forward contracts with exchange-traded futures. Why is the secondary market for futures more liquid than it is for forwards?
4. What are the differences between currency put and call options?
5. What is the nature of credit or counterparty risk when trading options?
6. What is the difference between writing and buying a currency option?
7. Compare futures margins with options premiums.
8. Identify the key parameters that determine the value of a currency option.
9. Explain how the put-call parity ties the currency options market to the forward market.
10. What is an option straddle strategy? How does it take advantage of exchange rate volatility?
11. What is meant by the intrinsic value and the time value of an option?

12. What are zero-premium options? Why are they more attractive to risk managers than plain-vanilla options?

PROBLEMS

1. **Reading futures prices (beginner).** Refer to Exhibit 8.2 for futures prices.
   a. What is the December 2018 futures price for Australian dollars and Japanese yen?
   b. What is the cross-rate for December 2018 Japanese yen price of the Australian dollar futures contract?

2. **Going long with Mexican peso futures contract (intermediate).** Soledad McArthur is the chief currency trader at the Magna Carta macro hedge fund. She decides on January 15 to go long by buying Mexican peso (MXN) March and June futures currently trading at US$0.11953 and US$0.11790.
   a. What does it mean to go long with an MXN futures contract? What is Soledad's implied exchange rate scenario?
   b. Assuming that the initial margin is set at 12.5% of the face value of the contract, what is the amount that Soledad has to deposit in the margin account (each contract has a face value of MXN 500,000)?
   c. If Soledad held the March futures to maturity and the spot exchange rate on that day was US$0.11878 = MXN 1, what would be the cash gain/loss incurred by Magna Carta? Assume that the margin account remains constant during the March futures holding period and that Magna Carta's opportunity cost of capital is 10%.
   d. On January 16, the inflation forecast released by Mexican authorities points to an upward acceleration of price movements. March and June MXN futures plummet by 4 and 6%, respectively. Should Soledad expect a margin call from the futures exchange? Explain what it would mean for Magna Carta.

3. **Speculating with futures (intermediate).** A trader for Prometheus Partners — a macro hedge fund — is debating how to structure his bet that the euro-zone will break up in the next six to nine months, resulting in a massive capital flight into refuge currencies such as the Swiss franc. On October 17, 2013, March 2014 futures on the euro and the Swiss franc are available at US$1.3605/€ and US$1.1617/CHF.
   a. Show how Prometheus Partners' trader can structure his speculative bet.
   b. Suppose that on January 17, 2014, Greece exits the euro. March 2014 futures on the euro plunge to $1.2417/€ while the CHF jumps to US$1.2777/CHF. Should our trader close his positions? Show profit/loss, taking into account that Prometheus Partners is required to maintain a 10% margin of contracts' face value and that its opportunity cost of funds is 6.5% per year.

4. **Speculating with currency options (beginner).** A hedge fund manager anticipates a weaker euro over the next 180 days. Both six-month put and call options on the euro are available with strike price at the money of US$1.33 = €1.
   a. Would you recommend the purchase of a put or a call option for speculative purposes?
   b. Under what exchange rate scenario would the purchase of a put currency option result into a cash-flow profit?
   c. Assuming that the option premium is US$0.02 per €, calculate the payoff at expiration of a put option with strike price at US$1.33 = €1 if the exchange rate at maturity stands at US$1.18 = €1.

5. **Speculating with currency options (beginner).** Referring to problem 3, Prometheus Partners is considering currency options as alternative instruments to speculate on the possible demise of the euro. March 2013 European put and call options are available on the euro at a strike price of $1.3700/€ with respective premiums of 2 and 3%.
   a. How could a speculative bet be structured around March 2013 option contracts?
   b. Explain what cash flows are involved and their timing. Show graphically the payoff profile of the option strategy that you recommend.
   c. What are the differences between speculating with futures versus options?

6. **Speculating and hedging with currency options (intermediate).** A trader at Credit Suisse First Boston is speculating on the movement of the Swedish krona (SEK). She is prepared to invest US$10 million in the transaction. The current spot rate between the krona and US$ is SEK 7.610 = US$1, while the 30-day forward rate is SEK 7.150 = US$1.
   A. If the trader at Credit Suisse First Boston believes that the Swedish krona will actually

depreciate in value against the US dollar, so that the spot rate will be SEK 7.950 = US$1 at the end of 30 days, what should she do? For this part of the question, use only the trader's view, the spot price, and the 30-day forward market price. If she is correct, how much profit will she earn from the transaction?

B. If the trader wishes to hedge her position after launching the initial strategy outlined in part A — in other words, protect against the market moving against her — she can buy one of two options, with prices as follows:

- Put option at SEK 7.800 = US$1.
- Call option at SEK 7.500 = US$1.

Prices of either put or call option are assumed to be the same at $US0.0795.

a. Which option should the trader buy today? Explain your reasoning. What will the end game profit be?

b. Draw a generic payoff diagram for the option that the trader should buy. Show the strike price and break-even point. You do not actually need to know the option premium to draw the diagram.

(Prepared by Phil Uhlmann.)

7. **Writing a straddle (advanced).** Assuming that Allied-Lyons was relying on a straddle strategy (refer to International Corporate Finance in Practice 7.3 for background information), explain graphically and numerically under what conditions Allied-Lyons could have generated speculative gains. For illustrative purposes, assume that on January 15, 1991, Allied-Lyons had written sterling calls and puts with identical strike prices of $1.25 = £1 and respective premiums of 2.70 cents and 3.13 cents per pound. Was Allied-Lyons bullish or bearish on the dollar? If the dollar were to rebound to 1.50 by March 1, how and when should Allied-Lyons hedge its otherwise speculative position? How would your answer differ if the straddle used American rather than European options?

8. **Writing a strangle (advanced).** Assuming that Allied-Lyons would write a strangle as a speculative strategy, rather than a straddle as in problem 7, would you consider it to be more or less speculative? Prepare a single graph contrasting the two approaches, assuming that to create a strangle, Allied-Lyons was writing put and call options at strike prices of $1.20 and $1.30 and premiums of 1.16 cents and 1.04 cents, respectively.

9. **Put-call parity (intermediate).** Assuming (1) that you can buy a pound sterling call with strike price of $1.50 for 3 cents, (2) that you can sell a sterling put at the same strike price for 4 cents, (3) that the prevailing forward rate is $1.54, and (4) that the annual risk-free rate in the United States is 6%, show how arbitrageurs can generate a riskless profit. Explain how you would expect the different prices to adjust.

10. **Valuing a September Canadian dollar (CAD) call option (intermediate).** On June 15, the premium on a September CAD put option is US$0.017 per CAD at a strike price of US$1.07. If the quarterly US interest rate is 1.25%, what is the price of a September CAD call option?

11. **Covered put options (intermediate).** Show graphically that writing a covered call option on sterling amounts to writing a naked put option on sterling.

INTERNET EXERCISES

12. **Futures Quotations (intermediate).** Log in to the Chicago Mercantile Exchange www.cmegroup.com and sketch two futures contract prices at the deepest discount to the US dollar from the shortest to the longest maturity. Is the line positively or negatively sloped? Why?

13. **Currency Options.** Log in to the Philadelphia Stock Exchange website www.phlx.com and identify the three most traded currency option contracts.

14. **Implied Volatilities for Currency Options.** Log in to the Federal Reserve Bank of New York website www.ny.frb.org/markets/impliedvolatility.html and identify the three most volatile currencies

15. **Open Interests.** Log in to the Bank of International Settlements website www.bis.org and find the current open interests for interest rate futures and currency options worldwide. Were those statistics markedly different five years ago?

REFERENCES

Briys, Eric, and Michel Crouhy. 1988. "Creating and Pricing Hybrid Foreign Currency Options." *Financial Management* (Winter): 59–65.

Derosa, David F. 1991. *Options on Foreign Exchange*. Chicago: Probus Publishing.

Dodd, Randall 2009. "Playing with Fire." *Finance and Development* 46(2).

Giddy, Ian H. 1983. "Foreign Exchange Options." *Journal of Futures Markets* 3(2): 143–166.

Grabbe, J. Orlin. 1983. "The Pricing of Call and Put Options on Foreign Exchange." *Journal of International Money and Finance* 2(3): 239–253.

Jacque, Laurent L. 2010. *Global Derivative Debacles: From Theory to Malpractice*. Singapore and London: World Scientific.

Marshall, John F., and Kenneth R. Kapner. 1992. *The Swap Market*, 2nd edition. Miami, FL: Kolb Publishing.

Popper, Helen. 1993. "Long-Term Covered Interest Parity: Evidence from Currency Swaps." *Journal of International Money and Finance* 12(4): 439–448.

Smith, Clifford W., Jr, Charles W. Smithson, and D. Sykes Wilford. 1989. "Managing Financial Risk." *Journal of Applied Corporate Finance* 1(4): 27–48.

APPENDIX 8A: PRICING CURRENCY OPTIONS[17]

European currency options can be priced by modifying the Black–Scholes stock option valuation model. Although we do not explain the theoretical derivation of the following option pricing model, the reader should simply recall that the intrinsic value of a call option at expiration time T is the difference between the spot exchange rate and the option exercise price if the option is in-the-money. Before expiration at time $t < T$, the value of the call option $p(t)^c$ is the present value of the option's expected intrinsic value at expiration. Garman and Kohlhagen (1983) proposed a valuation model for a currency call option with exercise price $E(T)$:

$$p(0)^c = [F(T) \times N(d_1) - E(T) \times N(d_2)]e^{-\lambda T} \quad (8.5)$$

where: $d_1 = \frac{\ln\left(F(T)/E(T)+(\sigma^2/2)T\right)}{\sigma\sqrt{T}}$

$$d_2 = d_1 - \sigma\sqrt{T}$$

where $F(T)$ is the forward rate prevailing at t for delivery at T (with $t < T$) and $e^{-\lambda T}$ is the continuous discounting or present value factor. Furthermore, λ is the domestic risk-free interest rate expressed on a continuous compounding basis; σ is the standard deviation of the continuously compounded annual rate of change of the exchange rate (proxy for the volatility of the underlying asset), generally approximated by calculating the standard deviation of $\ln[S(t)/S(t-1)]$ over T observations and multiplying correspondingly by $T^{.5}$; finally, $N(d)$ is the probability that a deviation less than d will occur in a normal distribution with a mean of zero and standard deviation of 1 (given d, this can be readily found from any standard normal probability table).

Using interest rate parity, the forward rate $F(T)$ can be expressed as $S(t)e^{\lambda T}e^{-\lambda^* T}$, where λ^* is the foreign risk-free interest rate. This allows us to restate the European currency option pricing formula (8.6) in terms of spot exchange rate $S(t)$:

$$p(t)^c = e^{-\lambda^* T}[S(t) \times N(d_1)] - e^{-\lambda T}[E(T) \times N(d_2)] \quad (8.6)$$

It should be emphasized that this currency valuation model assumes that changes in the exchange rate follow a lognormal distribution with constant variance, whereas empirical studies indicate that exchange rate changes tend to follow a longer-tailed probability distribution model than does the lognormal distribution.

As hinted in the introduction to this section, financial engineering has shown tremendous ingenuity in the past decade, with far too many exotic options to include in the present chapter. International Corporate Finance in Practice 8.5 offers a lexicon of these exotic options.

To illustrate pricing of European currency options, consider a slightly out-of-the-money call option on EUR with the strike at \$1.2 per EUR as of December 1, 2018. This option matures on December 31, 2019. The market quote on the premium is 2.45 US cents per EUR.

We can understand how the premium is calculated using the equation (8.5). The option pricing formula requires five inputs: strike (E(T)), forward rate (F), market implied volatility (σ), time to maturity (T), and the domestic risk free rate (λ). Maturity date is 395 days from the quotation date,

17 This section on option pricing requires familiarity with the Black–Scholes model and its application to currency options. It is technical and complex and can be skipped without loss of continuity. For further discussion see Derosa (1991).

which makes $T = 395/365 = 1.0822$. The observed EUR-USD spot rate and the forward rate out to December 31, 2019 observed on December 1, 2018 are \$1.1320 and \$1.1731, respectively. Also, implied volatility for the strike and maturity is 7.55%. The annualized domestic risk free rate from today to time T estimated using the overnight index swap rate is at 2.52% as of December 1, 2018.

From these inputs, we can calculate d_1 and d_2:

$$d_1 = \frac{\ln(1.1731/1.2) + .5 \times 0.0755^2 \times 1.0822}{0.0755\sqrt{1.0822}} = -0.2494$$

$$d_2 = -0.2497 - 0.0755 \times \sqrt{1.0822} = -0.3279$$

Consequently, it can be determined that $N(-0.2494) = 0.4015$, and $N(-0.3279) = 0.3715$. Now we have everything we need to calculate the price of the call option.

$$p(t)^c = [1.1731 \times 0.4015 - 1.2 \times 0.3715] \times e^{-0.0252 \times 1.0822} = 0.0245$$

Now, let's examine a put option on EUR instead. With the same strike of 1.2, the put option is slightly in-the-money. Consider that a put option on EUR that matures on December 31, 2019 with the strike at USD 1.2 per EUR is quoted at 5.07 US cents per EUR.

Using d_1 and d_2 calculated above, $N(-d_1)$ and $N(-d_2)$ can be determined as follows:

$$N(-d_1) = N(0.2494) = 0.5985$$

$$N(-d_2) = N(0.3279) = 0.6285$$

Now, the put option price can be calculated by:

$$p(t)^p = [1.2 \times 0.6285 - 1.1731 \times 0.5985] \times e^{-0.0252 \times 1.0822} = 0.0507$$

CASE STUDY 8.1. DAEWOO'S UNORTHODOX FUNDING STRATEGY

Daewoo Corporation, headquartered in Seoul, South Korea, was established in 1967 by an entrepreneur named Woo Choog Kim and soon became one of the largest corporations in all of Korea. Its 1987 unconsolidated annual sales amounted to some US\$5.6 billion, which made Daewoo the number four "chaebol" in Korea. Daewoo was mainly involved in three lines of activities: international trading, domestic and overseas construction, and textile goods manufacturing with 31 domestic and 16 foreign subsidiaries. It was the third largest exporter in terms of volume among South-Korea's seven General Trading Companies, was the number-two "general contractor", and was rapidly diversifying into industrial and consumer durables. As for its major rivals, the only check on Daewoo's explosive growth was its access to capital.

As the financing arm of Daewoo's International Trading division, the main responsibilities of the Foreign Exchange and Trade Finance Department were trade financing, treasury, and management of foreign exchange risk. At a time when the Bank of Korea was attempting to cool off the economy through a tight monetary policy, the Department was under mandate to raise as much money as possible to help solve the Daewoo's perennial capital shortage.

Mr. Y.D. Ahn had become the general manager of the Foreign Exchange and Trade Finance Department in 1985 after receiving his MBA from the Wharton School on a company scholarship. Charged with the task of raising capital for Daewoo, Mr. Ahn, with the help of three part-time dealers, soon turned to creative financing techniques. Indeed, an exciting opportunity presented itself at the end of 1987 when South-Korea's Ministry of Finance allowed the use of currency options by listing them as authorized financial tools in the Foreign Exchange Control Regulations. After a month of research and detailed discussions with a couple of banks, Mr. Ahn and his team concluded that writing "deep-in-the money" currency options could become a very effective method of raising funds.

Writing deep-in-the-money options

In early 1988, Mr. Ahn approached four American banks, Supreme Federal County Bank (SFCB), Trace Queens Bank (TQB), Financiers Guild Bank (FGB), and Fabricators Bremen Bank (FBB), with his new scheme. By the end of January, SFCB, FGB, and FBB had presented Mr. Ahn with their respective terms and conditions for Daewoo to write ¥ put/\$ call option at a strike price of ¥100/US\$1. SFCB was the first to give a letter of intent, and their representatives informed Mr. Ahn that no legal difficulties would arise from trading "deep-in-the-money" options as long as their options were backed by "real demand", — that is, legitimate underlying transactions.

Meanwhile, as options were quickly discovered by the financial community, Mr. Ahn hurriedly approached Mr. I.T. Shan, President of Daewoo Corporation, on February 3, 1988. Although it was relatively easy to explain options to his immediate superior, Managing Director (M/D) T.M. Kang, who was a former central bank official, more detailed explanations were needed for the President and for Mr. M.I. Park, the Vice President (V/P) and Treasurer. In these few briefings outlining the overall structure of the deals along with the associated risks, Mr. Ahn had to evaluate the advantages of the new product on the basis of a conservative 5% annual won-appreciation scenario and an 11.5% internal cost of capital. At that time, the rate of won-appreciation was expected to be more than 10% per annum, and Daewoo's internal rate of interest to be applied in managerial accounting was 14% per annum. On February 12, Mr. Ahn obtained final approval from the President of Daewoo Corporation. Permission to write the options, however, was contingent upon the total position being less than US$200 million and Mr. Ahn maintaining a very conservative approach, i.e., minimizing Daewoo's undue exposure to foreign exchange risk.

As shown in Exhibit A, Daewoo wrote four option contracts, two with FGB and one each with SFCB and FBB. The principal amount of each contract was ¥5 billion, or US$50 million, and the strike price was ¥100/US$. In fact, two deals had already been completed before final approval was received because Mr. Ahn and M/D Kang had decided to seize the opportunity before the market changed significantly. From the four contracts, Daewoo received a total sum of US$35.8 million in premiums, or 27.7 billion won, on ¥ 20 billion to be received in one year in exchange for US$200 million, which indicated that the negotiated premiums compared less than favorably with those quoted on the Philadelphia Exchange Market (Exhibit B). However, Mr. Ahn was in no position to reject a deal simply because of the high price: the "option-loan" market had already turned out to be a buyers'

Exhibit A. Writing options.

Option style: European yen-put/dollar-call
Contract amount: US$50 million (¥5 billion) each
Strike price: 100/US$
(In thousand US$, million won)

					Premiums Received		
					Amount	Amount	
Bank	**Contract**	**Expiry**	**Settlement**	**Date**	**(US$)**	**(won)**	**B/E[a] (¥/US$)**
SFCB	08-Feb-88	08-Feb-89	10-Feb-89	10-Feb-88	8,850	6,888	126.22
FGB	12-Feb-88	10-Feb-89	14-Feb-89	16-Feb-88	9,000	6,960	126.78
FGB	17-Feb-88	15-Feb-89	17-Feb-89	19-Feb-89	9,175	7,064	127.45
FBB	11-Feb-88	14-Feb-89	16-Feb-89	16-Feb-88	8,800	6,805	126.03
Total	...	...	...	...	35,825	27,717	126.62

			US$ LIBOR	
Date	**Yen/US$**	**Yen LIBOR**	**(1 year)**	**Forward Rate**
08-Feb-88	129.25	4.2500	7.1875	125.71
12-Feb-88	129.7	4.1250	7.0625	126.14
17-Feb-88	130.35	4.3125	7.3125	126.71
21-Feb-88	128.85	4.2500	7.1250	125.39

Notes: [a]The break-even (B/E) rates on the settlement dates were calculated based upon very "conservative" assumptions, specifically that the rate of won-appreciation be 5% p.a. and that the financing cost be 11.5% p.a., i.e., the "official rate".
[b]One-year forward exchange rates were calculated using the Interest Rate Parity theorem.
Daewoo wrote yen-put/dollar-call options and sold the yen forward against the dollar.

Exhibit B. Summary of results from the "options-loans".

		Forward Contracts			
Source	**Amount**	**Contract**	**Delivery**	**Rate (¥/US$)**	**Receivables**
SFCB	¥5 billion	17-May-88	10-Feb-89	122.46	$40,828,000
FGB	¥5 billion	25-Oct-88	14-Feb-89	124.66	$40,108,000
FGB	¥5 billion	28-Oct-88	17-Feb-89	125.45	$39,856,000
FGB	¥5 billion	01-Nov-88	16-Feb-89	123.98	$40,328,000
Total	¥20 billion	...	...	124.14	$161,120,000

market, and Mr. Ahn was especially encouraged by the growing expectations of a substantial won-appreciation against the dollar, which according to many forecasts would reach 680 won per dollar by year's end.

To hedge or not to hedge?

Mr. Ahn was also the convener of Daewoo's Foreign Exchange Rate Committee. With M/D Kang as chairman, the Committee met on the second business day of each month and determined the monthly won/dollar exchange rates for the coming 12 months to be used in various business plans of the Corporation. At the February meeting, the Committee revised their year-end rate from 720 won to 650 won per dollar, an appreciation of nearly 22%. Since the "option-loans" were denominated in US dollar, Daewoo would benefit from savings of roughly 18% if the predicted won-appreciation occurred.

The option contracts involved contingent exposures denominated in the Japanese yen, which on maturity, Daewoo could receive in exchange for the US dollar (see Exhibit B). Hedging the exposures would simply involve selling yen forward to match the Japanese yen bought on the option contracts. Still, Mr. Ahn felt that he should not hedge his yen position immediately. Indeed, since the Plaza agreement of September 1985, the US dollar had steadily depreciated against the Japanese yen and the major European currencies. Many people had expected the dollar to continue its depreciation, breaking the ¥120/US$ level in a few months. When the option contracts were written, the dollar rebounded to ¥129/US$ from its record low of just above ¥120/ US$ in early January. Personally, Mr. Ahn strongly believed that the dollar would still come back down below ¥120/US$ and that would be the time at which he should hedge. Because of this and his belief that the Japanese yen was the strongest currency at the time in terms of expected appreciation, he decided to write yen-put/dollar-call options.

Mr. Ahn even thought that the US dollar could fall as low as ¥100/US$ by the time the options matured. This was the second reason why he did not hedge his yen position immediately. If the dollar did fall that low, forward contracts for the purpose of hedging would turn out to be a big loss since the options would be left un-exercised. The last reason for leaving his exposure un-hedged was to guard against the possibility that Korea's Office of Bank Supervision and Examination (OBSE) would recognize the deal for what it was. OBSE was very emphatic about their dislike for any disguised foreign currency loans, and several previous deals had been denounced as such. The "option loans" had a good chance of being found out, and if they were hedged with forwards, there would be no excuse available. However, by leaving them open, Mr. Ahn could disclose them as hedging instruments for different exposures.

After signing the option contracts, Mr. Ahn had his dealers submit to the three banks documents substantiating the evidence of "real" demand. An E/L was submitted to SFCB representing the shipment of US$63 million worth of "Le Mans" passenger cars to be delivered to the Pontiac Division of General Motors. To both FGB and FBB, a license issued by the Korean Exchange Bank for overseas construction works in Africa amounting to US$420 million was submitted. Both the export and construction contracts were denominated in US dollar and were in no way connected to the Japanese yen. Even so, the E/L and the "license for overseas construction works" effectively served to provide proof of real demand for the yen-dollar option contracts. Soon after, SFCB sent notice to Daewoo that their lawyers had approved the E/L as an appropriate document. As there were no stated definitions of the nature of functional currencies or accounting currencies in the Foreign Exchange Control Regulations, Daewoo could claim that the transactions were simply a conversion of receivables denominated in the weak dollar into the stronger yen through the use of option contracts. As it turned out, the OBSE had previously accepted similar claims in past examinations of foreign banks.

After Daewoo successfully completed writing the options with the three banks, the market activity suddenly flared up, with many companies following Daewoo's path by structuring option contracts very similar to the "option-loan" scheme. Indeed Daewoo had engineered an ingenious way of raising financing now … and not to worry about its true cost until much later!

CASE STUDY QUESTIONS

1. What are "deep-in-the money" currency options? Why is writing "deep-in-the-money" currency options tantamount to short-term financing?
2. What are the mechanics for Daewoo of writing "deep-in-the-money" yen put/dollar call options?
3. Under what exchange rate scenario is the "option-loan" interest-free? What is Daewoo's cost of financing?
4. How would you measure the exposure incurred by Daewoo in writing "deep-in-the-money" options?
5. How should Daewoo hedge itself? How would it impact the financing cost?

PART THREE

International Financing

If globalization of financial markets has gone a long way toward eradicating differences in national cost of capital, they have not been entirely erased; this is why global financial markets are often characterized as being mildly segmented rather than fully integrated (Chapter 9). Part 3 outlines funding as a global procurement decision from both equity markets (Chapter 10) and debt markets (Chapter 11). Risk(s) arising from investing in or financing via fixed-income securities can be managed with currency, interest rate, and credit default swaps (Chapter 12). The idiosyncrasies of International Trade Financing are presented in Chapter 13.

The uniqueness of financing strategies and capital markets in two regions of the world that loom especially large on the global economy — namely, East Asia and the Middle East — is addressed in separate chapters: Chapter 26 profiles the idiosyncrasies of Asian finance and banking in the context of Japan, South Korea, and China, and Chapter 27 explores the mysteries of Islamic finance.

CHAPTER 9

The International Financial Sector and the Dynamics of Global Capital Markets

The creditors are a superstitious sect, great observers of set days and times.
— Benjamin Franklin

The growing internationalization of the financial services industry means that firms are confronted with a plethora of funding sources. International financing thus becomes a truly global exercise in procurement whereby firms in need of capital will search widely and exhaustively for competing domestic and foreign funding sources before comparing and ranking them according to their true costs. This chapter starts with a review of the functions performed by the international financial sector before shedding light on the key forces fueling the dynamics of emerging capital markets. Companion chapters will focus on international equity financing (Chapter 10), international debt financing (Chapter 11), international trade financing (Chapter 13), and the special circumstances of Asian finance (Chapter 26) and Islamic finance (Chapter 27).

This chapter argues that the dynamics of emerging markets are largely fueled by *disintermediation*, *securitization*, and, more broadly, *deregulation* of the financial sector. Indeed, the world economy is in the midst of a far-ranging restructuring in which national financial systems and capital markets are the handmaidens of enhanced resource allocation and operational efficiency that translates into a lowering of the cost of capital for all economic agents, be they firms, households, municipalities, or governments.

In this chapter you will gain an understanding of:

- What are functions performed by the financial sector in the overall economy.
- How banks compete with capital markets in channeling savings into productive investments.
- How financial *disintermediation* lowers the cost of capital available to firms and other borrowers.
- How *securitization* lowers the cost of consumer financing.
- How deregulation is eroding *segmentation* barriers and bridging the cost of capital differential across national capital markets.
- What the *emergence* process is for national capital markets and what its drivers are.
- Why the cost of capital differs from one country to the next — the notion that capital markets are to some degree segmented.

FINANCING AS A GLOBAL PROCUREMENT DECISION

At its simplest, firms need cash to finance new investments in property, plant, and equipment; to launch new products; to enter new markets; to acquire competitors or to simply increase their working capital. In most cases the major source of funds is the cash generated from operations net of interest and principal (re)payments on outstanding debt and dividends paid to shareholders. When these *internally* generated funds are insufficient, the firm will turn to *external* sources of funds. Such externally sourced financing can be procured from lenders in the form of *loans* and *leases*.[1] Lenders are *financial*

1 A lease is a contractual agreement between the owner of an asset (lessor) and the user of the asset (lessee) whereby the lessee has the right to use the asset in exchange for periodic tax-deductible payments to the lessor. Thus, leasing is an alternative source of debt capital that allows lessees to use assets such as computers, trucks, or aircraft without owning them. Leasing accounts for a significant portion — possibly as much as half — of all equipment financing.

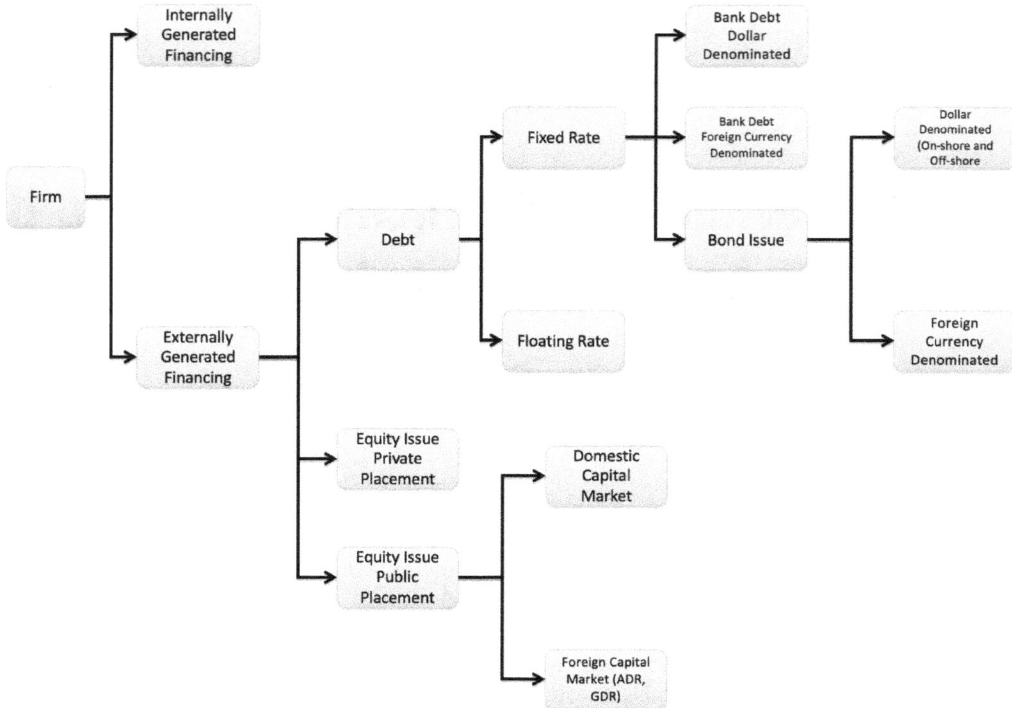

Exhibit 9.1. Alternative sources of financing.

intermediaries such as commercial banks, finance companies, or insurance companies that fund themselves by taking deposits from the public at large or issuing their own debt securities in capital markets.

Alternatively, external financing can be sourced directly from investors in the form of equity (stocks), debt (notes and bonds), or hybrids (convertible bonds and preferred stocks). As a practical matter, investors provide the money by purchasing the securities that the firm issues in capital markets. These securities can be either *short-term, medium-term or long-term bonds* raised from existing or new bondholders or *preferred and common stocks* sold to existing or new shareholders. New bond or equity securities can be sold on domestic or any foreign capital markets. Unlike bank loans or leases, all such securities are negotiable and tradable on an active secondary market (see Exhibit 9.1).

This external financing process is facilitated by investment banks, which assist the issuing firms in designing, pricing, and marketing the appropriate securities to be sold to investors in capital markets. Investment banks generally do not provide direct financing as commercial banks would; instead they may have to purchase the securities *wholesale* — so-called underwriting — before they are quickly *retailed* to investors. Investment banks are compensated by retailing securities at a somewhat higher price than the price they paid wholesale — this is called the spread. As globalization steadily erodes the barriers to cross-border financing, external financing is increasingly procured from international/foreign capital markets.

THE FINANCIAL SYSTEM AND FINANCIAL (DIS)INTERMEDIATION

The financial system's primary function is to mobilize savings from households and to allocate those funds among competing users (firms but also households, municipalities, and governments) on the basis of expected risk-adjusted returns. Thus, the financial system provides a conduit through which the cash surplus of savers is channeled to cash-deficient firms in need of financing. Without a financial system, entrepreneurs would have to fund their activities exclusively with their own personal savings (perhaps augmented with the savings of their family network) and their firm's internally generated excess cash-flows. Most of the cash surplus comes from the *household* sector — that is individuals like you and me who save more than they consume. Excess savings may also come from other firms, spendthrift municipalities or even governments.

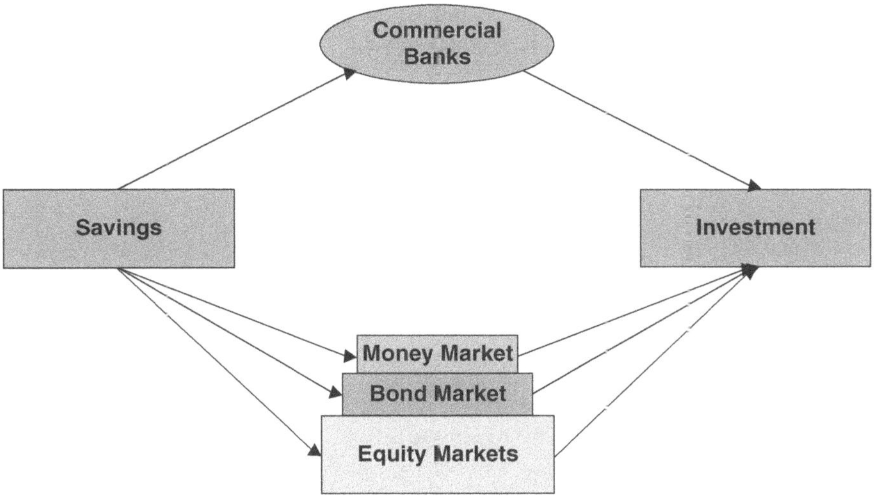

Exhibit 9.2A. Banks versus financial markets.

Cash-deficient firms however also compete for funds with deficit-ridden governments or municipalities and households in need of consumer finance to purchase a home or an automobile. Clearly, the economy at large will greatly benefit from this cash transfer if it is carried out efficiently and at a low cost and — most important — if the cash is invested in value-creating projects. This process can be carried out through two competing paths as described in Exhibit 9.2A.

Financial intermediaries

Financial intermediaries are primarily *commercial banks*, insurance companies and *venture capital firms* which act as conduits between the ultimate providers of capital (mostly households which have accumulated excess savings) and ultimate users of capital (primarily firms short of cash). Commercial banks provide the bulk of credit in the form of short to medium term loans with maturities ranging from 1 day to 10 years (see upper part of Exhibit 9.2A). In order to fund the loans that they extend to firms, banks get cash from depositors in the form of checking and savings accounts or from investors to which they sell short term negotiable certificates of deposit (CDs). Furthermore, in addition to carefully screening loan applicants and making informed credit-granting decisions financial intermediaries also *monitor* the performance of borrowers by gathering information on their performance and by implementing loan *covenants*. For performing this important function of financial intermediation banks are compensated in the form of a *spread* or difference between the interest rate they pay to depositors and the higher interest rate they charge on the loan granted to firms.

Today most corporate loans are made to firms that borrow against pre-negotiated *credit lines* whereby the bank stands ready to lending any amount up to the full credit line commitment. Thus, the corporate borrower has a credible option of taking down any amount between 0 and the full credit line for any period of time during the duration of the loan commitment. In addition to interest charged to the actual amount borrowed, the bank collects an *upfront fee* on the total amount of the credit line pledged as well as a commitment fee (*back-end fee*) for the unused portion of the credit line. As an example assume that Alaska airline negotiate a \$100 million one year line of credit at the annual rate of 7% with an upfront fee of 15 basis points and a back-end fee of 50 basis point. Should Alaska Airlines end up borrowing \$50 million for only 4 months it would be paying an interest of $\$100\text{ million}\times[0.07\times 4/12+0.0015+0.005\times 8/12]=\$\,2790{,}000$ or an annualized interest rate of 8.37%.

Once upon a time, banks were the only source of financing until capital markets first appeared in the nineteenth century. Still, to this day bank loans are the way most firms are financed in many parts of the world, and indeed Japanese, German, French, Indian, Chinese, and other emerging markets–based companies still rely heavily on bank financing.

Financial markets

Alternatively, firms can raise funds directly from savers by selling them securities such as stocks or bonds. Indeed corporate borrowing is increasingly in the form of negotiable and tradable securities issued in public financial markets (debt or credit

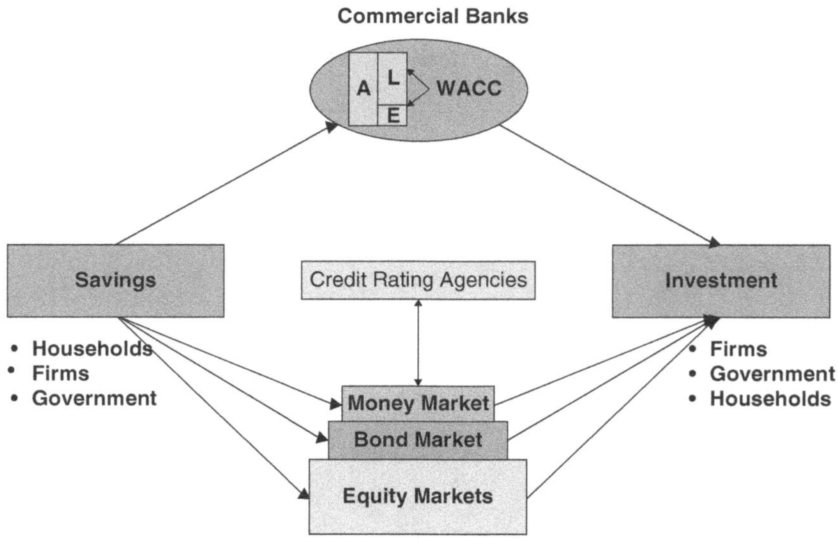

Exhibit 9.2B. Disintermediation and the rise of the commercial paper market.

markets — see lower part of Exhibit 9.2A) rather than in the form of nontraded illiquid loans provided by financial intermediaries. Financial markets encompass (1) the *money market* where debt securities of maturity of one year or less such as commercial paper are traded and (2) *capital markets* which cater for corporate *notes* (maturity between one and five years), corporate *bonds* with maturities exceeding five years and stocks.

Financial markets are further characterized as primary or secondary markets. *Primary* markets are the markets in which securities are sold to investors for the first time — this would be the case of a newly issued bond or an *Initial Public Offering (IPO)* when a privately held firm sells for the first time some of its equity to the public at large. The *secondary* market caters for already issued securities which are now traded — bought and sold — by investors.

The financial system also plays a critical role in reducing risk by enabling investors to hold diversified portfolios of financial assets (either individually or more likely through mutual funds). They also facilitate the *transfer of risk* from firms that are ill-equipped to bear risk (such as exporting firms exposed to currency risk) to other economic agents that are better endowed to bear risk (such as commercial banks, insurance companies, or hedge funds willing to be the counterparty to forward contracts or swaps). Financial *derivatives* such as forwards, swaps, or options on currencies, commodities, or interest rates are the primary instruments facilitating this risk transfer because they provide a reliable pricing mechanism; they also enable an efficient division of labor based on each economic agent's comparative advantage in risk-bearing.

Similarly to financial intermediaries, investors discriminate amongst competing borrowers by rewarding with lower (or higher) interest rate more (or less) financially healthy firms. Once the debt security is issued and start to trade investors provide a different kind of monitoring on borrowing firms by continuously bidding up or down the prices of notes and bonds or exerting corporate control in the form of threatened hostile takeovers and leveraged buy-outs for underperforming firms or outright bankruptcy for insolvent ones. This process both before and after credit is granted (debt security is issued) is greatly facilitated by credit rating agencies.

Credit rating agencies

When a firm issues a bond it makes to the investor a series of contractual promises — that is to pay interest and repay principal on time and in full. By assessing the credibility of these promises and issuing a notation credit rating agencies assist investors in better valuing bonds and the borrower in better gauging its cost of debt. Indeed, one of the key determinants of the cost of debt is its notation or credit rating. Credit rating agencies such as Standard & Poor's (S&P), Moody's or Fitch for years immemorial have provided credit rating on domestic and international bonds and their issuers whether they be corporations, municipalities or sovereigns. The rating is an overall assessment of the borrower's credit worthiness given the specifics of the debt

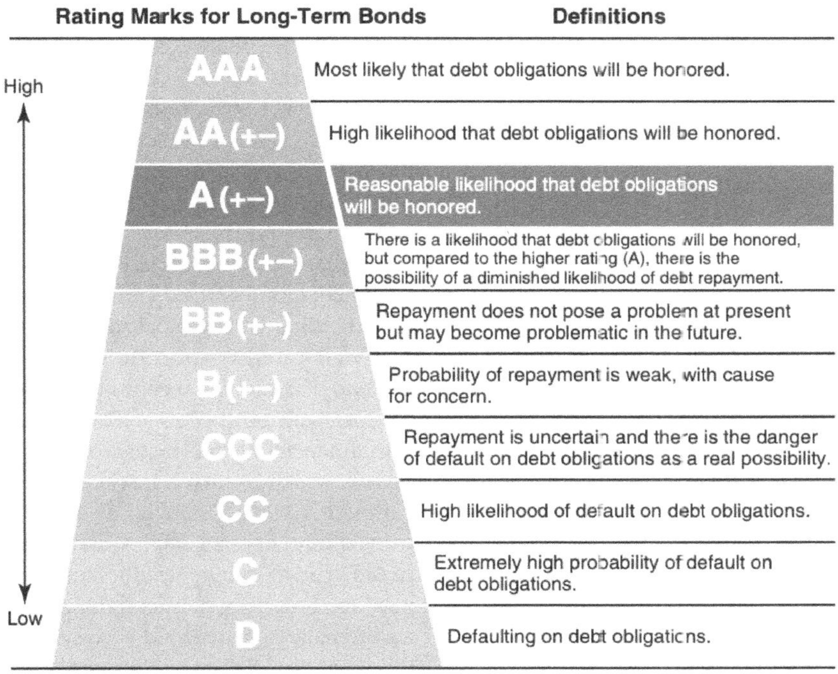

Exhibit 9.3. Standard and poor credit notations.

Note: Credit ratings range from AAA to D, and are further subdivided into a total of 20 ratings (see chart) by the use of plus and minus signs for ratings AA to B.

obligation — that is a gauge of the borrower's ability to pay interest and to repay principal on time and in full. *Credit risk* or *default risk* would materialize when the bond issuer fail to service the bond — specifically missing payment of promised coupons and/or failing to redeem the bond at its face value at maturity. The ratings are constructed on the basis of a comprehensive analysis of the firm's actual and projected cash-flows taking into account its long-term growth prospects.

Specifically, S&P assigns a triple AAA rating to bonds with the strongest financial health, followed by ratings of AA, A and BBB in declining order of financial strength. Any bond rated BBB or better is referred as an *investment grade* bond whereas any bond rated below BBB — that is BB, B and CCC is known as a *speculative-grade, high yield or junk* bond. Within each letter category S&P uses + or — modifiers to position a bond issue at the upper or lower end of the category (see Exhibit 9.3 for a definition of each category).

According to its rating, a bond will pay an interest rate higher than what government bonds offer for the same maturity (referred as the risk-free rate): the extra return is called the *credit spread* or the *yield spread* or the *credit risk premium*. For example, the US government pays 2.7% on 10 year treasuries whereas AAA-rated Proctor & Gamble pays 3.25% on its 10 year bonds — that is a credit spread of 3.25% – 2.7% = 0.55% or 55 basis points. South West Airline with a single A credit rating pays 4.1% on 10 year bonds or a credit spread of 1.4% or 144 basis points whereas BBB-rated GE pays 6.7% or a credit spread of 4%. As credit rating deteriorates, the yield of corporate bonds will increase reflecting the higher reward that investors are requiring to hold a riskier bond.

In sum, a well-functioning financial sector is critical to steady economic growth. By mobilizing savings and channeling those savings efficiently (low transaction costs) to the most deserving investment projects, the financial sector optimizes the allocation of scarce capital. Whether carried out by financial institutions or by financial markets, this intermediation process will be most effective when property rights are secure, contracts are easily enforceable in a timely fashion and at low cost, and meaningful accounting information is made available in a transparent way to all interested parties.

Banks versus capital markets: The rising tide of disintermediation

Financial intermediaries have been steadily losing market share in the global financial intermediation business to capital markets. This is not really a new phenomenon since financial markets have traded stocks and bonds for the past 150 years. What is relatively new is the rise of commercial paper as a lower-cost alternative to short-term bank loans. *Commercial paper* (CP) is a short-term unsecured promissory note of 270 days maturity (or less) issued by strongly rated companies (see Exhibit 9.2B).

> ***Q:*** Chlorox — the manufacturer of household cleaning products — is in need of \$250 million for working capital financing over the next 90 days. It has the choice between a) a one year credit line from Wachovia Bank at the yearly interest rate of 5.50% with a 0.5% commitment fee on unused fund versus b) a 3-month commercial paper at the annual rate of 5% with a 0.25% back-up credit line from Metropolitan Life Insurance co.
>
> ***A:*** Bank loan costs \$250 million $\times$ $[0.0550 \times 3/12 + 0.005 \times 9/12] = \$4{,}375{,}000$; commercial paper is cheaper at \$250 million $\times$ $[0.05 \times 3/12 + 0.0025] = \$\ 3{,}750{,}000$.

Commercial paper first appeared when financial deregulation of credit markets in the 1970s loosened the grip that traditional financial intermediaries held over household savings. CP could now be sold directly to newly established money market mutual funds (MMMFs),[2] which were in direct competition with commercial banks in collecting savings.[3] Not only could money market mutual funds offer most of the services that a bank checking or saving account offered, but they also paid a far more attractive interest rate. Household savings were now pooled by MMMFs and directly invested in CPs or other short term liquid and highly rated securities such as government treasury bills, thereby bypassing the more expensive financial intermediation of commercial banks (see International Corporate Finance in Practice 9.1).

Thus, a significant share of the overall financial intermediation business (short-term and medium-term lending by financial intermediaries to large and well-rated corporations) was abandoning the ship of commercial banks to transit through the cheaper path of the commercial paper market.[4] In sum, financial disintermediation lowers the cost of capital, which in turn boosts corporate borrowers' competitiveness. Financial disintermediation has successfully engulfed Anglo-Saxon countries, which already had a stronger tradition of relying on capital markets. Emerging markets countries — which had traditionally lagged behind — seem to be jumping on the disintermediation bandwagon (see International Corporate Finance in Practice 9.2).

In continental Europe and East Asia, powerful oligopolies of universal banks have delayed the rise of commercial paper, thereby protecting banks' franchises. This cost handicap should come as no surprise, as traditional financial intermediation is an inherently costly process because the intermediary's balance sheet adds a layer of cost in the process. Recall that banks convert short-term deposits (liabilities) that are redeemable at par and often on demand into *illiquid* loans (assets) that are placed at various risk levels of default. Indeed, banks will protect themselves against such default risk through proper capitalization as mandated by the Basel II.5 accord, thereby incurring a significant equity cost of capital in the process.

2 US Regulation Q, which prohibited banks from paying interest on checking accounts, was in force until March 1986. Its repeal greatly encouraged the success of MMMFs.

3 In the United States, investments in MMMFs are not insured by the Federal Deposit Insurance Corporation, unlike savings accounts with banks or savings and loans.

4 As commercial banks were losing in the 1970s the lucrative business of short-term and medium-term lending to large, well-rated corporations, they turned to recycling petrodollars to developing countries, mostly in Latin America. Taking the accumulating dollar balances of the Organization of Petroleum Exporting Countries (OPEC) and lending them through syndicated loans to sovereigns was at first a profitable activity before turning into a colossal financial crisis.

INTERNATIONAL CORPORATE FINANCE IN PRACTICE 9.1

The Equity Capital Cost of Financial Intermediation

The requirement that banks would hold a significant amount of (expensive) equity capital arises from the fear of systemic risk — that is the possible bankruptcy of a large financial institution which would trigger a chain reaction or domino effect whereby other major financial institution would soon collapse. One method to mitigate systemic risk is to force financial institutions to have enough equity capital to weather asset losses — from a non-performing loan to a debtor going bankrupt. The Basel II.5 — soon to be Basel III accord aims at strengthening the global financial system by mandating how much equity capital banks need to hold in order to meet time liabilities and to provide a safety "cushion" against loan losses. It therefore purports to level the playing fields for financial institutions by imposing standard capital adequacy ratios (CARs) across countries. CARs are similar to financial leverage and defined as:

$$\text{CAR} = \frac{Tier\ 1\ Capital + Tier\ 2\ Capital}{Risk - Adjusted\ Assets}$$

where Tier 1 capital is equity + retained earnings and Tier 2 capital is preferred stock + 50% of subordinated debt. Risk-adjusted assets refers to the bank's assets adjusted according to their intrinsic riskiness. Tier 1 capital has to account for at least 4% of risk-adjusted assets and combined Tier 1 and Tier 2 Capital have to exceed 8%. Cash held by a bank is not risky, and therefore the bank should not be required to hold any capital for cash. A loan to the Ukrainian government is indeed risky, and 8% in equity capital may not be enough in case of default: thus, Basel mandates that 150% of the face value of the loan should be protected by capital. In a nutshell, this illustrates the idea of risk-weighted assets, whereby the value of each asset is weighted by a risk factor corresponding to the default probability of the asset: thus, each asset is first multiplied by its corresponding risk factor before the total capital charge is set at 8% of risk-weighted assets. Banks regulators monitor and enforce CARs to protect bank depositors and other lenders thereby maintaining confidence in the financial system.

This standardized approach assigns capital separately to each asset on the basis of credit risk, but fails to recognize market risk and correlation between different types of securities. More sophisticated banks with well-functioning control systems are allowed to use "internal-based models" to determine market risk capital. This approach requires calculating a value-at-risk (V@R) measure of the bank portfolio and converting it into a capital requirement according to a formula spelled out in the 1996 amendment to the Basel I accord. Most large banks preferred to use V@R-based internal models which capture the benefits of diversification and generally lead to lower capital requirements.

FINTECH AND DISINTERMEDIATION 2.0.

Fin tech is a shorthand for ***fin**ancial **tech**nology*. The *fin* part refers to the usual financial products and services such as taking a business or consumer loan, making an investment, seeking advice to better manage one's pension fund, making a payment or buying insurance. The *tech* part describes the technologies used to deliver financial products and services.[5] Specifically:

"fintech is defined as the digital delivery of financial products and services through the internet, a mobile phone or other electronic device ... Fintech companies target customers which are underserved by the traditional financial services industry — typically individuals and small businesses. These entrepreneurial start-ups initially focus on a problem or pain point, related to financial services. Fintech then

5 The marriage of technology with financial services is nothing new: fintech 1.0 first started with the transatlantic cable laid between New York and London in 1858 which allowed for the nascent integration of European capital markets with North American ones through spatial arbitrage in stocks, bonds, currencies and commodities. One century later fintech 2.0 — with the introduction of computers and ATMs soon to be enhanced with the widespread use of personal computers — streamlined the cost of back-office operations and generally resulted into lower fees and commissions.

INTERNATIONAL CORPORATE FINANCE IN PRACTICE 9.2

A Money Market Colossus Rises

In just 4 years, a money-market fund created by an affiliate of China's Alibaba Group Holding Ltd. has become the world's largest, providing millions of the country's savers a high-returning place to park their money. Now, it is facing pressure from regulators to slow down. Fueled by contributions from some 370 million account holders, the fund, known as Yu'e Bao — which means *"leftover treasure"* — has grown rapidly to manage $211 billion in assets. It is more than twice the size of the next largest money-market fund, a US dollar liquidity fund managed by J.P. Morgan Asset Management, according to data from Morningstar Inc. Yu'e Bao's assets doubled in the past year alone, and the fund now makes up a quarter of China's money-market mutual fund industry. Its ascent has been an accidental byproduct of a sharp shift among Chinese consumers toward mobile payments. Yu'e Bao draws its funds from users of Alipay, an electronic-payments platform used by roughly one-third of China's population to make purchases on Alibaba's e-commerce sites and to pay for everything from cinema tickets to household bills.

Attracted by the fund's generous returns — Yu'e Bao's investments produce a seven-day yield of 4.02% — some investors have been sending chunks of their monthly paychecks to it, another reason for its growth. A year ago, the fund's yield was 2.3%, according to Tianhong Asset Management Co., an Ant subsidiary that manages the fund. Yu'e Bao's short-term yield dwarfs the 1.5% interest rate on one year Chinese bank deposits and even beats the 3.6% yield on 10-year Chinese government bonds. The fund invests most of its money in CDs issued by Chinese state-owned or state-supported banks. It also holds government bonds, bank-issued bonds and commercial paper. Data reviewed by The Wall Street Journal indicate Tianhong boosted Yu'e Bao's returns in recent years by increasing its allocation of funds to financial instruments with longer maturities. Such assets, however, tend to be less liquid than bank deposits and lower-yielding investments. About 40% of Yu'e Bao's investments mature in under 60 days, versus over 60% four years ago, according to Tianhong's reports.

The surge is making Chinese regulators nervous. In March, China's securities regulator called for "significantly stronger" risk controls at money-market funds to "prevent systemic risks caused by large-scale redemptions." The concern is that money-market funds could see sudden and large-scale redemptions by investors if, for example, returns drop, or during periods of broader market turmoil. If the funds are forced to liquidate large volumes of assets to raise cash, the moves could potentially destabilize the financial system. In early September, regulators issued new liquidity rules requiring money-market funds to boost their holdings of higher-quality assets, such as short-term debt securities, that carry top credit ratings. The regulator also labeled money-market funds as "systemically significant" and instructed them to curb their exposure to individual financial institutions. The new rules take effect on Oct l. Tianhong said it has various measures in place to prevent a liquidity crunch and believes the "probability of mass redemption is very low." It said most of the fund's customers have fairly small holdings of around $590 on average.

Source: *Wall Street Journal* (September 14, 2017); reprinted with permission.

leverages technology to offer a solution to this problem electronically that is less expensive, easier to use, faster and more convenient than traditional methods. That is the fintech value proposition: cheaper, easier, faster and more convenient".[6]

Because Fintech avoids building costly human customer relationships it has to rely on big data being substituted to soft information. Big data reaches far beyond the simple metrics such as credit score or loan to value ratio favored by traditional financial institutions to include customers' spending track records, educational profiles. … As it lowers the cost of financial services in general and financial intermediation in particular, countries which have embraced

6 King, Michael R. 2023. *Fintech Explained*. Toronto: University of Toronto Press, p. 2.

fintech will benefit from a lower cost of capital thereby boosting their economic competitiveness and the standard of living of their households.

Payments are the keystone of the financial service industry — sometimes referred as the "plumbing" of the financial system. Indeed, no financial service ever happens without payment. Underlying problems undermining the payment system are speed, convenience, lack of transparency and cost which technology can correct thus making the payment industry a good candidate for disruption. Indeed, payments fintech have addressed the pain points around money transfers, cashless means of payment, foreign exchange and international remittances.

Online lending or debt crowdfunding are digital platforms that allow individuals and businesses to borrow directly from other individuals bypassing traditional financial intermediaries such as savings and loans and/or commercial banks. By matching borrowers with lenders Peer-to-Peer (P2P) online portal/digital platform acts as financial intermediaries. By avoiding costly brick-and-mortar bank infrastructure fintech lenders enjoy lower fixed and operating costs which in turn permits them to offer smaller value loan thereby broadening consumer and small business access to credit. Each on-line lending platform would set the interest rates, terms of the loan and closing fees while enabling the transaction which is entirely automated. Most debt crowding portals typically quote a wide range of interest rates according to the credit worthiness of the applicant.

Borrowers are often individuals who would be spurned by traditional banks because of a sub-standard credit history or simply consumers that are seeking lower cost financing than offered by traditional financial institutions. Similarly, small and medium-sized enterprises turn to on-line lending when they are closed out of traditional bank financing. As expected, the default rate of P2P loans — which are typically unsecured — is much higher than the national average and hovers around 10%.

> *But who are the lenders? "The original P2P platforms raised money from the "crowd", with individual investors committing a small part to each loan (such as $100). These individuals would log on to the platform and find a list of borrowers looking to raise capital. Each borrower would have a borrowing target and a description of how they would use the proceeds. The online platform would assign a credit rating and interest rate on the loan which is the financial return to the lender. The retail investor could buy some of the loan during the subscription period with a dashboard showing how much had been committed.*
>
> *By investing a small amount in any given loan, individual investors could diversify their exposure by holding a portfolio and reduce their exposure to any given borrower. As demand for borrowing grew the capital available from individuals was insufficient to meet demand. Online platforms therefore expanded to accept investments from institutional investors such as hedge funds, money managers, banks and insurance companies".*[6]

Crowdfunding are digital platforms which allow small businesses and NGOs to raise *equity* capital or grants. Crowdfunding procures small amount of capital from a large number of individuals to finance a new business venture. It is subjected to the Securities and Exchange Commission Regulation Crowdfunding (Reg CF) which limits the amount to be raised to $1.07 million per year as well as the amount that each investor can contribute according to wealth and income.

Asset Management. Managing households' investment portfolio is a very lucrative business especially when it comes to high net worth individuals but also the ever-growing population of retirees who increasingly have to deal with *defined contribution* rather than *defined benefit* pension models. By relying on algorithms and digital platforms Robo-advising offer low cost portfolio construction and re-balancing which optimizes asset allocation between stocks, bonds and other asset classes according to investors' goal and risk tolerance. FinTech firms such as Wealthfront and Betterment offer sophisticated investment advice to the rapidly growing population of retirees at a fraction of the cost of traditional financial advisers.

FinTech-based financial services — because of their digital nature — are relatively easy to distribute and it can be done at a lower cost than traditional financial services would typically bear. As a result, FinTech is proving to be a formidable engine of financial inclusion as it reaches under-served and underbanked households and firms. To wit, consider the case of M-Pesa[7] — a Kenyan mobile phone-based

7 M stands for mobile and Pesa means money in Swahili.

money transfer service which was first launched in 2007 by Kenya's leading mobile-phone network operator Safaricom. Then, Kenya's was grossly under-banked with only 14% of its population having a bank account. M-Pesa introduced mobile payment strictly based on the use of a cell/mobile phone. Customers would first open an account stored on their phone to deposit money using a network of local agents from Safaricom. The money could then be used to make payment to merchant via text messaging, to transfer money to other M-Pesa clients and to make international remittances at a significantly lower cost than traditional banks would charge. Thus, any individual owning a cell-phone or having access to one could deposit money, make payments, transfer or receive money and all of which could be done without having access to a bank account. Effectively, individuals and small enterprises could join the formal economy and start accumulating savings even-though they did not have a bank account. By 2023 M-Pesa had 52 million customers principally in Kenya claiming a penetration rate of 90% of all mobile phone users. Interestingly, as a non-bank squarely providing financial services M-Pesa escapes — for the most part — the regulatory burden imposed on commercial banks by the Central Bank of Kenya. By broadening the scope of financial services and deepening the pool of savings, FinTech — M-Pesa style — is allowing the Kenyan economy to access domestic savings at a lesser cost.

Can FinTech displace banks? Clearly Fintech firms are benefiting from lighter regulation than banks and are not burdened by heavy legacy IT costs but banks can fight back by incorporating FinTech into their operations. For example, payments which has attracted the largest numbers of FinTech firms is home to Venmo — a well-known and very popular peer-to-peer stand-alone payment service owned by Paypal which enables individuals to make cash transfers immediately to other individuals domiciled in the same country or abroad using a smart-phone. However, a network comprised of the largest commercial banks in the US introduced in 2017 Zelle which is directly competing with Venmo.

BigTech and Disintermediation 2.0. So far, we have left out of the FinTech equation Big Tech firms such as Amazon, Apple, Alphabet, Meta and others. BigTech is crawling into the financial service industry but has yet to leverage its huge competitive advantage in big data. Amazon — as a platform where buyers and sellers are continuously browsing and transacting — is in a unique position to collect valuable data to guide advertising and product selection to customers most likely to be receptive. The same data can be used very effectively in granting credit as demonstrated by Ant Financial which is the financial arm of Alibaba — the giant e-commerce firm in China:

> *"through MYbank it grants credit to small businesses that sell on Alibaba's Taobao platform. Ant Financial uses both historical data and real time sales data on the platform, including ratings by customers, to grant credit lines to small businesses. With the help of machine learning techniques, it uses data available to assign credit scores to platform sellers. It has an automated process to offer credit lines to small business whose credit score exceeds a threshold ... The credit is withdrawn if the score of the seller drops below a minimum threshold".*[8]

The same logic applies to granting financing to buyers active on the same platform. Indeed, BigTech lurks as a formidable threat to FinTech and traditional banks:

> *"BigTech firms have all the technical know-how and up-to-date systems that FinTech aspires to. They have the scale of large banks. They have neither the legacy cost nor the organizational issues that banks have. And finally, they have access to data that neither banks nor FinTech firms have".*[9]

SECURITIZATION AND THE (LOWER) COST OF CONSUMER FINANCING

More than half of all lending is destined to households primarily for financing consumers' home purchases, automobiles, appliances, or credit cards. Consumer financing has been undergoing its own revolution paralleling the disintermediation story, which pits banks against capital markets. It is known as the *securitization* of consumer financing. First pioneered in the US residential mortgage market more than 50 years ago, the technology of securitization has truly revolutionized consumer finance in the United States and other common law[10] countries. It is making slower progress in most other countries in part

8 See Rene M Stulz "FinTech, BigTech and the Future of Banking" *Journal of Applied Corporate Finance* (Fall 2019), p. 95.

9 Idem.

10 Securitization is more problematic in *civil law* countries where the concepts of trust law have not existed. By contrast, *common law* countries (mostly the Anglo-Saxon world) have well-defined trust laws.

because these countries lack the sophisticated legal infrastructure that securitization requires. In this section we review first the architecture of the technology and explain its economic logic before illustrating its far-reaching potential for emerging countries.

A primer on securitization

Consumer financing was traditionally intermediated by commercial banks, thrifts, savings and loans, or finance companies. A consumer seeking medium- to long-term financing for purchasing a home or an automobile would apply for a mortgage or an automobile loan; if approved, the lender would fund the loan by using savings deposits or by securing financing of its own directly from the capital market. The consumer loan would stay on the financial intermediary's balance sheet for its entire life.

Securitization unbundled such traditional financial intermediation. By repackaging illiquid consumer loans such as residential mortgages, automobile loans, or credit card receivables — which were traditionally held by thrifts, finance companies, or other financial institutions — into liquid and tradable securities, securitization is a more elaborate form of disintermediation that typically results in a lower cost of consumer finance. It is generally estimated that in the United States prior to securitization (that is, prior to 1975), the average yield on a 30-year mortgage for a single family middle-income dwelling was equal to the yield on a 30-year Treasury bond + 285 basis points; after 30 years of securitization, the premium is down to less than 100 basis points, which amounts to gigantic savings in the cost of home financing, admittedly a major component of individual household budgets and a source of improvement in the standard of living.

As illustrated in Exhibit 9.4, a typical securitization transaction is structured around six basic building blocks:

1. *Origination* consists of managing the *credit-granting process* to consumers applying for a loan to facilitate the purchase of a home or an automobile or the use of a credit card. It is carried out by the financial institution that traditionally financed the transaction. In effect, the originator is charged with gauging the creditworthiness of the household or individual applying for a loan; this amounts to checking the applicant's source of income and outstanding liabilities to ensure the ability to make mortgage payments.

   For example, when a household applies for a mortgage to purchase a house, the lender would use simple rules such as: The applicant's after-tax income should be at least three times the monthly mortgage payment plus carrying costs of the house (insurance premium and real estate taxes), and the cash down payment should amount to 25–30% of the purchase price to approve the loan.

   As explained earlier, in a pre-securitization world the originator would have also provided the financing by using demand deposits or raising debt directly in the capital market. In a securitization world, originators are not the financiers. Their role is limited to processing a loan application, and, in fact, they will immediately sell the loan to a special purpose vehicle.

2. *Structuring* is the creation of a legal entity — generally known as a special purpose vehicle (SPV) — for the sole purpose of the transaction, which would use the loans/receivables as collateral for issuing new securities in the capital market. The SPV would typically purchase *without recourse* the loans/receivables from the originators at precisely the time it is issuing notes.

   It is important to note that the SPV is not a going concern; that is, it will not pursue other deals once it is set up. In other words, it *opens* for business for a very short period of time — long enough to raise debt financing from the bond market to purchase the loans from the originator — and immediately thereafter *closes* for business for however long the securities will take to be redeemed. During that period the SPV — like the sleeping beauty in the fairy tale — lies dormant until it is awakened when the notes are redeemed! Interestingly enough, an originator is often invited to also be one of the credit enhancers, admittedly the ultimate incentive to perform as a sound originator.[11]

   One of the crucial features of structuring is that the originator transfers the receivables to the SPV in what is known as a *true sale*. The SPV is thus said to be *bankruptcy remote* from the originator so that the receivables transferred are indeed removed from the originator's bankruptcy estate.

3. *Credit enhancing* is about improving the credit risk profile of the original loans by procuring insurance coverage against default from insurance carriers or commercial banks. Because default on consumer loans can be accurately gauged through

11 Originators are expected to approve loans only to creditworthy borrowers. If they double up as credit enhancers, they would end up paying for part or the totality of any defaulting loans that they should not have approved in the first place.

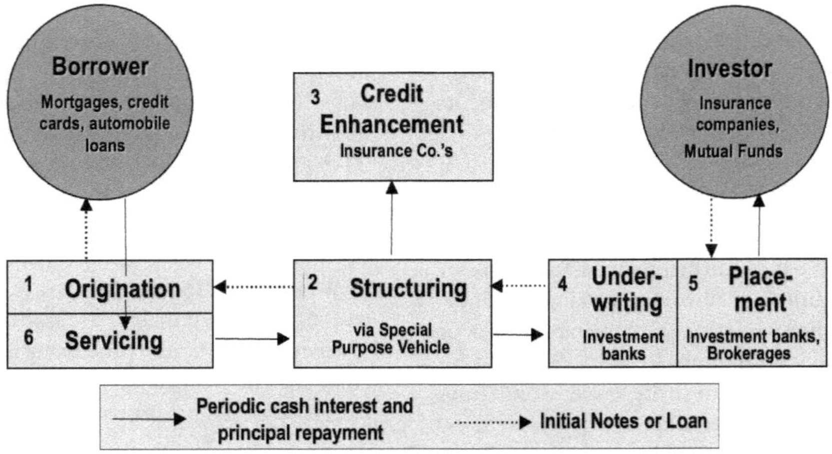

Exhibit 9.4. Structure of securitization transactions.

actuarial techniques,[12] it is relatively easy to price credit enhancement. Credit rating agencies such as Moody's and Standard & Poor's play a critical role in assisting credit enhancers to calibrate the cost of insuring a portfolio of collateral loans against default.

The fact that the SPV is not a going concern (the loan portfolio acquired at time of inception is frozen for the entire life of the SPV) also facilitates evaluating its credit risk, which in turns makes the pricing of credit enhancement easier and cheaper. Typically, securitization deals are credit enhanced to the best possible rating, which in turn enables the issuer to offer a lower yield to investors. Presumably the cost of credit enhancement is somewhat lower than the reduction in the yield courtesy of residual inefficiencies in capital markets.[13]

4. and **5.** *Underwriting and placing* the newly created securities with appropriate investors are activities carried out by the underwriting and placement bank syndicates and are no different from any debt securities issuance.

6. *Servicing* is the collection of the loans' interest and principal repayments to ensure the proper cash-flow disbursement to securities holders. The originator continues to collect interest payments and principal repayments, which are channeled through the SPV to be paid out to securities holders.

Subprime crisis, securitization, credit default swaps, and the AIG debacle

The subprime crisis of 2008 is often blamed on securitization for corrupting financial intermediation and bringing our financial system to the edge of the precipice. It seems that the roots of the problem lie primarily with data fed into the securitization machinery rather than with the architecture of the machinery itself. When (1) originators failed to do due diligence on applicants for mortgage financing, (2) credit rating agencies failed to properly assess credit risk and rated mortgage-backed securities above their intrinsic creditworthiness, and (3) credit enhancers failed to properly price their insurance guarantees (in part because of faulty information provided by credit rating agencies), securitization was indeed set up for failure. Although all three failures largely contributed to the subprime crisis, it is the debacle of American International Group (AIG) that is of course best remembered for nearly bankrupting the international financial system. Its collapse was in fact the result of AIG failing to properly price its guarantees (credit enhancements) to mortgage-backed securities and thereby accumulating contingent liabilities for which it had failed to reserve.

Credit enhancement is about providing some form of partial or full insurance against the risk of default and is concretized either through more traditional standby letters of credit or bond insurance or

12 Consumer loans have been tracked for generations in the United States and in other advanced economies, which means that time series of actual defaults going back more than half a century provide a very rich database from which to extract probability distributions about possible future losses. The same actuarial properties do not necessarily apply to business loans, which as a result are not good candidates for securitization.

13 Credit enhancement can also be provided with bond insurance, overcollateralization of the loan portfolio, and credit default swaps.

more recently through *credit default swaps* (CDSs). As a result, the credit-enhanced securities are better rated and can therefore be issued at a lower yield. Of course, credit enhancement makes sense only as long as its cost (often as low as 35 to 50 basis points) is less than the resulting reduction in interest rates paid out by the issuer of the mortgage-backed securities.

AIG, with its AAA credit rating, was a much sought after provider of such credit enhancements and indeed readily obliged by building over the previous decade a portfolio of credit default swaps that reached $500 billion in notional value by 2008. AIG would lend its strong credit rating to lesser-rated securities so that they could enjoy the AAA rating of the insurance carrier. AIG would receive a fee for providing the protection from default to investors. So far, so good. As for any insurance coverage provided by an insurance carrier (such as AIG), the two key questions to answer are: What premium should be charged? How much of that premium should be reserved to pay for future losses (rather than paid out as bonuses to staff or dividends to shareholders)? AIG — as a premier insurance carrier — should have been particularly well equipped to properly answer both questions. History showed otherwise!

As AIG believed that the risk of default on the mortgage-backed securities it was credit enhancing was minuscule, it was underpricing its insurance protection, over-insuring, and under-reserving. In the words of AIG Financial Products division president Tom Savage:

> *The models suggested that the risk [about credit default swaps] was so remote that the fees were almost free money. . . . Just put it on your books and enjoy the money.*[14]

Unsurprisingly, disaster struck AIG when default rates on subprime mortgage-backed securities started to accelerate in 2008 and AIG was asked to make good on its insurance policies.

International securitization

The transfer of the securitization technology to emerging markets started somewhat slowly in the early 1990s, in part because most candidate countries to this new technology lacked the sophisticated legal and regulatory infrastructure that is quintessential for such transactions. When the ultimate financier of the transaction happens to be an *emerged* market-based investor, a host of problems such as country risk and currency risk complicate the architecture of the transaction beyond the traditional credit risk evaluation. As a backdrop to the discussion we will use Thailand's Thai Cars Ltd. securitization deal, which was completed in August 1996. Thai Cars, a company related to the Tisco financial company, issued the first public securitized notes of Thai consumer loans — automobile loans and leases in this case. The transaction secured a AAA rating from the US rating agency Standard & Poor's with the insurance company MBIA Inc. providing the guarantee (see Exhibit 9.5).

As in a domestic securitization transaction, automobile leases and installment loans were *originated* by Tisco Leasing (for automobile leases) and Tru-Way

14 Brady Dennis and Robert O'Harrow, "A Crack in the System," *Washington Post*, December 30, 2008.

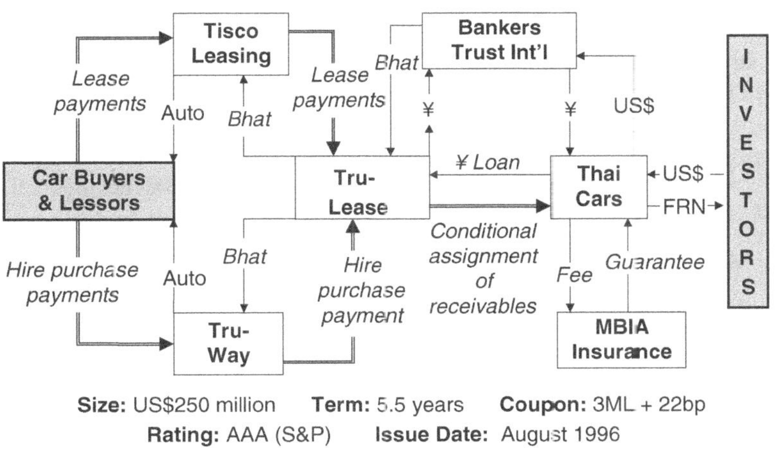

Exhibit 9.5. Securities backed by leases: Thai car's asset-backed floating rate note.

(for automobile installment loans). The loans were then sold to Tru-Lease, the special purpose vehicle that *structured* the collateral assets into tradable baht-denominated notes. Up to this point the transaction would be no different from a US securitization deal except that it was domiciled in Thailand.

Because the investors tapped to purchase the notes were international Eurobond[15] investors, the transaction required some creative financial engineering to resolve the unique problems raised by currency and credit risk. For example, to get around the currency risk issue, a second "twin" SPV — Thai Cars — was established in the Cayman Islands to issue US dollar–denominated notes. The link between the two SPVs — Tru-Way domiciled in Thailand and originating baht-denominated loans and leases and Thai Cars domiciled in the Cayman Islands and holding the same loans and leases but now denominated in US dollars — was a currency swap that transformed the currency denomination of the baht Tru-Way balance sheet into the US dollar Thai Cars balance sheet (see our later discussion of currency risk).

The deal was *credit enhanced* to AAA by the US insurance company MBIA Inc. for a mere 35 basis points. Thai Cars issued US$250 million of 5.5-year floating rate notes (FRNs) through ING Barings (which led the underwriting and placement syndicate) at a mere 22 basis points above three-month LIBOR (3ML). This translated into a 150 basis point reduction in the cost of baht financing, most of which was passed along to Thai consumers.

Currency risk. Structured barely a year prior to the Asian financial crisis, which engulfed the Thai baht[16] on July 2, 1997, this transaction had to address the challenge of exchange risk embedded in the transformation of Thai-denominated receivables into dollar medium-term notes. Bankers Trust International — domiciled in Hong Kong — swapped baht into yen and yen into dollars.[17] Why the bifurcation into yen first and dollars second rather than a straight swap of baht into dollars? The answer has to be found in the withholding tax levied by the Thai tax authorities on interest payments. Since interest rates in yen were close to 1% as opposed to the 6% or 7% for dollars, the amount of taxes paid would be considerably lower on yen-denominated interest payments than on dollar-denominated ones, hence the need for the baht/yen leg of the currency swap.

Credit risk. Securitization works well for consumer loans with an established track record because they make actuarial forecasts of losses reasonably reliable. This would be the case for countries with long experience in consumer financing such as the United States or the United Kingdom (but not generally the case for emerging market countries such as Thailand) where actuarial forecasts are predicated on long-dated time series. Such assessments are in turn necessary for credit enhancement, which brought this deal to a AAA rating and lowered the cost of capital for Thai Cars. The credit enhancer MBIA seems to have overlooked the unique characteristics of high net worth (or highly leveraged) borrowers who could afford luxury automobiles in Thailand (in the US$100,000 to US$300,000 range due to high import taxes) financed by Thai Cars; newly rich borrowers in Thailand didn't have much of a track record as users of consumer financing, and time series of default for such loans must have been exceedingly short, making it difficult to price credit enhancement (MBIA charged a surprisingly low 35 basis point).

Country risk. Last but not least, investors had to contend with the possibility of exchange controls, whereby the Central Bank of Thailand would block the timely payment of interest and principal. This is why such deals cannot be rated more highly than their sovereign unless some special arrangements are made. In this particular case, MBIA must have provided some degree of country risk enhancement (in addition to credit enhancement) for the ratings to have been seven notches higher than the sovereign ceiling (Thailand was single B rated).

This transaction clearly illustrates the benefits of securitization for emerging market economies even though not all conditions were satisfied in this instance. The deal did survive the Asian financial crisis and the devaluation of the Thai currency.[18]

---

15 Eurobonds are discussed in Chapter 11. These are bonds that are issued outside the country in whose currency they are denominated. For example, dollar Eurobonds are dollar-denominated bonds issued and traded outside the United States. The "Euro-" prefix has nothing to do with Europe or the euro as a currency.

16 The Thai baht depreciated by close to 50 percent against the US dollar within the first six months of its initial unpegging from the US$ on July 2, 1997. From 1984 to the onslaught of the Asian financial crisis, the Thai baht (THB) had been firmly pegged to the US dollar at THB 25 = US$1.

17 The reader will recall from Chapter 12 that a currency swap is very similar to a series of currency forward contracts. In this case the swap locked in the value of baht-denominated leases/receivables to the dollar.

18 The counterparty risk embedded in the currency swap could have been an issue had the other party to the swap (Japanese banks) and the swap guarantor (Bankers Trust International) defaulted when the baht abruptly plunged. They did not.

DEREGULATION

The past half century has experienced an accelerating worldwide effort at deregulating economic activity, with financial markets being a major beneficiary of this trend. A *financially repressed* system is generally defined as a system in which the amount and the price at which credit is allocated is determined directly or indirectly by the government; *deregulation* is thus characterized as the process of allowing market forces — rather than the government — to progressively determine who gets and grants credit and at what price. As countries loosen the shackles of financial repression, financing becomes more readily available at a lower cost. This process will typically develop along six dimensions:

1. Relaxation of credit controls.
2. Deregulation of interest rates.
3. Relaxation of controls on international capital flows.
4. Floating exchange rates.
5. Free entry into and exit from the financial services industry.
6. Privatization of financial institutions.

Each country has defined its own deregulation agenda and proceeds in its own peculiar way and at its own pace toward a freer financial system. Relaxation of exchange controls and cleaner float of the currency are critical for better integration with global capital markets, as unimpeded capital flows allow domestic firms to access the freer (less regulated), more liquid, and generally cheaper global pool of investable capital. This is sometimes referred to as hitching onto the globalization train! In a similar vein, governments that keep in place interest rate ceilings are also likely to pressure banks into lending to favored firms or industry sectors at preferential rates. In many instances governments can do so directly through state-owned banks. Privatization of state-owned banks and lower barriers to entry for foreign financial institutions are all characteristic of a lesser degree of financial repression. Closed economies whose financial intermediation process is heavily guided by the government give way slowly to open economies that allow a greater role for financial markets to provide a cheaper alternative to financial intermediaries. We consider next how *incomplete* markets may trigger *regulatory arbitrage*, which in turn brings about more *complete* markets and the dismantling of some — not all — regulatory walls with the landmark case of Denmark's Bull and Bear notes.

Kingdom of Denmark's bull and bear notes

On September 30, 1986, the Kingdom of Denmark issued French francs (FF) 800 million worth of equity-linked notes redeemable on October 1, 1991. The notes, which were listed on the Paris Bourse, were issued at par with a face value of FF 10,000 and an annual coupon rate of 4.5%. The issue was divided into two separate and equal tranches — one called *Bulls* (shown as R_1 in Exhibit 9.6) and the other *Bears* (shown as R_2 in Exhibit 9.6) — of FF 400 million each. The redemption value of both tranches would be a function of the value of the French stock market index CAC 40 on that day. For the Bulls notes, the redemption value was directly and positively related to the value of the French stock market index at the maturity of the notes and defined as R_1 = Par × 1.05 × (Index value at redemption/405.7). The redemption value of the bear notes, on the other hand, was inversely and negatively related to the value of the index and defined as R_2 = Par × 2.32 — R_1 (see Exhibit 9.6).[19]

More specifically, each Bear note combined a five-year, FF 450 annuity (4.5% of FF 10,000 of face value paid annually for five years) and a five-year put option on the stock market index with an exercise price of 896.45 (at the time of the issue, the stock market index stood at 405.7). The Bull note consisted of a five-year, FF 450 annuity plus a long position in the stock market index minus a five-year European call option with an exercise price of 896.45. The latter call option gave the Kingdom of Denmark the right to redeem/call the bull notes at FF 23,200 if the stock market reached 896.45, thus effectively putting a ceiling on the notes' value.

$$R1 = PAR \times 1.05.\ \frac{\text{Terminal Value Index}}{405.7}$$

$$\text{Maximum of } R1 = 2.32 \times PAR - 23.200$$

$$R2 = PAR \times 2.32 - R1$$

$$\text{Total Value} = 1/2\ (R1 + R2)$$

$$= (PAR \times 2.32) \times 1/2 = 11{,}600$$

Although both the Bear and Bull notes are risky equity-linked instruments for investors when held separately, for the issuer the total issue is *riskless* as long as both tranches are fully subscribed. This is because $(R_1 + R_2)/2$ = (Par × 2.32) × 1/2; that is, the cost is fixed. As shown by the dotted horizontal line in Exhibit 9.6, the average redemption value of the bull and bear notes is effectively fixed at FF 11,600

19 Par is the par value or face value of the note when issued: Par = FF 10,000.

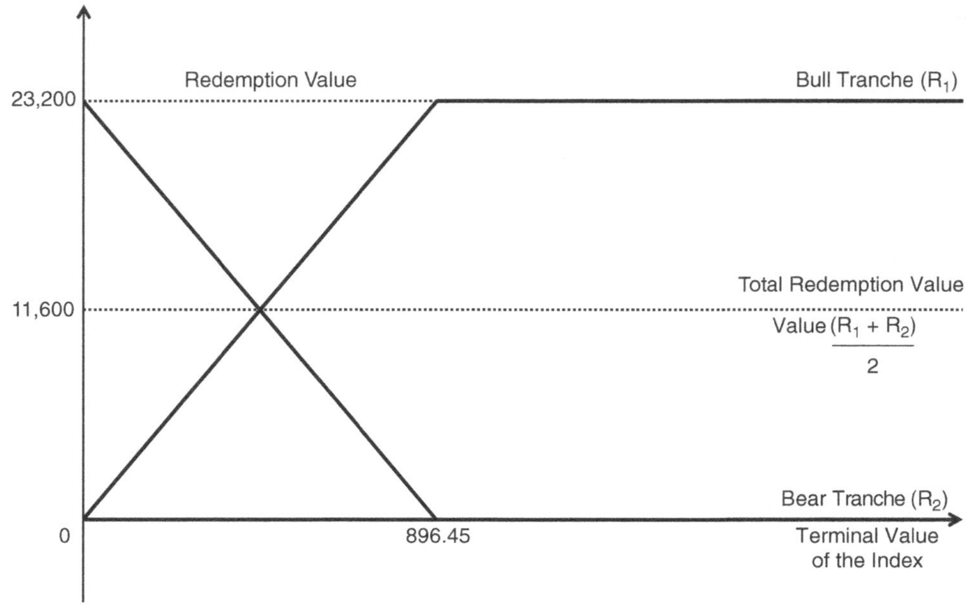

Exhibit 9.6. Kingdom of Denmark's bull-bear notes.

(or half of FF 23,200) per note. And the *effective cost* of this debt issue for the Kingdom of Denmark (rated as an AA credit) — given an initial cash inflow of FF 10,000 per note, five annual FF 450 coupon payments, and an average final "principal" repayment of FF 11,600 — turns out to have been 7.27%.[20]

At the same time these notes were issued, the AAA-rated French government was raising 5-year fixed-rate debt at approximately 8% and AA-rated French corporations were issuing debt at 8.90%. Thus, by issuing a package of Bull and Bear notes (instead of five-year straight bonds), the Kingdom of Denmark managed to reduce its cost of funds below the prevailing risk-free rate (the cost of debt faced by the French government) and 163 basis points below what its credit rating would have warranted. In short, the market priced the Bull and Bear notes at a premium, resulting in a lower cost of debt for the issuer.

Another way to view this financing transaction is that the Kingdom of Denmark was able to sell separately the components of the package (Bull and Bear notes) for more than the value of the package itself (the equivalent straight bonds). To understand why this might be possible, consider the French stock market conditions in September 1986. Equity prices were rising steadily but market participants were questioning such abnormal growth rates. Those already in the market needed protection against a stock price reversal; those outside the market wanted to enter with minimum risk.

One possible answer would have been futures and options contracts on a French stock market index. Portfolio managers could then protect their diversified holdings of French equity by simply buying put options on the stock market index CAC 40, and investors wishing to enter the equity market could buy futures contracts on the same stock market index, thereby creating a long position on French stocks without making a sizable investment. Unfortunately, French regulatory agencies had not yet approved the issuance and trading of these instruments: Regulation was clearly resulting in incomplete markets and an inefficient financial intermediation process. If these forbidden instruments could somehow be supplied to the market in contravention of existing regulation, they would clearly command a scarcity premium.

This is exactly what the Kingdom of Denmark offered under the guise of the Bull-Bear issue. Bear notes embedded long-term put options designed for that segment of the market (mostly wholesale investors) wishing to buy portfolio insurance. Bull notes were equity-linked bonds paying interest and offering a play on the upward market movement. They were sold to the segment of the market (composed mainly of retail investors) who wished to enter the market with reduced risk.

20 This is simply computed as the internal rate of return or yield to maturity of the bond set as an equality between the par value of the bond at time of issue and the present value of future interest payments and principal repayment discounted at the unknown yield to maturity.

Thus, the issuer was able to lower its cost of debt significantly by selling at a premium securities that were close substitutes to prohibited products for which there was an unmet market demand. The issuer took advantage of a *segmented* market that was not permitted to offer derivatives instruments on a stock market index. Had such instruments existed in September 1986, the Bull-Bear issue would probably not have been brought to market. Therefore, it should come as no surprise that, immediately after Denmark's French franc issue, similar notes were issued in Frankfurt, Zurich, and Tokyo — but none in New York and London. As the reader could guess, derivative instruments on stock market indexes existed in New York and London, but not in the other three markets. Each of the regulated markets thus moved one step closer to completeness, along the *emergence continuum* path that we introduce next.

MAPPING THE FINANCIAL SYSTEM/ CAPITAL MARKET EMERGENCE PROCESS

Most financial systems and capital markets are *segmented* from one another, at least to some degree, thus allowing for differences in the effective cost of capital among different countries. For this reason, rather than thinking in terms of a clear-cut dichotomy between *segmented* and *integrated* national financial systems and capital markets, it is more useful to position each country along a *continuum* ranging from extreme segmentation to complete integration, as illustrated in Exhibit 9.7.

Such a continuum would show the relatively newly hatched Tashkent or Ulaanbaatar stock exchanges at its segmentation extreme whereas the London and New York stock exchanges would appear at the opposite integration extreme.

The emergence continuum and the national cost of capital

The more segmented a given nation's capital market (positioned at the bottom of the continuum), the higher its cost of capital. As countries ascend the capital market emergence continuum, their financial markets grow, and they presumably avail themselves of a lower cost of capital. This is due to the fact that less regulated financial sectors build on a deeper pool of savings (both domestic and international), allowing for a healthy competition between financial intermediaries and capital markets (disintermediation) and greater reliance on securitized consumer finance. Thus, identifying the

The EMC Continuum

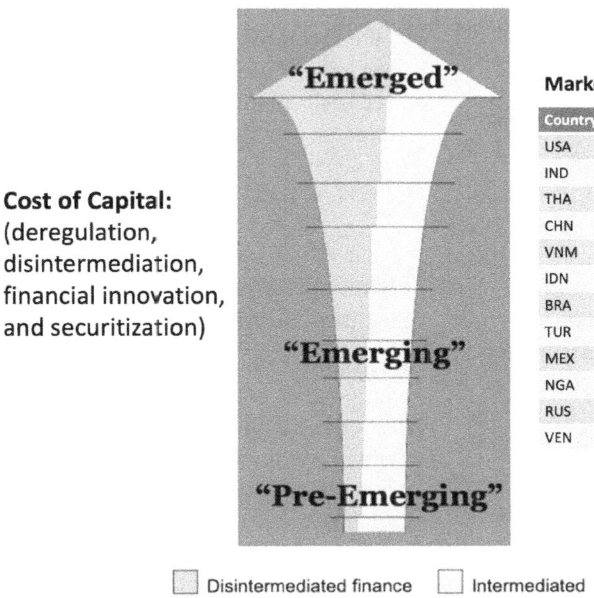

Market Capitalization / GDP

Country	2013	2023
USA	142.7%	194.5%
IND	120%	120%
THA	88.8%	119.4%
CHN	40.3%	65.1%
VNM	21.1%	62%
IDN	62.7%	46.9%
BRA	45.3%	42.4%
TUR	27.7%	41.4%
MEX	43.3%	32.1%
NGA	16.5%	14%
RUS	9.0%	6.6%
VEN	4%	4%

Exhibit 9.7. Capital markets ranked by market capitalization/gross national product.

drivers of this emergence process is of paramount importance to policy makers, since a lower cost of capital makes the country's national firms more competitive in the global marketplace. It also boosts the living standards of households through a lower cost of consumer financing, which will in turn keep wage inflation in check. As discussed earlier in this chapter, *disintermediation*, *FinTech, securitization*, and *deregulation* count as some of the key drivers of this process, and implementing policies that nurture them will go a long way toward accelerating the emergence process. The practical question of positioning a particular capital market along this continuum can be resolved by relying on a multidimensional scale that would include the following four variables:

1. *Market capitalization (MCAP)*[21]*/gross domestic product (GDP)* index as a proxy for the country's financial sector depth and maturity. For example, Vietnam may have a low MCAP/GDP ratio of 4% which means that its financial sector is still in its infancy, whereas Thailand at 95% is far more developed. Vietnam would therefore rank very low on the emergence market continuum whereas Thailand would be positioned in the middle with other middle-income countries.
2. *Disintermediation* index as a measure of the percentage of aggregate financing channeled by financial markets, as opposed to traditional financial intermediation provided by commercial banks. Presumably the allocational and operational efficiency is enhanced by a greater reliance on financial markets (especially the commercial paper market) than on financial institutions. For example, Germany may have a disintermediation index of 55% whereas the United Kingdom's index is higher at 78%.
3. *Global depositary receipts (GDRs) and American depositary receipts (ADRs)* index as a measure of the offshore market capitalization of national firms traded on the New York or London stock exchange as compared to total market capitalization (see International Corporate Finance in Practice 9.3 and Chapter 10 for further discussion). For example, Santiago (Chile), through a handful of major Chilean firms whose American depositary receipts (ADRs) are trading on the New York Stock Exchange while the original shares trade simultaneously on the Santiago stock exchange, may be characterized by an index as high as 35%, indicating a significant degree of market integration. When such firms are simultaneously traded on both exchanges, they force on the otherwise relatively segmented market of Santiago valuation rules that are more closely aligned with the highly efficient New York Stock Exchange.
4. *Market completeness* index capturing the degree of coverage of the matrix of financial market/product offerings (see Exhibit 9.8). As capital markets avail themselves of a fuller range of financial products, they benefit from a higher level of both allocational and operational efficiency that is welfare enhancing. The matrix is built on both the market dimension (left column) such as foreign exchange (FX or forex), commodities, and bonds, and the derivative product dimension (top row) of forwards, futures, swaps, and options. A complete market trading all derivatives in every market would fill all 25 cells in the matrix and would receive a perfect score of 100%. Most markets are incomplete and would fill some but not all of the cells in the matrix; therefore, they would receive a lower score than 100%. For example, the Paris Bourse at the time of the Bull-Bear notes issued in 1986 by the Kingdom of Denmark recounted in the previous section would have had a low score on the market completeness index. More generally, if we arbitrarily allocate equal weights of 0.04 (out of a maximum of 1.00) to each cell of the market (25 cells in total), Bangkok (BKK) would receive a score of 0.16 whereas São Paulo (SP) would get 0.40 out of a maximum of 1.00 for markets such as New York or London.

Three-dimensional (3D) segmentation map

Alternatively, one can map this segmentation/integration continuum in a three-dimensional space by decomposing the world's capital markets into three major components: (1) the equity market, (2) the debt market/money market, and (3) the foreign exchange market, which functions as a kind of transmission belt between national segments of the first two (see Exhibit 9.9). Unlike industrialized nations, which have efficient and well-functioning capital markets, emerging capital markets have burgeoning

21 Market capitalization of an entire country's stock market is simply the sum of the market values of all of the individually listed/traded companies.

INTERNATIONAL CORPORATE FINANCE IN PRACTICE 9.3

ADRs and the Segmentation of Capital Markets

American depositary receipts (ADRs) are US dollar–denominated negotiable instruments issued in the United States by a depositary bank on behalf of a foreign company. The investor in an ADR enjoys the benefits of share ownership in a foreign corporation without facing the cumbersome and otherwise onerous costs of investing directly in a foreign equity market. Such obstacles include costly currency conversions, opaque tax regulations, and unreliable custody and settlement in a foreign country. ADR programs also offer several advantages for the issuing company, which is often domiciled in an emerging market. Creation of a larger and geographically more diversified shareholder basis generally stabilizes share prices and provides additional liquidity. Raising of additional equity capital is also facilitated if the firm's home capital market cannot absorb a new issue. More exacting reporting and disclosure requirements enhance the profile and the attractiveness of the firm's stock from investors' perspectives. In sum, it is generally believed that ADR programs result in a lower cost of capital for the issuer.

Exhibit 9.8. Matrix of market completeness.

	Forwards	Futures	Swaps	Options	Other Derivatives
Foreign Exchange	BKK, SP	BKK, SP		BKK, SP	...
Interest Rate	SP	SP		SP	...
Commodities	BKK, SP	SP		...	...
Bonds	...	...		...	...
Stock	...	SP		SP	...

equity markets, embryonic debt markets (often with relatively short maturities), and mildly controlled foreign exchange markets. As discussed further later, in such emerging markets, debt financing continues to be provided predominantly by commercial banks and finance companies (which may also be major providers of equity financing). Let's turn now to each dimension of the world's capital markets space.

Equity market segmentation

A national capital equity market is defined as segmented from other countries' equity markets to the extent that a given security's rate of return in that particular market differs from that of other comparably risky securities traded in other national markets. Why are national equity markets segmented from one another? Segmentation may result from differences in financial reporting and disclosure requirements, in government tax policies, in regulatory obstacles to the introduction of financial innovations, in foreign exchange controls on financial account transactions (especially for the purpose of international portfolio investment), in restrictions (or lack thereof) on the amount of corporate control exercised by large investors, and in other forms of regulatory interference with the efficient functioning of national equity markets. Segmentation can also be caused by differences in investors' expectations stemming from informational barriers and differences in disclosure requirements among national equity markets.

Debt market segmentation

In efficient and integrated money markets, interest rates are free to adjust to changing expectations. As a result, they tend to respond so quickly to new information that opportunities for profitable arbitrage are quickly bid away. This is true of most industrialized countries with complete financial markets (that is, markets benefiting from

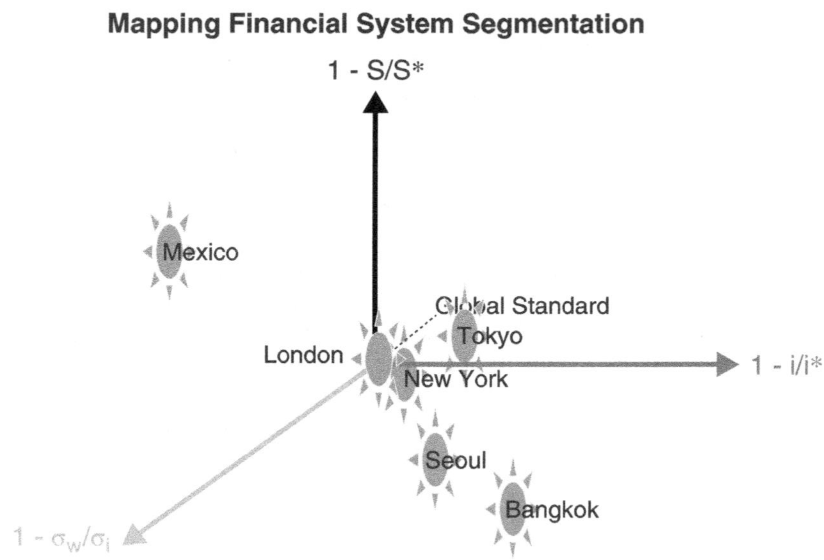

Exhibit 9.9. Space mapping of capital market segmentation.

well-functioning currency and interest rate futures, forwards, swaps, and options markets) and fully convertible currencies.

In such markets, a condition known as *interest rate parity* (see Chapter 6) is likely to prevail whereby large sophisticated borrowers and lenders such as commercial banks and money market mutual funds should be indifferent between borrowing or lending in the domestic or the foreign currency (when exchange risk is eliminated). Nominal interest rates for identical debt securities may still differ across currencies, but such differences should effectively be offset by anticipated depreciation of the currency with the lower real rates — a theory known as the *international Fisher effect.*

By contrast, segmented money markets are characterized by interest rate rigidities resulting from government-imposed distortions and controls, such as interest rate ceilings and mandatory credit allocations. When interest rate controls are coupled with exchange rate controls, arbitrage-motivated market forces are blocked, thus impeding interest rate parity and allowing for abnormal arbitrage opportunities to persist until the controls are lifted. As an example, the abolition of exchange controls in 1990 by the Central Bank of Thailand failed to narrow the interest rate differential between the Thai baht, whose rate ranged between 16% and 18%, and Eurodollars in Singapore and Hong Kong with rates between 6% and 8%. Quotas imposed on offshore borrowing by Thai commercial banks and major corporations arguably accounted for the continued interest rate difference.

Even among closely integrated financial markets, a "tiering" of credit markets between *onshore* (or domestic) and *offshore* (or Eurocurrency) segments continues to produce small but non-negligible segmentation residuals both within and across currency habitats (see Chapter 11 for further discussion of offshore or Eurocurrency markets). By and large, lower taxes, the absence of reserve banking requirements, and the reduced presence of other such market imperfections almost always lead to a greater degree of capital market integration in the offshore than in the onshore components of given debt markets.

Foreign Exchange Market Segmentation

In the 50-year history of the current floating exchange rate system, bilateral exchange rates have fluctuated over a wide range, with many appreciations and depreciations in a single year approaching 25% or more. The dollar itself has depreciated by as much as 50% in a single year against the Japanese yen or the euro. It is not uncommon for the price of a single currency to vary as much as 10% in a single day — as we witnessed during the subprime financial crisis.

Perhaps more perplexing than volatility itself is the evidence of prolonged periods of exchange rate over/undershooting. For the purposes of this chapter, currency over/undershooting is defined as long-term deviations of nominal exchange rates from their intrinsic equilibrium levels generally approximated by exchange rates consistent with *purchasing power parity* (PPP), which holds when exchange rate changes between two currencies over a given period are explained entirely by differences in underlying inflation rates over the same time period — see Chapter 7. In the case of the US dollar, such overshooting has been pronounced in relation to foreign currencies such as the yen, the pound, and the euro.

Most *segmented* capital market countries suffer from chronic balance of payments problems that are typically suppressed by an intricate web of exchange controls. In many newly industrializing countries, the quasi-convertible status of the currencies continues to be shrouded by a pervasive web of exchange controls running the gamut from light restrictions on visible trade transactions to byzantine controls on financial account transactions. Such restrictions may also sometimes take the form of two-tier and multiple-tier exchange rates or, in the case of hyperinflationary economies, government-mandated crawling pegs.

A mapping paradigm for emerging capital markets

As national capital markets loosen the regulatory shackles that create segmentation, the cost of capital should gradually edge lower toward its equilibrium value approximated by the United States' cost of capital, thus bringing about a truly integrated global capital market. This process is driven by the dismantling of controls in the debt and exchange markets and by the creation of an institutional setting that reduces equity market imperfections. But, until that process nears completion, world capital markets will continue to exhibit pockets of segmentation.

In Exhibit 9.10, we provide a map of capital market segmentation in a three-dimensional space by defining the origin of the axes as full integration. Each of the three axes gauges the degree of market segmentation exhibited by each of the three major financial markets — currency, debt, and equity — in the following fashion:

1. An index of currency over/undervaluation equal to 1 — S/S^* where S measures the nominal local currency price of one US dollar with S^* being the purchasing power parity equilibrium exchange rate similarly defined. If the currency is overvalued, $S < S^*$, the exchange market will be positioned between 0 and 1, and between 0 and −1 when undervalued. If the exchange rate is fairly priced, and thus financial markets are integrated (at least in an international sense), the exchange market will be positioned at the origin of the axis.

   Currencies such as the South African rand and the Brazilian real may at times be over-valued because of the currency carry trade, whereas the South Korean won or the Taiwanese dollar may at times be undervalued. For example, the Mexican peso in December 1994 and the Thai baht in July 1997 immediately before their respective financial crises were respectively overvalued by 20% and 35%. The Chinese yuan in 2012 was generally believed to be 25 to 30% undervalued. Even fully convertible currencies such as the Japanese yen or the euro may experience prolonged periods of overshooting or undershooting against their benchmark purchasing power parity equilibrium value.

> ***Q:*** The Mexican peso is currently trading at MXN 12 = US$1 when its fair value in PPP terms is generally believed to be at MXN 15 = US$1. Where would the peso be positioned along the foreign exchange market segmentation axis?
>
> ***A:*** The peso is overvalued and the index $1 - S/S^*$ can be readily computed as $1 - 12/15 = 1 - 0.80 = 0.20$. Thus, the peso would be positioned on the positive segment of the foreign exchange axis at 0.20.

2. An index of domestic interest rate overpricing/underpricing $1 - i/i^*$, where i denotes the controlled interest rate or nominal cost of debt financing (reflecting local debt market imperfections) and i^* the underlying equilibrium cost of capital.[22] The latter assumes the removal of interest rate controls of any kind as well as an institutional setting with conditions near market perfection.

   Such an index would range from a mildly negative to a positive number, depending on local market conditions. For Mexico the index was estimated as $1 - 0.76 = 0.24$.

22 Unlike PPP for exchange rates, there is no obvious theory for determining equilibrium interest rates. Econometric models, however, often fill the void.

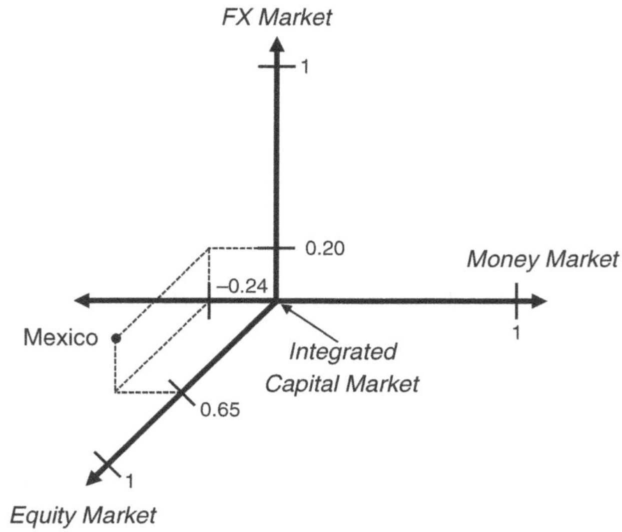

Exhibit 9.10: 3D segmentation mapping.

3. An index of relative market portfolio volatility, defined as $1 - \sigma_w/\sigma_i$ where σ_i and σ_w denote, respectively, the standard deviation of the market portfolio of a segmented emerging capital market i (σ_i) and the standard deviation of the world capital market portfolio (σ_w). Alternatively, the ratio of relative market portfolio volatility could be captured as the country beta, which measures the covariance of the local market portfolio with the world portfolio. As $\sigma_i \rightarrow \sigma_w$, the segmented capital market's "market portfolio" broadens and deepens and its volatility should decrease toward the volatility of the world market portfolio; similarly, as the local capital market becomes better integrated, its beta would tend toward 1.00.

   For example, the volatility of the Mexican market could be estimated at $\sigma_i = 0.46$ as compared to a world market volatility of $\sigma_w = 0.16$, resulting in an index of equity market segmentation of $1 - 0.16/0.46 = 0.65$. Thus, as illustrated with the case of Mexico, our map of capital market segmentation would allow us to position each country in a three-dimensional space.

The second policy question is the identification of the levers guiding this emergence process; as we argued before, moving gradually along this continuum would bring about a lower cost of capital, which is truly welfare enhancing: What can policy makers initiate in order to nurture this process? The consensus points toward economic liberalization/deregulation, disintermediation, FinTech and securitization as the major forces propelling capital markets toward a higher level of emergence.

SUMMARY

1. The financial system's primary function is to mobilize savings from households and to allocate those funds among competing corporate users on the basis of expected risk-adjusted returns. Thus, the financial system provides a conduit through which excess cash — primarily accumulated as savings by households — is channeled to firms primarily but also to households, municipalities, and government in need of cash or financing.
2. Financial intermediation can be carried out *indirectly* through commercial banks or other financial institutions or more *directly* through financial markets. Increasingly, borrowers bypass banks to connect directly with savers. This process is known as *financial disintermediation* and it lowers the cost of capital.
3. Securitization is a more elaborate form of disintermediation that typically results in a lower cost of consumer finance. It repackages illiquid consumer loans such as residential mortgages, automobile loans, or credit card receivables — which were traditionally held by commercial banks, thrifts, finance companies, or other financial institutions — into liquid tradable securities.

4. Most financial systems and capital markets are segmented from one another, at least to some degree, thus allowing for differences in the effective cost of capital from one country to the next. Capital markets are said to be *segmented* rather than *integrated*.
5. Globalization of capital markets means that national markets tend to become better integrated as deregulation, disintermediation, FinTech, securitization, and financial innovation relentlessly erode segmentation barriers. The world, though, is not flat yet!
6. Capital markets can be positioned along an *emergence continuum* ranging from extreme segmentation to complete integration. As countries ascend this continuum they avail themselves of a progressively lower cost of capital.

QUESTIONS FOR DISCUSSION

1. What are the principal sources of financing available to firms that find themselves in a cash-deficit situation?
2. What are the principal functions performed by the financial sector?
3. What does it mean to describe financing as a global procurement decision?
4. What are financial intermediaries?
5. What is financial disintermediation? Is it desirable?
6. What are the conditions for successful disintermediation?
7. What is the role played by credit rating agencies?
8. What is the role played by commercial paper in financial disintermediation?
9. What is securitization? Why does it lower the cost of consumer financing?
10. What are the unique risks inherent in an international securitization transaction?
11. What does it mean for financial markets to be "segmented"?
12. Explain how to map a given national financial system in a 3D space?
13. What makes emerging financial markets emerge?
14. Should securitization be blamed for the subprime crisis?

PROBLEMS

1. **Commercial paper (foundational).** Toro, the Wisconsin-based AA-rated manufacturer of snow-blowers and lawn mowers, anticipates that because of the seasonal nature of its business it will require an additional US$250 million for working capital during the second quarter (April, May, and June). The funding options are:
   - Bank loan from Wachovia Trust in the form of a one year line of credit for US$250 million at the annual rate of 6%. Wachovia charges a commitment fee of 0.5% on the unused portion of the line of credit.
   - Commercial paper issued for 90 days at the annual interest rate of 4.75%. Issuance cost, including the expense of a backup line of credit (credit enhancement), is 50 basis points of the amount issued.

   a. Compute the cost of each funding option.
   b. How do you explain the difference in funding cost?
   c. Would the funding cost faced by Toro be different if it were AAA-rated?
   d. Would you recommend that Toro select the cheaper funding option?
2. **Comparing financing options (foundational).** Maytag Limited — the manufacturer of white goods appliances — estimates that because of the seasonal nature of its business, it will require an additional $100 million of cash for the month of July. Maytag Limited has the following three options available for raising the needed funds:
   (a) Establish a one year line of credit for $100 million with a commercial bank. The commitment fee will be 0.5% per year on the unused portion, and the interest charge on the used funds will be 7% per annum. Assume that the funds are needed only in July and that there are 30 days in July and 360 days in the year.
   (b) Forego the trade discount of 2/10, net 40 on $100 million of purchases parts and sub-assemblies during July.
   (c) Issue $100 million of 30-day commercial paper at a 5.5% per annum interest rate. The total transactions fee, including the

cost of a backup credit line, on using commercial paper is 0.5% of the amount of the issue.

i. What is the dollar cost of each financing arrangement?

ii. Is the source with the lowest expected cost necessarily the one to select? Why or why not?

3. **The cost of financial intermediation (intermediate).** Weyerhaeuser, the lumber multinational company, is comparing the cost of alternative methods for financing its exports trade. US$500 million is needed for 180 days and can be sourced from Chicago Trust in the form of a bridge loan at a cost of 5.75%. Alternatively, Weyerhaeuser could tap the commercial paper market at the cost of 5.00% with an additional 35 basis points for a backup line of credit from Bank of America.

   a. Compare the cost of either financing option proposed to Weyerhaeuser.

   Weyerhaeuser's CFO is perplexed by the gap in financing cost, as he has just learned about Chicago Trust's ongoing commercial program at the rate of 5.25% with a letter of credit from Bank of America at the cost of 25 basis points. How could he reconcile the cost of financing difference given that Chicago Trust is required to keep a minimum equity capital at 10% of its book value (as per Basel II.5 agreement), that the cost of its equity capital is 17%, and that to break even Chicago Trust has to charge a spread of 150 basis points over its cost of funds? Assume that Chicago Trust's debt financing (as a percentage of debt + equity) is comprised of 25% of customers' deposits in checking accounts (which do not pay interest) and 60% of commercial paper.

   b. What is Chicago Trust's cost of capital? What is the minimum interest rate it should charge on a six-month loan to Weyerhaeuser? What is the net income generated by a loan to Weyerhaeuser? Does it account for the 10% capital adequacy ratio imposed by Basel II?

4. **Positioning Venezuela on the capital market emergence continuum (web exercise** — intermediate) By accessing the IMF monthly Financial Statistics and other pertinent websites:

   a. Compute for 2012 the ratio of the market capitalization of the Caracas (Venezuela) stock exchange to the country GDP.

   b. Does it rank ahead of or behind Argentina?

   c. What was Venezuela's positioning *vis-à-vis* Argentina on the emergence continuum in 2007 and 2002?

   d. How did Venezuela rank *vis-à-vis* Colombia in 2002, 2007, and 2012?

   e. How do you explain Venezuela's reversal of fortune over the past decades?

5. **Mapping Argentina's capital market segmentation (intermediate).** The Argentine peso (ARS) is officially trading at ARS 4.65 = US$1, with increasing volume of forex transactions channeled through the black market at ARS 6 = US$1. Interest rates on bank loans under tight supervision from the central bank are controlled with a benchmark prime rate of 12.50% when inflation is generally estimated at 21% annually. With recent nationalization of foreign-owned oil and utility companies, stock trading on the Buenos Aires Bolsa has declined sharply whereas the Merval index volatility has jumped to 37% compared to 16% on the New York Stock Exchange.

   a. Explain why Argentina's capital market is severely segmented from the global capital market (proxied by the New York Stock Exchange).

   b. Map in a 3D space Argentina's capital market.

   c. Assume that Argentina's central bank decides to let the ARS float unencumbered by exchange controls and that the exchange rate promptly falls to ARS 5.65 = US$1. How would Argentina's position in the 3D segmentation space adjust?

INTERNET EXERCISES

6. **Country Ratings.** Log in to Standard & Poor website www.standardandpoor.com to find the country rating of the Ukraine, Vietnam, Nigeria and Argentina. Are the ratings different for local currency and foreign currency? When were these country ratings last downgraded or upgraded?

7. **Corporate Ratings.** Log in to Standard and Poor website to find the credit ratings of Peugeot-Citroen, Volvo, Fiat-Chrysler and Toyota. When were these ratings last upgraded or downgraded.

REFERENCES

Acharya, Viral V., Thomas Cooley, Matt Richardson, and Ingo Walter, eds. 2010. *Regulating Wall Street, The Dodd-Frank Act and the New Architecture of Global Finance*. Hoboken, NJ: John Wiley & Sons.

Beim, David O., and Charles W. Calomiris. 2001. *Emerging Financial Markets*. New York: McGraw-Hill/Irwin.

Gorton, Gary B. 2010. "Questions and Answers about the Financial Crisis." NBER working paper #15787.

Jacque, L. L., and G. Hawawini. 1993. "Myths and Realities of the Global Capital Markets: Lessons for Financial Managers." *Journal of Applied Corporate Finance* 6(3): 81–90.

Jacque, L. L., and P. Vaaler, eds. 2001. *Financial Innovations and the Welfare of Nations*. Norwell, MA: Kluwer Academic Publishers.

Kratz, O. S. 1999. *Frontier Emerging Equity Markets Securities: Price Behavior and Valuation*. Norwell, MA: Kluwer Academic Press.

Schwarcz, Steven L. 1994. "The Alchemy of Asset Securitization." *Stanford Journal of Law, Business & Finance* (Fall). 1: 133–154.

Stulz, R. M. 1999. "Globalization of Equity Markets and the Cost of Capital." Paper presented at the SBF/NYSE Conference on Global Equity Markets in Paris, February.

Williamson, J., and M. Mahar. 1998. "A Survey of Financial Liberalization." *Princeton Essays in International Finance* (221).

CASE STUDY 9.1. HOW THAI AIRWAYS FOILS JET FUEL PRICE RISK

Shuvam Dutta

Songkran Piyavasti, the CFO of Thai Airways, was planning a round of capital raising to meet the airline's fleet expansion plans and needed to raise up to US$800 million in debt by June 2010. Traditionally, the company had financed its aircraft acquisitions through the issuance of baht-denominated debentures and bank loans from Thai banks. However, in the aftermath of the Asian financial crisis, the airline had sought to diversify its funding sources; it had raised debt from international capital markets through dollar- and euro-denominated loans from international banks, and it had increasingly used structured lease instruments to finance its capital expenditures.

Aircraft financing through structured leases

By the end of 2009, 56% of Thai Airways' fleet was financed by operating and financial leases. Net gearing (debt/equity ratio) of a number of Asian carriers, including this airline, was at a record high. With limited unpledged assets, unsecured loans were difficult to obtain without guarantees or government support. A stretched balance sheet, high capital expenditures commitments, and a net tightening of credit conditions pushed the carrier to seek off-balance-sheet financing in the form of leases.

Airlines were also entering into sale and leaseback transactions[23] through which they could effectively fund 100% of the value of the aircraft. In contrast, an airline would have to struggle to raise 85% of the value as the asset owner. Sale and leasebacks became an attractive source of off-balance-sheet financing for airlines because they aided in cash enhancement and provided flexible terms with no exposure to the residual value of the asset, which was typically not easy to realize through an asset sale in difficult market conditions.

What is lease financing?

As an alternative to traditional debt, lease financing allows Thai Airways to use an aircraft without actually owning it. A lease is a contractual agreement between the owner of the asset (lessor) and the user of the asset (lessee). The lessor can be the manufacturer of the asset, a financial institution, or an independent leasing company. If the lessor is not the manufacturer, the asset would be sold to the lessor, which in turn leases it to the lessee. In the airline industry most leases are financial leases, which are long-term contracts that extend over most of the

23 A sale and leaseback is a transaction whereby Thai Airways would first acquire an air-plane, and then sell it immediately to a leasing company, which would in turn lease it back to Thai Airways. Thai Airways thus becomes the lessee.

useful life of the asset and require the lessee — not the lessor — to be responsible for the maintenance and insurance costs of the asset. The advantage of leasing is that the lessee will not incur any initial large cash outlay to purchase the asset; however, the lessee will not benefit from tax-deductible depreciation expenses, which now accrue to the lessor. Instead, the lessee's annual payments to the leasing company are tax-deductible expenses for the lessee. Leases are off-balance-sheet items that do not impact the lessee's leverage ratio.

Fuel price volatility and airline performance

Fuel price volatility was plaguing the airline sector as fuel costs continued to increase. The volatility in the price of jet fuel led to unstable cash flows and increased operational and financial risks. It hindered management's ability to plan for the company's long-term business operations, investments, and financing strategies. (See Case Exhibits 9.1 and 9.2.)

As a major long-haul carrier providing international flights, Thai Airways had a higher rate of fuel burn than most of its peers and was thus more exposed to the volatility of fuel prices. Apart from fluctuating profitability, volatility in jet fuel threatened Thai Airways' credit rating and its ability to borrow at competitive rates.

It is in this context that Mr. Piyavasti met with Standard Chartered Bank in Bangkok and expressed his interest in a structured solution that would combine a fuel hedging derivative with a lease.

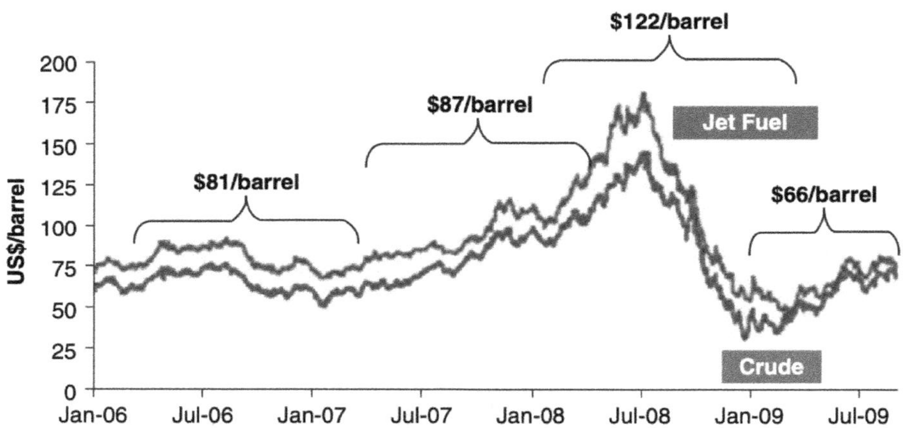

Case Exhibit 9.1. Average jet fuel price.

Source: International Air Transport Association (IATA), September 2009; Bloomberg.

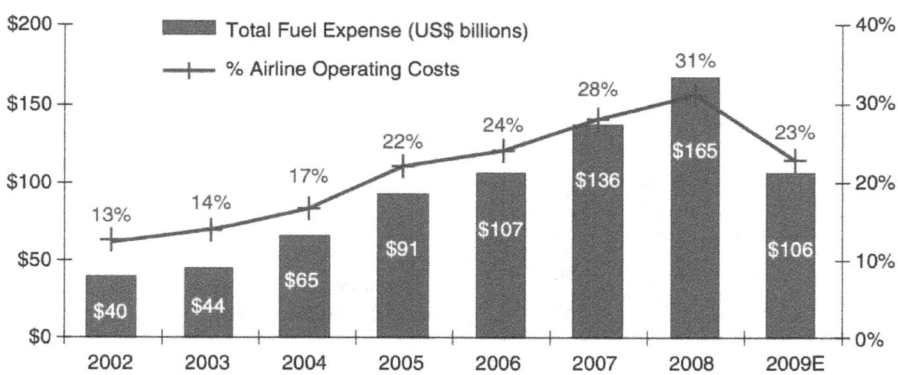

Case Exhibit 9.2. Fuel as percentage of airline operating costs.

Source: International Air Transport Association (IATA) News Update No. 24 as of June 2009.

Fuel oil insulated lease (foil): Combining aircraft financing with fuel risk management

Standard Chartered's bankers structured a product combining an aircraft operating lease and a jet fuel derivative such that lease payments could be reduced when fuel prices increased, thus enhancing the predictability, and reducing the volatility of cash flows.

This structured financing solution provided a dedicated asset-specific capital cost hedging solution where the quantum of fuel hedged would be consistent with the fuel consumption of the specific aircraft to which it related. The hedging product could be used as an overlay program on any existing aircraft operating lease and could be bundled with new aircraft operating leases. Tenors, notional amounts, and payouts could be tailored to match the airline's fuel hedging requirements and policy.

The bankers illustrated the payout profile of the lease with and without the solution, as shown in Case Exhibit 9.3. The underlying derivatives used in the structure were call and put options bought and sold at different strike prices.

The bankers also estimated that using this structure could have resulted in cost savings worth US$12 million per aircraft from 2004 to 2010. This analysis was done based on the typical value and fuel consumption profile of an Airbus A330.

After the meeting, Mr. Piyavasti pondered the lease repayment profile proposed by Standard Chartered, shown in Case Exhibit 9.4. Was this novel financing structure suitable for Thai Airways?

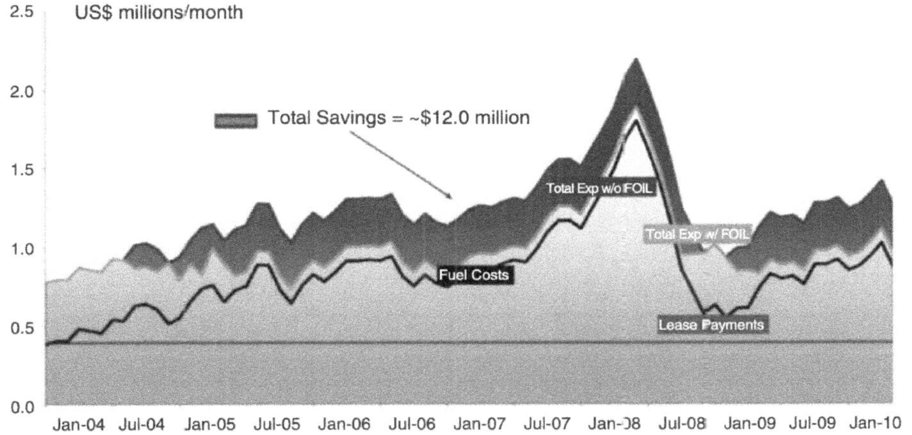

Case Exhibit 9.3. Historical total expenses per aircraft, January 2004 to May 2010.

Case Exhibit 9.4. Lease repayment profile.

WTI Price (US$)	Jet Fuel Price (US$)	Flexible Lease	Fixed Lease	Fuel Expense	Fuel + Lease (without FOIL)	Fuel + Lease (with FOIL)
30.00	40.00	780	390	423	813	1,203
40.00	50.00	780	390	529	919	1,309
48.00	58.00	780	390	614	1,004	1,394
50.00	60.00	760	390	635	1,025	1,395
60.00	70.00	654	390	740	1,130	1,395
70.00	80.00	549	390	846	1,236	1,395
80.00	90.00	443	390	952	1,342	1,395
90.00	100.00	337	390	1,058	1,448	1,395
100.00	110.00	231	390	1,164	1,554	1,395
110.00	120.00	126	390	1,269	1,659	1,395
120.00	130.00	20	390	1,375	1,765	1,395
122.00	132.00	0	390	1,396	1,786	1,396
130.00	140.00	0	390	1,481	1,871	1,481
140.00	150.00	0	390	1,587	1,977	1,587
150.00	160.00	0	390	1,693	2,083	1,693

Note: All figures in US$'000 unless otherwise stated.

Questions for Discussion

1. What is the nature of Thai Airways' exposure to oil price risk?
2. How could Thai Airways hedge its oil price exposure with traditional derivatives such as oil futures, forwards, options, and swaps?
3. How does FOIL as proposed by Standard Chartered Bank differ from traditional oil price hedges bundled with a loan or a note?
4. What is the West Texas Intermediate (WTI) oil price range within which Thai Airways is immunized against oil price risk? What is the cost of the hedge?
5. Why did Thai Airways end up choosing FOIL?

CHAPTER 10

Sourcing Equity Globally

DaimlerChrysler shares will trade in the U.S. in dollars, on the Deutsche Borse in Deutsche marks, and in 16 other markets around the world in whatever currency these markets would choose. We created for the first time a concept where equity could follow the sun.
— Richard Grasso, CEO of the New York Stock Exchange

The increasing integration of national capital markets offers access to new and cheaper sources of financing beyond those available to firms in their home markets. Thus going "global" rather than staying "domestic" when it comes to financing is increasingly becoming a way of life for many firms, whether they are domestic or multinational in their sales reach and regardless of where they are domiciled. Consider, for example, the global initial public offering (IPO) odyssey of Jazztel, an upstart Spanish telecom. Jazztel was considering an IPO on the New York NASDAQ (rather than the Madrid Bolsa) for funding its ambitious capital expenditure program, estimated at $750 million over the next 10 years. Following the liberalization of the Spanish telecom market on December 1, 1998, Jazztel became the first alternative service provider to challenge the giant monopolist Telefonica (a recently privatized Spanish state-owned telecom) by providing a full range of high-quality, tailor-made integrated voice, data, and Internet services at attractive prices. As a Spanish telecom company aiming exclusively at the domestic telecom market, one would have expected Jazztel's IPO to be launched on the Madrid Bolsa. Issuing equity on the US NASDAQ would, after all, require significant costs in the form of additional disclosures, not to mention restating financial statements according to US accounting principles. Yet Jazztel became the first Spanish company to achieve a simultaneous IPO on NASDAQ (United States) and on EASDAQ (Luxembourg) in December 1999. It raised €196 million at a market capitalization valuing Jazztel at approximately €917 million.

This chapter explores why so many firms like Jazztel decide to list their shares and raise equity financing on foreign capital markets. But first we conduct a grand tour of stock markets before showing that equity financing is no different from any capital procurement decision that is primarily guided by a cost of capital minimization rule.

In this chapter you will gain an understanding of:

- What the hallmarks of national equity markets are.
- How continuing mild degrees of capital market segmentation warrants foreign equity financing.
- Why foreign listings of a firm's shares may reduce its cost of equity capital.
- What are American depositary receipts (ADRs) and global depositary receipts (GDRs).
- What are the costs and benefits of listing and/or raising capital via ADRs and GDRs.
- What is the rationale for cross-listing shares in multiple stock markets.
- How corporate ownership and control shape governance systems and impact firms' valuation (Appendix 10A).

A GRAND TOUR OF EQUITY MARKETS

The revolutionary concept of the *joint stock company* is generally traced to the granting by the British crown of a royal charter to the Muscovy Company in 1557 giving it exclusive trading privileges with Russia. Not only did this allow for the pooling of capital, but it also *limited* shareholders' *liability* to their initial equity investment, created an independent legal entity that through its company seal could sue (and be sued), established a governance structure, and, last but not least, allowed *transferability* of interests. Sometime thereafter, in 1602, the Dutch East India Company (Vereenigde Oost-Indische Compagnie) issued stock shares that were *tradable* on the Amsterdam Bourse (see International Corporate Finance in Practice 10.1); the first modern stock exchange was born. Indeed, this innovation enhanced firms' ability to raise capital, as investors could easily dispose of their investment if necessary by readily selling their shares on the Bourse.

It was not until the late eighteenth century, however, that organized bourses or stock exchanges started to operate on a significant scale. Historical legacies and cultural differences shaped by national juridical traditions help to explain differences in idiosyncratic regulations, market structures, and trading patterns. Nevertheless, modern technology and the relentless rise of the digital economy act as the great cost of equity equalizers across national stock exchanges. After profiling major stock exchanges, this section sketches the key trends that are reshaping the global equity trading landscape.

Statistical market overview

US stock exchanges have long been the largest in the world, with a market capitalization in excess of $25 trillion, but are increasingly challenged by rising Chinese stock markets. Exhibit 10.1 lists the 25 largest stock markets in 2020 ranked by their *market capitalizations* — the sum of market values of all publicly traded companies on that exchange. Exhibit 10.1 also includes market capitalization in 2000, 2005, 2010 and 2015 for comparison purposes: The ranking by market capitalization remained relatively stable over the decade, but the reader will note how barely functioning stock markets 25 years ago — such as China or India — have vaulted into the big leagues.

This is the story of emerging capital markets that has transformed the world of international finance and that is depicted by the *emerging capital markets continuum* introduced in the previous chapter. The reader will recall that the ratio of market capitalization to gross domestic product (GDP) was deemed indicative of a given market level of emergence (see Exhibits 10.2A and 10.2B for both developed and emerging capital markets). Among developed markets, Anglo-Saxon countries such as the United States, the United Kingdom, Canada, and Australia tend to have a higher ratio of market capitalization relative to the size of their economies than continental Europe — most

INTERNATIONAL CORPORATE FINANCE IN PRACTICE 10.1

The World's Oldest Share*

The year is 1602 and the date is September 1. The Vereenigde Oostindische Compagnie (VOC) or Dutch East India Company, the world's first joint-stock limited liability company with freely transferable and tradable shares, just closed the public offering of its shares, giving subscribers the opportunity to participate in this new venture. The charter from the States-General of the Netherlands granted VOC a monopoly to carry out colonial activities in Asia — primarily the trade of spices in the early years. Until then it had been customary for a company to be set up for the duration of a single voyage and then to be dissolved on the return of the fleet. Indeed, investment in these expeditions was a high-stakes gamble because of the dangers of piracy, disease, and shipwreck, not to forget the volatility of supply, which could make the prices of spices tumble at the wrong time for the commercial success of the enterprise. The VOC eclipsed all of its rivals in the Asia trade and became inordinately profitable, distributing an 18% annual dividend for almost 200 years. It had two types of shareholders — the *partipanten* (common shareholders) and 76 *bewinhedders* (managing directors); their liability was limited to the paid-in capital that was deemed permanent during the lifetime of the company. Investors who opted to liquidate their stock holdings could do so at any time by selling their shares to others on the Amsterdam Stock Exchange.

Note: * In 2010 Ruben Schalk, a history student from Utrecht University, found the world's oldest share in the Westfries Archief in Hoorn. It dates from 1606 and was issued by the Dutch East India Trading Company Chamber of Enkhuisen.

Source: Ricklefs, M.C. 1991. *A History of Modern Indonesia Since c. 1300*. London: Macmillan.

Exhibit 10.1. The 25 largest stock exchanges.

Country	2000	2005	2010	2015	2020
United States[a]	15,214,600	17,000,864	17,283,452	25,067,540	41,569,862
Japan[b]	3,193,934	7,542,716	4,099,606	4,894,919	6,718,220
China[c]	1,204,387	1,456,852	6,739,156	11,372,894	18,344,886
United Kingdom	2,612,230	3,058,182	3,613,064	3,219,211	3,669,685
Euronext[d]	2,269,571	2,706,803	2,930,072	3,305,901	5,443,947
India[e]	148,063	1,069,046	3,228,455	3,001,305	4 732 245
Canada	770,116	1,482,185	2,170,433	1,591,929	2,608,377
Brazil	226,152	474,647	1,545,566	490,534	988,374
Australia	372,794	804,015	1,454,491	1,187,084	1,720,556
Deutsche Börse[f]	1,270,243	1,221,106	1,429,719	1,715,801	2,284,109
Switzerland	792,316	935,448	1,229,357	1,519,324	2,001,603
Spain	504,222	959,910	1,171,625	787,192	759,175
South Korea	148,361	718,011	1,091,911	1,231,200	2,176,189
OMX Nordic Exchange	114,918	802,561	1,042,154	1,268,042	2,110,440
Russia	38,921	548,579	949,149	393,238	694,739
South Africa	131,321	549,310	925,007	735,945	1,051,529
Taiwan	247,597	476,018	818,490	745,000	1,598,570
Singapore	155,126	257,341	647,226	639,956	652,615
Mexico	125,204	239,128	454,345	402,253	399,617
Malaysia	113,155	180,518	408,689	382,977	436,538
Indonesia	26,813	81,428	360,388	353,271	496,086
Saudi Arabia	67,171	646,103	353,410	421,060	2,429,102
Chile	60,401	136,493	341,799	190,352	184,549
Turkey	69,659	161,538	307,052	188,862	237,474
Norway	65,774	190,952	295,288	193,896	332,000

Notes: All figures in millions of US dollars.
[a] Includes NYSE Euronext and NASDAQ.
[b] Includes Tokyo and Osaka exchanges.
[c] Includes Shenzhen, Shanghai, and Hong Kong.
[d] Euronext includes Paris, Brussels, and Amsterdam exchanges.
[e] Includes Bombay Stock Exchange and National Stock Exchange India.
[f] Deutsche Börse is headquartered in Frankfurt.

Source: World Federation of Exchanges, International Monetary Fund, and the World Bank.

notably Germany, France, and Italy, which have ratios generally below 1.0, reflecting that their firms are far less likely to go public than their Anglo-Saxon counterparts and rely more heavily on bank financing.

Trading practices

At its most basic, equity markets enable continuous *share valuation* and facilitate the *marketability* and *transferability* of shares. Indeed, investors and traders who subscribe to a firm's IPO (primary market) will not hold their shares indefinitely and will rely on their marketability to reduce their holdings (secondary market) as they reallocate their stock portfolio. How this process is carried out or, in other words, how stocks are traded is important because it directly affects price discovery and market liquidity.[1] *Price discovery* is the process by which information is

1 Which in turn informs share valuation and facilitates their marketability.

Exhibit 10.2A. Market capitalization to GDP ratios — developed capital markets.

Country	2000	2005	2010	2015	2020
United States	1.5	1.3	1.2	1.4	1.9
Japan	0.7	1.0	0.7	1.1	1.3
United Kingdom	1.8	1.3	1.6	1.1	0.9
France, Netherlands, and Belgium[a]	1.2	0.9	0.8	0.9	...
Hong Kong	3.7	5.9	12.1	10.3	17.8
Canada	1.1	1.3	1.4	1.0	1.6
Australia	0.9	1.1	1.2	0.9	1.3
Germany	0.7	0.4	0.4	0.5	0.6
Switzerland	3.2	2.5	2.3	2.2	2.7
Spain	0.9	0.8	0.8	0.7	0.6
South Korea	0.3	0.8	1.1	0.9	1.3
Nordic countries[b]	1.1[c]	0.7	0.7	0.8	...
Taiwan	0.8	1.3	1.9	1.4	2.3
Singapore	1.6	2.1	2.9	2.1	1.9

Notes: All figures in millions of US dollars.

[a]NYSE Euronext (Europe) includes the GDP of France, Netherlands, and Belgium.

[b]NASDAQ OMX Nordic Exchange includes the following exchanges: Denmark, Sweden, Finland, Estonia, Latvia, Lithuania, Iceland, Armenia, and Norway.

[c]NASDAQ OMX Nordic Exchange did not exist in 2000. This figure is the sum of the Finland, Norway, Sweden, Denmark, and Slovenia exchanges.

Source: World Federation of Exchanges and International Monetary Fund.

Exhibit 10.2B. Market capitalization to GDP ratios — emerging capital markets.

Country	2000	2005	2010	2015	2020
China	1.0	0.2	0.7	0.7	0.8
India	0.3	1.3	2.0	0.7	1.0
Brazil	0.4	0.5	0.7	0.3	0.7
Russia	0.1	0.7	0.6	0.3	0.5
South Africa	1.0	2.2	2.5	2.3	3.1
Mexico	0.2	0.3	0.4	0.3	0.4
Malaysia	1.2	1.3	1.7	1.3	1.3
Indonesia	0.2	0.3	0.5	0.4	0.5
Chile	0.8	1.2	1.7	0.8	0.7
Turkey	0.3	0.3	0.4	0.2	0.3
Thailand	0.2	0.7	0.9	0.9	1.1
Colombia	0.1	0.3	0.7	0.3	0.4

Note: All figures in millions of US dollars.

Source: World Federation of Exchanges, International Monetary Fund, and the World Bank.

revealed and ultimately reflected in stock prices. To be efficient, the price discovery process has to prevent stock price manipulation by individual traders.

Market liquidity allows large trades to be carried out quickly, at low transaction costs, and without markedly impacting the price of the traded stock.

There are two principal trading systems to consider. In a *price-driven* market, transactions take place continuously through the day and *market makers* (also known as *dealers*) ensure market liquidity at all times. Market dealers quote both a *bid* and an *ask* price. The bid price is the price at which the dealer is willing to buy the share, and the ask/offer price is the price at which the dealer stands ready to sell the share. Market makers will adjust their quotes continuously to reflect new information related directly or indirectly to the share value, its inventory, and the supply and demand for the share. Thus, customers will simply shop around for the best quotes. The NASDAQ is the largest and best-known dealer market.

In less active markets, orders are batched together in an order book and auctioned off once or several times a day at prices for which supply of and demand for the shares are in equilibrium. This trading system is also known as *order-driven*. In yesteryears, stock exchanges were physical exchanges where brokers would negotiate verbally (and loudly) until a clearing price would match buy and sell orders. These were the heyday of colorful "open outcry" stock exchanges, which are increasingly morphing into computerized markets (or cohabiting with them). Today buy and sell orders are directly entered into a computerized trading system that will periodically match them off through a computerized auction. The highest bid/buy and the lowest sell/ask orders receive priority. This system provides the necessary liquidity when the auctioning takes place but is found lacking in between auctioning times, hence the current effort to marry the market-dealing function with the periodic auctioning process. The Tokyo Stock Exchange (TSE) combines floor trading with an automated trading system, and the Paris Bourse is fully automated; they are prime examples of auction-based or order-driven markets. However, by recording and making public quasi-instantly all orders, automated electronic trading systems may discourage traders from revealing their intentions, especially when they are finalizing large orders (block trades). This can impair the price discovery process.[2]

The NYSE is a unique and anomalous combination of a *price-driven* and an *order-driven* market. Each stock is assigned to a single specialist who acts both as a dealer (as in a price-driven market) and as an auctioneer (as in an order-driven market). The specialist (an actual human being) is physically located at one of the exchange trading posts on the NYSE trading floor and — as a dealer — will continuously post bid and ask prices. As an auctioneer, the specialist maintains the order book when orders are submitted by customers.

Market liquidity

Transaction volume is a good gauge of the liquidity of each market. More specifically, a measure of liquidity is given by the total number of stock market transactions over a given period — say a year — divided by the market capitalization at the end of the period; this important ratio is also known as the *turnover* ratio and sometimes as the *share turnover velocity* ratio. For example, in 2010 the turnover ratio reached 3.49 (or 349%) in the United States but was only 0.15 in Ukraine. This means that on average every US-listed stock traded 3.49 times in 2010 whereas in the Ukraine only 15% of all listed stocks traded once in 2010. Generally, a higher turnover ratio means a more liquid secondary market, lower transaction costs, and greater ease for investors to buy and sell stocks very close to currently quoted prices.

Exhibits 10.3A and 10.3B present turnover ratios for selected equity markets over the period 2000–2020; the range of turnover ratios is a good proxy for the degree of national equity market emergence first presented in the previous chapter. Large markets such as Brazil or Mexico are far more liquid than smaller markets such as Ukraine or Peru. Over the decade, many markets have shown signs of increasing liquidity consistent with the notion that these markets were ascending along the emergence continuum. Very low turnover ratios are generally synonymous with small and illiquid equity markets whose high transaction costs deter investors from trading actively; such markets are positioned very low on the emergence continuum.

> ***Q:*** What would be the turnover ratio of an equity market in which every listed stock traded once and only once during the year?
>
> ***A:*** Each listed stock would add to exactly the market's market capitalization, and therefore the ratio should be 1.00.[3]

2 For example, the Paris Bourse allows large trades to be negotiated "upstairs" outside its computerized trading system through bilateral telephone negotiation in the offices away from the trading floor.

3 The ratio would be 1.00 if all stocks were traded on the last day of the year when market capitalization is computed. Because each stock would presumably be traded at some time during the year at a price that may be different from what it is when market capitalization is computed, the turnover ratio would be close to but not exactly 1.00.

Exhibit 10.3A. Liquidity for developed capital markets.

Rank	Country	2000	2005	2010	2015	2020
1	United States	2.0	1.3	1.9	1.7	1.1
2	Japan	0.7	1.2	1.1	1.1	0.9
3	United Kingdom	0.7	1.4	1.0	1.1	0.2
4	Germany	0.8	1.5	1.0	0.8	0.8
5	France	0.7	0.9	0.4	0.6	N/A
6	Hong Kong	0.6	0.4	0.6	0.6	0.5
7	Canada	0.8	0.6	0.7	0.7	0.7
8	Australia	0.6	0.8	0.9	0.6	0.7
9	Switzerland	0.8	1.0	0.8	0.6	0.7
10	South Korea	3.8	2.1	1.7	1.5	2.4

Source: World Bank.

Exhibit 10.3B. Liquidity for emerging capital markets.

Rank	Country	2000	2005	2010	2015	2020
1	China	1.6	0.8	1.6	4.8	2.6
2	India	3.1	0.9	0.8	0.5	0.7
3	Brazil	0.4	0.4	0.7	0.9	1.4
4	Russia	0.4	0.4	0.9	0.3	0.4
5	South Africa	0.3	0.4	0.4	0.3	0.4
6	Mexico	0.3	0.3	0.3	0.3	0.2
7	Malaysia	0.4	0.3	0.3	0.3	0.6
8	Indonesia	0.3	0.5	0.5	0.2	0.3
9	Saudi Arabia	0.3	2.3	0.6	1.0	0.2
10	Chile	0.1	0.1	0.2	0.1	0.1

Source: World Bank.

Market efficiency

Equity markets are continuously processing new information as it becomes available. The question — hard to answer — is to what extent the processing of information is efficient and does result into reliable stock prices. Thus, in efficient equity markets the share price of firms would instantly adjust to the release of new and relevant information to the extent that such new information would impact the firm's future cash-flows.

A vivid illustration of the speed and scope of equity markets informational efficiency is Volkswagen's "diesel-gate": on Friday, September 18, 2015, the Environmental Protection Agency accused Volkswagen of cheating on emissions testing and ordered the recall of 482,000 diesel-powered cars sold in the United States that featured "defeat device" software. On Monday, September 21, Volkswagen AG's stock price opened 14% down, a reduction in market capitalization of €11.3 billion. On September 22, the company conceded that 11 million cars worldwide were fitted with the defeat devices. By the close of markets, Volkswagen's stock was down a further 24%, wiping out €28.3 billion from its market capitalization and prompting its CEO to resign shortly after. Cost of retrofitting diesel engines, mammoth fines, lost sales and legal cost had been incorporated in Volkswagen's future cash-flows in a matter of a few hours.

Are equity markets worldwide reliably efficient? Do they provide unbiased estimates of share prices? Empirical evidence indicates that — on balance — the more developed equity markets are informationally efficient. But, on occasions, stock markets can succumb to excesses as herd exuberance led to the internet stock bubble (1999–2002) or the sub-prime crisis (2007–2009).

Market concentration

Markets that are dominated by a few large firms offer fewer opportunities for risk diversification and active portfolio management. A simple measure of market concentration is the ratio of the sum of the 10 largest firms (in terms of their market capitalization) to the entire market capitalization. Switzerland, for example, is highly concentrated, with a ratio hovering around 70%, whereas both the NYSE and the TSE show market concentration ratios lower than 20%.[4]

The world's major stock markets

The New York Stock Exchange (NYSE) is the single largest stock exchange in the world, listing close to 3,000 firms, including 450 foreign listings; its unique specialist-centered floor-trading auction system has remained largely unchanged since 1792, unlike its closest competitor, the National Association of Securities Dealers Automated Quotation system (NASDAQ), which functions on an electronic price-driven trading system.

Europe has as many stock exchanges as it has sovereign nations, with the majority of them being small and illiquid. Unsurprisingly, mergers and consolidation of national stock exchanges in pursuit of greater liquidity have greatly simplified Europe's equity trading landscape in recent years. Only the United Kingdom and Germany have retained national autonomous stock exchanges; the London Stock Exchange (LSE) continues to be the hub of international finance and attracts many international listings through GDRs of more than 350 firms from as many as 50 different countries. The Deutsche Börse Group, through its ownership of the Frankfurt Stock Exchange, accounts for more than 75% of all German equity trading. To better compete with the LSE and the Deutsche Börse Group, Euronext was established in 2000 with the merger of the Amsterdam, Brussels, and Paris stock exchanges (Lisbon joined in 2002).[5] On a smaller scale the OMX — first established through the merger of the Stockholm and Helsinki exchanges in 2003 — now regroups the Copenhagen, Reykjavik, Talinn, Riga, and Vilnius stock exchanges.

The TSE — long the dominant Asian market (it overtook the NYSE briefly in the late 1980s) — has fallen on hard times with dramatically shrinking market capitalization after the bursting of its stock price bubble in 1991.[6] Reduced trading volume on the TSE after the 1991 crash triggered the exodus of many foreign firms delisting from its exchange and migrating to other more vibrant Asian stock exchanges such as Hong Kong; compared to as many as 125 multinational corporations (MNCs) listed on the TSE in the early 1990s, fewer than 10 foreign firms are now listed on its exchange.

The growth of Chinese stock markets in Shanghai and Shenzhen has largely mirrored China's phenomenal growth despite continued exchange controls on financial account transactions that hamper foreign portfolio investors. Most notable is the continued segmentation among Chinese firms' shares: (1) *A shares* are strictly held by Chinese individuals and institutions and traded on Chinese exchanges, (2) *B shares* are denominated in US dollars and available only to foreign investors but also traded on Chinese stock exchanges, and (3) *H shares* are traded only on the Hong Kong stock exchange in Hong Kong dollars and, therefore, are free of mainland China's currency controls. Hong Kong, however — long an independent heavyweight among Asian stock markets — is increasingly rejoining greater China's fold as its economy becomes more closely integrated with that of mainland China. The rest of developed Asia — South Korea, Taiwan, and Singapore — is host to some of the most vibrant and liquid stock markets. Meanwhile, emerging Southeast Asian stock exchanges — Thailand, Malaysia, Philippines, and Indonesia — are less active.

Similarly, India — with more than 2,500 companies' stock actively traded, primarily on the Bombay Stock Exchange (which accounts for close to 75% of all equity trading in India) — is enjoying a renaissance ever since restrictions on foreign ownership were relaxed in 1992 along with the increasing convertibility of the Indian rupee.

4 At the apogee of its stock valuation, Nokia accounted for more than 50 percent of the Helsinki (Finland) stock exchange market capitalization!

5 In 2002 Euronext acquired the London International Financial Futures and Options Exchange. In 2007 Euronext merged with the NYSE to form NYSE Euronext.

6 The Nikkei 225, the TSE's stock index, slumped from over 40,000 in 1990 to below 10,000 in 2012.

INTERNATIONAL CORPORATE FINANCE IN PRACTICE 10.2

Is Market Efficiency on Death Row in Saudi Arabia?

Government are prone to intervening in their currency market to prop up the value of their currencies or to slow down their appreciation. Government intervention in their stock market to shore up market indices is a much rarer occurrence. Yes, Asian countries such as Japan and China have indeed, on occasion, interfered with market forces to stem the precipitous descent of their stock market indices. Japan, for example, through its central bank and the Government Pension Investment Fund, has intervened in the TSE on average every three days since 2013 and, as of June 2015, held about 1.25% of exchange total market capitalization. This unorthodox policy is known modestly as PKO for *"Price Keeping Operations"* (not to be confused with "Peace Keeping Operations"!)

"Saudi Arabia is reported to have been spending billions of dollars to quietly prop up its stock market and counter sell-offs triggered by a series of recent political crises which have engulfed the kingdom. Typically, the Saudi government would place huge buy orders often in the closing minutes of negative trading days....

Rather than buying stocks directly and fully disclosing the transactions the Saudi government has routed its purchases through asset managers at Saudi financial institutions who run funds that don't need to reveal their clients. It is a strategy that the kingdom used last year after it launched an economic blockade of Qatar, following the arrest of and torture of prominent Saudis, a corruption crackdown and the detention of Lebanon's prime minister. ... The Saudi government has been keen to show the world that Saudi Arabia remains safe for foreign investors. The Saudi stand apart because they're geared to attract foreign investors to a market with little foreign ownership. Foreigners only own 4% stock on the Saudi market, where all the companies are Saudi-based with some government ownership. ... Antoine van Agtmael who coined the term "emerging markets" almost 40 years ago. ... said government intervention makes the Saudi stock exchange "more of a fake market and that kind of undermine the trust of investors in the long run".

Having a healthy stock market is especially important because the Saudi stock exchange known as the Tadawul will be included next year in global emerging market indices. That inclusion will result in billions of dollars of foreign capital entering the exchange, which currently has a market capitalization of $500 billion. ... To prop up the market, the government has bought stocks via its sovereign Public Investment Fund (PIF) ... Public data show that as of November 1, 2018 Saudi government-related entities owned about $200 billion in shares of companies listed on the local exchange. The actual value is billions of dollars higher due to the PIF's undisclosed buying ...

Since 2015, when his father became king, the prince, known widely by his initials "MBS" has placed the Tadawul at the center of his plans to modernize Saudi Arabia's economy. His government suggested taking the Saudi state oil company ARAMCO public on the exchange in what would the largest ever IPO which heightened the importance of making the market seems stable and safe to foreign investors. The murder of Saudi journalist Khashoggi inside the kingdom's embassy in Ankara is the latest geo-political incident to jolt the Saudi stock market. Government large scale intervention to paper over the cracks that are undermining market efficiency on the Tadawul is only adding fuel to the fire that is engulfing investors trust and confidence.

Abridged from the "Saudi Arabia Pumps Up its Stock Market After Bad News". *Wall Street Journal* (December 14, 2018).

GLOBAL EQUITY FINANCING AS A PROCUREMENT DECISION

Firms need cash to finance new investments in property, plant, and equipment in order to launch new products, acquire firms or simply increase their working capital. In most cases, the primary source of funds is the cash generated from operations net of interest and principal (re)payment on outstanding debt and dividends paid to shareholders. When these *internally* generated funds are insufficient, the firm will turn to *external* sources of funds. Such externally

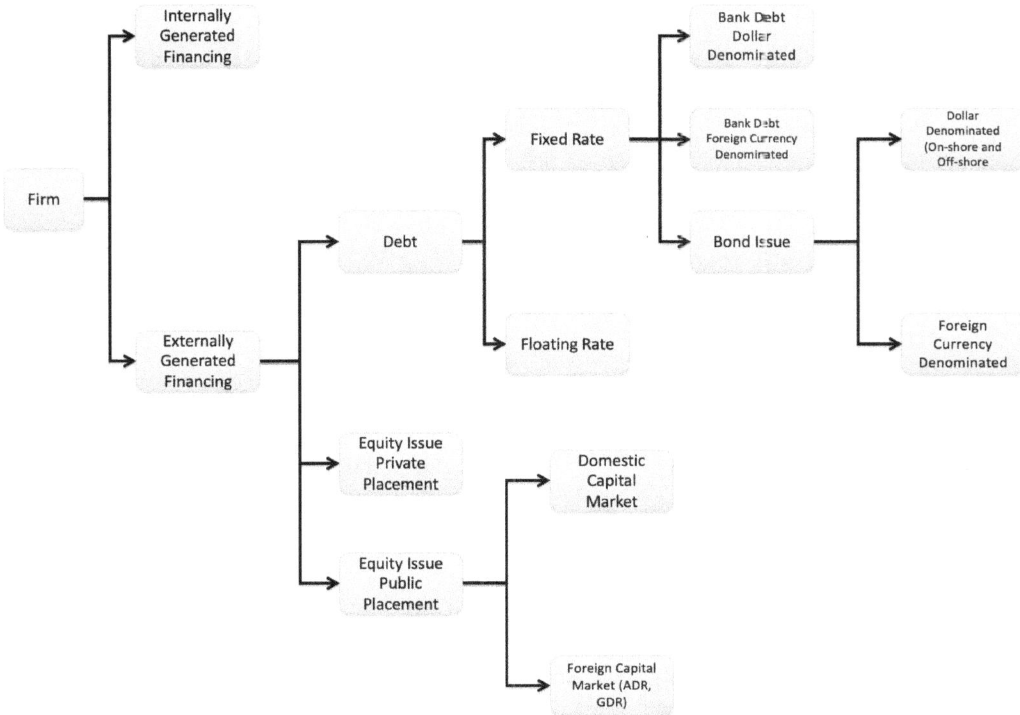

Exhibit 10.4. Alternative sources of financing.

sourced financing can be procured directly from investors in the form of *equity* (stocks), *debt* (loans or bonds), or *hybrids* (convertible bonds and preferred stock).

Once a firm has decided on external equity funding, the search is on for the lowest-cost sourcing option. The choice boils down to raising equity in the home market versus venturing into foreign equity markets (see Exhibit 10.4). This is the time when the firm has to take stock of where its home stock market is positioned along the emerging market continuum first introduced in the previous chapter. The lower a firm's home capital market is on the continuum,[7] the stronger the case for raising equity in a foreign market positioned at a higher level along the continuum. Clearly, there will be additional costs associated with listing one's stock on a foreign market and then raising equity in that market, but they should be well dwarfed by the savings due to a lower cost of equity capital. Thus, the case for sourcing foreign equity rests upon the premise that a firm domiciled in a smaller, illiquid, and segmented equity market can lower its cost of equity capital by accessing a larger, more liquid, and better-diversified pool of investors.

Next, we review the landmark case of Novo Industri, which illustrates how — for firms domiciled in segmented capital markets — their cost of equity capital will typically decline when foreign rather than domestic equity is raised.

INTERNATIONALIZING THE COST OF CAPITAL: THE LANDMARK CASE OF NOVO INDUSTRI[8]

Set in the very early years of globalization (1977–1981), the tale of Novo Industri highlights how a firm shackled to a segmented capital market was able to overcome its cost of capital handicap. Its success story was replicated by a flurry of other Nordic companies as well as other emerging market-based

7 Recall from Chapter 9 that the lower the positioning of a country's capital market on the emergence continuum, the higher presumably is its cost of capital.

8 This section is based on the seminal book by Arthur I. Stonehill and Kare B. Dullum, *Internationalizing the Cost of Capital: The Novo Experience and National Policy Implications* (New York: John Wiley & Sons, 1982).

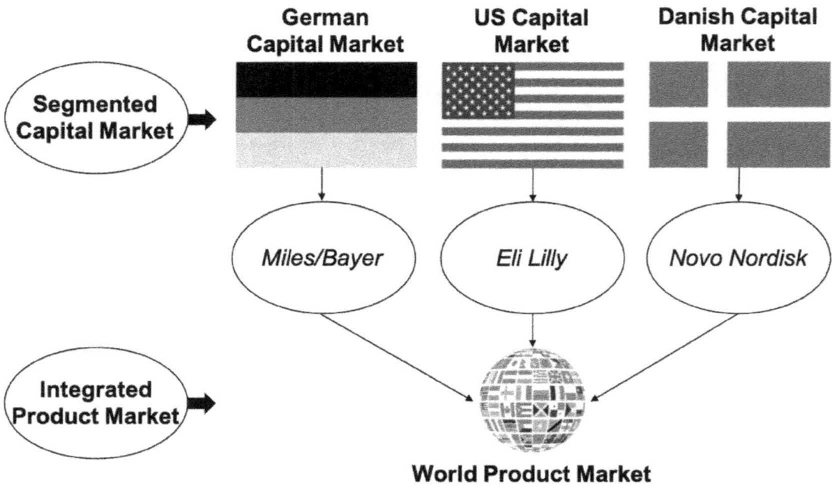

Exhibit 10.5. Geofinancing and the competitive motive.

firms that over the next two decades of the 1980s and the 1990s embarked on a similarly successful internationalization of their cost of capital.

Novo is a leading multinational manufacturer of industrial enzymes and insulin. Based in Denmark but generating 98% of its sales outside Denmark, Novo had to compete in the late 1970s with other multinationals such as Eli Lilly (US), Miles Laboratory (US-based but a subsidiary of Bayer of Germany), and Gist Brocades (Netherlands) in the context of a highly integrated global oligopoly. With nearly 100% of its shareholders being Danish nationals, Novo was at an increasing competitive disadvantage, as it was forced to source growing capital needs (Novo is a technological leader in its industry) from a highly illiquid and segmented Danish securities market (see Exhibit 10.5).

Why was the Copenhagen stock exchange segmented from other developed capital markets?

Danish regulation prohibited Danish investors from investing in foreign stocks, but foreign investors could invest in Danish stocks. Thus, Danish investors had no reason to track developments in foreign stocks or to incorporate such information in their valuation of Danish stocks. Because they could not sell foreign stocks to Danish investors, foreign brokerage firms had no reason to locate an office or staff in Copenhagen. This, in turn, reduced the propensity of foreign stock analysts to follow Danish securities, whose annual reports and financials were prepared in Danish. In a similar vein, there were few Danish security analysts tracking a small number of home-grown companies and, when they did, they issued reports in Danish (only one professional security analysis was published in Denmark — Borsinformation). In sum, strong informational barriers kept the Danish investment sphere separate from the rest of the world. Danish stocks, therefore, might have been priced correctly in the Copenhagen stock market cocoon, but they were certainly priced incorrectly in the broader context of a global stock market.

Taxation was another major segmentation barrier discouraging investors from holding Danish stocks. Capital gains accruing within two years of a stock purchase were taxed at the punishing marginal personal income tax of 75% whereas gains after two years were still taxed at the rate of 50%. By contrast, capital gains on bonds were tax free, which encouraged Danish investors to hold bonds rather than stocks, which, in turn, depressed stock prices.[9]

Indeed, Novo's price-earnings (P/E) ratio was traditionally around 5, while P/Es of its foreign competitors were well over 10. Danish investors were clearly valuing Novo very cheaply compared to US and other European investors' valuation of Novo's

9 Given the small size and closed/segmented nature of the CSE, Danish stock prices were highly correlated and volatile — or, in the terminology of modern portfolio theory, they exhibited a high level of "systematic" risk. Conversely, Danish stock prices were not closely correlated with world stock price movements and therefore offered a great opportunity for foreign investors to diversify internationally.

INTERNATIONAL CORPORATE FINANCE IN PRACTICE 10.3

Firm Value, P/E Ratio, and the Cost of Equity Capital

The reader may wonder why the inverse of a firm's P/E ratio is often used by managers as a gauge of its cost of equity capital. All that is needed is to go back to valuation basics to confirm formally what intuition makes plausible. Consider the firm's market value P as a perpetuity of constant earnings E discounted at the equity cost of capital k_e or $P = E/k_e$. The firm's value, however, is derived from future equity cash flows (ECF), not accounting earnings (E). Therefore, what is needed is to show how E is a reasonable proxy of the firm's equity cash flows. Recall further that equity cash flows are linked to earnings as follows:

$$\text{ECF} = \text{Earnings} + \text{Depreciation} - \text{Capex} - \Delta\text{WCR}$$

Assuming that accounting depreciation is equal to capital expenditures (Capex), or Depreciation = Capex, and that the change in net working capital requirement (WCR) is zero in steady state, or ΔWCR = 0, then ECF = E or residual equity cash flows to shareholders are equal to earnings, which confirms the firm's valuation as $P = E/k_e$. Solving for the cost of equity capital, we do find that it is equal to the inverse of the P/E ratio: $k_e = E/P = 1/(\text{P/E})$.

Numerical illustration: Novo P/E = 5 translated into a cost of equity capital of 1/5 = 20%, when its competitors with a P/E = 10 enjoyed a considerably lower cost of capital of 1/10 = 10%.

competitors, which resulted in a comparatively expensive cost of equity capital (the inverse of a firm's P/E ratio is often used as a rough proxy for its cost of equity capital; see International Corporate Finance in Practice 10.3). Admittedly, if the Copenhagen Stock Exchange (CSE) were well integrated with other major stock exchanges, one would expect foreign investors to rush in and buy undervalued Danish securities, making Novo's cost of capital comparable to that of its competitors.

How Novo internationalized its cost of capital

In order to overcome its cost of capital handicap, Novo undertook the following incremental steps:

- Overcoming the information gap was the first order of business for Novo, which was relatively unknown outside Denmark's investment community. Thus, Novo started to increase the breadth and depth of information disclosures and did so not only in Danish but also in English: In 1977, Grieveson, Grant and Co. — a UK brokerage firm that had been persuaded to follow Novo stock — issued the first professional security analysis report in English.
- To further close the information gap and raise a significant amount of long-term capital, which was not available in Denmark, Novo considered alternative equity sourcing strategies from international capital markets. In 1978, Morgan Grenfell successfully led a bank syndicate to underwrite and place a \$20 million Eurobond[10] convertible issue for Novo while Novo was listing its shares on the LSE to facilitate conversion and to gain visibility. Both policies were meant to lower information barriers as far as foreign investors were concerned while sourcing a significant amount of long-term capital at favorable terms compared to what they would have been in Denmark.
- As biotechnology was catching the fancy of the US investment community (with several sensational oversubscribed IPOs by start-ups such as Genentech and Cetus), Novo realized that with its proven record as an established biotech firm it should tell its story more forcibly. In April 1980, Novo organized a seminar in New York City attended by 40 journalists and financial analysts, which resulted in the purchase of Novo's stock and convertible debt by a few sophisticated professional investors on the LSE. As foreign interest in Novo shares started to snowball, initially on the LSE and then gradually on the CSE, Danish investors were only too happy to sell their shares, whose price was appreciating gradually.

10 Dollar Eurobonds are dollar-denominated bearer bonds issued outside the United States. See the next chapter for a detailed discussion of the Eurobond market.

By the end of 1980, Novo's stock price had more than doubled and foreign investors now owned more than 50% of Novo shares. Its P/E ratio had reached 16, which was in line with Novo's competitors but totally decoupled from valuation of other stocks on the CSE. It is only fair to conclude that Novo had freed itself from the depressed valuation metrics of its home capital market and was now valued by the international investment community for what it was: a high-growth biotech multinational that was a key player in the global oligopoly of insulin and industrial enzymes — and yes, with roots in tiny Denmark! The prize was now within reach: a large-scale equity issue at a now much-reduced "internationalized" cost of capital.

> ***Q:*** Can you gauge the reduction in Novo's cost of equity capital when its P/E ratio climbs from 5 to 16?
>
> ***A:*** Recalling that a firm's cost of equity capital can be approximated by the inverse of its P/E ratio (see International Corporate Finance in Practice 10.3), Novo's cost of equity capital went from 1/5 = 20% down to 1/16 = 6.2%.

- To ease the purchase of its stock by US investors, who could do so only on the LSE and the CSE, Novo sponsored an ADRs program (ADRs are discussed in the next section) in April 1981 and quoted its shares on the US NASDAQ. This was the penultimate step to set the stage for a US seasoned equity offering.
- Ensuring that one's stock is traded met many — but not all — of the requirements for a full-fledged equity offering: In early 1981, Novo, with the assistance of Goldman Sachs and a small coterie of international leading banks, prepared a prospectus for registration with the US Securities and Exchange Commission (SEC) paving the road for an eventual stock offering and a listing on the NYSE. One last segmentation barrier had to be overcome: reconciliation of Novo's financial statements with US generally accepted accounting principles (GAAP) and a more detailed level of disclosure that included industry segment reporting. For Novo — and perhaps worth emphasizing for any would-be firms contemplating an equity offering on an American exchange — this was the most onerous and time-consuming phase in this long journey.

By May 1981, Novo's stock price had reached 1,500 Danish Kroner (DKK) and foreign ownership now stood at 75%. On July 8, 1981, with the guidance of Goldman Sachs, Novo became the first Scandinavian firm to sell equity through a public issue as well as the first to list on the NYSE. Mission accomplished: Novo's stock valuation was now based on prevailing global standards for biotech multinationals and its new equity issue had just been able to capitalize on its rich stock price. At an issue price of DKK 1,399, Novo had achieved its ultimate objective of lowering its cost of capital to fund its long-term capital needs.

- Interestingly enough, although Novo had successfully overcome the segmentation barriers between the CSE and the NYSE, those very barriers had not disappeared. At best they had been mildly eroded: During the first half of 1981 the Danish investment community through reports from security analysts and other professionals consistently recommended "sell", whereas their US and British counterparts had a strong "buy" on the stock.

Further anecdotal evidence of market segmentation could be drawn from the dramatic 10% fall in Novo's stock price on the CSE when the new stock issue was announced on May 29, 1981. Indeed, Danish investors held bearish views for Novo's future prospects, and the 8% additional stock shares about to be issued meant stock price dilution — the glass was half empty for them! Later the same day, however, as Novo started to trade on the NYSE, it fully recovered its loss.[11] For US investors, the stock issue meant enhanced liquidity and greater visibility for Novo as the new issue was being aggressively marketed to institutional investors who had remained underrepresented prior to the new issue — the glass was half full.

WHY DO FIRMS CROSS-LIST?

As the Novo story amply demonstrates, the primary purpose for firms to list their shares on a foreign stock exchange is to reduce their cost of capital. Indeed, there is overwhelming empirical evidence[12] that when firms cross-list their shares their market value increases — in other words, their P/E ratios

11 Trading on the CSE opens six hours ahead of the NYSE. In the early hours of trading on that day, mostly bearish Danish investors were trading until bullish U.S. investors got into the act.

12 See Craig Doidge, G. Andrew Karolyi, and René M. Stulz, "Why Are Foreign Firms Listed in the US Worth More?," *Journal of Financial Economics* 71 (2004).

also increase, which is tantamount to a lower cost of equity capital.

Lowering the cost of equity capital

Most firms that embark on cross-listing their shares are domiciled in either smaller developed capital markets such as Nordic countries or in emerging capital markets such as Brazil, Mexico, or India. In both cases their shareholders are relatively undiversified in the sense that they have access to a limited set of domestic shares and therefore require a higher risk premium/rate of return on their investments. This premium is in turn reflected in a lower market value for a firm whose shares are exclusively locally traded. What typically prevents such investors from reaping the benefits of global portfolio diversification are foreign exchange controls that either prohibit or, at the very least, increase the cost of investing in foreign shares through discriminatory taxes in addition to higher transaction costs or simply limited access to proper information.

When raising capital on a US stock exchange or any other large, well-developed capital market, foreign firms are gaining access to a larger pool of investors, which spreads equity ownership across more shareholders domiciled in several geographical markets. Better-diversified investors accept a lower required rate of return on their equity investments, which results in richer value and therefore a lower cost of capital for the cross-listing firm. Clearly, the more segmented the home capital market of the issuer, the more significant the reduction in the issuer's cost of capital when it decides to cross-list its shares on more developed capital markets; such reduction is generally estimated at ranging between 1% and 3%.[13]

Numerical Illustration Bajaj Motors is an Indian firm listed on the Bombay Stock Exchange whose shareholdership is 100% domestic. Its beta against the Sensex 100 is $\beta = 1.15$, the risk-free rate is $r_F = 8\%$, and its risk premium is $r_M - r_F = 5.5\%$; its cost of equity capital k_E according to the capital asset pricing model is:

$$k_E = r_F + \beta(r_M - r_F)$$

$$k_E = 0.08 + 1.15 \times 0.05 = 13.75\%$$

Bajaj Motors decided to issue stock on the LSE. By raising equity capital on a much larger market, Bajaj Motors intended to attract globally diversified investors who would value its stock by reference to the LSE market portfolio, which is far more diversified than the Bombay Stock Exchange's domestic market portfolio — hence the company has a lower $\beta^* = 0.90$ against the LSE market portfolio. Assuming further a risk-free rate of $r_F^* = 6\%$ and a market risk premium[14] of $r_M^* - r_F^* = 4\%$ on the LSE, Bajaj Motors' new cost of equity capital is k_E^*:

$$k_E^* = 0.06 + 0.90 \times 0.04 = 9.60\%$$

Bajaj Motors' newly listed/issued stock on the LSE would become immediately more valuable, as globally diversified investors now discount its pro forma cash flows at a lower cost of equity.

Another (subtler) segmentation barrier lies in differences of shareholder protection. Firms domiciled in countries whose markets provide weak protection to minority shareholders may cross-list their shares in markets whose governance laws offer stronger investor protection. Indeed, by committing themselves to tighter accounting standards, more exacting disclosure requirements, and generally stronger investor protection safeguards, controlling shareholders and managers are less likely to appropriate funds or expropriate minority shareholders. Thus, bonding with stronger governance guidelines will encourage international investors to buy the firm's shares, thereby boosting its value and lowering its cost of capital.

Kookmin Bank — the largest South Korean bank, which had been severely bruised by the Asian financial crisis between 1997 and 1998 seemed to have listed on the NYSE in 2001 for precisely this reason. In the words of its president and CEO,

> *After Korea's financial crisis in 1997, many foreign investors were suspicious of Korean banks' books, and we wanted to clarify the situation by going abroad, especially on the NYSE. I think we have been fully tested in terms of accounting transparency and asset quality under more conservative US GAAP. Our primary purpose is to be as open as possible.*[15]

13 See Vihang R. Errunza and Darius P. Miller, "Market Segmentation and the Cost of Capital in International Equity Markets," *Journal of Financial and Quantitative Analysis* 35, no. 4 (2000): 577–600.

14 The risk premium on the LSE would typically be lower than on the BSE or other emerging capital markets, reflecting a much broader and better diversified market portfolio.

15 Cited in Geert Bekaert and Robert J. Hodrick, *International Financial Management* (Upper Saddle River, NJ: Prentice Hall, 2009), 448.

Enhanced corporate visibility is good for business

Many managers believe that listing their firms' shares on a major foreign stock exchange is an effective advertising strategy for its products. Indeed, a so-called road show and the continued media attention that the launching of an ADR or GDR program typically generates are likely to strengthen brand awareness. This would be especially true if the cross-listing firm is already operating in or exporting to the country where it is listing; indeed, as customers in the host country become better acquainted and more comfortable with the firm's products, sales volume will increase. For example, SAP — the leading German software company — introduced its ADR program on the NYSE in 1999 to enhance its market visibility and to better compete with its archrival Oracle.

Cross-border mergers and acquisitions may also benefit from an existing ADR or GDR program for the simple reason that the acquirer often pays for its acquisition with its own stock. Since foreign listing usually means a richer stock price, the acquirer would end up paying less for its acquisition. Furthermore, if the acquirer is listed only on its home stock market — say Mumbai or Johannesburg — shareholders of the acquired firm may balk at the idea of receiving stocks traded in a distant and often illiquid foreign stock exchange and may immediately sell them. If the acquirer's shares are already listed locally (that is, on the same stock exchange as the acquired firm) through an ADR or GDR program, the target shareholders are more likely to hold on to the acquirer firm's shares, thereby ensuring the success of the stock swap. In 2000, Stora Enso, the Finnish paper conglomerate, acquired the US firm Consolidated Papers for $5 billion, half of which was paid for through a stock swap. Stora Enso's ADRs rather than its Helsinki-traded shares were used as the currency to close the transaction.

HOW TO SOURCE EQUITY GLOBALLY

Raising equity in a foreign market is not markedly different from raising equity in your domestic market, but it will require that the issuer lists its shares in the foreign market. Firms may choose to list their stock in a foreign stock market either directly or through a depositary receipt (DR) program. Such listing can take place on an organized exchange such as the NYSE or the LSE, in an over-the-counter (OTC) market, or as a private placement. After listing on a foreign market, firms often decide on raising capital in the form of an equity issue. However, many foreign firms are primarily interested in broadening their shareholder basis and may not have an immediate interest in raising additional equity capital. The United States continues to be the country of preference for such foreign listings — mostly in the form of ADRs, with more than 450 companies listed and trading on the NYSE and as many on the NASDAQ. Daily trading in foreign shares amounts to as much as 10% of the NYSE turnover.

Equity listing

Foreign firms may choose a direct listing by issuing their ordinary shares in a foreign market that will trade in all respects like any domestic firms' shares. Thus, the issuing firm will have to meet all regulatory requirements of the host market's securities laws as well as its disclosure, reporting, and accounting rules. For example, listing on a US stock exchange requires extensive SEC registration materials as well as restating quarterly and annual financial reports in accordance with GAAP. This explains why, in the case of US stock exchanges, direct listing by foreign companies seems to be limited to Canadian firms: Canadian disclosure and reporting standards are very similar to US standards, which makes the dual listing process inexpensive. In most other cases, foreign listing is an arduous and onerous process, which explains why foreign firms generally elect a less costly path than direct cross-listing on a foreign market — in the form of an ADR or GDR program. (See International Corporate Finance in Practice 10.4.)

American Depositary Receipts

An ADR is a stock certificate traded in the United States representing a number of shares in a foreign company that are held on deposit with the custodian US depositary institution which issued the ADR. ADRs offer US investors significant advantages in the form of convenience and lower transaction costs compared to trading directly in the underlying stock on the foreign stock exchange.[16] Such advantages include the following:

- ADRs are listed and traded on a US stock exchange and therefore denominated in US dollars; they can

16 Listing on a U.S. capital market through an ADR program does not entail a new equity issue. The firm still has the same number of outstanding shares except that some are now traded on a U.S. capital market in the form of ADRs while fewer shares are now traded on its home market. The shares backing up the ADR program are sourced by the U.S. depositary institution's custodian from the firm's home stock market.

INTERNATIONAL CORPORATE PRACTICE IN FINANCE 10.4

Infosys ADRs and Capital Market Segmentation Between India and The United States

ADRs can have prices different from the value of the underlying assets, although in most cases they do not have significant deviations since arbitrage is possible. For example, if an ADR were selling at a premium to the underlying security, a financial intermediary could buy shares of the original stock in the home market and create new (cheaper) ADRs that would be sold at the premium price on the foreign market, thereby allowing the arbitrageur to make a quasi-instant and riskless profit.

Occasionally, however, price discrepancies do exist in this market. A particularly remarkable example is Infosys, an Indian information technology company trading in Mumbai (Bombay), and the first Indian company to be listed on an American exchange (NASDAQ). As of March 7, 2000, Infosys had experienced a huge increase in value, and its ADR was trading at $335, up from $17 (split-adjusted), the price at which it had been introduced to the US market just a year earlier. However, the enthusiasm of American investors appeared to be much greater than that of local Indian investors. The ADR was trading at a 136% premium to the Bombay shares.

In this case, official barriers prevented Americans from buying the shares trading in Bombay, so there was no way for American arbitrageurs to create new ADRs and thus to instantly profit from this relative valuation discrepancy.

Source: Adapted from Lamont, Owen A. and Richard H. Thaler. 2003. "The Law of One Price in Financial Markets." *Journal of Economic Perspectives* 17(4): 194–195.

be directly purchased through a US brokerage firm as any US shares would be, and price quotes are in US dollars.

- Dividends distributed by the foreign firm are collected and converted into US dollars by the custodian, which pays them directly to the ADR investors. Had the investors purchased directly the foreign underlying shares, they would need to repatriate distributed dividends after conversion into their home currency and clearing any withholding taxes levied by the foreign government.
- ADRs are usually a multiple or fraction of the underlying share to allow trading within a customary price range for US investors; for example, Japanese shares are often priced at a few yen per share and are therefore bundled into lots of 100 or more.
- ADRs are promptly settled within three business days like any US equity shares, unlike typically longer settlement practices in the domicile market of the underlying shares.

Depositary programs can be either sponsored or unsponsored by the issuing firm:

- *Unsponsored* programs are initiated by a bank (depositary institution) in response to market demand but without formal agreement from the issuing firm. In such instances the depositary institution will purchase securities in the foreign equity market, hold them on deposit, and issue against them DRs. The popularity of unsponsored ADRs was severely checked in 1982 when the SEC required that every ADR issue be registered, which ensured that the foreign issuing firm be at least informed of cross-border trading in its shares. The depositary institution was expected to file an F-6 form to formally register ADRs as a US security even though the SEC stopped short of imposing any significant disclosure requirements. Most unsponsored ADRs are now relegated to trading on the non-NASDAQ OTC market. These OTC shares are traded through *Pink Sheets*, an electronic bulletin board, or an electronic trading platform called PORTAL (an acronym for private offering, resale, and trading through automated linkages).[17]
- *Sponsored* ADR programs, by contrast, are issued by an exclusive depositary institution — usually a commercial bank such as Bank of New York or JP Morgan Chase — that is appointed by the foreign company under a formal agreement.

17 PORTAL was developed by the National Association of Securities Dealers to support the trading and to enhance the liquidity of private placements.

Exhibit 10.6. Types of ADR programs in the United States

	Use of existing shares to new shares		Raising capital with broader shareholder base	
	Level I	**Level II**	**Level III**	**Rule 144A**
Description	Unlisted program	Listed on a recognized exchange	Offered and listed on a recognized exchange	Private placement exchange to qualified institutional buyers
Trading	OTC: quoted on electronic bulletin board and *Pink Sheets*	NYSE, AMEX, or NASDAQ	NYSE, AMEX, or NASDAQ	Private placement market: quoted on PORTAL
US reporting 12g3-2(b) requirements	Exemption under Rule 12g3-2(b)	Form 20-F filed annually	Form 20-F filed annually; short exemption from reporting	Forms F-2 and F-3 may be used to provide for subsequent information offerings on request
Reconciliation	None	Partial	Full	None to US GAAP

Source: An Information Guide to Depositary Receipts by Citibank's Security Services Department (1995).

The depositary institution is first and foremost expected to issue deposit certificates in its home market (foreign market for the firm whose shares are listed as ADRs) and also to channel dividends to ADR holders and to distribute notices of shareholder meetings, voting instructions, and other relevant communications to facilitate shareholders' exercise of their voting rights. In turn the foreign issuer firm agrees to pay the depositary bank an appropriate administrative fee.

Sponsored ADR programs are further classified along three levels (see Exhibit 10.6) depending on the level of reporting that issuing firms commit to:

- *Level I.* The issuing firm does not comply with SEC registration or reporting requirements since it files with the SEC only those documents that it is required to file in its home country. This is the simplest and least expensive program, allowing the issuer to make its shares tradable in the United States. The shares, however, can be traded only in the OTC market.
- *Level II.* The issuing firm registers with the SEC and fully complies with all reporting requirements. Its shares can then be listed and traded on any official US stock exchange. Level II ADRs do not allow the listing firm to raise new capital in the United States but do allow it to access a wider shareholdership and presumably to lower its cost of capital.
- *Level III.* The listing firm complies with all securities laws as would any US-listed corporation. Accordingly, it is required to prepare its financial statements in accordance with GAAP and in compliance with all applicable SEC rules. By meeting these onerous requirements, not only are the firm's ADRs listed and traded on a US stock exchange, but it may raise capital through a public offering of its ADRs.
- *Rule 144a.* A nonregistered (Level I ADR) can also raise capital without meeting the costly reporting requirements of a Level III ADR. This can be done through a private placement with qualified institutional investors (QIBs) under Rule 144a, which excludes the much deeper pool of retail investors. Because QIBs are supposed to be financially sophisticated, the SEC imposes fewer reporting and registration requirements and waives the reconciliation of financial statements with US GAAP. In effect, Rule 144a makes access to US capital easier, faster, and cheaper than a Level III ADR issue would. However, private placement means reduced liquidity even though QIBs are allowed to buy and sell ADRs among themselves through PORTAL. (For a convoluted method of achieving many of the same goals see International Corporate Finance in Practice 10.5.)

Global depositary receipts

Foreign firms need not limit themselves to US capital markets — even though they account for a disproportionate share of such cross-listing. Other major capital markets in Europe such as London, Paris, or Frankfurt, or in Asia (Hong Kong or Tokyo) also play host to such cross-listing either directly or through GDR programs.

INTERNATIONAL CORPORATE FINANCE IN PRACTICE 10.5

Reverse Takeover

Also known as reverse mergers, a reverse takeover (RTO) is the acquisition of a public company by a private company to bypass the lengthy and costly process of listing on a stock exchange and, in effect, amounts to a disguised IPO. In an RTO, a private operating company will merge with a publicly listed nonoperational entity or shell. The public company being acquired is simply a legal entity or shell that has been stripped of all its assets. As a result of the merger, the private operating company's assets and liabilities would be transferred into the public shell company and the public shell company will become controlled by the shareholders of the private operating company. Any outstanding shares continue to be owned by the investors holding them, but the name and operations of the shell are morphed into the name and operations of the former private company.

For example, a former public Nevada (US) gaming company can re-emerge as a Chinese dairy company. The RTO process allows Chinese companies to gain exposure to the US capital and consumer markets as well as build a pool of US investors without subjecting themselves to the slow and costly meanders of listing through ADRs. The RTO is viewed by many as the back door to going public since an RTO enables a company to achieve instant listing and a cheaper seasoned (secondary) equity offering than an IPO would entail.[18] Chinese firms eager to get access to US capital markets without subjecting themselves to comprehensive regulatory and disclosure requirements have resorted to this back-door entry strategy. However, audited financial statements and significant disclosure requirements filed on Form 8-K are still required by the SEC. Investors beware!

---

18 Gabriel Nahoum, "Small Cap Companies and the Diamond in the Rough Theory: Dispelling the IPO Myth and Following the Regulation A and Reverse Merger Examples," *Hofstra Law Review* 35, no. 1865 (Summer 2007).

Global registered shares

If dual listing is a costly process, DaimlerChrysler AG took the concept to the next level by listing its ordinary shares simultaneously on 21 different national exchanges. As a result of the merger in 1998 between Daimler Benz and Chrysler to create a global automotive manufacturer, the newly established firm DaimlerChrysler decided to list itself as a global registered share (GRS), which would trade as seamlessly as its ordinary shares around the world. Both firms prior to their merger had experience with multiple listings through ADRs or GDRs, but this new facility was different and a first. Unlike an American or a GDR, a GRS is the actual share of the company — not a receipt backed by ordinary shares deposited in a trust; a global share became the only equity vehicle issued to all DaimlerChrysler stockholders. (See Exhibit 10.7 for a schematic depiction of how the facility would operate.) According to Karolyi (2003):

> *(1) the global share would be issued in registered rather than bearer form, eliminating the need for each share to be accompanied by dividend coupons, (2) a single, bilingual, multi-jurisdictional stock certificate representing the global shares would be developed that would satisfy applicable standards in Germany and the US, and (3) transfer agents and registrars would be appointed in Germany, the US and elsewhere to facilitate transfer and registration of shares.*

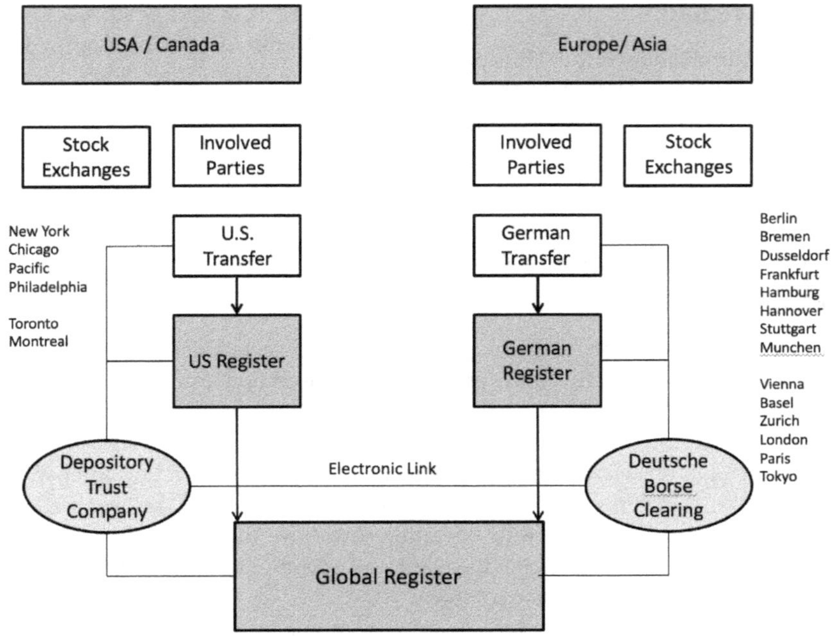

Exhibit 10.7. DaimlerChrysler GRS.

SUMMARY

1. Equity financing is first and foremost a procurement decision driven primarily by cost considerations — in this instance the cost of equity capital.

2. The largest stock markets are in the United States, China, Japan, and the United Kingdom and are characterized by relatively large market capitalization relative to their GDPs. This is unlike most European markets, where bank financing continues to play a relatively important role in companies' financing. China and India are rapidly making their way in the top league of capital markets.

3. Market liquidity is often gauged by the market's turnover, which is defined as the ratio of total volume of shares traded during the year to its market capitalization at the end of the year. Liquidity is highest in US capital markets. Emerging capital markets show steadily increasing liquidity as they mature.

4. The dynamics of capital markets can be visualized by positioning each national market along an emergence continuum stretching from frontier or pre-emerging markets such as Ulaanbaatar or Dhaka to emerging markets such as Jakarta or Lagos to developed markets such as Sydney or Zurich.

5. Markets in their early stage of emergence tend to be small, illiquid, inefficient, and handicapped by a high cost of capital. By ascending the emergence continuum, national equity markets avail themselves of a lower cost of capital. Segmented capital markets become progressively better integrated.

6. Many firms domiciled in emerging capital markets and many smaller developed stock exchanges continue to experience a cost of capital handicap *vis-à-vis* more developed and advanced capital markets such as US, UK, or Japanese stock exchanges. As a result, they often list and raise equity on a foreign stock exchange to overcome their cost of capital handicap.

7. The quest of Novo Industri for a lower cost of capital aligned with that of its key global competitors illustrates vividly how a firm domiciled in a segmented capital market — in this instance the CSE — can unshackle itself from a *segmented* market by listing on an *integrated* and developed stock exchange — in this case the NYSE.

8. Cross-listing on a foreign market may be achieved in different ways ranging from limited trading on the OTC market to full-fledged listing of the firm's original shares. In most instances cross-listing firms will choose an intermediate strategy through a DRs program.

9. US capital markets are the preferred destination of many cross-listing firms. ADRs are bank receipts collateralized by a multiple of foreign shares deposited with a foreign bank acting as a custodian. ADRs make it convenient and greatly reduce the costs of investing in foreign shares: They are denominated in US dollars, are traded in the United States like any other US shares, and pay dividends in US dollars. There are three types of ADR programs: Level I ADRs allow the stock to be traded OTC only, Level II allows exchange trading, and Level III allows all types of trading as well as capital raising.

10. By cross-listing, firms hope first and foremost to lower their cost of capital through their access to a larger, better-diversified pool of global investors who presumably will value their stock more richly. Additional motivations for cross-listing are to establish name recognition and to boost the firm's visibility in foreign markets in order to pave the way toward an equity offering. Furthermore, if strategic acquisitions are contemplated, having one's stock listed and traded in the target firm's market would greatly facilitate the financing of the acquisition of the target firm.

QUESTIONS FOR DISCUSSION

1. Explain the concept of "mildly segmented" capital markets.

2. How can one measure degrees of segmentation across national equity markets?

3. Why was Novo's P/E ratio so much smaller than its key competitors' P/Es? What were the implications for Novo's ability to compete in world markets?

4. Is the inverse of a firm's P/E ratio a reasonable proxy for its equity cost of capital?

5. How do you explain why firms often list their shares on foreign equity markets? Which equity markets are the primary hosts to foreign listing?

6. What is the difference between "sponsored" and "unsponsored" ADRs programs?

7. Why do firms sponsor ADR or GDR programs?

8. What is an ADR?

9. What is the difference between Level I, Level II, and Level III ADR programs?

10. What does it mean for a firm to internationalize its cost of capital?

PROBLEMS

1. **Honda's ADRs and the Law of One Price (introductory).** Honda shares trade on the TSE and on the NYSE as an ADR.
   a. Assuming that Honda stock closed at ¥2,177 and that ¥76.55 = US$1, at what price would you expect Honda to trade on the NYSE?
   b. If Honda trades at US$26.41, show how arbitrageurs could profit from the situation.
   c. How would you expect arbitrageurs to correct the disequilibrium?
   d. Explain what could be possible reasons for deviations from the Law of One Price.

2. **Ciments Lafarge's ADRs (introductory).** Ciments Lafarge trades on the Paris Bourse and on the NYSE as an ADR. If its shares trade for €80.40–81.20 on the Paris Bourse, what would you expect to be the quoted price of its ADR to a potential US investor? The euro is trading at 1.3075–1.3180, and one DR is equal to one-fourth of its share.

3. **MegaFon goes to London (introductory).** On November 28, 2012, MegaFon — the Russian telecom company — raised £1 billion on the LSE. The controversial Uzbek oligarch Alisher Usmanov owns 55.8% of MegaFon, which is the no. 2 Russian mobile phone operator company behind Mobile TeleSystems (MTS) but ahead of VimpelCom. Both MTS and VimpelCom are listed on the NYSE.
   a. The stock issue was in the form of GDRs at £20 per GDR. If MegaFon shares on the Moscow Stock Exchange are defined as five shares for one London GDR and the spot price prevailing on that day was RUB 49.47 = £1, at what RUB price were MegaFon shares trading in Moscow?
   b. Why do you think that MegaFon chose London rather than New York for its foreign listing debut?

4. **Investing in MegaFon's stock (intermediate).** Referring to the information presented in problem 3:
   a. Explain MegaFon's principal motivations in raising equity capital in London rather than in Moscow.
   b. Is the fact that MegaFon is almost exclusively a Russian and central Asian mobile phone operator a plus or a minus in listing on the LSE?
   c. As a pension fund manager based in San Francisco (US), would you rather invest in MegaFon's stock on the Moscow Stock Exchange directly or on the LSE through its GDR?

5. **MegaFon's cost of capital (intermediate).** MegaFon stock on the Moscow Stock Exchange trades with a beta of $\beta = 1.71$ while the risk-free rate and risk premium are, respectively, 6 and 7%.
   a. Compute MegaFon's cost of equity capital on November 1, 2012 (before its foreign listing).
   b. Compute MegaFon's cost of equity capital on December 1, 2012 (after its foreign listing). MegaFon's newly traded GDR on the LSE has a beta of $\beta = 1.61$ while the risk-free rate and risk premium stand at 3 and 4%, respectively.
   c. What are the costs and benefits for MegaFon of listing on the LSE?

6. **Salgacoar Shipping Ltd's cost of capital (A) — intermediate.** Salgacoar is an Indian shipping company that owns and operates 12 bulk dry cargo freighters. Headquartered in Goa (India), it specializes in shipping coal and iron ore primarily to South Korea. Its return on equity (ROE) is 17% with a book value currently at INR 15 billion. Its market capitalization on the Bombay Stock Exchange (BSE) is INR 22.5 billion with a $\beta = 1.31$. Risk-free and market return on the BSE are currently at 4.5 and 8%, respectively. Salgacoar Shipping was considering raising INR 5 billion on the Bombay Stock Exchange when its adviser at Standard Chartered Bank pointed out that the Hong Kong Stock Exchange was the world's premier equity market for shipping companies not only for Hong Kong flag carriers but also for Indonesian, Japanese, South Korean, and other Asian firms.
   a. Under what considerations should Salgacoar Shipping consider tapping the Hong Kong Stock Exchange for equity financing?
   b. What information would you like to have access to?
   c. What are the costs and benefits associated with raising equity in Hong Kong?
   d. The shipping stock index on the Hong Kong Stock Exchange is currently trading at a P/E of 17. What is your recommendation to Salgacoar Shipping?

7. **Salgacoar Shipping Ltd's cost of capital (B) — intermediate.** Salgacoar Shipping's CFO was preparing a final presentation to the firm's board of directors and wanted to bring additional validation to the decision reached in problem 6.
   a. Explain how the capital asset pricing model could be used in validating the equity financing decision to tap the Hong Kong versus the Bombay Stock Exchange. What information do you need?
   b. If the shipping industry index's β is 1.11 in Hong Kong with a risk-free and market risk premium of 3 and 6% respectively for the Hong Kong Stock Exchange, what would be the adviser's recommendation to Salgacoar Shipping?

8. **Salgacoar Shipping Ltd's cost of capital (C) — advanced.** Salgacoar Shipping's CEO expressed reservations about the equity financing recommendation that the firm's CFO was finalizing for presentation to the board (see problems 6 and 7). He generally agreed with the premise that larger, deeper equity markets may offer more favorable equity financing options but was concerned by the fact that his firm, because of its focused activities, was not directly comparable to the larger and more diversified shipping firms that made up the shipping stock index on the Hong Kong Stock Exchange. Do you share the CEO's skepticism? Explain.

INTERNET EXERCISES

9. **World Stock Market Indices (intermediate).** Log in to www.finance.yahoo.com to compare the performance of Japan TSE (Nikkei 225) with France Paris Bourse (CAC 40) and with the NYSE (S&P 500) over the last 5 years. Is the ranking the same if all three indices are measured in US dollar rather than in their respective local currency?

10. **Cost of Equity Capital.** Log in to the Wall Street Journal website http://online.wsj.com/mdc and find the stock price, dividend and earning per

share for Exxon, Royal Dutch Shell and Total. What is the cost of equity capital and dividend yield of each company?

REFERENCES

Addallah, Abed Al-nasser, and Christoph Ionnidis. 2010. "Why Do Firms Cross-List? Evidence from the US Market." *Quarterly Review of Economics and Finance* 50: 202–213.

Doidge, Craig, G. Andrew Karolyi, and René M. Stulz. 2004. "Why Are Foreign Firms Listed in the US Worth More?" *Journal of Financial Economics* 71: 205.

Gande, Amar. 1997. "American Depositary Receipts: Overview and Literature Survey." *Financial Markets, Institutions and Instruments* 6(5): 61–83.

Karolyi, G. Andrew. 2003. "Daimler-Chrysler AG, the First Truly Global Share." *Journal of Corporate Finance* 9: 409–430.

Kratz, Oliver S. 1999. *Frontier Emerging Equity Markets Securities Price Behavior and Valuation*. Norwell, MA: Kluwer Academic Publishers.

Lamont, Owen, and Richard Thaler. 2003. "Anomalies: The Law of One Price in Financial Markets." *Journal of Economic Perspectives* 17 (November).

Moel, Alberto. 2001. "The Role of ADRs in the Development of Emerging Capital Markets." *Economia* 2.

Oxelheim, Lars, *et al.* 1998. *Corporate Strategies to Internationalize the Cost of Capital*. Copenhagen, Denmark: Copenhagen Business School Press.

Saunders, Mark. 1993–1994. "American Depositary Receipts." *Fordham International Law Journal* 17: 48–83.

Stonehill, Arthur I., and Kare B. Dullum. 1982. *Internationalizing the Cost of Capital: The Novo Experience and National Policy Implications*. New York: John Wiley & Sons.

Wu, Congsheng, and Chuck C. Y. Kwock. 2002. "Why Do US Firms Choose Global Equity Offerings?" *Financial Management* (Summer): 47–65.

APPENDIX 10.A: SHAREHOLDERS' WEALTH MAXIMIZATION AND CORPORATE GOVERNANCE SYSTEMS AROUND THE WORLD

If *shareholders' wealth maximization* is the dominant gospel of financial management in Anglo-Saxon countries where capital markets and a dispersed shareholder base play the leading role in financing firms, this is not necessarily the case in other major capital exporting countries or emerging market countries, where banks, family groups, or even the state are the dominant owners and/or financiers. Indeed, understanding who actually owns a firm is key to figuring out where its control rests. For example, the Paris Bourse offers varying models of ownership-cum- control combinations: Renault and Air France are minority-owned (15%) by the French state,[19] LVMH — the luxury goods conglomerate — is 40% owned by its founder Bernard Arnault who through a holding company controls more than 75 luxury brands such as Louis Vuitton, Dom Perignon and Tiffany. Total Energy — the mammoth energy conglomerate is Anglo-Saxon style publicly-owned by an international and widely dispersed shareholder-ship.

Indeed *family-controlled business groups* often dominate the economy of emerging market countries such as India, Thailand, Indonesia or Mexico[20] but are also found in a few selected advanced countries such as Sweden, Belgium or France. In such instances, family-owned businesses hold controlling interest in publicly listed firms and may expropriate minority shareholders by abusing their power and appropriating unfairly more than their share of the firm's profits. In most cases, the architecture of family business groups is built around a pyramidal system where "an apex firm holds a controlling interest in two or more holding companies which, in turn, hold controlling interests in several operating firms in the next tier down. Further tiers can be added to maximize the control leverage of the apex firm — the more tiers the lower the percentage of capital the owners of the apex firm have to contribute to maintain control of the bottom tier firms. The controlling owners' actual cash-flows interest in firms lower in the pyramid is lower than in firms in higher tiers because of the pyramidal fractional ownership in the pyramid".[21] In most instances, the controlling family will issue two classes of shares: a class F share with multiple voting rights for family (F) members and a class G share with only one voting right for the general (G) public. An archetypical illustration of this pyramidal model with dual classes

19 Both companies were nationalized in 1945 and more recently privatized — Renault in 1996 and Air France in 1999.

20 For example, the Tata, Ambani and Birla families control far-reaching diversified conglomerates in India and so does Carlos Slim in Mexico and the Sophonpanich family in Thailand.

21 Ghemawat, Pankaj and Thomas M. Hout. 2010. "Differences in Business Ownership and Governance around the World". *Globalization Note Series*. IESE, p.2

of stocks is the Wallenberg family of Sweden which through its holding company Incentive is effectively controlling — among many other entities — three leading multinationals — ABB (electrical equipment), Ericsson (telecommunications) and Electrolux (home appliances).

In Japan, interlocking business groups formerly known as *keiretsu* focus on the health of the business group ahead of its individual firms and often emphasize market share more than share price maximization.[22] Initially, keiretsus were heavily networked structures with a main bank functioning as lead lender. The main bank's position was further reinforced through shareholding among affiliated companies themselves. Today, there are two main types of corporate groups in Japan: production-based corporate groups (vertical keiretsu) built around a major manufacturer such as Toyota and bank-based corporate groups (horizontal keiretsu) such as Mitshubishi. The membership of these corporate groups usually includes a number of foreign-affiliated firms. A production-based corporate group often consists of a major manufacturer and its much smaller supplier subcontractors. The unique role played by the web of reciprocal shareholding with group-affiliated companies as well as interlocking main bank in keiretsu is intimately linked to the notion of *relationship capitalism* in direct contrast with Anglo-Saxon *arm's-length* or *market-based* finance. Importantly, cross-holdings typically result in limited influence by affiliated firms' minority shareholders, which, in turn, insulates management from the disciplinary influences of the market for corporate control and threats of hostile takeovers.

Chaebols in South Korea mimic the Japanese model and may also maximize long-term growth more than short-term profits. In contrast to the *keiretsu*, South Korean *chaebol* are organized in a more hierarchical fashion under the control of a dominant shareholder or controlling family. They rely on pyramids and reciprocal cross-holding among group-affiliated firms to exercise management control with family members of the founder occupying often key managerial positions.

Even in Anglo-Saxon countries, there is no guarantee that managers will indeed manage the firm in the best interests of its owners/shareholders. After all, managers are human beings whose personal goals may not be congruent with the firm's overarching goal of value creation. Thus, managers may act in their self-interest rather than pursue policies aligned with the best interests of the firm's shareholders. For example, managers may use company resources to benefit themselves rather than their shareholders by squandering money on lavish offices, large personal staff, corporate jets, country club memberships, and other wasteful perquisites.

Clearly, *corporate governance*[23] — the charter that governs the relationship between the firm's owners and its managers — reflect varying firms' ownership and control patterns, as well as legal, cultural, and sociopolitical national idiosyncrasies. The central problem, however, remains how to strengthen corporate governance to best protect outside investors (often minority shareholders) from expropriation by the controlling shareholders to ensure that the former are fairly rewarded for their investment. Indeed, resolving the governance conundrum equitably has far-reaching implications for efficient allocation of corporate resources, corporate financing, realistic corporate valuation, efficient markets for corporate control (mergers & acquisitions) and development of capital markets. Fortunately, *corporate governance mechanisms were strengthened when* the United States passed the Sarbanes-Oxley Act of 2002 and the Dodd Frank Wall Street Reform and Consumer Protection Act in 2010. "These laws require a strong system of internal controls over financial statement reporting to be in place for the Board of Directors and management to be held responsible for errors in the financial statements and for the assessment of internal controls over financial statements by external auditors. The laws support majority corporate board membership by external, unrelated directors and require that significant board committees be chaired by external directors. The goal is for board members to take their fiduciary role as shareholder representatives seriously and be responsible to external stakeholders and not internal management".[24]

22 Chapters 26 and 27 are devoted to Asian and Islamic finance and banking (see book's website).

23 According to the OECD's definition, Corporate governance involves a set of relationships between a company's management, its board, its shareholders and other stakeholders . . . that provides the structure through which the objectives of the company are set, and the means of attaining those objectives and monitoring performance are determined . . . . [The] presence of an effective corporate governance system, within an individual company and across an economy, helps to provide a degree of confidence that is necessary for the proper functioning of a market economy . . . [and results in a lower] cost of capital.

24 Hass, S and P. Burnaby and M. Nakashima. 2018. "Toshiba Corporation — How Could So Much Be So Wrong?" *Journal of Forensic and Investigative Accounting* 10(2, Special Issue).

Needless to say, MNCs pursuing cross-border mergers and acquisitions or entering into joint-venture or licensing agreements with foreign firms should be well apprised of the nuances of national corporate governance systems. Similarly, asset managers, whether they are pension funds or hedge funds, need a keen understanding of how idiosyncratic local corporate governance may bias valuation.

CASE STUDY 10.1. JAZZTEL'S FOREIGN IPO

It was early November 1999 and Antonio Carro, CEO of Jazztel, was weighing with Miguel Salis and Christoph Schmidt, respectively Jazztel's CFO and its director of strategic planning and investor relations, the prospects for the company's next round of financing. Founded only two years earlier, Jazztel's objective was to become a leading independent telecom services provider in both Spain and Portugal. To do so, the company sought to provide a full range of telecommunication and data services through its own fiber-optic network linking Spain's primary metropolitan areas. Ultimately, the company planned to extend its services to Portugal. The challenge at hand was to source the necessary capital to complete the build-out of their infrastructure. Given the newly liberalized fixed-line telecommunications market and the growing importance of the Internet, Jazztel's plans to construct a state-of-the-art network held great potential; however, just 3.5 miles of the planned 3,800-mile network were operational. A significant amount of additional capital expenditure was required, and Mr. Carro was not certain as to the risk appetite of the market.

Market Deregulation and the Newly Competitive Landscape

Following the liberalization of the Spanish telecommunications market on December 1, 1998, Jazztel became the first alternative service provider to be granted a national license to provide facilities-based services (i.e., the company owns its own infrastructure). Prior to deregulation, the telecommunications sector was controlled by Telefonica S.A., the former state-owned monopoly. Although a large number of new service providers had entered the market since deregulation, Telefonica still dominated the sector, holding a 98.5% share of total minutes of traffic and a percent share of long-distance minutes.

Jazztel aimed to challenge Telefonica by providing a full range of high-quality, tailor-made integrated voice, data, and Internet services at attractive prices. Jazztel's primary targets were small to medium-sized firms — a market segment it felt was being underserved. Management believed that owning, operating, and controlling the high-bandwidth fiber-optic network that these valued-added services required would enable it to be a more reliable, low-cost service provider.

Although the European Union had initially set a January 1998 deadline for the full liberalization of the telecom sector across all member states, Spain was granted an extension to December 1998. In April 1998, the Spanish government passed a new telecom law establishing the basic regulatory framework for open competition. An independent regulatory body, the Comision del Mercado de las Telecomunicaciones (CMT), would both supervise and enforce the new legislation.

Jazztel, however, was not the only upstart to challenge Telefonica's monopoly. UK-based Colt Telecom Group plc, Esprit, and BT Telecomunicaciones (a subsidiary of British Telecommunications) appeared to be formidable entrants looming large over the Spanish competitive landscape, especially given their pan-European presence and prior experience in building networks. Colt, founded by Fidelity Investments, was a competitive local exchange carrier (CLEC) that had been granted a local B1 license for Madrid, Barcelona, and Valencia. It had already completed construction of a 40 km network covering the financial center of Madrid. However, like Esprit and BT Telecomunicaciones, Colt's primary focus was on servicing larger companies and multinationals that also operated on a pan-European basis.

New entrants were able to lease capacity from Telefonica (theoretically at cost) and then charge lower rates due to the heavily distorted legacy monopolist pricing structure, which allowed artificially high long-distance rates to subsidize local calls. The wide spread between Telefonica's cost base and the fees it charged to consumers provided an arbitrage opportunity for new entrants. Telefonica had taken steps to rebalance its tariff structure; in 1998 it doubled the costs of local calls while cutting the prices on long-distance and international calls by 12 and 13%, respectively. However, all such rate adjustments had to be approved by the government. Therefore, Telefonica had not been able to unilaterally or completely rebalance its tariff structure.

Jazztel's entry strategy

Jazztel was the first new entrant to conclude an interconnection agreement with Telefonica. The current one-year agreement was scheduled to expire on April 12, 2000. In May 1999 the company launched its indirect access services. Within a month it had built a customer base of nearly 50,000 clients. By November 1999 Jazztel counted approximately 250,000 indirect customers, well ahead of its initial estimates of 150,000 indirect clients.

Jazztel sought to build its own state-of-the-art high-bandwidth network in order to provide a wider array of value-adding services, which carried far higher margins than basic voice services via indirect access. Jazztel believed that owning, controlling, and operating its own network would enable it to be a lower-cost service provider. Management estimated that direct access services carried an average gross margin of 50%, whereas indirect access margins were a far lower 11% due to interconnection fees. Moreover, owning its own infrastructure was expected to afford greater control over the quality and range of these services.

Jazztel's network, known as the E1-4U Network, was being designed to pass through districts of high business density and high-volume telecommunications usage in Spain and Portugal and would be comprised of two integrated elements:

1. Local-access fiber-optic networks constructed in each of the major cities and most provincial centers, referred to as metropolitan area networks (MANs), that would link businesses and residential customers directly to the national network.
2. A 6,100 km nationwide fiber-optic backbone that would connect these local networks. This part of the network would be leased from Refne, the national railway company, and Iberdola, the second-largest electric utility in Spain.

Given management decision to lease backbone capacity, Jazztel's build-out amounted to the construction of 29 MANs. Essentially, MANs were fiber-optic rings constructed around a city. Customers were connected to Jazztel's network by fiber-optic lines linking their premises to the ring. Telecom traffic was routed within the city or onto the backbone for long-distance service. (See Case Exhibit 10.1 for an overview of Jazztel's network.)

In order to minimize speculative infrastructure investment, the company had developed a geographic mapping database to guide the construction of the network. The database covered 92 cities across Spain, including the locations of over 400,000 businesses within these cities. The database also provided information on telecom spending and existing telephone lines, enabling Jazztel to optimize the locations of the MANs by building the network so that it passed by as many target businesses as possible. The database took several thousand person-hours to construct.

Financing strategy

Venture capitalist and serial entrepreneur Martin Varsavsky provided Jazztel's initial operating capital of pesetas (Pts) 60 million in June 1998.[25] In February 1999 an additional €64.3 million of equity was raised from several private equity firms, such as Apax Partners and Advent International, which specialized in the financing of telecommunication firms.

In April 1999, Jazztel expanded its financing base, successfully raising a two- tranche high-yield issue of €203.4 million. The offering consisted of 100,000 dollar-denominated units and 110,000 euro-denominated units. Each unit was worth $1,000 and €1,000, respectively, and carried five warrants for the purchase of Jazztel stock. The 10-year notes carried a coupon rate of 14%.

Of the €203.4 million in proceeds, €79.4 million was placed in an escrow account to fund the first six biannual interest payments through 2001. No interest payments from company cash flow were scheduled until 2002. It was the largest such offering ever completed by a Spanish firm. Furthermore, the offering was two times oversubscribed.

In July, to further support its capital expenditures (capex) requirements, the company secured a €300 million senior secured credit facility from a syndicate of banks, including Argentaria SA, Barclays Plc, and Chase Manhattan Corp., among others. The facility entailed two tranches: a €200 million term loan and a €100 million revolving facility. The term loan (Tranche A) carried an interest rate of 3.75% over Euribor. The revolving facility (Tranche B) carried an interest rate of 2.50% over Euribor. Both facilities had an eight-year tenor. Both tranches were available subject to an extensive series of availability tests. Drawdown was monitored by ongoing operational and financial covenants, such as minimum coverage ratios and minimum annualized direct customer revenue levels.

25 The peseta (Pta) was Spain's national currency until Spain joined the euro-zone on January 1, 1999, adopting the euro as its currency at the exchange rate of Pta 166 = €1.

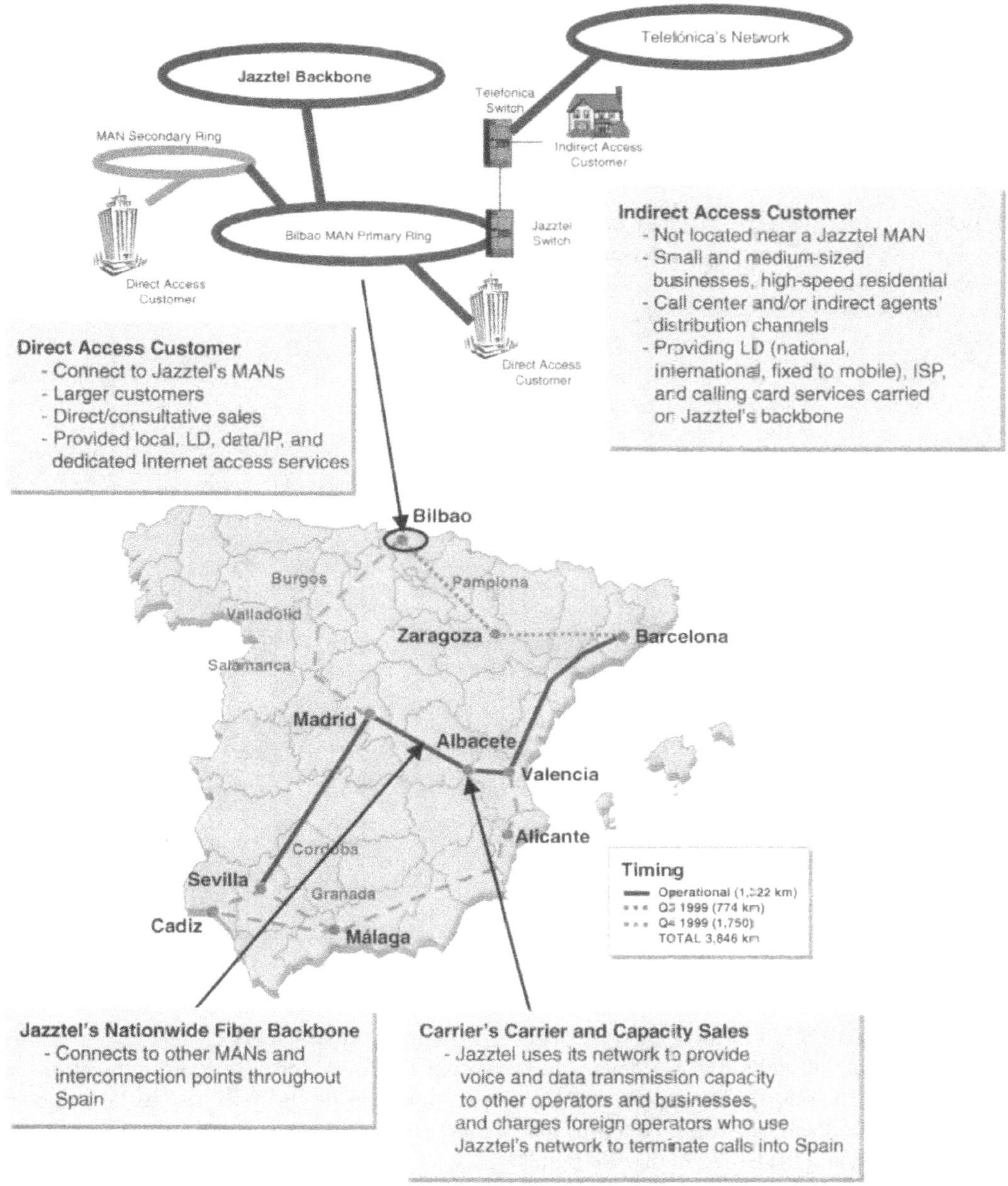

Case Exhibit 10.1. Jazztel's network.
Source: Jazztel.

Although owning its own network was expected to eventually lower operating costs, the required capital expenditure for the network build-out was formidable. Management expected cumulative capital expenditures to reach €566 million through 2003 with an additional €261 million required through 2008. Additional funding was required, and the timing seemed right for another round of financing.

Jazztel's initial debt offering had been assigned a rating of Caa2 by Moody's; however, management was hopeful that the company's favorable progress to date, in terms of customer acquisition and network build-out, would result in a debt rating upgrade, which in turn would lower future borrowing costs.

European debt markets appeared to be particularly attractive. In May KPNQwest BV had

Case Exhibit 10.2. Selected public offerings of corporate securities.

Date	Company	Instrument	Amount/Price	Market of Issue
July 1998	Colt Telecom Group	7¼5 8% fixed coupon 10-year senior notes. Callable 7/31/03 @ 103.81.	DM 600,000,000 @ 99.935% of face value	Euro nondollar
March 1999	Colt Telecom Group	2% fixed coupon 7-year notes convertible to 46.77 shares. Convertible/ callable @ 117.91. Convertible until 03/29/06.	€295,000,000 @ 100% of face value	Euro nondollar
May 1999	KPNQwest BV	7¼5 8% fixed coupon 10-year senior notes. Callable until 6/1/04 @ 103.56.	€340,000,000 @ 99.261% of face value	Euro-zone
June 1999	Energis Plc	9¾% 10-year notes. Callable until 6/15/04 @ 104.88.	US$200,000,000 @ 99.621% of face value	Eurodollar
June 1999	Energis Plc	9½% 10-year notes. Callable until 6/15/04 @ 104.88.	£125,000,000 @ 99.621% of face value	Euro nondollar
November 1999	Global Telesystems	11% 10-year bonds. Callable until 12/01/04 @ 105.50	€275,000,000 @ 100% of face value	Euro nondollar

successfully secured $805 million of 10-year debt in a combination of 450 million in US dollars and 340 million euros. The sale of notes represented the largest euro and nondollar offering ever completed (340 million euros), and the largest high-yield bond offering by a continental European issuer. The $450 million of 8¼8%, 10-year notes sold at 99.293 to yield 8.232% or 275 basis points more than Treasury notes of comparable maturities. The €340 million ($357 million) of 7¼8% notes sold at 99.261, for a yield of 7.23% or 325 basis points above the 10-year German bonds (see Exhibit 10.2).

Initial public offering

Equity financing was an option. Carro was well aware that several recent IPOs in the telecommunications sector had proven highly successful.

Global Telesystems Group Inc., a US-based owner and operator of telecommunications companies in Europe and Asia, saw its IPO share price increase 37% in its first day of trading. Teldafax AG, a German mobile telecommunications services firm, saw its IPO share price rise 52% in its first day of trading. (See Case Exhibits 10.3 and 10.4 for lists of selected IPO listings in the telecommunications sector and peer comparisons.)

If a public stock offering was to be pursued, Carro was unsure as to where the company should list (see Case Exhibit 10.5). The NASDAQ seemed to be the market of choice for new technology listings, but a local listing on the Madrid Bolsa would certainly further Jazztel's efforts to be seen as a pure Iberian player, thereby supporting its efforts to capture market share at the expense of foreign-owned

Case Exhibit 10.3. Comparative IPO listings.

Company	Country	IPO Market	Total Shares Offered[a]	IPO Date	IPO Price	Closing Price First Day	(%) Change
KPNQwest	Netherlands/	NASDAQ	44.0 million	11/09/99	$20.81	$28.71	43.3
	US	Amsterdam		11/09/99	€20.00	€30.30	51.5
GTS	US	NASDAQ[b]	11.1 million	02/05/98	$20.00	$27.31	36.6
		EASDAQ		02/05/98			
Colt	UK	NASDAQ	6.7 million ADRs (1 ADR = 4 ordinary)	12/10/96	$18.10	$19.75	9.1
Esprit[c]	UK	NASDAQ	4.8 million ADSs (1 ADS = 7 ordinary)	02/28/97	$12.00	$12.00	0.0
		EASDAQ		02/28/97			
Energis	UK	NASDAQ	75 million Ordinary (1 ADR = 5	12/09/97	$23.89	$24.25	1.5
		LSE	ordinary)	12/09/97	290 pence	292 pence	0.7
Viatel	US	NASDAQ	8.7 million	10/18/96	$12.00	$12.00	0.0
Mobilkom	Germany	Neuer Markt	480,000	03/10/97	DM 62.50	DM 98.00	56.8
Omnicom[d]	France	Nouveau Marche	518,000	07/10/97	Fr 215.00	Fr 258.00	20.0
Teldafax	Germany	Neuer Markt	8.5 million	07/01/99	DM 52.00	DM 61.00	17.3
Equant	Netherlands	NYSE Paris	26.1 million	07/21/98	$27.00	$43.81	62.3
				07/21/98	Fr 161.70	Fr 243.00	50.3

Notes: [a]Excluding overallotment.

[b]Moved to NYSE on 10/25/99.

[c]Acquired by Global Telesystems Group. Merger announced December 1998 at a price of $5.96 per Esprit ordinary share ($41.72 per ADS).

[d]Acquired by Global Telesystems Group. Majority stake purchased in April 1999 at a price of 195 euros (Fr 1,279) per share.

EASDAQ: A pan-European OTC exchange modeled after the NASDAQ. The two exchanges have similar listing requirements. By listing shares on the EASDAQ, European companies can also get access to American investors through the NASDAQ. The EASDAQ opened on November 27, 1997, and is based in Brussels. The exchange is controlled by 90 European banks. The NASDAQ holds a small stake in the exchange.

Nouveau Marche: A new exchange geared toward smaller start-up companies. Shares in the exchange trade twice a day. There are two daily pricing quotations, at 10:30 a.m. and 4:40 p.m. Paris time, where the market is based. A central order book is used for private client orders, and a separate market-making system is used for institutional investors. The exchange opened on March 21, 1997.

Neuer Markt: Opened on March 10, 1997, targeting midsize high-growth stocks. The exchange is controlled by Germany's largest banks through the Deutsche Boerse AG. The Neuer Markt is housed within the Frankfurt Stock Exchange. The Neuer Markt plans to hook up with the Nouveau Marche and other exchanges in Amsterdam and Brussels through the Euro NM, a pan-European exchange.

Source: Bloomberg.

Case Exhibit 10.4. European comparables (telecom stocks).

	Mobilkom AG (DM million)	Colt Plc (£ million)	Energis PLC (£ million)
Summary P&L Year-end 1998			
Revenues	1,485	215	221
EBITDA	281	(5)	34
Net income	141	(56)	(35)
Summary Balance Sheet Year-end 1998			
Cash and liquid securities	120	727	7
Net fixed assets	175	365	490
Total debt	57	789	157
Total equity	401	387	340
Current enterprise value			
Share price as of 5/21/99	DM 154.1	£14.53	£16.82
Shares outstanding (mn)	43	636	296
Market cap (mn)	6,657	9,305	4,979
Enterprise value (mn)	6,594	9,367	5,129
Financial ratios			
EV/Revenues	4.4×	43.6×	23.2×
EV/EBITDA	23.5×	25.7×	150.8×
EV/PPE	37.7×	n/a	10.5×
Beta	n/a	1.68	1.74

Source: Jazztel, NASDAQ.

Case Exhibit 10.5. Jazztel profit and loss statement (Euro '000).

	1999	2000	2001	2002	2003	2004	2005
Net revenue	21,794	150,972	319,352	456,368	541,734	581,590	614,387
Telecommunications cost	37,890	104,700	181,276	231,338	259,710	271,821	287,593
Gross margin	**−16,096**	**46,272**	**138,076**	**225,030**	**282,025**	**309,769**	**326,794**
Sales and marketing	16,401	18,901	21,058	24,516	33,933	37,748	40,468
General and administrative	27,087	38,679	51,759	67,952	75,663	79,970	84,759
Total SG&A	**43,488**	**57,580**	**72,817**	**92,467**	**109,596**	**117,718**	**125,228**
Depreciation and amortization	−9,688	22,651	35,510	44,398	49,980	55,250	59,910
EBIT	**−69,272**	**−33,960**	**29,749**	**88,164**	**122,449**	**136,801**	**141,656**
Interest expenses	5,205	8,233	15,054	28,668	40,718	38,249	30,740
EBT	**−74,477**	**−42,193**	**14,695**	**59,496**	**81,731**	**98,552**	**110,916**
Taxes	0	0	0	0	12,255	34,493	38,821
Net income	**−74,477**	**−42,193**	**14,695**	**59,496**	**69,476**	**64,059**	**72,095**

firms such as Colt and BT. Telefonica had been listed on the Bolsa since 1989 and was trading at a P/E multiple ranging between 7 and 9. However, a listing on the Bolsa would subject Jazztel to stricter listing requirements in terms of its projected profitability and ability to service its debt. Moreover, a Bolsa listing entailed trading restrictions such as price bands that sought to limit stock price volatility.

Carro weighed the pros and cons of his story to investors. As a new entrant, Jazztel could cherry-pick the segment of the relatively underdeveloped market that it wished to serve. Moreover, the company possessed an experienced and well-respected local management team that had successfully obtained first-mover advantage among the alternative carriers. However, Jazztel was a money-losing company with just three kilometers of its own network operational and a voracious need for capital going forward. Carro was uncertain as to how the company would be valued by investors. He wondered how Jazztel's IPO would be received by the market.

Questions for Discussion

1. What is/are the risk(s) faced by Jazztel in borrowing medium-term debt denominated in US dollars or euros, given its Iberian footprint?
2. Compare the effective cost of debt faced by Jazztel with the cost of debt for its European competitors.
3. What are the pros and cons of launching an IPO on the Madrid Bolsa?
4. What are the costs of listing on the NASDAQ or the EASDAQ?
5. Under what conditions should Jazztel pursue a foreign IPO?

11

Sourcing Debt from Global Bond Markets

If you can look into the seeds of time, and say which grain will grow and which will not, speak to me.
— Shakespeare

JetBlue Airlines was seeking to raise $250 million in a seven-year note to upgrade its aging fleet. Ms. Rousse — JetBlue's newly appointed CFO — was reviewing the different funding options offered by its investment bankers, which included a domestic dollar-denominated *zero-coupon bond* priced at 61%, a dollar-denominated *Eurobond* with a 7.25% annual coupon, and a *samurai bond* denominated in yen with a semiannual coupon of 4.00%. Last, a *floating-rate note* denominated in euros paying euro-LIBOR + 165 basis points was also being considered. Ms. Rousse was perplexed by the array of currency denominations and the significant differences in nominal interest rates, both of which complicated direct comparisons among the funding options.

Ms. Rousse was not alone in trying to make the best of this complicated world of bond financing in which a plethora of debt instruments with exotic names turns a seemingly simple debt financing decision into a challenging computational exercise, only to be qualified by global strategic considerations. She was particularly intrigued by the seemingly inexpensive samurai bond but could not help recalling one of her vivid B-school finance classes:

> *In a world of efficient currency markets and integrated capital markets, optimal currency denomination for long-term debt sourcing decisions becomes a matter of indifference since nominal interest rates reflect inflation rate expectations, which, in turn, determine the future spot exchange-rate adjustment path. In such an idealized world, the effective cost of debt across currency "habitats" should be equal.*[1]

Nearly a decade of hard work in various treasury positions had taught Ms. Rousse the hard facts of international finance:

> *Most financial markets are segmented from one another — at least to some degree — and the resulting discrepancies in cost of international debt instruments are what keep corporate treasurers busily employed. Indeed, a world of "mildly" segmented capital markets, characterized by "overshooting" exchange rates, and "distorted" interest rates due to credit rationing and "crowding out" by public borrowers, is generally the norm rather than the exception.*

In this chapter you will gain an understanding of:

- Global debt financing as a procurement decision.
- National and international debt markets.
- The different debt securities in which corporate borrowing can be structured.
- The difference between onshore (domestic) and offshore (Eurocurrency) bond markets.
- How to compute the effective cost of foreign currency–denominated debt.

---

1 If interest rates are *unbiased* predictors of future inflation and exchange rates obey the *purchasing power parity* rule, differentials in national interest rates should be exactly compensated by subsequent exchange rate changes. Of course the world of international finance is never that Cartesian! See Chapter 7 for an elaboration of this point.

- How currency swaps integrate national bond markets.
- How to reconcile the *hedge* motive with the *opportunistic* motive in denominating long-term debt.

THE INTERNATIONAL DEBT PROCUREMENT DECISION

Debt financing is no different from any other procurement decision, and when it is international, that only means there are far more financing sources to choose from (see Exhibit 11.1). Any firm, domestic or multinational, will first rely on *internally generated* funding resulting from cash flows generated by operations, net of interest and principal (re)payment on outstanding debt, and dividends paid to shareholders. *Externally generated* financing, in contrast, is broken down between equity and debt (including equity-linked debt). Debt can be sourced from financial institutions in the form of loans, also known as *intermediated* financing — mostly via commercial banks but also via finance companies, leasing firms, or national and supranational agencies such as the International Finance Corporation. Alternatively, debt can be sourced directly from fixed-income capital markets in the form of bond issues; this is called *disintermediated* financing. Debt can be issued in the firm's own domestic capital market, in a foreign capital market, or in the offshore/Eurobond market. Multinational corporations have the additional flexibility of raising debt either through their foreign subsidiaries, the parent company, or some dedicated international finance subsidiary domiciled in a tax haven or low-tax jurisdiction, such as Luxembourg, the Cayman Islands, or the Dutch Antilles.

Since money is perfectly homogeneous, the guiding criterion in deciding which financing source to tap is primarily the cost of debt. However, this criterion is not as simple to apply as it may first appear, since different debt funding options would typically be denominated in different currencies. For example, if the US-based air carrier JetBlue is seeking to raise $250 million, it will have to consider sourcing funds not only in US$ but also in €, ¥, £, Swiss francs, and so on, which offer different nominal long-term interest rates. Thus, JetBlue is not interested merely in the nominal cost of debt but rather in its effective cost — that is, the nominal cost of debt corrected by each currency's respective appreciation or depreciation *vis-à-vis* the US$ over the financing horizon — a difficult question to which we will return in more detail later in this chapter. But first we want to introduce the reader to the global debt market.

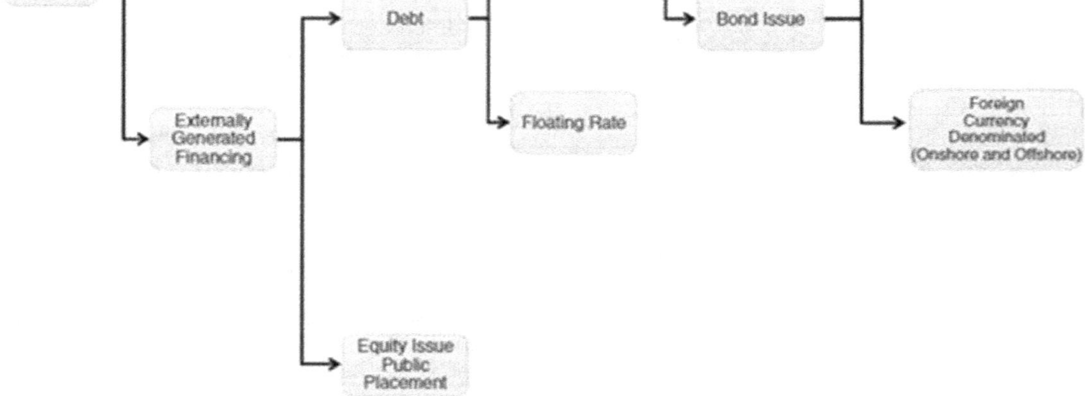

Exhibit 11.1. Sources of debt financing.

GRAND TOUR OF THE GLOBAL DEBT MARKET

Well-developed markets for fixed-income securities (a fancy name for bonds) are generally the hallmark of advanced industrialized economies. Their origin can be traced to the early stages of industrialization in England, France, Germany, and later the United States. By providing a viable and often cheaper financing option than banks, they have made possible the construction of railways and major infrastructural projects such as the Suez Canal and the Channel Tunnel. Today, they are most vibrant in countries that have relatively unfettered capital markets and few exchange controls.

The global bond market is comprised of three distinct tiers (see Exhibit 11.2):

1. *Domestic bonds* are issued locally by a locally domiciled borrower and are denominated in the local currency. For example, All Nippon Airways issues a ¥100 billion five-year bond with a 3% coupon in Japan. Japanese investors would primarily purchase the bonds although foreign investors are not excluded.
2. *Foreign bonds* are also issued locally and denominated in the local currency but the borrower is domiciled abroad. For example, Cathay-Pacific — the Hong Kong-based air carrier — issues ¥100 billion five-year notes with a 3% coupon in Japan. Here again, Japanese investors would primarily purchase the notes but not exclusively.
3. *Eurobonds* are issued and placed in a jurisdiction outside the country of the currency of denomination. For example, a $500 million 10-year Eurobond with a 5.75% coupon issued by Michelin SA — the French tire multinational company — would be sold anywhere but in the United States since it is denominated in US dollars.

Domestic bonds generally account for the bulk of a national bond market. Treasury bonds necessary to finance government budget deficits typically dominate national bond markets. State-owned agencies along with municipalities (local governments) are also key players. Corporate bond issues and asset-backed securities (bonds collateralized with assets such as mortgages or other types of financing instruments) constitute the rest of the market.

Foreign bonds are also issued in national *onshore* markets by firms domiciled in a foreign country. Foreign bond issuers are subject to the same disclosure requirements as domestic firms. Because the issuer is a foreign entity, investors may find that in case of default legal recourse is difficult and expensive. These bonds are typically designated by nicknames, such as *Yankee* bonds for bonds issued in the United States by foreign-domiciled issuers, and similarly *samurai* bonds (in Japan) or *bulldog* bonds (in the United Kingdom).

Typically, regulatory authorities in countries where foreign bonds are issued make legal distinctions between such foreign bonds and domestic bonds. For example, different tax rules may apply to the payment of interest, there may be different requirements as to the information to be disclosed for registration purposes, and a different calendar

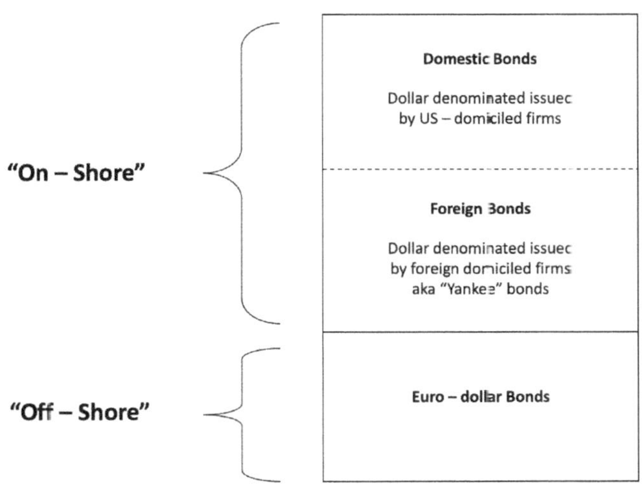

Exhibit 11.2. Market tiers for dollar-denominated bonds.

may dictate the timing of such issues with a queuing process favoring domestic issuers. Even if the rules are identical between domestic and foreign issuers, issuing foreign bonds may prove to be costly. For example, the massive Yankee bond market requires foreign issuers to satisfy the disclosure requirements of the US Securities and Exchange Commission (SEC), which in turn may necessitate that they restate their financial statements according to US generally accepted accounting principles (GAAP). To mitigate this cost handicap *vis-à-vis* the Eurobond market, the US SEC promulgated Rule 144A in 1990, which allows firms to raise debt through a private placement with "qualified institutional investors" without requiring either registration of the bonds or compliance with US GAAP.

Eurobonds allow the issuers to circumvent many of these national idiosyncratic obstacles. Eurobonds are typically (1) issued with the help of an international syndicate of banks, (2) placed simultaneously in a large number of countries outside the country of the currency of denomination, (3) offered in *bearer* form[2] and generally not subject to withholding tax (see International Corporate Finance in Practice 11.1 for an illustration). Eurobonds may not look all that different from domestic bonds — both are primarily medium-term, fixed-rate, and coupon-paying bonds issued by well-rated corporations or national and supranational sovereigns. Eurobonds, however, by targeting the *offshore* bond market[3] — rather than the *onshore* domestic market — avoid registration and disclosure requirements, thereby lowering issuing costs and circumventing mandatory withholding taxes.

Historically, the Eurobond market first evolved because (1) it allowed issuers to avoid regulatory interference from national governments, which traditionally impose tight restrictions on foreign issuers, often forcing them to get in a queue; (2) it reduced issuance costs by avoiding burdensome, time-consuming, and onerous disclosure requirements, such as those imposed by the US Securities and Exchange Commission on the sales of bonds within the United States; and (3) it offered both issuers and lenders an offshore quasi-tax-free space within which to connect. In fact, as *bearer* bonds, Eurobonds are the security of choice for any investor seeking anonymity and tax avoidance — a polite way to refer to tax cheats, mob gangsters, drug dealers and corrupt politicians of all colors and from all latitudes. Eurobonds are thus very popular with asset managers domiciled in tax havens, such as Switzerland, the Cayman Islands, or Hong Kong. The

2 A bearer bond is an unregistered bond; unlike a nominal bond, no record of ownership is kept. Bearer bonds are favored instruments for evading taxation or for money laundering.

3 *Offshore* means that Eurobonds cannot be issued onshore of the country whose currency is used for denomination purposes. For example, a sterling-denominated Eurobond could not be distributed in England and would typically be purchased by investors domiciled in tax havens or at least outside England.

INTERNATIONAL CORPORATE FINANCE IN PRACTICE 11.1

The First Eurobond

The first Eurobond in the amount of $15 million was issued in July 1963 by Autostrade — an Italian toll road authority — and was guaranteed by the Italian government. Sixty thousand bonds were issued with a face value of $250 each, and paid an annual coupon of 5.5% on July 15 of each year. The issue was underwritten and placed by the London merchant bank S.G. Warburg with Banque de Bruxelles S.A., Deutsche Bank AG, and Rotterdam Bank NV as co-managers. The bonds could not be offered to the general public because they were not registered in any of the European countries. Instead they were placed privately, mostly with Swiss banks. The dollar-denominated bonds would normally have been issued as Yankee bonds in the United States except that the Interest Equalization Tax decreed by President John F. Kennedy on July 18, 1963, imposed a 15% flat tax on the purchase price of long-term Yankee bonds by US investors.[4] The new concept of issuing bonds outside the country's currency of denomination was born: Autostrade bonds were sold anywhere but in the United States, hence this label of an "offshore" bond market.

4 This tax was meant to discourage capital outflows at a time when the US balance of payments was in deficit and the US dollar under pressure.

legendary "Belgian dentist" is a natural candidate to invest in such bonds. The reader may wonder why Belgian dentists have achieved such a level of notoriety in the Eurobond market: One has to surmise that dentistry is a very lucrative profession in Belgium and that personal income tax is very punitive, driving Belgian dentists to hide part of their assets in secret Swiss bank accounts and to invest them in bearer (anonymous) Eurobonds!

Euro Bonds, Eurobonds, and Euro Eurobonds. When the single currency was adopted by the European Union in 1999, 12 (and later 19) currencies disappeared and were replaced by the euro. Thus, issuers deciding to tap capital markets in the euro-zone will typically do so by denominating their bonds in euros, and these bonds would be known as *euro bonds*. Such euro bonds have nothing to do with *Eurobonds* discussed earlier in the chapter, which can be denominated in any convertible currency (including the euro) but are sold outside the country's currency of denomination. Last, a bond denominated in euros but sold outside the euro-zone is a *euro Eurobond*.

In sum, the reader will recall that a dollar-denominated Eurobond would be issued with the help of an international syndicate of banks and sold outside the United States even though it is denominated in US dollars. It would not be registered with the US Securities and Exchange Commission and would likely be listed in Luxembourg. It would be a bearer bond and not subject to any withholding tax on interest payments. Investors in such bonds may or may not report the interest income to tax authorities and, since the bonds are issued in bearer form, it is difficult for any tax jurisdictions to trace them.

Sovereign bonds. A special category of bonds which account for a disproportionate share of domestic, foreign and Eurobonds are Treasury or sovereign bonds issued by (sovereign) governments. In most advanced developed economies sovereign debt is considered of the highest quality, rated as AAA or AA and issued mostly in the sovereign's own domestic markets. Countries such as the United States, the United Kingdom or France — which have to finance their budget deficit — issue debt almost exclusively in their own domestic capital market and pay the lowest interest of any borrower. The case of emerging countries is different as most of them find it difficult to meet their financing needs from their own domestic markets. Therefore, they turn to the Eurobond market or to the foreign bond tier of major capital markets — mostly the US, Japan, the UK and the euro markets — to meet their financing needs. Because of less than stellar public finance, many emerging market economies are rated as non-investment grade (below BBB) and therefore borrow at significantly higher interest rates than the US, UK or French government would (see International Corporate Finance in Practice 11.2). They also have to borrow in a foreign currency thereby exposing themselves to foreign exchange rate risk. The difference in yields between say a dollar-denominated 10-year bond issued by Brazil and the US government is known as the *sovereign yield spread* and is the *risk premium* that investors require to hold 10-year dollar-denominated Brazilian bonds rather than a 10-year US treasuries.

Fixed-income securities

Each compartment of the global bond market offers debt securities, which can be structured in a number of different guises.

Zero-coupon bonds are sold at a deep discount from their face value, pay no interest (zero coupon), and are repaid in full at their principal value upon maturity; the reward to investors thus comes in the form of bond price appreciation, and depending on the tax jurisdiction in which they are issued, the annual appreciation in the value of the zero-coupon bond can be considered as taxable interest income.

Straight debt or level-coupon bonds pay a semiannual interest coupon (domestic bonds) or an annual interest coupon (Eurobonds) and are repaid at par (or close to it) upon maturity. Domestic bonds can be offered with maturities of 30 years, 100 years, or even as perpetual or quasi-perpetual bonds (e.g., Walt Disney issue of 100-year bonds dubbed "Sleeping Beauties"). Most Eurobonds mature in 10 years or less (in fact, they are often called Euro-notes). Bullet bonds require full principal repayment at maturity; a sinking fund would allow the issuer to repay principal in installments starting after a pre-agreed date well before the bond matures (see International Corporate Finance in Practice 11.3 for an illustration of the first ruble-denominated Eurobond).

Euro-Medium Term Notes (Euro-MTNs). Between short-term Euro-commercial paper (maturity of one year or less) and long-term bonds (maturity in excess of 10 years), Euro-MTNs are flexible debt instruments to raise medium-term funds. Like level coupon bonds, euro-MTNs have a fixed maturity and require periodic coupon interest payment. Unlike bonds the full amount of a Euro-MTN is not issued all at once — instead it is issued overtime in relatively small denomination ranging from \$5 million to \$25 million through a Note-Issuance facility (NIF) as a function of the borrower's needs.

INTERNATIONAL CORPORATE FINANCE IN PRACTICE 11.2

Sovereign Bonds: Argentina Sells $2.75 Billion of 100-Year Bond

A recent example of a sovereign bond is the Century bond issued by Argentina. After barely exiting a long period of being technically in default (2002–2016) the Argentine government issued on June 17, 2017, $2.75 billion of sovereign bonds maturing in 2117 with an annual coupon of 7.125%. The bond issue was privately placed in the US with proceeds earmarked to financing the Argentine government deficit and refinancing existing debt. Having averaged a default on its sovereign debt every 25 years since its founding, for Argentina to issue a century-long bond is quite a coup. For a country which is still rated (B+) below investment grade (a polite label for junk bonds) and which had defaulted on $80 billion of sovereign dollar-denominated debt as recently as 2002, re-entering global capital markets is unprecedented and betrays assets' managers myopic hunger for high yield. With an annual coupon of 7.125% it would take an investor a little over 1000/71.25 = 14 years to recover his/her principal coupon (pay-back period) — assuming that Argentina would not default during that period. Indeed, this sovereign bond issue offers a yield spread of 3.92% over 30-year US treasuries (there is no 100 year US Treasuries — only 30 year US Treasuries paying 3.2%). The yield spread of an Argentine sovereign bond reflects the additional compensation that investors require to hold Argentina Century bonds.

Within less than a year after the bond was issued Argentina found itself engulfed in yet again another financial crisis with the peso plunging by 50% during the first nine months of 2018: Argentina's Century bonds have lost value from 100% down to 73% reflecting a widening sovereign yield spread from 7.125% – 3.2% = 3.92% at time of issue (17/06/2017) to 9.72% – 3.2% = 6.52% on 30/09/2018. See Exhibit 11.3 showing the yield to maturity of Argentina 100 year bond versus the yield on US 30-year Treasuries and the sharp depreciation of the peso over that same period. The verdict is still out as to whether Argentina will weather this last crisis. The IMF having just approved a $50 billion bailout rescue package must believe that it will!

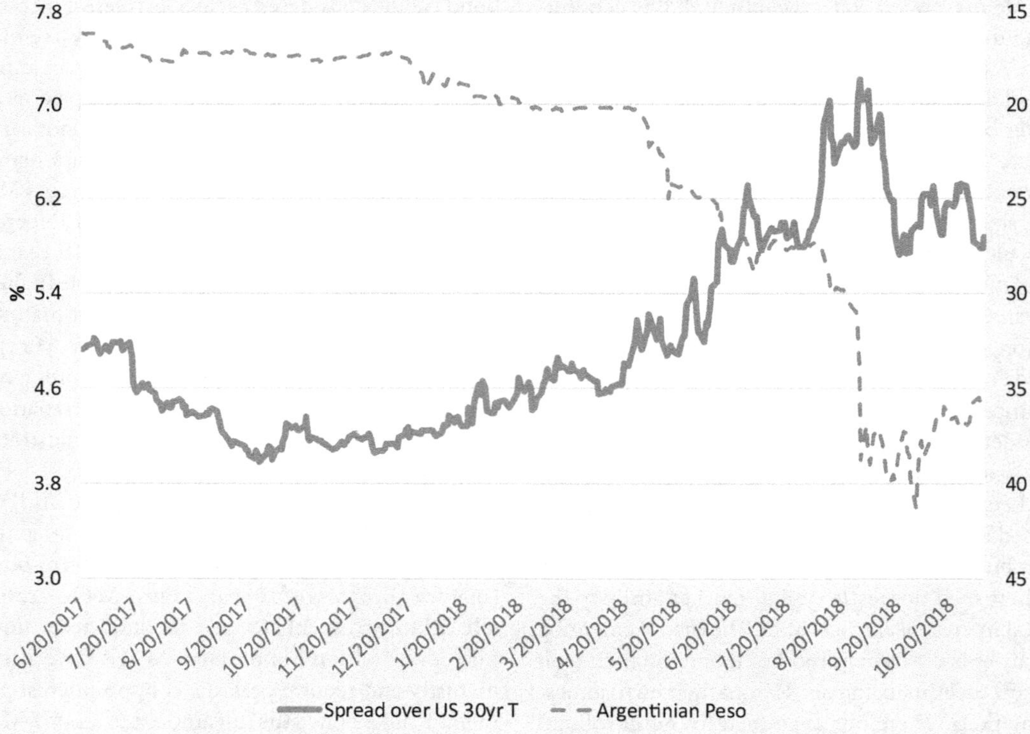

Exhibit 11.3. Argentina's century bond yield spread against 30-year US Treasury and peso price of one US dollar.

INTERNATIONAL CORPORATE FINANCE IN PRACTICE 11.3

Rushydro Has Successfully Placed Pioneering Ruble-Denominated Eurobonds

On October 28, 2010, RusHydro — Russia's largest power-generating company — announced that loan participation notes (LPNs) issued by the special purpose vehicle RusHydro Finance Ltd had been successfully placed. The proceeds of the LPNs would be used to fund RusHydro's investment program and operating activities. The volume of the issue was RUB 20 billion. The LPNs would mature in five years and have a coupon rate of 7.875% per annum. The issue received the following ratings: S&P: BB+, Moody's: Ba1, and Fitch: BB+. The consortium of underwriters and book runners included JPMorgan, Gazprombank, and Troika Dialog. The instrument is listed on the London Stock Exchange under Reg. S rule. This is the first ruble-denominated Eurobond issued by a Russian corporation and represents a milestone in the maturing of Russian capital markets.

Structured notes

Unlike bonds which call for a fixed coupon payment, structured notes pay variable interest which are indexed to a key benchmark rate such as the Secured Overnight Financing Rate (SOFR), the dollar-yen exchange rate, the price of crude oil etc ... The index formula is what makes the interest payment a "derivative" of an underlying economic variable(s) via a more or less complicated but generally creative formula. This asset class includes plain vanilla floating rate notes, inverse floaters, commodity-indexed bonds and dual index notes.

Floating Rate Notes (abbreviated as FRN and also known as floaters are medium-term notes (usually 5 years or less) that pay quarterly or semi-annual interest periodically adjusted and set on the basis of a widely used index, such as the Secured Overnight Financing Rate (SOFR). Depending on the creditworthiness of the issuer, the interest rate paid will reflect a credit spread over the index. FRNs account for close to 25% of all issuances in the Eurobond market. FRNs can be easily swapped into fixed-rate bonds thanks to a very liquid *interest rate swap* market (see Chapter 12).

INTERNATIONAL CORPORATE FINANCE IN PRACTICE 11.4

The LIBOR Scandal[5]

In 2012 the financial service industry was engulfed in a scam whose scale defied human comprehension. It revolves around the LIBOR (London Interbank Offering Rate) and widespread rumors swirling around bank traders alleged to have manipulated the most important figure in finance. Indeed the LIBOR is the key benchmark on the basis of which a plethora of financial products are priced and it underpins more than $350 trillion in financial contracts such as adjustable-rate mortgages, students' loans, asset-backed securities, floating rate notes, interest rate swaps, credit default swaps.... In effect, it determines the price that corporations and households will pay for their loan and the income that they will earn on their savings. A panel of sixteen major multinational banks with a presence in London were asked to submit a good faith *estimate* of the borrowing interest rate for short-term wholesale funds that they would face in the unsecured interbank market. Each contributing bank was asked to base its estimate on the following question:

> *At what rate could you borrow funds were you to do so by asking for and then accepting interbank offers in a reasonable market size just prior to 11 am London time?*

---

5 For an in-depth analysis of the LIBOR demise see Sheila Melvin and Ken Shotts' *Barclays and the LIBOR: Anatomy of a Scandal* (case ETH 03: Stanford Graduate Business School, 2013) and Michael H. Moffet's *Replacing LIBOR* (Thunderbird School of Global Management, Arizona State University, 2021).

Specifically, the LIBOR was calculated daily with an 11 am GMT fixing for five currencies (US dollar USD, Euro EUR, Japanese yen JPY, British Pound GBP and Swiss franc CHF) and seven tenors (overnight, one week, one, two, three, six, and 12 months). The British Bankers Association would collect the 16 estimates, discard the four highest and the four lowest and compute the average interest rate of the remaining eight estimates.

In June 2012, the LIBOR scandal exploded when the iconic Barclays bank admitted to repeated manipulation of its interest rate and agreed to paying $450 million in fine to the US department of Justice. ... The LIBOR scandal shortly thereafter engulfed several other leading banks — UBS, Deutsche Bank — with a total of $9 billion in fine as evidence of repeated intra-bank and inter-bank collusion became public.

Rate-rigging happened in two different ways. Early on, bank traders manipulated the daily estimate that Barclays was submitting to benefit ongoing positions especially with respect to interest rate swaps — overstating or understating the true rate at which Barclays could obtain short-term financing. Bank traders initially colluded with other Barclays traders but soon reached out to traders at other banks in the panel. In a similar vein, statistical analysis of LIBOR rates used for adjustable home mortgages showed that on the first day of the month when rates are reset the LIBOR tended to rise; this simply means that the mortgagee (home-owner) would have to pay more than he/she should and that the mortgagor collected a higher interest than they should have. The second form of rate manipulation was more strategic and was encouraged by senior bank officials. It aimed at understating the fair estimate of the interest rate that Barclays would pay when procuring short-term financing in order to project financial fortitude and strong credit worthiness. It was prevalent during the sub-prime crisis from 2006 to 2008.

LIBOR ceased publication on June 30, 2023 and was replaced in the case of the US dollar by Secured Overnight Financing Rate (SOFR). Similarly, risk free rates were introduced for the pound sterling (SONIA or Sterling Overnight Index Average), the Euro (ESTR or Euro Short Term Rate), the Japanese Yen (TONAR or Toyo Overnight Average Rate) and the Swiss franc (SARON or Swiss Average Rate Overnight). "SOFR is superior to LIBOR in a number of ways. SOFR is calculated on *actual documented transactions* whereas LIBOR was based on surveys of *possible transactions.* SOFR is based on secured transactions of government securities, truly risk-free. LIBOR was based on the unsecured borrowing of firms possessing credit risk. SOFR is calculated from transactions from the largest overnight financial market reflecting the opinion of thousands of buyers and sellers, including all forms of financial institutions and investors. LIBOR was based only on the perceived borrowing and lending costs between select commercial banks, a weak measure of market activity".[6]

6 See Moffet (2021).

FRNs can also be sourced from banks rather than capital markets as term loans[7] and would be termed *euro-credits*. If the euro-credit is extended in the form of a long-term line of credit, an additional fee for the unused portion of the credit is added to the spread. Such international bank loans are often arranged through *syndication* simply because the loan amount exceeds a single bank's lending limit. Syndication allows lending banks to spread the risk of large loans among the members of the syndicate. A lead managing bank (underwriter) working on behalf of the borrowing firm will assemble the bank syndicate, allocate the loan amount that each member bank is responsible for, and set the terms of the loan.

Interest payments on FRNs are indeed variable because they are reset periodically — usually every six months as the benchmark interest rate itself floats upwards or downwards. Consider for example a five-year $100 million floating rate note which pays SOFR + 50 basis points for six months: if the six-month SOFR on July 1, 2024 stood at 3.5% the FRN would pay on December 31, 2024 a semi-annual interest (or ½ of one year) of:

$$\$100 \text{ million } (0.035 + 0.005) \times \tfrac{1}{2} = \$2 \text{ million}$$

The next interest payment covering the first six months of 2025 would adjust to the new SOFR prevailing on December 31, 2024: assuming that

7 *Term loan* is a loan with a medium- or long-term maturity for a fixed amount and as an FRN would be priced as a spread over SOFR reflecting the credit risk of the borrower.

SOFR stood at 4% on December 31, 2024 the FRN would pay on June 30, 2025:

$100 million (0.040 + 0.005) × ½ = $2.25 million

and so on and so forth for the remaining eight semesters before the FRN would be redeemed. Because the coupon is reset every 6 months the face value of the FRN is not exposed to changing interest rates and for investors there is no market risk; in that sense FRNs are nearly as safe as cash as long as the issuer's credit risk remains steady. The borrower though faces *re-pricing* risk (roll-over risk) as the interest rate is reset on the basis of the benchmark rate — itself fluctuating with market conditions.

Inverse Floating Rate Notes (also known as inverse floaters or reverse floaters). Reverse floaters pay an interest amount which is inversely indexed to the reference/benchmark rate: it would increase when the reference rate decreases and conversely decreases when the reference rate increases. An example of an inverse floating rate note would be a $100 million note that pays a coupon at the rate of [7% — six month SOFR] to be reset every six months. Assuming SOFR = 3% for the previous six month period the inverse floater interest rate would be set at 7% — six month SOFR = 0.07 – 0.03 = 0.04 and the coupon payment received would be:

$100 million (0.07 – 0.03) × ½ = $2 million

Inverse floaters are often leveraged whereby either or both the fixed and/or the floating rate of the coupon formula are multiplied by a factor of two, three or four ... Leverage would simply magnify upward or downward the change in the coupon amount paid as a function of the multiplier applied. For example, consider an inverse floater that pays two times fixed interest rate set at 6% minus three times LIBOR. Assuming LIBOR = 3% such a $100 million inverse floater the interest paid would amount to:

$100 million (2 × .06 – 3 × .03) × ½
= $1.5 million

Commodity-indexed bond. Structured notes can also be designed for managing risk. Consider the case of a silver mining company whose risk profile is a direct function of the highly volatile spot price of silver. It finds it difficult to finance its operation simply because its revenue stream — linked to the price of silver — is highly volatile: instead of relying on straight debt one solution would be to issue debt whose principal repayment is tied to the spot price of silver. *Sunshine Mining Company* — a large US silver mining firm-issued 15 year $25 million silver-indexed bonds paying an annual interest of 8 ½ %. Each $1000 face amount bond was payable at maturity/redemption at the greater of $1000 or the market price of 50 ounces of silver. In effect the principal was indexed to the price of silver as long as the price of silver at redemption was higher than $20 per ounce. Sunshine Mining was able to borrow at below market interest rate by offering the bond-holder to partake in the upside potential of silver. Should the price of silver decline Sunshine Mining would become less profitable but would benefit from lower cost (below market rate) debt financing. Were the price of silver to rise above $20 per ounce Sunshine Mining would repay a larger principal (cost of debt would increase) but would gladly do so as it would benefit from stronger revenues. In effect Sunshine was offering investors a fixed-rate bullet bond + a European call option on silver with a strike price of $20 per ounce.

Dual-currency bonds pay interest coupon in one currency and principal redemption in another currency. JetBlue is considering issuing a dollar-denominated bond in the same amount of $250 million paying an annual coupon in yen of 6%. The advantage of a dual-currency bond for the issuer is that it avoids exchange rate risk on the principal ($250 million is borrowed and $250 million is repaid) and lowers its coupon yield relative to a plain-vanilla dollar-denominated issue. Thus, the exchange risk is limited to annual payment of interest coupons, which could be hedged through forward contracts by purchasing the appropriate amount of yen forward. Japanese investors like the idea of receiving a higher yield on the bond (say a straight yen bond issue would pay only 4% instead of 6%) even though the principal is denominated in a foreign currency.[8]

Convertible bonds allow issuers to lower their cost of debt by bundling a convertibility/call option with a straight debt instrument. The more value the call option holds for the investor (a function of the issuing firm's growth prospects), the lower the cost of the bond component. Debt coupled with warrants offers similar benefits to issuers and investors with the one difference that the convertibility call option (called a warrant) is readily separable from the bond itself and can be easily traded.

Contingent convertible bonds

The reader will recall that banks are required to hold a significant amount of (expensive) equity capital because of the fear of systemic risk — that is the

8 Here again the Japanese investor could readily hedge against a depreciation of the US dollar by selling forward dollar for yen in the exact amount of the principal.

possible bankruptcy of a large financial institution which would trigger a chain reaction or domino effect whereby other major financial institution would soon collapse (see International Finance in Practice 9.1). The principal method to mitigate systemic risk is to force financial institutions to have enough equity capital to weather asset losses — from non-performing loans to debtors going bankrupt. Thus, in the aftermath of the sub-prime crisis (2007–2009) the Basel III accord mandated minimal capital adequacy ratios (CARs) to provide a safety "cushion" against loan losses. CARs are similar to financial leverage and defined as:

$$\text{CAR} = \frac{\text{Tier 1 Capital} + \text{Tier 2 Capital}}{\text{Risk-Adjusted Assets}}$$

where Tier 1 capital is equity + retained earnings and tier 2 capital is preferred stock + 50% of subordinated debt. Risk-adjusted assets refers to the bank's assets adjusted according to their intrinsic riskiness. Tier 1 capital has to account for at least 4% of risk-adjusted assets and combined Tier 1 and Tier 2 Capital have to exceed 8%.

It is in this context of tighter capitalization requirements that contingent convertible bonds (also known as Cocos) were introduced to prevent the need for government-funded "*bail outs*" of financial institutions on the verge of bankruptcy. Because CoCos convert into equity at the discretion of the issuing bank they are part of Tier 1 capital under the label of Additional Tier 1 capital (AT1). Thus CoCos are fixed-income securities which may be forced to convert into a pre-specified amount of equity or simply written down should the issuer face difficult times. In good times they are simply high-yield bonds. The market for CoCos is worth around $275 billion. Private banks in Asia have historically been keen buyers, snapping up issuances for their ultra-rich clients.

Of primary interest to investors is the definition of the trigger which would force the conversion of Coco bonds into equity. In effect, CoCos allow a defaulting bank to replenish equity capital by bailing in. Typically, the trigger is defined as a threshold ratio of Tier 1 capital to risk-weighted assets. A more punishing but less frequently used is the ratio of the market value of equity to the book value of assets.

INTERNATIONAL CORPORATE FINANCE IN PRACTICE 11.5

"Death-spiral" of CoCo Bonds at Credit Suisse

When Swiss regulators decided to impose considerably tighter CARs on their two largest banks UBS and Credit Suisse with Tier 1 capital to exceed 10% and Tier 1 + Tier 2 capital to exceed 19%, Credit Suisse issued CHF16 billion of Cocos bonds to meet the additional 9% of non-equity capital. Triggers were (1) Tier 1 capital falls below 7% risk-weighted assets or (2) injection of public funds are necessary to keep Credit Suisse solvent.

Fast forward to the spring of 2023 when the Silicon Valley Bank bankruptcy in the United States unleashed mayhem in the banking industry which reverberated all the way to Switzerland. Credit Suisse faced a bank run which required the Swiss government to inject CHF 50 billion to keep it afloat and to force a hasty acquisition of Credit Suisse by its great rival, UBS. As part of the deal the *Swiss Financial Market Supervisory Authority* decided to write down around CHF16bn ($17bn) in Coco *bonds*.

When a bank goes bankrupt it is generally understood that senior bondholders have a right to payouts first, followed by more junior bondholders and then those who hold subordinated equity-linked bonds such as Cocos. Shareholders (equity) should take the first losses. When Banco Popular, a mid-sized Spanish lender, failed in 2017, it took about $1.4bn of CoCo bonds with it but shareholders were entirely wiped out first. The write-down of Credit Suisse's CoCos was more than ten times larger, making it the largest in history. But the real damage caused to the market was in upending the pecking order of claimants and placing shareholders above (rather than below) Cocos bondholders. Credit Suisse's bond issuance documents did state that Cocos bond buyers waived any right to re-imbursement in a "write-down event". This was confirmed by the Swiss Financial Market Supervisory Authority on March 19, 2023. Credit Suisse's shareholders were given approximately CHF 3 billion of UBS shares. How could Credit Suisse's shareholders — normally residual claimants on the bank cash-flows — find themselves in a more senior position to cocos bondholders? Will convertible contingent bonds survive as an asset class?

COST OF FOREIGN CURRENCY DEBT FINANCING

This section develops a quantitative framework for comparing the cost of different funding options.

A primer on bond valuation

The reader should recall from his or her first corporate finance course how to compare the cost of different bond financing options. This section revisits the key concepts of simple bond valuation by considering zero-coupon and level-coupon bonds. We use JetBlue's funding choices to illustrate the concepts:

- **Zeros** are issued in US dollars at \$61 and redeemed seven years later at \$100. No interest (zero coupon) is paid prior to redemption.
- **Dollar-denominated Eurobond** is issued at \$97, pays annual interest of \$7.25, and is redeemed in seven years at 102% of par.
- **Samurai bond** is issued at ¥100, pays a semiannual interest of 4% (¥2 every six months), and is repaid at 101% of par value in seven years. The exchange rate at time of issue is ¥100 = \$1. The exchange rate at time of interest payment or principal repayment is defined as the dollar price of one yen at time t, denoted as $S(t)$, and is unknown.
- **Floating rate note** is issued at euro-LIBOR + 165 basis points. Floating interest rate is reset every 6 months.

Remember that *zero-coupon bonds* are bonds that pay no (zero) coupon during their lives and are redeemed at par value. For example, a bond issued at 92% of par value and redeemed in one year is a zero-coupon bond whose yield to maturity (*ytm*) is:

$$92 = \frac{100}{(1+ytm)^1} \quad \text{or} \quad ytm = \frac{100}{92} - 1 = 8.70\%$$

Ms. Rousse at JetBlue was considering a dollar-denominated seven year zero-coupon bond issued at 61% and redeemable at 100% of par. Its yield to maturity would be given by[9]

$$61 = \frac{100}{(1+ytm)^7} \quad \text{or} \quad ytm = 7.32\% \qquad (11.1a)$$

More generally, the yield to maturity on a T-year zero-coupon bond is given by solving the following relationship:

$$P = \frac{Z}{(1+ytm)^T} \qquad (11.1b)$$

where P is the price of the zero-coupon bond today, and Z its value when redeemed at maturity, T years from now.

Level-coupon bonds pay a periodic interest coupon (typically every year in the Eurobond market or semiannually in most domestic bond markets) and principal at maturity. For example, JetBlue was considering a Eurodollar seven year bond to be issued at 97% of par, paying an annual 7.25% interest, and redeemable at 102% of par; its yield to maturity (or the internal rate of return) is calculated by setting the current price of the bond (\$97) equal to the present value of annual interest payments (\$7.25) from year one through year seven plus the principal repayment (\$102) at the end of year seven and solving for the internal rate of return or yield to maturity (*ytm*):

$$97 = \sum_{t=1}^{6} \frac{7.25}{(1+ytm)^t} + \frac{7.25+102}{(1+ytm)^7} \qquad (11.2a)$$
$$\text{with } t = 1, 2, \ldots, 6$$

which yields $ytm = 8.05\%$.

More generally, the yield to maturity on a level-coupon bond paying an annual coupon C over the next T years is given by solving for the yield to maturity (*ytm*) of the following bond equation:

$$P = \sum_{t=1}^{T-1} \frac{C}{(1+ytm)^t} + \frac{C+B}{(1+ytm)^T} \qquad (11.2b)$$
$$\text{with } t = 1, 2, 3, \ldots, T-1$$

where P is the bond issue price and B is the principal repayment at the end of year T.

9 The *ytm* is simply the interest rate at which the bond valued today at 66 has to be invested over the next seven years to grow into exactly 100; that is, $66\,(1 + ytm)^7 = 100$.

The reader will note that if the bond is issued at par (say $1,000) and repaid at par, then the yield to maturity is exactly equal to the coupon rate. Unfortunately, issuing fees and short-term fluctuations in interest rates will result in the issue price being (slightly) different from the bond par value.

All-in cost of debt versus yield-to-maturity of bonds

Although we use the yield-to-maturity as a measure of the cost of debt, the effective cost of debt financing to the borrower is slightly higher when issuance costs are taken into account. Indeed, the purchase cost of a bond to the investor is not exactly the net cash proceed the issuer receives — the difference being underwriting fees to investment banks managing the issue and registration cost to various regulatory agencies. JetBlue, in our earlier example, issuing a seven-year bond at a 3% discount from par and issuance costs of 150 basis points would receive a cash proceeds of 100 × (1 – 0.03 – 0.015) = 95.50. Therefore, the all-in cost for JetBlue of issuing this seven year bond is the internal rate of return of the bond equation (11.2a) found to be 8.35% The *all-in cost* to the borrower is always slightly higher than the 8.05% *yield-to-maturity* to the investor.

THE EFFECTIVE COST OF STRAIGHT FOREIGN DEBT

JetBlue was also considering issuing samurai bonds, which seemed to offer a considerably cheaper funding option. The cost in yen for a Japanese issuer can be solved similarly to the cost of dollar bond financing (see equation (11.2c)). For Jet-Blue, which is a US-based carrier and operates in US dollars, things get more complicated because neither the nominal coupon rate in yen nor the bond *ytm* in yen are anywhere close to JetBlue's effective cost of debt *YTM*[10] in US dollars.

Samurai bonds are issued at par of ¥100, which translates to $1. It will pay ¥2 of interest every six months, which translates to a dollar payment of [¥2 × $S(t)$] and principal repayment at maturity of ¥101 × $S(T)$. Therefore, its annualized yield to maturity in ¥ is simply[11]:

$$100 = \sum_{t=1}^{14} \frac{2}{(1+ytm)^t} + \frac{101}{(1+ytm)^{14}} \quad (11.2c)$$

or $ytm = 4.12\%$

In dollar terms, the *YTM* for JetBlue is a function of unknown exchange rates over the life of the seven year bond. The bond equation (11.2c) is simply restated by converting every interest and principal repayment at the corresponding exchange rate $S(t)$ defined as the dollar price of one yen at time t:

$$100 \times S(0) = \sum_{t=1}^{14} \frac{2 \times S(t)}{(1+YTM)^t} + \frac{101 \times S(14)}{(1+YTM)^{14}} \quad (11.3)$$

Implicit in the resolution of equation (11.3) is the availability of point estimates of future exchange rates $S(t)$ with t = 1, 2, …, 14 for 14 six-month periods. Unfortunately, most forecasters have shied away — and for good reason — from generating long-term exchange rate forecasts (see Chapter 15 for a full discussion of currency forecasting).

This is probably why corporate treasurers tend to be skeptical of point estimates of long-term forecasts in a market where so many have been wrong so often; they prefer to posit a constant annual average rate of appreciation/depreciation α% for the exchange rate.

Accordingly, let $S(t+1) = S(t)(1+\alpha)$

or with annual compounding

$$S(t) = S(0)(1+\alpha)^t \quad (11.4a)$$

$$\text{where } \alpha = \left(\frac{S(T)}{S(0)}\right)^{1/T} - 1$$

Substituting the above in equation (11.3) allows us to find the effective cost of yen financing for JetBlue by solving for *YTM*:

$$100 \times S(0) = \sum_{t=1}^{14} \frac{2 \times S(0)(1+\alpha)^t}{(1+YTM)^t} + \frac{101 \times S(0)(1+\alpha)^{14}}{(1+YTM)^{14}} \quad (11.4b)$$

10 Capital letters *YTM* refers to the effective yield to maturity when financing in a foreign currency; lowercase *ytm* refers to the yield to maturity when financing is denominated in the issuer's currency.

11 The solution to equation (10.2c) is the semiannual yield-to-maturity which should be annualized according to the formula: $(1 + \text{semiannual } ytm)^2 - 1 = \text{annual } ytm$.

which simplifies to:

$$100 = \sum_{t=1}^{14} \frac{2\times(1+\alpha)^t}{(1+YTM)^t} + \frac{101\times(1+\alpha)^{14}}{(1+YTM)^{14}} \quad (11.4c)$$

Unfortunately, this not an easy polynomial equation to solve, and we advocate a trial-and-error approach to finding the break-even rate of yen appreciation α^* that would bring the cost of samurai bond financing equal to dollar Eurobond financing. Very simple trial and error consists of computing the samurai bond *YTM* for as many different rates of yen appreciation (α) as necessary to identify the interval within which *YTM* moves from being lower to being higher than the $ytm = 8.05\%$ on the dollar Eurobond. Once the interval has been identified, the computation is repeated at smaller increments until the break-even value of α is reached:

Set α = 0.5%, 1%, 2%, 3%, ..., and find the corresponding $YTM(\alpha)$:

α = 0.5% per semiannual period $YTM = 5.15\%$

α = 1% per semiannual period $YTM = 6.17\%$

α = 1.5% per semiannual period $YTM = 7.19\%$

α = 2% per semiannual period $YTM = 8.21\%$

At $\alpha = 2\%$ the *YTM* is close to the dollar Eurobond financing with $ytm = 8.05\%$; therefore, we narrow further the numerical trial and error around 2%:

α = 1.85% per semiannual period $YTM = 7.90\%$

α = 1.90% per semiannual period $YTM = 8.00\%$

α = 1.923% per semiannual period $YTM = 8.050\%$

Thus, direct break-even analysis at which the *YTM* is equal to the *ytm* for the annual rate α^* of yen appreciation/depreciation can assist JetBlue in deciding between domestic dollar financing at the coupon rate of $i_\$ = 7.25\%$ versus ¥ financing with coupon rate of $i_¥ = 4\%$. Thus setting $YTM = ytm$ in equation (11.4b) and solving directly for α will yield the break-even value that was derived earlier by numerical trial-and-error iteration:

$$100 = \sum_{t=1}^{14} \frac{2\times(1+\alpha)^t}{(1+ytm)^t} + \frac{101\times(1+\alpha)^{14}}{(1+ytm)^{14}} \quad (11.4d)$$

which yields $\alpha^* = 1.923\%$.

Exhibit 11.4 illustrates how the cost of ¥ financing increases as a function of the annual rate of yen appreciation *vis-à-vis* the US dollar. At the break-even rate of $\alpha^* = 1.923\%$, the effective costs of domestic or foreign financing are equal. Beyond the break-even point, yen financing becomes more expensive than dollar financing. For example, for

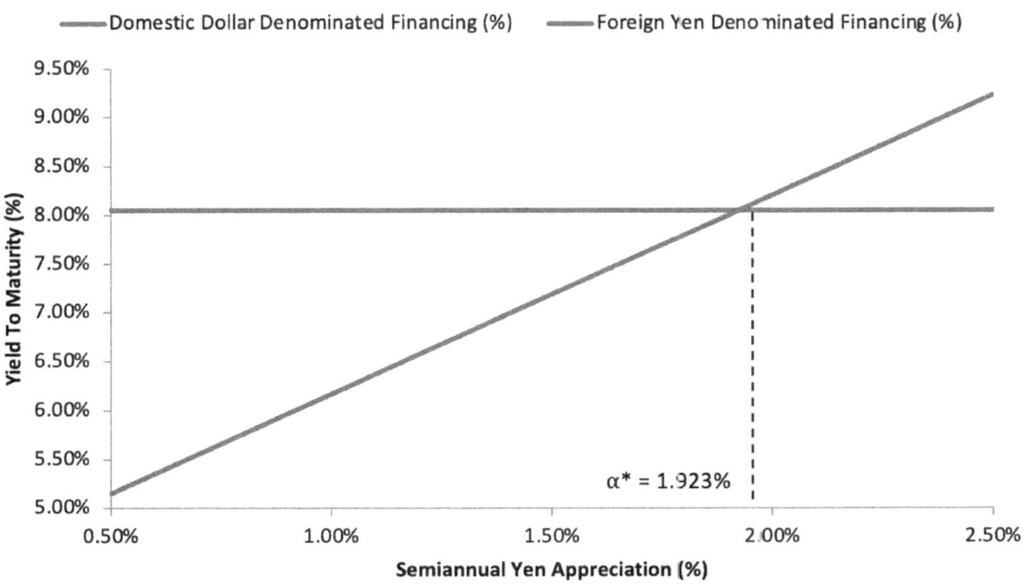

Exhibit 11.4. Break-even analysis.

$\alpha = 2.5\%$ the effective cost of yen financing climbs to 9.23%. Conversely, below the break-even rate of 1.923%, yen financing becomes increasingly cheaper than dollar financing as JetBlue would pay interest and repay principal in a cheaper currency (i.e., every yen owed costs fewer dollars to purchase). See International Corporate Finance in Practice 11.6 for the case of a bond issued and repaid at par.

INTERNATIONAL CORPORATE FINANCE IN PRACTICE 11.6

Special Case When the Bond Is Issued at Par and Repaid at Par

For such bonds issued in the domestic and foreign currency paying coupon at the annual rate of i_d and i_f, the *ytm* of such bonds in their respective currency is simply the coupon rate i_d and i_f. The break-even rate of the foreign currency appreciation/depreciation, which brings to equality the effective cost of financing in either currency, is found to be simply:

$$\alpha^* = \frac{(1+i_d)}{(1+i_f)} - 1 \quad \text{or approximately} \quad \alpha^* = i_d - i_f \tag{11.5}$$

Assuming the nominal interest rate on foreign debt to be less than that on domestic debt, foreign financing will be preferred if $\alpha < \alpha^*$ — that is, if the rate of appreciation of the foreign currency is less than the interest rate differential. Conversely, domestic financing should be preferred if $\alpha > \alpha^*$.

Q: Assuming JetBlue can finance at 7.25% through a seven year Eurodollar bond or through a seven year samurai bond at 4.25%, what would be the exchange rate scenario under which the samurai bond would be the preferred mode of financing? (Both bonds are issued and repaid at par.)

A: The break-even rate α^* of annual yen appreciation that brings the two bonds' *ytm* to equality is $\alpha^* = 7.25\% - 4.25\% = 3\%$. As long as the yen appreciates by less than 3% annually, samurai bond financing should be chosen.

The impact of taxation

Because tax rates on interest payments and capital gains/losses differ among countries and exchange gains and losses are not necessarily treated symmetrically, the effective cost of foreign debt should carefully reflect the tax situation of the borrower. Equations (11.4b) and (11.4c) can be adapted to specific tax situations, and break-even analysis can be carried out through numerical analysis. Generally, three polar cases will characterize most situations:

1. Exchange losses on the principal of a foreign currency debt may not be tax-deductible, as is the case in England. Domestic financing will be favored (sterling in this case for an England-domiciled issuer) as long as the foreign currency is expected to appreciate, because the exchange losses (unlike interest payments) are not tax-deductible.
2. By contrast, the tax laws in some countries, such as Sweden, encourage domestic companies to prefer foreign financing (under a scenario of foreign currency appreciation) by permitting unrealized exchange losses on foreign currency debt to be tax-deductible immediately, while taxes on exchange gains are deferred until realized.
3. The intermediate case, characteristic of the United States, is to make exchange losses on principal repayment tax-deductible when realized at the corporate income tax rate. The exchange gain will generally be taxable at the lower capital gains rate, which ceteris paribus should favor financing in a weak currency.

DEBT REFINANCING[12]

As exchange rates and interest rates fluctuate widely over the life of a bond, many firms may decide to prepay or refund their foreign currency–denominated debt with domestic currency in order to lessen their exchange losses due to foreign currency revaluations or to take advantage of currency overshooting. If we

12 This section is analytically more advanced and can be skipped without loss of the main lessons from this chapter.

assume the interest rates differential between two currencies anticipates exchange rate changes (*uncovered interest rate parity*) and issuing costs are equal, the decision to refinance foreign debt with domestic debt should be perfectly identical to the decision to refinance the existing debt with a new issue of foreign debt. Typically, though, market imperfections, prolonged exchange-rate overshooting, asymmetry in the tax treatments of exchange losses on early redemption of foreign currency principal, and violations of uncovered interest rate parity due to continued credit rationing or interest rate subsidies will force the borrowing firm perennially to consider the debt refinancing option in its global financing strategy. We discuss next how a firm should decide whether to exit a given financing instrument deemed to have become too expensive. Three methods are considered: (1) exiting a foreign bond by refinancing with a domestic bond, (2) exchanging a foreign bond for a domestic bond with a ready-made *currency swap*, and (3) using a series of forward contracts to lock in the cost of the existing foreign bond.

Straight debt

This method consists of raising domestic debt at the rate of i_d to refund foreign currency debt whose cost is increasing as a result of the foreign currency appreciation. Formally, if it takes $1 + \varphi$ units of domestic currency at time θ (with $\theta < T$ in a new bond issue) to refund one unit of foreign currency at the interest rate of i_d after meeting all flotation and prepayment costs, the effective cost of domestic debt refinancing necessary for refunding the foreign debt is the solution *ytm* to the following bond equation:

$$1+\varphi=\sum_{t=\theta}^{T-1}\frac{i_d(1+\varphi)}{(1+ytm)^t}+\frac{(1+i_d)(1+\varphi)^{T-\theta}}{(1+ytm)^{T-\theta}} \qquad (11.6)$$

with $t = \theta, \theta + 1, \ldots, T - 1$

where the first term is the present value of servicing the new principal of $\$(1 + \varphi)$ at the nominal interest of i_d over the remaining $T - 1 - \theta$, and the second term is the present value of interest and principal repayment in year terminal year T.

Similarly, the effective cost of not prepaying the foreign debt is given by solving for *YTM* in the following equation:

$$1+\varphi=\sum_{t=\theta}^{T-1}\frac{i_f(1+\varphi)(1+\alpha)^t}{(1+YTM)^{T-t}}+\frac{(1+i_f)(1+\varphi)(1+\alpha)^{T-\theta}}{(1+YTM)^{T-\theta}} \qquad (11.7)$$

where the foreign currency continues to appreciate at the annual rate of α over the remainder of the bond tenor $T - \theta$. Thus, the decision whether to hold or refund the foreign debt instrument at time θ is given by simple break-even analysis about whether *ytm* or *YTM* is larger. This can be solved through numerical methods, as we demonstrated in the previous section.

In a similar vein, two currency-derivative alternative solutions to the cumbersome debt-refunding strategy should be considered: currency swaps and long-term forward contracts. These techniques allow the issuer to change the currency denomination of its long-term debt portfolio without incurring the significant transaction costs associated with early redemption of principal and flotation costs. However, there are still many situations where limited currency convertibility will impair the availability of currency forwards or currency swaps.

Currency swaps

By exchanging (swapping) interest payment and principal repayment obligations at a fixed (once-and-for-all) exchange rate, borrowers can free themselves from a foreign debt obligation without incurring the additional cost of a prepayment penalty on the debt issue being retired and flotation costs on the new debt issue. In effect, the currency swaps amount to a series of forward contracts set at the prevailing spot exchange rate when the swap occurs and will tend to be cheaper than hedging each interest and principal repayment at the corresponding forward rate. The reader is further referred to the full discussion of currency swaps in Chapter 12.

Currency swaps in the framework of equations (11.6) and (11.7) are easy to interpret, since they allow the borrower to avoid both prepayment penalties and flotation costs if indeed domestic financing becomes cheaper than foreign financing.

Long-term forward contracts

Long-term forward contracts allow the borrower to lock in the domestic currency cost of servicing both principal and interest rate payments on the foreign debt instrument by entering into a series of forward purchase contracts[13] that match in both amount and maturity the cash flow associated with the foreign debt instrument.

---

13 By applying the interest rate parity first introduced in Chapter 6, it is relatively easy to compound long-term annual interest rates i_d and i_f to derive long-term forward rates $F(t)$ maturing in year t;

$$F(t)=\frac{S(0)\times(1+i_d)^t}{(1+i_f)^t}$$

Numerical illustration

Having borrowed samurai bonds at 4% (yield to maturity of 4.12%), JetBlue is experiencing severe exchange losses as the yen has appreciated from ¥100 to ¥85 = $1 over the first 4 years. JetBlue fears the yen will continue to appreciate over the remainder of the bond term. Should JetBlue lock in (hedge) its cost of yen financing by refinancing in dollars through a new bond issue at an effective cost of 7.26%, swapping into dollars for a new effective yield to maturity of 7.12% or buying yen forward to meet both interest and principal repayments? Forward rates are quoted as follows:

$$F(4.5)=\frac{1}{83.25},\ F(5)=\frac{1}{80.50},\ F(5.5)=\frac{1}{78},\ F(6)=\frac{1}{76},\ F(6.5)=\frac{1}{73},\ F(7)=\frac{1}{69.25}$$

for the remaining 3 years of six semiannual interest payments.

The corresponding dollar "hedged" yield to maturity is derived by solving the bond equation (11.3), where forward rates are substituted for unknown spot exchange rates:

$$100\times S(4)=\sum_{t=1}^{3}\frac{2\times F(t+4)}{(1+YTM)^t}+\frac{101\times F(7)}{(1+YTM)^7} \quad (11.3a)$$

with $t = 0.5, 1, 1.5, 2, 2.5, 3$.

Thus, the hedged yield to maturity on the remaining 3 years of semiannual payments and principal repayment should be compared with the yield to maturity of a dollar refinanced bond either directly or through a currency swap.

$$\frac{100}{85}=\left(\frac{2}{83.5}\times\frac{1}{(1+YTM)^{0.5}}\right)+\left(\frac{2}{80.5}\times\frac{1}{(1+YTM)^{1}}\right)+\left(\frac{2}{78}\times\frac{1}{(1+YTM)^{1.5}}\right)+\left(\frac{2}{76}\times\frac{1}{(1+YTM)^{2}}\right)+\left(\frac{2}{73}\times\frac{1}{(1+YTM)^{2.5}}\right)+\left(\frac{2}{69.25}\times\frac{1}{(1+YTM)^{3}}\right)$$

for a $YTM = 6.97\%$.

Clearly hedging the current samurai bond with forward contracts is the cheapest and preferred solution. The reader may wonder why the yield to maturity on a foreign bond hedged back in dollars would still be cheaper than a dollar-denominated bond. There are at least three good reasons for the discrepancy in yields: (1) Issuance cost may be lower on a foreign market, (2) credit spread — that is, the risk premium investors demand from a corporate bond — will vary slightly from market to market, or (3) forward rates of a long-term nature may deviate from their intrinsic interest rate parity value.

THE INTERNATIONAL DEBT FINANCING CONUNDRUM

So far our discussion of international debt financing has focused on selecting the currency denomination that minimizes the effective cost of debt. In fact, firms face a delicate balancing act between satisfying the *hedge motive* and satisfying the *opportunistic motive* to reach an appropriate solution. The hedge motive simply refers to the best attempt at matching the risk profile of the firm's cost stream (including debt servicing) with its revenue stream, whereas the opportunistic motive attempts to maximize cost savings by making bets on the future course of interest and exchange rates.

Thus, optimal long-term debt currency denomination should never be divorced from the overall currency configuration of the borrower's revenues and cost streams. When there is a structural imbalance between the currency denomination of cash inflows and cash outflows as a result of the firm's idiosyncratic involvement in input and output markets, choosing to denominate debt in the currency of cash inflows can create a *natural hedge* and should take precedence over a strict cost of debt decision criterion. In many cases, the firm will consider issuing debt in a currency that aligns its revenue stream with its debt servicing cost stream, even though it may not minimize its cost of debt — at least not in a narrow computational sense. In fact, the cost at which the firm borrows should reflect how the debt servicing obligations impact the borrower's risk profile. Very often, however, it does not.

The Asian financial crisis of 1997 comes to mind as a vivid illustration of how currency denomination decisions in sourcing debt should *not* be made. From our discussion of the international monetary system in Chapter 3, the reader will recall how Southeast Asian countries, such as Thailand and Indonesia, had long maintained pegged exchange rates against the US dollar. In Thailand, for example, the Thai baht had been pegged at THB 25 = $1 since 1984 and seemed unassailable because of the large foreign reserves the Bank of Thailand had accumulated over the years. Thus, for Thai companies the temptation to issue debt in US dollars at 6% rather than borrowing long term in Thai baht at 13% was indeed very enticing, since the dollar peg for the Thai currency seemed rock solid.

Many Thai companies, such as real estate developers whose franchises were strictly domestic (i.e., they would develop real estate projects in Thailand for Thai nationals), issued dollar-denominated Eurobonds to take advantage of the substantially lower dollar cost of debt (opportunistic motive). When the crisis hit with the devaluation of the Thai baht in July 1997, these firms suddenly faced debt-servicing burdens, which practically doubled while the revenue stream denominated in Thai baht remained unchanged. This was the case of the Thai real estate developer Somprasong Land, which defaulted on its $80 million Eurobond issue in February 1998. The currency mismatch between companies' baht-denominated revenue streams and their dollar debt financing costs had remained gaping as they neglected to heed the hedge motive. Indeed, on a number of occasions (see International Corporate Finance in Practice 11.7), bankruptcy has resulted from debt issuers' inability to reconcile a cost of debt minimization exercise with a more strategic understanding of the firm's long-term economic exposure to foreign exchange risk.

INTERNATIONAL CORPORATE FINANCE IN PRACTICE 11.7

"Budget" Laker Airways Crashes into Bankruptcy

The crash of Sir Freddie Laker's UK-based low-cost Skytrain had little to do with the failure of its navigational equipment or landing gear. Indeed, it can be largely attributed to misguided financial decisions that were exacerbated by adverse dollar appreciation. Laker mistakenly agreed to dollar invoicing in the installment purchase of McDonnell Douglas DC-10 aircrafts. The mortgage financing provided by the US Export-Import Bank and other financial institutions called for debt servicing and principal repayment in US dollars. Unfortunately for UK-based Laker Airways, the gross mismatch between revenues, evenly divided between dollar and sterling ticket sales, and costs, primarily comprised of fuel (priced in US dollars) and debt servicing and principal repayment (also denominated in US dollars), led to bankruptcy in 1982 when the pound plunged from US$2.25 to US$1.60. Laker management had naively projected total revenues on the basis of a stable exchange rate US$2.25 = £1, which resulted in a dramatic dollar revenue shortfall when sterling-denominated debt ticket sales had to be converted at US$1.60 = £1. Thus, Laker Airways was forced into bankruptcy.

Source: Adapted from Srinivasulu, S. L. 1983. "Currency Denomination of Debt: Lessons from Rolls-Royce and Laker Airways," *Business Horizons.* (September–October): 19–23.

SUMMARY

1. The international debt financing decision is similar to a global procurement decision. The borrower has to identify the different sources of financing, both domestic and foreign. Each funding source has to be priced so that the borrower can compare and select the cost-of-debt minimizing option.
2. The global bond market is segmented in two ways: (1) across different currency spaces (bond market in US dollars or Japanese yen and many others) and (2) between the domestic/onshore and the external/offshore tiers.
3. For major currencies, the bond market is comprised of (1) an internal/onshore market encompassing domestic bonds issued by domestic firms and foreign bonds issued by foreign-domiciled firms, and (2) an external/Eurobond offshore market.
4. Eurobonds are typically (1) issued by an international syndicate of banks, (2) placed simultaneously in a large number of countries except for the country of the currency of denomination, and (3) offered in bearer form and not subject to withholding tax.
5. The effective cost of bond financing is best measured by its yield to maturity. It is defined as the bond's internal rate of return and solved by setting the price of the bond equal to the present value of all interest payments and principal repayment.
6. The effective cost of issuing a bond in a currency that is different from the reference currency of the

borrower is complicated by the uncertainty with respect to the exchange rate prevailing at the time of interest and principal payments. Forecasting exchange rates — especially over the longer term — is a treacherous exercise.

7. The yield to maturity of a foreign bond can be solved by incorporating an exchange rate forecast into the bond equation. Forward rates — derived from the yield curves of the two currencies involved — can be used as forecasts. A simpler approach is to posit an annual rate of appreciation/depreciation for the foreign currency and search for the break-even rate at which the effective cost of foreign debt financing is equal to comparable domestic debt financing.

8. Cost comparison among different debt instruments should be embedded into a more strategic analysis of the borrower's cash inflows and cash outflows configuration. For example, a firm deriving significant revenue from a given export market may prefer to issue debt in the export market's currency. Similarly, a firm facing import competition from foreign-based rivals may decide to raise debt denominated in the home currency of these rivals. In such cases, a *hedge motive* dominates the *opportunistic motive* driven by simple cost considerations.

QUESTIONS FOR DISCUSSION

1. What are the key decisions firms face in establishing their debt financing policies? How do they differ between a domestic and a multinational firm?

2. Identify the principal sources of foreign debt financing. Are they available only to multinational corporations?

3. What are the differences between domestic bonds, foreign bonds, and Eurobonds?

4. Define what is meant by the offshore or Eurobond market.

5. What is the difference between a *bearer* and a *nominal* bond?

6. What is the difference between the euro bond market and the Eurobond market?

7. What are Yankee, samurai, panda or bulldog bonds?

8. What is meant by bond market segmentation?

9. What is the difference between the yield-to-maturity and the all-in-cost of a debt instrument?

10. What is the difference between the nominal and effective cost of foreign debt?

11. Explain how currency swaps can be used to compute the effective cost of foreign debt.

12. Discuss the key factors that should guide firms in determining which currency to borrow in.

PROBLEMS

1. **Yield-to-maturity on zeros (foundational).** Royal Dutch Shell — the Anglo-Dutch oil company — issues a dollar-denominated seven year zero-coupon Eurobond in the amount of US$1 billion at an annual yield of 6.5%.
   a. Where would the funds actually be raised? Who would the investors be? Would investors in such Eurobonds be primarily domiciled in the euro-zone?
   b. How much capital would Royal Dutch raise with this issue?
   c. If underwriting fees amount to 150 basis points of the bond issue's face value, how much capital would Royal Dutch receive?
   d. What is the all-in cost of debt faced by Royal Dutch Shell?

2. **Zeros versus perpetual bonds (foundational).** Consider the following two bond investment opportunities and compare their yields:
   a. Compute the yield to maturity (YTM) of a zero-coupon bond with a face value of €1,000 with nine years to maturity and currently selling at 48%.
   b. Compute the YTM of a perpetual bond with an annual coupon of €50 and currently selling at €1,120.

3. **Effective yield to maturity and exchange risk (foundational).** An investor is considering investing in one-year zero-coupon Eurobonds. He is comparing investment in either a British pound–denominated bond with a yield of 6.2% or a euro-denominated bond with a yield of 5.5%. The current exchange rate is €1.3408 per £.
   a. Identify likely investors in either bond.
   b. Under what exchange rate scenario would the two investment opportunities be equal?

c. Which investment would you recommend if you anticipate that the actual exchange rate one year later will be €1.3175 per £?

4. **Pemex's international financing (foundational).** Pemex — the Mexican state-owned oil company — is rated AA in Mexico for domestic bond issues but constrained in its international financing by Mexico's B country rating.
   a. What is the highest rating that Pemex can receive on international debt financing?
   b. Why do Pemex domestic and international debt ratings differ?
   c. What is/are the risk(s) that investors domiciled outside Mexico face when they invest in Pemex's international bonds?

5. **Sovereign bonds (foundational).** The Republic of South Africa issued $1.25 billion debenture at 97% of 100% par value with issuing cost of 65 basis points. The sovereign bond pays a coupon rate of 4.875%. The bond was rated BB+ and would be redeemed at par in 10 years.
   a. The US government pays a coupon of 1.50% for 10 year maturity treasuries. How do you explain the significantly higher interest rate paid by South Africa as compared with the US? What is South Africa's sovereign yield spread?
   b. What is the yield-to-maturity to investors purchasing this South African bond?
   c. What is the all-in cost of debt paid by South Africa?
   d. A little less than a year after the bond issue South Africa was downgraded to BB-: what would you expect would happen to bond's coupon rate and to its all-in cost?

6. **Zero-coupon Eurobonds for PepsiCo (foundational).** PepsiCo Overseas issues dollar-denominated zero-coupon Eurobonds at a price of 67.25%. The bonds are to be repaid at 100% three years hence.
   a. What is the bonds' yield to maturity?
   b. Would your answer be different if you assume semiannual rather than annual compounding?
   c. Where would the bonds be sold? Who are the likely investors?

7. **Walt Disney Sleeping Beauties Bonds (intermediate).** In July 1993, the Walt Disney Company issued a $300 million debenture paying a semi-annual coupon of 7.55%. The bonds were issued at 100% of par value, redeemable at par on July 15, 2093 and were rated AA — by Standard & Poor's. Underwriting, registration and other fees amounted to 1.25% or 125 basis point.
   a. Why were Walt Disney's Century bonds dubbed "*Sleeping Beauties*"?
   b. What is the all-in cost of the Sleeping Beauties bonds?
   c. Assume that one year later the coupon rate on similarly rated 100 year bond has increased by 50 basis points to 8.05%: what would you expect the market price of Sleeping Beauties bonds to be?
   d. Walt Disney had also considered a similar issue on the dollar Eurobond market at a coupon rate of 7.35% with issuing cost at 1.75%. What would be the all-in cost of this bond? How do you explain the lower coupon rate on Eurobond issue?

8. **Nominal versus effective cost of debt (intermediate).** Black & Decker — a US multinational manufacturer of small power tools — is considering financing a plant expansion in France with euro (€) Eurobonds. The bond issue would be a five year maturity instrument with a coupon rate of 7% to be paid semiannually, whereas the principal repayment occurs at maturity. A comparable financing in US dollars ($) would cost the borrower a coupon rate of 10%.
   a. Assuming the US dollar depreciates at a rate of 1% (0.5% semiannually), the effective tax rate of Black & Decker US is 35%, and the exchange losses on principal repayments are tax-deductible, which long-term financing option should be selected? On the date of the issue, €1 = $1.34.
   b. Would your answer change if exchange losses on principal repayment were not tax-deductible?
   c. A similar financing arrangement with bonds denominated in pound sterling at a coupon rate of 8.5% annually is possible. Should Black & Decker US consider such a financing option? Are there other considerations that could influence your recommendations?

9. **Currency denomination in international financing (intermediate).** Nokia — the Finnish manufacturer of cell phones — is considering alternative financing options to fund the $1 billion acquisition of US-based Magic Telecommunications.
   - A €-denominated Eurobond at an annual coupon rate of 4.80% over seven years with up-front fees of 2% to be issued and repaid at par.

- A seven year Yankee bond with a coupon rate of 5.75% to be issued at 98% with up-front fees of 1.25% and repaid at par.
  - **a.** What are the effective costs of financing in euros and in US dollars?
  - **b.** Under what exchange rate scenario would the two bond issues be equivalent (at time of issue €1 = US$1.33)?
  - **c.** Should the funding currency be selected on the basis of the currency of the parent or of the business unit that will be responsible be for servicing it? What financing option do you recommend Nokia should choose?

10. The peso Eurobond market (intermediate). The market for peso-denominated bonds issued outside of Mexico was initiated in 2004. The peso Eurobond market began with the issuance of a MXN $3,000 MM bond by the Inter-American Development Bank in April 2004, and the last issuance was a MXN $1,200 MM bond by the US Export-Import Bank in January 2008.

- **a.** Explain what peso Eurobonds are.
- **b.** What does their issuance reveal about the development of Mexican financial markets?
- **c.** Would you expect peso Eurobonds to be issued as bearer bonds?
- **d.** Who are likely investors in peso Eurobonds? Would you expect Mexican nationals to invest in such bonds?
- **e.** Would you expect the cost of issuing peso Eurobonds as compared to domestic peso bonds to be about the same? Should there be cost of debt differences? Explain.

11. Peso Eurobonds and Televisa's funding choices (intermediate). Televisa (TV) — the Mexican media conglomerate — was contemplating the issuance of peso-denominated Euro-notes. It would be the first such issue by a Mexican corporation in a market that was barely three years old. On October 2006, Televisa was upgraded by Standard & Poor's from BBB to BBB+ in its Global Scale. Local Scale grade remained AAA. Televisa's funding options included:

- Peso-denominated 8.49% senior unsecured Euro-notes due 2037.
- US dollar–denominated long bond issued in US capital markets as a 144A Reg. S. The bonds would have a maturity of 30 years and would be issued at a spread over the 30-year Treasury bond of 150 basis points. The Treasury rate at the time was trading at 4.836%, which resulted in an all-in rate of 6.336% for TV. The swap to pesos represented a spread over the 30 year Mexican treasury of 121 basis points (bps), 54 bps higher than the euro-peso spread negotiated in the transaction.
- Peso-denominated long bond issued in the local market (Certificado Bursatil). The local bond would compare very closely with the peso Eurobond, notwithstanding that TV has a 4.9% withholding tax impact on interest payments from issuing in a foreign capital market versus issuing in the local market.
  - **a.** What are the differences — if any — between a 30-year peso Euro-note and a peso-denominated bond? Which issue would you expect to cost less for Televisa?
  - **b.** What is the nominal cost for Televisa of borrowing US dollars? What would be the effective cost of US$ financing?
  - **c.** What is the cost of US$ financing swapped into MXN?
  - **d.** Which funding option do you recommend to Televisa?

12. Bond yields and exchange rate forecasts (advanced). On August 28, 2010, IBM International Finance NV — the Dutch Antilles-based international finance subsidiary of IBM Corporation — issued four $100 million equivalent tranches of Eurobonds respectively denominated in US dollars, pounds sterling, euros, and Swiss francs, and maturing on August 28, 2015, at par. Each bond pays semi-annual coupons at the rate of $8\frac{5}{8}$%, $11\frac{7}{8}$%, 10%, and $4\frac{3}{8}$%, respectively.

- **a.** On August 28, 2011, the market values of the bonds were at 99.88%, 97.25%, 95.63%, and 103%, respectively. Anticipating that the pound sterling would shortly depreciate, the treasurer of IBM was considering swapping both the euro and US dollar tranches for sterling. What is the minimum annual rate of sterling devaluation necessary to warrant such a reconfiguration of the currency denomination of the debt?
- **b.** Can you infer from the previous information the market expectations of the exchange rate relationships between US dollars, pounds sterling, euros, and Swiss francs? On August 28, 2011, the spot exchange rates were US dollar 1 = British pound 0.59 = euro 0.7990 = Swiss franc 1.0173.

13. **Use of artificial currency unit in long-term financing (advanced).** On December 1, 1970, the European monetary unit (EMU) was first used as a contractual device for the denomination of a bond issue floated by the European Coal and Steel Community. The value of the EMU was then fixed irrevocably in terms of the currencies of the six original European Economic Community (EEC) member countries for the duration of the bond issue, which had a 15-year maturity. The EMU was then defined as 3.66 Deutsche marks (DM) or 50 Belgian francs (BF) or 3.62 Dutch guilders (DG) or 625 Italian lira (LIT) or 50 Luxembourg francs (LF) or 5.55 French francs (FF). At the time of bond issue, 1 EMU = 1 US dollar on the basis of the then-prevailing exchange rates between the dollar and the six EEC currencies. Any subsequent devaluation or revaluation of one component currency could not alter the original relationship between the EMU and that currency. Finally, the investor had the right to choose the component currency in which payment of principal and interest were to be made by the borrowing entity.
    - **a.** Assume that a Belgium investor had purchased 25,000 EMU with a 7% coupon rate on December 31, 1970 (purchase of EMU-denominated bonds was made at par value). On December 17, 1971, the DM was revalued by 15%. Determine the interest payment received by the Belgian investor on December 31, 1971. Had the BF been devalued by 5% simultaneously with the revaluation of the DM, would the interest payment received by the Belgian investor be different?
    - **b.** Is the borrower protected against foreign exchange risk when denominating bonds with a multiple-currency clause such as the EMU?
    - **c.** Is the lender (bondholder) protected against foreign exchange risk when purchasing bonds that include a multiple-currency clause such as the EMU?
    - **d.** Do units of accounts that include a multiple-currency clause qualify as contractual exchange-sharing devices?
    - **e.** On December 2, 1985, the prevailing exchange rates were DM 2.5180 = BF 52.10 = DG 2.8125 = LIT 1,712 = FF 7.6805. What was the yield to maturity (YTM) of the EMU-denominated bonds purchased by our Belgian investor?

14. **Dual-currency bonds (advanced).** R.J. Reynolds is considering a 25-billion yen debenture to be issued at 101.50% of par. The five year, annual coupon bond would pay an interest rate of 7¾% denominated in yen, but the principal would be repaid in dollars, rather than yen, in the amount of $111.956 million.
    - **a.** What are the yields to maturity from the perspectives of the issuer, a US-based pension fund, and a Japanese insurance company that is considering the dual-currency bond as a possible investment? At the time of issue, the spot exchange rate stood at 136.90 yen = $1. Five-year forward contracts were also available at 97.60 yen (bid)–102.70 yen (offer) per dollar.
    - **b.** Should R.J. Reynolds prefer a straight $100 million Eurobond issued at 100.125% of par that pays an annual coupon of 10.125% and is redeemable at par?
    - **c.** Alternatively, R.J. Reynolds could issue 25 billion yen worth of Eurobonds at 100.25% of par with a 6.375% coupon. This bond is also redeemable at par. Under what exchange rate scenario would you recommend this last option to R.J. Reynolds? Note: All three debentures carry up-front fees of 1.875% of par.

15. **Mortgage financing and currency swaps (advanced).** Conoco-Norway — a subsidiary of Houston-based Conoco — christened the world's first floating oil-production platform built from concrete, which will also be the world's largest floating production facility. This innovative concrete platform was designed and built by Aker, the Norwegian engineering group. It cost 25 billion Norwegian crowns (NOK) and is being financed through a mortgage debt instrument at a subsidized rate of 11% over a period of seven years.
    - **a.** What is the monthly installment owed by Conoco? The standard expression for the amount M to be repaid each year on a one Norwegian crown loan for T years at the interest rate of i_f is:

$$M = \frac{i_f\left(1+i_f\right)^T}{\left(1+i_f\right)^T - 1} \times P$$

    - **b.** Given that the platform will tap the Heindrum oil field approximately 1,100 km off the coast of Norway, Conoco is considering swapping the NOK-denominated debt into a dollar-denominated debenture to reduce economic exposure. Two options are available: (1) a dollar-denominated mortgage at 8⅛% or (2) a dollar-denominated coupon bond at 8⅝%. What are the exchange rate scenarios that would warrant either swap? On May 10, 2012, $1 = NOK 6.24.

INTERNET EXERCISES

16. **Interest Rate Forecasts.** Log in to www.oecd.gov and identify the countries for which the OECD forecast the highest and lowest long term (10 year) interest rate. What is the OECD forecast for short term interest rates in Turkey and the United Kingdom? What is the current inflation rate in those two countries?

17. **Coupon Rates and Yield-to-Maturity.** Log in to Bloomberg website www.bloomberg.com/markets to find the coupon rate and the yield-to-maturity of one- and ten-year Australian and US government bonds. Why are the two rates different? Derive the no-profit one year and ten year no profit forward rates between the US and Australian dollars.

18. **Bond Financing.** Log in to the Bank of International Settlements website www.bis.org to find how much money had been raised in the Eurobond market in the current year. What are the two leading currencies of denomination used in Eurobond issues? Would have the answers been different five or ten years ago?

REFERENCES

Claes, Anouk, Mark J. K. DeCeuster, and Ruud Polfliet. 2002. "Anatomy of the Eurobond Market, 1980–2000." *European Financial Management* 8 (3): 373–386.

Giddy, Ian H. 1994. *Global Financial Markets*. Lexington, MA: D.C. Heath.

Jacque, Laurent L., and Pascal Lang. 1987. "Currency Denomination in Long Term Debt Financing: A Cross-Hedging Paradigm." *Journal of Operational Research Society* 38(2): 173–182.

O'Malley, Chris. 2015. *Bonds without Borders*. Chichester, United Kingdom: John Wiley & Sons.

Solnik, Bruno, and J. Grall. 1975. "Eurobonds: Determinants of the Demand for Capital and the International Interest Rate Structure." *Journal of Bank Research* 5(4 Winter): 218–230.

CASE STUDY 11.1. MCDONALD'S DIM SUM BONDS: "LOVIN' IT"

— Patrick J. Schena

The Fletcher School, Tufts University

On a warm May day in 2010, Marc Monyek, senior director of Asia Pacific Middle East finance for McDonald's, was sitting in his Oak Brook, Illinois, office when he received a call. Standard Chartered Bank presented him with an intriguing idea: Would McDonald's be the first multinational corporate issuer of Chinese renminbi (RMB) — denominated bonds in the fledging yuan market in Hong Kong?[14]

The Chinese government maintained a tight hold on both China's capital ac count and the value of the RMB. Beginning in 2005, Beijing permitted the RMB to appreciate in a carefully managed fashion. Since July 2005, the RMB had appreciated 20.5% against the US dollar (see Case Exhibit 11.1). However, much of this appreciation occurred between July 2005 and June 2008, when the RMB increased in value at an annual rate of about 6%. Since then, in response to the global financial crisis, the Chinese government had resumed a fixed peg to the US dollar at approximately RMB 6.8/US$1. While it was widely expected that China would eventually resume a managed float, there was no indication when precisely this would occur.

In an effort to gradually expand the international use of the RMB in both trade and finance, Beijing began actively promoting the development of an offshore RMB market in Hong Kong.[15] RMB deposits were growing with the increased use of the RMB to settle trade invoices with Chinese suppliers. Though small, the settlement and deposit volumes[16] were expected to grow rapidly. As the local deposit base increased, both Hong Kong and Beijing turned to building a market for longer maturities through the local issuance of RMB-denominated bonds, commonly referred to as "dim sum bonds".

14 See www.thefreelibrary.com/First+taste+of+dim+sum+bonds%3A+McDonald's.-a0271994123.

15 The RMB traded in Hong Kong is referred to as CNH to distinguish it from onshore RMB (CNY).

16 RMB deposits represented less than 2% of Hong Kong deposits at the time of the case.

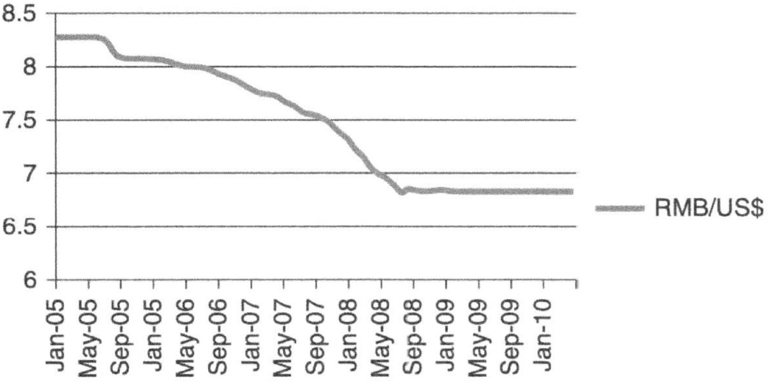

Case Exhibit 11.1. RMB/US$.

Marc had responsibility for financing the Asia operations of McDonald's and was quite aware of these developments; but how did they help with his onshore financing requirements? China was the company's fastest-growing market. With revenues doubling from $782 million to $1.5 billion between 2006 and 2010, the company maintained 1,300 outlets across China and some 60,000 employees.[17] The capital expenditures of McDonald's for 2010 were expected to be $2.4 billion. In China specifically, the company was planning on a rapid expansion to nearly double the number of its restaurants to 2,000 by the end of 2013. This included the introduction of a franchise model. Marc's immediate concern was to provide working capital for the near-term China expansion of McDonald's and the planned opening of as many as 175 restaurants in 2010 alone.

At the end of 2009 the long-term debt of McDonald's stood at US$10.6 billion. More than half of this was denominated in US dollars, but also included were loans and issues in euros, British pounds, yen, Swiss francs, and South Korean won (see Case Exhibit 11.2). The company was rated A3 by Moody's and enjoyed a solid credit outlook. Compared to its peers — Wendy's/Arby's and Yum! Brands — McDonald's boasted a higher ratio of earnings before interest, taxes, depreciation, and amortization (EBITDA) to revenues (35% compared to 12.1 and 21.3%, respectively) and a higher ratio of EBITDA to interest expenses (14.1× versus 3.1× and 7×).[18]

The proposed offering earned an A from the credit rating agency Fitch, and the deal was expected to raise RMB 200 million at a five year maturity in a target rate of approximately 3%. That compared favorably to the US$ borrowing costs for McDonald's. As a single-A borrower, McDonald's indicated spread above US Treasuries was approximately 150 basis points (see Case Exhibit 11.3, US Treasury Yield Curve). However, a 3% coupon would represent a substantial discount to fixed onshore RMB borrowing costs of 5.31%.[19] The deal would add approximately $30 million to the debt structure of McDonald's and would come on the heels of recent deals of Hopewell Highway Infrastructure Ltd, Bank of East Asia Ltd., and HSBC Holdings Plc's China. Marc agreed that the prospect of being the first multinational issue in the market was intriguing. The China expansion of McDonald's would certainly require continuing access to capital. RMB debt could be offset against the company's RMB assets and serve as a natural hedge.

However, the deal was not without its challenges. First, the RMB would be raised offshore in Hong Kong but used to fund onshore capital requirements in China. How easy would it be to repatriate the proceeds of the deal? Marc was advised that, for financial account purposes, all requests to transfer the deal proceeds onshore would undergo a case-by-case approval by China's State Administration of Foreign Exchange (SAFE). This process could take several weeks and add complexity, risk, and time

17 www.thefreelibrary.com/First+taste+of+dim+sum+bonds%3A+McDonald's.-a0271994123.

18 Standard & Poor's, "Risk-to-Price Commentary: McDonald's Corp," August 2010. http://www.standardandpoors.com/productsservices/articles/en/us/?assetID=1245219545545.

19 The Chinese government, to insure positive bank lending spreads, regulates onshore lending rates. The onshore RMB one-year benchmark lending rate in May 2010 was 5.31%. See also "How to Repatriate Dim Sum Proceeds" at www.financeasia.com/News/260645,how-to-repatriate-dim-sum-proceeds.aspx.

Case Exhibit 11.2. McDonald's schedule of long-term debt financing.

	Maturity Dates	Interest Rates as of Dec. 31, 2009	In Millions of U.S. Dollars	(%) Total
Fixed		5.6	4,677.6	
Floating		2.90	1,300.0	
Total U.S. dollars	*2011–2040*		5,977.6	*56.5*
Fixed		4.80	932.6	
Floating		1.80	683.9	
Total euros	*2011–2017*		*1,616.5*	*15.3*
Total British pounds sterling	*2020–2030*		*1,025.6*	*9.7*
Fixed		2.70	359.6	
Floating		3.80	793.3	
Total other currencies[a]	*2011–2021*		*1,152.9*	*10.9*
Debt obligations before fair value adjustments[b]			10,498.8	
Fair value adjustment[c]			79.6	
Total debt obligations[d]			10,578.4	

Notes: [a]Weighted-average effective rate, computed on a semiannual basis.
[b]Primarily consists of Swiss francs and South Korean won.
[c]The carrying value of underlying items in fair value hedges, in this case debt obligations, is adjusted for fair value changes to the extent they are attributable to the risk designated as being hedged. The related hedging instrument is also recorded at fair value in prepaid expenses and other current assets, miscellaneous assets, or other long-term liabilities.
[d]Includes notes payable, current maturities of long-term debt, and long-term debt included on the consolidated balance sheet.

Case Exhibit 11.3. US Treasury yield curve, May 2010.

Term	Yield
1 Month	0.1247
3 Months	0.1501
6 Months	0.2263
1 Year	0.3915
2 Years	0.8673
3 Years	1.3697
5 Years	2.2641
7 Years	2.9786
10 Years	3.5425
30 Years	4.4113

to the deal.[20] Second, the deal was very small when compared to the capital requirements of McDonald's and the company's usual capital acquisition strategy.

In fact, it would be its smallest debt issue since 2004, when it raised $25 million from 5.375% notes due in 2016. Was it cost-effective to do such a small placement? Finally, given the low interest rate, who would buy the notes? Would there be sufficient interest?

Despite the low interest rate, Marc was assured by Standard Chartered Bank that there would be sufficient demand from investors because of keen interest among foreigners for RMB exposure and

20 www.thelawyer.com/dim-sum-finance-tasty-morsels-for-law firms/1010136.article.

the general dearth of RMB-denominated investment products available to foreigners. In addition, the 3% yield was considerably higher than prevailing RMB deposit rates in Hong Kong. SAFE approval would remain an obstacle, but perhaps the deal would raise the company's profile both within the region and within the Chinese government.[21]

Marc needed to get back promptly to Standard Chartered Bank with an indication of interest. With the RMB forecast to continue to appreciate, did it make sense to issue RMB debt at this time? Was the offering big enough to do? Did the deal fit into the debt structure of McDonald's? Could the offshore RMB market be a recurring source of capital to fund the company's China growth strategy? Marc had his work cut out for him.

21 Jamil Anderlini, "McPanda Bonds Still Just a McGesture," *Financial Times*, August 20, 2.

Questions for Discussion

1. Does the RMB-denominated bond market domiciled in Hong Kong constitute a euro-RMB bond market?
2. How does the cost of financing in offshore RMB compare with US$ bond financing?
3. Would you recommend a dim sum bond issue to McDonald's?

CHAPTER 12

Currency, Interest Rate and Credit Default Swaps

Long term fixed income securities typically expose borrowers and investors to three quintessential risks: *currency risk* if the debt instrument is denominated in a currency different from the home currency of the borrower or investor, *interest rate risk* if the interest rate is reset periodically as a function of a fluctuating benchmark such as LIBOR or SOFR and *credit risk* should the borrower default. Each risk can be deftly reduced or eliminated with the use of appropriate swaps. This chapter examines how currency, interest rate and credit default swaps (CDSs) can be used by multinational corporations to lower the risk profile of their assets/liabilities portfolio and/or to reduce their financing costs. Exhibit 12.1 portrays the breakdown of swap transactions' notional amounts showing reduced activity in the CDS market since the sub-prime crisis and continued overall dominance of interest rate swaps.

By reading this chapter you will understand:

- What are currency swaps and how they are priced.
- What are interest rate swaps and how they are priced.
- What are CDSs and how they are priced.
- How to compute actual cash-flows — payments or receipts — characterizing different types of swaps.
- What are the factors underlying the economic benefits of swaps.

CURRENCY SWAPS

As pointed out in Chapters 6 and 8, the market for currency forward, futures and options rarely extends beyond one year and, when it does, its lack of depth and unattractive pricing (wide bid-ask spreads) discourage its use. Yet the foreign exchange risk exposure that arises from international trade transactions spanning several years or long-term debt financing denominated in foreign currency readily translates into a broad-based need for long-term forward contracts. Currency swaps — barely hatched in the early 1980s — have filled the vacuum (what economists call *market completion*) and have experienced a phenomenal growth, to the point that, more often than not, new debt issues are immediately swapped into a different currency (see International Corporate Finance in Practice 12.1 for the landmark IBM/World Bank "mother" of all currency swaps!). This section provides an operational definition of a currency swap before turning to its valuation. Corporate use of currency swaps as hedging tools in international financing and trade will be discussed later in Chapter 16.

What are currency swaps?

A fixed-to-fixed cross-currency swap is an agreement between two parties to exchange (swap), via the intermediation of a bank, the principal and interest payments associated with a *coupon bond*[1] denominated in one currency for the principal and interest payments of a similar coupon bond denominated in another currency. Specifically, a currency swap involves three sets of cash flows:

---

1 A coupon bond requires periodic interest payments, I (semi-annually or annually in most cases), with a balloon (full) principal repayment, P, at maturity, T. Its value at any point in time $t \le \tau \le T$ is equal to the present value, $B(\tau)$, of its outstanding cash flows discounted at the required rate of return, i. The yield to maturity can be expressed by solving for i in the following bond equation:

$$B(t) = \sum_{\tau=t}^{T} \frac{I}{(1+i)^{\tau}} + \frac{P(T)}{(1+i)^{\tau}} \qquad (7.7)$$

Further discussion of bond valuation techniques is provided in Chapter 11.

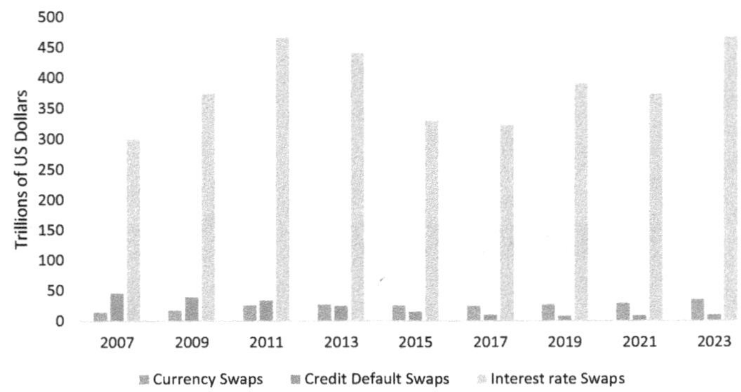

Exhibit 12.1 Global OTC derivatives market.
Notional Amounts Outstanding, Trillions of US Dollars.

INTERNATIONAL CORPORATE FINANCE IN PRACTICE 12.1
The IBM–World Bank Currency Swap

In previous years, IBM had borrowed in the capital markets of West Germany and Switzerland, acquiring fixed-interest-rate debt in Deutsche marks (DM) and Swiss francs (CHF). When the dollar appreciated sharply against these two currencies during 1981 and interest rates in West Germany and Switzerland had gone up, IBM enjoyed a substantial capital gain from the reduced dollar value of its foreign debt liabilities. The Deutsche mark, for example, depreciated from DM 1.93 in March 1980 to DM 2.52 per US$ in August 1981. Thus, a coupon payment of DM 100 had fallen in dollar cost from $51.81 to $36.68. By swapping its foreign interest payment obligations for dollar obligations, IBM could realize this capital gain immediately. This is similar to closing out a foreign exchange contract after a profit has accumulated. The World Bank, on the other hand, prefers to borrow in low interest rate countries such as West Germany and Switzerland but unfortunately it was close to the official borrowing limits in these currencies and yet it wishes to borrow more.

Clearly both parties would be better off if they could simply barter their liabilities through a cross-currency liability swap and that's precisely what they did: In August 1981, Salomon Brothers brokered a swap on a notional principal of $290 million. The World Bank issued two-dollar Eurobonds, one that matched the maturity of IBM's DM debt and one that matched the maturity of IBM's Swiss franc debt. The World Bank agreed to pay all future interest and principal payments of IBM's DM and Swiss franc debt, while IBM in turn agreed to pay future interest and principal payments on the World Bank's dollar debt. Thus, IBM was able to lock in the exchange gains without facing prepayment penalty and refinancing costs, while the World Bank gained immediate access to DM and SF financing. In effect IBM had converted its DM and CHF debt into dollar liabilities while the World Bank's dollar liabilities had morphed into DM and CHF.

(1) the initial exchange of principals at the inception of the swap, (2) a stream of interest payments made by each counterparty to the other during the life of the swap, and (3) the final re-exchange of principals at maturity of the swap. Both the initial and final (re exchange of principals are made at the initial spot exchange rate that prevails when the currency swap is first contracted. Currency swap contracts typically include the *right of offset* whereby each counterparty to the swap is entitled to offset any non-payment of interest or principal by withholding a comparable payment.

The currency swap effectively allows a company to transform an exposure in one currency into an exposure in a second currency. When combined with a debt issue, a currency swap allows a corporate borrower to convert the currency in which it initially raised funds into the currency in which the funds are ultimately needed, while achieving a lower all-in cost of capital than it would have by tapping the market directly (otherwise there would be no reason to follow this roundabout strategy). Viewed somewhat differently, a currency swap is similar in nature to a series of sales/purchases of forward contracts, and it has far-ranging implications for hedging long-dated forex exposure. (See Chapter 16 for further discussion.)

Cash-flow analysis of a currency swap

Consider the case of US-based Duke Power (DUK) and France-based Electricité de France (EDF) which both need five year financing in the amount of €100 million (or equivalent). Duke Power is AAA-rated in US capital markets but a novice in international financial markets. DUK can issue five year dollar-denominated straight debt at the effective rate of 5.25% annual coupon payments and bullet repayment at maturity. Its investment banker, however, suggests that a primary issue in euros (€) at the effective rate of 4.50% immediately swapped into US dollars would lower its effective cost of debt to 5.10%. The counterparty in this operation—AAA-rated Electricité de France (EDF) — is omni-present in the €-debt market but relatively absent from the $-bond market: it would also lower its cost of debt from 4.70% to 4.50% if it agreed to raise dollars first at the effective rate of 5.10% to be immediately swapped into euros. Exhibit 12.2 recapitulates DUK and EDF's cost of debt in the respective dollar and euro bond markets before entering into a currency swap. Each borrower has a cost advantage in the currency denomination in which it does not wish to borrow — DUK has a 20 basis points advantage in the €-debt market and EDF a 15 basis point advantage in the $-debt market. The currency swap will allow each party to transfer its cost advantage to the counterparty, thereby lowering its own cost of debt in the desired currency (dollar for DUK and euro for EDF). Here is how it would work:

Exhibit 12.2. DUK and EDF's respective cost of debt before (and after) the currency swap (percent per annum).

Borrower	Cost of Debt ($)	Cost of Debt (€)
DUK	5.25% (5.10%)	4.50%
EDF	5.10%	4.70% (4.50%)

Initial exchange at inception of the swap. DUK floats a €100 million bond issue and — assuming that the spot exchange rate is $S_{\$,€}(0) = 1.25$ — EDF issues a $125 million debenture. Both parties immediately swaps the bond proceeds and assume their counterparty's debt servicing obligations — DUK winds up with a five year dollar-denominated bond liability and EDF with a euro-denominated five year debenture.

Stream of annual interest payments. DUK services the dollar debt — initially raised by EDF — by paying a coupon of $125 million × 0.051 = $6.375 million. Similarly EDF pays an annual coupon of €100 million × 0.045 = € 4.5 million on the euro debt initially raised by DUK. The contractual exchange rates at which interest payments are exchanged is $S_{\$,€}(t) = 6.375/4.50 = 1.41$ with t = 1, 2, 3, 4, and 5. Exhibits 12.3A, 12.3B, and 12.3C portray graphically the exchange of cash flows at inception, during, and at maturity of the swap.

Re-exchange of principals at maturity of swap. Five years later — when both bonds are to be fully repaid — DUK delivers €100 million to EDF and receives $ 125 million from EDF. Bonds principals are de facto exchanged at the initial exchange rate of $S_{\$,€}(5) = 1.25$.

In sum, the currency swap enabled DUK to borrow indirectly $125 million at a lesser annual cost 5.10% than if it had borrowed directly at 5.25%. Similarly, EDF borrowed indirectly the euros it needed at a lesser cost of 4.50% than if it had borrowed directly at 4.70%. In effect

For DUK: *€ debt + currency swap "pay $-interest/receive €-interest" = $ synthetic debt*

For EDF: *$ debt + currency swap "pay €-interest/receive $-interest" = € synthetic debt*

Typically, a currency swap such as the one described between DUK and EDF involves a major commercial or investment bank, which brokers, structures and guarantees the deal, presumably eliminating counterparty risk and for which it would be compensated by a small spread.

> *Q:* Referring to the above DUK/EDF currency swap, explain how a 5 basis point would impact the post-swap cost of debt for both counterparties assuming that it would be shared equally.
>
> *A:* DUK would be pay a slightly higher dollar annual interest of 5.125% and EDF would similarly incur a slightly higher annual euro cost of 4.525%

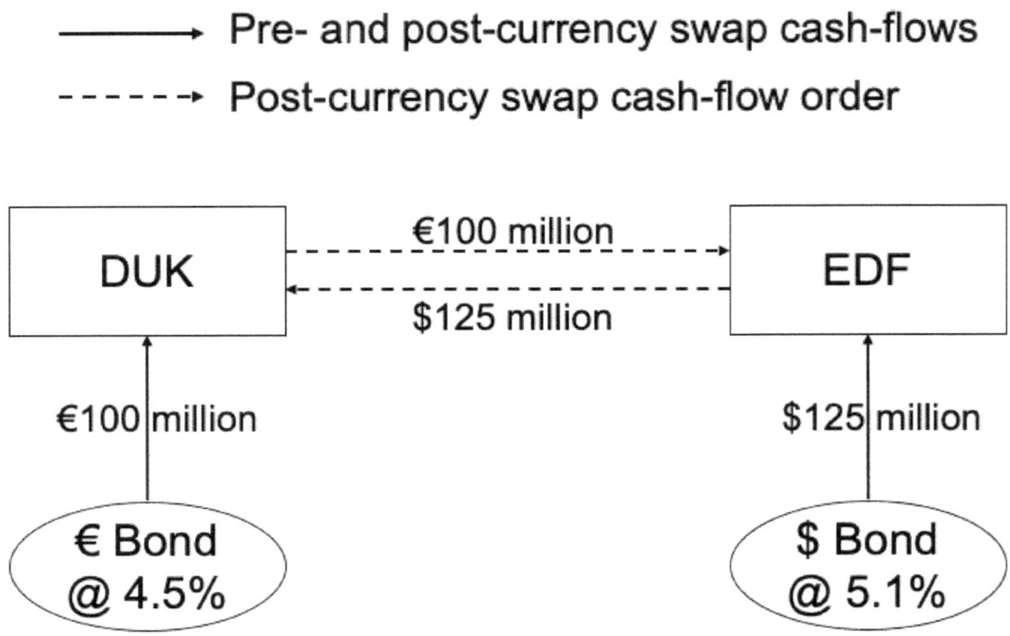

Exhibit 12.3A. Initial exchange of principal at inception of swap.

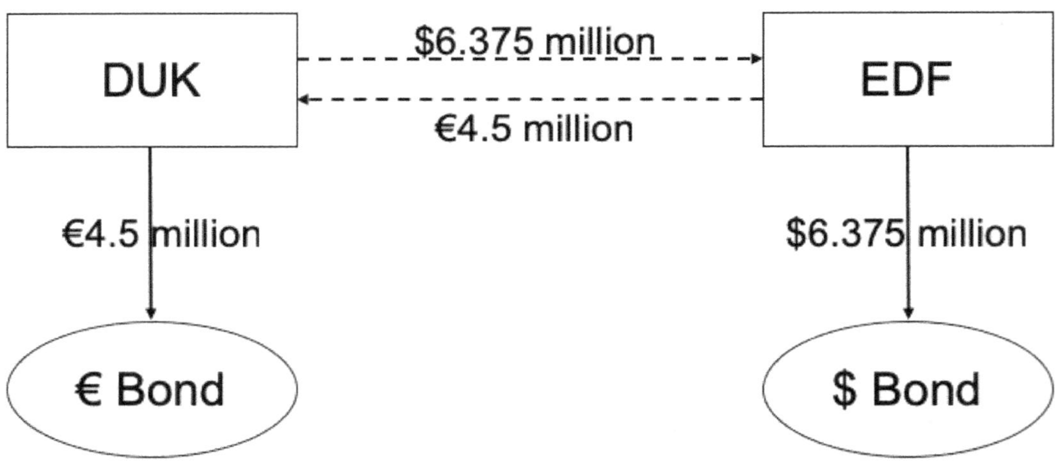

Exhibit 12.3B. Stream of annual interest payments by each party over the life of a swap.

The reader may wonder why the two issuers — both of which enjoy AAA ratings in their respective financial markets — face more favorable conditions in a foreign market where they are relatively unknown. If each borrower has saturated its home market through large-scale debentures, then by courting foreign investors, the borrower can capitalize on the unique benefits of portfolio diversification that it can offer those foreign investors. There are other reasons behind *capital market segmentation*

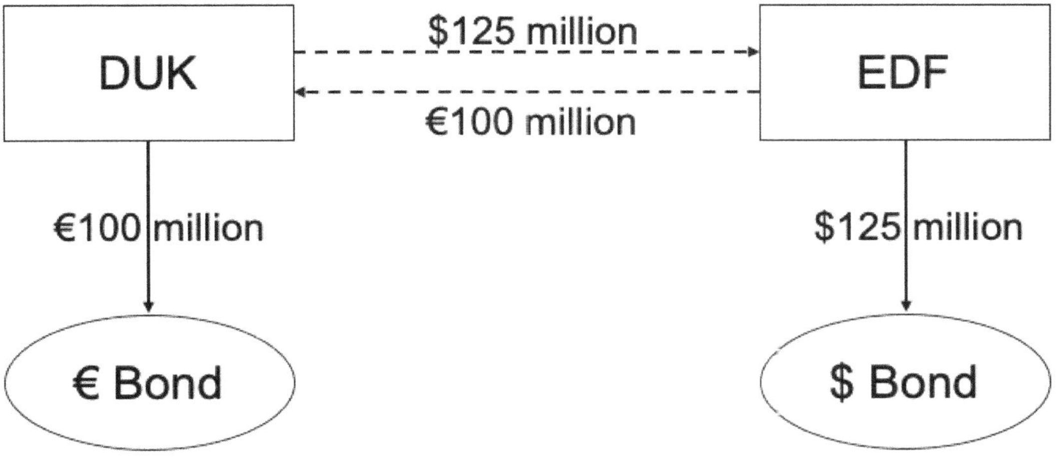

Exhibit 12.3C. Re-exchange of principal at maturity of swap.

such as differences in regulation governing investment by institutional investors and asymmetry in the tax treatment of interest income and capital gains/losses. All of these factors help explain arbitrage opportunities across different currency spaces. Of course, as more and more currency swaps are structured, differences in the cost of capital will be arbitraged away progressively in much the same fashion as interest rate parity aligns domestic, short-term interest rates when correction is made for the cost of covering exchange rate risk.[2]

Valuation of currency swaps

Bond valuation techniques can be used for deriving the net present value of the respective stream of assets (receipts) and liabilities (payments). At the inception of the currency swap, its net worth should be zero — that is, the net present value of the currency i-denominated bond $B_i(0)$ is equal to the net present value of the currency j-denominated bond $B_i(0)$ translated at the current spot currency i price of one unit of currency j, $S_{i,j}(0)$:

$$V_{swap}(0) = B_i(0) - B_j(0) \times S_{i,j}(0) = 0 \quad (12.1)$$

2 For empirical evidence on the arbitrage process relentlessly eradicating absolute differences in cost of capital financing, see Popper (1993).

If the net value of the swap is not zero, a compensatory payment would have to be made to the recipient of the higher net-present-value bondholder.

As soon as random news starts affecting the bond and currency markets, the value of each of the legs of the swap will immediately adjust to a new price. Therefore, it is possible to compute the net worth, $V_{swap}(t)$, as the algebraic difference between the asset and liability side using equation (12.1). This is nothing other than marking to market the value of the swap:

$$V_{swap}(t) = B_i(t) - B_j(t) \times S_{i,j}(t) \qquad (12.2)$$

As an illustration, we could value the DUK/EDF currency swap at the outset of year 2 (i.e., immediately after paying the year 1 coupon) assuming that 5 year interest rates in \$ and € coupon bonds of similar credit rating have moved to 5 and 4%, respectively, and that the € has appreciated to €1 = \$1.30. Expression (12.2) yields:

$$V_{swap}(1) = B_{\$}(1) - B_{€}(1) \times S(1)$$

where

$$B_{\$}(1) = \frac{6,375,000}{(1+0.05)} + \frac{6,375,000}{(1+0.05)^2} + \frac{6,375,000}{(1+0.05)^3} + \frac{131,375,000}{(1+0.05)^4} = 125,443,244$$

and

$$B_{€}(1) = \frac{4,500,000}{(1+0.04)} + \frac{4,500,000}{(1+0.04)^2} + \frac{4,500,000}{(1+0.04)^3} + \frac{104,500,000}{(1+0.04)^4} = €101,814,948$$

which yields the new value of the swap at $t = 1$:

$$V_{\text{swap}}(1) = \$125,443,244 - €101,814,948 \times 130$$
$$V_{\text{swap}}(1) = \$125,443,244 - \$132,359,432$$
$$V_{\text{swap}}(1) = -\$6,916,188 \quad (12.2 \text{ illustrated})$$

which results in a swap depreciation from the DUK point of view from $V_{\text{swap}}(0) = 0$ to $-\$6,916,188$. In other words, if DUK were to liquidate its currency swap it would incur a net dollar cash-flow cost of –$6,916,188.

INTEREST RATE SWAPS

A variant of the currency swap is the interest rate swap, in which both legs of the swap are denominated in the same currency. The most common type of interest rate swap is a *fixed to floating* coupon swap whereby fixed interest rate payments are exchanged for floating interest rate payments. Floating interest rates are generally pegged to an interest rate index such as the 6 month US dollar London Interbank Offered Rate (LIBOR).[3] Because principal amounts on the two legs of the swap are denominated in the same currency, principals need not be exchanged and instead are simply *notional amounts* used for calculating interest payments. Thus, only the difference between the interest payments is swapped when interest payments are due.

Reducing the cost of borrowing with interest rate swaps

Consider the case of GE and assume that the company has borrowed $100 million fixed rate three year debt at 5% and wants to take advantage of a lower cost floating rate note (FRN) as it believes that interest rates will hold steady or possibly head lower. Wells Fargo had previously issued a FRN indexed to LIBOR currently paying 3.25% and reset every six months. Because of a maturity mismatch between its assets and liabilities, Wells Fargo seeks to re-balance its assets/liabilities portfolio by increasing the relative weight of fixed-rate debt in its liabilities portfolio.

Instead of repaying its fixed rate debt and reissuing floating rate debt, GE enters on July 1, 2019 into an interest rate swap with Wells Fargo: GE would now pay the floating rate on the FRN to Wells Fargo while receiving the fixed 5% interest payment with which it meets its pre-swap fixed rate debt obligation. Each payment is based on a notional amount of $100 million and the swap agreement specifies that interest payments are to be exchanged every six months.

Specifically, the first exchange of interest payment would take place on January 1, 2020 — six months after the swap was entered into GE — the *"floating rate payer "* — will pay the six month LIBOR which prevailed six month earlier on July 1, 2019 on the swap notional principal or 0.0325/2 × 100 million = $1,625,000. Wells Fargo — the *"fixed rate payer"* pays the six month fixed interest on the same notional principal or 0.05/2 × 100 million = $2,5000,000. The second exchange of interest payments would be due on July 1, 2020 with GE paying the six months LIBOR prevailing six month prior on January 1, 2020 and assumed to be 3.50% on the same notional principal of $ 100 million or 0.0350/2 × $100 million = $1,750,000. Wells Fargo will pay the same fixed interest payment of $2,500,000 as it did on January 1, 2020.

Over the three years life of the swap there will be a total of six payments. The fixed interest payments made by Wells Fargo are always $2.5 million. The floating interest payments made by GE are based on the floating benchmark LIBOR as it stood six months prior to the payment date and — except for the first payment on April 1, 2019 — are unknown to the parties when the parties entered into the swap contract and have to be forecasted for valuing the swap. Exhibit 12.4 spells out the details of each payment to be made on the remaining five payments assuming that prevailing LIBOR is known on these dates.

As the *"floating rate payer"* GE exposes itself to interest rate risk or repricing risk; that is, when the interest rate is reset six months later, LIBOR may have substantially increased — possibly above the 5% interest rate that GE was paying before the swap.[4]

3 LIBOR was the London Interbank Offered Rate, defined by the British Bankers' Association as the mean of 16 multinational banks' offered interest rate on US dollar–denominated loans. This reference rate was widely used for loan agreement and financial derivatives valuation until it was replaced by the Secured Overnight Financing Rate (SOFR) in 2023.

4 Such a jump in short-term interest rates is very unlikely on a short-term basis, but such interest rates may gradually increase over the long term of the note to make the interest rate swap a costly proposition rather than a cost-saving one. Forecasting interest rates is certainly a treacherous endeavor, although interest rates are far less volatile than exchange rates.

Exhibit 12.4. Cash-flows to and from GE.

Dates	Six-month LIBOR (%)	Fixed interest rate payment received by GE from Wells Fargo*	Floating interest rate payment @ LIBOR made by GE to Wells Fargo	Net cash-flows to GE = interest cost saving due to IRS
July 1, 2019	3.25	...	...	...
January 1, 2020	3.50	−1,625,000	2,500,000	+875,000
July 1, 2020	3.75	−1,750,000	2,500,000	+750,000
January 1, 2021	4.00	−1,875,000	2,500,000	+625,000
July 1, 2021	4.25	−2,000,000	2,500,000	+500,000
January 1, 2022	4.50	−2,125,000	2,500,000	+375,000
July 1, 2022	...	−2,250,000	2,500,000	+250,000

Note: *Floating interest payment is based on LIBOR prevailing 6 month prior.

Indeed it turned out that LIBOR did increase from 3.25% to 4.50% over the life of the swap. For all practical purposes, once the swap is in place it is as if GE had borrowed a short-term floating rate note (in lieu of its pre-swap fixed rate liability) and Wells Fargo had issued a fixed coupon bond (in lieu of its pre-swap FRN).

Why do firms enter into interest rate swaps?

The reader may wonder what are the other motivations for two parties to enter into an interest rate swap beyond reducing the cost of debt. Interest rate swaps are the instrument of choice for financial institutions in managing interest rate risks in asset/liability management as well as hedging *repricing* risk or more generally hedging a firm's exposure to interest rate movements. In our earlier case, GE wanted to free itself from the rigidity of fixed interest rate loan and take advantage of lower floating interest rates. The counterparty could be any financial institutions that lends at a five year fixed rate to a AAA-rated construction company and is financed with floating rate commercial paper: It would want to eliminate its exposure to interest rate risk (it lends at a fixed rate money that it borrowed at a floating rate) by locking in its margin (the spread between the fixed interest rate at which it lends and the fixed interest rate at which it borrows) by swapping out of its floating rate debt into a five year fixed rate note. It would be a natural counterparty to GE, and Wells Fargo would just play matchmaker. Let's turn to a more elaborate analysis of IRS architecture.

Exploiting comparative advantage in the debt market through interest rate swaps

Consider the architecture of a basic "plain vanilla" interest rate swap (IRS). *Commercial Bank* — AAA-rated — needs to raise $100 million to fund recently booked variable rate construction loans. *AAA-Commercial Bank* could issue a five year level coupon bond at a fixed interest rate of 5% per annum but would prefer to secure variable rate financing through a floating rate note (FRN) costing six month LIBOR which better matches the maturity structure of its construction loan portfolio. *Industrial Firm* -BBB-rated — also has a funding gap of $100 million for its plant modernization program: it is considering a five year FRN at LIBOR + 0.50% which is cheaper than a level coupon bond at 6.50%. *BBB-Industrial Firm,* however, is concerned that short-term interest rates are on the upswing and would rather fund long term fixed assets with long fixed interest rate debt.

Clearly, *AAA-Commercial Bank* faces a lower cost of debt than *BBB-Industrial Firm* in either the floating or the fixed rate debt space. However, the spread differential between the two firms is quite different: *AAA-Commercial Bank* has a comparative advantage in the fixed rate debt market because it borrows fixed rate debt at 1.50% less than *BBB- Industrial Firm* could, whereas in the FRN market the spread differential is only 0.50%. *BBB-Industrial Firm* thus has a comparative (not absolute) advantage in the FRN debt space (see Exhibit 12.5 for a summary of quality spread differentials). Clearly the FRN market penalizes far less lower-rated borrowers than the fixed rate bond market does. One explanation is that the interest rate on floating rate notes are six month rates and usually gives the lender the opportunity to reconsider and increase the spread over LIBOR should the borrower's creditworthiness deteriorate over the prior six month period. Indeed the yield curve for BBB-rated borrowers tends to be more

	Fixed Rate	Floating Rate
AAA – Commercial Bank	5%	LIBOR
BBB – Industrial Firm	6.50%	LIBOR + 0.50%
Difference	1.50%	0.50%

Exhibit 12.5. Fixed and floating interest rates for IRS counterparties.

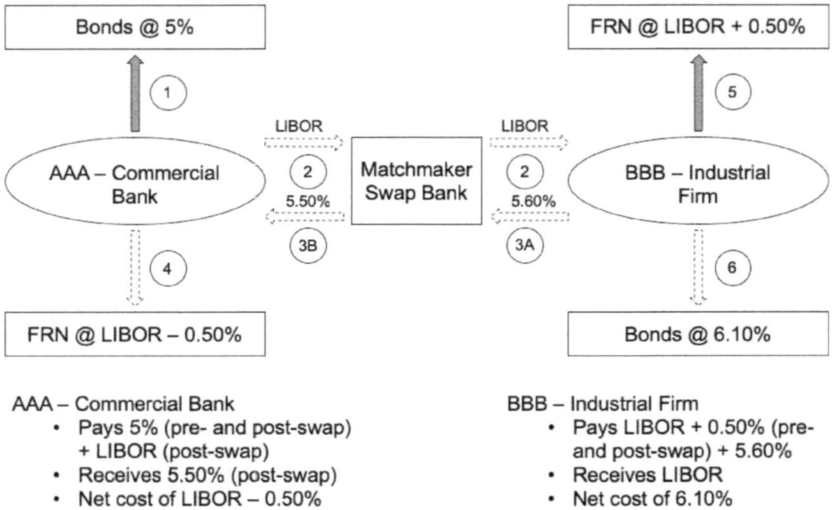

Exhibit 12.6. Architecture of an interest rate swaps.

steeply sloped than it is for AAA-rated borrowers resulting into a narrower spread for shorter maturities but wider yield spread for longer maturities. In this case the quality spread differential between fixed and floating rate debt of 1.5–0.5% is precisely the financing cost savings that the two counterparties to the interest rate swap will be able to share.

AAA-Commercial Bank, as a consummate user of the swap market, approaches *Matchmaker Swap Bank* which quotes an interest rate swap at 5.50–5.60% for LIBOR flat. *Matchmaker Swap Bank* searches and finds a counterparty in *BBB-Industrial Firm.* An agreement is signed whereby *BBB-Industrial Firm* commits to paying *Matchmaker Swap Bank* 5.60% of which the latter passes through to the *AAA-Commercial Bank* 5.50% — keeping a small commission of 0.10%. *AAA-Commercial Bank* in turns commits to paying LIBOR to *Matchmaking Swap Bank* which passes it to *BBB-Industrial Firm.* Interest rate payments are quoted on an annual basis but are exchanged on a semesterly basis.

AAA Commercial Bank has swapped a fixed rate debt for a *synthetic* FRN on which it pays LIBOR — 0.50%, which amounts to a saving of 50 basis points compared to directly tapping the FRN market. *BBB Industrial Firm* now pays 6.10% on a *synthetic* 5 year fixed interest bond instead of 6.50% had it raised debt directly from the bond market for a saving of 0.40%. The *Matchmaker Swap Bank* earns 0.10% for intermediating the swap. The interest rate swap saves both parties a total of 50 basis points + 40 basis points = 90 basis points or 0.90% by allowing each party to take advantage of its comparatively (not absolute) lower cost of debt in the market from which it did not want to source debt. Thus, *AAA- Commercial Bank* will raise 5 year fixed rate debt at 5% even-though it ultimately seeks a floating rate loan. Similarly, *BBB-Industrial Firm* issues a FRN at LIBOR + 0.50% even though it ultimately seeks to five year fixed interest bond. Exhibit 12.6 summarizes the pre-swap cash-flows (bold arrows) and post-swap cash-flows (dotted line).

The net results of this financial montage are as follows:

- *AAA Commercial Bank* pays 5% on 5 year fixed rate bond (pre-swap) — arrow 1 — and pays LIBOR to *Matchmaker Swap Bank* — arrow 2; it receives 5.50% from the latter — arrow 3B. Its net cost of synthetic FRN financing — arrow 4 — amounts to 5% + LIBOR — 5.50% = LIBOR — 0.50%
- *BBB Industrial* Firm pays LIBOR + 0.50% on FRN (pre-swap) — arrow 5 — and pays 5.60% to *Matchmaker Swap Bank* — arrow 3A; it receives LIBOR — arrow 2. Its net cost of synthetic bond financing — arrow 6 — amounts to LIBOR + 0.50% + 5.60% — LIBOR = 6.10%
- *Matchmaker Swap Bank* receives 5.60% from *BBB-Industrial Firm* and pays 5.50% *to AAA Commercial Bank* earning a 0.10% commission for arranging the swap.

By entering into an interest rate swap (IRS) both parties have — in effect — transform the cash-flow profile of their liabilities while reducing their funding cost by exploiting their counterparty's comparative advantage in their respective debt market:

AAA Commercial Bank: Bond + IRS "pay floating/ receive fixed interest payment" = synthetic FRN

BBB Industrial Firm: FRN + IRS "pay fixed/receive floating interest payment" = synthetic bond

> **Q:** Assuming that LIBOR stands at 3.25% and AAA-rated five-year bond yield 5.00%, explain what *AAA-Commercial Bank* pays/receives when it enters into an IRS with *Matchmaker Swap Bank.*
>
> **A:** Before the swap, it paid a fixed interest rate of 5.00% on a principal of $100 million or $5.0 million in two semi-annual payments of $2.5 million. After the swap, it receives from *BBB-Industrial Firm* S5.50 million annually in two semi-annual payments of $2.75 million and pays LIBOR = 3.25% or $3.25 million annually ($1.625 million every six months). Its net interest cost is $5.0 million + $3.25 million – $5.50 million = $2.75 million or two semi-annual payments $1.375 million The first payment is fixed for *AAA Commercial Bank* but subject to price resetting risk six months later as LIBOR fluctuates.

Valuing interest rate swaps

The terms of an interest swap are set so that the present value of the fixed interest cost leg is equal to the present value of the floating leg so that neither party would gain or lose from entering into the swap. The value of the fixed interest rate leg is easy to compute, since interest payments are contractually defined at the outset; but valuing the floating rate leg is complicated by the problem of not knowing what future short-term interest rates are going to be. By extracting forward interest rates from the zero-coupon yield curve, it is possible to generate market-based forecasts of what those future short-term interest rate are going to be. With that information, it is possible to value the floating rate leg of the swap the same way it is done for the fixed rate leg of the same swap.

The Swap bank

Interest Rate Swaps are typically brokered by a financial institution dubbed in our above example the *Matchmaker Swap Bank.* Typically, it would be a major commercial or investment bank whose primary role is to match the two counterparties to the transaction thereby acting as a *swap broker.* The intermediary bank — is likely to act also as a *market maker* willing to book one leg of the swap while searching for a counterparty. In warehousing one leg of the swap until a counterparty is found the Swap Bank takes on the risk that the matching leg of the swap may turn out to be more expansive than the warehoused swap's first leg.

As a market maker the Swap Bank quotes bid-offer interest rates at which it is willing to swap fixed interest debt for floating interest rate debt and vice-versa. The Swap Bank's bid rate is the (lower) fixed interest rate that it is willing to pay over a longer term maturity (ranging from two to 30 years) in exchange for receiving semi-annual payment at six month LIBOR. The Swap Bank higher offer/ask rate is the fixed interest rate that it will receive from the IRS counter-party to which it will pay six month LIBOR.

As a broker or a dealer/market maker the Swap Bank is compensated by collecting a spread between the interest payment it collects from one counter-party and the interest payment made to the other counterparty. Once the IRS is in place both parties will post a collateral to mitigate the risk of default by either counterparty.

INTERNATIONAL CORPORATE FINANCE IN PRACTICE 12.1

Caveat Emptor: The Procter & Gamble — Bankers Trust Leveraged Interest Rate Swap

On April 13, 1994 Procter & Gamble announced a one-time pre-tax charge of $ 152 million against net income. The loss resulted from the early closing of two seemingly innocuous *leveraged interest rate swaps* which Procter & Gamble had entered into with Bankers Trust as a way of reducing financing costs. Procter & Gamble alleged that it had been played, manipulated and deceived by Bankers Trust and initiated a lawsuit whose settlement allowed Procter & Gamble to pay a much reduced amount of $35 million.

Since the early 90s Procter & Gamble with the help of Bankers Trust had implemented a disciplined financing policy which achieved effective financing costs below the benchmark rate on 30 day average commercial paper.[5] At the core of this policy was the swapping of long term fixed rate debt into floating rate short term debt which allowed Procter & Gamble to capitalize on its wager that short term interest rates would continue to decline. Bankers Trust proposed a tailor-made interest rate swap meeting its client's special requirement which offered floating rate debt at 75 basis points below commercial paper rate. However, the attractive cost of debt was predicated on interest rate remaining stable or declining further. The actual swap that Procter & Gamble eventually agreed to was a far more complicated instrument than a plain vanilla swap.

The agreed interest rate swap had a term of 5 years and a notional amount of $200 million: for the first 6 months it called for Procter & Gamble to receive a fixed interest rate of 5.3% and pay to Bankers Trust a 30 day average CP floating interest rate minus 75 basis points. For the remaining 4.5 years the rate would be set on May 2, 1994 (the 6 month anniversary of the signing of the swap) according to a complex formula which added a spread to the base interest rate set at *30 day average commercial paper rate — 75 basis points*. Under the best circumstances the spread would be zero — a scenario corresponding to a stable or declining long-term interest rate which meant that Procter & Gamble would effectively pay 30 day average commercial paper rate — 75 basis points. Otherwise — should longer term interest rates rise — the spread and therefore the floating interest rate would very quickly reach astronomical level. Formally:

$$\text{Interest Cost} = \text{Interest Cost on 30 day commercial paper} - 75 \text{ basis points} + \text{spread}$$

where the spread is defined as but cannot be a negative number

$$\text{Spread} = [98.5 \times (5 \text{ year Treasury yield})/5.58\% - 30 \text{ year } 6.25\% \text{Treasury Bond price}]/100$$

In plain English the spread was linked to the difference between the *yield* on 5 year Treasury bond and the *price* of 30 year Treasury bond. Recalling that yield and bond price move in opposite direction when interest rate change the practical question to ask is which one of the yield and bond price will respond most to a change in interest rate. For example, a small interest rate hike by the Federal Reserve would result into a smaller increase of the 5 year yield but a deeper decline in the 30 year bond price and would therefore exacerbate their differential on which the spread was based.

Gauging risk through numerical analysis. To get a better sense of how the spread would respond to gradual interest rate increases Exhibit 12.7 tabulates this relationship: the first column shows the five year yield on Treasury rising from the prevalent level of 4.95% — when the swap was signed — to 6.45%; the second column estimates the corresponding price of a 30 year bond assuming a parallel shift

5 Commercial paper (CP) is an unsecured promissory note with a fixed maturity ranging from 1 to 270 days. CP is issued by large banks and corporations with strong credit ratings and is generally a cheaper source of short-term financing than bank financing. CP is largely bought by money market funds.

Exhibit 12.7. Simulations on the Procter & Gamble's leveraged swap.

Five-year Treasury Yields (%)	30-yr Treasury Price (%)	Spread (bp)	Leverage[i]	Net spread (bp)	$equivalent[ii]
4.95	103.02	−1905	—	−1830	$1.5M
5.35 (+40 bp)	97.61	−644	31	−569	$1.5M
5.55 (+60 bp)	95.07	−49	31	−124	$1.5M
5.65 (+70 bp)	93.85	+243	31	+168	−$3.36M
5.75 (+80 bp)	92.64	+535	31	+460	−$9.20M
5.95 (+100 bp)	90.30	+1110	30	+1035	−20.70M
6.45 (+150 bp)	84.86	+2505	29	+2430	−$48.60M

Notes: i. Leverage is defined as change in spread as computed by formula triggered by corresponding change in the five year fixed rate.

ii. The dollar equivalent shows the incremental annual interest cost resulting from the spread minus 75 basis points. At 4.95%, 5.35% and 5.55% the spread would be negative in effect zero because Bankers Trust had set a floor. Procter & Gamble would still reduce its floating rate by .0075 × $200 million = $ 1.5 million.

Source: Jacque, Laurent L. *Global Derivative Debacles: From Theory to Malpractice* (World Scientific, 2nd edition, 2015)

in the yield curve; the third column calculates the actual spread[6] and shows how it literally exploded with relatively minor change in interest rates; the fourth column computes the leverage embedded in the formula as the ratio of the *change in the spread/[corresponding change in five year yield on Treasury]* — in effect measuring the percentage change in the spread triggered by a one percent change in the five year interest rate. With a leverage ratio at "*31 times*" the swap was indeed a leveraged interest swap as Procter & Gamble discovered the hard way. The fifth and last column shows the corresponding interest payments which Procter & Gamble would actually be required to make. The reader will no doubt be flabbergasted to see the penalty corresponding to the annual spread to be added to the base interest rate rising from — $1.5 million to + $ 48.60 million when the five year yield on Treasury goes from 4.95% to 6.45%. That is an increase of only 150bp — which under normal circumstances should translate into an increase of $3 million in interest payment — would in fact be magnified 16 times and result into an interest cost increase of $48 million. So much for the power of leverage!

6 The spread had a floor of zero which effectively kept the interest rate at no less than 6-month CP – 75bp even though the spread would be negative until the 5-year interest rate reached approximately 5.58% (see the first three lines on Exhibit 12.7).

Combining currency swaps with interest rate swaps

Although historically currency swaps appeared first as *fixed interest rate cross-currency swaps*, most currency swaps today bundle an interest rate swap with a currency swap. In effect, a floating interest rate liability in one currency is transformed into a fixed interest rate liability in another currency (or vice versa — a fixed interest debt in one currency is transformed into a floating currency in another currency). All it requires is to combine an interest rate swap in the first currency — whereby the floating interest rate debt is morphed into a fixed interest rate debt — with a currency swap that in turn transforms the currency denomination of fixed interest rate debt in the first currency into a fixed interest rate debt in the second currency.

CREDIT DEFAULT SWAPS

CDSs were introduced in the mid-nineties as a new and more flexible form of bond insurance. CDSs are over-the-counter contracts whereby the buyer (insured) agrees to pay the seller (insurer) periodic fees (insurance premium) in exchange for receiving protection against default (event) of a loan or bond issued by a referenced entity such as a corporation or a sovereign nation. Thus, credit derivatives allow for the placement of bets on whether the referenced loan/bond or debtor will experience a negative "credit event". More specifically, the event triggering the payment of the loss is usually the debtor's default, bankruptcy or failure to pay. A "credit event" can also be a credit rating downgrade or restructuring of the debtor. The party speculating that the negative credit event will occur is said to take the "short" side of the wager ("buying" insurance); the party taking the "long" side of the bet ("selling" insurance) wagers that no credit event will occur during the contract specified period of time (see Exhibit 12.8). Unlike a bond insurance policy, whereby the buyer purchases protection on a loan/bond she/he owns, the buyer of a CDS may not have any material relationship with the debtor (a so-called "naked" CDS). Purchase of a credit swap is therefore motivated not only by hedging but also by arbitrage and speculative reasons. Banks or any unregulated entities writing CDSs ("selling" credit insurance) are not required to set aside loss reserves (as insurance companies would) but are nonetheless subject to regulatory capital and may hedge themselves by buying CDSs from third parties. Counterparty risk for anyone purchasing a CDS is a real issue, but one which is partially mitigated by the posting of a margin updated on a periodic basis — but not on a daily basis, as in the case of exchange-traded products.

As an illustration, consider the case of JP Morgan Chase seeking protection on January 2011 against the default of $1 billion of American Airlines five year bonds and thereby purchasing CDSs from Allianz — the German insurance company — for a semi-annual fee/premium of $10 million. This would amount to a 2% credit spread:

$$\frac{\$10 \text{ million} \times 2}{\$1 \text{ billion}} = 0.02$$

JP Morgan Chase is committed to making 10 payments through the life of the five year bond — as long as American Airlines is solvent. Should American Airlines default — as it did in September 2011 — Allianz will pay the full $1 billion to JP Morgan and JP Morgan will stop paying its semi-annual $10 million premium (note two premiums were already paid, on January 1 and July 1). Note further that JP Morgan Chase's motivation in buying CDSs may be twofold: (1) the bank may have invested in American Airlines five year bonds, in which case purchasing a CDS amounts to simple *hedging* of credit risk — that is, protecting against the risk that American Airlines may default or (2) the bank may bet on American Airlines default without owning any of American Airline debt in which case this amounts to simple speculation (the CDS is referred as a "naked" CDS because JP Morgan does not hold any of American Airlines bonds).

Purchasing CDSs may be likened to buying a put option on American Airlines bonds: the strike price is the notional value of American Airlines bonds — except that this strike price is only activated when the value of the underlying bond is impacted by a credit event (limited to bankruptcy, credit downgrading or restructuring — not an increase in interest rates); the premium, moreover, is paid periodically rather than upfront in full, as in the case of a put option.

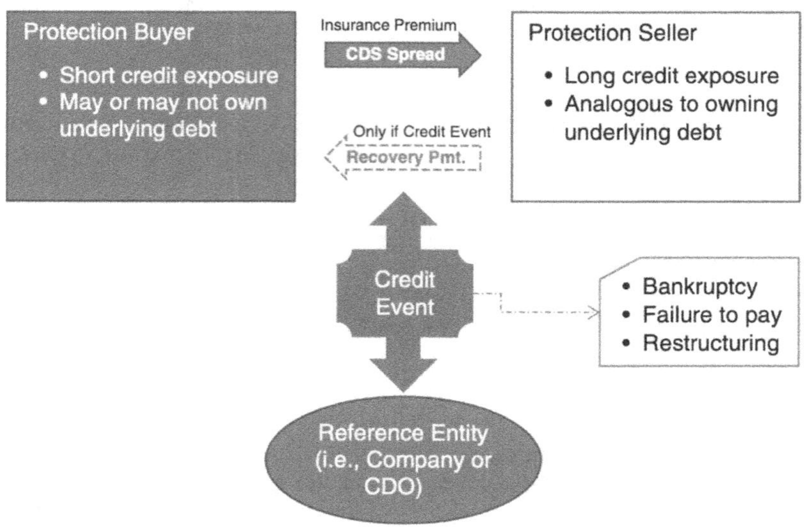

Exhibit 12.8. Credit default swaps.

CDS spreads and bond yields

The bond yield spread is the amount by which a bond yield exceeds the yield on a risk-free bond of matching maturity. For example, if American Airlines issues five year bonds paying 7% interest when five year US treasury bonds (which are risk-free) offer a 5% yield, the bond-yield spread on American Airlines AA-rated bonds is 7% – 5% = 2%. The 2% differential is the extra interest income that investors require to bear AA credit risk. If an investor in five year AA-rated bonds desires to protect his/her investment against default he/she may purchase a CDS which requires an annual premium of 2%. In effect the investor has transformed a risky AA bond into a risk-free bond yielding 7% – 2% = 5%. The 2% premium is known as the CDS spread and is equal to the bond yield spread:

$$\textit{CDS spread} = \textit{Risky bond yield} - \textit{Risk-free bond yield} = \textit{Bond yield spread}$$

Credit indices

First introduced by JP Morgan Chase and Morgan Stanley in 2001, credit indices are portfolios of individual CDSs and therefore reference a basket of selected credit instruments. The composition of the basket is set once for all at the credit index inception; it determines the value of the index as the weighted average of the value of the constituent credit-instrument components of the basket.

One of the leading provider of such Credit derivatives is the Markit Group Ltd that owns and administers multiple index products publishing their daily prices on its website. Markit's two principal families of credit index products are CDX and iTraxx. CDX is a set of credit indices which references North American and Emerging-Markets corporations whereas iTraxx references corporations in Europe and Asia. Both credit indices were instruments of choice in the saga of *JP Morgan's London Whale* debacle chronicled in International Corporate Finance in Practice 12.2. As an illustration JP Morgan would trade the *CDX.NA.IG.9* where *CDX* refers to credit index, *NA* refers to North America, and *IG* to investment grade — since the index tracks CDSs of 125 North American investment grade corporations. The number 9 refers to the year of issuance — in this case 2007. Indeed, Markit issues two series of this index each year, updating the composition of the constituent basket of its 125 firms every six months. Furthermore, the IG9 series offers varying maturities. For instance, JP Morgan Chase could bet on the IG9 five-year, which expired in 2012 (having been issued in 2007); similarly, the IG9 10-year would expire in 2017. A party going "long" (writing insurance) on the CDX.NA.IG9 five year is betting that the value of the index will increase over the five-year period. If one of the constituent reference firms in the basket goes bankrupt during that period, the long party will make a payment to the counter-party (short side) which purchased credit protection.

INTERNATIONAL CORPORATE FINANCE IN PRACTICE 12.2

JP Morgan London Whale

On July 13, 2012 JP Morgan Chase & Co announced a stunning trading loss of $6.2 billion which wiped out more than $25 billion of the bank's market capitalization. The losses originated from the bank's Synthetic Credit Portfolio (SCP) which is itself part of the Chief Investment Office (CIO). This derivative debacle represented a significant misstep -if not an outright stumble — for JP Morgan Chase Chairman and CEO Jamie Dimon. Once vaunted for his risk management prowess in steering the bank deftly through the subprime crisis, Dimon was generally regarded as one of most steadfast and savvy chieftains of the banking world. How did JP Morgan allow what began as a benign effort at hedging the bank portfolio to morph into a mammoth position in the credit market — which nicknamed it, half-mockingly, as the "London Whale"? Was it a deliberate attempt by the bank to bypass the Volcker rule in the new Dodd-Frank Act?[7] How could JP Morgan Chase, which decades earlier had pioneered

7 The Dodd–Frank Wall Street and Consumer Protection Act (Dodd-Frank Act, 2010) and more specifically its Volcker Rule bans "proprietary" trading by commercial banks operating in the United States whereby commercial banks used FDIC insured deposits and cash to engage in speculative trades — often involving derivative products — for the bank's own accounts.

the new Value-a-Risk (V@R) metrics and was known for its expertise in risk management, seem so dysfunctional in taming its synthetic portfolio? How did a savvy giant banking institution allow the *London Whale* to be savagely harpooned by hedge funds?

Within JP Morgan Chase (JPM), the Chief Investment Office (CIO) is charged with optimizing the management of the bank's excess cash from its wide deposit base. Indeed, the bank takes in far more deposits than it can profitably lend out — and therefore the CIO mandate is to invest this cash conservatively across the universe of fixed-income securities, upholding high credit and liquidity standards. With 140 traders and a back- and middle-office staff of 288 straddling the New York and London operations, the CIO was well-equipped to do so. In fact, at the end of 2011 the CIO was investing $350 billion of excess cash deposits in various fixed income securities. But the CIO mandate stretched out further as it was charged with managing a "macro-hedge" for the bank — presumably to mitigate its exposure to credit, and interest rate risks. It did so by constructing a synthetic credit portfolio (SCP) as a hedge against the credit risk of the bank's loan portfolio. Admittedly, this is a daunting task for an institution of this size, which required extensive reliance on financial derivatives such as CDSs.

In December 2011, Dimon instructed the CIO to reduce the bank's synthetic credit portfolio so that JPM could lower its Risk-Weighted Assets in preparation of impending Basel III and higher mandatory capital requirements. At the same time, Iksil and his team were asked to keep open the opportunity to benefit from unexpected corporate bankruptcies as they had done successfully in the past from American Airlines bankruptcy through purchases of CDSs. In an effort to reconcile these conflicting objectives, the SCP expanded on its strategy of buying CDSs on higher risk high yield bonds and bonds indices and financing it by selling CDSs on lower risk investment grade companies. By the end of March 2012, the SCP had ballooned into a notional value of $175 billion — 3.5 times greater than the $51 billion portfolio it held at the close of 2011. The breakdown of this mammoth notional portfolio shows long positions of $82 billion in the Investment Grade 9 index (estimated to comprise more than half of the market of that credit index), $71 billion in the iTraxx index and a short position of $22 billion in the high-yield index. Long positions mildly benefitted from improving credit markets but failed to compensate losses from the short position in high-yield credit indices: in Macris' words, the investment grade rally "lagged" the high yield rally. The investment grade positions were gaining less value than expected, whereas the high grade positions were losing more value than expected.[8] In other words, the marked-to-market gains that the SCP portfolio was able to post on the investment-grade credit protection it had been aggressively selling was insufficient to compensate the marked-to-market losses that it had to post on the high yield protection it had purchased. Alarmed by mounting paper losses the SCP was instructed to terminate the strategy and unwind the portfolio which ultimately resulted in a staggering loss of $6.2 billion.

The bank's oversized positions built over time did not go unnoticed. Bruno Iksil — JP Morgan Chase's point man for executing these trades — started to build a reputation as the trader who relentlessly pushed the CDS index down by selling more and more credit insurance whenever the index seemed to recover. Iksil — even though not necessarily identified by name — became known as the "London Whale"! The SCP's massive long positions in IG9 investment credit indices led to a decline in credit spreads from November 2011 to April 2012, when JP Morgan Chase traders were finally ordered to stop trading — "phones down".

Hedge funds' rationale for buying the insurance that JP Morgan Chase was selling was based on the notion the bank was selling *so much insurance* that it was artificially driving its price down. All it would take for the price of insurance to increase would be either for the bank to stop selling so much of it or for the credit markets to start deteriorating. For instance, a euro crisis, and a subsequent Grexit, triggering a European debt meltdown! Hedge funds felt that either or both alternatives were likely, which explains why they were willing purchasers of credit insurance on the cheap, on the bet that the value of credit insurance would reverse course and soon start to rise.

---

8 The value of high yield (high risk) bonds is far more elastic/sensitive to credit market sentiment than it is for investment grade/low risk bonds. Credit yield spreads respond accordingly.

Soon, however — as long anticipated by hedge funds — JP Morgan Chase's aggressive stance became unsustainable and was finally reversed, as the CIO mandated the Synthetic Credit Portfolio to curtail its exposure to the credit market. This was meant, in part as noted earlier, to reduce the bank's risk-weighted assets to meet impending Basel III's tighter capital-adequacy ratio requirements. Hedge funds which had accumulated credit protection at bargain cost incurred losses initially, as the London Whale was selling even more credit protection at increasingly underpriced cost. As soon as the London Whale stopped trading, these same hedge funds saw their position swing into positive territory, as the index was reversing to its intrinsic value. Several hedge funds –with Saba Capital Management in the lead, but also Blue Mountain Capital and Bluecrest Capital (both created by former JP Morgan traders) which had had the hunch and had been the ready buyers of credit insurance, were now ready for the kill: they were the big winners when JP Morgan Chase had to buy back the CDSs that it had sold on the cheap to close its positions.

The verdict is still out as to whether JP Morgan Chase, in view of a rapidly changing and constricting regulatory environment, was running a stealth hedge fund as a platform to continue its proprietary trading without admitting to it. The Volcker Rule intended to ban proprietary trading by banks on the grounds that FDIC-protected deposits at banks should not be used as a platform for pure speculative gambits which do not benefit their depositors.

TRADING CREDIT DEFAULT SWAPS

The cost of insuring a bond against default will fluctuate over the life of the bond as its creditworthiness changes. To facilitate their trading, CDS trade as bonds so that the periodic protection payments (premiums) remain fixed (similar to a bond's coupon). To account for the difference between the market value of the CDS and the original premium payment set when the CDS was first issued, a compensatory payment is made between the seller and the buyer. If the quoted spread is positive because the creditworthiness of the reference name has deteriorated (adding to the coupon) the buyer compensates the seller by paying — up-front — the expected present value of the credit spread over the remaining life of the CDS. Conversely, if the quoted spread is negative (subtracting from the coupon) the seller compensates the buyer by paying upfront the expected present value of the excess spread, over the remaining life of the CDS. Thereafter, the buyer of the CDS then pays the original premium, for as long as he/she holds the CDS.

SUMMARY

1. A fixed-to-fixed cross-currency swap is an agreement to exchange (swap), via the intermediation of a bank, principal and interest payments associated with a *coupon bond* denominated in one currency for the principal and interbest payments of a coupon bond denominated in another currency.
2. The currency swap effectively allows a company to transform an exposure in one currency into an exposure in a second currency. When combined with a debt issue, a currency swap allows a corporate borrower to convert the currency in which it initially raised funds into the currency it ultimately needs, while achieving a lower all-in cost of capital than it would have had by tapping the market directly (otherwise, there would be no reason to follow this roundabout strategy).
3. Interest rate swaps are a variant of the currency swap in which both legs of the swap are denominated in the same currency. The most common type of interest rate swap is a *fixed to floating* coupon swap, whereby fixed interest rate payments are exchanged for floating interest rate payments. Floating interest rates are generally pegged to an interest rate index such as the 6 month London Interbank Offered Rate (LIBOR). Because principal amounts on the two legs of the swap are denominated in the same currency, principals need not be exchanged and are simply notional amounts used for calculating interest payments. Thus only the difference between interest payments is swapped when interest payments are due.
4. CDSs are over-the-counter contracts whereby the buyer (insured) agrees to pay the seller (insurer) periodic fees (insurance premium) in exchange for receiving protection against default (event) of a loan or bond issued by a referenced entity such as a corporation or a sovereign nation. Thus credit derivatives allow for the placement of bets on whether the referenced loan/bond or debtor will experience a negative "credit event".

5. The event triggering the payment of the loss on a CDS is usually the debtor's default, bankruptcy, credit rating downgrade or its restructuring. The party speculating that the negative credit event will occur is said to take the "short" side of the wager ("buying" insurance); the party taking the "long" side of the bet ("selling" insurance) wagers that no credit event will occur during the contract specified period of time.

QUESTIONS FOR DISCUSSION

1. What is a cross-currency swap? How does it compare with a currency forward contract?
2. How do you value a cross-currency swap? Why does the net value of a cross-currency swap fluctuate continuously?
3. Why are cross-currency swaps compared to a series of long-dated forward contracts?
4. What is an interest rate swap?
5. How do you value an interest rate swap? Why does the net value of an interest rate swap fluctuate continuously?
6. What is a CDS?
7. How do you value a CDS?
8. Compare a CDS with bond insurance
9. Do you consider purchasing a CDS to be a speculative bet? What is the maximum gain you can hope? What is the maximum loss you should fear?
10. Would you consider the purchase of a CDS similar to the purchase or the underwriting of an option? Would it be a call or a put option?

PROBLEMS

1. **Currency swaps and the cost of debt (intermediate).** Michelin S.A., the French multinational tire manufacturer, needs to borrow $300 million to expand its US plant in Georgia. It can issue a US$-denominated five year note at 6% while a similar note denominated in euros would cost 4%. E.I. Dupont de Nemours Inc., the US chemical firm, wants to hedge its long-term euro exposure because of its Spanish operations and is considering issuing a €250 million five year note at 4.5%, whereas its cost of debt for a similar US dollar note issue is 5.5%.
   a. Explain how a currency swap could help both firms to lower their cost of debt. Given that both firms are AAA-rated, how do you explain such cost of capital differences?
   b. Given that at time of issue the exchange rate is US$1.20 = €1, explain pre- and post-swap cash flows.
   c. What are the annual cash-flow payments/receipts in years one through five?
   d. Show actual cash-flow payments by either firm at maturity of the loan, assuming that the exchange rate at the end of year 5 is exactly what was predicted by interest rate parity at the inception of the swap.
2. **Valuing currency swaps (advanced).** With reference to the NSP/KLM currency swap discussed in this chapter, answer the following questions:
   a. What is the implied forward exchange rate used throughout the life of the swap for exchanging cash flows?
   b. At the end of year 3 but immediately prior to swapping cash flows as a result of the euro appreciation against the US dollar to 1.80, the interest rate on 3 year €-denominated bonds has fallen to 4.85%. What is the value of the swap to (1) NSP and (2) KLM?
   c. Using the information provided in (b), discuss a macroeconomic scenario that would increase the value of the currency swap to NSP.
   d. What is the new implied forward exchange rate?
3. **Valuing cross-currency swaps (advanced).** Japan Airlines International (JAI) issues a five year US dollar–denominated 250 million bond yielding 5%. Preferring to keep its liabilities in its domestic currency, JAI immediately swaps the US$-denominated bond into a yen-denominated bond of matching maturity at the prevailing 2% interest rate. The current exchange rate stands at ¥100 = US$1. One year later, having just made the first coupon swap, the US$/¥ rate appreciates to ¥85 = US$1 and interest rates on five year notes decline, respectively, to 4% in the United States and 1% in Japan.

a. What is the value of the currency swap when JAI first contracts it?

b. Detail how the first interest payments are swapped before interest rate and exchange rate changes materialize.

c. How is the market value of the currency swap adjusting to these changes one year later?

4. **Interest rate swap (intermediate).** The Water & Sewer Department (WSD) of the City of Sacramento (California) has issued a floating rate note (FRN) maturing in seven years with an interest rate pegged to the US dollar six month SOFR + 0.25% (25 basis points). The Water & Sewer Department is concerned that short-term interest rates may be trending upward and decides to protect itself against price resetting risk. The swap desk at Wachovia Bank quotes a seven year interest rate swap whereby WSD would pay a fixed rate of 5% for the next seven years and receive SOFR, with both payments made semiannually.

   a. What is the nature of the swap offered by Wachovia Bank? How does it protect WSD against interest rate risk?

   b. Assuming that SOFR stands at 3.75%, compute the first payment and indicate the payment(s) that WSD makes/receives.

5. **CDSs (intermediate).** Mellon Bank sold a CDS to MetLife for the protection of seven year US$375 million mortgage-backed securities requiring a semiannual payment of 55 basis points. In case of default, settlement is to be made in cash.

   a. Default occurs on the anniversary of the seventh semiannual payment, at which point it is estimated that the reference bond value has slumped to 35 cents on the dollar; show the cash-flow payments and their timing for Mellon Bank.

   b. What was/were the risk(s) faced by MetLife when it purchased the CDS from Mellon Bank? How can it protect itself against such risk(s)?

   c. What does it mean for CDSs to be traded over-the-counter? Would you recommend that CDSs be traded on an organized exchange as currency or interest rate futures are?

6. **CDSs on sovereign debt (A) (intermediate).** Ian Maxwell is the chief investment officer for Glasgow's municipal workers' pension funds (GMWF). He is intrigued by the high-yielding sovereign debt issued by PIIGS countries. Most notably, Spain just issued five year treasury bonds at par paying a coupon of 6.25%. Spain as a sovereign is rated B but CDSs (CDSs) on Spanish debt for an annual premium of 285 basis points are available from AXA — an AA-rated French insurance company.

   a. What is a CDS on sovereign debt? How does it differ from CDSs on corporate debt?

   b. Spell out the cash flows — timing and amount — between GMWF and AXA, assuming that Spain does not default.

   c. A referendum held in Cata lonia in December 2013 leads to Catalonia seceding from Spain and precipitating Spain into default by the close of 2014. How would the cash flows between GMWF and AXA be changed? Again, be specific in timing and amounts.

7. **CDSs on sovereign debt (B) (intermediate).** Germany's new issue of comparable five year treasury bonds offers a much lower coupon of 3.10% than Spain's 6.25%. Germany is AAA-rated.

   a. Can the Spanish and German bonds be directly compared with the help of CDSs in spite of the wide difference in credit rating?

   b. Assuming that Ian Maxwell is instructed to invest only in AAA bonds, should he recommend investment in German or Spanish bonds?

REFERENCES

Jacque, Laurent L. 2015. *Global Derivative Debacles: From Theory to Malpractice*, 2nd edition. Singapore and London: World Scientific.

Marshall, John F., and Kenneth R. Kapner. 1992. *The Swap Market*, 2nd edition. Miami, FL: Kolb Publishing.

Popper, Helen. 1993. "Long-Term Covered Interest Parity: Evidence from Currency Swaps." *Journal of International Money and Finance* 12(4): 439–448.

Smith, Clifford W., Jr., Charles W. Smithson, and D. Sykes Wilford. 1989. "Managing Financial Risk." *Journal of Applied Corporate Finance* 1(4): 27–48.

CASE STUDY 12.1. THE DEMISE OF AIG

> *They thought they were selling insurance, when in fact they were betting the company's soul in a high-stakes game of Russian roulette.*
>
> — US Congressman Christopher H. Shays

At its apogee in 2007, American International Group (AIG) had 74 million customers, employed 116,000 people worldwide, and generated $110 billion in revenue with an asset base of US$1 trillion. Approximately half of its revenue came from general insurance — primarily property and casualty — with the other half generated by life insurance, financial services, aircraft leasing, and asset management. AIG traced its roots to Shanghai (China), where Cornelius Vander Starr established a small insurance agency in 1919 under the name of American Asiatic Underwriters. Not long after, as he started to represent US insurance companies in China, Starr opened an office in New York called American International Underwriters to directly underwrite US-owned risks in Asia. The firm grew by leaps and bounds, first in Asia and later in Latin America and Europe, but it struggled in the United States until Starr hired Maurice "Hank" Greenberg in 1962. Over the next four decades Greenberg masterminded AIG's phenomenal growth into one of the global giants of the insurance industry.

AIG and the rise of AIG financial products unit

The demise of AIG was probably seeded in the creation in 1987 of its Financial Products Unit dedicated to capitalizing on growing opportunities in the financial services sector; it was particularly focused on the trading and structuring of complex financial products such as interest rate and currency swaps. Most importantly, AIG Financial Products Unit's good fortunes owed as much to its financial engineering savoir-faire as to its ability to free-ride on its holding parent's AAA credit rating. Specifically, the unit became a major dealer in the over-the-counter derivatives market, with a notional portfolio reaching US$2.7 trillion. Indeed, because of the AAA rating of its parent, the unit had become a preferred counterparty for trading financial derivatives.

For the first 10 years of its existence, the Financial Products Unit prospered selling financial products such as plain-vanilla interest rate swaps, until it was approached by JPMorgan in 1998 with a proposal to credit-enhance (write insurance against default) collateralized debt obligations (CDOs). This new form of insurance on debt took on a life of its own as newly minted CDSs (CDSs): In exchange for a stream of premium-like payments from the debt holder, the Financial Products Unit would promise to reimburse the investor the principal value of the bond in case of default.

AIG, with its AAA credit rating, rapidly became a much sought-after provider of such protection. Over the next decade it built a portfolio of CDSs that had reached $500 billion in notional value by 2007. AIG lent its strong credit rating to lesser-rated securities that, as a result, would now enjoy the AAA rating of the insurance carrier. AIG received a fee for providing the protection from default to investors. Although similar in concept to bond insurance, CDSs were not subject to the same regulation as insurance products are: Most notably, when an insurance company sells a policy, it is required to set aside reserves that cannot be touched until a payout is necessary to settle a loss, whereas the sale of a CDS contract would not even require AIG to post collateral — at least as long as it maintained its AAA rating.

Credit default swaps versus bond insurance

CDSs were a new and more flexible form of bond insurance. They are over-the-counter contracts whereby the buyer (insured) agrees to pay the seller (insurer) periodic fees (insurance premiums) in exchange for receiving protection against default (event) of a loan or bond (loss). The event triggering the payment of the loss is usually the debtor's default, but it can also be a credit rating downgrade or the restructuring of the debtor that adversely alters a loan's seniority or maturity. CDSs are not easy to price; in principle, the fair value of a CDS premium is set such that the present value of a bond, risk-adjusted by the probability of a credit event for the reference entity (issuer of the bond), is equal to the risk-adjusted present value of premiums payment over the life of the CDS.

Unlike a bond insurance policy, whereby the buyer purchases protection on a loan/bond he or she owns, the buyer of a CDS may not have any material relationship with the debtor (so-called naked CDSs). Purchase of a CDS is therefore motivated not only by hedging but also by arbitrage and speculative reasons. In contrast, bond insurance is provided by regulated insurance carriers to entities that own the bond being insured. Bond insurance is clearly of a hedging nature, unlike CDSs, which allow anyone to place a bet on the risk of a firm's bond default. Banks or any unregulated entities writing CDSs are not required to set aside loss reserves (but are nonetheless subject to regulatory capital) and may hedge themselves by selling CDSs to third parties. Counterparty risk for anyone purchasing a CDS is a real issue that can be mitigated by the posting of margin, which should be updated on a periodic basis — but not on a daily basis as in the case of exchange-traded financial products.

Buyers of CDSs are not required to own the underlying bond being insured (naked position) and often purchase them for speculative reasons. The notional amount of outstanding CDSs is considerably larger than the actual amount of under-lying bonds on which the swaps are written. For example, at the time of its default Lehman Brothers owned $125 billion in bonds, but the notional amount of the CDSs written on those bonds approached $500 billion.

Securitization and credit default swaps

Between the subprime crisis of 2008 and the demise of the insurance colossus AIG stands the securitization revolution, which made consumer finance more accessible to American households. At its simplest, securitization transforms old-fashioned and illiquid automobile loans, home mortgages, and credit card receivables into liquid, tradable fixed income securities, which institutional investors such as pension funds can readily purchase.

Most importantly, the technology of securitization hinges on credit enhancement of the newly issued securities, also known as mortgage-backed securities (because they are collateralized by the cash flows of the original borrower's mortgage). Credit enhancement is about providing some form of partial or full insurance against the risk of default and concretized either through traditional bond insurance and more recently through CDSs. As a result, the credit-enhanced securities are better rated and can therefore be issued at a lesser yield. Of course, credit enhancement makes sense only as long as its cost (often as low as 35 to 50 basis points) is less than the resulting reduction in interest rates paid out by the issuer of the mortgage-backed securities.

At first, the AIG Financial Products Unit was reluctant to write CDSs, in part because the unit's continued success in its first decade of existence had been built on careful hedging to avoid risk whenever possible and had certainly avoided speculative bets of any sort. However, Gary Gorton — a finance professor on the faculty of the Wharton School at the University of Pennsylvania — had developed simulation models with real estate data going back to 1946 that showed that CDSs could be sold with a 99.85% chance of never having to pay out, which ultimately convinced AIG to enter the business. By the end of 2004, the unit had built a portfolio of CDSs with a notional value of US$290 billion, which, unlike most of the unit's other activities, was largely unhedged because — according to the words of AIG's global head of credit trading — "the likelihood of ever having to make a payment had to be greater than remote, even in recessionary market scenarios".[9]

The demise of AIG

In 2005 AIG's writing of CDSs continued at the same pace but the nature of debt being insured turned increasingly toward consumer debt. A significantly increasing percentage of consumer debt was subprime mortgages, which did not carry any guarantee from either Fannie Mae or Freddie Mac. Concerns were surfacing about the share of subprime mortgages in the overall portfolio of mortgage-backed securities that AIG protected by writing CDSs. In the spring of 2005, AIG lost its AAA credit rating pursuant to the discovery of earnings manipulation. The rating downgrade required AIG to post collateral for its CDS portfolio. Later that year, in the fall of 2005, housing prices showed a modest decline — AIG's descent into the subprime abyss had started.

The AIG Financial Products Unit's revenue (from insurance premiums) peaked in 2005 at $3.26 billion, with operating income accounting for 17.5% of the firm's total operating income. Unlike its many siblings in the extended AIG family, AIG Financial Products did not believe in proper reserving and capitalizing of the insurance products it was selling.

9 AIG Form 10-K for the period ending December 31, 2004, p. 181; cited in "AIG — Blame for the Bailout," Stanford Graduate School of Business, Case A-203, March 12, 2009.

As the president of AIG Financial Products so eloquently remarked:

> *The models suggested that the risk (about CDSs) was so re-mote that the fees were almost free money . . . Just put it on your books and enjoy the money.*[10]

Because of its faulty business model, AIG Financial Products misled itself, its parent, and its investors, reporting a profit margin of 83% in 2005, and unsurprisingly it lavished on its employees outlandish salaries and bonuses:

> *Mr. Cassano and his colleagues minted tidy fortunes during these high-cotton years. Since 2001, compensation at the small unit ranged from $423 million to $616 million each year, according to corporate filings. That meant that on average each person in the unit made more than $1 million a year.*
>
> *In fact, compensation expenses took a large percentage of the unit's revenue. In lean years it was 33%; in fatter ones 46%. Overall, AIG Financial Products paid its employees $3.56 billion during the last 7 years.*[11]

Had CDSs written by AIG been fairly priced? Had AIG properly reserved for potential losses? Had AIG been misled by its CDS valuation models that consistently showed a minuscule risk of default?

Questions for Discussion

1. What are CDSs, and do they differ from bond insurance? What was the role played by AIG in the market for securitized home mortgages — so-called mortgage-backed securities?
2. How did AIG use CDSs to credit-enhance mortgage-backed securities?
3. How did AIG's extensive involvement in the CDS business compare with AIG's traditional insurance activities such as property and casualty or life insurance?
4. How should AIG price CDSs? Is such pricing similar to pricing other insurance products?
5. How could AIG have avoided its infamous debacle? Who was to blame?

10 Brady Dennis and Robert O'Harrow, "A Crack in the System." *Washington Post*, December 30, 2008.

11 Gretchen Morgenson, "Behind Biggest Insurer's Crisis, a Blind Eye to a Web of Risk." *NewYork Times*, September 28, 2008.

CHAPTER 13

International Trade Financing

The propensity to trade, barter and exchange one thing for another . . . is common to all men, and to be found in no other race of animals.
— Adam Smith

If a good face is a letter of recommendation, a good heart is a letter of credit.
— Edward Bulwer-Lytton

Tata Motors of India's export manager, Raju Aneja, has just signed an export order for 1,000 Nanos — its new revolutionary minicar — with Atlas Distributors, a Vespa scooter dealership based in Casablanca (Morocco). The export sale is denominated in euros (€) and calls for payment of €20 million upon delivery — scheduled for approximately three months from the time of shipment. Tata Motors has never had any commercial dealings with Atlas but was envisioning a long-term relationship with the Moroccan firm. However, it was concerned about the importer's solvency. The Moroccan dirham was pegged to the euro and partially convertible. How should Tata Motors finance its export trade? Raju knew that this would be the first of many similar deals that Tata Motors was hoping to forge with other emerging market countries where the Nano was expected to meet with much commercial success.

In this chapter you will gain an understanding of:

- The different risks faced by exporters.
- The difference between documentary credit and a letter of credit.
- How trade documentation allows for hedging or significant mitigation of risks faced by exporters.
- The different methods of trade financing.
- How government agencies assist their national firms with subsidized financing and insurance schemes.

A BRIEF HISTORY OF INTERNATIONAL TRADE

From time immemorial, traders have been faced with four problems: (1) how to guarantee payment from a faraway buyer, (2) how to finance the physical transportation of merchandise from point A to point B — perhaps several hundreds or thousands of miles away and weeks or months away, (3) how to insure the cargo (risk of being lost at sea or to pirates), and (4) how to protect against price fluctuations in the value of the cargo across space (from point A to point B) and over time (between shipping and delivery time).

Ancient times

Trade carried over long distances is probably as old as the human species and has long been a source of economic power for the nations that embraced it. Indeed, international trade seems to have been at the vanguard of human progress and civilization: Phoenicians, Greeks, and Romans were all great traders whose activities were facilitated by marketplaces and money changers that set fixed places and fixed times for exchanging goods. Some historians even claim that some form of contracting with future delivery appeared as early as several centuries BC. At about the same time in Babylonia — the cradle of civilization — commerce was primarily effected by means of caravans. Traders bought goods to be

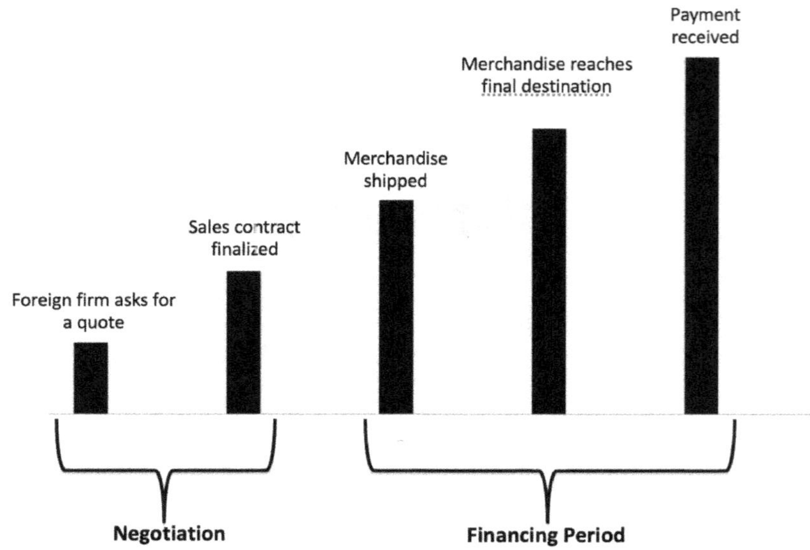

Exhibit 13.1. Time line of export transactions.

delivered in some distant location and sought financing. A risk-sharing agreement was designed whereby merchants-financiers provided a loan to traders whose repayment was contingent upon safe delivery of the goods. The trader borrowed at a higher cost than that of an ordinary loan to account for the purchase of an "option to default" on the loan contingent upon loss of cargo. As lenders were offering similar options to many traders and thereby pooling their risks, they were able to keep its cost affordable.[1]

Trade in early times was primarily of a barter nature. A caravan would convoy merchandise to a faraway foreign city and would exchange it for other merchandise of presumably equivalent value even though money had not been invented. The first breakthrough came with the introduction of money in the form of precious metals (gold and silver primarily) as numéraire and store of value. Our caravan would now deliver goods and receive money in exchange, which widened considerably the scope of trading opportunities. The caravan could now take that money to another city, purchase merchandise for money, and bring it back to its home city. Of course carrying precious metals over long distance was fraught with risks: pirates and highway robbers were always lying in wait ready to hijack the riches. The second breakthrough came with paper money in the form of drafts that allowed for compensation among the different branches of banking houses. In fact, merchant banking is the granddaddy of modern banking: documentary credit was born (discussed at great length in this chapter) and is still widely used today.

THE TRILOGY OF RISKS IN EXPORTING

Exporters are confronted with *credit, currency,* and *country risks* when completing international sales. These risks are best understood in the context of the time lag during which funds are tied up while the merchandise is in transit between the exporter's loading dock and the importer's showroom. The time line sequencing the events characterizing an international trade transaction is sketched in Exhibit 13.1. The exporter is approached by a foreign buyer and asked to quote prices or make a bid. Negotiations about price, modalities, and timing of payment occur between the exporter/seller and the importer/buyer. If negotiations are successful, a contract is signed. Physical shipment will follow but may be delayed several weeks if the merchandise has to be made to order or is simply not available in the seller's inventory. Depending on the logistics of transportation, it may be several weeks or months before the merchandise reaches its final destination and actual payment is received by the exporter. It is during this critical period stretching from the time of shipment until payment is received that the exporter will seek financing, duly aware of its precarious situation, having surrendered physical control of the

1 Jorion, P. 1995. *Big Bets Gone Bad.* San Diego, CA: Academic Press, p. 138.

export merchandise while awaiting the deferred payment: Can the buyer's promise to pay be trusted, or should a third party be brought into the transaction as a guarantor of expected payment and be trusted to deliver on its guarantees?

Credit risk arises when payment significantly lags the shipment of goods and the seller thus extends financing to the buyer. This is essentially the same risk that arises when carrying out a domestic sale — that is, assessing the likelihood of nonpayment or default, delayed payment, or partial payment by your customer. In fact, the exporter's predicament in making a credit-granting decision is no different from that of a banker adjudicating a loan application. However, there is one important difference in gauging credit risk in international sales — the *availability* of accounting and financial information about your client domiciled in a foreign country. If the information is indeed available, is it formatted in a *comparable* way to domestic information? Differing accounting standards make the reading, understanding, and analysis of foreign financial statements more complicated. Furthermore, national accounting conventions distort simple comparison of key accounting ratios[2] used in credit risk analysis. For example, a number of Latin American countries make large use of inflation accounting techniques,[3] which are generally not found in Organization for Economic Cooperation and Development (OECD) countries. Last but not least, how *reliable* is this information? This is really a question about the integrity of the auditing process of your client's accounting statements. Indeed, standards of transparency and accountability in emerging market countries may be much lower than in OECD countries, thereby undermining the reliability and truthfulness of foreign financial statements.

Depending on the country you are trading with, the availability, comparability, and reliability of the accounting data — upon which a probabilistic statement of timely payment in full is based — will be questionable. Other OECD advanced industrialized countries have a legal accounting and financial infrastructure that makes credit risk analysis reasonably congruent with what a US-based firm is used to in probing domestic clients. In such countries databases are widely available, and if the firm is listed on the national stock exchange credit risk analysis should be manageable. The problem really arises with emerging market countries, which may lack a credit bureau[4] and have a more rudimentary financial accounting reporting system whose enforcement is often lax and compromised by corruption or different degrees of cronyism. *Ex post*, or once export goods are shipped and payment becomes an issue, legal recourse may be slow and costly; here again the less developed the foreign country, the more cumbersome the recovery process becomes.

Currency risk arises from the possibility that the exchange rate prevailing when the sales invoice, if denominated in the importer's currency, is sent (the account receivable [A/R] is booked) may depreciate by the time payment is actually made. This is the *transaction* exposure to foreign exchange risk, which will be discussed at great length in Chapter 16. Most exporters prefer to invoice foreign customers in their own currency, thereby forcing exchange rate risk to their client. An abnormally high percentage of world trade continues to be denominated in US dollars, but exporting/importing firms domiciled in Brazil, Russia, India, China (BRIC), and other emerging market countries are increasingly able to invoice international trade transactions in their own currencies. This should not come as any surprise since these countries now enjoy close to or fully convertible currencies and are increasingly availing themselves of currency derivatives, which greatly facilitates hedging currency risks.

Unfortunately, many exporters conduct *credit risk* and *exchange risk* analysis independently when they should be approached conjointly. Many foreign distributors and importers find their operating margins squeezed or squashed when faced by an abrupt devaluation or depreciation of their currency. As the costs of imports skyrocket due to the devaluation, importers find themselves unable to pass through higher costs to their domestic customers. This is a typical case of economic exposure to exchange rate risk discussed in Chapter 18. Credit risk analysis should be made contingent on exchange rate scenarios: A foreign distributor may be perfectly solvent at the currently prevailing exchange rate but become insolvent if its currency depreciates by 30%.

2 Current and acid test ratios are widely used in gauging the liquidity of the buyer. The payables ratio, which measures how long on average it takes the buyer to pay up the suppliers, is also relevant.

3 Inflation accounting aims at correcting distortions due to historical accounting in situations of high inflation or hyperinflation. Price-level indexes are used to adjust accounts such as fixed assets and depreciation to reflect purchasing power parity losses.

4 A credit bureau is simply an independently run database that keeps records of all loans dispersed by various credit-granting institutions as well as the payment history of borrowing firms.

Country risk refers to the possibility of exchange controls blocking currency transfers for trade payment purposes. The importer, which may be otherwise perfectly able to effect timely payment, may in fact default on its international trade obligations because its country is facing an acute shortage of hard currency. Its central bank would enact controls on foreign exchange payment, thereby forcing our importer to default on its obligations to the exporter eagerly awaiting payment.

MANAGING CREDIT RISK

If the exporter is comfortable with the findings of its credit risk analysis, it will extend financing to the importer and will simply carry accounts receivable (accounts payable for the foreign buyer) on its books. The exporter is thus relying on the importer's promise to pay; in other words, the exporter will pray for his account *receivables* to be *received* in a timely fashion and paid in full on the due date! More often than not, trust between newly acquainted exporters and importers will be slight to nonexistent. Tata Motors certainly had had no prior relationship with Atlas Distributors nor had done any business in Morocco!

Cash in advance

In many situations, gauging a foreign buyer's creditworthiness becomes a treacherous exercise that discourages the exporter from directly extending credit. The exporter may thus demand *cash in advance* or *prepayment*, which ensures that payment is received before the goods are shipped (or well before they reach their destination). As one would expect, this is a relatively uncommon method of international payment because of the burden it places on the buyer. It certainly offers maximum protection to the exporter, but unless the transaction involves a specially made to order product or the buyer finds itself in a weak bargaining position *vis-à-vis* the seller, these draconian payment terms will be difficult to impose on the buyer.

Documentary letter of credit

When the exporter is unable to receive cash in advance but not quite willing to rely on the importer's promise to pay, he will turn to an *indirect* payment-cum-financing method based on an elaborate documentary credit machinery. The instrument of choice is the *letter of credit* (L/C), which is, in essence, a letter addressed to the exporter that is written and signed by an advising bank on behalf of the importer. In the letter, the issuing bank commits itself to honoring drafts drawn on itself by the exporter — as long as the latter meets the very specific conditions set forth in the letter of credit. The draft can be a *sight draft* or a *time draft*, depending on whether payment is due immediately when the exporter has met the terms of the L/C or payment is deferred. What makes documentary credit a somewhat cumbersome process is that it requires a documentary machinery that ensures that the exporter does satisfy the conditions necessary for the payment to be made; we will return shortly to the different documents that typically accompany a letter of credit.

Advantages to the exporter of using a letter of credit are significant, as the creditworthiness of the foreign bank issuing the letter of credit is substituted for the creditworthiness of the importer, which we know is more problematic to gauge. Presumably the creditworthiness of the bank is much easier to assess than that of the importer. Equally important, the L/C greatly facilitates financing, since the exporter's otherwise hazardous A/R is now guaranteed by a bank in good standing; the trade acceptance has now become a banker's acceptance. In other words, the short-term claim against the importer materialized by the *trade acceptance* (nothing more than a receivables confirmation by the importer that formally acknowledges its payment responsibilities) has morphed into a claim acknowledged/accepted by the bank against which it is held — so-called *banker's acceptance*.

Advantages to the importer of a letter of credit are first and foremost that since payment is only made in compliance with the L/C's stipulated conditions, the importer is able to ascertain that the proper goods (*certificate of inspection*) are being shipped on or before the agreed date (*bill of lading*). Furthermore, since an L/C is almost as good as cash in hand for the exporter, the importer finds itself in a strong bargaining position *vis-à-vis* the exporter to negotiate sales terms other than payment in advance or financing.

MANAGING CURRENCY RISK

Tata Motors had preferred to invoice the export sale in Indian rupees, thereby shifting the entire burden of currency risk to the Moroccan importer. After intense negotiation, though, it had to compromise, and it agreed to denominate the account receivable in euros. Tata Motors was keen on hedging its euro exposure and was also considering the cost of financing in euros at 5% annually for the estimated one year period elapsing between shipment and payment as an alternative to rupee financing at 10% annually. A third option of financing in Eurodollars at a yet lower interest rate of 3% per annum (p.a.) was intriguing but would expose Tata Motors to a third currency — the US dollar — which would seem to detract the firm from hedging its euro exposure. In sum, Tata had three financing options to choose from:

1. From a State Bank of India at the rate of i_{IN} = 10% p.a.
2. From a euro-land bank such as Credit Lyonnais at the rate of $i_€$ = 5% p.a.
3. From a US bank such as Citibank at the rate of i_{US} = 3% p.a.

Tata Motors will select the option that affords the largest amount of rupees now (rather than a year from now) while eliminating exchange rate risk. Let's consider the mechanics of each of the three hedging-cum-financing options.

1. *Rupee financing.* The rupee-denominated loan will be collateralized by the euro receivables. Specifically, Tata Motors will borrow the present value of the rupee counter-value of the euro receivables hedged through the forward contract at the forward rupee price of one euro for delivery in 90 days, $F(90) = 60$.

$$\frac{€20,000,000}{1+0.10} \times 60 = \text{INR } 1,090,090,090$$

Note that by borrowing rupees, Tata Motors is creating a rupee liability while holding a euro asset. To correct the currency denomination mismatch, Tata Motors is selling forward euros (creating a euro liability matching in amount and maturity its euro asset) for rupees (creating a rupee asset matching in amount and maturity its rupee liability). Thus, rupee financing is obtained while hedging is secured.

2. *Euro financing.* Tata Motors will borrow the present value of its euro receivable and immediately convert the euro loan proceeds into rupees at the spot rupee price of one euro, $S(0) = 63$.

$$\frac{€20,000,000}{1+0.05} \times 63 = \text{INR } 1,200,000,000$$

3. *Dollar financing.* This montage is somewhat more complex since Tata Motors needs a loan denominated in rupees but incurs a debt in a third currency ($), which is collateralized by a receivable denominated in euros. The currency mismatch between the dollar liability and the euro asset is addressed by selling forward the euro proceeds for dollars, thereby transforming the currency denomination of euro assets into dollars to neutralize the dollar liability. Specifically, €20,000,000 will be sold forward for dollars at the rate $F(365) = 1.45$ (dollar price of one euro for delivery in 365 days), the present value of which (discounted at the dollar interest rate) will be borrowed and immediately exchanged for rupees at the spot rate of $S(0) = 45$.

$$\frac{€20,000,000 \times 1.45}{1+0.03} \times 45 = \text{INR } 1,266,990,290$$

Simple numerical comparison shows that dollar financing is preferred because it yields the largest INR loan. Interestingly, more than 50% of international trade continues to be invoiced and financed in US dollars (see International Corporate Finance in Practice 13.1).

INTERNATIONAL CORPORATE FINANCE IN PRACTICE 13.1[5]

The Resilience of the US Dollar as the Dominant World Currency

The dollar is used globally as a unit of account, store of value and medium of exchange. At least half of cross-border trade invoices are in dollars. That is five times America's share of world goods imports, and three times its share of exports. The dollar is the preferred currency of central banks and capital markets, accounting for close to two-thirds of global securities issuance and foreign-exchange reserves.

The world's financial rhythm is American: when interest rates move or risk appetite on Wall Street shifts, global markets respond. The world's financial plumbing has Uncle Sam's imprint on it, too. Most international transactions are ultimately cleared in dollars through New York by American "correspondent" banks. America has a tight grip on the main cross-border messaging system used by banks, SWIFT, whose members ping each other 30m times a day. Another part of the us-centric network is CHIPS, a clearing house that processes $1.5trn-worth of payments daily. America uses these systems to monitor activity. Denied access to this infrastructure, an organization becomes isolated and, usually, financially crippled. Individuals and institutions across the planet are thus subject to American jurisdiction — and vulnerable to punishment.

America began to flex its financial muscles after the terrorist attacks of September 11, 2001. It imposed huge fines on foreign banks for money-laundering and sanctions-busting; in 2014 a $9bn penalty against BNP Paribas shook the French establishment. The US government has taken the weaponization of finance to a new level. It has used sanctions to throttle Iran, North Korea, Russia, Turkey (briefly), Venezuela and others. After America pulled out of a nuclear deal with Iran in 2018, European firms fled Iran, even as the EU encouraged them to stay. SWIFT quickly fell into line when America threatened action if it did not cut off Iranian banks after the reimposition of sanctions in 2018.

5 Abridged from "Dethroning the dollar" *The Economist* (January 18, 2020).

MANAGING COUNTRY RISK

Tata Motors of India had never dealt with a Moroccan firm before. We showed in the previous section how credit risk — lack of trust — had been addressed with an L/C issued by Atlas's bank — Banque pour le Commerce Maghrebin (BCM). Although well-rated in Morocco, BCM was not immune to country risk in the form of exchange controls if Morocco were to be engulfed in a severe balance of payments crisis. Under such dire circumstances BCM might not be able to effect the payment, because the convertibility of the dirham would be suspended.

Tata Motors had two options to hedge its exports trade against country risk: (1) It could require that the irrevocable letter of credit issued by BCM be confirmed by its Indian bank — the State Bank of India. In effect Tata Motors' draft would now be accepted by a domestic bank and its claim would escape the travails of country risk. By issuing an L/C, BCM transferred Tata Motors' credit risk away from the unknown Atlas Distributors and onto itself. By confirming the L/C, the State Bank of India was further transferring credit risk from Morocco back to India. Tata Motors would rest peacefully — it could definitely live with a claim confirmed by its main bank. (2) Alternatively, Tata Motors could purchase political risk insurance against nonpayment from the Export-Import Bank of India; see the last section of this chapter for further discussion of government programs for financing international trade.

THE MECHANICS OF TRADE FINANCING WITH A LETTER OF CREDIT[6]

Because of the complexity of payments-cum-financing in cross-border trade transactions, we detail next the multiple steps involved in the process and introduce the many documents that accompany such transactions. Thus, under a letter-of-credit financing scheme several transactions will happen almost concurrently (refer to Exhibit 13.2; each numbered transaction on the chart is explained next).

6 Letters of credit can be used for payment purposes only, and as such are effective tools for insulating the exporter form the risk of nonpayment. Most often letters of credit are bundled with financing, enabling the exporter to be paid at shipment time rather than much later.

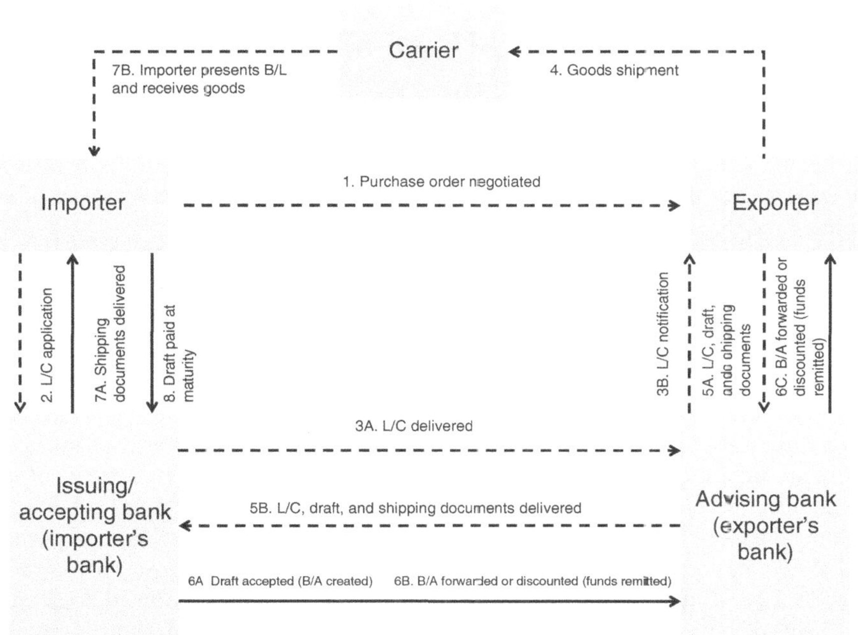

Exhibit 13.2. Cross-border trade financing steps.
Source: Adapted from Instruments of the Money Market (Federal Reserve Bank of Richmond, 1986).

- The importer Atlas Distributors (Morocco) orders goods — 1,000 Nanos — from the exporter Tata Motors (India). The two parties finalize a sales contract spelling out the terms governing the transaction that include a letter of credit accompanied by a time draft (1).
- Importer applies for an *irrevocable* L/C with his bank — Banque pour le Commerce Maghrebin (BCM) and names Tata Motors as its beneficiary (2).
- BCM issues the L/C and informs the advising bank (3A) — State Bank of India (SBI) — which notifies Tata Motors that the L/C has been issued and outlines what the stipulated terms are (3B).
- *Credit risk has been transferred from Atlas Distributor to BCM.* Tata Motors requests SBI to confirm the L/C for a fee,[7] thereby adding its guarantee to BCM's.
- *Tata Motors has insulated itself from Moroccan credit and country risk, which have morphed into SBI's credit risk.*
- Tata Motors arranges for shipment of the merchandise to Atlas Distributors through a common carrier (4), receiving from the carrier a bill of lading B/L (see International Corporate Finance in Practice 13.2).
- Tata Motors presents the documents stipulated by the L/C, including the B/L to advising bank SBI, along with a 365 day time draft[8] drawn on the L/C-issuing bank BCM (5A). Exporter's bank SBI presents the export documents as well as the draft to importer's bank BMC, which accepts the draft and takes possession of the export documents (5B).
- The accepted draft becomes a 365 day banker's acceptance B/A[9] which is a negotiable instrument (6A). B/A will be forwarded to Tata Motors via SBI. Tata Motors can hold it until maturity (no financing provided since Tata Motors waits 1 year to be paid) or it can ask BCM or SBI to discount it (financing provided and Tata motors receives immediately the present value of B/A — its receivable) (6B and 6C).

7 The exporter's advising bank will not confirm the L/C unless the foreign issuing bank makes it *irrevocable* — so that it cannot be cancelled or altered except with the agreement of all parties.

8 A *draft* is an unconditional order in writing signed by the exporter (drawer) and addressed to the importer (drawee) requiring them to pay on demand (sight draft) or at a later date (time draft) to the payee (usually the drawer).

9 When the draft is accepted/confirmed by the importer, it becomes a trade acceptance. If the trade acceptance is in turn confirmed by the bank, it becomes a banker's acceptance. Trade or banker's acceptances can be sold at a discount to money market investors and are therefore used for financing purposes.

INTERNATIONAL CORPORATE FINANCE IN PRACTICE 13.2

Documents in International Trade

Letters of credit (L/C) are referred to as documentary credit because they are accompanied by several key documents: bill of lading, commercial invoice, insurance certificate, and consular invoice, all of which play an important role in securing international transactions and avoiding unpleasant surprises for both the exporter and the importer.

An **ocean (or airway) bill of lading (B/L)** issued by the international carrier to the exporter is first and foremost a receipt of the merchandise and as such includes a short and simple description of the goods. Second, it is a contract between the exporter/consignor and the carrier that spells out the latter's obligation to transport the merchandise from the port of shipment to the port of destination for delivery to a consignee in exchange for certain freight charges. Last but not least, it is a document of title that establishes control over the merchandise. An order[10] bill of lading usually consigns the goods to the exporter because it wants to retain control over the goods until payment from the importer or the importer's bank has been received. At time of payment, the exporter will transfer/endorse the bill of lading to the consignee (usually the importer), who surrenders it to the carrier in exchange for the goods. Thus an order bill of lading is equivalent to holding the title to the goods and as such can be used as collateral for financing purposes.

A **commercial invoice** is used for customs declaration and determining import tariffs. As such it is an exhaustive, itemized description of the merchandise being shipped, including the quantity, grades, and per unit and total value of the goods involved. It lists exporter's and importer's names and addresses, the name of the vessel, point of shipment and destination, freight and insurance charges, as well as importer's fees and duties to be paid.

An **insurance certificate** is proof that the merchandise is insured by an insurance carrier against loss or damage. It must be signed by the insurance carrier (or an authorized representative) and issued in the name of the exporter or the consignee. The insurance value should be denominated in the same currency used in the invoice. Because most exporters have an umbrella or open policy covering all their exports, the exporter will have to issue a specific insurance certificate using the form provided by the insurance carrier. The certificate details the specifics of the export transaction and should conform with the information on the bill of lading, the commercial invoice, and the consular invoice.

A **consular invoice** is an official document filled by the exporter in consultation with a consular representative of the importer's country. Its primary purpose is to assist the customs officials in the importer's country in assessing the exact value of the imported merchandise for customs duties assessment.

- Importer's bank BCM notifies importer that documents have arrived. Importer Atlas Distributors endorses the draft (promissory note). Importer's bank releases export documents (including the bill of lading) which gives title of the goods to the importer, who may now claim the shipment (7A).
- Upon arrival of the goods, importer presents the bill of lading and collects them from the carrier by presenting the bill of lading (7B).
- Either advising or accepting bank may keep the B/A in their portfolio until the importer pays, thereby directly financing the trade transaction. Alternatively, they may choose to sell the B/A in the money market.
- Importer pays the time draft — now a banker's acceptance — upon maturity (8). Money market investors who had purchased the B/A are, in turn, paid off.

---

10 Most international trade transactions involve financing from third parties and therefore require that title of goods be assigned/transferred to third parties. Order rather than straight bills of lading allow for such transfer of title to third parties as necessary. A straight bill of lading consigns the goods to a specific party — usually the importer — and cannot be transferred; accordingly, it is used when no financing is required.

FINANCING EXPORTS

So far this chapter has addressed the key risks faced by exporters and how they can be hedged. It has also sketched the mechanics of international payments in a typical export transaction, showing specifically how hedging currency risk can be combined with trade financing. More specifically, exporters, like any other business firms, would need to finance their working capital, and exports-linked A/Rs are certainly an important component of working capital. In a different vein, for exporting to happen, providing financing to the buyer/importer will be required. More often than not, the exporter's home country offers subsidized financing to ensure that the exporter does win the sales contract. We now turn to the various financing techniques available to exporters, starting with transactions with low or no credit or country risk.

Discounting of accounts receivable

In many situations, exporters are dealing with affiliated parties such as sister affiliates in the case of intra-corporate trade or known nonaffiliated parties such as longtime distributors. The exporter would typically have an *open account* sales relationship — built over many years — with the foreign parties; trust is high and credit and country risk are deemed to be nil or very low in such cases. The exporter would naturally turn to its bank to fund its export trade, and the bank would oblige, often requiring that the A/R be pledged as collateral. The bank would thus discount the receivables *with recourse* to the exporter. In effect, the bank is providing a financing service at a cost that should reflect the exporter's overall credit risk rather than the specific credit and country risk attached to the A/R. Recourse means that the discounting bank in case of nonpayment — when accounts *receivable* are *not received* in a timely fashion — will simply exercise recourse against its client for the full payment of the A/R. Had the discounting bank discounted the A/R *without recourse*, the bank would now find itself collecting the A/R from the importer. In other words, it would charge the exporter for having to assume both credit and country risk associated with the A/R on behalf of the importer, and a significant risk premium would be added to the usual discount rate.

Q: Wachovia Bank is quoting to AAA-rated Weyerhaeuser Inc. — a US-based exporter of newsprint — an interest rate of 6% for discounting with recourse \$25 million of 90 day A/R from Mexico-based La Prensa. Wachovia typically adds a 150 basis point country risk premium for trade transactions originating from Mexico. How much financing will Weyerhaeuser receive?

A: Weyerhaeuser should receive the present value of the A/R discounted at the applicable rate. The proper discount rate should not include the country risk premium since the loan is made with recourse to US-based Weyerhaeuser and should reflect its AAA credit rating. Weyerhaeuser should thus receive \$25 million/(1 + 0.06/4) = \$24 639 million. In case of nonpayment, Wachovia will exercise its recourse directly against Weyerhaeuser.

Factoring and forfaiting

Many small to medium-sized firms may not have the resources to develop in-house expertise for carrying out exports trade. Thus they find it preferable to subcontract the credit investigation, collection, and financing activities to a third party — the so-called *factor*, which is a specialized financial institution often affiliated with a large commercial bank. During the negotiation between the exporter and a potential importer, the exporter will keep the factor abreast of all relevant information about the impending deal, and the factor in turn will tap its network of foreign affiliates to perform credit risk analysis on the potential importer.

Factoring is usually nonrecourse financing. It is clearly different from a bank loan collateralized by A/Rs since such loans are priced on the basis of the exporter's overall creditworthiness and allow the bank in case of nonpayment not only to seize the A/R but also to exercise recourse against the firm's entire assets. Often the agreement between the exporter and the factor involves the entire portfolio of exports transactions: For a servicing fee and a financing charge, the factor will immediately pay the discounted value of the export receivables' face value, thereby reflecting the cost of assuming all risks on behalf of the exporter. Factoring is prevalent for short-term export transactions involving consumer goods or light capital equipment with maturity of 180 days or less.

Forfaiting is a form of factoring applied to export transactions spanning a medium-term horizon — typically 2–5 years (but sometimes as long as 10 years) and generally involves capital equipment goods. Again, forfaiting is appealing to small to medium-sized firms that lack the export structuring experience and therefore prefer to turn over collection and financing to a specialized financial institution, often affiliated with a large commercial bank. The term *forfaiting* comes from *forfeiting* or surrendering legal rights of recourse against the exporter in case of nonpayment by the importer. These are situations when both credit and country risks are significant and the exporter has not secured the transaction through a documentary letter of credit. Typically, the exporter will involve the forfaiter during the negotiation of the exports' sale and will tailor the contract accordingly, in exchange for which the exporter will know the cost of financing before closing the transaction. In sum, through forfaiting the exporter transforms a credit sale — with attendant credit, currency, and country risk — into a cash sale fully protected from any recourse by the forfaiter in case of default at a cost that reflects the idiosyncratic risks of the transaction.

International leasing

In the case of export transactions involving big-ticket items such as aircraft or container ships, the financing may be provided in the form of an international lease. In effect the supplier/exporter sells the big-ticket item to a specialized leasing company/*lessor* (possibly domiciled in a third country — often a tax haven) for cash. The lessor in turn leases the equipment to the importer/*lessee*. (See International Corporate Finance in Practice 13.3) The leasing contract is similar to a domestic lease with the added complexity of the lessor and lessee being domiciled in different countries. More specifically, the contract spells out the *duration* of the lease (typically several years for big-ticket items), the *amount* of the lease payment to be paid periodically (quarterly, semiannually, or annually), and its *currency of denomination*.

International leasing has immediate advantages for the exporter, as it amounts to a *cash-on-delivery* export sale. Financing and subsequent credit risk and country risk are assumed by the leasing company, which owns the asset and has no recourse to the exporter in case of difficulties in collecting periodic payments on its lease (see International Corporate Finance in Practice 13.4 for an illustration of how financial engineering can mitigate credit risk).

The importer also benefits: The duration of the lease can be adapted to the economic life of the leased asset — three to six years for capital goods such as machine tools or delivery trucks and eight to 10 years for aircraft or container ships. The lease is not a debt and therefore does not constrain the lessee's borrowing capacity; it really amounts to *off-balance-sheet* financing.

INTERNATIONAL CORPORATE FINANCE IN PRACTICE 13.3

Aircraft Leasing

Traditionally, airline companies directly purchased aircraft from the manufacturer and arranged financing from banks, often credit enhanced by export credit agencies such as the Export-Import (Ex-Im) Bank (United States), Hermes (Germany), Coface (France), and others. Such traditional financing requires the airline company to put up at least 15% of equity toward the purchase. For example, in 2002 Credit Lyonnais — the French commercial bank — arranged a credit line in the amount of $1.1 billion for Scandinavian Airlines (SAS) to purchase 17 Airbus airliners. However, SAS had to tie up its own cash at 15% of the amount toward the acquisition. To avoid both cash contribution and heavy debt load, European airlines (lessees) have turned increasingly toward the leasing of aircraft to gain increased operating flexibility to renew their fleets. Entities such as Gecas and IFLC (lessors) acquire aircraft that they in turn lease to airlines such as Air France-KLM, which relies on this modus operandi for 40% of its fleet. Lessors, in turn, finance their acquisitions through innovative techniques such as the securitization of their lease portfolios.

INTERNATIONAL CORPORATE FINANCE IN PRACTICE 13.4

Floating Oil Insulated Lease (Foil)

Aircraft leases account for an overwhelming share of international leasing. Because oil price volatility is a major factor in the financial health of airlines, Standard Chartered Bank proposed to Thai Airways a novel approach for structuring leases by bundling a plain-vanilla operating lease with a fuel risk management program (combination of options on oil prices): The so-called Floating Oil Insulated Lease (FOIL) insulates Thai from its exposure to jet fuel prices (linked to the WTI oil price index). The lease without FOIL is set at US$390,000 per month regardless of jet fuel price. With FOIL the lease payment becomes US$ [390,000 + (85 – floating oil price) × 10,578], which is floored at 0 (oil price at $122 per barrel) and capped at 780,000 (oil price at $48 per barrel). In effect, when the oil price climbs from $85 to $122 per barrel, Thai pays a lower and lower lease (it decreases by $10,578 for every dollar that the WTI oil price settles above $85) to offset higher fuel charges. Conversely, when the WTI oil price declines from $85 down to $48 Thai sees its lease payments increase while benefiting from lower fuel charges. With FOIL, Thai Airways is a stronger lessee and should be able to better its lease terms.

PRE-EXPORT FINANCING

For exporters whose *future flow* receivables are recurrent with an established track record, structured financing or securitization may unlock access to steady financing at rates which may be lower than the firm's otherwise unsecured borrowing rates for working capital financing purposes. This is the case of natural resource exports such as natural gas, oil, and other minerals such as copper or bauxite (see International Corporate Finance in Practice 13.5).

Securitizing export receivables

The architecture of such structured export financing allows firms to access a broader pool of funds if their receivables are securitized. Such securitization deals are patterned after domestic securitization as introduced in Chapter 9. In a typical future flow securitization the exporter (originator) is typically domiciled in an emerging market country whose sovereign rating is less than stellar — say BBB or below (see Exhibit 13.3). Because of the country ceiling rule, such a borrower cannot be rated higher[11] (at least for international financing purposes) than its country of domicile even though its inherent creditworthiness may be several notches higher — say AA. However, it may sell/assign its future exports receivables (A/Rs) to an *offshore* special purpose vehicle (1),[12] which in turn issues debt instruments to international investors (2). The proceeds of the securities issued are remitted to the borrowing firm. Designated international customers (obligors) of the exporter sign an agreement to direct payables to the offshore SPV's escrow/collection account — rather than to the onshore originator/exporter — and pay accordingly as exports are shipped to them (3) and (4). The collection agent will in turn forward export proceeds to the SPV, which will in turn pay principal and interest to investors (5). Whatever is left is remitted to the exporter (6). Investors that would otherwise be exposed to country risk are now protected against risk of currency inconvertibility because the borrower obtained a legally binding agreement from obligors to make their payments directly to the offshore trust. Thus, the central bank of the borrower's country of domicile cannot interfere with the timely payment of interest and repayment of principal since obligors and investors are both beyond its jurisdiction and so is the payment of the receivables — typically denominated in a hard (convertible) currency — which is also carried

11 Firms typically receive two credit ratings: (1) a domestic rating for raising funds in the domestic market in domestic currency and (2) an international credit rating for raising funds internationally in a foreign currency. The latter rating, because it incorporates some measure of country risk, is constrained by the credit rating of its country of domicile (so-called country ceiling), which is often lower than its domestic credit rating.

12 The special purpose vehicle has to be domiciled outside or offshore the home country of the borrowing firm to hedge country risk.

INTERNATIONAL CORPORATE FINANCE IN PRACTICE 13.5

Mexicana de Cobre

Mexicana de Cobre (Mexcobre) — a recently privatized copper-mining company — is domiciled in BBB-rated Mexico. At the height of the sovereign debt crisis it was able to secure medium-term financing from a syndicate of international banks in the amount of $210 million at significantly more favorable terms than it was currently receiving. In effect it reduced by half the cost of its short-term financing from 23% to 11.5%. The three year term loan was collateralized by copper future export receivables staggered over a period of 36 months. The export receivables contracted with an AAA-rated Belgian metal-trading firm SOGEM were US dollar-denominated.

Mexicana de Cobre decided to hedge against volatile copper prices on the London Metal Exchange[13] in order improve its creditworthiness in the eyes of its foreign lenders. It entered into a copper price swap with Metallgesellschaft (one of the leading metal-processing firms) whereby for a period of three years it committed to paying/receiving every month the difference between the spot price of copper and $2,000 per metric ton times 4,000 metric tons of copper. In effect, the swap was tantamount to a portfolio of 36 forward contracts with maturity ranging from 1 to 36 months at a forward rate of $2,000 per metric ton. As is often the case in commodity price swaps, the physical transaction (in this case Mexcobre delivers 4,000 metric tons of copper to SOGEM, which pays the spot price) is unbundled from the financial transaction (Mexcobre and Metallgesellschaft agree to pay/receive the differential between the spot price and $2,000 times 4,000 tons every month).

Effectively, the swap transformed the risk profile of Mexcobre's top-line revenue, thereby enhancing its creditworthiness, which translated into a much-reduced cost of financing. Country risk — the risk that Mexcobre may be unable to remit dollars to its creditors — was mitigated by establishing an *offshore escrow account* in the state of New York (US) to which all export proceeds (corresponding to the monthly 4,000 metric tons) would be paid so as to service the loan and repay the principal. The central bank of Mexico would not be able to enforce exchange controls holding up the timely payment of interest and principal. This offshore escrow account in effect transformed a loan to a Mexican firm into a quasi-loan to a US firm as long as performance risk — the ability of Mexcobre to mine and ship 4,000 metric tons of copper every month — was not an issue.

13 Jacque, Laurent L. and G. Hawawini. 1993. "Myths and Realities of the Global Market for Capital: Lessons for Financial Managers," in *Journal of Applied Corporate Finance* (Fall). The deal was engineered by Dr. Gaylen Byker.

out offshore (see International Corporate Finance in Practice 13.5).

Thus, through securitization of future export receivables, firms domiciled in countries with low country ratings are able to finance their exports at lower rates than their sovereign ceiling would otherwise allow. The offshore escrow account is beyond the exporter's home country central bank control, and thus the risk of *currency inconvertibility* is avoided as long as importers are legally bound to make payment to the offshore escrow account.[14]

Market risk due to price and quantity uncertainty can be hedged through long-term contracts and/or commodity price swaps. Ultimately, investment-grade firms (in domestic currency terms) are able to *pierce* their country ceiling and finance their exports at much lower interest rates than their governments would. (See International Corporate Finance in Practice 13.6.)

In late 1998, Pemex, the Mexican state-owned oil enterprise, issued export-backed securities that were rated BBB by Standard & Poor's, thereby piercing Mexico's country ceiling by as much as three notches. Pemex saved as much as 337.5 basis points on what it would have had to pay on its senior unsecured debt.

14 Country risk cannot be entirely eliminated if the sovereign were to force the exporter to sell to domestic rather than foreign customers. This risk is higher for soft commodities (agricultural products) than it is for minerals and energy products.

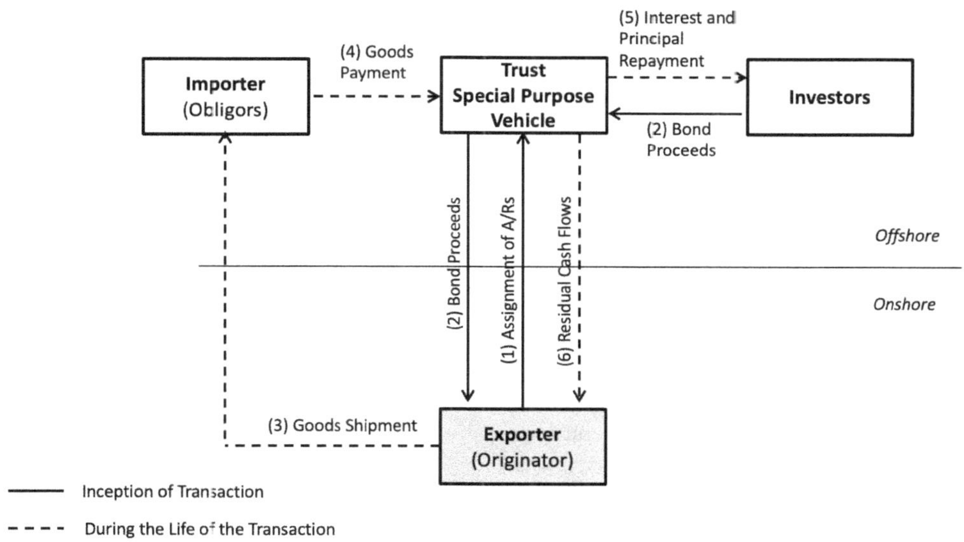

Exhibit 13.3. Basic future-flow securitization structure.

INTERNATIONAL CORPORATE FINANCE IN PRACTICE 13.6

The First Future-Flow Securitization: Telmex, 1987

In 1987, Citibank structured an innovative transaction for Telmex, then the monopoly phone company in Mexico. At the time, Mexico was restructuring its sovereign debt. International capital markets were essentially inaccessible to Mexican corporate debt issues. However, Telmex was able to issue investment-grade bonds via a securitization of its *future flows* of net international settlement receivables. These balances of net receivables arose when Telmex completed more calls for AT&T customers calling into Mexico than AT&T completed for Telmex customers calling from Mexico to the United States. Thus, Telmex was expected to be a consistent net exporter of telephone services to AT&T. Forecasting the magnitude of the exports was relatively easy given the market positions of AT&T and Telmex at the time. The crux of the financial innovation was to enable Telmex to capitalize its future flow of receivables through a Eurobond offering that was priced to reflect Telmex's ability to complete calls for AT&T and AT&T's ability to pay for these services.

Currency convertibility and *exchange rate risk* were mitigated by selling the dollar-denominated receivables to a US-domiciled trust and instructing AT&T to pay its Telmex invoices to the US-domiciled trust account. Because dollar-denominated Eurobonds were serviced by dollar-denominated receivables from AT&T and paid to a US-domiciled account, bondholders were not concerned by the risk of exchange controls that Mexico could impose or the risk of devaluation of the peso. The trust had become AT&T's new creditor with respect to the invoices owed to Telmex. Overcollateralization of the trust provided a layer of protection to the investors against variation in the value of Telmex's exports to AT&T. As the receivables liquidated and the notes issued by the trust amortized, the residual cash in the trust flowed back to Telmex. The basic structure of the transaction, which was designed by Citibank in 1987 has since been exploited by financial companies, mining companies, industrial companies, and other telecommunications companies. Fine points of each structure will differ due to differences in collateral, obligor risk, local and foreign laws, and the financial and operational characteristics of the originator.

Source: Adapted from Charles Austin Stone and Anne Zissu. 2001. "Engineering a Way Around the Sovereign Ceiling: Securities Backed by Future Flow Export Receivables," in *Financial Innovations and the Welfare of Nations*, edited by Laurent L. Jacque and P. Vaaler. Norwell, MA: Kluwer Academic Publishers.

GOVERNMENT-SPONSORED EXPORT CREDIT AGENCIES

Most countries have established some kind of government-sponsored agency such as the Export–Import Bank in the United States, Hermes in Germany, or Sinosure in China to provide subsidized trade financing to their national firms. Government assistance comes in several ways:

- Offering loans for specific international trade transactions to exporters at below-market rates, thereby enhancing their price competitiveness against foreign competitors.
- Providing financing to exporters when credit from normal commercial sources is simply not available because the transaction is deemed too risky.
- Providing loan guarantees to either the exporter or the importer to allow them to borrow at very favorable terms to fund the international trade deal (see International Corporate Finance in Practice 13.7).
- Providing insurance against credit risk, exchange rate risk, or country risk at preferential rates compared to commercial market sources or simply when no insurance is available commercially.

Such a subsidized form of export financing is ultimately paid for by the taxpayer on the grounds that such programs foster national employment and level the global playing field since most other exporting nations engage in similar free-trade-distorting practices. The rationale for such government assistance is rooted in *mercantilism* — an economic doctrine dating back to the 16th century that argues that the nation-state should maximize its export trade and minimize imports to generate a balance of payments surplus paid for in bullion (gold), thereby accumulating wealth.

SUMMARY

1. Exporters face three principal types of risks in selling to foreign entities: (1) credit risk or risk that the importer defaults on its payment obligations, (2) country risk or the risk that the importer's central bank authorities may hold up payments and thereby suspend its currency convertibility, and (3) currency risk or the risk of a loss due to devaluation of the foreign currency in which the sales invoice is denominated.
2. Documentary letters of credit allow the exporter to shift its credit risk exposure from an unknown foreign buyer to a better-known foreign bank that issues the letter of credit.
3. Confirmed letters of credit by the exporter's bank further insulate the exporter from its credit and country risk exposure to the importer's bank since a confirmed letter of credit is a claim against the exporter's domestic bank.
4. Small and medium-sized firms that do not have the in-house expertise to collect payments or to finance short-term export trade may subcontract those activities to export factors. Factoring is the

INTERNATIONAL CORPORATE FINANCE IN PRACTICE 13.7

Export–Import Bank Provides Largest Financing in History to Support US Solar Energy Exports

The Ex-Im Bank is providing loan guarantees amounting to a total of $573 million to Tempe (Arizona)-based First Solar Inc. for supporting exports to solar energy projects in Canada and India. In the case of Canada, the loan guarantees support for $455 million of commercial loans for the purchase of US-manufactured 40- and 50-megawatt (MW) solar-photovoltaic equipment to power electricity generation in the province of Ontario (Canada). The commercial loans have an 18 year repayment schedule and are backed by the sale of electricity to the Ontario Power Authority under multiple 20 year power purchase agreements. Similarly, the Ex-Im Bank is providing $75 million financing for First Solar exports of thin-film solar modules to the Indian Azure Power 5 MW solar project in the state of Rajasthan and similar projects in the state of Gujarat.

nonrecourse discounting of A/Rs concretized in promissory notes or trade acceptances.

5. Forfaiting is the medium-term equivalent of factoring. It is often associated with sales of capital equipment goods to foreign firms associated with significant credit and country risk.
6. Most industrialized nations provide some form of subsidies to their exporters in the form of (1) subsidized export credit, (2) loan guarantees to either the exporter or the importer to allow them to finance the export trade at favorable terms, and (3) insurance protection against country or currency risk.

QUESTIONS FOR DISCUSSION

1. What are the risks faced by exporters?
2. What is the relationship between credit and currency risk?
3. What is different about gauging the credit risk of a foreign buyer?
4. What are letters of credit? Distinguish between revocable and irrevocable letters of credit.
5. Explain how letters of credit are used for international trade financing purposes.
6. Why are confirmed letters of credit an effective hedge against country risk?
7. What is the nature of currency risk in international trade?
8. Identify the key documents accompanying an export transaction. Which specific functions do they perform?
9. What is the difference between a bank loan collateralized with A/Rs and factoring?
10. What is international leasing?
11. Explain why governments subsidize national exports.
12. Discuss the function performed by the bill of lading, commercial invoice, insurance certificate, and consular invoice.
13. Discuss the principal forms of government assistance provided by governments to their exporters.

PROBLEMS

1. **Cisco Systems' trade acceptances (A).** Cisco Systems (US) has sold to France-Telecom Internet servers for the amount of €10 million to be paid in three months. The transaction is secured by a trade acceptance from France-Telecom.
   a. What are the risk(s) faced by Cisco Systems?
   b. Explain what a trade acceptance is. How does it differ from a plain account receivable?
   c. Explain the different ways whereby Cisco Systems can hedge and finance this export transaction. The following conditions prevail when Cisco Systems is reviewing its different options:
      - Spot dollar price of one euro is 1.41.
      - Forward dollar price of one euro is 1.45.
      - Discount rate on trade acceptance are, respectively, 4% p.a. in euros and 6% p.a. in US dollars.

   d. Assume that Cisco Systems decides to ship the servers on open account to France-Telecom and to discount with recourse its receivables with Citibank at 5%. What additional risk (if any) is Cisco Systems assuming? France-Telecom is AAA-rated.
2. **Cisco Systems' trade acceptances (B).** Following a three month-long crippling strike, France-Telecom was downgraded to BBB.
   a. Should Cisco Systems reconsider its open account exports policy toward France-Telecom?
   b. Can Cisco Systems settle for a trade acceptance as outlined in problem 1, or should it require a bank acceptance proposed by Société Générale at an additional cost of 85 basis points?
   c. What is the all-in cost of relying on a bank acceptance rather than a trade acceptance?
3. **Cisco Systems' bank acceptances.** Cisco Systems has sold to Dhaka's municipal water and sewer company an integrated computer system to modernize its citywide billing procedure. The trade acceptance in the amount of US$5 million has been confirmed by Bangladesh's Commonwealth Commerce Bank (CCB). The transaction is secured by a letter of credit issued by CCB to Cisco Systems and confirmed by State Street Bank (US).
   a. Identify the different risks faced by Cisco Systems.

b. Explain the roles played by CCB and State Street Bank in mitigating these risks.
c. The trade acceptance can be discounted at 5% in addition to a fee of 1% of its face value. How much will Cisco Systems receive upon shipping the equipment? How much would Cisco Systems receive if it did not discount its trade acceptance?

4. **Bollywood Studio of India (BSI) exports to Cambodia (A).** BSI has sold to Cambodia's Angkor Wat Entertainment Inc. (CAWE) INR 10 million licensing rights to 10 of its recent films. Payment is due in six months. BSI can simply finance its exports by drawing on its credit line from the State Bank of India at the rate of 12% and purchase export credit insurance from the Ex-Im Bank of India at the cost of 175 basis points.
   a. What is/are the risk(s) faced by Bollywood Studio of India?
   b. What is the annualized percentage all-in cost of this method?
   c. Outline alternative export financing methods that BSI could consider. How do they mitigate the different risks faced by BSI?

5. **Bollywood Studio of India (BSI) exports to Cambodia (B).** BSI has been approached by a factor that offers to purchase the Angkor Wat Entertainment Inc. exports receivable at a 15% per annum discount plus a 150 basis points charge for a nonrecourse clause.
   a. What is the annualized percentage all-in cost of this factoring alternative?
   b. How does factoring compare to bank financing proposed in problem 4? Which method do you recommend? What is/are the risk(s) incurred by BSI under either method?

7. **Pemex's securitization of exports receivables.** By issuing US$500 million of BBB-rated future exports-backed securities through an offshore special purpose vehicle (SPV) domiciled in Luxembourg, Pemex was able to lower its cost of debt by 337.5 basis points as compared to direct unsecured international debt financing.
   a. Why are Pemex's exports-backed securities rated BBB when Pemex's international credit rating is a lower single B?
   b. Explain why securitization of its future oil exports receivables can help Pemex lower its cost of international debt.
   c. What are the assets being securitized? What is the role played by the SPV?
   d. What is/are the risk(s) faced by investors purchasing Pemex's future exports-backed securities?

INTERNET EXERCISES

8. **Exim Bank.** Log in to www.exim.gov and review the different programs that the US Exim Bank make available to US exporters. How do they compare to similar programs the French COFACE www.coface.com make available to French exporters.

9. **Foreign Trade Financing with Commercial Banks versus Exim Bank.** Access the website of a major international bank such as Citibank www.citibank.com or Bank of America www.bankofamerica.com and compare the trade financing services they offer with those offered by Exim Bank.

CASE STUDY 13.1. WARRICK PHARMACEUTICALS INC.

In May 2003, Warrick Pharmaceuticals Inc. (WPI) export manager and deputy international treasurer, Mr. Albert Brill was informed that accounts receivable in respect with shipments of pharmaceutical to Venezuela were overdue to the extent of over $3,000,000. Mr. Brill had been aware for a number of months of the deteriorating situation in the Venezuelan foreign exchange market and he considered that a review and appraisal of the situation was urgently called for (see Case Exhibit 13.1). Indeed the exchange market had now degenerated into a three-tiered system with the black market rate having plunged to Bolivars (VEB) 3300 to the dollar.

Warrick Pharmaceuticals Inc. — a Minneapolis based pharmaceutical company — had first entered the Venezuelan market in the early sixties supplying hospitals, pharmaceutical distributors and general importers with proprietary drugs and pharmaceutical products. The last 20 years had been an era of steady and expanding exports volume buoyed by the

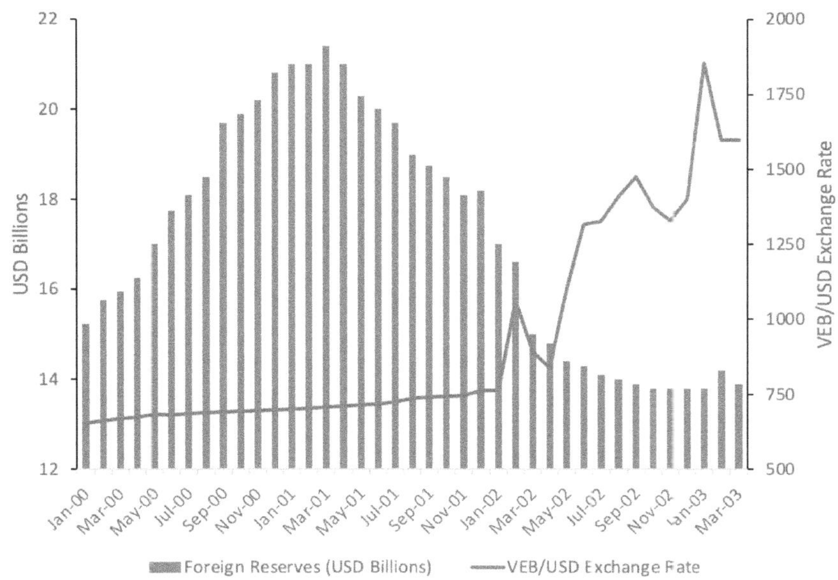

Case Exhibit 13.1. Venezuela's exchange rate and foreign reserves (2000–2003).

healthy state of the Venezuelan economy, to the point that Venezuela now accounted for nearly ten percent of WPI total export activities (but only two and a half percent of its total turnover). On the average WPI had been shipping monthly $600,000 worth of pharmaceutical to various distributors in Venezuela.

Because WPI was dealing with well established import houses and repeat orders, its usual practice was to draw a 90 day bill denominated in U.S dollars on the Venezuelan importers at the time of shipment and to send along with the export product the invoice, insurance certificate, bill of lading and consular invoice to the importer for acceptance. Most of the outstanding overdue bills were held by regional banks in Minnesota — primarily Wells Fargo — for collection with recourse to WPI and it seemed that the backlog of overdue accounts receivable were reaching such a level that additional bills may no longer be readily discounted.

Three tier foreign exchange market in Venezuela

Hugo Chavez's tenure as president of Venezuela had been tumultuous at best since his election in 1998. After repeated recalls, resignations, coups, and reappointments the political turmoil had taken its toll on the Venezuelan economy as a whole and its currency in particular. The short lived success of the anti-Chavez coup in 2001, and his nearly immediate return to office, had set the state for a retrenchment to his isolationist economic and financial policies.

On January 21, 2003, the Bolivar closed at a record low of VEB1891.50/$. The next day President Chavez suspended the sale of dollars for two weeks. Nearly instantaneously, an unofficial or black market for the exchange of Venezuelan Bolivars for foreign currencies (primarily US dollars) sprouted. As investors of all kinds sought ways to exit the Venezuelan market, or simply to obtain the hard currency needed to continue to conduct their businesses, the escalating capital flight caused the black market value of the Bolivar to plummet to VEB2500/$. As markets collapsed and exchange values fell, the Venezuelan inflation rate soared to more than 30% per annum.

Capital controls and CADIVI

To combat the downward pressures on the Bolivar, the Venezuelan government announced on February 5, 2003, the passage of the *2003 Exchange Regulations Decree*.

The decree took the following actions:

Set the official exchange rate at VEB1596/$ for purchase (bid) and VEB1600/$ for sale (offer).

Established the Comision de Administracion de Divisas (CADIVI) to control the distribution of foreign exchange. Request for foreign exchange related to imports transaction were classified in two categories: "preferential" with no advance deposit required and "non-preferential" with a 25% advanced deposit required at time of application. Pharmaceuticals were currently categorized as preferential along with food products, raw materials, equipment machinery and spare parts.

Implemented strict price controls to stem inflation triggered by the weaker bolivar and the exchange control-induced contraction of imports.

CADIVI was both the official means and the cheapest means by which Venezuelan citizens could obtain foreign currency. In order to receive an authorization from CADIVI to obtain dollars, an applicant was required to complete a series of forms. The applicant was then required to prove that they had paid taxes the previous three years provide proof of business and asset ownership and lease agreements for company property, and document current Social Security payments.

Unofficially, however, there was an additional unstated requirement for permission to obtain foreign currency — that authorizations by CADIVI would be reserved for Chavez supporters. In August 2003 an anti-Chavez petition had gained widespread circulation. One million signatures had been collected. Although the government ruled that the petition was invalid, it had used the list of signatures to create a database of names and Social Security Numbers that CADIVI utilized to cross-check identities when deciding who would receive hard currency. President Chavez was quoted as saying "Not one more dollar for the putschits, the bolivars belong to the people". In addition to the official process, through CADIVI, one could also obtain dollars through the *gray market*, or the *black market*.

The gray market: CANTV shares

In May 2003, three months following the implementation of the exchange controls, a window of opportunity had opened up for Venezuelans — an opportunity that allowed investors in the Caracas stock exchange to avoid the tight foreign exchange curbs. This loophole circumvented the government-imposed restrictions, by allowing investors to purchase local shares of the leading telecommunications company CANTV on the Caracas bourse, and then convert them into dollar-denominated American Depositary Receipts (ADRs) traded on the NYSE.

The Sponsor for CANTV ADRs on the NYSE was the Bank of New York, the leader in ADR sponsorship and management in the United States. The Bank of New York had suspended trading in CANTV ADRs in February after the passage of the exchange regulations decree, wishing to determine the legality of trading under the new Venezuelan currency controls. On May 26, after concluding that trading was indeed legal under the decree, the bank resumed trading in CANTV shares. CANTV's share price and trading volume soared in the following week.

The share price of CANTV quickly became the primary method of calculating the implicit gray market exchange rate. For example, CANTV shares closed at VEB7945/share on the Caracas bourse on May 26, 2003. That same day, CANTV ADRs closed in New York at $18.84/ADR. Each New York ADR was equal to seven shares of CANTV in Caracas.

The black market

A third method of obtaining hard currency by Venezuelans was through the rapidly expanding black market. The black market was, as is the case with black markets all over the world, essentially unseen and illegal. It was, however, quite sophisticated, using the services of a stockbroker or banker in Venezuela who simultaneously held US dollar accounts offshore. The choice of a black market broker was a critical one; in the event of a failure to complete the transaction properly there was no legal recourse.

If one wished to purchase dollars in the black market, he would deposit Bolivars in this broker's account in Venezuela. The agreed upon black market exchange rate was determined on the day of the deposit, and usually was within a 20% band of the gray market rate derived from the CANTV share price. One would then be given access to a dollar-denominated bank account outside of Venezuela in the agreed amount. The transaction took, on average, two business days to settle. The unofficial black market rate was VEB3300/$.

The export manager decision conundrum

As Mr. Brill was reviewing the deteriorating accounts receivable situation *vis-à-vis* Venezuela he was wondering about guidelines to be established for handling upcoming orders from Venezuela. Should a confirmed letter of credit be required of all new orders? Should distributors be asked to channel their payments through the gray or black market tiers of the exchange market? Should WPI suspend shipment until the backlog of overdue accounts receivable is resolved or should it consider local manufacturing in Venezuela (although WPI US manufacturing capacity had just been increased to serve expanding foreign markets)?

He was also concerned by the deteriorating competitive position of WPI products in Venezuela due in part to the increasing availability of locally manufactured substitutes. A state owned concern had recently signed a licensing agreement with the Japanese pharmaceutical company Fujisawa and a bilateral clearing agreement with China also resulted in cheaper alternatives to WPI well established brand name products. Other European competitors were enjoying subsidized exports financing which presumably allowed them to be paid promptly while offering generous payment terms to Venezuelan distributors.

CASE STUDY QUESTIONS

1. Define risk or risks in export transactions. Is WPI's policy of shipping on open account warranted?
2. Is WPI exposed to any of the above risks in its dealing with Venezuela? How could those risks be mitigated?
3. What is your outlook on the Venezuela foreign exchange situation?
4. Would a further devaluation of the Bolivar help WPI competitive position in Venezuela?
5. Would you advise Mr. Bril to use letter of credit for future WPI's exports to Venezuela. Detail the mechanics of such an approach. What would be its cost?

PART FOUR
Managing Foreign Exchange Risk

The exchange rate variable permeates all key financial management decisions and injects a considerable degree of variability into a firm's overall risk profile. Part Four starts by asking whether hedging a part or the totality of a firm's exposure to currency risk is indeed value-creating for the firm's owners and therefore warranted (Chapter 14). To the extent that exchange rate forecasting (Chapter 15) is indeed a treacherous activity in the context of clean floating exchange rates, we take a "total risk" view of risk management. Exporters/importers as well as multinational corporations and globally reaching financial institutions generally hedge their exposures to both transaction and translation exposure by using forwards, futures, options, or swaps. Measuring and managing transaction, translation and economic/operating exposures are discussed in Chapters 16, 17, and 18, respectively.

CHAPTER 14

The Case for Foreign Exchange Risk Management

It is part of wise men to preserve themselves today for tomorrow, and not risk all in one day.
Cervantes

The ever-increasing integration of the international economy, coupled with the heightened volatility of foreign exchange (FX or forex) rates, has elevated managing currency risk from a tactical, functional assignment to a *cross-functional* and truly *strategic* management responsibility. Indeed, since the demise of the Bretton Woods system of quasi-fixed exchange rates in 1973, the international monetary system has experienced exploding exchange rate volatility coupled with periods of prolonged over- or undershooting of currency values, which tends to wreak havoc on strategic plans when they are laid on shifting sands. As one author notes allegorically:

> *[I]n this era of floating exchange rates, no business in the industrial world may consider itself insulated from currency risk. For if business is a war without bullets, then that war is increasingly fought on a floating battlefield. Imagine an army that struggles mightily to take a hill only to find that the hill, overnight, has turned into a valley, and the plain, out of which the enemy had been beaten, is now the high ground. Currency is such a battleground. Every company may be such an army.*[1]

Indeed, managers who continue to ignore foreign exchange rate risk are a rapidly disappearing species! Simply put, foreign exchange risk management refers to the proactive management of currency exposures deemed to affect the firm's cash flows and stock price. Thus, its purpose is to increase the firm's value by stabilizing its cash-flow stream. Part Four of this book is about foreign exchange risk management, its *theory*, and *praxis* as understood from financial, managerial, and strategic perspectives. Accordingly, Part Four develops a risk-management framework and offers operational guidelines within which currency risk can be (1) consistently hedged across different risk situations and over time, (2) tightly integrated with other types of financial risk such as interest rate and commodity price risk, and (3) managed consistently with the firm's overall strategic plans so that the financial engineering dimensions of risk hedging are fully integrated with strategic management. (See International Corporate Finance in Practice 14.1 for how one management scholar sees foreign exchange risk management — not necessarily this author's view.)

Thus, the new imperative for the international treasurer is to involve himself or herself proactively with the strategic planning process so as to recognize early the impact of currency fluctuations on the firm's market share, profit margins, cash flows, and ultimately its value — a far cry from the more technical and mechanical task of hedging say yen-denominated account receivables, computing options premiums, or marking to market currency swaps. But first, we must define foreign exchange risk and make a case for managing it.

1 Millman (1990).

INTERNATIONAL CORPORATE FINANCE IN PRACTICE 14.1

Management Guru Peter Drucker's View of Foreign Exchange Risk Management

1. **Exchange rates are inherently unstable and will remain so.** Fixed exchange rates are not from Genesis. It must be accepted that governments mess with exchange rates.

2. **Predicting currency rates is a foolish game.** Talk and emotions often move exchange rates in unpredictable directions. Imponderables such as these make it dangerous to engage in rate-dependent financial maneuvers. In other words, you had better hedge.

3. **Not to hedge is to speculate.** Exchange rates are a cost of production that financial executives must manage. A multinational corporation (MNC) with 60% foreign sales had better sell forward this year's expected earnings.

4. **MNCs must take advantage of global markets.** Most MNCs still finance largely in one country. This is an increasingly dubious luxury. Managers should protect earnings by financing capital in the same currency.

5. **Finance managers cannot blame corporate losses on market volatility.** The company's business is not finance but making widgets. In the next violent currency fluctuation — and it will occur during the business life of everyone working today — many managers will find that corporate profits are down, say, 40% owing to foreign exchange. This will not be accepted, and the company will say, "You are paid to protect us from that."

Excerpted from keynote address by Peter Drucker, Chief Financial Officers Conference, sponsored by Business International, San Francisco, 1990.

DEFINING FOREIGN EXCHANGE RISK MANAGEMENT AND ITS OBJECTIVES

Risk is at the core of economic activity. Indeed, a firm becomes exposed to various kinds of risks in its quest to create a competitive advantage and ultimately value for its shareholders. However, *business* risk should be clearly distinguished from *financial* risk (of which foreign exchange rate risk is a major component), which can be hedged through appropriate market-traded instruments and techniques.

As a first approximation, foreign exchange risk can generally be defined as the additional variability experienced by a multinational corporation in its worldwide consolidated earnings due to unexpected currency fluctuations. By way of illustration, consider the 2024 earnings performance reported by a large U.S. multinational corporation — call it Omega — under the following three mutually exclusive scenarios (illustrated in Exhibit 14.1).

Under *situation 1*, characterized by stable exchange rates throughout the 2024 accounting period, Omega reports small variations in earnings per share. *Situation 2* relaxes the assumption of fixed exchange rates; that is, fluctuating exchange rates prevail over the accounting horizon. Omega now exhibits an *erratic* pattern in quarterly earnings, with attendant foreign exchange gains and losses. Finally, in *situation 3*, Omega is assumed to be conservatively managing its foreign exchange risk exposure, thus reporting a somewhat lower but definitely more stable (and rising) pattern of quarterly earnings. The significant earnings variability has been virtually eliminated at a substantial cost, namely, the cost of managing foreign exchange risk.

However, this focus on *accounting* values is increasingly challenged by a sounder emphasis on *economic* value, defined as the sum of future *free cash flows* discounted at the firm's cost of capital. Exchange risk should then be redefined as the *variance* component in the firm's overall free cash flows due to exchange rate volatility.

Exhibit 14.2 depicts the firm's value/pretax future free cash flows as a random variable whose variance captures its riskiness. Foreign exchange risk management aims at reducing the volatility of the firm's pretax cash flows — that is, lowering the variance of the probability distribution of the

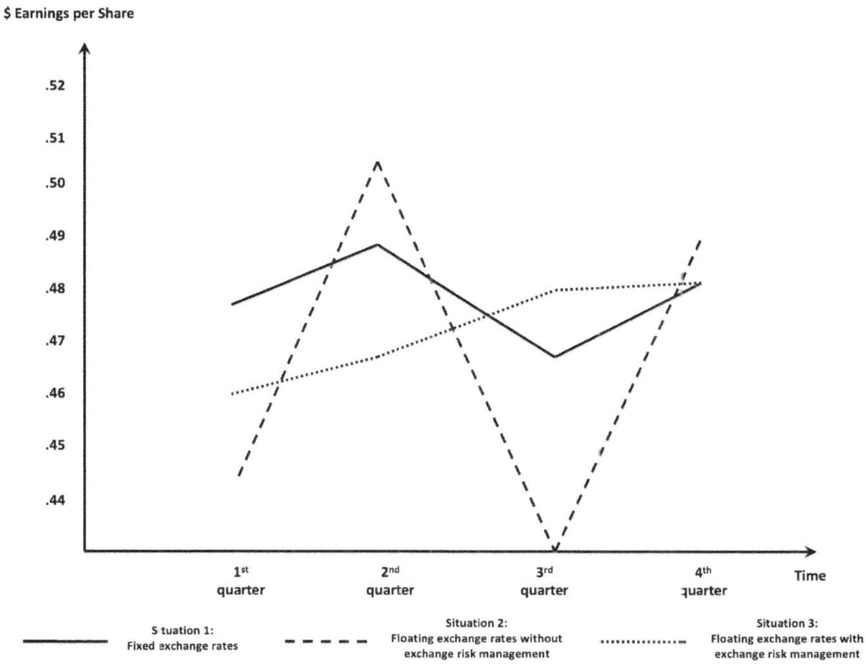

Exhibit 14.1. Omega's pattern of quarterly earnings.

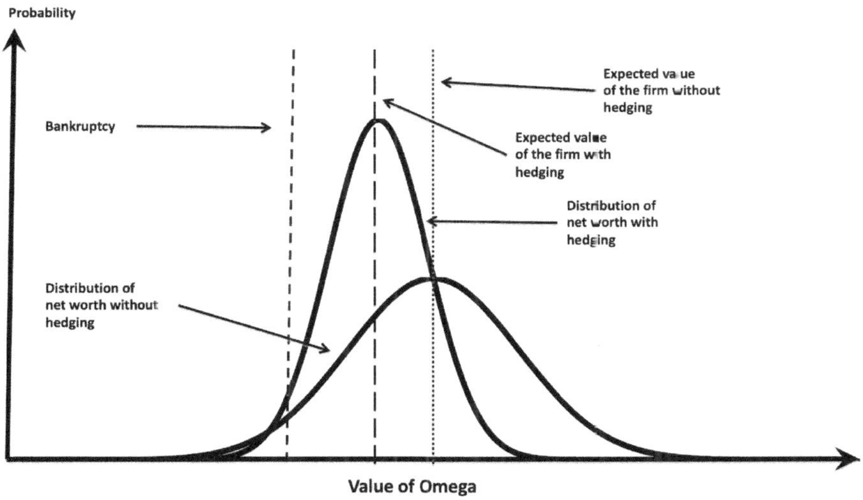

Exhibit 14.2. Omega's lower variance of net worth with hedging.

firm's value. This is generally achieved by creating cash-flow positions via borrowing and lending in foreign currency or through currency derivative contracts whose rise or fall in value — due to currency fluctuations — offsets the firm's underlying fall or rise in value due to those same currency fluctuations. Admittedly, reducing the firm's riskiness, however, is achieved only at the cost of hedging shown in Exhibit 14.2 as an inward shift of the firm's mean value accompanied by a tighter variance around the mean (see International Corporate Finance in Practice 14.2).

INTERNATIONAL CORPORATE FINANCE IN PRACTICE 14.2

What Is the Cost of Hedging?

When purchasing a currency option, it is easy to record the up-front cash-flow premium as the cost of hedging. Similarly, discounts on forwards or futures may seem reasonable measures of the cost of hedging. This is, however, a misleading approximation because the true cost of hedging is not known until the derivative contract matures, at which point its actual cost may turn out to be a cash-flow gain rather than loss or profit rather than cost. Thus, the accounting view of hedging as being a known *ex ante* cost — shown as a shift to the left in Exhibit 14.2 of the hedged value of the firm — though widely held — should be revisited in a cash-flow valuation perspective, because hedging may result in a shift to the right (windfall gain). More generally, derivative products are priced as the present value of future positive and negative cash flows and as such do not have a cost (zero present value).

But could it be that by *stabilizing cash flows*, hedging has a net positive — not negative — impact on the firm's pretax cash flows? And could it be that by stabilizing its cash flows (now deemed less volatile by investors) and therefore improving the firm's risk profile, hedging *reduces the firm's cost of capital* and enhances its ability to implement strategic plans now predicated on more dependable future cash flows?

CAN HEDGING CURRENCY RISK INCREASE THE VALUE OF THE FIRM?[2]

Hedging currency risk is warranted if it can be shown to increase the firm's value. Since the firm's value is equal to future cash flows discounted at the appropriate risk-adjusted cost of capital, value enhancement comes from either increased free cash flows, FCF(t) (numerator), or a decreased weighted average cost of capital (WACC) (denominator):

$$\text{Value of the firm} = \sum_{t=1}^{T} \frac{\text{FCF}(t)}{(1+\text{WACC})^t}$$

Hedging increases the firm's value by increasing the firm's net cash flows

Such benefits are generally attributed to a lower probability of bankruptcy and financial distress, decreased taxes, and lower agency costs.

Hedging adds value by reducing the cost of financial distress. Hedging currency risk aims to curb the volatility of the firm's free cash flows and therefore reduces the probability of the firm going bankrupt, with all the *direct* costs that it entails (lawyers' fees, bankruptcy proceedings, and reorganization). Bankruptcy or default arises from the firm's inability to cover its fixed costs, such as interest expenses. Hedging, by reducing the variance of the firm's cash flows, increases the likelihood that the firm will meet its debt service obligations necessary to continue operating. This is especially true of highly leveraged firms.

There are also important *indirect* costs associated with a high probability of default. Financial distress impacts all the firms' stakeholders — customers, suppliers, employees, and lenders — not only its shareholders. When bankruptcy looms large on its horizon, a firm may find it difficult to sell its products, thereby incurring lower revenues and further compounding its chances of default. This is especially true of firms selling quality products for which after-sales service is important, as customers may not be able to exercise their warranties against a bankrupt firm. In a similar vein, firms approaching bankruptcy may find it difficult to retain employees or to source materials from suppliers and may end up incurring higher costs as a result. Similarly, procuring capital becomes more expensive as lenders require a hefty risk premium to protect themselves against the borrower's "junk" credit status. Debt covenants can trigger a loan recall when the firm's income falls below a threshold and accounting ratios are violated. Refinancing can be difficult and costly. Here again, hedging currency risks reduces income volatility, enhances the firm's credit status, and reduces the likelihood of rating downgrades or that debt covenants will be triggered.

2 The argument presented in this section would also apply to hedging commodity price risks as in the case of oil or gas companies and interest rate risks as in the case of financial institutions.

Hedging adds value by decreasing taxes. If the firm faces a *linear* tax schedule, it pays a set percentage of its taxable income in taxes regardless of its income, and hedging does not matter. However, if the firm faces a *convex* tax schedule reflecting tax progressivity — a higher level of taxable income means a higher percentage of taxable income is paid in taxes — hedging can reduce taxes. Erratic taxable income before hedging means that some years the firm will earn a low income or incur a loss and be subject to a lower effective tax rate, and some years it will earn a higher income taxed at a higher rate (see International Corporate Finance in Practice 14.3). On average, the firm pays an effective tax rate as if it were facing a linear tax schedule. By hedging, the firm stabilizes its average income at a midpoint between the low- and high-income points (when the firm does not hedge) and therefore faces an effective tax rate that is lower due to the convexity of the tax schedule. Most countries, however, have a flat corporate income tax rate — for example, 21% in the United States — which translates into a linear, not convex, tax schedule. Nevertheless, *tax preference items* such as tax loss carryforwards, investment tax credits, and minimum alternative taxes do account for significant convexity of the effective tax schedules faced by most firms, which are always motivated to use the most valuable tax preference items first.

Hedging adds value by reducing agency costs between shareholders and managers. Managers are supposed to act as agents of the firm's shareholders, who are interested in the maximization of their wealth. However, managers through their wages, bonuses, and stock option plans have a great share of their wealth dependent on the firm's performance and survival. As relatively undiversified shareholders who cannot easily hedge their wealth individually, they naturally favor corporate hedging. Should the firm decide as a matter of policy against hedging currency risk, managers will resort to their second line of defense, which is to shun high-value-creating investment opportunities that they deem very risky. Since shareholders do not have direct information about the firm's investment opportunities, there is not much they can do to correct such a misalignment of incentives between diversified, less risk-averse shareholders and undiversified, more risk-averse managers. Hedging gives managers peace of mind, allowing them to pursue value-creating investment opportunities that they might otherwise shun.

Hedging increases the firm's value by decreasing the firm's cost of capital

Future cash flows are discounted at the firm's weighted average cost of capital (WACC), defined as

$$\text{WACC} = \frac{D}{D+E} k_D (1 - \text{Tax}) + \frac{E}{D+E} k_E$$

where the firm's after-tax cost of debt $k_D(1 - \text{Tax})$ and its cost of equity k_E are respectively weighted by percentages of debt $D/(D+E)$ and equity $E/(D+E)$ financing. D and E are market value of the firm's outstanding debt (D) and equity (E).

INTERNATIONAL CORPORATE FINANCE IN PRACTICE 14.3

Reducing Taxes with Risk Management

Consider the firm Omega exposed to currency risk: Its pretax income is volatile. Assume that in the absence of hedging, its pretax income I is low in year 1, $I(1)$, and high in year 2, $I(2)$ (see Exhibit 14.3). It pays corporate income tax at the corresponding tax rates: $T(1)$ the first year and $T(2)$ the second year. Its effective tax rate for the two years is the average of taxes on unhedged income $T(U) = [T(1) + T(2)]/2$ or the midpoint on the straight line connecting $T(1)$ and $T(2)$ on the graph as if Omega were facing a *linear* tax schedule. If indeed Omega faces a *convex* tax schedule (curved on the graph), hedging currency risk can help. By eliminating (or greatly reducing) its income volatility, Omega's hedging stabilizes its income in both year 1 and year 2 at (or close to) its average for the two years: $I(H) = [I(1) + I(2)]/2$. At this average income, however, Omega faces a lower tax rate $T(H)$ on the curved schedule due to its convexity. Hedging currency risk thus saves Omega the following amount of tax:

$$\text{Tax savings} = (\text{Pretax income})(\text{Tax rate}_{\text{Unhedged/linear}} - \text{Tax rate}_{\text{Hedged/convex}})$$

$$\text{Tax savings} = [I(1) + I(2)]/2 \times [\text{T(U)} - \text{T(H)}]$$

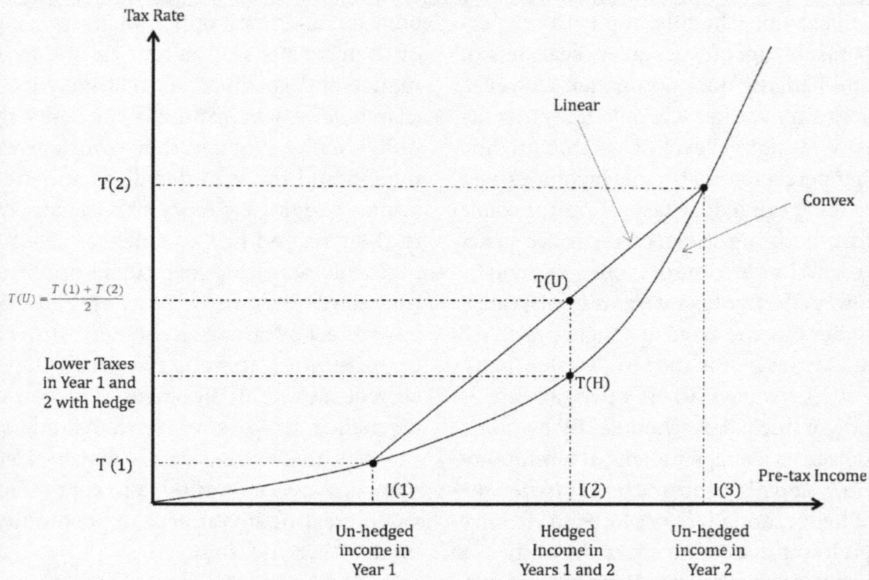

Exhibit 14.3. Omega's taxes with and without hedging, years 1 and 2.
Source: Adapted from Smithson *et al.* (1995, pp. 103–105).

Our earlier discussion has already established that hedging should credit-enhance the firm's risk profile by reducing the likelihood that debt covenants would be breached, which enables it to access debt financing at a lesser cost. The impact of currency hedging on the firm's equity cost of capital is less clear: Although a smoother stream of earnings should presumably result in a lower cost of equity, modern finance theory would argue that the firm's beta should remain unchanged since currency risk is diversifiable. In sum, a lower cost of debt combined with an unchanged cost of equity does amount to a lower weighted average cost of capital. Enhanced free cash flows discounted at a lower cost of capital do boost the firm's market value. Currency hedging is indeed value-creating.

WHEN IS HEDGING CURRENCY RISK IRRELEVANT?

And yet several arguments are often made against corporate hedging of currency risk. They are rooted in modern capital market theory, which defines foreign exchange risk as the *unsystematic* or *diversifiable* risk associated with a foreign currency-denominated revenue (or cost) stream. Modern capital market theory argues that under certain assumptions of market efficiency, foreign exchange risk management is totally superfluous. In this somewhat hypothetical world, the treasurers of multinational corporations abdicate the initiative of foreign exchange risk management to the shareholders, who, in turn, manage the unsystematic portion of exchange rate risk through efficient portfolio diversification. More specifically, we have the following:

- *Argument*: Shareholders are capable of diversifying currency risk better than managers. Indeed, shareholders, by holding an internationally diversified portfolio, are able to lay off this risk more cheaply than the firm itself. After all, shareholders could very well reduce the stock price volatility by holding part of their portfolio in the stocks of other multinational corporations that do business only in certain foreign countries.

  Rebuttal: Because individual investors face exchange controls, high transaction and information costs, multinational corporations can better reduce the burden of such market imperfections and segmentation than individual investors, since they are superiorly equipped to carry out currency diversification and to assume the responsibility of exchange risk management on behalf of their shareholders. For proprietorships, partnerships, and closely held corporations, whose owners are relatively undiversified and presumably risk-averse, the case for foreign exchange risk management is even more compelling. Similarly, firms that are highly leveraged will pursue conservative hedging to avoid surprises that may push them into bankruptcy.

- *Argument*: Hedging currency risk is costly and lowers the expected value of future cash flows (see inward shift of the mean value of probability distribution on Exhibit 14.2). It is not clear that lower cash-flow volatility reduces the cost of capital enough to compensate for the cost of hedging.

  Rebuttal: Hedging costs are not necessarily positive; for example, currency forward rates may be at a premium rather than at a discount. Furthermore, hedging boosts cash flows by reducing bankruptcy costs, taxes, and frictions between managers and shareholders. A less volatile income stream due to hedging reduces the firm's cost of debt and therefore its cost of capital.
- *Argument*: Managers cannot beat the market. In efficient markets, where forward rates are unbiased predictors of future spot exchange rates, hedging currency is at best a zero net present value (NPV) proposition.

  Rebuttal: In the real world, currency markets are often in temporary disequilibrium, with exchange rates prone to long-lasting periods of over- or undervaluation. Managers are in a far better position than shareholders to identify such disequilibrium situations and to take advantage of them through selective hedging. This may be — for example — the case of large and non-recurring currency exposure arising of a large exports contract or a cross-border acquisition.

FROM HEDGING TO MANAGING CURRENCY RISK

All too often, currency hedging is associated with surgical strikes aimed at neutralizing exposure to foreign exchange risk through a forward contract, a currency swap, or some fancy currency derivatives. And indeed, these are critical building blocks of any foreign exchange risk management (FERM) program. Currency hedging, however, is best embedded in a year-round and year-in, year-out management process, which is far more than the case-by-case use of derivative instruments to neutralize specific transactions, translations, or economic exposures. Such a process would typically incorporate the following steps. (See Exhibit 14.4 and International Corporate Finance in Practice 14.4.)

Steps 1 and 2 are the preliminary steps of (1) defining the firm's attitude toward risk and (2) establishing objectives that are congruent with the firm's risk aversion. These are indeed treacherous steps, as they require systematic introspection on the part of the firm's senior managers as well as consistency in dealing with different types of risk, whether it is exchange risk, interest rate risk, commodity price risk, or general liability risk. For example, aiming to keep free cash-flow volatility below a standard deviation of 10% with a probability of 95% would be consistent with a high level of risk aversion.

Step 3 focuses on the quintessential question of knowing *what is at risk*. Typically, firms are exposed to (1) *transaction exposure* arising from foreign currency-denominated and time-deferred contracts materializing exports, imports, or debt; (2) *translation exposures* resulting from the periodic consolidation of foreign subsidiaries' financial statements; and (3) *economic exposure* due to the sensitivity of the firm's value to unexpected exchange rate changes.

Step 4 requires forecasts of future exchange rates. Since currency forecasts are to be used for risk management purposes, they should be formulated in probabilistic terms — as a properly defined random variable — rather than as point estimates. Our pessimistic conclusion with respect to forecasters' ability to generate reliable forecasts is one of the rationales for foreign exchange risk management: To the extent that we cannot forecast exchange rates with great accuracy, it becomes imperative to manage exposure to foreign exchange risk.

Step 5 defines the *optimal* percentage of currency exposure consistent with the firm's degree of risk aversion to be routinely hedged through appropriate derivatives or hedging techniques. The firm commits to a policy of *selective hedging* rather than exhaustive hedging of all exposures all the time, which is characteristic of risk-paranoid firms.

Step 6 identifies alternative hedging policies and compares their costs as well as their impacts on pro forma budgets under multiple exchange rate scenarios.

Step 7 incorporates the FERM in the control process of foreign operations. In evaluating foreign operations and their managers, due consideration to hedging decisions needs to be incorporated into the monitoring process.

Step 8 closes the loop. To what extent have the FERM objectives set at the outset of the cycle been met? Simple variance analysis between *ex ante* objectives and actual *ex post* results should result in some soul-searching by managers and possibly lead to a recalibration of FERM objectives.

INTERNATIONAL CORPORATE FINANCE IN PRACTICE 14.4

Hedging at Porsche.[3] Best known for its performance sports cars Porsche also proved to be a savvy risk manager. At the company's annual press conference on November 28, 2008, Porsche reported a healthy €1 billion in operating profit (on a sales revenue of € 7.2 billion) with a hefty profit margin of 25%. It also reported foreign exchange gains of € 250 million — most of which were derived from large trades in US dollar put options which had benefited from the US dollar weakness. With a third of its revenues derived from exports sales to the US and a euro-denominated manufacturing base anchored mostly to Germany, Porsche had to weather a structural imbalance between dollar sales revenue and euro-denominated costs. Porsche had learnt the hard way that unchecked currency exposure could lead to bankruptcy; indeed, in the early 1990s, Porsche had faced the combined damages of a severe recession in the United States and Germany aggravated by a weak dollar with sales plummeting from 50,000 cars down to 14,000!

Porsche's hedging policy was built on an extensive portfolio of dollar put options; its notional value amounted to € 12 billion corresponding approximately to the company's three-year projected sales outside the eurozone. Put options were purchased *at the money* — that is their strike price was equal to the exchange rate prevailing at the time of purchase. In effect, the put options allowed Porsche — should the dollar depreciate — to lock in a floor exchange rate at which dollar sales revenue would be converted back into euros while keeping open the possibility of an appreciating dollar. For example, if on July 1, 2007, Porsche purchased one year dollar put options at the strike price of € 0.80 = $1 in the amount of $ 4 billion, one year later — assuming the dollar had weakened to € 0.70 — Porsche would exercise the put option: It would sell dollars at € 0.80 = $1 which it would purchase at the spot rate of € 0.70 thus netting € 0.10 per dollar or a profit of $4 billion × [0.80 – 0.70] = €40 million. This exchange gain would be added to the spot euro value of sales or $4 billion × 0.70 = € 2.8 billion. Conversely, had the dollar appreciated to 0.90 over the one-year exposure horizon, Porsche would simply walk away from its put option contract and repatriate its $4 billion sales revenue at the rate of € 0.90 for a total euro revenue of € 3.6 billion.[4]

Porsche was clearly focusing on its dollar asset *transaction* exposure rather than its *economic* exposure. Indeed, at about the same time, Porsche's key competitors Daimler-Benz and BMW steered away from transaction exposure management via derivatives to embark on ambitious foreign direct investment strategies building assembly operations in the US and thereby creating a *natural* hedge against their dollar-denominated revenues. Porsche — largely owned and fully controlled by the families Piech and Porsche — was very *risk-averse* but not quite *risk-paranoid* since it left itself open to upside potential foreign exchange gains while locking itself out of its downside risk exposure. It did, however, hedge 100% of its transaction exposure and did so three years out purchasing dollar put options at the money rather than selling forward dollar revenues for euro.

3 This illustration is drawn from Stephan Nagel case study "Hedging at Porsche" (WDI publishing — a division of the William Davidson Institute at the University of Michigan, 2014).

4 The reader will recall that a small upfront cash option premium would have been paid at the time of purchasing the put options.

Exhibit 14.4. The foreign exchange risk management process.

Step 1	Identify firm's attitude toward risk: Is management risk-paranoid or simply risk-averse?
Step 2	Establish objectives for foreign exchange risk management (FERM) — risk locking versus risk smoothing — and define appropriate performance indexes.
Step 3	Measure exposure to foreign exchange risk (on a rolling basis): accounting transaction and translation versus cash-flow economic/operating exposure. How does the firm compare with its key rivals?
Step 4	Identify currencies that are grossly over- or undervalued. Generate forecast for each currency in probabilistic terms. Forecasts should be continuously updated.
Step 5	Set optimal percentage of exposure to be hedged (as a function of firm's attitude to foreign exchange risk). Simulate pro forma budgets under multiple scenarios to gauge in probabilistic terms cash flow at risk. Measure also the impact of worst exchange rate scenarios on key performance indexes.
Step 6	Compare costs and benefits of applying different currency instruments and techniques. Set internal guidelines governing the use of currency derivatives for hedging purposes.
Step 7	Incorporate hedging policies in the performance evaluation system in setting budget and tracking performance.
Step 8	Compare results of FERM policies with FERM objectives. Variance analysis leads to recalibration of FERM objectives.

THE BUILDING BLOCKS OF FOREIGN EXCHANGE RISK MANAGEMENT

Chapters 15–18 of Part Four discuss in depth the following building blocks of currency hedging.

Forecasting foreign exchange rates

Chapter 15 provides a framework for generating foreign exchange rate forecasts. It explores the perplexing issues of forecasting *floating* exchange rates. *Market-based* forecasts are contrasted with *model-based* forecasts in an attempt to answer the ever-elusive question: "Can managers beat the forex market?" The somewhat different problem of forecasting *pegged yet adjustable* exchange rates is tackled in the appendix to Chapter 15, where a four-step forecasting framework, based on the estimation of macroeconomic indicators, is introduced. Our pessimistic conclusion with respect to forecasters' ability to generate reliable forecasts is one of the rationales for foreign exchange risk management: To the extent that we cannot forecast exchange rates with great accuracy, it becomes imperative to manage exposure to foreign exchange risk, which requires the firm to take stock of its exposure to currency risk.

Managing transaction exposure

Transaction exposure results from time-deferred foreign currency-denominated contracts, which materialize imports, exports, or international financing transactions. Changing exchange rate relationships over the life of the contract will result in windfall cash-flow gains or losses at the time of payment. More complex are transaction exposures resulting from international bids or transnational acquisitions fraught with uncertainty about their timing or magnitude. Indeed, bids on foreign projects may be lost, and transnational acquisitions may be blocked or delayed by host governments. How to eliminate or, as a second-best option, mitigate cash-flow losses that may result from transaction exposure to foreign exchange risk is described in Chapter 16. The cases of short- versus medium- or long-term contracts denominated in both convertible and inconvertible currencies are examined separately. The chapter systematically introduces the use of currency options and swaps. Throughout Chapter 16, decision rules are formulated algebraically to enable the decision maker to simulate, under alternative future spot exchange rates (break-even analysis), the relative cost of hedging versus not hedging currency risk.

Managing translation exposure

By contrast, *translation exposures* stem from the practice of consolidating foreign subsidiaries' financial statements with those of their parents. Such consolidation results in *unrealized* accounting gains or losses, as foreign currencies move up and down *vis-à-vis* the reference currency during the accounting period,[5] which may severely disrupt the steadiness of multinational corporations' foreign income streams. Even though no cash-flow losses are incurred, consolidated accounting income may exhibit erratic trends that will in turn affect the corporation's overall risk profile as perceived by its shareholders and the investment community at large. Chapter 17 shows how the accounting income of multinational corporations' foreign operations can be smoothed by combining a strategy of selective hedging through the forward market with adequate manipulation of translation exposures by local borrowing or leading/lagging intra-corporate payments. Later, Chapter 25 explores how currency risk can distort the performance-evaluation process of foreign subsidiaries by their parents. It constructs a *value-based contingent budgeting* model that builds on the concept of economic exposure and aligns shareholders' quest for wealth maximization with exchange-rate-dependent operating decisions by managers.

Managing economic/operating exposure

Accounting concepts of exposure to foreign exchange risk fail to incorporate the longer-term impact of exchange rate changes on the value of the multinational corporation. Chapter 18 sketches the link between the firm's value and exchange rates by tracing the impact of the inflation/devaluation cycle on the firm's cash flows. Its economic/operating exposure to foreign exchange risk primarily depends on (1) the *destination of its output* (i.e., export market vs. domestic market), as well as the *origin of its inputs* (imported vs. domestically sourced), and (2) the *pricing* response to the inflation/devaluation cycle by its key competitors.

The benefits of hedging are confirmed by the widespread practice of multinational corporations that selectively manage foreign exchange risk because they presume its benefits outweigh its costs (see the appendix to this chapter). That such costs are justified further presumes that corporate treasurers should be concerned — up to a point — with the smooth period-to-period earnings pattern so cherished by securities analysts. Without hedging, a volatile earnings stream can affect a firm's stock price and, in turn, by depressing its price-earnings ratio, can reduce its ability to raise funds at a reasonable cost, fend off hostile takeovers, or implement effectively a merger/acquisition strategy through a stock swap. Indeed, the readily established link between the variability of corporate earnings and the value of the firm justifies the moderate allocation of (scarce) cash resources to the hedging of exchange risk.

5 The reference currency is the common numéraire in which multinational corporations' financial statements are disclosed. U.S. multinational corporations naturally use the U.S. dollar as their reference currency; similarly, Swiss multinational corporations would use the Swiss franc as their reference currency, and so on.

SUMMARY

1. Exchange risk is defined as the *variance* component in the firm's overall free cash flows due to exchange rate volatility. Foreign exchange risk management (FERM) aims at reducing the volatility of the firm's pretax cash flows — that is, lowering the variance of the probability distribution of the firm's value. This is generally achieved by creating cash-flow positions through borrowing and lending in foreign currency or through currency derivative contracts whose rise or fall in value due to currency fluctuations offset the firm's underlying fall or rise in value resulting from those same currency fluctuations.
2. By stabilizing cash flows, currency hedging increases the firm's value by boosting its future free cash flows and reducing the cost of capital at which they are discounted. Increased cash flows induced by currency hedging are due to (1) lower operating and financial costs associated with a reduced likelihood of bankruptcy, (2) tax savings provided that the firm faces a convex tax schedule, and (3) reduced agency costs whereby risk-averse managers would not underinvest or shun positive NPV opportunities even if they are risky investments.
3. Currency hedging is much more than the use of currency derivatives to hedge case-by-case transactions, translations, or economic exposures. It is best embedded in a year-round and year-in, year-out multiple-step *management process* that includes most notably the setting of FERM objectives, measurement of what is at risk, generation of probability currency forecasts, cost comparison of alternative hedging policies, assessment of how they impact pro forma budgets, and variance analysis of FERM *ex post* results against *ex ante* objectives.

QUESTIONS FOR DISCUSSION

1. What is foreign exchange risk?
2. How does the firm's level of risk aversion impact its propensity to hedge currency risk?
3. What is the rationale for hedging currency risk?
4. Why is hedging value-creating?
5. Which types of firms are the best candidates for hedging currency risk?
6. Under what assumptions is hedging currency risk redundant?
7. What are the principal steps of the foreign exchange risk management process?

REFERENCES

Adler, M. and Dumas, B. 1983. International portfolio choice and corporate finance: A synthesis. *Journal of Finance* 38:925–984.

Allayanis, G. and Weston, J. P. 2001. The use of foreign currency derivatives and firm value. *Review of Financial Studies* 14 (Spring):243–276.

Bodnar, G., Giambona, E., Graham, J., and Harvey, C. 2019. A view inside corporate risk management. *Management Science* 65(November).

Davis, H. A. and Militello Jr., F. C. 1995. Foreign exchange risk management: A survey of corporate practices. *Financial Executives Research Report* 2(1) (January):1–3.

Froot, K. A., Scharfstein, D. S., and Stein, J. 1993. Risk management: Coordinating corporate investment and financing policies. *Journal of Finance* 48(5) (December):1629–1658.

Giambona, E., John, G., Harvey, C., and Bodnar, G. The theory and practice of foreign exchange risk management: Evidence from the field. *Financial Management* 783–832.

Jacque, L. L. 1981. Management of foreign exchange risk: A review article. *Journal of International Business Studies* 12(1) (Spring/Summer):81–101.

Jesswein, K., Kwok, C. C. Y., and Folks Jr., W. R. 1995. What new currency risk products are companies using and why? *Journal of Applied Corporate Finance* 8(3) (Fall):103–114.

Jin, Y. and Jorion, P. 2006. Firm value and hedging: Evidence from US gas and oil producers. *Journal of Finance* 61 (April): 893–919.

Millman, G. J. 1990. *The Floating Battlefield: Corporate Strategies in the Currency Wars.* New York: AMACOM, pp. 3–4.

Smithson, C. W., Smith Jr. C. W., and Wilford, D. S. 1995. *Managing Financial Risk.* Chicago: Irwin.

APPENDIX 14A: FOREIGN EXCHANGE RISK MANAGEMENT: WHAT DO FIRMS DO?[6]

- Firms continue to emphasize unduly the management of accounting exposures — not necessarily congruent with cash-flow-based value creation — simply because management compensation systems are heavily biased toward accounting results.
- While operating within the accounting model in daily exposure management, most managers understand that the accounting model does not capture the economic and competitive impacts that foreign exchange gains and losses have on their companies.
- Senior management is becoming aware of the complexity of exposures and the need to understand how they are managed, due to recent incidents involving the use of derivatives. In leading companies, treasury departments are working with management to define business and financial risks, to decide which of those risks the company is in the business of taking and which it wants to hedge, to decide where on the risk spectrum the company wants to be, to design hedging programs to fit the company's risk tolerance, and to define benchmarks to measure and control the hedging program.
- The two most widely used financial hedging tools are forward exchange contracts and over-the-counter options. Forward exchange contracts are used for hedging booked transaction exposures, while options are used extensively for committed off-balance-sheet transactions. Few companies are active in the futures market.
- More recently, the corporate practice of foreign exchange exposure management has become more systematic and less driven by day-to-day currency movements. The development of relatively inexpensive computer power has spurred the development of increasingly complex derivative financial instruments, technical currency rate

6 Abridged from Davis and Militello (1995).

trend analysis, and systems that help corporations identify exposures, simulate alternative exposure scenarios and hedging strategies, execute hedging transactions, and manage portfolios of hedging instruments.

- Foreign exchange risk management, interest rate risk management, and commodity risk management are becoming integrated because the hedging instruments are similar and the same personnel in the company have expertise in using them.

CASE STUDY 14.1. BIO-OILS ENERGY S.L

> *The use of vegetable oils for engine fuels may seem insignificant today but such oils may become, in the course of time, as important as petroleum and the coal-tar products of the present time.*
>
> — Rudolf Diesel, 1912

Christoph Schmid was sitting in his home office finishing reading a report on biofuels issued by the European Commission. He had found that report surfing on the Internet looking for interesting ideas to build up a new business. Just two months earlier, in November 2004, he had left his last venture, Jazztel plc, as one of the five founding partners and CFO. Jazztel today is one of the largest telecom operators in Spain. It reaches annual revenues in excess of €400 million and is listed on the Spanish stock exchange. After crunching a few numbers on potential biodiesel economics that he extracted from the report, he gave a call to Antonio Carro, his former partner and CEO of Jazztel. Christoph thought that, in the context of rapidly escalating oil prices and heightened concern about global warming, much attention will finally be redirected to renewable sources of energy such as wind power, solar power, and biofuels to create an enormous business opportunity. Antonio was thrilled about the idea, and they started immediately to work and to identify key drivers of the biodiesel business.

The promise of biofuels

Biofuels are renewable sources of energy that are alternatives to fossil fuels. Bio-ethanol is made from sugar cane, corn, wheat, or biomass and is a substitute for gasoline or can be readily blended with gasoline. Biodiesel is made from vegetable oils such as rapeseed, soybean, or palm oil and is a substitute for or can be readily blended with fossil diesel fuel.

Biofuels offer two key advantages in a carbon-constrained world: First, they reduce dependency on fossil fuels, which from resource and geostrategic perspectives is a major plus. Second, they contribute to reducing greenhouse gas emissions and other toxic elements like sulfur in the case of biodiesel. However, biofuels cost considerably more than fossil fuels and couldn't get off the ground if it weren't for generous tax subsidies. Prospects for biodiesels in Europe seemed particularly auspicious, with rising diesel consumption and favorable regulation earmarked by EU energy policy aimed at a non-mandatory blending target for biofuels set at 5.75% by 2010.

European Union member countries are given flexibility in meeting this target by implementing their own specific tax-incentive schemes — in effect subsidizing energy security by forgoing tax revenue. Germany has taken the lead in spurring biofuels by offering the most generous tax incentives in the EU; in 2005, it accounted for 50% of EU total supply of biofuels. However, it is expected that the EU will over time transition to a mandatory blending rate expected to reach 10% by 2020 while progressively reducing tax incentives. At current market prices, the European biodiesel industry was expected to increase from less than €2.5 billion to between €15 and €17 billion by 2010.

The project

The strategic challenge of successfully entering the biodiesel business was to choose a scale of operation that would guarantee cost competitiveness while securing a geographical location that in turn would facilitate the securing of an off-take sales contract. This was achieved ultimately after close to two years of protracted negotiation by securing a long-term lease from Cepsa, the second-largest Spanish oil company, for 30 hectares strategically located adjacent to the Cepsa-Huelva hydrocarbon refinery on the southern Atlantic coast of Spain close to the border with Portugal. Cepsa also signed an off-take agreement for a substantial share of total planned production capacity of 250,000 metric tons annually. The biodiesel produced by this new plant was to be blended with the fossil biodiesel currently produced at the Huelva refinery in accordance with EU and Spanish directives.

Needless to say, the strategic relationship with Cepsa would become the cornerstone of the entire project, as this off-take contract combined with an optimal geographical location contiguous to the core customer would enable the newly established Bio-Oils Energy project to secure the equity and debt financing necessary to build the plant. However, bargaining power with a quasi-unique and much larger customer could prove to be an uneasy long-term relationship.

Procuring vegetable oil

A variety of oils can be used to produce biodiesel, with rapeseed, palm, and soybean oils being the most commonly used; soybean oil alone accounts for about 90% of all fuel stocks. Rapeseed accounted for the bulk of European output but was deemed too expensive by Bio-Oils Energy, which decided to explore alternative procurement arrangements — most importantly, soybean oil from South America and palm oil from Southeast Asia.

Soybeans are native to Southeast Asia, but 45% of the world's soybean area, and 55% of production, is in the United States. The United States produced 75 million metric tons of soybeans in 2000, of which more than one-third was exported. Other leading producers are Brazil, Argentina, China, and India.

To produce soybean oil, the soybeans are cracked, adjusted for moisture content, rolled into flakes, and solvent-extracted with commercial hexane. The oil is then refined, blended for different applications, and sometimes hydrogenated. Soybean oils, both liquid and partially hydrogenated, are exported abroad, are sold as vegetable oil, or end up in a wide variety of processed foods. The remaining soybean husks are used mainly as animal feed.

Of concern to Bio-Oils Energy was the global oligopolistic structure of the vegetable oil business, which was 70% controlled by five major agribusiness conglomerates — also known as the ABCD&Gs, which stands for Archer Daniels Midland (United States), Bunge (Brazil), Cargill (United States), Dreyfus (France), and Glencore (Netherlands). Clearly arranging stable supply lines for the biodiesel plant was going to require a long-term relationship with the ABCD&G cartel, with contracts typically based on the Chicago Board of Trade (CBOT) or Kuala Lumpur–Malaysia Bursa commodity exchange quotations. Alternatively, Bio-Oils Energy was keen on exploring direct procurement with upstream local producers, either large-scale cooperatives or independent crushers; contracts would also be based on international commodities exchange quotations, but long-term bulk contracting could theoretically yield some discounting from world prices. Last but not least, some consideration was to be given to vertical integration, which would involve investing in large land tracts and the building of crushing facilities, all of which would require very substantial capital investment.

The offer

On February 21, 2007, Bio-Oils Energy was in the process of securing a second round of financing when it received a formal offer from a competing and well-capitalized bio-fuels operator for €21 million in cash contingent upon usual due diligence. In its initial round of financing Bio-Oils' Energy two original founders, Antonio Carro and Christoph Schmid, had raised €3 million from family and friends while conserving 80% ownership. The second, more ambitious round of financing was aimed at raising an additional €15 million of equity in cash by issuing an additional 1,700 shares beyond the existing 4,200 outstanding shares.

This second cash injection was contingent on Bio-Oils Energy arranging for an additional €110 million of debt financing at an average of Euribor + 100 to 200 basis points to be drawn as the refinery was being built and operations were being launched (€50 million in senior debt, €10 million in working capital line, €10 million in performance bond,[7] €30 million in factoring line,[8] and €10 million in value-added tax or VAT financing).[9]

7 A performance bond is an irrevocable bank commitment guaranteeing the fulfillment of a contractual obligation; that is, were Bio-Oils Energy to default on a forward purchase contract of soy oil with a commodity trading company, the said company would have the right to claim from the guaranteeing bank the full value of the posted bond. Said amount is negotiated *ex ante* by the two contracting parties and is different from the marked-to-market value of the forward contract.

8 Factoring line is a financing arrangement between Bio-Oils and its bank to discount without recourse all receivables guaranteed by buyer of biodiesel.

9 Value-added tax (VAT) financing is bridge financing provided by the bank to Bio-Oils Energy for the delayed reimbursement of VAT taxes paid on capex during the construction phase to be fully repaid by the Spanish state every June 30. For example, if Bio-Oils in phase 1 of the plant construction of €10 million is assessed a 16% VAT tax to be paid on January 1, the contractor bank will provide financing for €1.6 million for the period January 1 to June 30.

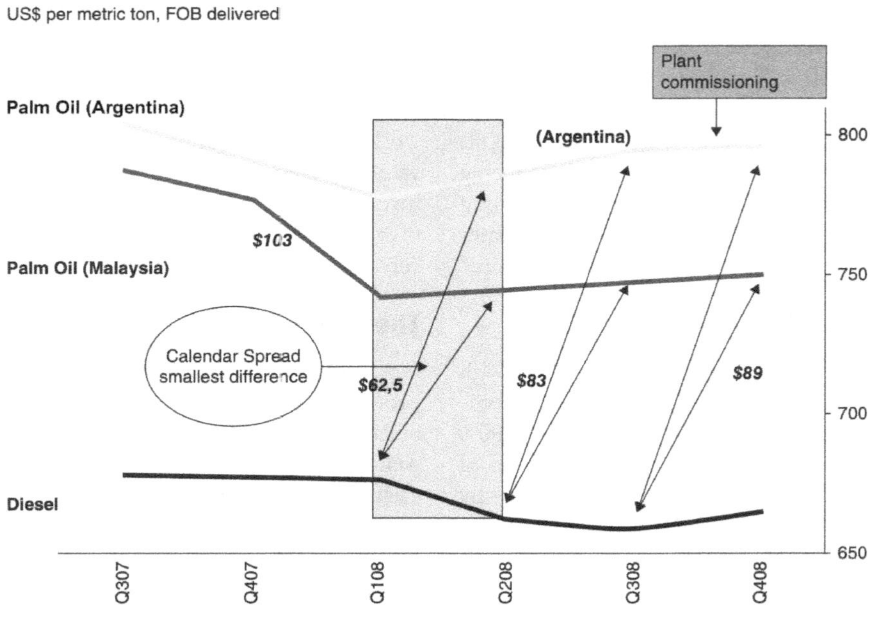

Case Exhibit 14.1. Calendar spread based on differential of forward rates.
Source: Reuters.

The hedging conundrum

Of major concern to Bio-Oils' owners and senior management were the explosive price increases that both the diesel and the vegetable oil markets had experienced in the prior five years. Several hedging alternatives were being considered: Diesel prices could be locked in with forward and futures contracts for as long as 12–18 months, whereas hedges for longer-term maturities could be envisioned with diesel price swaps. Similarly, vegetable oil prices could be hedged through short-term forward contracts in maturities ranging from six to 12 months.[10] A large commodity trading firm also offered to supply vegetable oil at diesel price (average price of last quarter) + a spread (see Case Exhibit 14.1). This was a novel pricing scheme that directly linked the vegetable oil and diesel markets' forward curves, as the metric of choice became a calendar spread rather than commodity-specific quotes. For Bio-Oils Energy, this contracting scheme allowed it to lock in significantly its future margin since the price of future diesel sales was directly linked (albeit with a calendar delay) to its vegetable oil cost.

Interestingly, the diesel forward prices were consistently below the vegetable oil forward prices, which makes the tax subsidy critical to the profitability of this venture. Diesel[11] markets were typically in backwardation whereas vegetable oil markets were in contango.

Diesel and vegetable oil prices seemed to exhibit some correlation (see Case Exhibit 14.2). Last but not least, financing would be denominated

10 Storage costs for vegetable oil are approximately $5 per cubic meter (vegetable oil density is 0.92 cubic meters per metric ton). The spot price of soy oil on February 21 was $595/mt (FOB Argentina) and palm oil was $555/mt (FOB Indonesia). Shipping costs run at $80/mt from Indonesia or Argentina for delivery at the Huelva refinery. Refining one metric ton of vegetable oil would yield one metric ton of biodiesel and 10% of glycerin, while 10% methanol is used as a catalyzer.

11 Thanks to the currently prevailing Spanish tax subsidy, Bio-Oils would be able to sell at 162% of pretax fossil diesel. This is due to the fact that the consumption tax levied on fossil diesel is waived for biodiesel refiners who collect the tax. This prevailing tax encouragement was available throughout the EU, albeit at varying levels country by country. Historically, Germany had the highest tax subsidy scheme until 2007, when it decided to scrap it entirely while imposing a mandatory blending requirement on fossil diesel refiners. Spain had legislation in place guaranteeing the existing tax subsidy until 2012.

Case Exhibit 14.2. Cross-correlation table (2001–2006).

	Brent	Diesel	Soybean Oil FOB Argentina	Soybean Oil FOB Brazil	Palm Oil FOB Malaysia	Rapeseed Oli Ex-Works Holland
Brent	1	0.89	0.51	0.55	0.55	0.84
Diesel	0.89	1	0.34	0.42	0.38	0.72
Soybean Oil FOB Argentina	0.51	0.34	1	0.94	0.93	0.67
Soybean Oil FOB Brazil	0.55	0.42	0.94	1	0.96	0.65
Palm Oil FOB Malaysia	0.55	0.38	0.93	0.96	1	0.55
Rapeseed Oil	...	...	...	...	...	...
Ex-Works Holland	0.84	0.72	0.67	0.65	0.55	1

in euros whereas cash flows from operations were dollar-linked. Fundamentally, Bio-Oils had to chart what was going to be its preferred risk profile. At one end of the continuum, Bio-Oils could lock in over the next five years its price risk exposure at a significant cost but would have access to bank financing at a somewhat lower cost of approximately 50 basis points. Alternatively, it could choose to remain more nimble and hedge more opportunistically, as the plant was nearing completion and actual refining operations were about to commence.

With the heightened volatility in oil markets and a barrel of crude at an all-time high of $67, combined with uncertainty in procuring a steady supply of vegetable oil, the offer was tempting. Christoph and Antonio were pondering the merits of this cash-rich offer (see Case Exhibit 14.3). After all, this project was barely two years old since inception and construction on the refinery had barely begun. Yet Christoph would have to report to the board the results of his objective analysis. It was going to be a long weekend.

Questions for Discussion

1. Should Christoph Schmid accept the offer?
2. What is the nature of risk that faces Bio-Oils?
3. How do you interpret the correlation matrix between fossil fuels and vegetable oils? What are the implications of the selection of vegetable oil for this project?
4. What are the different hedging options available to Bio-Oils Energy?
5. What is the relationship between hedging and value creation?

Case Exhibit 14.3. Business plan forecasts.

Balance Sheet (Thousand Euros)	**2005**	**2006**	**2007**	**2008**	**2009**	**2010**	**2011**	**2012**	**2013**	**2014**
Fixed Assets	0	0	39,446	44,946	40,154	35,555	31,100	26,782	22,636	18,706
Investments	0	0	42,075	52,850	53,375	54,164	55,188	56,470	58,071	60,073
Accumulated Depreciation	0	0	2,629	7,904	13,222	18,608	24,089	29,688	35,435	41,367
Total Fixed Assets	0	0	39,446	44,946	40,154	35,555	31,100	26,782	22,636	18,706
Inventory	0	0	22	14,408	22,061	19,589	20,382	20,858	21,223	21,774
Raw Materials	0	0	13	8,501	13,079	11,639	12,131	12,421	12,639	13,040
Finished Goods	0	0	9	5,907	8,982	7,950	8,251	8,437	8,584	8,734
Accounts Receivables	0	0	24	12,877	17,670	14,64	14,187	14,249	14,210	14,286
Tax	0	358	12,227	3,077	1,760	1,760	1,760	1,760	1,760	1,760
Cash	0	−880	16,617	6,920	39,916	57,166	64,292	76,264	84,209	99,582
Short Term Assets	0	−522	28,889	37,282	81,407	93,165	100,622	113,132	121,403	137,403
Total Assets	0	−522	68,335	82,228	121,561	128,720	131,721	139,914	144,039	156,108
Paid in Capital	0	0	7,884	7,884	7,884	7,884	7,884	7,884	7,884	7,884
Retained Earnings	0	−573	−611	12,695	42,882	68,658	87,864	103,169	116,307	128,125
Shareholder's Equity	0	−573	7,273	20,579	50,766	76,542	95,748	111,053	124,191	136,009
Long Term Bank Debt	0	0	35,116	37,669	31,286	24,904	12,139	6,382	0	0
Long Term Liabilities	0	0	35,116	37,669	31,286	24,904	12,139	6,382	0	0
Accounts Payables	0	51	8,219	9,280	13,949	12,457	12,960	13,295	13,583	13,891
Short Term Debt	0	0	17,728	12,682	11,000	8,250	6,188	4,641	0	0
Tax	0	0	0	2,018	14,560	6,567	4,686	4,542	6,265	6,208
Short Term Liabilities	0	51	25,947	23,980	39,509	27,274	23,834	22,478	19,848	20,099
Total Liabilities & Shareholders' Equity	0	−522	68,355	82,228	121,561	128,728	131,721	139,914	144,039	156,108

P&L (Thousand Euros)	2005	2006	2007	2008	2009	2010	2011	2012	2013	2014
Revenues	0	0	62	97,750	197,681	194,007	188,876	187,136	186,589	187,576
% Growth	*n.a.*	*n.a.*	*n.a.*	*156841%*	*102%*	*−2%*	*−3%*	*−1%*	*0%*	*1%*
Bio-diesel	0	0	62	97,750	197,681	194,007	188,876	187,136	186,589	187,576
Direct Costs	0	0	42	67,338	141,269	143,920	148,526	152,710	155,659	158,373
% Revenues	*n.a.*	*n.a.*	*68%*	*69%*	*71%*	*74%*	*79%*	*82%*	*83%*	*84%*
Gross Margin	0	0	20	30,412	56,412	50,087	40,350	34,426	30,930	29,203
% of sales	*n.a.*	*n.a.*	*32%*	*31%*	*29%*	*26%*	*21%*	*18%*	*17%*	*16%*
SG&A	0	819	1,620	4,673	4,763	4,857	4,953	5,053	5,156	5,262
Labour cost	0	119	530	1,393	1,441	1,492	1,544	1,598	1,654	1,712
Other SG&A	0	700	1,090	3,280	3,322	3,365	3,409	3,455	3,502	3,550
EBITDA	0	−819	−1,600	25,739	51,649	45,230	35,397	29,373	25,774	23,941
% of sales	*n.a.*	*n.a.*	*−2568.9%*	*26.3%*	*26.1%*	*23.3%*	*18.7%*	*15.7%*	*14%*	*13%*
Depreciation and Amortization	0	0	2,629	5,275	5,318	5,387	5,480	5,599	5,747	5,932
EBIT	0	−819	−4,229	20,464	46,331	39,843	29,917	23,774	20,027	18,009
% of sales	*n.a.*	*n.a.*	*−6789%*	*21%*	*23%*	*21%*	*16%*	*13%*	*11%*	*10%*
Financial Income/(Expense)	0	0	−894	−3,144	−3,207	−3,019	−2,480	−1,910	−1,259	−1,126
Taxes	0	−246	−5,085	4,013	12,937	11,047	8,231	6,559	5,631	5,065
NET INCOME/(LOSSES)	0	−573	−38	13,306	30,186	25,777	19,206	15,305	13,138	11,818
% of sales	*n.a.*	*n.a.*	*−61%*	*14%*	*15%*	*13%*	*10%*	*8%*	*7%*	*6%*
CAPEX	0	0	42,075	10,775	526	788	1,025	1,281	1,601	2,002
% of sales	*n.a.*	*n.a.*	*67552%*	*11%*	*0%*	*0%*	*1%*	*1%*	*1%*	*1%*

15

Forecasting Exchange Rates

I tell the future. Nothing easier. Everybody's future is in their face. But who can tell your past — eh? Nobody! . . . I can't tell the past and neither can you. If anybody tries to tell you the past, take my word for it, they're charlatans! Charlatans! But I can tell the future.
—Fortune-teller in Thornton Wilder's *The Skin of Our Teeth*, Act Two

Reliable estimates of future spot exchange rates are critical inputs to the decision-making process in international business for such key areas as (1) hedging overall corporate exposure to foreign exchange (FX or forex) risk, (2) protection of the value of expected profits from foreign subsidiaries, as well as of their remittances to the parent, (3) selection of the cheapest financing source, (4) optimization of multicurrency cash management, (5) evaluation of foreign long-term investment proposals, and (6) international sourcing/procurement decisions. Optimal decisions require reliable exchange rate forecasts over varying time spans. Similarly, for globally reaching financial institutions continuously optimizing their assets–liabilities portfolios in the time × currency space, exchange rate forecasts (along with interest rate forecasts) are also critical informational inputs.

This chapter considers the validity of generating *model-based* forecasts when *market-based* forecasts are available free of charge in the context of *floating* exchange rates. This is the old question, "Can we beat the market?" which essentially means, "Is the forex (FX) market truly efficient in the sense that it incorporates all currently available information?" The appendix to this chapter revisits the forecasting question when exchange rates are *pegged yet adjustable,* as it is still the case of many emerging market countries.

In this chapter you will gain an understanding of:

- Why evidence of FX market efficiency may invalidate model-based forecasts.
- Under what conditions forward exchange rates are reliable predictors of future spot exchange rates.
- What various methods are used in model-based exchange rate forecasting.
- How to measure the accuracy versus the correctness of various exchange rate forecasting models.
- When to use econometric versus technical analysis forecasting models.
- What the key steps are in forecasting pegged yet adjustable exchange rates (Appendix 15A).

MARKET-BASED FORECASTS

Market-based forecasts are as simple as taking today's spot or forward rates to be forecasts of future spot rates. They are provided by the FX market free of charge. For example, if on January 1, 2025, the 90 day forward dollar price of one euro is \$1.1315, one could surmise that the best forecast of the actual spot dollar price of one euro on April 1, 2025, would be indeed \$1.1315. Such forecasts are anchored in the theory that FX markets do indeed constitute efficient markets in an *informational* sense. Thus — if clearly established — the efficient market hypothesis would possibly invalidate the usefulness of building elaborate forecasting models and therefore the relevance of model-based forecasts.

The efficient market hypothesis

A FX market in which exchange rates fully and immediately reflect all available information is said to be efficient.[1] Three degrees of market efficiency are customarily distinguished[2]: (1) The *weakly* efficient market hypothesis says that series of historical exchange rates contain no information that can be used to forecast future spot exchange rates; (2) the *semi-strong* version of market efficiency holds that a large and competitive group of market participants has access to all publicly available information that can be the basis for the formation of expectations about future rates; and finally, (3) if the set of available information also includes private (such as insider) information about central bank intervention in the FX market, the market is said to be *strongly* efficient. Let us now review the evidence for and against the efficiency of the FX market and explain the forecasting implications of the hypothesis.

Is the FX market "weakly" efficient?

In essence, what is being investigated is whether a *past series of exchange rates* contains useful information for the prediction of future spot prices, thus implying that general patterns would repeat themselves at regular intervals. Indeed, if the FX market is shown to be *inefficient*, it would validate *technical* forecasting models, which use past exchange rates to forecast future exchange rates (see next main section on model-based forecasts). Of particular interest is the profitability of trading models such as various *filter rules* above and beyond a naive *buy-and-hold* strategy. If the market were efficient in the *weak form* sense, such trading models should not outperform a buy-and-hold strategy, which assumes market efficiency. Popular trading models are often built on a typical k percent filter rule, which would be defined as follows: If the exchange rate of a particular currency increases by at least k percent from its last trough, buy the currency and hold it until the exchange rate decreases by at least k percent from its peak, at which time one should sell the holding and short the currency (sell it forward). Maintain the short position until the currency price rises by at least k percent above a subsequent low. At this point, cover the short position and go long (buy forward). Exchange rate changes of less than k percent in either direction should be ignored.

Clearly, using a filter rule is profitable only if successive price changes are dependent in a statistical sense — for example, if a large increase in the exchange rate is followed by further increases more often than by decreases. This dependency is often associated with the price dynamics hypothesis, which posits that a subset of market participants (*market leaders*) are known or simply perceived by the rest of the market (*market followers*) to have earlier access to more timely and more accurate information concerning factors affecting future spot exchange rates and/or to have the use of more sophisticated forecasting models. Thus, when the price of a currency begins to fall (or to rise), market followers will jump on the bandwagon — that is, join in the selling (or the buying) pressure as they attribute the price change to be a signal that market leaders (who know better) have themselves begun to sell (or to buy). In so doing, market followers will be pushing the currency price down (or up) further until it overshoots its equilibrium level and the trend eventually reverses itself (see International Corporate Finance in Practice 15.1).

This view of exchange rate behavior supports the hypothesis that past exchange rates contain useful information in forecasting future exchange rates, since information only disseminates itself slowly among market participants, thus disproving the *weak form* of the efficient market hypothesis. Indeed, purchasing the appreciating currency after the first increase will, on average, yield abnormal gains. Such positive dependency will occur only if the FX market does not react instantaneously to the random arrival of new information — that is, when exchange rates adjust only gradually to such new information. In efficient markets of the weak form, however, a trading strategy such as the filter rule would not be expected to outperform a naive buy-and-hold strategy; yet a number of recent studies have shown otherwise.[3]

1 This concept of market efficiency should be clearly distinguished from the concept of market perfection. Market perfection is certainly a sufficient condition of market efficiency, but it is not a necessary one. As long as transactors take into account all available information, even large transaction costs that inhibit the flow of transactions do not in themselves imply that when transactions do take place, exchange rates will not "fully reflect" all available information.

2 This three-tier categorization of market efficiency was suggested by Eugene Fama for empirical testing purposes in the context of stock price. See Eugene Fama, "Efficient Capital Markets: A Review of Theory and Empirical Work," *Journal of Finance* 25, no. 2 (June 1970), 383–417. The distinction between semi-strong and strong forms of efficiency may not be as relevant to the forex market, where insider trading would be limited to private knowledge of central bank intervention.

3 In a comprehensive study spanning the period 1976–1990, Levich and Thomas found that simple trading rules consistently led to abnormal profits. See "The Significance of Technical Trading-Rule in the Foreign Exchange Market: A Bootstrap Approach," *Journal of International Money and Finance* 12, no. 5 (October 1993): 451–474.

INTERNATIONAL CORPORATE FINANCE IN PRACTICE 15.1

On Currency Overshooting

One explanation for currency overshooting that has received a considerable amount of attention in recent years is the possibility that currency markets may be characterized by temporary, rational bubbles (also known as "bootstraps", "sunspots", or "will-o'-the-wisp" equilibria).

At an intuitive level, bubbles are easy to understand, reflecting the familiar phenomenon of a self-reinforcing movement of the price away from its equilibrium level. Since time immemorial, laypersons have observed that in this type of situation, "everyone thinks that the price is too high, but no one expects it to fall yet". With hindsight, the most notorious price bubbles in history are blamed on investors' irrationality: market psychology, mass hysteria, and so forth. Take an example: Many people (including the majority of economists, traders, bankers, and politicians) believed that the US dollar was vastly overvalued on any reasonable criterion during the mid-1980s. Yet, in the face of this consensus, the high exchange rate was maintained for two years or more. Why? It is difficult to say with any confidence, but what is certainly true is that it was not obviously rational at the time to sell dollars, even if one shared the view that the dollar was overvalued. On the contrary, it made sense to hold dollars — as long as one believed the bubble would last, and as long as one was adequately compensated for the perceived risk that the bubble might burst. However, the more overvalued the currency, and the greater the probability the bubble will burst, the more rapidly it must rise so as to compensate for the increased risk. In other words, the critical question facing the investor in this type of situation is not the direction of the next major price movement, but its timing.

This picture of life inside a price bubble has probably been familiar to practitioners ever since the first caveman-speculator stored food in case of an exceptionally hard winter ahead. History records a number of spectacular events that were regarded as bubbles either at the time or fairly soon after they burst — for example, the Dutch Tulip Bubble, the Mississippi Bubble, the South Sea Bubble, and more debatably, the bull markets that preceded the Wall Street crashes of 1929, 1987, and 2008. In some cases, the bubbles were initiated by fraudsters who successfully duped irrational, or at least ill-informed, traders. However, that fact does not rule out the possibility that at some point a rational bubble mechanism may well have been at work in the market.

However, economists take comfort from being able to replicate the wisdom of the ages in mathematical models by simply adding a "bubble" term (what else?) in their equilibrium model. The bubble term can be defined as simply the extent of the deviation from the market fundamental equilibrium equation. Unfortunately, the theory has, as yet, nothing to say about how or why a bubble develops.

Source: Abridged from Laurence S. Copeland, *Exchange Rates and International Finance*, 2nd ed. (Reading, MA: Addison-Wesley, 1994).

Are forward rates good forecasters of future spot rates?[4]

This is tantamount to asking the question: Is the FX market "semi-strongly" efficient? Simply put, this theory postulates that the forward rate is the best, unbiased (in the statistical sense) predictor of the future spot exchange rate. Intuitively that means that the probability distribution of the future exchange rates $S(t)$ is centered on the forward rate — or that the forward rate is the mean value of all possible values that the future spot exchange rate may take. Most importantly, that does not mean that the future spot exchange rate will actually be equal to the forward exchange used as a predictor. Another rationale for this hypothesis is to consider how speculators who think that the forward rate is above their expectation of the future spot exchange rate will sell the foreign currency forward, thus bidding down the forward rate until it equals the expected

4 See Baillie and Bollerslev (2000).

future spot rate.[5] Conversely, speculators who see the forward rate undervaluing the expected future spot rate will buy foreign currency forward, thus bidding the forward rate up until the forward and expected future spot exchange rates become equal. If speculative demand for forward contracts were infinitely elastic and all speculators held homogeneous expectations with respect to the future spot exchange rate, the current forward exchange rate would be equal to the expected future spot rate. In statistical terms, the current forward rate is an *unbiased predictor* of the future spot exchange rate:

$$F(d) = E\left[\tilde{S}(t)\right] \tag{15.1}$$

where $F(d)$ is the dollar price of one unit of currency i for delivery d days forward (at time t) as quoted at time 0; $E[\tilde{S}(t)]$ is the mathematical expectation of the random variable $\tilde{S}(t)$ modeling the future dollar price of one unit of currency i to prevail at time t.

Empirical tests

Empirical evidence for or against this simple hypothesis has been provided by countless studies,[6] which have generally "regressed" the forward rate against the lagged spot rate. Unsurprisingly, the forward rate is found to be a *biased* predictor of the future spot exchange rate when the spot exchange rate $S(t)$ is regressed against the prior forward rate $F(d)$ set at time $t - d$ and maturing at time t:

$$S(t) = a + bF(d) + e(t) \tag{15.2}$$

If the forward rate were indeed an *unbiased* predictor, the linear coefficients a and b should be equal to 0 and 1, respectively, and the error term $e(t)$ should be normally distributed with mean 0, constant variance, and free from autocorrelation. Study after study has established the existence of a very significant bias; in fact, the forward rate is so biased that it may systematically predict future exchange rate movements in the wrong direction! One explanation is that currency traders and other market participants are not risk-neutral but rather risk-averse; in other words, they would not make decisions based simply on the mean of the probability distribution modeling the future spot exchange rate and would want to include some measure of risk such as variance around the mean — hence the idea of including a risk premium in equation (15.2) whose variability over time would account for the autocorrelation of residuals.

Perhaps more damning is the evidence of massive use of *carry trades* during the past two decades that have consistently delivered anomalous profits. A currency carry trade is simply a bet against the uncovered interest rate parity hypothesis, which claims that exchange rate changes will compensate for interest rate differentials between two currencies. This is the same as forward rates being construed as unbiased predictors of future spot exchange rates.[7]

Long-term forecast with forward rates

Because of a dearth of long-term currency forecasts, it is tempting to hypothesize long-dated forwards to be unbiased predictors of future spot exchange rates. Even though forward rates may not be actively quoted beyond maturity of 18 or 24 months, it is possible to compute synthetic forward rates with the help of the interest rate parity formula. All that is needed is the yield to maturity (YTM) of medium- or long-term bonds with the same credit rating in the respective currencies.[8] For example, assuming that the current spot US dollar price of one Australian dollar is $S(0) = 1.11$ and the YTM on 7 year US Treasuries is 5.75% and 8.21% for Australian treasuries, a simple annual compounding of the interest rate parity formula yields a seven year forward rate:

$$E\left[\tilde{S}(7)\right] = F(7) = \frac{1.11 \times (1 + 0.0575)^7}{(1 + 0.0821)^7} = 0.76$$

which is deemed the unbiased forecast of the spot rate $S(7)$ seven years hence.

More generally, the expected value of the future spot rate t years hence $\tilde{S}(t)$ is equal to the forward rate of matching maturity:

$$E\left[\tilde{S}(t)\right] = F(t) = S(0) \times \frac{(1 + i_{US})^t}{(1 + i_K)^t}$$

5 For a detailed explanation and illustration of speculation through the forward market, see Chapter 6.

6 For a comprehensive review, see Jussi-Pekka Lyytinen, "Currency Carry Trade — Betting against the Uncovered Interest Parity" (unpublished master's thesis, Helsinki School of Economics, 2007).

7 See Chapter 6 for a discussion of currency carry trade and how it contradicts uncovered interest rate parity (UIP). According to UIP, the future spot rate is equal to the no-profit forward rate derived from covered interest rate parity, which is the same proposition as $F(d) = E[\tilde{S}(t)]$.

8 A more sophisticated model would extract market-implied one year interest rate forecasts from zero-coupon yield curves and derive annual forward premiums/discounts to forecast future exchange rates.

where i_{US} and i_K are the respective t year YTM on US and foreign country k treasury bonds. No one would claim great accuracy for such forecasts (actually, there is no empirical test available to prove or disprove this hypothesis), but they do indeed exist as rational point estimates, which are in great demand for many strategic decision-making situations.

Perhaps the less than overwhelming evidence supporting the efficient market hypothesis should come as no surprise to the reader: If indeed exchange rates were to reflect fully and immediately all relevant information, one must wonder what the incentive would be for FX traders and forecasters to gather and process costly information. Only if the forex market is efficient in a *process* sense rather than in a *state* sense — that is, if some time is required for new information to get fully discounted into prices, or if a window of opportunity is opened during which traders can make abnormal profits — can we resolve this paradox.

In sum, the accumulating empirical evidence is fraught with the lack of a comprehensive testing of an exhaustive and uniform database and does not quite support the efficient market hypothesis. As a result, currently available information may be fruitfully used in making forecasts of future spot exchange rates. This is indeed comforting news for currency forecasters.

MODEL-BASED FORECASTS: TECHNICAL VERSUS ECONOMETRIC MODELING APPROACHES

If the FX market could be proven to be efficient beyond the shadow of a doubt, there would be little room left for currency forecasters. And yet there is a plethora of forecasting services that over the past 40 years have survived if not prospered; of course, this industry is characterized by low entry and exit costs, and there is no doubt that the population of forecasters has been in a continuing state of renewal. Indeed, successful forecasters face the burden of the efficient market hypothesis; that is, exchange rates will soon incorporate their forecasts, thereby rendering their value contribution as forecasters nil! Thus, successful forecasters, by making the FX market more efficient, are driving themselves out of business. There are two principal approaches to forecasting: (1) *technical models*, which are especially popular for short-term forecasting (one month or less), and (2) *econometric models*, which build on fundamental economic relationships. These are discussed next.

Technical forecasting

The very essence of technical forecasting is to unearth stable trends from time series of past exchange rates. The presumption is that these trends tend to repeat themselves, thereby allowing the forecaster to predict future currency prices or, more precisely, to provide *buy/sell* signals. Since no reference is made to exchange rate fundamentals, such as balance-of-payments statistics or interest rate policy, and since exclusive focus is put on extrapolation from past prices, technical models are in clear contradiction of the *weak form* of market efficiency.

Long associated with the forecasting of commodity and stock prices, it is relatively recently that technical analysis has been applied to currency forecasting. Worth mentioning though is that, unlike the case of commodity or stock markets, the FX market does not make available any information about trading volumes. It should be also noted that because technical analysis is not rooted in economic theory it is often looked down upon by academics and economists. And yet recent surveys of currency traders indicate that this forecasting method is widely used by FX dealers for short-term forecasting purposes.[9] As a result, if a large segment of the FX market relies on technical forecasting, it would be foolish for otherwise "rational" FX market participants to ignore technical forecasting signals followed by "irrational" currency traders.

Moving averages

There are many different methods actively used by technicians, including moving averages, momentum analysis, the Box and Jenkins method, and expert systems (which attempt to reproduce the reasoning of FX market participants through artificial intelligence software), not to mention the popular graphical method better known as *chartism*. For example, the *moving average* method consists of comparing the arithmetic mean of past exchange rates over a short time series (the short-term moving average, or SMA) — say, over a period of 15 days — with a longer-term moving average (LMA) — say, the arithmetic average of the past 60 days — where SMA(t) and LMA(t) at time t are respectively defined as:

$$\text{SMA}(t)=\frac{1}{15}\left[S(t)+S(t-1)+S(t-2)+\cdots+S(t-15)\right]$$

$$\text{LMA}(t)=\frac{1}{60}\left[S(t)+S(t-1)+S(t-2)+\cdots+S(t-60)\right]$$

9 See Allen and Taylor (1990) as well as Osler (2003).

and are continuously updated to reflect the past 15 or 60 periods. By definition, moving averages smooth erratic daily swings in currency prices, with the LMA trailing the SMA because the LMA gives less weight to recent currency prices than the SMA does.

This technical method provides a simple buy/sell rule: After a period of decline when a currency starts rising again, its SMA will increase faster than the LMA; when its curve crosses the LMA curve from below it will be deemed a buy signal (see *buy* signal in Exhibit 15.1, panel A). Conversely, when the pattern reverses itself — that is, when the SMA curve crosses the LMA curve from above — the currency should be sold (see *sell* signal in Exhibit 15.1, panel A). More generally, such a simple forecasting model would provide the FX trader with an anchor (the longer-term moving average line, which, by definition, tends to be smoother) against which short-term volatility can be put in its proper perspective.

Filter rules

The other very popular technical model, already discussed, is based on the mechanical application of *filter rules* such as "buy (long) currency *i* anytime its price exceeds its last trough by *x* percent" and, conversely, "sell (short) currency *i* whenever it falls by the same *x* percent from its last peak." Consider the case of an FX trader using the following filter rule: "Buy sterling if its dollar value increases by more than 5% above the last trough, and sell if it falls from the last peak by 5%." Exhibit 15.1, panel B, illustrates how the trader would start buying sterling when it crosses the 5% band at $1.5750 from the last low of $1.50 and would sell at $1.71 after retreating from a high of $1.80.

Chartism

Chartism is a forecasting technique based on a *visual nonlinear* price pattern and thus refrains from hypothesizing any *quantitative* relationships between past and future exchange rates. Of particular interest is the *head and shoulders* chart pattern, which (according to technical analysts) occurs when the second of a series of three peaks is higher (the "head") than the first and third (the "shoulders"), typically signaling a trend reversal. Exhibit 15.2 provides a dramatic illustration of the trend reversal experienced by the dollar against the German mark; specifically, by drawing the *neckline* between the two shoulders, it is possible to infer that, from the point in time when the second shoulder is crossed, the downward trend should at least match the distance between the neckline and the top of the head. Practically no selling (shorting) decision should be

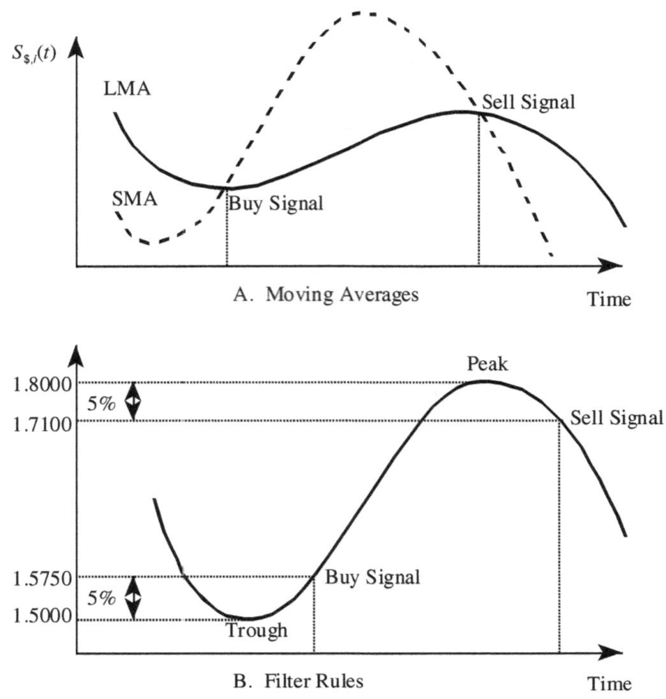

Exhibit 15.1. Technical forecasting.

Exhibit 15.2. Head and shoulders reversal pattern.

made until the price line clearly crosses and breaks below the neckline.

The gamut of currency charts extends far beyond the popular head and shoulders pattern to include such colorful configurations as *bearish (bullish) key reversal*, *breakaway gap*, *bearish rising (bullish falling) wedge*, and many others. In fact, the past 25 years have witnessed such a growing interest in chartism that most forex trading rooms will include at least one alchemist hunched over his or her keyboard attempting to extract a message from the entrails. Unfortunately, this author is not aware of any published empirical study proving or disproving the forecasting performance of chartists.

Econometric forecasting

After briefly sketching the nature of econometric forecasting, this section analyzes the type and the value of information services that the treasurers of multinational corporations may purchase from econometric forecasting services. Finally, it provides a framework for assessing their track records (see International Corporate Finance in Practice 15.2).

Exchange-rate econometric forecasting models are a systematic effort to uncover a functional relationship between a set of *explanatory/independent* (exogenous) variables, such as price-level differentials, interest rate differentials, or differentials in the growth rate of money supplies, and an *explained/dependent* (endogenous) variable, namely, the exchange rate. The functional relationship may involve only the *current* period values of the explanatory variables, or it may be of a *lagged* nature — that is, incorporate past-period values taken on by the explanatory variables. In this latter case, econometric modeling is clearly inconsistent with the efficient market hypothesis, whereas in the former case it is not necessarily so. As a matter of fact, one may be tempted to argue that econometric forecasting that disregards lagged functional relationships is assisting the market in correctly interpreting all currently available information, thus making it more efficient.

As an illustration, a simple forecasting model could express the percentage change in the US dollar price of one Japanese yen (explained/dependent variable) as a linear function of the expected differential in inflation rates and of the known differential in short-term interest rates (explanatory/independent variables) between the US and Japan:

$$\frac{S(t,t+1)-S(t)}{S(t)}=a\left[r_{\text{US}}(t,t+1)-r_{\text{JAP}}(t,t+1)\right]$$
$$+b\left[i_{\text{US}}(t,t+1)-i_{\text{JAP}}(t,t+1)\right]+e(t) \quad (15.3)$$

where a and b are positive linear coefficients arrived at through multiple regression analysis, and $r_{\text{US}}(t, t+1)$, $r_{\text{JPN}}(t, t+1)$, $i_{\text{US}}(t, t+1)$, $i_{\text{JPN}}(t, t+1)$ are US and Japanese inflation and interest rates, respectively, over the period $(t, t+1)$.[10]

10 The forecasted values of $r_{\text{US}}(t, t+1)$ and $r_{\text{JPN}}(t, t+1)$ could be generated by macroeconomic forecasting models, which will require several simultaneous equations rather than a single and all too often simplistic equation model; $i_{\text{US}}(t, t+1)$ and $i_{\text{JPN}}(t, t+1)$ are readily available from money market data for a variety of instruments.

INTERNATIONAL CORPORATE FINANCE IN PRACTICE 15.2

How Forecasting Prowess Helps Ingersoll-Rand Control a $2 Billion Portfolio of Currency Exposure

Ingersoll-Rand Co., a manufacturer of heavy industrial equipment based in New Jersey, has an extensive network of wholly owned subsidiaries around the world. As a result of operating production facilities in the Americas, Europe, and Asia, and sales subsidiaries in many locations, including the Philippines and Colombia as well as Japan, Ingersoll-Rand has diverse currency exposures to manage.

The treasury operation is labeled conservative and is not run as a profit center. Its goal is to hedge exposure, intracompany and third-party liabilities, expenses, and dividend programs. The treasury also provides currency guidelines when a subsidiary is bidding on a project. *Hedging operations, however, are centralized.* The treasury also functions as a corporate bank for the group; excess funds are pooled and swapped among subsidiaries, allowing the company to save some 20 to 25 basis points compared with commercial lending rates.

Currency forecasting plays an important role as a key input in the risk management program, according to its FX manager. The FX manager is responsible for generating the currency forecasts. He looks at — typically on a monthly basis — all the major currencies, plus a handful of exotics. Forecasts extend to a maximum period of one year. He relies on the weighted average of several consensus tallies to provide him with a general picture of the currency market. Furthermore, to get a feel for the market outlook in each country, he stays in regular telephone contact with overseas subsidiaries. Their contributions play an important part in his effort.

"I also look at technical resistance points", says the foreign exchange manager. "Regardless of whether you believe in them or not, markets do, and are moved by them". He further cautions that neither technical nor fundamental forecasts should be used in isolation. Instead, his forecast is a blend of all these factors. He also emphasizes the need to be flexible and open-minded when forecasting currencies, as well as to trust the knowledge and experience gained over time. "The general direction of the currency move may be correct, but timing isn't always easy to predict", he notes. Last but not least, he sees political developments as the toughest part in forecasting. They are difficult to predict — yet they may change everything.

Source: Adapted from *Finance & Treasury*, February 1993, pp. 7–8.

The specification of the model itself — that is, the nature of the functional relationship (not necessarily linear), as well as the choice of exogenous variables included — is generally a blend of economic theory (in this case a combination of the purchasing power parity and uncovered interest rate parity theories) with the model builder's experience, judgment, and intuition. Because single equation models as illustrated (equation (15.3)) feed by necessity on forecasts of some of the explanatory variables, econometric forecasters will often build simultaneous equation models that capture better the complex correlations among key economic variables. In that sense, econometric building is as much an art as a science, and accordingly, the reader should expect the various forecasting services to be highly idiosyncratic.

Suffice it to say, at this point, that structural equations (usually one for each currency forecasted) are extracted from time series of exogenous or endogenous variables — that is, from past observations. This means that if a drastic change in the structural relationship between independent and dependent variables (e.g., an oil price shock) were to occur and be disregarded in specifying functional relationships, the econometric model forecasting accuracy would be adversely affected.

One important feature of econometric forecasting models is the random error — $e(t)$ in equation (15.3) — that is always incorporated into this type of model.[11] It allows probability statements to be made about the forecasted variable — for example, there is a 95% chance that the future (90 days later) US dollar price of the Japanese yen will be bound between ¥74 and ¥77/US$. This feature is indeed attractive compared with a point estimate (as provided, for instance, by the forward exchange rate), especially when we recall that the information is to be used in a *risk management* context. A word of caution about the methodological soundness of econometric forecasting should be acknowledged, as one or several of the following conditions for a correct use of multiple regression analysis are all too often ignored: (1) the error term is normally distributed with zero mean and finite variance, (2) the variance of the error term is constant and finite (homoscedasticity), and (3) zero covariance exists between any two dependent variables (multicollinearity).

Last but not least, an attractive feature of econometric forecasting models is that they can be used interactively, as they are often made available by the vendor on a time-sharing basis. User-managers can thus input their own subjective assumptions and scenarios about explanatory variables and find out how the exchange rate (explained variable) responds. For strategic projects, the "what if" capability will prove critical in stress-testing the soundness of important decisions.

Assessing the track records of forecasting models

Potential users of such forecasting models must decide, first, whether it is worth the subscription fee (which may range anywhere from \$10,000 to \$250,000 per annum) to purchase such forecasting services and, second, which forecasting service to subscribe to. Before we attempt to answer either question, the reader should be reminded that at any single point in time, the forward exchange market provides unconditional point estimates of future spot exchange rates (the forecasting horizon is naturally given by maturities of forward exchange contracts — 30, 60, 90, 180, and 360 days)[12] and that this forecasting service is free of charge. Econometric forecasting services generally provide monthly, quarterly, semiannual and annual average exchange rates, rather than end-of-period estimates. Such point estimates usually come as unconditional forecasts, but provisions for conditional forecasts can easily be made.

Traditionally, the performance of currency forecasting services is assessed by measuring the extent to which the forecast surpasses the forward exchange rate in predicting the actual future spot exchange rate. Levich (1980) offers a methodological framework for conducting such performance analysis by focusing on the forecast error **E**(t), which is defined as the exchange rate forecast $S(t)^*$ minus the actual spot exchange rate $S(t)$:

$$\mathbf{E}(t) = S(t)^* - S(t) \tag{15.4}$$

One obviously desirable property of such a forecast error is that it be small in absolute value; however, this simple criterion needs to be qualified according to the sign of the forecast error. Consider the example of two alternative forecasts for the 90 days-hence dollar price of one pound sterling:

$$S(90)^{*I} = 1.48 \text{ and } S(90)^{*II} = 1.58 \tag{15.5}$$

whose accuracy is to be compared against the benchmark forward exchange rate:

$$F(90) = 1.50$$

Assuming that the actual exchange rate turns out to be $S(90) = 1.52$, the forecast errors associated with each forecast would be:

$$\mathbf{E}(t)^{I} = 1.48 - 1.52 = -0.04 \tag{15.6}$$

$$\mathbf{E}(t)^{II} = 1.58 - 1.52 = 0.06 \tag{15.7}$$

11 An econometric model must contain a stochastic element to permit statistical inference from the data. The usual procedure is to hypothesize a model of varying degrees of sophistication that should account for the phenomenon under review and then to add, almost as an afterthought, a disturbance or random-error term to which convenient statistical properties are ascribed. This residual random-error term represents in an indeterminate way all the factors that are ignored in the systematic part of the model. The major flaw of current forecasting efforts is probably the normality assumption of exchange-rate probability distribution that is generally made. Exchange rates are not normally distributed and were found to be best generated as non-normal members of the Pareto–Levy class of probability distributions by Westerfield, Janice M. 1977. "An Examination of Foreign Exchange Risk under Fixed and Floating Exchange Rate Regimes," *Journal of International Economics* 7(2): 181–200. The normality assumption is also refuted in Aggarwal, Raj. 1990. "Distribution of Spot and Forward Exchange Rates: Empirical Evidence and Investor Valuation of Skewness and Kurtosis," *Decision Sciences* 21(3): 588–595.

12 Alternatively, the synthetic forward exchange rate can be computed for any maturity — provided that information is available for relevant interest rates — with the help of the interest rate parity theorem.

This approach can be generalized to a given forecasting service whose performance is compared to the forward rate. The average forecasting accuracy is usually gauged by computing the square root of the mean squared error (RMSE) of the forecaster:

$$\text{RMSE} = \text{Square root of}\left(\frac{1}{N}\right)\times\left\{\sum_{t=1}^{N}\left[S(t)^{*}-S(t)\right]\right\}^{2}$$

where $S(t)^*$ and $S(t)$ are predicted versus realized exchange rates over N forecasting iterations. Since a positive error is no worse or better than a negative error, squared errors are averaged over all forecasts. Its square root is then measured against the square root of the forward mean squared error: the forecaster with the smaller RMSE wins!

Accurate versus useful forecasts

Even though the first forecasting error is smaller in absolute terms and therefore more accurate, the second forecast is superior because it leads the hedger to the correct decision. Indeed, both the actual and forecast rates were on the same right side of the forward rate. The forecast indicated an appreciation of the pound sterling and therefore would have led an investor who is long sterling not to hedge. Similarly, a speculator would have been prompted to buy pound sterling forward. Thus, the forecast turned out to be *correct* since it gave the right information for both hedging and trading.

> ***Q:*** Explain why the first forecast at $S(t)^{*I} = 1.48$ is more accurate but not useful for the hedger/speculator as compared to the second forecast of $S(t)^{*II} = 1.58$.
>
> ***A:*** The absolute error is only \$0.04 for the first forecast rather than \$0.06 for the second forecast. However, it anticipated a devaluation of the pound *vis-à-vis* its forward rate and would have prompted an investor therefore to hedge a long sterling position and a speculator to sell the pound forward; both transactions would have resulted in a loss.

COMPOSITE FORECASTS

The preceding methodological framework — dubbed *the right side of the market approach* — has clear limitations in the sense that it provides a currency-by-currency evaluation that compares each service against the forward rate but not against other forecasting services. More important, there is no way of knowing whether some combination of two or more services would be superior to a single service — hence the idea of a *composite* forecast that combines information from different forecasting models with the objective of outperforming any single forecast. Such a composite or portfolio forecast can be constructed by formulating a weighted average of single forecasting services. For example, for maturity t, the composite forecast $S(t)^C$ would be written as:

$$S(t)^{C} = \left(1-w^{1}-w^{2}\right)F(t)+w^{1}S(t)^{1}+w^{2}S(t)^{2} \tag{15.8}$$

where w^k is the estimate of the weight given to forecast $S(t)^k$ with $k = 1, 2$ and derived through econometric techniques analogous to optimal portfolio allocation.

The weighting scheme could assign equal weight to each forecast (arithmetic average) or could derive weights that minimize the composite forecast's average forecasting error subject to an acceptable level of the composite forecasting error's standard deviation. Interestingly, a composite forecast could include (and weigh heavily) the forward exchange rate for a particular currency and maturity combination as illustrated in equation (15.8). For example, if the previous composite weighted equally the forward rate and the other two forecasts, it would simply be expressed as:

$$S(t)^{C} = 0.33F(t)+0.33S(t)^{1}+0.33S(t)^{2} \tag{15.8, illustrated}$$

Indeed, composite forecasts are commercially available from independent firms such as the London-based Foreign Exchange Consensus Forecasts, which pools as many as 250 forecasters monthly and publishes a consensus forecast based on the mean value of all forecasts surveyed.

HOW TO USE CURRENCY FORECASTS

To determine which service a multinational corporation should subscribe to, criteria such as the nature of output in terms of number of currencies forecast, forecasting horizons, frequency of currency updates, and ability of the client to enter his or her own assumptions about potential states of the world, in addition to cost and forecasting accuracy, should be carefully weighted. Most important, though, the tasks for which currency forecasts are to be used will often dictate the type of forecasting services subscribed to:

- A corporate treasurer making hedging decisions about short-term foreign currency receivables or payables, short-term financing, and dividends repatriation will find *technical* forecasts of great help.
- A hedge fund manager involved in the currency carry trade and other speculative activities will also find *technical* forecasts useful adjuncts to his or her decisions.
- A strategic planner reviewing foreign market entry strategies, foreign direct investment, or foreign acquisitions will require long-term currency forecasts stretching possibly 7–10 years ahead. Long-term forwards and certainly econometric models will be most helpful — in fact, they may be the only forecasts available — and *econometric* forecasts will lend themselves to simulations and multiple scenario analyses answering "what if" questions.

SUMMARY

1. Does it make economic sense to forecast exchange rates? To couch the same question in more scholarly terms: Are foreign exchange markets efficient? That is, do market exchange rates (spot or forward, depending on which form of market efficiency we refer to) reflect all currently available information? If they do, it is clearly pointless to build elaborate forecasting models based on some kind of a lagged relationship between an explanatory (exogenous) variable (or a set of such variables) and the dependent variable (exchange rate) to be forecasted.
2. An extensive review of the various available empirical tests has led us to the conclusion that the burden of proof probably lies with proponents of the efficient market hypothesis, given the accumulating evidence that it is possible to beat the market.
3. The forward rate is a biased predictor of the future spot exchange rate even though it embodies all publicly available information. Indeed, the massive amount of currency carry trade during the past decade is irrefutable proof that forwards (based on interest rate differentials) are not unbiased predictors of future spot exchange rates. If they were, uncovered carry trades would merely break even.
4. Technical forecasting services seem to be able to beat the market consistently, and chartism is as popular as ever among forex players. Technical forecasts, however, provide directional forecasts — not point estimates.
5. Fundamental/econometric forecasting services have a dubious track record over short-term horizons but successfully offer (for a fee) unconditional forecasts of future spot exchange rates over the medium and long term in the form of quarterly averages rather than end-of-period point estimates.
6. Because of the statistical nature of econometric forecasting, the information provided by such models lends itself readily to probability statements (confidence intervals), which, in a risk management context, is a significant advantage over the daily point estimates freely generated by the forward exchange market.
7. The lack of definitive answers to the general question of forecasting exchange rates, however, is probably one of the most potent justifications for undertaking costly and at times highly constraining hedging policies against foreign exchange risk.
8. Composite forecasts combine information from different forecasting models with the objective of outperforming any single forecast. Such a composite or portfolio forecast can be constructed by formulating a weighted average of single forecasting services with weights reflecting each forecast's relative accuracy.

QUESTIONS FOR DISCUSSION

1. What are exchange rate forecasts used for?
2. What are market-based forecasts?
3. What is different about forecasting *pegged yet adjustable* foreign exchange rates?
4. How do you reconcile the efficient market hypothesis with the existence of model-based foreign exchange rate forecasting services?
5. What does it mean for forward rates to be *unbiased* forecasters of future spot exchange rates? What are the implications in risk management situations?
6. What is the difference between fundamental forecasting models and technical forecasting models?

7. What is the chartist approach to forecasting exchange rates?
8. How do you gauge the accuracy of a foreign exchange forecasting model?
9. What are econometric foreign exchange forecasting models?
10. What are composite forecasts?

PROBLEMS

1. **Long-term currency forecast.** South Korean treasury bonds maturing in seven years currently trade at 91% and pay an annual coupon of 7.5% while similar US Treasuries paying an annual coupon of 4.25% currently trade at 103%. Both bonds are redeemed at par. What would be your forecast for appreciation/depreciation of the South Korean won against the US dollar over the next seven years?
2. **Forecasting the Thai baht.** Pernod-Ricard — the French distiller — is exporting to Thailand and is concerned about the euro value of its Thai baht–denominated sales revenue. It considers two forecasts for the 90 day baht/euro exchange rate. The current spot rate is THB 40 = €1. The first forecast puts the baht at 45.50 whereas the second forecast is 41 and the forward rate is 42. Ninety days later the spot rate stands at 43.
   - **a.** Which forecast turns out to be more accurate?
   - **b.** Which forecast proves to be more helpful from a hedging perspective?
3. **Forecasting the Brazilian real (A).** As the chief economist of the Lusitania country fund with extensive holdings in Brazil, you have been approached by Third Eye, a professional currency forecasting firm that claims to have superior forecasting accuracy on the BRL/US$. Its forecasting track record is presented in the following table, which juxtaposes the firm's three month forecast at the outset (BGN), the forward 90 day forecast, and the actual exchange rate 90 days later (end of period, EOP).
   - **a.** Using the percentage-of-correct-forecasts methodology, is the forecaster demonstrating useful forecasting expertise?
   - **b.** Using the RMSE methodology, evaluate the forecasting performance of Third Eye.
   - **c.** Should you subscribe to the proposed forecasting service given that the forward rate is always available as a free-of-charge forecast?

Quarter	Year	Forecast (BGN)	Forward 3-Month	Actual EOP
Q1	2007	2.17	2.16845	2.044
Q2	2007	2.14	2.06985	1.9242
Q3	2007	1.95	1.94565	1.846
Q4	2007	1.90	1.8498	1.7587
Q1	2008	1.75	1.7793	1.7435
Q2	2008	1.75	1.783605	1.5958
Q3	2008	1.62	1.6426	1.9613
Q4	2008	1.70	1.9412	2.3309
Q1	2009	2.41	2.4183	2.3275
Q2	2009	2.35	2.3655	1.9541
Q3	2009	2.05	1.9886	1.7935
Q4	2009	1.80	1.7997	1.7405
Q1	2010	1.70	1.7813	1.7891
Q2	2010	1.75	1.825331	1.8122
Q3	2010	1.81	1.8434	1.7009
Q4	2010	1.75	1.719	1.66
Q1	2011	1.70	1.69095	1.6288
Q2	2011	1.67	1.66223	1.5678
Q3	2011	1.58	1.593646	1.8397
Q4	2011	1.66	1.875306	1.8657
Q1	2012	1.85	1.9015	1.8215
Q2	2012	1.77	1.85408	2.0793
Q3	2012	2.00	2.111898	2.0315
Q4	2012	2.00	2.05258	2.0669

4. **Forecasting the Brazilian real (B).** The chief economist of the Lusitania country fund believes that the firm will be better served in the long term by using a composite forecasting model combining the forward rate and the Third Eye forecast.
   - **a.** What are the pro and cons of using composite forecasts?
   - **b.** Propose two design methods for creating composite forecasts.
   - **c.** Calculate actual forecasts under both methods.
5. **Forecasting the Indian rupee.** As the Mumbai-based currency analyst for Infosys, you have been approached by 20/20, a professional currency forecasting firm that claims to have superior forecasting accuracy on the INR/US$. Its forecasting track record is presented in the following table, which juxtaposes the firm's three month forecast (BGN), the 90 day forecast, and the actual exchange rate 90 days later (EOP).

Quarter	Year	Forecast (BGN)	Forward 3-Month	Actual (EOP)
Q1	2007	44.50	44.60	43.51
Q2	2007	44.05	43.82	40.7463
Q3	2007	40.10	41.02	39.8025
Q4	2007	40.60	39.94	39.4113
Q1	2008	39.00	39.59	40.0788
Q2	2008	39.95	40.16	43.015
Q3	2008	42.78	44.58	47.00
Q4	2008	44.88	47.26	48.6775
Q1	2009	49.25	49.20	50.70
Q2	2009	51.00	51.75	47.925
Q3	2009	47.42	48.25	48.105
Q4	2009	47.25	47.98	46.52
Q1	2010	45.50	46.78	44.94
Q2	2010	45.50	45.12	46.4375
Q3	2010	45.05	47.02	44.94
Q4	2010	45.50	45.09	44.71
Q1	2011	44.24	45.36	44.59
Q2	2011	45.10	45.27	44.67
Q3	2011	45.00	45.11	48.9663
Q4	2011	46.00	49.88	53.1838
Q1	2012	53.00	54.53	50.9475
Q2	2012	51.00	51.98	55.83
Q3	2012	55.00	57.05	52.74
Q4	2012	54.50	53.31	54.895

a. Using the percentage-of-correct-forecasts methodology, is the forecaster demonstrating useful forecasting expertise?

b. Using the RMSE methodology, evaluate the forecasting performance of 20/20.

c. Referring to problem 3, which forecasting service has a more legitimate claim to forecasting accuracy?

INTERNET EXERCISES

6. **Forecasting a Pegged Exchange Rate (intermediate).** You are the chief investment strategist for the Tiger Emerging Market Fund (with access to the websites www.oanda.com and www.imf.gov), which has approximately 20% of its assets invested in the Buenos Aires Bolsa. It is January 2001 and Argentina will soon celebrate its tenth anniversary of a "happy" peg of the peso to the dollar. Should you be concerned?

7. **Forecasting Grexit (advanced).** Consider the case of Greece in the spring of 2010; its national currency, the drachma, was abolished when it joined the euro-zone and it officially adopted the euro as its currency. Apply the four-step forecasting procedure presented in Appendix 15A using quarterly International Monetary Fund's *International Financial Statistics* at www.imf.gov over the period 2001–2010. What conclusion do you reach? Do you believe that Greece will exit the euro-zone? If so, when?

REFERENCES

Allen, H., and Michael P. Taylor. 1990. "Charts, Noise, and Fundamentals in the London Foreign Exchange Market." *Economic Journal* 100(400): 49–59.

Baillie, R. T., and T. Bollerslev. 2000. "The Forward Premium Anomaly Is Not as Bad as You Think." *Journal of International Money and Finance* 19(4): 471–488.

Eun, Cheol, and Sanjiv Sabherwal. 2002. "Forecasting Exchange Rates: Do Banks Know Better?" *Global Finance Journal* 13(2): 195–215.

Giddy, Ian H., and Gunter Dufey. 1975. "The Random Behavior of Flexible Exchange Rates: Implications for Forecasting." *Journal of International Business Studies* 6(1): 1–32.

Klein, Michael W., and Nancy P. Marion. 1998. "Explaining the Duration of Exchange Rates." *Journal of Economics Development* 54(2): 387–404.

Levich, Richard M. 1980. "Analyzing the Accuracy of Foreign Exchange Advisory Services: Theory and Evidence." In *Exchange Risk and Exposure*, edited by R. Levich and C. Wihlborg. Lexington, MA: D.C. Heath.

Rosenberg, Michael R. 1996. *Currency Forecasting.* Chicago: Irwin. See Chapter 12 of this book for an up-to-date discussion of technical analysis for forecasting purposes.

Osler, Carol. 2003. "Currency Orders and Exchange Rate Dynamics: An Explanation for the Predictive Success of Technical Analysis." *Journal of Finance* 58(5): 1791–1819.

Takagi, Shinji. 1991. "Exchange Rate Expectations: A Survey of Survey Studies." *International Monetary Fund Staff Papers* 38(1): 156–183.

Taylor, Alan, and Mark Taylor. 2004. "The Purchasing Power Parity Debate." *Journal of Economic Perspectives* 18: 135–158.

APPENDIX 15A: FORECASTING PEGGED YET ADJUSTABLE EXCHANGE RATES

As discussed in Chapters 2 and 3, under *pegged yet adjustable* or *stabilized* exchange rates, central banks pledge to maintain exchange rates within a narrow margin around the par value. This par value is changed whenever the balance of payments of a country moves into fundamental disequilibrium and when various corrective policies such as internal deflation in combination with exchange controls prove economically ineffective or politically unacceptable. Under such conditions, a change in the exchange rate is a discrete, one-way adjustment of a not inconsiderable magnitude, with the new rate being expected to prevail for some time — until a new fundamental disequilibrium develops!

The general forecasting procedure developed in this appendix is essentially a *four-step sequence*.[13] First, through a review of selected economic indicators, the forecaster will identify which countries have balance of payments that are in fundamental disequilibrium.[14] Second, for the currencies of such countries, the forecaster will measure the pressure that market forces are exercising on prevailing exchange rates. Third, the level of central bank foreign exchange reserves gives an indication of the future point in time at which the central bank will no longer be in a position to defend the prevailing exchange rate. The fourth and crucial step is to predict the type of corrective policies that political governments are likely to implement: Will the country under pressure adjust through a manipulation of its exchange rate (devaluation or revaluation), or instead initiate, essentially for political reasons, a dilatory strategy, combining deflationary or inflationary measures with exchange controls and extensive international borrowing? In applying the four-step forecasting procedure, it is helpful to depict first graphically the trajectory that a currency under pressure is likely to follow. In Exhibit 15A.1, the status of a currency is mapped along two dimensions:

1. The vertical axis simply measures the exchange rate, defined as the local currency price of one US dollar.
2. The horizontal axis measures the severity of exchange controls.

13 The case of countries (primarily emerging-market countries) maintaining controlled exchange rates is somewhat different. Forecasting exchange rates under such conditions is a less perplexing proposition, since such countries are already faced with a fundamental disequilibrium in their balance of payments and are merely suppressing it through controls. The critical warning signal is no longer the absolute magnitude of the fundamental disequilibrium but rather the relative trend in the magnitude of the fundamental disequilibrium over time (worsening/improving). The forecasting procedure under such conditions would be essentially limited to steps 2 and 3 of the sequence outlined next.

14 In Chapter 4, we emphasized that from an accounting point of view a balance of payments always balances. Disequilibrium refers to a situation where the algebraic sum of current and financial accounts is in surplus or deficit and requires large-scale central bank intervention.

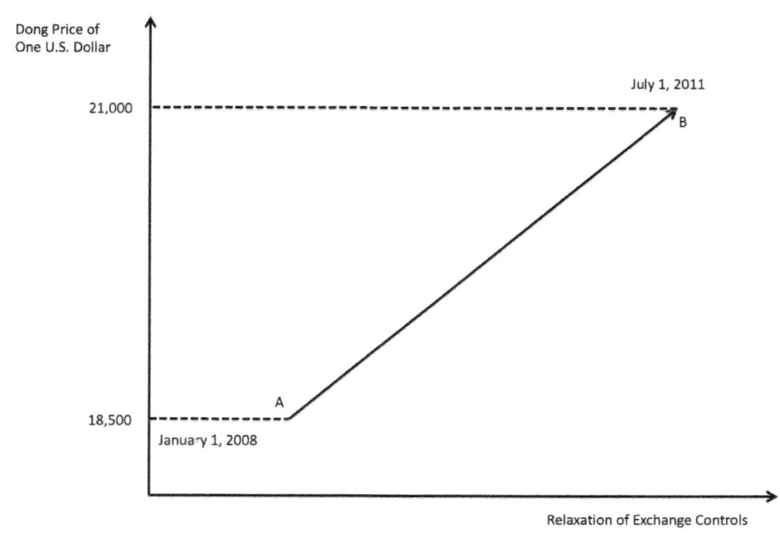

Exhibit 15A.1. Mapping pegged yet adjustable exchange rates.

Thus, the task of the currency forecaster is twofold: (1) a *quantitative forecast* (vertical axis) as a point estimate of the future spot exchange rate and (2) a *qualitative forecast* (horizontal axis) of the increasing or decreasing convertibility of the currency. For example, the Vietnamese dong, currently trading at 18,500 dong per dollar (A), is expected to depreciate over the next six months to 21,000 dong per dollar while the central bank of Vietnam moderately relaxes exchange controls on financial transactions (B).

Step 1: Assessing the balance of payments outlook

Through a review of selected economic indicators, the forecaster first identifies which countries have balance of payments that are in fundamental disequilibrium by developing an early warning system to pinpoint countries whose currencies are becoming potential candidates for adjustment. Like any early warning system, it should be carefully monitored for the early detection of meaningful variances from established patterns. We first define economic indicators that are critical in probing a country's balance-of-payments outlook: Such evidence will be provided by two "quick and dirty" indicators, (1) measuring the rate of depletion or growth in international reserves and (2) the coverage of import spending by export earnings.

Rate of Change in International Reserves: A country experiencing a widening deficit on its balance of payments, resulting from an overall imbalance in its current and financial accounts, must ultimately settle it by drawing down its central bank's liquid external assets of convertible foreign currencies (essentially US dollars), gold, and special drawing rights. These liquid assets, generally called international reserves, are analogous to the cash account of a firm's balance sheet and therefore disregard short-term liabilities that the country may have incurred through its public and/or private sector. Through depletion of its international reserves, a country will be able to finance a deficit on its balance of payments. Conversely, a country experiencing a surplus on its balance of payments will accumulate international reserves. Formally, an index, $\delta_i(t)$, measures the rate of depletion or growth in country i's international reserves:

$$\delta_i(t) = \frac{R_i(t) - R_i(t-1)}{R_i(t-1)}$$

where $R_i(t-1)$ and $R_i(t)$ measure the total amount of international reserves available to country at time $(t-1)$ and t, respectively. This index, however, ignores country i's borrowing potential as measured by its quota with the International Monetary Fund, standby arrangements, and swap agreements with other central banks.

A rate of growth $\delta_i(t)$ significantly at variance from zero clearly points to a disturbance in country i's balance-of-payments equilibrium. It generally reflects systematic central bank intervention, as the par value is being defended against downward (or upward) market pressures. A persisting trend away from zero will indicate that the disturbance is not of a random nature; that is, the disturbance is structural and likely to translate itself into fundamental disequilibrium.

Indicator of trade performance

Evidence of a deteriorating balance of trade is signaled by a lower coverage of import expenditures by export earnings.[15] More than the absolute size of the ratio itself,[16] the currency analyst will closely watch the downward or upward trends in this indicator of trade performance. Formally, the following ratio, $\theta_i(t)$, will be computed for country i at the end of period t:

$$\theta_i(t) = \frac{X_i(t)}{M_i(t)}$$

where $X_i(t)$ and $M_i(t)$ refer to the value of country i's exports and imports, respectively, during period t (year, quarter, or month). $\theta_i(t)$ measures in percentage terms the coverage of country i's imports by its exports during period t.

These two indicators provide good evidence on an *ex post* basis of a full-fledged disequilibrium in the balance of payments of the country under scrutiny. Of better forecasting value are indicators capturing underlying economic trends likely to induce a lagged disequilibrium in the balance of payments under study.

A deterioration in a country's balance of trade usually lags by as much as 6–18 months (depending on the nature of the country's foreign trade) a buildup of inflationary pressures, with the effect

15 Monthly or quarterly trade statistics are usually the first balance-of-payments statistics to be released by governments.

16 This ratio is traditionally low for countries enjoying a substantial surplus on their balance of invisibles. For example, Bangladesh balances its current account, traditionally in deficit from visible transactions (the visible balance of trade), with large-scale remittances from expatriate workers and earnings from tourism (invisibles). In such cases, this indicator should be redefined as the ratio of current account exchange earnings to current account exchange expenditures.

that the currency forecaster should refine the assessment of a country's balance-of-payments outlook by probing underlying trends in relative prices. Higher domestic prices usually undermine the competitiveness of a country's export products in the world marketplace. More specifically, if domestic inflation entrenches itself at a rate exceeding that of the country's major trading partners and to the extent that higher domestic prices are indeed translated into higher export prices, foreign demand for domestically produced goods will seek lower-priced alternatives; conversely, domestic buyers will shift their purchases to foreign (imported) goods.[17] The resulting deterioration of the balance of trade (higher imports and lower exports) will put pressure on the prevailing exchange rate, and devaluation will become necessary for the country to reestablish its trade position.[18]

Step 2: Measuring the magnitude of required adjustment

For the currencies of countries experiencing a fundamental balance-of-payments disequilibrium, the forecaster will measure the pressure that market forces are exercising on prevailing exchange rates. Once a currency has been singled out for adjustment, the currency forecaster will carry out the second step of the forecasting procedure — that is, assessing the magnitude of the change in the exchange rate required to bring the balance of payments back into equilibrium.

The percentage change in the exchange rate between country i's currency and country j's currency is approximated by a *trade-weighted* average of inflation rate differentials:

$$\frac{S_{i,j}(t)^{*}-S_{i,j}(t)}{S_{i,j}(t)}=r_i(t)-\sum_{j=1}^{n} w_i(t)^{j}\times r_j(t)$$

where $S_{i,j}(t)$ is the currency i price of one unit of currency j before devaluation or revaluation (that is, in the disequilibrium situation), whereas $S_{i,j}(t)^{*}$ is the equilibrium exchange rate predicted by the purchasing power parity hypothesis; $r_i(t)$ and $r_j(t)$ measure the rate of inflation experienced by countries i and j over the period starting with the last parity adjustment up to time t; and $w_i(t)^{j}$ is the percentage of trade that country i conducts with country j.

For example, if Vietnam last adjusted its exchange rate against the US dollar in 2021, in 2024 after 3 years of inflation at the rate of 12% annually against its three major trading partners — Thailand, China, and the United States, which experienced respective rates of inflation of 4%, 6%, and 1% — the dong is expected to devalue by:

$$\frac{S(2024)-S(2021)}{S(2021)}=36\%$$
$$-\left(0.25\times 12\% + 0.25\times 18\% + 0.50\times 3\%\right)=25\%$$

assuming that Vietnam does 25% of its international trade with Thailand, 25% with China, and 50% with the United States. Note that we are also assuming that Vietnam's other trading partners are ignored.

Market versus black market rates as an indicator of the future spot exchange rate

Under a system of controlled exchange rates, a good proxy estimate of what the equilibrium exchange rate should be is provided by the exchange rate quoted by the black market. However, black market rates tend to *overestimate* the extent of the needed devaluation to bring back the balance of payments into equilibrium and should be used in combination with the purchasing power parity rate.

Step 3: Timing adjustment policies

The level of central bank foreign exchange reserves gives an indication of the future point in time at which the central bank will no longer be in a position to defend the prevailing exchange rate. Once the pressure on a given currency has been estimated as the discrepancy between the forecasted (equilibrium) rate $S_{i,j}(t)^{*}$ and the actual prevailing rate of exchange $S_{i,j}(t)$, the currency forecaster will probe the resistance capacity of the country under pressure to adjust. The ability to resist or to delay the implementation of corrective policies is very much dependent on the overall amount of international reserves that can be spent to finance the deficit resulting from the fundamental disequilibrium of the balance of payments. An index, $\varphi_i(t)$, measuring the grace period can be computed as follows:

$$\varphi_i(t)=\frac{R_i(t)+R_i(t)^{*}}{D_i(t)}$$

where $\varphi_i(t)$ measures the number of periods t (usually months or quarters) during which country i can

17 This assumes that the demand is price-elastic.

18 This is the purchasing power parity hypothesis introduced in Chapter 7. Empirical tests indicate that inflation and devaluation do, in fact, tend to be linked over the long term.

afford to sustain a deficit of $D_i(t)$ per period, and $R_i(t)$ is the quantity of reserves (both owned and borrowed) available to country i. These are made up of holdings of foreign exchange, gold, and special drawing rights. $R_i(t)^*$ is the estimated amount of international liquidities that can be readily obtained from international sources (standby agreements), or from other central banks (swap agreements), or simply borrowed from international money and capital markets such as the Eurobonds market.

As time runs out, the index $\varphi_i(t)$ decreases, and the grace period, by the end of which adjustment policies can no longer be postponed, shortens dangerously.

Step 4: Anticipating the nature of adjustment policies

For a country whose balance of payments is in fundamental disequilibrium, devaluing (or revaluing) its currency or letting it depreciate (or appreciate) is ultimately a political decision. No matter how necessary a devaluation (or revaluation) may be from an economic point of view, political factors have the final word in deciding between the implementation of inflationary (or deflationary) policies and/or the imposition of exchange controls versus a change in the par value of the currency.

In the case of a structural balance-of-payments deficit, policy makers will first consider the implementation of an austerity plan or deflationary policy as a way of bringing the balance of payments back into fundamental equilibrium.[19] An appropriate combination of restrictive fiscal and monetary policies should presumably induce a reduction of aggregate domestic demand for both domestic and foreign-produced goods so that the demand for imports falls and the supply of exports rises. Such results may be easier to obtain if deflationary policies are combined with internal controls on wages and prices.[20] Furthermore, external controls, essentially on capital account transactions, should further reinforce the improvement in the balance of trade, which should follow a deflationary policy combined with internal controls

Clearly, deflation will work best when the income elasticity of demand for imports is large. For example, if a cut of 1% in national income reduces the volume of imports by 3% (income elasticity is 3), only half as much deflation is needed to secure a given improvement in the balance of trade (lower imports resulting from lower national income) as when the income elasticity is 1½. The effect of domestic deflation on exports is less clear; much will depend on the modus operandi of deflationary policies and on the state of world trade. When world trade is buoyant, it is important to have supplies available and to be competitive in delivery dates; deflation will definitely help by making additional manufactured goods readily available for exports. Conversely, when world trade slumps, there is no shortage of supply, and additional exports will be primarily achieved through reduced prices; deflation will be of little help.

The cost of such remedial action for external disequilibrium (deficit on the balance of payments) is predictable enough: unemployment, which, to say the least, is unlikely to arouse popular enthusiasm.

Devaluation

If a combination of deflation and controls does not work out as intended, or if the expected political cost of unemployment cannot be afforded by the government in power, or if a policy of large-scale borrowing has reached its limits, then the weapon of last resort will have to be used: devaluation. At this point, political factors will have to be reviewed in a qualitative manner by the currency analyst. In so doing, he or she should be able to determine how much longer a devaluation can be postponed for purely political reasons or even if devaluation is totally ruled out on a priori grounds by responsible decision makers. The fourth and crucial step is to predict the type of corrective policies that political decision makers are likely to implement: Will the country under pressure adjust through a manipulation of its exchange rate (devaluation or revaluation), or instead initiate, essentially for political reasons, a dilatory strategy, combining deflationary or inflationary measures with exchange controls and extensive international borrowing?

19 By deflationary policy is meant a combination of reduction of government spending and higher taxes (fiscal policy) and a tightening of monetary policy, inducing higher interest rates, which should discourage business investments and the financing of consumers' spending.

20 Restraint on wages should limit domestic demand and make export goods more competitive on foreign markets. A price freeze is somewhat similar to a devaluation of the domestic currency staggered over the life of the controls, but cannot be applied to export prices.

CASE STUDY 15.1. EUCLIDES ENGINEERING, LTD.

The submission of a bid to the Mexican government's agency in charge of the rural telephony project had been most disappointing. In early March 2009, Sam Finkel, manager of finance for the Telecommunication Systems Division at Euclides Engineering, was notified that Euclides had been underbid in Mexico to the tune of $13 million by the Swedish conglomerate LM Ericsson.

Euclides had entered the bidding contest for the installation of five cell towers for mobile telephone systems near Monterey, Mexico's second-largest industrial center. The bid submitted in March 2009 was in the amount of $67 million, to be paid in three equal installments on December 31, 2009, December 31, 2010, and December 31, 2011, with installation to be completed in the last six months of 2010.

Attached with the reply from the Mexican government was a photocopy of LM Ericsson's bid, which was virtually identical from the standpoint of technical specifications but varied in terms of payment:

1. *LM Ericsson*: equivalent of $54 million (denominated in Swedish krone (SEK) at the rate of SEK 9.10 = US$1). Same payment schedule as Euclides, but in three equal installments to be paid in Swedish krone.
2. *Euclides Engineering*: $67 million.

A second round of bidding was to be held on March 15, with the winner to be announced on April 1. Sam Finkel was concerned that a strong dollar had just about closed his export market, whereas Euclides used to be price competitive even when lavish export credits were offered by its foreign competitors. Sam felt that in spite of his new financial responsibilities, his background and the past 15 years of his career as a civil engineer with Euclides did not equip him with the financing skills that could close the gap between the two bids. Fortunately, Sam felt he could depend on his new assistant, Gerardo Wehmann, a Mexican national with graduate education in electrical engineering from Stanford and an MBA in international business from the Wharton School. Gerardo, who had gone over the files, felt that Finkel's consideration of the exchange rate had much to do with Euclides' problem. He decided to study the situation further. To begin, he examined the Swedish krone exchange rate forecasts put out by Bloomberg's consensus forecast. He also studied the forward rates and the rates on several options contracts as of March 3. These data are contained in Case Exhibits 15.1 and 15.2, respectively.

Questions for Discussion

1. In view of the US dollar–Swedish krone exchange rate, how can you explain the discrepancy between the US bid and the Swedish bid?
2. Can Euclides match the Swedish bid without changing its dollar price? How?
3. If you were to advise the Mexican government on how to compare bids denominated in different currencies, what would your advice be?

Case Exhibit 15.1. Exchange rate forecasts and quotations for end of year.

	12/2009	12/2010	12/2011
Forecast	7.78	7.21	7.08
Forward	9.07	8.98	8.96

Note: Exchange rates are expressed in SEK price for one US dollar.

Case Exhibit 15.2. Options quotations.

	Premium on Call Contract		Premium on Put Contract	
Strike Price	**12/2009**	**12/2010**	**12/2009**	**12/2010**
0.105	1.20	2.25	0.33	0.55
0.110	1.10	1.65	0.64	0.92
0.115	0.62	1.19	1.19	...
0.120	0.33	0.79	...	...
0.130	0.20	0.52	...	...

Note: Strike prices are expressed in US dollars per SEK, and premiums are in cents per SEK.

CHAPTER 16

Managing Transaction Exposure

Merchants have no country. The mere spot they stand on does not constitute so strong an attachment as that from which they draw their gains.
— Thomas Jefferson

In the early phases of internationalization, firms are primarily exposed to foreign exchange (FX or forex) risks of a *transaction* nature. Firms that are actively involved in exporting will find it necessary, for competitive reasons, to invoice accounts receivable in the currency of the foreign buyer. Similarly, firms actively *sourcing* components or finished products and services from foreign companies may have to accept being invoiced in the currency of their foreign supplier. In other words, their accounts payable would be in a foreign currency. Either way, whether a firm buys or sells goods in a foreign currency, sizable exchange losses may be incurred from unforeseen and abrupt exchange rate movements. These currency fluctuations can wipe out profits on export sales or eliminate cost savings on foreign procurements (see International Corporate Finance in Practice 16.1).

After showing how to measure and consolidate transaction exposure, this chapter introduces and compares various hedging techniques for the elimination or reduction of such transaction exposures. Whether they are short-term or long-term, known with certainty or contingent upon other events, different transaction exposures require different hedging mechanisms. A firm must assess its particular type of exposure, as well as its risk profile, before deciding on the appropriate technique and the percentage that should be hedged.

After reading this chapter, you should understand the following concepts:

- What *transaction exposures* are and how to measure and consolidate them.
- How to use *currency forwards*, *futures*, and *options* to manage short-term transaction exposures.
- How to use *money market hedges* and *currency swaps* to manage long-term transaction exposures.
- How international trade transactions can be financed and insulated from exchange rate risk.
- How to use currency options to manage uncertain transaction exposure, as is often the case in *international bidding* contests or in *cross-border mergers and acquisitions*.
- Why the cost of hedging will generally warrant only partial exposure rather than total risk elimination, and how to determine this *optimal hedge ratio*.

MEASURING TRANSACTION EXPOSURE

What is transaction exposure to foreign exchange risk? How can such exposure be measured? How should internal reporting systems be designed to keep track of it? Should such currency exposures be centrally consolidated by the multinational corporation? Many of the answers to these questions depend on the nature of the firm's degree of internationalization, and good answers to those same questions will lighten the burden of actually hedging transaction exposures.

Transaction exposure to foreign exchange risk arises from time-deferred foreign currency-denominated contracts. Such contracts materialize imports, exports, or international financing transactions with a well-defined maturity. Changing

INTERNATIONAL CORPORATE FINANCE IN PRACTICE 16.1

Dade Behring Inc. Knows Why It Is Hedging Its Transaction Exposure

If there is one thing Dade Behring Inc. guards assiduously, it is the company's credit rating. After staging a stunning bounce back in 2003, the Chicago-based medical diagnostic equipment manufacturer emerged from Chapter 11 protection after just two years to qualify for unsecured credit at the bargain interest rate of just 62.5 basis points above the London Interbank Offered Rate (LIBOR). Now, it carefully avoids bumps in the road that could upset its lenders and result in a credit downgrade. In the words of Dade Behring's treasurer, one potential sinkhole was the company's sizable exposure — 51% of its $1.6 billion annual revenues — to the vagaries of foreign exchange rate fluctuations. The company sells in more than 100 foreign countries with revenues denominated in 22 currencies, so hedging part or all of that currency exposure is no minor undertaking. Dade Behring takes a distinctly brainy approach to its foreign exchange risk management, hedging the euro (36% of its exposure), the yen (19%), and six other currencies (23%), relying on a sophisticated options strategy.

Source: Adapted from Treasury & Risk, November 2005.

exchange rates over the life of the contract will result in windfall cash-flow gains or in losses. More complex are transaction exposures resulting from international bids or transnational acquisitions: Do they create transaction exposures? What are their maturities? Indeed, bids on foreign projects may be lost, and transnational acquisitions may be blocked or delayed by host governments.

Central to the argument of this section is the premise that, whatever the degree of autonomy granted by a multinational corporation to its subsidiaries, their transaction exposures should be consolidated with the parent's — and their management should be tightly centralized at the enterprise decision center so as to avoid redundant hedging and to achieve economies of scale in foreign exchange risk management.

Matrix of net transaction exposure for exporting firms

For US-domiciled multidivisional firms whose business units may engage in thousands of import or export transactions and many international financing or portfolio investment operations, there is an imperative need to centralize the information concerning transaction exposures in each foreign currency for every maturity *at the comptroller's office*. To capitalize further on the benefits of consolidated information, each business unit should be encouraged to use a company-wide standardized maturity — for example, the 15th of each month or the third Tuesday of each month — to match the maturity of exchange-traded currency futures and options. In so doing, such corporations will be able to deal with their net transaction exposures on an *aggregate* basis, thereby avoiding duplication of protective measures and significantly reducing covering costs.

Consider the fictitious case of United Technologies (UT), whose wide business portfolio engenders multiple transaction exposures.

- Its Otis Elevator division books the exports sale of 20 high-rise elevator systems to the new NATO headquarters in Brussels in the amount of €400 million for delivery on June 30 and September 30, 2024.
- In 2024, its Carrier air-conditioner division procures compressors from Italy at the rate of €75 million for quarterly delivery starting March 31, 2024, and from Japan at the rate of ¥750 million in two installments due June 30 and September 30, 2024.
- UT's consumer finance division issued a one year €1 billion note at a coupon rate of 6% payable quarterly and a six month note in the amount of ¥100 billion carrying two quarterly payments at an annual coupon rate of 2% payable March 30 and June 30, 2024.
- Last, the Sikorsky division has delivered 10 patrol helicopters to the Japanese coast guard for ¥1 billion to be paid on June 30 and December 30, 2024.

United Technologies' treasury mandates a uniform billing date on the 30th of each month to avoid

Exhibit 16.1. Matrix of net transaction exposures (in millions of euros and yen).

	March 30	June 30	September 30	December 30
Euro	...	+400	+400	...
	−75	−75	−75	−75
	−15	−15	−15	−1,015
Net euro exposures	−90	+310	+310	−1,090
Yen	−500	−500	−500	−500
	...	+600	...	+600
Net yen exposures	−500	+100	−500	+100

mismatching of maturities and therefore simplifying the netting of gross exposures. This information can be conveniently stored in a matrix that will summarize by currency (read across the relevant row) and maturity (read down the relevant column) the corporation's asset and liability transaction exposures as indicated in Exhibit 16.1. UT will simply manage the net (rather than the gross) exposure in each currency for different maturities, largely reducing the total number of FX transactions. The challenge is to update *continuously* the information with the help of large-scale, computer-based management information systems, but the benefits of company-wide consolidation of transaction exposures are significant:

- Hedging fewer and considerably smaller net exposures is a source of significant cost savings.
- Business units are freed from the burden of FX management while retaining their autonomy in running their businesses.

Reinvoicing centers and the case of a multinational corporation

We now consider the case of a US multinational corporation (MNC) with several autonomous foreign affiliates, each undertaking international commercial and financial transactions on their own and thus opening themselves to transaction exposure. The problem then becomes one of aggregating corporate transaction exposures incurred by both the parent company and its affiliates. Most often, large multinational corporations will streamline their portfolios of transaction exposures held by both parent and foreign affiliates by establishing a *reinvoicing center*. Such reinvoicing centers are typically legal entities whose raison d'être is to channel all transactions in order to consolidate all transaction exposures and thereby minimize the MNC's overall hedging activities. Reinvoicing centers are preferably domiciled in low-tax countries with minimal regulatory interference such as Switzerland, Luxembourg, or Hong Kong. Individual foreign affiliates will now invoice all transactions in their own currency to the reinvoicing center which — in turn — will reinvoice the same transaction to the recipient affiliate in its own currency. Thus, every foreign affiliate works strictly in its own currency, having transferred all transaction exposures to the reinvoicing center. Expertise in foreign exchange risk management is no longer necessary in the treasury office of each foreign affiliate since it has been centralized at the reinvoicing center.

Consider again United Technologies' Otis division and how it can benefit from United Technologies' European reinvoicing center, which is domiciled for tax reasons in Lausanne (Switzerland). If Otis-Germany exports elevator cabins to its sister affiliate Otis-Sweden in the amount of Swedish krone (SEK) 120 million due in 90 days, it would have to manage its SEK transaction exposure on its own. Instead, Otis-Germany will directly invoice to the reinvoicing center its exports receivable in its own currency — the euro — for the amount of €24 million, equivalent to SEK 120 million at the spot rate prevailing on booking day. United Technologies' reinvoicing center will take title of the goods and assume the € transaction exposure (it therefore has a euro-denominated 90 day payable to Otis-Germany on its books). In turn, it will invoice the Swedish subsidiary in the amount of SEK 120 million and now has a 90 day SEK-denominated receivable from Otis-Sweden (an imports payable from Otis-Sweden's perspective denominated in its own currency — the Swedish krone).

Separately, Otis-Sweden ships cables to Otis-Netherlands in the amount of €16 million. Instead, the shipment will be directly invoiced to United Technologies' reinvoicing center in the amount of SEK 80 million, which now owes a 90 day SEK-denominated payable to Otis-Sweden but holds a euro-denominated receivable from Otis-Netherlands (Otis-Netherlands holds a euro liability exposure denominated in its own currency in the amount of €16 million). United Technologies' reinvoicing center will net the SEK and € exposure that is now reduced to SEK (80 – 120) million = –SEK 40 million and € (16–24) million = – €8 million.

The initial array of bilateral intra-corporate transactions without a reinvoicing center are now being consolidated with a reinvoicing center. The benefits for United Technologies are twofold:

1. It netted €-SEK cross transaction exposures, thereby reducing United Technologies' overall FX exposures and hedging costs.
2. It freed both German and Swedish subsidiaries from the task of managing their respective forex exposures by centralizing this task at UT's European reinvoicing center.

See International Corporate Finance in Practice 16.2 for more advantages of forex centralization.

> ***Q:*** Otis-Netherlands also independently sells suspension cable to LM Ericsson, the Swedish multinational corporation. The shipment is worth SEK 24 million to be paid in 90 days. How would this transaction impact United Technologies' overall FX exposures?
>
> ***A:*** Otis-Netherlands would invoice its reinvoicing center directly in euros for the equivalent amount of €4.8 million, and UT's reinvoicing center would hold an SEK receivable in the amount of SEK 24 million, which would further reduce its net SEK exposure to SEK (24 – 40) = –SEK 16 million as well as its net euro exposure to € (4.8 – 8) million = – €3.2.

INTERNATIONAL CORPORATE FINANCE IN PRACTICE 16.2

Medtronic Centralizes Exposure Management to Make Banks Take Notice

With $1.1 billion of foreign sales annually, Medtronic is neither the smallest nor the largest player on the FX market. Its approach to exposure management reflects the firm's overall size and its relative position in the market. The US-based manufacturer of pacemakers manages exposures in 20 currencies with a staff of three. Its web of operations starts with headquarters in Minneapolis, extends to four major assembly and manufacturing operations — in the Netherlands, France, Brazil, and Canada — and finally spreads to 20 sales operations in 20 countries. The majority of Medtronic's exposures are intracompany transactions.

The company is now in the process of centralizing its forex task. Some time ago, Medtronic established a global netting system through Bank Mendes Gans. The system nets out on a monthly basis the firm's global exposures, leaving the rest to be managed in Minneapolis. For tax reasons, Medtronic has preferred to keep the forex function in the hands of local entities. In addition, management felt that this kept local managers vigilant. "We were concerned that if they didn't feel the impact of currency, they would be reluctant to raise prices," the managers said. Hence, Minneapolis bills the Netherlands in dollars, and the Netherlands bills European, Middle Eastern, and African sales in euros. However, this will all soon change for three reasons: First, the Mendes Gans netting system makes managing consolidated exposure simpler than before. Medtronic is also in the process of shifting its intracompany billing. Soon the Netherlands will be billed in euros, local sales operations will be billed in local currencies, and Minneapolis will hedge the exposures.

Third, volume carries weight on the forex market. A company that does $500 million in foreign currency sales gets $500 million worth of attention from banks. A company that does only $1 million in foreign currency sales finds itself out in the cold. Medtronic believes that centralizing its foreign exchange can help the company get better treatment from the banks. "When you look at us in aggregate, we look like a nice business as far as foreign exchange goes. But when you look at the sales of our country operations, they are relatively small. By consolidating and doing a lot through one bank (via the netting system), we have a lot more leverage."

THE MECHANICS OF HEDGING TRANSACTION EXPOSURE

For independent exporters and importers, foreign exchange risk results from contracts that provide for deferred payment in a currency that is foreign to one of the parties involved. The party that signs the contract in a foreign currency is exposed to the risk that the exchange rate prevailing when the contract is signed may have changed when payment comes due. Specifically, exchange gains or losses arise from the difference between exchange rates prevailing on the day the accounting entry is recorded on the books of the exporter or importer, and the day, several months or years later, when the payment is actually made. If the actual payment received by the exporter is less than initially booked, an exchange loss will be recorded in the income statement; similarly, an importer having to pay more than initially recorded would record a loss on its income statement. The case of an exchange gain (higher payment received by the exporter or lower payment due for the importer) would be treated symmetrically, with the gain also recorded on the income statement.

The case of Sun Microsystems, a United States computer manufacturer, will illustrate the problems that arise from transaction exposure as well as the various hedging techniques available to alleviate the risk. On June 30, 2013, Sun Microsystems exports a supercomputer to France's Institut Pasteur for biomedical research. An export contract is signed that calls for payment in euros (€) to be paid in one year (365 days) on June 30, 2014. The accounts receivable materializing the export transaction is in the amount of $a(365) = €10{,}000{,}000$. At the outset of the transaction on June 30, 2013, the following spot and forward exchange rates — defined as the dollar price of one euro — are prevailing in the market: $S(0) = 1.25$ and $F(365) = 1.20$. Sun Microsystems can choose to deal with this transaction exposure by employing one of the following four strategies:

1. Do nothing.
2. Cover the transaction through a forward contract.
3. Cover the transaction through a money market hedge.
4. Cover through a currency option.

Let's now take a look at the mechanics of each policy.

Do nothing

Sun Microsystems may decide that its best course of action is to leave its euro exposure uncovered. To the extent that this is a conscious decision (rather than carelessness), it is viable. *Doing nothing* implicitly assumes that either the euro will remain stable over the next year or it may possibly appreciate. If the euro remains stable, the accounts receivable will not change in value over the course of the year. If the euro appreciates, Sun's accounts receivable will be worth more in one year's time. When the Institut Pasteur finally pays Sun in euros, Sun will convert the amount into dollars at a more favorable exchange rate. In Exhibit 16.2, line (1) depicts the amount of dollars that Sun will receive in one year (or the exports proceeds in dollars) as a function of the

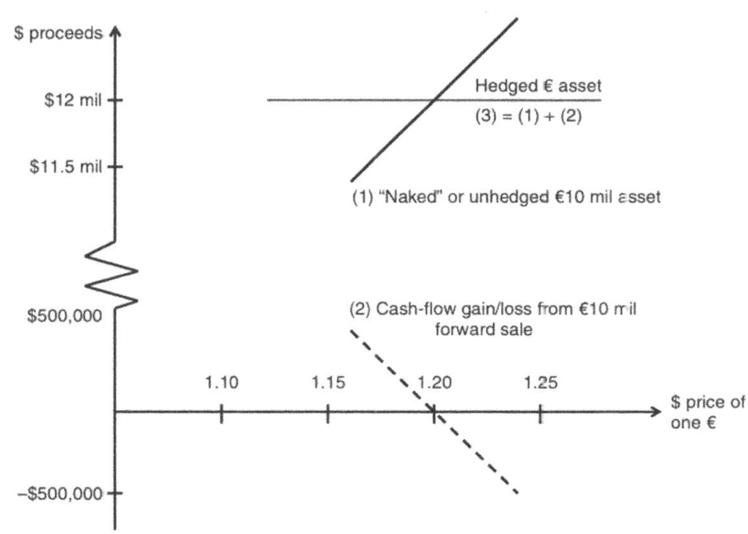

Exhibit 16.2. Hedging transaction exposure with forwards.

Exhibit 16.3. Numerical illustration of hedging transaction exposure with forwards.

The dollar value of hedged accounts receivable is the algebraic sum of the naked euro position (line 1) and the gain/loss of the forward euro sale (line 2), which yields a dollar amount of $12 million (line 3).

Dollar Price of 1 Euro	1.15	1.20	1.25
$ value of unhedged asset (line 1)	11,500,000	12,000,000	12,500,000
$ cash-flow gain/loss from forward sale @ F(365) = 1.20 (line 2)	500,000	0	-500,000
$ value of hedged asset (line 3 = line 1 + line 2)	12,000,000	12,000,000	12,000,000

dollar price of one euro in one year's time, $S(365)$; it is simply a linear function of the unknown one-year-hence spot exchange rate whose slope is the outstanding euro exposed asset, $a(365)$:

$$a(365) \times S(365) = 10{,}000{,}000 \times S(365) \quad (16.1)$$

The exact amount of dollars that Sun will eventually receive depends on where the spot exchange rate will fall in one year's time. Recall that the spot dollar price of one euro is 1.25 on June 30, 2013. If the euro appreciates above 1.25 by June 30, 2014, Sun will receive more dollars than the $12.5 million it expected (10,000,000 × 1.25).

Conversely, if the euro were to depreciate below 1.25, Sun would receive less than $12.5 million. This relationship is depicted by line (1) in Exhibit 16.2 and is illustrated numerically in the top row of Exhibit 16.3.

> A **forward contract** is an agreement between two parties to exchange currencies of different countries at a specified future date and at a specified forward rate. The contract is signed today, but cash flows are not exchanged until maturity regardless of what happens to the spot exchange rate. Here Sun sells forward €10,000,000 at $F(365) = 1.20$ to receive $12,000,000 1 year hence, $t = 365$. The forward contract valuation is determined at the forward rate by the interest rate parity theory (IRPT).

Covering through the forward exchange market

Let us now assume that Sun Microsystems decides to manage its transaction exposure instead of leaving it naked. Sun might choose to cover its foreign exchange risk arising out of its euro-denominated accounts receivable through a forward euro sale contract at the rate of $F(365) = 1.20$. In other words, when the contract is signed, Sun will enter into a forward contract to sell euros and buy dollars in 365 days. When the export contract matures (at time $t = 365$), Sun will receive:

$$\begin{aligned} a(365) \times F(365) &= (10{,}000{,}000) \times (1.20) \\ &= \$12{,}000{,}000 \end{aligned} \quad (16.2)$$

The forward sale contract coupled with the exports receivable will be an entirely self-liquidating operation. At maturity of the euro liability arising out of the forward contract, Sun simultaneously receives euros in payment for the exported goods *and* delivers these euros against dollars to fulfill its obligation under the forward contract. This is shown in Exhibit 16.2. The net result for Sun is the aggregate of the naked euro position (line 1) and the gain/loss of the euro forward sale (line 2) that yields a dollar amount of $12 million (line 3). This amount is independent of the final spot rate, and exchange risk has been fully eliminated.

What Is the Cost of Hedging Through a Forward Contract? As Exhibit 16.3 illustrates, covering a transaction through a forward contract eliminates the risk of a depreciating currency — the euro in the case at hand. However, this benefit comes at a cost, which can be calculated as the annual discount rate of selling forward the euro exports proceeds. The following formula captures this cost:

$$\frac{F(365) - S(0)}{S(0)} = \frac{1.20 - 1.25}{1.25} = -4.00\% \quad (16.2a)$$

Sun is able to know exactly the dollar amount to be received on June 30, 2014. The cost of this certainty is 4% of the face value of the export contract and is measured as the *annualized forward discount of the dollar vis-à-vis the euro*. It represents the nominal cost of covering or eliminating the exchange rate risk arising from accounts receivable denominated in a foreign currency. If the euro is at a deeper discount *vis-à-vis* the dollar (lower forward dollar price of one euro as compared to spot rate), the cost of covering increases. Conversely, if the euro is at a premium *vis-à-vis* the dollar, the hedging cost would actually be negative; that is, a net gain would accrue to Sun.

> ***Q:*** Assume that the forward rate on June 30, 2013, is $F(365) = 1.30$. How much would Sun receive from its €10,000,000 exports receivable? What is the annualized percentage cost of hedging?
>
> ***A:*** Sun would receive \$13,000,000 at an annualized negative cost (profit) of 4%.

By selling its expected exports proceeds forward, Sun was implicitly assuming that the euro would depreciate even further than indicated by the forward exchange rate. If, on June 30, 2014, the exchange rate turns out to be \$1.16 per €1 (instead of \$1.20 per €1), Sun will realize an opportunity gain. This gain can be calculated in the same manner as before:

$$\frac{F(365)-S(365)}{S(365)}=\frac{1.20-1.16}{1.16}=3.45\% \quad (16.2b)$$

Had Sun not covered itself against the foreign exchange risk and the spot exchange rate landed at 1.16, the firm would have incurred an exchange loss:

$$\frac{S(365)-S(0)}{S(0)}=\frac{1.16-1.25}{1.25}=-7.20\% \quad (16.2c)$$

Covering through the money market

The third strategy available to Sun is to cover itself through the money market. This is a symmetrical approach to covering through the forward exchange market and consists of using a combination of the spot foreign exchange market and money markets, sometimes known as synthetic forward contracts. Let's now outline the broad mechanics of a money market hedge.

The first step for Sun would be taken on June 30, 2013, when supercomputers are invoiced and shipped to France. Sun will borrow the present value of its exports proceeds from a European bank (or a bank willing to lend euros), immediately convert the loan proceeds into dollars, and invest them in a time deposit. Second, when the euro-denominated accounts receivable actually matures a year later, Sun simply pays off the euro debt it owes to the bank with its exports proceeds. Let's now take a closer look at each step in this transaction.

Step 1: Sun must first take out a loan from a European bank. The firm will borrow an amount equal to the present value of its exports proceeds. The reader may wonder why Sun borrows the discounted amount and not the total amount of the exports proceeds. The reason is simply that the loan principal plus interest due will equal exactly the exports proceeds in the amount €10,000,000 to be received in one year's time. The relevant interest rate for trade-financing operations prevailing in Europe on June 30, 2013, is $i_€ = 6\%$. Therefore, the euro amount actually borrowed at time $t = 0$ can be calculated as follows:

$$\left[\frac{a(365)}{1+i_€}\right]=\frac{10,000,000}{1+0.06}=€9,433,962 \quad (16.3a)$$

Step 2: Sun will now immediately convert the euro loan proceeds into dollars at the prevailing spot exchange rate. The spot dollar price of one euro on June 30, 2013, is $S(0) = 1.25$. The following formula captures the dollar present value equivalent of the euro loan. Sun, therefore, receives:

$$\left[\frac{a(365)}{1+i_€}\times S(0)\right]=9,433,962\times 1.25$$
$$=\$11,792,453 \quad (16.3b)$$

Step 3: Sun will now invest this dollar amount in a time deposit. If the relevant interest rate in the United States is $i_\$ = 3\%$, then the dollar-equivalent euro loan will grow to the following amount:

$$\left[\frac{a(365)}{1+i_€}\times S(0)\times[1+i_\$]\right]=11,792,453\times(1+0.03)$$
$$=\$12,146,226 \quad (16.3c)$$

In order to evaluate the advantages of a money market hedge against other hedging techniques, this dollar amount should be compared with the dollar amount that Sun would have received had it covered through the forward exchange market:

$$\left[a(365)\times F(365)\right]> or <\left[\frac{a(365)}{1+i_€}\times S(0)\times[1+i_\$]\right]$$

or \$12,000,000 < \$12,146,226. (16.4a)

Since the dollar proceeds are higher with the money market hedge than the forward cover, Sun should cover its transaction exposure through a money market hedge.

The covering decision and interest rate parity

Exhibit 16.4 graphically compares the different covered and uncovered export schemes. Each scheme is sketched as a function of the dollar price of one euro at time of payment $S(365)$. Uncovered exporting (line 1) is a positive linear function of $S(365)$ and appears as an upward-sloping straight line. The dollar proceeds Sun will receive when the export transaction matures at time $t = 365$ will depend on where the exchange rate falls. Covered exporting, either with a money market hedge (line 2) or a forward contract (line 3), is independent of the unknown exchange rate prevailing at time of payment and thus appears as a horizontal line.

In Exhibit 16.4 the intersection points between line (1) and line (2) *and* between line (1) and line (3) are particularly interesting. The no-profit forward exchange rate, $F(365)^*$, can be found at the intersection of (1) and (2), and the market-determined forward rate, $F(365) = 1.20$, is found at the intersection of (1) and (3). Specifically, the no-profit or synthetic forward rate is found by setting expression 16.4a as an equality and solving for $F(365)$:

$$F(365)^* = S(0) \times \frac{1+i_\$}{1+i_€} = 1.25 \times \frac{1+0.03}{1+0.06} = 1.2146 \qquad (16.4b)$$

The reader should recognize in expression 16.4b the *interest rate parity theorem* (IRPT). Clearly, if the theorem of interest rate parity held perfectly, options (2) and (3) would coincide and the market-determined forward rate, $F(365) = 1.20$, would be equal to the no-profit forward rate of exchange, $F(365)^* = 1.2146$. Chapter 6 discussed why the IRPT may not hold perfectly: In this particular case, exporters may have access to preferential government export financing schemes offering subsidized (rather than equilibrium market-clearing) interest rates, which would explain why options (2) and (3) differ. Under such circumstances, Sun should work out both covering strategies and choose the one yielding the maximum dollar amount on June 30, 2014. Only if the market forward exchange rate, $F(365)$, is equal to the no-profit forward exchange rate, $F(365)^*$, would Sun be indifferent between covering through the forward exchange market or through the money market.

The **IRPT** describes how money markets and interest rates tie in with spot and forward rates for two countries. In a strongly managed system, the forward rate is the driven variable, and the spot and interest rates are the drivers. The following formula captures this "no-profit" forward rate:

$$F(365) = S(0) \times \frac{1+i_\$}{1+i_€}$$

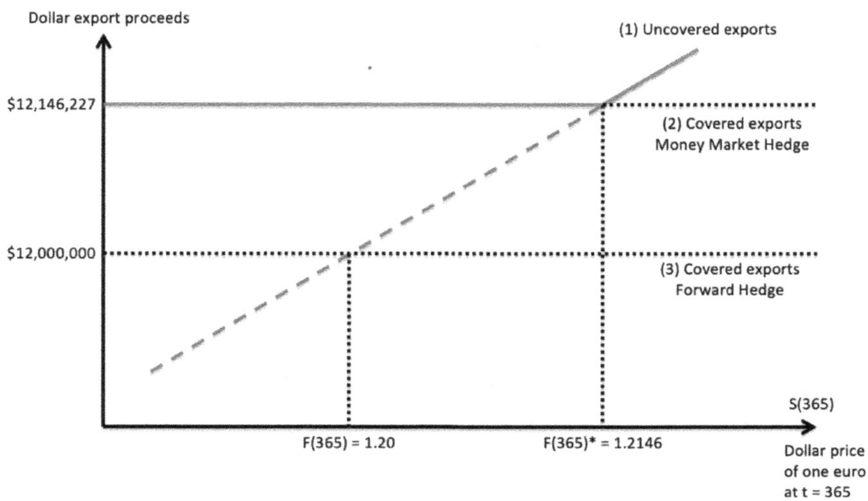

Exhibit 16.4. Dollar export proceeds under different hedging policies.

> *Remember:* Parity in this theorem does *not* refer to equality between nominal interest rates. Rates in different markets vary because inflation expectations are asymmetrical. Instead, parity can be found between the effective yields *corrected for the cost of eliminating forex risk.*

Finally, in reviewing Exhibit 16.4, the reader will readily conclude that in the best of all possible worlds, the exporter would lock in option (2) until $S(365) = F(365)^* = 1.2146$ and then switch to option (1) for $S(365) > F(365)^*$. The reader will have recognized the profile of a put option on euros combined with a naked euro position.

Let's now take a closer look at how currency options can be used to manage transaction exposure.

Covering with currency options and hybrids

Although forward contracts and money market hedges continue to dominate foreign exchange risk-management practices, these techniques are increasingly regarded as too restrictive. Indeed, mechanical or transaction-specific hedging may deprive a firm of favorable exchange rate movements and may place it at a comparative disadvantage *vis-à-vis* key competitors. Currency options and derivative foreign exchange products have become increasingly popular instruments with corporate treasurers because they allow firms to pay for the option to benefit from favorable exchange movements (see International Corporate Finance in Practice 16.3).

Hedging with currency options

Recall that currency options give the right (without the obligation) to buy (in the case of a call option) or sell (in the case of a put option) a specified amount of foreign currency at an agreed strike price for exercise on or even before the expiration date.

Returning to our question of how to cover a transaction exposure, an exporter would buy a *put* option at an exercise price $E(t)$ that could be higher than, equal to, or lower than the forward rate, hoping that the dollar would appreciate beyond the premium-adjusted strike price. The right (without the obligation) to sell euros at the strike price will work at a cost — the option premium — due at the outset of the transaction. Thus, the payoff function has the kinked curve profile first introduced in Chapter 8 and portrayed in Exhibit 16.5A.

Consider again Sun's export sale to the Institut Pasteur: delivery and the payment of €10 million, will occur on June 30, 2014, one year from the signing of the export order. Sun could sell forward all the proceeds for dollars at the rate of $F(365) = 1.20$ or consider the purchase of put options at the exercise price of $E(365) = 1.20$ (at-the-money) with a premium of $810,000. Exhibits 16.5A and 16.5B illustrate the net cash flows resulting from hedging with a put option. Exhibit 16.5A sketches how the naked position (line 1) combined with a put option (line 2) allows Sun to set a floor at $11,190,000 if the euro were to depreciate below 1.20 while also allowing Sun to partake in the benefit of a euro appreciation beyond 1.20 (line 3).

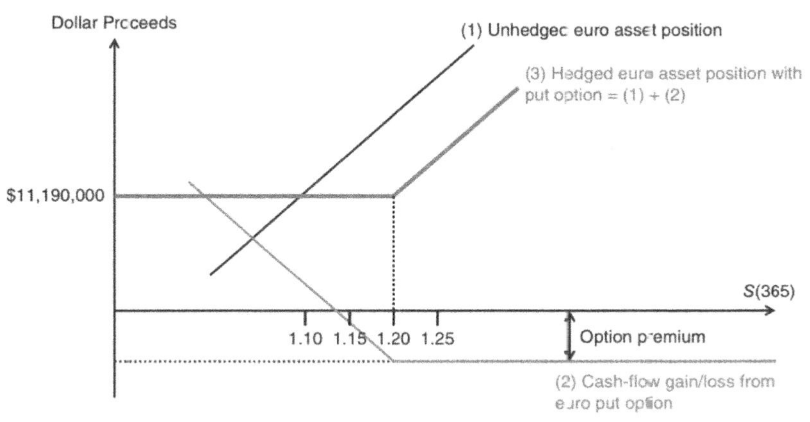

Exhibit 16.5A. Hedging with currency options.

Exhibit 16.5B. Numerical illustration of hedging with currency options.

S(365)	1.15	1.20	1.25
Euro naked position (line 1)	11,500,000	12,000,000	12,500,000
Premium $	810,000	810,000	810,000
Cash-flow gain/loss from euro put option with $E(365) = 1.20$ (line 2)	500,000	0	0
Hedged euro asset position after premium of $810,000 (line 3)	11,190,000	11,190,000	11,690,000

INTERNATIONAL CORPORATE FINANCE IN PRACTICE 16.3

Lufthansa's Unfriendly Foreign Exchange Skies

Hedging the purchase of big-ticket items in a world of currency overshooting can prove unnerving even for the most savvy and globally minded company. Consider the plight of Heinz Ruhnan, the chairman of the board of Lufthansa German Airlines who, in early 1985, after hard negotiations, had closed a deal for the purchase of 20 Boeing 737s for approximately 500 million US dollars. The contract called for delivery and payment in early 1986.

In early 1985, the US dollar had peaked against major European currencies, and indeed, the purchase of 20 Boeing 737s even for cash-rich and profitable Lufthansa was ill-timed. But who was to know that the US dollar had peaked and was going to tumble down in the next few months? Indeed, currency forecasters had wrongly predicted the depreciation of the US dollar as early as 1982, whereas, in fact, the dollar appreciation had confounded its doomsayers until early 1985.

Heinz Ruhnan was rightfully concerned that the US dollar could continue to climb. Thus, he locked in 50% of Lufthansa's dollar liability exposure with a forward contract at \$1 = DM 3.20. The US dollar did finally and precipitously depreciate against the Deutsche mark (DM), so much that, at delivery time, the dollar stood at \$1 = DM 2.30. Thus, the forward cover on half the transaction exposure cost Lufthansa \$250 million (2.30 – 3.20) = –DM 225 million in an opportunity sense. Better, had Lufthansa bought a call option on the US dollar at a strike price of \$1 = DM 3.20, it would have broken even (against an unhedged position) at \$1 = DM 2.90 after taking into account a hefty option premium of DM 150 million and would have saved itself DM 300 million at \$1 = DM 2.30.

Unfortunately for Heinz Ruhnan, the politicians focused on the fact that he had been half wrong, rather than half right: Indeed, the foreign exchange loss was as substantial as it had been embarrassing. Ruhnan was summoned by the transportation minister to explain the losses, while the press called for his dismissal on grounds of "reckless speculation." In fact, for a time, the airline's supervisory board considered not renewing his employment contract.

Source: Adapted from "Lufthansa: Where Options Would Have Made a Difference," *Intermarket*, November 1986, pp. 20–22.

We now consider the more general case of purchasing put options at various strike prices of $E(365) = 1.15$ (out-of-the-money [OTM]), 1.20 (at-the-money [ATM]), or 1.25 (in-the-money [ITM]) with respective premiums per euro of $p(1) =$ €0.0135, $p(2) =$ €0.0675, and $p(3) =$ €0.0905. Each payoff is sketched in Exhibit 16.6A.

The choice of the exercise price is the key decision when hedging with currency options. Choosing the price determines the risk profile of the hedging strategy and is a function of the decision maker's level of risk aversion. A risk-averse firm would be willing to pay a hefty up-front cash-flow premium to guarantee itself a favorable rate

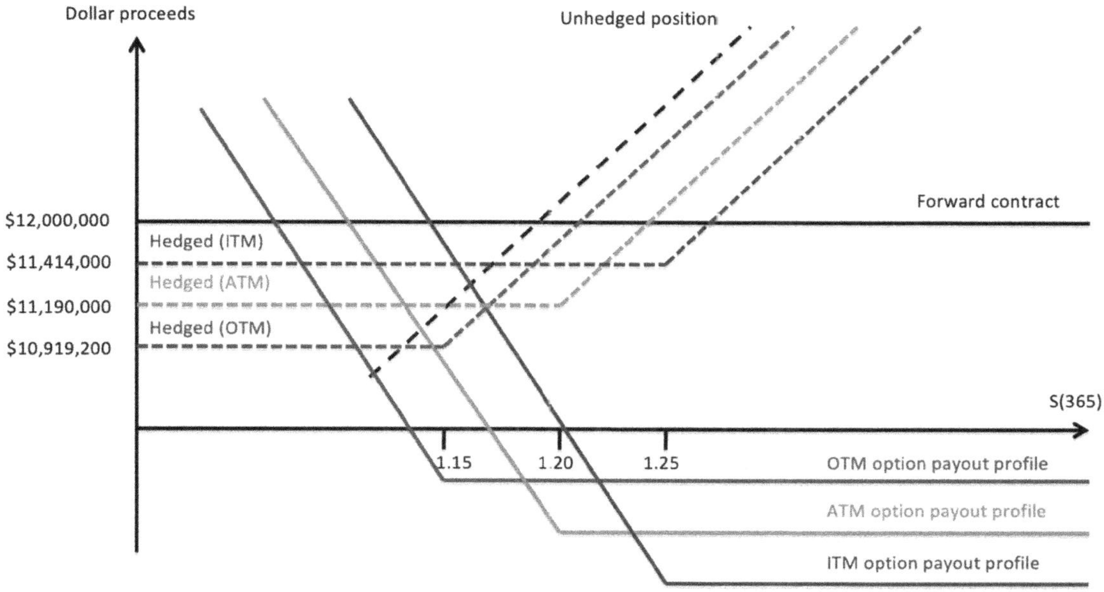

Exhibit 16.6A. Hedging with currency options (out-, in-, at-the- money).

Exhibit 16.6B. Numerical illustration of hedging with currency options.

S(365)	1.15	1.20	1.25
Euro naked position (line 1)	11,500,000	12,000,000	12,500,000
Out-of-the-money put option (*strike price* = 1.15)			
Premium ($)	580,800	580,800	580,800
Cash-flow gain/loss ($)	0	0	0
Hedged euro asset position	11,338,000	11,838,000	12,338,000
At-the-money put option (*strike price* = 1.20)			
Premium ($)	810,000	810,000	810,000
Cash-flow gain/loss ($)	500,000	0	0
Hedged euro asset position	11,190,000	11,190,000	11,690,000
In-the-money put option (p = 1.25)			
Premium ($)	1,086,000	1,086,000	1,086,000
Cash-flow gain/loss ($)	1,000,000	500,000	0
Hedged euro asset position	11,414,000	11,414,000	11,414,000

at or above the forward rate. The currency option is then said to be at-the-money or in-the-money. A more aggressive, less risk-averse firm would want to pay as low a premium as possible and be willing to lock in a far less favorable guaranteed rate below the forward rate. The currency option is then said to be out-of-the-money since the option buyer is betting that the euro will be appreciating and that he or she will not have to exercise the option. The reader will recall from Chapter 8 that purchasing a put option to cover an asset transaction exposure allows the hedger to lock in a minimum guaranteed exchange rate equal to the exercise price minus the premium.

Exhibit 16.7. Forward participation contracts.

Forward Participation Agreement	Guaranteed Minimum Rate	Participation Rate (α) (%)	Dollar Proceeds
Forward contract	1.20	0	12,000,000
Strategy I	1.12	26	...
Strategy II	1.08	49	...
Strategy III	1.02	65	...
Put option (premium €0.028)	1.08	100	...

Hedging with forward participation contracts

The major obstacle to using currency options is the large up-front premium. Corporate treasurers find that the painless forward contracts are often much easier to sell to their board of directors than costly currency options. The forward participation agreement offers a compromise solution. It allows the user to share in the upside potential of a currency option by receiving a fixed percentage (the participation rate) of any favorable currency appreciation irrespective of magnitude. Hence, the forward participation contract has proven popular with hedgers since it allows them to trade off the option premium for a reduced percentage α of the upside potential on the future exchange rate.[1] Clearly, the downside risk is limited to the strike price, but the exporter will partake (less than fully) in any upside potential if the foreign currency appreciates. What is perhaps most important is that no up-front cash premium is required from the exporter. The lower (less favorable) the threshold established, the higher the rate of participation. It should be emphasized, however, that forward participation contracts are binding, unlike currency option contracts. Regardless of what happens to the underlying transaction exposure, the buyer of a forward participation contract will have to take delivery.

Consider again the case of Sun selling a supercomputer to the Institut Pasteur. The one year euro asset position could be hedged via forward participation contracts, which would allow the US exporter to benefit from a potential upside movement in the value of the euro *vis-à-vis* the US currency without the disbursement of a hefty up-front option premium.

For instance, let us consider Sun's three alternatives of forward participation contracts. Strategy I offers a relatively generous guaranteed rate of €1 = \$1.12 if the dollar falls below the guaranteed rate, but Sun only participates in the euro appreciation to the tune of $\alpha = 26\%$. Strategies II and III offer lower guaranteed rates of €1 = \$1.08 and €1 = \$1.02 in exchange for higher participation rates of $\alpha = 49\%$ and $\alpha = 65\%$, respectively (see Exhibits 16.7 and 16.8).

Exhibit 16.9 illustrates the payoff of using a forward participation contract (strategy II) versus a forward rate contract at $F(360) = 1.20$ or an

1 Recall from Chapter 8 that a forward participation agreement is nothing but a put option whose premium is financed by writing a call option at the same strike price.

Exhibit 16.8. Hedging with currency options and forward participation agreements.

Exchange Rate Scenario	Outcome with Currency Option Contract	Outcome with Forward Participation Contract
(a) Euro appreciates $S(360) > E(360)$	Exporter abandons put option and receives after adjusting for premium cost $a(360) \times [S(360) - p(0) \times (1 + i)]$	Exporter receives $a(360) \times \{E(360) + \alpha \times [S(360) - E(360)]\}$
(b) Euro depreciates $S(360) < E(360)$	Exporter exercises put option and receives after adjusting for premium cost $a(360) \times [E(360) - p(0)(1 + i)]$	Exporter receives $a(360) \times [E(360)]$

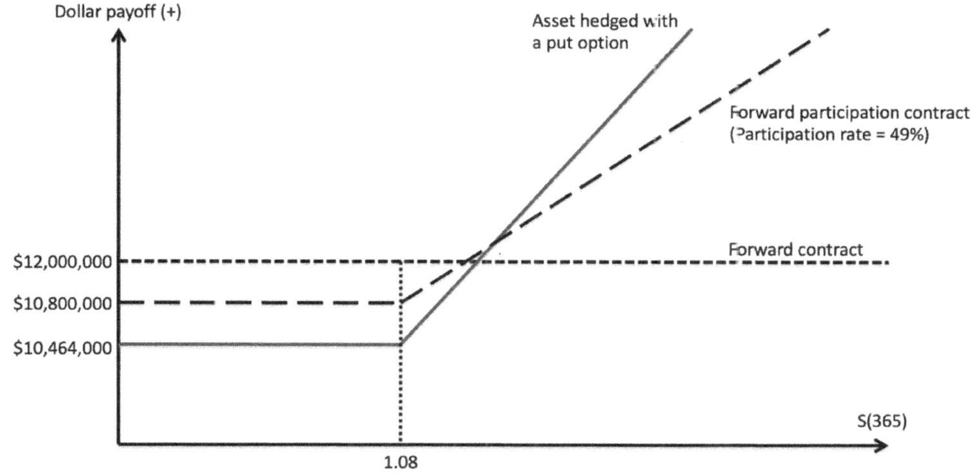

Exhibit 16.9. Hedging with currency options versus a forward participation contract.

out-of-the-money put option over a range of future spot exchange rates. Under a scenario of euro depreciation below the strike price of $1.08 = €1, the hedger benefits from a better floor protection than the out-of-the-money put option provides, although it is not as favorable as the forward contract would be. If the euro appreciates, however, beyond the strike price, the hedger keeps only 49% of the gain versus 100% with a put option. The hedger would abandon 51% of the upside potential to the bank in exchange for not paying any up-front cash premium. The self-financing property of forward participation contracts makes them indeed popular with corporate treasuries precisely for being seemingly costless hedging products.

> *Q:* Referring to the case of Sun's exports to France, what hedging policy should Sun favor if it were very bullish on the euro (expected the euro to appreciate)?
>
> *A:* Sun should opt for an out-of-the-money put option (low strike price and inexpensive premium) or a forward participation agreement at a low floor price and relatively high participation rate (strategy III).

Hedging, expectations, and risk aversion

Referring to a long (asset) position in a foreign currency, a hedger will lock in the proceeds through a forward contract whenever the hedger is *bearish* (pessimistic) on the value of the foreign currency. A put option, very much in-the-money, would achieve a favorable guaranteed rate while leaving open some upside potential. As the hedger becomes more aggressive (less risk-averse) and more *bullish* (optimistic) on the currency, the hedger should consider out-of-the-money put options or forward participation agreements, which offer low minimum guaranteed rates but high upside potential (high participation rate).

HEDGING AND FINANCING INTERNATIONAL TRADE

Exporters are often required to provide financing to their foreign clients but may themselves be in need of financing their exports receivables from external sources. So far, we have focused exclusively on hedging currency risk arising from time-deferred cash flows. Let's now return to the case of Sun Microsystems exporting supercomputers to the Institut Pasteur and expecting the payment of €10,000,000 one year later. More likely than not, Sun will need the funds now rather than a year from now and will consider alternative sources of short-term financing:

- From a US bank such as *State Street* at the rate of $i_\$ = 0.03$.
- From a euro-land bank such as *Credit Lyonnais* at the rate of $i_€ = 0.06$.
- From a third currency-based bank such as *Bank of Tokyo-Mitsubishi* at the rate of $i_¥ = 0.005$.

Sun will select the option that affords the largest amount of dollars now rather than a year from now, while eliminating exchange rate risk. Let's consider the mechanics of each hedging-cum-financing option.

- *Dollar financing*. The dollar-denominated loan will be collateralized by the euro receivables. Specifically, Sun will borrow the present value of the dollar counterparty of the euro receivables hedged through a forward contract at the rate of $F(365) = 1.20$.

$$\frac{a(365)\times F(365)}{1+i_{€}}=\frac{€10{,}000{,}000\times 1.20}{1+0.03}=\$11{,}650{,}485$$

  Note that by borrowing dollars, Sun is creating a dollar liability while holding a euro asset. To correct the currency denomination mismatch, Sun is selling forward euros (creating a euro liability matching in amount and maturity its euro asset) for dollars (creating a dollar asset matching in amount and maturity its dollar liability). This dollar financing was obtained while hedging was secured.

- *Euro financing*. Sun will borrow the present value of its euro receivable and convert immediately the euro loan proceeds into dollars at the spot exchange rate, $S(0) = 1.25$.

$$\frac{a(365)}{1+i_{€}}\times S(0)=\frac{€10{,}000{,}000}{1+0.06}\times 1.25$$
$$=\$11{,}792{,}452$$

  Note that by borrowing euros Sun is creating a euro liability that is perfectly matched by the euro-denominated export receivable whose proceeds will be used to pay off the loan.

- *Yen financing*. This montage is somewhat more complex since the debt is incurred in a third currency (yen), collateralized by a receivable denominated in euros while the loan proceeds are converted to dollars. The currency mismatch between the yen liability and the euro asset is addressed by selling forward the euro proceeds for yen, thereby transforming the currency denomination of euro assets into yen to neutralize the yen liability. Specifically, €10,000,000 will be sold forward at the rate $F(365)^* = 150$ (yen price of the euro), against which yen will be borrowed (the present value only of the loan principal is received) and immediately exchanged for dollars at the spot rate of $S(0) = 1/120$.

$$\frac{a(365)\times F(365)^*}{1+i_{¥}}\times S(0)$$
$$=\frac{10{,}000{,}000\times 150}{1+0.005}\times\left(\frac{1}{120}\right)=\$12{,}437{,}811$$

The simple numerical comparison shows that the yen financing is preferred. In practice, the comparison will be extended to more than three currencies with simple software routines assisting the treasury offices of firms or banks.

ELIMINATING FOREIGN EXCHANGE RATE RISK IN LONG-TERM CONTRACTS

When international trade transactions extend over several years, forward exchange contracts will not usually be available. Covering through the money market, however, is often possible, and the rapid development of the currency swap market during the 1980s made long-dated synthetic forward contracts readily available.

Consider the case of Boeing, the American aircraft manufacturer. Boeing has signed a major export order with the United Kingdom's Virgin Airlines calling for the annual delivery of four 747-400 jet airliners over the next five years starting on January 1, 2011. The schedule of sterling-denominated cash flows is summarized in Exhibit 16.10, rows (1) and (2).

Exhibit 16.10. Hedging with synthetic forward contracts.

(1) Payment Time		Year 1 (%)	Year 2 (%)	Year 3 (%)	Year 4 (%)	Year 5 (%)
(2) Sterling payment (in millions)		100	100	100	100	100
(3) UK interest rate	Simple	9.00	9.30	9.50	9.70	9.80
(4) US interest rate	Simple	8.00	8.20	8.40	8.50	8.60
(5) Synthetic Forward exchange rate		1.7339	1.71477	1.69752	1.67329	1.65489
(6) US dollar payment (in millions)		173.39	171.477	169.752	167.329	165.489

Presumably, Boeing would want to protect itself against the possible depreciation of the pound sterling over the 5 year exposure horizon and would consider the following options.

Hedging with synthetic forward contracts or money market hedges

The first solution would be to sell pounds forward for corresponding maturities of 1–5 years against US dollars. However, given the long-term nature of the dollar transaction exposure, outright forward contracts will not readily be available — but money market hedges (synthetic forward contracts) should be easy to structure.

For example, Boeing would hedge its £100 million five year receivable by borrowing its present value, £100 million/(1 + 0.0980)^5, immediately converting the proceeds at the spot rate of 1.75 for dollar proceeds of [£100 million/(1 + 0.0980)^5] × 1.75, which will, in turn, earn interest at the rate of 8.60% for a total dollar amount 5 years hence of [£100 million (1 + 0.0860)^5/(1 + 0.0980)^5] × 1.75 = \$165.489 million. In effect, it is as if Boeing had sold £100 million at a synthetic forward rate of 1.75 × (1 + 0.0860)^5/(1 + 0.0980)^5 = 1.6564. Boeing can similarly hedge its sterling exports receivable for years 1, 2, … , 4. More generally, for year t, the corresponding forward rate $F(t)^*$ can be computed as the no-profit synthetic forward rate:

$$F(t)^* = S(0)\times\left[\frac{(1+i_\$(t))}{(1+i_£(t))}\right]^t \quad \text{with } t=1,2,\ldots,5 \tag{16.5}$$

where $i_\$(t)$ and $i_£(t)$ refer to annual US and UK interest rates for a t-year horizon as shown in rows (3) and (4) of Exhibit 16.10.

For example, a five year money market hedge using the information in the last column of rows (3) and (4) of Exhibit 16.10 is found to be:

$$F(5)^* = (1.75)\times\left[\frac{(1+0.0860)}{(1+0.0980)}\right]^5 = 1.6564$$

which indicates that the pound sterling is at a forward discount for the five year term of: (1.6564 – 1.75)/1.75 = –0.0535.

Thus, for each maturity t = 1, 2, … , 5, Boeing will sell forward its sterling exposure at the corresponding synthetic forward rate of $F(t)^*$:

$$\begin{aligned} a &= a(t)\times S(0)\times\left[\frac{(1+i_\$(t))}{(1+i_£(t))}\right]^t \\ &= a(t)\times F(t)^* \end{aligned} \tag{16.6}$$

which for year t = 5 yields dollar proceeds of:

$$a(5) = 100{,}000{,}000 \times (1.6548) = \$165{,}489{,}000$$

Similarly, synthetic forward rates for years 1, 2, 3, and 4 are shown in row (5) of Exhibit 16.10 with actual dollar proceeds presented in the bottom row (6).

Hedging with currency swaps

As discussed in Chapter 12, the absence of an active market for long-term forward contracts was partially responsible for the explosive growth in currency swaps. The situation just discussed could readily lead Boeing to hedge its series of transaction exposures with the help of a currency swap.

The solution here is to consider the five (sterling) cash flows as constant annuities corresponding to the principal and interest payments on a fictitious mortgage-style loan whose face value or notional amount would have to be determined.[2]

Once the notional amount is computed, the currency swap allowing Boeing to transform its sterling-denominated cash flows into dollar-denominated cash flows should be easy to figure out.

If we refer to row (2) of Exhibit 16.11, it is possible to compute the present value of a notional principal corresponding to five constant annuities whose present value is found by discounting their face value of £100 million at the corresponding zero coupon[3] rate; see row (3) of Exhibit 16.11.

Boeing is left with swapping its sterling-denominated notional loan for an equivalent dollar-denominated loan, also repayable in five constant annuities. The notional principal, $P(0)$, of such a sterling-denominated loan would be:

$$\begin{aligned} P(0) &= \frac{100m}{1+0.09}+\frac{100m}{(1+0.0931)}+\frac{100m}{(1+0.0953)^3} \\ &+\frac{100m}{(1+0.0975)^4}+\frac{100m}{(1+0.0987)^5} \\ &= 382{,}923{,}500 \end{aligned} \tag{16.7}$$

2 This is analogous to a mortgage loan whose interest payments and principal repayments are amortized in equal installments.

3 Zero-coupon rates are used because each annuity is considered as a zero-coupon bond (no intervening interest payments are made between time of issue and time of repayment of the bond).

Exhibit 16.11. Hedging with currency swaps.

(1) Payment Time		Year 1 (%)	Year 2 (%)	Year 3 (%)	Year 4 (%)	Year 5 (%)
(2) Sterling payment (in millions)		100	100	100	100	100
(3) UK interest rate	Simple	9.00	9.30	9.50	9.70	9.80
	Zero-coupon	9.00	9.31	9.53	9.75	9.87
(4) US interest rate	Simple	8.00	8.20	8.40	8.50	8.60
	Zero-coupon	8.00	8.21	8.42	8.53	8.64
(5) Synthetic Forward exchange rate		1.7339	1.7148	1.6975	1.6733	1.6549
(6) US dollar payment (in millions)		173.39	171.48	169.75	167.33	165.49

with its US dollar counterpart $P(0)^*$ readily computed as:

$$P(0)^* = P(0) \times S(0) = 382{,}923{,}500 \times 1.75 = \$670{,}116{,}125$$

As in the case of the fictional sterling loan, the dollar loan can be construed as equal to the sum of present values found by discounting the corresponding US zero-coupon yield of each annuity, shown in row (4) of Exhibit 16.11. Since the US loan would be repaid in constant dollar-denominated annuities $A(t)$, we can solve

$$\$670{,}116{,}125 = \frac{A(1)}{(1+0.08000)} + \frac{A(2)}{(1+0.08208)^2} + \frac{A(3)}{(1+0.08423)^3} + \frac{A(4)}{(1+0.08531)^4} + \frac{A(5)}{(1+0.08644)^5}$$

with $A(1) = A(2) = A(3) = A(4) = A(5)$, and find each constant annuity equal to $A(t) = \$169{,}823{,}810$.

As in the case of a one year money market hedge, Boeing would borrow £382,923,500 with repayment structured as a five year annual mortgage (annual payment of £100 million), thereby creating sterling-denominated liabilities matching in amount and maturities its £ receivables. Boeing would use the matching amount of its £ receivables to pay back the loan. The £ loan proceeds would be swapped immediately into a dollar-denominated five year mortgage in the amount of $670,116,125 with the swap counterparty committing to annual payment of $A(t) = \$169{,}823{,}810$.

Thus, the design of this currency swap on the basis of two fictitious loans would allow Boeing to transform constant pound sterling–denominated annuities into constant US dollar annuities, resulting in a constant unified forward rate of[4]:

$$F(t) = 1.6982 \quad \text{with } t = 1,2,\ldots,5$$

In contrast to the first approach based on a synthetic and maturity-specific forward rate, currency swaps have the practical advantage of resulting in a constant forward rate across all maturities of payments. The reader is further referred to International Corporate Finance in Practice 16.4 for another illustration of how long-dated transaction exposures can be hedged with currency swaps.

4 The constant unified forward rate is simply derived as the exchange rate which equates the $ annuity to the £ annuity: £100 m × 1.6982 = $169.82 m.

INTERNATIONAL CORPORATE FINANCE IN PRACTICE 16.4

Walt Disney's Yen Phobia

In 1983, Walt Disney Productions launched an ambitious new theme park: Tokyo Disneyland. The park was operated by an independent Japanese company that paid yen royalties of 5% of gross income to Walt Disney Productions. The yearly yen-denominated royalties represented a significant transaction exposure for Walt Disney Productions for years to come. In early 1985, Walt Disney Productions became concerned about the significant exchange risk embedded in this transaction exposure. Specifically, the very predictable stream of yen royalties was expected to grow throughout the 1980s and beyond while the dollar value of this future stream of royalties was expected to decline as a result of the anticipated depreciation of the yen.

The firm considered a range of hedging techniques, including forward exchange contracts, futures, and currency options. None of these traditional hedging tools, however, allowed Disney to deal with yen transaction exposures beyond 12 to 18 months. Alternatively, Disney considered creating a yen-denominated liability by swapping ten year European currency unit (ECU)-denominated bonds[5] with a sinking fund, the all-in costs of which were denominated in yen. Indeed, this indirect yen financing was cheaper than a similar yen-denominated ten year term loan but most important, it created a series of long-dated yen liabilities that neutralized the expected string of yen-denominated royalty receivables.

Since royalties were paid semiannually by Tokyo Disneyland, the yen would be used to retire the long-term debt, thanks to the sinking fund attached to the ECU-denominated Eurobonds. The exchange rate used in converting yen into dollars had been set once and for all at ¥241 to the dollar when the proceeds of the yen financing had been exchanged for dollars at the time of the bond issue; in effect it was the forward rate at which all yen royalty receivables had been hedged over the period 1985–1995. Unfortunately for Walt Disney Productions, as early as September 1985, the dollar embarked on its precipitous descent, and it was not long before the yen appreciated to 150 yen to the dollar. Yen-denominated royalties had been locked in at a rate that overvalued the US dollar considerably, thus depriving Walt Disney of the benefits of the yen appreciation.

Source: Adapted from W. Carl Kester, *The Walt Disney Company's Yen Financing*, Harvard Business School Case Study 9-287-058.

---

5 The ECU is a basket of European currencies that had joined the European Monetary System in 1979. It is the ancestor of the current euro. See Chapters 2 and 3 for further discussion.

Optimal currency invoicing

As mentioned earlier, foreign exchange risks can always be eliminated by invoicing in a firm's own domestic currency. However, this solution is not necessarily good for customer-supplier relations, as it shifts the burden of hedging onto the customer. Furthermore, the fact that the other party is made to bear the exchange risk will normally be reflected in the price at which the transaction will be concluded. The importer that insists on being invoiced in its own currency as a passive trouble-free policy is in fact paying for shifting the foreign exchange risk to the exporter. The importer may be paying more than if it had been prepared to be more flexible in the choice of currency denomination.

Compromise solutions are available in the nature of contracts denominated in currency units that allow for the parties to share the burden of a change in the exchange rate between contracting time t_c and payment time t_p.

Contracts denominated in both parties' currencies (50–50 basis)

Consider the case of Mitsubishi Heavy Industries, which sources iron ore from Newmont Mining, the US mining conglomerate. For consistency of supply, the Japanese company signs a five year contract, fixing both price and quantity to be purchased from Newmont Mining. If the contract is denominated in dollars ($), at $100 per metric ton, a depreciation

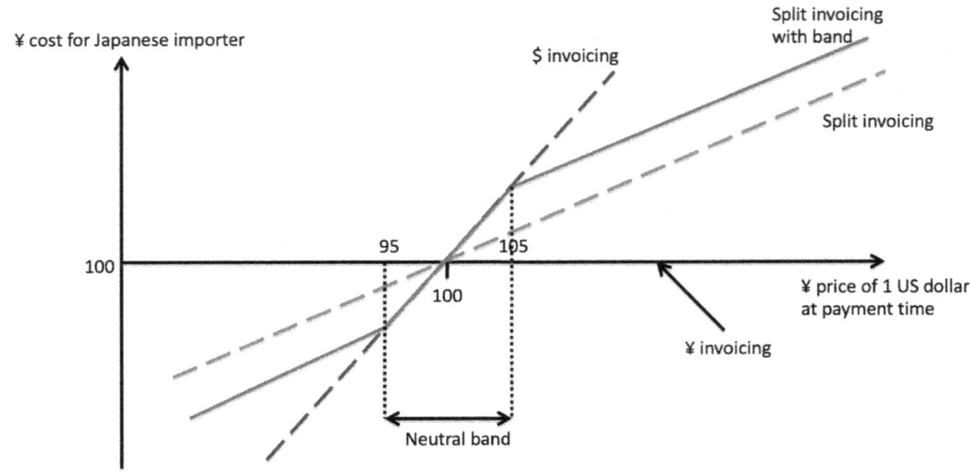

Exhibit 16.12. Split currency invoicing.

of the Japanese yen (¥) between contracting and payment time would be totally supported by the Japanese importer. Conversely, had the contract been denominated in Japanese yen at ¥10,000 per metric ton, a depreciation of the Japanese yen would, in this case, be fully supported by the US exporter.

Under such circumstances of a purely bilateral contract, it is conceptually appealing to price a metric ton of iron ore at $50 plus ¥5,000, assuming, as before, that the prevailing exchange rate is ¥100 = $1 at contracting time. Consider the following two scenarios under alternative contracting schemes:

Scenario 1. The Japanese yen depreciates between contracting and payment from $1 = ¥100 to $1 = ¥125. Under the first contracting scheme (denominated in dollars), the US firm receives $100 per metric ton of iron ore as anticipated at contracting, but the Japanese importer pays ¥12,500 per metric ton of iron ore, which is ¥2,500 per unit more than anticipated at contracting time. The Japanese importer fully absorbs the exchange loss. Had the contract been denominated in Japanese yen, at ¥10,000 per metric ton, the US firm would only receive $80 per metric ton, which is $20 less per unit than anticipated at contracting time.[6]

In the case of a contract pricing the metric ton of iron ore at $50 plus ¥5,000, the Japanese importer would pay at time t_p ¥6,250 plus ¥5,000, which is still an exchange loss of ¥1,250 per metric ton of iron ore as compared to the price that was envisioned at time t_c, but is an improvement over the ¥2,500 loss that would have been incurred had the contract been denominated in dollars. Conversely, the US exporter receives $50 plus $45, which is still a loss of $5 per unit as compared with the price envisioned at time t_c but is an improvement over the $20 loss that would have been incurred had the contract been denominated in ¥. Under this last contracting scheme, both parties have shared equally in the exchange loss.

Scenario 2. The Japanese yen appreciates between time t_c and t_p from $1 = ¥100 to $1 = ¥90. The exchange gain reaped by each party can be worked out under the same three alternative contracting schemes. The result found will be entirely symmetrical with those reached in the case of a depreciation of the Japanese yen.

Split currency invoicing with neutral band

A related invoicing method often used in the case of a bilateral trade relationship, as illustrated in the previous section, is to combine (1) a 50–50 split invoicing contract with a base exchange rate of ¥100 = $1 with (2) establishing around the base exchange rate a neutral band of arbitrary width of, say, +/−¥5, within which the exchange gains/losses are fully assumed by the importer. Within the neutral band of ¥95 to ¥105 per $1, the Japanese importer absorbs the full extent of the dollar exchange rate change. Outside the neutral band, the exchange loss or gain is equally shared between both parties. All four invoicing methods are depicted graphically in Exhibit 16.12, which shows how the yen cost of one

6 As the Japanese yen depreciates from $S(t_c) = 100$ to $S(t_p) = 125$, the US dollar price of Japanese yen decreases from 1/100 = 0.01 to 1/125 = 0.008.

dollar's worth of imports is linked to the ¥ price of one $ at payment time.

However, the idea of a 50–50 split of foreign exchange risk is clearly unsuitable for products or services such as airfare or shipping rates that are actually or potentially traded multilaterally. In such cases, two compromise solutions involving the use of a third country's currency or an artificial currency unit as a basis for contract denomination can be envisioned.

Contract denominated in a third country's currency (dollar or euro invoicing)

For non-US trading parties, denominating longer-term contracts in US dollars or euros may have attractive properties. Although the burden of foreign exchange risk is neither eliminated nor even shared, it may be compensated by the returns in convenience that trading companies exporting to and importing from a great many countries will derive from a uniform dollar invoicing. Such returns in convenience concern the netting of accounts receivable and accounts payable denominated in dollars; this results in substantially smaller transaction costs because only the algebraic balance of accounts receivable and accounts payable is eventually converted from the dollar into the domestic reference currency, or vice versa. If dollar-denominated accounts receivable exceed dollar-denominated accounts payable (a positive algebraic balance), the difference should be converted from dollars into the domestic reference currency and conversely for a negative algebraic balance. Furthermore, by transacting in only one foreign currency, the trading firm will be able to develop a significant expertise in exchange rate forecasting that a multiplicity of foreign exchange dealings would preclude. Using only one foreign currency should also allow the firm to get much better rates, because the scale of its exchange transactions will be significantly larger than if it were fragmenting exchange transactions in several currencies. Finally, the exchange market for dollars against any single currency is usually much deeper and less volatile than between currencies of nations that are only insignificant or minor economic partners.

EXCHANGE RATE RISK IN INTERNATIONAL BIDDING

So far, the discussion has proceeded on the restrictive assumption that a transaction is immediately materialized by a contract. This assumption is undoubtedly true for an export order received on a particular date, filled from existing inventory, and delivered within a fixed period of time. The assumption also holds for an importer who commits to the purchase of foreign goods to be paid for at a future point in time. But consider the situation in which it is necessary to quote prices in another currency contingent on the customer's acceptance, as is often the case for exporters tendering bids on big-ticket items such as aircraft, weapons systems, or power plants. Similarly, a firm bidding for a foreign company — so-called cross-border mergers and acquisitions — may not know for some time if indeed the bid has been won and that it has cleared all regulatory obstacles in the foreign country; this is another case of a sizable transaction exposure contingent on decisions or events beyond the control of the bidding firm. Therefore, it is impossible to enter into a contractual hedge whose maturity and amount would exactly match the projected transaction that has yet to materialize.

Covering contingent exposures with options on forwards or futures

The introduction of currency options has greatly simplified the covering of contingent exposures. For example, at bidding time, an exporter/tenderer holding a contingent foreign currency exposure may simply use a put option on the foreign currency that will reach maturity when the contract is expected to be awarded. If and when the bid is awarded, the exporter may either enter into a forward contract (or money market hedge) or buy another option or relevant hybrid hedging product. If the bid falls through, the exporter/tenderer may exercise the option if it is in-the-money and enjoy a cash profit or — if the option is out-of-the-money — just abandon it. This two-stage process affords the bidder flexibility and good protection against exchange rate surprises. It is clearly a better strategy than hedging through a forward contract, as the story of Air Products in International Corporate Finance in Practice 16.5 clearly illustrates.

Alternatively, our exporter may use a currency option on a futures contract, as available on the Chicago Mercantile Exchange. A futures put option contract is similar to a currency option insofar as it allows the option holder to sell the underlying asset (a currency futures contract in this case rather than the currency itself) at an agreed price — the strike price.[7] However, unlike the currency option, exercise

7 For very large transactions, options on forward contracts would have to be negotiated with a bank.

INTERNATIONAL CORPORATE FINANCE IN PRACTICE 16.5

Air Products Double Whammy

In May 2000, Air Products & Chemicals reported an after-tax charge of $300 million. Most of the charge was attributed to a stunning foreign exchange loss arising from Air Products' failed bid to acquire the UK-based BOC Group PLC. To hedge its *contingent* sterling transaction exposure (BOC would have to be paid for in pounds sterling) Air Products had purchased a forward sterling contract whose market value declined dramatically by the time the acquisition fell through. Had the transaction closed — as it was expected to — Air Products would still have incurred a sizable loss on its sterling forward purchase contract, but it would have paid less for BOC because of the decline in the value of the pound sterling. Simple purchase of a call option on sterling instead of a more speculative forward contract would have protected Air Products for the very modest cost of an up-front premium.

Source: Adapted from the *Wall Street Journal*, May 11, 2000, A4.

of the currency futures option does not involve the payment of cash equal to the exercise price. Instead, upon exercise, the owner of the futures option simply acquires a long or short position, with the futures price equal to the exercise price of the option. This two-step hedge better reflects the realities of many international bids since actual shipment or delivery would typically lag by several weeks or months the actual resolution of the bid — that is, when the tendering firm actually finds out if it won. Thus, exercise of a put option on a dollar futures contract would result — in the preceding case — in a *short* dollar futures position, since the exporter is hedging a dollar asset position. When the futures position acquired is marked to market at the close of the day, the option holder is free to liquidate the position if the exports contract had failed to materialize.

Numerical illustration

Dassault Aviations S.A., the French defense contractor, tendered a bid on the sale of 20 Rafale jet fighters to the Kingdom of Thailand. The bid was entered on April 1, 2019 — along with competing tenders from Israel, Sweden, and the United States — in the amount of US $500 million. The result of the bidding contract would be announced on June 1, 2019, and delivery-cum-payment would take place on September 1, 2019.

At bidding time, market conditions were as follows:

- Spot euro price of one dollar: $S(0) = 0.86$.
- Forward euro price of one dollar for delivery in 150 days: $F(150) = 0.88$.
- Put dollar option on a euro future contract maturing on September 1 with exercise price of 0.88 and exercise date of June 1. It carried a premium of €0.0264 per US$ or 3% of exercise price $E(60, 90) = 0.88$. Exercising the put option on the 60th day would give the option buyer the right to sell dollars for euros for delivery 90 days later at the rate of €0.88 = $1 (150 days from the day the put option was purchased).

In sum, Dassault Aviation S.A. purchased dollar put options to sell dollars forward at the guaranteed effective future exchange rate of €0.8536 per dollar (0.88 – 0.0264).

Scenario I: On June 1, 2019, the dollar has appreciated to $S(60) = 0.92$, and the forward € price per $1 is now $F(90)^* = 0.95$.

- *Assume bid is awarded.* Dassault Aviation S.A. abandons its option and simply sells dollars on the forward market at the rate of €0.95 per dollar for an effective rate of €0.95 – €0.0264 = €0.9236 per dollar received once the currency option premium has been subtracted from the prevailing forward exchange rate.
- *Assume bid is lost.* Dassault Aviation S.A. abandons the put option and loses the up-front currency option premium of €0.0264 per dollar.

Scenario II: On June 1, 2019, the dollar has depreciated *vis-à-vis* the euro to $S(60) = 0.82$ and the forward € price per $1 is now $F(90) = 0.84$.

- *Assume bid is awarded.* Dassault Aviation exercises the put option at the rate of €0.88 and will be

INTERNATIONAL CORPORATE FINANCE IN PRACTICE 16.6

The Shared Currency Option Under Tender (Scout)

Unrelated to the Boy Scouts of America, this product — introduced by Midland Bank — attempts to alleviate the FX contingent exposure supported by a tenderer. The contract awarder, typically an overseas government or corporation, buys an option from Midland and then splits the premium among the tenderers. On the contract date, the successful tenderer is also awarded the option, giving that firm full exchange cover. In the case of four tenderers for a contract with an estimated maximum value of $50 million to be awarded in three months' time, each firm's share will be only a quarter of the normal premium. When the contract and its associated option are finally awarded to one of the four, the other three will each have paid in premium only $312,500 instead of the full $1.25 million. The buyer exercises the option on behalf of the successful tenderer. If the award of the contract does not take place or is delayed beyond the expiration date of the option, then any profit available by exercising the option would be distributed pro rata among all the tenderers.

The advantages to the tenderers are twofold:

1. Full option cover on a successful bid but at a fraction of the normal price for each tenderer.
2. The ability to bid more aggressively because hedging costs are fixed and cheap, being split as many ways as there are tenderers willing to share the option.

The advantages to the contract awarder are as follows:

1. More competitive bids, as each tenderer's full hedge costs are fixed in advance.
2. A larger number of bids possible with potential tenderers no longer deterred by exchange risk.
3. Reduced risk that foreign exchange losses will lead to the bankruptcy of a successful bidder before construction is completed or goods delivered. SCOUT cover could be made a condition of the tender.

Source: Adapted from *Euromoney*, May 1997, 262–263.

selling dollars forward on June 1 with delivery of $500 million slated for September 1 at the rate of 0.88 – 0.0264 for a euro amount of $500 million × 0.8536 = €426.80 million. Clearly, Dassault Aviation would have avoided a significant exchange loss.

- *Assume bid is lost.* Dassault Aviation exercises the put option to receive a forward dollar sale contract at 0.88, which would be liquidated at the rate of 0.84 minus the option premium for a total cash-flow gain of $500 million (0.88 – 0.0264 – 0.84) = €6,800,000.

See International Corporate Finance in Practice 16.6 for an alternative handling of option premiums among bidders.

HOW MUCH TO HEDGE TRANSACTION EXPOSURE

So far, the chapter has discussed at great length how to hedge transaction exposure. In practice, firms have to decide how much to hedge. Should all exposures be fully hedged all the time? Such firms would be characterized as "risk-paranoid" — typically overpaying for hedging products in order to enjoy the peace of mind of no exchange rate surprises.

Most firms will hedge only a percentage of their transaction exposure and may focus on exposures in currencies that have exhibited steady patterns of volatility. Such risk-averse firms will carefully weigh the costs and benefits associated with their hedging policies — see the case of General Motors presented in International Corporate Finance in Practice 16.7.

Although there are formal decision models that attempt to determine the *optimal hedge ratio* to apply to specific transaction exposure as a function of the firm's level of risk aversion and the currency's volatility, these models are seldom implemented in practice. The principal reason is that it is difficult to measure scientifically a firm's level of risk aversion. At best one can argue that the larger the firm, the stronger its credit rating, and the less leveraged it is, the less risk-averse it will tend to be and therefore the less

INTERNATIONAL CORPORATE FINANCE IN PRACTICE 16.7

General Motors' Transaction Exposures

General Motors (GM) hedges 50% of all significant commercial exposures — where *commercial* refers to cash flows associated with ongoing operations such as receivables and payables. Exposure in a given currency is deemed hedgeable if its *implied risk*, defined as face value of exposure × annual volatility of the currency pair, exceeds \$10 million. Such exposures are hedged with forwards for the first 6 months and options for maturities of 6–12 months. For example, if GM–North America had forecasted a 12 month exposure in sterling of \$600 million equivalent and given sterling annual volatility of 15%, the sterling implied risk would be equal to \$600 million × 0.15 = \$90 million and would warrant a 50% hedge since it exceeds the threshold of \$10 million. GM–North America would therefore hedge \$600 million × 0.50 = \$300 million. Last but not least, capital expenditures are fully hedged with forwards to their anticipated payment date (100% hedge ratio), provided that their amount exceeds \$1 million or that implied risk equivalent accounts for at least 10% of the unit's net worth.

Source: Adapted from Desai, Mihir A. 2005. "Foreign Exchange Hedging Strategies at General Motors: Transactional and Translational Exposures." *Harvard Business School Case Study* 9: 205–095.

it will hedge. Conversely, a firm with a poor credit rating (or one that is coming out of bankruptcy) with a heavy debt burden will tend to play it very safe when it comes to currency risk and will hedge a much higher percentage of outstanding exposures.

Similarly, a small firm (or a privately held firm whose owner's wealth is undiversified) with little experience in international business and dealing with a relatively large transaction exposure — as measured by its overall level of sales — will adopt a very conservative, risk-averse approach to currency risk; in other words, it would hedge most if not its entire transaction exposure.

SUMMARY

1. Multinational corporations, whose parent company and foreign affiliates may be involved in thousands of cross-border trade operations, will tightly centralize its handling of transaction exposures, perhaps through an international reinvoicing center.
2. A comprehensive management information system will allow the firm to carry out systematic bilateral and trilateral netting by establishing reinvoicing centers, thus avoiding unnecessary duplication of covering costs. Residual after-tax transaction exposures should be dealt with using the techniques developed in this chapter, given ceiling transaction exposures that the headquarters' treasury is willing to undertake in each foreign currency.
3. Eliminating foreign exchange risks in international trade and financing transactions is straightforward whenever the maturity of the contract (materializing the transaction) is of relatively short duration (less than a year) and denominated in the currency of a country that looms large in international trade. Foreign exchange products such as forwards, currency options, and hybrids are readily available and efficiently priced.
4. The full-fledged exporter whose portfolio of export sales is both large and well diversified may, in contrast, be prepared to play the long-run averages (that is, not cover) or, at the very least, cover its transaction risks more selectively.
5. For long-dated transactions (two years and beyond), the market for currency swaps has grown at a rapid pace over the past decade and is affording international firms deep and well-functioning quasi-forward exchange markets for long-dated transactions.
6. In trading between or with emerging market countries with embryonic foreign exchange markets and limited forex hedging products, it is recommended that commercial contracts be denominated in a currency unit acceptable to both parties, such as a third national currency like the US dollar or the euro.

7. For the occasional big-ticket item exporter, covering foreign exchange risk should be carefully scrutinized, and its cost should be worked into the initial bidding. If the exports contract calls for multiple-step delivery to and payment from a foreign party operating in a less developed country whose currencies are not traded on the forward exchange market, the exporter may turn to institutional insurance guarantees that major industrialized exporting countries generally provide for long-term and large-scale transactions — for example, Coface in France and Britain's Exports Credits Guarantee Department program.

QUESTIONS FOR DISCUSSION

1. What is transaction exposure to foreign exchange risk?
2. Why is hedging transaction exposure generally warranted?
3. What are the benefits of netting transaction exposures?
4. When is the establishment of a reinvoicing center warranted?
5. What is the difference between hedging with forward contracts and with money market hedges? When would you expect their respective costs to be somewhat different?
6. Compare the pros and cons of using forwards and currency options versus forward protection agreements for hedging transaction exposures.
7. Why should firms consider financing international trade in a third currency that is neither the exporter's nor the importer's currency? Show how financing and hedging can be effectively bundled.
8. What is different about hedging long-term transaction exposures?
9. Why do firms generally hedge less than their full exposure? What does it say about their attitude toward risk?
10. What is different about hedging contingent transaction exposures? What are the most appropriate instruments and techniques for hedging transaction exposures?

PROBLEMS

1. **Electrolux transaction exposure (easy).** The Swedish manufacturer of home appliances exports €175 million of vacuum cleaners every month to Carrefour, the French retailer. Payment is due at the end of each month. Electrolux also imports monthly small electrical motors from Italian manufacturer Finmeca in the amount of €50 million due at the end of each quarter. Electrolux pays a quarterly interest of €35 million on its €-denominated outstanding commercial paper on March 30, June 30, September 30, and December 31 and a balloon principal repayment of €250 million on March 31 and September 30 of each year.
   a. Show Electrolux's net monthly € transaction exposure for a typical year.
   b. Electrolux decides on January 1st of this year to swap its €-denominated commercial paper into Swiss franc–denominated commercial paper. How would its € transaction exposure be impacted?
2. **Bombardier's exports receivable (A-easy).** Bombardier — Canada-based defense contractor — signed a sales contract for the delivery by the end of 2008 of five Dash 8 twin-engine turboprops to Alaska Airlines for the sum of US$75 million. It was November 2, 2007, and the Canadian dollar (CAD) had just hit another record — jumping to CAD 1 = US$1.0717. Indeed, the Canadian dollar, fueled by the high price of commodity exports (primarily oil), had been the best-performing currency for the year, appreciating by 25% against the US dollar. One-year forwards were currently quoted at CAD 0.9386/0.9409 = US$1 whereas the spot exchange rate stood at CAD 0.9344/0.9351.
   a. Is the US dollar at a premium or discount *vis-à-vis* the Canadian dollar?
   b. What is the nature of Bombardier's exposure to foreign exchange risk?
   c. How can Bombardier hedge its dollar exposure? Illustrate your answer graphically.
3. **Bombardier's exports receivable (B-easy).** Royal Bank of Canada had just revised its forecast, saying that the CAD would further rise to CAD 1 = US$1.08 before declining below parity by the middle of 2008. The currency desk at Royal Bank of Canada offered the following quotes for currency options. Indeed, Bombardier was now inclined to consider currency options as a possible hedge.

Call Option for November 2, 2008		
Strike Price	**Bid Price**	**Ask Price**
93.50	1.68	1.73
94.00	1.45	1.50
94.50	1.24	1.29
95.00	1.06	1.11

Put Option for November 2, 2008		
Strike Price	**Bid Price**	**Ask Price**
93.50	1.74	1.79
94.00	2.00	2.05
94.50	2.29	2.34
95.00	2.60	2.65

Note: to get the CAD option premium, multiply the bid or ask price (expressed in percentage) by the face value of the contract.

a. Should Bombardier use call or put options in this case? Would you recommend a higher or lower strike price compared to the forward rate?
b. What is the cost for Bombardier to hedge with currency options as opposed to forward contracts? Be specific as to the timing of cash flows.
c. If indeed the currency forecast offered by the Royal Bank of Canada turned out to be correct, which hedging policy would have been best? Sketch your answer graphically.

4. **Sony's royalties payment (easy).** The US sales subsidiary of the Japanese consumer electronics giant Sony Inc. is committed to paying a fixed lump sum of money (royalties) set at 2.5% of its US revenue to its parent on December 31 of the previous year. On January 1, 2014, the royalty payment is fixed at US$5.75 million, payable December 31, 2014.

   The treasurer of Sony-Japan wonders whether he should cover the royalty payment in the forward exchange or the currency options market. The spot exchange rate on January 1, 2014, is 85 yen to the dollar; 360 day forward contracts on the US dollar are selling at a 1.5% annual discount, and December option contracts are available for a 3.6% cash premium for a strike price of 85 yen per dollar.

   a. Sketch the hedging options available to Sony-Japan. What would be the yen proceeds under each?
   b. A recently released econometric forecast projects annual inflation rates in the United States and Japan at 5 and 1%, respectively, in 2014. Furthermore, the Japanese balance of trade is projected to run a surplus of $160 billion and the US balance of trade to run a deficit of $435 billion for 2014. Should Sony-Japan hedge its dollar receivables? How? Is the information provided sufficient to reach a meaningful decision? What are the other covering techniques that should be considered?

5. **Currency risk in the travel industry (intermediate).** Ulysses Travel Ltd (UTL) is a Boston-based travel operator that specializes in tour and holiday packages with destinations in Spain, Italy, and Greece where vendors (hotels and transportation companies) accept payment in € only. UTL was firming its bookings in late October 1, 2013, for the following summer season (June–September 2014), although payment in the amount of €65 million was not due until April 1, 2014. UTL had to decide on prices to charge its clients in October so that brochures could be printed in the fall and customers could start booking their travel and hotel reservations in the following spring. Holidaymakers, however, decided on their travel plans only in late spring and, being US nationals, they were quoted prices in US dollars. UTL had to decide how to manage its upcoming € payment. Six-month forward contracts were quoted at €0.6271 = US$1 whereas the spot exchange rate stood at €0.6298 = US$1. UTL could borrow/lend US$ at 2.70%/2.55% annually and € at annual rates of 1.85%/1.65%.

   a. What is the nature of Ulysses Travel's exposure to currency risk?
   b. How could UTL hedge its exposure?

6. **John Deere's Chinese acquisition (intermediate).** The US farming equipment giant just won approval from the Chinese authorities for the acquisition of Shen-Zhen Excavators Ltd. — a medium-sized Chinese manufacturer of small earthmoving equipment (Bobcat style) — for yuan (CNY) 615 million with payment due in six months. The current spot and six month forward rates are respectively CNY 6.75 = US$1 and CNY 6.50 = US$1. Hong Kong and Shanghai Bank's currency desk further advises John Deere that

over-the-counter six-month European put and call options are available at respective premiums of 2.4 and 3% for a strike price equal to the forward rate. Interest rates in CNY and US$ are, respectively, 10 and 4% on an annual basis. Sketch John Deere's alternative hedging options. What would be your recommendation given that the Chinese currency is heavily stabilized by the Bank of China?

7. **Dinky Toys' cross-border acquisition (intermediate).** Dinky Toys, Inc. (DTI) of Pennsylvania has just purchased a Thai company that manufactures plastic beams and sockets for children's construction toys. The purchase price is 120,000,000 Thai baht (THB) with payment due in six months. The current spot exchange rate is THB 43 = $1, and the six-month forward rate is THB 45 = $1. Annual short-term interest rates are 12% in Thai baht and 4% in US dollars.
   a. Is the Thai baht at a premium or a discount? Compute the semiannually implied interest rate. Does it point toward an appreciation or depreciation of the Thai currency? The baht fluctuated within a range of THB 37 to 46 = $1 over the past 18 months.
   b. Compare the cost of alternative ways in which DTI could deal with its transaction exposure. Assume that DTI can lend at the given interest rate and borrow at 1% per annum above the lending interest rate. Sketch graphically your answers. What is your recommendation?
   c. Six-month call and put options with exercise price of THB 46.50 are available for 3 and 2.4% annual premiums, respectively. Explain how DTI could use an option strategy to manage its transaction exposure.

8. **Moulinex exports financing (intermediate).** On February 15, 2024, Moulinex, a French manufacturer of kitchen utensils, concluded a major exports contract with British retailer Tesco. It expects export proceeds of 100 million pounds sterling (£) to be paid on August 15, 2024.

   Financing of the export transaction can be arranged in three ways: (1) through the French banking system in euros (€) at a yearly interest rate of 5%, (2) through the British banking system in sterling (£) at a yearly interest rate of 7%, and (3) through the Eurodollar market in US$ at a yearly interest rate of 3%.

   On February 15, 2024, exchange rates are quoted as follows:

   $S(0) = 1.2505$ (€ price of one £ for immediate delivery)

   $S(0)^* = 1.2818$ (US$ price of one € for immediate delivery)

   $F(180) = 1.2818$ (€ price of one £ for delivery in 180 days)

   $F(180)^* = 1.2617$ (US$ price of one € for delivery in 180 days)

   a. What is the nature of Moulinex's exposure to foreign exchange risk before financing is taken into account? How can it be hedged?
   b. How can € or £ financing be combined with hedging? Which currency offers the cheaper financing?
   c. What would be the rationale for financing exports to the United Kingdom in US$? What is/are the additional risk(s) incurred by Moulinex? Can they be hedged?
   d. How should the transaction be financed?

9. **Zanussi exports financing (intermediate).** The Italian manufacturer of household appliances Zanussi is exporting dishwashers to Canada and extending 180 days credit to its Canadian wholesaler. The exports proceeds are denominated in Canadian dollars (CAD) and are worth CAD 24 million. To finance its working capital, Zanussi is investigating several financing sources: Banco di Roma would finance the deal in euros at an annual interest rate of 6%; Canadian Imperial Bank of Commerce, a leading Canadian commercial bank, would extend a loan at an annual rate of only 4%. Forward CADs are selling at a premium of 2.25% (on an annual basis *vis-à-vis* the euro) to the spot rate of €1 = CAD 1.31. The Eurodollar market could finance the loan in US$ at an annual rate of 3%. Finally, forward dollars are selling at a premium of 3.5% *vis-à-vis* the euro with a spot rate of €1 = US$1.33.
   a. What is the nature of Zanussi's exposure to risk(s) before financing is taken into account? How could it/they be hedged?
   b. How can € or CAD financing be combined with hedging? Which currency offers the cheaper financing?
   c. What would be the rationale for financing exports to Canada in US$?
   d. What are the additional risk(s) incurred by Zanussi? Can it/they be hedged?
   e. How should the transaction be financed?

10. **Hedging helicopter exports with collars (intermediate).** Eurocopter — the European defense contractor — exports 25 single-engine light helicopters known as Ecureuil (squirrel) to the Japanese Coast Guard with payment to be made in six months in the amount of ¥50 billion. Concerned with the high volatility of the €/¥ exchange rate relationship, Eurocopter is considering the use of a ¥ put option at the strike price of ¥108 = €1 at a premium cost of 2%.
    a. Explain how a put option allows Eurocopter to hedge its ¥ exposure. What is the cost of the hedge, and when is it incurred?
    b. Show graphically the € proceeds in six months as a function of the ¥ price of one € at payment time.
    c. To neutralize the cost of buying a put option, Eurocopter decides to sell a ¥ call option at the strike price of ¥100 = €1 for a premium exactly matching the cost of the put option. Show graphically the € export proceeds over the range of ¥75 to ¥110 = €1.
    d. How would a forward contract at the rate of ¥108 = €1 compare with a ¥ put option or a collar?
    e. At what exchange rate would € proceeds be the same under a forward or put option hedge?

11. **Currency and commodity price risk (intermediate).** Metallgesellschaft (MG), a leading German metal processor, has scheduled the delivery of 20,000 metric tons of copper for August 10, 2013, to Quelle, a German distributor of industrial supplies. On May 10, 2013, copper is quoted at 4,821 pounds sterling (£) per metric ton for immediate delivery and at £4,838 per metric ton for delivery on August 10, 2013, on the London Metal Exchange (LME) or in Hamburg (Germany). Monthly storage cost will run at £7 for a metric ton in London and 15 euros (€) in Hamburg, payable on the first day of storage.

    Exchange rate quotations are as follows: The pound sterling is worth €1.25 on May 10 and is selling at a 2.8% annual discount. The opportunity cost of capital for Metallgesellschaft is estimated at 6% annually, and the pound sterling is expected to depreciate at a yearly rate of 2.8% throughout the next 12 months.
    a. What is the nature of price risk(s) facing MG in procuring 20,000 metric tons of copper from the LME?
    b. Compute the euro cost on May 10, 2013, for Metallgesellschaft of the following options:
        - Buy 20,000 metric tons of copper on May 10 and store it in London until August 10.
        - Buy a forward contract of 20,000 metric tons on May 10, 2010, for delivery in three months. Cover sterling payable by purchasing forward pounds sterling on May 10, 2010.
        - Buy 20,000 metric tons of copper on August 10, 2010.
    c. Can you identify other options available to Metallgesellschaft? Which one would you recommend?

12. **Lufthansa hedges the purchase of 20 Boeing jets (A-advanced).** In January 1985, Lufthansa German Airlines purchased 20 Boeing 737 long-distance aircraft for US$500 million payable to Boeing exactly one year later. Because the US currency had been steadily rising against the Deutsche mark (DM) since 1980 to reach DM 2.30 = US$1, Heinz Ruhnan, chairman of Lufthansa, had decided to hedge 50% of Lufthansa's exposure with a forward contract at DM 3.20 = US$1.
    a. What are the other hedging strategies available to Lufthansa?
    b. Compare graphically the 50% hedge strategy to the other approaches identified under part a.
    c. If one year interest rates available to Lufthansa are 5 and 8% in DM and US$, respectively, explain how Lufthansa could structure a synthetic forward contract.

13. **Lufthansa hedges the purchase of 20 Boeing jets (B-advanced).** Heinz Ruhnan could have considered the use of currency options.
    a. What would be the advantage of using a currency option to hedge currency risk? Should Lufthansa buy or write an option? Should it be a call or a put option?
    b. At-the-money options cost 6%. What would be the cash cost to Lufthansa to fully hedge its exposure with a currency option? When would its cost be incurred?
    c. Sketch graphically a currency option hedge and compare it with a forward contract hedge. Would you expect Lufthansa board of directors to be favorable to a currency option hedge?
    d. Would you advise the use of a forward participation agreement? At what price?

14. **Boeing finances the sale of 20 Boeing jets to Lufthansa (C-advanced).** Boeing is seeking short-term financing for its export sales to Germany. The Overseas Private Investment Corporation (OPIC) offers subsidized US$ financing at 6.75%, which still compares unfavorably to DM financing at 5.00%.
    - **a.** What would be the risk incurred by Boeing in structuring DM financing? Could it be hedged?
    - **b.** Which financing would you recommend to Boeing?
    - **c.** UBS, a leading Swiss bank, offers an even better rate of 4.15% in Swiss francs (CHF). Would you recommend CHF financing, assuming the forward CHF/US$ is trading at a rate exactly consistent with interest rate parity?

15. **Merck (US) acquires Banyu (advanced).** On August 3, 1983, Merck, the giant US-based pharmaceutical company, reached an agreement with Banyu for the friendly acquisition of 50% of Banyu's stock for $313.5 million at a price of ¥670 per share. It was estimated that for the transaction to be executed, it would take approximately 60 days for the Japanese Ministry of Finance to approve it and another 30 days for the bureaucratic obstacles to be overcome. Yet the outcome would still be in doubt, since this foreign acquisition would be the first in the annals of Japan's mergers and acquisitions.

    Advise the treasury of Merck as to the proper hedging strategy that should be structured. On August 2, 1983, the spot, 60-, and 90-day forward yen/dollar exchange rates were respectively $S(0)$ = ¥243.35, $F(60)$ = ¥241.85, and $F(90)$ = ¥241.02 with respective 30-, 60-, and 90-day interest rates to remain flat over the next 90 days. Available American options on spot and futures are listed as:

Put and Call Option Premiums

Strike Price	90-Day Call Premium (%)	90-Day Put Premium (%)
230	5	1
228	4	2
226	3	3
224	2	4
220	1	5

REFERENCES

Beidleman, Carl R., John L. Hilley, and James A. Greenleaf. 1983. "Alternatives in Hedging Long Date Contractual Foreign Exchange Exposures." *Sloan Management Review* 24(4): 45–54.

Bilson, J. F. O. 1983. "The Choice of an Invoice Currency in International Transactions." In *Economic Interdependence and Flexible Exchange Rates*, edited by J. S. Bhandari and G. H. Putnam. Cambridge, MA: MIT Press.

Eaker, M. R., and D. M. Grant. 1985. "Optimal Hedging of Uncertain and Long Term Exchange Exposure." *Journal of Banking and Finance* 9(3).

Einzig, Paul. 1968. *A Dynamic Theory of Forward Exchange*, 2nd edition. New York: St. Martin's Press.

Giddy, I. H., and G. Dufey. 1995. "Use and Misuse of Currency Options." *Journal of Applied Corporate Finance* 8(3): 49–57.

Jacque, Laurent L., and John M. Cozzolino. 1986. "Foreign Exchange Risk Management and International Re-Insurance." *Managerial Finance* 13(1): 18–22.

Jacque, Laurent L., and Charles S. Tapiero. 1987. "Premium Valuation in International Re-Insurance." *Scandinavian Actuarial Journal* 50–61.

Jacque, Laurent L. 1996. *Management and Control of Foreign Exchange Risk*. Boston: Kluwer Academic Press.

CASE STUDY 16.1. HEDGING CURRENCY RISK AT TT TEXTILES

Rajesh Chakravarthi
Executive Director, the Bharti Institute of Public Policy at the Indian School of Business

It was a hot March morning in Kolkata in the year 2009. Sanjay K. Jain — Joint MD of TT Textiles — watched the sunlight stream in through his office window pane. But his mind was elsewhere, tracking the movements of the Swiss Franc (CHF) in the last few months and the world events that had caused them. It had touched 1.17 CHF/US$ from the previous year's record of 0.96 CHF/US$. That was good news for him. Or was it? The irony of the situation was not lost on him. Of all the different currencies that vied for his attention in the normal course of things, the Swiss Franc would hardly have a chance. And yet it was the movement of the CHF that weighed on his mind most heavily these days.

As an exporter to more than 30 countries, TT Textiles was no newcomer to the area of currency risk. TT Textiles usually used forwards to manage currency risks. However, during 2006–2007, when the Indian rupee (INR) was expected to appreciate to an unprecedented high of INR 35/US$1, the company was considering longer-lasting currency hedges, including a three-year currency swap deal based on the historical stability of the Swiss franc (CHF) against the US dollar.

TT Textiles

TT Textiles Ltd. was founded in 1949 by the family of Dr. Rikhab Chand Jain. It was India's first knitwear company to go public. It is a vertically integrated textile company with a presence in the entire cotton chain, from fiber to yarn to knitted fabric and garment. Its manufacturing facilities are located in all major garment centers such as Tirupur, Kolkata, Delhi, Varanasi, Saharanpur, and Kanpur. It has its ginning units in Gondal, Gujarat, and it has branches for cotton in Jalna, Maharashtra. The company's core businesses are in agricultural commodity, cotton, yarn, fabric, and garments, with markets spread all over the world as follows: About 75% of TT Textiles' revenues come from exports and at any particular point in time it would have an exposure of roughly US$25 million. The life of a typical export transaction in the industry — particularly like the ones that TT Textiles is party to — is less than three months. TT Textiles has enjoyed a margin of 5 to 6% in its business.

More generally, the textile and clothing industry has traditionally been an export-oriented industry in India. It contributes 4% to the overall gross domestic product (GDP) of India and makes up 14% of the industrial production and 14% of total exports of goods. But more importantly, India earns about 27% of its total foreign exchange through textile exports. It is also the second-largest employer after agriculture, providing direct employment to 35 million people and indirect employment to 45 million people. Being a mature industry, the textile industry is marked by relatively low margins — varying from 3% to 12%, depending on where in the value chain a specific company operates.

Currency derivatives in India

Currency derivative products have been relatively new entrants in India. Most Indian companies depend on their banks to hedge currency exposures. The currency market is one of India's biggest financial markets, with turnover on the spot and forward markets together yielding around US$12 billion a day in late 2006. Since September 2008, there have been both forex forwards as well as futures markets in the country, trading the INR/US$. Derivatives on other currencies are not traded. The rupee-dollar forward market is an over-the-counter (OTC) market, the trades on which are settled through the Clearing Corporation of India Ltd. (CCIL), which is the clearinghouse for foreign exchange (forex) and interest rate trades in India. This minimizes the credit risk associated with these agreements in the Indian market. By late 2006, the forward market turnover was nudging US$2 billion a day. Foreign institutional investors (FFIs) are able to do transactions on the currency derivatives market that can be characterized as hedging of the currency risk exposure on their Indian investments.

In addition to the domestic rupee-dollar forward market, there is active trading for cash-settled rupee-dollar forwards in Hong Kong, Singapore, Dubai, and London on what are termed nondeliverable forwards (NDF) contracts. For foreign institutional investors who have limited access to the forward market on the domestic INR-US$ markets, the NDF market does not suffer from the constraints imposed by capital controls. However, for domestic investors, this leads to limited participation by financial institutions in the onshore currency forward market.

Currency options are relative newcomers to India's financial markets. The Reserve Bank of India (RBI) launched trading in rupee options on July 7, 2003. On the first day it witnessed brisk activity, trading volumes of US$ 200–225 million with foreign as well as Indian banks like Standard Chartered, HSBC, ABN Amro, SBI, IDBI, ICICI Bank and IndusInd entering into major transactions. Large corporate houses like Reliance, HCL, Murugappa and L&T were also not far behind. In order to simplify procedural requirements for the small and medium enterprises (SME) sector, RBI granted flexibility for hedging underlying as well as anticipated and economic exposures without going through the rigors of complex documentation formalities. In order to ensure that SMEs understand the risks of these products, only banks with which they have a credit relationship are allowed to offer such facilities.

TT Textiles' hedging strategy

Currency hedging is of prime importance in a commoditized industry like the textile industry, which operates on razor-thin margins. In a hypercompetitive globalized environment, the problem of thin margins is compounded when there are adverse currency movements, and thus currency hedging assumes prime importance. The story was no different for TT Textiles, for which exports formed a major chunk of its revenues. In the textile industry, hedging currency risks has traditionally been through forwards, where the company has an estimate of the future sales and takes a conservative estimate of the US$/INR movement to hedge against unfavorable currency movements. TT Textiles was no different in that it used forwards for safeguarding against adverse currency movements. The options market was not considered attractive by the SME players as the option premiums were substantially high and the industry margins were quite low, making forwards the most popular of all the instruments used by the company.

In late 2006, when the INR was surging against the dollar, the Indian textile industry was reeling under severe currency pressures. While the rupee was hovering around the INR 45/US$1 mark, bankers were forecasting that the rupee would continue to appreciate, some even anticipating unprecedented levels like INR 35/US$1, and the industry was looking for solutions in order to stay afloat in these testing times. The appreciation in the rupee was particularly galling because it was driven by foreign portfolio investment flows to India rather than by a strong current account and low inflation; other competing countries such as Pakistan and Bangladesh did not experience such appreciation, and Indian exporters were losing out in competitiveness. For a low-margin industry like textiles, this threatened the very viability of the exporters. "Our competitiveness for the time being has gone away," said P. D. Patodia, chairman of the Confederation of Indian Textile Industry. The association estimates that for every 1% fall in the value of the dollar compared with the rupee, profit falls by 1.2%. "Some exporters will be permanently damaged and not all will survive," said Subir Gokarn, chief economist for Standard & Poor's Asia-Pacific.

There were two basic approaches that the companies could take:

1. Hedge against the upward movement of the rupee against the dollar. Forward US dollar contracts were available for up to 365 days with quotes as follows:
   - Three-month: 40.05 INR to 1 US$
   - Six-month: 39.82 INR to 1 US$
   - Twelve-month: 39.80 INR to 1 US$
2. Hedge through synthetic forward contracts or so-called money market hedge. TT Textiles could lend/borrow in INR or US$ at the respective annual interest rates of 12.75 and 7.75%. Two- and 3-year interest rates were also available at the respective levels of 13 and 15% and 5.5 and 6.5%.

Unorthodox hedging with a 3-year currency swap

Around this time, several private banks started offering attractive derivative products and many exporters were signing up for such deals. TT Textiles had until then been much more familiar with forwards as instruments of hedging foreign currency exposure, and it was only now being introduced to a new instrument called currency swaps. Currency swaps enabled the company to limit its exposure to fluctuations in the US$/INR exchange rate. The proposed swap was however on the US dollar and Swiss franc, as traditionally these two currencies had stable exchange rates in comparison to the rupee and the dollar.

Terms of the currency swap. The core of this transaction was a combination of swap plus options. The start date for the swap was October 19, 2006, and the expiration date was October 15, 2009, with the delivery date being October 19, 2009. The parties to the swap were ABC Bank and TT Textiles. The currencies under the swap were the INR and the Swiss franc (CHF). The notional principal amount of the contract was INR 225 million = US$4,965,791.22 = CHF 6,306,554.84. While TT Textiles was lending INR 225 million to ABC Bank, in turn ABC Bank was lending CHF 6,306,554.84 to TT Textiles; there was no actual exchange of cash. Since the deal was done at the going spot rate, the values of these two monies were the same. The interest would be on notional principals. There was, however, an interest rate differential/arbitrage as the Swiss franc had a much lower interest rate than the rupee. As TT Textiles was making a rupee loan, it would receive a higher interest rate and since it had taken a Swiss franc loan, it would pay a lower interest rate. Similar to a carry trade, the contract implied that TT Textiles would receive a net fixed interest of 1.77% semiannually on the notional amount of INR 225 million and would not pay any interest on the notional amount of CHF 6,306,554.84 to ABC Bank. (See Case Exhibit 16.1.)

With a payout of INR 2 million every six months (interest differential) and a credit limit of INR 80 million to cover margins and mark-to-market losses granted on the basis of the strength of its balance sheet, it would be hard for TT Textiles to resist the ABC Bank offer. So, TT Textiles was virtually assured of earning INR 12 million over the life of the deal. This was much-needed cash that would provide a buffer against the squeeze in margins that the appreciating rupee would imply for TT Textiles.

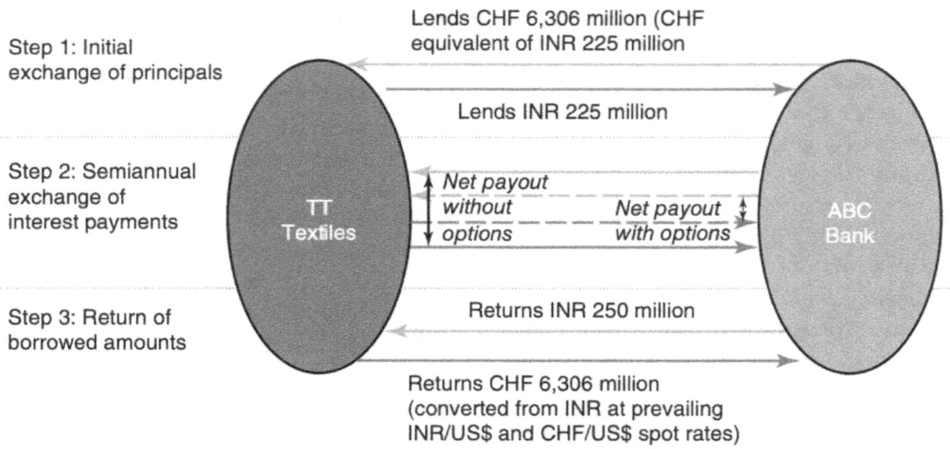

Case Exhibit 16.1. Currency swap-cum-option between TT Textiles and Standard Chartered bank.

Switzerland has a steady economy, and the Swiss franc has been a stable currency, having never gone below the CHF 1.09 = US$1 mark in over a century.

Going in for such a deal would provide TT Textiles with a much-needed buffer against the rupee's appreciation. Every April and October, TT Textiles would get a check for INR 2 million while it would pay nothing until October 2009. The final settlement in October 2009 would take place with the repayment of the initial loans. ABC Bank would return INR 225 million (including the last interest payment of INR 2 million) while TT Textiles would return the amount of CHF 6,306,554.84. In terms of INR, TT Textiles would end up paying: [CHF 6,306,554.84 × (INR/US$ divided by CHF/ US$)]. The source of risk here would be the two unknowns: the INR/US$ exchange rate and the CHF/US$ exchange rate.

Currency options

When the swap deal was designed in 2006, it was based on the fact that historically the US dollar had never gone below the exchange rate of 1.09 CHF, making the latter a very stable currency. But Dr. Jain was still unsure, and he says:

> *Although I was assured again and again that it has never happened in the history of currency markets that the CHF had fallen to below the 1.09 mark, I wanted to be doubly sure that I was safe. So, they offered us a cut-off mark of 1.04 CHF/US$, although our payouts would be reduced as well.*

While this was the central swap deal, options were thrown in to sweeten the deal. Within the window of September 15, 2009, to October 15, 2009, the swap had a partial barrier on the CHF/US$ rate of 1.04, which meant that, if the CHF/US$ rate fell below 1.04, then the payouts would be according to the spot rate. There was no barrier of any form on the INR/US$ rate.

The range for the INR/US$ rate was fixed between 45 and 46.25 (see Case Exhibit 16.2). At maturity:

- If the rate was above 46.25 (i.e., INR depreciates further), TT Textiles had the option of buying US$4,965,791.22 at 46.25.
- If the rate was below 45 (i.e., INR appreciates further), TT Textiles had the obligation to buy US$4,965,791.22 at 45.
- TT Textiles would buy at the spot rate if the US$/INR rate was between INR 45.00 and INR 46.25.

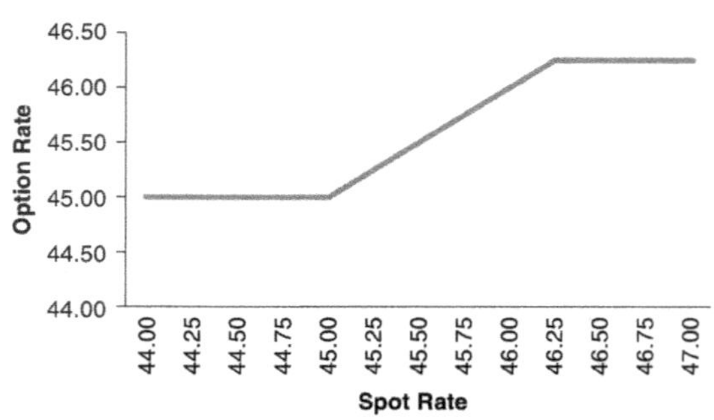

Case Exhibit 16.2. INR/US$ range.

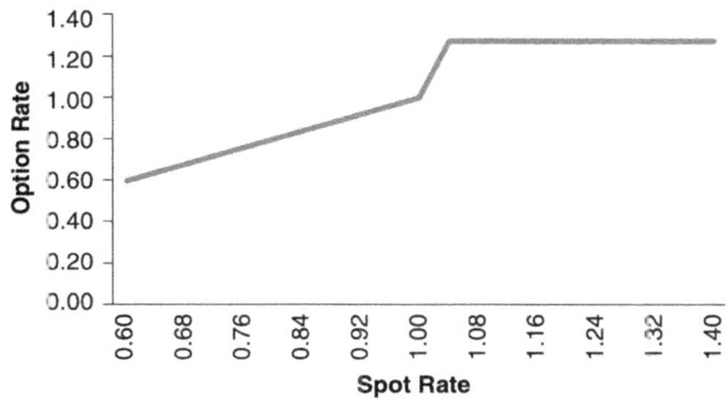

Case Exhibit 16.3. CHF/US$ range.

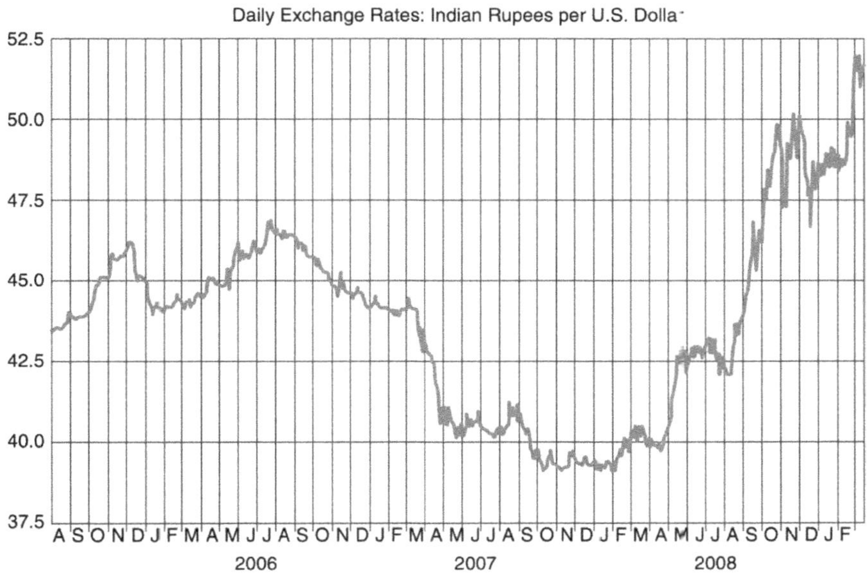

Case Exhibit 16.4. Exchange rate movement (2004–2009) of US$/INR.

The range for the CHF/US$ was fixed between 1.04 and 1.27 (see Case Exhibit 16.3). At maturity:

- If the rate fell below 1.04 during the window, TT Textiles would have to make the payout of CHF 6,306,554.84 at the spot rate.
- If the rate was between 1.04 and 1.27 during the window, TT Textiles had the right to sell CHF 6,306,554.84 at 1.27.
- If the rate was above 1.27 on maturity, TT Textiles had an obligation to sell CHF 6,306,554.84 at 1.27.

Forex markets in turmoil

The rupee in 2007

In 2007–2008, the net FII capital inflow into India shot up to US$ 20.3 billion, which was a key driver for an appreciating rupee, from INR 45/US$ to INR 39.60/US$ in the year end (see Case Exhibit 16.4), and the overall bullish outlook for the Indian economy as evident from the rising Sensex levels, which went from under 5,000 in early 2004 and peaked just above 21,000 in January 2008. This had a damaging impact on the Indian exporters as a rising rupee shrank margins drastically, especially for mid-sized players who did not have economies of scale in production and sophisticated currency risk hedging positions. The woes of the exporters weren't limited to the rise of the rupee against the US$. Domestic inflation and rising raw material prices placed further strains on the already dwindling profits. For instance, there was a rise in cotton prices globally which made the procurement of good quality raw material expensive. *"Our competitiveness for the time being has gone away,"* said P.D. Patodia, chairman of the Confederation of Indian Textile Industry.

The association estimates that for every 1 per cent fall in the value of the dollar compared with the rupee, profit falls by 1.2 per cent. "*Some exporters will be permanently damaged and not all will survive,"* said Subir Gokarn, chief economist for Standard & Poor's Asia-Pacific.

The tide turns in 2008

The rupee, however, swung completely in the opposite direction the following year when the financial meltdown led to massive FII capital outflows from the emerging market economies. FII outflows in India exceeded US$11.1 billion during the first nine and a half months of calendar year 2008, of which US$8.3 billion occurred over the first six and a half months of the financial year 2008–2009. This led to severe rupee depreciation in the year 2008 with the rupee touching INR 50 per dollar. At the same time the stock market collapsed, and the Sensex crashed from close to 21,000 in January to just over 8,600 in November, 2008.

Furthermore, during the course of the year, global recession in major textile importing economies like the US, European Union and Japan adversely affected textile exports from India. Anti-dumping, safeguard duty and other protectionist measures adopted by various countries proved to be a stumbling block for export.

The rollercoaster ride

It all started in a perfectly expected manner for TT Textiles when it received the first cheque of INR 4.5 million from ABC Bank. As the rupee started falling, the belief got stronger that the rupee was going to strengthen if only to get back to where it was. So TT Textiles started increasing its exposure to this instrument. "It seemed like a reasonable risk to take if the franc hasn't breached 1.10 level against the US dollar for 20–25 years," said a forex consultant. The options with knock-ins meant that if the franc breaches a level below this, say 1.09 to the dollar, then the company has to pay the difference.

By the end of 2007, the US started showing signs of recession. But the belief that the US was decoupled from India was strong among the Indian corporations and investors, which got reflected in the inflating Indian stock market. In January 2008, the rude shock came in the form of a major crash in the Indian stock market when the Sensex showed decrements to the order of 2000 points. At that time, the US$-INR exchange rate was close to 39.60 INR/US$. As the stock market crash led to panic amongst foreign investors, the FDI outflows from the Indian economy grew, which made the exchange rate creep up to 41 INR/US$ and eventually back to the 50 INR/US$ mark. The exchange rate movement of INR-US$ can be found in Exhibit 16.4. During this time, as Jain jocularly points out:

> *Firms started selling when the rupee was at 39 INR/US$ and then at 41 INR/US$ and so on and so forth because the economic forecast was nervous enough to predict the range within a couple of rupees or so. After 46 INR/US$ they gave up selling and when it finally stabilized at 50 INR/US$ no one was selling because by then the prediction had turned to 55 INR/US$! And thus the corporations went on over-hedging their futures.*

The Swiss Franc

However, in Europe the situation was completely different as the European economy had not yet showed signs of recession and investments in Europe were still considered relatively safer while the same could not be said for the US. Due to this factor, the CHF started becoming stronger than the US$ and the CHF/US$ rate — which had never breached the 1.09 mark historically — started decreasing and eventually crossed the strike rate of 1.04 that was specified in the swap deal of TT Textiles, and continued its downward trend to fall below 1. The projected losses for TT Textiles if the CHF/US$ rate touched 0.93 were estimated to be around INR 45 million and with further decrement in the dollar rate, the losses were expected to cross INR 55–63 million. The exchange rate movement of CHF-US$ is shown in Case Exhibit 16.5.

At the same time, the overall economic situation presented liquidity challenges to the banking sector and forced it to invoke margin calls on the counterparties. TT Textiles was also under tremendous pressure as sales were hit hard and hence on the swap deal TT Textiles demanded extra credit limit over and above the INR 45 million credit limit already granted by ABC bank. However, ABC bank did not entertain this request and in fact argued for removal of the existing credit limit as well.

The crisis comes to a head

As ABC bank entered into similar agreement with a host of other counterparties, there was an increasing pressure on its derivatives desk to recover the money

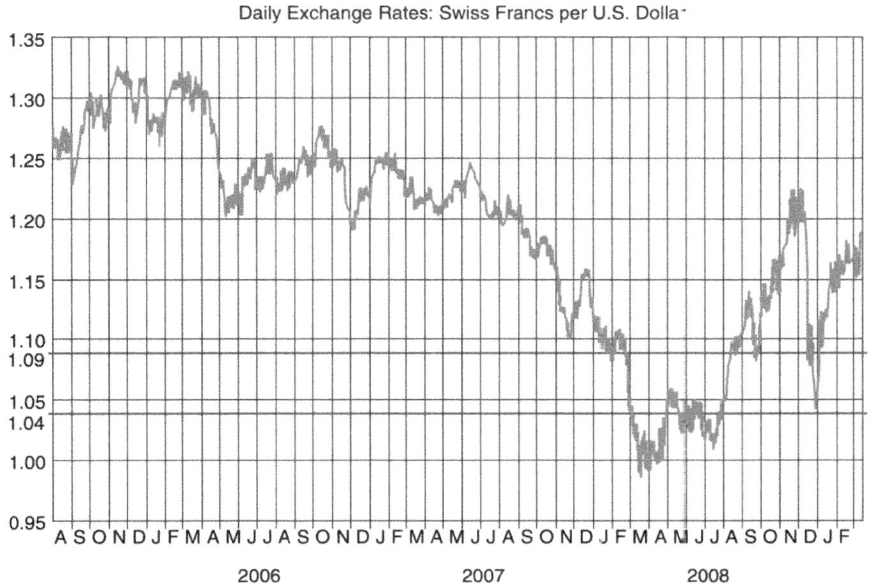

Case Exhibit 16.5. Exchange rate movement (2004–2009) of US$/CHF.

from them. The situation was further aggravated by the fact that most of the corporate players had entered the deal considering it an extremely safe bet. They had been benefitting consistently until then and these sudden and unforeseen events came as a rude shock to them. Under these circumstances, bankers from ABC bank came up with a few suggestions. The first suggestion was that TT Textiles should enter option contracts to seek protection but the option contracts available were extremely high-priced at that time due to the unstable economic environment. The other suggestion was to cut down on existing positions to reduce the existing exposure of TT Textiles.

Jain sought opinions from a host of financial experts about their expectation from the CHF/US$ exchange rate, but he was not able to form a clear view as there were diverse opinions due to lack of clarity on the underlying reasons for the happenings. The CHF kept getting stronger *vis-à-vis* US$ and touched the 0.96 mark. At this point, mounting panic even generated a speculation that this rate could well reach the 0.90 level. Some firms started cutting down their losses to the extent of 50 per cent of their initial positions in the instrument at this point. The knockout option in the contract was dependent on the event that the exchange rate touches the 1.04 mark during the last one month of the deal.

The shorting of the Swiss Franc

The dollar started reversing from 0.96 CHF/$ and gained momentum to reach the 1.17 CHF/$ level in a matter of months (see Case Exhibit 16.5). At this point, Jain faced an interesting situation. The position still showed a mark-to-market loss which made the decision to square it off difficult. Circumstances indicated that he should hold the security till maturity since the general belief was that the rate would not slide back to the 1.04–1.05 CHF/$ levels again in the near future. He decided in favor of carrying out a reverse transaction when the CHF/US$ exchange rate was 1.17 CHF/$. This meant that if the rate fell below 1.17 CHF/$, TT Textiles would cover the existing position at the lower rate, say 1.12 CHF/$. These range-bound deals made some money for TT Textiles during that period.

While the rates stood at 1.17 CHF/US$, the special month of the deal, i.e., September 2009, was almost still six months away. The instrument carried the clause which made TT Textiles liable to losses only if the CHF/US$ exchange rate touched the 1.04 CHF/US$ mark during the special month.

With recession hitting the US and the subsequent weakening of the dollar in 2008–2009 the CHF-US$ exchange rate had sunk to the unprecedented bottom of 0.96CHF/$. Now, having bounced back from such low rates, it posed a

Catch-22 situation for TT Textiles and for Jain. He had two choices; he could continue on the swap deal of CHF-US$ which was supposed to expire in October 2009 or he could get out of the swap deal at this favorable juncture and get rid of any uncertainty. By getting out of the position, on one hand he might forego attractive returns on the swap if the dollar remained at a high rate, but he could also gain protection against any adverse movement of the dollar.

Time to decide

The sun had shifted but the furrows on Jain's forehead lingered. Having witnessed the most unexpected behavior of the supposedly steady exchange rate relationship between US$ and CHF, he was still undecided about the right course of action. Should he close out his positions, taking a hit to the order of INR 9–19 million or should he trust that the US$ would be able to maintain its current position and thus run the risk of exposing his firm to losses to the tune of INR 55–63 million. Time was running out and the critical decision had to be made.

Questions for Discussion

Refer to Case Exhibits 16.4 and 16.5 to answer questions 1 through 5.

1. What is the nature of TT Textiles' exposure to foreign exchange risk?
2. How could TT Textiles protect itself against currency risk? Sketch the different options available, quantify them, and compare them graphically.
3. What makes the currency swap an attractive solution for TT Textiles? Would you characterize it as a hedge?
4. What is the role played by currency options attached to the currency swap? Is TT Textiles purchasing or writing those options?
5. What would be the outcome at the expiration of the swap? Formulate alternative exchange scenarios before quantifying the costs or benefits of the currency swap as a possible hedge.
6. What is your advice to Mr. Jain as the last month window is approaching?

CHAPTER 17

Managing Translation Exposure

If a man will begin with certainties, he will end with doubts, but if he will be content to begin with doubts, he shall end in certainties.
— Francis Bacon

Multinational corporations are required to report periodically their worldwide performance from both parent and foreign subsidiaries in the form of simple statistics such as consolidated earnings and the much awaited and closely studied earnings per share (EPS). This chapter examines how this periodic consolidation process requires the parent firm to translate the assets and liabilities of its foreign subsidiaries into its reporting currency. Thus, *translation exposure* refers to the impact of exchange rate fluctuations on the parent firm's consolidated financial statements. After reviewing translation methods and conditions warranting the hedging of translation exposure, basic hedging techniques are analyzed; specifically, *contractual* hedging with forward contracts or currency options is compared with *financial* hedging through local borrowing.

After reading this chapter you should understand:

- What translation exposure is and when it should be hedged.
- How translation exposure is measured under alternative methods.
- When hedging translation exposure is warranted.
- How to hedge translation exposure with forward and currency options.
- How to hedge translation exposure through borrowing in the exposed currency.
- What the true cash flow cost of hedging is.

WHAT IS TRANSLATION EXPOSURE?

Translation exposure to foreign exchange (FX or forex) risk arises from the practice of periodically consolidating or aggregating the parent's and the foreign subsidiaries' balance sheets and income statements. Reporting consolidated worldwide net income is in fact the result of a complex accounting process of aggregating — or translating — all domestic and foreign subsidiaries' results with their parent's. Unfortunately for the firm's controller — the individual in charge of this task — foreign subsidiaries prepare their results in the currency of the country in which they operate (for example, yen for a Japanese subsidiary), which is different from the parent's reference currency (for example, US dollars for a US-domiciled multinational corporation). This means that the foreign subsidiary's accounting results will have to be converted/translated from the foreign currency into the parent company's currency, which is typically the currency in which the multinational corporation's stock is listed and traded. Because exchange rates may have changed since the last translation was completed, the multinational corporation's consolidated net worth may increase or decrease with each reporting cycle. This risk is rooted in the translation exposure resulting from foreign affiliates' ongoing operations. This accounting process is carried out according to detailed rules mandated by the official accounting authority — in the United States the Financial Accounting Standards Board (FASB) — which stipulate the following:

- The exchange rate to be used for translating specific balance sheet and income statement accounts.
- The disposition of any resulting translation gains and losses either through the income statement or accumulated on the balance sheet's equity account of the parent firm.

If all accounts on both the foreign subsidiary's balance sheet and its income statement were uniformly translated at the same rate, there would be no loss or gain for the parent to report. But because exchange rates used in translating will differ according to the nature of the accounts on the financial statements and will fluctuate from period to period, the resulting imbalance will result in so-called translation losses or gains.

Thus, translation exposure is defined as the net balance (assets minus liabilities) of foreign currency-denominated accounts (carried on the subsidiary's balance sheet) that is restated in dollar terms on the basis of the *current exchange rate prevailing at time of consolidation*. Such items are said to be *exposed*. The dichotomy between exposed and non-exposed accounting items is provided by FASB Statement No. 52 which was restructured and codified as FASB Accounting Standard Codification (ASC) 830. Non-*exposed* accounting items are translated into dollar terms on the basis of historical exchange rates that prevailed when the asset was first acquired or when the liability was first incurred. For example, FASB ASC 830 mandates that all assets and liabilities of foreign subsidiaries be translated at the current rate (all accounts are therefore *exposed*). This amounts to translation exposure being simply the foreign subsidiary's net worth and is also known as the *all-current* method of translation; a formal derivation of this important result is presented in the appendix to this chapter.

SHOULD TRANSLATION EXPOSURE BE HEDGED?

At the core of the debate over hedging translation risk is the fact that translation losses and gains — however large they may be — are *unrealized, non-cash flows* in nature and without tax implications. Yet we know that value creation is driven by cash flows — not by accounting profits. Furthermore, depending on whether translation losses or gains flow directly through the income statement or are accumulated in the owners' equity account may further exacerbate investors' anxieties. Is it then legitimate for sophisticated multinational corporations to concern themselves with translation exposure hedging?

It would seem that such activity is at best an attempt to deceive investors through accounting gimmickry rather than being motivated by value creation unless it can be shown that hedging translation exposure — by modifying/lowering the risk profile of the firm — is indeed resulting in a higher stock price, which in turn lowers the cost of equity capital. In capital markets that are truly efficient this will not be the case; in capital markets that are not quite fully efficient, investors will reward firms that are producing smoother earnings streams. If this is true, hedging translation exposure is value creating, and therefore warranted.

There are two special situations where hedging translation exposure will have more direct cash-flow implications:

- *Loan covenants*. If the firm has to satisfy a loan covenant that requires that a threshold metric such as debt/equity ratio not be crossed because of unchecked translation losses accumulated to the parent's sub-equity account, then direct cash-flow implications may result in the form of a higher cost of debt. Failure to meet such loan covenants may lower the firm's credit rating, reduce its borrowing capacity, or force it to renegotiate lending conditions at less favorable terms.
- *Credit rating*. A debt/equity ratio unduly damaged by a string of translation losses (thereby depleting the owners' equity account) may result in a firm's debt rating being downgraded. The firm, therefore, may face an increased cost of debt financing and/or restricted access to financial markets.

ALTERNATIVE TRANSLATION METHODS

We now review different translation guidelines as they have evolved over time for US-based multinationals; they can be categorized as follows:

- The *current/noncurrent* method, widely used until 1976, required all current and/or short-term accounts to be translated at the current/closing exchange rate. Translation exposure is simply the foreign subsidiary's *net working capital*. Translation gains or losses flow through the parent's income statement and are directly added to or subtracted from its EPS.
- The *monetary/nonmonetary* method, embodied in FASB Statement No. 8 (1976–1981), required all

monetary accounts (as opposed to real/physical ones) to be translated at the current/closing exchange rate. Resulting gains or losses flow through the parent's income statement and are directly added to or subtracted from its EPS.

- The *all-current* method, currently mandated by FASB ASC 830 (known as FASB Statement 52 from 1981 to 2009) requires *all* accounts to be translated at the current/closing rate. Translation exposure is simply the foreign subsidiary's *owners' equity* or *net worth*. Resulting gains or losses bypass the income statement to be accumulated into the parent's balance sheet in a sub-equity account designated as *cumulative translation adjustment*. When the foreign subsidiary operates as an extension of its parent with little autonomy, its "functional" currency is deemed to be the US dollar, in which case translation follows the rules of FASB Statement No. 8.

US-based multinational corporations currently follow the *all-current* method of translation as mandated by the Financial Accounting Standards Board ASC 830, discussed in this chapter at greater length. Unfortunately, different countries still live by somewhat different accounting rules — a continued source of capital markets' segmentation. However, under the auspices of the International Accounting Standards Board (IASB), countries are working toward harmonizing national accounting standards by promulgating International Financial Reporting Standards (IFRS), which should greatly facilitate international portfolio investment by making it easier to compare companies domiciled in different countries. Translation rules under IASB Statement No. 21 are fairly close to those upheld by the US FASB ASC 830, and they are being progressively adopted by a growing number of countries. We now turn to an in-depth discussion of the three principal methods of translating foreign currency-denominated financial statements. It should be mentioned that at least in the United States the *current/non-current* method and the *monetary/non-monetary* methods of translation are not currently in use.

The current/noncurrent method

The current/noncurrent method was the traditional method most widely used by US-based multinational corporations until 1976 when the Financial Accounting Standards Board promulgated its controversial Statement No. 8. This method was first recommended by the American Institute of Certified Public Accountants (AICPA) as early as 1939. Under this method, current assets and liabilities are translated at the exchange rate in effect at the time of consolidation (the current rate). Non-current assets and liabilities are translated at the exchange rates prevailing when the assets and liabilities were first acquired, incurred, or otherwise recorded in the foreign subsidiary accounts (noncurrent or historical rates). Most income statement items are linked to current assets or liabilities and therefore are translated at the current rate. A major exception is depreciation, which — linked tonon-current assets — is translated at the historical rate when the asset was first acquired.

Under the current/noncurrent method, the translation exposure is defined as the algebraic difference between current assets and current liabilities. Translation losses and gains flow through the parent's income statement and impact its EPS. The firm, though, has the discretion of deferring translation gains. One criticism often leveled at this method is that long-term debt is translated at the historical exchange rate when it was first incurred whereas — like short-term debt — it would be more realistic to value it at the current exchange rate.

Let's consider the case of Sun Microsystems' French subsidiary Marianne S.A., whose euro-denominated pro forma balance sheet for December 31, 2024, is presented in Exhibit 17.1A (see column 2). On October 1, 2024, when the pro forma balance sheet is prepared, the dollar price of one euro stands at $S(0) = 1.25$. In column 3, Marianne S.A.'s balance sheet is translated at a constant exchange rate — that is, $S(0) = S(90) = 1.25$. In column 4, translation is carried out at a depreciated rate of $S(90) = 1.00$ and all current assets and liabilities shrink in dollar terms. The last column shows actual translation losses item by item. The reader will verify that the total translation loss is equal to the net translation exposure measured in euros (*exposed* assets minus *exposed* liabilities) in the amount of €3,000 times the change in the exchange rate of 1.00–1.25.

The monetary/non-monetary method and FASB Statement No. 8 (1976–1981)

The monetary/nonmonetary method was first developed and widely publicized by the National Association of Accountants (NAA) in 1960 before being formally adopted in 1976. Under this method, the segmentation of accounts into *exposed versus non-exposed* accounts is based on their financial

Exhibit 17.1A. Translation under the current/noncurrent method (in '000s).

	€-Denominated Balance Sheet	Translated at Constant Rate $S(0) = S(90) =$ 1.25	Translated Under Depreciated Rate $S(90) = 1.00$	$ Translation Gain/Loss
Assets	25,000	31,250	...	...
Cash and marketable securities	4,000	5,000	4,000	−1,000
Accounts receivable	5,000	6,250	5,000	−1,250
Inventory	3,000	3,750	3,000	−750
Property, plant, and equipment	13,000	16,250	16,250	0
Liabilities and owners' equity	25,000	31,250	...	...
Accounts payable	7,000	8,750	7,000	−1,750
Short-term debt	2,000	2,500	2,000	−500
Long-term debt	12,000	15,000	15,000	0
Owners' equity (net worth)	4,000	5,000	4,250	−750
Net translation exposure in €	3,000	...	...	...
Net translation gains/losses in $	...	...	...	−750

versus physical characterization. Monetary assets and liabilities are translated at the current/closing exchange rate, whereas non-monetary assets and liabilities are translated at the historical rate when the asset was first acquired and the liability first incurred. Monetary assets and liabilities are those representing a contractual right or obligation to receive or pay an agreed amount of local currency units. By contrast, non-monetary assets and liabilities are defined as those whose value may vary in terms of the local currency, such as inventory. Translation exposure under this translation method is thus the algebraic difference between monetary assets and monetary liabilities. If the subsidiary is highly leveraged, the net exposure will tend to be negative, as total (monetary) liabilities may far exceed monetary assets and result in a translation gain (rather than loss) when the currency depreciates.

FASB Statement No. 8 eliminated much of the discretion that US-based multinational corporations had previously enjoyed until then in translating their foreign affiliates' financial statements into a reference currency. The most dramatic consequence of FASB Statement No. 8 was that exchange gains or losses resulting from both the conversion and translation process were to be included in the parent's net income for the accounting period in which the exchange rate change actually occurred and therefore directly impacted its EPS. FASB unequivocally rejected the distinction between realized and unrealized exchange gains or losses, as well as other income-smoothing devices that resulted in the deferral or amortization of exchange gains and losses. Accordingly, the implementation of FASB's Statement No. 8 produced large swings in reported EPSs of multinational corporations that resulted from significant translation gains and losses. Under pressure from publicly listed multinational corporations, a new statement, FASB Statement No. 52, replaced Statement No. 8 in December 1981. In 2009, to simplify users' access to foreign currency translation rules FASB Statement No. 52 was codified into FASB ASC 830.

Let's return to the case of Sun Microsystems' French subsidiary Marianne S.A., whose euro-denominated pro forma balance sheet for December 31, 2024, is presented in Exhibit 17.1B (see column 2). The reader will verify that under FASB Statement No. 8 the total translation loss is equal to the net translation exposure measured in euros (exposed monetary assets minus exposed monetary liabilities) multiplied by the change in the exchange rate. It is the amount that, subtracted from (in the case of a loss) or added to (in the case of a gain) the common equity account, will make the parent firm's balance sheet balance.

Note that the net translation exposure is now of a liability nature. Under the scenario of a depreciating euro, this liability yields a sizable translation gain

Exhibit 17.1B. Translation under the monetary/non-monetary method, FASB Statement No. 8 (in '000s).

	€-Denominated Balance Sheet	Translated at Constant Rate $S(0) = S(90) = 1.25$	Translated Under Depreciated Rate $S(90) = 1.00$	$ Translation Gain/Loss
Assets	25,000	31,250	...	...
Cash and marketable securities	4,000	5,000	4,000	–1,000
Accounts receivable	5,000	6,250	5,000	–1,250
Inventory*	3,000	3,750	3,750	0
Property, plant, and equipment*	13,000	16,250	16,250	0
Liabilities and owners' equity	25,000	31,250	...	...
Accounts payable	7,000	8,750	7,000	–1,750
Short-term debt	2,000	2,500	2,000	–500
Long-term debt	12,000	15,000	12,000	–3,000
Owners' equity (net worth)	4,000	5,000	8,000	...
Net translation exposure in €	–12,000	...	...	...
Net translation gains/losses in $	...	...	...	+3,000

Note: *Accounts translated at the constant/historical rate $1.25 = €1.

rather than a loss as would have been the case under the current/noncurrent method:

$$\text{Translation loss/gain} = \text{Net exposure} \times (\text{Closing rate} - \text{Historical rate})$$
$$\text{Translation loss/gain} = \text{€ net worth} \times [S(90) - S(0)]$$
$$\text{Translation loss/gain} = -\text{€}12{,}000 \times (1.00 - 1.25) = \$3{,}000$$

> **Q:** Assume that Marianne S.A.'s short-term debt is in fact a loan from its parent and that it is denominated in dollars. How would the net euro translation exposure change?
>
> **A:** The €2,000 in short-term debt would no longer be considered an exposed item since it is already denominated in dollars; the net exposure becomes –€10,000.

The current rate (or closing rate) method and FASB ASC 830 since 2009 (also known as FASB Statement No. 52 from 1981 to 2009)

This is the simplest method, because all assets and liabilities accounts — but not equity — are uniformly translated at the current rate that prevails at the time of consolidation. It is also the most universally used translation method. It is especially appealing in the case of affiliates operating in countries that require local currency accounts to be periodically adjusted for inflation,[1] provided that — in turn — the current/closing exchange rate generally reflects inflation differentials according to purchasing power parity.

Under this method, the local currency *translation exposure* is simply the *net worth* of the affiliate as expressed in local currency. Resulting translation losses and gains no longer flow through the parent's income statement and therefore do not impact its EPS. This, presumably, reduces the incentive for multinational corporations to engage in controversial translation hedging. Instead, translation losses or gains are accumulated to a sub-equity account, referred to as a *cumulative translation adjustment* account, which is supposed to attract less scrutiny from investors and remove their impact on the firm's earnings. However, any *transaction* gains or losses would continue to flow through the income statement; this includes unrealized transaction losses or gains arising from marking to market outstanding transaction exposures that will not mature within the accounting period.

Let's consider again the case of Sun Microsystems' French subsidiary Marianne S.A., whose euro-denominated pro forma balance sheet for December 31, 2024, is presented in Exhibit 17.1C (see column 2). Thus, under the current rate method,

1 That is, general price-level accounting substituted for historical cost accounting.

Exhibit 17.1C. Translation under the all-current method, FASB ASC 830 (in '000s).

	€-Denominated Balance Sheet	Translated at Constant Rate $S(0) = S(90) = 1.25$	Translated Under Depreciated Rate $S(90) = 1.00$	$ Translation Gain/Loss
Assets	25,000	31,250	...	...
Cash and marketable securities	4,000	5,000	4,000	−1,000
Accounts receivable	5,000	6,250	5,000	−1,250
Inventory	3,000	3,750	3,000	−750
Property, plant, and equipment	13,000	16,250	13,000	−3,250
Liabilities and owners' equity	25,000	31,250	...	...
Accounts payable	7,000	8,750	7,000	−1,750
Short-term debt	2,000	2,500	2,000	−500
Long-term debt	12,000	15,000	12,000	−3,000
Owners' equity (net worth)	4,000	5,000	4,000	−1,000
Net translation exposure in €	4,000	...	...	...
Net translation gains/losses in $	...	...	...	−1,000

Notes: Translation loss/gain = Net exposure × (Closing rate – Historical rate)
Translation loss/gain = € net worth × [S(90) – S(0)]
Translation loss/gain = €4,000 × (1.00 – 1.25) = – $1,000

the translation exposure held by Sun Microsystems' French subsidiary is nothing other than its net worth. The last column shows actual translation losses item by item. The reader will verify that the total translation loss is equal to the net translation exposure measured in euros (exposed assets minus exposed liabilities) multiplied by the change in the exchange rate, $S(90) - S(0)$. It is the amount that, subtracted from (in the case of a loss) or added to (in the case of a gain) the common equity account, will balance the parent firm's balance sheet.

Functional currency

Under special circumstances, FASB ASC 830 calls for translation rules similar to those mandated by FASB Statement No. 8. Generally, a *functional* currency is defined as the primary currency of the foreign subsidiary's economic environment or the currency in which cash inflows and outflows tend to be denominated. Specifically, when there is a high degree of interdependence between a given foreign subsidiary and its US parent firm and relatively low managerial autonomy of the former *vis-à-vis* the latter, the subsidiary's functional currency is deemed to be the US dollar rather than the local currency (see International Corporate Finance in Practice 17.1). In such cases its balance sheet would be restated in US dollars using the monetary/nonmonetary translation rule, with translation losses and gains flowing through the income statement.

Hyperinflationary countries

Similar guidelines also apply to foreign subsidiaries operating in hyperinflationary economies, which are defined as experiencing a cumulative rate of inflation of 100% over a three year period. Indeed, over the years several counties have endured punishing hyperinflation: Countries like Venezuela, Argentina, Brazil, Iran, Israel, and Turkey come to mind. Under such conditions, the current/closing exchange rate would result in a puny valuation of fixed assets, which are typically carried at historical cost in the local currency and would thus be restated into US dollars at a much-depreciated exchange rate. This is what accountants refer to — half jokingly — as the case of the "disappearing plant." Clearly — in this case — restating *non-monetary* fixed assets carried on the books at historical prices at the historical exchange rate produces a more realistic valuation in dollar terms. Because the currency of hyperinflationary countries is not considered to be stable enough to be used as their functional currency, FASB ASC 830 requires the US dollar to be their functional currency and mandates that the monetary/nonmonetary method be used for restating local currency balance sheets and income statements in US dollars.

INTERNATIONAL CORPORATE FINANCE IN PRACTICE 17.1

General Motors–Canada's Functional Currency Is the US Dollar

As a core supplier of General Motors (GM) in the United States, GM Canada finds its manufacturing activities closely integrated with its US parent. As a result, its functional currency is deemed to be the US dollar rather than the Canadian dollar, which means that its financial statements are translated into US dollars using the monetary/nonmonetary method and that resulting translation losses and gains flow directly through GM's consolidated income statement. Because of large pension liabilities (exposed monetary liabilities) and significant US dollar–denominated receivables (therefore excluded from exposed monetary assets), GM is generally short Canadian dollars and would therefore incur translation losses should the Canadian dollar appreciate against the US dollar — which has been the case for the past five years.

THE MECHANICS OF CONTRACTUAL HEDGING

The essence of hedging is to substitute, at the outset of the exposure horizon, a *known* cost of buying protection against exchange rate risk for an *unknown* translation loss. In a sense, the hedger is trading the uncertainty of an accounting loss that may never materialize for the certain cost of eliminating translation risk. This latter cost resembles an insurance premium. It should be emphasized, however, that unlike an insurance premium, which is a certain cash outflow, the cash-flow component of the cost of hedging is never known with certainty to the hedger at the outset of the exposure horizon.[2] This point, often overlooked by practitioners, will be formalized in the following pages. More prosaically, the rationale behind the hedging concept is to neutralize unrealized exchange losses consolidated in the parent company's sub-equity account by generating cash-flow hedging profits that flow first through the income statement before finding their way into the retained earnings account.

Hedging through the forward market (hereafter referred to as *contractual hedging*) is a flexible technique that leaves unhampered the financial management of foreign affiliates operating in depreciation/devaluation-prone environments. It consists of the timely and adequate forward sale or purchase of the exposed currency. The cost of contractual hedging can be accurately measured, as the following discussion will clarify.

2 Except for multinational corporations that are using currency options to hedge their translation exposures.

Revisiting the concept of translation losses and gains

When practiced under conditions of floating exchange rates, periodic consolidation of the parent's and foreign subsidiaries' financial statements for the purpose of uniform performance reporting will generally give rise to exchange losses or gains.

Consider again the case of Sun Microsystems Inc., a US-based multinational corporation, which wholly owns its French affiliate, Marianne S.A. As of July 1, 2024, Sun's treasurer forecasts that its euro translation exposure will be €50 million as of October 1, 2024.[3] If the exchange rate (defined as the dollar price of one €) remains constant at \$1.25 over the exposure horizon (third quarter of 2024), no exchange loss or gain will be incurred. The odds are, however, that the exchange rate will fluctuate over the exposure horizon; the euro may depreciate to \$1.20 by quarter-end, for example. In this case the following translation loss will be incurred:

$$€50{,}000{,}000(1.20 - 1.25) = -\$2{,}500{,}000 \quad (17.1a)$$

It should be emphasized that this is not a cash-flow loss and that, as such, it will not be tax deductible. It doesn't appear in the income statement. Instead, it is accumulated in the balance sheet of the parent in a sub-equity account labeled as a *cumulative translation adjustment* account. If the exchange rate appreciates back to \$1.25 by year-end,

3 Translation exposures that should be hedged are only pro forma magnitudes. As such, they are subject to uncertainty. This point is sometimes overlooked by treasurers who may use the exposure existing at the outset of the hedging horizon as a proxy measure for the end-of-period exposure.

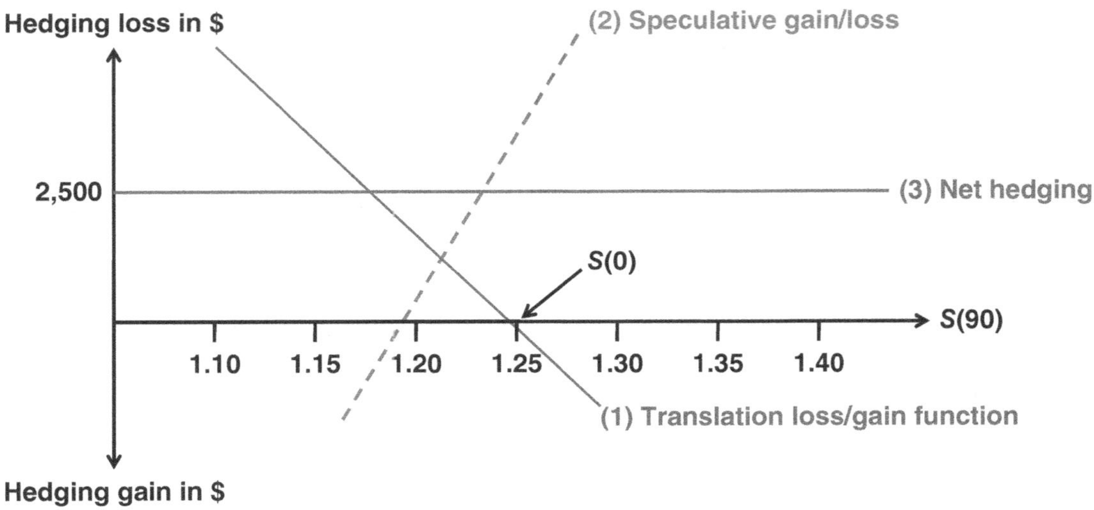

Exhibit 17.2. Net hedging gain/loss function under the contractual approach.

the third-quarter loss will be fully offset by the fourth-quarter gain, provided that the net translation exposure has not changed. More generally, this uncertain exchange loss or gain can be expressed as a function of the end-of-period exchange rate:

$$\text{Translation gain/loss} = €50{,}000{,}000[S(90) - 1.25] \qquad (17.1b)$$

where $S(90)$ denotes the spot dollar price of one euro on day 90 of the translation exposure (see Exhibit 17.2, line (1)).

Hedging with forward contracts

How to do away with such randomness in the parent's sub-equity account is precisely what the technique of contractual hedging is all about. By entering into a forward exchange contract — matching the translation exposure in both currency denomination and maturity — the hedger hopes to generate a cash-flow gain that, aggregated with the expected translation loss, will eliminate the uncertainty resulting from the translation exposure at a known cost, the cost of hedging. This is indeed something of a paradox: How, by engaging in what is seemingly an outright speculative transaction (whose outcome is clearly uncertain at the outset of the exposure horizon), can the hedger hope to eliminate the chance of a translation loss?

The paradox is — at least seemingly — easy to resolve. First, recall the purpose of forward speculation. Assume, for instance, that Sun's treasurer enters into a forward euro sale contract in which he agrees to deliver €50,000,000 on September 30 at a price of \$1.20 (the forward exchange rate). If the prevailing spot exchange rate on September 30 is \$1.15, a net cash-flow gain of 50,000,000(1.20 – 1.15) = \$2,500,000 will accrue to Sun.[4] More generally, if the spot exchange rate prevailing on the delivery date is again denoted by $S(90)$, the speculative gain/loss as depicted graphically in Exhibit 17.2 as line (2) and can be formulated as:

$$\text{Speculative gain/loss} = \$50{,}000{,}000[1.20 - S(90)] \qquad (17.2)$$

Net contractual hedging function

The proof is now about to be completed: The outcome of a contractual hedging policy is nothing other than the algebraic sum of the translation loss/gain function and the speculative gain/loss function that we define as the *net hedging* function:

$$\text{Net hedging cost} = \text{Translation loss/gain} + \text{Speculative gain/loss}$$

$$\text{Net hedging cost} = 50{,}000{,}000\left[S(90) - 1.25\right] + 50{,}000{,}000\left[1.20 - S(90)\right] \qquad (17.3a)$$

In general, the net hedging cost is independent of the future spot exchange $S(90)$, but its

4 Sun will purchase €50,000,000 on the spot market at the rate of \$1.15 = €1 to meet its forward sale obligation.

composition in terms of the mix between *unrealized* translation loss/gain and speculative *cash-flow* gain/loss will depend on what the future spot exchange $S(90)$ turns out to be. This reduces itself to:

$$\text{Net hedging cost} = 50{,}000{,}000(1.20 - 1.25) = -\$2{,}500{,}000 \quad (17.3b)$$

Clearly, by hedging only the €50,000,000 net exposure, the treasurer will not compensate exactly for a translation loss by a speculative gain, but will limit the net hedging cost (on a percentage basis) to the forward discount on the euro. In so doing, the treasurer removes all uncertainty as to the outcome of the hedging strategy: He substitutes for an unknown translation loss a *known* net hedging cost.

In our example, the cost of contractual hedging is simply the euro exposure multiplied by the difference between the 90 day forward rate and the spot exchange rate as prevailing at the outset of the exposure horizon (generally known as the 90 day forward discount). The uncertainty that resulted from the end-of-period exchange rate, $S(90)$, has all but disappeared, since the hedging cost function is no longer a function of the unknown end-of-period exchange rate. This is further evidenced by the horizontal line (3) in Exhibit 17.2, portraying the hedging cost as the sum of the translation line (1) and speculative line (2).

The paradox of translation hedging

Our risk-averse treasurer did avoid the potentially adverse effects of one currency bet (translation risk), but to do so he entered into a second currency bet (forward speculation). However, the nature of the currency bets are markedly different, since the first will never be realized in a cash-flow sense whereas the second one (the contractual hedge using a forward contract) will always be fully realized in a cash-flow sense.

To illustrate this paradox, consider the following two situations:

1. The euro appreciates to \$1.30 by year-end — $S(90) = 1.30$. By referring to Exhibit 17.2, the reader can check that Sun incurs an unrealized gain of 50,000,000(1.30 – 1.25) = \$2,500,000 as shown on line (1), whereas the forward contract created a cash-flow loss of 5,000,000(1.20 – 1.30) = –\$5,000,000 as shown on line (2). The net hedging cost is still, however, \$2,500,000 – \$5,000,000 = –\$2,500,000, as shown on line (3).
2. The euro depreciates to $S(90) = 1.15$ by quarter-end. The translation loss as shown in line (1) amounts to 50,000,000(1.15 – 1.25) = –\$5,000,000, whereas the speculative gain as shown in line (2) is 50,000,000(1.20 – 1.15) = \$2,500,000. Again, the net translation cost is the same amount, –\$5,000,000 + \$2,500,000 = –\$2,500,000. Sun would undoubtedly prefer the second situation where the net hedging cost hides a large cash-flow gain to the first situation where a large translation gain compensates for a large cash-flow loss.

> ***Q:*** Assume that the exchange rate at the end of the quarter is 1.21. Explain the composition of the net hedging cost.
>
> ***A:*** It is mostly translation loss 50,000,000(1.21 – 1.25) = –\$2,000,000 and some speculative loss 50,000,000(1.20 – 1.21) = –\$500,000. The net hedging cost is still –\$2,500,000.

Hedging with currency options

An elegant alternative to hedging translation exposures with forward contracts is to resort to the purchase of currency options. The direct benefit of this approach is that it eliminates the uncertainty of the cash-flow cost of hedging. At worst, the cash-flow cost would be limited to the option premium to be paid at the outset of the exposure horizon. At best, the option expires in-the-money and the hedger benefits from the cash-flow gain. The speculative function is reformulated as:

$$\text{Speculative gain/loss} = -875{,}000(1+0.015) + 50{,}000{,}000\,\text{Max}\left[0;1.20 - S(90)\right] \quad (17.4)$$

where \$875,000 is the premium cost of a put option contract[5] on the €50,000,000 translation exposure at the exercise price of $E(90) = 1.20$, and 1.5% is the US interest rate (option is paid up front). Max[0; 1.20 – $S(90)$] sums up the cash value of the put option at expiration: If $S(90) > 1.20$ the option is out-of-the-money, will not be exercised, and has zero value. If $S(90) < 1.20$, the put option is exercised, and the cash-flow gain is equal to 1.20 – $S(90)$. The kinked profile of the speculative function is sketched in Exhibit 17.3.

The net hedging function (line (3) on exhibit 17.3) would again be defined by aggregating the translation gain/loss function (equation (17.1a) or

5 A positive (asset) translation exposure is assumed. A call option would be necessary to hedge a liability translation exposure.

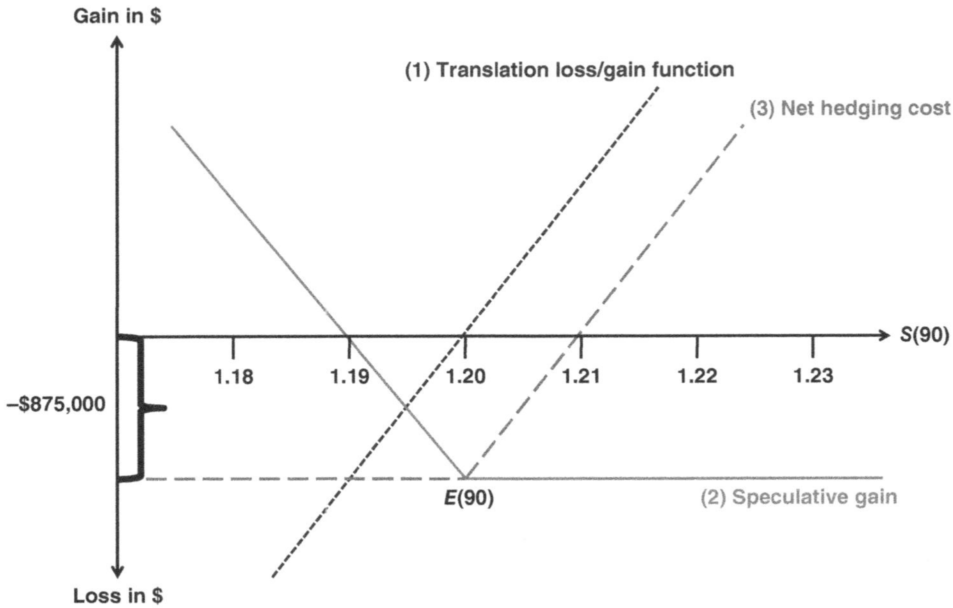

Exhibit 17.3. Translation hedging with currency option.

line (1) on exhibit 17.3) with the speculative gain/loss function (equation (17.4) or line (3) on Exhibit 17.3):

$$\text{Hedging cost} = 50{,}000{,}000\left[S(90) - 1.25\right] + 50{,}000{,}000\,\text{Max}\left[0; 1.20 - S(90)\right] - 875{,}000(1 + 0.015) \tag{17.5a}$$

which reduces itself to:

$$\text{Hedging cost} = 50{,}000{,}000[1.20 - 1.25] - 875{,}000(1 + 0.015)\ \text{for}\ S(90) < 1.20 \tag{17.5b}$$

$$\text{Hedging cost} = 50{,}000[S(90) - 1.25] - 875{,}000(1 + 0.015)\ \text{for}\ S(90) \geq 1.20 \tag{17.5c}$$

From Exhibit 17.3, it is readily observed that for actual exchange rates that are in excess of the exercise price of $E(90) = 1.20$, the translation gain is left unchanged and a small cash-flow cost (the option premium) is incurred; conversely, for an actual rate $S(90)$ below $E(90) = 1.20$, a cash-flow gain is incurred, thereby neutralizing the translation loss and stabilizing the net hedging cost at the option premium cost. For firms that are subject to strict debt–equity covenants, currency options are effective instruments for limiting the impact of exchange losses on cumulative translation (sub-equity) accounts (see International Corporate Finance in Practice 17.2).

INTERNATIONAL CORPORATE FINANCE IN PRACTICE 17.2

Black & Decker's Translation Exposure Paranoia

Black & Decker, the US-based multinational corporation of hardware and houseware products, has always consistently hedged its translation exposure. With more than 50% of its assets overseas, Black & Decker believes that changes in owners' equity position due to foreign exchange translation should not be viewed as merely paper (unrealized) gains and losses. Indeed, when foreign currencies depreciate against the US dollar, translation losses will reduce equity and raise the leverage (debt/equity) ratio. This, in turn, would increase Black & Decker's cost of debt financing and/or restrict its access to the capital market.

Black & Decker favors the use of currency options over forward contracts for hedging translation exposure because currency options allow for the management of both the equity account and the leverage ratio. Exhibit 17.4 shows how the use of currency options allows for maintaining the leverage ratio below a threshold ratio of 37%, as mandated in Black & Decker's debt covenant. Under a no-hedge policy, leverage would increase when the currency depreciates (sub-equity account depleted as a result of translation losses) and would decrease when the currency appreciates. With a forward hedge, leverage remains constant (as the sub-equity account remains unchanged as translation loss/gain is neutralized by cash-flow gain/loss). With an option hedge, leverage decreases — paralleling the no-hedge strategy — when the currency appreciates (put option expires out-of-the-money). When the currency depreciates and the put option is exercised, leverage would remain constant — paralleling the forward hedge.

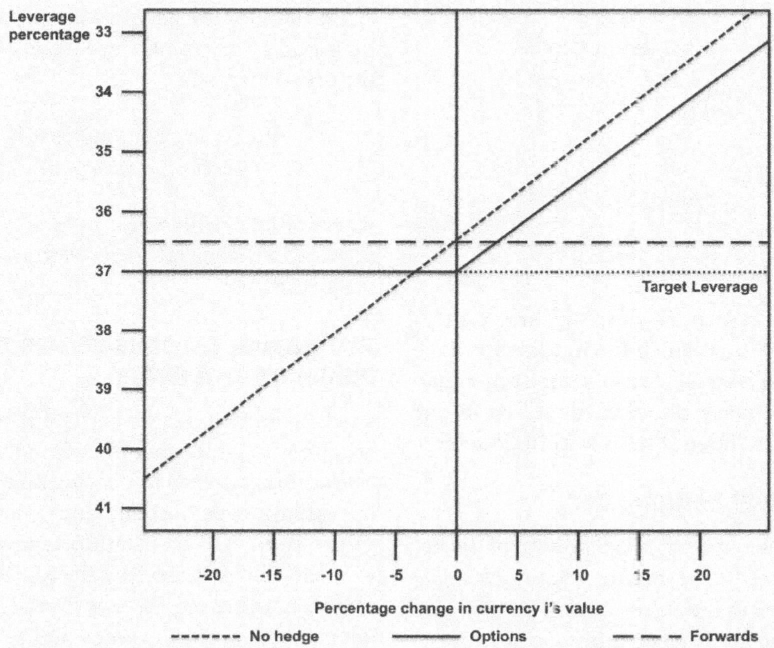

Exhibit 17.4. Black & Decker's translation exposure paranoia.

THE MECHANICS OF FINANCIAL HEDGING

An alternative approach to contractual hedging consists of eliminating balance sheet exposure by arbitraging *exposed* versus *non-exposed* accounting items. Clearly, the flexibility of contractual hedging, which only entails either a forward sale or the purchase of a put option, is lost insofar as financial hedging generally results in a significant disruption of the foreign subsidiary's financial management. However, in countries whose exchange markets do not offer forward or option contracts, this approach would be the only one available.[6]

6 The reader will remember that forward contracts are available for a handful of convertible currencies but are thinly traded for tightly managed currencies as found in several emerging market countries.

Interest rate arbitrage

If we recall that translation exposure is the difference between *exposed assets* and *exposed liabilities*, an intuitive method of financial hedging is to create an *exposed* liability (through local borrowing) matching the amount of the net exposed assets (translation exposure) and to immediately channel the offsetting local currency asset into an *unexposed* account (for example, by investing it in a devaluation-safe money instrument).

Returning to the case of Sun Microsystems Inc., whose French affiliate Marianne S.A. projects as of October 1, 2024, a net euro translation exposure of €50 million on December 31, 2024. Marianne S.A. borrows €50 million/(1 + 0.11/4) at the interest rate of $i_f = 0.11/4$ (note the present value rather than the nominal value of the exposure is borrowed), and immediately converts the loan proceeds at the prevailing spot rate $1.25 = €1 into a dollar-denominated asset returning $i_d = 0.075/4$. After taking into account the dollar cost of repaying the €50 million loan at the unknown spot rate $S(90)$, the dollar gain (or loss) resulting from this interest rate arbitrage operation can be formulated as:

$$\begin{aligned}&\text{Interest rate arbitrage gain/loss}\\&\quad= \text{\$ proceeds of €loan invested}\\&\quad\text{in \$-denominated assets} - \text{\$cost of repaying}\\&\quad\text{both principal and interest of € loan}\\&\quad= \frac{50{,}000{,}000}{1+\frac{0.11}{4}}\times(1.25)\times\left(1+\frac{0.075}{4}\right)\\&\qquad-\frac{50{,}000{,}000}{1+\frac{0.11}{4}}\times S(90)\times\left(1+\frac{0.11}{4}\right)\end{aligned}\tag{17.6}$$

The reader will note that the break-even exchange rate $S(90)^*$ at which the interest arbitrage gain/loss function is equal to zero is none other than the no-profit exchange rate first identified in our earlier discussion of interest rate parity in Chapter 6.

The net financial hedging cost

Proceeding by analogy with the definition of the net *contractual hedging* function, a net *financial hedging* function is defined as the algebraic sum of the translation loss and the interest rate arbitrage functions:

$$\begin{aligned}&\text{Financial hedging cost} = \text{Translation gain/loss}\\&\quad+\text{Interest rate arbitrage gain/loss}\\&= 50{,}000{,}000\times[S(90)-1.25]\\&\quad+\frac{50{,}000{,}000}{1+\frac{0.11}{4}}\times(1.25)\times\left(1+\frac{0.075}{4}\right)\\&\quad-\frac{50{,}000{,}000}{1+\frac{0.11}{4}}\times S(90)\times\left(1+\frac{0.11}{4}\right)\end{aligned}\tag{17.7a}$$

which simplifies itself to:

$$\begin{aligned}&\text{Financing hedging cost } H_f\\&= 50{,}000{,}000\times1.25\times\left(\frac{1+\frac{0.075}{4}}{1+\frac{0.11}{4}}-1\right)\end{aligned}\tag{17.7b}$$

or in more general terms:

$$\begin{aligned}&\text{Financing hedging cost } H_f\\&= e(t)\times S(0)\times\left[\frac{1+i_d}{1+i_f}-1\right]\end{aligned}\tag{17.8}$$

where $e(t) = €50{,}000{,}000$ is the pro forma translation exposure.

Thus, provided that the euro translation exposure is properly projected, the hedging cost will be known at the outset of the accounting period and is again found to be equal to the percentage forward premium or discount, since expression 17.8 can be readily written as:

$$\begin{aligned}&\text{Financing hedging cost } H_f\\&= e(t)\times[F(t)^* - S(0)]\end{aligned}\tag{17.9}$$

where $F(90)^* = S(0)\times(1+i_d)/(1+i_f)$ is the synthetic forward exchange rate derived from the interest rate parity theorem.

Arbitraging exposed versus non-exposed balance sheet items

At this point it might be useful to examine the accounting significance of hedging through interest rate arbitrage. When borrowing takes place in a local (devaluation-prone) currency, the present value of the projected translation exposure creates an *exposed* liability that offsets the translation exposure. However, the cash proceeds from a loan kept in the devaluation-prone currency add to exposed assets unless the proceeds are immediately converted into a *non-exposed* asset — for example, by investing in a devaluation-safe reference currency like the US dollar. Local borrowing is thus a necessary but not sufficient condition for financial hedging to succeed. That is, creating an offsetting exposed asset has to be matched by transforming the *exposed* asset item into a *non-exposed* asset item. There are four different methods for achieving the same goal:

1. Increase *exposed* liabilities and increase *non-exposed* assets — for example, borrow locally and invest the proceeds in marketable securities denominated in devaluation-safe currencies as discussed earlier.
2. Decrease *exposed* assets and increase non-*exposed* assets — for example, sell marketable securities denominated in the local currency and invest them in marketable securities denominated in devaluation-safe currencies.

INTERNATIONAL CORPORATE FINANCE IN PRACTICE 17.3

The Razor Company's Edge Turns Out to be a Poor Hedge!

Gillette, which has some 60% of its sales coming from outside the United States, experienced a staggering loss in its shareholders' equity account, which shrank from \$4.8 billion to \$2.1 billion over the period 1997–2001. Admittedly, not all was the result of translation losses: 20% of the \$2.7 billion loss or \$540 million consisted of translation losses directly traceable to the appreciation of the US dollar over that period. Surprisingly, Gillette hedges its translation exposures only in countries where interest rates are lower than in the United States or — equivalently — in countries whose currencies sell at a forward premium against the US dollar. This allows Gillette to lock in a net negative hedging cost (i.e., a gain) equal to the foreign currency's forward premium. As a result, translation exposures in the United Kingdom, Argentina, and Brazil, whose currencies were at a discount, were not hedged. Because these currencies did depreciate, they accounted for the brunt of Gillette's losses, whereas Japanese, Taiwanese, and Swiss operations were fully hedged over that same period. Obviously, Gillette did not believe that forward rates are good predictors of future exchange rates!

Source: Adapted from Ronald Fink, "Natural Performers," *CFO* Magazine, June 1, 2003.

3. Decrease *exposed* assets and decrease non-*exposed* liabilities — for example, use up cash or discount accounts receivable denominated in devaluation-prone currencies to prepay accounts payable denominated in devaluation-safe currencies, or to prepay dividends to the parent company.
4. Increase *exposed* liabilities and decrease non-*exposed* liabilities — for example, borrow locally to retire medium- or long-term debt denominated in devaluation-safe currencies or to prepay accounts payable denominated in devaluation-safe currencies, or to prepay dividends to the parent company.

Whatever the technical device used, the hedging entity will incur costs (not necessarily positive) for adjusting the segmentation of the exposed affiliate's balance sheet into *exposed* versus non-*exposed* items. Regardless of the technique used, the formulation of the net cost of financial hedging proposed in expression 17.8 remains valid, provided that the following substitutions are carried out:

- i_f becomes the cost of increasing *exposed* liabilities or the opportunity cost of reducing exposed assets.
- i_d becomes the return from increasing non-*exposed* assets or the cost savings from reducing non-exposed liabilities.

Numerical illustration

Consider the pro forma December 31, 2024, balance sheet of the French subsidiary of Sun Microsystems as of October 1, 2024, detailed in Exhibit 17.5. Accounts receivable can be discounted at an annual

Exhibit 17.5. Balance sheet of French subsidiary of Sun Microsystems in € (December 31, 2024).

Assets	**25,000,000**	**Liabilities & Networth**	**25,000,000**
Fixed assets	13,000,000	Long-term debt to parent (denominated in \$)	1,000,000
Accounts receivable (denominated in \$)	5,000,000	Long-term debt (denominated in €)	11,000,000
Inventory of finished goods	3,000,000	Accounts payable (denominated in €)	7,000,000
Marketable securities (denominated in €)	3,000,000	Accounts payable (denominated in \$)	2,000,000
Cash	1,000,000	**Net worth**	**4,000,000**

rate of 12%. Dollar-denominated accounts payable can be prepaid with savings of 10%. Six-month treasury bills denominated in US dollars yield 7½% annually, and € can be borrowed at an annual rate of 11%. Spot and 90 day forward € are available at \$1.25 and \$1.20, respectively. Which hedging strategy should be implemented?

Contractual hedging

A preliminary step is to compute Sun Microsystems' net translation exposure in euros, determined as the difference between *exposed* assets and *exposed* liabilities:

Exposed assets	= Fixed assets (13,000,000) + Inventory of finished goods (3,000,000) + €-denominated marketable securities (3,000,000) + Cash in €(1,000,000)
	= €20,000,000
Exposed liabilities	= €-denominated long-term debt (11,000,000) + €-denominated accounts payable (7,000,000)
	= €18,000,000
Net translation exposure	= €20,000,000 – €18,000,000 = €2,000,000

Contractual hedging can be carried out by selling 90 days forward the € amount corresponding to Sun Microsystems' net translation exposure. The cost H_c incurred by this contractual hedge is (expression 17.3):

$$H_c = 2{,}000{,}000 \times (1.20 - 1.25) = -\ \$100{,}000$$

It should now be compared with the cost of financial hedging.

Financial Hedging Sun Microsystems can essentially borrow from two sources and should presumably choose the least costly one. By discounting accounts receivable, the French affiliate of Sun Microsystems is borrowing from its customers at an annual rate of $i_€^1 = 0.12$, which is slightly more expensive than the French banking system $\left(i_€^2 = 0.11\right)$. The offsetting increase in non-*exposed* assets (investment in US Treasury bills at $i_{US}^1 = 0.075$) or decrease in non-*exposed* liabilities (prepayment of dollar-denominated accounts payable at $i_{US}^2 = 0.10$) should be tailored to maximize return (or to minimize costs). Accordingly, Sun Microsystems–France should borrow the net present value of its net euro translation exposure from the French banking system and use it to prepay its dollar-denominated accounts payable. The net cost of financial hedging amounts to (expression 17.7):

$$H_f = 2{,}000{,}000 \times 1.25 \times \left[\frac{1 + \frac{0.10}{4}}{1 + \frac{0.11}{4}} - 1 \right] = -\$6082.73$$

Financial hedging should be implemented as long as the unknown cash-flow component of either approach is not taken into account in the comparison. Most firms, however, should weigh the cost of possible impaired managerial flexibility that is associated with financial hedging when deciding on a hedging policy.

SUMMARY

1. Exchange rate fluctuations may severely disrupt a multinational corporation's foreign income stream or deplete its owners' equity account. Even though no cash-flow losses (or gains) are involved, consolidated accounting income may exhibit erratic trends that will, in turn, affect the corporation's overall risk profile as perceived by its shareholders, creditors, and the investment community at large.
2. Different translation guidelines can be categorized as follows: (1) The *current/noncurrent* method requires all current/short-term accounts to be translated at the current/closing rate. Translation exposure is simply the foreign subsidiary's *working capital.* Translation gains/losses flow through the parent's income statement and directly impact its EPS. (2) The *monetary/nonmonetary* method requires all monetary accounts (as opposed to real/physical ones) to be translated at the current/closing rate. Resulting gains/losses flow through the parent's income statement and directly to its EPS. (3) The *all-current* method requires all accounts to be translated at the current/closing rate. Translation exposure is simply the foreign subsidiary's *net worth.* Resulting gains/losses bypass the income statement to be accumulated in the parent's balance sheet.
3. At the core of the translation risk hedging debate is the fact that translation losses/gains — however large they may be — are unrealized, non-cash flows in nature and without tax implications. Yet we know that value creation is driven by cash flows, not by accounting profits. Thus, hedging is warranted if it can be shown that hedging

translation exposure — by modifying/lowering the risk profile of the firm — is indeed resulting in a higher stock price, which in turn lowers the cost of equity capital. In capital markets that are truly efficient this will not be the case. In capital markets that are not quite fully efficient, investors will reward firms that are producing smoother earnings streams.

4. The essence of hedging is to substitute, at the outset of the exposure horizon, a *known* cost of buying protection against exchange risk for an *unknown* translation loss. In a sense, the hedger is trading the uncertainty of an accounting loss that may never materialize for the certain cost of eliminating translation risk.
5. Multinational corporations' stream of accounting income can be smoothed through the use of forward contracts or currency options, or — alternatively — through skillful local borrowing (by foreign affiliates) and leading or lagging of international payments.
6. Special attention should be devoted to the cash-flow costs of translation exposure hedging, and a risk management model should be formulated to keep translation hedging costs within a preapproved cash budget.

QUESTIONS FOR DISCUSSION

1. What is translation exposure? How does it differ from transaction exposure?
2. Is hedging translation exposure warranted when financial markets are efficient?
3. Spell out specific conditions when translation exposure hedging is warranted.
4. Compare the three principal translation methods: Where are resulting gains and losses reported?
5. What is a *functional currency*? How does its choice determine applicable translation rules under FASB ASC 830?
6. Do translation losses negatively impact the firm's cost of capital?
7. How can forwards and options be used to hedge translation exposure?
8. What is the true cost of translation exposure hedging?
9. How can a company alter its translation exposure?
10. What is the cost of translation hedging when currency options are used?

PROBLEMS

1. **Pax Americana measures its Mexican peso translation exposure (A-easy).** The US-based multinational Pax Americana Inc. is concerned by the impact of the anticipated Mexican peso devaluation upon its net consolidated earnings, as well as on the net worth of its Mexican affiliate Mexicana Ltd., whose pro forma balance sheet for December 31, 2024, is listed in Exhibit 17.6. On January 1, 2024, the prevailing spot Mexican peso (MXN) price of one US$ is MXN 12.5 = US$1.
   a. Measure the translation exposure in peso terms that will be outstanding by December 31, 2024, using the current/noncurrent, monetary/nonmonetary, and all-current methods.
   b. What would be the translation loss or gain incurred by Pax Americana if the exchange rate at time of consolidation had depreciated to MXN 15 = US$1? Show how this gain/loss would be reported under each method.
2. **Pax Americana hedges its Mexican peso translation exposure (B-easy).** Referring to Pax Americana's translation exposure described in problem 1:
   a. Identify the alternative hedging methods available to Pax Americana.
   b. Show how Pax Americana could hedge its MXN exposure if 1-year peso forward contracts trade at MXN 14 = US$1.
   c. What is the cost of hedging through forward contracts? Is it tax-deductible?

Exhibit 17.6. Pro forma balance sheet of Mexicana Ltd. as of December 31, 2024.

Assets (MXN '000s)	**2,300,000**	**Liabilities & Equity (MXN '000s)**	**2,300,000**
Net fixed assets	700,000	Current liabilities	300,000
Cash and liquid assets	500,000	Long-term debt	1,200,000
Receivables	300,000		
Inventories	800,000	Owners' equity	800,000

d. An alternative approach is for Mexicana Ltd. to borrow Mexican pesos and convert them immediately to US dollars. Explain how the latter approach effectively eliminates Pax Americana's exposure in pesos. What is the cost of this approach, assuming that pesos can be borrowed/lent at 8.5% per annum and US dollars return 3.5% annually on the Eurodollar market?

e. Which hedging method should Pax Americana select? Compare the two methods graphically.

3. Firestone's euro exposure (intermediate). On July 1, 2024, the Dutch subsidiary of Firestone Company–USA has a projected net translation exposure of €50,000,000 for July 1, 2025. Because of the euro-zone's buoyant balance of trade and a relatively low rate of inflation, the euro is widely expected to revalue by 4 to 6% *vis-à-vis* the US dollar during the next 12 months.

a. Should the international treasurer of Firestone hedge its net exposure in euros?

b. The prevailing dollar price of one euro is €1 = $1.32, and one year forward contracts for euros sell at a 1.5% premium. Show how Firestone could hedge its € exposure.

c. At-the-money € put options are also available at a 1.75% premium. Would you advise Firestone to use currency options to hedge its € exposure?

4. Motorola's Argentine peso translation exposure (intermediate). US-based Motorola has a wholly owned subsidiary in Argentina that assembles consumer electronics products for sale there. The net worth of the Argentine subsidiary is currently Argentine peso (ARS) 250 million. Because of recent labor strikes in Buenos Aires, Motorola's treasurer is concerned that the peso could depreciate by as much as 20% against the dollar from its present level of ARS 4.5 per US$1. The treasurer believes that this exposure should be hedged with a forward contract. The 3 month forward exchange rate is ARS 5 = US$1. Motorola uses the current method to translate foreign currency financial statements into dollars.

a. What is the functional currency of Motorola's Argentine subsidiary?

b. Do you agree with the treasurer about the need to hedge? What are the arguments for and against hedging this exposure?

c. What is the cost of hedging?

5. Archimedes SA's money market hedge. On December 31, 2024, Archimedes SA, the Philippine affiliate of a US irrigation equipment manufacturing company, is projecting its Philippines peso (PHP)-denominated balance sheet for December 31, 2025, as shown in Exhibit 17.7. The current exchange rate is PHP 40 = $1.

a. What is the peso translation exposure under the monetary/nonmonetary and all-current methods?

b. One-year peso forward contracts are available in the United States at a 9% discount. Show how the all-current peso translation exposure can be hedged, assuming that cash-flow exchange losses are tax-deductible at 21% from normal corporate income.

c. Explain how refinancing the long-term debt in dollars at 5% in lieu of the prevailing 10% interest rate on peso-denominated long-term debt would result in an alternative translation hedge. How does it compare with the contractual hedge introduced in part b?

6. Sun Microsystems' functional currency (intermediate). Referring to Sun Microsystems' French subsidiary (see Exhibit 17.5), Marianne S.A., assume that due to the close production integration between US and French operations the US dollar is deemed to be the functional currency for consolidation purposes. What is Sun Microsystems' pro forma translation exposure? Assuming that the € is expected to revalue by 10% over the exposure horizon, show what gains/losses would be incurred by Sun Microsystems and where they would be reported.

Exhibit 17.7. Pro forma balance sheet of Archimedes SA as of December 31, 2025 in PHP 000s.

Assets	**540,000**	**Liabilities**	**540,000**
Cash	60,000	Accounts payable	30,000*
Accounts receivable	120,000	Short-term debt	55,000
		Long-term debt	200,000
Inventories	120,000		
Net fixed assets	240,000	Owners' equity	255,000

Note: *Denominated in US$ (imports of components from US parent).

7. **Galileo's functional currency (intermediate).** The US multinational manufacturer of drilling and seismic instruments Galileo Ltd. (GLL) is reviewing the rapid deterioration of the Venezuelan economy and how it may impact its consolidated accounts. The bolivar (VEF) is currently officially trading at VEF 4.5 = US$1 but, with cumulative inflation over the past three years approaching 125%, another maxi-devaluation is widely anticipated.
   a. Referring to the GLL-Venezuela pro forma balance sheet shown in Exhibit 17.8, determine GLL's translation exposure in bolivars. Would your answer be different if Venezuela's cumulative inflation over the past three years had been 75% instead of 125%?
   b. Assuming that the bolivar will depreciate by year-end to VEF 6 = US$1, what would GLL's translation loss be? How would it be reported?
   c. GLL-Venezuela borrows an additional VEF 30,000,000 to pay dividends to its US parent. How would GLL's bolivar exposure be changed?

8. **Hewlett-Packard's Indian financing-cum-hedging conundrum (intermediate).** Following the successful introduction of Copernicus, its latest line of laptop computers, in May 2024, Hewlett-Packard-India (HPI) was facing working capital financing problems: It needed rupee (INR) 5 billion over the next six months, which could be readily sourced from the Indian money market at the annual rate of 10% (interest rate payable semi-annually) or from the Eurodollar market through a one year zero-coupon note issued at 95%.
   a. Find the break-even exchange rate(s) that would leave HPI indifferent between rupee and dollar financing. The current spot rupee price of one US$ is INR 50 = US$1. Illustrate your answer graphically.
   b. Forward rupee contracts are available at a 4.5% annual discount from the dollar standpoint; should HPI consider covered dollar financing?
   c. Illustrate your decision graphically. Are the rupee and dollar money markets integrated?
   d. Prior to initiating new financing, the comptroller of HP-USA projected a net asset translation exposure of INR 9 billion. Explain how the two financing alternatives introduced in question a would impact HP's rupee translation exposure.
   e. HPI was also considering the non-recourse discounting of six month US$-denominated accounts receivable (A/R) in the amount of US$50,000,000. How much financing would be generated? What would its impact be on HP's rupee translation exposure?
   f. How could HP hedge its rupee translation exposure? Which method do you recommend?

Exhibit 17.8. Pro forma balance sheet of Galileo-Venezuela as of December 31, 2015 in VEF 000s.

Assets (VEF '000s)	500,000	Liabilities (VEF '000s)	500,000
Cash	60,000	Accounts payable	80,000
Accounts receivable	140,000	Short-term debt	55,000
Inventories	100,000	Long-term debt	150,000
Net fixed assets	200,000	Stockholders' equity	215,000

9. **Hippocrates hedges its translation exposures (A-advanced).** Hippocrates Inc. is a leading US-based manufacturer of medical imaging systems such as MRI machines with headquarters offices and manufacturing facilities in St. Paul, Minnesota. Its Mexican manufacturing and assembling affiliate, domiciled in Mexico City, services the entire Latin American market. The French affiliate is domiciled in Paris and services the entire euro-zone area. As of January 1, 2024 the two affiliates' balance sheets are prepared in Mexican pesos (MXN) and euros (€), respectively (see Exhibit 17.9). Current exchange rates are MXN 12.5 = US$1 = €0.80.
   a. What is Hippocrates' translation exposure to the Mexican peso and the euro, taking into account intracorporate transactions?
   b. Would denominating in US$ all intracorporate transactions between sister affiliates or between affiliates and their parent materially affect Hippocrates' translation exposures? How?

10. **Hippocrates' balance sheet consolidation (B-advanced).** Referring to information provided in the preceding problem:
   a. Prepare a consolidated balance sheet for Hippocrates Inc. using current exchange rates.
   b. Assuming that the Mexican peso will depreciate by 15% in 2024, what would be the translation gains or losses to Hippocrates? Where would they appear on the consolidated statements? (Assume that for pro forma purposes both the Mexican and French affiliates' balance sheets remain unchanged at the end of 2014.)

Exhibit 17.9. Nonconsolidated pro-forma sheet for Hippocrates Inc., December 31, 2024 (in '000 currency units).

	Parent	Mexican Affiliate	French Affiliate
Assets			
Cash	$1,500	MXN 1,420	€1,200
Accounts receivable	2,500[a,b]	2,800[a,c]	1,500
Inventory	5,000	6,200	2,500
Property, plant, and equipment	2,400	...	...
Goodwill	3,600	...	...
Net fixed assets	12,000	11,200	5,600
Total assets	$27,000	MXN 21,620	€10,800
Liabilities and Net Worth			
Accounts payable	$3,000	MXN 2,500[a]	€1,700[c]
Notes payable	4,000	4,200	2,300[b]
Long-term debt	9,000	7,000	2,300
Common stock	5,000	4,500	2,900
Retained earnings	6,000	3,420	1,600
Total liabilities and net worth	$27,000	MXN 21,620	€10,800

Notes: [a]The parent firm is owed MXN 1,320 by the Mexican affiliate. This sum is included in the parent's accounts receivable. The remainder of the parent's accounts receivable is denominated in dollars, and the remainder of the Mexican affiliate's accounts payable is denominated in pesos.
[b]The French affiliate owes its parent €1,000. Notes payable are US$ denominated.
[c]The Mexican affiliate has MXN 800 of accounts receivable (peso-denominated) owed by its sister French affiliate.

c. Assuming that the US$ is the functional currency of Hippocrates' Mexican operation, prepare revised consolidated statements. What would be the impact of a 15% peso devaluation on the consolidated statements, and where would it appear? (Assume again that for pro forma purposes both the Mexican and French affiliates' balance sheets remain unchanged at the end of 2024).

INTERNET EXERCISES

11. **ASC 830.** Log in to the Financial Accounting Standard Board website www.fasb.org and review ASC 830: how should financial statements of subsidiaries operating in hyperinflationary countries be translated? How is hyperinflation defined according to ASC 830?

12. **Proctor & Gamble Foreign Exchange Risk Management.** Access Proctor & Gamble website www.proctorgamble.com and search the firm's annual report/Form 10K: how does the company manage currency risk?

REFERENCES

Aggarwal, Raj. 1991. "Management of Accounting Exposure to Currency Changes: Role and Evidence of Agency Costs." *Managerial Finance* 17(4): 10–22.

Arnold, Jerry L., and William W. Holder. 1986. *Impact of Statement 52 on Decisions, Financial Reports and Attitudes.* Morristown, NJ: Financial Executives Research Foundation.

Brayshaw, R. E., and Ahmed E. K. Eldin. 1989. "The Smoothing Hypothesis and the Role of Exchange Differences." *Journal of Business Finance and Accounting* 16(3): 621–635.

Financial Accounting Standards Board. 1981. *Statement of Financial Accounting Standards No. 52.* Norwalk, CT: Financial Accounting Foundation.

Garlicki, T. Dessa, Frank J. Fabozzi, and Robert Fonfeder. 1987. "The Impact of Earnings under FASB 52 on Equity Returns." *Financial Management* 16(3): 36–44.

Houston, Carol O. 1990. "Translation Exposure Hedging Post FASB 52." *Journal of International Financial Management & Accounting* 2(2 and 3): 145–170.

Jacque, Laurent L. 1979. "Why Hedgers Are Not Speculators." *Columbia Journal of World Business* 14(4): 108–116.

APPENDIX 17A: ACCOUNTING VALUATION AND THE CONCEPT OF TRANSLATION EXPOSURE

At a given point in time, the accounting value[7] of a multinational corporation Z is formally defined as the aggregate of both the parent's and its affiliates' net worth. For instance, at the outset of the accounting period $[0, t]$, its total net worth $W(0)$ would be expressed as:

$$W(0) = W_P(0) + \sum_{i=1}^{N} W_i(0) \qquad (17.10)$$

where $W_p(0)$ is the net worth of the parent company measured in reference currency terms at the beginning of the accounting period, and $W_i(0)$ is the net worth of affiliate i also measured in reference currency terms at the beginning of the accounting period.

Similarly, at the end of the accounting period, Z's aggregate net worth $W(t)$ becomes:

$$W(t) = W_P(t) + \sum_{i=1}^{N} W_i(t) \qquad (17.11)$$

where $W(t)$, $W_p(t)$, and $W_i(t)$ are defined as in equation 17.10, but measured at the end of the accounting period.

From first accounting principles, the reader will recall that Z's net income, I, earned over the period $[0, t]$, is simply Z's change in aggregate net worth (assuming that no dividends are paid):

$$I = W(t) - W(0) \qquad (17.12)$$

Z's worldwide net income, I, can be further disaggregated into a parent (p) domestic net income component, I_p, and a foreign (f) net income component, I_f:

$$I = I_P + I_f \quad \text{with} \quad I_p = W_P(t) - W_P(0)$$

and

$$I_f = \sum_{i=1}^{N} I_i = \sum_{i=1}^{n} \left[W_i(t) - W_i(0) \right] \qquad (17.13)$$

where I_i is the net income of Z's affiliate A_i expressed in reference currency terms, measured over the accounting period $[0, t]$.

All accounting magnitudes (net worth and net income) have been carefully defined in reference currency terms. If this is perfectly legitimate when dealing with the net worth and net income of Z's parent company and domestic affiliates, how can we account for the net worth and net income of Z's foreign affiliate A_i in reference currency terms? After all, Z's affiliate A_i operates in country i; that is, it generates revenues and incurs costs denominated in currency i and presumably also maintains its accounting books in currency i.

The answer is simple. We have assumed away an important step in our chain of reasoning — the translation or restatement of A_i's financial statements from currency i into Z's reference currency. This should present little difficulty so long as the exchange rate, expressed as the reference currency price of one unit of currency i, remains constant throughout the accounting period — that is, $S_{\$,i}(t) = S_{\$,i}(0)$. If this is indeed the case, a simple relationship will obtain between the net reference currency income I_i that Z derives from A_i's operations and the change in A_i's net worth as expressed in local currency i over the accounting period:

$$I_i = [w_i(t) - w_i(0)] \times S_{\$,i}(0) \qquad (17.14)$$

where $w_i(0)$ and $w_i(t)$ are A_i's net worth as measured at the beginning and the end of the accounting period in currency i terms.[8]

We now relax the assumption of a constant exchange rate throughout the accounting period, with $S_{\$,i}(t)$ different from $S_{\$,i}(0)$. The net reference currency income I_i^* that accrues to Z because of its operations in country i through its affiliate A_i will have to reflect the fact that A_i's accounting value or net worth as measured at the beginning and end of the period should be translated at different exchange rates:

$$I_i^* = w_i(t) \times S_{\$,i}(t) - w_i(0) \times S_{\$,i}(0) \qquad (17.15)$$

The exchange gain or loss suffered by Z because of a change in the exchange rate used for translation purposes can now be formulated as the difference between I_i^* and I_i. These are the net reference currency incomes that Z derives from its affiliate

7 Needless to say, a firm's *accounting* value is always different from its *market* value as derived from its stock price.

8 Lowercase letters are used for accounting magnitudes measured in *local* currency i as opposed to capital letters that refer to *reference* currency magnitudes.

A_i's operation under the exclusive assumptions of, respectively, a constant and a non-constant translation exchange rate over the exposure horizon [0, t]:

$$\text{Translation exchange gain or loss} = I_i^* - I_i \tag{17.16}$$

From expressions (17.15) and (17.16), the translation exchange gain or loss $T[S_{\$,i}(t)]$ becomes:

$$T[S_{\$,i}(t)] = w_i(t) \times S_{\$,i}(t) - w_i(0) \times S_{\$,i}(0) - [w_i(t) - w_i(0)] \times S_{\$,i}(0) \tag{17.17}$$

which simplifies itself to:

$$T[S_{\$,i}(t)] = w_i(t) \times [S_{\$,i}(t) - S_{\$,i}(0)] \tag{17.18}$$

At the outset of the accounting period (0), the projected translation exchange gain or loss that Z will incur from its affiliate A_i's operation is a function of its net worth *projected* at the end of the period, $w_i(t)$, as well as the end-of-period exchange rate $S_{\$,i}(t)$. In an accounting sense, the projected net worth $w_i(t)$ is Z's translation exposure in currency i. This definition, however, is based on a key assumption that was implicitly made throughout our presentation of the concept of translation gain or loss — namely, that all balance sheet items of affiliate A_i are uniformly translated using the end of the accounting period exchange rate $S_{\$,i}(t)$. This translation method, called the *current method*, is used by US multinational corporations as well as for the consolidation of their foreign branches (as opposed to foreign subsidiaries) and is mandated by Financial Accounting Standards Board Statement No. 52.

More generally, however, the accepted practice for translating the accounts of foreign subsidiaries into reference currency terms is to differentiate between so-called exposed and non-exposed balance sheet items. *Exposed* items, such as cash, marketable securities, or accounts receivable, are translated at the current exchange rate that prevails when accounts are consolidated. Non-*exposed* assets, such as fixed assets or long-term debt, by contrast, are translated at the rate that prevailed at the outset of the accounting period.[9] Formally, the currency i value of Z's affiliate A_i should be disaggregated as

$$w_i(t) = [a_i(t) + a_i^*(t)] - [l_i(t) + l_i^*(t)] \tag{17.19}$$

where $a_i(t)$ and $a_i^*(t)$ are, respectively, A_i's non-exposed and exposed assets as measured in currency i. Similarly, $l_i(t)$ and $l_i^*(t)$ are, respectively, A_i's non-exposed and exposed liabilities as measured in currency i.[10]

The reference currency valuation of the net worth of Z's affiliate A_i should incorporate the dichotomy in exchange rates used in translating the two categories of balance sheet accounts:

$$W_i(t) = [a_i(t) - l_i(t)] \times S_{\$,i}(0) + [a_i^*(t) - l_i^*(t)] \times S_{\$,i}(t) \tag{17.20}$$

Note that the equality $W_i(t) = w_i(t) \times S_{\$,i}(t)$ holds only if all balance sheet items are translated at current exchange rates. To reiterate, this is the accepted practice of US multinational corporations consolidating balance sheets of their worldwide operations for public disclosure to their shareholders.

The translation gain or loss introduced in expression (17.20) should be reformulated, after making use of expressions (17.19) and (17.20), as

$$T[S_{\$,i}(t)] = [a_i^*(t) - l_i^*(t)] \times [S_{\$,i}(t) - S_{\$,i}(0)] \tag{17.21}$$

The concept of translation exposure itself should now appear fairly obvious: It is formally defined as the algebraic difference between exposed assets and exposed liabilities. Thus, we can write:

$$e_i(t) = a_i^*(t) - l_i^*(t) \tag{17.22}$$

where $e_i(t)$ is Z's projected translation exposure in currency i resulting from affiliate A_i's operations in country i.

The translation exposure, as defined in expression (17.22), is clearly a pro forma magnitude. Its accuracy depends on the accuracy of pro forma financial statements, and it is normally derived from projected balance sheets of foreign affiliates. The segmentation of accounts into exposed versus non-exposed items results from the translation method used: It generally leads to different measures of translation exposures and thus to different expected translation losses or gains. Similarly, the disposition of translation gains/losses incurred by the parent company will depend on the translation method used.

Although the discussion of the concept of translation exposure was cast in terms of balance

9 Or, to be more precise, the exchange rate that prevailed when the asset was first acquired or the liability first incurred. The segmentation between exposed and nonexposed items is somewhat arbitrary and depends on the accounting method mandated. See the "Alternative Translation Methods" section.

10 A word of caution is in order: $a_i(t)$ and $l_i(t)$ no longer refer, as previously, to currency i-denominated assets and liabilities maturing at time t. Rather, they simply denote the value of the portfolio of currency i-denominated assets and liabilities as measured at time t.

sheets, the translation of income statements would follow the same principles: Revenue and expense items associated with exposed assets or liabilities should be translated at the current period's exchange rate (or averages of current exchange rates over the base reporting period). Conversely, items associated with non-exposed asset or liability terms, such as depreciation charges, should be translated at the corresponding historical exchange rate.

Currency i versus country i — Translation exposure

The concept of translation exposure introduced in the "Alternative Translation Methods" section focused on the set of exposed currency i-denominated assets and liabilities (country i translation exposure). It left out the portfolio of currency i-denominated assets and liabilities that country j-based affiliate A_j may be holding because of cross-border trade or financing operations ($i \neq j$). Thus, an exhaustive measure of Z's overall currency i translation exposure, denoted as $\hat{e}_i(t)$, would include not only country i translation exposure, but also the balance of the whole portfolio of currency i-denominated exposed assets and liabilities held by any country j-based entity affiliated with corporation Z.

Accordingly, currency i translation exposure can be calculated by adding up country i translation exposure to all the currency i-denominated transaction exposures. Formally, this can be expressed as:

$$\breve{e}_i(t) = e_i(t) + \sum_{j=1}^{n} e_{i,j}(t) \qquad (17.23)$$

where $e_i(t)$ is Z's translation exposure in currency i and $e_{i,j}(t)$ the currency i-denominated (before tax) transaction exposure incurred by any entity j, including its parent, associated with corporation Z. The latter exposures are not maturity t specific, but they are simply valued at time t.

In closing our discussion of methodological guidelines for measuring transaction and translation exposures, we should emphasize again the challenge of designing and operating in real time a management information system that keeps track of all exposures all the time. At the very least, what is needed is a 12 month rolling forecast of (1) transaction exposure by currency and (2) balance sheet and income statement for each subsidiary so that the impact of exchange rate movements and management decisions can be easily simulated and evaluated.

CASE STUDY 17.1. WILKINSON SWORD'S TRIALS AND TRIBULATIONS IN TURKEY

It was late December 2000 and Banu Ozcan, president and general manager of Wilkinson Sword–Turkey S.A., frowned as she examined the monthly foreign exchange (forex) exposure statement about to be sent to Wilkinson Sword's US headquarters (see Case Exhibit 17.1). Having recently won approval for a US$12 million capital expenditure request for the launch of the new Quattro shaving system in Turkey, Ozcan was concerned by the modalities of its financing.

Wilkinson Sword–Turkey

The Turkish subsidiary, formed in 1971, was the first manufacturing operation of Wilkinson Sword (known in the United States as Schick[11]) in the Middle East. Very early on, through skillful marketing, Wilkinson Sword had established a dominant position in the Turkish market for shaving instruments. Over time, in part through continued tariff protection, savvy advertising, and product innovation, Wilkinson Sword had maintained and consolidated its quasi-oligopolistic hold on Turkey. This policy had been adhered to over the years in spite of difficult macroeconomic conditions, including bouts of hyperinflation and currency devaluation, which had affected the Turkish economy. In 1975, the Turkish government imposed foreign exchange controls prohibiting repatriation of funds. As a result, the subsidiary's earnings accumulated in Turkey. Foreign exchange restrictions were lifted in 1980, and repatriation of profits and dividends has been allowed since, although limitations on such remittances have been increasing. As of 2000, all payments of royalties, fees, dividends, and profits

11 Wilkinson Sword is commercialized in the United States, Europe, and Australia under the Schick brand name. It is a subsidiary of Energizers Holdings.

Case Exhibit 17.1. Wilkinson Sword–Turkey financial statements.

Profit and Loss Statement (TRL in Trillions)	1999	2000	Budget 2001[12]
Sales	80.0	104.0	120.0
Cost of goods sold	40.0	56.0	60.0
Interest expense	4.0	10.0	8.0
Marketing and other expenses	20.0	20.R	28.0
Profit before tax	16.0	17.2	24.0
Profit after tax (Turkey)	8.0	8.8	12.0
Profit U.S. after translation loss $in millions	$4.0	$2.8	$6.8

Balance Sheet (TRL in Trillions)

	1999	2000	Budget 2001
Current Assets			
Cash	2.0	2.0	2.0
Accounts receivable	16.0	19.20	24.0
Inventories	24.0	28.8	32.0
Other	0.8	0.8	0.8
Fixed assets (net)	14.0	20.0	28.0
Total assets	56.8	70.80	86.80
Current Liabilities			
Loans payable ($-denominated)	8.0	12.8	16.0
Accounts payable (50% $-denominated)	16.0	18.0	20.8
Intercompany payables ($-denominated)	4.0	8.0	14.8
Other	4.8	8.0	7.2
Long-term debt	—	—	—
Capital stock	12.0	12.0	12.0
Retained earnings	12.0	12.0	16.0
Total liabilities & equity	56.8	70.80	86.80

were subject to government approval. A progressive tax was levied on all remittances in excess of 12% of registered capital, with a 25% tax levied on remittances greater than 20% of registered capital.

While Wilkinson Sword was still in 2000 the sole local manufacturer of razors and blades, reductions in tariffs as Turkey was under pressure to comply with World Trade Organization (WTO) guidelines and to ready itself for European Union membership application had made imports increasingly competitive in recent years. Although Wilkinson Sword held 90% of the Turkish razor and blade market, Gillette (the world market leader in shaving systems) and BIC (the French multinational leader in ballpoint pens, disposable lighters, and razors) had made preliminary advances into the market in the past 3 years; BIC was also manufacturing lighters in Ankara for which it held a dominant position in the Turkish market. BIC and Gillette, however, were late entrants and still minor players in the razor blades market, where they competed through imports only.

Ozcan expected increased competition in 2001 and felt that the introduction of the Quattro shaving system in 2001 was crucial for Wilkinson Sword's future in Turkey.

The financing decision

Ozcan's pro forma financing needs amounted to US$12 million for the coming year, computed as follows. Half of the request would cover the cost of importing and installing new machinery and

12 Pro-forma 2001 budget without US$12 million of capital expenditure.

equipment for the local plant. About US$4 million was budgeted for additional net working capital requirements. The remainder would be applied to the promotion campaign. The need for additional working capital was partially due to increased unit volume, but because of continuous high inflation in Turkey, ever increasing sums were required to finance accounts receivable. Also, stiffer competition in recent months had forced Ozcan to extend more liberal credit terms to the 6,000 outlets in Wilkinson Sword–Turkey's distribution network.

Two principal sources of financing were available: One was through the extension of intercompany receivables from the parent company to the Turkish subsidiary. This credit would be denominated in dollars at an annual interest cost of 7.5%. The second source of financing was local bank debt denominated in Turkish lira (TRL), with interest costs at present running at an annual rate of 45%. The choice would be determined by the treasurer's office at US corporate headquarters in close consultation with Banu Ozcan.

Turkish hyperinflation

The abnormally high interest rate for financing in Turkish lira resulted from Turkey's ongoing battle with hyperinflation. Indeed, over the prior 30 years, Turkey had been governed by 22 governments that had consistently attempted to slay the dragon of hyperinflation and failed. Even though the Turkish economy never experienced hyperinflation like Argentina or Israel in the period of global inflation from 1973 to 1994, the country fell into a unique situation after 1994 when inflation culminated at 100%, which severely penalized the Turkish economy until the end of the 1990s (see Case Exhibit 17.2). By December 1999, Turkey launched yet another

Case Exhibit 17.2. Hyperinflation statistics in Turkey, 1995–2001.

	Turkey		U.S.	
	CPI	WPI	CPI	Exchange Rate (EOP)
1995M3	84.9265	90.2029	99.312	41,919.4
1995M6	95.2432	97.8363	100.434	43,204.1
1995M9	110.293	107.029	100.354	47,786.9
1996M3	152.304	149.066	101.316	68,476.2
1996M6	174.16	172.342	102.598	79,804.9
1996M9	197.772	192.447	102.759	88,911.5
1996M12	229.041	221.744	103.48	104,757
1997M3	270.042	263.809	102.037	124,991
1997M6	310.085	302.863	101.957	144,418
1997M9	375.495	356.78	102.198	170,471
1997M12	456.008	423.438	101.636	199,937
1998M3	532.479	490.633	99.9532	235,817
1998M6	590.869	535.143	100.033	261,123
1998M9	677.497	591.963	99.2318	275,141
1998M12	773.964	653.192	98.4303	307,228
1999M3	870.802	727.268	98.27	361,922
1999M6	970.619	804.462	100.354	412,949
1999M9	1,112.93	914.286	102.598	453,668
1999M12	1,306.39	1,064.1	102.438	527,613
2000M3	1,462.04	1,207.79	104.843	581,034
2000M6	1,539.58	1,261.34	107.247	616,594
2000M9	1,657.79	1,316.11	107.808	664,548
2000M12	1,816.32	1,411.64	109.171	677,621

ambitious stabilization program, this one backed by the International Monetary Fund (IMF), to reduce inflation to single-digit levels in the medium term. The program relied on three main areas of policy adjustment: a rapid reduction of the fiscal deficit, structural reforms (especially privatization)[13] and the adoption of a rigid crawling-peg exchange rate regime. The new exchange rate policy — in place on January 1, 2000 — predetermined the monthly pace of lira depreciation in line with the government's wholesale inflation target (20% in 2000) against a basket consisting of US$1 plus €0.77 until June 2001.

13 Revenue raised from the proceeds of privatization would be used to retire expensive domestic debt, thereby lowering the government's interest burden. The government raised US$7.6 billion in 2000 and was targeting US$6.1 billion in 2001. Progress has been good, with the sale of a 51% stake in Petrol Ofisi (POAS) and a 31.5% public share offering of the state oil refinery TUPRAS, raising US$2.3 billion. In addition, the winning bid of US$2.5 billion for one of two new mobile telephone licenses for sale was four times the government's minimum bid. Last but not least, the sale of a 20% equity stake in Turk Telekom was expected to raise another US$2 billion by the end of the year.

At first, the program was quite successful. Interest rates fell sharply below expected levels, inflation significantly slowed down, and production and domestic demand started to increase. Indeed, the financial markets' confidence in the stabilization program helped to reduce interest rates on government securities: Yields on short-term Turkish lira-denominated treasury bills averaged less than 40% in the first 6 months of 2000 compared with an average of close to 110% in 1999. In spite of its early success, by November 2000 Turkey had relapsed into a banking crisis that resulted in significant capital outflows and dented the central bank's reserves. The current-account deficit widened considerably from 0.7% of gross domestic product (GDP) in 1999 to 5.5% of GDP (US$11 billion) in 2000. Indeed, strengthening demand in Turkey's main export markets in the EU and Russia and a recovery in the tourism sector were not expected to be sufficient to overcome the price disadvantage that was facing many Turkish exports in low-value-added sectors (such as textiles) as real currency appreciation was taking its toll (see Case Exhibit 17.3).

Case Exhibit 17.3. Macroeconomic projections for Turkey (% unless otherwise indicated).

	1999[a]	2000[b]	2001[c]	2002[c]
Real GDP growth	−5.1	6.0	4.0	4.6
Industrial production growth	−5.2	4.0	4.2	4.5
Gross agricultural growth	−4.6	1.0	2.0	2.0
Unemployment rate (average)	7.3	8.3	9.0	9.5
Consumer price inflation				
Average	65.1	54.9	29.3	20.9
Year-end	68.8	38.9	22.7	21.0
Short-term interbank rate	73.5	43.4	40.3	31.9
Consolidated general government balance (% of GDP)	−11.0	−10.3	−4.8	−4.5
Exports of goods FOB (US$ bn)	29.3	29.5	30.9	33.1
Imports of goods FOB (US$ bn)	39.8	51.8	53.4	56.1
Current-account balance (US$ bn)	−1.4	−11.1	−9.3	−8.3
% of GDP	−0.7	−5.5	−4.4	−4.1
External debt (year-end; US$ bn)	102.1	109.8	130.8	138.9
Exchange rates				
TRL/US$ (av.)	418,783.0	628,101.1	765,774.4	947,642.0
TRL/¥100 (av.)	367,651.8	585,314.6	736,321.5	929,060.8
TRU€ (av.)	446,164.1	578,685.2	723,656.8	995,024.1

Notes: [a]Actual.
[b]Economist Intelligence Unit estimates.
[c]Economist Intelligence Unit forecasts.

Translation exposure

Wilkinson Sword's corporate guidelines called for foreign exchange exposure measurement and management to be closely related to subsidiary financial planning. Each subsidiary manager prepared an annual budget with detailed balance sheet, cash-flow statement, and profit/loss statement. This budget established performance goals for subsidiary managers and provided the basis for a comparison with actual results. A capital spending budget was also developed by each manager. Once budgets were approved, the treasurer's office arranged for proper financing in close consultation with subsidiaries' general managers.

Every month, the treasurer's office at the US parent received an updated quarterly and yearly pro forma exposure statement from each of Wilkinson Sword's foreign subsidiaries prepared according to Financial Accounting Standards Board (FASB) Statement No. 52. Wilkinson Sword's reporting system took into account intracorporate payables and receivables, and dollar- or other currency-denominated assets or liabilities. "Exposed" liabilities were subtracted from "exposed" assets to yield a net translation exposure position. If this exercise resulted in a positive number, the company was vulnerable to a foreign exchange loss should the local currency depreciate. If Wilkinson Sword had a net asset position in a currency, the first step would be to use forward or futures markets to cover part of the exposure, if such markets existed.

Liquid and well-functioning forward and futures markets existed for about a dozen major currencies. However, such currency derivatives are not readily available to offset exposed positions in other currencies. The bulk of Wilkinson Sword's foreign exchange losses were incurred in currencies for which no forward or futures market existed, such as the Turkish lira. In such a situation, Wilkinson Sword's treasurer would consider several alternative means of reducing exposure. One technique would be to repatriate the maximum amount of retained earnings permissible under local law. A second would be to have the subsidiary pay royalties or fees to the parent or other subsidiaries. A third would be an adjustment in the terms of intrasystem transactions between the subsidiary and the rest of Wilkinson Sword. If all else failed, the subsidiary could convert any liquid assets into hard inventory commodities. This last technique, however, impinges upon the normal operations of the subsidiary. The normal procedure in such cases is to take a long-run approach that emphasizes maximum dividends repatriation and an increase in local debt.

Decision time

Over the years Wilkinson Sword has experienced major foreign exchange losses in Turkey, and the short-term outlook for continued depreciation of the Turkish lira was indeed forbidding. Yet the Turkish subsidiary had been consistently profitable and remained in a dominant market position, with over 90% of the local market. Banu Ozcan, who had been president of Wilkinson Sword–Turkey since 1994, intended to maintain that market position and achieve her budgeted level of sales and profits for 2001. In order to do so, however, she would need additional capital to finance the introduction of the Quattro shaving system. She hoped that the new product launch would be financed at the most favorable terms.

Questions for Discussion

1. How would you characterize Turkey's foreign exchange market? What is your outlook for the Turkish lira? What does it mean for Wilkinson Sword's competitive position in Turkey? Why did Wilkinson Sword approve the capital request from its Turkish subsidiary?
2. What is Wilkinson Sword–Turkey's translation exposure without Quattro? How would each financing option impact Wilkinson Sword's translation exposure in Turkish lira?
3. How should the launch of Quattro in Turkey be financed?

CHAPTER 18

Managing Economic Exposure

God does not play dice with the universe.
—Albert Einstein

The abrupt devaluation of the Argentine peso in January 2002 nearly bankrupted Aerolíneas Argentinas, the country's national air carrier. Argentina's currency board had enshrined the parity between the Argentine peso (ARS) and the US dollar at ARS 1 = US$1 for an entire decade (1991–2002), and when it collapsed, the newly floating Argentine peso rapidly devalued by 200% to ARS 3 = $1. As a result, Aerolíneas Argentinas experienced an immediate tripling of its largely US dollar–denominated costs, which consisted primarily of jet fuel expenses, debt financing, and lease payments on airplanes. Unfortunately for Aerolíneas Argentinas, the collapse of the peso induced a deep recession that resulted in a sharp contraction in domestic airline ticket sales as Argentinians' disposable income shrank. Aerolíneas Argentinas — which had been lulled into a false sense of security with the seemingly matched currency denomination of its revenue and cost streams for as long as the ARS 1 = US$1 peg held — was now unable to pass through exploding costs into higher airfares to regain its profitability. It had to seek bankruptcy protection from its creditors.

The sorry tale of Aerolíneas Argentinas is very revealing: It illustrates how a myopic focus on what was apparently a *zero* short-term and long-term transaction exposure to the US dollar had failed to alert its managers to how the firm's intrinsic value would be severely impaired by an abrupt drop in the value of the peso. What is needed is a holistic concept of exposure to foreign exchange (FX or forex) risk that goes beyond contractually defined transaction exposures and extends into the future to better gauge how the firm's expected cash flows and, therefore, its value would be impacted by changing currency values.

Accordingly, this chapter introduces a different concept of exposure — one that is rooted in a future cash flows-based valuation of the multinational corporation. More specifically, economic exposure measures the extent to which a given currency price change affects the value of the firm. Formally, so-called *economic or operating exposure* to a given foreign currency i is redefined as the percentage change in the firm's dollar value $\Delta V_\$(t)/V_\$(t)$, proxied by its market capitalization, that results from an unexpected 1% change in the dollar value of foreign currency i, $\Delta S_{\$,i}(t)/S_{\$,i}(t)$. It is akin to an elasticity concept $\boldsymbol{\varepsilon}$ as defined in microeconomics. Thus, the firm's economic exposure *vis-à-vis* foreign currency i is expressed as

$$\boldsymbol{\varepsilon} = \frac{\Delta V_\$(t)\,/\,V_\$(t)}{\Delta S_{\$,i}(t)\,/\,S_{\$,i}(t)} \tag{18.1}$$

After reading this chapter you will understand:

- How to recognize the different categories of operating exposures to FX rate risk.
- What key factors are shaping operating exposure to FX risk.
- How to measure operating exposure to exchange rate risk using regression analysis.
- How marketing, pricing, manufacturing, and financial strategies can mitigate operating exposure to FX risk.

A Taxonomy of Economic Exposures

Let us start by profiling the two archetypical cases of economic exposure to exchange rate risk that capture most real-life situations. Vivid illustrations of how mismatched cash inflows and outflows can result in drastic losses for these two cases, dubbed respectively the *import competitor* and the *global competitor*, are provided next.

THE CASE OF THE IMPORT COMPETITOR

Gillette-Argentina is the wholly owned affiliate of Gillette-USA, the Boston-based, multinational market leader in disposable razors and shaving systems. Its Argentine operations, first established in the 1960s, have enjoyed a monopolistic hold on the local market in excess of 90% of market share. The ride, though, over the years has been a bumpy one with long periods of hyperinflation combined with crippling price controls that at times were killing operating margins and making Gillette-Argentina a questionable venture. When President Menem finally established a currency board in 1991 and passed a law guaranteeing the par value of the Argentine peso to be one US dollar, Gillette-Argentina breathed a sigh of relief and looked forward to long-term monetary stability.

Ten years later the peso was still firmly anchored to the US dollar, but Gillette-Argentina had lost its controlling market share, which was now down to less than 70%, with imports of BIC and Schick razor systems having conquered the balance (30%) of the local market. By being a local manufacturer, Gillette-Argentina seemed to be in the driver's seat, sourcing 100% of its inputs (raw materials and labor services) domestically and selling 100% of its output domestically; yet it had struggled to remain competitive with imports of close substitute razor systems. A fully matched revenue-cost stream (in terms of currency denomination) should have insulated its operating margins from the vagaries of the FX market. What happened? The story is about the divorce between the *nominal* exchange rate — pegged at ARS 1 = US$1 — and the *real* (purchasing power parity (PPP)) exchange rate — driven by the difference in the rates of inflation between Argentina and the United States. It reveals a gaping overvaluation of the Argentine peso.

Argentine inflation-indexed costs: Gillette-Argentina experienced annual price increases of its inputs averaging 7.5% per year over the currency board era (1991–2002).

Under normal circumstances it would have *passed through* higher costs in its sales price to maintain its operating margins. In other words, if Gillette's costs increased by 7.5% in a given year it would simply reflect the increased cost burden by increasing its sales prices by the same 7.5%. Unfortunately, life is never that simple.

Overvalued peso-indexed sale revenues: Gillette had to contend with import-competing products that looked increasingly attractively priced in Argentine peso terms. Assuming that BIC and Schick — based in France and Germany, respectively — experienced zero inflation and maintained their respective prices fixed in dollar and therefore peso terms, Gillette-Argentina could not increase its prices without losing market share — which eventually it had to do. Consumers are sensitive to price differentials, and they were willing to substitute BIC and Schick razors for Gillette ones. This was a classic situation of a *price-elastic local demand* for razors.

Gillette's predicament stemmed from the fact that Argentine inflation should have triggered a steady depreciation of the Argentine peso to maintain its PPP *vis-à-vis* the US dollar. Failure to allow market forces to correct for creeping Argentine inflation through a cheaper peso resulted into a bulging *overvaluation of the Argentine peso*[1] (see Exhibit 18.1).

> ***Q:*** Why would a steady devaluation of the peso in line with inflation have helped Gillette-Argentina's competitiveness in Argentina?
>
> ***A:*** Imports from BIC and Schick would have to be priced at a higher peso price reflecting the devaluation of the peso (it would now take more pesos to purchase one US dollar). Gillette-Argentina itself would have to increase its peso sale price simply to recoup its higher cost due to inflation in Argentina. However, if the exchange rate were devalued to reflect exactly the differential in rates of inflation between Argentina and the United States, the resulting price increases by Gillette and its import competitors would balance each other out!

Economic/operating exposure: Gillette-Argentina's true economic exposure to exchange rate change was deceptive. At first sight, peso-denominated sales revenues matched peso-denominated expenses and should have insulated Gillette-Argentina from any economic or operating exposure to exchange rate

1 Chapter 7 provides a full-length discussion of purchasing power parity or real exchange rates as well as the concept of over/undervalued exchange rates against PPP benchmarks.

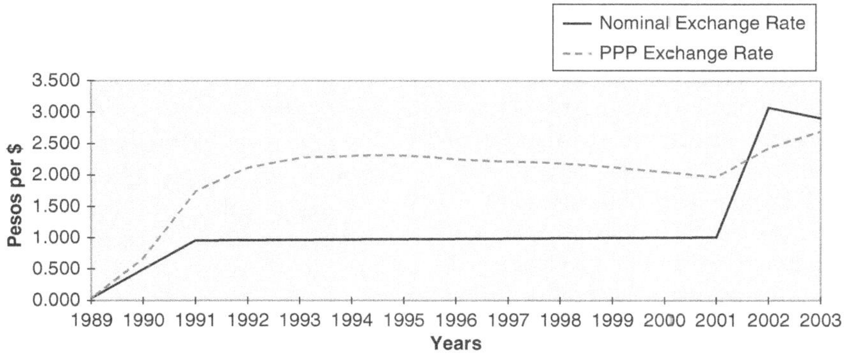

Exhibit 18.1. Nominal and PPP exchange rates — Argentina.

risk, especially since there was no nominal exchange rate risk. Clearly, this simplistic analysis leaves out the cost structure of Gillette-Argentina's key competitors and how an overvalued peso progressively distorted their competitive advantage: BIC and Schick certainly did not experience any increases in their costs. Exhibit 18.1 charts both the nominal and the real (PPP derived) peso-dollar exchange rate over the 1991–2002 period. As inflation in Argentina reached an annual rate of 7.5%, the peso became increasingly overvalued (see top dashed line). In effect, Gillette-Argentina's tale of economic exposure to exchange rate risk is directly portrayed in this graph:

- Gillette's revenue stream is indexed to the nominal exchange rate (flat line).
- Its cost stream is indexed to the PPP/real exchange rate (top dashed line), which is essentially Argentine inflation during that period (if US, French, and German inflation are assumed to be zero); it clearly shows how operating margin is increasingly negative and indexed to the peso overvaluation.[2]

Gillette was not the only company to suffer excruciating cash-flow pains from the grossly overvalued peso. The entire Argentine economy suffered increasing unemployment and was imploding; the ineluctable finally happened when the peso was at last unshackled and the currency board dismantled in 2002. The peso promptly collapsed from 1 to 3 pesos to the dollar, which made imported razors three times more expensive in Argentina. Gillette-Argentina was finally able to pass through its higher peso costs by raising its peso price, and started to regain market share.

THE CASE OF GLOBAL EXPORTERS

Rolls-Royce, the British jet-engine manufacturer, suffered a loss of £58 million in 1979 on worldwide sales of £848 million — approximately 7.5% of its gross revenue. The company's annual report for 1979 blamed the loss on the dramatic appreciation of the pound sterling against the dollar, from £1 = $1.71 to £1 = $2.12 by the end of 1979:

> *The most important factor in the loss was the effect of the continued weakness of the U.S. dollar against sterling. The large civil engines which Rolls-Royce produces are supplied to American air frames Because of U.S. dominance in civil aviation, both as producer and customer, these engines are usually priced in U.S. dollars and escalated accordingly to U.S. price indices.*

A closer look at Rolls-Royce's competitive position in the global market for jet engines reveals the sources of its dollar exposure. For the previous several years, Rolls-Royce export sales had accounted for a stable 40% of total sales and had been directed at the US market. This market is dominated by two US competitors, Pratt and Whitney Aircraft Group (United Technologies) and General Electric Company's aerospace division. Since the clients of its mainstay engine, the RB 211, were US aircraft manufacturers (Boeing's 747SP and 747–200 and Lockheed's L1011), Rolls-Royce had little choice but to use the dollar in the currency denomination of its export sales.

Indeed, Rolls-Royce won some huge engine contracts in 1978 and 1979 that were fixed in dollar terms. Rolls-Royce's operating costs (wages, components, and debt servicing), on the other hand,

2 Peso overvaluation refers to the gap between the PPP and the nominal exchange rates. Cumulative Argentine inflation over the period 1991–2002 meant that it should have cost more than one peso to buy one US dollar.

were almost exclusively incurred in sterling, unlike General Electric and Pratt-Whitney, which enjoyed perfectly matched, dollar-denominated cash inflows and cash outflows. Rolls-Royce exports contracts were mostly pegged to an assumed exchange rate of about $1.80 for the pound,[3] and Rolls-Royce officials, in fact, expected the pound to fall further to $1.65. Hence, they did not cover their dollar exposures. If the officials were correct and the dollar strengthened, Rolls-Royce would enjoy windfall profits. When the dollar weakened instead, the combined effect of fixed dollar revenues — which converted into fewer pounds than initially planned — and of sterling costs resulted in FX losses in 1979 on Rolls-Royce's US engine contracts that the *Wall Street Journal* estimated to be equivalent to $200 million.

Now fast-forward to 2004 — 25 years later

Rolls-Royce is still based in the United Kingdom (some would say shackled!). The firm still supplies major aircraft manufacturers such as Boeing and Airbus with engines in a market almost exclusively priced in US dollars. With a strong pound, the same fundamental mismatch between dollar-denominated revenues and pound-denominated costs still squeezes Rolls-Royce's operating margins. Today, however, there are some significant differences[4]:

- Rolls-Royce now owns sizable manufacturing facilities in the United States such as the former Allison Engine in Indianapolis, thereby creating a "natural hedge" by matching some of the dollar revenue with dollar costs. It has also systematically increased its sourcing of parts and subassemblies from US-based firms, and — with non-US suppliers — it has forced dollar contracting or some form of risk sharing.
- Rolls-Royce has a systematic and long-term hedging program with about $9 billion of cover in place.

  This means we sell forward dollars in a controlled way, taking advantage of periods when the rate is favorable and we don't necessarily have to rush in and take extra cover if an order comes in and the dollar weakens . . . in theory we could go three and a half years without taking further cover. In reality, that could leave us exposed in four years' time if the dollar remained weak.

  In fact, Rolls-Royce's hedging policy has been so effective that its average dollar/sterling exchange rate change has been limited to 10 cents over the past 15 years whereas market fluctuations have been 70 cents.
- Rolls-Royce relies on dollar-denominated financing for a significant part of its overall funding strategy, effectively neutralizing the effect of exchange rate fluctuations and preserving its competitiveness in its key export markets. When the pound appreciates against the dollar, the lower effective cost of funding export operations provides Rolls-Royce with a windfall gain, which offsets losses on dollar exports revenue. Conversely, when the pound sterling depreciates against the US dollar, windfall exports profits are partly neutralized by a higher cost of servicing and repaying dollar debt.

GENERALIZATION

The impact of the exchange rate fluctuations on the operating cash flows of a fictitious firm — call it Omega — is primarily determined by the nature of the output markets served by Omega and the market origin of its inputs. Thus, measurement of economic/operating exposures should start with a qualitative analysis of how the firm's future free cash flows are shaped by inflation-cum-currency appreciation/depreciation both in *absolute* terms and in *comparison* to its key competitors. This section identifies the various polar cases of economic exposures by disaggregating cash outflow and cash inflow according to their destinations or origins.

Revenues

The output of Omega can be directed to the local market or exported to foreign markets. In serving its local market, Omega may be primarily competing with other domestic firms. The important question is whether domestic competitors are operating under the same cost constraints as Omega. If they were to have an imports-dependent and therefore different procurement policy than Omega, a devaluation of the home currency would hurt them (and benefit Omega); conversely, overvaluation of the home currency (local inflation not matched by devaluation) would help them and would put Omega at a

3 In pricing export contracts, Rolls-Royce had to make some forecasts of what the exchange rate would be at times of payment, typically staggered over several quarters. It seemed to use the exchange rate prevailing at the time of signing as its best forecast of the future exchange rates to prevail at times of delivery and payment.

4 Helen Massy-Beresford and Max Kingsley-Jones, "Dollar Defense," *Flight International*, February 22–28, 2005.

competitive disadvantage. This would be especially true for relatively undifferentiated products facing a price-sensitive/elastic domestic demand. Similarly, if Omega is in direct competition with imports from firms located in foreign countries that are operating under different cost constraints, devaluation of the home currency should help Omega's domestic market position. Overvaluation of the home currency, however, would in effect subsidize import-competing products and jeopardize Omega's market position (see previous discussion of Gillette-Argentina as an import competitor).

As an exporter Omega would benefit from its home currency depreciation, especially if it is facing a price-sensitive foreign demand in its exports market. If Omega's export products are well differentiated (low price elasticity of exports demand and/or few substitutes), it may *pass through* only a fraction of the home currency's depreciation, thereby generating windfall profits. Should Omega's product lines be relatively undifferentiated, the following questions should be asked of its competitors: Are they local firms or exporters based in other countries? To what extent do their cost structures differ from Omega's? This classification of the nature of end markets served by Omega is represented schematically in Exhibit 18.2. Clearly, the impact of the exchange rate changes can be expected to result in inherently different cash inflows depending on whether Omega is primarily geared to serving its domestic market (with or without import competition), its export market, or some combination thereof.

Costs

The inputs used by Omega may be either imported or sourced locally. In the latter case, a distinction has to be made between domestically sourced inputs that themselves may or may not be facing import competition. Needless to say, for firms whose pricing policy is constrained by imported competing products, the ability to switch opportunistically to imported inputs might be critical in surviving periods of currency overvaluation. In effect, Omega would simply be aligning/matching its cost structure with its competitors' when it works to its advantage (the reader is referred to the tale of Gillette-Argentina in the 1990s). The classification of sources of inputs available to Omega is summarized diagrammatically in Exhibit 18.2. Again, the qualitative analysis should be carried out comparatively with each key competitor. In this respect, economic exposure measurement should be closely aligned with industry analysis as practiced in strategic management.

Generally, Omega will use one or more inputs sourced domestically (with or without import competition present) in combination with one or several imported inputs. In addition, Omega is confronted with only two combined demands: a foreign demand (export market) coupled with a domestic demand (absence of import competition) or a foreign demand (export market) coupled with a domestic demand facing import competition.

A word of caution about *sector versus economy-wide inflation* and *currency pass-through*. Analysts would often argue that if exchange rate changes reflect inflation rate differentials (PPP world), the firm's economic/operating exposure coefficient should be zero — the firm's value would not change — as the exchange rate change simply corrects for change in nominal cash flows due to the impact of inflation. Beyond the obvious rebuttal that PPP never holds in the short or medium term, even if it did, it is unlikely that the impact of inflation on the firm's cash flow would be close to the average

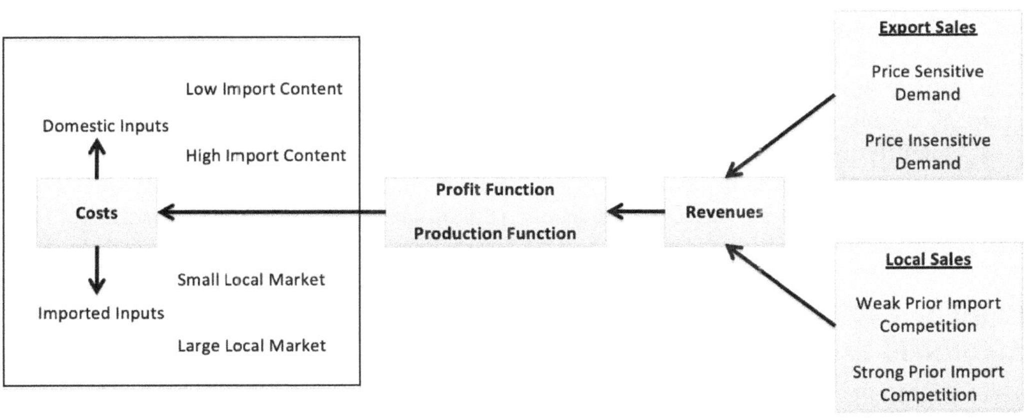

Exhibit 18.2. Mapping taxonomy of economic exposures.

rate of inflation. Inflation rates are simply weighted averages of different sectoral rates of inflation. Each sector of the economy experiences inflation at its own pace, reflecting idiosyncrasies of its industry: Industrial chemicals, for example, may suffer from 7.5% inflation when oil prices spike on the world market, whereas building materials experience a small deflation of −2.5%, reflecting a housing construction slump.

To gauge a firm's economic exposure to inflation, focus should be on industry-wide, not economy-wide, inflation. Furthermore, attention should be paid to how the firm's key competitors are themselves passing through inflation — a far cry from focusing on economy-wide inflation. PPP exchange rates, however, track economy-wide not industry-wide inflation, and even if they did, each firm *pass-through* exchange rate changes in its own idiosyncratic way. Currency pass-through is simply the degree to which a firm chooses to reflect exchange rate changes in its own pricing of exports goods. An exporter may reflect 100% of its home currency depreciation, 0% (ignoring it altogether), or any coefficient between 0 and 100%, depending on market conditions. For example, if the exporter faces a very price-elastic foreign demand, it will speedily reflect 100% of its home currency depreciation and lower its export prices in the foreign market in order to capture increased market share as its customers happily switch to the cheaper imports. Conversely, our exporter may in be in a dominant market position facing weak competitors and decide to reflect only 33% of its home currency depreciation, thereby earning a windfall profit as long as foreign demand is price-inelastic (see further discussion of this point in the section on pricing and product differentiation).

In sum, the analysis of economic/operating exposure to the inflation/devaluation cycle should be carried out at the industry level — indeed a different story from macroeconomic analysis — with careful attention given to how price inflation and currency pass-through of key competitors shape their pricing policies. Quantifying such exposures remains a treacherous task, and firms are often better off developing a qualitative grasp of their operating exposure in relation to their peers.

TOWARD AN OPERATIONAL MEASURE OF ECONOMIC EXPOSURE

The previously detailed description of how each case of economic exposure responds to the changing relationship between inflation and exchange rate fluctuations illustrates how complex the task of measuring economic exposure really is. However, when cash flows and underlying competitive circumstances are relatively stable over time, it is possible to use a statistical technique known as *regression analysis* to measure economic exposure. Specifically, the objective is to quantify the sensitivity of the firm's net cash flows to changes in nominal exchange rates.

Economic exposure as a regression coefficient[5]

Formally, we posit a linear relationship between foreign affiliate Omega's free cash flows $FCF_{\$}(t)$ converted into dollar terms at the exchange rate, $S_{\$,i}(t)$ during the corresponding period:

$$\Delta FCF_{\$}(t) = \alpha + \beta \Delta S_{\$,i}(t) + e(t) \qquad (18.2)$$

where $\Delta FCF_{\$}(t) = FCF_{\$}(t) - FCF_{\$}(t-1)$ measures Omega's foreign affiliate dollar-equivalent free cash flows during the period $[t-1, t]$, and $e(t)$ is the random error term with mean of 0. Most relevant to our purpose is the value of the β coefficient, which captures the elasticity (sensitivity) of cash flows to the exchange rate. For example, if $\beta = -0.15$, it would mean that for a 10% drop in the value of currency i, the net cash flows of Omega in reference currency terms actually increase by 1.5%. Thus, Omega is negatively exposed to exchange rate risk in an economic sense, albeit to a small degree. Of course, regression analysis will also provide important information on how statistically significant the β coefficient is — the so-called t-statistic — as well as the fraction of the overall variability of Omega's net cash flows that can be attributed to exchange rate change (the so-called R-squared or R^2). This last piece of information warrants close attention, since a low R^2 may indicate that we are focusing on the wrong source of risk.

Consider an example in which the β coefficient is 1.2 and the R^2 is 0.08. At first glance, we would conclude that there is a significant degree of economic exposure (a 12% change in cash flows for every 10% change in the exchange rate) when, in fact, an R^2 of 8% indicates that only a small fraction of Omega's cash-flow variability can be attributed to exchange rate risk. Perhaps one should look to interest rate risk or commodity price risk as possible alternative sources of explanation (more on the last two sources of risk follows).

5 See Adler and Dumas (1984) and Garner and Shapiro (1984).

Multiperiod exposure

So far, our economic exposure model has assumed for the sake of simplicity that exchange rate fluctuations affect only current-period t cash flows. More realistically, exchange rate changes will affect cash flows over several periods, since pricing and sourcing decisions typically *lag* exchange rate changes. This is the elusive *pass-through* question formally introduced in the earlier part of this chapter. To address this quintessential question, it is possible to modify equation (18.2) by incorporating *past* exchange rates as explanatory variables in the regression equation as follows:

$$\Delta FCF(t) = \alpha + \beta_1 \Delta S_{\$,i}(t) + \beta_2 \Delta S_{\$,i}(t-1) \cdots + \beta_T \Delta S_{\$,i}(t-T+1) + e(t) \qquad (18.3)$$

The practical question is how far back one should go in estimating equation (18.3). Depending on industry practices (e.g., equipment goods versus consumer nondurables), we may limit the relevant period to two to six quarters with $T = 1, 2, \ldots, 6$. The reader should also keep in mind that regression analysis allows for simple experiments whereby the number of periods can be increased to determine whether the equation explains more of the cash-flow variability as captured by a higher R^2.

Economic exposure to financial risk: Smith, Smithson, and Wilford's model

The aforementioned methodology can be extended to capture the sensitivity of the firm's cash flows to other sources of financial risk, such as interest rate risk (especially for financial institutions) and commodity price risk (important for energy and mining companies). Indeed, there are many parallels to be drawn between FX risk management and the management of interest rate and commodity price risks. Equation (18.2) would thus be generalized as

$$\Delta FCF(t) = \alpha + \beta_{FX} \Delta S_{\$,i}(t) + \beta_{INT} \Delta i_{US}(t) + \beta_{COM} \Delta S_{\$,COM}(t) + e(t) \qquad (18.4)$$

where explanatory variables (regressors) $i_{US}(t)$ and $S_{\$,COM}(t)$ are the change in US prime interest rate and the spot dollar price of the relevant commodity, respectively (for instance, petroleum for Exxon, copper for Kennecott, natural gas for Enron, etc.). β_{FX}, β_{INT}, and β_{COM} are the respective regression coefficients that measure exposure to exchange rate (FX), interest rate (INT), and commodity price (COM) fluctuations.

This approach relies on the ability of the firm to generate the necessary data to assess the sensitivity of cash flows to relevant economic variables. This *flow* approach is especially well suited to firms that engage in extensive financial planning *simulations* and will generally nurture a very helpful cross-fertilization among the various *functional* departments. Specifically, sales, procurement, and treasury should exchange information so as to make the planning process as all-encompassing and cross-functional as possible, allowing exchange rate *contingent* forecasts to be built into pricing and procurement decisions.

Stock versus flow measure of economic exposure

Many of the aforementioned results can also be derived from stock prices, which are readily available from capital market sources. This is the so-called *stock* (as opposed to *flow*) approach to measuring economic exposure. It is akin to the capital asset pricing model (CAPM) theory, which measures betas as proxies for a firm's exposure to different types of financial risk. Equation (18.4) would be rewritten as

$$r(t) = \alpha + \beta_{TB} \Delta P_{TB}/P_{TB} + \beta_{FX} \Delta S_{\$,i}(t)/S_{\$,i}(t) + \beta_{CCM} \Delta S_{\$,COM}(t)/S_{\$,COM}(t) + e(t) \qquad (18.5)$$

where $r(t)$ is the rate of return on Omega's equity value, and β_{TB}, β_{FX}, and β_{COM} are estimates of Omega's value sensitivity (elasticity) to a 1% change in the price of US Treasury bills $\Delta P_{TB}/P_{TB}$; the dollar value of foreign currency i, $\Delta S_{\$,i}(t)/S_{\$,i}(t)$; and the dollar value of the relevant commodity, $\Delta S_{\$,COM}(t)/S_{\$,COM}(t)$.

Smith, Smithson, and Wilford (1989), who operationalized this approach, provide some illustration of how the method would capture the economic exposure of one financial institution (Chase Manhattan Bank), one industrial firm (Caterpillar), and one energy company (Exxon) to the price of a 1 year T-bill; the dollar value of one Deutsche mark (DM), pound sterling (£), and Japanese yen (¥); and the price of West Texas Intermediate (WTI) crude oil. The findings are summarized in Exhibit 18.3. The values of the parameters are the β coefficients, which measure each firm's exposure to the different financial risk variables with their statistical significance (t-statistic) reported in the adjoining column.

Thus, Chase Manhattan is positively exposed to the 1 year price of T-bills[6] with $\beta_{TB} = 2.598$: Banks

6 One-year T-bill prices move in the opposite direction than interest rates.

Exhibit 18.3. Measuring exposures to interest rates, FX rates, and oil prices.

Percentage Change in	Chase Manhattan Parameter Estimate	*t*-value	Caterpillar Parameter Estimate	*t*-value	Exxon Parameter Estimate	*t*-value
Price of 1-year T-bill	2.598*	1.56	−3.221**	1.76	1.354	1.24
Price of DM	−0.276	0.95	0.344	1.07	−0.066	0.35
Price of sterling	0.281	1.16	−0.010	0.38	0.237*	1.50
Price of yen	−0.241	0.96	0.045	0.16	−0.278**	1.69
Price of WTI crude	0.065	1.21	−0.045	0.77	0.082***	2.33

Notes: *Significant at 90% single-tailed.
**Significant at 90%.
***Significant at 95%.
Source: Smith Jr., Clifford W., Charles W. Smithson, and D. Sykes Wilford. 1989. "Managing Financial Risk," *Journal of Applied Corporate Finance* 1(4): 27–48.

benefit from accepting short-term deposits at a lower interest rate to fund longer-term loans. Exxon is marginally positively exposed to the price of petroleum with a $\beta_{WTI} = 0.082$ and would benefit from an increase in the value of the pound sterling with a $\beta_{£} = 0.237$. Perhaps counterintuitive is the finding that Caterpillar is not significantly exposed to the price of the yen.[7] This last result may have something to do with a methodological flaw associated with the stock method of exposure measurement. Since share prices are used as informational inputs, we typically measure the hedged rather than the naked exposure of the firm, as stock prices reflect not only the firm's preexisting exposure but also the hedging policies put in place by its management. Thus, Caterpillar's low exposure to the value of the yen is probably the result of skillful hedging and of offshoring its production facilities, which has successfully neutralized the firm's cash-flow sensitivity to the value of the yen.

History does not necessarily repeat itself

Numerical estimation of operating exposure is greatly improved by the regression analysis just presented. However, it is important to emphasize that this methodology assumes that the sensitivity of future cash flows to exchange rate changes (or other sources of risk) is identical to its past sensitivity. If abrupt changes were to impact the firm's operating and competitive environment, a regression-based exposure estimate would have to be re-estimated with new data that better represent the new relationships between the firm's cash flows and exchange rate changes. In sum, history does not necessarily repeat itself and linear extrapolation of past relationships into the future should be carefully monitored. For example, Caterpillar's only key global competitor for decades was Japan-based Komatsu. When South Korea–based Daewoo also became a global player, Caterpillar was now a member of a ménage à trois, and its stock price was no longer solely influenced by the value of the yen but also the value of the won. In this case, the time series used for estimating exposure would have to be reformatted to include data with Daewoo and Komatsu.

MANAGING OPERATING EXPOSURE

We next consider alternative risk-mitigating policies, ranging from flexible and easily reversible hedges to longer-term more permanent hedges, such as offshoring production facilities.

Contractual hedging

The first line of defense in managing operating exposure to currency risk is to put in place a long-term contractual hedging program relying on forwards, options, and swaps to neutralize projected net transaction exposure. The objective is simply to correct the mismatch between the currency denomination of revenues and costs. For *global exporters* such as Rolls-Royce or Porsche, which are *long* the

7 It is common knowledge that Caterpillar's only global competitor is the Japanese firm Komatsu. A strong yen hurts Komatsu's export competitiveness, and conversely a strong dollar (i.e., weak yen) hurts Caterpillar's export competitiveness.

currency of their key export market (the currency in which sales are priced) and *short* the currency of their manufacturing cost base (the country in which they are domiciled), it simply means selling forward short-term, medium-term, and if at all possible long-term export proceeds. This would be no different than traditional transaction exposure management except that the firm is now working with longer-term and *projected* exposures rather than shorter-term, *contractually defined* and therefore known transaction exposures. Clearly, such hedging policies will work best for firms that enjoy stable export revenue in terms of both volume and currency distribution. Furthermore, contractual hedging has the obvious advantage of leaving key operating decisions such as sourcing, pricing, and manufacturing decisions unperturbed. In other words, contractual and financial hedging decisions would be made by the treasurer alone (see International Corporate Finance in Practice 18.1 for an illustration of how Porsche deals with its lopsided exposure to the US dollar).

Flexible sourcing policy

Currency mismatch between export revenues and manufacturing costs can often be corrected by sourcing key parts or subassemblies from suppliers domiciled in the same currency space as the firm's customers, thereby creating a natural hedge against operating risk. If the source of risk originates from the lower cost structure of key competitors, it will require sourcing from some of the same firms or countries from which these competitors procure. In fact, it may simply mean outsourcing from a low-cost country such as Mexico or China. A flexible sourcing policy simply ensures that if the currency basis of the firm's key competitors becomes unduly cheap/undervalued it would benefit as much as its key competitors — in other words, avoid facing a cost handicap. International Corporate Finance in Practice 18.2 illustrates how Whirlpool effectively dealt with such a situation.

INTERNATIONAL CORPORATE FINANCE IN PRACTICE 18.1

Porsche Powers Profit with Currency Plays

Porsche, the German sports car manufacturer, has 100% of its manufacturing activities domiciled in the euro-zone (mostly Germany). Close to 50% of its sales revenue, however, is derived from the US market and therefore denominated in US dollars. Many European carmakers with significant sales in the United States were reeling from a weak dollar, but Porsche AG seemed to have charted a different path — leveraging the weak dollar to rev up its results. Investment analysts believe that financial engineering in the form of sophisticated currency bets are turbocharging Porsche's profits. One equity analyst estimates that as much as 75% of the company's pretax profits — amounting to €800 million ($1.07 billion) that Porsche reported for the fiscal year ending July 31, 2004 — came from skillfully executing currency options. Indeed, Porsche's transaction exposures arising from sales to the US market are fully hedged through July 31, 2007, and the automaker is working to extend its protection well beyond that date. "Fully hedged" refers to the purchase of dollar put options that aim to protect all of the company's earnings from dollar depreciation.

Although Porsche remains secretive about its hedging techniques, informed observers believe that the carmaker essentially bets on a weak dollar by buying deep-in-the-money dollar put options to exchange dollars for euros at an artificially high exchange rate for the euro — for example, $1.15 to one euro. If the dollars on the open market fail to appreciate to that level — by remaining at $1.30 for one euro — Porsche gets a hefty cash payout by exercising the put option at expiration. Conversely, if the dollar strengthens beyond the put option's strike price, dollar-denominated sales result in a windfall profit. Porsche would then simply allows its dollar put options to expire unexercised, and the only losses it incurs are the premiums it has paid for buying those options. Although those premiums are high — around 2% annually of the total amount that Porsche wants to hedge or $20 million on hypothetical US revenue of $1 billion — Porsche can afford them, since its profits are among the highest in the industry.

Source: Adapted from the *Wall Street Journal*, December 8, 2004, C3.

INTERNATIONAL CORPORATE FINANCE IN PRACTICE 18.2

Whirlpool Outsources from Italy

In the early 1980s Whirlpool, the leading US manufacturer of white goods (washing machines and refrigerators), was feeling pressure from cheaply priced imports from Europe — most notably Italy — and East Asia. Whirlpool was then a typically domestic firm in that its entire output was sold in the United States, and manufacturing and sourcing were entirely US-based as well. As the US dollar become grossly overvalued in PPP terms against European and East Asian currencies, imports from these countries became progressively cheaper — in effect subsidized by the US Federal Reserve Bank's high interest policy, which had resulted in an expensive dollar. In effect, Whirlpool had to price its products in line with imports that were primarily indexed to the expensive dollar, whereas Whirlpool's US manufacturing costs were tied to significant US inflation. Thus, Whirlpool's costs were rising while revenues were shrinking in line with an appreciating dollar that translated into cheaper and cheaper imports. Whirlpool's operating exposure was severely hurting its profitability.

Although Whirlpool was tied to its US manufacturing base, it decided to source compressors and other key subassemblies from Italian firms in order to take advantage of the expensive dollar, which made importing these components very inexpensive. In effect Whirlpool was aligning part of its cost structure with its key Italian competitors. "If you cannot beat them, join them!"

Moving manufacturing overseas

The next stage in reducing exposure to operating risk is to shift manufacturing to the firm's export market. Here again the objective is to match closely the revenue and the cost streams' currencies of denomination. It is a longer-term and firmer commitment than the flexible sourcing discussed in the previous section in the sense that investing in bricks and mortar would be costly to reverse. This is the well-documented case of Japanese car manufacturers, whose domestic manufacturing cost basis — the yen — experienced a meteoric rise over the past 40 years *vis-à-vis* Japan's key export market — the United States: The yen rose from ¥360 = $1 in 1971 (before the collapse of the Bretton Woods system of pegged exchange rates) to ¥80 = $1 in 2011. A Honda Civic, for example, worth ¥3,600,000 in 1971, was sold for ¥3,600,000/360 = $10,000 in the United States at the 1971 exchange rate; it would be worth at a more recent exchange rate ¥3,600,000/80 = $45,000 if it were manufactured and exported from Japan. Of course, Honda Civics have long been manufactured in the United States and are still sold for under $20,000. Over that period Toyota, Nissan, and Honda have all shifted a larger and larger percentage of their manufacturing to US production sites (see International Corporate Finance in Practice 18.3).

Pricing

Sharp swings in currency values confront firms with difficult and urgent pricing decisions. Let's return to the situation of a *global exporter* whose domestic cost base is severely increased *vis-à-vis* its exports revenue because of the home currency appreciation. This has been the case over the years of many Japanese firms in the automotive, consumer electronics, or industrial machinery industries. Japanese exporters have three choices:

1. Keep *dollar price constant* and ignore the yen appreciation to protect market share in their export market. Operating margins will be severely damaged and the exporter may have to subsidize its exports business (that is, absorb a loss).
2. Maintain *yen price constant* and fully pass through the yen appreciation, which means increasing the dollar price by the full amount of the yen appreciation to protect operating margins. The risk is that their market share may plummet when customers decide to turn to cheaper substitute products. Market response to such price increases is a function of the price elasticity of US demand for Japanese imports. If the Japanese product is unique and uniquely differentiated from competing products, price elasticity may be zero or very low, and a full pass-through of the yen appreciation will yield no loss of market share. Conversely, if consumers have ready access to comparable substitute products, price elasticity of demand will be high and Japanese exporters will lose significant market share.

INTERNATIONAL CORPORATE FINANCE IN PRACTICE 18.3

Moving Manufacturing Overseas

The Japanese government has been pulling out all the stops to protect its exporters from a strong yen through heavy-handed intervention in the FX market — buying dollars to slow down the appreciation of the yen. But Japan's big manufacturers have made themselves more immune to currency swings by steadily moving manufacturing to their key export markets. Indeed, not so long ago, executives at Japan's big electronics and auto companies were terrified by recurring *endaka*, or yen strength, that damaged their profits by reducing the value of overseas sales when translated into yen. Japanese exporters still dread the rising yen, and the Ministry of Finance has bought dollars at a record pace to cap the yen's strength.

Toyota and other exporters began reducing their exposure to exchange-rate swings more than a quarter of a century ago by expanding production abroad, a move that recently has been picking up speed. Honda now makes 75% of the cars it sells in the United States in North American factories, up from 60% a decade ago. Nissan opened a $1 billion factory in Canton, Mississippi, to make pickup trucks, sport-utility vehicles, and minivans. With the plant, Nissan planned to nearly double its production capacity in North America to 1.35 million vehicles a year by 2004 from about 700,000 previously. "We're making an effort to take FX out of the equation as much as possible," says Nissan spokesman Gerry Spahn.

Source: Adapted from "Japanese Firms Practice 'Yen' Damage Control," *Wall Street Journal*, September 26, 2003, p. A7.

3. Decide on a partial pass-through of the yen appreciation, depending on the competitive landscape and their actual operating margins.

Product differentiation

Global exporters such as Japanese or European firms have invested heavily in research and development (R&D) to differentiate their products, hoping to shift to a segment of the market characterized by lower price elasticity. Witness Japanese carmakers introducing in the 1980s luxury brands such as Toyota's Lexus line.

> ***Q:*** Nintendo 3DS is priced at $200 in the US market. Assuming that the Japanese yen has appreciated from 125 to 100 to the dollar, should Nintendo increase its price by the percentage of yen appreciation? Estimates show that the Nintendo 3DS faces a demand characterized by a price elasticity of –0.05.
>
> ***A:*** The yen appreciates by (125 – 100)/125 = 20%. By increasing its price to $200 × (1 + 0.20) = $240 Nintendo would suffer a reduction of 20% × (–5%) = –1.00% in the number of 3DS units sold, which is negligible. Very low price elasticity of the demand for its export products would justify Nintendo's full passthrough of the yen appreciation.

Let us consider next the pricing challenge of the *import competitor* and return to the example of Gillette-Argentina struggling to maintain its market share. The pricing options are similar to those available to the global competitor:

- Ignore Argentine inflation and maintain peso prices constant to defend market share against US-based competitors. Gillette would suffer from severely squeezed margins but hold on to its market share. It has to be willing to subsidize its sales if need be — in case the peso becomes grossly overvalued.
- Pass through Argentine inflation, increasing prices by 7.5% annually and assuming price elasticity estimated at –1.5, suffering a reduction in units sold of 7.5% × (–1.5) = –11.25%.
- Partially pass through Argentine inflation at the rate of, say, 33% or at 7.5% × (0.33) = 2.5% per year, resulting in a more modest decline in units sold of 2.5% × (–1.5) = –3.75%.

Ultimately, the import competitor will have to make a judgment call based on its assessment of (1) how long the peso overvaluation is sustainable and (2) how costly it would be to regain market share once the overvaluation gap is bridged.

Financial hedging

For global competitors domiciled in countries of *ever-rising* currencies or competing with firms domiciled in countries with *sinking* currencies, it is relatively easy to construct a long-term hedge by borrowing in the currency of exposure. For example, a Japan-based firm such as Honda would simply issue long-term debt in US dollars, thereby saving on financing cost[8] to compensate for squeezed margins due to an ever-rising yen. This approach rests on the assumption that the uncovered interest rate differential of dollars versus yen is dwarfed by the percentage appreciation of the Japanese yen *vis-à-vis* the US dollar. In a similar vein, Chrysler Corporation has maintained a significant percentage of its long-term debt in Japanese yen over the years to better match the cost structure of its key Japanese competitors.

SUMMARY

1. Economic/operating exposure to FX risk measures how the firm's expected future free cash flows are affected by unexpected exchange rate movements. It is akin to an elasticity coefficient and measured as the percentage change in the value of the firm triggered by a 1% change in the value of its home currency.
2. If PPP holds exactly, and market (output) prices and production (input) costs move in line with overall inflation, then there is no operating exposure to exchange rate changes. Because PPP never holds on the short or the medium term then operating/economic exposure has to be measured and managed. Even if PPP held, sectorial prices in input and output markets have a life of their own; that is, they are divergent from average inflation because firms' pricing policies do not necessarily pass through fully or immediately any inflation and exchange rate changes.
3. Economic/operating exposure can be gauged qualitatively, but it is difficult to measure precisely. The critical variables underlying economic exposure include market origin of inputs, market destination of outputs, supply and demand elasticity conditions, substitutability of inputs, likely pricing, and sourcing reactions of key competitors.
4. A *regression-based* method under certain conditions yields precise estimates of the firm's sensitivity to exchange rate fluctuations and to other economic variables.
5. Managing economic exposure is by necessity a multifaceted, all-encompassing corporate effort that will cut across contractual hedging, financing, pricing, sourcing, marketing, and production strategies.
6. Exchange rate considerations in the form of carefully *simulated* plans should be woven into the design of proactive — rather than reactive — sourcing, marketing, and production strategies. At the very least, economic exposure management should strive to *neutralize* the impact of adverse exchange rate movements when competitive advantage cannot be leveraged from the opportunities presented from currency appreciation or depreciation.
7. Pricing (by choosing to pass through less than the full extent of currency appreciation/depreciation) and product differentiation (to lessen exposure to highly price-elastic demand) are the key parameters within a firm's marketing mix that can be adjusted to cope with economic exposure to exchange rate risk.
8. Product sourcing (by purchasing more components and subassemblies overseas) and plant location (by allocating production among plants according to their relative cost structures or by positioning new plant facilities in low-cost countries) allow global competitors to respond more flexibly to the constantly evolving map of competitive advantages.
9. Financial hedging allows global competitors domiciled in countries of *ever-rising* currencies or competing with firms domiciled in countries with *sinking* currencies to construct a long-term hedge by borrowing in the currency of exposure.

8 Lower interest payment and principal repayment denominated in US dollars and costing far fewer yen due to the appreciation of the Japanese currency.

QUESTIONS FOR DISCUSSION

1. Explain what economic/operating exposure is. Why does it matter?
2. What is the difference between economic/operating and transaction exposure to currency risk?
3. How can operating exposure to currency exposure be measured?
4. What are the limitations of relying on the PPP framework to gauge firms' economic/operating exposure to FX risk?
5. What does it mean for operating exposure to be measured by a "regression coefficient"?
6. Why is operating exposure to currency risk more difficult to manage than transaction exposure?
7. What is the role played by currency pass-through in exports pricing for managing operating/economic exposure?
8. How can contractual and financial hedging be harnessed to reduce operating exposure to currency risk? What are the limitations of this approach?
9. How can marketing policies be used to manage operating exposure to currency risk?
10. How can manufacturing policies be used to manage operating exposure to currency risk?

PROBLEMS

1. **Embraer exports to the United States (easy).** Embraer is a Brazilian aircraft manufacturer. It exports fifty 120-passenger jets to regional airlines primarily in the United States and Western Europe. Sales contracts are US$ denominated and average $100 million per plane. Its book of future exports sales is projected as far as 2015 with average annual sales of US$3.5 billion. Many sales are still in the negotiation phase. In 2010 alone, the Brazilian real surged from BRL 2.1 to BRL 1.6 = $1. Embraer's manufacturing costs are 80% domestic with the remaining 20% corresponding to imports.
   a. What is the nature of Embraer's exposure to exchange risk?
   b. How would you advise Embraer to manage its exposure?
2. **Currency risk in the travel industry (intermediate).** Kuoni, a leading Swiss tour operator, sells package tours to Sri Lanka for French and Swiss tourists. On January 1, 2022, Kuoni sent its printed catalog to French, Belgian, and Swiss travel agencies quoting prices of €7,500 and CHF 10,000, respectively, valid throughout 2022 on their fortnight package tours to Sri Lanka. The cost incurred by Kuoni, on a unit basis, is distributed as follows: CHF 5,200 for administrative and travel costs and SLR 13,000 (Sri Lankan rupees) for residential costs. The exchange rate is SLR 10 to CHF 1.

   On August 15, 2022, the Swiss franc is revalued by 15% *vis-à-vis* the euro. However, because of earlier booking, the CHF revaluation cannot be passed through before January 1, 2023.
   a. Assuming that Kuoni sells 500 trips every 15 days evenly divided between France and Switzerland, assess the impact of the Swiss franc revaluation upon the profitability of Kuoni in 2022.
   b. On March 30, 2022, an inflationary wage settlement in Sri Lanka results in an increase of 25% in the SLR cost of residential expenses that takes effect immediately. Assuming that the French demand for such services is characterized by a price elasticity of 1.5 and an income elasticity of 2, assess the impact of fully passing through the CHF revaluation in a year in which the French real national income is expected to increase by 8%.
3. **Leather goods in Portugal and the single currency (easy).** Portugal's leather footwear industry has suffered from an expensive euro while its rate of inflation since the launch of the euro in 1999 has exceeded the euro-zone average by an annual average of 3.5%. Over the period 2007–2012, sales revenue for the industry at large has declined by approximately a third. As the newly appointed minister for trade and industry, develop a strategic plan to revive the Portuguese leather footwear industry.
4. **Walmart as a Chinese retailer (easy).** In 2024, China experienced an inflation rate of 11% against 1% in the United States, whereas the renminbi appreciated from RMB 6.7 to RMB 6.3 = $1 during the same period. Walmart, the US retailer, has large operations in China, sourcing 70% of the products it sells in China from local suppliers with

the remainder being primarily imported from the United States.

a. How is Walmart's dollar profit impacted by the change in the real value of the Chinese currency?
b. Should Walmart refinance a US$1 billion revolver loan currently priced in US$ at 4% in RMB at 7%?

5. **Renault SA builds Logans in Romania (intermediate).** In a move toward becoming a major car producer in Eastern Europe, Renault in 2004 purchased the Romanian firm Dacia for €211 million to build Logans in Romania. The pact calls for Renault to start producing as many as 100,000 Logans a year, primarily for sale in Romania, at an old Dacia factory located some 120 km northwest of Bucharest in the Arges. The Logan is a modern, robust entry-level vehicle aimed at emerging markets and priced very moderately at Romanian leu (RON) 15,000. The company had already invested nearly that much in Hungary for an engine plant and small-scale assembly operation from which Dacia would source its engines at the equivalent of €1,250 (but actually denominated in Hungarian forint, which is pegged to the euro). Since 2007, when the RON stood at RON 3.50 = €1, inflation in Romania has run at an annual rate of 9% (against 1.5% in the euro-zone) while the leu has steadily depreciated at an annual rate of 5% against the euro.
   a. Assess Renault-Dacia's operating/economic exposure to inflation/devaluation. The exchange rate stood at RON 4.45 = €1 on January 1, 2012. Until Romania joined the European Union in 2007, Dacia as the national state-owned automobile manufacturer enjoyed a quasi-monopolistic hold on its domestic protected market.
   b. With Romania's tentative plan to join the euro-zone by 2017, it was announced that the RON might be pegged to the euro at a new rate of RON 5.00 = €1 as of January 1, 2012. Would this new exchange rate arrangement benefit or penalize Renault-Dacia?
   c. As a general manager of Renault-Dacia, you are preparing for a summit meeting with the governor of Romania's central bank and the minister of finance. How would you make the case against this new currency plan?
   d. Transylvania Cars Ltd is the newly appointed distributor in Romania of South Korean Hyundai automobiles, which are to be imported from Turkey, where subcompact models are assembled. How should your diagnosis in part a of Renault-Dacia's economic exposure be revised?

6. **Renault-Dacia as an exports platform (intermediate).** The company is now positioning itself to take advantage of Romania's relatively low wages to use its Dacia plant as an export platform to neighboring East European countries such as Bulgaria, Belarus, and mostly Ukraine. Production would be ramped up by 25,000 vehicles over the next five years.
   a. For its newly mounted exports push, Dacia is targeting Ukraine, where ZAZ — the Ukrainian car company — accounts for more than 50% of the market. Do you believe that Dacia is well-positioned to penetrate the Ukrainian automobile market? Ukraine has recorded an annual rate of inflation of 15% over the past five years, but the Ukrainian hryvnia is on a free float and generally considered to be fairly valued. Spell out the macroeconomic conditions for successful entry.
   b. Skoda — the low-cost subsidiary of the German automotive firm Volkswagen (VW) — is the #2 brand sold in the Ukraine, accounting for 20% of the market. Skoda's subcompact, the Yeti, is currently manufactured in Slovakia, which joined the euro-zone on January 1, 2009. Compare Dacia's potential for success with that of Skoda. What is your assessment of Renault-Dacia's currency exposure in its export sales to Ukraine?

7. **Financing exports to Vietnam (intermediate).** Minneapolis-based Norwest Bank has granted a 3 year fixed-interest dollar-denominated loan in the amount of US$25 million to Water Irrigation Systems Inc. for a major export sales to Danang Mutual, a large farming cooperative in central Vietnam.
   a. Is Norwest exposed to currency risk? What is the nature of its exposure?
   b. The loan is extended with recourse to Water Irrigation Systems, which has a solid AA credit rating. Is Norwest protected against exchange rate risk?
   c. Should the interest rate charged by Norwest Bank reflect exchange rate risk? Should other risk(s) be considered?

8. **Air Algérie (advanced).** The national Algerian flag air carrier operates a web of 63 routes

mostly to Europe and the Middle East. Its fleet is financed in euros to the tune of €2.5 billion, and ticket sales are overwhelmingly to Algerian nationals (80%). The Algerian currency — the dinar (DZD) — is currently pegged to the euro at DZD 100 = €1.

a. How would a 25% devaluation of the dinar impact Air Algérie's cash flows?

b. In 2024, Air Algérie sold 10 aging airplanes and used the proceeds to pay down partially its € debt. It decided to lease rather than purchase its new fleet of seven jumbo jets. Would Air Algérie's new exposure to currency risk be materially altered as a result?

c. Would you advise Air Algérie to negotiate lease payments inversely tied to the price of jet fuel?

9. Showa Shell (advanced). Showa Shell Sekiyu K.K. is the 50% owned Japanese subsidiary of the oil giant Royal Dutch Shell. Unlike giant multinationals such as Exxon or Royal Dutch Shell that are vertically integrated from oil exploration and extraction all the way to distribution, Japanese oil companies are primarily engaged in downstream activities — namely domestic refining and distribution operations through company-owned service stations. Such activities are almost exclusively focused on the Japanese market, which offers very stable market conditions in terms of price controlled by the Japanese government and quantity sold (relatively stable with a 12.5% share of the Japanese market). International dealings are limited to importing petroleum products whose prices are set in dollars.

a. Map out the cash flows configuration characteristic of a Japanese domestic oil refiner and distributor such as Showa Shell. What is the nature of Showa Shell's exposure to FX risk?

b. Showa Shell experiences spikes in operating costs due to jumps in the price of oil or the yen price of the dollar. Such spikes squeeze operating income since Showa Shell is not able to translate or pass through immediately its higher costs into higher prices (because of governmental price controls). How should Showa Shell protect itself from such occurrences?

c. Would your answer be different if Showa Shell sourced all crude oil from (1) its parent Royal Dutch Shell or (2) the spot oil market?

REFERENCES

Adler, Michael, and Bernard Dumas. 1984. "Exposure to Currency Risk: Definition and Measurement." *Financial Management* 13(1): 41–50.

Ahn, Mark J., and William D. Falloon. 1991. *Strategic Risk Management: How Global Corporations Manage Financial Risk for Competitive Advantage*. Chicago: Probus.

Bartram, Sohnke M., Gregory W. Brown, and Bernadette A. Minton. 2010. "Resolving the Exposure Puzzle: The Many Facets of Exchange Rate Exposure." *Journal of Financial Economics* 95: 148–173.

Bodnar, Gordon M., Bernard Dumas, and Richard C. Marston. 2002. "Pass-Through and Exposure." *Journal of Finance* 57: 199–231.

Campa, Jose Manuel, and Linda S. Goldberg. 2005. "Exchange Rate Pass-Through into Imports Prices." *Review of Economics and Statistics* 87: 679–690.

Campa, Jose Manuel, and Linda S. Goldberg. 2006. "Distribution Margin, Imported Inputs and the Sensitivity of the CPI to Exchange Rates." Federal Reserve Bank of New York Staff Report no. 247.

Dufey, Gunter. 1972. "Corporate Finance and Exchange Rates Variations." *Financial Management* 1(2): 51–57.

Flood, Eugene, Jr., and Donald R. Lessard. 1985. "On the Measurement of Operating Exposure to Exchange Rates: A Conceptual Approach." *Financial Management* (Spring): 25–36.

Garner, C. Kent, and Alan C. Shapiro. 1984. "A Practical Method for Assessing Foreign Exchange Risk." *Midland Corporate Finance Journal* 2(3): 6–17.

Hekman, Christine R. 1985. "A Financial Model of Foreign Exchange Exposure." *Journal of International Business Studies* 16(2): 83–99.

Jorion, Philippe. 1990. "The Exchange Rate Exposure of US Multinationals." *Journal of Business* 63(3): 331–345.

Luehrman, Timothy A. 1990. "The Exchange Rate Exposure of a Global Competitor." *Journal of International Business Studies* 21(2): 225–242.

Oxelheim, Lars, and Claes Wihlborg. 1987. *Macroeconomic Uncertainty: International Risks and Opportunities for the Corporation*. Chichester, UK: John Wiley & Sons.

Smith, Clifford W., Jr., Charles W. Smithson, and D. Sykes Wilford. 1989. "Managing Financial Risk." *Journal of Applied Corporate Finance* 1(4): 27–48.

Sundaram, A., and V. Mishra. 1991. "Currency Movements and Corporate Pricing Strategies." In *Recent Developments in International Banking and Finance*, volume 5, edited by Sarkis J. Khoury. New York: Elsevier.

CASE STUDY 18.1. PEUGEOT CITROËN SA'S ECONOMIC EXPOSURE TO THE SOUTH KOREAN WON

The severe economic downturn engulfing the eurozone was taking a severe toll on the French automobile industry, which experienced an overall fall of 14% in personal car sales during the first 6 months of 2012. More specifically, Peugeot's and Renault's sales dropped by 20 and 17%, respectively, in the European Union, where they record most of their sales, whereas the South Korean Hyundai group's sales in France increased by 30% over that same period. The slump pushed Peugeot into the red, forcing it to implement far-ranging cost-cutting measures, including the closure of its assembly operations in Aulnay-Sous-Bois and the layoff of 3,000 employees — the first automobile plant closure in France in 20 years. To add insult to injury, Hyundai recently announced that it was hiring 1,000 workers to ramp up its production at its assembly plant in Nosovice (Czech Republic) in order to reach full capacity. Hyundai's successful expansion in Europe seems to rest on its offering competitively priced vehicles — especially the i30 hatchback, its most popular model, which ranks among the 10 best-selling models in its midsize segment. Rival automakers in Europe, however, have attributed Hyundai's success to the South Korean won's weakness against the euro and a free-trade agreement that South Korea signed with the European Union (EU) as recently as May 2011.

The newly elected French socialist government did not take long before accusing the South Korean car manufacturers Kia Motors and Hyundai Motor Company of dumping their cars on the French market.[9] Kia and Hyundai are the two main subsidiaries of the South Korean *chaebol* Hyundai Motor Group, which is the world's fifth-largest automaker by sales. According to ACEA, the European automobile association, Hyundai and Kia together sold 391,511 cars in the European Union during the first six months of 2012, up 17% from the previous year, and now capture 5.9% of market share, up from 4.7% the year before. Dumping is an illegal predatory pricing policy whereby a firm would sell in exports markets at prices below what it charges in its home market.

Such discriminatory pricing policies are often cloaked in the veil of currency fluctuations; for example, an exporter may fail to reflect the appreciation of its home currency to keep market share in the export market or may cut prices in the export market faster than the depreciation of its home currency would warrant.

Vania Mareuse, deputy CFO at PSA Peugeot Citroën SA, was convinced that his firm was directly exposed to the South Korean won (KRW) depreciation against the euro. More specifically, he believed that the following chain of relationships would make a compelling case for managing Peugeot's economic exposure to the South Korean currency: (1) A depreciation of the won resulted in lower manufacturing costs at Hyundai's EU assembly operations in the Czech Republic because of its heavy reliance on imports of parts, components, and subassemblies from its South Korean parent. Such cost savings (2) were in turn passed through partially in lower € sticker prices to European consumers, and as a result (3) Hyundai gained market share in France and the European Union at the expense of French car manufacturers, (4) which suffered from rapidly falling profits and therefore stock market value.

Of course, gauging the numerical exposure of the Peugeot group to the South Korean won would depend on a number of assumptions and a fair amount of guesswork. Mareuse's colleagues in the strategic planning group had developed confidential strategic profiles of Peugeot's key competitors in Europe and were able to provide much-needed estimates of some of the key input variables. On average, South Korean cars sold in Europe incorporated 60% of South Korean content, whether that meant parts or subassemblies such as power trains or engines sourced from South Korea. With more than half of all Hyundai cars sold in the European Union assembled in the Czech Republic (itself a member of the EU but not of the euro-zone), a won depreciation resulted in a substantial reduction in the cost of goods sold. On average, 50% of cost savings were reflected in lower sticker prices. A more difficult linkage to assess was the actual price elasticity of French consumer demand. Peugeot's dealers estimated that a 5% reduction in Hyundai sticker prices triggered an increase in sales to the tune of 15%, with resulting lost sales equally divided between Peugeot

9 Hyundai offers a 7 year car warranty on the models it sells in Europe but only a 3 year warranty on the same cars sold in South Korea.

and Renault. Peugeot's profit margins had declined to €3,000 per vehicle during the first 6 months of 2012.

Questions for Discussion

1. Sketch diagrammatically cash flows for Peugeot-France versus Hyundai's operations in the Czech Republic. Assume that the Czech koruna is pegged in perpetuity to the € in anticipation of the Czech Republic becoming a member of the euro-zone.

2. Assuming a 25% devaluation of the South Korean won, estimate how much Hyundai car sales would increase in the EU.

3. Assuming that, due to Hyundai's sales gain, French car manufacturers' losses are equally shouldered by Renault and Peugeot and that the first-year profit and loss are capitalized as a perpetuity discounted at Peugeot's cost of capital of 15%, what would be Peugeot's loss in market capitalization?[10]

4. How could Peugeot mitigate its exposure to the South Korean won?

5. How would an annual depreciation of the Czech koruna of 2.5% in excess of its inflation change Peugeot's economic exposure?

10 Peugeot's market value can be measured as a constant perpetuity of earnings in 2012, whose present value is simply: earnings (2012)/0.15. Should the perpetuity grow annually at the rate of g, Peugeot's market value would then be equal to earnings (2012)/(0.15 – g).

PART FIVE

Cross-Border Valuation and Foreign Investment Analysis

Part 5 develops a valuation framework for cross-border investments that uniquely incorporates the different variables such as foreign exchange risk, country risk, asymmetric tax treatment, and different inflation rates. As a preliminary, in chapter 19 we outlined the organizational modalities within firms entering foreign markets and when cross-border valuation issues arise. Chapter 20 contrasts metrics such as net present value of asset-based cash flows or equity-based cash flows versus adjusted present value and real options metrics, and reviews the necessary adjustments to be made to the cost of capital used at a discount rate in international valuation. The framework is applied to cross-border mergers and acquisitions in Chapter 21 and large-scale infrastructural project finance in Chapter 22. Taking the perspective of asset managers manning the desks of mutual funds, pension funds, hedge funds, or sovereign wealth funds, global investing in stocks and bonds is addressed in Chapter 23, which gauges the limit of geographical diversification in the context of increasingly integrated capital markets.

CHAPTER 19

Foreign Market Entry Strategies and Country Risk Management

The International Corporation operates in a kind of vacuum. . . . It is constantly exposed to the danger of expropriations, discriminatory legislation, and the hatred and opprobrium of the people and the countries whom on the whole it serves. It seems to be one of the unfortunate facts of society that being merely useful is a poor source of either prestige or legitimacy.

—Kenneth E. Boulding

Tata Motors' launch in India of the much-awaited low-priced Nano minicar in 2008 is opening new opportunities for the budding automotive firm. Jamshed Contractor, Tata Motors' newly appointed senior vice president for international operations, is narrowing down strategic options for Africa. Nigeria and South Africa stand out as potentially lucrative markets; with populations over 225 million and approaching 65 million respectively and gross domestic product (GDP) per capita higher than most African nations, Nigeria and South Africa could be the early targets of market entry, although both countries already have multiple, albeit small-scale, automotive manufacturing operations — mostly in the form of local assembly subsidiaries of global car companies.

What entry strategy should Tata Motors pursue: exporting to test African consumers' appetite for the Nano, manufacturing under license to speed up market penetration while keeping entry cost to a minimum, or a bolder full-fledged entry *en force* through foreign direct investment? In many ways, this early decision would serve as a blueprint for other national foreign markets for the Nano. South Asia, Latin America, and Central Asia are all pre-emerging or emerging markets and good candidates for the Nano. In each situation, Jamshed Contractor would have to prepare a detailed and comparative analysis of alternative entry modes, which Tata Motors would carefully review at its next board of directors meeting.

This chapter introduces sequentially the different modes of entry that domestic firms can choose from — a choice that, by necessity, ought to be guided by (1) an understanding of the multinational corporation's *sources of competitive advantage* and (2) a careful assessment of the target market's *country risk*.

After reading this chapter you will understand:

- What the contractual modes of foreign market entry are.
- What the pros and cons of international licensing are.
- What the difference between licensing and franchising is.
- What the theories motivating foreign direct investment are.
- What country risk is and how to mitigate it.
- How a cost-benefit analysis of foreign direct investment informs country risk forecasting.

CONTRACTUAL MODES OF FOREIGN MARKET ENTRY

Most firms shy away from foreign markets, if anything, because they are *geographically* and *culturally* distant. For those firms that are more intrepid and venturesome, foreign market entry will take different modes, which this section explores in a sequential format.

Random exporting

Many small to medium-sized firms whose sales scope is domestic will stumble into export sales. An inquiry from a foreign distributor or department store about one of the firm's products can be triggered by web advertising or manning a kiosk at an international fair and may lead to a foreign sale. The firm is simply reacting to an opportunity knocking at the door, and such export sales are appropriately qualified as *random* exports. And this may be the end of it. In such a case the export sale is a one-time occurrence, and the occasional exporter — focused on its domestic sales territory — may not think much of it if the export sale is not repeated. Conversely, our firm may wake up to this foreign call and start thinking more systematically about export sales. Presumably the effort will be focused first on the export market from which the unsolicited first order came.

Systematic exporting

Having discovered the potential for random export sales, the firm would first want to repeat the sale and secure a foothold in that export market. The practical question is whether the newborn exporter has much managerial expertise in negotiating a more permanent relationship with its newfound export partner. Indeed, many idiosyncratic tasks would have to be completed to secure financing for and payment from a foreign customer domiciled in a distant foreign land whose credit risk may be hard to gauge. More specifically, the exporter has to assess its potential client's *credit risk* (the possibility that the client may default), *currency risk* (the possibility that the importer's foreign currency in which the invoice is denominated may have depreciated by payment time), and *country risk* (the possibility of exchange controls delaying actual payments).

Indirect exporting

The exporting firm may decide that export sales require in-house expertise that would be simply too costly and time-consuming to develop organically. Our exporter therefore may decide to subcontract the entire exporting process to a firm specializing in such activities, generally known as an export management company (EMC). In effect, under such an arrangement, the export sale would look very much like a domestic sale in the sense that the sale is made to another domestic firm, the EMC, which assumes the responsibility of carrying the goods to the foreign client. The exporter has de facto subcontracted the exporting activities to a third party with the necessary expertise. Our exporting firm may be eager to develop other export markets using one or several EMCs with expertise for certain countries and certain lines of products. Our exporter is now effectively reaching export markets but has surrendered management control over the exporting process and — most importantly — has little say in selecting a distributor, shaping the marketing policy, or setting the pricing of its product at the foreign point of sale.

Should this first indirect export strategy prove successful, the firm will start thinking seriously about regaining some control over the exporting process — that is, internalizing some of the idiosyncratic activities that make export sales unique. In a way, the success of EMCs is also their demise, which is why special attention should be given to the termination/cancellation clause of the contract signed between the exporter and the EMC. A strong cancellation clause allows the exporter to exercise tighter control over its agent and exit the relationship if the EMC fails to perform according to plan or the exporter desires to regain selective control over the exporting process. On its side, the EMC must be assured that it will be adequately rewarded for investing in and securing a successful foothold in a foreign market on behalf of the exporter.

Semi-indirect exporting

Having secured distributors through the hard work of its EMC, the exporter will be inclined to interface directly with its foreign distributor, thereby eliminating the EMC as an intermediary. In effect, the exporter now needs to assume the *transfer* activities whereby its goods travel safely from its factory's loading dock to its foreign distributor's warehouse. Packaging, shipping, financing, insurance, customs documentation, clearing, and ultimately timely payment are now tasks that the exporter is internalizing — possibly by hiring an export manager reporting to its sales manager. The foreign marketing activities continue to be outsourced to the foreign distributor, which controls, among other things, the choice of distribution channels, advertising, pricing, and after-sales service. Clearly, our exporter is now much closer to its export market but still unable to learn directly about the foreign market and consumer demand idiosyncrasies, which are relayed and screened by the foreign distributor keen on protecting its position.

Here again, a very successful distributor encourages the exporter to want to either bypass it or take it over. The drive for full control of the exporting process only grows stronger with the distributor's success, and inevitably the exporter will seek at some point to establish its fully owned and controlled marketing branch or subsidiary. Typically, the distributor would have protected its position by negotiating ex ante a contract that makes early termination difficult and costly for the exporter.

Direct exporting

The last stage of full internalization of the exporting process is direct exporting. It requires significant resource allocation to establish and staff a foreign sales *branch* or *subsidiary* with, among other things, adequate warehousing facilities. A foreign subsidiary is incorporated in the host country and therefore is a legally self-standing entity, whereas a foreign branch is considered, for liability and tax purposes, an extension of the parent exporting company.[1] The exporter now fully controls the foreign marketing activities and thus is able to make its own decisions on advertising, distribution channels, and pricing. By directly engaging with the end consumer, the exporter is now able to learn fully about its foreign market and therefore be more responsive to its changing conditions.

International licensing

Broadly defined, international licensing refers to contractual arrangements whereby a domestic firm — the *licensor* — makes available its intangible assets such as patents, technological know-how, trade secrets, or trademarks to a foreign company — the *licensee* — in return for royalties. Some foreign markets that would otherwise have been promising candidates for export sales may be difficult to penetrate through direct sales because of high tariff walls. Local manufacturing by proxy may be the only viable mode of market entry. Our firm would thus seek a local partner with adequate manufacturing know-how to become its licensee. Such international licensing relationships are fraught with the risk of losing control over one's proprietary technology and need to be carefully protected by a strong licensing contract.

1 See Chapter 25 for a full discussion of the tax implications of operating as a branch versus a subsidiary in a foreign country. One important consideration is that a branch allows losses (often important in the early years of operations) to be immediately netted against the parent's taxable income.

Advantages of licensing

Licensing is a low-cost (or no-cost) way of generating incremental income on technology that has already been paid for. For firms with limited managerial, technical, and financial resources available for pursuing international sales, licensing is an inexpensive entry mode and is particularly suitable for small and medium-sized firms deterred by highly uncertain foreign sales. Often licensing as an entry mode into a foreign market allows for the circumvention of import barriers, which increase the cost (in the case of ad valorem tariffs) or limit the quantity (in the case of quotas) of export sales to said market. In the case of certain products, high transportation costs relative to the value of the product are also a hindrance to competitive exports, and licensing provides an economic solution. When a foreign country is closed to imports and foreign direct investment, as is often the case for military equipment or telecommunications gear, licensing to foreign companies may be the only way to meet host government requirements mandating that these products be manufactured by local companies.

Disadvantages of licensing

The foremost downside of international licensing is that the licensor surrenders managerial control over the manufacturing and marketing of its products to a foreign-domiciled licensee. In situations where the licensee fails to perform according to expectations, the licensor has limited recourse unless it is willing to terminate the licensing contract.

A more subtle risk of international licensing is that the licensor may have created a competitor in third markets. Once your licensee is armed with your technology, it may be difficult to rein him in should he forcibly enter third markets where the licensor is present solely via export sales.[2]

Last but not least, licensing income — though of low risk because it is pegged to sales revenue rather than earnings[3] — is modest, with royalties rarely exceeding 5% of sales. Furthermore, licensing agreements usually expire within 7–10 years, leaving

2 Sometimes this is no fault of the licensee, which may be selling to independent distributors that in turn export to third markets or even the home market of the licensor.

3 Royalties are defined as a percentage of sales revenue (top line) rather than a percentage of profit (bottom line). Sales revenue is typically a far steadier cash-flow stream than residual profits, which makes royalties a very dependable, low-volatility income stream for the licensor.

INTERNATIONAL CORPORATE FINANCE IN PRACTICE 19.1

Xerox's Historic Licensing Blunder

In 1956, Xerox Corporation, facing tremendous growth prospects for its new copying technology in the US market, felt it could not begin to tackle the rest of the world and therefore joined forces with the United Kingdom-based Rank Organization to form a 50–50 joint venture known as Rank Xerox (RX). Xerox gave the venture an *exclusive license in perpetuity* to manufacture and sell all xerographic machines outside North America. During the following 15 years the basic agreement changed little, although it was repeatedly adjusted with regard to both the equity and profit splits, as well as the markets in which RX had exclusive sales rights. RX's share capital by 1968 was $53.8 million, of which the Xerox contribution was $32.6 million (although the voting split was still 50–50). The more important adjustments concerned the marketing arrangements.

In 1963, RX sold marketing rights for Latin America back to Xerox in return for a 5% royalty on all subsequent net sales and rentals earned in Latin America, plus a payment to Rank of 7,500 shares of Xerox stock worth approximately $3.3 million at that time. By 1971, Xerox had paid RX royalties of between $2.6 million and $6.6 million for the privilege of marketing its own products in the western hemisphere since 1964, even though Rank had readily acknowledged in 1963 that it had been unable to increase sales in the area. Xerox had to invest about $20 million in Latin America to make the sales and rentals out of which the 5% royalties were paid to RX.

The original agreement was amended again and again in an apparent further effort to correct the original mistake. By 1971 Xerox had paid Rank $7.5 million in stock for the right to stop paying the Latin American royalties. In other words, besides the investment Xerox has had to make to market its own products successfully in Latin America, it has had to pay Rank a total of between $10 million and $14 million over a 5 year period for the privilege of doing so. Xerox's freedom to expand in the lush European (and Japanese) markets was sharply constrained by having to work through RX. Even with control at the director level, RX was a UK firm that had to work through some of the world's toughest capital outflow controls, which in turn severely constricted RX's expansion outside the United Kingdom. Even the Rank chairman was quoted as being surprised at the Xerox decision to license all of its products to RX. In total, the 1956 agreement and the subsequent efforts to correct it had, by 1971, cost Xerox shareholders as much as $200 million.

technology and trade secrets vulnerable once the contract has lapsed.

Licensing contract

A carefully crafted licensing contract should offer protection to the licensor, keeping in mind that legal documents are only as good as their enforceability. In international commercial disputes there are several mechanisms for resolving conflicts. A licensing contract should include the following four elements: definition of the technology package; conditions for using the technology, including territorial and sublicensing rights; compensation; and termination of contract.

1. *Technology package*. The contract should describe the scope of the industrial property being licensed (patents, trademarks, or know-how), as well as spell out the process for transferring necessary know-how to the licensee. Such contracts often detail proprietary equipment and intermediate goods or subassemblies that will be supplied by the licensor over the life of the license.
2. *Territorial rights*. The licensor often grants an exclusive license[4] for the purpose of developing sales in a given target market. Unfortunately, nothing prevents the licensee from exporting to third markets, and tight clauses delineating territorial rights may be hard to enforce in the licensee's country. Host countries are seldom inclined to curtail exports business!

4 A licensor may prefer to grant a nonexclusive license to reserve the opportunity to license other firms in that same country or even to enter the market on its own accord at a later point. A strong licensee would insist on an exclusive license.

3. *Compensation.* Payment is based on royalties and fees for technical assistance provided to the licensee. The licensor may stipulate a minimum amount of sales or require a minimum royalty payment as a strong motivation for the licensee's selling efforts. Royalties, however, may be delayed or blocked because the licensee's country of domicile is experiencing balance-of-payment difficulties and shortage of hard currencies. Under such a scenario the licensor may require that after 18 to 24 months, blocked royalties, which presumably have been deposited in an escrow account, would be automatically converted into an equity interest in the licensee.[5] Such a clause would spur the licensee in finding creative solutions to expedite remittance of royalties to the licensor.

4. *Performance provisions and (early) termination.* Setting numerical goals will allow the licensor to monitor the licensee in terms of the following benchmarks: (1) Are quality standards being upheld by the licensee? (2) Is the target market's sales potential being fully exploited? Failure to deliver on either the production or sales goals should trigger penalties in the form of additional fees or termination of the contract. (See International Corporate Finance in Practice 19.1 for the costs of an in-perpetuity agreement.)

International franchising

International franchising is a form of licensing whereby the *franchisor* licenses a business system and other property rights such as brand names — rather than technology — to a foreign firm, the *franchisee.* It is most readily used in service industries such as fast-food restaurants, car rentals, hotels and motels, and real estate brokerage. The franchisee does business under the franchisor's trade name and logo, implementing tight operating guidelines as set by the franchisor (see International Corporate Finance in Practice 19.2). As with a licensing agreement, the franchisor is compensated by the periodic payment of royalties defined as a percentage of the franchisee's sales revenues. Many US household names such as Kentucky Fried Chicken, McDonald's, Avis, and Century 21 have expanded globally through franchising, giving this mode of foreign market entry a distinctly American flavor!

5 The licensing contract should include a simple valuation rule such as the price/earnings ratio or market/book value ratio to avoid unnecessary haggling over the terms of the conversion.

FOREIGN MARKET ENTRY THROUGH FOREIGN DIRECT INVESTMENTS

Contractual modes of foreign market entry offer a low-cost but low-return solution (limited to royalties) as the exporter or the licensor/franchisor is unable to realize the full sales and profit potential of its products. They also pose a significant control risk to the exporter or the licensor who operates internationally by *proxy* through a foreign distributor or licensee. The most carefully crafted contracts with foreign distributors, licensees, or franchisees are never foolproof, and even if they were their enforceability is always challenging.

By manufacturing abroad, the firm reasserts its control over final sales since it is able to keep abreast of market developments and to adapt product designs and manufacturing logistics faster to changing local tastes and/or competitive landscapes. Fundamentally, foreign direct investment entails the

INTERNATIONAL CORPORATE FINANCE IN PRACTICE 19.2

Domino's Pizza in Japan

In geographically and culturally distant Japan, Domino's Pizza chose the franchising route, thereby shifting the burden of adapting its product-cum-delivery system to its Japanese master franchisee, Y-Higa Corporation. From the time the first Domino's unit opened in Tokyo's affluent Azabu district, Domino's Japanese operations have consistently been its most successful foreign operation. Interestingly, Domino's Japanese locations do not provide on-premises restaurants. Given the price of real estate in Japan, Domino's operates in small spaces and relies exclusively on home delivery, which required design of special three-wheeled Honda scooters that can easily maneuver in the Tokyo's traffic.

transfer of an entire enterprise to the foreign target market, whereas exporting is limited to the transfer of the finished product and licensing is limited to the transfer of technology and other intellectual property. Beyond the obvious transfer of money to enable the acquisition of land and the construction of manufacturing and warehousing facilities in the country of entry, the firm transfers its knowledge assets — that is, managerial, technical, and technological know-how — and its marketing and financial skills and expertise in the form of an enterprise that it fully controls. Presumably, this enables the investor to more fully exploit its competitive advantage in the target market.

One of the immediate advantages of foreign direct investment is that, in many industries, local production allows the firm to be more cost-competitive than exporting would have been,

INTERNATIONAL CORPORATE FINANCE IN PRACTICE 19.3

Why Do Firms Invest Abroad?

Foreign direct investment is motivated by (1) procuring raw materials, so-called *resource seekers*; (2) sourcing products at a lower cost or *cost minimizers*; and (3) penetrating local markets or *market seekers*.

From time immemorial **resource-seeking firms** have sought access to natural resources that were either not available or only available in limited supply in their home country. Oil and mining companies as well as agribusiness ventures emerged as powerful foreign direct investors in the nineteenth century and often grew under the mantle of the British, Dutch, and French colonial empires. British Petroleum, Compagnie Francaise des Pétroles (Total), Union Minière du Katanga, Rio Tinto, Anaconda, Kennecott, and United Fruit trace their roots back to the industrial revolution and are often portrayed as the villains of international business. As such, they have been targets of political risk, nationalization, and expropriation. The physical output of their activities is typically exported for further processing in their downstream operations or simply sold on world markets. More recently the relentless drive by Chinese state-owned companies to secure access to foreign sources of energy, minerals, and other natural resources follows the same economic logic of their yesteryear Western counterparts.

Cost minimizers (by offshoring) primarily search for lower labor costs and establish assembly operations in low-wage countries such as Mexico, China, Vietnam, or India. This is especially true of labor-intensive manufacturing processes characteristic of consumer electronics, garments, or footwear but also includes service operations such as back-office operations in the financial services industry or software development in information technology.

Market seekers are manufacturers exploiting a competitive advantage based on proprietary products, manufacturing methods, and marketing policies, and favor foreign direct investment as a mode of foreign market entry over exporting or licensing. This is the case of high-technology industries for which protecting firm-specific proprietary expertise is paramount and licensing is deemed hazardous, as well as firms that face intense cost pressures requiring tight control over foreign operations. Such firms are often found among the few key players of global oligopolies that protect themselves from competition by erecting entry barriers rooted in economies of scale or in capital intensity, research and development, and advertising outlays. Interestingly, strategic rivalry among oligopolistic firms explains the sequencing of foreign direct investment, as rivals often imitate what a firm does in an oligopoly. Consider a US oligopoly dominated by three key players: I, II, and III. If firm I decides to enter the Indian market, firms II and III will fear that firm I may displace their exports business to India, giving firm I a first-mover advantage; firms II and III would follow the lead of firm I and invest in India — a form of oligopolistic reaction aimed at ensuring that a rival does not gain a commanding position in any one market.

because of significant savings on transportation costs and customs duties. This is especially the case of industries whose products' ratio of value to transportation costs is low, making manufacturing close to your final demand highly desirable. In fact, foreign direct investment is often triggered by changes in tariff policies by the host country, which may increase duties on finished products but reduce them on subassemblies and parts. India, for example, maintains a punitive tariff on finished cars at 166% but lowered duties on parts and subassemblies to 25%, thereby encouraging local assembly by foreign firms. Similarly, investment entry often creates *marketing* advantage, as local production — being close to your customers — facilitates product adaptation to local preferences and purchasing power. It also enables speedier and more reliable delivery to distributors, as well as better provision of after-sales services. Of course, with higher control over the entire value chain comes a much larger commitment of corporate resources and higher exposure to risk. In short, foreign direct investment has the *highest risk-return* ratio among foreign market entry strategies. (See International Corporate Finance in Practice 19.3 on investing abroad.)

Once the decision to manufacture abroad has been made, the firm still needs to decide whether it will go it alone or team up with a joint venture partner, and whether it will build its own production facilities or acquire a going concern. The *greenfield* or *de novo* entry mode is analyzed at great length in Chapter 20. Alternatively, the acquisition route speeds up the process, giving almost instant access to manufacturing facilities as well as to an existing marketing and distribution network. Chapter 21 discusses in further detail the necessary strategic and financial analysis leading to such acquisitions.

COUNTRY RISK

The principal drawback of foreign direct investment is that it is directly exposed to the vagaries of the host country's government policies. An important component of the decision-making process is therefore that investors closely scrutinize the foreign investment climate of the target country before investing. Uncertainty about the government's future policies and how it may arbitrarily change the *rules of the game* is an investor's paramount concern. Indeed, investors prefer constraining rules of the game that are well understood and stable to laxer rules of the game that may be subject to erratic changes.

Defining country risk

Country risk refers to how uncertainty about the host country's foreign investment climate (rules of the game) impacts the value of the multinational firm's investment in that country. Country risk may be divided more specifically into four subcategories to which multinationals are exposed in varying degrees depending on the nature of their business activities and the idiosyncrasies of the host country.

Macropolitical risk results from the instability of the host country's political system, which may in turn jeopardize the investor's profitability and its survival. Civil wars or terrorism in countries such as Pakistan or Nigeria illustrate this class of risk, which results in business interruptions and impaired profitability for prolonged periods of time.

Ownership/control risk refers to adverse policies implemented by the host country government in the form of expropriation or nationalization of a foreign investor's plant and equipment — as well as interference in the managing of its operations. The history of international business is replete with cases of expropriation or nationalization with or without compensation by populist governments and often target industries that loom large on the host country's economic horizon such as mining, telecommunications, or banking. Venezuela recently nationalized its foreign-owned oil companies yet again (see International Corporate Finance 19.4). Post World War II, Communist takeovers in Eastern Europe also resulted in blanket nationalization of all private-sector interests; even post-Soviet Russia has selectively expropriated foreign energy and mining interests. Government limits to foreign managerial control may force the multinational investor to divest the majority stake in its subsidiary, thereby surrendering not only its majority interest but also its full managerial control to a local business partner. In a similar vein, abrupt *repudiation* of contracts or licenses by host countries or their state-owned enterprises without proper compensation of the foreign direct investor is tantamount to expropriation (see International Corporate Finance in Practice 19.5).

Operations risk results from uncertainty about government policies regarding the rules of the game

INTERNATIONAL CORPORATE FINANCE IN PRACTICE 19.4

Venezuela Nationalizes Its Oil Industry Yet Again

Venezuela expropriated foreign oil interests for the second time in the past 30 years: President Hugo Chavez, on May 1, 2007, transferred operating control of Venezuelan oilfields from international oil companies to the government-owned oil conglomerate Petroleos de Venezuela (PVDSA). ExxonMobil, ConocoPhillips, Total, British Petroleum and Statoil were in effect nationalized with a derisory offer of compensation that they turned down. A decade later, in August 2018, Conoco announced that (PVDSA) had agreed to a $2 billion judgment handed down by an International Chamber of Commerce tribunal. PVDSA was granted a five year payment schedule with the first $500 million payment due within 90 days but given its state of dilapidated finances it is not clear how much payment it will be able to make. PVDSA did require some gentle (or no so gentle) nudging to settle: after winning the arbitration ruling in April 2018 Conoco seized PVDSA's oil inventories, cargoes and terminals on several Dutch Caribbean islands effectively choking Venezuelan oil exports which happen to be the lifeline to the otherwise moribund economy. But that's not all — ConocoPhillips is also pursuing a separate arbitration case through the World Bank's International Center for Settlement of Investment Disputes which may result into another very large settlement of perhaps $6 billion. Will Venezuela ever pay? In spite of being endowed with the largest oil reserves in the world, Venezuela's oil production has plummeted to the lowest level in decades and — without oil exports revenues — the country is close to sovereign default.

Source: Adapted from Krauss, Clifford "Venezuela Agrees to Pay $2 Billion over Seizure of Oil Projects" *New York Times* (August 20, 2018).

governing day-to-day operations. Changes in local procurement requirements may force the multinational subsidiary to source components from a domestic firm at a higher cost. Domestic firm may also require the subsidiary's managerial assistance in bringing its product quality up to the multinational corporation's standard. This would in turn tax the multinational investor's resources and result in higher final prices for its products. Imposition of price controls on finished products when labor costs or other inputs costs are left unchecked will squeeze operating margins and impair the subsidiary's profits. Labor laws may force the multinational subsidiary to restrict its employees' workweek to 35 hours as the French socialist government did in the early 2000s; this may in turn be disruptive and costly to the company's manufacturing schedules. More generally, any unanticipated change in the regulatory environment may adversely impact the productivity and profitability of the multinational investor's local operations.

Transfer risk refers to any unanticipated host country policy change that impacts the flow of money, goods, and technology between the subsidiary and the rest of the multinational enterprise system. Most obvious are withholding tax increases on dividend remittances to the parent company and/or sharp increases on ad valorem tariff duties on key imported parts, components, or subassemblies. Blocked funds in times of balance-of-payments difficulties will halt all payments in convertible currencies for dividends, royalties, and management or technical fees by the subsidiary to its parent as well as for imports of various inputs.

Managing country risk

There are several hedging strategies that can be implemented by a proactive foreign direct investor that — to different extents — will mitigate the adverse impact of country risk on a proposed investment.

Negotiating the environment

The key is to negotiate an agreement that spells out the rights and responsibilities of both parties *ex ante* — that is, before the investment is implemented and when the investor retains its full bargaining power. For example, the investor commits to exporting 25% of the project output or creating 250 new skilled jobs annually over the next 5 years. The host government, for its part, will not impose punitive tariff duties on

INTERNATIONAL CORPORATE FINANCE IN PRACTICE 19.5

Once Bitten and Twice Shy" Unless You Are Peugeot Woeing Iran

At its worst, country risk is generally associated with adverse policies implemented by the host country government in the form of expropriation or nationalization of a foreign investor's plant and equipment. The extra-territorial reach of economic sanctions imposed by a third-party sovereign is a different form of country risk although it may have consequences similar to expropriation and nationalization without compensation. The imposition of such sanctions against Iran is a vivid illustration of how biting such sanctions can be. To wit, consider the trials and tribulations of the French car manufacturer Peugeot in Iran. Peugeot had long had a dominant position in Iran with as much as 30% market share. It exited Iran in 2012 because its minority shareholder GM was barred by the US government from doing business with Iran and could not associate with any firm dealing with Iran. Only a few short weeks after the 2016 milestone nuclear deal between the West and Iran was signed, Peugeot re-entered the much coveted Iranian market — admittedly the last emerging market frontier for automotives — through a 49% joint venture with Iran Khodro Industrial Group — itself 14% owned by the Iranian government. It committed to investing €400 million over a five year period to ramp up car manufacturing to 200,000 units with a 40% local content within a three year span. And yet, with the United States Trump administration repudiating the nuclear deal and re-imposing far-ranging economic sanctions against Iran, Peugeot had no choice but to hastily withdraw yet again from Iran as it did on August 8, 2018. In fact, the United States was re-instating extra-territorial "secondary sanctions" which are designed to dissuade non-US firms from doing business with Iran. It is unlikely that Peugeot will recover any funds already invested or that it will be able to regain control of the technology transferred to its joint venture partnership. In fact, Iran threatened to impose a fine on Peugeot for reneging on its contract. One may wonder why should a French multinational corporation with zero activities in the US be forced to abide by US economic sanctions. Is it because Peugeot does have plan to re-enter the US market from which it has been absent since 1991? Or is it the fear of not being able to access the US financial system or procure loans and services from US financial institutions or to clear US dollar denominated transactions in its far-flung web of international activities?

the imports of parts or subassemblies, change local procurement laws beyond existing requirements, or subject the proposed investment to discriminatory taxation. More specifically, a well-crafted investment contract will spell out the letter and the spirit of the following key items:

- *Taxation*. Tax rates, taxable income, tax holidays, and ancillary taxes.
- *Imports*. Restrictions on imports of key inputs such as subassemblies versus local procurement requirements.
- *Remittances*. Rules pertaining to access to foreign exchange for payment of management fees, dividends, royalties, and so on to the parent company. This includes the way in which blocked funds (in case of balance-of-payments crises) can be invested in local currency assets so as to earn a return, providing at least some protection against loss of purchasing power due to local inflation or currency devaluation.
- *Local financing*. Access to the domestic banking system or local capital market, including concessionary/subsidized financing from the host government.
- *Labor laws*. Allowing the use of expatriate managers or technicians for operating the local subsidiary by expediting their work permit documents as necessary.
- *Corporate governance*. Host country restrictions on ownership and/or control of the local subsidiary, and guidelines for planned divestiture from investment and exit modalities.
- *Protection of intellectual property rights*. Host countries may be less than forthcoming in protecting

patents, trademarks, copyrights, proprietary technologies, or manufacturing processes that are the foundation of multinationals' source of competitive advantage.

- *Conflict resolution.* An investment contract is only as good as its enforceability. Host governments change and may not uphold the prior commitments of previous administrations. Specific guidelines about binding dispute resolution mechanisms such as an international arbitration court would smooth the process should conflict arise between the two parties (see International Corporate Finance in Practice 19.6).

Obviously, such agreements are easy to frame and agree upon in year 0 of the investment, but once the project is under way, the dynamics of shifting perceptions and expectations may soon put the investor and its host at loggerheads. The next main section details a costs/benefits analytical framework that should facilitate smoother management of this process.

Structuring the investment

From its inception, raising the maximum amount of capital from local sources (as opposed to parent or third-party foreign lenders) reduces the investor's exposure as well as the host country's propensity to expropriate. Loading up on local debt (including financing from government-owned financial institutions) even though it may be more expensive than international financing is an excellent deterrent against hostile actions by the host country. In the same vein, financing from multilateral lending agencies such as the International Finance Corporation or regional development banks should deter the host country from initiating expropriation. Few governments want to be responsible for the default of one of those agencies' debtors and thereby risk antagonizing such lenders of last resort!

Local equity participation from an institutional/passive investor such as an insurance company would be an effective hedge against political risk without diluting the foreign investor's managerial control of its local operations. In fact, in many situations where the host country requires majority local ownership, it seldom requires that ownership be coupled with effective local managerial control. If the host country's capital market is well developed, floating equity to local shareholders is another way of building up good local citizenship credentials. To the extent that shareholdership is widely distributed among local investors, the multinational corporation will preserve its managerial control of local operations.

INTERNATIONAL CORPORATE FINANCE IN PRACTICE 19.6

Bilateral Investment Treaties (BITs)

Foreign direct investors embroiled in a dispute with a host country could either directly sue the host country or rely on their home government to press claims against their host. Neither approaches is likely to be favorable to the aggrieved investor given the asymmetry in bargaining positions between the investor and its host. Recourse to local courts may be impaired by government officials' xenophobia and distorted by the host government interference in the judicial process. To correct this imbalance *Bilateral Investment Treaties (BITs)* were first introduced in the early 1960s to provide a legal charter governing the relationship between foreign direct investors and their host governments. It typically includes guarantees against expropriation, nationalization and for unhampered management of operations as well as free transfer of means. Most importantly, it established an international arbitration tribunal where investors could bring claims against their host for violating investment treaties standards. This international legal machinery for resolving disputes through *conciliation and arbitration* was considerably strengthened by the creation in 1965 of the *International Centre for Settlement of Investment Disputes (ICSID)* under the auspices of the World Bank. By establishing a third party, supra-national and presumably unbiased legal entity through which disputes between aggrieved investors and their host are adjudicated, the World Bank aimed at improving a host country's "investment climate". By formalizing the "rules of engagement" between investors and their host nation states BITs would lessen "political risk" and therefore encourage the flow of foreign direct investment to emerging market countries believed to be so instrumental in fostering economic development.

Q: What is the necessary percentage of equity capital that a multinational corporation needs to own to exercise managerial control of its local operation?

A: To play it safe, one may believe that the multinational investor needs to own at least 51% of its local subsidiary to control it. In fact, it all depends on the ownership of the other 49%. An insurance company or a pension fund would typically be a passive "sleeping" investor with no interest in managing the joint venture as long as dividends are steadily distributed. In fact, as little as 20 to 25% of the total equity investment may be sufficient to exercise managerial control as long as the other 75–80% is held by several passive investors.

Political risk insurance

Corporate assets can be insured against political risk in the case of expropriation due to war, insurrection, terrorism, or revolution. Business income insurance policies also compensate the investor for any losses due to business interruptions arising from political violence. For example, insurance would cover losses due to a terrorist attack that disables a manufacturing plant for four months and results in loss of income (interest payments and other contractual obligations, including salaries, have to be met) until the plant is rebuilt. Similarly, restrictions on repatriation of dividends, royalties, or other contractual payments due to currency inconvertibility can be insured against.

Most countries that are home to multinational corporations offer political risk insurance. The

INTERNATIONAL CORPORATE FINANCE IN PRACTICE 19.7

When Midamerican Energy Holdings (Formerly Known as Calenergy) Collects Political Risk Insurance[6]

In the mid-1990s CalEnergy — the US energy concern — entered, through its two Indonesian subsidiaries Himpurna and Patuha, into a far-ranging contractual agreement to develop and operate a geothermal field for 42 years on behalf of Pertamina, Indonesia's state-owned natural resources company. The contract was signed with the Indonesian state-owned electricity utility company PT (Persero) Perusahaan Listruik Negara (PLN) — itself a wholly owned subsidiary of Pertamina. Under the terms of the contract, PLN committed to pay as an off-taker a US dollar-denominated tariff for available electricity for a period of 30 years. The contract was signed at a time when, after three decades of President Suharto's rule, Indonesia was perceived to be an investor-friendly host country in spite of wide-ranging corruption.

In the summer of 1997, the Indonesian economy was shattered by the Asian financial crisis, which sent the Indonesian rupiah plummeting from IDR 2,400 to as low as IDR 16,000 = US$1. In September 1997, the Indonesian government decided unilaterally to suspend further development of the two power projects, even though one of them was close to coming on stream. Faced with dollar-denominated tariff obligations that now translated into stratospheric rupiah electricity prices, PLN started to default on its obligations to purchase electricity from both Himpurna and Patuha. CalEnergy wasted no time in bringing the breach of contract to an arbitration hearing in Jakarta as called for in the contracts. PLN defended its actions on the grounds that the contracts had fraudulently extracted concessions from the Indonesian government to benefit members of the Suharto clan under accusations of KKN (a Bahasa Indonesian acronym for corruption, collusion, and nepotism).

The international proceeding was held under the auspices of the United Nations Commission on International Trade Law (UNCITRAL) rules, which found in favor of the plaintiff and awarded damages in the amount of US$392 million and US$171 million to Himpurna and Patuha, respectively. However, the plaintiff was unable to collect the damages. Fortunately, Calenergy had purchased political risk insurance from OPIC and Lloyds of London to protect against expropriation of the company investments in Himpurna and Patuha as well as material breaches by PLN of the energy sales contract. CalEnergy, unable to enforce the ruling of the arbitration proceeding, filed insurance claims and by November 1999 collected from OPIC and Lloyds of London a total amount of US$290 million.

6 Mark Kantor, "International Project Finance and Arbitration with Public Sector Entities. Why Is Arbitration a Fiction?" *Fordham International Law Journal*, 24(4), 2000.

Overseas Private Investment Corporation (OPIC) in the United States, Hermes in Germany, Coface in France, and the Export Credits Guarantee Department in the United Kingdom are some of the best-known quasi-government-sponsored political risk insurers. In 1988 the World Bank created the Multilateral Investment Guarantee Agency (MIGA) to promote international trade and foreign direct investment. It now insures a portfolio of several billion dollars of corporate assets. Since the early 1990s, private political insurance schemes have emerged as an alternative to government schemes, thereby deepening the market of political risk insurance coverage. Lloyds of London, US-based American International Group (AIG), and London-based Nelson Hurst PLC are some of the more prominent players in this industry (see International Corporate Finance in Practice 19.7).

COSTS/BENEFITS OF FOREIGN DIRECT INVESTMENT TO HOST COUNTRIES[7]

The value creation from foreign direct investment is carefully gauged by the investing firm through a thorough *feasibility* study and *financial* analysis (see Chapter 20 on international capital budgeting). After all, corporate resources in the form of capital, technology, and management know-how have an opportunity cost, and if they are deployed to host country A, they are no longer available for alternative use in other countries. What investors often neglect to understand is the host-country perspective: What really is the investment impact on the welfare of the recipient country? How is the costs/benefits ratio to the host country changing over the life of the prospective investment? By adopting the recipient country's metrics and first measuring the projected impact, the investor is better able to communicate and negotiate with host country officials the implementation modalities of the proposed investments and presumably can better manage its exposure to country risk. As one would expect, the value-creation metrics of a proposed investment as gauged by a multinational investor may significantly differ from the welfare impact measured by the recipient country. The ability of the investor to proactively manage this gap will go a long way toward mitigating country risk.

The national income effect

Foreign direct investment in the form of a manufacturing subsidiary should positively impact the recipient economy's GDP. At its simplest, the net benefits contributed by the proposed investment are equal to *output — inputs*, also known as the project's *value added*; output is the sales revenue generated by the project whereas inputs are the raw materials, parts, subassemblies, components, and the like necessary to produce the output. Value added is nothing other than the contribution made by the firm's factors of production to the manufacturing process. It amounts to the sum total of payments made to labor and capital in the form of wages, salaries, interest, rent, and profit:

$$\begin{aligned}Benefits &= Output - Inputs = Value\ added\\ &= Payments\ to\ factors\ of\ production\end{aligned}$$

The conventional measure of net value added as compiled in national income statistics often overstates the true contribution of a project because it does not take into account the *opportunity cost* of the factors of production involved in the project. Clearly the factors of production have to be used more productively in the proposed project than in their prior use; otherwise, this is only a reshuffling of factors of production without any additional income creation: In such cases the opportunity cost of factors of production is equal to their previous use and the benefits derived from the project are nil. Conversely, were factors of production previously idle (for example, labor was unemployed), their opportunity cost would be zero and the project's implementation would now enable the firm to fully realize their potential:

$$\begin{aligned}Benefits &= Payments\ to\ factors\ of\ production\\ &\quad - Opportunity\ costs\end{aligned}$$

Most projects are not implemented in a vacuum and would typically have significant indirect benefits or costs, also known as *externalities*, for the recipient economy. For example, by sourcing subassemblies or parts from local firms, the proposed project may allow these firms to capture economies of scale, thereby improving their competitiveness. Negative externalities may include air or water pollution with additional health care costs supported by the local community. For example, a coal power station

7 This section draws on the excellent discussion in Franklin R. Root, *International Trade and Investment*, 7th edition (Cincinnati; OH: South-Western Publishing Company), 1994, pp. 627–640.

project may first appear to be highly beneficial to the host country, but when the cost of treating the adjacent lake of fly-ash externalities[8] is factored in, the project may no longer be beneficial. Thus, the net benefits accruing to the host country are:

Benefits = Value added – Opportunity costs of Payments to factors of production + Externalities[9]

The cost side is generally measured by the sum total of all payments made to foreign factors of production that are used by the proposed project and would include dividends remitted to the parent company along with royalties, interest payments, and management fees:

Costs = Payments to foreign factors of production

The benefits-to-costs ratio should be convincingly in excess of one — not only in the early life of the project but throughout its entire life; otherwise the host country may want to change the *rules of the game* to improve the ratio to its advantage.

The balance of payments effect

Many emerging-market economies are often burdened by heavy foreign debt service and maintain only partially convertible currencies. As such, they are likely to be sensitive to the foreign exchange implications of any proposed foreign direct investment. The obvious benefit is the one-time capital inflow necessary to launch the project and fully or partially finance the manufacturing affiliate. Once up and running, the project may generate new exports revenue (a net foreign exchange inflow) or its output may readily substitute for imports (a net foreign exchange savings):

Benefits = Capital inflow + Exports sales + Imports substitution

On the cost side, the manufacturing affiliate will make payments to foreign factors of production in the form of dividends, royalties, interest, and management fees. It may also import some of its raw material inputs, subassemblies, or components. By positively impacting the host country's income, it may indirectly induce a higher level of imports for the host country. Last but not least, the investor may at some point divest from its investment or, more subtly, decapitalize its manufacturing affiliate by repatriating residual cash flows in excess of net after-tax income:

Costs = Payment to foreign factors of production + Imports[10] *+ Divestment*

Discounting future benefits and costs

So far, the framework introduced has focused on a one-period assessment of all of the proposed investment's benefits and costs accruing to the host country. Clearly foreign direct investments have a multiyear economic life, and such analysis must capture their lifelong benefits and costs. This is achieved by discounting all future benefits and costs at an appropriate rate, one that reflects the cost of capital of the factors of production committed to the project — the so-called weighted average cost of capital (WACC). Note that the discount rate applied to the project's net cash flows by the host country is likely to be lower than the discount rate applied by a foreign investor simply because the latter will typically add a risk premium to account for country risk. Thus, the project initially discounted at the host government's lower cost of capital will be very beneficial to the host country (high net present value). However, as the project matures and becomes more profitable, the initial benefits of large capital inflows are increasingly dwarfed by increasing remittances to the parent company. Exhibit 19.1 portrays how the project's net present values differ markedly between its rendition by the foreign investor (lower at first but steadily increasing) and the host country (higher at first but declining over time). The gap is a leading indicator of potential future conflict between both parties. As this analysis is reiterated over time, the gap will typically be *positive* in the early years (until point A in Exhibit 19.1), favoring the host country, before turning *negative* and widening significantly (beyond point A as shown as the hatched area in Exhibit 19.1).

Another source of disagreement between foreign direct investors and recipient countries has to do with the fact that welfare economics — the lens through which the host country would gauge a proposed foreign direct investment — adjusts nominal prices

8 The by-product of burning coal for power generation is fly ash — a light, toxic carcinogen. It is typically weighted down with gray water and forms a sludge that accumulates into desolate wastelands often referred to as "fly-ash lakes."

9 *Positive* externalities add to the net benefits whereas *negative* externalities are subtracted from the net benefits.

10 This term would include indirect imports triggered by higher local income through the marginal propensity to import.

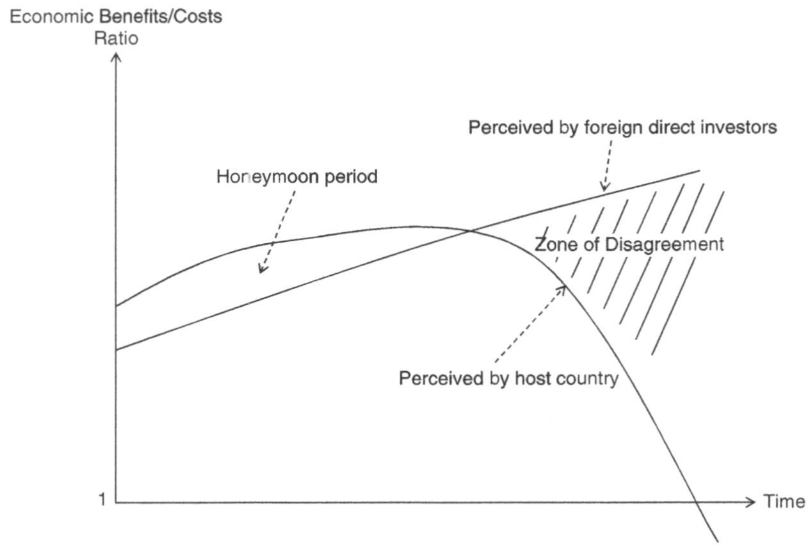

Exhibit 19.1. Dynamics of foreign direct investment's costs/benefits.

Exhibit 19.2. Profit viewed by investor and host country.

Income Statement	Investor's Income Statement (Market Prices)	Shadow Price Adjustments	Host Country's Social Income Statement (Shadow Prices)
Sales of irrigation pumps	200.0	–50.0	150.0
Costs of goods sold	140.0	–40	130.0
Local labor	60.0	–30.0	30.0
Imported raw materials	60.0	+20	80.0
Local raw materials	20.0	+0.0	20.0
Overhead	15.0	+0.0	15.0
Interest	10.0	+1.65	11.65
Remitted abroad	5.0	+1.65	6.65
Paid locally	5.0	...	5.0
Profit	35	...	–6.65

for various sources of market imperfections. Welfare economics gauge the different cash flows according to their *intrinsic* rather than *nominal* value, thereby reflecting their economic scarcity. This is what economists refer to as *shadow prices*. For example, an *overvalued* exchange rate understates the true value of imported parts or subassemblies, which are essentially subsidized by the host country central bank's policy. It also understates the true cost of remitting dividends to the foreign-domiciled parent company. Conversely, exports revenues are understated if the exchange rate is overvalued. Tariff duties protecting the project's output price also distort its true contribution to the host country. Increasingly, multilateral advising and lending institutions such as the International Finance Corporation encourage recipient countries to adjust this type of cost/benefits analysis by substituting shadow prices for nominal market values.

Numerical illustration

Black & Decker — the US multinational of handheld power tools — is negotiating with the government of Bangladesh for an assembly plant to manufacture handheld irrigation pumps. Exhibit 19.2 shows the future plant's pro forma income statement in Bangladeshi taka (BDT) prepared under current market conditions (see column 2). At net earnings of BDT 35 million, the project is clearly profitable.

However, the Bangladeshi Ministry of Trade and Investment revisits the proposed project and makes adjustments to the income statement reflecting price distortions due to tariff protection (33% ad valorem), exchange rate overvaluation, and the opportunity cost of factors of production. Tariff protection allows Black & Decker to sell its irrigation pumps for 33% more than it would if it were directly competing with imports. The projected revenue is discounted accordingly to BDT 200 million/(1 + 0.33) = BDT 150 million. The currently 33% overvalued[11] taka BDT 75 = US$1 is reset at its purchasing power parity rate of BDT 100 = US$1, which increases the cost of imported parts (see column 3 in Exhibit 19.2). Imported parts will show an increase of 33% when restated at the PPP exchange rate and so will interest payments to foreign lenders. Assembly workers will be hired from a pool of employed labor at half the wages offered by Black & Decker and therefore have a 50% opportunity cost.

In sum, the project shows a much lower return when proper adjustments have been made for price distortions. The project, which would appear profitable and beneficial to Bangladesh when appraised in private-sector metrics, now becomes unprofitable and detrimental to the host country. Clearly, Black & Decker needs to reengineer its proposal by (1) pricing below the cost of imported substitutes, and (2) finding locally procured parts and subassemblies.

SUMMARY

1. Most small to medium-sized firms whose sales scope is domestic will stumble into exports sales. A product inquiry from a foreign distributor or a department store triggered by web advertising or manning a kiosk at an international fair may result in a foreign sale. Having discovered the potential for export sales, the firm would first want to repeat its foreign sale and secure a foothold in this export market. This may be achieved by subcontracting the entire exporting process to an exports management company or by directly contracting with a foreign distributor. Ultimately the exporter may want to better control its export market by establishing its own sales subsidiary.
2. International licensing refers to contractual arrangements whereby a domestic firm — the *licensor* — makes available its intangible assets such as patents, technological know-how, trade secrets, or trademarks to a foreign company — the *licensee* — in return for the payment of royalties.
3. International franchising is a form of licensing whereby the franchisor licenses a business system and other property rights such as brand names — rather than technology — to a foreign firm (the franchisee) in exchange for the periodic payment of royalties.
4. Country risk refers to uncertainty about the host country's *rules of the game* toward foreign direct investors. Of particular concern to investors are macropolitical risk, ownership/control risk, operating risk, and transfer risk.
5. Hedging country risk is achieved *ex ante* by negotiating an investment agreement with the host country and/or *ex post* by purchasing political risk insurance against expropriation, currency inconvertibility, or blocked funds.
6. What investors often neglect to do is understand how the host country gauges the investment impact on its national income and balance of payments. How is the costs/benefits ratio to the host country changing over the life of the prospective investment? By adopting the host country's metrics and first measuring its projected impact, the investor is better able to communicate and negotiate with host country officials the implementation modalities of the proposed investments and presumably to better manage its exposure to country risk.
7. A proposed investment's *nominal value added* as measured by private-sector firms is typically adjusted by host countries for externalities, such as pollution cleanup costs or price distortions induced by currency over- or undervaluation and tariff barriers.

QUESTIONS FOR DISCUSSION

1. Why do firms often follow a sequential strategy in entering foreign markets?
2. Discuss the different challenges facing an exporting firm.
3. What are the pros and cons of international licensing as a mode of foreign market entry?

11 (PPP rate – overvalued rate)/overvalued rate = (100 – 75)/75 = 0.33. See the appendix to Chapter 2 for a discussion of purchasing power parity. Bangladesh had suffered from cumulative inflation over the past several years that had not been compensated by a commensurate devaluation of the taka, hence the 33 percent rate of overvaluation.

4. What are the key elements that a licensing contract should include? What are the clauses that may be the most difficult to enforce?
5. What are the differences between licensing and franchising?
6. Identify the key motivations for foreign direct investment.
7. How do host countries gauge the costs and benefits of foreign direct investments over the life of a project? Why should foreign direct investors understand how such analysis is carried out and the results it delivers?
8. Define country risk. Compare the exposure to country risk faced by an exporter, a licensor, a franchisor, and a foreign direct investor. How can such firms mitigate their exposure to country risk?

INTERNET EXERCISES

9. **Political Risk Insurance (intermediate).** Access the Overseas Private Insurance Corporation website www.opic.org and find the different risks that US firms can cover through OPIC insurance programs. Are all foreign countries covered by OPIC insurance programs?
10. **World Bank's Political Risk Insurance (intermediate).** Access the World Bank's Multilateral Investment Guarantee Agency website www.miga.org and identify the different risks that businesses can cover through MIGA insurance programs. Under what conditions are projects eligible for direct or indirect financing from/through MIGA?
11. **Lloyd's of London Insurance Market (advanced).** Access the Llyod's of London website www.llyod.com and identify the different types of political risks that it can insure. What is uniquely different about the Llyod's of London as compared with public — government or multilateral — and private insurers?

REFERENCES

Dixon, Jay and Paul Alexander Haslam. 2016. "Does the Quality of Investment Protection Affect FDI Flows to developing Countries? Evidence from Latin America." *The World Economy* 39(8): 1–29

Fladmoe-Lindquist, Karen, and Laurent L. Jacque. 1995. "Control Modes in International Service Operations: The Propensity to Franchise." *Management Science* (July).

Root, Franklin R. 1994. *Entry Strategies for International Markets*. New York: Lexington Books.

Root, Franklin R. 1994. *International Trade and Investment*. 7th ed. Cincinnati, OH: South-Western.

Rummel, R.J. and David Heenan. 1978. "How Multinationals Analyze Political Risk." *Harvard Business Review* 56: 67–76.

Salacuse, Jeswald W. 2013. *The Three Laws of International Investment: National, Contractual, and International Frameworks for Foreign Capital*. Oxford University Press.

CASE STUDY 19.1. CARREFOUR'S INDIAN ENTRY STRATEGY

> *It is the last and a very big frontier, Brazil is done, China is done. India is the last Shangri-La of retail. Where will Tesco and Wal-Mart get their growth?*
>
> —Sunil B. Mittal, chairman and managing director, Bharti Enterprises Ltd.

Albert Montgolfier is the deputy head of Carrefour's strategic planning department. He has been charged with a review of Carrefour's options with respect to the Indian market and would submit his preliminary recommendations to Carrefour's board meeting next April 2007. India had been on Carrefour's radar for some time now and, as late as 2004, Carrefour had been close to entering the Indian market through franchising but decided to defer any strategic move. Bharti Enterprise recent announcement, in late November 2006, of a large scale joint venture with WalMart[12] changed the competitive landscape in a major way and Albert knew that Carrefour could not defer and temporize for ever as time was of essence. For "Big Box" retailers — the likes of Walmart, Ahold, Tesco or Carrefour — India was the last uncharted frontier. Indeed with more than 1.1 billion people, half of them 25 years

12 According to Sunil Mittal "Government policy allows foreign equity in back-end wholesale, logistics and real estate, so we'll do a joint venture partnership in those areas and we will own the retail business 100% until the government allows FDI there and then we'll do a joint venture with our partner."

or younger, an economy growing at an annual rate of 8–10% and no major retail chain to speak of, India represented in 2006 a US$250 billion market potential widely expected to double within 10 years. Retail was estimated to contribute 14% of India's GDP employing 21 million people and was indeed a mainstay of the Indian economy — only second to its agricultural sector.

Yet, India's retail sector was highly fragmented with as many as 12 million outlets — owner-operated general or convenience stores also known as *"kirana"* shops which included handcart and pavement vendors. This unorganized sector accounted for more than 95% of Indian retail and generally operated in floor space of 500 square feet or less.

The dearth of organized major retail chains when viewed in a context of a booming economy and an emerging middle class numbering a quarter of a billion people provided a tantalizing opportunity for both domestic firms and multinational retail giants except that India was closed to Foreign Direct Investment (FDI) in retailing. Yet India, long shackled by an over-zealous bureaucracy, had since 1991 steadily relaxed restrictions on FDI in most sectors of its economy including real estate and wholesale trading– but not retailing — which raised speculation as to if and when entry by major foreign retailers would be allowed. An encouraging omen was the lifting of restrictions for single-brand retailers.

Indian firms for their part were in the early stage of major investment to take advantage of legal entry barriers which — for the time being — kept at bay formidable multinational retailers. For example, the Tata group owned the West Side group and was developing a retail chain for consumer goods under the name of Croma. Croma was partly a joint venture with Woolworth which owned the wholesale operation (allowed under FDI law) and supplied the retail stores owned by the Tata group. In a similar vein, Reliance Industries announced in 2006 an ambitious plan to invest US$5.5 billion over five years to open 1,000 hypermarkets and 1,500 convenience stores.

As in the cases of all major markets "Big Box" retailers were perceived by existing "moms-and-pops" corner stores as a tsunami which would devastate the sector and throw out of work millions of people. Carrefour had waged the same battle over and over again starting with France in the 1960s before turning to similarly atomistic retail sectors in Spain, Brazil, Thailand, China and many others. For public authorities the policy conundrum was not easy to resolve: on the one hand modern large scale retailers brought economies of scale efficiency gains to distribution and lower prices to end consumers by streamlining the supply chain. For food products greater sanitation through a modern cold chain for fresh produces and much reduced waste were obvious welfare benefits for the consumer. On the other hand, large scale retailers would displace millions of "moms and pops" store adding to the 40 millions or so of unemployed. Large scale demonstrations by threatened shopkeepers would only become more militant as more pressure was being applied on the Congress party currently in power.

Even if FDI restrictions were lifted Carrefour was well aware of the daunting hurdles that it would face especially in the food sector which accounted for approximately half of its revenue. Absence of modern logistics and a dilapidated infrastructure would be a major part of the challenge. With lacking proper storage facilities and refrigerated trucks, the world's second largest producer of fresh produces was estimated to lose to spoilage and waste as much as a third of its output.[13] To make matter worse, India was weighted down by a byzantine system of government-mandated middlemen who deployed an army of agents collecting various transit fees along the way from the original farmer to the final consumer.[14] Needless to say, this cascade of fees levied from the farm to the retail store shelf increased the cost of the product as much as five-fold. Would Carrefour be able to exploit the same competitive advantage that it had honed in other markets starting in France in the 1960? One of its recent success stories was Thailand for which financials are provided in the case appendix.

Could Carrefour defer yet again its entry in the Indian market or should it devise a modular entry strategy which would allow to position itself for the day when restrictions on FDI in retailing would be finally lifted?

---

13 There were fewer than 5000 cold storage facilities providing enough capacity for 10% of what India produced.

14 Nationwide there were approximately 415,000 government licensed traders and 210,000 licensed commission agents who hawk farmers' goods on their behalf and take a cut of the transaction.

Balance Sheet (in millions of Thai Baht)			
2006		**2006**	
Current assets		**Liabilities**	
Cash and securities	2,960	Trade payables	29,836
Trade receivables	540	Other current liabilities	10,725
Inventories	12,310	Long-term borrowings	7,840
Other current assets	15,034	Other long-term liabilities	3,604
Capital assets		**Owners' equity**	**24,342**
Fixed assets	33,671		
Intangible assets	6,754		
Financial assets	5,078		
Total assets	**76,347**	**Liabilities and owners' equity**	**76,347**

Notes:

1. Mostly loans to other companies, including loans to nonconsolidated affiliated companies and deferred and recoverable taxes.
2. Short-term debts and accruals

Income Statement (in millions of Thai Baht)	
Year 2006	
Net sales	**154,905**
Cost of sales	(125,072)
Gross margin from operations	**29,833**
Selling, general, and administrative expenses	(22,184)
Depreciation, amortization and provisions	(4,020)
Financial income, net of expenses	1,609
Income before taxes	**5,238**
Income taxes	(1,637)
Income adjustments (due to consolidation of accounts)	(362)
Net income	**3,289**

CASE STUDY QUESTIONS

1. Referring to Carrefour's financials for Thailand (see appendix) please compute the Days Sales Outstanding ratios for A/Rs and its payment deferral ratio for A/Ps. What is Carrefour's cash conversion cycle? What does it mean for Carrefour' working capital requirement and financing needs? How would you characterize Carrefour's competitive strategy in Thailand?
2. Would Carrefour be able to replicate its strategy in India? What do you see as the principal obstacles?
3. Would you advise Carrefour to enter India now or await a full liberalization of FDI for retailers?
4. Should Carrefour decide to enter India now what mode(s) of entry would you recommend?
5. What are the costs and benefits to the Indian economy of Carrefour's entry in the retailing industry as a foreign direct investor?

20

International Capital Budgeting

Merchants have no country . . . the mere spot they stand on does not constitute so strong an attachment as that from which they draw their gains.
—Thomas Jefferson

One of the most vital decisions firms make is the capital investment decision — selecting value-creating investment projects that will increase the current market value of the firm. As the firm expands the geographical scope of its activities, it will consider entering foreign markets, retooling foreign assembly operations, offshoring, or even acquiring foreign businesses. The primary motivation for these important decisions is undoubtedly strategic, but ultimately each "go" decision will have to be validated by a feasibility study that includes traditional financial analysis. This is a complex exercise fraught with many more unknowns. This chapter develops a framework for directly comparing contending foreign investment proposals in a way that systematically incorporates the many complicating factors that uniquely shape each project under review.

By reading this chapter you will understand:

- What the foreign direct investment process is within which capital budgeting is embedded.
- What the differences are between valuing international projects and valuing domestic ventures.
- How to identify relevant cash flows for an international project.
- Why it is crucial to value the project in the host country's *local* currency terms first and then in the investor's *reference* currency.
- What the rationale is for discounting *residual equity cash flows* (ECFs) at the firm's *equity cost of capital.*
- How to account for the many risk factors likely to impact the project.

THE FOREIGN DIRECT INVESTMENT DECISION-MAKING PROCESS

Multinationals rarely stumble into specific foreign projects. Instead, they rely on a systematic *search-and-discovery* process before they choose specific projects to evaluate in greater detail. At its simplest, multinationals strategize about where they want to be one, two, or five years from now, having first taken stock of where they are currently. Think of a 3D global strategy space in which the firm can map its international trajectory in terms of (1) where (which country), (2) how (mode of entry and operation), and (3) what (which product line). For example, 3M — the US nondurable consumer multinational — may have a marketing subsidiary in Vietnam for office products only (i.e., tapes, Post-it Notes, etc.) and be aiming to establish a manufacturing minority joint venture for its medical imaging business within three years; what 3M does for Vietnam, it will also do for another 120 national markets. Once the 3D global strategy space is fully populated, the challenge is to transform it into actionable investment proposals:

- *Phase I: Global scanning.* Multinationals will rely on "listening posts" or "data-gathering antennae" — in effect a business intelligence system. These may be law or accounting firms with which the multinational has a retainer agreement, or they could be investment banks, distributors, and licensees. These are partners who will be asked to do a simple task: keep their eyes and ears open for local businesses that may be up for sale, firms in an adjacent line of business that may be desirable joint-venture partners, and so on. At this early stage, the multinational is interested in generating a large pool of somewhat unstructured investment proposals from an opportunity set as global as possible. It is not yet interested in studying any of them in depth.

- *Phase II: Ranking*. The next step is to slim down this long list of viable investment proposals without expending unduly large resources. Often multinationals rely on a simple screening algorithm to eliminate most proposals from further analysis. Since the pool may at any given time include more than 100 ill-defined and ill-formulated proposals, the algorithm will focus on highly discriminating parameters.

One cluster of such parameters is generally referred to as *multiplicative stopping variables* that take on a value of 0 or 1, depending on whether the project should be stopped (overall score brought down to 0). For example, an investor may not consider projects in countries that allow minority joint ventures only; in this case, a project requiring a minority ownership position would receive a 0 score for its country ownership/control variable, which as a multiplicative parameter would bring the project score to 0 and effectively remove this proposal from the pool. Local procurement rules, political risk index failing to exceed a threshold amount, and others would be examples of stopping variables, which eliminate the project.

The second cluster of *additive variables* will provide an actual ranking. These parameters include size of the market, annual rate of growth, degree of industry concentration, and availability of concessionary financing, with each variable being assigned a score from 1 to 5; each variable is in turn weighted according to its presumed contribution to the overall attractiveness of the project. For example, a scoring function built on two stopping and three additive variables would be formulated as

$$\text{SCORE} = s_1 s_2(\alpha a_1 + \beta a_2 + \gamma a_3) \tag{20.1}$$

where a_1, a_2, and a_3 are additive variables ranging from a low of 1 to a high of 5, and s_1, s_2 are stopping variables taking on value of 0 or 1.

The weights α, β, and γ range from 1% to 99%, adding up to 100%, and can be changed to see how the ranking varies. If the ranking is relatively invariant to changing weights, the ranking will be easily adopted; however, if the ranking were to change markedly with different weights, further analysis is necessary. Thus, this scoring rule allows for a rough ranking of the entire pool and yields a short list of desirable projects warranting further study. Depending on the size of the multinational, the slimmed-down list may be as short as five to seven major foreign market entry proposals or may reach as many as 20 to 25. See a Carrefour algorithm in International Corporate Finance in Practice 20.1.

- *Phase III: Feasibility study*. The investor now commits significant resources to an in-depth evaluation or *feasibility study* of each proposal designated as a finalist by the ranking phase. Market surveys, pilot studies, and product testing will be prerequisites for a full-blown financial analysis. As a result, detailed pro forma sales forecasts will be generated to anchor the actual valuation exercise; logistical and production surveys will verify the feasibility of the project proposal and facilitate cost projections. Ultimately, the feasibility study will deliver financial metrics gauging the project's attractiveness, such as its payback period, its net present value (NPV), or its internal rate of return (IRR). This is the *"go or no-go"* decision that concludes the process.

A PRIMER ON EVALUATING INVESTMENT OPPORTUNITIES

The basics of evaluating investment opportunities, also known as capital budgeting, involves three steps:

1. Estimating relevant cash flows.
2. Calculating a *figure of merit* or metrics — a summary statistic quantifying the attractiveness of the project under review.
3. Comparing the figure of merit against an acceptance criterion — the so-called "go or no-go" decision.

The reader will recall from his or her first corporate finance course several contending yet widely used metrics — such as the *payback period* or average rate of return — but more likely metrics built on discounted cash flows (DCFs) to yield the NPV or the IRR of the investment proposal under review. Clearly, taking into account the time value of money is a far better metric, but it requires an appropriate discount rate. This discount rate is the investor's cost of capital. More specifically, DCFs may focus on free cash flows (FCFs) discounted at the firm's weighted average cost of capital (WACC).

INTERNATIONAL CORPORATE FINANCE IN PRACTICE 20.1

Ranking Algorithm

Consider, for example, the case of Carrefour S.A. — the French retailer — that has been eyeing Eastern Europe for possible market entry in Russia, Belarus, Ukraine, and Romania. These are attractive target countries that have been under the retailer's radar. Specifically, Carrefour would use two stopping variables and three additive variables for the screening algorithm:

Stopping variables: (1) s_1 = currency convertibility for remitting royalties, management fees, and dividends: $s_1 = 1$ if convertible in the past three years and $s_1 = 0$ if unconvertible at any time during the past three years, and (2) s_2 = country risk notation: $s_2 = 1$ for investment grades equal to or higher than BBB, and $s_2 = 0$ for below investment grade BBB.

Additive variables: (1) a_1 = GDP annual growth with coefficient of $\alpha = 30\%$: $a_1 = 3$ if GDP growth rate > 5% for the past 3 years, $a_1 = 2$ if between 3 and 5%, $a_1 = 1$ if between 1 and 3%, and $a_1 = 0$ if <1%.

(2) a_2 = Car ownership/100 citizens with coefficient of $\beta = 50\%$ $a_2 = 3$ if >25/100, $a_2 = 2$ if between 15/100 and 25/100, $a_2 = 1$ if between 5/100 and 15/100, and $a_2 = 0$ if less than 5/100.

(3) a_3 = Country risk notation with a coefficient of $\gamma = 20\%$: $a_3 = 3$ if AAA, $a_3 = 2$ if AA, $a_3 = 1$ if A, and $a_3 = 0$ for any grade below A.

Carrefour would rank the four Eastern European countries as follows:

$$\text{SCORE}_{\text{Russia}} = 1 \times 1(0.3 \times 3 + 0.5 \times 1 + 0.2 \times 0) = 1.4$$

$$\text{SCORE}_{\text{Belarus}} = 0 \times 0(0.3 \times 2 + 0.5 \times 0 + 0.2 \times 0) = 0$$

$$\text{SCORE}_{\text{Ukraine}} = 1 \times 1(0.3 \times 3 + 0.5 \times 2 + 0.2 \times 1) = 2.1$$

$$\text{SCORE}_{\text{Romania}} = 1 \times 1(0.3 \times 2 + 0.5 \times 2 + 0.2\ '\ 2) = 2.0$$

and may decide to investigate Ukraine further. The algorithm would be fed updated information continuously, thus providing a rough yet inexpensive ordering of potential target markets. For large MNCs, the scoring would encompass as many as 75 countries at any time over several major product lines; thus, the ranking algorithm may cover 75 × 5 = 375 potential investment opportunities if the multinational has five major product lines.

$$NPV = \sum_{t=1}^{T} \frac{FCF(t)}{(1+WACC)^t} \tag{20.2a}$$

or on residual equity cash-flows (ECFs) to shareholders discounted at the firm's cost of leveraged equity cost of capital (LEC).

$$NPV = \sum_{t=1}^{T} \frac{ECF(t)}{(1+LEC)^t} \tag{20.2b}$$

The basic difference between these two approaches is the treatment of financing costs. In the first approach, based on FCFs, financing costs are not charged against operating cash flows; instead they are accounted for in the debt component of the WACC nested in the denominator of the NPV formula. Clearly this is a simplistic assumption, which assumes among other things that the capital structure of the project is invariant over its life (the proportion of debt in overall financing remains constant) and the tax rate at which interest expenses are tax-deductible does not change over the life of the project. This is almost never true!

The second approach, based on residual ECFs to shareholders, charges specific financing costs against operating cash flows and uses the LEC as a discount rate. It certainly allows for a more accurate

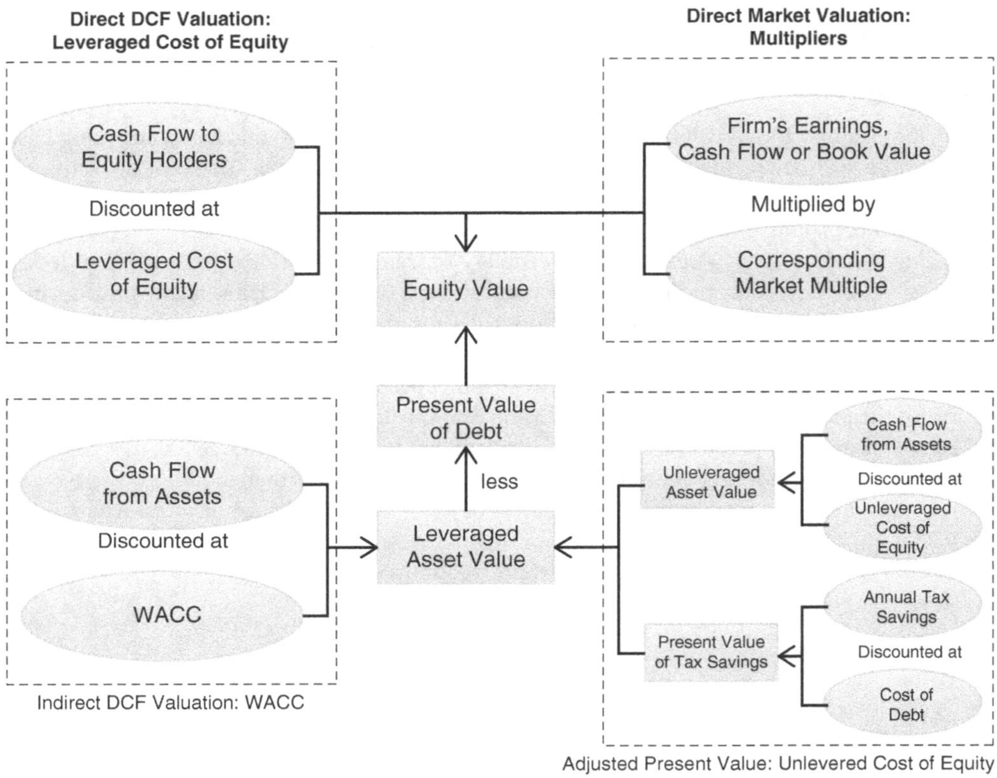

Exhibit 20.1. Alternative valuation methods.

accounting of the project's debt financing, as its costs generally vary over its life.[1]

Exhibit 20.1 offers a synoptic summary of these two valuation models — lower left-hand side for FCFs/WACC and upper left-hand corner for ECFs/LCE (leveraged cost of equity). It also includes *valuation by comparables* based on ratios such as price/earnings or market value/book value (upper right-hand corner), as well as *adjusted present value* (APV in lower right-hand corner), which breaks down projects between operating cash flows (discounted at an all-equity cost of capital) and side benefits such as a tax shield from debt financing or concessionary financing (both of which are discounted at the lower cost of debt). The APV method is further discussed in the appendix to this chapter.

1 Under this approach, the capital structure of the project may also be changing, which would require an adjustment of the equity cost of capital since the leveraged beta used in computing the cost of equity will also change. See Chapter 22 on project finance for an illustration of this method.

WHAT IS DIFFERENT ABOUT EVALUATING FOREIGN INVESTMENT PROPOSALS?

Evaluation of foreign projects is complicated by the idiosyncrasies of the host country's contextual environment. Foreign direct investors may be subject to a whole series of operating constraints — such as price controls, local procurement rules, discriminatory taxation, and exchange controls — that would be unheard-of in their home country. Indeed, such constraints will uniquely impact the project's cash flows and will have to be carefully woven into its analysis. To better capture such intricacies, a four-step analytical framework is proposed next: (1) graphical map of the *noncontrollable* contextual forces shaping the project's cash flows, (2) cash-flow projections in *local* currency terms from the project/subsidiary perspective, (3) cash-flow projections from the parent's perspective in *reference* currency terms, and (4) risk analysis. We start with a general discussion, but the reader should keep in mind the elaborate case discussion to follow, which illustrates the key principles presented in this section: Renault — the French

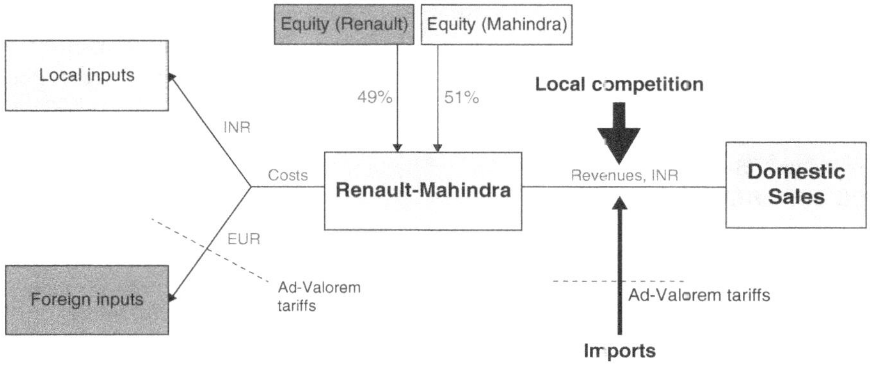

Exhibit 20.2. How contextual forces shape local currency cash flows.

automobile manufacturer — is contemplating entry in the Indian market to manufacture and distribute passenger cars.

Step 1: Mapping contextual forces shaping project's cash flows

To better grasp the strategic focus of the project, it is recommended to start with a graphical mapping of the project's cash flows to understand how noncontrollable factors will shape them over time:

- On the *revenue side*, identify key competitors: Are they domestic firms or are they foreign-based import competitors? Are these firms' cost structures similar to our project's cost structure? Is pricing subject to government price controls?
- On the *cost side*, identify where inputs are sourced from and whether they are subject to local procurement rules. For domestically procured inputs, are they subject to price controls? Or if they are imported, what are the tariff duties or quotas currently in place? Is the exchange rate fairly valued, or is it overvalued, thereby providing a de facto subsidy to foreign sourced inputs or to import competitors?

This preliminary exercise is similar to the economic exposure analysis presented in Chapter 18, although the analysis here is broadened beyond the impact of exchange rates and inflation on the firm's local and reference currency cash flows to include other contextual factors (see Exhibit 20.2 for an illustration in the context of the Renault joint venture with Mahindra & Mahindra).

Step 2: Forecast project's cash flows in local currency terms

All too often foreign investment analysis is directly prepared in the investor's reference currency. Although this is clearly the ultimate objective of such an analysis, skipping the local currency cash-flow analysis amounts to making simplistic assumptions about how the local reference currency exchange rate will behave over the life of the investment — in effect, it assumes that today's exchange rate when the project is first analyzed is a good estimate of future exchange rates.[2] It also distorts sensitivity or multiple-scenario analysis, which incorporates changing exchange rates over the life of the project for both its revenue and its cost side. Indeed, such exchange rate changes typically impact the project's local currency cash flows *asymmetrically*. This is why it is critical to forecast a project's cash flows in local currency terms first.

Before jumping to numerical pro forma cash flows, it is also recommended to model the cash-flow statement by explicitly incorporating in both revenue and cost cash flows different contextual factors — in effect the graphical mapping and qualitative analysis of step 1. For example, if a project sells exclusively in the domestic market in direct competition with imports, a 30% currency devaluation may provide a significant boost to local sales. Thus, the exchange rate variable should be factored into the revenue cash flow to show how sales revenue is benefiting from a 30% depreciation through the price elasticity of local demand (imports become more expensive and price-elastic local demand will favor the domestic product). The same project may depend on imported subassemblies for which tariff duties and the exchange rate can be identified as defining exogenous variables that would subsequently allow

2 Exchange rate forecasts over the life of the investment could be used. Typically, such analysis incorporates the exchange rate prevailing today when the pro forma financials are prepared instead of incorporating exchange rate forecasts.

for simulation of this cost factor, as the ad valorem duty may be reduced, and the exchange rate devalued in the early life of the project.

Step 3: Restate local currency subsidiary/project's cash flows in reference currency

At its simplest, all that is required is to convert projected local currency cash flows into the investor/parent company's reference currency using exchange rate forecasts. Appropriate adjustment must also be made for taxation of both a *transfer* nature for cash flows exiting the host country and also at the home country level. What complicates this third step is that what matters is the project's *incremental* contribution to the multinational investor's entire activity portfolio of activities. In other words, what is needed is a careful assessment of the firm's global *cash flows with the project* minus its *cash flows without the project*, or what is referred to as incremental cash flows. The project's local currency cash flows as assessed in step 2 are a good place to start but it requires a number of adjustments.

- *Sales cannibalization.* Existing sales by sister subsidiaries to the new host country may be displaced as the new project comes on line. Thus, pro forma sales of the new project may overestimate the actual sales contribution by the proposed project to the multinational investor.
- *Incremental sales by sister-affiliates.* The project may benefit from additional sales of parts or subassemblies to the new subsidiary and thereby sister-affiliates may be able to reap economies of scale due to longer production runs.
- *Royalties and management fees.* These fees paid by the new subsidiary to the parent company are tax-deductible expenses to the local subsidiary, but they are net income to the parent.

Exchange rate forecasts

Local currency cash flows are restated into the reference currency by applying an exchange rate forecast for the corresponding period. Chapter 15 on exchange rate forecasting established how treacherous such an exercise may be. The fact that forecasts over the long term are required only compounds the difficulty. If the host country benefits from a relatively well-developed bond market with long maturities, forward rates are reasonable forecasts to use. Typically, long-term forward rates are not quoted directly, but synthetic forward rates can be derived from the interest rate parity theorem. As an illustration, assume a US multinational is evaluating a project in Thailand: If the current spot dollar price of one baht (THB) is THB 32 = US\$1, and the 7 year interest rate on US and Thai government bonds are 5 and 8.5%, respectively, then the 7 year forward rate can be derived as:

$$F(7) = \frac{1}{32} \times \frac{(1+0.05)^7}{(1+0.085)^7}$$

$$F(7) = \frac{1}{43} \text{ or THB 43=US\$1}$$

Similarly, the forward rate for years 2, 3, … , 6 would be derived using the same formula with the appropriate exponent. For many emerging market countries, however, bond markets are still embryonic and interest rates are available for only very short-term maturities; it will then be necessary to posit forecasts based on subjective assumptions about the future rate of inflation in the target country to generate a purchasing power parity–based exchange rate forecast.

Taxation

As mentioned before, taxation is a three-tiered sequence for an international project. The host country will tax the project but often offer tax inducements in the form of time-limited tax holidays: Local-currency cash flows are adjusted accordingly in step 2. Transfer taxes, such as withholding tax on dividend remittances, as well as royalties or other management fees, are reflected in reference-currency cash flows as shown in step 3. Last but not least, the investor's home country also taxes remittances but typically grants credit for taxes already paid and may allow consolidation with other foreign source income generated by the investor's other international activities (see further discussion of international taxation in Chapter 25).

Step 4: Discounting and risk analysis

After-tax reference-currency cash flows should be discounted at the investor's worldwide leveraged cost of equity capital. The NPV of the base case of the foreign investment proposal should then be adjusted for risk in two ways:

1. Add a risk premium to the firm's cost of equity capital. The last section of this chapter develops a methodology for computing the project-specific risk premium. The parent's after-tax

INTERNATIONAL CORPORATE FINANCE IN PRACTICE 20.2

Renault's Foray in Romania to Build Logans

As part of its strategy to become a major car producer in Eastern Europe, Renault invested €211 million to acquire a majority interest in Dacia — Romania's only car manufacturer — to build Logans. The investment called for Renault to start producing as many as 100,000 Logans annually (with 25% earmarked to neighboring East European countries) at an old Dacia factory located some 120 km northwest of Bucharest in the Arges. The Logan is a modern, robust, entry-level vehicle aimed at emerging markets and priced very moderately at €5,000.

In addition to snaring a dominant role in Romania's 100,000 cars a year domestic market, Renault is also positioning itself to take advantage of Romania's relatively low wages and to use its Dacia plant as an export platform. "I can assure you, we're not going into Romania just for this initial assembly project," says Robert Genet, president of Renault International. The agreement marks an important step in Renault's aggressive eastern expansion. Renault had already invested nearly €500 million in Hungary for an engine plant and small-scale assembly operation from which Dacia would source its engines at the equivalent of €1,250 (but actually denominated in Hungarian forint — freely floating against the euro). Renault's main competitor in the Dacia deal was France's PSA Peugeot Citroen; earlier on, Italy's Fiat S.p.A. had also been interested.

net incremental ECFs based on the most likely scenario should be discounted at the *cost of equity + risk premium*.

2. Adjust cash flows themselves for specific types of country risk. Local-currency cash flows should be adjusted for (1) *operational risk* (any change in the competitive and contextual environment that will impact the project, such as price controls, local procurement requirements, labor laws, antipollution regulation, etc.); (2) *expropriation risk* (sometimes creeping but real), which directly impacts the equity position of the investor and would be captured by the terminal value; and (3) *transfer risk,* which will constrict the smooth flow of royalties, management fees, and dividend remittances from the foreign subsidiary to its parent. Such transfer risk may manifest itself as an increase in withholding taxes or other impediments to the timely payments of remittances, devaluation of the local currency, or even blocked funds due to inconvertibility of the local currency.

These cash-flow adjustments and risk analyses can be structured in several nonexclusive ways:

- *Break-even analysis* focuses on one key environmental variable[3] at a time — annual percentage increase or decrease in sales, annual percentage cost overrun due to local inflation in the cost of goods sold (COGS) as a percentage of sales, annual exchange rate devaluation — and asks the following question: What is the threshold/break-even value of this variable that brings the project's NPV down to zero?
- *Multiple scenarios* are defined as plausible alternative schematic futures markedly different from the base case scenario. For each scenario the project's NPV is computed and compared to the base case scenario's NPV. If plausible, the investor may decide to reengineer the project differently to mitigate the bluntness of such adverse scenarios. This would be a form of hedging, which comes at a cost to the investor.

Reaching a decision

Investment decisions of strategic importance, such as entering a new market (see International Corporate Finance in Practice 20.2) or building a plant in a foreign country, would typically be made by the firm's board of directors. The board will carefully consider the results of the project's financial analysis and will rely on its valuation model as a vehicle for simulation and discussion purposes rather than as a solution provider. This is why it is especially important to make the architecture of the valuation model as transparent and objective as possible and to separate it from cash-flow forecasts themselves, which are by

3 A more formal approach to identifying variables that are good candidates for break-even analysis is to take the partial derivative of the project NPV = $f(x, y, z)$ with respect to all exogenous variables x, y, and z and to focus on variables to which the project NPV is most sensitive.

nature more subjective. By submitting the project to a variety of stress tests, the board will gain a better grasp of its vulnerability under downside scenarios.

CASE STUDY: RENAULT INVESTS IN INDIA

French automobile manufacturer Renault was considering entry into the Indian car market through a 49/51% joint venture with Mahindra & Mahindra (M&M), the Indian truck, sport-utility vehicle, and motorcycle manufacturer. The proposal called for building a new plant in Nashik, close to Mumbai, with a capacity of 50,000 vehicles a year by 2009, to be increased to 110,000 by 2013 (with increments of 15,000 per year after the first year).

The construction would start in 2008, last for one year, and cost 20 billion Indian rupees (INR), or approximately €500 million. The cost would be financed by INR 6 billion in equity (shared between Renault [49%] and M&M [51%]) and by INR 14 billion in debt. Subsidized financing would be provided by the State of Gujarat in the amount of INR 7 billion, at the rate of 7% over five years. The remaining INR 7 billion would have to be borrowed in the euro debt market at 6% per annum. The initial capital expenditures could be depreciated for income-tax purposes over a 10 year schedule.

India requires a 40% local content, and Renault would import engines and powertrains from its Spanish plant in Valencia at the cost of €1,333 (CIF),[4] subject to a 20% ad valorem tariff. Renault's plant in Valencia would benefit through economies of scale from a reduction of 1.5% in COGS in its €200 million revenues. Labor cost would account for 20% of the final INR sale price of the Logan. Renault would be paid a licensing fee of 5% per car sold from 2009 onward and would repatriate 49% of INR ECF in the form of cash dividends.

The Logan is a modern, robust, entry-level vehicle aimed at emerging markets and priced very moderately at €5,000 or INR 200,000 in India; it will be in direct competition with the well-established Maruti,[5] which sells for US €4,000 or INR 160,000. Renault said it expected the Indian market to grow to more than two million vehicles per year by 2012. For 2006, Indians bought 1.14 million vehicles. According to an automotive expert, "The Indian market is all about small cars and getting the price right," and he predicted that Renault's possible entry could heat up the competition in the low-cost sedan and hatchback market that Maruti has dominated.

After an initial investment of INR 20 billion, annual capital expenditures were expected to amount to 50% of each year's accounting depreciation; working capital requirement would amount to 15% of sales revenues. The exchange rates prevalent at the time of the initiation of the project (2008 year-end) were €1 = US$1.33 = INR 40.

Step 1: Mapping out the architecture of project's local currency cash flows

Exhibit 20.2 depicts the cash flows of the proposed 49/51 joint venture between Renault and Mahindra & Mahindra. The revenue side (right-hand side of the graph) shows projected sales revenue in INR with strong domestic competition from Suzuki and others, as well as increasing imports. On the cost side, note the breakdown of cash outflows to domestic sources for locally procured inputs, subject to Indian inflation, and of foreign-sourced components, including subassemblies such as power trains imported from Spain, subject to the changing €/INR exchange rate $S(t)$ and ad valorem tariff duty (which may be increased or decreased at the will of the Indian government).

Step 2: Forecasting local currency cash flows for stand-alone project

The task is to project annual sales revenue and costs over the period 2008–2013, including the initial investment, the project's annual cash flows during its economic life, and its terminal value in 2013. This is an exercise in financial planning identical to what the reader already learned in his or her first corporate finance class. The forecasting methodology most helpful in such instances is the *percentage-of-sales* forecasting model, which assumes a constant relationship between key cost factors and annual sales revenues.

Initial investment

- Building the manufacturing facility will cost INR 20 billion; plant and equipment will be depreciated over 10 years at the annual rate of

4 Cost, insurance, and freight. The seller is responsible for the cost of shipping up to the destination port and insuring the cargo, and invoices the buyer accordingly. The buyer pays for the cost of merchandise plus insuring it as well as the cost of transportation (freight).

5 Marutis are manufactured by Suzuki in a 54/46% joint venture with the Indian government. Suzuki-controlled Maruti currently has over 50% of the 1.14 million Indian automotive market, down from about 65% 5 years ago and 90% a decade ago.

INR 20 billion/10 = INR 2 billion. Of the INR 20 billion spent in building the plant and purchasing the equipment, INR 6 billion will be provided by equity investment from Renault (49%) and M&M (51%). The balance will be debt financing in the form of a subsidized INR-denominated loan from the State of Gujarat (INR 7 billion) at 7% over five years and a €-denominated term loan at 6% per annum (INR 7 billion).

Annual net income during project life

- *Sales revenues.* The proposed plant will manufacture $q(1) = 50{,}000$ Logans in its first year of operation in 2009 with production ramping up to 110,000 units by 2013. At a price of INR 200,000, sales revenue is equal to unit price $p(1)$ in year 1 times quantity sold $q(1)$ in year 1 or

$$\text{Sales }(1) = p(1) \times q(1) = 200{,}000 \times 50{,}000 = \text{INR 10 billion in 2009}$$

By 2013, sales revenue sales(t) will grow to

$$\text{Sales }(5) = 110{,}000 \times 200{,}000(1 + 0.025)^5 = \text{INR } 24{,}284 \text{ billion}$$

as output increases to 110,000 units. The sales unit price of the Logan reflects annual price increases in line with inflation at 2.5%.[6]

- *Operating expenses* are divided between locally procured parts — subassemblies as well as labor costs amounting to 25% of sales — and imported power trains from Renault's sister-subsidiary in Valencia, Spain. INR-denominated cogs[7] are assumed to rise more slowly than Indian inflation at the annual rate of 1%, whereas €-denominated imports are subjected to an ad-valorem tariff[8] and exchange risk. Domestic cogs(t) are calculated as

$$\text{cogs}(t) = 0.25 \times p(0) \times [1 + 0.01]^t \times q(t)$$

where the third term reflects cumulative inflation after t years over the base year unit price. Imported COGS(t) are similarly calculated as

$$\text{COGS}(t) = 1{,}333 \times q(t) \times (1 + 0.20) \times S_{\text{INR},€}(t)$$

where the base price of €1,333 is adjusted by a 20% ad valorem tariff duty and $S_{\text{INR},€}(t)$ is the INR price of one € when the powertrains are imported.

- *Selling, general, and administrative expenses* (sg&a) are quasi-fixed costs increasing very slowly at the annual rate of 1%:

$$\text{sg\&a}(t) = \text{sg\&a}(1) \times (1 + 0.01)^t$$

The joint venture will also pay a licensing fee (royal) set at 5% of sales to the Renault parent to account for the use of Renault's technology:

$$\text{royal}(t) = 0.05 \times \text{sales}(t)$$

- *Depreciation* is a noncash-flow charge based on straight-line depreciation at the annual rate of

$$\text{dep}(t) = \text{INR 20 billion}/10 = \text{INR 2,000 million}$$

- *Interest expenses* are comprised of an INR-denominated component at the rate of 7% on a principal of INR 7 billion and a €-denominated component at 6% on a €-denominated principal of €7 billion/40:

$$\text{int}(t) = 0.07 \times 7\text{bn} + (0.06 \times 7\text{bn}/40)S_{\text{INR},€}(t)$$

The second interest payment is subject to exchange rate risk because the INR may weaken against the €. $S_{\text{INR},€}(t)$ denotes the INR cost of one € at time t, when the annual interest payment is made.

With corporate income tax rate tax(t) projected at 34% for the life of the project, earnings after tax eat(t) are shown as the "bottom line" of Exhibit 20.3A. It is computed as follows:

$$\text{eat}(t) = [\text{sales}(t) - \text{cogs}(t) - \text{COGS}(t) - \text{sg\&a}(t) - \text{royal}(t) - \text{dep}(t) - \text{int}(t)][1 - \text{tax}(t)] \quad (20.3)$$

Annual equity cash flows during project life

We are now ready to assemble revenues and cost cash flows derived from pro forma income and balance sheet statements (not shown here) in a simple formula showing equity cash flows ecf(t):

$$\text{ecf}(t) = [\text{sales}(t) - \text{cogs}(t) - \text{COGS}(t) - \text{sg\&a}(t) - \text{royal}(t) - \text{int}(t)] \times [1 - \text{tax}(t)] + \text{dep}(t) - \Delta\text{wcr}(t) - \text{capex}(t) \quad (20.4a)$$

where

- *Working capital requirement*, wcr(t), is accounts receivables + inventory −accounts payables and is set at 15% of sales, which means from year to year

6 The Logan's base price is adjusted annually for 2.5% inflation to reach in year t the price of 200,000 $(1 + 0.025)^t$ with $t = 1, 2, \ldots, 5$.

7 Local currency-denominated revenue and costs (such as cogs) are denoted in lowercase whereas costs incurred in foreign currency (€) are denoted by capital letters (such as COGS).

8 An ad valorem tariff duty is a tariff computed on the basis of the value of the imports declared to customs authority. *Ad valorem* is the Latin term for "according to the value."

Exhibit 20.3A. Renault-Mahindra joint venture: Pro forma income statement (INR).

	2008	2009	2010	2011	2012	2013
Sales in '000 units	0	50	65	80	95	110
INR, price per unit[a]	0	200,000	205,000	210,125	215,378	220,763
Sales revenue, million INR	**0**	**10,000**	**13,325**	**16,810**	**20,461**	**24,284**
cogs — domestic at 25.0% of sales[b]	0	2,500	3,365	4,245	5,166	6,132
COGS — imported[c]	0	3,445	4,591	5,791	7,049	8,366
Gross profit	0	4,055	5,370	6,774	8,245	9,786
sg&a[d]	0	1,750	1,768	1,785	1,803	1,821
Royalties at 5.0% of sales	0	500	666	841	1,023	1,214
Depreciation[e]	0	2,000	2,000	2,000	2,000	2,000
EBIT[f]	0	(195)	936	2,148	3,419	4,751
Interest expense on EUR loan @ 6.0%[g]	441	452	464	475	487	499
Interest expense on INR loan @ 7.0%[h]	490	490	490	490	490	490
EBT[i]	(931)	(1,137)	(18)	1,183	2,442	3,761
Taxes at 34%	0	0	0	402	830	1,279
Earnings after tax	**(931)**	**(1,137)**	**(18)**	**781**	**1,612**	**2,483**
Future $S_{INR,EUR}(t)$[j]	42.03	43.08	44.15	45.26	46.39	47.55

Notes: [a] Price per unit increase at 2.5% per annum.
[b] Domestic cogs is 25.0% of sales and increases at 1.00% per annum.
[c] COGS subject to 20.0% ad valorem tariff at unhedged exchange rates.
[d] Increases at a rate of 1.0% per annum.
[e] 10-year straight-line depreciation.
[f] Earnings before interest and taxes.
[g] Interest on principal of INR 7.0 billion.
[h] Interest on principal of €7bn/40.
[i] Earnings before taxes.
[j] Spot INR price of 1 euro increases at the rate of 2.5% per annum.

the change in wcr is set at 15% of the change in sales or Δ wcr(t) = 0.15 Δ sales(t).

- *Capital expenditures*, capex(t), such as additional machinery or retooling of existing equipment, is defined as 50% of budgeted depreciation: capex(t) = 0.50 dep(t). Capex is indeed a cash outflow whereas depreciation is a noncash-flow charge that reduces taxable income.

Equation (20.4a) can be simplified by applying the percentage-of-sales forecasting model as[9]

$$\begin{aligned}\text{ecf}(t) = \Big[&\text{sales}(t) - 0.25\times q(t)\times p(1)\times(1+0.01)^t \\ &-1{,}333\times q(t)\times(1+0.20)\times S_{\text{INR},€}(t) \\ &-1{,}750(1+0.01)^t \\ &-0.005\times\text{sales}(t) - \text{interest}(t)\Big] \\ &\times\big[1-\text{tax}(t)\big] + \text{dep}(t) \\ &-0.15\times\Delta\text{sales}(t) - 0.50\times\text{dep}(t) \quad (20.4\text{b})\end{aligned}$$

Terminal value

Valuation is based on reasonably accurate projections of a project's future cash flows — five years in this instance. This is an exercise fraught with uncertainty

9 The reader will note that cogs and wcr are now a linear function of sales, and capex is a linear function of depreciation. This new formulation clearly simplifies the financial planning exercise since all that is needed is a sales forecast.

Exhibit 20.3B. Renault-Mahindra joint venture: Pro forma cash-flow statement.

	2008	2009	2010	2011	2012	2013
Net income	**(931)**	**(1,137)**	**(18)**	**781**	**1,612**	**2,483**
Depreciation	0	2,000	2,000	2,000	2,000	2,000
Change in net working capital[a]	0	(1,500)	(499)	(523)	(548)	(573)
Net cash provided by (used for) operating activities	(931)	(637)	1,484	2,258	3,064	3,909
Capital expenditures[b]	(20,000)	(1,000)	(1,000)	(1,000)	(1,000)	(1,000)
Net cash provided by (used for) investing activities	(20,000)	(1,000)	(1,000)	(1,000)	(1,000)	(1,000)
Issuance/repayment of debt[c]	14,354	(700)	(700)	(700)	(700)	(700)
Issuance of equity	6,304	0	0	0	0	0
Net cash provided by (used for) financing activities	20,658	(700)	(700)	(700)	(700)	(700)
Equity cash flows to JV	**(273)**	**(2,337)**	**(216)**	**558**	**1,364**	**2,209**

Notes: [a] Change in net working capital set at 15.0% of sales.

[b] With the exception of 2008, capital expenditure is assumed to be 50% of depreciation.

[c] Of this debt, 7 billion is denominated in INR while €175 million is subject to exchange rate risk. Debt provisions require INR 700 million repayment every year for 20 years.

that becomes fuzzier as one pierces further into the future. That's why we assign a relatively short economic life to any given project. The question then becomes how to account for the value most likely to be created beyond the cutoff point of five years. One widely used method is to treat the project as a very slow-growing perpetuity beyond year T, whose value is simply $\text{ecf}(T)(1+g)/(k_E - g)$ where $\text{ecf}(T)$ is the ECF in terminal year T, k_E is the cost of equity capital, and g is the perpetual rate of growth, which is generally kept below the projected rate of economic growth and/or rate of inflation.[10] Another approach is to assume that the project would be sold to a third party at a price based on the price-earnings ratio or net ECFs prevailing in the industry. For example, if the current price-earnings ratio for the industry is 7, the terminal value in year T would simply be earnings after tax in year $\text{EAT}(T) \times 7$. (See Exhibit 20.3B.)

Step 3: Discounting reference currency incremental cash flows at the firm's cost of equity capital

Dividend remittances to the parent set at 49% of the project's local currency $\text{ecf}(t)$ have to be translated into reference currency at the forecasted exchange rate $S(t)$ and adjusted by all incremental cash flows induced from this new project. The project will not displace any exports to India but will allow the Spanish subsidiary to benefit from economies of scale, which creates significant synergistic benefits $\text{SYN}(t)$ that would otherwise not have been available. Additional incremental cash flows will include royalties to Renault-parent — a tax-deductible expense to the project in India but a net cash contribution to the parent. Overall, the net incremental equity cash flows $\text{ECF}(t)$ contributed to Renault-parent by its Indian joint venture are comprised of: (1) its 49% share of INR-denominated equity cash flows[11] $\text{ecf}(t)$ plus 5% royalties, which are both subject to India's withholding tax of w_{IN} before being converted into € at the then-prevailing spot exchange rate $S(t)$, and (2) the synergistic benefits accruing to the sister-affiliate in Spain, $\text{SYN}(t)$:

$$\text{ECF}(t) = \left[0.49\text{ecf}(t) + 0.005s(t)\right] \times (1 - w_{\text{IN}})S(t) + SYN(t) \qquad (20.5)$$

10 A word of caution is in order: Should the terminal value of the project become a very significant percentage of the total value of the project — say 50–75% — skepticism should be applied to the valuation results, and the assumptions underlying the determination of terminal value should be revised conservatively.

11 Renault may choose to repatriate 49% of profits or decide to reinvest excess cash flows locally. Their valuation would follow the same approach as outlined earlier and would take into account the INR rate of return and the future exchange rate at which they would be ultimately repatriated.

Exhibit 20.3C. Renault-Mahindra joint venture: Equity cash flows valuation.

	2008	2009	2010	2011	2012	2013
INR equity cash flows to JV	(273)	(2,337)	(216)	558	1,364	2,209
Terminal value of JV in INR[a]						16,195
Future $S_{INR,EUR}(t)$	42.0	43.1	44.2	45.3	46.4	47.5
49.0% equity cash flows to Renault in euros	(3)	(27)	(2)	6	14	23
Add: Royalties	0	12	15	19	22	26
Improved operations in Valencia	0	3	3	3	3	3
Gross equity flow to Renault in euros	(3)	(12)	16	28	39	51
Minus: 10.0% withholding tax	0	0	(2)	(3)	(4)	(5)
Plus: Terminal value of JV in euros						167
Net of tax equity cash flows to Renault in euros	**(3)**	**(12)**	**14**	**25**	**36**	**213**
Net present value discounted at 10.8%	150.7					

Notes: [a] Growth rate in INR net equity cash flows at 1.0%; annual depreciation of 3.5% after the terminal year, resulting in a net growth rate: $g = 1.0\% - 3.5\% = (2.5\%)$.

The total NPV created by the project is calculated as the sum of:

$$NPV = -\text{ Initial investment}(0) + PV(\text{Incremental equity cash flows}) + PV(\text{Terminal value})$$

$$NPV = -INV(0) + \sum_{t=1}^{T} \frac{[0.49ecf(t) + 0.05sales(t)] \times (1 - w_{IN})S(t) + SYN(t)}{(1+k_E)^t} + \frac{1}{(1+k_E)^5} \times ECF(5) \times \frac{1+g}{k_E - g} \quad (20.6)$$

where the discount rate $k_E = 10.8\%$ is the investor's LEC whose determination is detailed in the next main section, and $g = 1\% + (-2\%) = -1\%$ is the annual growth rate of terminal ECFs, reflecting a 1% annual growth rate in nominal INR cash flows offset by a –2% annual INR depreciation starting after the terminal year of the project. (See Exhibit 20.3C.)

Step 4: Risk analysis

The analysis of the proposed project has proceeded on the assumption of a base or most likely scenario. Indeed, with an NPV = €51 million, an IRR = 25.5%, and payback period of 3.6 years, Renault-Mahindra is undoubtedly an attractive project. However, no firm would be naive enough to expect to actually achieve such results since much of the analysis has proceeded on the basis of sophisticated guesswork about revenues and costs fed into an admittedly scientific algorithm. In all likelihood, the project analysis would be subjected to a comprehensive risk analysis, which can be carried out in two principal ways:

1. By *adjusting cash flows* — the numerator of the NPV model. This is what we propose in the remainder of this section.
2. By *adjusting the discount rate by a risk premium*. See the next section for an elaboration of an appropriate risk premium to embed in the discount rate or leveraged cost of equity.

Most firms would subject the most likely scenario to systematic sensitivity analysis, searching for break-even threshold values on key environmental parameters. In a similar vein, many firms will simulate what would happen to the project's NPV under several "what if" scenarios. This is why — as pointed out earlier — it is especially important to keep the subjective assumptions separate from the architecture of the project to allow a systematic *stress-testing* of said assumptions.

Sensitivity analysis

The first step is to select the right variables to submit the project to sensitivity analysis. *Operating* and *transfer* variables are natural candidates for such an exercise — more specifically, percentage of projected sales actually sold, local procurement rules,

Exhibit 20.3D. Sensitivity analysis.

Valuation Sensitized to Percentage of Projected Sales

	Percentage of Projected Sales				
	100%	95%	90%	85%	80%
	150.7	113.0	75.3	36.2	(3.9)

Valuation Sensitized to INR Rate of Depreciation

	INR Rate of Depreciation				
	0.0%	2.5%	5.0%	7.5%	10.0%
	233.9	150.7	80.7	21.5	(48.3)

Valuation Sensitized to Tariff Duties

	Tariff Duties				
	30%	35%	40%	45%	50%
	119.8	104.4	89.0	73.5	57.6

Valuation Sensitized to Withholding Tax

	Withholding Taxes				
	10%	15%	20%	25%	30%
	150.7	146.6	142.5	138.5	134.4

Valuation Sensitized to Percentage of Projected Sales and Exchange Rate

Exchange Rate Devaluation	Percentage of Projected Sales				
	100%	95%	90%	85.0%	80%
0.0%	233.9	191.3	147.4	103.5	58.4
2.5%	150.7	113.0	75.3	36.2 **80.5**	(3.9)
5.0%	80.7	47.7	13.8 **88.0**	(26.8)	(73.5)
7.5%	21.5 **96.9**	(15.4)	(55.4)	(95.9)	(137.0)
10.0%	(48.3)	(83.2)	(118.9)	(154.5)	(190.2)
12.5%	(110.3)	(141.3)	(172.4)	(203.4)	(234.5)

Note: Breakeven percentages of projected sales are shown in gray boxes for respective INR for 2.5%, 5.0%, and 7.5% rate of depreciation.

rate of withholding tax, tariff duty imposed on key imported subassemblies, exchange rate at which dividends and royalties are remitted, and so on.

The "what if" questions could be as simple as asking: What would happen to Renault-Mahindra's NPV if only 90% of projected sales materialized? Or if tariff duties on imported subassemblies were increased from 30% to 50%? Or if the INR depreciated at the faster pace of 5% than the currently projected pace of 2.5% per year? Or if withholding tax was increased from 10% to 20%? Exhibit 20.3D shows the result of such an analysis for several key variables. For example, the top panel of Exhibit 20.3D derives the project NPV if actual sales are only 95%, 90%, and so on of projected sales. Similarly, the second panel shows the project NPV assuming that the INR depreciates by 5%, 7.5%, or even 10% instead of the base case of 2.5%.

As it is often the case, the project's NPV seems to be particularly vulnerable to a deviation in the sales revenue from the base case scenario. In fact, at 80.5% of projected sales, the project barely *breaks even* — its NPV drops to 0. Further analysis would question the unit price projections as well as the number of units sold as sales; revenue is simply price times quantity. Similarly, the tariff duty shows the project to be very exposed to an increasing level of trade protection by the Indian government, which may be the result of lobbying by Indian manufacturers of subassemblies or parts.

> **Q:** If the INR were to abruptly depreciate by 25% in year 1 of operations, by what percentage would you expect the project's NPV to change?
>
> **A:** The easy and almost obvious answer would be to expect the project's NPV to drop also by 25%. This would be true if we had assessed the project directly in euros rather than factoring the exchange rate variable singularly into each cash flow — both INR- and euro-denominated. In reality, the impact of a 25% INR is almost never a 25% decrease on the project's NPV. In fact, should the project be partially export-oriented, it may very well show an increase rather than a decrease in its NPV simply because the devaluation would make exports sales more competitive. Conversely, if the project is heavily dependent on imported parts, as in the case of Renault-Mahindra, its NPV may decrease by more than 25%.

As a result of the sensitivity analysis, the investor may want to seek stronger commitments from the host-country government on those variables (such as tariff duties) that were found to be most sensitive or may decide to structure the project differently to mitigate what it sees as excessive exposure to various factors of country risk.

Multiple scenario analysis[12]

In the sensitivity analysis introduced in the preceding subsection, only one variable was changed at a time. What would happen to the project's NPV if several of the key variables turn out to be better or worse than expected in the base case scenario? This is the very idea of multiple scenario analysis. Indeed, a useful complement to one-variable or unidimensional sensitivity analysis is to test the project's attractiveness under alternative scenarios for which the project's NPV is computed. For example, the bottom panel of Exhibit 20.3D shows the project's NPV under joint assumptions with respect to the actual level of sales (as a percentage of projected sales) and INR depreciation. As an illustration, if the INR depreciates annually by 5%, the project's NPV will remain positive as long as the *break-even* point of 88% of projected sales is realized.

More generally, scenarios are defined here as schematic multidimensional representations of the future: An effort is made to visualize likely alternative future operating environments for the project. The exercise has to be kept reasonably simple by focusing on only the most important environmental/contextual variables, often referred to as *make-or-break* variables or variables having the most direct impact on the project's success or failure. For example, such scenarios could be designed as *laissez-faire globalization* or *national champions* for the Indian automobile industry.[13] The approach is similar to one-variable sensitivity analysis except now *joint* assumptions are made about several key contextual variables that are not controlled by the investor: Tariff duties, local procurement rules, and local ownership requirements are examples of make-or-break variables.

- *A laissez-faire globalization scenario* would assume that foreign-manufactured automobiles could be imported without duties, and so would all imports of subassemblies by automobile manufacturers in India. Local ownership requirements would be abolished, and so would local procurement rules. In sum, the Indian government would allow the full sweep of globalization to unleash market forces.
- *A national champions scenario* would mandate that local procurement of all subassemblies and parts must increase to 100% over the next three years. Indian-owned automobile manufacturers would receive concessionary financing, would be granted 5 year tax holidays on the launch of new models, and would be exempt from tariff duties for key imported parts in the first three years.

Probabilities are often assigned to each scenario. For example, in the Renault-Mahindra project, the *base case* could be given a 50% probability, *national champions* a 35% chance, and *laissez-faire globalization* probability of only 15% with respective NPVs of €150.5 million, €168 million, and €141 million. The expected value of the project would then be calculated as a probability-weighted average of NPVs under alternative scenarios:

$$NPV = 0.50NPV^{base\ case} + 0.35NPV^{laissez\text{-}faire\ globalization} + 0.15NPV^{national\ champion}$$

$$NPV = 0.50 \times 150.7 + 0.35 \times 168 + 0.15 \times 141 = €155.30 \text{ million} \quad (20.7)$$

A *Monte Carlo simulation* is a more scientific methodology that combines sensitivity analysis

12 For a seminal discussion of multiple scenario analysis, see Robert E. Linneman and John D. Kennell, "Shirt-Sleeve Approach to Long-Range Plans," *Harvard Business Review*, March–April 1977.

13 Plausible scenarios should be preferred to a Manichaean view of the future — an all-pessimist scenario versus an all-optimist scenario!

with probability distribution of key informational inputs and their correlations. The goal is to generate a probability distribution of the project's NPV. Several steps are required:

- Formulate a probability distribution for each key input underlying the cash flows. For example, variable cost could be assumed to follow a normal distribution and would require an estimate of its mean and variance.
- For each simulation, one outcome is randomly drawn from each probability distribution. This allows the computation of the project's NPV for this particular simulation.
- Repeating the previous steps hundreds if not thousands of times generates a probability distribution for the project's NPV, which in turn allows the investor to formulate probability statements about the project's NPV. For example, there is a 71% chance the project's NPV will exceed \$62 million or there is a 90% chance the project's NPV will fall between \$30 million and \$121 million.

There are several software packages that can be used conjointly with Excel to derive the end product of the Monte Carlo simulation — a probability distribution of the project's NPV. Clearly one of the challenges of running a Monte Carlo simulation is the formulation of reliable probability distributions for each key input; this is a difficult task when the analyst is dealing with a new project in a country in which he or she has limited experience.

GLOBAL COST OF EQUITY CAPITAL

The discount rate to be used in cross-border valuation is a critical statistic because it draws a boundary line between "go" and "no-go" projects *ex ante* and is a key determinant of *ex post* successes versus failures. The proposed formula to derive this discount rate is based on the capital asset pricing model (CAPM) and its beta coefficient for the purpose of computing the equity cost of capital, and it incorporates an *across-the-board country risk premium* to capture the idiosyncratic risks attached to such projects.

Understandably, not all equity investments are carried out in countries that enjoy the benefits of a well-developed capital market. Thus, the difficulty of deriving an accurate cost of equity and a meaningful beta for a project in less than fully developed markets should not be underestimated. Yet markets are indeed emerging, and many of the larger investments are carried out in countries that are enjoying reasonably well-developed capital markets, such as Indonesia, China, and Mexico. In such cases, the CAPM methodology should definitely be used for gauging the risk of the target investment proposal. We propose next a *two-factor* operational methodology, which expands on the *one-factor* CAPM methodology for refining the computation of the levered cost of equity capital. Let's first recall that, as a one-factor model, the CAPM offers a familiar formula for computing the levered cost of capital:

$$\text{Cost of equity capital} = \text{Risk-free interest rate} + \text{Firm's levered beta} \times \text{Risk premium}$$

When applied to a foreign equity investment, several complications arise: How do you estimate the beta of a foreign project? What are an appropriate equity risk premium (factor 1) and country risk premium (factor 2)?

Estimating the project's beta

There are three principal methods for deriving an estimate of a foreign project beta:

1. *Local betas adjusted by country betas.* The target project's local beta $\beta_{\text{local firm } k}$ would be derived through regression of the project's returns against the local stock market index return. It would then be adjusted by the country beta defined against the MSCI (formerly Morgan Stanley Capital International) World index or the investor's home country stock market index $\beta_{\text{country } k}$ to yield the project market risk beta $\beta^{k}_{\text{market risk}}$:

$$\beta^{k}_{\text{market risk}} = \beta_{\text{country } k} \times \beta_{\text{local firm } k} \tag{20.8}$$

Analysts largely prefer this two-step estimation to a direct estimation of the project beta against the investor's home market stock index, and it is reasonably operational. It does assume, however, that there are no significant covariance (off-diagonal) relationships between the local firm and the global portfolio index (proxied by the MSCI World index). This is generally the case for projects and firms whose activities are clearly grounded in the local economy; it would not be the case for an export-oriented business, such as raw material extractive ventures.

Estimates of applicable *country betas* are available for a fee from a number of financial data providers. For emerging markets that are still segmented from the global financial market, low country betas will reduce the equity risk premium, since the target firm's returns have a low correlation to the global portfolio. This means the degree of systematic risk for a foreign project or firm may well be lower (rather than higher) than the systematic risk of comparable US projects or companies. As emerging markets become better integrated into the world economy, their economic fortunes will more closely correlate to the global portfolio, resulting in progressively higher country betas and lower benefits of diversifying into such markets.

When a *greenfield* or *de novo* project is being evaluated (no historical data is available),[14] the use of proxies based on comparable firms is recommended, and they should be local companies to the extent possible. The betas of such *pure plays*[15] may, however, need to be adjusted for a different level of leverage. This can be readily achieved by first un-levering the pure play's beta and then re-levering it to the appropriate degree of the proposed project's leverage.

It should be noted, however, that even if local betas are available, the market portfolio index against which they are derived may not be representative of a well-diversified economy. This could severely bias the value of the project's local beta. Indeed, equity markets in young emerging countries are all too often small, illiquid, and dominated by a handful of big market capitalizations.

2. *Direct estimation*. Alternatively and whenever possible, it is recommended that the target firm's equity beta be derived by regressing its stock price returns against the MSCI World index returns or the investor's home country stock index returns. This requires the target investment firm's cash flows to be restated in US dollars at appropriate exchange rates.
3. *Industry proxy*. If local proxies are not directly available, an often-used alternative is an estimate of the foreign/parent firm's beta. The estimate is obtained by computing the corresponding US industry or sectoral beta[16] and multiplying it by the foreign market beta relative to the US index. This approach rests on two somewhat tenuous assumptions: (1) The beta for an industry in the United States against the US market portfolio will have the same relative beta in each foreign market. In other words, the firm has the same risk relative to the risk of the local market as a comparable firm would have in the US market. This is a questionable assumption, considering that national markets have different industries and different weightings of industries in their indexes, (2) The only correlation with the US market of a foreign company in the same industry comes through its correlation with the local market and the local market's correlation with the US market.

Estimating the equity risk premium

Using the US equity risk premium as a proxy for an emerging country equity risk premium would understate it and result in an unreasonably low cost of equity capital. One approach to correct for this bias is to adjust the US equity premium by the ratio of the emerging market stock price volatility to the stock price volatility of the US market. Using the standard deviation ratio:

$$\frac{\sigma_{\text{market } k \text{ index}}}{\sigma_{\text{U.S. market index}}}$$

as a conventional measure of stock price volatility, we can formulate the equity premium for a given emerging market k as[17]

$$\text{Equity risk premium for country } k = \frac{\sigma_{\text{market } k \text{ index}}}{\sigma_{\text{U.S. market index}}} \times \text{US equity risk premium} \qquad (20.9)$$

Estimating country risk and appropriate corporate exposure

Country risk is traditionally measured as the yield spread between the emerging market's sovereign bonds and the US Treasury bonds of similar maturities (a 10 year horizon is often used). Of some importance is whether all firms are equally exposed to country

14 It is not possible to regress the project's pro forma cash flows' returns against future market portfolio returns.

15 A pure play refers to a firm whose characteristics — line of activity, size, market scope, production function — are similar to those of the new project being contemplated.

16 Adjusting for differences between the target firm and sectoral proxy in operating leverage (ratio of fixed to total costs) and financial leverage (ratio of debt to debt plus equity) can be readily performed using the Hamada equation.

17 Orthodox finance theory would resist this double adjustment by the country beta (systematic risk) and the standard deviation ratio (total risk). Note that the country beta will lower the equity risk premium, as segmented emerging markets are low-beta countries, whereas the variance ratio is typically superior to one. An alternative approach used by a number of financial analysts is to adjust the US equity risk premium by the foreign country's ratio of stock price volatility to its sovereign bond price volatility. Implicitly, this assumes that investors are comparing equity versus bond investment in country *k* as opposed to comparing equity investment in country *k* versus the United States.

risk. If not, what exposure index should be used to adjust the country risk premium? What is proposed next is to gauge the degree of exposure to country risk by measuring the relationship between a firm's returns and country risk premiums, in the same spirit as the concept of a beta coefficient for market exposure.[18] By regressing the firm's returns against the sovereign bonds' returns, the coefficient will provide a specific measure of country risk exposure if one accepts the notion that sovereign bond price fluctuations mark to market the country risk premium.[19] The reader will note that the beta $\beta^k_{\text{country risk}}$ measuring sensitivity of the project to country risk is different from the notion of a country beta $\beta_{\text{country } k}$ introduced earlier.

The equity cost of capital

As a benchmark discount rate, we recommend the use of the levered cost of equity capital k_e derived from a two-factor CAPM, which explicitly incorporates the target investment firm's exposure to equity market risk and country risk:

$$k_e = r_{\text{free}} + \beta^k_{\text{market risk}} \times \frac{\sigma_{\text{market } k \text{ index}}}{\sigma_{\text{U.S. market index}}} \times \text{Equity risk premium} + \beta^k_{\text{country risk}} \times \text{Sovereign yield spread} \tag{20.10}$$

Implementation

The information necessary to implement the preceding methodology requires access to project and country betas, sovereign yield spreads, target investment firm returns/cash flows, and US/foreign market index returns. The initial setup of the appropriate database would be reasonably time-consuming but not necessarily onerous given that most constituents' statistics are widely available.

Numerical illustration

Referring to the Renault-Mahindra joint venture, the risk-free rate for Renault is the French capital market risk-free rate of 4.91%. Using Mahindra & Mahindra as a pure play, the relevant market risk and country risk betas are estimated as

1. *Market risk factor.* Mahindra's beta versus SENSEX is $\beta_{\text{local firm } k} = \beta_{\text{M\&M}} = 1.068$. The beta of SENSEX (India) versus CAC-40 (France) is $\beta_{\text{country } k} = \beta_{\text{India}} = 0.304$. Standard deviation of CAC-40 and SENSEX 30 are respectively $\sigma_{\text{CAC40}} = 9.4\%$ and $\sigma_{\text{SENSEX30}} = 27\%$. French risk premium × $(\sigma_{\text{SENSEX}}/\beta_{\text{CAC40}}) = 14.36\%$.
2. *Country risk factor.* India's sovereign yield spread is 5% with $\beta^k_{\text{country risk}} = \beta^{\text{MM}}_{\text{Indian sovereign}} = 0.81$. This yields an adjusted country risk premium of 5% × 0.81 = 4.05%.

The appropriate discount rate can be readily computed as

$$k_E = r_{\text{FREE}} + \beta^{\text{MM}}_{\text{SENSEX}} \times \beta^{\text{SENSEX}}_{\text{CAC40}} \times \sigma_{\text{SENSEX}} / \sigma_{\text{CAC40}} \times \text{French risk premium} + \text{Sovereign yield spread} \times \beta^{\text{MM}}_{\text{India sovereign}}$$

$$k_E = 4.91\% + 0.0325 \times 14.36\% + 5.00\% \times 0.81 = 10.80\%$$

Thus, 10.80% was the risk-adjusted cost of equity capital used in the financial analysis of the Renault–Mahindra & Mahindra joint investment proposal.

OPTIMAL WORLDWIDE CAPITAL STRUCTURE

The cost of equity capital is, in part, a function of the firm's financial leverage — that is the mix of debt and equity it procures to fund its operations. As the firm increases its degree of leverage, equity capital becomes more expensive simply because shareholders — as residual claimants on the firm operating cash-flows — are rewarded after (more) debt holders and therefore are holding a riskier claim. For a domestic firm it is customary to establish a *target* capital structure which corresponds to the degree of leverage at which the firm minimizes its WACC. But what about a multinational corporation operating in far flung foreign markets which runs the gamut from bank-dominated and tightly regulated to capital market-friendly financial systems. Should a US-based multinational with a well-defined target capital structure choose to:

- Replicate worldwide in every country its US capital structure for the sake of consistency.
- Be a good citizen and follow local capital structure norms prevailing in each country.
- Be opportunistic and select whatever capital structure to exploit host country's concessionary financing, tax shelters or other market imperfections which may result into lower cost and risk and minimize the multinational's cost of capital.

18 See Damodaran, A. 2003. "Country Risk and Company Exposure: Theory and Practice," *Journal of Applied Finance* (Fall/Winter), for a discussion of this methodology.

19 Here again in the case of a de novo project the analyst will have to fall back to a pure play to derive an estimate of $\beta_{\text{country risk}}$.

Most parent multinational companies would guarantee formally or informally (so-called *letter of comfort*) their foreign subsidiaries' debt obligations which means that the latter can choose whatever degree of financial leverage it sees fit as lenders will assess the parent's credit worthiness — not its subsidiary. Thus, it is the parent's capital structure which is relevant and the design of the subsidiary's capital structure only matters to the extent that it impacts its parent's capital structure.

In the unlikely case that parent company would be willing to allow its foreign subsidiary to default then the latter should adopt a capital structure that minimizes the likelihood of such default. Indeed, its creditors will scrutinize the subsidiary's credit worthiness — not the parent company's. The subsidiary should choose independently a mix of debt and equity which reduces the chance of bankruptcy and minimizes its financing costs. In reality, no MNCs would allow their foreign affiliates to default because they know that it would severely damage their reputational capital and impair access to future financing.... Unless of course, for no fault of its own, a parent company is unable to enforce a promise of guarantee to its subsidiary perhaps because of exchange controls or other regulatory hindrances.

In light of the above considerations the first and second set of guidelines for designing foreign subsidiaries' capital structure do not seem warranted. Why should a MNC's foreign subsidiary replicate its parent capital structure and forego access to subsidized local financing which would otherwise lower the firm's WACC. Similarly, why should a foreign subsidiary follow local capital structure norms when — with the backing of its parent — it can capitalize on cheap concessionary financing and the tax deductions of interest payments (especially when the corporate income tax is higher in the host country than in the home country). Instead, foreign subsidiaries should fully avail themselves of the benefits of subsidized financing even if their leverage ratio may come to far exceed their parent's target leverage.

Among key determinants of a foreign subsidiary's capital structure country risk plays also an important role. If the parent company fears possible expropriation or nationalization it would favor local financing over parent financing. Should the host government decide to nationalize or expropriate the MNC's local subsidiary the latter would simply default on its local loans. High degree of financial leverage of foreign affiliates is an effective hedge against political risk and a powerful deterrent against expropriations. In the case of large scale extractive projects which historically have been prone to expropriations, investors may prefer the architecture of project finance discussed in detail in Chapter 22. As sponsors of such projects, MNCs will provide a very small amount of equity financing leaning instead on debt financing from a worldwide web of lenders including international development agencies, foreign banks, state-owned enterprises as well as customers. Debt servicing is directly tied to the project's cash-flows insuring a close alignment of the multi-partite lending consortium with the project success. Any attempt to expropriate such a project would antagonize not a single investor but a microcosm of the world financial community.

SUMMARY

1. Evaluation of foreign investment projects such as retooling an existing foreign plant, entering *de novo* a foreign market, or acquiring a foreign company is complicated by a number of factors unique to the host country.

2. Multinationals, however, rarely stumble into specific foreign projects. Instead they rely on a systematic search-and-discovery apparatus before choosing specific projects to evaluate in greater detail. Continuous global scanning through listening posts such as foreign affiliates, foreign distributors, and local accounting firms will generate a pool of investment proposals that will be slimmed down to a handful of projects warranting a feasibility study for which a four-step evaluation model is recommended:

   Step 1: Map out in a simple diagram the proposed project's cash flows in the local currency and identify unique competitive and contextual factors shaping these cash flows. Such factors may include price controls, local procurement requirements, and ad valorem tariff duties on imports.

   Step 2: Formulate the project's cash-flow statement in the local currency. This is an exercise in financial planning similar to what would be done for a domestic project, but special care should be taken to incorporate unique host country operating constraints.

   Step 3: Formulate in the parent's reference currency the incremental cash-flow contribution made by the proposed project. This will involve first converting the local currency project's cash flow at the forecasted exchange rate and, second, measuring incremental cash flows such as the cannibalization of existing exports sales, special remittances in the form of royalties, and management fees charged to the foreign project. Discount incremental reference-currency cash flows at the risk-adjusted equity cost of capital.

Step 4: Conduct risk analysis either through adjusting the discount rate with a varying risk premium (simple enough but also simplistic) or adjusting cash flows themselves for operational or transfer risks. This latter approach is best achieved by building multiple scenarios or conducting stress tests, sensitivity analyses, and break-even analyses.

3. The discount rate to be used in cross-border valuation is a critical statistic since it draws a boundary line between "go" and "no-go" projects. It is based on both the capital asset pricing model (CAPM) and its beta coefficient for the purpose of computing the equity cost of capital, and it incorporates an *across-the-board country risk premium* to capture the idiosyncratic risks attached to such projects.
4. When the CAPM is applied to foreign equity investment, several complications arise: How do you estimate the beta of a foreign project? What are an appropriate equity risk premium (factor 1) and country risk premium (factor 2)? The use of the levered cost of equity capital k_e derived from a two-factor CAPM, which explicitly incorporates the target investment firm's exposure to equity market risk and country risk, is recommended.

QUESTIONS FOR DISCUSSION

1. What are the different metrics used in gauging the attractiveness of capital projects such as plant modernization, product launch, or acquisition of a business unit?
2. What are the key phases involved in making foreign direct investment decisions?
3. What is different about evaluating foreign projects?
4. When evaluating foreign projects, why is discounting residual cash flows to equity holders ECFs at the equity cost of capital preferable to discounting free cash flows FCFs at the weighted cost of capital?
5. Why is it important to first forecast the project's local currency cash flows?
6. Identify different kinds of risk encountered when operating a subsidiary in a foreign country.
7. What are incremental cash flows, and why should they be incorporated into the evaluation of a foreign project?
8. What are the different methods available for incorporating risks into foreign projects' evaluation?
9. Is shortening the required payback period an appropriate method for accounting for risk in foreign projects?
10. Give a simple example of how break-even analysis can be used in evaluating foreign projects.
11. Why is adjusting the risk premium in the cost of equity capital in discounting reference currency cash flows simple, albeit simplistic?
12. What is adjusted present value and what are the unique benefits it brings to valuing foreign projects?
13. What are real options and how can they be used in valuing foreign projects? How does this methodology differ from traditional DCFs?

PROBLEMS

1. **Puma invests in the Philippines (intermediate).** The leading German sport equipment company, Puma, is reviewing a proposal to establish a sport shoe manufacturing plant in the Philippines. The investment will require initial capital of Philippine pesos (PHP) 50 million. The investment life is five years. Consider the proposed investment particulars:
   - Sales are projected to reach PHP 20 million the first year and to grow at the annual rate of 5% over the next five years.
   - Earnings before interest and tax, currently at PHP 15 million, will grow at the same rate as sales.
   - The inflation rate in the Philippines is currently 7%, and it is 2% in the United States. These rates are expected to remain constant during the next five years.
   - The corporate tax rate in the Philippines is 25%, and the withholding tax rate on dividend remittances is 10%.

- Annual capital expenditure is equal to 50% annual depreciation expense.
- Working capital requirement equals 10% of sales.
- The terminal value of the plant at the end of the fifth year is expected to be PHP 15 million.
- The spot exchange rate is PHP 50 per €1.
- The company's cost of equity capital is 15%.

  a. Should the company set up the manufacturing plant in the Philippines, assuming that 100% of its sales are destined to the Philippine market?

  b. Assuming that 100% of sales are expected to be exported to Japan, explain how you would adjust your analysis. What additional information is required to reach a decision?

  c. What are the risks involved, and how would you account for them in your financial analysis?

2. Kubota invests in Vietnam (A) — intermediate. Kubota — the Japanese manufacturer of tractors and small earthmoving equipment — is considering building an assembly plant in Da Nang (Vietnam). The initial investment would amount to dong (VND) 200 billion (US$10 million) and would be financed partly (50%) by a loan from the Vietcong Bank in VND at the subsidized rate of 6% over five years with bullet principal repayment at the end of year 5 and partly (30%) by a revolver from Mitsubishi-Tokyo Bank at TIBOR + 120 basis points. The balance of the initial investment is in the form of equity provided by Kubota-Japan.

Output is planned at 5,000 small bulldozers per year. Sale price is VND 200 million/unit. Power train and chassis would be imported from Japan for VND 100 million cif/unit. Locally sourced parts and labor cost amount to VND 75 million/unit.

Kubota-Vietnam is granted a corporate income tax holiday and will pay a 5% royalty to its Japanese parent. Kubota estimates that the project will displace 750 units that are currently exported directly from Japan to Vietnam. Export sales have a profit margin of 15%.

Assume that VND 20,000 = ¥100 over the life of the project and that the TIBOR floating rate revolver can be swapped in a 5 year fixed-rate loan paying 3.5%.

a. Map out the project's cash flows and identify the different risks that may derail it.

b. What is the operating exposure of the project to a devaluation of VND?

c. Would you recommend that Kubota invest in Japan? Kubota applies a cost of equity capital set at 14% for this kind of project.

3. Kubota invests in Vietnam (B) — advanced. Referring to the information provided in problem 2, evaluate the following:

a. How would a 30% ad valorem tariff on power train and chassis imposed by the Vietnam government impact Kubota's decision?

b. How would an 8% annual rate of inflation in Vietnam but no devaluation of the VND against the ¥ impact Kubota's decision?

c. How would a 30% corporate income tax imposed by Vietnam impact Kubota's decision?

d. How would a 10% withholding tax on all cash remittances by Kubota-Vietnam to its parent impact Kubota's decision?

e. How would a composite scenario based on assumptions a through d change Kubota's decision?

4. Kubota invests in Vietnam (C): Social costs/benefits versus private-sector analysis (intermediate). Vietnam's Ministry of Industry is conducting its own analysis of the proposed project to assemble small-scale bulldozers by Kubota for sale in Vietnam.

a. Explain what the economic framework used by the Vietnamese authorities in scrutinizing the project should be.

b. Assuming that the VND is overvalued by 30% and that the opportunity cost of employing Vietnamese labor is only 50% of the nominal labor cost incurred by Kubota-Vietnam, assess the project impact on the host country's economy and its balance of payments. Start with conditions described in Problem 2. Iterate by introducing sequentially conditions presented in Problem 3.

c. How should Kubota use the result of your analysis for negotiating its proposed investment with Vietnamese authorities?

5. Renault invests in Romania (A) — foundational. Refer to International Corporate Finance in Practice 20.2 on page 560 relating the French carmaker Renault's entry into the Romanian automobile market. The year is 2004 and Romania is barely gaining associated status in the European Union. Full membership is a couple of years away. As the chief investment analyst for Renault, you are charged with the preparation of an in-depth analysis of the investment proposal and making a go/no-go recommendation.

a. Describe briefly your methodological approach to strategic investment of this nature. Be specific.
b. Map out the architecture of the project. Be specific as to the currency denomination of each cash flow and other environmental variables likely to impact cash flows.
c. Outline the different phases of the financial analysis leading to the Renault board of directors' eventual decision.
d. Which valuation metric is most appropriate for Renault to reach a decision?

6. **Renault invests in Romania (B) — intermediate.** Referring to Problem 5 and information provided in International Corporate Finance in Practice 20.2 about Renault investment in Dacia, prepare a five year pro forma cash-flow statement for the project. Car sales are expected to reach 75,000 units in the first year of the project and will sell in leu (RON) for 20,000 or the equivalent of €5,000. Initial investment ear marked for the Dacia project is €500 million with an equity contribution from Renault of €150 million. The balance of the investment would be financed by a RON 800 million loan from the Romanian government at 7% per annum denominated in leu and €150 million from BNP Paribas, the French commercial bank, at 5%.
   a. Show relevant cash flows in both local and reference currencies for valuation purposes. Assume that labor costs are RON 8,000 per vehicle; selling, general, and administrative expenses are 10% of sales; working capital is 5% of sales; and engines are imported from Hungary at the cost of RON 6,000 per unit (imports are paid in Hungarian forint).
   b. Explain how you would determine the appropriate discount rate for valuing the project. Renault's P/E is 11 and its beta is 1.1. Bucharest's stock exchange index beta *vis-à-vis* the Paris Bourse is 0.60. The Bucharest stock exchange is twice as volatile as the Paris Bourse. Renault is financed with 40% debt. Romania's sovereign debt is at 400 basis points over French 10 year euro-denominated treasuries. Spell out your assumptions.
   c. Explain how you would account for the different kinds of risks faced by Renault in investing in Dacia and show some simple results to help you decide whether to invest.

   Note: The Romanian leu (RON) stood at €1 = RON 4 in January 2004, with inflation having declined from 25% in 2000 to 10% at the end of 2003.

7. **Licensing versus foreign direct investment (intermediate).** Novo — the Danish biotech multinational — is considering alternative modes of entry into the Indonesian market. It could (1) license the Indonesian state-owned pharmaceutical agency known as Farma and receive royalties at 5% of sales revenue or (2) start a greenfield operation in Bandung and repatriate profits as they are earned. In either case the proposed venture will generate sales revenue of rupiah (IDR) 25 billion and earnings after tax of IDR 2.5 billion. Sales revenues are as volatile as 10 year Danish treasuries yielding 5%, while earnings after tax are as volatile as the Copenhagen stock market index yielding 10%. Explain how you would formulate a comparison of either mode of entry. What additional information, if any, would be required to complete your financial analysis?

8. **Offshoring (A) — intermediate.** Cardiex is a world-leading manufacturer of implantable defibrillators based in Maastricht (Netherlands). Gustav Lund, Cardiex's senior vice president for production and logistics, is trying to decide whether to offshore the assembly of defibrillators to the Philippines. Medtronic — Cardiex's key competitor — offshored more than a decade ago by opening a plant in Shen-Zhen (China). Moving operations to the Philippines would allow Cardiex to take advantage of considerably cheaper labor costs resulting in lower cost of goods sold (currently at 72% final sales in Maastricht and expected to fall to 67% in the Philippines).
   a. What are the strategic factors that militate in favor of domestic manufacturing versus offshoring given that Cardiex's sales are strictly focused on the European Union with 60% to Benelux and Germany?
   b. Discuss the analytical framework that you would develop to compare the two contending options.
   c. What are the additional factors and risks that need to be taken into account to reach a decision?

9. **Offshoring (B) — advanced.** Referring to information provided in problem 8, Cardiex's sales in the European Union are projected to remain stable at €100 million for the next five

years. Show pro form income and cash-flow statements for Cardiex manufacturing in the proposed offshore plant in the Philippines. Depreciation of property, plant, and equipment for the new facilities is straight-lined over 10 years for an initial investment of €35 million. Selling, general, and administrative expenses are 8% of final sales while working capital is at 10% of final sales. The Philippines' Ministry of Industry offers a tax holiday on the first five years of corporate income, and a subsidized PHP 2,000 million five year loan with interest-only at 7%. Cardiex is expecting to sell its plant at the end of 5 years for €17.5 million. Assuming that Cardiex would incur closure costs of €5 million at its Maastricht plant, would you advise Cardiex to move assembly to the new Philippines site? Assume that Cardiex's risk adjusted cost of equity capital for this project is 11.8% and that the exchange rate PHP 50 = €1 remains stable over the next 5 years.

10. **Offshoring (C) — advanced.** Referring to the information provided in problems 8 and 9, inflation in the Philippines is expected to run at an annual rate of 8% over the next five years while the peso, currently trading at PHP 50 = €1, is expected to depreciate at the rate of 5% against the euro over the same period.
    a. Does this confirm your recommendation reached in Problem 9?
    b. Cardiex fears that labor wage inflation in excess of the 8% inflation already projected would jeopardize the economic logic of offshoring (labor costs account for 50% of cost of goods sold). What is the maximum increase in labor wages that would keep the offshoring plan worthwhile?
    c. How would the imposition of an 8.5% ad valorem tariff by the European Union on the importation of assembled defibrillators from the Philippines change your recommendation?

INTERNET EXERCISES

11. **Country Risk Premium.** Log in to Professor Aswath Damodaran's website http://www.stern.nyu.edu/~adamodar/pc/datasets/ctryprem.xls and identify the three countries with the highest and lowest country risk premia. Is the data consistent with the country rating?

REFERENCES

Copeland, Thomas, and Peter Tufano. 2004. "A Real-World Way to Manage Real Options." *Harvard Business Review*, March.

Damodaran, Aswath. 2004. "Country Risk and Company Exposure: Theory and Practice." *Journal of Applied Corporate Finance* (Fall/Winter).

Lessard, Donald R. 1996. "Incorporating Country Risk in the Valuation of Offshore Projects." *Journal of Applied Corporate Finance* 9, issue 3 (Fall): 52–63.

Luehrman, Timothy. 1997. "Using APV: A Better Tool for Valuing Operations." *Harvard Business Review*, May–June.

Shapiro, Alan C. 1978. "Financial Structure and the Cost of Capital in the Multinational Corporation." *Journal of Financial and Quantitative Analysis* (June), 211–226.

Stonehill, Arthur and Thomas Stitzel. 1969. "Financial Structure and Multinational Corporations." *California Management Review* 91–96.

Stulz, René. 1995. "The Cost of Capital of Internationally Integrated markets: The Case of Nestlé" *European Financial Management* 1, 11–22.

APPENDIX 20A: ADJUSTED PRESENT VALUE

The approach to capital budgeting developed in this chapter is to estimate after-tax incremental ECFs to shareholders and to discount them at the firm's leveraged cost of capital. This approach assumes that all components of the ECFs have the same systematic risk. When it comes to international projects, this key assumption may be less tenable simply because of concessionary or subsidized financing offered by the host government and the importance of royalties and management fees in remunerating the investor equity contribution. An alternative approach is to value a project by assuming first that it is *all equity financed* and then to add the *side benefits* stemming from debt financing and other contractual cash flows. Since these different cash-flow streams have widely different risks, they should be discounted at appropriately different rates. This valuation method is known as *valuation by parts* or *adjusted present value* (*APV*):

APV = NPV of project if all equity financed
+ NPV of financing side effects
+ NPV of royalties and management fees

The total value created is thus the sum of the following components:

- The project's reference currency cash flows after taxes $ECF(t)^*$ but before financing costs, discounted at the project's *unlevered* cost of equity k_e^*. The unlevered cost of equity capital is derived from the capital asset pricing model (CAPM) as introduced in equation (20.10) using the project's unlevered beta (β^U):

$$\text{NPV of project if all equity financed} = -\text{INV}(0) + \sum_{t=1}^{T} \frac{ECF(t)^*}{(1+k_e^*)^t}$$

The cost of unlevered equity capital should be adjusted for country risk as shown in equation (20.10).

- Tax savings due to local debt financing, computed as tax rate (t) × interest rate (k_D) × amount of debt (D)[20] and discounted at the cost of debt before tax k_D. If some of the debt D^* is available at concessionary (lower) rate k_D^*, the tax savings should reflect the lower interest rate but should be discounted at the market cost of debt. This is known as the *tax shield*:

$$\text{NPV of tax shield} = \sum_{t=1}^{T} \frac{t \times (k_D \times D + k_D^* \times D^*) \times S(t)}{(1+k_D)^t}$$

where $S(t)$ is the reference currency price of one unit of local currency prevailing in year t when the tax savings are accrued.

- Interest cost savings (or penalties) equal to the difference between the market interest rate k_D and the subsidized interest rate k_D^* applied to the amount of subsidized debt D^*.[21] Since this subsidy is no more and no less risky than the interest payments, it also discounted at the pretax market interest rate k_D:

$$\text{NPV of subsidized financing} = \sum_{t=1}^{T} \frac{(k_D - k_D^*) \times D^* \times S(t)}{(1+k_D)^t}$$

- Royalties and other contractual payments such as management fees, also discounted at the parent's lower pretax cost of debt.[22]

$$\text{NPV of royalties} = \sum_{t=1}^{T} \frac{\text{royalties}(t) \times (1-t) \times S(t)}{(1+k_D)^t}$$

Note that for the tax shield, other interest subsidies, and other contractual payments remittances, the parent's pretax cost of debt is used to reflect the greater certainty of these cash-flow streams.

Renault–Mahindra & Mahindra case revisited. The reader is referred to the proposed joint venture between Renault and Mahindra & Mahindra presented in Exhibits 20.3A, 20.3B, and 20.3C and summarized at the top of Exhibit 20A.1.

We simplify somewhat the financials of the project assuming that all financing INR 14 million is INR-denominated — half at the market interest rate of 7% and half at the subsidized 4% interest rate. Terminal value is now assumed to be 10 times the all-equity-financed cash flows in terminal year 5. Taking the perspective of Renault, the project's APV is shown to be the sum of:

- €-denominated after-tax *all-equity-financed cash flows* €58 million (lines 1 to 3) discounted at the *unlevered* cost of equity[23] found to be 8.9%.
- *Tax shield* €22 million due to tax-deductible interest payments on both market-rate and subsidized-rate debt (lines 4–7) discounted at the 7% market interest rate.
- *Subsidized financing* €18 million (lines 8–10) discounted at 7%.
- *Royalties* €62 million to Renault (lines 11–13) discounted at the 7% market interest rate.

$$\text{APV} = €58\,\text{million} + €22\,\text{million} + €18\,\text{million} + €62\,\text{million} = €160\,\text{million}$$

20 The tax savings due to debt financing result from the fact that interest payments are tax-deductible. If debt in the amount of D is borrowed for 1 year at the rate of k_D the present value of debt cash inflows and outflows are $D - [(1 + k_D)/(1 + k_D)]\ D$. Since interest payments are tax deductible, the PV of tax cash-flow cost savings is $t \times k_D \times D/(1 + k_D)$. The NPV of borrowing D is thus $D - [(1 + k_D)/(1 + k_D)]\ D + t \times k_D \times D/(1 + k_D) = t \times k_D \times D/(1 + k_D)$.

21 Here again the NPV cost of borrowing D at the subsidized interest rate k_D^* is $D - [(1 + k_S)/(1 + k_D)] \times D = [(k_D - k_D^*)/(1 + k_D)] \times D$.

22 Strictly speaking these cash flows are part of the project equity cash flows. They are singled out simply because of the important role they play in international projects.

23 This requires un-levering the levered equity beta. See in Chapter 22 the section on adjusting the discount rate for a discussion of this procedure.

Exhibit 20A.1. APV of Renault–Mahindra & Mahindra joint venture.

	Year 0	Year 1	Year 2	Year 3	Year 4	Year 5
Recall:						
efc(t) = INR all-equity free cash flow[a]	(20,000)	(629)	1,119	1,895	2,709	3,563
Terminal Value = efc(5) × 10[b]	0	0	0	0	0	35,627
$S_{€,\,INR}(t)$	1.0/42.0	1.0/43.1	1.0/44.2	1.0/45.3	1.0/46.4	1.0/47.5
(1) Renault's € all-equity free cash flows: 0.49 $EFC_{INR}(t) \times S_{€,\,INR}(t)$ (1 − .10)	(210)	(6)	11	18	26	33
(2) Terminal Value = EFC(t = 5) × 10	. . .	. . .	. . .	. . .	. . .	331
(3) Present Value ($EFC_€(t)$) at 8.9%	58	. . .	. . .	. . .	. . .	. . .
(4) Interest Expense on INR 7bn @ 7.0%	0	490	490	490	490	490
(5) Interest Expense on INR 7bn @ 4.0%	0	280	280	280	280	280
(6) Tax Shield = Total Interest Expense × 0.34 × $S_{€,\,INR}(t)$	0	6	6	6	6	6
(7) Present Value of Tax Shield at 7.0%	22	. . .	. . .	. . .	. . .	. . .
(8) Interest Expense on INR 7bn Concessionary Loan at 7.0%	0	490	490	490	490	490
(9) Savings from Concessionary Financing (7% − 4%) INR 7bn × $S_{€,\,INR}(t)$	0	5	5	5	5	4
(10) Present Value of Concessionary Financing Subsidy @ 7.0%	18	. . .	. . .	. . .	. . .	. . .
(11) INR Royalties	0	500	666	841	1,023	1,214
(12) € Royalties = INR Royalties (1 − .10) × $S_{€,\,INR}(t)$	0	10	14	17	20	23
(13) Present Value of the Royalties at 7.0%	62	. . .	. . .	. . .	. . .	. . .

Notes: [a] See Exhibits 20.3A, B, C.
[b] Terminal value based on terminal year efc(5) × 10.

By separating a project's different value side effects, APV estimates the contribution of each of them in a simple and easy way. The APV model's advantage over other discounted cash-flow models is clearly its informational content and flexibility. It is often favored by academics for its conceptual elegance but seldom used by financial managers.

APPENDIX 20B: REAL OPTIONS

— Martin B. Rietzel

Flexibility, discounted cash flows, and real options

As seen before, multinationals are exposed to multifarious uncertainty when making international capital budgeting decisions. In particular, cross-border investments or investments with very long lives are subject to complex uncertainty since more factors can change or an increased number of events can occur over the life of the project.

Confronted with this volatile environment, *flexibility* is desirable. This is the flexibility to postpone decisions until the company has more information available to limit risk while still preserving the option to play (i.e., exploit future opportunities). In analogy to financial options, capital budgeting problems can be treated as options as well. But since capital budgeting is concerned with real assets as opposed to financial assets, the options are called *real options*.

Budgeting capital as real options rather than by just *discounting cash flows* (DCF) brings additional advantages. The problem with the DCF method is that it assumes that management has to make all the decisions at the beginning of the project. Often, however, a large investment consists of a series of smaller commitments over the life of the project. Thus, real options allow for modeling that is closer to the realities of the project.

Quantifying real options

Overall, the reasoning for using real options in capital budgeting is convincing and intuitive, but there are downsides, too. Indeed, the limited use of real options in real-life business problems is for a reason. First, the valuation of real options is more difficult than that of financial options because statistical data about the different variables might be limited. Contrary to liquid financial markets, where transparent information is a given, it will often be difficult to find real assets comparable to the one that is to be valued. Second, unlike the analysis of financial options, the analysis of real options can soon become very complex. Even a simple project may consist of different options at different times, demanding a wide range of variables.

But despite these obstacles, even simplified real option pricing methods can bring valuable insights when making capital budgeting decisions. Rather than to determine a reliable and exact value, these methods force management to think about the different risks inherent in the investment. Thus, real option valuation does not replace the DCF method; its value lies in giving management an additional perspective on the factors that it should consider before making the capital budgeting decision. Additionally, although real option analysis requires simplifications and might be far from reality, the same is true for the widely used DCF method.

What are real options?

The mechanics of real options are analogous to those of financial options. Like the latter, real options can be divided into call and put options and into American-style and European-style options. Remember that a call option gives the right but not the obligation to buy an asset at a specific price. In the context of real options an example would be the right to increase the scale of a production plant at a specified price if sales go well. A put option gives the right but not the obligation to sell an asset. In this case, the right to sell a production plant if sales demand is low would be an example of a real put option. Thus, while a real call option reserves the right to exploit emerging opportunities without prior commitment, a real put option limits the risk of an investment.

American-style options give the right to exercise at any point in time until expiration date, whereas European-style options can be exercised only at the date specified. However, in a real option context, unlike with financial derivatives, management very often will not have contractual obligations to wait until a specific date to make a capital budgeting decision. Management will be able to start earlier if it thinks that the conditions are right. Given this enhanced flexibility, American-style options are more valuable than European options and closer to reality in capital budgeting problems.

There are a number of real option examples that illustrate the value of flexibility that management can consider when making capital budgeting decisions:

- *Option to defer.* A property developer that is holding a lease on land with the option to exploit it can wait to see if the conditions justify major investments.
- *Time-to-build option.* A pharmaceutical company can see its R&D activities as a series of outlays with the option to evaluate the progress and abandon the project after each stage.
- *Option to alter the operating scale.* A mining company, for instance, can adjust the size of its operations in response to commodity price levels.
- *Option to abandon* In capital-intensive industries such as airlines and shipping, the option to resell assets if demand declines reduces risk substantially.
- *Option to switch.* In the event of a change in the price of raw materials or consumer tastes, management can change its output or input mix (i.e., sell different products or manufacture the same products with different components).
- *Growth option.* Sometimes an early investment is necessary to reserve the right to play. Multinational corporations, for instance, often test a market first before fully committing to it.
- *Multiple interacting options.* Most real-life projects involve a combination of the aforementioned options. Management will consider upward maximizing calls and downward protecting puts to deal with opportunities and risks.[24]

24 Trigeorgis, L. 1993. "Real Options and Interactions with Financial Flexibility." *Financial Management* 22(3), 204.

Modified Renault–Mahindra case

In order to demonstrate how a simple real option can be valued, a modified version of the earlier example of Renault and Mahindra will help. Recall that Renault invested about €500 million in a plant in India. Now assume the project consists of two phases. Phase 1 requires an investment of €250 million and will lead to a constant capacity of 50,000 cars per year. For Phase 2, Renault will have to spend an additional €250 million to increase capacity by another 50,000 vehicles to a total of 100,000 per year.

Therefore, the risk profile of the project has changed. The initial commitment has been reduced to €250 million but with the option to double plant capacity in any of the five following years for another €250 million. By seeing this investment in two stages, Renault would limit its risk exposure by, in a worst-case scenario, losing only the up-front investment for the first phase instead of the entire €500 million. However, depending on how the different uncertain market factors develop, Renault could still ramp up the factory to the scale it had in mind originally. This means that Renault could wait and see what happens to the underlying uncertainties and then decide what the best decision is. This flexibility is intuitively valuable to Renault, but how valuable? To calculate the value of the option to double capacity in any of the next 5 years, the value of the project without this option has to be compared to that with this option.

For simplicity, assume that the first phase leads to: $NPV_{Phase\ 1}$ = €230m – €250m = –€20m.[25] Since the NPV is negative, Renault would not go on with this project if it consisted only of the first phase. However, since there is the option to conduct a second phase later when there is more information available, management will reconsider its decision depending on the value of the project including this option. (See Exhibit 20B.1.)

Phase 2 represents a call option where the €250 million required as an investment is nothing other than the exercise/strike price *K*. Notice that the option premium in this case is the negative present value of Phase 1.[26] It is an expected loss that is necessary in order to have the option to implement Phase 2 if conditions turn right. Thus, only if the PV of the expected cash flows of Phase 2 exceeds the strike price and premium will the option come into the money.

The volatility of both project phases' PVs will depend on the four uncertainties identified earlier:

1. Car sales.
2. INR/US$ exchange rate volatility.
3. Tariff duties.
4. Withholding tax.

The already mentioned, Monte Carlo simulation technique helps merge the respective probability distributions of the four variables into a single probability distribution. The standard deviation of this curve will serve as a metric for the volatility needed in option valuation.

25 Also notice that the same applies for investing the entire €500m up front in both project phases to have twice the capacity: NPV = €460m – €500m = –€40m.

26 Investing in Phase 1 is a precondition for obtaining the option for Phase 2. As with financial options, where the option premium is the price of a contract, the negative NPV of Phase 1 is the cost associated with the option to expand the project. It is, however, important to consider that the performance of Phase 1 can turn out better or worse than –€20m. In a worst-case scenario the loss will reach the total €250m.

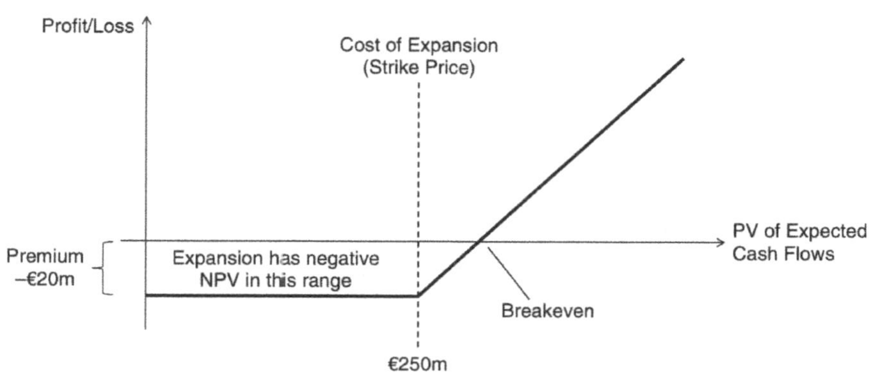

Exhibit 20B.1. Profile of the Phase 2 call real option.

As a first step to comparing real options with financial options, the price drivers of a financial option can be mapped to those of a real option to understand the similarities:

- **Stock price *S*.** The present value of a project's operating assets to be acquired corresponds to the stock price of a financial option.[27] Unlike financial options, where there is a liquid market to determine the price of the asset, in the case of real options the present value of the project without options is the best unbiased estimator of the market value of the project. Assume a DCF valuation has identified a PV for each project phase without options to be €230 million.
- **Exercise price *K*.** The capital expenditure required to acquire the project assets of Phase 2 gives the strike price. In this case capital expenses of €250 million are necessary to build Phase 2 of the project.
- **Time to expiration *t*.** This is the length of time the decision may be deferred. Time is valuable because the longer the time before the option expires, the more can be learned and happen before a decision has to be made and therefore the chances that the option will come into the money are higher. Renault will be able to exercise the option at any time within the next 5 years.
- **Risk-free rate of return r_f.** The time value of money of the project can be used here and is given at 4.91%. It is important to note that since the cash flows rather than the discount rate are risk adjusted (the PV of €230 million already accounts for the project's risks), the risk-free rate is accurate.
- **Standard deviation of returns on stock σ.** A good approximation of the volatility of a real asset is the riskiness of the project assets (i.e., the volatility of the present value of the project). A Monte Carlo simulation combines the several sources of uncertainty (sales volume, INR/US$ exchange rate volatility, tariff duties, and withholding tax) into a single representative uncertainty. Higher variance is a price driver because in a highly volatile scenario the price of the asset swings up or down more heavily and thus there is a greater chance that the option will come into the money than in a lower-volatility scenario. Assume the Monte Carlo simulation has given a 60% standard deviation of the project's PV.[28]

27 This is not the capital expenditure required for the project but its underlying present value.

Now, with this information, the value of the real option hidden in this project can be calculated in four steps.[29] *First*, compute the base case PV using the traditional DCF approach. *Second*, model how the present value from the base case develops given the underlying uncertainty of the project. *Third*, incorporate the expansion option into the binomial model by analyzing the value maximizing decision for each limb of the lattice. *Fourth*, subtract the PV of the project without the option from that of the project including the option to obtain the option value.

Step 1: Estimation of the PV if the project had no flexibility

The project without the option would look like the following: Renault would have to spend €250 million to get a capacity of 50,000 cars per year or a total of €500 million for 100,000 cars per year. Since the PV is only €230 million for Phase 1 (or €460 million for both phases combined if invested up front), the NPV of the project is negative and Renault's management would reject the investment. Another way to say this is that the option is out-of-the-money.

Step 2: Modeling of the evolution of the PV with a binomial model

Generally, option pricing theory, including the Black–Scholes–Merton model, is based on a concept called geometric Brownian motion (GBM).[30] This can be directly applied to value real options with binomial lattices or trees. The binomial model is based on the assumption that the value of an asset can evolve in two (therefore binomial) ways. It can either go up "*u*" or down "*d*." Luckily, it is not necessary here to go into the details of the mathematical theory behind the model. All that is needed for the

28 A weakness, however, that is important to be aware of when transferring financial options pricing methods to real options is the assumption of lognormal distributions that are used in the valuation of financial options. In contrast to these, the uncertainties of a business project may follow other distributions.

29 Koller, T. et al. 2010. *Valuation: Measuring and Managing the Value of Companies*, 5th edition. Hoboken, NJ: John Wiley & Sons, pp. 697–702.

30 Brownian motion is the random movement of particles in a liquid or gas. In finance, GBM refers to the standard assumption that the value of an asset varies according to a random stochastic process similar to particles in a fluid. The Black-Scholes model, for example, also applies this assumption.

binomial valuation approach is to calculate the following up and down values using the drivers of the project's option value identified earlier:

- Up movement: $u = e^{\sigma\sqrt{\Delta t}} = e^{0.6\sqrt{1}} = 1.82$ (using the standard deviation of 60% identified earlier and setting the number of years per movement, Δt, to 1). The factor u corresponds to the future value of the favorable state in the next period divided by the present value and can be understood as the factor by which the present value of the underlying asset increases from one period to the next as a function of volatility and time.
- Down movement: $d = \frac{1}{u} = 0.55$ corresponds to the future value of the unfavorable state in the next period divided by the present value.[31]
- Risk-neutral probability:

$$p = \frac{(1 + r_f - d)}{u - d} = \frac{(1 + 4.91\% - 0.55)}{1.82 - 0.55} = 0.39^{32,33}$$

31 d is the inverse of u since the value decrease is defined by the same but negative exponent of u : $d = e^{-\delta\sqrt{\Delta t}}$.

32 p can be tested by deriving any PV in the lattice from the expected PV of the next period and discounting it at the risk-free rate. The expected PV of a period is simply the "up PV" times the "up probability" plus the "down PV" times the "down probability" from the next period. For example, for the initial PV:

$$PV_{t=2008} = \frac{(\text{"up PV"}_{t+1} \times p) + [\text{"down PV"}_{t+1} \times (1-p)]}{(1 + r_f)} = \frac{(419 \times 0.39 + 126 \times 0.61)}{(1 + 4.91\%)}$$

33 Koller et al., *Valuation*, pp. 691–700.

The starting point of the binomial model is the PV of the project's first phase of €230 million identified earlier. This value will go up by the factor u or down by the factor d because of the underlying volatility. Therefore, the PV of €230 million can either go up to €419 million or down to €126 million in the first period, multiplying the PV by the factors u and d, respectively. The same method applies to the periods that follow. The resulting binomial lattice (Exhibit 20B.2) shows how the PV of Phase 1 of the project without optionality (the underlying asset) evolves over the next periods. For management it is a way to consider the upside potential and downside risk of the project.

Management knows that it would have to invest €250 million for the expansion. The problem is that in 2008 the PV of the expansion is only €230 million. Thus, as the NPV is negative; management would wait until next year to see what the expansion is worth now. It could be more or less than the initial value. The €419 million in 2009 clearly exceed the up-front investment while in the case of €126 million the NPV remains negative. In general, if the PV exceeds €250 million in a given period, management would invest; otherwise it would wait with the decision for the next period. The upper half of the lattice leads to scenarios in which this condition is met (in light gray) and management would opt for Phase 2 (the option is in-the-money). At any point in the lower half (in dark gray), management would not exercise the option (it remains out-of-the-money).

Step 3: Modeling of the flexibility with a decision tree

Based on the binomial lattice shown in Exhibit 20B.2, this step consists of eventually deriving the value of the project with the option at the time of deciding

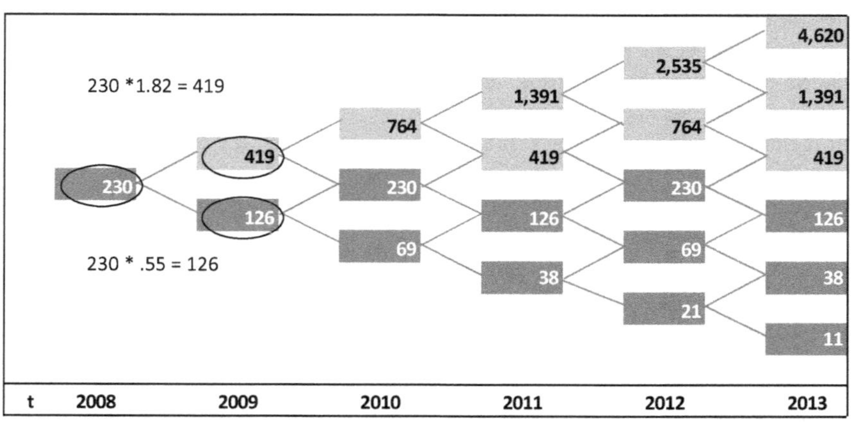

Exhibit 20B.2. Binomial lattice with GBM.

on the investment at all, in 2008. This is done by analyzing whether an expansion of production capacity by 100% for an investment of €250 million is worth more than simply sticking to Phase 1 of the project for any possible scenario. Thus, while the prior lattice simply showed the evolution of Phase 1's PV, the decision tree shown in Exhibit 20B.3 now incorporates the option value at each decision point.

To calculate the option value at each of these points, start with the last period. For example, for the second value from before, compare the PV of €1,391 million (simply Phase 1) to twice this value minus the investment of €250 million (Phases 1 + 2):

Max{€1,391m or [€1,391(1 + 100%) – €250m]} = €2,533m[34]

Using the assumption that management would at any given time want to maximize the project's NPV, in this case doubling capacity is the solution since €2,533 million exceeds €1,391 million.

After computing all the values for the last period in the same way as earlier, the whole tree can be solved backward (a process often called backward induction). This is done by applying the risk-neutral probability identified earlier because any value in a given period is derived from the expected PV of the next period (i.e., the two possible PVs in the following period weighted by their respective probabilities p for an up movement and "1 – p" for a down movement) and discounted at the risk-free rate. For example, for the second value from before in 2012, multiply the two corresponding limbs of 2013 with the risk-neutral probabilities of an up movement and a down movement, respectively:

$$PV_t = \frac{(\text{“up PV”}_{t+1} \times p) + (\text{“down PV”}_{t+1} \times (1-p))}{(1+r_f)}$$

$$= \frac{(€2{,}533\text{m} \times 0.39) + €588\text{m} \times (1-0.39)}{(1+4.91\%)}$$

$$= €1{,}289\text{m}$$

All values follow the same process. After identifying the values for 2012, those for 2011 and so on can be filled the same way until arriving at a single value in 2008.

Step 4: Estimation of the option value

Recall that the NPV of the project's Phase 1 without the option to expand was negative with NPV = €230m – €250m = –€20m. However, starting with Phase 1 and having the flexibility of expanding with Phase 2 adds value to the project. Incorporating the option increases the project's NPV to €357m – €250m = €107m. Renault's management would therefore start with Phase 1 and wait with Phase 2 until the conditions are right. This will be the case in the first period that the PV of Phase 1 in the binomial lattice exceeds the strike price (i.e., the option comes into the money). For example, the earliest scenario in which Renault's management would want to exercise the option would be in 2009, if the first movement was up. In summary, the NPV of the total project changes from –€40 million (when

34 Note that there is a linear relationship, since doubling production capacity doubles PV.

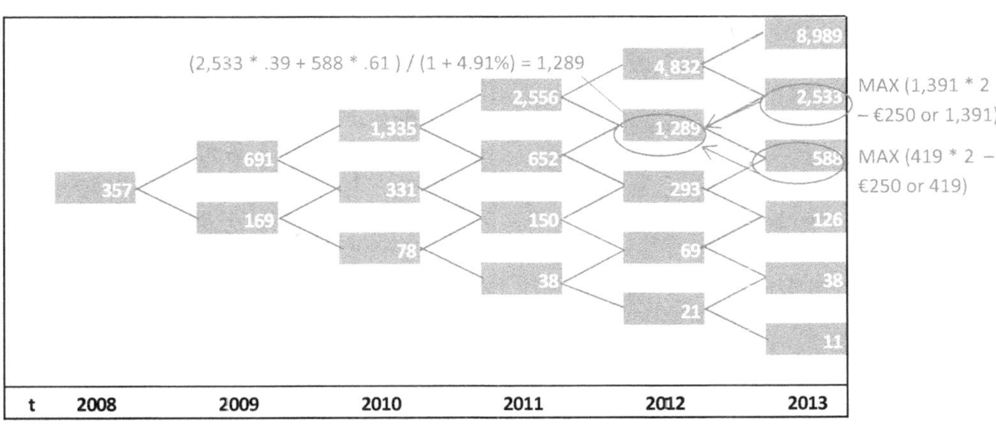

Exhibit 20B.3. Option valuation with backward induction.

investing €500 million up front) to €107 million if the project is undertaken with the flexibility of two phases.

To conclude, while real option analysis does not replace the DCF method, it adds a different perspective to budgeting capital. As seen in this case, real option analysis allows better decisions to be made than by solely employing DCFs because it considers the value inherent in the flexibility of deferring decisions until conditions are right. Relying exclusively on the DCF method brings the danger of potentially underestimating a project's true value and forgoing a good investment opportunity. It is important to note that while real option analysis is far from perfect and, like all other available methods, is based on simplifications, the combination of different methods is still the best approach in the search for an accurate picture of the complex reality of a real-life project.

APPENDIX 20C: APPRAISING CROSS-BORDER SOCIAL PROJECTS[35]

Farmers without Borders (FWB) is a US based NGO domiciled in Saint Paul, Minnesota. Its mission is to assist family-operated farms in emerging market countries to boost their performance by offering educational training and assistance in securing irrigation equipment and appropriate fertilizers. It specializes in coffee, cocoa and sugarcane farming. In a typical year, FWB would review up to 5–7 one million dollar + proposals, narrow down the list to two finalists before funding one project. This year FWB has slimmed down the list of viable projects to a sugarcane venture in northern Vietnam and a coffee venture in southern Vietnam. Both projects involve 100 small family farms exploiting a two-acre parcel of land. This note develops a methodological framework to guide NGOs into making sound decisions when target projects operate in a foreign currency rather than the US dollar.

Appraising a social project 1.0. Unlike private sector projects for which pro-forma cash-flows can be readily compared by applying metrics such as NPVs or IRRs social projects are primarily motivated by the benefits accruing to the recipient farmers in the form of higher incremental income. One simple approach would be to estimate the farmer's incremental income resulting from FWB's assistance — that is farmers' income with FWB assistance and farmers' income without. Such incremental benefits would be tabulated against the cost of assistance incurred by FWB to gauge the relative attractiveness of the project and compare it with competing ones.

Sugarcane for domestic market (Vietnam). Assume that FWB is considering assisting 100 sugar-cane farms in Northern Vietnam by providing educational training including how and when to use fertilizers, pest control chemicals as well irrigation hardware to boost yields and therefore farmers' income. Fertilizers and pest control chemicals would have to be imported at the annual cost of $40 per acre. Farmers would sell sugar-cane to a local sugar mill. Sugarcane would be crushed and sugar milled for domestic consumption — that is sugar would be sold in Vietnam only. Once educational training and irrigation equipment is installed (in year 1) farmers consolidated revenue in Dong (VND) are shown in Exhibit 20C.1 for years 2 to 5.

Exhibit 20C.1. Farmers income measured in millions of Dong.

Year	1	2	3	4	5
Income with	50	85	105	115	120
Income without	50	55	60	65	70
Incremental	0	30	45	50	50

Given the initial investment by FWB of VND 50 million, the project social returns would be measured as a rough first approximation as the *gross Return on Investment* (*ROI*) defined as the ratio of cumulative *incremental* income to farmers measured in VND million of 30 + 45 + 50 + 50 = 175 accruing to farmers divided by the initial cost of VND 50 million or a ratio of 175/50 = 3.50. Thus, for every Dong spent by FWB each sugar cane farm earns an additional 3.50 Dong. In relative terms, a ratio of 3.50 does not tell us much unless we can compare it to a benchmark — for example FWB has a historical record of averaging a ratio of 1.35 on assistance projects to farmers.

Appraising a social project 2.0. This metrics ROI is easy enough to compute but it is somewhat simplistic for several reasons:

35 This appendix builds on the excellent discussion on how to measure the impact of social investments developed in Hawawini and Vialet, *Finance for Executives*, 7th edition. Cengage, pp. 313–317.

Exhibit 20C.2. Net incremental income for sugar cane farmers in VND millions.

Year	1	2	3	4	5
Incremental Sales	0	30	45	50	50
Incremental Costs	0	10	15	20	20
Net Incremental Income	0	30	30	30	30

Exhibit 20C.3. Net incremental income for coffee farmers in VND million.

Year	1	2	3	4	5
Incremental Sales	0	27	40	45	45
Incremental Costs	0	10	15	20	20
Net Incremental Income	0	17	25	25	25

1) It is based on gross incremental income rather than net incremental income. This can be easily corrected by tabulating the incremental costs that farmers will incur to generate incremental income — see Exhibit 20C.2.

2) It disregards the time value of money and does not take into account the risk associated with more distant net incremental income — that is the fact that incremental income earned in later years is less valuable than when it is earned today or in the very proximate future. This shortfall can be remedied by discounting future incremental income at an appropriate discount rate. Hawawini and Vialet (2022) recommend — as a proxy — to use the average yield-to-maturity of social impact development bonds currently at 5.75%

3) It is somewhat simplistic because it encompasses arbitrarily only the first five years of the project; in all likelihood- the benefits of FWB assistance would extend beyond the first five years as the benefits of learning to become a more productive farmer are acquired for the longer term if not in perpetuity.[36]

Coffee for exports. FWB is considering another project in the hills of Southern Vietnam — providing educational assistance to 100 coffee farmers whose crop are entirely destined to exports markets. For each coffee farmer the incremental costs and benefits are tabulated in Exhibit 20C.3. The initial cost of training coffee farmers and equipping them with adequate irrigation equipment is VND 50 million resulting in a gross ROI of 3.14 still above the average but below the sugar-cane project.

Exposure to foreign exchange risk. So far, we have assumed that either coffee or sugar cane farmers are impervious to the value of the Dong on the foreign exchange market. Indeed, these ROIs are both computed in the Vietnamese currency — the Dong — whereas FWB is a US domiciled NGO committed to allocating its limited resources to the most deserving project. As indicated earlier sugar cane farmers earn Dongs generated by domestic sales that is sales to Vietnamese consumers but 66% of their costs are exposed to exchange rate risk. For example, a 10% devaluation of the Dong in year 2 of the project would jolt two-thirds of sugar cane farming cost and the resulting ROI would decrease significantly as a result. On the face of it the sugar cane (SC) project dominates the coffee project — at least under the assumptions of a fixed exchange rate at VND 25,000 = USD1 over the life of either project. This is however, a highly improbable scenario. Should the Dong depreciate against the US dollar the sugar cane farmers would experience a significant increase in their cost of imported fertilizers and pest control which would negatively impact the attractiveness of the project. Coffee (CF) farmers on the other hand would benefit from richer exports sale revenue as each USD of exports revenue converts back into a larger number of Dongs resulting in a far more attractive project.

Formally, the net ROI on either project ($ROI(\alpha)_{SC}$ and $ROI(\alpha)_{CF}$) can be formulated as a function of the present value (PV) of net incremental income which is itself a function of the annual rate α of Dong depreciation/appreciation

$$PV_{SC}(\alpha) = \Sigma\,\{Sales\,(t) - Opex\,(t) \times [0.33 + 0.66\,(1+\alpha)^t]\}\,/(1+.0575)^t$$

$$PV_{SC}(\alpha) = \frac{30-10\left[0.33+0.66(1+\alpha)^2\right]}{(1+0.0575)^2} + \frac{45-15\left[0.33+0.66(1+\alpha)^3\right]}{(1+0.0575)^3} + \frac{50-20\left[0.33+0.66(1+\alpha)^4\right]}{(1+0.0575)^4} + \frac{50-20\left[0.33+0.66(1+\alpha)^5\right]}{(1+0.0575)^5}$$

36 Assuming that the net incremental income continue in perpetuity at a constant rate of VND 30 million per year, the project would accrue additional incremental income of Terminal Value (5) = 30/.0575 = 521 at the end of year 5 or in present value term 521/(1 + 0.0575)^5 = 521/1.3225 = 393.

$$PV_{CF}(\alpha) = \Sigma \{Sales(t) \times (1+\alpha)^t - Opex(t)\}/(1+0.0575)^t$$

$$PV_{CF}(\alpha) = \frac{27(1+\alpha)^2 - 10}{(1+0.0575)^2} + \frac{40(1+\alpha)^3 - 15}{(1+0.0575)^3} + \frac{45(1+\alpha)^4 - 20}{(1+0.0575)^4} + \frac{45(1+\alpha)^5 - 20}{(1+0.0575)^5}$$

where Sales (t), Opex (t) are respectively sales revenue and operational expenditures for year t. ROI(α) would thus be redefined as

$$ROI(\alpha) = \frac{PV(\alpha) \text{ of net incremental income}}{\text{initial cost}}$$

Reaching a decision. Exhibit 20C.4 graphs $ROI(\alpha)_{SC}$ and $ROI(\alpha)_{CF}$ (measured on the vertical axis) as a function of the annual rate α of Dong depreciation/appreciation (measured on the horizontal axis): as expected the $ROI(\alpha)_{SC}$ for the sugar cane project declines as the Dong depreciate whereas the $ROI(\alpha)_{CF}$ for the coffee project increases due to richer exports sale revenue as each USD of exports revenue converts back into more Dongs.

At the break-even point of $\alpha^* = 2.47\%$ FWB would be indifferent between the two projects; beyond the break-even rate of α^* FWB would prefer the coffee project and conversely below the break-rate α^* the sugar cane project dominates. Clearly incorporating exchange rate in the projects' evaluation shows how sensitive the decision is to future exchange rate scenarios.

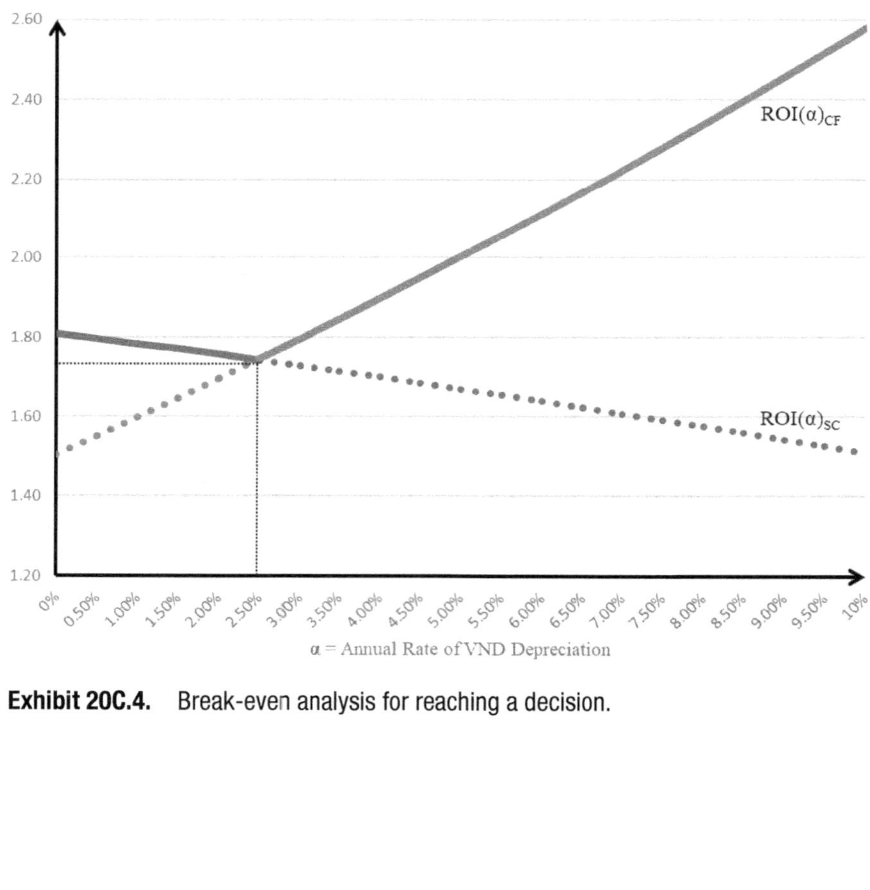

Exhibit 20C.4. Break-even analysis for reaching a decision.

CHAPTER 21

Cross-Border Mergers and Acquisitions

The price of pig
Is something big,
Because its corn, you'll understand,
Is high-priced too, because it grew
Upon the high-priced farming land.
If you don't know why that land is high,
Consider this: its price is big
Because it pays thereon to raise
The costly corn, the high-priced pig.
— H. J. Davenport

International acquisitions are a relatively easy and fast mode of foreign market entry. Globalization, buttressed by deregulation, lower entry barriers, and privatization, has fueled cross-border mergers and acquisitions (M&A). Walmart, for instance, in 2011 completed the acquisition of Massmart as a mode of entering the South African market. Ciments Lafarge — the world leader in cement and construction materials — had reviewed the acquisition of state-owned Hoang Thach Cement in Vietnam.

But there is another dimension to mergers and acquisitions in industries that have become global oligopolies: Global players merge with or acquire other global players rather than local players. Witness the hyperactivity of M&A in the automotive industry — not always bearing fruit! DaimlerChrysler stands as the worst-ever cross-border merger (1998). General Motors' acquisition of Swedish Saab (1990) or Ford's takeover of Jaguar (1989) did not fare much better. But Renault's bold purchase of Nissan (1999) is generally hailed as a success. Tata Motors' outright takeover of Jaguar Land Rover in 2008 has already turned the corner of profitability and so has Fiat's move to revive bankrupt Chrysler initiated 10 years ago. But wait: Geely (Mandarin for lucky) — the Hangzhou-based company — paid $1.3 billion for Volvo in 2010. The Swedish carmaker lost $2.6 billion in the 2 years prior to the acquisition with global sales of only 335,000 cars, down 27% from their peak. Geely — one-sixth the size of Volvo and primarily a low-cost, low-end domestic producer — has already begun to revive the fortunes of a global premium brand. Cross-border M&As work in mysterious ways.

After reading this chapter you will understand:

- What the industrial logic of mergers and acquisitions is.
- How the landscape of cross-border M&As is changing.
- What the international acquisition process is.
- How to value a cross-border acquisition.

A BRIEF HISTORY OF MERGERS AND ACQUISITIONS

Much of the action in the market for corporate control has historically been centered in the US economy, where hyperactive stock markets have been enablers for reallocation of corporate assets whether they be entire firms or simply business units. Business historians generally stereotype six M&A waves.

The first wave lasted from 1893 to 1904 and consolidated basic manufacturing and mining industries.

The second wave — the decade following World War I and extending until the 1929 crash — emphasized vertical integration; Ford Motor Company, for example, took control of steel mills and railroads to support its assembly lines. After World War II, conglomerate-style M&As — that is, acquisition of firms in unrelated industries — became the flavor of the day with the rise of ITT, Litton Industries, and LTV. The fourth wave from 1974 to 1989 is remembered as the era of hostile takeovers fueled by leveraged buyouts (LBOs) and the issuance of junk bonds; it was also marred by so-called greenmail — a sort of ransom paid to corporate raiders threatening to take control of companies. The fifth wave, in the 1990s, saw the creation of global giants through friendly M&As seeking to gain economies of scale or scope to better compete in the world economy. The recent decade — the sixth wave — has witnessed the emergence of new players — hedge funds, private equity firms, and sovereign wealth funds (SWFs) — whose metrics and strategic objectives differ from more traditional corporate M&As.

It is only in the past 25 years that cross-border M&As have taken on a life of their own, reshaping the industrial map of the global economy. See Exhibit 21.1 for a list of recent major cross-border M&As; almost all of them were driven by the economies of scale imperative — that is, key players in global oligopolies buying out a direct competitor. Indeed nearly all of the largest cross-border

Exhibit 21.1. The 16 largest cross-border M&As of the past decade.

Deal Announcement Date	Acquirer	Acquirer Country	Target	Target Country	Deal Value ($Billion)	Industry Sector	Deal Type
10-Aug-23	VinFast Auto	Vietnam	Black Spade	USA	23	Automotive	H-Acq[a]
13-Jun-23	Bunge	USA	Viterra	Switzerland	18	Agriculture	H-Acq
31-May-22	DSM	Netherlands	Firmenich	Switzerland	21	Food and Beverage	H-Acq
5-Mar-21	Altimeter Growth Corp.	US	Grab Holdings	Singapore	48.6	Technology	H-Acq
29-Oct-18	Atlantia & Grupo ACS	Italy, Spain	Abertis	Spain	22	Infrastructure	H-Acq
9-May-18	Vodafone	UK	Liberty Global	US	21.8	Telecommunications	H-Acq
25-Apr-18	Comcast	US	Sky plc	UK	39	Telecommunications	H-Acq
19-Apr-18	Takeda	Japan	Shire	Ireland	62	Pharmaceuticals	H-Acq
17-Jan-17	British American Tobacco	UK	R.J. Reynolds	US	49.4	Tobacco	H-Acq
16-Jan-17	Essilor	France	Luxottica	Italy	58.5	Eyewear	H-Acq
16-Aug-16	LindeAG	Germany	Praxair	US	85	Chemicals	H-Acq
18-Jul-16	Softbank	Japan	ARM Holdings	UK	32	Semiconductors	V-Acq[b]
23-May-16	Bayer	Germany	Monsanto	US	54.5	Agribusiness	H-Acq
3-Feb-16	ChemChina	China	Syngenta	Switzerland	43	Chemicals	H-Acq
16-Sep-15	AB InBev	Belgium	SAB Miller	UK	107	Beverages	H-Acq
4-Aug-15	Shire	Ireland	Baxalta	US	32	Pharmaceuticals	H-Acq
27-Jul-15	Teva	Israel	Actavis Generics	US	40.5	Pharmaceuticals	H-Acq
8-Apr-15	Royal Dutch Shell	Netherlands & UK	BG Group	UK	70	Oil and gas	H-Acq
17-Nov-14	Actavis	Ireland	Allergan, Inc.	US	70.5	Pharmaceuticals	H-Acq
14-Oct-12	Softbank	Japan	Sprint	US	21.6	Telecommunications	H-Acq

Note: [a & b] H-Acq = Horizontal Acquisition. V-Acq = Vertical Acquisition.

M & As in the last decade seems to obey a geographical diversification imperative and are labelled "horizontal" acquisitions.

THE INDUSTRIAL LOGIC OF MERGERS AND ACQUISITIONS

There are many motivations for firms to merge and acquire other businesses — mostly, but not always, grounded in the logic of value creation. In *horizontal* M&As, two firms in the same line of business join forces. The domestic US merger of American Airlines and US Airways would be a horizontal merger and so would the cross-border merger between Air France and KLM — both international air carriers based respectively in France and the Netherlands. Increased market power combined with significant operating economies made for a compelling industrial logic in both cases.

Vertical mergers refer to a firm acquiring a supplier or distributor depending on whether the merger is carried out upstream or downstream along the value chain. Conoco's acquisition of pipelines connecting oil fields in Alaska to refineries in California would be deemed a vertical merger. Securing access to key raw material inputs — for example an aluminum producer acquiring a bauxite mining firm — is a primary rationale for such vertical acquisition. When firms operating in adjacent product lines combine operations, the merger is labeled *congeneric*. Caterpillar's acquisition of Bucyrus and Citibank's merger with Travelers are instances of M&A between two firms in the same industry offering different but related products or services.

Conglomerate mergers refer to transactions involving firms in unrelated lines of business. The acquisition of NBC Universal by General Electric (GE) was a good example of a conglomerate acquisition. Emerging market economies are often dominated by family-controlled business groups, which typically grow through conglomerate-style M&As. In all the cases previously mentioned (with the exception of conglomerate M&As), the primary motivation was operating economies resulting from synergy.

In most acquisitions the buyer ends up paying a significant *control premium* above the target firm's current stock price. Therefore, the target firm's shareholders are the clear and immediate beneficiaries of the acquisition. It is less clear that the acquiring firm benefits. Successful acquisitions boil down to a simple proposition: *Do the operating economies and various synergies accruing to the combined firms compensate the buyer for the control premium?*

The process of M&A itself is a multistep exercise: The acquiring firm must first identify a suitable target; then establish a price (or price range), often with the help of an investment bank; and finally, decide how it will pay for it. Will it be an all-cash deal, or will the acquirer offer its own stock, bonds, or any combination thereof as payment? In practice, if both parties agree on the terms of the transaction (making it a friendly merger), the target firm's shareholders are asked to tender their stock to the acquirer in exchange for cash, bonds, the stock of the acquiring firm, or a combination thereof.

ARE CROSS-BORDER ACQUISITIONS DIFFERENT?

Before elaborating on the valuation methodology appropriate to cross-border acquisitions, this section highlights the unique features of cross-border transactions.

Acquisition as a mode of foreign market entry

If the taxonomy of mergers and acquisitions presented in the previous section is generally valid for domestic and "mega" cross-border M&As, it remains that the driving motivation for international acquisitions is grounded in foreign market entry. In Chapter 20, we presented a foreign direct investment decision model outlining how multinational companies routinely *introspect, search, and screen* before foreign direct investing. The choice then becomes *greenfield* or *de novo* investment — whereby the multinational company builds its operations from the ground up — versus a strategic acquisition of an existing company (see International Corporate Finance in Practice 21.1), which amounts to a shortcut. By choosing the latter the acquirer gets instant gratification since the acquired firm is a going concern with existing production facilities, a workforce, a management in charge, a tested product portfolio, and a distribution network. By acquiring a going concern with known cash flows and readily available financial statements, uncertainty about valuation is considerably reduced; however, for the acquirer the question remaining is whether it is paying a fair price.

INTERNATIONAL CORPORATE FINANCE IN PRACTICE 21.1

When Walmart Goes Hunting in Africa

Walmart, also known affectionately as the "Beast of Bentonville," acquired South African Massmart for the bargain price of $4.1 billion, which, quite clearly, doesn't quite qualify for your "everyday low price." Massmart is a food retailer with 288 stores in 14 countries in sub-Saharan Africa; it offers a lot of products besides food, which dovetail nicely with the expanding range of products that Walmart sells elsewhere. Walmart, which has built its recent success on world-class logistics, is said to be particularly keen on Massmart's low-cost distribution system. In effect, the bid for Massmart is an attempt to gain a first-mover advantage by the world's largest retailer, which belatedly recognized that South Africa is one of the few remaining growth markets. And what if it all goes wrong, as it might? The great thing about being one of the cash-richest multinationals is that you can go on an expensive safari (as much as $4.1 billion), return empty-handed, and barely notice!

Source: Adapted from *The Economist*, September 30, 2010.

Host government barriers

Foreign takeover of local firms may unleash emotional reactions from various constituencies in the host country (see International Corporate Finance in Practice 21.2). If the target firm is an iconic brand or considered a strategic asset, host country barriers to outright acquisition by foreign interests are to be expected. In many cases ownership/control restrictions directed at foreign acquisitions are already the law; transportation, utilities, and mining are often restricted. When China National Offshore Oil Company (CNOOC) — the Chinese government-owned oil company — was finalizing its all-cash acquisition[1] of Unocal (2005), the US Congress derailed the deal on the grounds that it

1 The bid at $18.5 billion topped ChevronTexaco's $17.1 billion. The US Congress claimed that since $13 billion came directly from the Chinese government the transaction would violate free market principles.

INTERNATIONAL CORPORATE FINANCE IN PRACTICE 21.2

When Cross-Border M&As Run into the Wall of Economic Nationalism

A wave of cross-border mergers is sweeping Europe. But as globalization and no-holds-barred industrial restructuring gather strength on the continent, France is holding on to its jingoistic biases and resisting economic integration on "strategic" grounds. The latest affront to Europe's free marketers came as France derailed a bid for Suez, a French electric and water utility, by Enel, an Italian rival. Conveniently, the French government brokered instead a merger between Suez and state-owned Gaz de France — both French companies — creating a group with annual sales of $76 billion. France's creation of an energy colossus came just days after Spain's government had made clear in no uncertain terms that a bid by E.ON, a giant German gas and electricity provider, for Endesa, a Spanish utility, was unwelcome. Indeed, across Europe, more and more countries are resorting to economic nationalism, which runs counter to the liberalizing forces and open markets that the European Union is supposed to foster. France published a list of 11 sectors in which it intended to reserve the right to veto takeovers on the grounds of national security. Recently, rumors of a takeover by PepsiCo of Danone, a French dairy giant, unleashed a torrent of vitriol from leading French politicians. The American suitor rapidly backed off. Yogurts are not your obvious strategic industrial sector, but Yankee flavors may clearly be unpalatable to French diets — definitely a matter of national interest!

Source: Adapted from *The Economist*, May 1, 2006.

would give China access to sensitive US deep-sea exploration drilling technology.

The long arm of extra-territorial antitrust

Before closing, any merger or acquisition deal must clear an antitrust review process by relevant government authorities (US Department of Justice in the case of United States-domiciled firms). The process is lengthy and its outcome uncertain as the regulator needs to be convinced that the merger (especially in the case of a horizontal merger) is not anti-competitive. Often, the merging parties are asked to shed strategic assets to win approval from the regulator. If the merging parties are US-domiciled but with major international activities, other countries affected by the merger will become an integral part of the review process and may reach a different conclusion from the US regulator. To wit, on July 3, 2001, the European Commission blocked a $45 billion deal between General Electric (GE) and Honeywell — barely two months after the US Department of Justice had "blessed" the merger. GE was seeking *"cockpit to tail"* solutions to the commercial aircraft industry by acquiring Honeywell — the worldwide supplier of avionics and non-avionics equipment. The European Commission resisted the combination of GE's dominant position as a leading manufacturer of aircraft engines for large and regional jets seconded with mammoth financial leasing capability (GE Capital) with Honeywell — the leading manufacturer of corporate jet engines and the only manufacturer of regional jet engines (along with GE). The remedy asked by the European Commission was no less than GE divesting from its financial leasing arm or Honeywell's shedding off its entire aerospace business portfolio. Indeed M&A transactions involving multinational corporations are subjected to a *multi-partite* onerous if not convoluted review process (see International Corporate Finance in Practice 21.3).

INTERNATIONAL CORPORATE FINANCE IN PRACTICE 21.3
The Glencore Xstrata Merger Saga

Glencore and Xstrata were two giant commodity-based companies with global reach. Both firms were domiciled in Switzerland – primarily for tax reasons since in both cases their activities occurred outside Switzerland. When they first announced their "merger of equals," both firms were publicly listed on the London Stock Exchange. Xstrata is one of the largest mining and metals companies and is a dominant producer of zinc, copper, tungsten, and thermo-coal with activities in more than 20 countries and a workforce of 70,000. Its largest shareholder is Glencore International plc with a stake of approximately 34%. Glencore itself is a leading integrated producer, trader, and marketer of both mineral and agricultural commodities. It is involved in the refinement, processing, storage, and transportation of these commodities with a workforce of 60,000 and operations in more than 30 countries. Glencore, though, had no mining activities. The economic logic of the merger is primarily one of vertical integration whereby Glencore would secure access to minerals.

In the first week of 2012 Glencore announced plans to merge with Xstrata in an all-share deal offering 2.8 Glencore shares for one share of Xstrata thereby valued at US$61.3bn. After opposition of key shareholders (principally the SWF of Qatar), on September 28 Glencore improved its offer to 3.05 shares which now valued Xstrata at US$50.8bn. The initial offer represented a 15.2% premium to Xstrata's closing share price on February 1, 2012 whereas the revised offer represented a 21% premium over the average Xstrata-Glencore price ratio during the period between Glencore's IPO in 2011 and February 1, 2012.

Q: *Why would an enhanced acquisition bid result in a lower valuation for Xsrrata?*

A: *Glencore pays with its own shares. Yes, it offers to give more of its share to acquire one Xsrata share but, 6 months after the initial bid, Glencore shares' price is down and this results in a lower equity valuation for Xstrata.*

With Xstrata came a prize — Las Bambas copper mine located 150 km north-west of Tintaya in southern Peru. It is an open-pit mine situated at an altitude 4000 meters above sea level. The copper ore reserves are estimated at 7.2 million metric tons and average production is expected to be 480,000 metric tons of copper concentrate for the first 10 years (with a 20 year life expectancy for the mine).

Mega cross-border mergers and acquisitions are subjected to regulatory scrutiny and approval. In a transaction of this sort the European Commission's Directorate-General for Competition and the US Justice Department are expected to be major gate-keepers and would have to approve the deal before it could go forward. In fact, both regulators "blessed" the transaction fairly easily with minor divestments required. However, the Ministry of Commerce of the People's Republic of China (MOFCOM) raised strenuous objections arguing that the merger created a firm which would be the world's largest commodity trader as well as the fourth largest mining conglomerate and that the combined entity would have too great a control over global copper prices. Even though Xstrata has no mining operations in China, Glencore is actively involved in sales and trading with China which gives the latter a great deal of clout over the former. This quickly led to protracted negotiations and it was not until April 16, 2013 that MOFCOM finally approved the merger — 16 months after the merger had been first announced. The approval was contingent upon Glencore divesting 100% of Las Bambas copper project to a purchaser approved by MOFCOM no later than September 2014 with completion by June 2015. Las Bambas would be sold for no less than the higher of (1) *fair value of the mine determined by two investment banks chosen by Glencore* or (2) *total costs incurred by Xstrata and Glencore in developing the mine up to the date of sale.* Importantly, MOFCOM had to approve the purchaser — a not so subtle hint that a Chinese acquirer would have to be involved. This requirement would, in turn, rule out an international bidding process thereby reducing the potential for a sale at a substantial premium to fair market value. If Glencore were unable to complete divestiture of Las Bambas it would be required to appoint a divestiture trustee to sell by way of auction its interest in one of Tampakan (Philippines), Freida River (Papua New Guinea), El Pachon (Argentina) or Alumbrera (Argentina) copper mining projects at *no minimum price.*

On April 13, 2014, Glencore Xstrata announced that it had agreed to sell Las Bambas mine to a Chinese consortium led by MMG Ltd which is itself 74% owned by state-controlled China Minmetals in an all cash-deal worth \$5.8 billion. The sale gave China greater control over raw materials that its industry craves. Indeed, China accounts for 40% of world demand for copper and Las Bambas was projected to produce annually 480,000 metric tons of copper concentrate for at least the next 10 years. The announcement brought to closure a lengthy and tortuous negotiation with China and removed the last stumbling block to Glencore completing its merger with Xstrata. Peru — which would have to live with a new landlord — was only marginally involved in this multi-partite negotiation.

Currency values and acquisition timing

By definition, cross-border M&As involve a foreign exchange (FX or forex) transaction: Target firm B is to be paid for in currency B by the acquiring firm A, whose reference currency is currency A. More often than not, currency B may be mispriced *vis-à-vis* currency A — either overvalued or undervalued in purchasing power parity terms — which would in turn distort the economics of the transaction. Assume that the acquisition target is a Vietnamese firm valued at dong 100 billion and that the dong is currently overvalued by 35% *vis-à-vis* the US dollar. The acquirer would end up paying 35% more than the target is worth intrinsically. Should the acquirer delay its acquisition until after the dong's devaluation? The question then becomes how long the wait will be. Generally, overvalued currencies — often found in emerging market countries that maintain stabilized exchange rates against the US dollar or other reserve currencies — typically adjust within a foreseeable cycle, and the acquirer may — if otherwise possible — wait to close the acquisition until the target firm's currency is devalued in line with its intrinsic value. The reader is referred to our discussion of forecasting pegged yet adjustable exchange rates in Chapter 15 for answers about the timing of devaluations/revaluations or more general currency adjustments.

Q: The Chinese yuan is currently widely believed to be undervalued by 30 to 35% *vis-à-vis* the US dollar and 40 to 45% *vis-à-vis* the euro. Should US firms or euro-zone domiciled firms delay or accelerate their acquisition strategy of Chinese firms?

A: The yuan is relatively cheap for foreign investors, and if one believes that the yuan is indeed on an appreciation path, acquisitions — if anything — should be speeded up (not delayed).

Sovereign wealth funds

The past decade has seen the emergence of new key players in the global market for corporate control: SWFs are established as "savings funds for future generations" by governments of either oil-rich countries (United Arab Emirates, Norway, Saudi-Arabia, Kuwait, Russia) or East Asian nations with current account surpluses such as China, Singapore, and Hong Kong. SWFs were once contented with passive international portfolio investments but are now increasingly acquiring illiquid foreign assets in the form of partial or minority equity positions. Unlike private equity firms committed to an early exit strategy, SWFs are patient long-term investors whose motivation may go beyond simple financial returns and may — it is feared — be to further national geopolitical interests. In most cases such concerns are ill-conceived as there is little to fear from Norway's, Singapore's, or Qatar's geopolitical ambitions to be furthered by their SWFs. But Russia and China are a different story, somewhat reminiscent of French or British colonial multinationals of yesteryears.

Acquisitions of privatized firms

In the last quarter century more than a trillion dollars of state-owned firms were privatized, providing unique opportunities for foreign companies to enter countries and industries that had been hitherto closed to the private sector in general and foreign firms in particular. The challenge in completing the acquisition of state-owned firms is the valuation of *going concerns* that operated under a very different set of rules until their privatization: Protected or monopolistic market protection, bloated payrolls, and antiquated and generally inefficient operating conditions make it difficult to extrapolate into the future existing financials to generate cash-flow forecasts for valuation purposes. Major adjustments have to be made to top-line/sales revenues and operating expenses to reflect the deregulated markets that often accompany privatization. In the same vein, modernization/rationalization of the production apparatus delivers efficiency gains due to new equipment, streamlined operations, and labor cost savings, which result in a markedly different cost structure.

Private equity firms are now accounting for more than a third of all cross-border acquisitions and are increasingly vying for opportunities with multinationals (see International Corporate Finance in Practice 21.4). Unlike strategic corporate acquirers, private equity firms have shorter investment horizons anchored to early exit strategies and tight financial goals. Traditionally, private equity firms' acquisition style is tantamount to LBOs; however, the subprime crisis has put a dampener on aggressively leveraged cross-border acquisitions.

INTERNATIONAL CORPORATE FINANCE IN PRACTICE 21.4
Celanese AG

Celanese AG — a German manufacturer of industrial chemicals — was acquired in December 2003 by Blackstone, the US titan of private equity, for $650 million in equity and $2.43 billion in debt. The deal was finalized as a tender offer at €32.50 per share (a premium of 13% over the previous quarterly stock price average) and closed in April 2004. Celanese AG was delisted. As early as September 2004, Celanese issued €513 million in senior discount notes that were used to pay Blackstone a special dividend of €500 million.[2] By January 2005 — less than a year after taking Celanese private — Blackstone took it public again at a value corresponding to 3.5 times what it had paid for it by executing an €800 million initial public offering, and paid itself another extraordinary dividend of €800 million. In the end Blackstone made six times its initial investment of $650 million over a three year period — a mind-boggling rate of return of 273%. Blackstone had correctly predicted an upswing in the chemical industry cycle while aggressively streamlining Celanese's operations.

2 Lenders to an LBO-style private equity transaction typically include a "cash sweep" covenant in the loan agreement requiring that all cash available be used to pay down the debt. Blackstone had negotiated an atypical loan that allowed it to borrow additional monies to pay itself a special dividend, also known as a leveraged dividend recapitalization transaction.

VALUATION OF FOREIGN ACQUISITIONS

Valuation of foreign acquisition targets is generally easier than the case of greenfield projects for the simple reason that actual financial statements for the going concern are readily available. This undoubtedly facilitates cash-flow forecasts, which are central to any valuation exercise. However, metrics should take into account whether the acquisition target is privately held or publicly listed, as the availability of a stock price greatly facilitates valuation for bidding purposes. Further complications arise when the target is a business unit or an *equity carve-out* of a larger parent company (see International Corporate Finance in Practice 21.5 describing Lenovo's acquisition of IBM's PC business).

There are two principal steps involved in valuing a foreign acquisition target:

1. Value target as a stand-alone pre-acquisition play V^{pre} in local currency.
2. Value target having incorporated the various value-creating enhancements in local currency that the acquisition will bring to the target V^{post}.

Establishing an upper bound for V^{post} will require that valuation be carried out in local currency first (currency of target firm) and reference currency second (currency of acquirer) so as to capture the incremental benefits of the acquisition to the bidder before — last step — being reconverted in the local currency for bidding purposes. The second step — worth emphasizing — reflects the tax burden of transferring equity cash flows back to the parent so that the final local currency bid (reference currency upper-bound valuation converted back into local currency) fully incorporates all incremental benefits of the acquisition on the value of the bidder. Needless to say, this is an important and necessary step — one that is often ignored in cross-border acquisition. Presumably, $V^{post} > V^{pre}$, and the difference between the pre- and post-acquisition values of the target is precisely the price range within which the acquirer can negotiate.

Acquisition target is privately held

This is often the case of family-owned closely held firms. Indeed, conglomerate-style business groups in emerging market countries are often privately held. In such cases the obvious missing statistic for valuation is the stock price, as it is always a useful starting — but not final — reference point in pricing an acquisition target.[3] Valuation by *multiples* of earnings (E); earnings before interest and tax (EBIT); earnings before interest, tax, depreciation, and amortization (EBITDA);[4] book value (BV); and so on will prove useful frameworks, however simplistic they may be. The valuation approach requires finding comparable publicly listed firms to be used as proxies, which means firms that are similar in terms of product portfolio, size, leverage, and so on relative to the firm of interest. Once a reasonably close comparable has been identified, it is easy to apply the multiple to the metric of choice and derive the target firm's value.

The most widely used valuation by the comparables method is the price/earnings (P/E) ratio (see International Corporate Finance in Practice 21.5). In basic terms, the P/E ratio is a measure of what the market is willing to pay (P) for each dollar of earnings per share (E). Assume that firm A is privately held by an Indian family (P^A not available but E^A = INR 5 is known) and comparable to firm B, which is publicly listed and whose stock is currently trading at 65 with a $(P/E)^B = 11$. By applying the $(P/E)^B = 11$ to firm A's earnings $E^A = 5$, its stock price is simply derived from:

$$(P/E)^A = (P/E)^B = 11 \text{ or } P^A = E^A \times (P/E)^B$$
$$= 5 \times 11 = \text{INR } 55$$

Valuation by P/E multiples assumes similar financial leverage since earnings are exclusive of interest payments. When leverage between the target firm and comparables is different, EBIT or EBITDA would be preferred because they are both exclusive of interest charges. Furthermore, because of notable differences between national accounting standards, it is important to use proxy firms domiciled in the country of the acquisition target — not in the country of the acquirer.

Multiples of EBITDA — an imperfect proxy for free cash flows — are often used by private equity firms to size up foreign acquisition targets. Returning to the previous example, assume that firm A's EBITDA = INR 8 and that firm B's EBITDA

3 This is also the case in the acquisition of government-owned firms that are being privatized.

4 Earnings (E) = Earnings before Interest, Tax, Depreciation, and Amortization (EBITDA) – Interest (I) – Tax (T) – Depreciation (D) – Amortization (A) = Earnings before interest and tax (EBIT) – Interest – Tax.

INTERNATIONAL CORPORATE FINANCE IN PRACTICE 21.5

P/E and the Cost of Equity Capital

P/E is widely used as a basis for valuation by comparables and as a proxy for a firm's cost of equity capital. It is simple and simplistic but in fact consistent with valuation through discounted cash flows if some strong assumptions are made. Let's say a firm has a P/E = 10. If the firm's cash flows are assumed to be a perpetuity with equity cash flows approximated by earning (ECF) = E, then its value is $P = E/k_E$, where k_E is the cost of equity capital. But earnings are not quite equity cash flows:

$$ECF = E + Depreciation - Capital\ ecpenditures - Change\ in\ net\ working\ capital$$

If depreciation is assumed to be equal to annual capital expenditures and if net working capital is assumed to be in steady state (i.e., change in net working capital = 0), then E = ECF, $P = ECF/k_E$, $P = E/k_E$, or $k_E = 1/(P/E)$. The firm's cost of equity capital is simply the inverse of its P/E ratio.

multiple is 6. This information would lead to value firm A at:

$$(P/EBITDA)^A = (P/EBITDA)^B = 6 \text{ or}$$
$$P^A = EBITDA^A \times (P/EBITDA)^B = 8 \times 6 = INR\ 48$$

This valuation is lower than the valuation derived from the P/E multiple and may reflect differences in leverage between the two firms.

The market/book (M/B) ratio is also widely used and will provide a useful complement to the P/E ratio derived value. Referring to the previous example, assume that firm A's book value is INR 45 per share and that firm B, currently trading at 65, has $(M/B)^B = 1.3$. Firm A's market value per share is derived as

$$(M/B)^A = (M/B)^B = 1.3 \text{ or } M^A = B^A \times (M/B)^B$$
$$= 45 \times 1.3 = 58.5$$

Acquisition target is publicly listed

Under normal market conditions, the current stock price or historical price average over the previous one to 3 months provides an easy starting point for valuing the pre-acquisition target V^{pre}. Typically, the acquirer pays a premium over the current stock price so that shareholders will willingly tender their shares to the acquirer. The premium amount that the acquirer is willing to pay — post-acquisition V^{post} — pre-acquisition V^{pre} — is determined by the value-creating enhancements that the acquisition will bestow on the target firm.

As a first step, the premium could be determined in part by deriving the target's value on the basis of comparables to unveil possible market inefficiencies or undervaluation of the target. The second step is to ensure that equity cash flows, discounted at the levered cost of equity in the target currency, reflect the benefits (sometimes costs) of acquisition enhancements and/or adjustments of the target firm's cash inflows and cash outflows (such as reduced operating expenses due to modernization of equipment and streamlined operations).

Such an analysis will provide an upper bound for how much the acquirer is willing to pay. If the acquirer pays the upper price, it would simply mean that all the value created by the acquisition would accrue to the acquired firm, not the acquiring firm. Any price paid between the pre-acquisition value of the target and the upper bound simply results in some sharing of the value created by the acquisition between buyer and seller.

CIMENTS LAFARGE ENTERS VIETNAM

Ciments Lafarge — the French cement multinational conglomerate — had been on the prowl for a major acquisition in Vietnam for some time to complement its already dominant positions in Thailand and Malaysia. Vietnam was the missing piece in the multinational firm's Southeast Asian portfolio. Somehow Ciments Lafarge had entirely ignored the opening of the Vietnamese economy in the 1990s and was now going to be a late entrant. A successful acquisition, however, would hasten its entry, and Ciments Lafarge was closely scrutinizing the partially privatized Hoang Thach Cement Company (HTC), which was part of the state-owned Vietnam National Cement Corporation.

HTC is located about 100 km east of Hanoi on the Ba Dack River with a total installed capacity of 2.3 million tons of cement per year. It employs approximately 2,700 employees, who work on three shifts. The factory uses rotating kiln technology for cement production; it is a relatively integrated process from the mining of limestone and clay to the crushing, heating at 1,450°C, and processing in the kilns. The kilns produce clinker, which is mixed with additives such as gypsum and milled to become Portland cement. The factory, built in the early 1980s with Soviet technology, had been somewhat neglected, and lack of proper maintenance had taken its toll on product quality and on operating expenses. HTC seemed to be your typical poorly managed state-owned company. Lack of systematic maintenance, along with operating inefficiencies, low motivation, and poor employee morale appeared to be widespread throughout the company, impairing its performance. Ciments Lafarge was contemplating investing Vietnamese Dong (VND) 1,600 billion (approximately €100 million at the exchange rate of VND 16,000 = €1) to modernize its operations.[5] Output would rise from 2.3 to 3.1 million tons of cement per year while payroll would decline to 1,950 employees, resulting in the lowering of cost of goods sold (COGS) from 42% to 39% of sales.

The immediate challenge for Guillaume Tel — the senior vice president overseeing strategic acquisitions for Ciments Lafarge — was to formulate a bid price at a premium over the current stock price that would be attractive enough to convince the Vietnam National Cement Corporation to sell its 49% stake in its Hanoi operations by completing HTC privatization. Based on its current stock price on the Ho Chi Minh stock exchange, HTC was valued at V^{pre} = VND 1,710 billion (€107 million) or a stock price of VND 171,000 with 10 million shares outstanding. At least one P/E of a comparable publicly listed cement company indicated that HTC might be overvalued by as much as 15%. Guillaume Tel's task was to establish an upper bound for HTC at which the acquisition would still make sense.

> ***Q:*** The Sai Son Cement Company — one of HTC's major Vietnamese competitors — is currently trading at a P/E of 8.3 on the Ho Chi Minh stock exchange. Siam Cement, the leading Thai cement manufacturer, is trading on the Stock Exchange of Thailand at a P/E of 7.1, while Ciments Lafarge on the Paris Bourse enjoys a P/E of 11. Given HTC's earnings per share of VND 18,000, what should its value be? It is currently trading at VDN 171,000 for a P/E = 171,100/18,000 = 9.5.
>
> ***A:*** Valuation by comparable P/Es would yield $18{,}000 \times P/E^{\text{Sai Son}} = 18{,}000 \times 8.3 = 149{,}400$ on the Ho Chi Minh exchange. A similar valuation on the Stock Exchange of Thailand (SET) and Paris Bourse would yield 18,000 × 7.1 = VND 127,800 and 18,000 × 11 = VND 198,000. The wide price range may reflect differences in leverage, accounting standards, and liquidity among the three stock markets.

Ultimately, Ciments Lafarge believed that *incremental after-tax value* in euros contributed to the multinational group was the appropriate metric to apply to such a transaction. Equity cash flows to the acquirer reflecting value enhancements would thus be discounted at the levered cost of equity capital. It would yield the post-acquisition upper value bound V^{post} for the range of bid prices within which Ciments Lafarge should negotiate. The pro forma VND income statement and VND and euro cash-flow forecasts reflecting increased output and operating efficiencies are presented in Exhibits 21.2, 21.3, and 21.4, respectively, and yield an upper bound of V^{post} = VND 420,480 per share (or €262.8 million for the entire firm). Let's now recapitulate the key steps.

Step 1. Value HTC as a *stand-alone* Vietnamese firm to establish a floor price. The stock price provides a fair value of V^{pre} = VND 171,000 per share or €107 million using the prevailing exchange rate of VND 16,000 = €1. In addition, valuation by P/E multiples would yield a price range of VND 127,800 (based on Thai Siam Cements comparable) and VND 198,000 (based on French Ciments Lafarge comparable).

Step 2. Value HFC as an *acquisition target* in local currency VND with revised revenue reflecting an increase in output from 2.3 to 3.1 million metric tons (mmt) per year and sales price increasing annually at the rate of 5%. Operating expenses (Opex) due to productivity gains and reduction in the workforce are expected to decline from 42% to 39%. Sales, general, and administrative expenses (SG&A) are

5 It generally costs $125 to $150 of capex to produce one metric ton (mt) of cement. Given lower-cost conditions prevailing in Vietnam, the 800,000-ton expansion of the plant is reckoned to cost $125/mt or $125 × 800,000 × 16,000 = VND 1,600 billion.

Exhibit 21.2. Valuation of Hoang Thach Cement Company (1).

Pro Forma Income Statement (Millions of Vietnamese dong)						
	Notes	**2008**	**2009**	**2010**	**2011**	**2012**
Sales volume[a]	Q	2.3	2.7	3.1	3.1	3.1
Actual sales as % of full capacity		100	100	100	100	100
Price in VND/metric ton increasing at 5.0% p.a.	P	928,000	974,400	1,023,120	1,074,276	1,127,990
Sales revenue	**Q × P**	**2,134,400**	**2,630,880**	**3,171,672**	**3,330,256**	**3,496,768**
Opex		(896,448)	(1,104,970)	(1,300,386)	(1,332,102)	(1,363,740)
Opex as % of sales		42.0	42.0	41.0	40.0	39.0
Gross profit/margin		1,237,952	1,525,910	1,871,286	1,998,153	2,133,029
Gross margin as % of sales		58.0	58.0	59.0	60.0	61.0
SG&A[b]		(220,000)	(222,200)	(224,422)	(226,666)	(228,933)
SG&A % of sales		10.3	8.4	7.1	6.8	6.5
SG&A % of growth			1.0	1.0	1.0	1.0
Licensing fees		(53,360)	(65,772)	(79,292)	(83,256)	(87,419)
Licensing fees as % of sales		2.50	2.50	2.50	2.50	2.50
EBITDA		964,592	1,237,938	1,567,573	1,668,231	1,816,677
EBITDA as % of sales		45.2	47.1	49 4	50.7	52.0
Depreciation		(250,000)	(250,000)	(250,000)	(250,000)	(250,000)
Depreciation as % of sales		11.7	9.5	7.9	7.5	7.1
EBIT		**714,592**	**987,938**	**1,317,573**	**1,438,231**	**1,566,677**
EBIT as % of sales		33.5	37.6	41.5	43.2	44.8
Interest expense[c]		(300,000)	(300,000)	(300,000)	(300,000)	(300,000)
Taxable income		414,592	687,938	1,017,573	1,138,231	1,266,677
Less: Income tax		(124,378)	(206,382)	(305,272)	(341,469)	(380,003)
Tax rate		30.0	30.0	30.0	30.0	30.0
Net income		**290,214**	**481,557**	**712,301**	**796,762**	**886,674**
Net income as % of sales		13.6	18.3	22.5	23.9	25.4

Notes: [a] In millions of metric tons at 100% capacity.
[b] SG&A is a quasi-fixed cost increasing at 1.0% per annum.
[c] Interest-only interest expense on a principal of 2 trillion Vietnamese dong (VND) at 15.0%.

quasi-fixed costs increasing slightly at an annual rate of 1%. Licensing fees to the parent Ciments Lafarge are set at 2.5% of sales. See Exhibit 21.2 for HTC pro forma income statement in VND.

Increased plant capacity from 2.3 to 3.1 million ton per year as well as modernization require capital expenditures (capex) of VND 1.5 billion. These expenditures would be distributed over years 2008–2012, set at a high of 200% of accounting depreciation in 2008 and declining to a low of 40% of accounting depreciation in 2012 when capex is limited to maintenance. Change in working capital

Exhibit 21.3. Valuation of Hoang Thach Cement Company (2).

Pro Forma VND Cash-Flow Statement (Millions of Vietnamese dong)						
	Notes	**2008**	**2009**	**2010**	**2011**	**2012**
Net income		**290,214**	**481,557**	**712,301**	**796,762**	**886,674**
Minus: Capital expenditures		(500,000)	(400,000)	(300,000)	(200,000)	(100,000)
Capex as % of depreciation		*200.0*	*160.0*	*120.0*	*80.0*	*40.0*
Plus: Depreciation		250,000	250,000	250,000	250,000	250,000
Minus: Change in WC		(100,000)	(90,000)	(80,000)	(70,000)	(60,000)
Change in WC as % of sales		*4.7*	*3.4*	*2.5*	*2.1*	*1.7*
Equity cash flows		**(59,786)**	**241,557**	**582,301**	**776,762**	**976,674**
Terminal value in 2012 at 7.5 × E		0	0	0	0	6,650,052
Equity cash flows + Terminal value		**(59,786)**	**241,557**	**582,301**	**776,762**	**7,626,726**
NPV discounted at 10.5% in VND		**5,725,728.7**	. . .	. . .	. . .	. . .
NPV discounted at 10.5% in euros		**357.9**	. . .	. . .	. . .	. . .

would decline progressively from a high of 4.7% of sales in 2008 to a low of 1.7% of sales in 2012. Terminal value is computed on the basis of a P/E ratio arbitrarily set at 7.5 for the terminal year's equity cash flows.[6] Using a discount rate of 10.50%,[7] the value of HFC restated in euros at the exchange rate of VND 16,000 = €1 prevailing in 2008 is found to be V^{post} = €357.9 million or VND 572,000 per share (see Exhibit 21.3). This bid price is often mistakenly considered as the upper range that the acquirer should be willing to pay. However, it does not reflect the true incremental contribution to the foreign acquirer because it does not incorporate royalties,[8] side payments, or the necessary transfer tax adjustments that should be made for remittances paid to the foreign acquirer.

Step 3. Value incremental contribution made by the acquisition target after the remittance adjustments (exchange rate and transfer taxes) have been fully incorporated. Restate after-tax local currency cash flows in *reference currency* terms. This restatement should take into account remittances of royalty payments (2.5% of sales subjected to a 10% withholding tax) in addition to equity cash flows taxed at the higher rate of 20% as imposed by the central bank of Vietnam on all dividends repatriation. Exchange rates used for translation reflect the expected 8% annual devaluation of the dong from a base rate of VND 16,000 = €1 in 2008. Using a 10.5% discount rate, HFC would be valued at V^{post*} = €262.2 million or VND 420,480 per share (see Exhibit 21.4).

For Ciments Lafarge, a negotiation price range lies between the pre- and post-acquisition of VND 171,000 to VND 420,480. Interestingly for Ciments

6 See Chapter 20 for a detailed discussion of the mechanics of cash-flow-based valuation. Note that this method of discounting VND cash flows first before converting their present value into the reference currency is second best to the method presented in Chapter 20 whereby cash flows are converted directly into the reference currency at the forecast exchange rate. The approach presented here is warranted in the case of a target firm whose cash flows are entirely local currency denominated with little or no import competition. Should the target firm be directly or indirectly exposed to international competition, the method developed in Chapter 20 would be preferred.

7 The equity cost of capital for Vietnamese investors is approximated by the inverse of the P/E ratio or 1/[P/E] = 1/9.5 = 10.50%.

8 For valuation purposes, royalties are cost to the target firm but additional revenue to the acquiring firm.

Exhibit 21.4. Valuation of Hoang Thach Cement Company (3).

Pro Forma Euro Cash-Flow Statement (millions); VND Cash Flows (millions)						
	Notes	**2008**	**2009**	**2010**	**2011**	**2012**
VND per euro	...	16,000	17,280	18,662	20,155	21,768
Percentage devaluation	...	...	8.0	8.0	8.0	8.0
Equity cash flows (VND)	...	**(59,786)**	**241,557**	**582,301**	**776,762**	**976,674**
Less: 20% withholding tax	20%	0	(48,311)	(116,460)	(155,352)	(195,335)
Net equity cash flows for remittance (VND)	...	(59,786)	193,246	465,841	621,409	781,339
Net euro equity cash flows remitted	A	(3.7)	11.2	25.0	30.8	35.9
Licensing fee remittance (VND)	2.5%	53,360	65,772	79,292	83,256	87,419
Minus: 10% withholding tax (VND)	...	(5,336)	(6,577)	(7,929)	(8,326)	(8,742)
Net licensing fee	...	48,024	59,195	71,363	74,931	78,677
Net euro licensing fee remitted	B	3.0	3.4	3.8	3.7	3.6
Terminal value in 2012 at 7.5 × E	C	0.0	0.0	0.0	0.0	305.5
Net equity cash flows to Ciments Lafarge (euros)	A + B + C	**(0.7)**	**14.6**	**28.8**	**34.5**	**345.0**
NPV discounted at 10.5%	...	**€262.2 million**	...	..	...	...

Lafarge, the impact of a 10 and 20% withholding tax on remitted cash flows to the French parent coupled with the devaluation of the dong over the investment horizon considerably lower the upper bound within which it should negotiate. If the analysis had stopped with step 2 — which most managers typically do — the upper range for the acquisition bid would have been misleadingly VND 572,000 per share. All too often an international acquirer would value HFC as a stand-alone firm, incorporating modernization and cost-restructuring benefits but ignoring royalties and the impact of currency misvaluation and transfer taxes. Ultimately what should matter to Ciments Lafarge is the incremental contribution of HFC to the value of the entire group — not its value as a stand-alone Vietnamese target.

Last but not least, the acquirer would want to test the sensitivity of its bid price range to key noncontrollable contextual factors. Exhibit 21.5 highlights the upper range bid price sensitivity to exchange rate devaluation ranging from 8 to 16% with domestic Vietnamese inflation stable at 5% per annum. Similarly, sensitivity analysis shows low exposure to an increase of withholding tax on dividends but higher exposure to corporate income tax. Of most concern is the sensitivity of the project to capacity utilization when a drop in actual sales of 20% triggers a reduction in value of 39%. For a cross-border acquisition between world players in the context of a global oligopoly, please see International Corporate Finance in Practice 21.6.

Exhibit 21.5. Valuation of Hoang Thach Cement Company (4)

NPV discounted at 10.5%	**265.2**

NPV Sensitized to Exchange Rate Devaluation

	Exchange Rate Devaluation				
	8.0%	10.0%	12.0%	14.0%	16.0%
	265.2	248.2	232.6	218.2	205.0

NPV Sensitized to Cash-Flow Withholding Tax

	Cash-Flow Withholding Tax				
	16.0%	18.0%	20.0%	22.0%	24.0%
	268.7	267.0	265.2	263.5	261.7

NPV Sensitized to Corporate Tax Rate

	Corporate Tax Rate				
	26.0%	28.0%	30.0%	32.0%	34.0%
	281.4	273.3	265.2	257.1	249.0

NPV Sensitized to Sales Price Growth Rate

	Sales Price Growth Rate				
	5.0%	6.0%	7.0%	8.0%	9.0%
	265.2	280.4	296.0	312.0	328.5

NPV Sensitized to Actual Sales as Percent of Capacity

	Sales as Percent of Capacity				
	100.0%	95.0%	90.0%	85.0%	80.0%
	265.2	239.9	214.7	189.4	164.1

NPV Sensitized to Actual Sales as % of Capacity and Exchange Rate

		Sales as Percent of Capacity				
		100.0%	95.0%	90.0%	85.0%	80.0%
Exchange Rate Change	8.0%	265.2	239.9	214.7	189.4	164.1
	10.0%	248.2	224.3	200.4	176.5	152.6
	12.0%	232.6	210.0	187.3	164.7	142.1
	14.0%	218.2	196.8	175.4	153.9	132.5
	16.0%	205.0	184.7	164.3	144.0	123.7

INTERNATIONAL CORPORATE FINANCE IN PRACTICE 21.6

Lenovo Buys IBM PC Division[9]

When East meets West and a little-known upstart buys its most famous rival, three times its size. . . . It actually happened when Beijing-based Lenovo — China's market leader in personal computers with $3 billion in sales — announced on December 7 its acquisition of IBM's $9 billion personal computer business for $1.75 billion in cash, stock, and assumed liabilities. This bold move instantly propelled Lenovo onto the world stage, and it is now playing in the big leagues in third place behind Dell and

9 This section draws from John Ackerly and Mans Larsson, "The Emergence of a Global PC Giant: Lenovo's Acquisition of IBM's PC Division" (manuscript, Harvard Business School, December 2005).

Hewlett-Packard. Lenovo would be owned by the Chinese government (46%),[10] public investors (35%), and IBM (19%). Interestingly, the new company would be managed out of New York (rather than Beijing) primarily by former IBM executives (including the CEO) with a total workforce of 19,000 (10,000 of them based in China). Lenovo also acquired the right to use the IBM logo for 5 years and the ThinkPad brand permanently.

Industrial Logic

On the face of it, the acquisition makes good economic sense. As a low-cost manufacturer, Lenovo specializes in the consumer segment of the PC market with a 26% share of the Chinese market. Big Blue is a global player that focuses on the business segment of the PC market with a global sales force of 30,000. "The complementary nature of their business across geographies, products, and areas of functional strength opened a number of win-win opportunities for buyer and seller. . . . The deal offered significant opportunity for revenue synergies, [and] the cross-border combination was viewed as a 'cost-play' by the parties involved."[11]

IBM will hold an equity stake of 19% in the new Lenovo and its CEO will be the CEO of the company. In essence IBM is outsourcing its PC business to Lenovo, while Lenovo is outsourcing its management and sales to IBM.

---

10 Senior American politicians attempted to block the deal on national security grounds. Indeed, prior to the deal the Chinese government — through the Academy of Sciences — was the majority owner of Lenovo. It was then alleged that the Chinese government, by acquiring sensitive American technologies, could use IBM's facilities to spy. In reality Lenovo was acquiring mature technologies, commoditized products with no clever applications and no military use.

11 Ackerly and Larsson, "Emergence of a Global PC Giant," 3.

SUMMARY

1. International acquisitions are a fast-paced foreign market entry strategic alternative to greenfield or de novo foreign direct investment.

2. Mergers and acquisitions are generally characterized as either *horizontal* (the firms are direct competitors in one product market), *vertical* (acquirer is buying control of upstream or downstream activities), *congeneric* (the firms are in sectorially contiguous yet distinct product/market segments), or *conglomerate* (the firms are in unrelated industries). If this taxonomy is generally valid for domestic and mega cross-border M&As, it remains that the driving motivation for international acquisitions is grounded in foreign market entry.

3. Multinational corporations find themselves increasingly competing with private equity firms and SWFs in the pursuit of international acquisitions. Each contending acquirer has markedly different objectives, which typically results in different bidding price ranges.

4. The acquisition target should be valued first as a *stand-alone* firm in local currency (currency of target firm), which will establish a floor price for bidding price purposes. If the target is not publicly listed, valuation by comparables is recommended.

5. The target firm should then be valued as an acquisition target with all revenues and costs carefully adjusted for the value-enhancing benefits of the transaction. This should be carried out first in local currency terms and then further adjusted to incorporate the incremental impact of the proposed acquisition on the acquiring firm. This last step is critical and should reflect all remittances to the acquirer adjusted for transfer taxes and exchange rate translation. The result of this last step will be reconverted into local currency to establish the upper range of the acquisition price bid.

QUESTIONS FOR DISCUSSION

1. Discuss the logic for mergers and acquisitions. Are cross-border M&As substantially different from domestic M&As?
2. What is meant by a control premium? Who are the primary beneficiaries in M&As?
3. What are the pros and cons of international acquisition as a mode of foreign market entry?
4. What is unique about valuing cross-border acquisitions? What valuation methodology would you recommend?
5. Contrast cross-border acquisitions carried out by multinationals, private equity firms, and SWFs.
6. What is the appropriate discount rate to use in valuing foreign companies?
7. Discuss the pros and cons of valuation by multiples in cross-border acquisitions.
8. What is the value range within which the acquirer should set the acquisition premium?

PROBLEMS

1. **How should private equity firms value cross-border acquisitions? (A).** Ulysses, a Boston-based private equity firm, specializes in transportation with a focus on emerging capital markets. It has identified Salgacoar Ltd., a family-owned business group headquartered in Goa (India). Salgacoar is involved in three businesses — iron ore mining in the State of Goa, ocean-going freighters, and hotels. Each division is cash-flow positive. Its shipping division generated earnings after taxes of INR 4 billion. Two publicly listed shipping companies on the Mumbai stock exchange have P/E multiples of 8 and 9.2, respectively. Maersk, the giant Danish shipping and container company, is listed on the Copenhagen Stock Exchange and has a P/E of 13.5.
   a. What is your value estimate for Salgacoar's shipping business? Spell out the assumptions that you are making in answering.
   b. If it turned out that Salgacoar had signed a three-year charter for 70% of its fleet, how would you adjust your response to part a?
2. **How should private equity firms value cross-border acquisitions? (B).** Referring to background information provided in problem 1 assume that Ulysses did purchase Salgacoar's shipping business at a P/E multiple of 10 for cash, that Salgacoar's shipping business will grow its earnings at the annual rate of 2.50%, and that all earnings are paid as dividends, at what exit price will Ulysses have to sell Salgacoar in five years to guarantee to its investor a rate of return of 25%? The current exchange rate stands at US$1 = INR 50, and the INR is expected to depreciate at an annual rate of 1.25% over the next five years.
3. **LBO (intermediate).** Referring to background information provided in Problem 1, assume now that the transaction was financed by a jumbo loan for 80% of the purchase price. The loan is INR-denominated at 12% with interest payment tax-deductible at the rate of 30% and repaid in full in a lump sum payment at exit time.
   a. What is a LBO? What are the pros and cons of LBOs in cross-border acquisitions?
   b. Assuming that Ulysses did purchase Salgacoar's shipping business at a P/E multiple of 10, that Salgacoar's shipping business will grow its earnings at the annual rate of 2.50%, and that all earnings are paid as dividends, at what exit price will Ulysses have to sell Salgacoar in five years to guarantee to its investor a rate of return of 25%? The current exchange rate stands at US$1 = INR 50, and the INR is expected to depreciate at an annual rate of 1.25% over the next five years.
4. **Bidding for Salgacoar (intermediate).** Maersk is preparing an offer to acquire the privately held Indian shipping company Salgacoar. In addition to the background information provided in problem 1, Maersk believes that by giving access to its global logistical network, Salgacoar would be able to lower its operating expenses by 10%. However, Maersk has to contend with 10% withholding tax levied by the Indian government on all dividend remittances. What is the price range within which Maersk should formulate its acquisition bid? Assume that Maersk's cost of equity capital for international acquisition is 10.5%, that acquisition targets are valued for the first 5 years only, and that terminal value is based on Maersk's P/E multiple.
5. **Cross-border valuation with concessionary financing (intermediate).** Referring to Ciments Lafarge's acquisition, explain how the valuation of the Hoang Thach Cement Company would differ if instead of an all-cash deal the transaction had been financed with a VND 1 billion loan from the State Bank of Vietnam at a subsidized interest rate of 10% to be amortized over 5 years.

6. **Which cost of capital? (advanced).** Guillaume Tel of Ciments Lafarge was unsure about the legitimacy of applying a discount rate of 10.5% to value the acquisition of Hoang Thach Cement Company. After all, Ciments Lafarge's company-wide WACC was estimated at 9% and the country risk premium applied to Vietnam was set at 365 basis points.
   a. How was the 10.5% discount rate derived? How would you justify its use?
   b. Should a country risk premium be added to the 10.5% discount rate?
   c. What appropriate discount rate should be applied to the valuation of Hoang Thach Cement Company?
7. **Timing cross-border acquisition (intermediate).** GE Capital — a global leader in automobile leasing — started to scrutinize possible acquisitions in Thailand in the early 1990s when the THB was pegged to the US dollar at THB 25 = US$1. With healthy economic growth at better than 7.5% per year and a rapidly expanding car manufacturing industry, Thailand was indeed ripe for a strong market entry by GE. Ultimately, GE Capital delayed its acquisition of Tisco automobile leasing operations until 1998 — more than a year after the historic devaluation of the baht had unleashed the Asian financial crisis. GE Capital closed its acquisition at a much-devalued baht of THB 57 = US$1. Time being of the essence, had GE Capital waited too long and itself fallen victim of the Asian financial crisis?
8. **Costs/benefits analysis (advanced).** How should Vietnam gauge the proposed cross-border acquisition described in problems 5 and 6?
   a. What are the costs and benefits of Ciments Lafarge's proposed acquisition on Vietnam's balance of payments?
   b. What are the costs and benefits of Ciments Lafarge's proposed acquisition on Vietnam's gross domestic product?
   c. How is your analysis evolving over time? What could the acquirer do to maintain a positive costs/benefits ratio?

INTERNET EXERCISES

9. **Mergers & Acquisitions in Energy.** Access the Institute for Mergers, Acquisitions and Alliance (IMAA) website https://imaa-institute.org/mergers-and-acquisitions-statistics/ and identify the three largest cross-border M&As involving energy companies in the last 20 years. Is the Energy sector the most active sector by value of transactions and/or number of transactions over the last 20 years?
10. **Mergers & Acquisitions in Europe.** With the help of the imaa website identify the two largest life-science/pharmaceuticals European M&As during the last 20 years. What were the value of the transactions. Which sector in Europe was the most active by value of transactions over that same period. Can you explain?

CASE STUDY 21.1. ETIHAD'S PROPOSED ACQUISITION OF MALAYSIA AIRLINES

— Shuvam Dutta

A significant strategic shareholding in Malaysia Airlines (MAS) had become available in the market. As the flag carrier of Malaysia with a fleet of 85 aircraft traveling to 103 destinations worldwide, the airline was trading at an equity value of US$1,316 million as of March 30, 2010. MAS was led by a strong management team with a proven track record. Over the past few years, the management had undertaken a strategic business transformation resulting in a significant positive turnaround of performance, including Malaysian ringgit (MYR) 2.3 billion in cost savings from 2006 to 2008 and steady revenue growth from MYR 9 billion in 2006 to MYR 15 billion in 2008.

Etihad Airlines was a Middle Eastern carrier looking to extend its route network beyond its hub in Dubai, and it hoped to gain access to lucrative routes to Singapore, Hong Kong, and Australia. Etihad's bankers at Standard Chartered advised them to consider a 20% to 25% investment stake in MAS, hand in glove with an operating alliance.

Etihad Airways was established as the flag carrier of the United Arab Emirates in July 2003 by royal decree with an initial paid-up capital of United Arab Emirates dirham (AED) 500 million provided by the Abu Dhabi Investment Authority. As of January 2010, the airline operated passenger and cargo services to 85 destinations around the world from its home base in Abu Dhabi.

Malaysia Airlines is partially privatized with Khazana Nasional, the Malaysian SWF, holding a residual equity stake in the airline. Malaysia Airlines operates flights in Southeast Asia, East Asia,

South Asia, Middle East, and on the Kangaroo Route between Europe and Australasia. It operates transpacific flights from Kuala Lumpur to Los Angeles via Tokyo. It flies to 87 destinations in over six continents. Malaysia Airlines has existing code share agreements with American Airlines, Cathay Pacific, and Japan Airlines, among others.

As an international airline, Malaysia Airlines was exposed to the effects of foreign exchange rate fluctuations because of its foreign currency–denominated operating revenues and expenses. Its largest exposures were to the US dollar, followed by the euro, British pound, Japanese yen, and Australian dollar. Approximately 58% of the airline's sales and almost 65% of the airline's costs are denominated in foreign currencies. The airline's trade receivables and trade payables balances had similar exposures. The airline was also exposed to fuel price volatility, partially mitigated by entering into jet fuel hedges.

The bankers articulated several strategic benefits arising from the potential acquisition. The transaction would ensure major presences in two of the highest-growing air traffic regions in the world (Asia and the Middle East) and allow Etihad to leverage consistently growing tourism and trade between Asia and the Middle East. The acquisition would grant Etihad access to a complementary route network — 30 out of 56 unique MAS destinations in Asia did not overlap with Etihad's routes. Importantly, it would give Etihad an opportunity to significantly strengthen its competitive position on the important Kangaroo Route (London/Dubai to Sydney via Kuala Lumpur/Singapore). Last, it would create a politically appealing alliance between two Islamic nations' flag carriers.

Etihad's management asked its bankers to value the target based on trading and transaction comparables. Based on a current share price of US$0.64, MAS was trading at an equity value of US$1,316 million, which was at the lower end of its 12 month trading range between US$1,092 million and US$2,074 million — an attractive entry price. On the other hand, research analysts were suggesting that prices could fall further, reducing equity value to as low as US$910 million, which made the current price less attractive than it seemed initially. However, based on comparable trading multiples, the airline was undervalued relative to its Southeast Asian peers, which were trading on higher multiples based on their enterprise value/EBITDA ratios in 2010 and 2011. Market indicators, though, often do not serve as the best indicators for successful bid prices, as airline mergers and acquisitions (M&A) transactions in Asia cleared the market at significant premiums to traded value — reflecting high investor interest in the market, acquisition synergies, and control premiums. Thus, if precedent transactions were an indicator, the target could be valued at over twice its current market value. (See Case Exhibit 21.1.)

Etihad's management now wanted to embark on a more detailed due diligence of the airline, culminating in a discounted cash-flow valuation of the airline based on the projected financials shown in Case Exhibit 21.2. Malaysia Airlines was trading at a levered beta of 1.06, with a market risk premium of 9.38% above a risk-free rate of 3.68%. Its cost of debt based on outstanding bonds, loans, and leases was 3.9%. Etihad on the other hand was trading at a cost of equity of 10.5% and a cost of debt of 2.4%. Based on these assumptions and the cash-flow projections provided in Case Exhibit 21.2, the deal team proceeded to value the acquisition.

Questions for Discussion

1. What is a fair value for MAS as a stand-alone firm?
2. What would be the synergistic benefits for Etihad of acquiring a strategic minority stake in Malaysia Airlines?
3. How much should Etihad bid for MAS shares?

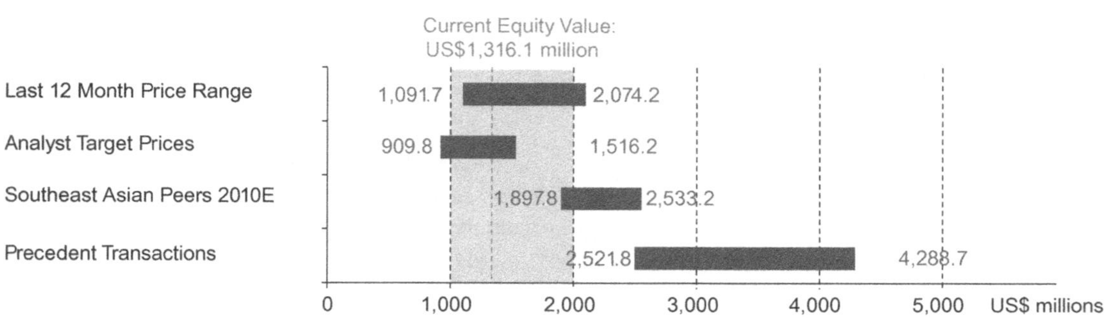

Case Exhibit 21.1. Precedent transactions.

Case Exhibit 21.2. Historical and projected financials for Malaysia Airlines.

	Historical Financials					Projected Financials		
(In Millions of MYR)	2007A	2008A	2009A	2010E	2011E	2012E	2013E	2014E
Profit & Loss								
Revenues	14,630.2	15,035.3	11,309.9	12,971.7	14,038.5	15,192.1	16,439.3	17,787.6
Operation expenses	14,031.9	14,855.2	11,866.6	12,473.8	12,591.4	13,620.2	14,442.8	15,345.5
— Fuel cost	4,915.8	6,531.6	3,497.3	4,330.0	4,335.1	4,509.8	4,619.9	4,763.0
— Depreciation	2,082.5	1,890.8	1,846.7	1,751.4	1,305.6	1,588.6	1,683.7	1,775.8
— Others	7,033.6	6,432.8	6,522.6	6,422.4	6,950.6	7,521.7	8,139.2	8,806.8
EBITDA	2,680.8	2,070.9	1,290.0	2,249.2	2,752.8	3,160.5	3,680.1	4,217.9
EBIT	598.3	180.1	(556.7)	497.9	1,447.2	1,571.9	1,996.4	2,442.1
Net profit	795.5	244.3	490.3	177.3	1,145.1	1,193.9	1,554.2	1,996.7
Balance sheet								
Gross debt (includes off-balance-sheet debt)	8,256.2	8,938.2	7,390.2	6.081.0	7,898.5	10,157,5	10,318.9	9,681.5
Net debt (includes off-balance-sheet debt)	3,821.9	5,366.4	4,725.4	4,133.5	4,662.1	5,774.9	4,539.2	2,210.0
Cash	4,434.3	3,571.7	2,664.9	1,947.5	3,236.4	4,382.6	5,779.7	7,471.6
PP&E	9,457.7	9,984.0	8,182.6	6,764.9	8,594.8	11,070.0	11,572.3	11,440.3
Total assets	17,458.5	17,590.8	13,598.3	11,983.3	15,362.0	19,264.5	21,467.7	23,356.2
Shareholders' equity (excluding MI)	3,934.9	4,185.7	735.7	913.0	2,058.1	3,252.0	4,806.2	6,802.8
Cash flow								
Cash flow from operating activities	4,108.5	939.3	(47.7)	925.6	2,606.9	2,951.1	3,421.6	3,973.0
Cash flow from investing activities	(2,245.2)	(2,922.6)	(1,306.0)	(1,693.2)	(2,942.4)	(4,480.2)	(2,230.1)	(1,747.1)
Cash flow from financing activities	986.3	489.6	862.5	50.3	1,624.5	2,675.2	205.6	(534.1)

22

Project Finance

The objects of a financier are, then, to secure an ample revenue; to impose it with judgment and equality; to employ it economically; and when necessity obliges him to make use of credit, to secure its foundations in that instance, and forever, by the clearness and candor of his proceedings, the exactness of his calculations, and the solidity of his funds.

—Edmund Burke

Investments in large-scale infrastructure projects such as oil, gas, utilities, transportation, and mining constitute a growing portion of foreign direct investment. Indeed, one of the most daunting tasks of the twenty-first century is how to finance the surge of such infrastructural investments necessary to sustain population growth while improving living standards. This chapter explores the unique architecture of project finance that is playing a pivotal role in enabling infrastructure projects.

Project financing of single-purpose, large-scale infrastructural business undertakings has a long history that predates the limited liability corporation. An often-cited venture involves the English Crown, which reportedly negotiated a loan in 1299 from the House of Frescobaldi — a leading Italian bank of that era — to finance the development of the Devon silver mines. The lender had full control of the mines for the first year, during which time it would pay itself back by appropriating as much silver ore as it could mine. There was no provision for interest payment, forbidden then by canon law, and the British Crown offered no guarantee as to the quality or the quantity of silver that could be extracted during that first year. This mode of financing would be known today as a *production payment loan* — a forebear of project finance as we know it today. Another rudimentary mode of project finance was used in charting commercial ships in the sixteenth and seventeenth centuries. Each voyage was a finite-life project, with investors providing financing to be fully returned with profits (if successful) upon the vessel's return when both cargo and ship would be sold.

Much later, the Suez (1869) and Panama (1914) canals were project finance transactions, as was the development of North Sea oil fields. Very recently the Hopewell Partners Guangzhou Highway in China, the Petrozuata (1998) heavy oil crude projects in Venezuela, and the Ras Laffan liquefied natural gas venture in Qatar (1997) were project finance transactions much celebrated in the media.[1]

After reading this chapter you will understand:

- What makes project finance unique and how it differs from traditional corporate finance.
- What the risks faced by such projects are and how the unique governance structure of project finance allows for a superior allocation of those risks.
- How to value projects.

WHAT IS PROJECT FINANCE?

Project finance generally refers to the long-term financing of stand-alone, single-purpose, capital-intensive, large-scale infrastructural and industrial projects whose debt servicing and principal repayment are solely secured by the project's future cash flows (rather than the equity sponsors' balance sheets). As seen in Exhibit 22.1A, the architecture of project finance is independently housed in a *special*

1 Other projects have also attracted much media attention — such as Motorola's Iridium project, the Channel tunnel (Eurotunnel), and the Euro-Disney theme park in France — but for the wrong reasons: financial distress!

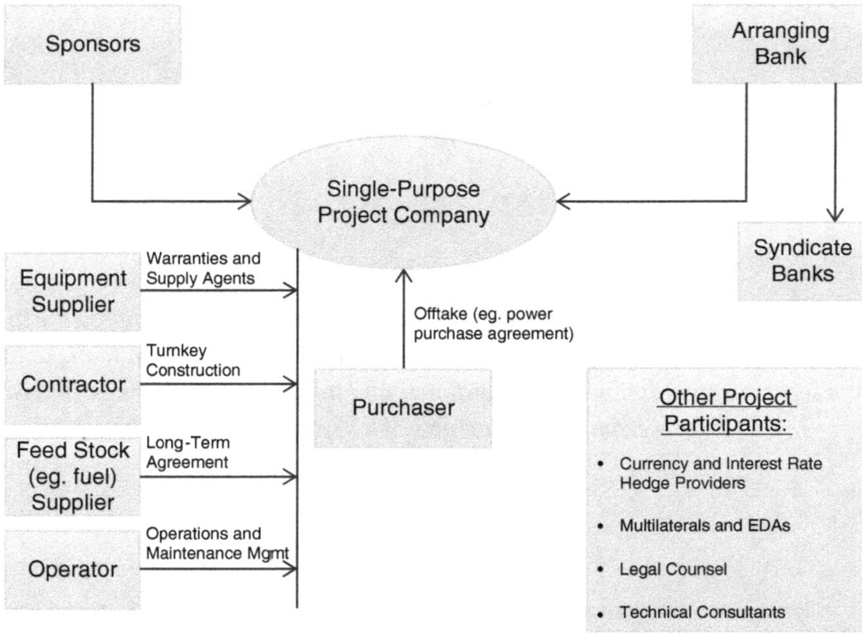

Exhibit 22.1A. Project finance — Sample structure.

purpose entity (more commonly known as the project company) and financed by a small number of equity investors/sponsors as well as a syndicate of lending financial institutions — primarily commercial banks.

Candidates for Project Finance

Natural resources (mines, oil wells, and gas fields) as well as infrastructure (power plants, toll roads, pipelines, airports, and telecommunication systems) are generally good candidates for a project finance solution. A further differentiation is between stock versus flow-type projects: mining ventures in copper, oil, or gas are good examples of *stock projects* (sometimes referred to as "wasting" assets), which deplete the natural resource and use the revenue proceeds from the output of the mine or well to service the debt and pay dividends to equity sponsors. *Flow-type projects* such as toll roads, pipelines, or power plants rely on the project's infrastructural assets[2] to generate the revenue necessary to service creditors and reward equity sponsors. By their very nature such ventures commonly require large-scale indivisible investments in a single-purpose asset that will often exceed $1 billion.

Project Finance Versus Corporate Finance

Large multinationals, however well capitalized, will often balk at such mammoth investments and will eschew the corporate finance approach for the project finance one. Such project-financed ventures require the establishment of a legally independent, self-standing entity defined earlier as a *special purpose entity* that houses the project and is off-balance-sheet and bankruptcy-remote from the equity sponsoring firms.

In a traditional corporate-financed investment, the firm's balance sheet becomes available in its entirety to repay debt providers. Thus, lenders provide capital to the entire firm rather than to an individual project, however large it may be. In a project-financed transaction, debt financing providers have limited or no recourse to the balance sheet of the equity sponsors. Because projects are self-standing and legally independent entities, the loans are generally *non-recourse* to the equity sponsors. Thus, lenders are restricted to the project cash flows for interest and principal (re)payment[3]; in case of financial distress lenders would have no recourse against the equity sponsors' cash flows.

2 For example, in the case of a pipeline, the pipeline would be the asset rather than the oil flowing through it, whereas the oil would be the (wasting) asset in the case of an oil well.

3 Lenders may have partial recourse to equity sponsors' cash flows during the project construction phase. Typically, such limited recourse will be voided when the project becomes operational.

This is why project finance is also referred to as a form of *off-balance-sheet* financing in the sense that neither the project's assets nor its liabilities appear on the equity sponsor's balance sheet. Lenders are given a lien on the project's entire asset portfolio ensconced in the special purpose entity but no more. Thus, should the project fail to comply with loan covenants, lenders are able to take over the project. Bankruptcy of a project-financed venture would therefore not contaminate sponsors' balance sheets, and conversely equity sponsors' financial distress would not spill over onto the project-financed assets. This is the very idea of *bankruptcy remoteness*.

LEVERAGE AND NON-RECOURSE FINANCING

Financing can be generally sourced from multilateral lending agencies such as the International Finance Corporation or regional development banks, commercial banks, and capital markets. Public agencies offer the advantage of political risk insurance, loan guarantees, and a certain halo effect (see International Corporate Finance in Practice 22.1) that will, in turn, facilitate the securing of financing from both banks and capital markets.[4] Most characteristically, project finance tends to be highly leveraged, especially in the early phase of operations, with a debt-to-assets ratio often peaking at 65% to 80%. Lenders — primarily commercial banks — look to cash-flow projections as collateral for the loan, which makes *ex ante* feasibility studies and due diligence with respect to the project's economic viability especially important.

4 Host countries are less likely to expropriate projects partially financed by the World Bank or other multilateral lending agencies for the simple reason that they may need those agencies for other purposes. Also, commercial banks co-lending with international agencies are subject to lower capital reserve requirements under Basel II capital adequacy ratios rules, which in turn reduces the cost of lending.

INTERNATIONAL CORPORATE FINANCE IN PRACTICE 22.1

Petrozuata

Petrozuata[5] is a $2.4 billion oil-field development project in Venezuela consisting of three parts: inland oil wells to extract heavy crude, two pipelines to transport the crude to the coast, and a refinery to produce syncrude. Petrozuata was indeed a true project finance deal: a single-purpose capital investment (integrated production/transportation/refining facility) constituting a stand-alone entity with a finite life of 35 years and a mammoth price tag of $2.4 billion. Its two equity sponsors are Conoco (50.1%), owned by DuPont, and Maraven (49.9%), a subsidiary of PVDSA (Venezuela government–owned energy conglomerate), which would provide $975 million in equity financing. Market risk was mitigated by an off-take agreement with Conoco — one of the sponsors (rated AA) — but oil price risk remained unhedged (the project would break even as long as crude prices would remain above $8.63 per barrel). The project was financed in 1997 by syndicated bank loans for $450 million and a $1 billion bond offering in the Rule 144A market.[6] Recourse to equity sponsors was waived once construction was completed. By channeling the dollar-denominated oil revenues through an offshore escrow account domiciled in the United States and governed by New York state law, the bond offering achieved an investment grade rating that "pierced the sovereign ceiling"; in other words, the project received a higher debt rating than Venezuela did on its long-term foreign currency obligations.[7] Bankers Trust acted as the trustee and disbursed funds according to a strict hierarchy (cash waterfall) — operating expenses first, debt servicing second, and dividends distribution to equity sponsors last, provided that the project's debt service coverage ratio remained above the threshold of 1.35×.

5 See Esty, Benjamin C. 1999. "Petrozuata: An Effective Use of Project Finance." *Journal of Applied Corporate Finance* 12(3): 26–42.

6 Rule 144A allows non-US-domiciled entities to sell bonds to US qualified institutional investors without satisfying SEC disclosure requirements.

7 Venezuela's sovereign rating stood at B or five notches below investment grade at BBB–.

ON ALLOCATING RISKS

Because project-financed transactions are complex transactions fraught with many risks, their proper identification and allocation are crucial to the project design. Indeed, risk allocation needs to be codified into legally binding contracts between the project company and its many participants. A typical project finance transaction may link as many as 15 different parties through 50 or more contracts governing the relationships between the project company and (1) construction contractors, (2) project operator(s), (3) inputs suppliers, (4) output purchasers (known also as off-takers), and (5) various creditors. Financing itself will be distributed among multiple parties such as commercial banks, bond investors, export-import banks, and multilateral institutions to ensure wide risk allocation. Thus, the project company is at the nexus of a complex web of contractual relationships that strive to allocate a variety of project-specific risks to those parties best suited to appraise them and control them, and most important best endowed to bear them. This is why project finance is often referred to as "contract finance." (See International Corporate Finance in Practice 22.2.)

During the *construction phase* of the project (typically 2–3 years), risk exposure is at its greatest as mammoth capital expenditures are made while little or no operational cash inflows can be expected. Is the project technologically viable and environmentally friendly? Are the natural resources indeed accessible? Will the contractors complete the project on time and within budget? These are some of the big question marks that make the construction phase so treacherous for lenders. Construction loans will include tight covenants in the form of completion guarantees enshrined in an engineering, procurement, and construction (EPC) contract, with the contractor obligated to build and deliver the project facilities on a turnkey basis — that is, ready for immediate use. Such contracts are generally underwritten and guaranteed by the project's equity sponsors. Typically, these guarantees are *several* rather than *joint*[8] and only as good as the sponsors' creditworthiness. Thus, if any mishap were to occur during this phase in the form of delays or cost overruns, the sponsors might have to increase their equity participation to ensure project completion.

Post-completion risk refers to the entire gamut of risks once the project is up and running. This risk phase encompasses the full economic life of the project — as long as 20 to 35 years. First and most important is market risk, which will directly impact the revenue (top line) of the project: Recalling that *sales revenue* = *price per unit* × *quantity sold*, market risk can be decomposed as price risk (especially crucial in commodity projects) and quantity risk (demand for output may fall below projection). Off-take agreements with the project's customer(s) in the form of long-term purchase contracts for a fixed amount at a fixed price (or more often with a guaranteed minimum price) will mitigate market risk.[9] However, with any long-term contracts, the question of their enforceability has to be closely scrutinized with special attention given to the creditworthiness of off-takers. Off-takers may also be asked to take a minority equity position in the project.

---

8 A *several* guarantee obligates the sponsor only to the extent of its share of the project rather than to the full project (as would a *joint* guarantee).

9 A "take-or-pay" contract obligates the off-taker to pay for products or services at a pre-agreed price whether or not the off-taker actually takes the product or service. In a "take-and-pay" contract, the off-taker pays at a pre-agreed price for only the product or service taken.

INTERNATIONAL CORPORATE FINANCE IN PRACTICE 22.2

When Project Finance Fails: Aguas Argentinas S.A. (AASA)

As part of its bold privatization program, in 1993 the government of Argentina auctioned off the concession to supply water and sanitation services for the greater metropolitan district of Buenos Aires. Thus, the concessionaire would be granted the rights to operate the assets (water and sewer plants as well as water and sewer lines) but the assets would remain under public ownership. The bid was won by Aguas Argentinas S.A. (AASA) — a project finance firm sponsored by a consortium led by the French water company Suez-Lyonnaise des Eaux (25.30%), the Soldati group (20.7%), Sociedad General Aguas de Barcelona (12.6%), the Meller family (10.80%), and others. The Soldati group and the Meller family were local partners with strong political ties to Argentina's president at the time, Carlos Menem. At first the project was portrayed as a poster child for privatizing utilities. AASA had reduced tariffs by 26.9% from inception and improved bill collection from 55% to 95% by mid-1995 while increasing its customer reach. The project showed solid profitability from day one with return on equity from 1994 to the peso crisis in 2002 averaging 20% (more than twice what similar projects earned in developed economies). The lead sponsor, Suez-Lyonnaise des Eaux, alone collected $171 million in dividends on an initial investment of $34.14 million (annualized return of 22.7%) on top of a 6% gross margin management fee.

On the eve of the peso crisis in January 2002, AASA had accumulated $706.12 million in loans from the World Bank's International Finance Corporation, the Inter-American Development Bank, the European Investment Bank, and a bank syndicate led by ING Barings. The peso devaluation of 300% in January 2002 led to a gross domestic product (GDP) contraction of 12%, with wholesale inflation reaching 110%. To alleviate the impact of the crisis on the Argentine population, the government declared that all utility tariffs would be invoiced and collected in the newly devalued Argentine peso and frozen at that level. On April 11, 2002, AASA suspended debt payments and tried to restructure its outstanding loans. On July 17, 2003, claiming $1.7 billion, Suez-Lyonnaise des Eaux filed arbitration proceedings against the government of Argentina in the World Bank's Centre for Settlement of Investment Disputes under the bilateral investment treaty between France and Argentina.

AASA fell victim to the peso crisis of 2002. How could an otherwise well-crafted project finance venture that had carefully allocated risks among its many participants miss in a most basic way to hedge currency risk? The project was deriving 100% of its revenue from Argentine consumers by collecting tariffs in Argentine pesos (ARS) while financing 100% of its operation in US dollars. Granted, Argentina had passed a law and established a currency board enshrining the ARS 1 = US$1 parity, which gave the project sponsors the false sense of having safely matched the currency denominations of their revenue and cost streams. How could otherwise savvy multinationals be gullible enough to believe that the law would survive a decade of Argentine inflation leading to a 40% to 50% overvaluation of the Argentine peso on the eve of its collapse? Once Argentina allowed the peso to devalue, it plunged by 200%, triggering a deep recession and fueling inflation. AASA found itself in the classic economic exposure squeeze — deriving revenues in devalued pesos[10] and facing debt servicing denominated in dollars. At ARS 3 = US$1, the financing costs had tripled while peso revenues stayed stagnant because tariffs had been frozen by the government. AASA had made no attempt to use a currency swap or other hedging techniques to protect itself against a major devaluation. Default was the only exit strategy.

10 Although AASA had managed tariff increases of 80% between 1994 and 2001, it was now not only facing frozen tariffs, but also weak demand coupled with difficulty of collecting its water bills, as the Argentine population rate of poverty had significantly increased with the crisis.

Supply and throughput risk may similarly result from price and quantity uncertainties and would therefore impact the cost side of the project. Most intractable are (1) *sovereign risk*, which includes inflation, currency convertibility (or lack thereof), exchange rate devaluation (or revaluation; see Corporate Finance in Practice 22.2), price controls, adverse changes in tax laws or royalty rates, and creeping or outright expropriation, and (2) risk of *force majeure* or an act of God such as an earthquake, tornado, fire, or a terrorist act. By inviting state-owned enterprises to become equity sponsors, the project may significantly mitigate sovereign risks. In a similar vein, establishing an offshore escrow account[11] domiciled in a reliable tax jurisdiction that channels all export proceeds from the project will significantly reduce the risk profile of the project by ensuring that lenders' debt claims are met on a priority basis. A lower risk profile in turn results in lower financing costs.

Anatomy of Project Finance: The Case of the Ras Laffan Liquefied Natural Gas Company

The State of Qatar granted development and exploration rights for its offshore gas North Fields to Qatar General Petroleum Corporation (QGPC), which in turn formed a joint venture, Ras Laffan Liquefied Natural Gas Company Ltd, with Mobil Corporation to exploit these rights. Mobil and Qatar General Petroleum Corporation were the primary equity sponsors of Ras Laffan, which was set up as a *bankruptcy-remote special purpose entity* to develop the gas reserves of Qatar's North Fields. Its core asset was indeed a single-purpose, large, capital-intensive, and wasting asset.

Ras Laffan construction was completed on the basis of typical EPC contracts, which were fixed-price, date-certain, and turnkey. Although severe penalties would apply to contractors for failing to meet the terms of the EPC contracts, responsibility for the construction loan ultimately fell on the equity sponsors. Indeed, the initial construction phase was financed primarily by debt with guarantees provided by Mobil and Qatar General Petroleum Corporation. The sponsors were therefore fully liable for the debt servicing and principal repayment of the construction loan. The reader may be wondering why during this construction phase the financing was provided *with recourse* to the sponsors when it was emphasized earlier that debt financing in project finance is nonrecourse. This is simply due to the fact that lending during the construction phase is much riskier, since there are no cash inflows to secure the loan until the project is up and running and becomes fully operational.

The project company in this case was jointly owned by state-owned Qatar General Petroleum Corporation (63%) and Mobil (25%), with minority stakes from off-takers Korea Gas (KOGAS) (5%) and Japanese trading companies Nissho Iwai (3%) and Itochu (4%). The inclusion of QGPC as a state-owned majority local partner mitigated sovereign risk. Similarly, minority equity stakes by primarily long-term customers provided additional risk mitigation against counterparty risk. Seventy-five percent of the liquefied natural gas (LNG) output was sold to a single buyer, Korea Gas, through a long-term take-or-pay contract with a minimum floor price set at a crude-oil equivalent of $18.60 per barrel (see Exhibit 22.1B).

This large energy capital-intensive project was funded with $1.35 billion in non-recourse loans (except during the construction phase), which simply means that under no condition could the creditors recover their loans from either Mobil or Qatar Petroleum. As noted earlier, the off-takers — the utility firm Korea Gas and the liquefied natural gas marketers Nissho Iwai and Itochu — also took minority equity positions in the project to mitigate counterparty risk.

VALUING PROJECT FINANCE: THE ESTY MODEL[12]

Much of the negotiation between various lenders — whether they are banks or institutional investors — and equity investors about the terms of financing is based on the valuation of the project finance — hence the close attention generally devoted to this exercise. Unfortunately, large-scale infrastructure projects do not readily lend themselves to traditional valuation methodologies based on cash flows from assets (asset cash flows, ACF) discounted at the

11 Most but not all project financings are international projects whose revenue streams are derived exclusively from export revenues. This is generally the case for extractive or energy projects but would generally not apply to infrastructure projects such as toll roads that generate local currency revenues. For an illustration of how an offshore escrow account mitigates country risk, see the Mexicana de Cobre case discussed in Chapter 11.

12 This section draws from Benjamin C. Esty "Improved Techniques for Valuing Large-Scale Projects," *Journal of Project Finance* 5 (Spring) 1999: 9–25.

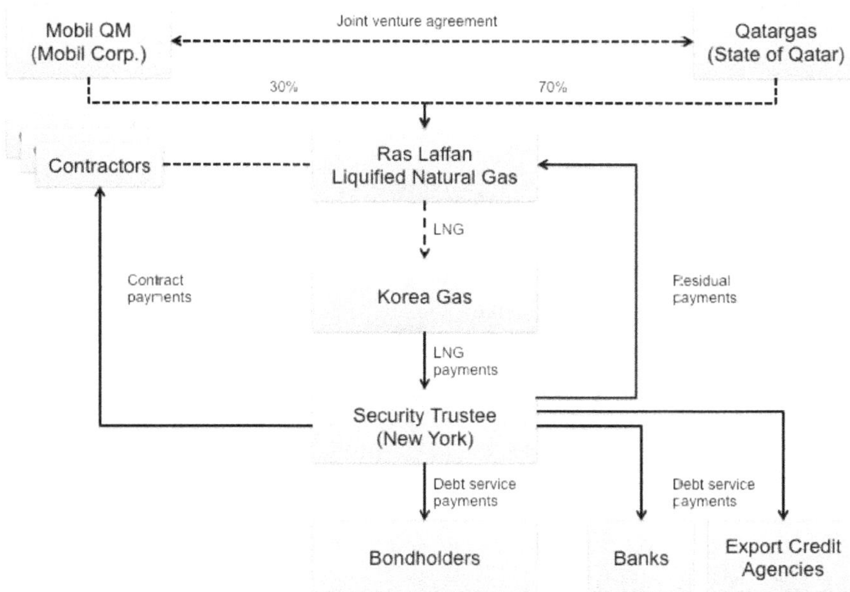

Exhibit 22.1B. Ras Laffan: Natural gas project finance.

weighted average cost of capital (WACC). As we explained in Chapter 20 on international capital budgeting, this widely used valuation framework rests on two simplistic assumptions that fare poorly in a cross-border transaction such as international project finance: (1) that the effective tax rate at which interest payments are tax-deductible is constant over the life of the project and (2) that the capital structure remains invariant over the valuation horizon.

Valuation framework

Traditional ACF/WACC valuation requires the estimation of an after-tax cost of debt k_D to compute the weighted average cost of capital:

$$\text{WACC} = \frac{D}{D+E} k_D \left(1 - \text{Tax}\right) + \frac{E}{D+E} k_E$$

where D and E are the respective amount of debt and equity financing and k_E is the cost of equity. Since a constant WACC is used for the entire economic life of the project, a constant tax rate has to be assumed. Because of multiple levels of taxation (the host country may offer tax holidays for the early years, or there may be transfer taxes such as withholding tax on royalties and dividends paid to equity sponsors and home country income taxes), it is difficult to estimate a constant tax rate at which interest payments are tax-deductible. Thus, it is far more accurate to have actual interest payments subjected to effective (and adjusted annually) rates of taxation and deduct them directly from top-line revenues instead of collapsing the cost of all debt financing in the after-tax cost of debt in one invariant WACC. Such an approach will require a valuation model predicated on residual cash flows to equity sponsors (equity cash flows, ECF) discounted at the levered cost of equity (LCE).[13]

Similarly, it is unrealistic to assume a stable capital structure for the entire project finance life as is required in the traditional ACF/WACC valuation method. One complicating feature of project finance is the changing level of leverage. Most project finance schemes are characterized by a high level of leverage in the early years with the ratio rising very rapidly from 0% to a peak of 65 to 80% within a couple of years. As debt is progressively paid off, the leverage ratio is driven back down to 0% over the project life. Discounting ACFs at the same WACC computed on the basis of an unchanging capital structure (debt and equity weights are constant in the WACC) clearly distorts the valuation process. Indeed, pegging the WACC to the peak leverage ratio (as is often done) would greatly undervalue the project, thereby

13 Levered cost of equity refers to the cost of equity derived from the capital asset pricing model, which requires an estimate of the firm's beta. A levered beta — and by association a levered cost of equity — indicates that financial risk due to leverage is duly incorporated into the cost of equity. A highly leveraged firm has a higher cost of equity than an all-equity-financed firm.

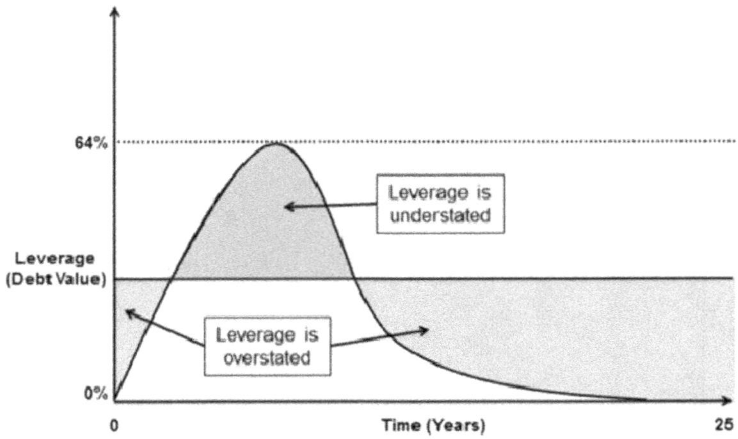

Exhibit 22.2. Leverage and equity cost of capital.

Source: Adapted from Esty, Benjamin C. 1999. "Improved Techniques for Valuing Large-Scale Projects." *Journal of Project Finance* 5 (Spring): 9–25.

putting lenders in a stronger bargaining position than they should actually be in.[14] Clearly, the correct approach is to use multiple leveraged equity costs of capital adjusted yearly to reflect the actual leverage of the project (see Exhibit 22.2). Here again it is far more accurate to work with residual equity cash flows (net of interest payments) discounted at a yearly adjusted cost of equity capital rather than with cash flows from assets that include interest payments and are discounted at an invariant WACC.

Modeling project finance cash flows

The first step is to estimate equity cash flows (ECF) by focusing on cash available for debt servicing (CADS), which is simply free cash flows from which debt servicing (both principal and interest payments) and the escrowing of funds in anticipation of debt servicing (EWDS)[15] are subtracted. We develop a numerical example to illustrate how this valuation model actually works.

Referring to the Ras Laffan project (see Exhibits 22.3A, 22.3B, and 22.3C, where each cash-flow column is numbered 1 through 22), equity sponsors contributed $500 million in year 0, while debt financing in the amount of $1.35 billion at the interest rate of 10% was raised in years 1 and 2. Revenue from LNG sales (column 1) started in year 2 and is assumed to grow at an annual rate of 2.0% in years 2 to 5, 1.0% in years 6 to 10, and remain stagnant for the remaining life of the project. Operating expenses (2) are keyed to revenue at the rate of 38%. With capital expenditures (4) at $500 million and $1,350 million in years 0 and 1, straight-line depreciation (5) starts in year 2 at the constant level of $200 million through year 11. Earnings before interest and taxes (EBIT) (3) is computed as:

$$\text{EBIT} = \text{Revenue} - \text{Operating expenses} - \text{Depreciation}$$

Net operating cash flows (NOCF) are derived from EBIT (3) by adding back non-cash-flow depreciation (5), deducting host country cash taxes (6) at 25% with a tax holiday in years 0 through 5, capital expenditures (CAPEX) in the amount of $500 million and $1.35 billion in years 0 and 1 (4), and change in net working capital or ΔWCR (7) assumed to be 1% of revenue[16]:

$$\text{NOCF} = \text{EBIT} + \text{Depreciation} - \text{Cash taxes} \\ - \text{Capex} - \Delta\text{WCR}$$

14 A lower value for the project allows the lenders to exact more favorable terms from the sponsors in terms of interest rate and covenants simply because a weaker/poorer project is deemed riskier.

15 EWDS stands for **e**scro**w**ing for **d**ebt **s**ervicing. By forcing the project manager to set aside cash to cover (in this case) the next six months of interest and principal repayment, lenders are simply protecting themselves.

16 Change in working capital requirement (ΔWCR) is defined as change in accounts receivable plus change in inventory minus change in accounts payable. In this case we made a simplifying assumption and set ΔWCR equal to 1% of sales instead of showing a pro forma balance sheet for the project.

Exhibit 22.3A. Qatar LNG project finance (1) (millions of dollars).

	Revenues[a]		Operating Expenses[b]	EBIT[c]	Capex[d]	Depreciation[e]	Cash Taxes[f]	ΔWCR[g]	NOCF[h]
Year	1	Royalties	2	3	4	5	6	7	8
0					500.0		0.0		(500.0)
1					1,350.0		0.0		(1,350.0)
2	700.0	35.0	266.0	269.0		200.0	0.0	7.0	462.0
3	714.0	35.7	271.3	278.4		200.0	0.0	7.1	471.2
4	728.3	36.4	276.7	287.9		200.0	0.0	7.3	480.7
5	742.8	37.1	282.3	297.7		200.0	0.0	7.4	490.3
6	750.3	37.5	285.1	302.7		200.0	75.7	7.5	419.5
7	757.8	37.9	288.0	307.7		200.0	76.9	7.6	423.2
8	765.4	38.3	290.8	312.8		200.0	78.2	7.7	426.9
9	773.0	38.7	293.7	317.9		200.0	79.5	7.7	430.7
10	780.7	39.0	296.7	323.1		200.0	80.8	7.8	434.5
11	780.7	39.0	296.7	323.1		200.0	80.8	7.8	434.5
12	780.7	39.0	296.7	523.1			130.8	7.8	384.5
13	780.7	39.0	296.7	523.1			130.8	7.8	384.5
14	780.7	39.0	296.7	523.1			130.8	7.8	384.5
15	780.7	39.0	296.7	523.1			130.8	7.8	384.5

Notes: [a] Revenue grows at 2.0% for years 2–5; 1.0% for years 6–10; and 0.0% for years 11–15.
[b] Operating expenses are at 38.0% of revenues.
[c] EBIT = Revenues – Operating expenses – Depreciation.
[d] Capital expenditures.
[e] Straight-line depreciation over 10 years.
[f] Taxes @ 25%; waived for years 1–5.
[g] Change in working capital requirement.
[h] NOCF = Net operating cash flows = EBIT – Capex + Depreciation – Cash taxes – Change in working capital requirement.

Net operating cash flows will now be adjusted by a special escrowing for debt servicing or EWDS (9) whereby lenders direct the project firm to set aside six months of principal and interest payments. This yields the amount of cash available for debt servicing CADS (10)[17]:

$$\text{CADS} = \text{NOCF} - \text{EWDS}$$

Total debt servicing (13) is derived from principal repayment (11) and interest payment (12). Finally, equity cash flows available to the project's sponsors or ECF (15) is derived as:

$$\text{ECF} = \text{NOCF} - \text{EWDS} - \text{Principal repayment} - \text{Interest payment}$$

17 Strictly speaking, cash available for debt servicing (CADS) includes the cash escrowed EWDS. The escrow account is simply providing an additional buffer or insurance in case operational cash flows fall short and put debt servicing in jeopardy.

The debt servicing coverage ratio (DSCR) is an important ratio computed as (cash available for debt servicing)/(debt servicing), and is set at an absolute level of 1.35 below which the project cannot fall or else it will risk default. It is also a key covenant to the loan/bond contract that is carefully monitored by creditors.

Adjusting the discount rate

We emphasized that one of the complicating features of valuing project finance is the project's changing leverage over its life. We advocated the ECF/LCE method, whereby the cash flows are exclusive of interest payments and would be discounted at the leveraged cost of equity. This method would require that the discount rate reflect the corresponding leverage for that year's particular cash flows. Annual discount rates would thus have to be calculated.

Exhibit 22.3B. Qatar LNG project finance (2) (millions of dollars).

Year	Escrow for Debt Servicing[i]	Cash Available for Debt Servicing[j]	Principal Outstanding	Interest Payment[k]	Total Debt Servicing	Debt Servicing Coverage Ratio[l]	Equity Cash Flows[m]
	9	10	11	12	13	14	15
0	...	...	0.0	0.0	0.0	...	(500.0)
1	100.0	0.0	1,500.0	0.0	0.0	...	50.0
2	187.5	274.5	1,500.0	150.0	150.0	1.8×	124.5
3	180.0	291.2	1,425.0	142.5	217.5	1.3×	73.7
4	172.5	308.2	1,350.0	135.0	210.0	1.5×	98.2
5	165.0	325.3	1,275.0	127.5	202.5	1.6×	122.8
6	132.5	287.0	1,200.0	120.0	195.0	1.5×	92.0
7	155.0	268.2	1,175.0	117.5	142.5	1.9×	125.7
8	147.5	279.4	1,100.0	110.0	185.0	1.5×	94.4
9	140.0	290.7	1,025.0	102.5	177.5	1.6×	113.2
10	170.0	264.5	950.0	95.0	170.0	1.6×	94.5
11	...	454.5	800.0	80.0	230.0	1.9×	204.5
12	...	384.5	600.0	60.0	260.0	1.5×	124.5
13	...	384.5	450.0	45.0	195.0	2.0×	189.5
14	...	384.5	300.0	30.0	180.0	2.1×	204.5
15	...	384.5	150.0	15.0	165.0	2.3×	219.5

Notes: [i] Escrow amount at all times: six months of interest and principal repayment.
[j] Cash available for debt servicing = NOCF – Escrow for debt servicing.
[k] Interest payment at 10.0% of principal outstanding.
[l] Cash available for debt servicing/total debt servicing.
[m] ECF = EBIT – Tax + Depreciation – ΔWCR – Debt servicing – Escrow for debt servicing. In year 0, sponsors contribute $500.0 million in equity to the project.

Fortunately, the capital asset pricing model allows for a relatively easy assessment of the leveraged cost of equity, provided that appropriate adjustments are made to the project's levered beta, β^L. According to the capital asset pricing model, the cost of equity capital k_E is equal to the risk-free rate r_F plus the risk premium:

$$k_E = r_F + \beta^L \times (r_M - r_F) \qquad (22.1)$$

where r_M is the rate of return on the market portfolio. The appropriate beta coefficient is the levered beta that corresponds to the project's level of indebtedness.

The reader will recall from a first corporate finance course that the levered beta in fact embodies core asset or business risk (exclusive of financial leverage as if the project was all equity financed) around which is wrapped financial risk reflecting the project leverage. Thus, we can rewrite the cost of equity by highlighting the two components of risk embedded in the levered beta, with the first term capturing the unlevered (all-equity-financed) business risk embodied in the unlevered beta β^U and the second term capturing additional financial risk due to leverage[18]:

$$k_E = r_F + \beta^U \times (r_M - r_F) + (\beta^L - \beta^U) \times (r_M - r_F) \qquad (22.2)$$

As leverage changes from year to year, the levered beta will have to be adjusted. This can be readily done by peeling off financial risk (from the levered β^L to the

18 Equation (22.2) readily simplifies itself to equation (22.1) if factored out!

Exhibit 22.3C. Qatar LNG project finance (3) (millions of dollars).

Year	Total Equity	Total Debt	Leverage Ratio[n]	Constant Leveraged Cost of Equity[o]	Project Valuation Using Constant Leveraged Cost of Equity k^E	Leverage-Adjusted Cost of Equity k_E^p	Project Valuation Using Leverage-Adjusted Cost of Equity Capital k^E
	16	17	18	19	20	21 (%)	22
					NPV = −18.1		NPV = 119.7
0	500.0	0.0	0.00	20.0%	(500.0)	20.0	(500.0)
1	500.0	1,500.0	0.75	20.0%	41.7	19.4	41.9
2	500.0	1,500.0	0.75	20.0%	86.5	18.8	88.2
3	500.0	1,425.0	0.75	20.0%	42.7	18.2	44.7
4	500.0	1,350.0	0.73	20.0%	47.3	17.6	51.3
5	500.0	1,275.0	0.72	20.0%	49.3	17.0	56.0
6	500.0	1,200.0	0.71	20.0%	30.8	16.4	37.0
7	500.0	1,175.0	0.70	20.0%	35.1	15.8	45.0
8	500.0	1,100.0	0.69	20.0%	22.0	15.2	30.4
9	500.0	1,025.0	0.67	20.0%	21.9	14.6	33.2
10	500.0	950.0	0.66	20.0%	15.3	14.0	25.5
11	500.0	800.0	0.62	20.0%	27.5	14.5	46.1
12	500.0	600.0	0.55	20.0%	14.0	14.4	24.8
13	500.0	450.0	0.47	20.0%	17.7	14.3	33.3
14	500.0	300.0	0.38	20.0%	15.9	14.2	31.9
15	500.0	150.0	0.23	20.0%	14.2	14.1	30.4

Notes: [n] Leverage ratio = Total debt/(Total equity + Total debt).
[o] Assumes that leverage is not reflected in project beta.
[p] Leverage-adjusted cost of equity reflects declining leverage of the project.

unlevered beta β^U) and then re-levering the unlevered beta β^U to the new level of leverage β^{L*}.

The practical method for adjusting the levered beta to the appropriate leverage is derived from expressing the entire firm asset beta β^{asset} as the leverage-weighted average of the debt β^{debt} and equity beta β^L:

$$\beta^{\text{asset}} = \frac{D}{D+E} \times \beta^{\text{debt}} + \frac{E}{D+E} \times \beta^L \quad (22.3)$$

The debt beta measures the correlation of the returns on debt with the returns on the market portfolio: When debt is considered low risk or riskless it would be quasi-inelastic to the market rate of return and therefore its beta can be reasonably assumed to be zero, and equation (22.3) reduces itself to:

$$\beta^{\text{asset}} = \frac{E}{D+E} \times \beta^L \quad (22.4)$$

thereby establishing a simple relationship between the firm's levered equity beta β^L and the asset unlevered beta β^{asset}. It is therefore easy to (1) peel off the effect of leverage from β^L to derive β^{asset} with equation (22.4) and (2) relever β^{asset} (unlevered β^U)using again equation (22.4) to yield the new levered β^{L*} corresponding to the new leverage ratio $[E/(D+E)]^*$.

For example, if in year 5 the project β_5^L is 0.80 corresponding to a leverage of 0.60, in year 6 with leverage down to 0.55 the new levered β_6^L is down to 0.76. Assuming a risk-free rate of 5% and a market rate of return of 15%, the equity cost of capital would correspondingly be adjusted from 17% to 15.5%. Multiple discount rates reflecting annually changing leverage[19] are shown in column 21 of Exhibit 22.3C.

19 This numerical example is based on book values of debt and equity for computing leverage ratios. A better approach is to use market value of equity.

Valuation metrics

Discounting ECFs at the LCE will yield the net present value (NPV) of the project. Column 19 shows a constant discount rate that ignores annually changing leverage with resulting NPV in column 20. Column 21 shows multiple discount rates reflecting annually changing leverage with resulting NPV shown in column 22. Unsurprisingly, after peaking early in the life of the project, multiple discount rates tend to be lower than the single discount rate (assumed to be pegged to the peak leverage ratio) and result in a higher valuation NPV = $119.7 million (as opposed to NPV = –$18.1 million if LCE remains invariant at 20%), which, consequently, should lead to more favorable financing terms.

Stress-testing

Valuation is a judgmental exercise that rests upon subjective assumptions over a very distant time horizon. With project finance, numbers are just bigger, and the time frame is much longer than with other investment decisions. It is therefore imperative to complement a *base case* scenario analysis with *break-even* and *sensitivity* analysis based on variables proxying the different sources of risk. In the case of the Ras Laffan project, much would depend on reliable revenue streams. These, in turn, rest upon reliable forecasts of LNG prices and quantities sold. Also, sovereign risk may derail the project: Would Qatar's taxation of the project uphold the tax waiver for the first 5 years? Exhibit 22.4 summarizes NPVs, under a base case scenario and alternative scenarios combining LNG prices, inflation-driven increases in operating costs, and Qatar's tax policy. Similarly, simple break-even and sensitivity analyses are developed around the aforementioned three key variables and show how much of an LNG price decline the project could sustain before breaching the floor DSCR.

SUMMARY

1. Project finance generally refers to the long-term financing of stand-alone, single-purpose, capital-intensive, large-scale infrastructural and industrial projects whose debt servicing and principal repayment are solely secured by the project's cash flows (rather than by the equity sponsors' balance sheets).
2. Project-financed ventures differ markedly from corporate-financed ones because they require setting up a legally independent, self-standing entity known as a *special purpose entity* that is off-balance-sheet and bankruptcy-remote from the equity sponsoring firms.

CONSTANT LEVERAGED COST OF EQUITY

NPV (Constant Leveraged Cost of Equity) Sensitized to % of Sales

100%	95%	90%	85%	80%
(18.1)	(343.4)	(588.5)	(777.2)	(925.6)

NPV (Constant Leveraged Cost of Equity) Sensitized to COGS (% of Sales)

38.0%	39.0%	40.0%	41.0%	42.0%
(18.1)	(43.3)	(68.5)	(93.7)	(118.9)

NPV (Constant Leveraged Cost of Equity) Sensitized to Tax Holiday (Years)

1	2	3	4	5
(169.7)	(123.0)	(82.7)	(48.0)	(18.1)

NPV (Constant Leveraged Cost of Equity) Sensitized to Royalties (% of Sales)

5.0%	4.0%	3.0%	2.0%	1.0%
(18.1)	(43.3)	(68.5)	(93.7)	(118.9)

ADJUSTED LEVERAGED COST OF EQUITY

NPV (Adj. Leveraged Cost of Equity) Sensitized to % of Sales

100%	95%	90%	85%	80%
119.7	(338.7)	(669.5)	(913.6)	(1,098.3)

NPV (Adj. Leveraged Cost of Equity) Sensitized to COGS (% of Sales)

38.0%	39.0%	40.0%	41.0%	42.0%
119.7	88.5	57.4	26.3	(4.9)

NPV (Adj. Leveraged Cost of Equity) Sensitized to Tax Holiday (Years)

1	2	3	4	5
(41.7)	6.0	48.1	85.7	119.7

NPV (Adj. Leveraged Cost of Equity) Sensitized to Royalties (% of Sales)

5.0%	4.0%	3.0%	2.0%	1.0%
119.7	88.5	57.4	26.3	(4.9)

Exhibit 22.4. Stress-testing with invariant versus leverage-adjusted cost of equity.

3. Project finance is fraught with multiple risks, the allocation of which is codified into legally binding contracts between the project company and its many participants. A typical project finance transaction may link as many as 15 different parties through 50 or more contracts governing the relationships between the project company and the (1) construction contractors, (2) project operator(s), (3) inputs suppliers, (4) output purchasers (known also as off-takers), and (5) various creditors.
4. Project finance tends to be highly leveraged, with the debt-to-value ratio often peaking at 65% to 80% in the early years. Most financing is procured from multilateral lending agencies and commercial banks. Because projects are self-standing and legally independent entities, the loans are generally *non-recourse* to the equity sponsors, which simply means that lenders are restricted to the project cash flows for interest and principal (re)payment; in case of financial distress, lenders would have no recourse against the equity sponsors' cash flows.
5. Valuation of project finance is the basis on which negotiation of financing terms between lenders and equity sponsors is conducted. It is best carried out on the basis of residual equity cash flows to equity sponsors discounted at the levered cost of equity capital rather than the more widely used approach of discounting net operating cash flows at the weighted average cost of capital.
6. Project finance is characterized by a rapidly changing degree of financial leverage, generally peaking at 65 to 80% in the early life of the transaction. This invalidates any valuation based on cash flow from assets discounted at an invariant WACC, and it requires a yearly adjustment in the levered cost of equity capital.
7. Failure to account for the varying level of leverage often results in an undervaluation of projects (if the discount rate is pegged to the peak level of leverage), which in turn bolsters the lenders' bargaining power at the expense of the project sponsors.
8. To give themselves an ample safety buffer against bankruptcy, lenders scrutinize the debt servicing coverage ratio (cash available for debt servicing/debt servicing) and generally constrain project finance through a loan covenant to show at all times a DSCR in excess of 1.35.
9. Because valuation of project finance is very sensitive to assumptions about future cash flows, it is recommended to complement a base scenario analysis with break-even and sensitivity analysis around key variables that proxy the different risk factors.

QUESTIONS FOR DISCUSSION

1. What is project finance? Identify the sectors of the economy where project finance type deals are most likely to be found.
2. What are the advantages of using *project finance* rather than *corporate finance* for funding large-scale infrastructure investments?
3. Compare the risks faced by equity sponsors during a project-financed venture's construction phase versus the operational phase. Are the risks faced by lenders the same?
4. Why is construction financing provided with recourse to the sponsors?
5. What are non-recourse loans, and why are they important to the architecture of project finance?
6. Why is escrowing for debt servicing a requirement of project finance? Are equity cash flows to sponsors inclusive or exclusive of cash escrowed for debt servicing?
7. Why do off-takers play a critical role in project finance? What is off-taker risk?
8. How should the changing leverage be taken into account in valuing project finance?

REFERENCES

Beidleman, C. R., D. Fletcher, and D. Vesbosky. 1990. "On Allocating Risk: The Essence of Project Finance." *Sloan Management Review* (Spring): 47–55.

Esty, B. C. 1999. "Improved Techniques for Valuing Large-Scale Projects." *Journal of Project Finance* 5 (Spring): 9–25.

Finnerty, J. 2007. *Project Financing: Asset-Based Financial Engineering*. Hoboken, NJ: John Wiley & Sons.

Sawant, R. J. 2010. *Infrastructure Investing: Managing Risks & Rewards for Pensions, Insurance & Endowments*. Hoboken, NJ: John Wiley & Sons.

CASE 22.1. CLEAN INFRA LTD PROJECT FINANCE

— Shuvam Dutta

The Indian power sector has seen significant investments in recent years; however, there still remain approximately 400 million people in the country without electricity, representing close to 35% of the country's population. The overall energy shortage in the country is immense; power supplies are estimated to be at about 10.3% of what the Indian economy needs, with the peak shortage being as high as 12.7%. These shortages have led to the emergence of the power sector as a critical bottleneck for economic growth and poverty alleviation efforts in the country.

As a result, the government of India is actively seeking to address these shortages and is also striving to achieve a good balance in its energy mix between conventional and renewable energy sources in order to mitigate the adverse impacts of climate change. Against this backdrop, the Indian government has provided the impetus for the growth of renewable energy sources (RES). Traditionally, the RES capacity addition has largely been driven by wind, biomass, and small hydroelectricity projects. Solar power, though technically feasible for a long time, has not seen much growth because of very high capital costs and lower efficiency. Recently, however, solar power has enjoyed renewed attention due to decreasing costs, increasing conventional fuel prices, and heightened concern about climate change.

In 2008, the prime minister launched the National Solar Mission, which envisions 20,000 MW of power generation from solar energy by the end of 2017. This is part of a broader plan to ensure that 5% of the energy requirements of the country will be met from renewable sources. In accordance with this policy, many Indian states have specified a set percentage of the total electricity purchases by state electricity boards to be made from renewable sources, ranging from 1 to 10% over the next few years. Regulators have also determined preferential minimum tariff levels for procurement of energy from such sources. Such tariff floors have been set separately for individual renewable sources on a normative cost-plus basis against benchmarked capital, fuel, interest rate, and operation and maintenance costs. The tariff has been determined primarily by targeting a minimum return on equity of 15%.

Even under the most optimistic assumptions, solar projects will need strong regulatory support on tariffs for several years to come in India. However, with a reduction in capital costs, the price of solar energy has declined significantly, with the trend expected to continue and thereby progressively reduce the future subsidy burden. Further, the relatively expensive solar power purchased from the energy providers is being bundled with cheaper thermal power and sold at a very competitive bundled rate to state electricity boards. Given the overall power shortage and obligations to buy a certain percentage of power from renewable sources, a state would have little incentive to default on payments and forgo its access to attractively priced power. Last, the government has sanctioned a US$88 million grant to fund a Solar Payment Security Account, which is meant to cover shortfalls due to default by state electricity boards. Hence, the government has matched its commitment to promoting renewable energy generation with a policy that creates a viable business model for power developers, while reducing credit risk for lenders participating in the sector.

The International Finance Corporation (IFC), which is the private-sector development arm of the World Bank, aims to catalyze clean energy investments in India as part of its broader strategy of climate change and inclusive growth. In the Indian market, the IFC plays an important role by providing debt and equity financing to sponsors that have a good track record and a long-term commitment to the renewable energy business. The IFC's support, provided to developers at a critical stage in their growth, in turn encourages other financiers to provide support for renewable energy projects. Thus, companies supported by the IFC are able to broaden and diversify their sources of funding. Over time there is a strong demonstration effect of the viability of investments in the sector, resulting in a crowding-in of other investors.

Clean Infra Ltd, a leading producer of renewable energy in India, is developing several renewable energy projects (solar, wind, and small hydroelectricity) across India. Clean Infra has significant experience in executing greenfield renewables projects in the country. (See Case Exhibit 22.1.) Hudson Clean Energy Partners is a private equity firm making privately negotiated investments in the clean energy industry. Global in scope, Hudson is dedicated to investing exclusively in renewable power, alternative fuels, and energy-smart technologies. These two entities formed a joint venture to build a 20 MW photovoltaic solar power plant, which the IFC was considering financing.

Case Exhibit 22.1. Clean Infra Ltd's uses and sources of funds (in millions).

Uses	INR	US$	Percentage (%)
Project EPC[20] cost	1,595.9	29.0	89
Land cost	14.9	0.3	1
One-time development costs	108.7	2.0	6
Working capital	7.1	0.1	0
Financing cost	74.1	1.3	4
Total uses	**1,800.6**	**32.7**	**100**
Sources	**INR**	**US$**	**Percentage**
IFC loan	450.2	8.2	25
Other lender–I	360.1	6.5	20
Other lender–II	450.2	8.2	25
Total debt	**1,260.4**	**22.9**	**70**
Equity	540.2	9.8	30
Total sources	**1,800.6**	**32.7**	**100**

The project is located in the city of Jodhpur in Rajasthan. The plant has been awarded a license to supply solar power to the grid at a competitively bid tariff of US$0.17/kWh to be sold to NTPC Vidyut Vyapar Nigam (a public agency designated by the Indian government for the purchase of solar power) under a 25-year power purchase agreement (PPA).

The IFC is among the few long-term financiers of the nascent solar sector in India. The IFC possesses extensive in-house technical expertise and growing global project experience in the solar sector. It is working closely with Clean Infra/Hudson to structure the project appropriately to mitigate implementation risks and other related risks and has arrived at a tentative approximation of project costs and capital structure based on discussions with the client and other lenders supporting the transaction.

As part of its due diligence, the IFC's investment team built financial projections to assess the project's ability to service debt, as measured by the debt service coverage ratio (DSCR). The DSCR is calculated as cash flow available for debt service divided by total interest and principal payments due for the year. A DSCR of less than 1 would mean a negative cash flow. For example, a DSCR of less than 1, say 0.95, would mean that there is only enough cash available to cover 95% of annual debt payments. As per its base case projections summarized in Case Exhibit 22.2, the IFC estimated that the project would generate a minimum DSCR of 1.36 and an average DSCR of 1.45 over the first 10 years of operation. Seventy percent of the project would be funded by debt at a cost of 12% with the remaining 30% funded by equity at an estimated cost of 24%. The corporate tax rate was 33%. The IFC was planning to support the project through a US$8.2 million loan, payable over 15 years with an average maturity of 9.5 years. The loan would charge a fixed interest rate of 12%. The interest rate was benchmarked to the INR swap equivalent of the six-month LIBOR rate. The transaction would additionally require up-front fees of 1% of the IFC loan, a commitment fee of 1.5 percent per annum, and a prepayment fee of 2%. Loan covenants required the project to maintain a minimum DSCR of at least 1.3×, current ratio of at least 1.2×, and ratio of maximum liability to tangible net worth of 2.5×. As security, the IFC wanted a first-ranking security over movables, immovables, land, contracts, and cash flows, and a pledge on 100% of paid-up equity share capital until the physical completion of the project.

However, several risks could affect the economics of the project and increase risks for lenders:

- Solar radiation is a variable resource that directly influences the plant load factor and the power output of the plant.
- The availability of solar radiation will vary so that a power plant's generation will also vary seasonally and from year to year.

20 EPC stands for Engineering Procurement and Construction.

Case Exhibit 22.2. Base case projections summary.

	Units	2013 (%)	2014 (%)	2015 (%)	2016 (%)	2017 (%)	2018 (%)	2019 (%)	2020 (%)	2021 (%)	2022 (%)	2023 (%)
Income Statement												
Revenue	US$ mn	0.56	6.16	6.12	6.08	6.03	5.99	5.95	5.91	5.87	5.83	5.79
EBITDA	US$ mn	0.51	5.56	5.48	5.40	5.32	5.24	5.16	5.07	4.98	4.89	4.80
Profit after tax (PAT)	US$ mn	0.04	0.85	0.88	0.95	1.03	1.12	1.22	1.33	1.44	1.56	1.68
Balance Sheet												
Total assets	US$ mn	33.24	33.54	33.09	32.60	32.06	31.49	30.92	30.33	29.82	29.39	29.03
Equity	US$ mn	9.87	10.72	11.60	12.55	13.57	14.69	15.91	17.24	18.68	20.24	21.91
Liabilities & equity	US$ mn	33.24	33.54	33.09	32.60	32.06	31.49	30.92	30.33	29.82	29.39	29.03
Cash Flow												
Cash generated from operations	US$ mn	0.07	2.34	2.61	2.68	2.76	2.85	2.95	3.06	3.17	3.29	3.41
Ratios												
EBITDA margin	%	90.7	90.2	89.5	88.9	88.2	87.5	86.7	85.8	84.9	84.0	83.0
PAT margin	%	7.4	13.8	14.3	15.6	17.0	18.7	20.5	22.5	24.6	26.7	29.0
Current ratio	× (times)	0.4	1.1	1.5	1.9	2.3	2.6	2.9	3.2	3.2	4.0	4.2
Long-term debt-to-equity ratio	× (times)	2.2	1.9	1.6	1.4	1.2	0.9	0.8	0.6	0.4	0.3	0.2
DSCR	× (times)	2.00	1.36	1.37	1.37	1.36	1.36	1.37	1.37	1.42	1.47	1.53

- Output in any given year can be significantly higher or lower than the long-run mean, and there is uncertainty in estimating the extent of this variation around the mean.

Structuring project finance for the clean energy sector involves quantifying and structuring around these uncertainties. In most cases the uncertainty of a generation estimate can be expressed as a distribution of outcomes, and certainty of power plant output above a certain value can be expressed with a certain level of confidence or a P value.

The IFC required recommendations from an energy consultant on what would be the levels of radiation available at 50% (P_{50}),[21] 75% (P_{75}), 90% (P_{90}), and 99% (P_{99}) confidence levels. Base case projections were based on radiation availability at a 50% confidence interval (P_{50}). Debt repayments had to be sculpted to achieve a minimum debt service coverage ratio of 1.30 at P_{50} levels of radiation. Furthermore:

- There were some concerns over the efficacy of thin film panels in high-temperature areas such as Rajasthan. High-temperature environments may result in higher module degradation and less than estimated generation, which in turn would affect project revenues.
- Interest rates could be reset upward during the life of the project, increasing the amount of debt to be serviced.

Sensitivity analysis yielded the DSCRs under these stressed conditions shown in Case Exhibit 22.3 (P is probability of loss of frame).

Case Exhibit 22.3. Debt service coverage ratios under stressed conditions.

Scenario	20 MW Average DSCR	Minimum DSCR
Base case	1.90	1.37
reduced P to P_{90}	1.68	1.22
reduced P to P_{99}	1.50	1.10
Degradation, worst case: 1.05% for first 10 years and 0.78% thereafter	1.87	1.36
Increased interest rates: 12.0% for IFC and 12.5% for other lenders	1.86	1.33

There were other structural risks that had to be assessed/mitigated before IFC's Credit Committee could underwrite the debt.

- If the power off-taker, NTPC Vidyut Vyapar Nigam, defaulted under its payment contract with Clean Infra/Hudson, the project might not be able to service its debt. Electricity boards and power distribution companies were facing high budget deficits, which could deteriorate to bankruptcy.
- The tariff that made the project feasible could be afforded by power consumers only if the government maintained its subsidy for renewable energy, making the project vulnerable to changes in government policy toward renewables.
- The power purchase agreement required that the project be commissioned within 12 months, which is a tight construction time line. In case of a delay, the project's tariff would be revised downward.
- Hudson was owned by a private equity fund that typically monetized its investments over a five- to seven-year horizon, which implies that equity ownership of the project may change hands before the debt holders are repaid.

At the same time, the project enjoyed several advantages: It was backed by an experienced sponsor with a good track record of implementing similar projects in India. The project financing was structured with reasonable leverage to withstand adverse shocks. Last, the project would have strong developmental impact in promoting the development of renewable energy infrastructure and would pave the way for the financing of future solar projects.

All of these issues would be discussed in an investment review meeting to decide IFC's involvement in this project.

21 One of the big risks for solar projects is the variability of fuel source. Thus, to protect them- selves against generation shortfalls and possible loan defaults, lenders and investors have implemented production requirements on potential projects which involve the calculation of probabilities expressed as P values (the "P" stands for probability). For instance, P90 denotes the level of annual solar-driven electricity generation that is forecasted to be generated with a 90% confidence interval.

Questions for Discussion

1. What are the key characteristics that qualify this project as project finance?
2. Develop a graphical map of the project's relevant cash flows.
3. What are the risks faced by the sponsors? Differentiate between the Indian and the US sponsor's situations.
4. Assuming that the base case scenario holds, what return could Hudson Clean Energy Partners expect from its investment should it decide to exit the project at the end of the seventh year? Assume that INR 50 = US$1 at the inception of the project.
5. Would you advise the IFC to invest in this project? Are there any covenants you would recommend the IFC require to be included in the loan agreement?

23

Global Investing

Trust not all your goods to one ship.
— Erasmus

But divide your investments among many places for you do not know what risks might lie ahead.
— Ecclesiastes 11:2

One of the many faces of globalization is the surging flow of cross-border portfolio investment into foreign stocks and bonds searching for higher yields and capital appreciation (but not managerial control). This phenomenon is rooted in the rekindling of Adam Smith's *invisible hand* — the dismantling or at the very least the loosening of capital controls — and powered by the explosive growth of emerging capital markets and fast-paced privatizations of state-owned companies. This chapter explores the financial logic behind global investing in the context of increasingly integrated capital markets, with a focus on stocks.

Consider, for example, the predicament of Dr. James Breech, who is the founder and CEO of Cougar Investments — a globally diversified mutual fund based in Toronto (Canada). One of his important investors is the municipal workers pension fund of the City of Toronto, which gave Cougar Investments a mandate to manage 250 million Canadian dollars (CAD). Recently Dr. Uhlman, the CFO of the City of Toronto's pension fund, has been questioning the tenets of Cougar's international diversification strategy. Quite simply, in spite of a respectable 9.2% performance for the last 12 months, simple domestic investment in Canadian stocks over that same period would have yielded a significantly higher return of 13.7%, not to mention that over that same period the CAD appreciated on a trade-weighted basis by 6.7%.[1] Investing strictly in Canadian stocks might have been simpler, less risky, and less costly: no fears about perennial currency risk or concern about transaction costs. Dr. Breech would have some explaining to do. Should the gospel of international portfolio diversification be revisited? Had globalization eroded the traditional benefits of international investing? Was simple tracking of Canadian stock market indexes, which was gaining increasing popularity, the way of the future? Should Dr. Breech think of early retirement if passive investment through simple tracking of stock market indexes made asset managers redundant?

By reading this chapter you will understand:

- What the basics of international portfolio management are.
- What the benefits of international diversification are.
- How to manage currency risk in international portfolios.
- How to invest internationally.
- What the new landscape of the global asset management industry is.

1 The return on the internationally diversified portfolio at 9.2% would have been approximately 6.7% higher had the CAD remained stable during the last 12 months.

- How is ESG investing re-shaping asset management.
- What alternative investments and the search for alpha (see the appendix to this chapter) are.

THE BASICS OF INTERNATIONAL PORTFOLIO MANAGEMENT

The old adage "Don't put all your eggs in one basket" is the cornerstone of investing. At its simplest, it calls for diversifying any investment pool across several asset classes rather than one.[2] The objective is to reduce the risk of the overall stock portfolio while maintaining its return or — equivalently — to increase return for a given level of risk. Presumably this is achieved by investing in several stocks across industries whose price movements are less than perfectly correlated. Portfolio risk is reduced through skillful diversification, which means adding high-return stocks that exhibit little correlation to stocks already in the portfolio. Because stock returns tend to be far less correlated across countries than within a given country, it stands to reason that international diversification (adding foreign stocks to a domestic portfolio) will deliver far greater risk reduction than simple domestic diversification. Thus, by expanding the universe of available stocks through *international* diversification, it is possible to reduce the level of risk for a given level of return.

In a pathbreaking study, Solnik (1974) showed that a fully diversified US stock portfolio is only 27% as risky as one representative US stock and that a portfolio of only about 20 stocks will reduce the risk of an entire portfolio to the level of non-diversifiable risk (also known as systematic risk). Exhibit 23.1 portrays the reduction in portfolio risk as additional stocks are added to the portfolio. The vertical axis is the ratio of the portfolio variance to the variance of a typical stock, whereas the horizontal axis measures the number of stocks in the portfolio. As more stocks were added to the portfolio of US stocks its variance declined to 27% of the variance of a typical US stock. However, if the portfolio variance declined quickly at first it stabilized once the portfolio had included about 20 stocks. Thus, 73% of a typical stock variance can be eliminated through diversification.

But wait — diversification in US stocks is only half as good as diversifying the portfolio internationally. Indeed, the same portfolio's total risk as measured by its variance can be further reduced to only 12% of the riskiness of a representative US stock, and this can also be achieved again with as few as 20 foreign stocks (see Exhibit 23.2). The same study shows that the benefits of international diversification are even greater for investors domiciled in non-US stock markets. For example, a Swiss investor can only reduce the portfolio risk of a strictly Swiss portfolio to 44% of the risk of a representative Swiss stock. This result should be expected since US capital markets account for approximately 40% of world capitalization and therefore offer the largest benefits of domestic

2 Asset class refers to a group of reasonably homogeneous assets in terms of their risk-return distributions; technology stocks, high-yield bonds, commercial real estate, investment trusts, and macro-hedge funds are all different asset classes. This chapter deals primarily with stocks, but the concept of asset class would reach far more broadly to include commodities, real estate properties, timberland, works of art, and so on, which may not be traded on capital markets.

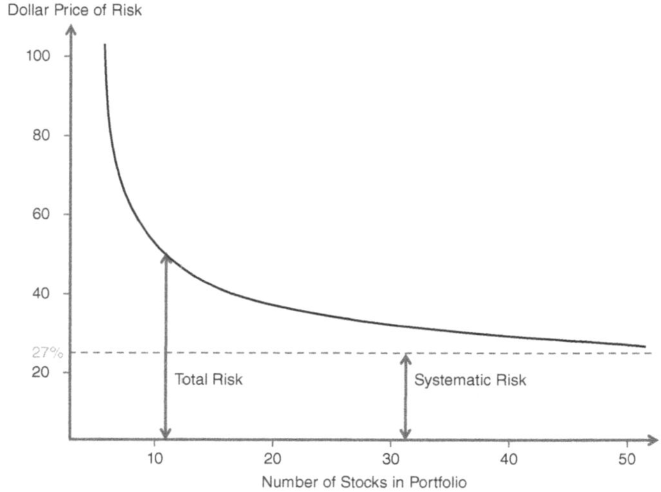

Exhibit 23.1. Portfolio risk reduction through diversification.

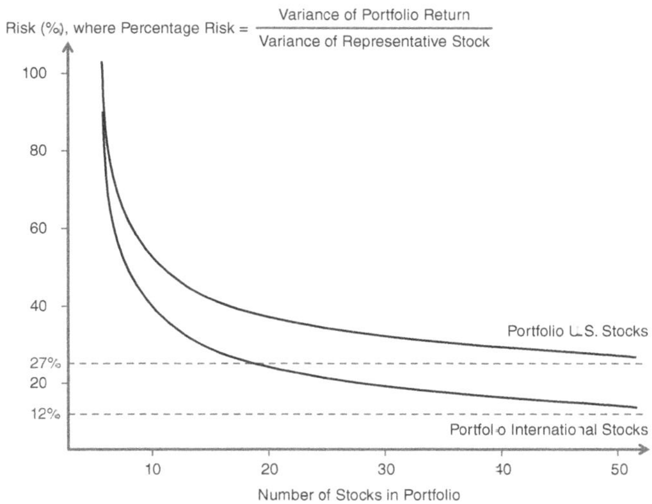

Exhibit 23.2. Portfolio risk reduction through international diversification.

diversification to their resident investors, who can select from the largest array of investable stocks.

Benefits of portfolio diversification

This section reviews the metrics of portfolio investing to better understand the benefits of international diversification. Consider an investor searching for the optimal allocation between domestic (*D*) stocks and foreign (*F*) stocks. Let's assume that the domestic stock is the US market portfolio, proxied by the Standard & Poor's 500-stock index (S&P 500) with expected return $r_D = 6\%$ and risk $\sigma_D = 13\%$, and that the foreign stock is the Indian stock market portfolio, proxied by the Bombay Stock Exchange 30-stock index (BSE 30) with return $r_F = 10\%$ and risk $\sigma_F = 20\%$. In both cases risk and return are measured as the historical standard deviation and average return of the index values over the prior three years (see International Corporate Finance in Practice 23.1 for a primer on measuring risk).

INTERNATIONAL CORPORATE FINANCE IN PRACTICE 23.1

Measuring Risk and Return

The total *rate of return* of an asset over a given period — say a year — is equal to the change in its price and whatever cash-flow income it produces such as dividends per dollar of investment. The rate of return of an asset is assumed to be distributed as a normal random variable $N(\mu;\sigma^2)$ whose probability distribution is fully described by its mean μ and variance σ^2 (or standard deviation σ). *Standard deviation* measures the historical dispersion of an asset return from its mean. It is often used by investors as a gauge of expected risk or volatility. A volatile stock will have a high standard deviation — say 50% — and will see its return widely dispersed from its mean, whereas a blue-chip stock will have a low standard deviation — say 10%. Because it is measured in the same unit as expected return (%), it is preferred to *variance,* which is measured as a squared percentage (%)[3] and therefore is more difficult to interpret. Let's consider the actual case of the average return and historical risk of domestic and foreign stocks over the period 2007–2011.

3 Asset class refers to a group of reasonably homogeneous assets in terms of their risk-return distributions; technology stocks, energy stocks, high yield bonds, commercial real estate investment trusts, and macro hedge funds are all different asset classes. This chapter deals primarily with stocks, but the concept of asset class would reach far more broadly to include commodities, real estate properties, timberland, works of art, and so on which may not be traded on capital markets.

Year	Domestic Stock (S&P 500) (%)	Foreign Stock (BSE 30) (%)
2007	3.53	47.15
2008	−38.49	−52.45
2009	23.45	81.03
2010	12.78	17.43
2011	0.00	−24.64
Average return	0.26	13.70
Standard deviation	23.49	53.65

Beta (β) coefficient

A relative measure of risk is given by a stock's beta, which measures volatility not in absolute terms as standard deviation does but in comparison to the stock market as a whole. Betas are calculated by regressing a stock's return against the stock market's return; it gauges the responsiveness of a stock's price to market swings. A stock with a beta of 1.2 would see its price increasing or decreasing by 1.20% on any 1% move in the stock market price. Conversely, a defensive stock with a beta of 0.7 would appreciate by only 0.70% on any 1% increase in the value of the market portfolio.

Sharpe ratio

A common method for evaluating a portfolio's risk-adjusted performance is to compute its Sharpe ratio, defined as the portfolio's excess return: portfolio return r_p minus risk-free rate r_f divided by its standard deviation σ_p:

$$\text{Sharpe ratio} = \frac{r_p - r_f}{\sigma_p}$$

Simply put, the Sharpe ratio measures the portfolio's excess return per unit of risk — a metric that portfolio managers find very useful since it allows direct comparison between different risk/return combinations. As one would expect, international diversification can often help. For example, if a Vietnam country fund has an expected return of 21% with a standard deviation of 34% when the US risk-free rate is 4%, its Sharpe ratio would be (21% – 4%)/34% = 50%. How does it compare with a Turkey country fund, which has an expected return of 12% and a standard deviation of 20%? With a Sharpe ratio of (12% – 4%)/20% = 40%, the Turkey country fund is less desirable than the Vietnam country fund.

One of the drawbacks of the Sharpe ratio is that it focuses on the portfolio's total risk when most asset managers are actually measured against a benchmark. Thus a ratio directly measuring the investor's performance against the reference benchmark is preferred; such is the information ratio, defined as the excess return of the portfolio r_p against the benchmark return r_b divided by the standard deviation of returns in excess of the benchmark's return $\sigma_{p,b}$ (also known as the tracking error):

$$\text{Information ratio} = \frac{\left(r_p - r_b\right)}{\sigma_{p,b}}$$

Asset managers often take active bets to beat the market (or any specified benchmark) and generate excess returns, also known as alpha, when compared to the market/benchmark beta return; their actual performance has to be adjusted by the actual risk incurred and is better measured by their information ratio.

Let's first compute the return and risk of such an internationally diversified portfolio assumed to be invested 60% in a domestic stock ($w_D = 60\%$) and 40% in a foreign stock ($w_F = 1 - w_D = 40\%$). Its overall rate of return r_P is simply the weighted average of the rate of return of the two component stocks comprising the portfolio:

$$r_P = w_D r_D + w_F r_F = 0.60 \times 0.06 + 0.40 \times 0.10$$
$$= 0.076 \qquad (23.1)$$

The domestic stock portfolio offers a lower rate of return but is less risky than the foreign portfolio. Our investor may be tempted to invest more capital in the foreign stock portfolio but understands that doing so would expose him or her to a higher level of risk. How much more risk depends in turn on how the two domestic (D) and foreign (F) stock portfolios move together — the statistical concepts of covariance and correlation (see International Corporate Finance in Practice 23.2). Covariance and correlation measure the extent to which the prices of two assets move together. Thus, the degree to which the risk of a portfolio can be reduced through diversification is a function of how much or how little the prices of the assets in the portfolio co-vary and are correlated.

For a two-stock portfolio invested in domestic stock and foreign stock in the relative proportion of w_D and $w_F = 1 - w_D$, the overall riskiness of the portfolio is measured by the variance of the portfolio return $\text{Var}(r_P)$ (or its standard deviation σ_P), defined as follows:

$$\text{Var}(r_P) = \sigma_P^2 = w_D^2 \sigma_D^2 + w_F^2 \sigma_F^2$$
$$+ 2\,\text{Cov}(w_D r_D, w_F r_F) \qquad (23.2)$$

where $\text{Cov}(w_D r_D, w_F r_F)$ is the covariance between the return on the domestic and foreign stocks and is defined as a function of the correlation coefficient ρ_{DF} and respective standard deviations σ_D and σ_F of the domestic (D) and foreign (F) stocks. The portfolio risk can be further expressed as

$$\text{Var}(r_P) = \sigma_P^2 = w_D^2 \sigma_D^2 + w_F^2 \sigma_F^2$$
$$+ 2 w_D \sigma_D w_F \sigma_F \rho_{DF} \qquad (23.3)$$

where ρ is the correlation coefficient between the domestic and foreign stocks. Recalling that $\sigma_D = 13\%$ and $\sigma_F = 20\%$ are the respective standard deviations of the domestic and foreign stock indexes and assuming that the correlation coefficient ρ is 0.50, then:

$$\text{Var}(r_P) = \sigma_P^2 = (0.60)^2 \times (0.13)^2 + (0.40)^2 \times (0.20)^2$$
$$+ 2(0.60) \times (0.13) \times (0.40) \times (0.20) \times (0.50)$$
$$= 0.01872 = (0.426)^2$$

INTERNATIONAL CORPORATE FINANCE IN PRACTICE 23.2

Computing Covariance and Correlation

Using historical returns of both the domestic stock $r_{t,D}$ (with mean r_D) and foreign stock $r_{t,F}$ (with mean r_F) with $t = 0, -1, -2, \ldots, T$, covariance is readily derived as:

$$\text{Cov}(r_D, r_F) = \frac{\sum_{t=0}^{T} (r_{t,D} - r_D)(r_{t,F} - r_F)}{T - 1}$$

Using the historical returns of both the domestic and foreign stock portfolios presented in International Corporate Finance in Practice 23.1, their covariance is found to be:

$$\text{Cov}(r_D, r_F) = 10.73\%$$

Thus — if you have already computed the standard deviation of both domestic and foreign stocks — it is easier to calculate covariance first and then derive correlation:

$$\rho_{DF} = \frac{\text{Cov}(r_D, r_F)}{\sigma_D \sigma_F} = \frac{10.73\%}{23.49\% \times 53.65\%} = 79\%$$

Correlation and risk reduction

Clearly, the overall portfolio risk is sensitive to the correlation coefficient ρ, which in the preceding example was assumed to be 0.50. But what would the portfolio's overall risk be if the correlation between the domestic and the foreign stock were to increase to a maximum of 1 or decrease to a minimum of −1?

- *Perfect correlation*: ρ = 1. The worst case is the situation of perfect correlation of 1 when diversification offers no benefits whatsoever. Note that in the case of perfect correlation the portfolio's total risk reduces itself to squaring the weighted average of each component stock's standard deviation[4]:

$$\begin{aligned}\mathrm{Var}(r_P) &= \sigma_P^2 = \left(w_D^2\sigma_D^2 + w_F^2\sigma_F^2 + 2w_D w_F \sigma_D \sigma_F\right)\\ &= \left(w_D\sigma_D + w_F\sigma_F\right)^2\\ \sigma_P &= w_D\sigma_D + w_F\sigma_F = 0.60\times0.13+0.40\times0.20 = 0.16\end{aligned}$$

- *Intermediate correlation*: $-1 < \rho < 1$. In this case the portfolio's total risk σ_P is always less than the weighted average of each component stock's standard deviation. Intuitively this important result should not be surprising, since in the case of zero diversification benefits (correlation equals 1), the standard deviation is itself equal to the weighted average of each stock's standard deviation. Therefore, with correlation less than 1 and benefits of diversification, the portfolio's standard deviation has to be less than the weighted average of each stock's standard deviation. Formally, we want to prove that:

$$\begin{aligned}\sigma_P &= \left(w_D^2\sigma_D^2 + w_F^2\sigma_F^2 + 2w_D\sigma_D w_F\sigma_F\,\rho_{DF}\right)^{.5}\\ &= \left[w_D^2\sigma_D^2 + (1-w_D)^2\sigma_F^2\right.\\ &\quad \left.+2w_D\sigma_D(1-w_D)\sigma_F\rho_{DF}\right]^{.5} < \left\{\left[w_D\sigma_D + (1-w_D)\sigma_F\right]^2\right\}^{.5}\end{aligned}$$

which is equivalent to:

$$\begin{aligned}&\left[w_D^2\sigma_D^2 + (1-w_D)^2\sigma_F^2 + 2w_D\sigma_D(1-w_D)\sigma_F\rho_{DF}\right]^{.5}\\ &\quad< \left[w_D^2\sigma_D^2 + (1-w_D)^2\sigma_F^2 + 2w_D\sigma_D(1-w_D)\sigma_F\right]^{.5}\end{aligned}$$

and verified as long as $\rho_{DF} < 1$.

For most capital markets, correlation will range from 0.30 to 0.90, but if asset classes other than stocks are considered, correlation can fall farther or even become negative (see next section for further data on correlation among national capital markets).

- *Negative correlation*: ρ = −1. The benefits of portfolio diversification are at their greatest here, and portfolio variance reduces itself to[5]

$$\begin{aligned}\mathrm{Var}(r_P) &= \sigma_P^2 = \left(w_D^2\sigma_{D2} + w_F^2\sigma_F^2 - 2w_D w_F\sigma_D\sigma_F\right)\\ &= \left(w_D\sigma_D - w_F\sigma_F\right)^2\end{aligned}$$

and σ_P = absolute value of $(w_D\sigma_D - w_F\sigma_F)$.

Exhibit 23.3 maps the polar cases of correlation at 1 and −1, depicting the risk-return profile of our portfolio under different degrees of diversification between the domestic (*D*) and foreign stock (*F*) by increasing w_F from 0 to 1. *D* shows a portfolio invested w_D = 100% in the domestic stock — the S&P 500 index in our case. Similarly, a portfolio fully invested in the foreign stock is represented by point *F* — the BSE 30 index. Assuming perfect correlation (i.e., a correlation coefficient of 1) between the domestic and the foreign stock, the risk-return trade-off is a straight-line *DF* portraying an increasing degree of international diversification as it moves from *D* to *F* (w_D declines from 1 to 0 as w_F increases from 0 to 1). In the opposite case of a coefficient of correlation equal to −1, the losses on one asset can fully offset the gains on the other. For this to happen, all that is needed is that portfolio weights be properly set. In this case — for $w_D = 0.58$ and $w_F = 0.42$ — the portfolio risk $\sigma_P = 0$. As we vary the portfolio composition, the risk level will linearly decline from *D* to *M*, bounce off the vertical axis, and increase linearly to *F*.

Efficient frontiers

For all the intermediate cases of correlation ranging from −1 to +1, equations (23.1), (23.2), and (23.3) for the overall portfolio's risk and return allow us to derive and plot both returns and standard deviations for varying combinations of domestic and foreign assets ranging from 100% invested in the S&P 500 US portfolio ($w_D = 1$, $w_F = 0$) to 100% invested in the foreign portfolio BSE 30 ($w_D = 0$, $w_F = 1$). The resulting plot is shown in Exhibit 23.3. The graph of risk and return is referred to as the *efficient frontier*: It allows the investor to find the level of return it can aspire to for a given level of risk.

As the level of risk increases, the allocation between the domestic and foreign assets will increasingly favor the higher-yielding foreign assets. Note that starting with 100% of domestic assets, an

4 Basic algebra reminds us that $(a + b)^2 = a^2 + b^2 + 2ab$ and $[(a + b)^2]^{1/2} = a + b$.

5 The reader will recall from elementary algebra that $(a - b)^2 = a^2 + b^2 - 2ab$.

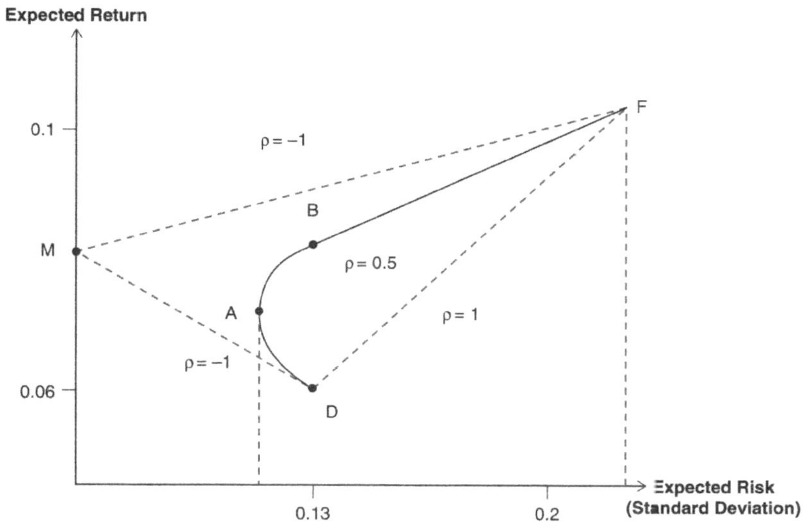

Exhibit 23.3. Efficient frontier under varying asset weights.

initial substitution of foreign assets will both reduce risk and increase return before point A is reached in Exhibit 23.3. Beyond point A, it is necessary to increase risk in order to yield increasing returns. In effect, at point B — corresponding to $w_F = 24\%$ of foreign stock, the overall riskiness of the portfolio is 13% — the same as for the 100% US portfolio — but with an improved rate of return of $w_P = 0.76 \times r_D + 0.24 \times r_F = 0.76 \times 0.06 + 0.24 \times 0.10 = 0.07$ courtesy of international diversification. Traveling from point D (100% domestic portfolio), returns steadily increase while the overall risk declines — a situation that is a win-win for the investor and has much to do with the level of correlation between the two assets in the portfolio. The portion of the graph DA offers greater benefits of diversification the lower the level of correlation. Thus, if the investor's objective is to minimize risk, Exhibit 23.3 shows this can be readily achieved by moving to the leftmost point on the graph, which corresponds to $w_F = 18\%$ being allocated to foreign assets.

Optimal portfolio allocation

In real-life situations, the universe of investable stocks is far larger than the stylized world of a simple domestic and foreign stock portfolio used for pedagogical purposes. The universe would include all domestic and foreign stocks and bonds but also other asset classes such as real estate, commodities, and so on. Portfolio choice could easily number (N) in the hundreds. In practice, though, the investment set may be limited to country stock market and bond indexes. The optimization algorithm remains one of *constrained maximization* — that is, find the percentage w_i to invest in asset i that will maximize the overall portfolio's rate of return r_P for a given level of acceptable risk σ_P:

$$\text{Max}\, r_P = \sum_{i=1}^{N} w_i r$$

$$\text{subject to}\, \sigma_P = \sum_{i=1}^{N} w_i^2 \sigma_i^2 + 2\sum_{i=1}^{N} \sum_{j=1}^{N} w_i w_j \rho_{ij} \sigma_i \sigma_j$$

$$= \text{acceptable level of risk and} \sum_{i=1}^{N} w_i = 1.$$

Using spreadsheet software (such as the Solver function in Excel) is the easiest way to find the optimal portfolio in terms of the maximum level of return for each level of risk; the result can be readily graphed into the efficient frontier similar to the one shown in Exhibit 23.3. As the reader would expect, the computational complexity explodes with the number of assets included in the universe; fortunately, however, there are powerful software models to solve large-scale constrained optimization problems.

Informational inputs

The implementation of this optimization algorithm requires the portfolio manager to forecast the risk and return for each asset as well as the matrix of correlation among all assets. Estimates of future asset returns are often based on historical returns but could also be derived from firms' pro forma cash flows for stocks and macroeconomic data for bonds. Estimates of assets' risk are derived from past prices data and, when available, from options' implied volatilities. Similarly, estimates of correlation coefficients for all currency pairs are derived primarily from historical data.

THE GAINS FROM INTERNATIONAL DIVERSIFICATION

Our discussion of international portfolio management in the previous section highlighted the importance of the correlation coefficient between the domestic stock market (home market for investors) and the foreign stock market: The lower the correlation coefficient, the more international diversification can reduce the portfolio risk and the greater the potential gains from international diversification. Therefore, it is important to study the empirical evidence measuring the correlation between national stock markets. Exhibits 23.4A and 23.4B illustrate such opportunities by tabulating the risk-return characteristics of major capital markets in both developed economies and BRIC countries (Brazil, Russia, India, China) for the periods 1990–2000 and 2001–2010. The reader will note wide differences in the rates of return (column 2) and the levels of risk (measured by the standard deviation of monthly returns and shown in column 3) across countries. All foreign capital markets are less than fully correlated with the US market portfolio (column 4). BRIC countries generally (but not always) offer significantly higher returns and are generally more volatile/riskier than developed capital markets; they do, nevertheless, exhibit a lower degree of correlation with the US market portfolio than developed markets. However, correlation is generally higher for the period 2001–2010 than it was for the period 1990–2000, reflecting the steadily increasing degree of capital market integration.

Exhibit 23.4A. International risk-return trade-off and correlation (1990–2000).

Country/Index	Annualized Returns (%)	Standard Deviation of Returns (%)	Correlation with US Market	Market Risk (Beta) from US Perspective
United States	17.4396	4.1859	1.0000	1.0000
Canada	12.2403	6.6870	0.6982	0.7905
Australia	6.5214	2.8493	0.5446	0.5444
Hong Kong	20.2740	7.4625	0.5005	1.1439
Japan	(4.8610)	7.2190	0.3769	0.6248
Belgium	13.8116	2.3472	0.5366	0.5928
Austria	1.3010	2.3461	0.3330	0.5353
Denmark	9.4909	4.5935	0.5800	0.5489
France	16.8363	3.4972	0.5531	0.7832
Germany	16.4751	4.7732	0.5332	0.7731
Italy	5.9907	3.8170	0.3351	0.5126
Netherlands	22.5250	2.8690	0.5627	0.7092
Norway	5.9477	5.1029	0.5920	0.7591
Spain	18.5894	4.5624	0.5181	0.8439
Switzerland	20.9663	3.2454	0.5747	0.7395
United Kingdom	14.2476	3.4462	0.6459	0.6638
Brazil	278.4103	9.8077	0.2518	1.6153
Russia	4.4952	16.1855	0.4828	2.6337
India	14.3709	7.2794	0.0680	0.1756
China	32.1543	3.2840	(0.0035)	(0.0221)
MSCI EAFE Index	6.5760	3.5518	0.5907	0.6611
MSCI World Index	10.5152	3.6058	0.8500	0.8223

Exhibit 23.4B. International risk-return trade-off and correlation (2001–2010).

Country/Grouping	Annualized Returns (%)	Standard Deviation of Returns (%)	Correlation with US Market	Market Risk (Beta) from US Perspective
United States	1.4123	6.0372	1.0000	1.0000
Canada	6.5833	3.0341	0.8245	0.7773
Australia	9.7913	4.0809	0.8121	0.6691
Hong Kong	7.8586	4.2920	0.7360	1.0039
Japan	(1.8220)	6.4447	0.6422	0.7918
Belgium	3.0089	4.2213	0.7771	0.8593
Austria	13.0875	6.8051	0.7037	0.9852
Denmark	7.0456	4.0489	0.7316	0.8671
France	(1.5085)	5.6054	0.8847	1.0525
Germany	0.7226	3.3006	0.8641	1.2402
Italy	(4.7676)	7.2870	0.8437	1.0829
Netherlands	(2.4229)	4.9844	0.8277	1.1333
Norway	8.4224	7.1059	0.7908	1.2219
Spain	4.3280	8.6156	0.8079	1.0197
Switzerland	(0.2375)	2.8095	0.7896	0.7182
United Kingdom	3.3313	5.1756	0.8767	0.8151
Brazil	16.3287	5.7118	0.7244	1.1813
Russia	20.5765	7.7076	0.5928	1.2922
India	19.9058	4.4521	0.6261	1.0293
China	3.0792	7.6601	0.3034	0.5599
MSCI EAFE Index	3.9281	7.4300	0.8917	1.0106
MSCI World Index	2.9015	6.4860	0.9723	1.0138

The empirical results presented in Exhibits 23.4A and 23.4B from a US investor's standpoint are generalized in the form of a world matrix of cross-country correlations among national stock markets' returns. The data are presented separately for high-income countries first (Exhibit 23.5A) and then for emerging market countries (Exhibit 23.5B) before being combined into one single matrix (Exhibits 23.6A and 23.6B).

Correlations tend to be higher between national markets whose economies are not only geographically contiguous but also integrated. It is, therefore, not surprising to find that Canada's and the United States' capital markets are highly integrated with a correlation coefficient of 0.72; Japan and Italy, on the other hand, exhibit a low level of correlation at 0.23. The reader will also note that correlation tends to be lower between emerged and emerging capital markets and even lower among emerging capital markets.

Since the matrix of correlation is a critical informational input into optimizing geographical diversification in portfolio allocation, one important question to ask is: Is the matrix reasonably stationary over time? In other words, can historical correlation be used as a reliable predictor of future correlation? Several empirical studies, such as Goetzmann *et al.* (2005), have concluded that:

- Correlation across national markets has been creeping upward over the past quarter of a century. This finding should not be surprising since over the same period the world economy has become increasingly integrated courtesy of globalization. As national economies become more open to international trade, foreign direct investment, and foreign portfolio investment, one would expect a continuing increase in the correlation of stock returns. This powerful trend is illustrated in Exhibits 23.6A and 23.6B, which show the world

Exhibit 23.5A. Matrix of correlation coefficients, high-income countries (December 31, 2000–December 31, 2010).

Country Name	Australia	Canada	France	Germany	Hong Kong	Italy	Japan	Netherlands	South Korea	Switzerland	Spain	Taiwan	UK	USA
Australia	1.0000	0.7404	0.7950	0.7359	0.6691	0.7403	0.6743	0.7619	0.6683	0.7350	0.7393	0.6005	0.8055	0.8121
Canada	0.7404	1.0000	0.7463	0.7104	0.7369	0.7100	0.6666	0.7497	0.6756	0.6717	0.6559	0.6271	0.7682	0.8245
Hong Kong	0.6691	0.7369	0.6657	0.6610	1.0000	0.6549	0.6246	0.6699	0.6644	0.6137	0.6735	0.6533	0.6923	0.7360
France	0.7950	0.7463	1.0000	0.9393	0.6657	0.9254	0.6388	0.9219	0.6987	0.8588	0.8671	0.5799	0.9089	0.8847
Germany	0.7359	0.7104	0.9393	1.0000	0.6610	0.8606	0.5973	0.8942	0.7241	0.8436	0.8185	0.5697	0.8522	0.8641
Italy	0.7403	0.7100	0.9254	0.8606	0.6549	1.0000	0.6064	0.8517	0.6780	0.7848	0.8679	0.5530	0.8756	0.8437
Japan	0.6743	0.6666	0.6388	0.5973	0.6246	0.6064	1.0000	0.6217	0.6002	0.6194	0.5656	0.4978	0.6379	0.6422
Netherlands	0.7619	0.7497	0.9219	0.8942	0.6699	0.8517	0.6217	1.0000	0.7141	0.8383	0.7991	0.6028	0.8722	0.8277
Sou th Korea	0.6683	0.6756	0.6987	0.7241	0.6644	0.6780	0.6002	0.7141	1.0000	0.6318	0.7035	0.6775	0.6532	0.6932
Spain	0.7393	0.6559	0.8671	0.8185	0.6735	0.8679	0.5656	0.7991	0.7035	0.7468	1.0000	0.5714	0.8237	0.8079
Switzerland	0.7350	0.6717	0.8588	0.8436	0.6137	0.7848	0.6194	0.8383	0.6318	1.0000	0.7468	0.4526	0.7993	0.7896
Taiwan	0.6005	0.6271	0.5799	0.5697	0.6533	0.5530	0.4978	0.6028	0.6775	0.4526	0.5714	1.0000	0.5356	0.5819
UK	0.8055	0.7682	0.9089	0.8522	0.6923	0.8756	0.6379	0.8772	0.6532	0.7993	0.8237	0.5356	1.0000	0.8767
USA	0.8121	0.8245	0.8847	0.8641	0.7360	0.8437	0.6422	0.8277	0.6932	0.7896	0.8079	0.5819	0.8767	1.0000

Exhibit 23.5B. Matrix of correlation coefficients, emerging market countries (December 31, 2000–December 31, 2010).

Country Name	Argentina	Brazil	Chile	China	Colombia	Egypt	India	Indonesia	Malaysia	Mexico	Philippines	Russia	South Africa	Thailand	Turkey	Vietnam
Argentina	1.0000	0.4479	0.4653	0.2231	0.4590	0.3929	0.4654	0.4984	0.4173	0.6414	0.4797	0.5792	0.4166	0.5134	0.4109	0.1434
Brazil	0.4479	1.0000	0.6802	0.3606	0.4028	0.3772	0.6423	0.4678	0.5121	0.6619	0.3814	0.6207	0.6240	0.6294	0.4863	0.2395
Chile	0.4653	0.6802	1.0000	0.3302	0.3726	0.3676	0.5719	0.5384	0.5197	0.5967	0.4671	0.5279	0.4905	0.5769	0.5226	0.2319
China	0.2231	0.3606	0.3302	1.0000	0.2451	0.1663	0.3372	0.2957	0.3521	0.2673	0.2534	0.2872	0.2944	0.2014	0.2198	0.2714
Colombia	0.4590	0.4028	0.3726	0.2451	1.0000	0.4158	0.4402	0.4383	0.4279	0.4690	0.4182	0.4601	0.4311	0.3731	0.3688	0.1495
Egypt	0.3929	0.3722	0.3676	0.1663	0.4158	1.0000	0.4392	0.5057	0.3251	0.4434	0.3719	0.4700	0.3905	0.4486	0.3882	0.1609
India	0.4654	0.6423	0.5719	0.3372	0.4402	0.4392	1.0000	0.6494	0.5380	0.5793	0.5532	0.5374	0.6114	0.6331	0.5038	0.3642
Indonesia	0.4984	0.4678	0.5384	0.2957	0.4383	0.5057	0.6494	1.0000	0.5831	0.6073	0.5960	0.5403	0.4676	0.5725	0.3212	0.2929
Malaysia	0.4173	0.5121	0.5197	0.3521	0.4279	0.3251	0.5380	0.5831	1.0000	0.5224	0.4939	0.4241	0.3827	0.5204	0.3254	0.2091
Mexico	0.6414	0.6619	0.5967	0.2673	0.4690	0.4434	0.5793	0.6073	0.5224	1.0000	0.5285	0.6930	0.6224	0.5517	0.4650	0.3710
Philippines	0.4797	0.3814	0.4671	0.2534	0.4182	0.3719	0.5532	0.5960	0.4939	0.5285	1.0000	0.3473	0.3683	0.5158	0.3115	0.2504
Russia	0.5792	0.6207	0.5279	0.2872	0.4601	0.4700	0.5374	0.5403	0.4241	0.6930	0.3473	1.0000	0.5672	0.5402	0.4846	0.3091
South Africa	0.4166	0.6240	0.4905	0.2944	0.4311	0.3905	0.6114	0.4676	0.3827	0.6224	0.3683	0.5672	1.0000	0.5160	0.4555	0.2475
Thailand	0.5134	0.6294	0.5769	0.2014	0.3731	0.4486	0.6331	0.5725	0.5204	0.5517	0.5158	0.5402	0.5160	1.0000	0.4552	0.1219
Turkey	0.4109	0.4863	0.5226	0.2198	0.3688	0.3882	0.5038	0.3212	0.3254	0.4650	0.3115	0.4846	0.4555	0.4552	1.0000	0.2588
Vietnam	0.1434	0.2395	0.2319	0.2714	0.1495	0.1609	0.3642	0.2929	0.2091	0.3710	0.2504	0.3091	0.2475	0.1219	0.2588	1.0000

Exhibit 23.6A. World correlation matrix coefficients, 1990–2000.

Country Name	Australia	Brazil	Canada	China	France	Germany	India	Indonesia	Japan	Mexico	Russia	South Africa	Switzerland	Turkey	UK	USA
Australia	1.0000	0.2849	0.6064	(0.0083)	0.5308	0.5497	0.1858	0.4520	0.4527	0.4988	0.3011	0.4567	0.4775	0.1844	0.5769	0.5446
Brazil	0.2849	1.0000	0.2280	0.0333	0.1876	0.1641	0.3146	0.2007	0.2145	0.4176	0.5172	0.3277	0.2517	0.1571	0.1994	0.2518
Canada	0.6064	0.2280	1.0000	0.0383	0.5374	0.5544	0.2063	0.4911	0.3831	0.6035	0.5458	0.5750	0.4773	0.2504	0.5129	0.6982
China	(0.0083)	0.0333	0.0383	1.0000	(0.0351)	0.0315	0.1845	0.0925	0.0371	0.1154	0.1699	0.0578	(0.0205)	0.0304	0.0242	(0.0035)
France	0.5308	0.1876	0.5374	(0.0351)	1.0000	0.7766	0.1636	0.4275	0.3088	0.4316	0.4339	0.3931	0.6725	0.2649	0.6894	0.5531
Germany	0.5497	0.1641	0.5544	0.0315	0.7766	1.0000	0.0940	0.4837	0.2820	0.3801	0.3998	0.4417	0.6055	0.2659	0.5904	0.5332
India	0.1858	0.3146	0.2063	0.1845	0.1636	0.0940	1.0000	0.2211	0.1293	0.3096	0.2417	0.1822	0.0610	0.1499	0.0743	0.1166
Indonesia	0.4520	0.2007	0.4911	0.0925	0.4275	0.4837	0.2211	1.0000	0.2973	0.2983	0.4554	0.3507	0.4897	0.2648	0.4065	0.4236
Japan	0.4527	0.2145	0.3831	0.0371	0.3088	0.2820	0.1293	0.2973	1.0000	0.3647	0.2189	0.3611	0.2708	(0.0688)	0.2727	0.3769
Mexico	0.4988	0.4176	0.6035	0.1154	0.4316	0.3801	0.3096	0.2983	0.3647	1.0000	0.5057	0.5173	0.3062	0.3006	0.4966	0.5582
Russia	0.3011	0.5172	0.5458	0.1699	0.4339	0.3998	0.2417	0.4554	0.2189	0.5057	1.0000	0.4901	0.4811	0.4732	0.5440	0.4828
South Africa	0.4567	0.3277	0.5750	0.0578	0.3931	0.4417	0.1822	0.3507	0.3611	0.5173	0.4901	1.0000	0.3357	0.2624	0.4717	0.4441
Switzerland	0.4775	0.2517	0.4773	(0.0205)	0.6725	0.6055	0.0610	0.4897	0.2708	0.3062	0.4811	0.3357	1.0000	0.1485	0.6760	0.5747
Turkey	0.1844	0.1571	0.2504	0.0304	0.2649	0.2659	0.1499	0.2648	(0.0688)	0.3006	0.4732	0.2624	0.1485	1.0000	0.1789	0.1637
UK	0.5769	0.1994	0.5129	0.0242	0.6894	0.5904	0.0743	0.4065	0.2727	0.4966	0.5440	0.4717	0.6760	0.1789	1.0000	0.6459
USA	0.5446	0.2518	0.6982	(0.0035)	0.5531	0.5332	0.1166	0.4236	0.3769	0.5582	0.4828	0.4441	0.5747	0.1637	0.6459	1.0000

Exhibit 23.6B. World correlation matrix coefficients (December 31, 2000–December 31, 2010).

Country Name	Australia	Brazil	Canada	China	France	Germany	India	Indonesia	Japan	Mexico	Russia	South Africa	Switzerland	Turkey	UK	USA
Australia	1.0000	0.6838	0.7404	0.3396	0.7950	0.7359	0.6516	0.5479	0.6743	0.6947	0.5912	0.6601	0.7350	0.5784	0.8055	0.8121
Brazil	0.6838	1.0000	0.7384	0.3606	0.6947	0.6727	0.6423	0.4678	0.5299	0.6619	0.6207	0.6240	0.5780	0.4863	0.6987	0.7244
Canada	0.7404	0.7384	1.0000	0.3145	0.7463	0.7104	0.6814	0.5657	0.6666	0.7462	0.6883	0.6870	0.6717	0.5129	0.7682	0.8245
China	0.3396	0.3606	0.3145	1.0000	0.2483	0.2483	0.3372	0.2957	0.2866	0.2673	0.2872	0.2944	0.2540	0.2198	0.2322	0.3034
France	0.7950	0.6947	0.7463	0.2483	1.0000	0.9393	0.6083	0.4557	0.6388	0.6880	0.5484	0.5831	0.8588	0.6447	0.9089	0.8847
Germany	0.7359	0.6727	0.7104	0.2483	0.9393	1.0000	0.5925	0.4736	0.5973	0.7040	0.4972	0.5262	0.8436	0.6055	0.8522	0.8641
India	0.6516	0.6423	0.6814	0.3372	0.6083	0.5925	1.0000	0.6494	0.5996	0.5793	0.5374	0.6114	0.5725	0.5038	0.6222	0.6409
Indonesia	0.5479	0.4678	0.5657	0.2957	0.4557	0.4736	0.6494	1.0000	0.4928	0.6073	0.5403	0.4676	0.4773	0.3212	0.5101	0.5277
Japan	0.6743	0.5299	0.6666	0.2866	0.6388	0.5973	0.5996	0.4928	1.0000	0.5605	0.5330	0.5836	0.6194	0.5420	0.6379	0.6422
Mexico	0.6947	0.6619	0.7462	0.2673	0.6880	0.7040	0.5793	0.6073	0.5605	1.0000	0.6930	0.6224	0.6528	0.4650	0.6891	0.7512
Russia	0.5912	0.6207	0.6883	0.2872	0.5484	0.4972	0.5374	0.5403	0.5330	0.6930	1.0000	0.5672	0.4682	0.4846	0.5698	0.5928
South Africa	0.6601	0.6240	0.6870	0.2944	0.5831	0.5262	0.6114	0.4676	0.5836	0.6224	0.5672	1.0000	0.5943	0.4555	0.6194	0.6070
Switzerland	0.7350	0.5780	0.6717	0.2540	0.8588	0.8436	0.5725	0.4773	0.6194	0.6528	0.4682	0.5943	1.0000	0.5122	0.7993	0.7896
Turkey	0.5784	0.4863	0.5129	0.2198	0.6447	0.6055	0.5038	0.3212	0.5420	0.4650	0.4846	0.4555	0.5122	1.0000	0.5832	0.6040
UK	0.8055	0.6987	0.7682	0.2322	0.9089	0.8522	0.6222	0.5101	0.6379	0.6891	0.5698	0.6194	0.7993	0.5832	1.0000	0.8767
USA	0.8121	0.7244	0.8245	0.3034	0.8847	0.8641	0.6409	0.5277	0.6422	0.7512	0.5928	0.6070	0.7896	0.6040	0.8767	1.0000

matrixes of correlation for the periods 1990–1999 and 2000–2009.

> *Q:* Which country's stock exchange shows the lowest correlation with the rest of the world's major markets?
>
> *A:* China. This is due to the relative inconvertibility of the renminbi and the slow integration of the Chinese capital market with other major capital markets.

- Market volatility itself varies over time and tends to be *contagious* at times of financial turmoil. Indeed, the degree of cross-country correlation tends to spike at times of high volatility such as the 1987 crash, the 1997 Asian financial crisis, and the 2008 subprime meltdown.

These findings indicate that benefits from geographical diversification are not what they used to be but are still superior to domestic diversification. Such benefits are greatest for investors domiciled in smaller (primarily emerging) capital market countries. For investors based in developed capital markets, emerging capital markets continue to offer significant diversification benefits — certainly superior to those offered by other developed capital markets.

> *Q:* Venezuela's stock exchange showed a correlation of 0.56 with the United States over the period 1990–1999. Would you expect that after 10 years of the Chavez rule this coefficient would increase or decrease over the next decade, 2000–2009?
>
> *A:* As Venezuela's economy is increasingly marred by high inflation, a depreciating currency, tightening exchange controls, and nationalization of foreign-owned companies, the Caracas stock exchange is increasingly decoupling itself from world capital markets, which means lower correlation with US and other capital markets.

TRIALS AND TRIBULATIONS IN FOREIGN EQUITY INVESTING

Investing in foreign stocks is fraught with pitfalls that may dim the allure of international diversification:

- *Currency risk.* Foreign stocks are generally traded and pay dividends in the currency of the home country in which the firm is legally domiciled and incorporated. For example, if you are a fund manager with Cougar Investments based in Toronto (Canada) and you allocated funds to purchase 250,000 stocks of the Siam Commercial Bank traded on the Stock Exchange of Thailand for THB 30 per share when the spot exchange rate was CAD 1 = THB 30, you may find that a stock price appreciation of 12% over the past 12 months was wiped out by a depreciation of 12% in the value of the Thai baht. Worse, a THB depreciation of 20% would not only eradicate the stock price appreciation but also result in a negative return in your base currency (see next section for further discussion of currency hedging in global investing).
- *Market risk.* Stock prices do fluctuate, and foreign markets — especially emerging capital markets — are subject to sharper price swings than more mature and liquid developed markets. If you ever attempted to time stock investing and have been less than successful in your home market, you may find that timing foreign markets is even more stressful!
- *Illiquid and inefficient markets.* Most foreign markets — especially recently emerging markets — have significantly lower trading volumes than most developed stock markets. The number of listed firms is also considerably smaller, with a few stocks accounting for the bulk of market capitalization. Price manipulation and insider trading may be poorly monitored by supervisory authorities, resulting in a less informationally efficient market. In many emerging markets the larger corporations are part of family-controlled business groups. Foreign investors may consequently find themselves in a minority position facing a coalition of majority controlling shareholders who may expropriate them (see Chapter 26 on Asian finance for further discussion).
- *Information barriers.* Differences in language and accounting standards complicate the valuation of foreign stocks and their comparability to domestic stocks. Often the information is prepared only in the native language, which restricts access to particular foreign stocks and the speed with which sensitive information about them can be processed. Furthermore, the amount and the quality of information about activity and performance of foreign stocks are often limited and unreliable. The auditing process that supposedly guarantees the reliability of financials is not necessarily as independent and objective as it is in the more advanced capital markets.

- *Higher transaction costs and withholding taxes.* Brokerage costs on foreign stock exchanges are typically higher than in the largest stock markets and often include stamp taxes.[6] From a low of 0.10 of 1% in the United States, the brokerage fees can rise to 0.50 to 1.0% in more illiquid markets. The size of an order may also indirectly impact transaction costs, with a large order in a relatively illiquid market driving up the price of the trade. Once a foreign stock has been acquired, it has to be held in custody by a local financial institution, which in turn reports to a master custodian domiciled in the investor's home country. This typical two-tiered custodial arrangement adds to the cost of investing in foreign stocks.

CURRENCY RISK IN GLOBAL INVESTING

Investing in a foreign stock is a two-step exercise: (1) purchase the foreign currency on the spot exchange market to (2) invest it in the foreign listed stock. Upon divestment — say one year later — the stock is sold, and the foreign currency proceeds are converted back into the investor's home currency. In effect, our investor has acquired two different assets: a foreign currency and a foreign stock. This raises a perplexing question: Should the currency risk component of the total return be hedged through traditional methods such as forward or option contracts or should the currency risk be considered an integral part of international diversification and left unhedged?

Let's return to the earlier example of Canada-based mutual fund Cougar Investments allocating CAD 10 million to invest in shares of Thailand-based Siam Commercial Bank (SCB). Cougar Investments would first purchase Thai baht (THB) at the spot rate of CAD 1 = THB 30 for total proceeds of THB 300 million, and second, invest in shares of Siam Commercial Bank worth THB 30 for a total investment of 10 million shares. One year later, SCB stock has appreciated by 20% to THB 36 and Cougar's stock investment is now worth THB 360 million. The Thai baht, however, has depreciated by 5% to CAD 1 = THB 31.5. Thus, the proceeds from the sale of SCB shares are now worth only THB 360 million/31.50 = CAD 11.428 million, thus yielding a net return to Cougar Investments of r_F = (CAD 11.428 million – CAD 10 million)/CAD 10 million = 11.428%, which can also be expressed as

$$r_F = (1+0.20)(1-0.05)-1 = 11.4\%$$

or formally:

$$r_F = \left(1+r_{\text{Foreign Stock}}\right)\left(1+r_{\text{Foreign Currency}}\right)-1$$
$$r_F = r_{\text{Foreign Stock}} + r_{\text{Foreign Currency}} + r_{\text{Foreign Stock}} \times r_{\text{Foreign Currency}}$$

often approximated as

$$r_F = r_{\text{Foreign Stock}} + r_{\text{Foreign Currency}}$$

if the last multiplicative term is negligible.

Hedging currency risk is motivated by investors' quest to minimize risk for a given return. From equation (23.2), the overall risk of investing in the foreign stock is given by the variance of its return:

$$\sigma_P = \left[\text{Var}\left(r_{\text{Foreign Stock}} + r_{\text{Foreign Currency}}\right)\right]^{.5}$$
$$= \Big[\sigma^2_{\text{Foreign Stock}} + \sigma^2_{\text{Foreign Currency}} + 2\,\sigma_{\text{Foreign Stock}}\,\sigma_{\text{Foreign Currency}}\,\rho_{\text{Foreign Stock, Foreign Currency}}\Big]^{.5}$$

where $\rho_{\text{Foreign Stock, Foreign Currency}}$ is the correlation between the return on the foreign stock and the return on holding the foreign currency.

Consider the case of the SCB share price, whose return's standard deviation in THB is 23%. The standard deviation of the CAD price of one THB is 10%, whose correlation with SCB stock return is –0.10. The standard deviation of the return on owning SCB shares, in CAD terms, is thus equal to:

$$\sigma_{\text{SCB}} = \left[0.23^2 + 0.10^2 + 2\times 0.23\times 0.10\times -0.10\right]^{.5} = 24.15\%$$

If exchange risk increases the risk of holding shares in SCB from the perspective of a Canadian investor, currency risk is not additive — in other words, 24.15% is less than the sum of 23 and 10%. In fact, if the correlation between SCB and the CAD/THB returns is sufficiently negative (SCB stock price and the CAD/THB move in opposite directions), the last term would negate the currency risk altogether. This would generally be the case with firms that are strong exporters or are competing primarily with imports. A devaluation of their home currency boosts their exports' competitiveness and their capacity to withstand competition from imports: Their returns would clearly be negatively correlated with the exchange rate. Conversely, if the SCB stock price in THB and the CAD/THB exchange rate

6 Stamp taxes are a transaction duty charged on the purchase or sale of stocks. In a pre-electronic world, transactions were materialized by paper documents that required a stamp to be purchased from the tax collector to be legally valid.

were positively correlated — that is, they moved in the same direction — a more credible case could be made to hedge the currency risk exposure to reduce the overall risk faced by Cougar Investments.

> ***Q:*** Cougar Investments purchased 100,000 shares of Infosys, the Indian software company; the standard deviation of Infosys's return is 28% whereas the standard deviation of the CAD price of one Indian rupee is 19%. Should Cougar Investments hedge its portfolio investment, given that the correlation coefficient between stock and currency prices is –0.50?
>
> ***A:*** By computing the standard deviation of the CAD return of investing in Infosys stock, we find that the negative correlation due to the strong exports orientation of Infosys better than negates its currency risk: $\sigma_{\text{Infosys}} = [0.28^2 + 0.19^2 - 2 \times 0.28 \times 0.19 \times 0.50]^{.5} < 0.28$. By hedging currency risk, Cougar would incur costs — that is, reduce its return — while maintaining the risk at 28% since the standard deviation of the exchange rate and its correlation with the rupee return of holding the Infosys stock are now zero.

Should Cougar Investments have hedged the CAD value of its 10 million shares position in SCB? A forward contract at a small 2.5% discount would have protected Cougar's return at $r_F = (1 + 0.20)(1 - 0.025) - 1 = 17\%$. This is a debate that has long divided asset managers. Many believe that currency risk is an integral part of international diversification and any effort at hedging currency risk undoes, at least partially, the benefits of international diversification. Others argue that removing currency risk allows asset managers to focus on selecting stocks, which is supposed to be their comparative advantage; thus, a number of funds will systematically hedge their currency position. Still others contend that selective hedging coupled with skillful stock selection will optimize the returns on international portfolio investment.

There is no question that at times currencies are grossly overvalued or undervalued and timely hedging may be successful: The Mexican peso crisis of 1994, Southeast Asian currencies during the Asian financial crisis of 1997, and the Argentine peso crisis of 2002 would certainly have warranted selective hedging. However, as the international monetary system moves steadily toward more flexible exchange rates with milder degrees of central bank intervention, clear situations of grossly misvalued currencies due to pegged exchange rates become fewer and farther apart.

ALTERNATIVE MODES OF INVESTING IN FOREIGN EQUITY

If the case for international portfolio diversification is a relatively easy one to make, its implementation is not as straightforward. Fortunately, there are many ways to invest directly or indirectly in foreign stocks:

- Purchase foreign stocks directly on your domestic exchange if they are listed or indirectly through an *American depositary receipt* or a *global depositary receipt*.
- Purchase foreign *stocks* on their own exchange, which requires the intermediation of a foreign broker and additional transaction costs, including the need to purchase the foreign currency in which the stock is traded.
- Invest in a globally diversified *mutual fund*, which is a low-cost method of gaining exposure to foreign stocks.
- Invest in increasingly popular *index-tracking funds*, which is an even cheaper strategy than investing in international mutual funds. These funds are simply portfolios of shares replicating a stock market index such as the S&P 500, the CAC 40, or the Nikkei 225 and were conceived as a response to the notion that stock markets are efficient. Indeed, if stock prices do reflect all available information, it would be impossible to beat the market and the best you could do would be to buy the market through an index-tracking fund, thereby minimizing fees, trading costs, and stamp taxes.

Foreign stock market index-tracking funds are indeed extremely low-cost investment vehicles that allow investors to get exposure to foreign markets. Overall, exchange-traded funds control US$1.5 trillion in assets (hedge funds account for close to $3 trillion). State Street's US$88 billion SPDR fund, for example, mimics the S&P 500 and has a total cost of only 0.09%. Last but not least, exchange-traded funds greatly facilitate risk management since most underlying indexes are also traded on the derivatives market as futures and options. For example, if Cougar Investments were to invest in an exchange-traded fund mimicking the Japanese Nikkei 225 stock market index, it could readily protect the value of its investment by buying put options on the Nikkei 225. Effectively, the put option's strike price would establish a floor price for Cougar Investments in the Japanese stock market.

> ***Q:*** Cougar Investments has purchased ¥10 billion in the Nippon Millennium fund — an exchange-traded fund that tracks the Nikkei 225 — at ¥9,000 per share. Cougar decided to protect its investment against a possible correction in the Nikkei 225 by buying a put option on the Nikkei 225 at a strike price of ¥8,750 for a 1% premium. What is the value of Cougar Investments' Japanese holding if the Nikkei 225 increases to 10,000 or falls to 8,000?
>
> ***A:*** With the Nikkei 225 reaching 10,000, shares of the Nippon Millennium Fund will also climb to ¥10,000 and the put option will be left unexercised; the net value of Cougar Investments' holding, however, has to account for the cost of the put option premium (1% × 8,750 = ¥87.50) at ¥10,000 – ¥87.50 = ¥9,912.50. Conversely, should the Nikkei 225 drop to 8,000, Cougar Investments will exercise the put option at ¥8,750 and Cougar Investments' holding in the Nippon Millennium Fund will stabilize at the option strike price minus the option premium or ¥8,750 – ¥87.50 = ¥8,662.50.

- Invest in *closed-end country funds* to gain direct exposure to a specific country. Such funds are dubbed "closed-end" because they issue a fixed number of shares against an initial capital offering. Their shares then trade on the stock market of the country where the initial capital was raised, such as the New York Stock Exchange or the Paris Bourse. Because closed-end country funds manage a fixed amount of capital, they do not have to worry about the constant inflow or outflow of funds or an untimely redemption, which are a way of life for open-ended mutual funds. This gives fund managers greater latitude to invest in relatively illiquid stocks, which are often the hallmark of emerging capital markets.

Theoretically, shares in a closed-end country fund should reflect the value of the underlying stock portfolio — net asset value (NAV) — but in fact they generally trade at a significant discount or premium to the net asset value of the underlying shares held by the fund.[7] Closed-end country funds assume that foreign stock markets are not efficient and that savvy portfolio managers should be compensated for beating the market because they deliver alpha returns to investors beyond the beta returns from passive investment in the market portfolio.

- Do *not* invest in the stocks of multinationals traded on your domestic stock exchange. They should provide significant international diversification to the extent that such firms are themselves a portfolio of foreign firms. Theoretically, investing in the stock of a multinational company, which has operating subsidiaries in as many as 20 or more different countries, should be an inexpensive proxy for investing in the stocks of these 20 foreign companies. Somewhat counterintuitively, multinationals' stocks, however, turn out to be poor substitutes for international diversification through direct portfolio investment in foreign stocks. Indeed, share prices of multinationals continue to be dominated by domestic factors of their home capital markets.

THE NEW LANDSCAPE OF GLOBAL INVESTING

Daunting challenges and the rise of formidable new entrants playing by different rules are reshaping the global asset management industry.

Changing demographics

One of the most daunting challenges of the twenty-first century will be to provide adequate income for an ever-larger population of retirees who live increasingly longer lives thanks to modern medicine and widely available healthcare. In many countries, the active population pays the retirees' pensions in a *pay-as-you-go* system of *defined benefits*. As the pyramids of age narrow at the base (smaller active workforce) and broaden at the top (larger passive retired population), the pay-as-you-go system shows increasing stress as the tax burden of funding retirees becomes necessarily heavier on the workforce. Many countries are shifting to the Anglo-Saxon system of funding pensions through the accumulation of savings, which in turn must be invested.

7 Closed-end funds have been historically at both significant premiums and discounts to their NAVs. However, their values tend over time to revert to their mean NAVs. A closed-end fund at a significant discount may reflect illiquidity of its stock portfolio, compounded by exchange controls on possible repatriation of the funds. Conversely, a significant premium may indicate a very desirable stock portfolio in a country that allows foreign portfolio investment only through a closed-end fund as South Korea did for many years.

However, the investment objectives of a graying population tend toward a more income-oriented, less risky approach than that of a younger population, which has a higher tolerance for risk and a stronger appetite for savings accumulation and capital growth and will target investment opportunities accordingly. It is generally estimated that in the United States alone more than two-thirds of all investable assets in 2015 were directly or indirectly controlled by household retirees who demand financial products (and advice) that emphasize income generation and principal protection. Indeed, as baby boomers move into retirement, they face new financial risks triggered by the decline of defined benefit pensions and health care coverage. As a result, retirees are increasingly interested in financial products that limit their exposure not only to market risk but also to *health care and longevity risk* — that is, the risk of living beyond life expectancy in poorer health and requiring heavier health care expenses. And yet the traditional *home-country bias* whereby asset managers overweight domestic investments is being progressively eroded due to relentless globalization and the lure of emerging capital markets. Global investing in search of higher alpha, even at the cost of higher risk, is increasingly the norm rather than the exception.

The new power brokers

Four actors — *Asian and petrodollar central banks, sovereign wealth funds, hedge funds*, and *private equity firms* — are looming increasingly large on the world financial markets stage. Their rapid growth since 2000 — with total combined assets under management exceeding $10 trillion — gives them increasing clout, but the relative opacity of their activities raises important public policy concerns. Without a doubt, their collective impact is amounting to a seismic shift in global financial markets. These four new players are largely responsible for a

> *broadening and diversification of the global investor base in terms of geographies, asset classes, and investment strategies as well as boosting liquidity. Each has longer investment horizons than traditional investors, enabling them to pursue higher returns (albeit with more risk). They have brought new dynamism to private capital markets and have given a considerable boost to financial innovation. They may also catalyze financial development in emerging markets. All these developments improve the functioning of global financial markets but also pose risks.*[8]

Asian or petroleum-exporting countries' central banks

Fueled by soaring trade surpluses and by the tripling price of oil since 2000, these central banks have amassed a treasure chest in excess of $6.5 trillion of foreign exchange reserves. China leads the pack with a foreign exchange treasure chest of US$3.05 trillion as of 2018, followed by Japan (US$1.25 trillion), Switzerland (US$ 0.80 trillion), Saudi Arabia (US$ 0.50 trillion), Taiwan (US$0.46 trillion) and Russia (US$ 0.46 trillion). By and large, they are sleeping giants and cautious investors in global financial markets, holding the bulk of their assets in conservative fixed-income securities overwhelmingly denominated in US dollars such as US Treasury bills and bonds. Increasingly, these actors are using their foreign exchange reserves to endow sovereign wealth funds.

Sovereign wealth funds

Unlike central banks' exceedingly conservative investments, these state-owned so-called *sovereign wealth funds* have diversified their portfolios *internationally* across equity, fixed income, real estate, and to a lesser extent alternative investments such as hedge funds and private equity firms. Their portfolio allocation strategies continue to be fairly traditional, more akin to pension funds or university endowment corporations and they tend to be passive investors rather than wild-eyed speculators. According to the International Forum of Sovereign Wealth Funds[9]:

> *SWFs are defined as special purpose investment funds or arrangements, owned by the general government. Created by the general government for macroeconomic purposes, SWFs hold, manage and administer assets to achieve financial objectives, and employ a set of investment strategies which include investing in foreign financial*

8 McKinsey Global Institute, "The New Power Brokers: How Oil, Asia, Hedge Funds and Private Equity Are Reshaping Global Capital Markets," October 2007.

9 Cited in Reinart and Keyfeths. 2016. "Sovereign Wealth Funds." *Harvard Business School Case Study* 9-717-003, p. 1.

assets. SWFs are commonly established out of balance of payments surpluses, official foreign currency operations, the proceeds of privatization, fiscal surpluses and/or receipts from commodity exports. This definition excludes inter alia, foreign currency reserve assets held by monetary authorities for the traditional balance of payments or monetary policy purposes, operations of state-owned enterprises, government-employee pension funds, or assets managed for the benefit of individual.

Assets under management by SWFs are estimated at approximately US$15 trillion with two principal overarching objectives: *stabilization* of government revenues (in the case of commodity-exporting countries) and *savings* for future generations (endowment of government pension funds). The oldest and now third largest sovereign wealth fund is the Abu Dhabi Investment Authority (ADIA), with assets in 2024 reportedly exceeding US$ 1.05 trillion. In the same league as ADIA one would count Norway's Government Pension Fund (US$1.55 trillion), China Investment Corporation (US$ 1.3 trillion), Kuwait Investment Authority (US$ 969 billion) Saudi Arabia's SAMA (US$ 1.34 billion), and Singapore's Government Investment Corporation (US$770 billion). Similar to but separate from sovereign wealth funds, those same countries have established *government holding corporations* such as Temacek in Singapore and Khazanah in Malaysia, which centralize the management of government shareholdings in national companies. Many of these funds operate more like private equity firms or conglomerates as they become active shareholders keen on maximizing the long-term value of their investment portfolios.

Hedge funds

Hedge funds' global assets under management exceed US$ 5 trillion, but when accounting for leverage their gross investments are closer to US$ 8 trillion. Hedge funds are unregulated pools of money that are aggressively managed with a great deal of flexibility. In fact, hedge funds are not necessarily "hedged" or safe investments and are certainly not meant for the fainthearted investor. The "hedge" misnomer is generally traced to the modest fund started by Alfred W. Jones in 1949 with $100,000, which he invested in common stocks hedged by short sales. Like mutual funds, hedge funds are financial intermediaries that attempt to channel savings into productive investments, thereby seeking to protect capital and to deliver hefty rewards to high net worth individuals, pension funds, endowments, and other investors who have entrusted their money (see International Corporate Finance in Practice 23.3).

Unlike mutual funds, which are tightly regulated in the simple investment strategies they can pursue, the fees their managers can collect, and the reporting requirements they must abide by, hedge funds can pursue complex strategies, including borrowing heavily, using all sorts of derivative products, as well as short selling, and do it all in almost total secrecy with very limited disclosure requirements. According to a study in Tremont's "TASS Asset Flows Report," as of the second quarter of 2005 more than two-thirds of the $1 trillion managed by hedge funds at the time were accounted for by four strategies:

1. *A long/short equity hedge fund* (31%) invests in common equity partially or fully hedged by short sales, futures, or options, thereby largely immunizing the fund returns from market price risk.
2. *An event-driven fund* (20%) capitalizes on perceived mispricing of securities arising from significant events such as mergers, acquisitions, reorganizations, and bankruptcies.
3. *A macro hedge fund* (10%) places leveraged bets on currencies, interest rates, or commodities, on the basis of its forecasting of geopolitical trends or macroeconomic events.
4. *A fixed income arbitrage fund* (8%) identifies temporary pricing abnormalities in bond markets and arbitrages them away through leveraged convergence trades. See discussion in International Corporate Finance in Practice 23.4 of how LTCM turned this strategy into a moneymaking machine.

There is no limit on the fees that hedge fund managers can pay themselves (15 to 30% of profits), although fees will usually be waived when losses are incurred and not recouped — sometimes known as high-water marks. In sum,

Hedge funds are investment pools that are relatively unconstrained in what they do. They are relatively unregulated (for now),

INTERNATIONAL CORPORATE FINANCE IN PRACTICE 23.3

Long-Term Capital Management[10]

Long-Term Capital Management (LTCM) was a hedge fund like no other. Its relentless delivery of low-volatility, outsized returns for the first 4 years of its existence was unparalleled. LTCM would search for market imperfections or pricing abnormalities that it would exploit through paired/hedged trades. At its simplest, the trading strategy was built on buying long assets perceived to be slightly undervalued and selling short very similar assets considered as slightly overvalued.[11] LTCM would then wait for the spread to narrow as convergence in prices was believed to be ineluctable. LTCM spectacular returns were built on parsimonious use of its equity capital and powered by extremely high leverage. However, when the Asian financial crisis triggered a capital flight to quality and liquid assets, illiquid assets became even more illiquid. LTCM found itself blatantly exposed to liquidity risk as the long side of its portfolio was comprised primarily of illiquid assets. LTCM's classic bets on convergence between on-the-run and off-the-run 30-year Treasuries diverged instead of converging, thereby triggering collateral calls from lenders as their periodic marking-to-market showed losses rather than gains. LTCM's demise and near collapse in the fall of 1998 was as calamitous as its rise had been spectacular.

At its apogee in early 1998, with debt of US$125 billion and off-balance-sheet over-the-counter derivatives exposure in excess of US$1 trillion piled up on a puny equity capital base of US$4.7 billion, Long-Term Capital Management had perfected financial leverage to a science. But when the crisis struck, LTCM's opaque web of over-the-counter derivatives without any proper posting of collateral and margin accelerated its precipitous collapse and stoked fear of systemic risk — that is, of a domino effect engulfing the entire global financial system — so much so that the New York Federal Reserve Bank coerced 14 major Wall Street firms, which were LTCM's main creditors, to come to its rescue with a bailout package of US$3.6 billion.

10 See Laurent L. Jacque *Global Derivative Debacles: From Theory to Malpractice.* 2nd edition World Scientific (Singapore and London 2015).

11 A good example of this strategy is the quasi-arbitrage of on-the-run for off-the-run 30-year US Treasuries. On-the-run 30-year Treasuries are newly issued bonds auctioned off by the US government every 6-months, are very liquid, and slightly overvalued. By contrast, off-the-run 29.5-year Treasuries — that is, Treasuries that were issued more than 6 months ago — are illiquid because they trade infrequently and are perceived as slightly undervalued.

charge very high fees, will not necessarily give you your money back when you want it, and will generally not tell you what they do. They are supposed to make money all the time, and when they fail at this, their investors redeem and go to someone else who has recently been making money. Every three or four years, they deliver a once-in-a-hundred-year flood.[12]

Private equity firms

Private equity is a general term that commonly refers to investing in a firm that is not traded on capital markets. It encompasses three investment vehicles: venture capital, leveraged buyouts (LBOs), and distressed investing funds. *Venture capital* provides early stage financing to entrepreneurs and start-up companies. *Leveraged buyouts* acquire larger, mature, and generally public companies using a considerable amount of debt — often bank-financed (leverage). They take them private to better manage them in order to increase their value before taking them public again after three to five years. *Distressed investing* — also known as vulture or special situations investing — focuses on investing in the equity and/or debt of firms or sovereigns in financial distress or bankruptcy (see International Corporate Finance in Practice 23.4).

12 In the more direct language of Cliff Asness of AQR Capital cited in *New York Magazine*, April 9, 2007.

INTERNATIONAL CORPORATE FINANCE IN PRACTICE 23.4

Vulture Funds "Didn't Cry for Argentina"

Hedge funds or private equity firms investing in distressed debt pursue a high stake strategy. Distressed debt securities trade at a deep discount to their face value, are typically rated below investment grade and face a high probability of becoming worthless. There are two very different types of distressed debt — *corporate* distressed debt and *sovereign* distressed debt. A fund investing in the former would likely involve itself in turning around the company and, if successful, nursing it back to health; in the process it could avail itself of substantial returns as the value of deeply discounted bonds may rebound closer to their face value. By contrast, hedge funds investing in distressed sovereign debt are unlikely to become materially involved in restructuring the country's public finance. Instead their strategy is entirely based on legal recourse with a simple modus operandi: purchase distressed debt at deep discount, refuse to participate in restructuring and pursue full value of debt often at face value plus interest, arrears and penalties through litigation if necessary.

The saga of Argentina since its massive default in 2001 on US$83 billion of sovereign debt — the largest recorded at the time — is a vivid example of how hedge funds specialized in distressed debt have emerged as pugnacious adversaries of defaulting sovereigns. By 2004, Argentina had restructured[13] most of its defaulted debt with 93% of bondholders having reluctantly agreed to a 65% write-down (so called haircut) and to swapping the defaulted bonds for new bonds in the form of GDP-linked securities.[14] The original bonds however did not include a "collective action clause" whereby any restructuring approved by a majority of bondholders could be forced on the recalcitrant minority of bondholders. Indeed 7% of original defaulted bonds were owned by investors who refused the terms of the restructuring and decided to hold out instead — preferring to seek full payment through litigation.

This militant group of holdouts were mostly hedge funds — dubbed "vulture" funds by their foes — including — most notably — Gramercy and Elliott Capital. Gramercy — for example — had a stated strategy of *"seeking to generate high, uncorrelated returns that are tail risk aware by investing in distressed and defaulted emerging markets corporate, sovereign or quasi-sovereign publicly traded securities"*. Interestingly, hold out hedge funds were not the original investors in Argentine bonds first issued in the 1990s; instead they had accumulated sizeable positions in defaulted bonds by purchasing them during the subprime crisis at a deep discount — as low as 6 cents on the dollar in the case of Elliott Capital. Having rejected any compromise offer to restructure the holdout bonds the funds secured in 2014 an injunction from New York State courts which forbade Argentina to pay interest on the restructured debt as long as holdout investors had not been paid in full; it also barred any bank with operations in the US from enabling interest payments. As result Argentina was forced to default on its restructured bonds. The newly elected center right president Macri quickly embarked on a more conciliatory stance *vis-à-vis* the vulture funds hoping to engineer Argentina's re-entry into international capital markets to ease pressure on the country budget deficit which stood at 7% of GDP. In early 2016 Argentina settled with holdouts funds: Elliott capital is rumored to have walked away with US$2.4 billion in payment of debt with face value of US$617 million which it purchased for only $117 million — a rich payoff and a historic victory for investors who chose long lasting litigation over restructuring. Within months Argentina was back to the US capital markets issuing 100 year — so called Century — bonds. Our serial defaulter had been amnestied!

Source: Adapted from Moffet, Michael M. 2016. "Argentina and the Vulture funds." *Case Study TB0395 Thunderbird School of Global Management*.

---

13 Restructured bonds would typically combine (i) a reduction in the principal of the original bond, (ii) a lower interest rate and (iii) a stretched out maturities of principal repayment. Haircut on restructured bonds is the ratio of the restructured to the original bond's net present value.

14 GDP warrants were attached to the restructured bonds as a sweetener. In effect bondholders would receive normal periodic interest payment plus whatever capital gains resulted from exercising the GDP warrants expiring in the money. These GDP warrants are akin to call options on Argentina's GDP growth rate. Every year — if Argentina had grown faster than the "strike" GDP growth rate — bondholders would receive a windfall gain as if they were shareholders in Argentina Inc.

Although private equity is the smallest of the four new power brokers, it exercises outsized influence on the governance of public firms by revolutionizing corporate ownership. Prior to the private equity revolution, there were two principal forms of ownership: (1) family-owned or closely held and (2) dispersed public ownership across many shareholders. By offering a new hybrid model, private equity is opening new funding options and governance structures that put healthy pressure on publicly held corporations in fear of being taken private.

ESG INVESTING

The acronym ESG which stands for *Environmental, Social and Governance* first came to prominence in 2004 when a report entitled "who cares win" — commissioned by the United Nations — was published by a consortium of eighteen leading financial institutions from nine countries.[15]

It is a framework aiming at measuring the impact — positive or negative — that public firms have on their environment and their stakeholders — employees, managers, customers, communities and shareholders. It is sometimes referred as *stakeholders capitalism* — that is managing the firm for the benefits of all its stakeholders to create longer term value rather than maximizing profits to create value solely for the benefits of equity investors which is also known as *shareholders capitalism*. It incorporates environmental, social and governance factors alongside financial metrics in guiding investment decisions. Specifically:

- Environment — that is the impact that the firm has on the environment as measured by its carbon footprint, greenhouse gas emissions, pollution reduction, water and waste management.
- Social — that is the social impact that the firm has within itself as well as the broader community by implementing objectives of enhanced employee welfare, racial and gender equality as well as inclusion in its hiring practices.
- Governance — that is how a firm's institutional structures and processes foster accountability and transparency towards its stakeholders as well as how it protects them against corruption, breaches of cybersecurity and invasion of privacy.

15 The December 2015 Paris Agreement, which made specific commitments to address the challenge of climate change was signed by representatives of 197 countries. Each country had to establish Sustainable Development Goals (SDGs) setting benchmarks for addressing environmental and social challenges.

ESG rating agencies enable investors to screen and compare firms according to their performance on environmental, social and governance criteria.[16] Such ratings are analogous to the credit worthiness assessment provided by credit rating agencies such as Standard and Poor, Moody or Fitch. The major difference though is that credit ratings are clearly defined as probability of default whereas ESG ratings are multi-dimensional and ill-focused. According to the Economist "The ESG ratings agencies are an acme of inconsistencies. A study of six of them found that they used 709 different metrics across 64 categories. Only 10 categories were common to all of them and they do not include such basics as green-house gas emissions". Characterizing ESG ratings as "aggregate confusion" a recent study identified three distinct sources of divergence: "*scope divergence* refers to the situation where rating are based on different sets of attributes. One rating agency may include lobbying activities, while another may not, causing the two ratings to diverge. *Measurement divergence* refers to a situation where rating agencies measure the same attribute using different indicators. For example, a firm's labor practices could be evaluated on the basis of workforce turnover or by the number of court cases brought against the firm. Finally, weight divergence emerges when rating agencies take different view on the relative importance of different attributes. For example, the labor practice indicator may enter the final rating with greater weight than the lobbying indicator. The contribution of scope, measurement and weight indicators are intertwined making it difficult to interpret the divergence between two ESG ratings".[17]

Advocates of ESG investing point to the massive flow of investable money which in the last 5 years has found its way into ESG-compliant funds which are estimated to amount to as much as a third of all assets under management. Recent empirical research provides credible evidence that firms which perform well on the ESG scoreboard outperform their peers. Stepped up demand for ESG-labelled stocks results in higher stock prices, higher P/E ratios and therefore a lower cost of equity capital; this virtuous cycle

16 In March 2021, the European Union's Sustainable Finance Disclosure Regulation (SFDR) required mandatory disclosure obligations for EU-based financial market participants and financial advisors. The SFDR standardizes ESG disclosures, clarifies the definition of sustainable initiatives, and establishes standards of evidence in support of such claims.

17 Berg, Florian, Julian F. Kolbel and Roberto Rigobon. 2022. "Aggregate Confusion: The Divergence of ESG Ratings." *Review of Finance*, 1315–1344.

should boost ESG-firms' competitiveness in the market place and further enhance their value.

ESG investing has been criticized for *greenwashing* — that is disguising firms' ESG track record by deceptively advertising that its products, processes and policies are environmentally friendly. One of the most flabbergasting case of greenwashing is Diesel-gate: Volkswagen — until 2015 — had been rated as more ESG-compliant than its peers when it was revealed that it had used from 2009 to 2015 an emission software — so-called "defeat device" — to hide that its diesel engines were polluting at a much higher rate than advertised. Volkswagen was fined $14.3 billion and paid another $19 billion in financial settlements, penalties and buy-back costs or in total about 33% of its market capitalization prior to the scandal. More recently, DWS — the investment arm of Deutsche Bank with $ 600 billion of assets under its management — was fine $25 million by the German regulator for deceptively distorting its ESG investment process and failing to enforce anti-money laundering monitoring policies.

Fees for ESG guided funds can be significantly higher than for mainstream funds.

INTERNATIONAL FINANCE IN PRACTICE 23

X : Oil Industry Tests Out ESG-Linked Financing[18]

Fossil-fuel companies are not generally regarded as the "poster boys" of the ESG investment craze and yet the oil-and-gas industry is increasingly relying on the rapidly growing pool of ESG-linked financing. To wit, pipeline giant Embridge Inc., driller Tamarack Valley Energy Ltd, oil water services company Aris Water Solutions Inc and well operator Presidio Petroleum have sold more than $3 billion in sustainability- linked bonds (SLBs) during the last two years. Unlike green bonds which often offer a *greenium* to issuers able to raise bond financing at a slightly lower coupon rate than their "twin" vanilla bonds, sustainable-linked bonds pay a coupon rate at a *premium* compared to the yield offered by comparable plain vanilla bonds.

Such bonds require the borrower to set goals linked to ESG metrics — so-called *Key Performance Indicators* such as a quantifiable drop in greenhouse gas emissions to be met over the life of the bond. Failure to deliver on such key performance indicators triggers penalties for the bond issuer such as a stepped-up coupon rate. SLBs should be distinguished from ***Green*** bonds which are *use-for-proceeds* bonds to finance specific ESG-compliant projects. Thus, issuers of sustainability-linked bonds can use the bond proceeds as they see fit and therefore do not lose control over budget priorities. Clearly contingent bonds such as sustainability-linked bonds tied to ESG metrics are powerful constructs. What is debatable is how are such ESG targets actually measured, who monitors the ex-post performance of the borrower and who enforces the penalties? ... The jury is still out!

18 Morenne, Benoit. 2023. "Oil Industry Tests Out ESG-Linked Financing." *Wall Street Journal*, January 8.

SUMMARY

1. The old adage "Don't put all your eggs in one basket" is the cornerstone of investing. At its simplest, it calls for diversifying any investment pool across several asset classes rather than one. The objective is to reduce the risk of the overall stock portfolio while maintaining its return or to increase return for a given level of risk. This is presumably achieved by investing in several stocks whose price movements are less than perfectly correlated.

2. Risk reduction through portfolio diversification is a function of how strongly correlated the different assets in the portfolio are.

3. International diversification yields greater benefits than domestic diversification because foreign markets exhibit a low level of correlation with the investor's home market.

4. As a result of greater capital market integration — courtesy of globalization — the world matrix of cross-country correlation has been steadily creeping upward. Accordingly, the higher degree of correlation means reduced benefits from cross-border portfolio diversification. Increased correlation is due to deregulation, higher capital mobility, freer international trade, and greater internationalization of firms.

5. Geographical diversification through direct purchasing of foreign stocks on their home exchange can be cumbersome and costly because of a lack of familiarity with foreign capital markets, currency risk, and multiple layers of transaction costs and taxes. Fortunately, the same geographical diversification benefits can be attained indirectly by trading ADRs or GDRs or by investing in closed-end or open-end country mutual funds — in effect by trading at home.
6. Hedging currency risk in foreign portfolio investing is a controversial issue, as many asset managers believe that the currency dimension is part and parcel of the benefits of international diversification.
7. The landscape of global investing is being rapidly redrawn with the shift in demographics (e.g., an aging population) combined with the rise of the new power brokers — Asian central banks, sovereign wealth funds, hedge funds, and private equity firms.

QUESTIONS FOR DISCUSSION

1. What are the key metrics of investment analysis?
2. Compare the Sharpe ratio with the information ratio.
3. What are the key factors reshaping the asset management industry?
4. Identify the new players in the global asset management industry.
5. What is the nature of the benefits to be derived from investing in foreign stocks? How can they be measured?
6. What are the key barriers to investing in foreign stocks? How can they be overcome?
7. Discuss the major risks involved in foreign stock investing. How can they be hedged?
8. Should currency risk be managed independently or conjointly with market risk?
9. How do you measure the correlation between two market indexes? What does it mean for two markets to be negatively correlated?
10. Why is globalization reducing the gains from international portfolio diversification?

PROBLEMS

1. **Risk and return (foundational).** Consider the following information on the expected return and risk of two country funds — the Taiwan country fund (asset 1) and the Ukraine country fund (asset 2):

$$E(r_1) = 10\%, \sigma_1 = 14\%$$
$$E(r_2) = 16\%, \sigma_2 = 20\%$$

   a. Calculate the expected return and risk of portfolios invested in the following proportions. Assume a correlation of $\rho = 0.35$.

Asset 1 (%)	Asset 2 (%)
100	0
80	20
60	40
50	50
40	60
20	80
0	100

   Using the expected return and risk calculations for all the portfolios, plot the efficient frontier.

   b. Assuming now $\rho = -1$, $\rho = 0$, and $\rho = +1$, repeat part a.

   c. What do you conclude about the role played by correlation in risk reduction?

2. **Correlation in global investing (foundational).** The standard deviation of Infosys in Indian rupees (INR) is $\sigma_I = 8.5\%$, and the standard deviation of the US\$/INR exchange rate is $\sigma_s = 5.5\%$.

   a. If the correlation between Infosys's asset return, in INR, and the exchange rate movement is $\rho = 0$, calculate the amount of risk that can be attributed to currency risk.

   b. If the correlation between Infosys's asset return, in INR, and the exchange rate movement is $\rho = 0.25$, calculate the amount of risk that can be attributed to currency risk.

   c. If the correlation between Infosys's asset return, in INR, and the exchange rate movement is $\rho = -0.25$, calculate the amount of risk that can be attributed to currency risk.

   d. What can you conclude from these cases about the impact of the level of correlation between the asset return in local currency and the exchange rate movement on the risk of a foreign asset measured in dollars?

3. **Currency risk in foreign equity (intermediate).** During the first quarter of 2012, the Brazilian real depreciated from BRL 1.65 to BRL 1.85 = US$1. Shares of Petrobras trading on the New York Stock Exchange in the form of American depositary receipts (ADRs) declined from US$31 to US$26 over the same period.
   a. How much did Petrobras shares lose in US$ terms and in BRL terms?
   b. Since Petrobras ADRs are traded in the United States in US$, are they exposed to exchange rate risk — the risk that the BRL will depreciate against the US$?
   c. Explain how you could hedge the US$ price of Petrobras shares against exchange rate risk.
   d. If BRL can be sold or purchased forward at a 6% discount against the US$ for delivery on December 31, 2012, under what exchange rate scenario would you hedge your investment in shares of Petrobras? What would be the value of your hedged investment if you expect that shares of Petrobras will appreciate by 10% by the end of 2012? What additional information do you wish to have access to so as to make a better-informed recommendation?

4. **Hedging currency risk in foreign equity investing (intermediate).** Cougar Investments holds 10,000 shares of Embraer and 25,000 shares of Bank Itau, currently worth BRL 100 and BRL 40, respectively. Both stocks have an expected return in Brazilian reals of 12% for 2012 with a similar level of risk at 15%. Embraer is a leading exporter of aircraft and the correlation between its share price in reals and the Canadian dollar is = –0.50, whereas Bank Itau is primarily oriented to the Brazilian market and shows a correlation with the exchange rate of +0.65.
   a. What is the risk faced by Cougar Investments on its Brazilian stock holdings?
   b. Given a widely anticipated 15% depreciation of the real against the Canadian dollar, would you advise Cougar Investments to hedge its currency exposure? Explain your rationale.
   c. One-year forward contracts on the BRL trade at a 7.5% discount. What would be your expected return on either investment with or without a currency hedge?
   d. Would consideration of the correlation between Embraer and Bank Itau's BRL return change your recommendations?

5. **Optimal international portfolio diversification (advanced).** Kaiwa is a US-based value fund considering investing overseas to benefit from international diversification. It is contemplating investing in the South Korea country fund that offers an expected return of 13% for a level of risk measured by the standard deviation of its return equal to 11%. Kaiwa's current portfolio offers a lower return of 9% for a level of risk of 7%.
   a. Assuming a correlation coefficient of 0.57 between the South Korea country fund and the US Kaiwa fund, how would a repositioning of 33% of Kaiwa into the South Korea country fund impact its expected return and level of risk?
   b. What would be the risk/return profile of a portfolio 66% invested in the South Korea country fund?
   c. Sketch in a risk/return space the preceding two portfolio configurations as well as a portfolio 100% invested in Kaiwa and 100% invested in the South Korea country fund.

INTERNET EXERCISES

6. **Oil Stocks (intermediate).** Access Bloomberg website www.bloomberg.com and track the price of the multinational oil company Total (TOT) stock price over the last five year. What is Total's P/E, dividend yield and beta? Compare Total stock price performance inclusive of dividends distribution with the best performing Global Energy fund over the last five years.
7. **Mutual Funds (intermediate).** Access Morningstar website www.morningstar.com and identify the two best performing *Indian Equity* mutual funds using the last five years as reference period. What is their market capitalization? Did the dollar price of the Indian rupee add to or detract from the fund performance. What are the criteria used by Morningstar to award a five-star ratings to these two funds?
8. **Yield Curves.** Access www.bloomberg.com and sketch the 30 year yield curve for Japanese and Australian government bonds of one, two, five, 10, 20 and 30 years.
9. **Sovereign Wealth Funds.** Access the International Monetary Fund-sponsored *International Forum of Sovereign Wealth Funds* www.ifswf.org and explain what are the Santiago Principles.

REFERENCES

Abken, Peter A., and Milind M. Shrikhande. 1997. "The Role of Currency Derivatives in International Diversified Portfolios." *Federal Reserve Bank of Atlanta Economic Review*, Third Quarter, 34–59.

Bookstaber, Richard M. 1997. "Global Risk Management: Are We Missing the Point?" *Journal of Portfolio Management* (Spring).

Dimson, Elroy, Paul Marsh, and Michael Staunton. 2002. *Triumph of the Optimists: 101 Years of Global Investment Returns*. Princeton, NJ: Princeton University Press.

Errunza, Vihung, Ked Hogan, and Mao-Wei Hung. 1999. "Can the Gains from International Diversification Be Achieved without Trading Abroad?" *Journal of Finance* 54 (December): 2075–2107.

Goetzmann, William, Lingfeng Li, and Geert Rouwenhorst. 2005. "Long-Term Market Correlations." *Journal of Business*, 78(1): 1–38.

Jorion, Philippe. 1989. "Asset Allocation with Hedged and Un-Hedged Foreign Stocks and Bonds." *Journal of Portfolio Management* 15 (Summer), 49–54.

Longin, Francois, and Bruno Solnik. 2001. "Extreme Correlation of International Equity Returns." *Journal of Finance* (April).

Solnik, Bruno. 1974. "Why Not Diversify Internationally Rather Than Domestically?" *Financial Analysts Journal* (July/August).

Solnik, Bruno, and Denis McLeavey. 2009. *International Investments*. 6th edition. Upper Saddle River, NJ: Pearson.

APPENDIX 23A: IN SEARCH OF ALPHA AT GLOBAL THEMATIC PARTNERS (GTP)[19]

Some global investors look at the markets by country or region, whereas others think in terms of industry and market capitalization. Global Thematic Partners' preferred method of organizing and distilling the vast universe of listed equities into a coherent and actionable opportunity set is to think in terms of themes. The result is a dynamic approach to portfolio construction that allows GTP to be flexible, nimble, and focused in our search for the most attractive risk/reward opportunities available worldwide.

The S-curve

GTP believes that major shifts in economics, social science, and — above all — natural science are highly nonlinear developments; therefore, seeking inflection points and uncovering hidden optionality are hallmarks of our focus on thematic investment. We trace the evolution of our themes using the s-curve, which is well suited to model the profile of their expected chronologies (see Exhibit 23A.1).

Sigmoid functions, or s-curves, can be used to represent the progression through time of a variety of phenomena. They have been used to elucidate topics ranging from the rise and fall of nations to the growth potential of individual companies, and they often model the diffusion within an economy of such factors as innovation prevalence, infrastructure construction, and technology adoption. An initial, experimental phase is followed by a frenzy of growth once a tipping point is reached — which may be due to a decrease in cost, increased demand, an increase

19 Global Thematic Partners is the brainchild of its founder Dr. Oliver S. Kratz.

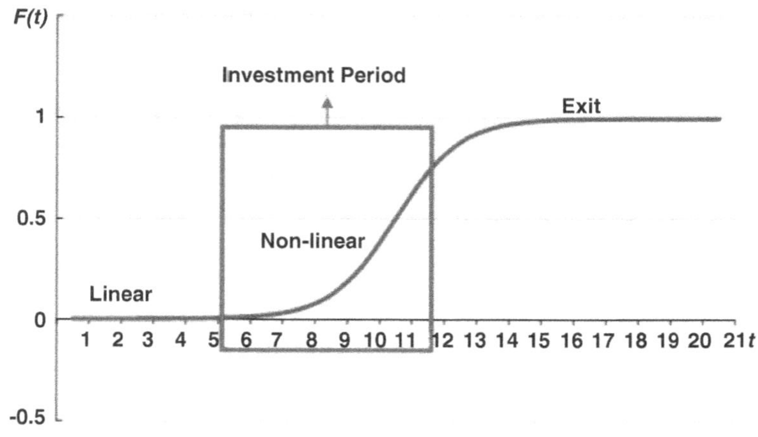

Exhibit 23A.1. The sigmoid.

in quality or reliability, network effects as a critical mass is attained, or a combination of these factors. Growth then moderates once saturation is attained, and the curve levels out at a new steady state.

Stock prices often exhibit nonlinear rallies and downturns corresponding to paradigm shifts in investor thinking due to new information or discrete events. As the underlying fundamental s-curve is identified by investors, both the evolution of investor beliefs as well as valuation models and the stock price itself should follow an s-curve pattern. Therefore, being an early adopter of disruptive information about inflection points presents an opportunity for *alpha* generation. Typically, the optimal investment entry point is just before the function begins to accelerate into an exponential-like stage. GTP searches for emerging sigmoid characteristic functions in industries, economic data, technology, and behavioral patterns before they are identified by others and incorporated into market expectations.

Thematic framework

In our experience, s-curve situations can be classified as arising from one or more of the following three categories, each representing a foundational explanation for asset mispricing:

1. *Scarcity*. Certain assets are scarce, valuable, and not easily replicable or substitutable. We focus on scarcity that is fundamental, as opposed to acute. Many products in the world are valuable but not scarce, while others are scarce but not valuable; the combination of these attributes is particularly powerful for those who control them. These desirable qualities may not be fully valued by the market, especially when a short-term surplus exists.

2. *Discontinuity*. Discontinuities arise from when, at any given time, there are situations around the world representing temporary, unstable equilibria whose disruption is a question not of if, but of when. Such situations present an attractive opportunity for the patient investor, as the equilibrium shift is often highly consequential for valuation.

3. *Behavioral finance*. Investors tend to fear the unknown, shying away from assets with uncertain probability distributions in favor of situations they perceive as more straightforward. Such fears may give rise to a herding mentality that classifies certain companies as un-investable, causing their market prices to deviate from a true clearing price due to a dearth of buyers. These situations can provide an attractive diversification benefit, as broad market movements often have little bearing on key idiosyncratic drivers of the stock performance of these companies.

Each theme requires a distinct grouping of the measurable *catalysts* that arise from one of these three situations. Nonoverlapping catalysts between themes provide a diversification benefit; however, some catalysts are themselves correlated (for example, urbanization for our Global Agribusiness theme and public health threats for our Security theme), so the diversification is only partial. These overarching catalysts are not themes in themselves; they are descriptive umbrella concepts that are too broad to be specific catalysts for an individual theme. Nevertheless, stepping back with a degree of abstraction allows us to identify some key tailwinds that will move our thematic theses forward.

Key catalytic tailwinds

The benefits of economic growth are generating profound consequences around the world at all levels. At the low end, newfound disposable incomes and increased redistribution in frontier countries are creating opportunities for our Bottom Billion theme. This burgeoning consumer class has important implications for the Sufficiency theme. Rising income levels at the middle class stratum catalyze the Global Agribusiness theme, as diets shift to more meat and dairy products. Importantly, the distribution of new wealth is increasingly unequal, accruing to highly skilled workers (represented in the Talent and Ingenuity theme) and resource owners (Asymmetric Negotiators). At the high end, wealth creation quickly begets a desire for wealth protection, which feeds into our Security theme.

Development through diffusion of technology

We believe that agrarian development lays the foundation for urbanization and economic development, so the Global Agribusiness theme plays a pivotal role. Moving away from subsistence farming has consequences for land use, time use, and logistics that directly transform the lives of the Bottom Billion. We believe some of the most important developments in infrastructure and trade over the next decade will occur in and around the Indian Ocean. Growing infrastructure needs with high costs give rise to a need for public-private partnerships to share risk and raise capital.

Resource constraints

At the core of our Sufficiency theme is the fact that infinite growth in a finite system is impossible, and the earth's constraints are becoming binding as the planet fills up. Increasing demand, fueled today by the emerging middle class and tomorrow by the Bottom Billion, presents the ultimate opportunity for Asymmetric Negotiators, who control finite resources. Growing consumption presents a myriad of challenges throughout the Global Agribusiness supply chain and opens the door for Talent and Ingenuity companies — which face their own constraints of skilled professionals — to develop new solutions. Finally, heightened competition and shortages relate to our Security theme, as they increase the prevalence of conflict, unrest, and war.

Innovation

As the abundance of capital increases and the share of equity value attributable to intangibles grows, Talent and Ingenuity become more critical to generate sustainable abnormal returns. Scientific breakthroughs and the declining cost of computing are increasing the Personalized Medicine opportunity set at an accelerating rate. The era of Sufficiency will challenge corporations and consumers to dramatically reform a broad range of common practices as total throughput levels off or declines. And the unique needs and price points of the Bottom Billion require complete reinvention of many products and services, as well as their marketing, distribution, and service mechanisms.

Imbalances

Leverage, capital flows, and rapid cost inflation are creating a variety of Disequilibria situations around the world, including among sovereigns. Cash-strapped governments may turn to public-private partnerships to help fund needed spending and may also attempt to raise taxes and confiscate wealth, creating opportunities in Security. These situations often result in opportunities in our Distressed Companies theme, as well as for Supply Chain Dominance firms with strong balance sheets to capture market share. Heightened risk perception and market distress beget demand for Market Hedge firms.

Regulation and negative feedback loops

Despite convergence efforts in many areas, regulation remains a complicated and often conflicting patchwork that seems more likely to expand than to moderate. Perceived windfall returns are at particular risk, especially those seen as stemming from a nation's natural resources endowment (with implications for Asymmetric Negotiators) or from market power (Supply Chain Dominance).

Themes: Our beliefs for the next five years

We hold the following nine beliefs for the near future:

1. Personalized Medicine and the advent of affordable genomics will fundamentally change medical treatment options. Prediction and prevention will increasingly replace treatment of disease. Gene sequencing is becoming affordable for broader scientific studies.
2. Food shortages are more likely to occur in the future. The factors of food production are showing diminishing returns at the same time that caloric needs are rising. Global Agribusiness supply chains require debottlenecking and large investments.
3. The poorest three billion people (the Bottom Billion) in the global economy will move toward participation in global commerce. This will not be a sleepy and gradual process.
4. The center of strategic focus is moving from the Atlantic Ocean to the Indian Ocean.
5. Large, dominant franchises in industry — Supply Chain Dominators — are more likely to capture opportunities in margin and market share.
6. Government finances are not realistic. Insolvency is often confused with illiquidity. Market Hedges against "inflating the debt problem away" need to be considered.
7. Regulation and uncertainty give rise to maximum pessimism and reduction of expectations. Such Disequilibria in expectation gives rise to Distressed valuations in companies and sectors that are more likely than not transitory.
8. Resources are constrained and biocapacity is limited. Companies that are net creditors of natural resources and biocapacity are Asymmetric Negotiators — both will become more highly valued assets.
9. Physical, data, biological, and wealth preservation Security is an exponentially more important

consideration in a rapidly urbanizing, densely populated, networked, and wealthier, yet more fragile, world.

Theme reflexivity and the research process

Shared tailwinds and linkages between our themes mean that much of our fundamental research has wide implications across the portfolio. A deeper understanding of one theme frequently brings with it added depth for one or more other themes; processing new information and deducing its impact on our various thematic hypotheses is one of our key skills as global investors. Therefore, although each theme has a research analyst who serves as a theme captain, all analysts are generalists and perform research on stocks across all of our themes. For example, deep research into Personalized Medicine has led us to companies doing pioneering work in crop bioengineering that remain off the radar of most agribusiness investors.

Conclusion

As the world becomes more connected and more complex, the importance of an integrative approach to making decisions and interpreting events continues to increase. Our search for opportunities at the knee of the s-curve continues, and we find that they are abundant. Even as market efficiency increases due to improved information transmission, regulatory changes, and learning from the past, we believe that the prevalence of disequilibria is actually increasing, due in large part to unintended consequences of government policy that seeks to maintain financial stability and dampen the amplitude of the business cycle in a global environment of increased perceived volatility.

CASE STUDY 23.1. INVESTING IN SUSTAINABILITY-LINKED SOVEREIGN BONDS

It had been an acrimonious board meeting for the Orbis' Global Sovereign Bond Fund. Orbis is a mid-sized global fixed — income securities fund with $14 billion under management. It is domiciled in Philadelphia and works closely with chief-investment-officers at endowment funds of liberal arts college. Its charter calls for a performance on par with US treasury funds but with a lower volatility. At its last board meeting two non-executive independent directors had questioned Orbis's commitment to its ESG-compliant investment policy which had focused exclusively on strongly-rated ESG sovereigns but had yet to invest in green bonds or sustainability-linked sovereign bonds SLB per se. Another non-executive independent director had questioned Orbis' avoidance of sovereign bonds denominated in the issuing country's currency. Several other directors had pointed to the changing fixed-income sovereign landscape and the need for Orbis — now 12 years old — to dust off its investment policy.

Saheba Sahni — as Orbis' lead portfolio manager — had argued convincingly to the board that Orbis' portfolio better than met its ESG objectives but perhaps it was time to consider an increasingly vibrant segment of the sovereign bond opportunity set — so-called sovereign sustainability-linked bonds — even though investment yields on such bonds were generally at a premium *vis-à-vis* comparable sovereign bonds with strong ESG metrics. Unlike ***Green*** bonds which are *use-for-proceeds* bonds to finance specific ESG-compliant projects, issuers of sustainability-linked bonds can use the bond proceeds as they see fit and therefore do not lose control over their budgetary process. Saheba was pondering if such bonds did indeed constitute a different asset class? Perhaps, it was time to take a closer look at the newly-minted and first in class offering of sustainability-bonds issued by the Republic of Chile and the Republic of Uruguay. In 2022, Chile and Uruguay issued the world's first sovereign SLBs in the amount of $3 billion (at a yield of 5.3%) and $1.5 billion (yield: 5.75%), respectively; interestingly, the Chilean bond issue was actually denominated in Pesos rather than US dollar and offered a slightly higher yield (85 bps) than a comparable dollar-denominated issue. Both bonds offered slightly higher field than comparable plain vanilla bonds. The greenium generally associated with green bonds did not seem to apply to these two SLSBs. A foray into local currency (rather than US dollar or euro) denominated sovereign bonds would constitute a major departure from Orbis' established investment policy but several of these bonds offered very attractive yield and potential for capital appreciation.

Republic of Chile 1.75bn Sustainability-Linked Bond (SLB) in local currency. As of 21 July 2023:

Fitch Ratings has assigned an 'A-' rating to Chile's Chilean peso (CLP) 1.75bn Sustainability-Linked Bond (SLB) in local currency. The bond carries a coupon of 5.3% and matures in 2037. Proceeds from the issuance will be used for general government purposes. Similar to the other recent USD- and EUR-denominated SLB issuances, the new bond is tied to sustainability performance targets related to Chile's greenhouse gas emissions reduction and a rise in the share of women on company boards. If Chile does not meet targets, it will be required to pay investors a higher coupon. The bond could see an annual coupon step-up of 15bps starting in 2027 if it fails to deliver on either of its social or environmental targets, and 30bps if it falls short of both.

ESG — Governance: Chile has an ESG Relevance Score (RS) of '5' for both Political Stability and Rights and '5' [+] for the Rule of Law, Institutional and Regulatory Quality and Control of Corruption. Theses scores reflect the high weight that the World Bank Governance Indicators (WBGI) have in our proprietary Sovereign Rating Model (SRM). Chile has a high WBGI ranking at 73.5, reflecting its long track record of stable and peaceful political transitions, well established rights for participation in the political process, strong institutional capacity, effective rule of law and a low level of corruption.

Republic of Uruguay $1.5 billion 5.75% sustainability-linked bonds due 2034. It is the first sustainability-linked bond issuance by Uruguay and only the second ever by a sovereign. Sustainability-linked bonds are designed to motivate issuers to meet ambitious sustainability targets, which are measured by key performance indicators (KPIs). Unlike green bonds and other ESG-labeled bonds, the proceeds of these offerings are not directed to specific projects. Instead, sustainability-linked bonds provide that if the specified KPI is not achieved, the issuer will be subject to a step-up in the coupon rate on the bond.

In this issuance, Uruguay innovated by becoming the first issuer to include a coupon step-down if it overperforms on the pre-defined targets by a certain threshold. The targets contemplated by Uruguay's bonds include achieving a reduction in aggregate greenhouse gas emissions, expressed in CO_2 equivalent per real GDP unit, by 2025 compared to 1990 and maintaining or increasing the native forest area covering Uruguay's territory by 2025 compared to 2012.

Total demand for the bond was $3.96 billion, greatly exceeding the $1.5 billion Uruguay decided to issue. The yield spread between this bond and the US Treasury bond used as a benchmark is 170 basis points. If the bond's goals are met, its spread will narrow by up to 30 basis points. Uruguay has made impressive progress towards reaching its KPIs having reduced its greenhouse gas emissions per GDP unit by 41% (compared with a 1990 baseline) and having retained 100% of its native forest area (compared with a 2012 baseline).

Questions for Discussion

1. What are sovereign bonds? How is the issuer's country risk measured?
2. What is the difference in risk profiles between dollar versus local currency denominated sovereign bonds?
3. Why do local currency versus US dollar-denominated sovereign bonds offer different yield?
4. How are ESG metrics applied to sovereign bonds?
5. Do sustainability-linked sovereign bonds constitute an asset class?
6. Why do sovereign SLBs offer a somewhat higher yield than comparable strongly ESG-compliant sovereign bonds? Why don't they enjoy the small *greenium* often associated with green bonds?
7. How should Orbis decide between in The Republic of Chile's and the Republic of Uruguay SLSBs?

PART SIX

Managing the Multinational Financial System

Chapter 24 shows how financial decisions could be optimized by leveraging the multinational enterprise system through skillful timing and adjustment of intra-corporate transactions. Finally, central to the successful implementation of a global strategy, multinational corporations need financial planning, budgeting, and control systems that incorporate the unique operating circumstances of each and every foreign subsidiary while ensuring that strategic goals are duly achieved (Chapter 25 to be found on the companion website).

24

Managing the Multinational Financial System

Through its propensity to nestle everywhere, settle everywhere, and establish connection everywhere, the multinational corporation destroys the possibility of national seclusion and self-sufficiency, and creates a universal interdependence.

—Stephen Hymer

As much as 40% of all international trade is transacted within the multinational corporation — so-called *intra-corporate trade*. This allows globally reaching firms to exploit their multinational enterprise system through skillful transfer pricing of cross-border shipment of parts or subassemblies, timely leading and lagging of payments among sister subsidiaries, comprehensive multilateral netting of payments, and consolidation of liquidities to reduce financing costs and take advantage of centralized cash management. This comprehensive optimization exercise in value creation is, however, severely constrained by national regulations, tax laws, and tariff duties.

After reading this chapter you will understand:

- What the key principles of international taxation are.
- How to exploit the multinational financial system's potential.
- How to organize the international finance function by using reinvoicing centers and international finance subsidiaries.
- How to design a global remittance strategy.
- How to optimize global cash management.

A PRIMER ON INTERNATIONAL TAXATION

By its very nature, a multinational corporation has considerable flexibility in designing and operating its financial system, with minimization of global tax liabilities as one of its important objectives. This flexibility, however, is severely constrained by national tax regimes that differ widely as to *what* they tax and *how* they tax their "corporate citizens", understood as national corporations domiciled within their borders.

The territorial reach of taxation: National versus worldwide systems

A country with a *national territorial tax reach* taxes all income generated within its own borders but no more. France, Germany, and the Netherlands apply a variant of the national tax regime. Thus France-domiciled retailer Carrefour would pay corporate income tax to the French government on income strictly generated in France; Carrefour's subsidiary in China will not pay corporate income tax to the French government on its corporate income generated in China but would obviously pay taxes to the Chinese government.

Worldwide system

A worldwide system is the case of countries like the United States and Japan that taxed their "corporate citizens" on their worldwide income — not just on their domestic income — *but only when profits are repatriated*. Such countries had an extraterritorial reach (beyond domestic borders) in defining what to tax. For example, US-domiciled Walmart — another globally reaching retailer with profitable operations in China — would pay taxes to the US government on its corporate income generated in China. Thus, Walmart, unlike its French rival, paid taxes on both its US and China corporate income. Of course, the extraterritorial reach of the US Internal Revenue Service was not limited to China — it was worldwide and encompassed all of Walmart's foreign-generated income. Effectively, Walmart's corporate income would be taxed twice — first by China and second by the United States, which may severely undermine Walmart's competitiveness unless some relief against double taxation was granted by the US government.

As pointed out earlier, taxation of foreign-source income under the worldwide tax regime is mitigated by the *deferral* rule whereby active foreign-source income is taxed only when dividends (or other form of earnings) are repatriated to the home country. One important implication is that multinational corporations had a strong incentive to delay as long as possible the repatriation of dividends and would instead decide to reinvest in other lower-tax jurisdictions (see International Corporate Finance in Practice 24.1). An important exception to this deferral rule is passive income (interest, royalties, insurance) — also known as *Subpart F income* — which is immediately taxable when accrued rather than when repatriated. (See later discussion of reinvoicing centers.)

Foreign tax credit as relief against double taxation

Multinational corporations seldom paid taxes twice on the same foreign-source income, courtesy of bilateral tax treaties. Typically, the parent multinational will benefit from a tax credit for taxes already paid to host countries by its foreign subsidiaries, as well as withholding taxes on transfer payments such as dividends and royalties remitted by the subsidiary to its parent. Two situations can arise:

1. The foreign subsidiary pays corporate income taxes at a higher rate than does its US parent. The parent company does not owe taxes on its active foreign-source income to the US Internal Revenue Service, but it cannot use its excess tax credit toward offsetting US tax liabilities on income earned domestically. It can, however, use its excess tax credit to offset any tax liabilities from other foreign-source income being taxed at a lower rate by a host government than the US rate. Additionally, if not used fully in the year it is accrued, the foreign tax credit can be carried backward one year and forward 10 years.

   Consider the case of a US-domiciled multinational firm whose foreign subsidiary earned the foreign currency equivalent of \$10 million. It is taxed at the corporate income tax rate of 50% whereas the US parent paid only 34%. The foreign subsidiary remits dividends subject to a 10% withholding tax. After tax, the parent nets \$10 million × (1 – 0.50) × (1 – 0.10) = \$4.5 million — an effective tax rate of 55%, which is considerably higher than the US tax rate. No taxes are due to the US government. In fact, the firm has a tax credit of \$10 million × (0.55 – 0.34) = \$2.1 million, which can be used to offset US taxes due on foreign-source income from subsidiaries taxed at a rate lower than 34%.

2. The foreign subsidiary is now taxed at a lower rate — say 15% — than its US parent is — say 34%. The US parent owes an additional 19% (34% – 15% = 19%) on this foreign-source income, but only when earnings are repatriated as dividends to the parent firm (for a more radical policy to dodge the extraterritorial reach of US taxation see International Corporate Finance in Practice 24.2).

> ***Q:*** Medtronic is taxed at 21% in the United States, but its Irish subsidiary is subject to a lower corporate income tax of 12.5%. Its earnings are constituted entirely of royalty fees paid by Medtronics' seven European affiliates. What are the total US taxes due on a \$100 million pretax income generated by the Irish subsidiary.
>
> ***A:*** The TJCA repealed US income taxes on active foreign source income but Medtronics' Irish subsidiary corporate income is passive and would be deemed subpart F foreign income. As such, it would be taxable at the full 21% rate whether the earnings are declared and distributed as dividends or not. Medtronic owes corporate income tax to Irish tax authorities at the 12.5% rate or \$100 million × 0.1250 = \$12.5 million. It also owes the US Internal Revenue Service \$100 million × 0.21 = \$21 million. However, it will claim a tax credit (the United States has a tax treaty with Ireland) of \$12.5 million of taxes already paid in Ireland and therefore pay only \$21 million – \$12.5 million = \$8.5 million.

An alternative method of granting relief for double taxation is to allow the foreign tax payment

INTERNATIONAL CORPORATE FINANCE IN PRACTICE 24.1

Corporate Inversions and the Lure of Tax Havens

One radical strategy to evade the extraterritorial reach of the US worldwide tax regime is corporate inversion — sometimes referred to as expatriation. In a typical inversion, a US-based multinational corporation forms a new subsidiary in a tax haven such as Bermuda. This newly established entity becomes the parent company of both the US-based operations as well as the corporation's foreign operations. Shares of the US parent multinational are exchanged for shares of the new Bermuda-domiciled parent multinational. The stock transfer transaction itself may be deemed a tax event by the US Internal Revenue Service, and shareholders and the former parent will pay capital gain taxes on the difference between the fair market value of the new shares and their tax basis.[1] When Tyco undertook a corporate inversion and relocated its parent company to Bermuda in 1997, its financial performance improved dramatically: Tyco's average tax rate declined significantly from an average of 50% in the early 1990s to under 20% in 1999.

In a similar vein, Stanley Works — a leading US toolmaker that later merged with Black & Decker — announced in February 2002 that it was relocating its headquarters to Bermuda. It claimed that its effective worldwide tax rate would drop by 9%. The day following the announcement, Stanley Works' market capitalization jumped by $200 million or an increase of 5%. Tax savings were real and duly incorporated in Stanley Works' stock price.

1 Alternatively, the new Bermuda-domiciled parent could have acquired Tyco's US assets, triggering capital gains tax on the difference between Tyco's US assets' fair market value and their tax basis (net book value after cumulative depreciation).

to be treated as a business expense deduction against the parent's taxable income in lieu of a direct full credit. For example, in the case of Medtronic being taxed in Switzerland at the lower rate of 15%, its US parent would charge the $15 million in Swiss tax against its US corporate income, reducing it to $100 million – $15 million = $85 million and then paying taxes at 34% on the $85 million, amounting to $85 million × 0.34 = $29 million. This is an amount markedly larger than the tax due under a direct full credit.

Withholding tax

Withholding tax is a tax collected by foreign tax authorities on *foreign-source income* that is repatriated by a subsidiary to its multinational parent corporation. Typical examples are withholding taxes levied on remittances of dividends, interest income, and royalties — all deemed passive income. For example, Medtronic-France remits to its US parent a dividend of €25 million. France withholds 5% or collects a tax of €25 million × 0.05 = €1.25 million, in addition to a corporate income tax of 31% it had already collected. Both taxes, if they amount to a higher effective US tax rate than 34%, are eligible for a tax credit to offset tax liabilities on other foreign-source income.

Foreign sales branch or subsidiary

Upon entering a foreign market, the multinational corporation can choose to operate either as a sales branch or as a subsidiary. A foreign branch is considered an extension of the parent exporting company. This has important implications for liability and tax purposes. The foreign branch's corporate earnings are consolidated with the parent company's, and as such, they become immediately taxable by the tax authorities of the parent's home country of domicile. Conversely, if the branch incurs losses, they become immediately tax-deductible for the parent. A foreign subsidiary is incorporated in the host country and is therefore a legally self-standing entity. Its corporate earnings are tax-deferred as long as they are not repatriated as dividends, but its losses cannot be netted against the parent's profits. Multinationals that enter new foreign countries may expect losses in the early years as their operations get off the ground and may choose the branch status as their preferred organizational form until the operations become profitable, at which point they will switch status to that of a foreign subsidiary.

Ad valorem tariff duties

Tariff taxes are akin to withholding taxes except that they are levied on the cross-border shipment of goods and services rather than the repatriation of money. *Ad valorem* (Latin for "according to the value") tariff duties are set as a percentage of the value of the imported goods. They are normal business expenses that are tax deductible by the subsidiary incurring them. To the extent that the importer has any discretion in disguising the value of the imports declared to custom authorities, it may be able to reduce the cost of the duty. More generally, such taxes collected by national custom authorities on cross-border shipment of goods also constrain the multinational enterprise system's flexibility and nimbleness.

Current US tax regime: Tax Cuts and Job Acts (2017)

In December 2017, the US tax code was overhauled with the passing of *Tax Cuts and Job Acts (TCJA)* which impacts both domestic and international taxation of worldwide activities of US-domiciled multinational corporations as well US operations of foreign companies. Most significantly, the US tax rate applicable to *domestic* corporate income is lowered from 34% to 21% but the TCJA does not tax the dividends that foreign subsidiaries of US multinationals declare to their US parent. This is a major departure from the prior tax code which — as noted earlier — taxed the *active* foreign source income of multinationals on a worldwide basis after having deducted foreign income taxes already paid. Subpart F passive income however, continues to be taxed as it was under the prior tax code. Overall little tax revenue was collected by the United States because taxes deemed on active foreign source income were deferred until the dividend income was actually distributed by foreign subsidiaries to their US parent.

As a result of the deferral rule, US multinationals as of 2017 accumulated close to $3 trillion of untaxed active income which remained in low-tax jurisdictions or tax havens awaiting repatriation; indeed the TCJA created a new and very favorable "deemed" repatriation tax of 15.5% for cash and marketable securities (and 8% for non-cash assets) with the actual tax payments staggered over an 8-year period: 8% for each of the first 5 years, 15% in the sixth year, 20% in the seventh year and 25% in the eighth year. This transition tax over untaxed prior foreign source income is due regardless of whether the funds are actually repatriated.[1]

Has the TCJA moved the US *worldwide* taxation regime closer to a *territorial* system? Indeed on the face of it, the repeal of taxes on foreign source income[2] transforms the US tax system into a modified territorial regime which would provide a strong incentive to US multinational to shift investment and reported income to low tax counties except for two provisions in the new tax code which practically amount to a form of *global minimum tax*[3]:

- First, a 10.5% minimum tax[4] without deferral is imposed on *Global Intangible Low-Taxed Income* (GILTI) — defined as profits earned abroad that exceed 10% of the adjusted basis in tangible property. It is intended to discourage moving intangible assets such as intellectual property rights to low tax jurisdictions.
- Second, the TCJA imposed a new *Base Erosion and Anti-abuse Tax* (BEAT)[5] at a 10.5% rate on the sum of the corporation's taxable income plus deductible payments (excluding costs of goods sold) made to foreign affiliates. It is meant to limit the ability of both foreign-resident and US-resident multinationals to shift profits out of their US affiliates. Thus, BEAT taxes the gross deductible payments (other than costs of goods sold) going out of the country, not the part of such payments that exceeds arms-length pricing. If it works as intended, BEAT will hurt the significant number of big businesses that use global supply chains, even if they're not engaging in abusive transfer pricing.

The complexity and intricacies of the new tax regime will certainly force multinationals to revamp their global tax strategy while testing the ingenuity of deft tax attorneys and creative financial engineers!

1 Unlike the deferral tax rule which was in place until 2017.

2 A major exception is that subpart F passive income continued to be taxed on a current basis.

3 This section draws from D. Shaviro *"The new non-territorial US tax system"*. Oxford University Center for Business Taxation WP 18/06, 2018 and *"Taxing Business under the TCJA: The good, the Bad and the Ugly"*. Anonymous working paper, 2018

4 To be increased to 13.25% in 2026.

5 According to Shaviro (2018) "the BEAT is a classical minimum tax in the sense that (i) it creates an expanded tax base, (ii) imposes a tax on this base at a rate below that of the regular tax and (iii) makes the resulting liability payable only to the extent that it exceeds regular tax liabilities".

THE MULTINATIONAL FINANCIAL SYSTEM

Unique to the web of international business activities that firms weave around the globe is the making of a complex multinational enterprise system that gives the firm unique opportunities to move money across borders from one subsidiary to the parent or to another subsidiary. For example, in the aftermath of the 1997 Asian financial crisis, countries such as Thailand and Indonesia imposed tight credit policies in the form of punishing interest rates to steady their currencies and to curb inflation. The foreign subsidiaries of many multinationals operating in these countries were able to bypass such restrictive policies by tapping into the internal financial market of their parent; in effect, procuring low interest rate financing from other parts of the multinational financial system provided them with a significant competitive advantage over local firms and enabled them to capture market share. Let's consider first the architecture of the multinational enterprise's financial system before showing how its skillful optimization will create value in its own right.

The architecture of a multinational's financial system is largely shaped by its global strategy. Many multinational corporations implement a *multidomestic* strategy whereby each foreign subsidiary is independent from its parent and sister affiliates and relatively self-contained in the sense that inputs are sourced from local suppliers and output is sold domestically. This is the case of manufacturers of consumer nondurable products, such as processed food or drinks that require a high degree of product adaptation to local market preferences and idiosyncrasies. For such firms the multinational financial system is anchored in the *equity and debt linkages* that tie foreign affiliates to their parent. These linkages are typically established when the subsidiary is first set up and the parent provides the necessary capital to fund it. More often than not, the parent will also transfer its technology and manufacturing know-how to its infant subsidiary after the subsidiary has signed a licensing contract requiring annual royalty payments and a management service agreement also requiring management know-how fees to be paid to its parent (see Exhibit 24.1).

The debt and equity linkages are likely to be upgraded over time as the parent provides additional capital to its subsidiary: They result in periodic *financial flows* such as dividends on equity ownership and interest payments on outstanding debt (see lower part of Exhibit 24.1). For multinationals implementing a multidomestic strategy, the financial system is relatively simple, with the repatriation of foreign earnings being the primary challenge, especially when the host country imposes exchange controls that may trap earnings in the foreign subsidiary (see later discussion of how to design a global remittance strategy).

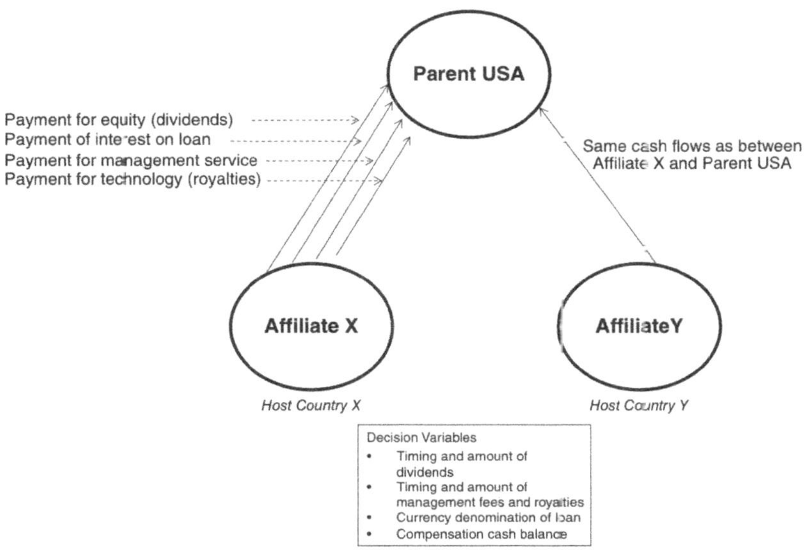

Exhibit 24.1. Typical financial links in a multinational enterprise implementing a multidomestic strategy.

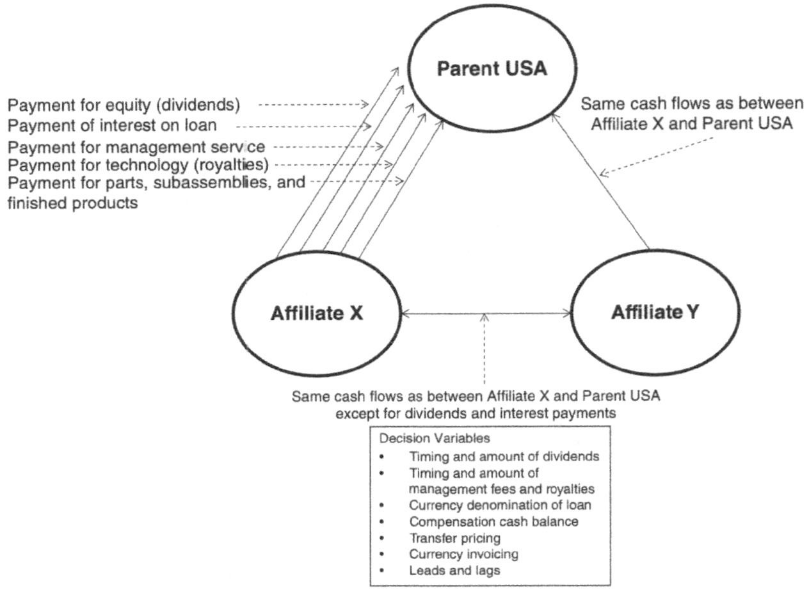

Exhibit 24.2. Typical financial links in a multinational enterprise implementing a global product rationalization strategy.

Multinationals pursuing a worldwide *production rationalization* built on an international division of labor designed to capture economies of scale will establish *operational linkages* to coordinate intra-corporate trade in materials, parts, subassemblies, and finished products among the national subsidiaries and the parent. The resulting multinational financial system is decidedly more complex than that of multinationals pursuing a multidomestic strategy, as it creates a different kind of financial flow — namely, payments for goods and services (see Exhibit 24.2). This is often the case for manufacturers of industrial products and consumer durables, which achieve economies of scale by specializing foreign affiliates in the production of one or several parts or subassemblies that are then assembled by sister affiliates for distribution worldwide. However, production rationalization strategies have to balance the significant cost savings against higher transportation costs, tariff duties, and higher coordination expenses due to more complex logistical systems that are also more vulnerable to exogenous shocks such as strikes or inclement weather and are susceptible to crippling the entire system.

A more tightly integrated multinational corporation allows it to better exploit its multinational financial system, as it now has additional levers at its disposal to reposition funds: *transfer pricing*[6] in the form of *over-invoicing* of shipments to a foreign subsidiary domiciled in a high-tax country to reduce its taxable income or leading payments/dividend remittances ahead of a currency devaluation, or *under-invoicing* in order to pay lower tariff duties on key imported subassemblies. These allow for skillful global tax minimization and therefore enhanced value creation. Optimizing the multinational financial system, however, is constrained by the regulatory framework in terms of taxation and tariff duties, to which we turn next.

EXPLOITING THE SYSTEM'S POTENTIAL TO MINIMIZE GLOBAL TAX LIABILITIES

The premise is that the multinational financial system will increase the value of the firm beyond what it would be if financial transactions were carried out on a strictly *arm's-length* basis as if the parent and its foreign subsidiaries were unrelated parties transacting

6 Transfer pricing refers to the price at which goods or services are exchanged/sold between two independent parties such as nonaffiliated firms. When the transaction is carried out between the subsidiaries of the same parent multinational, there is discretion for manipulating the actual price up (over-invoicing) or down (under-invoicing) and therefore shifting income out of high-tax countries.

solely through *external* channels. Exploiting the *internal* channels opened by the multinational financial system enables the corporation to (1) minimize global tax liabilities, (2) enhance earnings remittance from foreign subsidiaries, and (3) optimize global cash management.

Transfer pricing

Cross-border movement of goods and services avails the multinational corporation of the unique opportunity to shift income between various parts of the system in order to (1) reduce its global corporate income taxes, (2) minimize tariff duties, and (3) evade exchange controls. The weapon of choice is the transfer price set in carrying out cross-border transactions between sister subsidiaries.

Numerical example

Consider the case of Honda's European motorcycle operations (see Exhibit 24.3). Honda manufactures 100,000 engines in Ireland (corporate tax rate of 12.5%) and assembles its Integra motorcycle line in Spain (corporate tax rate 30%). Official *Organization for Economic Cooperation and Development* (OECD) transfer price guidelines call for Honda-Ireland to invoice its Spanish sister affiliate as if they were unrelated parties — also known as arm's-length transfer pricing. Each engine would be sold for €3,000. However, Honda may prefer to charge a higher transfer price by invoicing each engine at €3,600, thereby reducing Honda-Spain's taxable income by €600 (taxed at 30% for a saving of €600 × 0.30 = €180) and commensurately increasing its corporate income tax in Ireland by €75 per engine at a lower tax rate of 12.5% or €600 × 0.125 = €75. The result is a consolidated net tax saving of €105 per engine or a total saving of €10.5 million (see Footnotes at the bottom of Exhibit 24.3 for numerical details).

As the reader would expect, nation-states are very wary of tax games multinationals play. They regularly suspect that multinationals are skillfully shifting income from high-tax jurisdictions to low-tax jurisdictions. To deter such practices, many countries have enacted tax legislation that sets specific rules governing transfer pricing. Both Article 9

Exhibit 24.3. Tax effect on high versus low transfer price (€ millions).

	Honda-Ireland (Tax @ 12.5%)	Honda-Spain (Tax @ 30%)
Arm's-Length Transfer Price		
Revenue	300[1]	440
Less: Cost of goods sold (COGS)	200	300[1]
Gross profit	100	140
Less: Operating expenses	20	20
Income before taxes	80	120
Less: Taxes	10[2]	36[2]
Net income	70[3]	84[3]
High Transfer Price		
Revenue	360[1]	440
Less: Cost of goods sold (COGS)	200	360[1]
Gross profit	160	80
Less: Operating expenses	20	20
Income before taxes	140	60
Less: Taxes	17.50[2]	18[2]
Net income	122.50[3]	42[3]

[1]Honda-Ireland sales revenue is Honda-Spain cost of goods sold since it imports all parts from Ireland to assemble and distribute the Integra motorcycle in Spain.

[2]Honda's combined taxes were reduced from 10 + 36 = 46 to 17.5 + 18 = 35.5.

[3]Honda's combined net income increased from 70 + 84 = 154 to 122.5 + 42 = 164.5.

of the OECD Model Tax Convention and Section 486 of the US Internal Revenue Code mandate that transfer prices be set on an *arm's-length* basis — as if the two transacting parties were unrelated entities (not affiliates of the same parent company). As with many good principles, the devil is in the details! Primary methods for setting such intra-corporate transfer prices are:

- *Comparable uncontrolled price* based on observable independent market transactions between unrelated parties. If the product or service being transferred is *undifferentiated* and *commodity-like* for which there is an open market and active trading, the rule is easy to implement and certainly easy enough for the tax authorities to audit. This would be the case of energy, mining, and agribusiness products.
- *Resale price* method. The transfer price is set on the basis of the final price at which the product would be sold to an independent reseller and from which is subtracted an appropriate profit margin. However, if the marketing subsidiary is adding substantial value to the product, either by the unique nature of the distribution services it provides or through physical transformation/alteration of the product, the profit becomes difficult to establish. This method is most applicable to the case of a manufacturing company — parent or subsidiary of a multinational — selling to a foreign subsidiary a product for local distribution.
- *Cost plus*. The transfer price is set as the sum of the seller's cost and a profit markup based on verifiable benchmarks. In most situations, firms have sophisticated cost-accounting systems that establish the cost basis unambiguously. However, if the product is idiosyncratic enough to the corporation, there is considerable discretion for the firm to set the price as it sees fit and, if tax authorities were to audit, it may be difficult to challenge the price for lack of an objective benchmark against which to compare.
- *Comparable-profit method*. This method requires access to comparable firms that also engage in intra-corporate trade and whose transfer pricing practices can be used as a benchmark. If the firm engages in idiosyncratic activities, it may not be possible to find comparables.
- *Negotiated or advance pricing agreements*. Given the uncertainty about the enforceability of the transfer pricing method, a number of multinationals seek to negotiate an agreement *ex ante* with the tax authorities. Once agreed upon, such advance pricing agreements are less likely to be challenged during an audit by the respective taxing authorities, thereby assuring compliance and avoiding future litigation and costly penalties (see International Corporate Finance in Practice 24.2 about GlaxoSmithKline's $3.4 billion settlement with the US Internal Revenue Service).

Since transfer pricing involves two tax jurisdictions, such agreements ought to be negotiated with the tax authorities of the jurisdictions within which the selling and purchasing parties are domiciled. In 2007, US retailer Walmart announced that it had negotiated the first bilateral advance pricing agreement on imported products from China with the US Internal Revenue Service and China's State Administration of Taxation (Walmart-China is the procurement arm of Walmart-USA, as well a major retailer in China). Under this approach, the multinational corporation gives up value-creating benefits from using the flexibility of its system in exchange for the quasi-certainty of avoiding costly future audits of its transfer pricing policies.

Tax havens

Many multinationals have established foreign subsidiaries in tax havens for the express purpose of accumulating corporate earnings and deferring taxes while the money awaits reinvestment somewhere in the world or repatriation to the parent firm. *Tax haven subsidiaries* have much to do with the tax deferrals on foreign-source income that many countries allow. A tax haven subsidiary typically owns the equity of the multinational corporation's foreign operating subsidiaries and is in turn 100% owned by the parent multinational. Dividends would be remitted to and accumulated by the tax haven subsidiary instead of the parent. As long as the pool of corporate earnings is not remitted as dividends to the parent, it benefits from the tax-deferral treatment. These dividends may never in fact be taxed by the parent company's tax authorities as long as they are not repatriated. In the meantime, as the multinational expands its worldwide operations it can readily tap into the pool of funds parked tax free in the tax haven subsidiary. Some companies have gone one step further and reincorporated their parent in a tax haven; this is known as corporate inversion (see International Corporate Finance in Practice 24.1).

Reinvoicing centers

Reinvoicing centers are special-purpose administrative units that channel intra-corporate trade

INTERNATIONAL CORPORATE FINANCE IN PRACTICE 24.2

Glaxosmithkline and the IRS Finally Find Relief with Zantac

When it comes to transfer pricing, even the most seasoned tax professionals can find themselves with a stomachache. This is precisely what happened when UK-headquartered GlaxoSmithKline (GSK) received from the US Internal Revenue Service a bill for back taxes in the amount of no less than $5 billion claiming that GSK-UK had overcharged its US subsidiary. Indeed, for 14 years, GlaxoSmithKline (GSK) had disagreed with the IRS about the transfer prices the US subsidiary of GSK paid its UK parent for Zantac — a product designed to treat stomach ailments and ulcers. On September 11, 2006, GSK and the IRS agreed to a $3.4 billion settlement, the largest in IRS history.

A transfer price should be equal to the price that would be charged in an arm's-length transaction to be determined according to a number of methods (Treasury Regulation Section 1.482). In this situation, the IRS approves the *resale price method* when the purchase and resale of a tangible product are involved, and the reseller does not add substantial value to goods that are distributed by physically altering them before resale (packaging, repackaging, labeling, or minor assembly are not considered physical alteration). In the GSK case, the fundamental issue in setting the transfer price was whether the research and development process completed in the United Kingdom was more valuable than the marketing and advertising effort in the United States. Since the UK corporate tax rate at 28% is lower than the US tax rate at 40% (if state taxes are added to the 35% federal corporate income tax rate), GSK-UK would benefit by setting its sales price to GSK-USA as high as possible, retain as much profit in the United Kingdom (taxed at the lower rate), and minimize US income and therefore US taxes. Overall, GSK would reduce its global tax liabilities.

Source: Adapted from Burnett Sharon and Darlene Pulliam. 2008. "GlaxoSmithKline and the IRS Finally Find Relief with Zantac," *CPA Journal*, June.

(cross-border shipments of parts, components, subassemblies, and finished products among sister subsidiaries) to facilitate the netting of all foreign currency transaction exposures held by the multinational's various foreign branches or subsidiaries. Reinvoicing centers are desirable for multinationals that pursue a tightly integrated global production rationalization strategy built on an international division of labor among various parts of the multinational enterprise system. By centralizing cash management and consolidating hedging policies, reinvoicing centers are the source of significant savings.[7] In the absence of a reinvoicing center, bilateral trading between sister affiliates would require at least one of the parties involved to trade in a foreign currency with attendant costs. With a reinvoicing center, each subsidiary trades directly with the center in its own currency and the reinvoicing center becomes the sole counterparty to each subsidiary's intra-corporate trading. This allows the reinvoicing center to consolidate the multinational's intra-corporate foreign exchange trading and to reduce its hedging costs.

> ***Q:*** What is a tax haven?
>
> ***A:*** A tax haven is a financial center or country that applies a very low or zero tax rate on corporate income and dividends remittance. It also offers a stable currency, no risk of exchange controls, and a well-functioning legal and operational infrastructure for the financial services industry. Much sought after tax havens include the Cayman Islands, Bermuda, the Bahamas, and the Dutch Antilles in the Caribbean; the Isle of Man, Jersey, and Guernsey; Luxembourg, Liechtenstein, and Switzerland in Europe; and Singapore and Hong Kong in Asia.

Reinvoicing centers are typically domiciled in low-tax jurisdictions or tax havens to minimize tax liabilities on the earnings that they accumulate. Because they function as a conduit for multinationals' intra-corporate trade, skillful manipulation of transfer prices between selling/purchasing

7 For a discussion of the mechanics of bilateral and multilateral netting and how it reduces systemwide hedging costs, see Chapter 16 as well as the last section of this chapter.

subsidiaries and the reinvoicing center allows for minimizing tax liabilities in high-tax jurisdictions and the accumulation of profits in the reinvoicing center. In many situations the multinational's country of domicile will defer taxes on the earnings of the reinvoicing center until the latter repatriates dividends to the parent. However, under the US tax code, reinvoicing centers' earnings are deemed *passive income* and considered *Subpart F income*, which means that such earnings are immediately taxed whether they are repatriated or not. Nevertheless, earnings accumulated by reinvoicing centers can be offset by excess foreign tax credit generated by highly taxed sister subsidiaries elsewhere in the multinational enterprise system.

DESIGNING A GLOBAL DIVIDENDS REMITTANCE STRATEGY

In designing a global earnings remittance strategy, multinationals are confronted by three challenging issues: *how much* of the earnings to remit to the parent, *when* to remit, and *how* to remit. When the foreign subsidiary operates in a relatively uncontrolled monetary environment that allows full currency convertibility characteristic of OECD countries, the question of how much to remit is only one variable among a complex set of variables, including firmwide taxation and financing requirements. However, the minimization of global tax liabilities would most likely be the overwhelming

INTERNATIONAL CORPORATE FINANCE IN PRACTICE 24.3

Apple's "offshore" piggy-bank and the art of perfecting tax evasion. Why would cash-rich Apple decide to fund its stock buy-back and dividend program by selling $17 billion of bonds in the largest corporate offering on record when it holds in excess of $100 billion in cash. The reason is simply that Apple cash hoard is mostly "offshore" and therefore has never been subjected to US corporate income tax. In effect, a recent US Senate investigation showed that Apple sheltered at least $74 billion from US income taxes between 2009 and 2012 by using an arcane web of offshore dummy companies.

The center-piece of Apple's global tax evasion policy is its Irish subsidiary Apple Operations International (AOI) which is a holding company for most of Apple's foreign entities and is incorporated in Ireland. Apple houses its intellectual property in AOI by capitalizing it as an intangible asset on its balance sheet, and charge it out as a tax-deductible royalty payment to end-customers thereby siphoning income from high tax countries where its products are sold into Ireland — a low tax country where it amasses its profits. However, AOI is not considered as a tax resident in Ireland because it is neither managed nor controlled there: indeed, through an elaborate tax stratagem involving several *"mailbox"* subsidiaries in tax havens known as the *"Double Irish"* AOI didn't pay a dime to a single government anywhere, not even Ireland. Over the years, these untaxed "offshore" profits — also known as stateless money — accumulated to $102 billion — the precise cash hoard Apple chose not to "repatriate".

To add insult to injury it turns out that Apple wouldn't have to repatriate it because in fact the money is already safely invested with US banks. The Irish mailbox subsidiary, on whose books this money is for accounting purposes, transferred it to bank accounts in New York. The funds are managed by an Apple subsidiary in Reno, Nevada while Apple's accountants in Austin, Texas, keep the books. Apple is no exception and in fact US corporations have stashed away $ 1.6 trillion untaxed profits in "offshore" subsidiaries. That explains another corporate mystery. When Congress, after heavy lobbying by the largest US corporations, declared a "repatriation holiday" in 2004 to encourage the "return" of $300 billion to be invested in the US, nothing really happened. The "repatriated" profits were taxed at the bargain rate of 5.25% as opposed to the statutory rate of 34%. The companies made some adjustments on their books but there were no new investments nor hiring because the money had already been deployed in the US.

Post Scriptum. In 2016 The European Union fined Apple $13 billion plus interest in back tax to Ireland and instructed Ireland to close the "Double Irish" loophole also known as a base erosion and profit shifting (BEPS) tax tool. By 2019 Ireland had steadfastly refused to collect taxes from Apple which held $246 billion in its offshore accounts.

Source: Adapted from *The New York Times* "For US companies money "offshore" means Manhattan". (May 21, 2013).

concern. In many emerging market countries, however, that have yet to achieve full convertibility of their currencies, the ghost of earnings trapped in the foreign subsidiary's host country looms large (see International Corporate Finance in Practice 24.4 for the case of multinationals operating in China). In such situations earnings remittance dwarfs other financial considerations, and the answer to the question of *how much* to remit is generally *100%* of earnings. The best strategy is to plan proactively for earnings remittance by establishing, upon inception of the subsidiary, less conspicuous alternative channels to the obvious dividends route.

INTERNATIONAL CORPORATE FINANCE IN PRACTICE 24.4

After Earning Cash in China, The Trick Is Getting It Out

US companies have plowed billions of dollars into China with high hopes of capitalizing on the country's fast-growing economy. Few of them, however, contemplate the flip side: getting that money back out. Big corporate investors such as General Motors, industrial-gear maker Emerson Electric Co., and fast-food restaurant operator Yum Brands Inc. have long counted on China to fuel their growth. The country is now GM's biggest market, and the carmaker plans to invest as much as $7 billion more there by 2016. But, as their Chinese profits accumulate, some companies are finding that bringing that money home is a costly and time-consuming process. "It's like the 'Hotel California'", said Daniel Blumen, cofounder of consulting firm Treasury Alliance Group. "Everybody goes into China in a hurry, but then they find it's not so easy to get out".

Most countries regulate big movements of corporate cash. But in countries with a freely convertible currency, that often means little more than routine approval from tax authorities. In China, which closely regulates the conversion of its yuan into dollars or euros, the hurdles to withdrawing profits include an array of taxes and regulatory gray areas. The process can be especially frustrating for those who might need the money most urgently. Cash-strapped Eastman Kodak Co., which recently filed for protection under Chapter 11 of the US Bankruptcy Code, has about $320 million in China, and it is likely to need at least some of it to pay its creditors. But Antoinette McCorvey, Kodak's chief financial officer, said during a conference call in November that the photography icon wanted to remove as much of its China cash as it could "once various government requirements are met", and thought it would take several months for Kodak to repatriate its money.

That is because China, which has gradually been deregulating foreign investment since the 1980s, has put up barriers to limit the sort of capital flight that occurred in countries such as Thailand, Indonesia, and Malaysia during the Asian currency crisis of the late 1990s. "Trapped cash will always be a concern", said Sam Xu, executive director in JPMorgan Chase & Co.'s treasury services group, which advises companies on cash management. He added that recent steps China has taken to loosen its currency controls, aimed at promoting the yuan as a global currency, haven't made it easier for foreign companies to extract their profits. "It is very likely that it will take a long time before China's capital account is completely open", Mr. Xu said. In fact, the problem could get worse. China's slowing economy might encourage authorities there to make it more difficult for companies to take out profits, said Wei Shu, lead economist of Deloitte Touche Tohmatsu's transfer-pricing practice in China, which advises companies about cross-border transactions. "If the economy is not as good as it was in the past, the (Chinese) tax authorities could get more tax revenues from foreign companies", he said. Corporations that want access to their China cash have a few options, according to several experts. None is very straightforward, but the least complex is for a company's Chinese unit to pay dividends directly to its foreign parent.

First, the subsidiary has to put aside about 10% of its profits in a so-called enterprise reserve, capped at 50% of a company's total investment in the country, to protect against future losses. That can be a substantial sum for a company such as GM, which has invested billions in China. Then, the company must set aside another, unspecified percentage of profit for employee welfare. The sum is based on a number of factors, some of them murky. "It's a little bit of a gray area", said Alvin Chan, a director at tax and accounting advisory firm Nair & Co. The rest, already taxed at China's corporate rate of 15 to 25%, is subject to an additional 10% withholding tax.

Another way to move money: Foreign companies can charge their Chinese unit royalty fees or charge them for services. China also taxes those payments, and it insists that the payments have a legitimate business purpose that is supported by documentation. "It's a cumbersome process and not exactly tax-efficient", said Herbert Parker, chief financial officer of stereo equipment manufacturer Harman International Industries, which has been investing in China since 2000. He said the process is manageable, but that companies need to plan in advance. One reason is that the rules companies must follow to get government approval to repatriate Chinese funds can be a bit of a moving target. "There's a difference between the regulations as written and the laws and regulations as they are practiced", said George Kelakos of Kelakos Advisors LLC.

Source: The *Wall Street Journal*, February 15, 2012. Reprinted with permission.

Dividends

Remitting dividends is the natural compensation for the parent company's initial equity investment. It is also the most scrutinized and least welcome movement of funds by central bank authorities in emerging market countries that maintain selective controls on foreign exchange transactions. Yet more than 50% of all foreign earnings are remitted in the form of dividends. By adhering to a worldwide dividends *payout ratio*, multinationals establish a pattern of consistent and periodic dividends remittance in the eyes of otherwise recalcitrant central bank authorities. For example, if each foreign subsidiary is expected to pay 75% out of its earnings year in and year out,[8] the multinational may be more successful in convincing the host-country central bank that these payments are ordinary rather than arbitrary transactions. Repatriated earnings, however, are taxed three times — first by the host country (corporate income tax), again by the host country when remitted as dividends through a withholding tax, and a third time by the parent's home country (if its tax rate exceeds the foreign subsidiary's tax rate). As such, dividends are the least desirable mode of repatriating funds to the multinational parent.

Fees and royalties

By signing licensing (or franchising) agreements[9] with their foreign subsidiaries for the use of the parent's technology, patents, and trademarks, payments in the form of royalties create legitimate and complementary channels for remitting earnings to the parent. Royalties are typically less objectionable to emerging market countries' central banks and sail more smoothly through their exchange control machinery. Similarly, padded fees for management assistance and allocation of overheads are normal tax-deductible business expenses for the foreign subsidiaries, which can be used as disguised dividends. Such channels should be established on the very first day of operations to ensure consistency.

When exchange controls tighten and devaluation or depreciation looms closer on the horizon, multinationals may resort to emergency policies such as over-invoicing and/or leading payments to speed up remittances and avoid exchange losses or preempt exchange controls.

Overinvoicing and underinvoicing

As discussed earlier, over-invoicing is simply the practice of overcharging a foreign affiliate for goods or services above the normal transfer price to repatriate the difference between the over-invoiced and the normal price. For example, Nokia is facing delays in repatriating $5 million of dividends from its Vietnamese operation because of a deteriorating

8 Dividend payments are cash transactions whereas earnings are accounting constructs. A foreign subsidiary may report bountiful earnings and be cash poor; in such situations the subsidiary may still want to declare the dividends but wait to make the actual payment just to set the transaction in motion with the central bank.

9 See Chapter 19 for a discussion of licensing and franchising as foreign market entry strategies. Interestingly, multinational corporations routinely sign licensing agreements with their wholly owned affiliates.

balance-of-payments situation. Nokia also sells $50 million in parts and components to its Vietnamese subsidiary for assembly. It may over-invoice its subsidiary by 5% (from $50 million to $52.5 million) and over a course of 2 years repatriate the $5 million in trapped dividends. This presumes that central banks expedite the payments of imported parts and components that are deemed essential for local operations even when they freeze dividend remittances.

> ***Q:*** Nokia-Vietnam exports $100 million worth of assembled cell phones to Nokia-Singapore for distribution through Southeast Asia. Singapore has a perfectly convertible currency, but Vietnam does not. How can Nokia-Vietnam adjust its export price to repatriate $5 million of trapped dividends to Nokia-Singapore?
>
> ***A:*** Nokia-Vietnam can under-invoice Nokia-Singapore by 5%, thereby shifting income out of Vietnam. Nokia-Vietnam would generate only $95 million in sales revenue (instead of $100 million if the transaction were fairly priced), whereas Nokia-Singapore pays only $95 million and therefore accrues an excess profit of $5 million, which is simply disguised repatriated dividends.

Leading and lagging payments

Time may be of the essence in effecting earnings remittances when controlled exchange rates are subjected to devaluation pressures. The multinational may decide to lead (accelerate) its payment to take advantage of a better exchange rate. Such practices may be more difficult to carry out in the case of periodic/annual payments such as royalties or dividends but are usually easier to do for payments of goods. Consider the case of Nokia, which assembles cell phones in Vietnam for local sales as well as for sales in Cambodia and Laos. The parts are shipped from Malaysia and invoiced in US dollars. Typically, Nokia-Vietnam pays its accounts payable (A/P) on a 90-day cycle, and its current balance is $25 million. The Vietnamese dong is currently trading at VND 18,500 = $1 and is widely expected to devalue to VND 21,500. By leading its payment — that is, paying early on the 30th day rather than on the 90th day — its $25 million A/P will actually be $25 million × 18,500 = VND 462,500 million. If it waited 90 days, it might have had to pay $25 million × 21,500 = VND 537,500 million. Leading the A/P payment avoids a loss of $25 million × (21,500 − 18,500) = VND 75,000 million.

CENTRALIZING CASH MANAGEMENT

Centralizing cash management is an intuitively straightforward concept. Consider the case of Nestlé-USA — the subsidiary of the Swiss nutrition multinational. Its California-based Nescafé subsidiary projects a cash balance of $260 million for the month of April 2024, earning a paltry 1.75% per annum from its bank deposits. Buitoni, Nestlé's New Jersey–based pasta subsidiary, projects a cash deficit of $160 million and would have to bridge it by drawing on its line of credit at the cost of 6.75%. By consolidating both cash positions between its Nescafé and Buitoni subsidiaries, Nestlé-USA has a net cash balance of $100 million and will save itself [(6.75% − 1.75%) × 160 million]/12 = $666,666. The same logic applies at an international level. For example, Nestlé–South Korea has a dollar-equivalent deficit of $75 million and faces short-term borrowing interest rates in South Korea of 9% per annum. Consolidation of cash balances between the two countries' operations would allow Nestlé–South Korea to borrow from Nestlé-USA at the much lower rate of 1.75%.

Of course, netting on a cross-border basis raises issues of foreign exchange conversion cost and currency risk. Last but not least, let's assume further that Nestlé-Argentina is short $10 million for the same period and could draw on Nestlé-USA at 1.75% rather than borrowing in Argentina at the rate of 12%. The Argentine peso has been depreciating, and speedy transfer in and out of Argentina may be held up by the country's central bank. This, of course, would make Nestlé-USA pause before consolidating cash management between its Argentine and US subsidiaries. Let's consider next *why*, *how*, and *when* globally centralized cash management is warranted.

Cash management and working capital

The basic goals of cash management are (1) to speed up collection of accounts receivable while slowing down the disbursement for accounts payable, (2) to shift cash from subsidiaries that have excess liquidities to subsidiaries facing a cash deficit, and (3) to maximize the return on consolidated cash balances. Both multinationals and domestic firms are thus confronted with the same management conundrum of optimizing each subsidiary's working capital requirement relative to operating needs — namely, accounts receivable (A/R), inventory (INV), accounts payable (A/P), and ultimately cash, which are all components of the subsidiary's cash conversion cycle. The aim is to minimize the amount of time (measured in days) when cash is trapped in inventory and receivables, while extracting the longest possible delay in paying suppliers provided that supplier financing is cheaper than bank financing:

$$\text{Cash conversion cycle (ccc)} = \text{Average collection period (A/R)} + \text{Inventory conversion period (INV)} - \text{Payables deferral period (A/P)}$$

where

- The *average collection period* (ACP) is the average number of days the firm's customers take to pay after the sale is booked. It is measured as (A/R)/(sales/365). The ACP is also commonly known as *days sales outstanding* (DSO).
- The inventory conversion period (ICP) measures how long it takes for the firm to convert raw materials into finished goods and actual sales; denoting cost of goods sold as COGS it is measured as INV/(COGS/365).
- Payables deferral period (PDP) is the average number of days the firm takes to pay its suppliers; it is computed as (A/P)/(COGS/365).

The cash conversion cycle is a direct proxy for the cash requirement. Most firms have a positive ccc; the longer the ccc, the more working capital has to be short-term financed. Some firms operate with *negative* working capital (corresponding to a negative ccc) and therefore generate cash rather than use cash as part of their daily operations. This is the case of firms such as Dell (computers), Delta Air Lines, and Amazon.com, whose customers prepay their purchases. Large retailers such as Carrefour S.A. are firms that have financed long-term investments on the back of recurring negative working capital. For example, Carrefour sells for cash (or very short-term credit through credit cards) and therefore holds very small A/R balances (DSO is less than 1.5 days). As a mammoth purchaser, it leverages its economies of scale in procurement by extracting from its suppliers very long credit terms at zero cost for its purchases (high A/P balances and a PDP in excess of 85 days). As a retailer, Carrefour prides itself on moving its merchandise fast, thereby keeping a relatively small inventory at all times and an ICP of less than 20 days. In sum, Carrefour's cash conversion cycle is an astonishing ccc = 1.5 + 20 − 85 = −63.5 days, which generates a significant amount of cash that can be invested short-term rather than used to finance working capital.

Why is centralized cash management value-creating?

Each subsidiary holds cash and marketable securities to be able to meet day-to-day cash disbursements (the so-called transaction balance) and to protect against emergency cash needs that arise out of unanticipated deviations from the cash budget (so-called precautionary balance). A centralized global cash management policy allows the multinational firm to operate with a smaller worldwide aggregate amount of cash than it would if cash management were decentralized at the national subsidiary level. Indeed, each subsidiary can limit itself to holding transaction balances while precautionary balances are centralized, enabling the excess liquidity of certain subsidiaries to offset the cash shortages of others. As a result, by relying on the firm's *internal* (rather than external) financial market, short-term financing costs can be reduced. Similarly, as precautionary cash balances are pooled globally, returns on larger-scale short-term investments may be enhanced by reducing fees and accessing wholesale rather than retail yield on jumbo certificates of deposit.

Q: Otis-Spain is in a cash deficit of €250 million and can arrange a short-term loan from Banco de Santander at the annual rate of 6%. Otis-Germany earns 3% on its €300 million short-term investment, and Otis-Switzerland — its central cash depository — earns 4% on its €100 million consolidated cash balance. What are the benefits of centralized cash management for Otis?

A: If Otis left each subsidiary to fend for itself, Otis-Spain would pay an annual interest of €250 million × 0.06 = €15 million, and Otis-Germany would earn €250 million × 0.03 = €7.5 million. By centralizing cash management, Otis consolidates its short-term investments and earns a higher interest of 4% because it invests on a significantly larger scale. However, it will lend to Otis-Spain at the same rate of 4%, allowing its Spanish subsidiary to save on interest payments: €250 million × (0.06 − 0.04) = €5 million. Otis-Germany keeps a smaller cash balance earning 3%, and Otis's central cash depository can either earn a higher 4% on behalf of the group or help another subsidiary besides Otis-Spain reduce its short-term financing expenses.

We first review the fundamentals of cash planning before considering how centralized cash management can be value-creating when the multinational corporation pursues either a *multidomestic decentralized* strategy or a *globally integrated* strategy of *production rationalization*.

Cash planning

As part of the *planning* process, multinational corporations set a basic strategy, select a course of action with associated financial goals, and prepare various *budgets* to achieve those goals. Cash planning and budgeting are therefore a subpart of financial planning whereby the firm prepares and periodically updates pro forma financial statements — income statement, balance sheet, and cash-flow statement — with maturities ranging from one month or three months up to five years. Efficient cash management in turn builds on careful cash planning, which starts at the subsidiary level as the treasurer projects cash flows over future days, weeks, months, and beyond by constructing a comprehensive *cash budget*.

Typically, the pro forma cash budget is prepared in spreadsheet form, which facilitates the simulation of net cash positions under different assumptions that are usually anchored around sales revenue and cash collection of accounts receivable.[10] These simulations in turn help the treasurer estimate more precisely the amount of cash that should be held as transaction and precautionary balances. Cash budgeting itself is closely derived from working capital management, and guidelines formulated by the parent firm offer targets for each subsidiary's working capital requirement and cash conversion cycle.

Centralized cash management for multidomestic firms

For multinational firms that pursue multidomestic, decentralized, and more autonomous strategies in foreign countries, their working capital and cash management policies will be shaped in part by host-country business norms.[11] The parent firm, however, will establish company-wide guidelines aimed at minimizing the cash conversion cycle while maximizing the cash balances of each subsidiary, which will attempt to implement them as best as it can. Centralizing cash management in such cases amounts to finding a cost-efficient mechanism for netting cash balances across the entire multinational system.

Significant economies of scale can be realized by asking customers to pay directly into the firm's account with a subsidiary branch of a multinational bank. The bank in turn aggregates cash balances across all of the firm's subsidiaries, leaving each of them with the strictest minimum transaction cash balances. Banks with large international branch networks provide the multinational firm with electronic and quasi-instantaneous transfer and consolidation of cash balances — usually crediting the firm's account with same-day value. Thus, excess cash balances beyond the individual subsidiary's transaction cash balances are centrally pooled while each subsidiary continues to receive credit for interest earnings on its own share of the centralized cash balance.

Centralized cash management for globally integrated firms

The key difference between cash management for globally integrated firms and multidomestic firms is the extensive web of *intra-corporate* and cross-border shipment of parts, subassemblies, and finished products. Such highly integrated firms require a sophisticated approach to bilateral and multilateral netting among sister subsidiaries in order to reduce gross transaction costs in the form of foreign exchange conversion and hedging fees. Once this *prepayment* consolidation of transactions has been implemented, the same principles of centralized cash management outlined in the previous section apply to the net cash balances of each subsidiary.

Bilateral netting

The simplest form of cross-border netting is the bilateral offset of payables and receivables between sister subsidiaries domiciled in different countries (see Exhibit 24.4). For example, consider United Technologies' Otis European division and intracorporate trade between its German and British subsidiaries. Otis–Germany exports electrical motors for elevators to its sister affiliate Otis–United Kingdom in the amount of €120 million. Otis–United Kingdom ships suspension cables to Otis–Germany worth £80 million. To settle these transactions (in the absence of netting) Otis–United Kingdom would purchase €120 million to remit to Otis–Germany and Otis–Germany would purchase £80 million to remit to Otis–United Kingdom. Total foreign exchange transacted, and funds

10 Actual sales and actual sales collection are not fully under the firm's control. For example, an economic recession may account for a missed sales target or sluggish collection of accounts receivable.

11 Typically, payment terms for receivables and payables tend to follow local/host-country practices rather than global benchmarks.

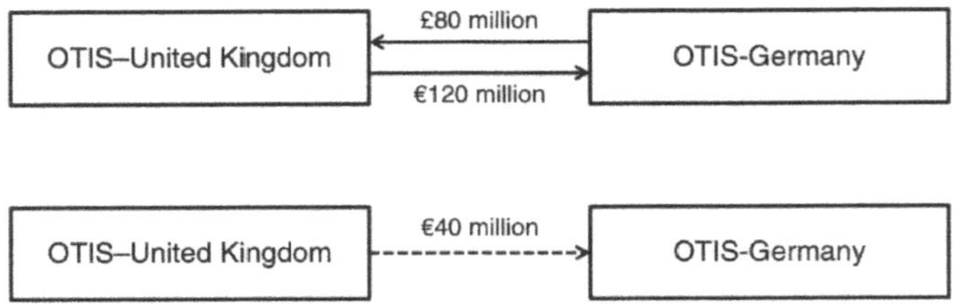

Exhibit 24.4. Bilateral netting of payables.

transferred — assuming €1 = £1 = $1 — would be equivalent to $200 million.

To offset their respective payables through bilateral netting, however, the sister subsidiaries would first determine which was the net payer and which was the net receiver. In this case Otis–United Kingdom is the net payer in the amount of €120 million − £80 million = $120 million − $80 million = $40 million. Thus, Otis–United Kingdom would need to purchase only €40 million with pound sterling, thereby relieving Otis–Germany of any currency exchanges or transfers. Bilateral netting in this case results in the following percentage of payables offset:

Gross payables and foreign exchange transacted (before netting)	**$200 million**
Net payables and foreign exchange transacted (after netting)	$40 million
Foreign exchange conversion and fund transfer avoided	$160 million
Percentage of payables offset	80%

The direct cost reduction resulting from bilateral netting comes from two sources: the cost of converting one currency into another (executing the foreign exchange transaction) and the cost of transferring funds across the border.

Multilateral netting

Circumstances often require multilateral netting arrangements without any obvious opportunities for bilateral netting. Let's return to the example of Otis's European division, whose subsidiaries in Germany, the United Kingdom, Sweden, and Poland are engaged in ongoing intracorporate trade of parts, components, and subassemblies (see Exhibit 24.5A). Otis–Germany will be paid €500 million by Otis–Sweden, but it owes Otis–Poland zlotys (PLN) 250 million; meanwhile it holds net payables to Otis–United Kingdom in the amount of £300 million, which in turn owes Otis–Sweden SEK 200 million. Finally, the British and Polish subsidiaries owe their Swedish sister subsidiary SEK 200 and 300 million, respectively. The benefits of multilateral netting are derived in the same manner as in the case of bilateral netting — by establishing whether a given subsidiary is a net payer or receiver *vis-à-vis* its sister affiliates.[12]

In this case, Otis–United Kingdom is a net receiver of $100 million while Otis–Sweden's receipts and payments cancel each other out (read down the Otis–United Kingdom total payments of $200 million and across Otis–United Kingdom line total receipts of $300 million and similarly for Sweden).

12 Here again exchange rates are assumed to be €1 = £1 = SEK 1 = PLN 1 = $1.

Exhibit 24.5A. Otis's matrix of intracorporate payments.

	Paying Subsidiaries				
Receiving Subsidiaries	**S**	**G**	**UK**	**P**	**Total**
Sweden (S)	0	. . .	200	300	500
Germany (G)	500	. . .	0	. . .	500
United Kingdom (UK)	. . .	300	0	. . .	300
Poland (P)	. . .	250	. . .	0	250
Total paid	**500**	**550**	**200**	**300**	**1,550**

Otis-Germany and Otis-Poland are net payers of $50 million each. Thus, the total offset from multilateral netting amounts to 94%, as shown in Exhibit 24.5B.

Before multilateral netting, gross payables would have amounted to $1,550 million (Exhibit 24.5C). After multilateral netting, the payments are only $100 million (Exhibit 24.5D). Consequently, substantial savings arise from *not* having to convert currencies or transfer $1,450 million.

There are two ways of settling intracompany accounts to capitalize on the benefits of multilateral netting: (1) by direct settlement or (2) through a clearing center.

Direct settlement

The company-wide netting center, usually embedded in the reinvoicing center or nested at the parent/regional treasury office, computes the net amount owed by the debtor subsidiaries. The debtor subsidiaries in this case are Otis-Germany and Otis-Poland, and they are directly responsible for purchasing foreign exchange and remitting the funds to the creditor subsidiaries through their own bank networks. Direct settlement is often viewed as cheaper and easier to run than a clearing center. More importantly, it preserves a higher degree of autonomy for the subsidiary, which maintains control over currency trading and the selection of banking partners for transferring funds and other cash management activities.

Clearing or reinvoicing center

By allowing each subsidiary to handle its own net payments, currency conversions, and hedging of

Exhibit 24.5B. Otis's gross and net intracorporate payments.

Gross payables and foreign exchange transacted (*before netting*)	**$1,550 million**
Net payables and foreign exchange transacted (*after netting*)	$100 million
Foreign exchange conversion and fund transfer avoided	$1,450 million
Percentage of payables offset	94%

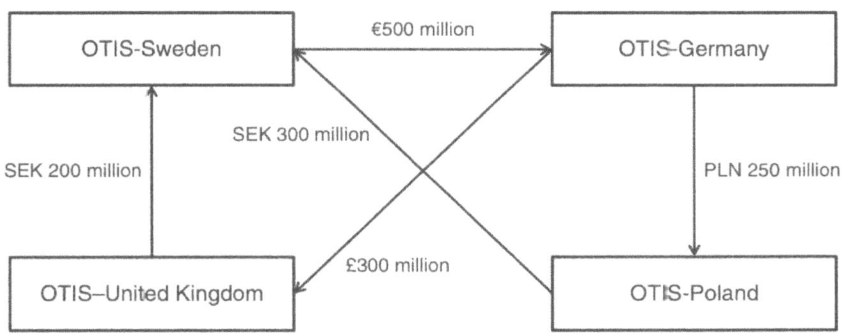

Exhibit 24.5C. Multilateral payables before netting.

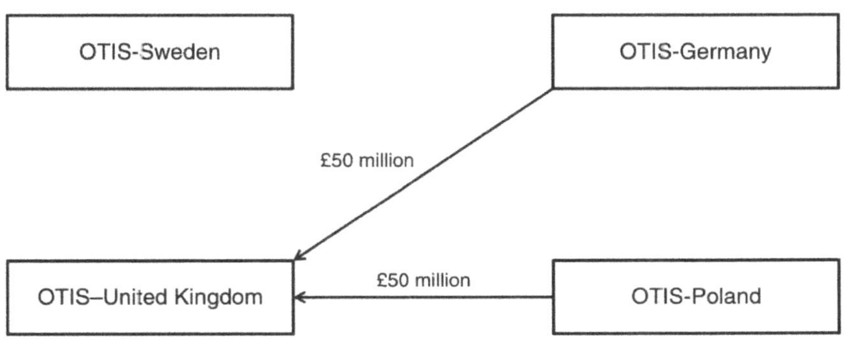

Exhibit 24.5D. Multilateral payables after netting.

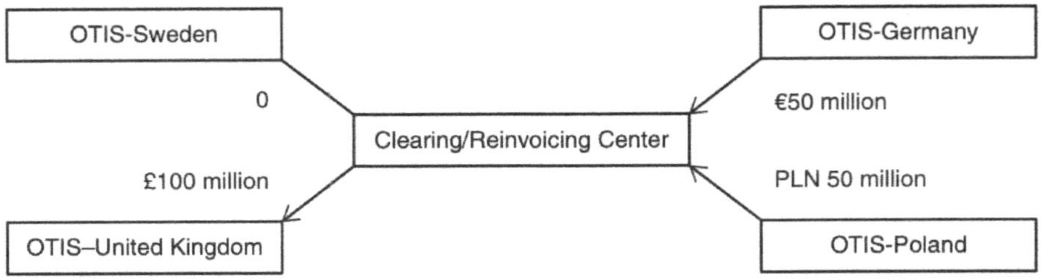

Exhibit 24.6. Multilateral netting through clearing/reinvoicing center.

transaction exposures, the multinational fails to capitalize on significant economies of scale that arise from consolidating payments through multilateral netting. To eliminate these inefficiencies, many firms — especially those with complex and intricate intracorporate trade flows — prefer to channel payments through a clearing center or reinvoicing center (see Exhibit 24.6). This settlement technique allows the net payers to pay their debts in their currency to the clearing center, which in turn purchases the foreign exchange to pay the net creditor subsidiaries in their own currencies. Thus, both the net payers and the net receivers pay or are paid in their own currencies in one single payment from the clearing center (as opposed to several payments under the direct settlement method). This reduces consolidated fund transfer costs for the company as a whole. Furthermore, neither debtors nor creditors need to engage in currency trading or currency hedging since they make payments or receive payments in their own currencies. Indeed, both currency trading and hedging activities are centralized in one location — the clearing or reinvoicing center — where treasury expertise and economies of scale can be leveraged to get the best rates.

How centralized cash management reduces precautionary cash balances

One of the key benefits of multilateral netting and centralized cash management through netting and a cash depository center is that a multinational corporation's investment in precautionary cash balances can be significantly reduced without jeopardizing its ability to meet unforeseen cash needs. To illustrate how this can be accomplished, let's return to the case of United Technologies' Otis European division and how it can benefit from its European cash depository center[13] domiciled in a low-tax jurisdiction — Lausanne (Switzerland). As explained earlier, each subsidiary keeps both a transaction cash balance to meet budgeted cash needs and a precautionary cash balance to meet unexpected cash needs that may arise during the cash budget cycle. The transaction cash balance required by each European subsidiary is assumed to follow a normal probability distribution independent from other sister subsidiaries with known mean μ and variance σ^2. The precautionary cash balance is assumed to fall within three standard deviations from the mean of the transaction cash balance which means that there is less than ½ of one % chance that the affiliate need for cash would exceed its available cash balance.

The maximum precautionary total cash balance is thus set at the mean of the transaction cash balance (μ) plus three standard deviations (σ) from the mean. For example, Otis–Germany maintains a transaction cash balance of €240 million as well as a precautionary cash balance of €300 million (three standard deviations) for a total of €540 million. Similarly, its sister affiliates Otis–Sweden and Otis–United Kingdom hold transaction cash balances of Swedish krone (SEK) 330 million and £100 million, respectively, while maintaining precautionary cash balances of SEK 210 million and £120 million (three standard deviations) for respective totals of SEK 540 million and £220 million. From Exhibit 24.7 it can be concluded that Otis-Europe will maintain total transaction cash balances of $670 million with a precautionary amount totaling $630 million[14] or a total of $1,300 million.

Let's assume that precautionary transaction cash balances (tcb) are necessary to maintain normal day-to-day operations in each country. If, instead of holding decentralized precautionary cash balances in each of its European subsidiaries, Otis consolidated them in its central cash depository unit in

13 Central cash depositaries are often coupled with a reinvoicing center.

14 To keep the numerical illustration simple, we are assuming the following exchange rates: €1 = £1 = SEK1 = $1.

Exhibit 24.7. Benefits of centralizing precautionary cash balances.

Subsidiary	Mean Transaction (μ)	Standard Deviation (σ)	Total Balance ($\mu + 3\sigma$)
Germany	240	100	540
Sweden	330	70	540
United Kingdom	100	40	220
Total Europe	670	. . .	*1,300*

Lausanne (Switzerland), it could make funds available to any subsidiary in case of emergency. Because the demand for cash by each national subsidiary is normally distributed, the consolidated demand for cash at the centralized location will also be normally distributed with a mean equal to the sum of each subsidiary mean demand for cash:

Mean of Otis–Europe portfolio's tcb
= Mean of Germany's tcb
+ Mean of Sweden's tcb
+ Mean of United Kingdom's tcb
$= 240 + 330 + 100 = 670$

By pooling precautionary cash balances in one location, Otis would be able to hold a much smaller amount corresponding to three standard deviations from the mean of its portfolio of transaction cash balances (tcb) or, assuming no correlation among the three European subsidiaries':

Standard deviation of Otis–Europe portfolio's tcb
= [(Standard deviation of Germany's tcb)^2
+ (Standard deviation of Sweden's tcb)^2
+ (Standard deviation of United Kingdom's tcb)^2]$^{1/2}$
= (\$100 million^2 + \$70 million^2
+ \$40 million^2)$^{1/2}$ = 128 million[15]

which is substantially less than \$1,300 million – \$670 million = \$630 million. Clearly the savings in the centralized precautionary cash balance results from the fact that the precautionary cash balance of each national subsidiary is less than fully correlated with the others. Such savings would decline as correlation increases. Conversely, as correlation becomes negative savings would even exceed the \$630 million corresponding to the case of zero correlation.

15 If random variables a, b, c are uncorrelated, $\text{Var}(a + b + c) = \text{Var}(a) + \text{Var}(b) + \text{Var}(c)$ and standard deviation $(a + b + c) = [\text{Var}(a) + \text{Var}(b) + \text{Var}(c)]^{1/2}$.

Who benefits from globally centralized cash management?

Not all multinationals are good candidates for tightly centralized global cash management. As emphasized earlier, much depends on the *global strategy* pursued by the firm and, most important, the *geographical footprint* of its foreign operations (see Exhibit 24.5A).

- Multinationals implementing a global strategy built on an international division of labor and production rationalization in developed market economies (convertible currencies) are the best candidates for implementing efficient global cash management since they can systematically net intracorporate transactions. Excess cash balances from surplus subsidiaries can be easily channeled to deficit ones, and overall cash balances can be consolidated at the group level for *wholesale* rather than *retail* investment. In addition to benefits from systematic multilateral netting, substantial savings in financing costs and enhanced yield will be value-creating for the multinational. Multidomestic multinationals are not able to achieve significant savings from multilateral netting but can still achieve significant savings by centralizing cash management regionally or globally.
- Conversely, if a multinational firm's subsidiaries generate excess cash but operate in countries marred by exchange controls, it will be difficult to move excess cash balances to cash-poor sister affiliates. Thus, the multinational will be unable to exploit its system's potential and redeploy excess cash where it is most needed. As a result, it will incur unnecessary short-term financing costs when it is in a cash deficit situation and will fail to harvest good returns from investing consolidated cash balances.

SUMMARY

1. Multinational corporations are taxed at three levels: (1) host country's taxation of local subsidiaries' profits, (2) host country's taxation of remittances (dividends, management fees, or royalties)

through withholding levies, and (3) home country's taxation of foreign-source income.

2. A country with a *national territorial tax reach* taxes all income generated within its own borders but no more; that is, foreign subsidiaries of a multinational corporation headquartered in such countries would not be taxed on the foreign subsidiaries' income. *Worldwide tax system* countries tax their "corporate citizens" on their worldwide income — not just on their domestic income — *but only when profits are repatriated.* Such countries have an extraterritorial reach (beyond domestic borders) in defining what to tax.

3. Upon entering a foreign market, the multinational corporation can choose to operate either as a sales branch or as a subsidiary. A foreign branch is considered an extension of the parent exporting company and its earnings are consolidated with the parent company's; as such it becomes immediately taxable by the tax authorities of the parent's country of domicile. Conversely, if the branch incurs losses, they become immediately tax-deductible for the parent. A foreign subsidiary is incorporated in the host country and is therefore a legally self-standing entity; its corporate earnings are tax-deferred as long as they are not repatriated as dividends.

4. Many multinationals have established reinvoicing centers domiciled in tax havens for the express purpose of accumulating corporate earnings and deferring taxes while awaiting reinvestment somewhere in the world or final repatriation to the parent firm. Such *tax haven subsidiaries* have much to do with tax deferral of foreign-source income that many countries allow on the foreign income that their national corporations earn abroad. Dividends would be remitted to and accumulated by the tax haven subsidiary instead of the parent. As the multinational expands its worldwide operations, it can readily tap into the pool of funds parked tax free in the tax haven subsidiary.

5. A more tightly integrated multinational corporation is able to better exploit its multinational financial system as it now has additional levers at its disposal to reposition funds: *transfer pricing* in the form of *overinvoicing* of shipments to a foreign subsidiary domiciled in a high-tax country to reduce its taxable income, *leading* payments/dividend remittances ahead of a currency devaluation, or underinvoicing in order to pay lower tariff duties on key imported subassemblies allow for skillful global tax minimization and therefore enhanced value creation.

6. Firms hold cash balances for transaction purposes to meet their day-to-day cash needs and for precautionary purposes to deal with unanticipated cash needs. A globally centralized cash management policy allows the multinational firm to operate with a smaller worldwide aggregate amount of precautionary cash than it would if cash management were decentralized at the national subsidiary level.

7. *How much* earnings to remit to the parent, *when* to remit, and *how* to remit: Remitting dividends is the natural compensation for the parent company's initial equity investment. It is also the most scrutinized and least welcome movement of funds by central bank authorities in emerging market countries that maintain selective controls on foreign exchange transactions.

QUESTIONS FOR DISCUSSION

1. What is the difference between territorial and worldwide tax regimes?
2. How is foreign-source income treated by the tax authorities of a multinational's home country?
3. What is tax deferral, and how is it applied to foreign-source income?
4. What guidelines are to be followed by multinational corporations in setting cross-border transfer prices?
5. What is Subpart F income?
6. What is the economic logic for corporate inversion?
7. What are reinvoicing centers? How do they differ from tax havens? How do multinational corporations take advantage of reinvoicing centers?
8. How can leading and lagging intracorporate payments be used to create value for the multinational corporation?
9. How should multinationals structure their global earnings remittance strategy?
10. How is centralized global cash management implemented?

PROBLEMS

1. **Branch or subsidiary for St. Jude Medical's new foreign operations.** The Minneapolis-based medical instruments firm is considering starting an assembly operation in Bratislava (Slovakia) and is hesitating between establishing it as a *branch* or a *subsidiary*. The proposed venture will be assembling medical instruments for distribution in Eastern Europe and is expected to incur losses in its first few years of operation, although it should be slightly cash-flow positive in years 4 and 5. Slovakia taxes both resident firms and branches of foreign firms at the same rate of 28% and levies a withholding tax of 10% on dividend remittances. The United States has a federal tax rate of 34% on worldwide income when earnings are repatriated but gives credit for taxes paid to foreign governments. Does it matter to St. Jude Medical how it chooses to operate in Slovakia?

2. **Taxation of foreign source income (A).** Fluor Inc. is a US-based global engineering and construction company. Its Brazilian subsidiary earned $112 million in 2012, which is taxed at the Brazilian corporate income tax of 30%. Dividends repatriated to the US parent are further subjected to a 10% withholding tax. Corporate income tax in the United States stands at 34% and is applicable to foreign-source income.
   a. Assuming that Fluor Inc. decides not to repatriate dividends from its Brazilian subsidiary in 2012, what is the total amount of taxes paid by Fluor in both Brazil and the United States on its profit of $112 million?
   b. How does repatriation of 100% of profit earned in Brazil in the form of dividends change Fluor's global tax bill?
   c. Assuming that Fluor operated in Brazil as a branch rather than a wholly owned subsidiary, how would its global tax bill be different?

3. **Taxation of foreign source income (B).** Referring to problem 2, consider the case of Fluor's wholly owned subsidiary in Ireland, which is taxed at the corporate income tax rate of 12.5%. Fluor-Ireland earned $27 million in 2012.
   a. How much in taxes is Fluor-USA liable for on its earnings generated by Fluor-Ireland?
   b. Assuming that Fluor decides to repatriate 100% of profits earned in Ireland, would Fluor's global tax bill change?
   c. Assuming that both Fluor-Brazil and Fluor-USA decide to repatriate 100% of their profits to their US parent, what would be Fluor's global tax bill?

4. **Transfer pricing and tax avoidance.** Electrolux — the Swedish multinational manufacturer of household appliances and white goods (refrigerators and washing machines) — manufactures compressors in Kiev (Ukraine) for assembly and distribution the Poland. Corporate income tax rates are, respectively, 30 and 50% in Ukraine and Poland. Make reference to income statements of both affiliates (Exhibit 24.8) in answering the following:
   a. Show how a manipulation of the transfer price between the Ukrainian subsidiary and its Polish sister subsidiary can reduce Electrolux's consolidated taxes. Assume that the Polish subsidiary's cost of goods sold is entirely accounted for by the compressor imports from Ukraine.
   b. The European Union applies a 20% ad valorem tax on manufactured goods from Ukraine. Explain how this tax helps or hinders income shifting between the sister subsidiaries.

Exhibit 24.8. Electrolux's income statements.

	Electrolux-Ukraine (30%)	Electrolux-Poland (50%)	Electrolux Consolidated
Revenue	300	440	440
Less: Cost of goods sold	200	300	200
Gross profit	100	140	240
Less: Operating expenses	20	20	40
Income before taxes	80	120	200
Less: Taxes	24	60	84
Net income	56	60	116

c. Intracorporate trade is conducted on 90-day credit terms. Electrolux-Ukraine expects the zloty to appreciate in the next three to six months; in which currency would you recommend that the exports shipment to Poland be denominated? Should Electrolux-Poland lead or lag its payment? Should Electrolux-Ukraine lead or lag collection?

INTERNET EXERCISES

5. **Transfer Pricing and Tax Evasion.** Access accounting firms websites such as www.pwc.com and www.kpmg.com to research the current status of The European Union combat against tax evasion by Google, Apple, Facebook and Amazon.

REFERENCES

Bartelsman, Eric J., and Roel Beetsman. 2003. "Why Pay More? Corporate Tax Avoidance through Transfer Pricing in OECD Countries." *Journal of Public Economics* 87, 2225–2252.

Clausing, Kimberly A. 2003. "Tax-Motivated Transfer Pricing and US Intrafirm Trade Prices." *Journal of Public Economics* 87, 2207–2223.

Lessard, Donald R. 1979. "Transfer Prices, Taxes and Financial Markets Implications of International Financial Transfers within the Multinational Firm." In *The Economic Effects of Multinational Corporations*, edited by Robert G. Hawkins. Greenwich, CT: JAI Press.

Robbins, Sydney M., and Robert B. Stobaugh. 1973. *Money in the Multinational Enterprise.* New York: Basic Books.

25

International Control Conundrum

Forewarned, forearmed; to be prepared is half the victory.
— Cervantes

You can't manage what you can't measure.
— William Hewlett

As the comptroller of the French multinational BIC S.A. — known for its stationery products, shavers, and lighters — Jean de la Fontaine was perplexed by the performance of BIC's Thai subsidiary. The past three years had delivered declining returns on equity (ROE), now standing at 7.8% when the aggregate ROE for the group hovered around 12.5%, and yet a steadily appreciating Thai baht had allowed the Thai subsidiary to remit an increasing stream of dividends to its French parent. Profit margins — now at barely 1% when BIC averaged 2.5% worldwide — had been especially battered by increasing imports competition from China, and BIC-Thailand had missed its sales budget two years in a row. Was BIC applying the right metrics for evaluating its foreign operations?

This chapter develops a framework for evaluating the performance of a multinational corporation's (MNC's) foreign subsidiaries. Translating a company's diverse and far-flung set of activities into a set of objective numbers is crucial for assessing performance and planning future actions. Designing effective management control systems for domestic firms is fraught with problems of information asymmetry and goal incongruence between corporate parent and subsidiary units. In an international setting, the problems are further complicated by exchange rate fluctuations between the foreign subsidiary's local currency and the parent firm's reference currency. To be reliable, management control systems for MNCs must somehow incorporate a multiplicity of contextual factors that are somewhat tied to the local environments in which they operate, such as exchange rate fluctuations, price controls, differential rates of inflation, segmented capital markets, and foreign exchange controls.

After reading this chapter you will understand:

- How planning, budgeting, and control systems are used by MNCs.
- What an economic value added (EVA)–based performance measurement system is.
- How to incorporate exchange rates into the budgeting and control process by mapping the *currency space* predicated on the concepts of exchange rate and inflation pass-through.
- How to develop a *contingent* budgeting and control model based on EVA as the sole performance numéraire.

A PRIMER ON MANAGERIAL CONTROL

As part of the *planning* process, MNCs set a basic strategy, select a course of action with supportive pro forma financial statements for associated financial goals, and prepare various *budgets* to achieve those goals. *Control* is the process by which management ensures that the plan is actually executed and is appropriately modified as circumstances change; as such, it increases the likelihood that all units of the firm are working together to achieve the goals set at the planning stage. A good budgeting system thus supports both planning and control, and planning without an effective control system is a recipe for disaster.

Ultimately budgets must define financial goals that can serve as *benchmarks* for evaluating the subsequent performance of the firm. Indeed, failure to meet such financial goals should trigger careful scrutiny of each subsidiary or business unit before the course can be corrected and the firm's strategic path redirected. Thus, the control process is at the core of any successful implementation of the firm's strategic plans. Traditionally, firms rely on two sets of tools for control purposes — a panoply of rates of return and budgetary variance analysis.

Rate(s) of return

If indeed the notion of a rate of return would seem a natural yardstick for measuring performance, it begs the question "Rate of return on what?" The simplest gauges of performance are *rate of return on sales* or *profit margin* (PM), *return on assets* (ROA), and *return on equity* (ROE). By far the most widely used and popular yardstick is the rate of return on equity, which is simply defined as:

$$ROE = \frac{\text{Net income}}{\text{Shareholders' equity}}$$

ROE measures the dollar amount of net income (accounting profits) generated by each dollar of equity capital contributed by the owners/shareholders of the firm. As such, it is a good gauge of the efficiency with which a firm employs shareholders' capital. It is often rewritten as:

$$ROE = \frac{\text{Net income}}{\text{Sales}} \times \frac{\text{Sales}}{\text{Assets}} \times \frac{\text{Assets}}{\text{Shareholders' equity}}$$

where each component is an important ratio in its own right:

$$ROE = \text{Profit margin} \times \text{Asset turnover} \times \text{Financial leverage}$$

Since:

$$ROA = \text{Profit margin} \times \text{Asset turnover}$$

then:

$$ROE = ROA \times \text{Financial leverage}$$

The reader will note that *profit margin = bottom-line profit/top-line sales* is a summary gauge of the firm's income statement. Similarly, *asset turnover = sales/assets* shows how the firm manages the asset side of its balance sheet by indicating the amount of assets necessary to support the level of sales. Finally, *financial leverage = assets/equity = (debt + equity)/equity* summarizes the liability side of the balance sheet by showing the proportion of total assets financed by equity. As an illustration, the multinational BIC S.A. reported the following results for France (domicile of the parent company), Thailand, and the worldwide group. Clearly, BIC-Thailand was a laggard in the group.

Metric	BIC-France (%)	BIC-International (%)	BIC-Thailand (%)
Profit margin	4.0	6.0	1.0
Return on assets	9.0	10.7	4.0
Return on equity	11.0	12.5	7.8

Budgeting and variance analysis

Simply put, budgetary variance analysis is based on the comparison of actual performance, whether it be measured by sales, operating expenses, or accounting income as recorded *ex post* (once the budgetary cycle is completed), and the corresponding budgeted amount as forecast *ex ante* (at the outset of the budgetary cycle). Differences between actual and budgeted amounts are then explained in terms of price and/or volume variance, which can in turn be traced to *environmental* variables that are generally *noncontrollable* by the reporting subsidiary's managers. Noncontrollable environmental variables could include a nationwide strike, flooding, imposition of price controls, and so on.

Clearly, operating managers should be held responsible only for budgetary variances that are deemed to have resulted from variables over which they do have control. Thus, any difference between projected and actual results is traced to changes in factors deemed either *exogenous* or *endogenous* to the business unit management. Management, however, is held responsible only for budgetary variances resulting from endogenous factors. BIC-Thailand had missed its sales budget by 2% in 2010 and 3.5% in 2011, claiming that Chinese imports — buoyed by the appreciating Thai baht — were able to underprice BIC's lighters and shaving products manufactured in Thailand. Should BIC-Thailand be held to the same standards as other sister subsidiaries, or should allowance be made for the special circumstances under which it was competing?

Exhibit 25.1A. Calculating EVA

Economic value added = Net sales
– Operating expenses, including depreciation (including taxes but excluding interest expense)
= Net operating profit after depreciation – Capital charges for both debt and equity employed
= Economic value added

EVA-based performance numéraire

The preceding metrics are primarily rooted in accounting profits but can be adapted to cash-flow-derived measures of value creation. Economic value added (EVA) measures the net operating results after taxes less a charge for the capital employed to generate those profits. Positive EVA indicates that value has been created for the firm's shareholders; negative EVA signifies value destruction. It is consistent with free cash-flow measures and can be readily used in capital budgeting as well as for performance measurement and control purposes.

Unlike similar conventional accounting measures of profit derived from an individual firm's income statement, EVA first takes into account the cost of *all* capital — that is, not only the cost of debt capital (readily visible as interest expense in the income statement), but also the cost of equity capital. Second, EVA is not constrained by generally accepted accounting principles (GAAP), thereby allowing managers to capitalize research and development (R&D), marketing, training, and related costs into the asset base that has been committed to the profit-generating project.[1] In its most elementary formulation, EVA is calculated as in Exhibit 25.1A.

Capital charges are equal to the firm's capital employed, multiplied by the weighted average cost of capital (WACC). The WACC equals the sum of the cost of each of the components of capital — both short- or long-term debt and shareholders' equity — weighted for their relative proportions in the firm's target capital structure. Thus, in its unadjusted form, EVA is equivalent to net operating profit after tax (NOPAT) minus the cost of debt and equity capital used to generate that income. The income (or loss) left represents the absolute value created (or destroyed) for shareholders of the firm.

Some clarification of EVA accounting methodology provides additional insight on how this performance measure compares with others commonly used. First, EVA accounting capital is the sum of all of the firm's financing, apart from non-interest-bearing operating liabilities, such as accounts payable, accrued wages, and accrued taxes. That is, invested capital equals the sum of shareholders' equity and all interest-bearing debt, both short-term and long-term maturities. Second, EVA accounting commonly leads to certain adjustments to net operating profit after tax (NOPAT) and capital-cost components. EVA proponents have identified over 160 possible adjustments for managers to consider implementing. From a practical standpoint, however, only eight adjustments are commonly implemented when shifting from GAAP to EVA accounting approaches, listed in Exhibit 25.1B.

EVA proponents argue that these accounting adjustments reduce most of the distortions in managerial incentives introduced by GAAP accounting and align performance measurement more closely with value creation. Other mechanisms such as EVA-based stock option plans used in conjunction with EVA accounting also act to curb managerial gaming with performance measures. Together, these EVA accounting standards and supplementary incentives schemes play a part both in *ex ante* budgetary negotiations between senior and midlevel managers and in the *ex post* review of their performance. Variance metrics for BIC-Thailand (except for the cost budget) confirm the underperformance unveiled by previous profit margin and ROE:

	BIC-France (%)	BIC-International (%)	BIC-Thailand (%)
Variance from sales budget	1.0	0.50	−3.0
Variance from cost budget	0.5	−1.00	−2.0
Variance from EVA	−1.5	−0.75	−3.5

1 R&D and marketing expenses are traditionally expenses when incurred in the income statement. By capitalizing these expenses first and then amortizing them over their economic lives, EVA provides a more realistic picture of actual performance.

Exhibit 25.1B. Examples of typical EVA Accounting adjustments to GAAP

Accounting Area	GAAP Treatment	Nature of EVA Adjustment
Marketing and R&D costs	Expense	Record as asset and amortize
Deferred taxes	Record as asset and/or liability	Reverse recording of asset and/or liability to reflect cash-basis reporting
Purchased goodwill	Record as asset: Amortize over up to 40 years	Reverse amortization to reflect original asset amount
Operating leases	Expense	Record asset and amortize; record liability and related interest
Bad debts and warranty costs	Estimate accruals	Reverse accruals to reflect cash-basis reporting
Last in, first out (LIFO) inventory costing	LIFO permitted	Convert to first in, first out (FIFO)
Construction in progress	Record as asset	Remove from assets
Discontinued operations	Include in assets and earnings	Remove from assets and earnings

THE INTERNATIONAL CONTROL CONUNDRUM

Senior managements of most multinationals routinely claim that, "The performance of our foreign subsidiaries is judged on precisely the same metrics as our domestic operations" — namely, *rate(s) of return* and *variance analysis of budgets*, which are admittedly the mainstays of the control process. Indeed, both domestic corporations and MNCs face problems of *goal incongruence* and *information asymmetry* between the corporate parent (or principal) and its foreign subsidiaries (agents). The problem of goal incongruence assumes that the corporate *principal* and its individual business unit *agents* are self-interested utility maximizers, but with different risk preferences and therefore different organizational strategies and performances. For example, corporate-wide goals emphasizing high returns on sales or investments may be inconsistent with the goals of individual business units operating in new product markets that may seek to maximize sales revenue.

If substantial, such differences may induce inconsistent product pricing, capital investment, and personnel compensation schemes to the detriment of corporate-wide performance. Reduction of the agency problem typically comes from the corporate parent, either by incurring monitoring costs to see that business units follow less preferable corporate policies, or by incurring design costs to set up incentives that make it preferable for business units to follow corporate policies.

The international control conundrum with foreign exchange risk

Complicating the design of international control systems is the exchange rate variable used for translating local currency budgets into reference currency terms. For the purposes of this chapter, it is convenient to distinguish among three budgetary systems used with varying degrees of success by MNCs, depending on whether the currency framework favors the point of view of the parent company (*ethnocentric*), the subsidiary (*polycentric*), or some compromise combination (*geocentric*).

Ethnocentric perspective: Firms favoring a reference currency perspective argue that the parent company is accustomed to thinking in terms of its own currency rather than in terms of the local currency of its subsidiary. This indeed facilitates comparison of financial performance among different subsidiaries. Technically, exchange rates enter the budgeting control process at two levels: in *drafting* the operating budget and in measuring or *tracking* results. Accordingly, an ethnocentric control system arbitrarily uses the initial spot exchange rate in setting up the operating budget and the ending exchange rate to measure the performance by tracking. Clearly, under such circumstances, local managers will bear the full responsibility for exchange rate changes during the period and, as a consequence, may be expected to behave in an overly risk-averse manner. A potentially harmful consequence of such a system may be the padding

INTERNATIONAL CORPORATE FINANCE IN PRACTICE 25.1

Levi's

Levi Strauss & Company (Levi's) compares in US dollar terms its foreign operations' actual performance against planned performance using the initial exchange rate. Actual performance is restated using the initial exchange rate so that the impact of exchange rate changes is removed from the performance evaluation process.

Furthermore, in order to give its operating managers a greater incentive to bring about the implementation of the strategic plan, Levi's offers them a bonus package made up of (1) an annual cash incentive tied to short-term goals and (2) a three-year incentive scheme tied to longer-term goals. Worth emphasizing is that short-term evaluation focuses on annual earnings and return on investment (traditional *ex post* accounting information), whereas long-term performance reward is tied to shareholder value as measured by Levi's stock price (a cash-flow-based concept).

Reconciling the performance of managers and units led Levi's to split managers' bonus package: Two-thirds is based on the performance of the unit as measured by accounting data, whereas one-third is tied to a standard employee-appraisal system that includes ratings for individual objectives such as staff development, market share, and so on.

of budgets,[2] as well as decentralized hedging by local managers eager to reduce their perceived exposure to exchange rate risk (which is generally suboptimal from the parent MNC's point of view).

Polycentric perspective: Other MNCs, by contrast, take the view that because foreign transactions are carried out in a foreign environment and are effected in the foreign currency, a local currency perspective ought to prevail. When performance evaluation is based strictly on local currency, foreign currency translation gains and losses[3] that result from fluctuating exchange rates are generally dissociated from the subsidiary's performance, thereby transferring the responsibility of foreign-exchange risk management to the treasury at headquarters. Specifically, initial spot exchange rates are used both to set budgets and to track performance, thus removing incentives for local managers to incorporate anticipated exchange rates into operating decisions or to react swiftly to unanticipated exchange rate changes during the life of the budget. (See International Corporate Finance in Practice 25.1.)

Geocentric perspective: In a seminal paper, Lessard and Lorange (1977) recommended that projected exchange rates be incorporated into both the budgeting and the tracking processes. This approach allows the subsidiary to negotiate an *internal forward rate*[4] with its parent that best reflects its anticipation of exchange rate changes. Such internal forward rates are expected to foster goal congruence between home-country parent and foreign subsidiaries as well as fairness for operating managers, since they will receive neither blame nor credit for variances in performance attributed to exchange rate surprises. Local management is shielded from unforeseen exchange rate changes, since the parent company acts as a banker, literally buying the foreign currency–denominated budget of its subsidiary at a prespecified forward rate.

However, the management of the foreign subsidiary is still held responsible for forecasting errors and is thus motivated to adjust managerial decisions to contingencies as they arise during the budget year. Lessard and Sharp (1984) developed a contingent budgeting method for the MNC, which features multiple scenario development, review for possible surprise deviations in existing exchange rates, and implied adjustments to costs and operating cash

2 By deflating sales/inflating costs or overstating currency depreciation — so-called budget padding — managers hope to improve their performance and reduce budgetary variance.

3 Translation exposure measurement and hedging are discussed in Chapter 17.

4 Internal forward rates could simply be market-based prices and — when not available — derived from interest rate parity. Managers may prefer to forecast the future exchange rate (see Chapter 15) or negotiate an ad hoc price having less to do with objective forward/forecasted rates.

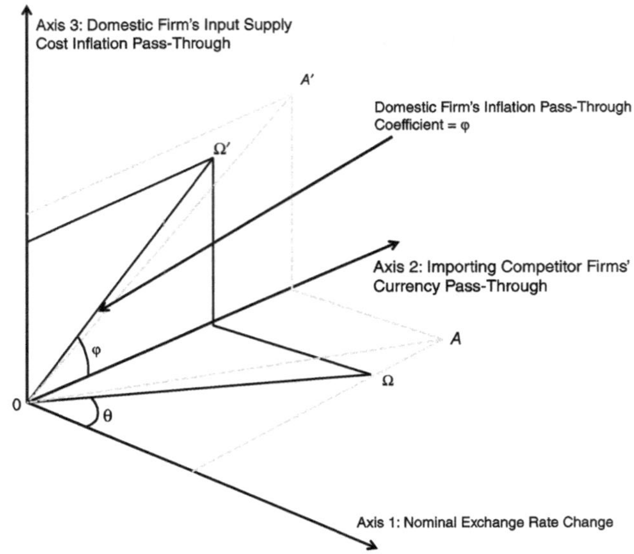

Note:
If θ = 1, the domestic firm's importing competitors pass through fully the exchange rate change; see parity line 0*A*.
If φ = 1, the domestic firm is able fully to pass through input supply cost inflation into output prices; see parity line 0*A*′.

Exhibit 25.2. Mapping the Currency Space in Product Markets

flows related to such surprises. Multiple scenarios, however, may still miss the mark if actual operating conditions differ from discrete scenarios formulated *ex ante*; budgetary variance analysis flounders when actual conditions "fall between the cracks" of these discrete scenarios. An improvement to this approach would be to establish an objective, continuous link between any surprises that may arise in actual operations and managerial response that optimizes the subsidiary's performance based, for example, on EVA-measured performance.

Currency space mapping

Contingent budgeting based on an EVA framework rests largely on management's ability to chart alternative scenarios, which adequately schematize future market conditions for the MNC's foreign subsidiaries. While alternative scenario methodologies are not new to strategic management, they do not take into account exchange-related factors. Factoring in such factors is central to accurately assessing the performance of foreign subsidiaries that may be experiencing exchange rate–induced economic turbulence such as imports competition. Importantly, it allows the MNC parent to lift the veil of exchange rate volatility to better focus on true operational performance. In order to reduce the *information asymmetry*, we introduce a three-dimensional mapping paradigm that facilitates the *joint multiple scenario* design by the MNC parent and its subsidiary to anchor the exchange rate–inflation relationship to the firm's product market micro-operating environment.

The foreign subsidiary's currency space map builds on the purchasing power parity (PPP) theory, which holds that changes in the exchange rate linking two countries' currencies may be explained by their underlying differential in inflation rates (see Chapter 7 for a discussion of PPP). If, for example, in 2024, Venezuela were to experience inflation at the annual rate of 45% whereas the US inflation rate were limited to 5%, according to PPP, the Venezuelan bolivar would depreciate against the US dollar by 0.45 – 0.05 = 0.40. In practice, PPP is a useful gauge of real currency values over the long term, but it is seldom a reliable predictor of nominal exchange rates in the short term. For emerging economies, nominal exchange rates are often overvalued in PPP terms before experiencing traumatic adjustments, as with the Mexican peso devaluation of 1994, the Thai baht devaluation of 1997, the Brazilian real in 1999, the Turkish lira in 2001, the Argentine peso in 2002, and the Burmese kyat in 2012.

This PPP-based perspective on exchange rate change is formalized in the currency space map depicted in Exhibit 25.2. *Axis 1* scales the *actual* economy-wide percentage of nominal exchange rate appreciation or depreciation experienced over time. If $S(0)$ and $S(t)$ denote the local currency i price of one unit of reference currency[5] at times 0 and t, respectively, then the index Δ of exchange appreciation ($\Delta < 0$) or depreciation ($\Delta > 0$) is given by:

$$\Delta = \frac{S(t) - S(0)}{S(0)} \tag{25.1}$$

Axis 2 measures the effective nominal exchange rate appreciation or depreciation *experienced* by the MNC's foreign subsidiary in pricing sales over this same time period. In effect, it captures what an economy-wide exchange appreciation or depreciation really means for the firm's sales revenue. For example, this foreign subsidiary may face rival importers that pass through on average only $\theta\% < 100\%$ of any economy-wide nominal exchange rate change, Δ. The pass-through coefficient is defined as:

$$\theta = \left(\Delta \cdot \ slope\overline{0\Omega}\right) \tag{25.2}$$

Thus, an exchange rate pass-through coefficient is simply measured by the slope of line $\overline{0\Omega}$ relative to Axis 1 in the two-dimensional space formed by Axes 1 and 2. Line $\overline{0\Omega}$ depicts a full pass-through of the nominal exchange rate change when it lies at $\theta = 45°$ angle relative to Axis 1, shown as line $\overline{0A}$.

If the firm operates in an autarkic economy, its inflation pass-through would be directly constrained by either governmental policies or industry-specific sectoral price rigidities. In most countries, however, international trade looms large on the national scene. Thus foreign-based competition, depending on how well established it is, will generally play a critical role in constricting sectoral domestic inflation, simply because consumers faced with a choice between a domestically produced product and a cheaper imported substitute tend to purchase the latter. In effect, local manufacturers will avoid losing market share by matching their pricing with the prices of imports. Specifically, for the MNC's subsidiary, whose output price increases are constrained by an import competitor's exchange rate pass-through policy θ and whose input i experiences price inflation at the rate of Π_i, the inflation pass-through coefficient would be defined as:

$$\varphi = \frac{\sum_{i=1}^{N} w_i \times \Pi_i}{\theta \times \left[S(t) - S(0)\right] / S(0)} \tag{25.3}$$

where w_i is the percentage of supply costs sourced from sector i with $\sum w_i = 1$.

In a fluid economy, where increased cash-flow costs can be fully passed through into the output selling price, the pass-through coefficient φ would be equal to 1. As explicit or implicit industry-specific sectoral price controls constrict the foreign subsidiary's discretion to pass through higher costs into higher prices, its overall pass-through coefficient may, at times, be considerably larger than 1.

The third axis of Exhibit 25.2 measures the percentage change in input costs, which is the numerator of equation (25.3). The foreign subsidiary pass-through coefficient is, therefore, depicted by the slope j in the two-dimensional space formed by Axes 2 and 3. If $\varphi > 1$, then the foreign subsidiary can pass through fully its increase in input costs into higher output prices, thereby generating excess returns. Conversely, if $\varphi > 1$, then the foreign subsidiary fails to pass through input costs into adequately higher output prices and it will consequently suffer negative operating margins. Input costs depend chiefly on the mix of domestic versus foreign sourcing options available to the foreign subsidiary. If currencies are properly valued and if the foreign subsidiary's competitors fully pass through exchange rate changes, then the operations of the foreign subsidiary will rest on the 45° parity line $\overline{0A'}$. Windfall gains will be generated when the foreign subsidiary operates below the $\overline{0A'}$ boundary parity line.

> ***Q:*** In 2024, BIC-Thailand is forecasting 12.5% inflation for all inputs procured domestically. During that same period the THB is expected to depreciate by $\Delta = 10\%$ while competing imports from China are expected to pass through only 50% of the THB depreciation in pricing their products in Thailand — that is, increasing their THB prices by $0.50 \times (0.10) = 5\%$. Position BIC-Thailand in the currency space.
>
> ***A:*** On axis 1, Thailand is positioned at −10%; on axis 2, BIC-Thailand is positioned at $(0.50) \times (0.10) = 5\%$. On axis 3, BIC-Thailand is facing 12.5% cost inflation. In sum, BIC-Thailand experiences a pass-through coefficient of j = 0.125/0.05 = 2.5. BIC-Thailand can pass through only 0.05/0.125 = 40% of its costs' increase if it wants to maintain market share. Its profit margin will be severely squeezed.

5 The reference currency is the parent MNC's currency, whereas local currency is the subsidiary's currency.

EVA-BASED CONTINGENT BUDGETING AND PERFORMANCE ASSESSMENT

Working through all three dimensions of the currency space map forces the MNC parent and the managers of its foreign subsidiary to be explicit about the key variables shaping the near-term environment of the foreign subsidiary. This helps mitigate agency problems in the MNC and enhances goal congruence. Instead of relying on an *ex ante* budget forecast and *ex post* budget variance analysis, the MNC parent assesses the subsidiary's ability to deliver optimal managerial responses contingent on a particular scenario as schematized in terms of exchange rate, inflation, and currency pass-through rates.

Modeling optimal managerial performance

Parent and subsidiary will start off by charting multiple scenarios and then work out what, under each scenario, should be the foreign subsidiary's optimal managerial response. When exchange rates, inflation, and all the other dimensions of the host country environment materialize, management will revisit the discrete scenarios as sketched *ex ante* and ascertain what should have been the subsidiary's optimal EVA-based performance. Variance analysis can then be carried out against a contingent EVA budget in terms of what had been initially agreed between parent and subsidiary management and what actually occurred.

In practice, the multiple scenario analysis advocated here is often difficult to implement when the actual (*ex post*) scenario turns out to be different from the *ex ante* multiple but discrete scenarios sketched at the outset of the budgeting cycle. This points to the need to formalize the relationship between the currency space map — from which the actual scenario is drawn — and the optimal managerial response. Here, microeconomics can help by providing an objective (profit) function tailored to the idiosyncrasies of the firm and directly linked to the concept of economic exposure to exchange risk. This approach — to the extent that it emphasizes EVA rather than mere accounting profits — is consistent with value-based strategic management. *Ex ante*, parent and subsidiary management will agree on an EVA model, which spells out what the optimal local management response should be under alternative scenarios. The objective is to substitute for an elaborate forecasting exercise, which may be purely speculative in nature, an understanding of what the subsidiary management's optimal response should be to alternative scenarios.

Consider again the case of the BIC-Thailand (subsidiary) and BIC S.A., its French parent. We develop for illustrative purposes an optimal managerial response model for this firm using EVA-based performance measures. Assume that the subsidiary is facing strong competition from China-based imports in its Thai market. Assume further that its production function is characterized by *increasing returns to scale* captured through the percentage reduction in average cost for each additional unit sold. Finally, assume that it sources all of its inputs domestically with the option of switching to foreign-sourced inputs.

The cash-flow operating revenue generated over period $(0,t)$ by the foreign subsidiary is influenced by the pricing policy implemented by Chinese import competitors. It is also assumed that Chinese imports reflect a pass-through rate $\theta(t)$ for an exchange rate change $\Delta S(t)$ with the local price and income elasticity of demand at $\in$ and at η. Therefore, the quantity sold $q(t)$ by the foreign subsidiary reflects demand response to both a change in price $\theta(t) \times \Delta S(t)$ and how much demand (as measured by income elasticity η) responds to a change in national income ΔY:

$$q(t)=q(0)\times\left[1+\in\times\theta(t)\times\Delta S(t)\right]\times\left[1+\eta\times\Delta Y\right] \tag{25.4}$$

where $q(0)$ is the amount produced in the base period while discretionary pricing will reflect a change from $p(0)$ to $p(t)$ defined as:

$$p(t)=p(0)\times\left[1+\vec{\theta}(t)\times\Delta S(t)\right] \tag{25.5}$$

where the firm's discretionary pass-through policy $\vec{\theta}(t)$ may differ from import competitors' pass-through policy $\theta(t)$. The cash-flow operating revenue generated at time t is then simply $p(t) \times q(t)$.

The total percentage decrease or increase in average operating cost is simply the per unit percentage decrease or increase in average cost, multiplied by the number of additional units sold. Thus, average operating cost over the period $(0,t)$ is given as:

$$c(t)=\sum_{i=1}^{N}c_i(0)\times\left[1-\delta\times\Delta q(t)\right] \times\left[1+\lambda\times w_i\times\Delta\Pi_i+(1-\lambda)\times\Theta\Delta S(t)\right] \tag{25.6}$$

where δ is the scale elasticity coefficient and $\Delta q(t)$ the change in quantity produced. Furthermore, the base operating cost $c_i(0)$ should be adjusted by the inflation pass-through coefficient for λ percent of locally sourced inputs and for the pass-through policy Θ of foreign suppliers as applicable to (1 – λ) of imported inputs.

Cost of capital employed: The debt component

In addition to operating costs, we need to take into account a charge for capital employed at a rate that compensates relevant debt and equity investors. This rate of compensation is embodied in the firm's WACC. The WACC, however, requires adjustment to reflect two factors: (1) the mix of domestic debt (d) and foreign-denominated debt (F) at the respective rates of k_D^d and k_D^F, and (2) the degree of capital market segmentation between the parent's home capital market and its foreign subsidiary's host capital market.

Assuming that α percent of debt is sourced domestically, then the blended cost of debt, k_D, is defined as:

$$k_D = \alpha \times k_D^d + (1-\alpha) \times k_D^F \qquad (25.7)$$

Caution should be exercised, however, in computing the cost of foreign-sourced debt, k_D^F, since the nominal cost of foreign debt, k_D^{F*}, seldom approximates the effective cost of financing when exchange gains or losses are recognized. Accordingly, we formulate the cost of foreign-sourced debt as:

$$k_D^F = k_D^{F*} + \left(1 + k_D^{F*}\right) \times \frac{F(t)^* - S(0)}{S(0)} \qquad (25.8)$$

where the effective cost of debt is expressed as the sum of the nominal cost of debt adjusted by the cost of a forward cover that is the percentage exchange gains or losses approximated by the forward (no-profit) exchange rate $F(t)^*$.[6]

This last adjustment is critical for many emerging-country capital markets that may maintain exchange rates at overvalued levels, thereby disguising the true cost of debt financing. Failure to correct such distortions would result in reporting an inflated performance, thereby misrepresenting the value that is actually being created by the foreign subsidiary.

> ***Q:*** BIC-Thailand borrowed on January 1, 1997, through a 2-year note at a yearly interest rate of 5% in the amount of \$10 million from Singapore-based Standard Chartered Bank. It could have borrowed the same amount in THB at 12%. The Thai currency has been pegged to the US dollar at THB 25 = \$1 since 1984. BIC-Thailand showed return on equity of 8% in 1997 (net equity was \$25 million at the outset of 1997) before plunging to –10% in 1998 as a result of the THB devaluation to THB 50 = \$1. What should have been the debt financing charge in computing EVA for 1997 and 1998?
>
> ***A:*** BIC-Thailand should have reported an interest charge of 5% × \$10 million + 7% × \$10 million both years. Five percent accounts for the nominal interest charge and 12% – 5% = 7% accounts for the forward premium to hedge against a THB devaluation. As a result, BIC-Thailand would have shown a lower and more realistic ROE in 1997 but a higher (and also more realistic) ROE in 1998 as a hedge against the THB depreciation would have smoothed its performance over that time period.

Cost of capital employed: The equity component

Several factors are considered in accounting for discrepancies in the business risk and financial risk between the foreign subsidiary and its parent. Applying the capital asset pricing model (CAPM), we obtain the following cost of equity, k_E, for the foreign subsidiary[7]:

$$k_E = r_{\text{free}} + \beta^k_{\text{market risk}} \times \frac{\sigma_{\text{market } k \text{ index}}}{\sigma_{\text{U.S. market index}}} \times \text{U.S. equity risk premium} + \beta^k_{\text{country risk}} \times \text{Sovereign yield spread} \qquad (25.9)$$

- r_{free} estimates the long-term risk-free rate.
- The beta for the foreign subsidiary with respect to the MNC parent's benchmark portfolio, $\beta^k_{\text{market risk}}$, is estimated by computing the beta of the foreign subsidiary relative to a local market portfolio, $\beta_{\text{local firm}}$, and then multiplying the result by the foreign country beta $\beta_{\text{country } k}$. This is a reasonable approach to computing the foreign subsidiary's

6 The no-profit forward rate is, in the absence of actively traded forward contracts, derived from the interest rate parity theorem (see Chapter 6).

7 See Chapter 20 for further discussion of country risk adjustment for the cost of equity capital.

relevant cost of equity capital if the foreign subsidiary is previously geared to its local market.

- Equity risk premium for country $k = \frac{\sigma_{\text{market } k \text{ index}}}{\sigma_{\text{U.S. market index}}} \times$ US equity risk premium whereby we adjust the referent market equity risk premium[8] by using the standard deviation ratio $\frac{\sigma_{\text{market } k \text{ index}}}{\sigma_{\text{U.S. market index}}}$ as a conventional measure of stock price volatility.
- $\beta^k_{\text{country risk}} \times$ Sovereign yield spread is a measure of country risk. Country risk is traditionally measured as the yield spread between the emerging market's sovereign bonds and the US Treasury bonds of similar maturities (a 10-year horizon is often used). Of some importance is the question as to whether all firms are equally exposed to country risk and — if not — what is the appropriate exposure index to use in adjusting the country risk premium. Thus, what is proposed is to gauge the degree of exposure to the country risk by measuring the relationship between a firm's returns and country risk premium — in the same spirit as the concept of a beta coefficient for market exposure. By regressing the firm's returns against the returns of sovereign bonds, the coefficient will provide such a firm's specific measure of country risk exposure if one accepts the notion that sovereign bond price fluctuations mark to market the country risk premium.

Weighted average cost of capital employed

The total capital cost, $f(t)$, to be charged against free cash flows can now be formulated as

$$f(t) = k_D \times \frac{D}{D+E} \times (1-T) + k_E \times \frac{E}{D+E} \qquad (25.10)$$

where D and E are the adjusted market value of debt and equity financing, respectively, and where k_D and k_E are the effective cost of debt and equity financing adjusted for capital market segmentation, as given earlier in equations (25.7) and (25.9).

Measuring EVA-based performance

With terms capturing cash-flow revenues, operating costs, and capital costs characterizing the foreign subsidiary's situation, we can now formulate the EVA-based performance as:

$$EVA(t) = \{[p(t) - c(t)] \times q(t) - d(t)\} (1-T) + d(t) - f(t) \qquad (25.11)$$

where $d(t)$ is tax-deductible accounting depreciation at the corporate tax rate T.[9] Since $d(t)$ is a non-cash-flow charge, it is added back to the after-tax income to derive EVA, which is a cash-flow gauge of the foreign subsidiary's performance. If the decision variables at the discretion of the local management are limited to pricing at $\vec{\theta}$, a sourcing mix of $\vec{\lambda}$, and a financing mix of $\vec{\alpha}$, then optimal management performance is defined by taking the derivative of the EVA function with respect to these variables:

$$\frac{\partial EVA(t)}{\partial \theta} = 0, \quad \frac{\partial EVA}{\partial \lambda} = 0 \text{ and } \frac{\partial EVA(t)}{\partial \alpha} = 0 \qquad (25.12\text{a–c})$$

subject to a probabilistic constraint of:

$$\text{Prob}\{(1-\omega) \times e(t) \times [\tilde{S}(t) - S(0)] \leq L\} \geq P$$

Translation losses as a constraint

Here, the constraint placed on the optimization exercise simply reflects the MNC parent's tolerance for translation losses resulting from holding a pro forma translation exposure, $e(t)$.[10] It is formulated as the probability statement that by hedging ω percent of the pro forma translation exposure $e(t)$ — or retaining $(1 - \omega)$ percent unhedged — the translation loss should not exceed a dollar amount L, arbitrarily set by management with a probability of P reflecting the firm's level of risk aversion. This stochastic constraint placed on optimizing the subsidiary's cash-flow performance accounts for the fact that at the outset of the operating cycle, translation losses are not known

8 Orthodox finance theory would resist this double adjustment by the country beta (systematic risk) and the variance ratio (total risk). Note that the country beta will lower the equity risk premium, as segmented emerging markets are low-beta countries whereas the variance ratio is typically greater than 1.

9 In choosing the appropriate corporate tax rate, T, we take the following approach. From the foreign subsidiary's perspective, EVA-based performance is assessed using the foreign subsidiary's local corporate tax rate. From the parent MNC's perspective, EVA-based performance is assessed using the parent's corporate tax rate. Of course, national tax treatment of MNC income differs. A slightly more refined decision rule for the MNC parent, assuming it is US-based, would be to use the MNC parent's corporate tax rate unless it is lower than the foreign subsidiary's local corporate tax rate. In this case, foreign-sourced income pooling principles apply. See Chapter 24 for further elaboration of the tax treatment of foreign source income.

10 Statement No. 52 of the US Financial Accounting Standards Board indicates that translation exposure is the foreign subsidiary's net worth exclusive of asset or liability items denominated in the MNC parent's currency, such as dollar-denominated debt. See Chapter 17 for a discussion of translation exposure management.

with certainty since they are a function of the end-of-period exchange rate $\tilde{S}(t)$.

By removing translation effects from the optimal performance model, we directly link operations by the foreign subsidiary to MNC shareholder value creation or destruction, and thereby enhance goal congruence between MNC parent and foreign subsidiary. Many other decisions undertaken by the foreign subsidiary (e.g., stretching the maturity structure of accounts receivable or sourcing inputs from imports) will similarly influence the translation loss constraint and could also be incorporated into a more sophisticated model of foreign subsidiary value creation or destruction.

This model rests on management's ability to generate a number of informational inputs such as income and price elasticity, currency pass-through, and an adequate rendering of the production function attributes like the degree of increasing returns to scale. There are well-accepted methodologies for deriving estimates for these informational inputs. Once informational inputs have been generated, management may estimate the foreign subsidiary's cash flows as a prelude to developing a quantitative model as illustrated here.

Contingent budgetary variance analysis

Equipped with such an EVA model of its Thai operations, the French MNC is no longer dependent on discrete multiple scenario analysis; it can utilize instead a continuous model for contingent budgetary variance analysis. Sales and production budget proposals will be based on varying estimates of the Thai subsidiary's cost of capital $f(t)$, exchange rate changes $\Delta S(t)$, and corresponding pass-through policy $\theta(t)$ implemented by its China-based competition over the operating cycle $[0,t]$. *Ex post*, it should be relatively easy to compute what should have been the Thai operation's EVA, given the actual exchange rate changes $\Delta S(t)$, a reliable estimate of capital costs $f(t)$, and the imports competition pass-through policy $\theta(t)$, all of which may be derived from examination of sectoral time series using multiple regression techniques. Following equation (24.11), we estimate optimal unit price $p(t)$, unit cost $c(t)$, quantity sold $q(t)$, depreciation $d(t)$, and cost of capital $f(t)$ to derive the economic value added or destroyed over the relevant time period, $EVA(t)$. We provide a summary example of such computations and their interpretation in Appendix 25A.

Once such a model has been set up, the focus of the control process can shift to management's ability to respond optimally to various contingencies. For example, BIC's Thai subsidiary's managers may examine the EVA implications of sourcing more of its shaving systems and lighters inputs from abroad — France or China instead of Thailand — in light of a China-based competitor's expected pass-through of forecasted baht appreciation against the Chinese yuan.

This reduces many control problems in the budgeting process. It nurtures a fruitful dialogue between the MNC parent and its foreign subsidiary by forcing onto paper the architecture of the foreign subsidiary's operations and how it relates to its competitive environment. By freeing the control process from its usual arbitrariness, the model should foster a more congruent system. Furthermore, by routinizing the control process, the MNC may be able to decentralize control without losing coordination among MNC units. The challenge then becomes one of designing an EVA performance model under assumptions that best characterize the nature of the competitive environment and the strategic focus of a given foreign subsidiary. This can be done objectively, especially if the MNC's foreign subsidiary has been doing business for some time in a particular locale; a track record of performance is then readily available. Important informational inputs such as pricing measures, income and price elasticity, and cost responses to various levels of sales may again be estimated through regression analyses of time series.

A similar philosophy may be applied to resolving the thorny issue of allocating unwanted translation gains or losses between MNC parent and foreign subsidiary. A contingent translation budget may be associated with the EVA model we sketched earlier, although some of the linkages between these two models still require further work. For the moment, however, we might briefly explore how the contingent translation budget might work with the EVA model.

Assume that the MNC parent will tolerate some maximum amount of translation losses above which it will then constrain the foreign subsidiary's operating decisions. To put the concept of a contingent translation budget into operation, the foreign subsidiary's pro forma balance sheet would be modeled with each accounting entry formulated as a function of the firm's position in the currency space. The equation is:

$$\text{Translation Budget} = e(t)\times\left[S(t)-S(0)\right] \quad (25.13)$$

where $e(t)$ is the pro forma translation exposure, defined as:

$$e(t)=a(t,\theta,\lambda,\alpha)-l(t,\theta,\lambda,\alpha) \qquad (25.14)$$

and $a(t, \theta, \lambda, \alpha)$ and $l(t, \theta, \lambda, \alpha)$ are pro forma exposed balance sheet items.[11] In fact, operating decisions as embodied in θ, λ, and α will influence the amount of exposed assets and liabilities. It may affect translation gains or losses so substantially as to violate the stochastic constraints in equation (25.12), and thereby bound operating decisions θ, λ, and α. Translation effects, which are often a source of conflict and result in myopic decision making, are removed from the cash-flow model and relegated to simply imposing boundary conditions on the foreign subsidiary's discretionary policies.

SUMMARY

1. In an international setting, problems of goal incongruence and information asymmetry are exacerbated by exchange rate fluctuations between the reporting foreign subsidiary's local currency and the MNC parent's reference currency.
2. A currency-space map is designed to nurture a dialogue between MNC parent and subsidiary, thereby mitigating the information asymmetry problem.
3. This sets the stage for operationalizing an EVA-based contingent budgeting framework. In the context of an MNC parent–foreign subsidiary reporting relationship, the budgeting framework directly aligns operating decisions with shareholder value creation. In the process, it enhances goal congruence not just between a single foreign subsidiary and its MNC parent, but throughout the MNC's network of foreign operations. It also promotes the development of common criteria for evaluation of all foreign and domestic operations by controlling for local exchange, inflation, and competitor pass-through policies, and by measuring performance with a single EVA-based measure.
4. Our framework deals with central issues in budgeting and performance assessment affected by fluctuating exchange rates, yet it is not meant to be an exhaustive treatment of all factors affecting the international control conundrum.
5. Exchange rate translation effects within the MNC may also be a source of conflict between headquarters and subsidiary units and may result in myopic decision making. In our framework, these effects are removed from the cash-flow model and relegated to simply imposing boundary conditions on the foreign subsidiary's discretionary policies. This implies that translation policy is *not* part of the budgeting and performance assessment process.
6. The model can also be extended to incorporate the thorny problem created by the transfer-pricing practices affecting the cost of product inputs imported from sister MNC affiliates. Transfer pricing policies may have a substantial impact on the allocation of operating profits between subsidiary and parent. In a foreign context, the interactive effect of fluctuating exchange rates and poorly conceived and executed transfer pricing policy distorts the budgeting and performance assessment processes and blunts managerial motivation. This way, performance assessment of a foreign subsidiary buying from or selling to MNC affiliates would better reflect the adroit management of factors within rather than outside its control.

QUESTIONS FOR DISCUSSION

1. Identify the metrics used in evaluating a firm's performance.
2. Why is EVA a better metric for gauging performance?
3. What is variance analysis? What role does it play in the control process?
4. Why do exchange rates complicate the performance evaluation of a multinational corporation's foreign operations?
5. What are "internal" forward rates? How are they used in the international control process?
6. What is a currency space map? What role does it play in the international control process?
7. What are "pass-through" coefficients? What do role do they play in the international control process?
8. What is different about an EVA-based contingent budgeting and control system?

11 So-called exposed balance sheet accounts are translated from the local currency into the reference currency by using the current exchange rate $S(t)$ prevailing at time of consolidation.

REFERENCES

Borkowsky, S. 1999. "International Managerial Performance Evaluation: A Five Country Comparison." *Journal of International Business Studies* 30, 533–555.

Ehrbar, A. 1999. "Using EVA to Measure Performance and Assess Strategy." *Strategy & Leadership* 27, 20–24.

Jacque, L. 1995. "Oligopolistic Pricing and Asymmetric Currency Pass-Throughs: Empirical Evidence from Japanese Exports." *Advances in International Banking and Finance*, 6.

Jacque, L. 1996. *Management and Control of Foreign Exchange Risk*. Boston, MA: Kluwer Academic Publishers.

Jacque, L., and P. Lorange. 1984. "The International Conundrum: The Case of 'Hyperinflationary Subsidiary.'" *Journal of International Business Studies* 15, 185–201.

Jacque, Laurent L., and Paul Vaaler. 2001. "The International Control Conundrum with Exchange Risk." *The Journal of International Business Studies* 32.

Lessard, D., and P. Lorange. 1977. "Currency Changes and Management Control: Resolving the Centralization/Decentralization Dilemma." *Accounting Review* (July), 628–637.

Lessard, D., and D. Sharp. 1984. "Measuring the Performance of Operations Subject to Fluctuating Exchange Rates." *Midland Corporate Finance Journal* 2, 18–30.

Miller, K. 1998. "Economic Exposure and Integrated Risk Management." *Strategic Management Journal* 19, 497–514.

O'Donnell, S. 1999. "Compensation Design as a Tool for Implementing Foreign Subsidiary Strategy." *Management International Review* 39, 149–165.

Roth, K., and S. O'Donnell. 1996. "Foreign Subsidiary Compensation Strategy: An Agency Theory Perspective." *Academy of Management Journal* 39, 678–703.

APPENDIX 25A: APPLYING THE EVA-BASED CONTROL SYSTEM

This appendix provides an example of how the EVA-based control framework may be implemented in the course of budgeting negotiations for the coming fiscal year between foreign subsidiary and parent management in an MNC. Consider the following stylized facts as a basis for the illustration.

A Thailand-based foreign subsidiary of a US-based MNC produces automobile components for sale to Thailand-based automobile assemblers. The MNC has subsidiary operations in several industries in several countries. It is May 1997 and the fiscal year for the MNC begins on July 1, 1997 and ends on June 30, 1998.

During negotiations over the budget for the upcoming fiscal year, the foreign subsidiary management team proposes a temporary expansion of its Thailand-based production facilities to accommodate an anticipated short-term increase in demand for automobile components in the coming fiscal year. Given increasing returns to scale in production, the proposal for temporarily increasing production will also drive down unit costs in the face of stiff competition from rivals in Thailand linked to Japan-based MNCs importing similar components. The foreign subsidiary holds a substantial percentage share of the overall market and is interested in retaining its percentage share over the coming fiscal year. Its components are produced from two inputs, both sourced from the US MNC parent. The proposed plant expansion will be completed over one month (June 1997), and expanded production will commence at constant monthly production levels on July 1, 1997, ending on June 30, 1998. Starting July 1, 1998, production will resume at the previous fiscal year's (1996–1997) levels.

Both foreign subsidiary and parent managers will evaluate this project in EVA terms *ex ante* for budgeting purposes in May 1997, and *ex post* for performance evaluation purposes in July 1998. As we summarize these processes, recall the equation (equation (24.11)) used to compute the EVA produced by a given project:

$$EVA(t) = \{[p(t) - c(t)] \times q(t) - d(t)\}(1 - T) + d(t) - f(t) \qquad \text{(25.11, repeated)}$$

Here the time index t spans the 1997–1998 fiscal year. To obtain this EVA estimate, we first make estimates of quantity $q(t)$, average unit pricing $p(t)$, average unit cost $c(t)$, capital costs $f(t)$, tax (T), and depreciation expenses $d(t)$ terms. These pro forma inputs for budget negotiation prior to the commencement of the fiscal year are provided in Exhibit 25A.1. Changes in key model variables and optimal EVA results used in *ex post* performance assessment are provided in Exhibit 25A.2. We conclude the appendix with a discussion of how our variance analysis would be applied to evaluate the subsidiary manager's performance.

Exhibit 25A.1. EVA evaluation of project: *Ex ante* May 1997 budgeting meeting.

Term	Definition	Estimate	Comment
$q(0)$	1996–1997 annual production level	100,000 units	Based on historical production data furnished by subsidiary management
$\Delta Y(t)$	Anticipated change in income in 1997–1998	0.08	Anticipated 8% growth in gross domestic product in Thailand in 1997–1998
η	Anticipated income elasticity of demand	1.25	Anticipated temporary increase in the demand in 1997–1998 for automobile components (and finished automobiles) in Thailand implies positive income elasticity term. Income elasticity term swamps any price elasticity effects (ε), which may be ignored in this example
$q(t)$	Anticipated production level in 1997–1998	110,000 units	$q(t) = q(0)[1 + \eta \times \Delta Y]$ (truncated equation 24.4)
$p(0)$	1996–1997 average unit pricing	1,000 baht	Based on historical production data furnished by subsidiary management. Subsidiary sells single automobile component made of two inputs of equal value. Both component inputs are sourced from MNC parent (US). One component input may be, but is not currently, sourced locally (Thailand) (switching option)
$\theta(t)$	Anticipated discretionary exchange pass-through rate in 1997–1998	0.4	Though sectoral government price controls may permit up to 50% pass-through ($\theta(t)$), subsidiary chooses to pass through only 40% in order to match rival's anticipated 1997–1998 pass-through rate (θ) of 40%. This allows subsidiary to match rival's unit pricing and retain market share
$\Delta S(t)$	Anticipated percentage change in baht/dollar exchange rate in 1997–1998	0.4	Anticipated depreciation of baht from 25 baht/US dollar to 35 baht/US dollar in 1997–1998 (40% depreciation)
$p(t)$	Anticipated average unit pricing in 1997–1998	1,160 baht	$p(t) = p(0)[1 + \theta(t) \times \Delta S(t)]$ (equation (24.5))
$c(0)$	1996–1997 average unit costs	800 baht (for final component made of inputs $i = 1$ and 2)	Based on historical production data furnished by subsidiary management. Automobile component made of two inputs, each costing 400 baht. Both component inputs currently sourced from the MNC parent (US). One component input may be, but is not currently, sourced domestically (Thailand) (switching option for 50% of component inputs)
δ	Anticipated 1997–1998 scale elasticity	0.9	Anticipated average unit cost reduction of 10% from increase in 1997–1998 production level of 10%
$\Delta q(t)$	Anticipated percentage change in annual production for 1997–1998	0.1	Anticipated increase in production levels from 100,000 units in 1996–1997 to 110,000 units produced in 1997–1998 (10% increase)
λ	Anticipated percentage of locally sourced inputs to produce automobile	0.0	Subsidiary currently sources both inputs from MNC parent (US). One of the inputs may be, but is not currently, sourced locally (switching option for 50% of inputs). Anticipated continuation of policy

(*Continued*)

Exhibit 25A.1. *(Continued)*

Term	Definition	Estimate	Comment
w_i	Anticipated percentage cost contribution of locally sourced inputs to final automobile components produced in 1997–1998	0	Subsidiary currently sources both inputs from MNC parent (US), although one of the inputs may also be sourced locally (switching option for 50% of inputs). Anticipated continuation of this sourcing strategy in 1997–1998
$\Delta\Pi_i$	Anticipated price inflation related to each locally-sourced input used in manufacture of final auto components made in 1997–1998	.1 (for input i = I, which may be, but is not currently sourced locally)	Subsidiary currently sources both inputs from MNC parent (US), although one of the input s may also be sourced locally (switching option for 50% of inputs). Anticipated "shadow" price inflation rate of 10%
c(t)	Anticipated average unit cost in 1997–1998	844 baht	$c(t) = \sum_{i=1}^{2} c_i(0) \cdot [1-\eta \cdot \Delta q(t)][1+\lambda \cdot w_j \cdot \Delta\Pi_i + (1-\lambda) \cdot \Theta(t) \cdot \Delta S(t)$ (Equation 6)
D	Anticipated debt capital to be employed in project	12.5 million baht (June 1997)	
E	Anticipated equity capital to be employed in project	12.5 million baht (June 1997)	Anticipated debt capital contribution for overall capital employed from May 1997 to finance plant facilities expansion
k_D	Anticipated rate of debt capital	.1	Anticipated equity capital contribution for 50% of overall capital employed from May 1997 to finance plant facilities expansion
k_E	Anticipated rate on equity capital	.2	Assumed by authors. Computational details available on request
T	Anticipated corporate tax rate 1997–1998	.3	Assumed by authors. Computational details available on request
f(t)	Anticipated capital charge for 1997–1998 plant expansion project capital	3.38 million baht	Based on historical production data furnished by subsidiary management. $f(t) = \left[k_D \cdot \frac{D}{D+E} \cdot (1-T) + k_E \cdot \frac{D}{D+E}\right] \cdot [D+E]$ (Equation 10)
d(t)	Anticipated tax-deductible depreciation in 1997–1998	2.5 million baht	Based on actual and estimated depreciation expenses furnished by subsidiary management
EVA(t)	Anticipated economic value created (destroyed) by proposed project for 1997–1998 fiscal year	32.13 million baht 918.000 dollars (at 35 baht/ dollar)	$EVA(t) = \{p(t) - c(t) \cdot q(t) - d(t)(1 - T)\} + d(t) - f(t)$ (Equation 11)

The onset of the Asian financial crisis in Thailand in mid-1997 and the substantial devaluation of the baht from BHT 25/US \$1 to approximately BHT50/US \$1 dollar undermines many of the budgetary assumptions and estimates agreed to earlier by subsidiary and MNC parent management teams. A review of key changes and their impacts on the original EVA estimate are provided in Exhibit 25A.2.

The exhibits provide three measures of EVA: (1) *ex ante* anticipated EVA (32.13 million baht); (2) *ex post* optimal EVA (5.05 million baht); and (3) *ex post* actual EVA (4 million baht). The two *ex post* EVA measures remain positive, though much reduced, even after the impact of the 1997 crisis. For purposes of our analysis, the important issue for MNC management is not necessarily whether the subsidiary managers are able to generate a positive EVA, but how well they perform relative to the optimal EVA response indicated by the model.

At the *ex post* performance assessment in July 1998, the MNC parent should use the optimal *EVA*(*t*) of 5.05 million baht to assess the subsidiary rather than the *ex ante* EVA anticipated prior to the onset of the crisis in May 1997 (32.13 million baht). The 5.05 million baht result accounts for many macro- and microeconomic factors largely outside the control of the subsidiary management team — for example, $\Delta Y(t), \eta, \Delta S(t), \Delta q(t), w_i$, and $\Delta \Pi_i$. The key discretionary terms are the exchange rate pass-through $[\theta(t)]$, component input switching $(\vec{\lambda})$, and funding source $(\vec{\alpha})$ terms. *Ex post* actual *EVA*(*t*) results of 4 million baht are substantially below the optimal 5.05 million baht level and should be cause for closer scrutiny by the MNC parent.

Transaction costs such as the costs of switching suppliers and lowering production levels may provide subsidiary and MNC parent management with a partial explanation for some *EVA*(*t*) variance from the optimal response indicated by our model. The MNC parent management may then decompose residual variance into components linked to the subsidiary's actual production levels, average unit pricing, average unit costs, and average capital costs. This information may be used to refine the EVA model further for future use in *ex ante* budgeting and *ex post* performance assessment.

Exhibit 25A.2. EVA evaluation of project: *Ex Post* July 1998 Performance Evaluation Meeting

Term	Definition	Estimate	Comment
$\Delta Y(t)$	Actual change in income in 1997–1998	−0.10	Actual 10% reduction in real income in Thailand in 1997–1998
η	Actual 1997–1998 elasticity of demand	2.0	Precipitous fall in baht/dollar exchange rate and real income stifles demand for automobile components (and finished automobiles) in Thailand. Crisis conditions exacerbate income elasticity, particularly for durable goods. Income elasticity term swamps any price elasticity effects (ε), which may be ignored in this example
$q(t)$	Actual production level in 1997–1998, given change in $\Delta Y(t)$ and η	80,000 units	$q(t) = q(0)[1 + \eta \times \Delta Y]$ (truncated equation (24.4)).
$\theta(t)$	Actual discretionary exchange pass-through rate in 1997–1998 average unit pricing	0.3	Rival passes through smaller-than-expected percentage of actual 100% baht/dollar depreciation. Subsidiary matches rival's pass-through rate (θ) of only 30% of actual depreciation in order to match rival's unit pricing and retain market share
$\Delta S(t)$	Actual percentage change in baht/dollar exchange rate in 1997–1998	1.0	Devaluation of baht from 25 baht/US dollar to approximately 50 baht/US dollar in mid-1997, and remaining unchanged throughout rest of 1997–1998 fiscal year (100% depreciation)

(*Continued*)

Exhibit 25A.2. *(Continued)*

Term	Definition	Estimate	Comment
$p(t)$	Actual average unit pricing in 1997–1998 given change in $\theta(t)$	1,300 baht	$p(t) = p(0)[1 + \theta(t) \times \Delta S(t)]$ (equation (24.5))
$\Delta q(t)$	Actual percentage change in annual production level for 1997–1998	−0.10	Expected decrease in production levels from 100,000 units in 1996–1997 to 79,200 units to have been produced in 1997–1998 given changes summarized previously (21% decrease)
λ	Actual percentage of locally sourced inputs to produce automobile components in 1997–1998	0.5	Subsidiary previously sourced both inputs from MNC parent (US). Crisis results in switch to domestic supplier (50% of inputs) in 1997–1998
w_i	Actual percentage cost contribution of locally sourced inputs to final automobile components produced in 1997–1998	1.0	Component produced by subsidiary has only two inputs. One is sourced locally in response to crisis in 1997–1998. It represents 100% of overall cost contribution from locally produced inputs
$\Delta\Pi_i$	Actual price inflation related to each locally sourced input used in manufacture of final auto components made in 1997–1998	0.25 (for input $i = 1$, which is sourced locally in response to crisis)	Subsidiary switches one component input to domestic (Thailand) sourcing. Experiences 25% price inflation for this locally sourced input. This 25% increase in domestically sourced inputs is still lower than 30% increase of 100% depreciation passed through in foreign-sourced input prices
$c(t)$	Actual average unit cost in 1997–1998 given changes	1,204 baht	
$EVA(t)^*$	Optimal economic value created by proposed project for 1997–1998 fiscal year given changes in $p(t)$, $c(t)$, $q(t)$ and $f(t)$	5.05 million baht (101,000 dollars (at 50 baht/dollar))	$EVA(t) = \{p(t) - c(t) \cdot q(t) - d(t)(1 - T)\} + d(t) - f(t)$ (Equation 11)
$EVA(t)$	Actual economic value created by project in 1997–1998 fiscal year	4 million baht (80,000 dollars (at 50 baht/dollar))	Actual project performance results provided by subsidiary management

CHAPTER 26

Asian Finance and Banking[1]

The Japanese firm is less interested in short-term profits and more interested with the long-run .... The company's capacity to think in long-range terms is made possible in part by their relative higher reliance on bank loans than on the sale of securities to meet their capital requirements.
— Ezra Vogel in *Japan as Number One*

The dynamic growth that propelled East Asian firms onto the world stage in the period after World War II led academics and practitioners to search for new business paradigms. The Japanese corporate form in particular was studied for its ability to foster both competitiveness and good governance. First published in 1979,[1] Ezra Vogel's work, *Japan as Number One*,[2] was among the first to focus attention on corporate business and financial practices in East Asia through a decidedly Japanese lens. This research spurred a reconsideration of the nature and raison d'être of the firm as understood by the Anglo-American capitalistic model and to question the paramount role of shareholders. In the following years, with the subsequent rapid development of the People's Republic of China (PRC), the Republic of Korea, and the Association of Southeast Asian Nations (ASEAN) bloc and their integration into the global economy, the idiosyncrasies of Asian finance and banking assumed added complexity and a new relevance.

Beyond its original Japan-centric focus, the story of Asian finance and banking developed into a subplot within the broader drama of emerging market financial development. Common themes — financial repression, government-directed lending, bank dominance, and an underdeveloped institutional infrastructure for capital market finance — linked the evolution of regional financial systems with those of other emerging markets. As importantly, defining features set Asian economies apart: a historical legacy of functioning capital markets in selected countries, prolonged periods of rapid economic growth, the catalytic effects of financial crises, an emerging regional identity, and an embrace of global competitiveness.

In subsequent years, the pace of economic growth, the volume and speed of international capital flows, and the pressures of global competition challenged all Asian governments to balance support for corporate development with the need for financial stability and economic sustainability. In turn, the global influence of the Asian corporation advanced,[3] while the pace of change in Asian finance continued briskly. A dynamic regulatory and capital market milieu demanded that regional financiers, policy makers, and global financial managers respond promptly to both challenges and opportunities. It required an understanding not only of Asia's financial roots, but more importantly the factors that informed risks and that influenced and drove change. This chapter seeks to explore these roots by relating key conceptual themes of corporate finance to the institutional context as it has evolved in East Asia.

- In this chapter you will gain an understanding of:
- The development legacy of corporate finance and governance in East Asia.
- Bank dependence and the role of relationship capital.

1 This chapter was written by Professor Patrick Schena (The Fletcher School, Tufts University).

2 Ezra Vogel. 1979. *Japan as Number One: Lessons for America.* Cambridge, MA: Harvard University Press.

3 The representation of Asian firms in the Fortune 500 increased 25 percent between 2006 and 2010 to 147 entries.

- Financial disintermediation, specifically the transition from bank-centric to capital market finance.
- The causes and consequences of market failure and financial crisis.
- The relationship between corporate ownership structures, business organization, and corporate governance.
- Corporate governance decisions and their impact on a firm's value.
- Capital market development and its implications for the cost of capital.

ASIAN FINANCE: COMMON HISTORICAL ROOTS, DIVERSE PATHS

As early as 1932, Berle and Means[4] warned of the governance challenges posed to the modern corporation by a broadly diffuse shareholder base paired with a loosely aligned management team. Fundamental to this critique was the question of the operating objective of the corporation; that is, why, or in whose interest, did the firm exist? Focused as it was on a largely Anglo-American financial context, the very question assumed a well-developed capital market infrastructure, arm's-length shareholders, and a legal system rooted in the *common law* tradition. The constructs of modern corporate finance, such as modern portfolio theory and the capital asset pricing model, extend from this legacy of developed financial markets. In fact, they rest on qualifying assumptions about the availability of information, frictionless transacting, risk-free alternatives, and common investor expectations, which to the extent they exist do so in developed capital markets.

We begin this exploration of Asian finance by challenging this very foundation in order to better understand how financial systems develop and adapt to circumstances when capital markets are underdeveloped, as they were for much of Asia's development journey, or when they fail, as they did during the Asian financial crisis (1997) and more recently during the subprime crisis (2008) and again during the COVID-19 crisis (2020). Featured prominently in this story is heavy-handed government involvement in financial development and institutional reform.

Circa 1950, **China** had just emerged from 40 years of warlordism, unstable republican government, colonial occupation, war, and revolution and was settling into a prolonged period of Communist rule, nationalization, and economy by command. Functioning as a Japanese colony for over 50 years, the **Korean** peninsula in 1950 spun into a downward spiral of division and war. In the north, the resurgent Stalinism we know today took root. In the south, a series of civilian governments struggled to engineer the economy out of poverty and ruin. **Japan** had been the dominant colonial power in the region for nearly 60 years. It had risen on the backbone of a military-industrial complex consisting of large family-owned conglomerates — *zaibatsu*. By 1950, American occupiers had dismantled many of the prewar structures and reorganized the *zaibatsu* in order to prevent the reemergence of concentrated economic power.

In the following years, inspired by the Japanese model, governments from South Korea to Singapore relentlessly pursued rapid economic growth by mobilizing private saving and directing it to preferred economic sectors. The result is what is often referred to as the "Asian economic miracle". The roots of this transformation can be traced to economic rebirth in the aftermath of World War II and feature several common themes. Defeat and destruction had forced a reordering of traditional politico-economic elites, while reconstruction, financed by US aid, rekindled rapid economic growth. Abundant labor and a sociocultural tradition of self-cultivation and improvement rooted in a form of industrial neo-Confucianism all contributed to this enterprise.[5] However, this apparent commonality of conditions and circumstances belies country-specific development paths,[6] which, as we will show, preordained a diversity of responses and outcomes that undermined the very presumption of a single Asian model.

Led by Japan, East Asian governments focused on building institutions and advancing policies that nurtured rapid economic growth. Post-reconstruction, Japan's per capita gross national product (GNP) grew at an annual rate of nearly 10% during the 1960s before beginning to slow down in the 1970s. Similarly, between 1965 and 1990 GNP

4 Berle, Adolf A. and Gardiner C. Means. 1932. *The Modern Corporation and Private Property,* 2nd edition. Transaction Publishers (New York: Harcourt, Brace & World, 1967).

5 Vogel, *Japan as Number One.*

6 Path dependence refers to the influence of preceding circumstances, events, and conditions on the trajectory and determination of economic outcomes.

per capita across Asia grew at a rate of 5.3%, led by Hong Kong, Singapore, Taiwan, and South Korea, whose average GNP per capita ranged from 5.7% to 6.8%. Though Japan enjoyed better productivity gains, generally growth in the region was attributable to large and rapid increases in investment and factor accumulation. China, by contrast, was delayed by the failed economic policy experiments of the Maoist period, but emerged as a transitional economy in 1979, and assumed a pace of growth that would ultimately exceed that of her neighbors.

Growth strategies varied, but the more structured, top-down approaches, such as those pursued by Japan's Ministry of International Trade and Industry (MITI) or South Korea's Central Planning Board (CPB), dominated, with government technocrats providing specific direction on industrial policy, including the identification and selection of targeted industrial sectors. The primary goal of industrial policy was rapid and sustained economic growth. The process required a concerted effort to mobilize labor and capital to respond to the pace of government-directed investment and the expansion of global demand. The focus was domestic production initially for import substitution.[7] However, over time government policies across the region embraced a strong export orientation that was facilitated by a mercantilist agenda and exchange rates pegged to the US dollar. As growth expanded and the targeted industrial sectors — shipbuilding, steel, autos and automotive parts, and later consumer electronics — blossomed, the composition of Asian exports became more diversified.

To finance such aggressive growth, governments required large amounts of capital. The model was invariably to curb domestic consumption in favor of mobilizing savings via the banking system. An important consequence of this form of *government-directed* finance was the repression of financial markets and the rapid expansion of banks. By mandating low interest rates and savings and implementing tight currency controls, governments locked in bank spreads and guaranteed returns on capital. Protectionist measures erected entry barriers to foreign banks and further enhanced domestic bank dominance. Such levels of government support nurtured a high level of intimacy among banks, corporations, and their government, thereby buttressing implicit guarantees during times of financial distress.

> *Q:* What is meant by financial repression?
>
> *A:* Financial repression occurs when governments intervene in the resource allocation process, via setting interest rates on different financial products and other controls, to channel savings to financial institutions such as banks, insurance companies, or pension funds that then facilitate government-directed lending.

To facilitate this process, governments founded development banks — the Japan Development Bank in 1954, the Korea Development Bank in 1954, and the China Development Bank in 1994 — whose raison d'être was to support large-scale debt financing for infrastructure or government-sponsored industrial development.

China

During the pre-reform era prior to 1978, corporate investment in China was financed through interest-free budgetary grants and the retained earnings of Chinese state-owned enterprises (SOEs). Chinese state-owned banks lent in limited fashion to support the working capital requirements of SOEs. By the time China embarked on reform in the early 1980s, the government had restructured the banking system and created four specialized commercial banks — the Bank of China,[8] the Industrial and Commercial Bank of China, the China Construction Bank, and the Agricultural Bank of China — whose primary functions were deposit taking and lending guided by government policies. In the following 20 years, bank assets grew rapidly as the Chinese economy expanded, with the ratio of loans to GDP increasing from 50% in 1978 to 100% by 1997.

South Korea

In Korea, banks were nationalized in 1962 after the military coup of General Park Chung Hee. They remained under state control for 20 years until 1982. This enhanced the ability of the government to control bank lending and to direct credit according to the national industrial plan. In addition to a purely lending function, the banking system — the principal

7 Import substitution policies encourage the domestic manufacturing of goods that substitute for imports. Such policies are also meant to save foreign exchange, thereby alleviating pressure on the current account of the nation's balance of payments.

8 The Bank of China should not be confused with the People's Bank of China. The former is a state-owned commercial bank, whereas the latter is the central bank of the PRC.

transactions bank system — also performed a degree of statutorily mandated monitoring and credit control aimed at improving the capital structure of South Korea's business conglomerates, also known as *chaebol*.[9] This effectively established the lead bank of the lead *chaebol* company as the group's principal transactions bank. Under this arrangement, the bank was to review the entire *chaebol* group's plans for capital structure improvement, set credit ceilings, monitor their compliance, and ultimately ensure that it was aligned with government industrial plans.

Japan

Banks in Japan, unlike those in China or South Korea, had remained private financial institutions. Despite the dissolution of the *zaibatsu*, centripetal forces brought many of the prewar alliances back together, though in a different guise. These new business organizations — *keiretsu* — have evolved over the years. In their emergent years, they were heavily networked structures with a main bank functioning as lead lender. The main bank's position was further reinforced through a web of reciprocal shareholding with group-affiliated companies as well as interlocking shareholding among affiliated companies themselves. As a result, the main bank's role was considerably broader than that of its counterparts in other Asian countries, and its ability to impact corporate decision making, especially during periods of client financial distress, decidedly more decisive.

Such extra-banking functions — including monitoring and governance — are intimately linked to the notion of *relationship capitalism*. When compared with Anglo-Saxon *arm's-length* or *market-based* finance, relationship- or bank-based financing internalizes traditional financial channels (from the perspective of the *keiretsu*) as capital circulates within a tightly knit web of related firms and institutions. In such closed systems, arm's-length market mechanisms are incomplete or in some cases missing. Transparency and open access by third-party nonaffiliated firms are sacrificed in favor of the intimacy of a formal business relationship and an informal financing relationship under which proprietary information (e.g., transaction accounts data) is used to make decisions with regard to risk and capital allocation.

9 The term Korean *chaebol* derives from same traditional Chinese characters — 财发 — as the Japanese *zaibatsu*.

ADAPTIVE RESPONSES: CRISES AND INSTITUTIONAL CHANGE IN ASIAN FINANCE

The combined impact of government-directed investment, financial repression, and bank dominance, while contributing to rapid economic growth, constrained the ability of firms to access alternative sources of capital and therefore to manage their costs of capital more nimbly. The concentration of financing within the banking sector left corporate balance sheets across the region heavily dependent on bank debt and financial systems vulnerable to bank failure. Pressure to liberalize interest rates and to facilitate access to alternative sources of capital was, however, building as the result of Asian firms' increasing dependence on exports, the demands of global competitiveness, and foreign pressures for access to local markets, including entry by foreign financial institutions. Thus, repressive financial practices would eventually melt away as growth slowed and financial markets were progressively deregulated. As a result, increased volatility of interest rates and exchange rates exposed firms to new forms of risk that required them to rethink and reengineer their financial and risk management practices.

Disintermediation

Until the 1960s, Japan's central government maintained a budget surplus, which effectively stunted an active market for Japanese government debt.[10] However, between 1965 and 1983 central government deficits ensued and national debt expanded from 5% to more than 50% of GNP. Initially, the government financed bond issuance through bank purchases and provided liquidity to banks through a repurchase program, which allowed them to manage their asset base. However, as the volume of public debt grew, the government rescinded the repurchase program. This put considerable pressure on bank balance sheets and operating profitability. Pressure by the banking industry led the government to permit secondary market sales of Japanese government bonds. By 1979, banks were net sellers of Japanese government bonds into an evolving secondary market, thus setting the stage for eventual bond market deregulation.

10 Bond markets greatly benefit from active government bond financing. Governments, however, issue treasury bonds only if they run a deficit on their budget. For many years Asian countries enjoyed budget surpluses rather than deficits and therefore did not need to issue treasuries.

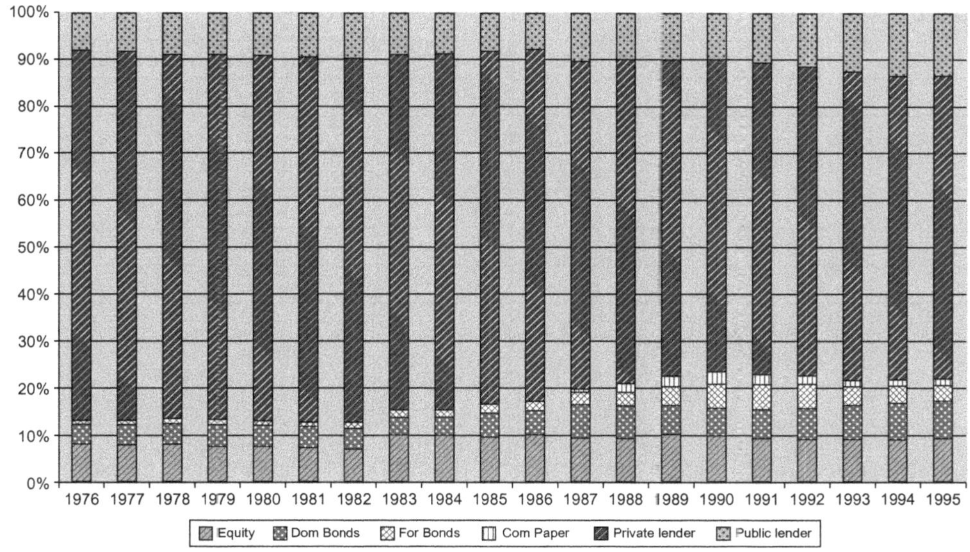

Exhibit 26.1. Financing patterns of Japanese firms.

By the 1970s the pace of Japanese economic growth began to subside, reducing corporate demand for bank borrowings. In parallel, both domestic and foreign pressure began to mount to liberalize access to the domestic bond market, and interest rates were progressively decontrolled. Similarly, foreign exchange controls were relaxed, allowing Japanese borrowers access to relatively less regulated, less expensive offshore Eurobond markets. As a result, the hollowing out of domestic capital markets became an authentic threat that led to the progressive deregulation of the corporate bond markets.

With slowing sales revenue, Japanese firms reduced their use of external bank financing, relying instead increasingly on internal financing. Over time as bond and foreign exchange markets were further deregulated and pricing improved, Japanese firms increased their use of direct external finance and issued bonds in domestic and overseas securities markets. Exhibit 26.1 documents this path characterized by progressive yet limited bank disintermediation[11] beginning in 1982 that was brought about by the emergence of more flexible and cost-effective capital market–based funding alternatives.

11 Savings can be channeled to borrowers either through financial intermediaries such as banks, which take deposits from savers and lend to borrowers, or directly through financial markets. Such disintermediated finance bypasses the middleman — financial institutions — and is generally deemed cheaper. See Chapter 8 for a full discussion of disintermediation.

In South Korea the link between reform and disintermediation is less stark, though distinguishable. Recall that its banking sector was state-owned in the 1960s and the 1970s, which facilitated credit allocation to support South Korea's rapid growth. By the early 1980s, South Korea was experiencing growing balance-of-payments current account deficits and a sizable buildup in corporate indebtedness, including debt to foreign banks. This prompted a series of financial reforms, such as privatization of banks and allowing *chaebol* to own and operate nonbank financial institutions (NBFIs). Additional reforms sought to reduce *chaebol* dependence on bank debt while promoting the expanded use of capital markets through bonds, commercial paper, and new issues of equity. Banks continued to maintain a statutory credit oversight function over the *chaebol*, but lacked a true means to enforce credit constraints. The *chaebol* continued to expand their financing and bypass credit controls imposed by banks, while shifting financing from banks to nonbank financial institutions and capital markets. NBFIs were less regulated than banks and enjoyed more freedom in managing asset portfolios and in setting borrowing and lending rates, thereby enabling *chaebol* to bypass their lead lenders on their way to accumulating large volumes of debt.

The Asian financial crisis as a catalyst for reform

By the time the Asian financial crisis hit in 1997, several Asian countries had initiated regulatory reform

Exhibit 26.2. Rate of return on invested capital (ROIC) of *Chaebol* bankruptcies.

	ROIC (%)		ROIC Less Prime Rate (12%) (%)	
Chaebol	1992–1996	1996	1992–1996	1996
Hanbo	3.0	1.7	−9.0	−10.3
Sammi	2.9	3.2	-9.1	-8.8
Jinro	2.7	1.9	-9.3	-10.1
Kia	18.9	8.7	6.9	-3.3
Dainong	6.8	5.5	-5.2	-6.5

Source: Giancarlo Corsetti *et al.* 1999. "What Caused the Asian Currency and Financial Crisis?." *Japan and the World Economy* 11: 318.

of their financial sectors. However, deregulation was for the most part only partial, incomplete, and iterative. Fixed income (bond) markets were underdeveloped, and exchange rates across the region were in most cases de facto pegged to the US dollar. Many of the countries in the region experienced increased capital inflows, including short-term bank borrowings and foreign direct and portfolio investment. Increased liquidity led to significant asset price appreciation. With the increased use of leverage — especially in the form of short-term, foreign currency–denominated debt — and declining investment efficiency, corporate fundamentals deteriorated. Therefore, conditions existed to promote rapid capital withdrawal in the presence of an external shock. That spark occurred first in Thailand and then spread like wildfire throughout Southeast Asia — Indonesia, Malaysia, the Philippines, Taiwan, and Hong Kong — and South Korea.

South Korea Financial distress first manifested itself as a domestic debt crisis, and then mushroomed into a currency crisis, as it was spurred by overexpansion and the large buildup of corporate debt. Warning signs first appeared in early 1997, when, for the first time, several underperforming *chaebol* failed. These included Hanbo in January 1997, Sammi in March, Jinro in April, and then Kia in October — all earning returns on invested capital (ROIC) substantially below the South Korean prime rate (as proxy for cost of capital), as illustrated in Exhibit 26.2. The crisis's vicious spiral was compounded by foreign banks refusing to roll over short-term foreign credits, which put undue pressure on South Korea's balance-of-payments current account and its banking system, and ultimately led to corporate bankruptcies and bank failures.

Japan In contrast to the South Korean experience, financial distress in Japan presented itself through the banking system, in part the result of responses to disintermediation. During the late 1980s Japan had experienced rapid asset price appreciation in the equity and property markets. The impacts of this bubble spawned Japan's so-called "lost decade' and continued to the prolonged period of deflation that has plagued Japan's economy and capital markets since. As large corporate borrowers diverted capital needs to financial markets, banks expanded their lending to small and midsize firms, as well as to the real estate and construction sectors. Credit standards were relaxed, resulting in a decline in asset quality, collateral value, and creditworthiness. The deterioration in asset quality contributed to capital depletion in the banking sector and also made it difficult to accelerate its cleanup. To make matters worse, large global banks demanded higher premiums from Japanese banks borrowing in the global interbank markets. The resulting credit squeeze had profound consequences for the real economy in Japan and rapidly became contagious to other Southeast Asian nations heavily dependent on Japan's capital exports.

The aftermath of the Asian financial crisis: Restructuring and reform

Prior to the Asian financial crisis of 1997, the pervasiveness of dollar invoicing had made exchange rate stability a high-priority policy objective. This was attributable in part to an embryonic domestic local currency bond market and sketchy yield curves. With the absence of long-term bonds, it was difficult to price longer-term forward exchange contracts, as well as interest rate and cross-currency swaps, which in turn undermined the development of a full-fledged currency derivatives market. Without effective markets in forwards and swaps, governments

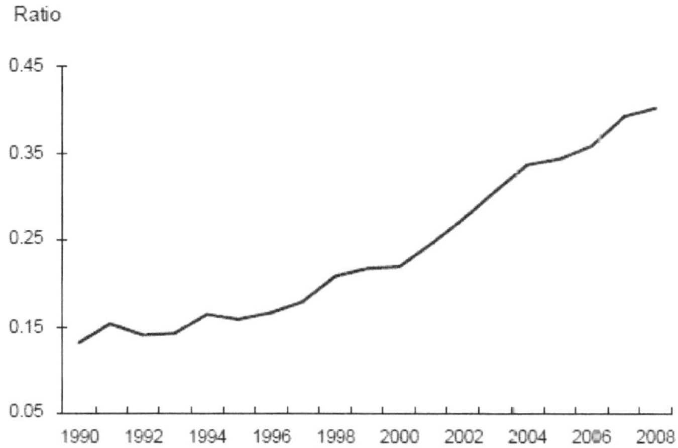

Exhibit 26.3. Ratio of foreign exchange reserves to GDP, developing Asia, 1990–2008.

Source: Donghyun Park and Andrew Rozanov. 2010. "Asia's Sovereign Wealth Funds and Reform of the Global Reserve System," Asia Development Bank, April. Authors' estimates based on data from CEIC Data Company Ltd. and International Monetary Fund, *International Financial Statistics* online database, both downloaded June 15, 2009.

implemented the next best policy of informal hedging by maintaining exchange rate stability via fixed exchange rates. The financial crisis ripped through Asia like a hurricane, dismantling pegged exchange rates and creating havoc throughout the region.

As crisis conditions waned, policy makers across the region began to take stock of the primary causes and consequences of financial distress. Crisis assessment brought attention to the extensive use of debt, specifically bank finance, and the resultant overdependence on banks. Linked to this were both the heavily leveraged state of corporate balance sheets and the underdeveloped state of local currency debt markets. At the macroeconomic level, fixed exchange rate regimes had provided a false sense of security against exchange rate volatility and contributed to the heavy use of short-term foreign currency debt by banks and corporations alike. Accentuating this was the use of short-term proceeds to fund longer-dated assets, thereby contributing to dual-currency and maturity mismatches.

In setting a reform agenda for the post-crisis period, key first steps — corporate restructuring, bank recapitalization, governance reform, and capital market development — were matched by a concerted effort to reduce immediate exposure to currency shocks and renewed risks of contagion. Most Asian nations embarked on a policy of systematic accumulation of foreign exchange reserve assets made possible by large current account surpluses that were often induced by undervalued exchange rates. Between 1998 and 2006, reserves of Asian central banks grew at an average annual compounded rate of over 19%, accumulating to over $3.1 trillion by 2006.[12] This foreign exchange reserve was intended to serve as a buffer against currency volatility and sudden capital outflows (see Exhibit 26.3). This explosion in reserve holdings by Asian central banks has challenged governments with a new problem: how to invest excess reserves efficiently. To address this dilemma, most regional governments have followed the early lead of Singapore and established *sovereign wealth funds* as a means to earn enhanced returns on reserves in excess of what is required to support the monetary base. More strategically, regional governments also seek relief from an overreliance on the US dollar as a primary reserve currency. In this regard, China has taken initial steps to promote an expanded international scope for its currency — the renminbi.

12 McKinsey Global Institute, "The New Power Brokers: How Oil, Asia, Hedge Funds, and Private Equity Are Shaping Global Capital Markets," October 2007.

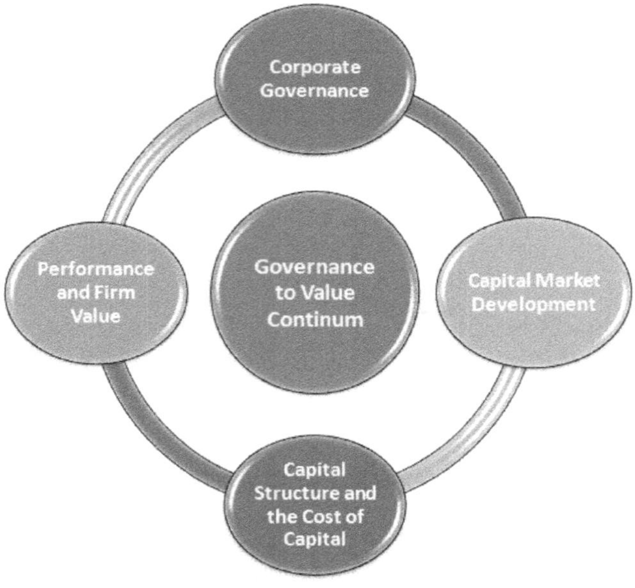

Exhibit 26.4. Governance to value continuum.

BUSINESS ORGANIZATION, CORPORATE OWNERSHIP, AND GOVERNANCE

To understand the transition in Asian finance from financial intermediation or bank dependence to financial disintermediation via deepening capital markets, we propose to trace the path to market-based finance along a continuum that links patterns of business organization, ownership, and governance through the increased reliance on market-based finance to the valuation of stocks and bonds. We refer to this framework as the *governance to value continuum* (see Exhibit 26.4).

Capital markets perform several important informational, allocational, and valuation functions, most notably capital (re)allocation and price discovery. In equity markets, in particular, shareholder rights[13] are allocated and exchanged on the basis of their price. Critical assumptions with respect to pricing are that investors are risk averse, that information is freely available to all investors, and that markets are complete and competitive in processing that information.

Price discovery is the process by which information is revealed and ultimately reflected in stock prices. To be efficient, the price discovery process has to prevent stock price manipulation by individual traders. Thus an efficient price discovery process, whether for equity or for debt securities, is critical to a realistic measurement of a firm's cost of capital. The cost of capital (discount rate) in turn is a critical variable in valuing the free cash flows of the firm and ultimately establishing firm value. In functioning markets for corporate control, it enables a would-be acquirer to price control rights in a firm based on structural changes the acquirer might make to the firm's operations and, ultimately, its stream of cash flows. Thus, the risks associated with structural weaknesses in a firm's practice of corporate governance, in efficient markets, should ultimately affect the value of the firm. The management of an undervalued entity, in the presence of a market for corporate control, becomes vulnerable to a loss of control (hostile takeover); therefore, it may take remedial action to protect its independence by improving governance in order to increase the firm's share price and restore value to shareholders.

The real world, however, is far removed from this ideal model: Asian capital markets have been plagued by illiquidity, limited availability of information to accurately price securities, and high transaction costs; they also lack a broad, diversified investor base with a differentiated appetite for risk. Therefore, to understand the link between such market imperfections and capital market efficiency, we suggest a construct — the microstructure of the

13 Shareholder rights generally consist of two broad types. *Control* rights permit shareholders to elect management and influence managerial decision making via the board process. *Cash flow* rights entitle shareholders to a proportionate share of any distributions by the firm, including both cash (e.g., dividends) and stock distributions.

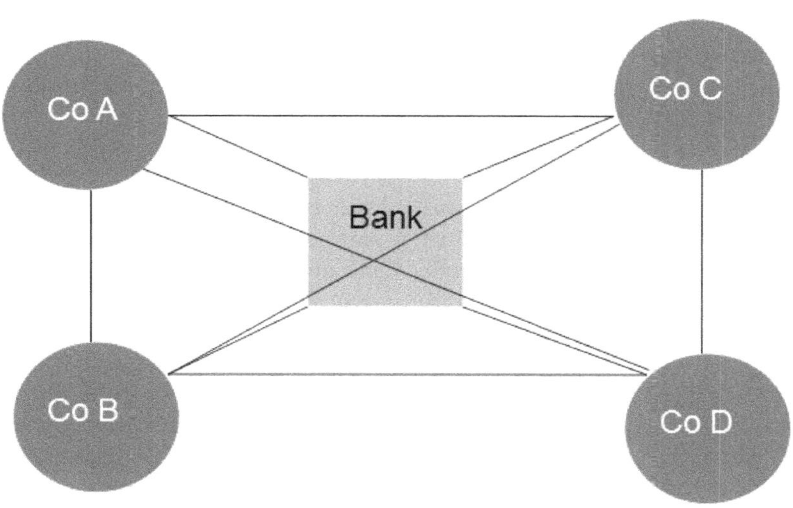

Exhibit 26.5. Intermarket Keiretsu structure.

capital market — which is an agency view[14] of capital market organization and development that focuses specifically on the role of information. It seeks to explain how capital markets produce and disseminate information, assess and reallocate risks, monitor the performance of corporate assets and reorganize them when necessary, and cope with the problems of incentives associated with asymmetries in the availability of information and the delegation of tasks among agents in the capital market. Fundamental to this concept is the mitigation of asymmetric information between and among all actors, and, broadly defined, aligning the interests of key stakeholders. It is especially useful in an Asian context where extra-market measures or institutions (e.g., banks) have been employed, sometimes in conjunction with market solutions, to mitigate the governance impacts of information or incentive gaps.

Corporate ownership and business organization

Despite a broadening of the investor base and the deepening equity markets, corporate control in Asian firms has remained concentrated in the hands of governments, banks, families, or conglomerate business groups. Indeed, in Asia, business groups are diversified across industries and generally consist of multiple independent enterprises. They are relationship-bound and, not uncommonly, reinforced through family or kinship groups. In addition, in most instances, because of their dominant position in the local economy, they are indebted to national governments for favorable regulatory regimes, protectionist policies, and, more tangibly, preferential access to capital and other resources. In emerging economies, business groups may also help affiliated firms overcome barriers or imperfections in markets for capital (i.e., capital constraints), and serve as a source of portfolio diversification in the absence of market mechanisms to diversify risk and uncertainty. Specifically, group structures allow member firms to share risks by smoothing income flows and reallocating capital among affiliates in the form of a self-contained (i.e., internal) capital market.[15]

The structures of group firms has varied depending on idiosyncratic path-dependent modes of corporate development: In some cases, groups have been linked loosely via cross-holdings or share interlocks; in other instances, a parent-subsidiary or dominant shareholder relationship defines the organizational and governance structure of the group.

14 Agency costs result from the delegation of decision making by a principal to an agent and represent the aggregate of expenditures by the principal to monitor the agent, the agent to bond to the role or transaction, and any residual losses resulting from the failure of either. See also Sheard, P. 1989. "The Main Bank System and Corporate Monitoring and Control in Japan," *Journal of Economic Behavior and Organization* 11: 399–422.

15 Khanna, T. and Y. Yafeh. 2005. "Business Groups and Risk Sharing around the World." *Journal of Business* 2005.

Japan Interlocking shareholding is a form of interfirm share ownership or cross-holding, involving a reciprocal exchange of property rights — control rights and ownership rights of the firm's residual cash flows. In Japan, this model has included an implicit agreement to waive control rights in favor of management, to withhold or delay the sale of shares to third parties, and/or to consult with the firm if there is a need to sell — all of which amounts to a de facto concentration of share ownership. Furthermore, cross-holdings typically result in limited influence by minority shareholders, which, in turn, insulates management from the disciplinary influences of the market for corporate control and threats of hostile takeovers.

Business groups in Japan, known as *keiretsu*,[16] are institutionalized interfirm relationships based on networks of "dense transactions" — both trading and financial in nature — and are buttressed by a web of interfirm cross-shareholding. *Vertical keiretsu* are hierarchical networked structures dominated by a large manufacturing firm (e.g., Toyota Motor Company and its supply chain). Intermarket or horizontal *keiretsu* run across industries and include trading and financial firms.[17]

Once central to the organization of the *keiretsu* was the role of *bank as shareholder*. In this capacity, banks transcended the lending relationship to establish a base of long-term, stable shareholding of affiliated firms. Thus, banks as stable shareholders were likely to support management in cases of minority shareholder dissidence or hostile takeover. Exhibit 26.5 portrays the networked structure of the *keiretsu* whereby affiliated firms (e.g., Co. A, Co. B, Co. C, and Co. D) hold shares in each other, while at the same time holding shares in the group's main bank. Likewise, under this structure, the main bank reciprocated by holding the equity of each of its group's affiliates.

South Korea In contrast to the *keiretsu*, South Korean *chaebol* — popularized in many K-dramas — are organized in a more hierarchical fashion under the control of a dominant shareholder or controlling family. Six groups, including Hyundai, Samsung, and LG, were founded during the period of Japanese colonialism. Eleven more arose during the US occupation between 1945 and 1948. Four groups, including Daewoo, were formed during the 1960s.[18] They each benefited from government-led investment and grew rapidly on the back of government-directed finance. The *chaebol* generally share a stylized structure of family ownership and management that is highly centralized through the office of the chairman, which retains for itself corporate functions, including responsibility for finance and investment decisions. *Chaebol* are diversified, vertically integrated, and, like Japanese *keiretsu*, they engage in cross-shareholding among independently listed companies — sharing majority ownership, but with different minority shareholders.

Unlike *keiretsu*, however, *chaebol* are not permitted to hold shares of banks. Neither can banks hold equity positions in corporations. Rather, under the somewhat unbalanced regulatory reordering noted earlier, *chaebol* are permitted to own positions in nonbank financial institutions (NBFIs) such as merchant banks and investment firms. During the 1980s, South Korea's principal transactions banks were tasked with monitoring and managing credit growth among the *chaebol*. To circumvent such control, the *chaebol* used affiliated NBFIs to access credit markets and continued to amass balance sheet liabilities.

Exhibit 26.6 illustrates the hierarchical form of the *chaebol* with control emanating from the chairman's office. Independent companies, with different minority shareholders but under the common control of the dominant *chaebol* family, are linked through share-interlocks and cross-debt guarantees facilitated by group financing companies. This form of business organization is suggestive of an *internal* (to the group) *capital market*, analogous to investment and financing functions in large, multidivisional firms. However, it differs in the use of cross-loan guarantees. For example, Firm A may guarantee a bank loan by a third party to sister affiliate Firm B, while Firm B reciprocally guarantees a bank loan for Firm A. In a second example, the relationship between the two affiliates can be slightly more arm's-length or triangular. Under this scenario Firm A makes a deposit in a *chaebol*'s NBFI, which on-lends to Firm B of the same *chaebol*.

China Unlike the post-war formation of corporate groups in Japan or Korea, corporate structures in postrevolutionary China took shape much later.

16 See Gerlach, Michael. 1992. *Alliance Capitalism: The Social Organization of Japanese Business.* Berkeley: University of California Press, for a comprehensive analysis of the Japanese *keiretsu.*

17 *Ibid.*

18 Lim, W. 2010. "The Emergence of the Chaebol and the Origins of the Chaebol Problem." In *Economic Crisis and Corporate Restructuring in Korea: Reforming the Chaebol,* edited by Stephan Haggard *et al.* Cambridge, UK: Cambridge University Press.

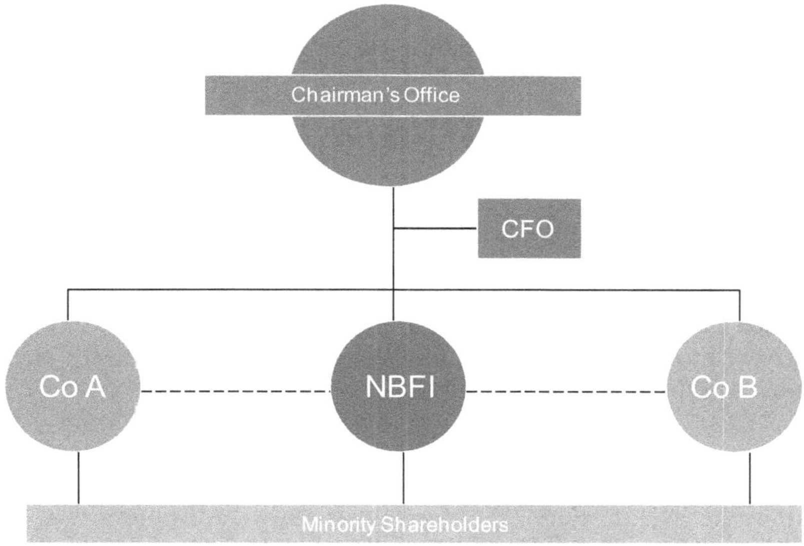

Exhibit 26.6. *Chaebol* structure.

In fact, during much of China's post-1949 experience, government entities controlled economic activity and financed investment and production via the state budget. A series of economic reforms during the 1980s and 1990s established the basis for *corporatization* — the transformation of state-owned *assets* into state-owned *corporations* — and resulted in a complex ownership framework that at once offered the prospect for a diversified shareholder base, but de facto protected the ownership interests of the government. Chinese government ownership is thus defined through restrictive (i.e., nontradable) share classes — state-held shares and "legal person" shares — that are separate and distinct from Chinese tradable (A and B) share classes. The resultant Chinese corporate structure, dominated by the Chinese SOE, is in some ways a derivative of this dominant shareholder model, with government agencies serving the interests of the state, as well as their own bureaucratic interests, as lead shareholder.

On reflection, business groups in Asia have served to relieve constrained access to resources and capital, help manage capital costs to group firms, and provide a form of mutual insurance or risk sharing. By facilitating their affiliates' access to capital, business groups could substitute an *internal* capital market for deep and liquid equity and debt markets as found in Anglo-Saxon countries. Beneficial evidence of this exists among affiliated firms in Japan, South Korea, and Thailand that exhibit smoother operating performance (i.e., lower operating volatility) than among non-group firms in the same countries. However, conversely such tightly knit business organizations can also distort governance mechanisms and undermine the very foundation of the microstructure of capital markets in the region.

CORPORATE GOVERNANCE

According to the OECD's definition, *Corporate governance involves a set of relationships between a company's management, its board, its shareholders and other stakeholders . . . that provides the structure through which the objectives of the company are set, and the means of attaining those objectives and monitoring performance are determined . . . . [The] presence of an effective corporate governance system, within an individual company and across an economy, helps to provide a degree of confidence that is necessary for the proper functioning of a market economy . . . [and results in a lower] cost of capital.*

Governance in an arm's-length, market-based system, dominated by rules, is rooted in transactions based on impersonal, explicit agreements, under a corporate legal or securities regulatory regime, which the state (as a third party) can enforce. *Rules-based governance* is predicated on disclosure and transparency and so relies heavily on *public information*. Fixed, front-end transaction costs are generally high in order to initiate a public offering, for example, or to secure a credit rating. However, marginal costs of enforcement are relatively small.

In the absence of well-functioning and developed capital markets, governance is dominated by necessity by *private information* that is used to facilitate private transactions that are mutually enforcing sometimes outside the legal system. Under such systems, government, banks, and corporations become closely linked in an implicit, idiosyncratic fashion, to engage jointly in the allocation of capital. Referred to in the Asian context as *relationship capitalism*, as a form of governance, it is often characterized by low fixed transaction costs, but high marginal and switching costs related to the efforts required to identify, screen, and qualify each new partner.

Japan

The archetype of relationship governance might well have been Japan's *keiretsu* model structured around the Japanese main bank. The main bank was synonymous with the key stakeholder relationship and was typically a firm's largest shareholder and/or largest creditor. Key to the relationship was active monitoring of client firm activities by the bank, where the monitoring was integrated and the intensity of the monitoring activity contingent on the financial health of the borrower.

Indeed, Japanese banks were most actively engaged as monitors when they had material assets, particularly loans, at risk and the client have included exhibited poor operating performance. Remedial actions varied, but might typically include changing senior management, appointing bank directors, and replacing outside directors, as well as restructuring and/or downsizing operations. In the most extreme cases, active bank monitoring and intervention were expected to reduce the costs of bankruptcy and financial distress as banks coordinated renegotiation of claims, formulated recovery plans, hired new management to improve monitoring, implemented restructuring, supplied new capital, maintained liquidity, and managed asset sales. Main banks were most active in such restructuring activities when the level of their financial exposure were high, the bank had a long history of support for the client, the firm's long-term prospects were solid, the regulatory authorities were encouraging of the action, and the bank's image benefitted. The case of Mazda (see International Corporate Finance in Practice 26.1) is a well-studied example of activist monitoring by Sumitomo Bank to materially impact the operating performance of its client. Of particular relevance was the bank's support for Toyo Kogyo Co. through public statements of its intent to continue lending. Such overt signals reduced uncertainly (i.e., asymmetric information) with respect to the intent of the principal lender, immediately relieved liquidity pressure on Toyo, and demonstrated Toyo's ability to continue raising capital at a reasonable cost.

As financial markets deepened in Japan and client firms increasingly turned to market-based sources of capital, the foundations of the main bank system began to erode. Over time, constraints imposed by the main bank structure reduced firms' flexibility and became costly. The rise of capital market finance resulted in creditor de-concentration as the banks' share of creditor debt became diluted. As a result, banks became less effective and flexible in participating in restructurings or exchanging their claims. By the mid-1990s, weak bank capitalization undermined their ability to maintain adequate reserves against risky loans and to raise new capital. As Japanese firms continued to migrate to direct capital-market-mediated finance, bank-intermediated financing thus became progressively less dominant, with consequences for both governance and corporate control.

Indeed, during the years of Japan's rapid growth and extending well into the 1990s, Japan's 20 largest banks had owned over 22% of the Tokyo Stock Exchange by market capitalization. Cross-shareholdings for much of this period remained constant at approximately 33% of all listed shares. From the perspective of formal governance structures, boards of directors were large — averaging between 25 and 40 members. Directors were overwhelmingly insiders (i.e., managers) with operating responsibility, and therefore were incapable of independent and objective self-monitoring. Outside directors, being few in number, were often not independent, but rather were drawn from the ranks of retired company executives or government, bank, and group member firm' officials. Lastly, annual shareholder meetings, as a shareholder monitoring and control vehicle, were ineffectual. They tended to be formal, quite short in duration, and frequently planned by firms to be held many on the same day to discourage shareholder attendance. More sinister — in some cases — was managements' use of *sokaiya* — hired "meeting keepers" — to maintain order and to prevent unanticipated issues from disrupting the planned meeting agenda.

As the role of bank-based finance receded in Japan, there has been a systematic decline in the ratio of cross-holdings — falling from some 70% of the entire Tokyo Stock Exchange market capitalization

INTERNATIONAL CORPORATE FINANCE IN PRACTICE 26.1

Toyo and the Japanese Main Bank

Toyo Kogyo Co., Ltd was the manufacturer of Mazda automobiles. In 1973, the Arab oil embargo drove up energy prices. Toyo was heavily dependent on export sales to the United States, and its export ratio, the highest among Japan's five major automakers, made it very vulnerable to fluctuations in foreign exchange rates. Furthermore, Toyo's labor force was strongly unionized and had been recently awarded a 30% increase in wages. However, the productivity of labor was relatively low (70%) compared to industry peers. Compounding Toyo's challenges was a family-centric, autocratic senior management, which lacked strong managerial skills at middle and lower levels and basic cost controls at the corporate level. Between 1973 and 1974, Mazda's domestic sales declined from 18,000 to 11,000 units per month. Within 1 year of the embargo, Mazda's US sales had declined by 60%. Slumping sales negatively impacted operating cash flows, resulting in a significant increase in debt to finance operating shortfalls.

Sumitomo Bank was Toyo's main bank and, along with Sumitomo Trust and Hiroshima Bank, its major lender. As of March 1974, Sumitomo had $234 million in loans outstanding to Toyo and owned approximately 4% of Toyo's outstanding equity, ranking as its second largest shareholder. As Toyo's condition deteriorated in late 1974, Sumitomo moved aggressively to restructure Toyo. It placed seven executives in Toyo to monitor and supervise Toyo's operations and eventually forced a transition in senior management. To ensure no disruption in liquidity, Sumitomo Trust, a key member of the lending group, advised all other lenders that it would continue to provide liquidity to Toyo. With this public expression of support, all lenders continued to lend, thereby ensuring Toyo's solvency. Sumitomo's next step was to lead the search for a strategic partner for Toyo that could provide industry-specific experience. This eventually led the group to Ford becoming a major shareholder.

Source: Adapted from Richard Pascale and Thomas P. Rohlen, "The Mazda Turnaround." *Journal of Japanese Studies* 9(2): 219–263.

in 1990 to just over 30% by 2022.[19] With this has come increased evidence of a reduced scope of bank-based monitoring and governance, accompanies by strengthening of market-based incentive and control systems as institutional shareholdings have correspondingly increased. For example, there has been progress in Japan in reducing the size and increasing the operating effectiveness of corporate boards. In addition, board responsibilities have, in some cases, been divided into strategic and operating components to better monitor the firm's different managerial functions. These advances have been coupled with an increase in the appointment of independent directors and an expanded internal audit function.[20] Finally, incentive stock options, as a market-based device to better align the interests of managers and shareholders, first permitted in 1997, have gained wide acceptance among Japan's large publicly traded firms. Notwithstanding progress, the Asian Corporate Governance Association recommends additional efforts in several key areas: Corporate boards and their committees must continue to expand participation by independent board members. Independent staffing to support the corporate audit function should be expanded and be further distanced from insiders' control. Not least, independent compensation committees should be more widely used and increased transparency brought to executive compensation ACGA, 2008.

As a core component of corporate monitoring and control, relationship governance regimes have been severely blamed for contributing to the Asian financial crisis of 1997. The South Korean *chaebol* organizational form, in particular, has been criticized for enabling self-interested behavior, cross-firm subsidies, unfettered discretion in investing activities, and excess risk taking. Indeed, the fact that such weak organizational structures, combined with

19 https://asia.nikkei.com/Business/Business-trends/Japan-s-cross-shareholdings-drop-to-new-low-on-investor-pressure.

20 For further evidence, the reader is referred to the example of Asahi Glass Company in International Corporate Finance in Practice 26.4.

the inefficient or ineffective exercise of corporate governance, accentuated crisis conditions is beyond question. In the case of South Korea specifically, the interfirm structures that facilitate capital allocation via internal markets, under lax governance, have enabled controlling shareholders-managers to reallocate capital from better-performing group firms to poorly performing firms. For example, a *chaebol* group firm (Firm A) may be encouraged to undertake a low-value-creating net present value (NPV) project that otherwise benefits an affiliated group firm (Firm B) via the sale of equipment or the provision of services. Such low-return investment activity is not in the interest of the minority shareholders of Firm A, whose wealth under such circumstances is reduced as a result of the low-yielding investment.

Globalization as a catalyst for governance reform

In the immediate aftermath of the Asian financial crisis, a regionwide focus on corporate restructuring, spurred by the International Monetary Fund, moved specifically to remedy governance gaps exposed during the prior years of economic and financial distress. These included not only those related to debt issuance and borrowing, but also measures related directly to improving information quality (e.g., accounting standards), transparency (e.g., disclosure requirements), and monitoring and control (e.g., board independence). This was in conjunction with greater capital market openness and in anticipation of higher levels of global market integration as local capital markets developed and foreign capital placed greater demands on issuers for information and the protection of investor rights, particularly those of minority shareholders. Progress in the broad imposition and enforcement of governance standards has varied. China, Indonesia, and the Philippines are among the weakest performers. Hong Kong and Singapore, by contrast, exhibit among the highest levels of regulatory compliance, corresponding to their relatively higher levels of capital market development and global market integration.

In the absence of a strong domestic governance and enforcement regime, can firms independently adopt (i.e., opt into) more rigorous governance standards by listing their shares internationally? Growing firms require continuing access to large pools of permanent capital at the lowest possible costs in order to maintain an efficient growth trajectory. When operating in underdeveloped markets, *cross-listing* (i.e., to issue equity in more developed markets) as a means to overcome constraints on capital access is certainly an option. Such markets offer access to a broader shareholder base that is able to provide capital on a larger scale, and at a potentially lower cost, than available domestically owing to the diversification benefits offered to investors (see Chapter 10 for further discussion). In doing so they must weigh the added costs of implementing such measures (e.g., audit, disclosure costs) against the expected benefits (e.g., reduced capital constraints and presumably a lower cost of capital.

However, in choosing to cross-list, firms must conform to disclosure and related governance requirements as defined by foreign regulatory authorities and commit to making individual decisions to adhere to the governance regime of the foreign market in which they list. This practice is referred to as *bonding* (i.e., demonstrating good governance via the cross-listing decision), and has been put to wide use by Asian firms. Chinese SOEs in particular have sourced equity extensively from foreign markets as part of share-issuance privatization schemes designed to extend capital access, while maintaining a degree of state ownership and control (see International Corporate Finance in Practice 26.2).

INTERNATIONAL CORPORATE FINANCE IN PRACTICE 26.2

PetroChina

PetroChina was incorporated in 1999 as part of the restructuring of China National Petroleum Corporation (CNPC), assuming most of CNPC's domestic oil and gas assets and liabilities. It was established under China's Company Law with a board of directors, a supervisory board, and four board committees. PetroChina went public as a share issuance privatization in April 2000 in Hong Kong and New York, issuing shares representing 10% of its capital. British Petroleum plc. took 20% of the offering. The company raised $3.4 billion out of an expected $10 billion.

In reorganizing as part of its dual-listing program, PetroChina opted for governance standards required by both the Hong Kong Stock Exchange (HKSE) and the New York Stock Exchange (NYSE), including requirements related to disclosure (e.g., it adopted International Financial Accounting Standards and was audited by PricewaterhouseCoopers), director independence, and other procedural matters (conforming to HKSE "Best Practices", adopting procedural rules for shareholder meetings, etc.). The company also linked executive compensation to performance via an incentive compensation scheme. Motivated in large part by the continuing need for large amounts of capital, PetroChina thus conformed in spirit to conventions of corporate governance more stringent than those otherwise enforced in China.

These changes notwithstanding, the functional reality resulting from them did not eliminate risks to minority shareholders. Ten percent of the capital raised in the offering was returned to CNPC, which controlled 90% of PetroChina and, through staff transfers, dominated management (e.g., Ma Fucai, chairman of PetroChina, was president of CNPC). This position would allow CNPC to influence key financial decisions (such as dividend policy), operating decisions, and those related to services and products for which PetroChina had limited alternative sources other than its parent. Of particular concern to foreign investors, legal recourse would be constrained by the lack of treaties that would permit enforcement of overseas judgments. Finally, senior management remained members of the Chinese Communist Party (CCP), including Ma, who was elected as an alternate member of the Central Committee of the CCP at its 16th Party Congress.

Source: Adapted from Sang Xu and Mary Ho. 2002. "PetroChina: International Corporate Governance with Chinese Characteristics," Centre for Asian Business Cases, University of Hong Kong, HKU183, February 15.

Exhibit 26.7. Disintermediation in Asia (2001–2010).

Market	Domestic Credit		Domestic Capital Markets		(%) Increase in Capital Markets
	2001	2010	2001	2010	
China	65.86	54.16	34.14	45.84	34
Hong Kong	28.83	13.43	71.16	86.57	22
Indonesia	54.48	35.23	45.51	64.77	42
Japan	57.60	47.45	42.40	52.56	24
Korea, South	49.24	32.41	50.76	67.59	33
Malaysia	40.82	33.53	59.18	66.47	12
Philippines	40.68	24.26	59.32	75.74	28
Singapore	33.00	20.20	67.00	79.79	19
Thailand	67.54	48.74	32.46	51.26	58

Source: Asian Bond Online.

CAPITAL MARKET DEVELOPMENT

The transition from relationship to rule-based governance is closely tied to the deepening of capital markets that accompanies an increasing level of disintermediation.

Among the most critical factor inputs and products of capital markets is information. The very efficiency of capital markets rests on their ability to disclose information and the speed with which information is processed. Thus, capital market development is intimately linked with the evolution of legal and regulatory structures that promote timely disclosure and dissemination of information, enhance liquidity, reduce investor uncertainty, and promote investor confidence.

Disintermediation

Earlier in this chapter, we noted regional responses to the financial crisis that beset Asia in the late 1990s. These included initiatives to reduce dependence on debt generally, and bank debt specifically, while actively encouraging the development of local currency capital markets. This broad-based process of disintermediation swept Asia in the following decade. Exhibit 26.7 documents the expansion of capital market finance between 2001 and 2010.

Moreover, International Corporate Finance in Practice 26.3 highlights the role of private, non-bank institutions in China — Alibaba for example — in offering money market services.

In particular to note are the relatively greater advances made by the countries most afflicted by the Asian financial crisis. China, as one example, has demonstrated large-scale increases in the use of both equities and bonds, reflecting successful governance reforms, as well as concerted measures to develop both local currency equity and bond markets.

Equity market

The development role of equity financing encourages information flows from management to shareholders and other stakeholders, and can also help better align the interests among them — the hallmark of good governance. Equity market development also supports effective investment allocation by promoting the transfer of savings from short- to long-term (permanent) investment and facilitates the funding of large, indivisible projects characterized by

INTERNATIONAL CORPORATE FINANCE 26.3

A Money Market Colossus Rises

In just four years, a money-market fund created by an affiliate of China's Alibaba Group Holding Ltd. has become the world's largest, providing millions of the country's savers a high-returning place to park their money. Now, it is facing pressure from regulators to slow down. Fueled by contributions from some 370 million account holders, the fund, known as Yu'e Bao- which means *"leftover treasure"*-has grown rapidly to manage $211 billion in assets. It is more than twice the size of the next largest money-market fund, a US dollar liquidity fund managed by J.P. Morgan Asset Management, according to data from Morningstar Inc. Yu'e Bao's assets doubled in the past year alone, and the fund now makes up a quarter of China's money-market mutual fund industry. Its ascent has been an accidental byproduct of a sharp shift among Chinese consumers toward mobile payments. Yu'e Bao draws its funds from users of Alipay, an electronic-payments platform used by roughly one-third of China's population to make purchases on Alibaba's e-commerce sites and to pay for everything from cinema tickets to household bills.

Attracted by the fund's generous returns-Yu'e Bao's investments produce a seven-day yield of 4.02%-some investors have been sending chunks of their monthly paychecks to it, another reason for its growth. A year ago, the fund's yield was 2.3%, according to Tianhong Asset Management Co., an Ant subsidiary that manages the fund. Yu'e Bao's short-term yield dwarfs the 1.5% interest rate on one-year Chinese bank deposits and even beats the 3.6% yield on 10-year Chinese government bonds. The fund invests most of its money in certificates of deposits issued by Chinese state-owned or state-supported banks. It also holds government bonds, bank-issued bonds and commercial paper. Data reviewed by The Wall Street Journal indicate Tianhong boosted Yu'e Bao's returns in recent years by increasing its allocation of funds to financial instruments with longer maturities. Such assets, however, tend to be less liquid than bank deposits and lower-yielding investments. About 40% of Yu'e Bao's investments mature in under 60 days, versus over 60% four years ago, according to Tianhong's reports.

The surge is making Chinese regulators nervous. In March, China's securities regulator called for "significantly stronger" risk controls at money-market funds to "prevent systemic risks caused by large-scale redemptions". The concern is that money-market funds could see sudden and large-scale redemptions by investors if, for example, returns drop, or during periods of broader market turmoil. If the funds are forced to liquidate large volumes of assets to raise cash, the moves could potentially destabilize the financial system. In early September, regulators issued new liquidity rules requiring money-market funds to boost their holdings of higher-quality assets, such as short-term debt securities, that carry top credit ratings. The regulator also labeled money-market funds as "systemically significant" and instructed them to curb their exposure to individual financial institutions. The new rules take effect on Oct l. Tianhong said it has various measures in place to prevent a liquidity crunch and believes the "probability of mass redemption is very low". It said most of the fund's customers have fairly small holdings of around $590 on average.

Source: *Wall Street Journal* (September 14, 2017); reprinted with permission.

Exhibit 26.8. Bonds versus equity in Asian capital markets in percentage of total financing.

Market	2010	
	Bonds	Equity
China	10.65%	23.49%
Hong Kong	7.91	63.25
Indonesia	30.98	14.53
Japan	28.02	14.38
Korea, South	34.27	16.49
Malaysia	23.45	35.73
Philippines	31.82	27.50
Singapore	21.36	45.64
Thailand	16.20	16.25

economies of scale. It advances pricing efficiency by establishing asset pricing benchmarks and channeling liquidity (i.e., portfolios flows) between markets. Lastly, it provides an exit strategy for investments by entrepreneurs and venture capitalists, while establishing a basis for liquidity in financing innovation.

As Exhibit 26.8 suggests, equity as a source of capital remained relatively underutilized across Asia, except in the most developed markets — e.g. Hong Kong and Singapore. In most of the region, equity capital was handicapped by overregulation, a dearth of independent institutional investors, and various structural market features that have hampered effective price discovery. With regard to regulatory constraints, many Asian countries have controlled or rationed access to equity capital either by requiring issuers to issue at a predetermined par value versus market value (e.g., Japan, Korea, and Taiwan)[21] or by simply requiring regulatory approval for an issuing sequence in any given year (e.g., China). Such measures were designed to influence the supply of shares and mitigate downward pressure on equity prices as the local equity market expanded. The danger, of course, would be the hollowing out the local market, as the ablest local firms decide to issue equity more cheaply in foreign markets.

Conversely, the equity market issuing experience in Asia between 2000–2008 and 2009–2018 has in fact be quite robust. Average equity capital raised by Asian companies across the two periods increased from US$45 billion to US$67 billion, buoyed by new listings by Asian companies due primarily to a significant increase in the role of public equity markets China.[22] Moreover, with respect to growth companies, advanced markets in Asia — Japan, Korea and Hong Kong — have all experiences an increase in listings. Outpacing the global average are Korea and Japan where 90% of initial public offerrings in the decade ending 2018 were by growth companies.[23]

In China, a legacy of corporatization has left the Chinese government as the major shareholder of many SOEs, with economy-wide ownership levels in excess of 50%. Despite a very rapid and pronounced expansion of private listings in China, global market capitalization among the top 100-listed Chinese companies remains dominated by state or mixed ownership firms.[24] For domestic listings in particular, this concentration has presented challenges with implications for shareholder value. To reduce its ownership, the Chinese government must continue to sell off its holdings. However, that prospect depresses share prices on Chinese stock exchanges. To address this challenge, China as early as 2004 began a series of reforms that required SOEs to develop share compensation schemes under which existing shareholders would be compensated in a predefined manner as the government continued to sell off previously non-tradable shares (NTSs). Notwithstanding, an overhang of government-owned shares will continue to put subtle pressure on the market values of Chinese listed shares with side effects including increased volatility (see Exhibit 26.9).

Nurturing equity markets for entrepreneurs and venture capitalists

The challenge of financing entrepreneurship through capital markets, including specifically private equity, is linked inexorably to the development of public equity markets. Given that the primary objective of any private equity investor is to *exit* the investment efficiently and at the highest possible price, public equity markets offer a liquidity channel to the extent they are accessible to small and medium-sized enterprises and venture-backed firms. Among the

21 Par issuance requires firms to issue new shares at the firm's predetermined par value as opposed to the firm's then-prevailing market value. If, as under usual circumstances, market value exceeded par value, this represented a form of severe underpricing and served as a significant disincentive to firms to issue new equity.

22 https://www.oecd.org/corporate/ca/OECD-Equity-Market-Review-Asia-2019.pdf.

23 *Ibid.*

24 https://www.piie.com/research/piie-charts/2023/chinas-state-vs-private-company-tracker-which-sector-dominates.

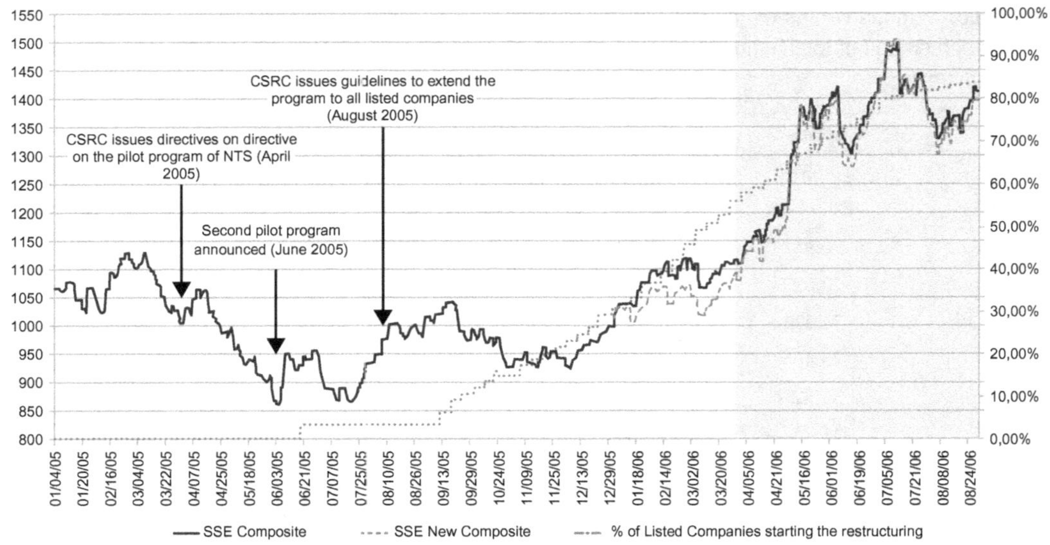

Exhibit 26.9. Market performance and progress of NTSs reform.

Source: Andrea Beltratti and Bernardo Bortolotti. 2006. "The Non-Tradable Share Reform in the Chinese Stock Market," Working paper, September 13.

specific equity market reforms undertaken across markets has been the introduction and promotion of "second" markets. These markets are designed to facilitate public listing of local small and medium-sized enterprises (SMEs). They generally have lower issuing requirements and are designed to offer an exit channel for entrepreneurs and private equity investors. For issuers, especially SMEs, they offer access to permanent local currency sources of capital and so encourage the active use of equity. From the perspective of equity market development, second markets can mitigate hollowing out by establishing a framework for firms to issue equity in local currency and advance the implementation of rules-based governance practices in order to increase investor participation. Enhanced trading liquidity and stock valuation in turn improve the supply of investable securities and further promote the participation of local institutional investors. Specific examples of second markets in Asia include Mothers, an affiliate of the Tokyo Stock Exchange, established in 1999; Growth Enterprise Market (GEM) in Hong Kong, established as both "an exit ground and a venue for further fund raising"; and ChiNext, a second market in China that is designed to relieve access constraints for SMEs.

Market regulation and globalization

In addition to market-inhibiting domestic policies and regulations, Asian policy-makers placed restrictions on investment in domestic equities by foreigners. The rationale for such regulations was to protect against price instability and loss of control to foreign investors when equity markets are shallow. The disadvantage was to restrict the liquidity and market discipline that domestic, and especially foreign, institutional investors can provide. Thus, there is a sequencing issue evident in the decision to allow access to a local equity (or any capital) market to foreigners: Markets must be of sufficient depth and demonstrate adequate liquidity at the time of opening to foreign investors to withstand sudden inflows (and outflows) of new capital.

Evidence of such market segmentation between local and foreign shareholders through either regulation or separate share classes of ownership became widespread in Asia's equity market development experience. South Korea, Thailand, Indonesia, Malaysia, and Taiwan imposed such restrictions as did China. Where restrictions have been lifted and the differentiation among share classes reduced or abolished, Asian equity markets have demonstrated a higher degree of correlation[25] with markets in North America and Europe. For example, over the 25-year period ending 2024 Japanese and Korean equity markets have exhibited

25 A correlation coefficient measures to the degree co-movement between two equity market indexes. A correlation coefficient of 1 signifies perfectly synchronous movement in index values. Increasing levels of correlation between 0 and 1 imply greater degrees of market integration with major capital markets.

Exhibit 26.10. Chinese classes of shares.

Security	Listing Market	Currency	Headquarters	Investors
A shares	Shanghai and Shenzhen	RMB	PRC	Domestic
B shares	Shanghai and Shenzhen	Shanghai — US$ Shenzhen — H KD	PRC	Foreign and Domestic
H shares	Hong Kong	HKD	PRC	Foreign
ADRs	New York — NYSE	US$	PRC	Foreign
N shares	New York	US$	PRC	Foreign
Red chips	Hong Kong	HKD	Hong Kong	Foreign

Source: Matthews International Capital Management, LLC, 2004 with author updates.

a correlation of approximately 0.7 with those in the US.

Cases of market segmentation offer a useful means to understand the benefits of portfolio diversification to foreign investors. Among Asian examples, foreign investors have consistently paid premiums (i.e., have accepted lower rates of return) for the same securities (and same underlying cash flows) traded in share classes segmented by residency. Such pricing differences can be in part explained by overseas demand for investments, especially in large firms with good credit ratings when general demand for international investment is high. Market segmentation continues to persist in the case of China. Chinese equity is divided into multiple share classes based on ownership eligibility and incorporation. As indicated in Exhibit 26.10, A shares are denominated in renminbi and traded in China by Chinese residents. B shares were originally intended only for foreign investors. They are listed in US or Hong Kong dollars and also trade in China. H shares are shares of Chinese-incorporated firms listed in Hong Kong and trade in Hong Kong dollars. Red chips represent firms with Chinese operations that are incorporated internationally, as in Hong Kong. In each case, voting and distribution rights are based on listing market regulations. With regard to voting rights in particular, while these generally conform to "one-share-one-vote", some markets — e.g., NYSE — permit dual class structures.[26]

Unlike in other cases in Asia, where foreign-eligible shares trade at a premium to resident-only shares, in China, foreign-eligible B shares and H shares have in the past traded at significant discounts to resident A shares. There are several arguments to explain what appears to be a pricing anomaly. At the firm level, there is evidence that the B shares of firms with weaker governance have traded at a discount to dual-listed shares of firms with stronger governance. At the system level, because few alternatives exist for Chinese investors to diversify their portfolio holdings, the demand for A shares has been less responsive to price changes than the demand for B or H shares, which substitute for each other and for red chips. Such price discrepancies are moderating as China's equity markets become more integrated with Hong Kong and other major stock exchanges via enhanced trading platforms such as Shanghai-Hong Kong Stock Connect, through which foreign investors may participate in the A-share market. Notwithstanding, the so-called AH premium has persisted among the most liquid Chinese companies with both A and H-shares eligible to be traded under the Stock Connect Scheme.[27]

Debt markets

The informational role of local currency debt markets, while similar with respect to information processing, governance, and pricing of equity markets, is more fundamental and complementary to the market for derivative securities, and therefore for the pricing and management of risk. Well-functioning debt markets define reference rates across maturities in local currency. Secondary debt markets promote

26 In recent years China has experimented with dual class structures on a limited basis. See for example, https://www.ecgi.global/publications/blog/chinas-experiment-dual-class-equity-structure#:~:text=Consequently%2C%20as%20of%20November%202023,has%20been%20dormant%20in%20China.

27 The Hang Seng Stock Connect China AH Premium Index tracks the average price difference of A over H shares for companies with listings in both markets. The top 50 constituents of the index and the associate A/H price ratio of each is available at https://www.hsi.com.hk/static/uploads/contents/en/dl_centre/factsheets/ahpremiume.pdf.

liquidity and pricing efficiency based on risk profiles (maturity, reinvestment, credit, etc.). Governance regimes that protect creditor rights, built on comprehensive and enforceable company law, securities law, contract law, and bankruptcy law, encourage active investor participation, while information channels — rating agencies, accounting/disclosure rules by firms — establish reliable databases for measuring probabilities of default risk. Most critically missing, in the absence of local currency debt markets, is a market-determined term structure of interest rates, also known as the *yield curve*. Because derivative securities (futures, options, and swaps on equity, interest rates, and foreign exchange) are priced using a market reference rate, the lack of a yield curve hampers the development of local derivatives markets (and so risk management). Ultimately the best of local issuers may be encouraged to issue externally, thus hollowing out local markets, while those who are unable to issue foreign currency debt become overly reliant on banks and are thereby vulnerable to bank health and subject to potentially higher costs of capital.

In Asia, a legacy of underdeveloped capital markets marred by illiquidity, lack of depth of secondary market trading, and poor legal infrastructure accentuated the strains of the crises in the late 1990s, exposing deep risks posed by the heavy reliance on bank debt. This was further underscored by borrowings in currency and maturity combinations that left entire financial systems vulnerable to steep and rapid changes in interest rates and currency values. Debt dependence varied across countries. It was highest or increasing among the most deeply affected crisis economies. These included Indonesia, Thailand, and South Korea, where leverage was on average four times that of Asian economies such as Taiwan, Malaysia, and Singapore, which exhibited low debt use. In the wake of the crisis, Asian governments, acting serially or through regional institutions, focused on the underdevelopment of local currency debt markets as a particular cause of debt concentration across the region. In response they launched a series of reforms and institutional structures to nurture market development.

The Asian Bond Market Initiative, sponsored by ASEAN and including Japan, China, and South Korea, took aim at microstructure issues, and provided an institutional framework through which regional financial policy-makers could examine global best practices and offer policy options on such matters as settlement and clearing, as well as strengthening local credit rating institutions. The launch of the Asian Bond Fund (ABF), a regional local currency bond fund, helped to validate the investment thesis for local currency–denominated debt and to provide improved liquidity and pricing. On the supply side, international financial institutions, most notably the Asian Development Bank, have issued bonds denominated in local currencies of different maturities to facilitate the establishment of domestic yield curves. In addition to governance reforms aimed at protecting bondholders, new regulations enhanced disclosure standards (e.g., Thailand), minority shareholder rights (e.g., South Korea and Thailand), and bankruptcy protection (e.g., Indonesia and Thailand). Finally, policy-makers devised and executed market-based solutions to both acquire and dispose of non-performing loans (NPLs) in order to improve bank balance sheets and remove bad loans from the banking system. Creative bond market solutions have included the securitization of distressed loans in both domestic and global markets, including the Korea Asset Management Corporation (KAMCO) highlighted in International Corporate Finance in Practice 26.4.

These various reforms and initiatives have contributed to material change in the region's outstanding issuances of local currency bonds since 1999, which has extended to the present. Exhibit 26.11 presents the comparative issuing experience in local currency bond markets in Emerging Asia from 2010 through 2023. Importantly, issuer diversity has also expanded, as approximately one-third of total outstanding bonds are corporate issuances. Supporting this growth have been improvements in issuer credit quality and the emergence of a broader institutional investor base of pension funds with local currency liabilities. Similarly, the maturing of an asset management industry in the region, including the development of mutual funds, has enhanced liquidity and price discovery in these markets.

Despite definite progress in reducing debt concentration and bank dependence, the development of national bond markets has nonetheless varied. As illustrated in Exhibit 26.12, development has been uneven, and, except in the case of the most developed markets, e.g., Hong Kong, South Korea, Singapore and more recently China, local bond markets remain heavily laden with government issues. China is especially noteworthy. The PRC has made extensive use of leverage to fuel its growth over the last 25 years, significantly expanding use of both government and corporate bonds.

INTERNATIONAL CORPORATE FINANCE IN PRACTICE 26.4
KAMCO

The Korea Asset Management Corporation (KAMCO) was established in 1962 to manage and dispose of the bad debts of the Korean Development Bank (KDB). In 1998 Kamco was owned 34% by the South Korean government, 31% by 24 commercial banks, and 31% by the KDB. Prior to the financial crisis in South Korea, banks typically funded long-term local currency investments with short-term foreign currency loans from offshore banks. When the crisis hit, this combined currency-maturity mis-match jeopardized local banks, forcing recapitalizations by the government and resulting in large volumes of non-performing loans (NPLs). In 1997, KAMCO received the additional mandate to acquire, manage, and dispose of these distressed assets as quickly and efficiently as possible, while maintaining sufficient liquidity to continue to purchase NPLs.

In 1998, to raise additional external capital, KAMCO launched an issuance of asset-backed securities (ABSs) backed by its NPL portfolio. This was then the largest ABS issued in South Korea and the first international NPL-backed offering in Asia outside of Japan. Under the deal, KAMCO sponsored a multitiered asset-backed security that securitized a portfolio of its NPLs, with each loan carrying full recourse to the originating bank. Among the ancillary objectives of the offering was to develop interest in South Korean debt, particularly NPLs, and to develop South Korea's ABS markets. At the time, KAMCO's loan book consisted of 135 NPLs to South Korean corporations, denominated in US dollars (90%) and yen. The aggregate outstanding principal of the debt was $395.3 million, dominated by loans originated by the KDB. Fitch and Moody's both rated the issuance BBB+, i.e., similar to their rating on KDB debt. Pricing was estimated at 200 basis points over LIBOR, which was relatively cheap compared to the few other comparables then trading.

Source: Adapted from George Chacko and Jacob Hook et al. 2004. "KAMCO and the Cross-Border Securitization of Korean Non-Performing Loans." *Harvard Business School Publishing*.

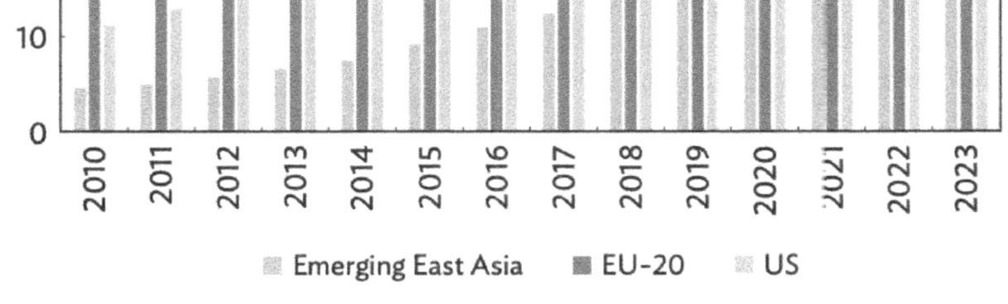

Exhibit 26.11. Outstanding local currency bonds.

Source: Asian Bond Online, https://asianbondsonline.adb.org/documents/abm_mar_2024.pdf.

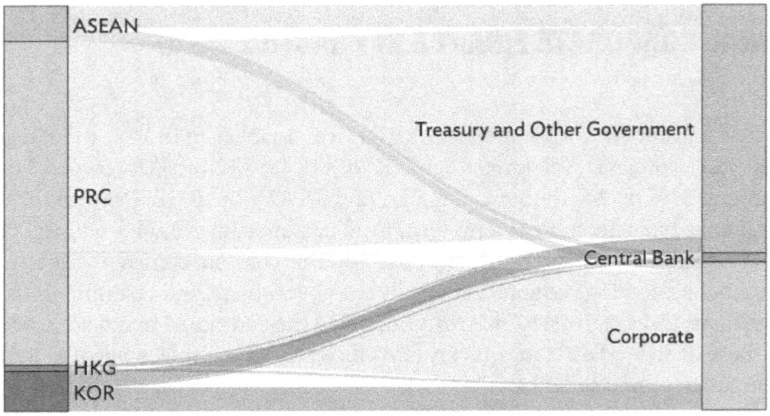

Exhibit 26.12. Outstanding local currency bonds by market.

Source: Asian Bond Online, https://asianbondsonline.adb.org/documents/abm_mar_2024.pdf.

CAPITAL STRUCTURE AND THE COST OF CAPITAL

Discussions of capital structure generally focus on the relative use of debt versus equity. Certainly, differences in taxability and return structures between these two sources of capital warrant separate consideration and treatment in understanding the financial policy of the firm and in analyzing its cost of capital. However, intraclass differences — those between intermediated and market-based debt, for example — are likewise important, as they can have impacts not only on the cost of capital, but also on governance and control.

Let us reconsider Vogel's description of capital structure choice (i.e., the use of bank debt by Japanese firms) that was presented in the preamble to this chapter. Because bank debt is short-term and carries a lender option to renew, and because a firm can convey private information to banks (as opposed to public bondholders), it had been argued that Japanese firms carried relatively more debt than non-Japanese firms. In addition, because the Japanese main bank held equity in the firms to which it lent, it was able to align its interests more closely with those of shareholders. Finally, as the bank acquired and produced information about the firm, it was able to affect managerial actions and to mitigate agency effects either *ex ante* or *ex post*, as the Toyo case demonstrated. During Japan's high growth period and extending into the 1990s (i.e., while the main bank relationship dominated Japanese finance), the use of bank debt in Japan was in fact been shown to constrain managerial discretion, mitigate agency costs, and so lower the cost of capital.

If bank debt was advantageous, why then were Japanese firms keen to embrace capital market finance? Here the argument returns to managerial discretion. In fact, while mitigating agency effects, banks can place operating constraints on management and so impose hidden costs of monitoring (i.e., agency costs) of their own. For large, well-established, and successful firms, able to leverage their reputations, capital market finance, specifically bond issuance in either local or global bond markets, offers the potential to access larger pools of capital at lower cost. In the case of Japan, the deregulation of bond markets was also advantageous to firms that did not have an established main bank relationship or otherwise had no access to preferential government-sponsored financing. Thus, for firms able to access capital markets, when afforded the choice, Japanese firms opted to reduce systematically their use of bank debt and increase their use of market-based sources of capital. In conjunction with this shift, they likewise opted to reduce cross-shareholdings in order to free up capital for more productive uses. This shift in capital structure patterns commenced with the deregulation of Japan's domestic bond markets in the mid-1980s, and accelerated through the next decade.[28]

Recent evidence on the financing policies of emerging market firms, including those domiciled

28 Hoshi, T. and A. Kashyap. 2001, *Corporate Financing and Governance in Japan: The Road to the Future.* Cambridge, MA: MIT Press.

in East and Southeast Asia, suggests that there have been substantial reductions in debt ratios since the early 1990s. Indeed, the leverage ratios of emerging market firms, including those in Asia, have dropped by more than 10% since the late 1990s. Furthermore, as capital markets developed, and as integration of emerging markets with the world economy has advanced, country characteristics have become less important than firm-level characteristics in explaining financing decisions. In the early 1990s, within the same country there were limited differences in corporate leverage policies. More recently, firm-level variables now explain a substantially larger share of the variation across firms with respect to emerging-market capital structure determinants. These are now comparable to determinants in developed markets, and the explanatory role of the country of origin has been diminished. For emerging market firms, in Asia as elsewhere, this suggests that those with sufficient access to capital markets are able to make discrete choices in leverage use and overall financing policy, and that firm-level characteristics, including size, profitability, and asset tangibility, rather than country variables, best inform capital structure decisions in the region.[29] In fact, with the development of local currency markets, improving company fundamentals since the crises and better credit quality permit more firms access to local currency capital.

Consistent with the development of local capital markets in non-Japan Asia, well-established local firms likewise have begun to move away from bank debt toward market-based bond financing. Furthermore, large, globally competitive Asian firms have accessed major bond markets and issued debt denominated in US dollars, euros, yen, or British pounds at competitive costs of debt. In 2010, for example, over 50 Asian corporations and banks raised their first overseas debt, as the region's share of global bond issuances tripled since the financial crises in 1997.[30]

However, given the uneven level of local bond market development in non-Japan Asia and a still relatively low level of equity market capitalization, bank debt continues to be an important source of local capital. As both the corporate and banking sectors stabilized in the decade after the crises, the volume of bank deposits expanded, enabling banks to rebuild and maintain sources of local currency capital. Moreover, the quality of bank assets (especially loans to corporations) also improved steadily. However, bank operating costs have remained relatively high across the region (with cost-to-income ratios averaging between approximately 40 and 55%). This places a floor under the cost of capital for firms without sufficient access to local or global capital markets (i.e., those that do not have the discretion to make firm-level capital structure choices with respect to sources of capital), and suggests a rather bifurcated profile of corporate finance.

Over time, the continued development of Asia's capital markets will allow Asian firms greater funding flexibility and better access to growing pools of local currency capital. As the microstructure of these markets improves and the markets themselves mature and deepen, capital costs are expected to decline as the functioning of the secondary market steadily improves, with better liquidity, improved governance, lower information barriers, and so reduced agency costs.

PERFORMANCE, VALUE, AND THE PRACTICE OF CORPORATE FINANCE

The final link in the continuum chain connects capital market access and capital structure choice back to governance. Its focus is the practice of corporate finance, specifically performance and value creation. Value-accretive activities — effective cost management, efficient capital investment, sound financial policy making — are reflected in strong corporate performance. In contrast, value-reducing actions are reflected in poor performance, and leave managements vulnerable to the disciplining effects of capital markets with the threat of hostile takeovers. Undoubtedly, capital markets in East Asia have matured institutionally and deepened significantly since the crisis years. In many cases, the architecture of the economic and financial policies that facilitated rapid economic growth — government-sponsored finance and relationship-based lending practices — has weakened. But are development trajectories converging toward a single paradigm? There is, in fact, a discernible evolution from relationship-based to market-based finance driven in large part by increasingly unrestricted flows of capital. In order to build globally competitive industries and national firms, it is argued that emerging market countries must dismantle the regulatory and institutional infrastructure

29 Fernandes, N. 2011. "Global Convergence of Financing Policies: Evidence for Emerging-Market Firms." *Journal of International Business Studies* 42: 1043–1059.

30 Miller, M. 2011. "Asia's Bond Market Boom Looks Set to Continue." *Institutional Investor*, April 11.

of relationship finance and build market-based institutions that foster competitiveness. Such a process is predicated on rules-based corporate governance and improved capital market transparency, accountability, and efficiency — all grounded in enforceable corporate and securities laws.

The gradual liberalization of domestic markets to global investors or overseas equity issuances, including the foreign listings of firms such as PetroChina, exposes East Asian corporations to the scrutiny of the global investment community that requires reliable sources of information about their holdings and is concerned about the protection of minority shareholder rights. The value these investors attach to the quality of management is reflected in share prices and extends to global markets for corporate control that leave management teams vulnerable to the market discipline of the collective actions of global shareholders. The globalization of product markets likewise requires a concerted approach to innovation, productivity, and profitability in order to perform effectively in such increasingly competitive markets.

It is interesting that, despite the general consistency in curricula of corporate finance globally, the tools of modern corporate finance (e.g., capital asset pricing model to estimate costs of equity, discounted cash-flow analysis for capital budgeting, and weighted average cost of capital to measure overall cost of capital) are rather unevenly applied in practice throughout Asia. Perhaps not dissimilarly to other regions, the practical application of these analytical constructs or best practices is more a function of the size of the firm, the complexity of its capital budget and financial structure, and importantly the level of development of local capital markets. This implies that firm-level characteristics, rather than broad generalizations of sophistication, help explain the way corporate finance is practiced in East Asia.

In spite of continued weaknesses with respect to corporate governance, many East Asian firms have become effective global competitors. This suggests that independently strong firms have overcome gaps or barriers in domestic markets by cultivating good governance, thereby enhancing corporate performance, and ultimately driving tangible increases in corporate value.

The case of Asahi Glass illustrates how the imperative of global competitiveness, combined with deft financial policy and strong corporate governance in the broader context of reform and restructuring in Japan, can drive corporate performance and hence value (see International Corporate Finance in Practice 26.5).

INTERNATIONAL CORPORATE FINANCE IN PRACTICE 26.5
Asahi Glass Company

Asahi Glass Company (AGC) is a Japanese multinational manufacturer of flat glass, chemicals, electronics, and displays. With annual sales of ¥1.3 trillion in 2002, it enjoyed the largest global market share in most of its product categories. Its overseas operations included more than 200 subsidiaries and affiliates in 25 countries and generated ¥52.4 billion in overseas operating profit. In 2002 the company split into four business units operating internationally. AGC is a member of the Mitsubishi group. Its main bank was Mitsubishi Bank and its successor Bank of Tokyo–Mitsubishi (BOTM). The bank was Asahi Glass's seventh-largest shareholder (with 3.8% share ownership). Reciprocally, the company owned 0.9% of Mitsubishi Tokyo Financial Group. Asahi Glass's banking relationship was an important component of its financing strategy, especially in overseas markets where it had limited access to capital market debt. However, like many Japanese firms, it began to make aggressive use of capital markets finance in the 1980s. The company in 2002 was rated A2 (Moody's) and A– (Standard & Poor's). Management was very conscious of its credit ratings and sought to protect them by careful management of its exposure to both business and financial risk.

To compete more effectively on a global basis, Asahi Glass began in 1999 to take a portfolio approach to capital investment strategy and resource allocation. The company delegated significant investment discretion to unit management, forcing managers to become more sensitive to the unit's capital structure and credit risk. To complement these measures, it took steps to align manager and shareholder interests through incentive compensation schemes. At the corporate level, it instituted a series of governance reforms that focused on making executive decision-making more efficient. The company's board of directors was streamlined from 20 to seven members. Two independent directors were added to the board. The scope of board meeting agendas was reduced as more authority was delegated to unit presidents. In focusing on its global operating and financial strategies and restructuring corporate governance, Asahi Glass also reevaluated its strategic holdings and, in particular, its cross-holding relationship with BOTM. The yield on its bank assets was approximately 1%. Management believed that this capital could be better deployed to higher-yielding investments and so began to steadily reduce its cross-holdings (from ¥224.5 billion in 1997 to ¥137.5 billion in 2003), finally announcing in 2003 a mutual divestiture with its banks, dismantling a key component of the main bank system.

Source: Adapted from Desai, Mihir A. and Egawa, M. 2004. "The Continuing Transformation of Asahi Glass: Implementing EVA." *Harvard Business School Publishing.*

SUMMARY

1. Our earliest thinking about finance in East Asia was colored by views of the uniqueness of Japan's story and its success at leveraging bank loans (i.e., a bank-centric model) to mobilize capital for rapid economic growth.
2. Relationships — among firms, banks, and government — were substituted for rules-based or market-based governance and gave managers the flexibility to think in long-range terms. The model was emulated by many of the countries of East and Southeast Asia in various forms and degrees.
3. However, Asia's outward-looking economic model, driven by access to global product markets and embracing of global competition, has outgrown a financial infrastructure that represses local markets for capital.
4. The crises that plagued Asian finance in the 1990s were both a harbinger and a catalyst for change. The by-products of financial repression — concentrated bank debt, underdeveloped local capital markets, ineffective governance, and high costs of capital — put firms at risk and required active responses at both the system level (i.e., government policy) and corporate level. Policymakers and corporate financial officers have responded.
5. Governance reforms and active measures to promote the development of local capital markets have given firms more tools with which to manage capital structure. Likewise, creative CFOs have, under their own initiative, responded independently by opting for governance regimes that provide them greater access to large pools of permanent capital at globally competitive costs.
6. Change continues as demographic shifts evolve, the pace of economic growth slows, regional economies become further integrated into the global economy, and global capital continues to flow into the region's financial systems.

QUESTIONS FOR DISCUSSION

1. What is the role that government-directed finance played in the economic development of Asia?
2. What are the functions performed by the main bank in Japanese finance?
3. What are the differences between the Japanese *keiretsu* and the South Korean *chaebol*?
4. What is the difference between relationship-based governance and rules-based governance? Why is it important to the development of capital markets?
5. What is meant by relationship banking? Why is it prevalent in East Asia?
6. Why is the absence of well-functioning bond markets in Asia a hindrance to the development of a complete derivatives market?
7. What is the logic of having multiple classes of shares list on Chinese stock exchanges?
8. What have been the major governance reforms promulgated in the aftermath of the Asian financial crisis?

REFERENCES

"ACGA White Paper on Corporate Governance in Japan." 2008. Hong Kong: Asian Corporate Governance Association, May.

Allen, F., J. Qian, and M. Qian. 2005. "Law, Finance, and Economic Growth in China." *Journal of Financial Economics* 77(1): 57–116.

Baxter, R. A. 2009. "Japan's Cross-Shareholding Legacy: The Financial Impact on Banks." *Asia Focus*, Federal Reserve Bank of San Francisco, August.

Corsetti, G. *et al.* 1999. "What Caused the Asian Currency and Financial Crisis?" *Japan and the World Economy* 11:305–373.

Gerlach, M. L. 1992. *Alliance Capitalism: The Social Organization of Japanese Business*. Berkeley: University of California Press.

Ghosh, S. R. 2006. *East Asian Finance: The Road to Robust Markets*. Washington, DC: World Bank.

Goswani, M., and S. Sharma. 2011. "The Development of Local Debt Markets in Asia." IMF Working Paper WP/11/132, June.

Herring, R. J., and N. Chatusripitak. 2000. "The Case of the Missing Market: The Bond Market and Why It Matters for Financial Development." Financial Institutions Center, Wharton School, University of Pennsylvania, pp. 1–8.

Hoshi, T., and A. Kashyap. 2001. *Corporate Financing and Governance in Japan: The Road to the Future*. Cambridge, MA: MIT Press.

Lemmon, M., and K. V. Lins. 2003. "Ownership Structure, Corporate Governance, and Firm Value: Evidence from the East Asian Financial Crisis." *Journal of Finance*, pp. 1445–1468, August.

McGuinness, P. B., and K. Keasey. 2010. "The Listing of Chinese State-Owned Banks and Their Path to Banking and Ownership Reform." *China Quarterly*, pp. 125–155, March.

Mitton, T. 2002. "A Cross-Firm Analysis of the Impact of Corporate Governance on the East Asian Financial Crisis." *Journal of Financial Economics* 64(2): 215–241.

Overholt, William H., Guonam Ma and Cheung Kwok Law. 2016. *Renminbi Rising*. Chichester, United Kingdom: John Wiley & Sons Limited.

Walter, Carl E., and Fraser J. T. Howie. 2011. *Red Capitalism: The Fragile Financial Foundation of China's Extraordinary Rise*. Hoboken, NJ: John Wiley & Sons.

27

Islamic Banking and Finance[1]

"Allah has allowed trading and forbidden riba (usury)"
—Koranic verse

The rapid growth of Islamic finance is testament to the diversity of global finance and the relevance of cultural and religious factors. Modern Islamic finance started in earnest in 1975 amidst considerable skepticism about its viability. Today, assets of Islamic institutions exceed $5 trillion, and most large Western financial institutions are involved in one way or another in the Islamic sector. Some, like HSBC, Standard Chartered, Citibank, Deutsche Bank and BNP Paribas have dedicated subsidiaries. Following the example of the Dow Jones Islamic Market Index (DJIM), there are other indices, such as the FTSE Shariah Index series, Tjomson Reuters Global Islamic Indices, and others that provide investors with benchmarks to track the performance of Shariah-compliant investments and facilitate the creation of investment products such as mutual funds, exchange-traded funds (ETFs), and other financial instruments that adhere to Islamic principles. Following the 2008 global financial meltdown, Islamic banks, unlike their conventional counterparts emerged relatively unscathed, which in turn provided greater legitimacy to this alternative form of finance.

All these developments may seem puzzling. Indeed, it is often said that the Islamic world has a hard time integrating in the global economic system. More specifically, how could practices rooted in the Middle Ages thrive in the age of technology-driven global finance? How could institutions suspicious of interest operate within a global, interest-based, financial system? And how could a phenomenon often considered to be a facet of political Islam experience its most rapid growth just as political Islam is under siege?

This chapter will:

- Summarize the fundamentals of the Islamic faith and explain how they have come to shape modern Islamic finance.
- Describe how the Islamic finance sector has evolved and changed during its short history.
- Explain the architecture of the main Islamic products.
- Identify firms that are acceptable investment vehicles for Islamic asset management.
- Profile and contrast key banks in the Islamic world.
- Discuss the impact of the global financial meltdown on Islamic finance.

THE UNDERLYING PRINCIPLES OF ISLAMIC FINANCE

Islam literally means surrender — that is believers (faithful) surrender to the will of *Allah* (as God is referred to in Arabic). The terms of Man's surrender to his God were revealed to Allah's messenger on earth — *Mohammed,* through the sacred scriptures-the *Koran*. If the tenets of the Islamic faith can be conceived as a pyramid the *Koran*, considered by Muslims to be God's word as conveyed to the Prophet Mohammed would stand at the top. Below it are the *Hadith* and the *Sunna*. Often used interchangeably, the first, commonly translated as the Traditions of the Prophet, actually refers to his words and deeds, as reported by a chain of transmission going all the way to the Prophet's companions, while the second refers to the righteous path established by those words and deeds.

1 This chapter was written by Professor Ibrahim Warde (Fletcher School, Tufts University).

As for issues and questions not addressed by those primary sources, the proper Islamic view can be obtained through *ijmaa* and *qiyas*. Ijmaa means consensus, and is based on the notion that the communal mind of Muslim scholars of a particular era provides assurance of freedom from error. Qiyas refers to reasoning by analogy or by logical inference based on primary sources. Jurists, through devout and careful reflection and effort (*ijtihad*) can derive appropriate rulings, by figuring out how the Prophet and his four immediate successors — the "right-guided caliphs" — would have acted, or what the accumulated wisdom of the community would prescribe. The *Shariah*, literally the path to water, is the Divine Law derived from all these sources.

Any religion that has survived for 14 centuries, and that has some 1.9 billion followers spread in every part of the globe must have some measure of flexibility and diversity. Not surprisingly, in various matters, including economic ones, there are disagreements as to what the Shariah dictates. The further down the pyramid, the broader the possible interpretations. The Koran, a short, specific text, is considered divine and eternal since it is the revealed word of God. The Hadith — a collection of short narratives that were not set down in writing until two to three centuries later — provide a first area of controversy. A great number of Hadiths were deemed apocryphal, typically fabricated to support a particular political faction or opinion, and a long process of authentication did not dispel all doubts about the veracity of certain texts. Specific narratives are often characterized as strong or weak, depending on the nature of the prevailing consensus about their truthfulness.

Such disagreements explain why different schools of jurisprudence (*fiqh*) developed over the years, each contributing different interpretations. By the tenth century, four main schools emerged within the orthodox Sunni tradition (The Shia had their own, separate schools): Hanafi, Shafii, Maliki and Hanbali. Every Sunni is in theory a follower of one of these schools. In classical Muslim society, four *qadis* (judges) in each major city would apply one of these four traditions to fill in areas of the law that were left undiscussed in the Koran and Hadith. Over the years however, each school found particular favor in certain localities, hence the geographical concentration of adherents that can be found nowadays.

To help understand the connection between religious principles and Islamic finance, one should also be aware of the distinction between *ibadat* and *muamalat*. Ibadat (acts of worship) refer to relations between man and God, such as prayer and fasting, are immutable, whereas muamalat (transactions) which refer to relations between man and man, and are open to evolution and change. Thus, in the realm of muamalat, which covers economic and financial dealings, there is considerable room to develop and change the law, albeit within limits set by the Koran and Hadith, in order to fulfill the *maqasid* (objectives) of the *Shariah* (Islamic law), which are to facilitate human interaction and promote justice and prosperity.

Such flexibility is made possible by the existence of adaptive mechanisms within the Islamic tradition. More specifically, three principles allow for departures from existing norms: *'urf* (local custom), *maslaha* (the public interest), and *darura* (necessity). The Shariah can thus be accommodated to societal developments, and allow for innovation, exceptions and loopholes, provided they are properly justified.

Riba (interest or usury)

At the core of Islamic finance is the prohibition of *riba*, a word meaning increase, and often translated as interest (see Box 27.1). In fact, it is not necessarily about interest as such, and it certainly is not exclusively about interest. It really refers to any unlawful or undeserved gain. Though there have been disagreements about what constitutes such gain, the prohibition was never in doubt.

The Koran declares that those who disregard the prohibition of riba are at war with God and his Prophet. That prohibition is explicitly mentioned in four different revelations of the Koran (2:275-81, 3:129-130, 4:161 and 30:39), expressing the following ideas: despite the apparent similarity of profits from trade and profits from riba, only profits from trade are allowed; when lending money, Muslims are asked to take only the principal and even forgo that sum if the borrower is unable to repay; riba deprives wealth of God's blessings; riba is equated with wrongful appropriation of property belonging to others; Muslims should stay away from it for the sake of their own welfare. Most other religions (among them Christianity and Judaism) as well as secular traditions (such as traditional Greek philosophy) had comparable misgivings, but over time distinctions appeared between "interest", a moderate, economically justified remuneration of capital, and "usury", an excessive, sometimes extortionary rate. No comparable evolution occurred among Islamic theologians. In most cases (including in the United States until 1980), a "usury ceiling" was established, separating lawful interest from unlawful usury in each state.

INTERNATIONAL CORPORATE FINANCE IN PRACTICE 27.1

Riba and the Time Value of Money

A question that often arises is how the time value of money is recognized if riba is forbidden in Islamic finance. Indeed the time value of money is an important concept in conventional finance — the value of $1 today is more than the value of $1 in the future. The postponement of consumption involves a sacrifice and thus the individual should be compensated for waiting. This increase in value is, however, considered to be riba and therefore prohibited under Islamic law ... Despite arguments against the time value of money, Islamic finance does allow for $1 today to be worth more than $1 tomorrow as long this is the result of investing/bearing risk rather than lending as there can be no notion of interest rate under Shariah law. The key point of differentiation is that time by itself cannot create value but investing and therefore bearing risk with associated profits (and losses) can create value.

Source: Abridged from Sapp, M. 2010. "A Note on Islamic Finance" 910N15. Richard Ivey School of Business, University of Western Ontario.

Gharar (uncertainty, risk or speculation)

A lesser known yet in the contemporary world of finance equally significant prohibition, is that of *gharar*. The question of gharar was generally ignored in the early writings on Islamic finance. It is only in the 1980s, with the pioneering work of Nabil Saleh and a handful of other specialists that serious work started appearing on this fundamental though ill-understood concept.[2] Unlike riba, which has parallels in all major religious traditions, gharar is unique to Islam, a religion steeped in commerce. It is also particularly relevant in today's financial environment.

The word gharar itself is not mentioned in the Koran, though etymologically related words, meaning deception or delusion with a connotation of peril, risk or hazard, are. It is however frequently mentioned in the Hadith. As in the case of riba, the prohibition is unequivocal though the concept lends itself to different interpretations. In most works on Islamic finance, it is translated as uncertainty, risk or speculation. Equating gharar with risk or uncertainty can be misleading, since it would be nonsensical, especially in a society of merchants to prohibit such things which are beyond human control. Furthermore, Islam does not even advocate the avoidance of risk. Indeed, incurring commercial risk is approved, even encouraged, since it provides the justification for profit.

Qadi Iyad, the 11th century Maliki scholar, defined *gharar* as "that which has a pleasant appearance but a hated essence". When it comes to commercial transactions, many deals look seductive but are fraught with hidden flaws, especially when transactions are aleatory, or conditioned on uncertain events. It is hard to resist the lure of easy money, hence the temptation to seek shortcuts and misrepresent to others (and often to oneself) the pitfalls of uncertain transactions. Such built-in ambiguities in turn lead to disputation and discord within the community. In the Hadith a range of transactions are forbidden: selling a fish in the sea, what is in the wombs and the contents of the udders, a runaway slave, etc. When it comes to foodstuffs, grapes cannot be sold until they become black, nor can grain be sold until it is strong. Merchants must be in possession of foodstuffs before selling them, at which time they must weigh them. There are also prohibitions against the "sale of gharar". Among such transactions are the "sale of the pebble" (the sale of an object determined by the throwing of a pebble), or the stroke of the diver.[3] Based on these hadiths, Frank Vogel has arranged those prohibitions in a spectrum, according to the degree of risk involved: pure speculation, uncertain outcome, unknowable future benefit, and inexactitude. He concluded that "a possible interpretation of the gharar hadiths is that they bar only risks affecting the existence of the object as to which

2 See Saleh, N. 1986. *Unlawful Gain and Legitimate Profit in Islamic Law.* Cambridge University Press (a second edition was published by Kluwer Law International in 1992) and Vogel, Frank E., and Hayes III, Samuel L. 1998. *Islamic Law and Finance: Religion, Risk and Return.* Cambridge, MA: Kluwer Law International.

3 Vogel, Frank E., and Hayes III, Samuel L. 1998. *Islamic Law and Finance: Religion, Risk and Return.* Cambridge, MA: Kluwer Law International, pp. 87–88.

the parties transact, rather than just its price." In the hadiths, such risks arise either (1) because of the parties' lack of knowledge (jahl, ignorance) about that object; (2) because the object does not now exist; or (3) because the object evades the parties' control. As explained by Maxime Rodinson:

> *Any gain that may result from chance, from undetermined causes, is here prohibited. Thus, it would be wrong to get a workman to skin an animal by promising to give him half the skin as reward, or to get him to grind some grain by promising him the bran separated out by the grinding process, and so on. It is impossible to know for certain whether the skin may not be damaged and lose its value in the course of the work, or to know how much bran will be produced.*[4]

In sum, a distinction is drawn between the risk connected to normal business transactions, and the kind of uncertainty that can be used by one party to take advantage of another. Clearly, since the early days of Islam, the worlds of commerce and finance have changed considerably though human nature — with its ever-present temptation to get something for nothing — has not. In today's financial environment, gharar is pervasive since it encompasses deceptive ambiguity, asymmetrical information, risk-shifting strategies and all forms of excessive and unnecessary risk-taking which are akin to betting and speculation.

To quote Nassim Taleb, *the glib snake oil façade of knowledge* promoted by finance professionals is a way designed to obfuscate and encourage investors to take risks they don't understand.[5] George Akerlof's "lemon theory" discusses the consequences of asymmetrial information — an endemic problem in finance since those who devise and sell complex instruments have an edge over those who buy them. Former business school professor John Kay, noting that "*it became increasingly hard to understand the nature of the underlying risk*" of such instruments describes the gulf between the theory and the reality. He writes:

> *The financial economics I once taught treated risk as just another commodity. People bought and sold it in line with their varying preferences. The result, in the Panglossian world of efficient markets, was that risk was widely spread and held by those best able to bear it. Real life led me to a different view. Risk markets are driven less by different tastes for risk than by differences in information and understanding. People who know a little of what they are doing pass risks to people who know less. Since ignorance is not evenly distributed, the result may be to concentrate risk rather than spread it.*[6]

Finally, gharar incorporates the prohibition of the kind of risk that is akin to outright speculation. Indeed, unlike conventional economics which has a benign attitude towards speculation, Islam forbids speculation and gambling (*qimar*). Three passages in the Koran prohibit Maysir,[7] a game of chance played in pre-Islamic days (2:219, 5:90, and 5:91).[8] In every instance, the prohibition is associated with that against wine drinking. The primary reason for condemning Maysir is that it causes enmity and distracts the faithful from worship.

All this explains the importance in the Shariah of seeking clarity, simplicity and avoiding unnecessary complexity. As for necessary and unavoidable risk, it must be based on equitable risk-sharing among those involved.

THE EVOLUTION OF ISLAMIC FINANCE

Modern Islamic finance is a young industry rooted in a very old tradition. It appeared as the result of specific historical circumstances, and later evolved through a complex process of trial-and-error. It was also shaped by broader competitive and political-economic factors. Although religion

4 Rodinson, M. *Islam and Capitalism*. London: Penguin, p. 16.

5 Nicholas Taleb, N. 2008. "The Fourth Quadrant: A Map Of The Limits Of Statistics. *The Edge*, September 15. http://www.edge.org/3rd_culture/taleb08/taleb08_index.html. See also Nicholas Taleb, N. 2007. *The Black Swan, The Impact of the Highly Improbable*. New York: Random House and *Fooled by Randomness: The Hidden Role of Chance in Life and in the Markets*, 2nd edition. New York: Random House, 2008.

6 Kay, J. 2007. "Same old folly, new spiral of risk." *Financial Times*, August 13.

7 A game of chance played by Arabs. The derivation is either from yusr (facility or ease, i.e., ease with which wealth could be attained) or from yasara (dividing anything into parts or portions).

8 Koran 2:219 "They ask thee about intoxicants and game of chance. Say: In both of them is a great sin and (some) advantage for men, and their sin is greater than their advantage. And they ask thee as to what they should spend. Say: What you can spare. Thus does Allah make clear to you the messages that you may ponder."

5:90 "O you who believe, intoxicants and games of chance and (sacrificing to) stones set up and (dividing by) arrows are only an uncleanliness, the devil's work; so shun it that you may succeed."

5:91 "The devil desires only to create enmity and hatred among you by means of intoxicants and games of chance, and to keep you back from remembrance of Allah and from prayer. Will you then keep back?"

was by definition central to Islamic finance, other variables — political, economic, social, cultural, demographic, etc. — also played a significant role.

The current state of the Islamic sector can best be understood by tracing its evolution through three distinct phases: the early years (1974–1991); the era of globalization (1991–2001); and the post-September 11 period (after 2001).

Early years (1974–1991)

Modern Islamic finance appeared in the early 1970s, at the confluence of two important developments in the Islamic world: the rise of pan-Islamism and the oil boom. The rise of pan-Islamism marked a new phase of the "Arab cold war" that had been raging since the 1950s. Its dominant figure was Egypt's President Gamal Abdel Nasser who was then a champion of pan-Arabism and the Third World's struggle against Western colonialism. Following the 1958 revolution in Iraq, Saudi Arabia emerged as the main Arab ally of the United States. King Faisal (1963–1975) sought to trump Nasser's pan-Arabism by founding a pan-Islamic movement, the Muslim World League, and used the pilgrimages to Mecca to forge ties with Islamic leaders, both inside and outside the Arab world. He also extended substantial amounts of aid to non-Arab Islamic countries in Asia and Africa.

Saudi Arabia's standing grew following the disastrous June 1967 war, after which a humbled Nasser embarked on a more moderate course. The year 1970, which was also the year Nasser died, saw the formal creation of the Organization of the Islamic Conference (OIC), which brought together 44 countries. It was under the auspices of the OIC that the idea of updating traditional Islamic banking principles — an endeavor that had preoccupied a few Islamic scholars, particularly in India and Pakistan, for a number of years — took center stage. Research institutes focusing on Islamic economics and finance sprouted throughout the Islamic world. A related development was the rapprochement between Saudi Arabia and Egypt now led by Anwar Sadat (1970–1981), which created a linkage between the Arab-Israeli conflict, and the price, indeed the availability, of oil. Soon, the price of oil would quadruple.

By the early seventies, the balance of power between oil producers and consumers and between governments and oil companies had shifted. Because of uninterrupted economic growth and the increased reliance on oil — at the expense of other energy sources — worldwide demand was very strong. Oil producers realized that with high inflation and a falling dollar, their oil receipts were steadily dwindling (in real terms, the price of oil, which had remained stagnant for decades, was going down). At the same time, oil-producing countries had become more assertive and better equipped to negotiate with oil companies. The October 1973 war between Arabs and Israelis triggered the first round of increases in oil prices along with an oil embargo in October 1973 against countries supporting Israel (including the United States).

In the wake of the quadrupling in oil prices, the 1974 OIC summit in Lahore voted to create the inter-governmental Islamic Development Bank (IsDB), which was to become the cornerstone of a new banking system inspired by religious principles. The sudden change in the financial fortunes of oil-exporting countries, many of them Islamic, was conducive to assertiveness and experimentation. The paradigm of modern Islamic banking was established in those years, through what Monzer Kahf called *the new alliance of wealth and Shariah scholarship.*[9]

What were the main tenets of Islamic finance? The realm of finance should be linked directly to the real economy, and governed by the principles of risk sharing and profit-and-loss sharing; interest-based lending (generally considered to be riba) should be replaced by Islamic financing contracts based on equity, sale or leasing; transactions involving speculation or gharar (a notion encompassing excessive or avoidable risk, deceptive ambiguity, and risk shifting) should be avoided, as are transactions involving haram (religiously forbidden) activities and unethical behavior; transactions must be clear and transparent and must fulfill social and developmental goals; leverage should be limited; certain conventional practices (such as short-selling) are not allowed; and financial innovations must be monitored by religious scholars.

Since riba was defined as interest, Islamic banking became synonymous with interest-free banking. The prevailing belief was that interest-based banking would be primarily replaced by profit-and-loss sharing (PLS) schemes. Instead of functioning on the basis of interest, Islamic banks would form partnerships based on profit-and-loss sharing with both depositors and would-be borrowers, through

9 Kahf, M. 2004. "Islamic Banks: The Rise of a New Power Alliance of Wealth and *Shari'a* Scholarship." In *The Politics of Islamic Finance*, edited by Clement M. Henry and Rodney Wilson. Edinburgh University Press.

the traditional Islamic practice of *mudaraba* (commenda partnership or trusteeship finance), discussed later. Another product, the old Islamic sale-based technique of *murabaha*, was, in its updated form, expected to play a subsidiary role; it became instead the most commonly-used product.

In 1975, the Dubai Islamic Bank, the first modern, non-governmental, Islamic bank came into existence. Islamic finance gathered momentum as a few countries (Pakistan in 1979, Iran and the Sudan in 1983) announced that their banking system would be entirely Islamicized. Another notable development, though one barely noticed at the time, also took place in 1983 when Malaysia introduced an Islamic banking legislation and created Bank Islam Malaysia Berhad (BIMB). Malaysia did not seek to Islamicize its financial sector, but rather to encourage a dual banking structure whereby an Islamic sector would coexist with the conventional one. Unlike Islamic finance in the Gulf, it was primarily driven by the developmental goals of the Malaysian government. The Islamic sector in Malaysia would greatly expand in later years, albeit with little interaction (until the post-September 11 era) with the Gulf-centered Islamic banks.

The performance of the first Islamic banks was disappointing: the profit-and-loss sharing model proved to be unworkable; the global recession and the sudden decline in oil prices throughout the 1980s had a devastating effect on the physical assets in which they were heavily invested. Furthermore, the Islamic sector was indirectly affected by financial scandals, such as those of Egypt's Islamic Money Management Companies (IMMCs) and the collapse of Bank of Credit and Commerce International (BCCI). None of these institutions was an Islamic bank, but the constant reference to their Islamic origins and character had a negative impact on the Islamic banking sector.

In later years, the international political economy changed beyond recognition, as it entered the age of globalization, the widely used catch-all concept encompassing a wide range of phenomena: the end of the Cold War and the emergence of a unipolar world, deregulation and increased openness of markets, the growing role of finance, the acceleration of technological change, etc. The fall of the Berlin War in November 1989 and the disintegration of the Soviet Union in December 1991 marked the end of the cold war. In the battle of ideas, of capitalism and the market economy over socialism and central planning. Within the Islamic world, the first Gulf War, following the invasion of Kuwait by Iraq, marked the beginning of a new regional order. The changes leading to a New World Order were accompanied by an ideological shift, which accelerated the transformation of finance. Many of the assumptions, indeed the founding principles, underlying the 1970s ijtihad crumbled. In particular, the world of international finance, which had not changed much in the fifties, sixties and seventies, underwent a veritable revolution in the eighties, one that has accelerated since.

The era of globalization (1991–2001)

This is when Islamic finance entered its second stage. In a departure from the early ideals, Islamic institutions moved toward more pragmatism and started focusing on ways of replicating conventional finance, albeit through Shariah-compliant contracts and within limits set by Shariah advisers. Largely driven by the oil boom, Islamic finance was also bound to be transformed by the collapse of oil prices in the 1980s. The attempt to create a new, fundamentally different financial order based on profit-and-loss sharing had failed. Islamic banks had been instead achieving the same goals as conventional banks, albeit through Islamic contracts and within the limits imposed by religious advisers. This new phase can be defined by its pragmatism, diversity, multi-polarity and convergence with conventional finance.

Financial deregulation allowed the creation of a wide range of new products. Just as it helped to create products to meet financial, legal or tax needs, financial engineering helped to devise products that would comply with religious precepts. Deregulation also had the effect of downgrading the role of interest: whereas conventional banks initially relied almost exclusively on "net interest income" (the difference between the interest charged to borrowers and the interest paid to depositors), they now relied on other sources of profits (from fees, proprietary trading, etc.) that were not directly linked to interest. Another factor was the rise of Islamism, which put pressure on governments throughout the Muslim world to allow for religiously-inspired financial products and institutions.

A new ijtihad gradually developed to deal with the changing position of Islamic finance within the international political economy and the new world of deregulated finance. Islamic finance grew more decentralized, diverse and pragmatic. New forms of Islamic finance also came into existence outside of the networks created by the first Islamic banks. This growing convergence led to the creation of Islamic units by many conventional banks. Western banks, such as Citibank and HSBC, created Islamic banking subsidiaries, respectively, in Bahrain (Citi Islamic) and in Dubai (HSBC Amanah). The late 1990s also saw the creation of the DJIM, which tracked companies whose products and financial practices did not violate Islamic law.

Post September 11, 2001

The third phase in the evolution of Islamic finance started after the September 11 attacks. The "global war on terror" which became the overarching theme of international relations had a significant but paradoxical impact on Islamic finance. The growing integration of Islamic finance in the global economic system was temporarily set back, as Islamic financial institutions found themselves suspected of funding terrorism.[10] But soon afterwards, the Islamic finance industry experienced dramatic growth and major transformations. Criticisms of Islamic banks were no doubt an important factor in the serious effort at rationalizing and streamlining Islamic finance. In parallel, the perception that Islam was under siege resulted in greater religiosity, which in turn drove an increase in demand for Islamic products.

Notable developments include countless new commercial and regulatory initiatives as well as the convergence of the Arab and the Malaysian models of Islamic banking. Coming under attack had the effect of greatly concentrating the minds of Islamic bankers and their regulators. As a result, efforts at international coordination and standardization grew more serious and better focused. The year 2002 alone saw the appearance of sovereign ijara (leasing) sukuk and the creation of coordination and standard-setting mechanisms such as the Islamic Finance Services Board (IFSB), the International Islamic Financial Market (IIFM), the Liquidity Management Center (LMC) and the Islamic International Rating Agency (IIRA). The Accounting and Auditing Organization for Islamic Financial Institutions (AAOIFI), though in existence since 1991 was greatly re-energized in its effort to harmonize accounting and auditing rules and create standard Islamic contracts. In 2005, International Islamic Centre for Reconciliation and Commercial Arbitration for Islamic Finance Industry was launched in Dubai in order to settle financial and commercial disputes.

The growth of Islamic finance shows no signs of abating. Initially scarce, Islamic financial products have multiplied in recent years, attracting a growing number of customers. No longer confined to the outer fringes of global finance, Islamic finance has also gone mainstream. Most major financial institutions are now involved in one way or another in Islamic finance, as are global consulting, accounting and information companies. Islamic financial institutions have spread all over the world. Within the Islamic world, Islamic financial institutions have become major economic players. Worldwide, they have become part of the financial landscape.

10 Warde, I. 2007. *The Price of Fear: The Truth behind the Financial War on Terror*, London: I.B.Tauris.

ISLAMIC FINANCING PRODUCTS

Most of the products offered by conventional financial institutions have some Islamic counterpart. Importantly however, the underlying contracts are often fundamentally different. Consider the case of *sukuk*, or *Islamic bonds*. From an investor's standpoint, the two are quite similar: they offer a fixed return at periodic intervals, they can be traded on the secondary market, and they will be redeemed at a certain date. Yet the underlying financial transactions are not the same: the conventional bond is an interest-bearing instrument with principal due at maturity, whereas the typical *sakk* (plural sukuk) represents a share in an underlying asset (typically real estate), and the periodic return usually represents a lease payment (see Box 27.2).

Thus, though Islamic products were often created to mirror conventional ones, their implications (for example, in the case of default or liquidation) are by no means identical. The contractual documentation is also usually significantly different. For example, a conventional leasing contract is typically a short one, incorporating all the elements of the lease, whereas the Islamic documentation for a comparable transaction is likely to include several contracts, in line with the Shariah principles of simplicity and clarity: a contract for the lease proper; another for the option to purchase the equipment (more likely to be a "promise" or *waad*), another for the agency agreement between lessor and lessee[11]; etc. Furthermore, the "fine print" in an Islamic contract is likely to include specific ethical and profit-and-loss-sharing features designed to prevent predatory practices.

To understand Islamic products, it is important to be aware of a number of building blocks. In the

11 In Islamic finance, the equipment owner must perform specific responsibilities, yet in practice he appoints the lessee as his agent through an agency (*wakala*) contract to perform such tasks as maintaining or repairing the equipment.

INTERNATIONAL CORPORATE FINANCE IN PRACTICE 27.2

Turkey to Sell Its First-Ever Islamic Bond

Turkey is gearing up to sell its first bond compliant with Islamic law, targeting emerging market investors as the country tries to diversity its funding sources. The sale of a dollar-denomination sukuk, is due to be completed on Tuesday and could raise more than $1billion, said one investor. About half, or $13 billion, of the Middle East's $24.3 billion of bonds sold in the first six months of 2012 were sukuks, according to data provider Dealogic, compared with $3 billion in Islamic bonds in the year-ago period out of $13 billion in deals. Conforming with Shariah law, which prohibits interest payments, sukuks also have attracted interest from investors outside of the region, including Malaysia and Indonesia, which have large Muslim populations.

In the sukuk, Turkey will sell certificates to investors, who will then lease them back to the issuer at a fee. This fee takes the place of a traditional interest rate. "Turkey is looking to broaden its investor base, and this makes good sense for the borrower", said Jeremy Brewin, head of the emerging-market division at Abiba. A banker involved in the deal said there has been strong demand for Turkey's debut sukuk offering, with orders ballooning to $6 billion. More than half of the orders came from the Middle East, $1 billion from Asian investors and the rest from the US and Europe, the banker said.

The sukuk will yield about the same as comparable Turkish government bonds, which pay an interest rate of 2.87%, according to market participants. Initial price guidance on the sukuk, maturing in 5½ years, is between 1.9 and 2.0 percentage points above the midswap rate, a benchmark in bond deals, which is about 1%.

Source: Peker, E., T. Falconer, and C. Dean. 2012. "Turkey to Sell Its First-Ever Islamic Bond." *Wall Street Journal* September 18, C4.

classical Islamic tradition theory, the only straightforward loan was the *qard hasan* (literally good loan) or interest-free loan and the only common form of deposit was *al-wadiah* (safekeeping). Typically, the qard hasan was given for benevolent non-business-related purposes, though it could be to distressed merchants, while al-wadiah was akin to the contemporary practice of renting a safe deposit box at a bank to store one's valuables. A significant update of traditional Islamic practices was necessary to replicate the offerings of modern banks. Thus, Islamic bankers have devised new products and instruments by updating or combining contracts that go back to classical Islam, by creating products that pose no religious objections, or by invoking custom (*'urf*), overriding necessity (*darura*) or the general interest (*maslaha*) to justify the creation of various instruments.

This section discusses the two main types of contracts: *equity like* (or profit-and-loss-sharing) *instruments, or debt-like instruments which are sale-based, and leasing* (or ijara) *based contracts.*

Equity-like instruments (residual claims)

When it first came into existence, Islamic finance purported to offer an alternative model, based on partnership finance. The basic idea was that instead of lending money at fixed rate of return, the banker would form a partnership with the entrepreneur, *sharing in a venture's profits and losses*. Under such an equity-based model, the bank provides finance, while the entrepreneur carries out the business venture whether trade, industry or service, with the objective of earning profits. Profits are shared in a predetermined ratio; losses are borne by the bank. The partnership could be of one of two types: *mudaraba* (commenda partnership or finance trusteeship) and *musharaka* (longer-term equity-like arrangements).

Mudaraba is an association between the *rabb-el-maal* (financier) and the *mudarib* (entrepreneur) where profits and losses are shared based on an agreed-upon ratio. The mudaraba can be restricted (if the contract specifies a particular line or place of business for the mudarib) or unrestricted. The specifics of the mudaraba are straightforward: the rabb al-maal, in the role of the limited partner, entrusts money to the mudarib who as managing trustee is to utilize it in an agreed manner. After the operation is concluded, the rabb al-maal receives the principal and the pre-agreed share of the profit. The mudarib keeps for himself the remaining profits. The rabb al-maal also shares in the losses, and may be in a position of losing all his principal.[12] His liability is exclusively limited to the provided capital, just as that of the entrepreneur is restricted solely to his labor. In other words, the mudarib cannot be made to make financial contributions in the case of losses. He would have lost only his time and efforts. However, if negligence, mismanagement or fraud can be proven, the entrepreneur may be financially liable. Under certain circumstances, for example if the mudarib has engaged in religiously illicit activities (speculation or the production of forbidden goods or services), or if the bank has demanded a collateral as a condition for its investment, the mudaraba or musharaka contracts can be considered null and void.

Musharaka is similar in its principle to mudaraba, except for the fact that the mudarib too often takes an equity stake in the venture. It is in effect a joint-venture agreement whereby the bank enters into a partnership with a client in which both share the equity capital, and sometimes the management, of a project or deal. In both the mudaraba and the musharaka cases, the bank would receive a contractual share of the profits generated by business ventures (see Box 27.3). Another product, commonly used in investment and asset management arrangements is wakala (agency), whereby investors appoint an agent (such as a financial institution) to manage their funds or assets in accordance with Islamic principles. The agent invests the funds on behalf of the investors and earns a fee for his services. The profits generated from the investment are shared between the investors and the agent based on a pre-agreed profit-sharing ratio.

Debt-like instruments (Fixed claims) are more controversial. They include:

Murabaha (sales-based or cost-plus financing). An individual desires to purchase a product today but can only pay for it later (in a lump sum or an installment plan). An Islamic bank would purchase the product on behalf of the individual and resell it at a cost-plus to said individual. Payment at cost-plus though is differed in time according to a pre-agreed schedule. The difference between the purchase price and cost-plus resale price is the equivalent of the interest earning that the bank would collect on a conventional loan. Thus, a murabaha transaction can be broken up into different steps. First is the agreement whereby the bank promises to sell and the client promises to buy the good. Second is the actual purchase of the commodity. Often, the bank appoints the client as its agent for purchasing the commodity on its behalf, and an agency agreement is signed by both parties. The bank is then the owner of the commodity. Third is the sale of that commodity by the bank to the buyer, to whom the ownership and risk of possession are actually transferred. The first step is not an actual sale, but a promise (waad), while the next two steps are sales. At the end of the process, the relation between the bank and the client will be that of creditor and debtor.

For example, if a business needs $100 million to buy machinery, it could borrow money at 8% a year to purchase it, or it could have the bank buy the machinery on its behalf, and pay the bank $108 million a year later. Beyond the bottom line, parallels abound: in both cases, the prior due diligence consists in examining the client's creditworthiness; the purchased asset serves as collateral, and the bank can also require other guarantees from the client; after the deal is completed, the relationship of the client to the bank is that of debtor; and in case of non-repayment, comparable recourses are available.[13] Regulators as well as conventional bankers are thus usually comfortable with such transactions. But this is also precisely why murabaha and other mark-up schemes are criticized — on the grounds that such contracts may disguise the interest through semantic games to the point that some have characterized them as "hiyal" (ruses).

Theological debates around murabaha revolve primarily around the justification for, and the extent of, the bank's remuneration.[14] In Islam, the

12 Cizakça, M. 1996. *A Comparative Evolution of Business Partnerships: The Islamic World & Europe*, with Specific Reference to the Ottoman Archives. Leiden: E.J. Brill. pp. 4–6.

13 An important difference however is that if the bank's customer has acted in good faith, and that his financial distress is attributable to factors beyond his control, the bank has to show forbearance.

14 There have been numerous attempts to establish common norms and standard contracts for murabaha transactions by organizations such as the Islamic Finance Services Board (IFSB) and the Accounting and Auditing Organization for Islamic Financial Institutions (AAOIFI). This has contributed to a noticeable increase in cross-national transactions, though country-specific and product-specific murabaha contracts persist.

INTERNATIONAL CORPORATE FINANCE IN PRACTICE 27.3

Case of a Diminishing Musharaka

The most popular form of Shariah-compliant Islamic mortgage financing is the "diminishing partnership" (or musharaka mutanaqisa). Under such a contract, the borrower/customer enters into a partnership with the bank for the purchase of a property. Over time, the customer buys off the bank's share.

The numerical example below, which leaves out taxes, insurance and other fees, assumes a home worth $300,000. The customer invests 20% ($60,000) and the bank 80% ($240,000) of the home value. The two parties will agree to a partnership period (in this case, 15 years or 180 months) and a fixed monthly payment consisting of a fair market value rental amount and a contribution to equity. In other words, the bank rents out its share of the property to the customer. In order to buy off the bank's share over time, the customer will make an additional payment constituting a contribution to equity. The relative shares of ownership will thus shift according to these accumulated contributions. The customer's share will gradually increase and that of the bank will decrease commensurately (which is why the rent component will steadily diminish). At the end of the 15-year partnership period, the bank's share will be down to zero and the customer will wholly own the property.

At any given time, the customer and the bank will know exactly their respective percentage of ownership. In the event of the sale of the home to a third party (or any other change in terms) they will be in a position to share in the profits and the losses. Of course, the specifics of the deal will depend on relevant laws, the bank's policies and the customer's needs.

Month	Rent ($)	Contribution to Equity ($)	Fixed Payment ($)	Bank's Share ($)
				240,000
1	1,600	694	2,294	239,306
2	1,596	698	2,294	238,608
3	1,592	702	2,294	237,906
4	1,588	706	2,294	237,200
5	1,584	710	2,294	236,490
…	…	…	…	…
176	74	2,220	2,294	8,878
177	60	2,234	2,294	6,649
178	44	2,250	2,294	4,394
179	30	2,264	2,284	2,130
180	14	2,130	2,144	0

justification for profit is risk-taking, and thus the amount of the profit is directly related to the risk incurred: the greater the risk, the greater the profit. Since the deal involves two sales transactions (one consisting in buying the goods from the manufacturer; the other in selling the goods to the "borrower"), the main difference with a conventional banking loan is that there is a period during which the financial institution owns the goods. During that time the bank bears the risks of ownership: the goods may be damaged or destroyed; the seller may go bankrupt; etc. The longer the period of ownership, the greater the risk. For Shariah scholars, the best murabaha is the one where the financier purchases the commodity directly or through an agent, and then truly assumes ownership risk before selling it to the customer. Yet from a prudential standpoint, neither the banks nor their regulators want to be subjected to ownership or inventory risk. The period of ownership will therefore be more symbolic than real (since the duration can theoretically be of just a few minutes or even just one second), and the profit of the bank, as murabaha is generally practiced, will likely correspond to the prevailing rate of interest for the period involved.

Ijara or leasing is also technically a sale contract, since it is understood from the standpoint of classical Islamic fiqh as the sale of usufruct (manfaa) and as such its rules closely follow those of ordinary sales. Yet as one of the fastest growing activities of Islamic financial institutions, it also presents enough distinctive characteristics to warrant being discussed separately. The principle of ijara is virtually identical to conventional leasing: the bank leases an asset to a third party in exchange for a specified rent. The amounts of payments are known in advance and the asset remains the property of the lessor. The profits of the lease are justified though because the financial institution owns the asset and, therefore, assumes risk for its performance. Although initially directed primarily at businesses, ijara is increasingly used in retail finance, primarily for home mortgages, cars and household needs. In recent years, leasing contracts have also been commonly used for big ticket items such as aircraft or ships and have become essential building blocks in project finance.

In order to avoid the elements of riba and gharar, there are a few differences between ijara and conventional leasing. The law views some benefits and burdens of the property as belonging naturally and unchangeably to the lessee, others to the lessor. For example the law provides that the duty to repair the goods always fall on the lessor since the repair benefits him as the owner. Also, the usufruct is not something existent and tangible, but a stream of use extending into the future, which is risky and unstable. Islamic law thus gives broad scope to the lessee to cancel the lease if the usufruct proves less valuable than expected. Finally, the price at which the asset may be sold to the lessee at the expiration of the contract cannot be predetermined. In practice however, numerous compromises have been arrived at, often because national regulation does not allow sufficient flexibility to accommodate Shariah-compliant leases.

A number of reasons account for the rapid growth of leasing: it is an acceptable instrument in the eyes of most scholars; it is an efficient means of financial intermediation; by financing assets, it is a useful tool in the promotion of economic development; it is a well-established instrument that lends itself to standardized mechanisms and procedures; most importantly, and unlike sales contracts such as murabaha, an ijara contract can be sold at any price on the secondary market. It is thus a flexible mode of financing that lends itself to securitization and secondary trading and to collaboration with conventional institutions. This explains why ijara sukuk are by far the most popular form of sukuk.

Istisnaa (*commissioned finance or construction loan*) calls for one party to contract with a purchaser to manufacture a product or build a facility; purchaser will pay in advance, at completion or in installment according to a pre-determined completion calendar and product/project specifications. According to Esty

> *the most common contract is referred to as "a back-to-back" istisnaa which includes a bank as a financial intermediary. Under the first istisnaa the purchaser enters into an agreement with the bank to purchase the asset (machinery, plant, airport etc.) upon completion. Under the second istisnaa contract the bank agrees to pay the manufacturer ("hire-to-purchase" contract) to build the asset in question. As an intermediary the Islamic bank accepted the manufacturer's performance risk and the purchaser's payment risk. Typically the istisnaa contracts have maturites equal to the construction period and fixed rates that are set on the day the contracts are signed. For complex assets such as manufacturing plants, the contracts may last two or three years.*[15]

As such istisnaa are appropriate for construction financing and often used in project finance but it is does not provide long term permanent financing (see Box 27.4).

15 Benjamin Esty's The International Investor: Islamic Finance and the Equate Project (Harvard Business School: case study 9-200-012, 2003), p. 7.

INTERNATIONAL CORPORATE FINANCE IN PRACTICE 27.4

The Equate Project: When Islamic and Traditional Finance Co-Habit

In August 1994 Union Carbide Corporation — the US chemicals multinational — and Petrochemicals Industries Company — a Kuwaiti state-owned enterprise — launched the construction of a $2 billion petro-chemical complex in Kuwait known as the Equate Petrochemicals company. As a project finance part of the funding had been earmarked for a tranche of Islamic finance which would be provided according to the principles of Sharia law. The rationale to include a tranche of Islamic finance was to make the project more socially acceptable in Kuwait and therefore mitigate its exposure to sovereign risks. Equate financing in the amount of $1 billion closed on September 15, 1996 and included two term tranches — a $400 million regional bank tranche and a $600 million international bank tranche to which Islamic financing contributed $200 million or 20% of the total. One of the challenges of using the Istisnaa financing structure was the selection of assets that the project's sponsor would be willing to relinquish to the Islamic financier since the latter had to assume ownership with all attendant risks to be allowed to provide funding in accordance with Islamic law.

Source: Based on Esty, B. 2003. "The International Investor: Islamic Finance and the Equate Project." *Harvard Business School: Case Study 9-200-012.*

SHARIAH COMPLIANT ASSET MANAGEMENT

Investing in equities rather than fixed income securities (bonds) is at the heart of Islamic asset management. The question is how to identify firms which are shariah compliant and therefore acceptable securities for investment purposes. One of the most significant innovations in Islamic finance was the introduction of standardized investment screens. Investment screens were pioneered by the Dow Jones company when it established in 1999 Dow Jones Islamic Market (DJIM) Indexes. Other companies have followed suit, among them Standard & Poor's (since 2007) and FTSE (since 2008). Although every screening company has its own standards and methodologies, the underlying logic of screening stocks for Shariah compliance is the same.

Drawing on classical Islamic jurisprudence on the mixture of permissible and impermissible, the halal and the non-halal, and a hadith on resolving the "how much is too much question", a number of criteria and ceilings were devised. The hadith in question stated that "The dividing line between a majority and a minority is one-third, and the third as a portion is considered to be much".[16] The Dow Jones methodology was established by its own Shariah Board. There are now more than 100 Dow Jones Islamic indexes, applying the same filters to different sectors, regions and asset classes.

There are typically three levels of screening to determine Shariah compliance. The first is the primary sector of activity of the company. Always excluded are companies involved in gambling, pornography, alcohol, pork, and conventional finance. Beyond such sectors, different screening companies differ in their methodology. The hospitality industry (hotels and restaurants) is often screened out because of its reliance on alcohol sales, and so are controversial or "sinful" sectors such as weapon or tobacco manufacturers.

After a firm's activities are deemed acceptable, more specific financial filters (primarily based on debt and interest income) typically based on the "one-third rule" are applied. The first criterion is the level of debt: companies whose total debt divided by 12-month average market capitalization is 33% or more are screened out. Companies can also be screened out for ethical lapses.

Another aspect of the screening is the recommended purification. The logic is that dividends from companies that pass the sectoral and financial screens, but still receive interest payments or have a small (less than 5%) involvement in illicit activities, must be purified. What it means in practice is that the investors are made aware of the percentage of

16 Elgari, Mohamed A. 2002. "Islamic Equity Investment." In *Islamic Finance: Innovation and Growth*, edited by Simon Archer and Rifaat Abdel Karim. London: Euromoney, pp. 153–154.

> ***Q:*** Is investing in western-style private-equity funds compliant with Shariah law?
>
> ***A:*** As their name indicate private-equity funds take equity positions in firms in the hope of turning them around by shedding assets and through more efficient use of corporate resources to allow the PE firm to exit its investment at a significant profit. However PE firms rely on significant leverage and use of debt to enable their investment and even though the investment itself is not in debt, debt is an integral part of the transaction.

company income that is tainted, the recommendation being that they donate such amounts to charity.

Screens were initially used for the benefit of mutual fund investors, by following the logic of socially-responsible funds, who select funds on the basis of criteria other than performance (for example the environment, labor, or political preference). Islamic screens are now used beyond mutual funds for all sorts of investments, such as private equity and other funds, even to decide whether an Islamic institution should be doing business with a certain company. The indices are heavily weighted towards technology, energy, resources, infrastructure, pharmaceuticals, telecommunications and consumer goods.

It should be noted that ethical business is also high on the agenda of other religions and interfaith groups. Shariah-compliant mutual funds have generally done quite well despite the fact that screening mechanisms can hinder performance (since they rule out certain well performing stocks) and add to the cost of managing the fund. They have done especially well during the turmoil of 2007–2008, helped in part by their systematic exclusion of financial stocks that were battered by the crisis.

ISLAMIC BANKING

The mudaraba principle in banking

Early pioneers of Islamic finance envisioned banks as functioning on the basis of the *double mudaraba* principle. On the liabilities side of the balance sheet, the depositor is the *rabb-el-maal* and the bank is the *mudarib*. On the asset side, the bank is the *rabb-el-maal* and the client is the *mudarib*. The principle of partnership finance is certainly seductive since in theory there would be a harmony of interests among depositors, financial institutions and entrepreneurs. The bank would essentially be a venture capitalist financing promising entrepreneurs. Partnership finance was supposed to bring a wide range of economic benefits to society, through mobilization of savings, productive investment and more generally economic development. It was regarded as vastly superior to the classical interest-based banking model. In addition to objections about riba, there are economic and financial misgivings to interest-based lending: it is unjust because the risk is borne primarily by the borrower; it favors already established businesses, and those who can provide collateral, and it offers no assurance of a direct link to the real economy. Furthermore conventional, interest-based banking is only marginally concerned with the success of the ventures it finances. In contrast, under profit-and-loss sharing, Islamic institutions as well as their depositors link their own fate to the success of the projects they finance. The system allows a capital-poor, but promising entrepreneur, to obtain financing. The bank, being an investor, as opposed to a lender, has a stake in the long-term success of the venture. The entrepreneur, rather than being concerned with debt-servicing, can concentrate on a long-term endeavor that in turn would provide economic and social benefits to the community.[17]

Report card on Islamic banking

The first Islamic banks plunged with great enthusiasm (and virtually no experience) in mudaraba. The result was, to put it mildly, disappointing, and as a result, virtually all institutions (except perhaps in the Sudan, Pakistan and Iran, the three countries which at least in theory have Islamicized their entire banking system) decided to steer clear from profit-and-loss sharing, and focus instead on sale-based, or mark-up transactions. Thus, except on the liabilities side of the balance sheet, the ideal of partnership finance has not really materialized. Maybe banks simply cannot be good venture capitalists. Indeed, banking and venture capitalism are completely different businesses; a good banker is not necessarily a

17 Kamali, M. H. 2005. *Equity and Fairness in Islam.* Cambridge, UK: The Islamic Texts Society, p. 104.

good venture capitalist and vice versa. Most venture capitalists are entrepreneurs by background, concerned with the growth of a business rather than the repayment of loans. It is also questionable whether it is a good idea to use the money of small depositors to invest in new business ventures, which are risky by definition. In a free enterprise system, most new businesses fail, and most new products never find a market. Another difficulty of Islamic institutions is that they operated in their early years in an environment where the necessary "ecosystem" of venture capitalism (the network of professional support and stakeholders such as corporate investors, venture capital firms, angel investors, tech hubs, incubators and accelerators, in addition to a legal infrastructure that provides for flexible corporate options, as well as a bankruptcy system that provides for efficient exit strategies for failed ventures) was lacking.

Despite all this, the profit-and-loss sharing and risk-sharing logics of Islamic finance have not disappeared entirely. On the liabilities side of the balance sheet, the mudaraba logic still prevails, since all investment accounts, usually referred to as Profit-sharing investment accounts (PSIA) are mudaraba contracts, where the depositor is the rabb al-maal and the bank the mudarib. Investment accounts come in two forms. They can be general accounts which are based on the overall performance of the bank: investors do well if the bank does well overall, and vice versa. The return paid is determined by the yield obtained from all the activities of the bank. After deducting such administration costs as wages, provisions, and capital depreciation, the bank pools the yields obtained from all ventures, and the depositors, as a group, share the net profits with the bank according to a predetermined ratio that cannot be modified for the duration of the contract. Different banks have different policies concerning the calculation and disbursement of profits. Increasingly, as a way of "smoothing" the returns (to avoid wide fluctuations, which can have negative consequences as extremely high returns can attract deposits but also create expectations that cannot be met, while very low returns can result in depositors leaving the bank in droves), banks have been creating a profit equalization reserve. So the sharing of the profit could take the form of 50% for the bank; 30% for profit equalization reserves and 20% for the depositor. (In a few instances, the remuneration can as a result of such smoothing parallel that of conventional savings accounts.) Some banks do the calculation and disbursement monthly, others quarterly, others still semi-annually or even annually. The other type of mudaraba account is the special investment account, where the same logic applies, except that the partnership between the account holder and the bank will be limited to a specified asset or group of assets. Depositors can reap profits from a venture's success, but risk losing money if investments perform poorly.

On the asset side of the balance sheet, the most common profit-and-loss sharing product is the diminishing musharaka which is increasingly used to finance Islamic mortgages. This is for example how a diminishing musharaka mortgage (which also includes an element of ijara) would work: the client forms a partnership with the bank, with the bank providing 80% of the purchase price, and the client 20%. Over a period of 10 years, the client will make periodic payments to the bank, progressively increasing his ownership share, while the bank will make its profit from the rent paid by the client for the share the bank owns.

The first Islamic banks appeared in the Arab world. First was the Dubai Islamic Bank in 1975. The following years saw the creation of Islamic banks in Kuwait, Jordan, Bahrain, Egypt and the Sudan. Then Islamic banks started appearing all over the world. Significant differences appeared across countries in the importance, status and characteristics of Islamic financial institutions. Their role in national economies ranges from essential to insignificant. Their "special character" may or may not be recognized by regulators. In some countries, they are strongly encouraged by the authorities; in others they are barely tolerated. Domestic factors and the diversity of national circumstances (including of course the impact of indigenous forms of Islam) have inevitably added to differences across countries.[18]

Even those countries that fully Islamicized their financial systems — Pakistan, Iran, the Sudan — did so under different religious, political, economic and cultural circumstances. In most cases, Islamicization did not occur in a carefully thought out application of Islamic principles and jurisprudence, but in an ad hoc manner and under the pressure of events. As a result, paradoxes abound, and the evolution of Islamic finance often runs counter to common perceptions and stereotypes.

Despite recent strides in harmonization and streamlining there is still a great deal of diversity and pluralism to the Islamic sector. Perceptions of

18 For a general discussion of the recent evolution of economic Islam in different countries, see Nasr, V. 2009. *Forces of Fortune: The Rise of the New Muslim Middle Class and What It Will Mean for Our World.* New York: Free Press.

Islamic finance in the West cannot be separated from general perceptions of Islam as a monolithic, unchanging and somewhat fossilized belief system. In reality, Islamic finance reflects the diversity of a 1400-year-old, 1.5 billion strong religion spread over every continent. Islamic financial institutions come in all shapes and forms: banks and non-banks; large and small; specialized and diversified; traditional and innovative; national and multinational; successful and unsuccessful; prudent and reckless; strictly regulated and freewheeling, etc. Some are virtually identical to their conventional counterparts, while others are markedly different. Some are driven solely by religious considerations; others use religion as a way of sidestepping regulation, as a shield against government interference, as a tool for political change, or simply as a marketing ploy.

National idiosyncrasies in Islamic banking

Despite the growing trend towards harmonization of rules and practices, there is a great deal of diversity within Islamic finance. A quick look at the leading Islamic institutions reveals the heterogeneity of the industry. Large government-owned Iranian banks, that are subject to sanctions and have few interactions with non-Iranian Islamic banks, hold the top spots. Then there are Gulf Cooperation Council (GCC) banks, themselves a heterogeneous group, including some of the earliest Islamic banks such as Kuwait Finance House and Dubai Islamic Bank, and more recent ones, such as Abu Dhabi Islamic Bank and Saudi Arabia's Al-Rajhi. The majority of GCC banks have a domestic focus, though another of the largest banks, Bahrain-based, Saudi-owned Al-Baraka group, had from the beginning a transnational focus. The top ranks of Islamic banks also include Malaysian banks, such as Bank Islam Malaysia Berhad (BIMB), had little contact with GCC banks. The largest Islamic institutions by assets also include Western-based institutions, such as the UK-controlled, but Dubai-based, HSBC Amanah.

Examples abound of how deeply embedded Islamic financial institutions are in their institutional and cultural framework. Saudi Arabia was founded as a "fundamentalist" Islamic state, in the sense that its society and institutions were based on a strict and "purist" interpretation of Islam. Paradoxically, this has made the issue of Islamic banking and finance politically sensitive. The reason is that by the time Islamic banks came into existence, Saudi Arabia was a wealthy state — to a large extent a "rentier" economy, living off its oil production and the substantial revenues from its foreign investment and fixed income. Its economy was thus heavily dependent, directly and indirectly, on interest. Creating Islamic ("non-interest") banks would make existing banks un-Islamic, in a country where the rulers have repeatedly had to fend off accusations of impiety. Although Saudi Arabia played a central role in creating and promoting the Islamic finance industry, it did not initially encourage the growth of Islamic institutions at home. It is only in recent years, mostly due to consumer demand, that Islamic finance came to play a growing role in the national economy — making Saudi Arabia one of the latecomers in the Islamic sector.

In Egypt, the story of Islamic finance is equally complicated: in the late 1970s the government promoted Islamic banks as part its new alliance with Saudi Arabia and as a counterweight to left-wing and Nasserite opposition. Yet the collapse of Islamic Money Management Companies IMMCs, companies that were not linked to the emerging Islamic banking sector cast suspicions on the entire Islamic sector and unleashed a political crisis. Political fears of the Muslim Brotherhood also led the government of Hosni Mubarak to stifle the growth of Islamic banks. In Turkey in the 1980s, a secular, but cash-strapped government allowed the creation of Islamic banks though they were not allowed to use the word Islam in their name, or to refer explicitly to their Islamic character. Initially called Special Finance Houses, they are now known as Participation Banks. In Jordan, the policy toward Islamic banks has reflected the accommodative policy toward Islamic groups in general. In Malaysia and Indonesia, Islamic finance has reflected the more syncretic brand of Islam, the developmental nature of government policies, as well as a variety of domestic considerations.

The United Kingdom, home to more than 2 million Muslims, has repeatedly announced its intention of becoming a global hub of Islamic finance. The reasons are political (the integration of an often disenfranchised community) and economic (attracting foreign investment to the UK). A number of tax and regulatory changes have been undertaken to fulfill that goal. Especially notable is the introduction of a new sukuk regime similar to that for conventional securitizations, adding sukuk to the London Stock Exchange, and finally the issuance of sovereign sukuk in June 2014. Other non-Islamic countries issuing sukuk include Luxembourg that same year include Luxembourg and South Africa.

Singapore, another country where Muslims are only a small minority (about 14% of the population) also announced its intention of becoming a hub of Islamic finance but has yet to issue sukuk. Countries and issued. In recent years, countries as diverse as Australia, France and South Korea have altered their legislation to become more hospitable to Islamic finance, in particular on sukuk issuance.

Islamic banking — Arab or Malaysian style?

Two main models can be identified, one associated with the Gulf (I'll refer to it as the Arab model), the other with Malaysia. The Arab ijtihad was primarily driven by the surpluses generated by the oil boom of the mid-to-late 1970s whereas the Malaysian effort was driven by the developmental imperative, combined with domestic political factors, principally the promotion of the (Muslim) Malay majority. In other words, the Gulf countries, flush with oil money, were concerned with asset management while Malaysia focused on generating financing for the economy and transforming the country from agricultural backwater to industrializing nation.

Another fundamental difference between the two systems is that the Arab model had evolved in disorganized fashion while the Malaysian model was based on a directive, top-down, approach. In the first case, the Shariah guidance model was fragmented and decentralized. Banks could do whatever their Shariah Board allowed them to do, and some were even not subject to central bank supervision. Thus the Kuwait Finance House was placed under the authority of the Ministry of Finance. In contrast, Malaysia sought consistency by creating a Shariah Board within its Central Bank, whose decisions would supersede those of individual Shariah Boards.

The Malaysian model of Islamic finance was more innovative and forward-looking, though religiously controversial. Certain Malaysian practices were not deemed acceptable to Shariah boards in more conservative Arab states, in particular the widespread use of bay' al-dayn (trading of debt). Malaysia's posture could be explained in terms of its traditions and broader political economy. Mahathir Mohammed, Malaysia's long-serving prime minister (1981–2003, and then again 2018–2020), sought to harness Islam to his goal of economic growth. His approach to Islamic finance was highly pragmatic. Rather than using what was historically acceptable as a starting point, he challenged the Malaysian ulema to an ijtihad designed to generate new ideas. Religion, rather than being an obstacle to change, was to be an engine of growth and modernization and a tool to promote financial innovation. An Islamic financial system that could offer a growing array of sophisticated financial services was part and parcel of the effort to turn Kuala Lumpur into a leading regional, if not international, financial center.

The Malaysian model came into its own in the 1990s. The dual banking logic, as well as other Malaysian innovations such as Islamic insurance (takaful or mutual insurance) had also taken root. Another singular characteristic of the Malaysian system is that Islamic products were geared to Muslims as well as to non-Muslims. Muslims would have the opportunity to invest according to their religious beliefs, while non-Muslims, especially for Chinese minority which controls most of the country's wealth, would have an extension of choice in money-management. The message of Malaysian leaders was that industrialization and productivity were fully compatible with piety, and that welfare in this world was fully compatible with salvation in the next.

Scholars in the Arab world considered their Malaysian counterparts too lax in their religious interpretations. As a result, Arab and Malaysian Islamic banks evolved along separate paths, and had minimal interaction until 2001.

ISLAMIC FINANCE AND THE GLOBAL FINANCIAL MELTDOWN

By the time of the 2008 financial meltdown, Islamic finance had become part of the mainstream of global finance. The trend was driven primarily by a desire on the part of global financial institutions to tap the wealth of the Islamic world, and broaden the scope of financial instruments. Indeed, in the first years of the new millenium, the paradigm of global finance, as epitomized by major Wall Street firms with their focus on financial innovation, commanded near-unanimous support where it mattered, that is among financial regulators, economics and finance professors, the financial community at large and the media. In those years, Islamic banks were usually on the receiving end of lectures essentially asking them to adopt newfangled financial derivatives.

All this changed with the 2007–2008 financial crisis. The crisis could be divided into three phases. In the first one, the decline in US real estate prices drew attention to subprime loans, which it turned out, had through the miracle of securitization found their way onto the balance sheets of major international financial institutions. In the second phase, losses suffered by such institutions triggered claims for which major Wall Street firms and other companies such as insurer

AIG were utterly unprepared. Indeed through highly lucrative and unregulated credit derivatives known as "credit default swaps", high-flying financial firms had in effect insured countless institutions (and one another) against defaults, and now they had to pay up. As the world's leading global financial institutions discovered the time-bombs on their balance sheets (in the form of toxic assets and unfunded liabilities), they realized that they were essentially insolvent: the ensuing credit freeze caused a global financial meltdown which soon spread to the real economy. The third phase of the financial crisis was thus a global economic recession — which would have turned into a depression were it not for massive government intervention worldwide. It is only then that Islamic banks started to feel the effects of the meltdown.

Why did Islamic institutions escape the first two phases relatively unscathed? Quite simply because many of the practices that caused the financial freeze would not pass muster with Shariah Boards. Indeed, neither the securitization of subprime loans (which is a sale of debt) nor credit default swaps (which are the sale of promises — forbidden in Islam — and are rife with gharar) are acceptable.

Similarly, negative Islamic attitudes toward short-selling appeared vindicated by the role short-selling played in many episodes of the financial crisis. Indeed, major financial centers subsequently placed strict limits on short selling of financial stocks. Some old-fashioned principles such as the distrust of excessive leverage and of open-ended innovation proved well-founded. As for the systematic vetting of new products by Shariah advisers, it played a checks and balances role, and proved a useful corrective to the groupthink that had overtaken conventional finance.

When the financial tsunami hit, bringing conventional finance to its knees, just as there was a mood of soul searching within mainstream finance, a sense of self-confidence — indeed triumphalism — overtook Islamic finance. Some did not hesitate to present Islamic finance as a panacea that would solve all the world's economic ills, and as the model that conventional banks should adopt to get out of their predicament.

Yet soon afterwards, the extension of the crisis from the financial realm to the real economy exposed the vulnerability of a sector that is mostly asset-backed, though its inherent conservatism mitigated somehow the effects of the economic downturn. This showed that Islamic finance was not after all a panacea, and that a faith-based system is not automatically immune to the vagaries of finance.

On balance however, the Islamic sector weathered the financial meltdown better than the conventional sector. If nothing else, there was an acknowledgement within conventional circles that the principles and strictures of Islamic finance were not without merit. This in turn created a renewed sense of self-confidence within the Islamic sector, which also weakened the hand of those who equated progress with uncritical imitation of conventional banks. Perhaps most significantly, the financial meltdown suggested that the quest for an alternative system of finance was not as far-fetched as it first appeared.

FUTURE TRENDS: CONVERGENCE WITH ESG AND SUSTAINABILITY

The excesses of financialization, especially in the wake of the Great Financial Crisis of 2008 have exposed governance failures, unethical practices, and lack of transparency, which highlighted the need for reform toward more responsible and sustainable business practices. In that context, the ESG movement, stressing the need to include environmental, social and governance in financial decision making, gathered steam. The December 2015 Paris Agreement, which made specific commitments to address the challenge of climate change was signed by representatives of 197 countries. Each country had to establish Sustainable Development Goals (SDGs) setting benchmarks for addressing environmental and social challenges. In March 2021, the European Union's Sustainable Finance Disclosure Regulation (SFDR) required mandatory disclosure obligations for EU-based financial market participants and financial advisors. The SFDR standardizes ESG disclosures, clarifies the definition of sustainable initiatives, and establishes standards of evidence in support of such claims.

These developments converged with well-established Islamic finance principles discussed earlier, which called for the inclusion of moral and religious considerations in financial decisions. These were based on the Koranic concept of "vicegerency", known as "khilafah" in Arabic, which states that humans are appointed as stewards or trustees to manage and safeguard God's creation in a responsible fashion (Koran, 2:30). In finance and economics, the concept emphasizes the ethical and responsible use of wealth and resources, and stresses the importance of accountability, fairness, and sustainability. More specifically, vicegerency encourages ethical investment practices, such as the avoidance of exploitative transactions, and the promotion of social welfare through charitable giving and economic empowerment. It also underscores the importance of utilizing financial resources in a manner that upholds justice, equity, and sustainability.

Green Sukuk and Sustainability Sukuk are the main new instruments that appeared after 2015, combining Islamic finance principles with environmentally friendly and sustainable investment goals. A whole ecosystem has developed around Islamic regulatory bodies and Shariah boards of individual Islamic financial institutions to create new standards designed to ensure transparency and credibility, and prevent "greenwashing". These initiatives have included developing a liquid and robust market for these instruments, in addition to creating awareness, encouraging investor education, and promoting collaboration among various stakeholders.

Green Sukuk have been used to finance environmentally friendly projects such as renewable energy initiatives, energy-efficient buildings, and sustainable water management systems. Sustainability Sukuk go beyond just environmental considerations to include social and governance aspects as well. Funds raised through Sustainability Sukuk can be used for projects that promote social welfare, community development, or good governance practices. Another significant component is the tracking and reporting the environmental and social impacts of funds raised as a way of maintaining the confidence of investors and stakeholders.

Notable Green Sukuk include the $814 million Green Sukuk issued in 2019 by ACWA Power, a Saudi-based developer, and operator of power and water desalination plants, a $59 million Green Sukuk issued in 2018 by Tadau Energy, a Malaysian renewable energy company to finance a large-scale solar project. The most significant Sustainability Sukuk was the $1 billion Islamic Development Bank's Sukuk issued in 2018 to finance projects aligned with the United Nations Sustainable Development Goals (SDGs) and structured to target social and developmental projects.

Issuance of a great variety of Sukuk, by governments, state-owned enterprises, and private sector entities many of them Green or Sustainable, has since accelerated, primarily in Malaysia and Gulf Cooperation Council (GCC) countries — Saudi Arabia, United Arab Emirates, Kuwait, Bahrain, Oman, and Qatar — but also in other countries, such as Turkey and Indonesia.

SUMMARY

1. What were the main tenets of Islamic finance? The realm of finance should be linked directly to the real economy, and governed by the principles of risk sharing and profit-and-loss sharing; interest-based lending (referred to as *riba* or usury) should be replaced by Islamic financing contracts based on equity, sale or leasing; transactions involving speculation or *gharar* (a notion encompassing excessive or avoidable risk, deceptive ambiguity, and risk shifting) should be avoided, as are transactions involving *haram* (religiously forbidden) activities and unethical behavior; transactions must be clear and transparent and must fulfill social and developmental goals; leverage should be limited; certain conventional practices (such as short-selling) are not allowed; and financial innovations must be monitored by religious scholars.
2. Islamic finance purports to offer an alternative model, based on partnership finance whereby instead of lending money at fixed rate of return, the banker would form a partnership with the entrepreneur, *sharing in a venture's profits and losses*. Under such an equity-based model, the bank provides finance, while the entrepreneur carries out the business venture whether trade, industry or service, with the objective of earning profits. Profits are shared in a predetermined ratio; losses are borne by the bank. The partnership could be of one of two types: *mudaraba* (commenda partnership or finance trusteeship) and *musharaka* (longer-term equity-like arrangements).
3. In a Murabaha contract (sales-based or cost-plus financing) an individual desires to purchase a product today but can only pay for it later (in a lump sum or an installment plan). An Islamic bank would purchase the product on behalf of the individual and resell it at a cost-plus to said individual. Payment at cost-plus though is differed in time according to a pre-agreed schedule. The difference between the purchase price and cost-plus resale price is the equivalent of the interest earning that the bank would collect on a conventional loan.
4. *Ijara or leasing* is also technically a sale contract, since it is understood from the standpoint of classical Islamic fiqh as the sale of usufruct (manfaa) and as such its rules closely follow those of ordinary sales. The principle of ijara is virtually identical to conventional leasing: the bank leases an asset to a third party in exchange for a specified rent. The amounts of payments are known in advance and the asset remains the

property of the lessor. The profits of the lease are justified though because the financial institution owns the asset and, therefore, assumes risk for its performance. Ijara is increasingly used in retail finance, primarily for home mortgages, cars and household needs as well for big ticket items such as aircraft or ships.

5. For commissioned finance or construction-type loan the most common contract is referred to as "a back-to-back" *istisnaa* which includes a bank as a financial intermediary. Under the first istisnaa the purchaser enters into an agreement with the bank to purchase the asset (machinery, plant, airport etc.) upon completion. Under the second istisnaa contract the bank agrees to pay the manufacturer ("hire-to-purchase" contract) to build the asset in question. As an intermediary the Islamic bank accepted the manufacturer's performance risk and the purchaser's payment risk. Typically, the istisnaa contracts have maturities equal to the construction period and fixed rates that are set on the day the contracts are signed. For complex assets such as manufacturing plants, the contracts may last two or three years".

6. Investing in equities rather than fixed income securities (bonds) is at the heart of Islamic asset management. The question is how to identify firms which are *shariah* compliant and therefore acceptable securities for investment purposes. One of the most significant innovations in Islamic finance was the introduction of standardized investment screens such as Dow Jones Islamic Market (DJIM) Indexes first introduced by the Dow Jones company in 1999.

7. Islamic finance is often characterized as following one of two main models: one associated with the Gulf (dubbed as the Arab model), the other with Malaysia. The Arab ijtihad was primarily driven by the surpluses generated by the oil boom of the mid-to-late 1970s whereas the Malaysian effort was driven by the developmental imperative, combined with domestic political factors, principally the promotion of the (Muslim) Malay majority. In other words, the Gulf countries, flush with oil money, were concerned with asset management while Malaysia focused on generating financing for the economy and transforming the country from agricultural backwater to industrializing nation.

8. Why did Islamic institutions escape relatively unscathed the 2008 sub-prime financial crisis? Quite simply because many of the practices that caused the financial meltdown such as the securitization of subprime loans (which is a sale of debt) nor credit default swaps (which are the sale of promises — forbidden in Islam — and are rife with gharar) would not pass muster with Shariah Boards. Similarly, negative Islamic attitudes toward short-selling as well as distrust of excessive leverage and of open-ended innovation proved well-founded. As for the systematic vetting of new products by Shariah advisers, it played a checks and balances role, and proved a useful corrective to the groupthink that had overtaken conventional finance.

REFERENCES

Khan, S. R. 1988. *Profit and Loss Sharing: An Islamic Experiment in Finance and Banking*. Karachi: Oxford University Press.

Rodinson, M. 1979. *Islam and Capitalism*.

Vogel, F. E. and S. L. Hayes III. 1998. *Islamic Law and Finance: Religion, Risk and Return*. Cambridge, MA: Kluwer Law International.

Warde, I. 2007. *The Price of Fear: The Truth behind the Financial War on Terror*. London: I.B.Tauris.

Warde, I. 2010. *Islamic Finance in Global Finance*, 2nd edition. Edinburgh University Press.

QUESTIONS FOR DISCUSSION

1. Explain what is *Ijara or leasing* and how it can be reconciled with the principles of Islamic finance. Is it appropriate to refer to Ijara as *debt-like* financing?

2. Is there such a thing as an Islamic bond?

3. Explain how the concept of a diminishing *Musharaka* is used in Shariah-compliant real-estate finance.

4. How is the *sukuk* construct used in Shariah-compliant long-term financing?

5. What is the key financial innovation that has greatly facilitated the growth of Islamic style asset management?

6. Is private equity-style investing consistent with the cardinal principles of Islamic finance?

7. Why did Islamic financial institutions escaped relatively unscathed from the 2008 sub-prime crisis. What are the key lessons that financial regulators should draw from this episode.

APPENDIX 27.1: EMIRATES FINANCIAL PROJECTIONS

Fleet Expansion and Required Capex FYE 2011E – FYE 2013E

	Aircraft Delivery from FY 2011 – FY 2013				
Aircraft Type	FYE Mar 2011	FYE Mar 2012	FYE Mar 2012	3 Years Total	Cost per plane
A380-800	7	7	11	25	235.0
B777-300ER	1	16	14	31	170.0
Total	**8**	**23**	**25**	**56**	**235.0**

(USD in million)	Acquisition Cost and Capex from FY 2011 – FY 2013			
Aircraft Type	FYE Mar 2011	FYE Mar 2012	FYE Mar 2013	3 Years Total
A380-800	1,645.0	1,645.0	2,585.0	5,875.0
B777-300ER	170.0	2,720.0	2,360.0	5,270.0
Total Cost	**1,815.0**	**4,365.0**	**4,965.0**	**11,145.0**
% Cash Payment				
PDP @ 30% of two year delivery	1,309.45	1,489.5	1,846.5	4,645.5
Balance @70% at delivery	1,270.00	3,055.5	3,475.5	7,801.5
Capex	**2,580.0**	**4,545.0**	**5,322.0**	**12,447.0**

Three Year Pro Forma Key Model Outputs [1]

(USD in million)	Historical FYE March					Projected FYE March			CAGR
Key Financials	2006A	2007A	2008A	2009A	2010A	2011E	2012E	2013E	2010A-2013E
Profit & Loss									
Revenues	6,173.3	7,942.8	10,566.5	11,779.8	11,831.3	12,273.4	13,090.8	14,241.6	6.4%
% Growth	*26.6%*	*28.7%*	*33.0%*	*11.5%*	*0.4%*	*3.7%*	*6.7%*	*8.8%*	
EBITDAR	1,625.5	2,069.2	2,649.1	2,256.0	2,896.3	3,015.6	3,142.8	3,422.5	5.7%
% Growth	*10.3%*	*27.3%*	*28.0%*	*(14.8%)*	*28.4%*	*4.1%*	*4.2%*	*8.9%*	
% Margin	*26.3%*	*26.1%*	*25.1%*	*19.2%*	*24.5%*	*24.5%*	*24.0%*	*24.0%*	
EBITDA	995.9	1,277.1	1,674.7	1,222.2	1,777.1	1,854.5	1,904.3	2,075.2	5.3%
% Growth	*3.5%*	*28.2%*	*31.1%*	*(27.0%)*	*45.4%*	*4.4%*	*2.7%*	*9.0%*	
% Margin	*16.1%*	*16.1%*	*15.8%*	*10.4%*	*15.0%*	*15.1%*	*14.5%*	*14.6%*	
Balance Sheet									
Total Debt	3,052.0	3,631.6	3,734.6	4,495.6	5,337.7	5,536.0	8,330.8	11,907.8	
Net Debt	557.5	1,127.0	914.0	2,544.0	2,476.0	3,081.3	5,712.6	9,059.5	
Cash	2,504.6	2,504.6	2,820.6	1,951.6	2,861.8	2,454.7	2,618.2	2,848.3	
Cash Flow									**3 year Capex**
Capex						2,580.0	4,545.0	5,322.0	12,447.00

CASE STUDY 27.1. WHEN EMIRATES AIRLINE TAPS ISLAMIC FINANCE[19]

Sheikh Ahmed bin Saeed Al Maktoum, chairman of Emirates Airline, rang the bell at the Nasdaq Dubai Stock Exchange to signal the start of trading for a secondary share offering issued by the carrier. At the back of his mind, he wondered whether the airline should raise debt capital on the back of this share offering to fund its aircraft acquisition program over the next five years amounting to over US$24 billion. For this size of financing requirement, careful planning and timing of fund raising was required in order to maximize investor interest and minimize funding costs.

Qatar Airways, another Gulf-based carrier, had issued an Islamic bond (Sukuk) which had been performing quite well. The company had just raised $1 billion from the sale of 10-year amortizing Islamic bonds at a rate of 3.875%, and $750 million from 12-year amortizing bonds at a coupon of 4.5%. That's not a big return for investors. However, investors stood to make a much bigger profit if the yields were compressed still further in the marketplace below the issue coupon. Then the value of the bond itself rises in mathematical proportion, delivering a profit to the owner rather like a rising share price.

Everybody was wondering how long current low interest rates, partially driven by quantitative easing by central banks in response to the global financial crisis, will last. When interest rates go up, bond prices go down. The small upside potential to holding bonds may then be massively outweighed by the downside risk of losing a lot more money, making it difficult to attract investors without rewarding them with a higher coupon rate. Hence, Emirates had a small window of opportunity to launch Sukuks at very low interest rates.

Standard Chartered Bank was mandated to advise the airline on its capital raising plan and they presented ideas on various funding options for Emirates. Recognizing that the airline will need both long- and short-term plans, as well as to tap different financing sources, they presented a multi-prong strategy to finance capital expenditure of this scale. They believed that the optimal long-term solution for Emirate would be to develop an asset-based funding platform centered around an Islamic enhanced equipment trust certificate ("EETC") issuance. Concurrently, they wanted Emirates to establish a corporate bond issuance platform by issuing an Islamic bond or Sukuk.

The Islamic product structures are described below:

Islamic enhanced equipment trust certificate

An equipment trust certificate (ETC) is a financial security used in aircraft finance. It is a debt instrument that allows a company to take possession of an asset and pay for it over time. The debt issue is secured by the equipment or physical assets, as the title for the equipment is held in trust for the holders of the issue. When the debt is paid off, the equipment becomes the property of the issuer, as the title is transferred to the company. An enhanced ETC, also known as a double ETC, is similar to a conventional ETC except that the security has been divided into two or more classes of securities, each with different payment priorities and asset claims. The more senior certificates (those with highest priority) have a higher credit rating and may obtain an investment grade rating for the particular issue. EETCs issues are similar to securitization transactions in that ownership remains with a separate trust rather than the operator.

EETCs can potentially achieve significantly higher ratings (up to three full categories above the airline's rating) through overcollateralization and structural enhancements, including liquidity facility. Funding costs are lowered as a result of enhanced credit ratings. The instrument has the flexibility in terms of structure to fit various investment profiles (short/long duration, fixed/floating coupon, bullets/amortizing payments, senior/junior tranches). Furthermore, Islamic execution would ensure participation of local Islamic investment houses which constitutes a considerable pool of liquidity in the region.

The instrument also has some limitations which require prior consideration. It is typically backed only by the most modern and desirable aircraft within a carrier's fleet. The instrument needs to be supported by a liquidity provider with a short-term debt rating at least consistent with the highest rating sought on the relevant EETC. Legal review for EETC transactions in non-US jurisdictions is generally complex and time-consuming.

19 This case was written by Shuvam Dutta.

Islamic EETC Structure

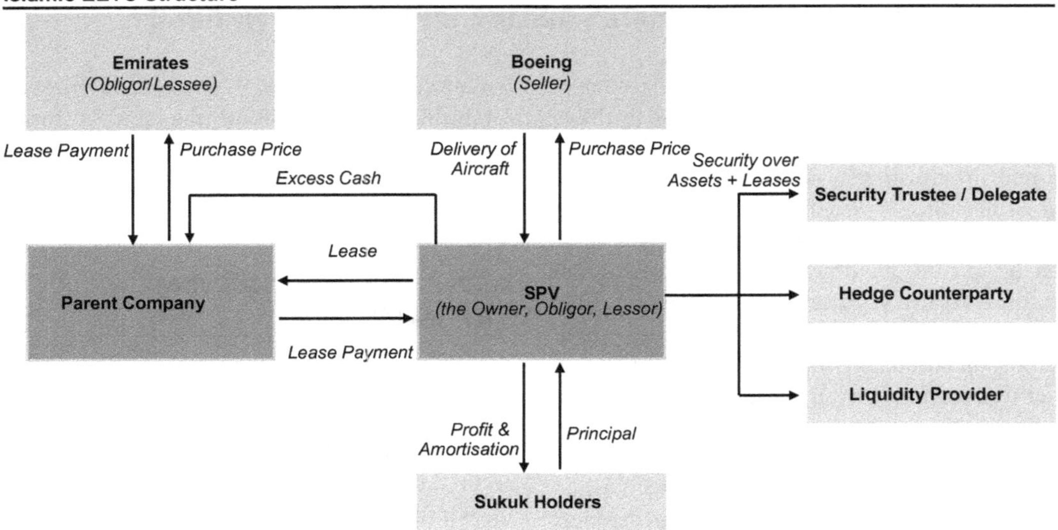

Issuance of Sukuk

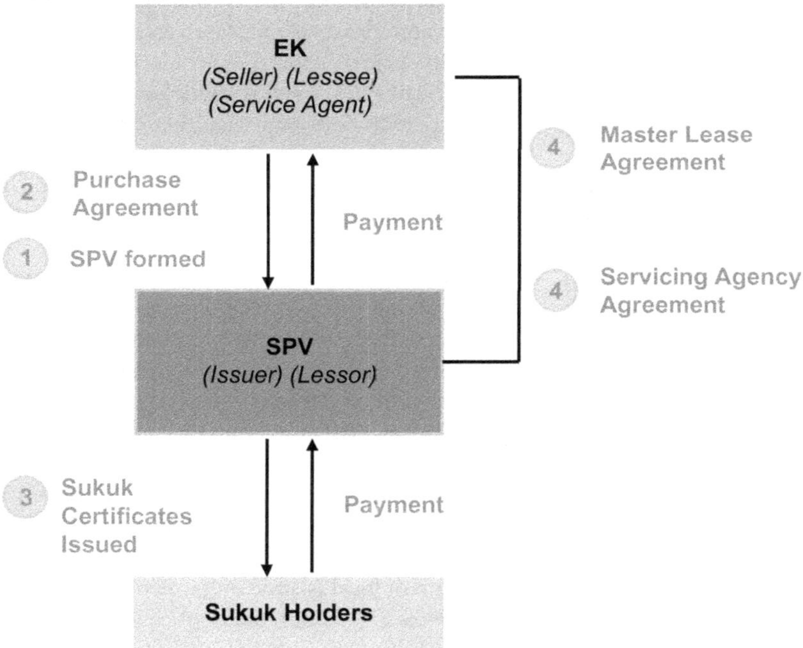

Islamic bond (Sukuk)

The Sukuk is an Islamic financial certificate, similar to a bond in Western finance that complies with Sharia. Since the traditional Western interest paying bond structure is not permissible under Sharia, the issuer of a Sukuk sells an investor group the certificate, who then rents it back to the issuer for a predetermined rental fee. The issuer also makes a contractual promise to buy back the bonds at a future date at par value.

Standard Chartered anticipated substantial demand for such an issuance by Emirates on the back of the Company's strong financial performance, a successful equity offering and the oversubscription observed on recent quasi-sovereign bonds/Sukuk issues from the region. They believed a 5 year deal will receive the most interest from investors, as this remains the "sweet spot" for investors and appetite decreased drastically for longer maturities. A Sukuk would allow Emirates to tap liquidity from both conventional and Islamic investors. However, a Sukuk would require Emirates to have available unencumbered assets for structuring purposes. If Emirates feels that it may not have unencumbered assets for structuring, a conventional bond issuance would be a better option than the Sukuk.

The Emirates leadership had to choose between competing Islamic finance options, after carefully assessing the advantages and limitations of each product. It also needed to compare Islamic debt products with conventional debt products to understand whether they need to tap one or both markets. Concurrent with the above Islamic products, Emirates could potentially establish a corporate bond issuance platform, or tap into the syndicated loan markets for a revolving credit facility, to address more immediate short-term funding needs. They could also retain funding flexibility through asset-based financing options such as finance leases and operating leases. The company needed to decide on the optimal mix of debt products to fund its capital expenditures.

QUESTIONS

1. Discuss the different financing options available to Emirates Airlines. What are their pros and cons given the unique requirements of aircraft financing?
2. How do you explain that Sukuk are referred to as Islamic bonds when interest payments are forbidden by Sharia law?
3. How would you compare the effective cost of traditional/western versus Islamic financing options? What is your final recommendation to Emirates?

Appendix: Answers to Selected Problems

CHAPTER 2

1. a) +30%; b) −23.21%.
2. a) −21% and +27%; b) 97.75 to 102.25.
3. a) 0.25; b) 3.7 to 4.3; c) 3.4 and 3.15 to 3.66.
4. 0.94, 1.25, +32.91%.
5. a) A round-trip (triangular arbitrage) would yield a risk-free profit of KRW 0.0135 per KRW 1 traded; c) profit of KRW 0.0093 per KRW 1 traded.
6. The prevailing exchange rate would have to be adjusted as follows:
   - Preferential imports: $S_{R,\$}(t) \times 1.03$
   - Semi-preferential imports: $S_{R,\$}(t) \times 1.06$
   - Essential imports: $S_{R,\$}(t) \times 1.09$
   - Nonessential imports: $S_{R,\$}(t) \times 1.11$
   - Luxury imports is $S_{R,\$}(t) \times 1.14$

   where $S_{R,\$}(t)$ is the rupee price of one US$ at time t.
7. a) −43.14%; b) profit of $13.88.

CHAPTER 3

2. −50%, +100%.
3. FF 5 = $1; FF 4.95 to FF 5.05.
4. −58.33%, 140%.
6. CFA 655
8. b) −25.85%.

CHAPTER 5

1. US$1.489 billion.
2. 0.084% or 8.4 bp.
3. US$255.049 million.
4. a) US$0.00084 per ruble transacted; b) RUB 0.800 per U.S. dollar transacted.
5. THB 23.85 = SGD 1.
6. THB price of one BRL is 17.89.
7. 0.30; 0.43%; 0.48%.
8. b) 1.06%, 0.45%, 0.29%, 0.15%; c) €0.8064–0.8071
9. net profit of DKR (6.47 − 6.04) or DKR 0.43 per euro sold forward.
10. NYC dollar price of one yen is: $0.012642 < [S_{\$,¥}(t)^*]^{NYC} < 0.012674$.
11. €2,498.
13. £30,000; £29,944 per £100 million transacted.
15. a) After the devaluation YPF should trade at 19.21 × (1/0.036) = ARS 533

    b) For each YPF stock purchased at ARS 521 in Buenos Aires and sold in New York City at ARS 533 the trader would earn a profit of ARS 12

CHAPTER 6

1. Invest in U.S. dollar.
2. INR 0.01970.
3. a) Invest in $; b) borrow in £; d) £0.001906 per £ transacted.
4. b) Invest in euros; d) keep investing in euros; e) 13.3%.
6. a) Carry trade is warranted as long as BRL does not depreciate beyond BRL 1.9600 = $1; c) break-even exchange rate is lowered to BRL 1.9446 = $1.
7. a) Covered euro-dollar loan is preferred.
8. a) 90 days forward rate: US$0.7407 = ARS 1; implicit annualized interest rate = −103.7%;

b) profit of US$0.2407 per ARS sold forward; reduced to US$0.2361 with a 20% margin; c) yes, profit of US$0.0593 per ARS purchased forward.

9. a) One year forward at ¥95.478 = US$1; c) the money market hedge through the purchase of UAZ is cheaper; d) no.

10. a) As long as the ¥ does not appreciate below 98.05; b) borrow in Eurodollar at 2.15% and invest on a covered basis in ¥ at 0.40%.

12. a) Borrow Japanese yen at 1.875% from Deutsche Bank's Tokyo office and invest in Citibank N.A. certificate of deposit at 3.56% for a net profit of 0.015 per yen borrowed. Alternatively, Louise could borrow yen at 1.875% and invest in króna at 14.5% for a net profit of 0.114 per yen borrowed. b) Carry trade would end up as a loss. c) Carry trade would turn into a huge loss.

13. a) $1 + i_d < (1 + i_f)\,[(1 - \tau_d)(1 - \tau_s)(1 - \tau_f)(1 - \tau_F)]$ $F\$,£(90)/S\$,£(0)$.

14. b) Effective yield is $k = 5.79\%$; d) US$0.2512 = ZAR 1.

15. a) The bank's home-made forward contracts will be slightly different from prevailing market rates at 1.5050–1.5083.

CHAPTER 7

1. The lira is very slightly undervalued by 0.3911%.
2. a) 1.0777; b) overvalued by 7.77%.
3. a) 13.99; b) ARS 3.5002 = US$1; overvalued.
4. a) 1.7241; b) grossly undervalued.
5. a) 2.26 and 3.75; b) undervalued; c) 5.10.

CHAPTER 8

1. b) AUD 1 = ¥79.93.
2. b) US$7,470.63; c) $499; d) yes.
3. a) Go long/purchase CHF futures, go short/sell €; b) US$0.1188 per € transacted minus the cost of putting up a margin of US$0.0022; profit of $0.1160 per CHF minus a margin of US$0.0019.
4. c) US$0.13.
5. a) Euro put option.
6. a) Profit of $0.0140 per SEK sold forward.
9. Arbitragers will buy the synthetic forward contract at 1.49 (combining a put and a call option) and sell the market forward at 1.54, netting a profit of US$0.05 per pound sterling transacted.
10. $0.047.

CHAPTER 9

1. a) Cost of bank loan = $3.9375 million; Cost of commercial paper = $3.218 million
3. a) Bank loan costs $14,375 million but commercial paper is cheaper = $13.750 million; b) Chicago's cost of capital is 3.01% and it earns 224 basis points.
5. a) 6.62%; b) 7.21% for Argentina; c) Argentina was well ahead of Venezuela in both 2002 (101% versus 4.26%) and 2007 (33.24% versus 3.6%); d) Colombia was well ahead of Venezuela in all three years.
6. b) Argentina would be positioned at 0.4898 on the interest rate axis, at 0.2250 on the foreign rate axis, and at 0.5676 on the equity axis.

CHAPTER 10

1. a) US$28.44; b) profit of ¥155 per ADR traded.
2. US$26.76.
3. a) One MegaFon share is worth RUB 989.4/5 = RUB 197.9 in Moscow.
5. a) 17.97%; b) 10.00%.
6. d) With P/E = 8.82, Salgacoar has a significantly higher cost of equity capital than its peers on the Hong Kong stock exchange (P/E = 17) and should therefore list/issue equity in Hong Kong.
7. a) Salgacoar's cost of equity is 14.98% compared with an industry average of 11.33%. b) The cost of equity capital k_E^* for the shipping industry on the Hong Kong Stock Exchange is 9.33%. Salgacoar should raise equity capital on the HKSE.

CHAPTER 11

1. b) $644 million; c) $629 million; d) 6.85%.
2. a) 8.50%; b) 4.46%.
3. b) €1.3319 = £1.
6. a) 14.14%; b) 14.14%.

9. a) $k_¥ = -3.00\%$, $k_\$ = 2.30\%$; b) $k_\$ = 9.60\%$.

11. c) Swapping dollar debt into pesos would cost 54 basis points more than a peso Euro-note: 8.49% + 0.54% = 9.03%.

13. a) BF interest payment = (25,000)(3.66)(0.07) (50/3.66)(1 + 0.15) = 100,625
b) No, c) Yes, d) No, e) DM.

15. a) M = NOK 425,351,862; b) NOK appreciates by less than 2.7%.

CHAPTER 12

1. At the swap inception there is no net cash-flow exchange between the two firms since principals are equal to \$300 million = €250 million × 1.20. Thereafter Michelin pays annual interest in the amount of \$300 million × 0.055 = \$16.5 million in years 1 through 6 and repays principal of \$300 million in year 6. Similarly, DuPont services €250 million debt at the rate of 4.0 percent, paying an annual coupon of €10 million and repaying principal in year 6.

3. c) $B_\$(1)$ = 259.08 million, $B_¥(1)$ = 22,079.17 million; ¥ value of currency swap = 22,021.80 − 22,079.17 = −57.37 million.

5. At time of default Mellon Bank incurs a loss of US\$243.75 million.

6. b) Effective yield on Spanish bonds is 3.40%; c) GMWF will pay the annual premium of €28.5 per €1,000 on January 1, 2013, and January 1, 2014. Upon default at the close of 2014, AXA would be liable for the full face value of the insured bond.

7. b) Invest in Spanish bonds protected by CDSs.

CHAPTER 13

1. c) Hedged € financing \$13.86 million, hedged \$ financing \$14.29 million.

2. c) 11.09%.

3. c) Cisco receives upon shipment \$4,790,000 at an all-in annualized cost of 7.72%.

4. b) 17.04%.

5. a) 20.05%; b) bank financing is cheaper at 17.04%.

CHAPTER 15

1. The U.S. dollar would appreciate by 44.11% against the KRW over the next seven years.

2. a) The forward rate is more accurate. b) The first forecast is more helpful for hedging.

3. a) Accuracy rate is 37.50%; b) RMSE for Third Eye is 0.2164 but only 0.1738 for the forward rate.

5. a) Accuracy rate is 58.3%; b) RMSE for 20/20 is 2.6687 but only 2.3520 for the forward rate.

CHAPTER 16

1. a) For each month, transaction exposures would be netted as either asset (+) exposures arising from export receivables or liability (−) exposures arising from import payables or interest/principal repayment on debt.

January	+€175 million
February	+€175 million
March	+€175 − €50 − €35 − €250 = −€160 million
April	+€175 million
May	+€175 million
June	+€175 − €50 − €35 = +€90 million
July	+€175 million
August	+€175 million
September	+€175 − €50 − €35 − €250 = −€160 million
October	+€175 million
November	+€175 million
December	+€175 − €50 − €35 = +€90 million

b) € transaction exposures reduce by €35 million at the end of each quarter and €250 million on March 30 and September 30.

2. a) US\$ at a slight premium; b) US\$-denominated transaction exposure; c) forward hedge yields CAD 70.395 million.

3. a) US\$ put option; b) A put option requires an up-front cash payment; for example, should Bombardier choose a strike price of CAD 0.94 = US\$1, which is slightly higher than the forward rate, it would pay a premium of (\$75 million) × 0.0015 = CAD 112,500; c) Put option.

4. a) (i) Do nothing—the ¥ proceeds would be a function of the December 31, 2013, spot ¥ price of US$1. (ii) Hedge its royalties receivable by selling forward its US$ receivables; the forward ¥ price of US$1 is at a 1.5% discount or $(F - 85)/85 = -0.015$ or $F = 85(1 - 0.015) = 83.7250$. ¥ proceeds to be received one year hence thus amount to US$7.5 million × 83.7250 = ¥627.9375 million. (iii) Purchase a US$ put/¥ call option at the strike price of ¥85 = US$1. ¥ proceeds thus amount to US$7.5 million × 85(1 – 0.035) = ¥615.1875 million if the ¥ were to appreciate/dollar to depreciate. Otherwise Sony-Japan would receive US$7.5 million × $S(360)$ × (1 – 0.035), reflecting the closing spot price $S(360)$ adjusted for the cost of the put option.

5. a) Forward hedge yields $103.65 million versus money market hedge $103.75 million.

6. a) Forward hedge locks in cost at $94.62 million versus b) money market hedge at $88.51 million, c) CNY call option would cost an up-front premium of $2,733,333 but low CNY volatility would favor money market hedge.

7. a) –4.44%; b) uncovered = THB 120,000,000 × $S_{\$,THB}(180)$; forward cover = $2,666,667; money market hedge = $2,685,388.

8. a) £ asset exposure can be hedged through a forward or a money market hedge; b) £ financing yields €120.82 million, whereas € financing yields €120.70 million; c) $ financing yields €119.98 million; d) £ financing.

9. a) CAD asset transaction exposure; b) CAD financing yields €17.96 million whereas € financing yields €17,987 million; c) $ financing yields €18.36 million; d) $ financing.

CHAPTER 17

1. a) Translation exposure under monetary/nonmonetary method is MXN 100,000, current/noncurrent method is MXN 1,300,000, and current method is MXN 800,000; b) translation losses of MXN 1,333, MXN 17,333, and MXN 10,666, respectively.

2. a) Sell MXN forward or borrow present value of MXN translation exposure; c) –10.71%; d) approximately –5%; e) financial hedging.

4. c) Nominal cost of hedging is –10%. If forecast of a 20% depreciation for the ARS proves correct, cash profit would be of 2.33¢ per ARS sold forward.

5. a) –PHP 75,000 and +PHP 285,000 respectively; b) nominal cost of hedging is 9% but cash-flow cost is unknown at hedging time.

6. Translation exposure is now €9,000,000, resulting in an unrealized gain of US$1,125,000.

7. a) –VEF 85,000 and +VEF 215,000 respectively; b) translation gain of US$4,722; c) –VEF 115,000,000.

8. a) 51.13; b) $F_{\$,INR}(180) = S_{\$,INR}(0)(1 - 0.045/2) = (1/50)(0.9775) = 1.9550$¢ or $F_{INR,\$}(180) = 1/F_{\$,INR}(180) = 1/0.019550 = 51.1$; INR financing is cheaper; c) INR and $ money markets are mildly segmented d) INR financing leaves INR translation exposure unchanged whereas $ financing results into an increase by a full amount of the loan e) INR 2,435,460,000 of financing would be generated f) Money market hedge.

9. a) French subsidiary's € translation exposure = €5,551; Peso translation exposure = MXN 9240; b) US$ denomination of intra-corporate transactions would materially affect translation exposure as such items would no longer be counted as part of either the MXN or € translation exposure. Specifically, the French affiliate € transaction exposure would be left unchanged since notes due to the parent are already US$ denominated and MXN payables due to sister affiliate in Mexico are already denominated in MXN. Net MXN exposure of 9240 – 800 – 1320 + 1320 = MXN 8440.

CHAPTER 18

2. a) Profit margin reduction of 5.68%; b) 11.07% increase in the number of tours sold.

7. a) Not directly; b) yes; c) no.

CHAPTER 20

1. a) With NPV of equity cash flows = €0.95 million, Puma should invest in the Philippines.

2. c) NPV of equity cash flow to parent discounted at 14% is Yen 25,492,803.

6. b) Cost of equity capital = 9.14%.

7. Both licensing and greenfield operations generate in present value terms IDR 25 billion, but

greenfield investment requires sizable up-front investment.

9. Offshoring at €45.918 million is less value-creating than staying put in the Netherlands at €54.850

CHAPTER 21

1. a) $(P/E)^{Salgacoar} = 8$ or $P/4 = 8$ or $P =$ INR 32 billion; $P^* = 4 \times 9.2 =$ INR 36.8 billion; $P^{**} = 4 \times 13.5 =$ INR 54 billion; b) Such a contract would improve considerably the firm's risk profile, thereby boosting Salgacoar's value and putting it in the upper INR 32 to 56 billion price range.

2. INR 93.840 billion.

3. $P^* =$ INR 44,682,891 for a P/E of 9.9.

4. a) Value of Salgacoar as a stand-alone target: INR 32 to 36.5 billion; b) INR target value as an integral part of the Maersk shipping conglomerate: $V_{INR}^{POST} = 54,373,081,025$ billion; c) US$ target value to Maersk: $V_{US\$}^{POST} = \$996,239,117$.

CHAPTER 23

2. a) 0.543; b) 0.540; c) 0.547.

3. a) –16.2% in US$, +5.96% in BRL terms; b) No d) US$30.14.

4. c) Without a currency hedge, return on investing in Bank Itau would show an appreciation in BRL of 12%, more than erased by the 15% depreciation on the Brazilian currency, for a net loss of –3%. With a hedge, Bank Itau would still return 12% in BRL minus 7.5% hedging cost, for a net positive return of 12% – 7.5% = 4.5%. In neither case would the Bank Itau stock price respond to the BRL devaluation. The case of Embraer is different because part of the BRL depreciation is compensated for by an appreciation of its BRL stock price.

5. a) Return increases to 10.23% and risk to 9.10%. b) return of 11.55% and risk of 10.56%. c) A. Kaiwa =100%, South Korea = 0%; B. Kaiwa = 67%, South Korea = 33%; C. Kaiwa = 33%, South Korea = 67%; D. Kaiwa = 0%, South Korea = 100%.

Kaiwa	Korea	Correlation	Return	Std Dev
100%	0%	0.57	9.0%	7.0%
67%	33%	0.57	10.3%	7.4%
33%	67%	0.57	11.6%	8.9%
0%	100%	0.57	13.0%	11.0%

CHAPTER 24

2. a) BRL equivalent of US$33.60 million; b) US$41.44 million.

3. a) US$3.75 million; b) US$5.805 million still owed to the US; c) $41.44 million in taxes have already been paid on account of profits earned in and repatriated from Brazil. Fluor should use its tax credit of $3.36 million arising from having paid taxes in excess of the mandatory U.S. rate of 34% on repatriated earnings from Brazil to reduce the $5.805 million owed on account of earnings repatriated from Ireland, resulting in $2.445 million still owed to the U.S.

Glossary

accounting exposure *See* translation exposure.

accounts payable Cash owed by a firm to its suppliers for purchases made on credit and not yet paid; reported in the firm's balance sheet as a current liability. Also known as payables and trade creditors.

accounts receivable Cash owed to a firm by its customers for sales made on credit and not yet paid; reported in the firm's balance sheet as a current asset. Also known as receivables and trade debtors.

adjusted present value (APV) A valuation method according to which the value of a firm's assets is equal to the sum of (1) their value, assuming that they are financed only with equity capital (unlevered value), and (2) the present value of the tax savings provided by the portion of the assets financed with debt.

ad valorem duty A cross-border tax or customs duty levied as a percentage of the assessed value of goods entering a country.

after-tax cost of debt The cost of the debt component in the firm's cost of capital. It is calculated as: (Pretax cost of debt) × (1 – Marginal corporate tax rate).

agency problem Governance problem arising from the separation of ownership and control of a firm.

algorithmic trading Trading conducted by computer models rather than by human traders. With foreign exchange widely considered as an asset class, hedge funds and other institutional investors are increasingly relying on automated trading models that seek and act instantly on market opportunities to generate alpha.

all in cost The percentage cost of a loan or bond calculated as the internal rate of return that takes into account placement fees and all relevant transaction costs.

allowance for bad debts Provision made by the firm for the possible uncollectibility of accounts receivable.

American depositary receipt (ADR) A bank receipt collateralized by a multiple of foreign shares deposited with a foreign bank acting as a custodian. ADRs make it convenient to invest in foreign shares and greatly reduce the costs of investing in such shares; they are denominated in U.S. dollars, are traded in the United States like any other U.S. shares, and pay dividends in U.S. dollars. By cross-listing their stocks on foreign stock exchanges through issuance of ADRs and their close cousins, global depositary receipts (GDRs), firms hope first and foremost to lower their cost of capital through their access to a larger, better-diversified pool of global investors who presumably will value their stock more richly.

American terms Foreign exchange quotations for the U.S. dollar, expressed as the number of U.S. dollars per unit of non-U.S. currency.

appreciation In referring to exchange rate changes, a one-time increase in the foreign exchange value of a currency that is pegged to other currencies or to gold. Also called revaluation.

arbitrage Refers to comparing the price of the same asset — currency in the case of the foreign exchange market — in two distinct physical locations. If prices are different, buy where it is cheaper and sell where it is more expensive. Arbitrage makes sense as long as the price differential exceeds the transaction costs incurred in carrying out the transaction.

arm's-length transfer price The price at which an unrelated buyer and seller freely agree to carry out a transaction. Used as a benchmark by tax authorities in gauging the fairness of transfer prices applied to intracorporate transactions between related companies such as foreign subsidiaries of multinational corporations.

artificial currency unit *See* currency basket.

ask (offer) rate The price at which a market maker is willing to sell a currency.

asset-backed security (ABS) A derivative security that typically includes second mortgages and home equity loans based on mortgages, in addition to credit card receivables and auto loans.

asset class A group of securities that exhibit similar characteristics, behave similarly in the marketplace, and are subject to the same laws and regulations. The three main asset classes are equities (stocks), fixed income (bonds), and cash equivalents (money market instruments). Similarly, artifacts, currencies, real estate, and commodities qualify as different asset classes.

at-the-money A term used to refer to a call option or a put option whose strike price is equal (or virtually equal) to the current price of the asset on which the option is written.

back office A bank's back office is responsible for making actual payments, record keeping, reconciling transactions concluded by the front office, and getting confirmation from counterparties.

backwardation A relationship in which spot or cash prices are higher than futures (or forward) prices.

balance of payments An accounting record of all officially recorded economic transactions between residents of one country and the rest of the world (residents of other countries) over a stated period of time.

balance of trade A subaccount of the balance of payments recording the net flow of goods (exports minus imports).

balance sheet hedge A hedging strategy whereby a foreign subsidiary's translation asset exposure is matched by an offsetting equal liability exposure created through borrowing in the local currency. As a result, any exchange rate change leaves the translated value of a foreign subsidiary unchanged in the parent's reference currency.

barrier option A normal option that is activated/deactivated when the spot exchange rate crosses a specified threshold/barrier rate.

banker's acceptance A draft accepted by a bank that constitutes an unconditional promise by the bank to make payment on a draft when it is presented for payment.

barter An exchange of goods or services directly between two parties without the use of financial instruments such as currency or credit.

Basel Accord Agreement initially reached in 1988 under the aegis of the Bank for International Settlements (domiciled in Basel) between the central banks of 12 major countries on how banks should be regulated and capitalized (so-called capital adequacy ratios) to stave off systemic risk.

basis point One-hundredth of a percentage point (0.0001).

bearer bond A bond on which the coupon and principal are payable to whoever has possession of the bond certificate, which protects the bond owner's anonymity. Eurobonds are typically bearer bonds.

beta (β) coefficient A relative measure of a stock's risk; beta measures volatility not in absolute terms as standard deviation does but in comparison to the stock market as a whole. Betas are calculated by regressing a stock's return against the stock market's return; beta gauges the responsiveness of a stock's price to market swings.

bid-ask spread A dealer's profit margin; it is the difference between a bid and an ask quoted price.

bid price The price at which a market maker in an asset will buy the asset.

bill of lading (B/L) Issued by the international carrier to the exporter, it is first and foremost a receipt of the merchandise and as such it includes a short and simple description of the goods. Second, it is a contract between the exporter/consignor and the carrier spelling out the latter's obligation to transport the merchandise from the port of shipment to the port of destination for delivery to a consignee in exchange for certain freight charges. Last but not least, it is a document of title that establishes control over the merchandise.

black market Any private market that operates in contravention of government restrictions. Such illegal markets may involve the exchange of currencies or goods at prices that are outside government-mandated levels, the trading of prohibited goods, or trading between individuals and/or institutions that are not approved by the government.

blocked funds Funds in one country's currency that may not be exchanged freely for foreign currencies because of exchange controls.

branch A multinational corporation's foreign operation that is not incorporated in the host country, in contrast to a subsidiary.

Bretton Woods international monetary system In the Bretton Woods system, each national currency was pegged/fixed to gold at a par value publicly known to all market participants. Gold was defined as $35 per ounce of gold. A modicum of flexibility was built into the system allowing each exchange rate to fluctuate within a narrow tunnel of +/−1 percent (later reduced to +/−0.75 percent) around the par value. National central banks acted as custodians of par value to be enforced through central bank intervention in the currency markets.

bulldog bonds British pound sterling–denominated foreign bonds issued in London by non-UK-domiciled firms.

call option A contract giving the purchaser the right, but not the obligation, to buy a particular asset such as a foreign currency at a stated strike price on or before a stated date.

capital account Subset of the balance of payments showing net changes in the domestic private sector's holdings of foreign financial assets or in foreign holdings of domestic financial assets.

capital asset pricing model (CAPM) A theoretical model according to which a security's expected return is equal to the risk-free rate plus a risk premium. Widely used to estimate a firm's cost of levered equity capital.

capital controls Governmental restrictions (such as prohibitions, taxes, or quotas) on the acquisition of foreign assets or foreign liabilities by domestic citizens, or the acquisition of domestic assets or domestic liabilities by foreigners.

capital expenditure (capex) A firm's new investment in fixed assets such as property, plant, and equipment (PPE).

capital flight Movement of funds out of a country because of political risk.

capital market integration National capital markets are integrated when there is no difference in their cost of debt or equity financing. *See also* capital market segmentation.

capital market segmentation Refers to the fact that the cost of capital varies from one national capital market to another. By contrast, integrated capital markets are markets for which the cost of capital would be the same. In the case of bond markets, nominal yields on national bonds should vary as they reflect different inflation expectations. However, exchange rate adjustment may equalize effective yields across different currencies, bringing about closer bond market integration.

carry trade Interest rate arbitrage without hedging against exchange rate risk. Typically, it involves borrowing in a low interest rate country such as Japan or the United

States and investing in a higher interest rate country such as Australia, Brazil, or Turkey. The effective yield of the carry trade is unknown at the outset of the transaction since it depends on the actual exchange rate (left unhedged) at the maturity of the transaction.

cash flow from assets (CFA) Net cash flow generated by a firm's assets. Also referred to as free cash flow.

central bank A country's official monetary authority charged with the conduct of monetary policy and responsible for price stability and orderly transactions in the foreign exchange market.

central bank intervention Refers to a country's central bank sales or purchases of its own currency (in exchange for a convertible currency) to steer the price of its currency downward (in the case of sales) or upward (in the case of purchases).

certificates of deposit (CDs) Negotiable instruments issued by a bank and payable to the bearer. CDs pay a stated amount of interest and mature on a stated date, but may be bought and sold daily in a secondary market.

chartism A forecasting technique based on graphing historical exchange rates to identify trends from which one can extract future currency prices. It is a primary tool of technical analysis.

Chicago Mercantile Exchange The world's largest market for trading standardized futures and option contracts on commodities, currencies, and fixed income securities.

clean float Refers to floating exchange rates without any central bank intervention.

collateral Any assets pledged as a guarantee to a lender in case the borrower defaults.

commercial paper A short-term, unsecured debt instrument of maturity of 270 days or less issued by a corporation and sold at a discount from its maturity value.

comparative advantage The notion according to which the world is better off when each nation specializes in manufacturing the goods that it can produce most inexpensively.

conglomerate merger A combination of unrelated businesses for which there are no obvious synergies.

consolidation In the context of accounting for multinational corporations, the process of preparing a single reporting currency financial statement, which combines through translation financial statements of foreign subsidiaries that are in fact measured in different currencies.

contango A relationship in which spot or cash prices are lower than futures (or forward) prices.

contractual exposure *See* transaction exposure.

controlled exchange rates An exchange rate regime whereby all currency transactions are channeled through the central bank, which arbitrarily fixes the rate at which foreign currencies are sold or bought.

control premium The difference between the acquisition price and the preacquisition target firm's market value.

convertibility Freedom to exchange a currency for any other currency without government restriction or controls. Originally the term meant the ability to be exchanged for gold. *Current account* convertibility connotes the freedom to buy and sell foreign exchange in relation to trade in goods and services. *Capital account* convertibility connotes a similar freedom in relation to direct investment or trade in financial assets.

Convertible contingent bond CoCos are fixed-income securities which may be forced to convert into a pre-specified amount of equity or simply written down should the issuer face difficult times. In good times they are simply high-yield bonds.

convertible currency A currency that can be exchanged freely for any other currency without government restrictions.

corporate governance Legal and financial organizational structure through which a firm's shareholders set its strategy and control its performance.

cost, insurance, and freight (CIF) Exporter's quoted price, including the cost of packaging, freight, and insurance premium, paid by the importer in respect of the goods from the time of loading in the country of export to their arrival at the named port of destination.

cost minimizers (offshoring) Entities that primarily search for lower labor costs and establish assembly operations in low-wage countries such as Mexico, China, Vietnam, or India. This is especially true of labor-intensive manufacturing processes characteristic of consumer electronics, garments, or footwear but also includes service operations such as back-office operations in the financial services industry or software development in information technology.

cost of capital The return expected by investors for the capital they supply to firms. Also, the highest return on an alternative investment with the same risk as the investment under consideration.

cost of equity Rate of return required by the firm's owners on their equity capital used to finance the firm's assets or a particular project. *See also* capital asset pricing model (CAPM).

cost of goods sold (COGS) The cost of the goods the firm has sold during the accounting period; reported in the income statement as expenses.

cost synergies Cost reductions resulting from combining the operations of two or more firms.

counterparty risk The potential exposure any individual firm bears that the second party to any financial contract may be unable to fulfill its obligations under the contract's specifications. For example, the risk that one party in a currency swap does not meet its contractual obligation. *See* currency swap.

countertrade A type of international trade in which parties exchange goods directly rather than for money. Also known as barter.

country risk Refers to how uncertainty about the host country's foreign investment climate (rules of the game) impacts the value of the multinational firm's investment in that country. Of special concern to investors are macropolitical risk, ownership/control risk, operating risk, and transfer risk.

coupon The periodic interest payment on a bond. Many bond certificates come with literally detachable coupons that must be removed and presented for payment, usually annually or semiannually.

covenant Agreement in a syndicated loan or bond contract imposing restrictions on the borrower's future conduct. Such covenants may involve, for example, the agreement to maintain a given balance sheet ratio in the future or impose restrictions on dividends distribution, asset sales, or additional debt issue.

covered interest rate parity Interest rate parity combines interest rate arbitrage (which requires comparison of the yield on two similarly risky securities denominated in different currencies) with a forward cover against exchange risk. Thus, interest rate parity does not mean equality of nominal interest rates; it means equality of interest rates in different currencies adjusted for the cost of a forward cover against exchange rate risk.

crawling peg An exchange rate system whereby the exchange rate is adjusted/devalued periodically (as often as every few weeks) to reflect the currency loss of purchasing power due to fast-paced domestic inflation. The system has been used over the years by countries suffering from hyperinflation.

credit default swap (CDS) An over-the-counter contract whereby the buyer (the insured) agrees to pay the seller (the insurer) periodic fees (insurance premium) in exchange for receiving protection against default (event) of a loan or bond (loss). The event triggering the payment of the loss is usually the debtor's default but can also be a credit rating downgrade or restructuring of the debtor. CDSs were introduced in the mid-1990s as a new and more flexible form of bond insurance.

credit enhancement Refers to providing some form of partial or full insurance against the risk of default and concretized either through a more traditional standby letter of credit or bond insurance, or more recently through credit default swaps (CDSs). As a result, the credit-enhanced securities are better rated and can therefore be issued at a lower yield.

creditors Parties to whom a firm owes money, including lenders and suppliers.

credit rating Rating that provides an overall assessment of a borrower's credit risk. *See* credit rating agency.

credit rating agency An agency, such as Standard & Poor's or Moody's Investors Service, that provides credit ratings for a fee paid by the issuer of the security (stocks or bonds) rather than by the investor.

credit risk The risk that a borrower will be unable to service its debt. *See* debt service.

cross-border acquisition A purchase in which one firm acquires another firm located in a different country.

cross-listing The listing of shares of common stock on two or more stock exchanges.

cross-rate An exchange rate between two currencies, neither of which is the U.S. dollar.

cumulative translation adjustment (CTA) account An entry in a translated balance sheet in which gains and/or losses from translation have been accumulated over a period of years.

currency basket The value of a portfolio of specific amounts of individual currencies. Also called currency cocktail and artificial currency unit. The special drawing right is a currency basket.

currency board A currency board exists when a country's central bank commits to back its money supply entirely with foreign reserves at all times. Thus the country's bonds and notes are convertible on demand into a foreign currency – usually the U.S. dollar – at a fixed rate.

currency futures contract A currency forward contract that has a standardized contract size and a standardized delivery date; it is traded on futures markets.

currency swap By exchanging (swapping) interest payment and principal repayment obligations at a fixed (once-and-for-all) exchange rate, borrowers can free themselves from a foreign debt obligation without incurring the additional cost of prepayment penalty on the debt issue being retired and flotation costs on the new debt issue. In effect, the currency swaps amount to a series of forward contracts set at the spot exchange rate prevailing when the swap occurs and will tend to be cheaper than hedging each interest and principal repayment at the corresponding forward rate.

current account Those items in the balance of payments involving imports and exports of goods and services, as well as unilateral transfers (gifts).

current/noncurrent method Translation method widely used until 1976 that required all current/short-term accounts to be translated at the current/closing rate. Translation exposure is the foreign subsidiary's working capital. Translation gains or losses flow through the parent's income statement and are directly added to or subtracted from its earnings per share (EPS).

current (translation) method The *all-current method* currently mandated by FASB Statement No. 52 (1981) requires all accounts to be translated at the current/closing rate. Translation exposure is the foreign subsidiary's net worth. Resulting gains or losses bypass the income statement to be accumulated into the parent's balance sheet in a subequity account designated as *cumulative translation adjustment*.

dealers Individuals or institutions that trade securities that they own.

debt service The timely and full payment of interest on borrowed funds as well as the repayment of the borrowed funds.

debt-to-equity ratio Total interest-bearing debt divided by owners' equity. A measure of financial leverage.

delta The ratio of a change in the option price to a small change in the price of the asset on which the option is written.

depreciation A decrease in the market value of a currency with respect to a second currency or a real asset.

devaluation A decrease in the official value of a currency with respect to a second currency or a real asset.

direct financing When firms raise funds by issuing securities that are held by ultimate savers (household sector) instead of financial intermediaries.

dirty float Refers to floating exchange rates with significant central bank intervention.

discounted payback period rule Rule whereby the project is accepted if its discounted payback period is shorter than a given cutoff period, or rejected if the payback period is longer than the cutoff period.

disintermediation A process in which savers withdraw deposits from financial intermediaries (like commercial banks and thrift institutions) and lend directly to investors and consumers by purchasing debt instruments such as commercial paper, bonds, and Treasury bills.

divergence indicator system One aspect of the European Monetary System that measured the departure of a country's economic policies from the European Community (EC) average. The measure of divergence was based exclusively on the movement of a country's exchange rate with respect to the European currency unit (ECU), which represented the community's average exchange rate. In the event of excessive divergence (see Chapter 3), the country was expected to alter economic policy to conform with the EC average.

diversifiable risk Risk that can be eliminated through portfolio diversification. Same as unsystematic risk or company-specific risk.

dividend The portion of a firm's net profit paid out to its owners in cash.

documentary letter of credit (L/C) *See* letter of credit (L/C).

dollarization The use of the U.S. dollar as the official currency of a country.

draft An unconditional written order requesting one party (such as an importer) to pay a specified amount of money at a specified time to the order of the writer of the draft. Also called a bill of exchange. Personal checks are one type of draft.

earnings after tax (EAT) Revenues minus all expenses, including interest and tax expenses. Same as net income, net profit, and bottom line.

earnings before interest and tax (EBIT) The difference between the firm's operating profit and any extraordinary items reported in its income statement.

earnings before interest, tax, depreciation, and amortization (EBITDA) Revenues minus all operating expenses, excluding depreciation expenses and amortization.

earnings multiple Share price divided by the firm's earnings per share. Same as price-to-earnings (P/E) ratio. Used to value a firm or to approximate its cost of equity capital.

earnings per share (EPS) Earnings after tax divided by the total number of shares outstanding.

econometric forecasting model A systematic effort to uncover a functional relationship between a set of *explanatory/independent* (exogenous) variables, such as price-level differentials, interest rate differentials, or differentials in the growth rates of money supplies, and an *explained/dependent* (endogenous) variable, namely, the exchange rate. The functional relationship may involve only the *current*-period values of the explanatory variables, or it may be of a *lagged* nature – that is, incorporate past-period values taken on by the explanatory variables.

economic exposure Exposure rooted in future expected cash-flows-based valuation of the multinational corporation. Economic or operating exposure to a given foreign currency *i* is defined as the percentage change in the firm's dollar value $\Delta V_{\$}(t)/V_{\$}(t)$ (often proxied by its market capitalization) resulting from an *unexpected* 1 percent change in the dollar value of foreign currency *i*, $\Delta S_{\$,i}(t)/S_{\$,i}(t)$. It matters because it links changes in exchange rates directly to the firm's cash flows and therefore to its value.

economic value added (EVA) Net operating profit after tax (NOPAT) minus a charge for the capital consumed to achieve that profit.

economies of scale The ability of a firm to reduce its average costs of production by increasing the volume of production; it is often a motivation to acquire other companies.

effective corporate tax rate The tax rate at which a firm actually pays its taxes, which may differ from the statutory corporate tax rate.

efficient market A market in which all relevant information is immediately reflected in market prices. The term is most frequently applied to foreign exchange markets and securities markets.

entry barriers Barriers that are costly enough to discourage potential competitors from entering a particular market or industry.

equity beta The beta of a firm's common stock. *See also* levered beta and market beta.

equity capital Funds contributed by shareholders that are equal to the difference, at a particular date, between what a firm's shareholders collectively own, called assets, and what they owe, called liabilities. Same as equity funds, net asset value, owners' equity, or shareholders' equity or funds.

equity cash flows Free cash flows minus interest payment and debt principal (re)payment. Equity cash flows are residual cash flows available to the equity owners of the firm.

equity risk premium The average annual return of the market expected by investors over and above riskless debt.

ESG investing The acronym ESG stands for ***"Environmental, Social and Governance"*** It is a framework aiming at measuring the impact — positive or negative — that public firms have on their environment and their stakeholders — employees, managers, customers, communities and shareholders. It is sometimes referred as ***"stake-holders capitalism"*** — that is managing the firm for the benefits of all its stakeholders to create longer term value rather than maximizing profits to create value solely for the benefits of equity investors which is also known as ***"shareholders capitalism"***. It incorporates environmental, social and governance factors alongside financial metrics in guiding investment decisions.

euro A new currency unit that replaced the individual currencies of 12 European countries belonging to the European Union. Also known as the single currency.

Eurobank A bank, or bank department, that bids for time deposits and makes loans in currencies other than that of the country where the bank is located.

Eurobond A bond underwritten by an international syndicate of banks and originally offered for sale outside the country in whose currency it is denominated – for example, a U.S. dollar–denominated bond that is originally offered for sale to investors outside the United States. Not to be confused with bonds denominated in euros.

Euro-commercial paper Short-term notes (30, 60, 90, 120, 180, 270, and 360 days) sold in international money markets.

Eurocurrency The currency in which securities issued outside the jurisdiction of a particular country are denominated. Not to be confused with the new currency launched by the European Union in 1999, the euro.

Eurocurrency market The money market for borrowing and lending currencies that are held in the form of deposits in banks located outside the countries in which those currencies are issued as legal tender.

Eurodollar A dollar-denominated deposit in a bank outside the United States.

Eurodollar bonds Bonds denominated in U.S. dollars that are sold simultaneously to investors outside the United States.

European Central Bank (ECB) Central bank that conducts monetary policy of the eurozone. Its goal is to safeguard the stability of the euro and minimize inflation in the eurozone.

European currency unit (ECU) An artificial currency unit created by the European Monetary System prior to the euro, which was designed to function as a reserve currency numéraire. It was the predecessor of the euro.

European Monetary System (EMS) A monetary accord among 15 European countries (same members as the European Union) from 1979 to 1999 that reestablished a system of pegged exchange rates between themselves, reminiscent of the Bretton Woods system.

European option An option that can be exercised only at its maturity.

European Union (EU) The official name of the former European Economic Community (EEC) as of January 1, 1994.

exchange controls Governmental restrictions (such as prohibitions, taxes, quotas, or government-set prices) on the purchase of foreign currencies by domestic citizens or on the purchase of the local domestic currency by foreigners.

exchange rate The price of a unit of one country's currency expressed in terms of the currency of some other country.

exchange rate mechanism (ERM) The means by which members of the European Monetary System formerly maintained their currency exchange rates within an agreed-upon range with respect to the other member currencies.

exchange rate pass-through The degree to which firms adjust the prices of imported and exported goods as a result of exchange rate changes. A full pass-through means that the full extent of the exchange rate change is reflected in the price of traded goods. For competitive reasons, firms often choose to pass through less than 100 percent of the exchange rate change.

exercise price *See* strike price.

export credit insurance Provides assurance to the exporter or the exporter's bank that, should the foreign customer default on payment, the insurance company will pay a major portion of the loss.

Export-Import Bank (Ex-Im Bank) A U.S. government agency created to finance and otherwise facilitate imports and exports.

expropriation Official government seizure of private property, recognized by international law as the right of any sovereign state, provided that the expropriated owners are given prompt compensation and fair market value in convertible currencies. *See also* nationalization.

face value The fixed amount of a bond that has to be paid back to bondholders at the maturity date of the bond. Same as principal, par value, or redemption value.

factoring Refers to specialized firms, known as factors, purchasing receivables at a discount on a nonrecourse or recourse basis from exporting firms. It is a relatively expensive form of exports financing.

fair market value An estimate of the amount that could be received on the sale of an asset under normal market conditions (as opposed to an emergency or liquidating sale).

FASB 8 Set of accounting rules enacted by the Financial Accounting Standards Board requiring U.S. companies to translate foreign affiliate financial statements by the temporal method (monetary/nonmonetary). FASB 8 was in effect from 1976 to 1981. It is still used under specific circumstances.

FASB 52 Set of accounting rules enacted by the Financial Accounting Standards Board requiring U.S. companies to translate foreign subsidiary financial statements at the current exchange rate (closing rate) and to accumulate resulting unrealized gains or losses to a subequity account on the parent company's balance sheet. FASB 52 became effective in 1981.

feasibility study In-depth evaluation of each proposal designated as a finalist by firms in their global search for investment opportunities. Market surveys, pilot studies, and product testing will be prerequisites for a full-blown financial analysis. As a result, detailed pro forma sales forecasts will be generated to anchor the actual valuation exercise; logistical and production surveys will verify the feasibility of the project proposal. Ultimately, the feasibility study will deliver financial metrics gauging the project's attractiveness, such as its payback period, net present value, or internal rate of return. This is the basis for the "go or no-go" decision that concludes the process.

financial disintermediation The process whereby savings are channeled to borrowers *directly* via the use of a market-traded security rather than *indirectly* through a financial intermediary via a loan from a commercial bank. Disintermediation is the hallmark of more sophisticated financial systems as found in OECD countries and are widely believed to lower the cost of capital.

financial distress Situation arising when a firm finds it increasingly difficult to service its debt.

financial engineering Those basic building blocks, such as spot positions, forwards, swaps, and options, used to construct positions that provide the user with desired risk and return characteristics.

financial intermediaries Institutions such as commercial banks that act as links between the ultimate recipients of capital (primarily firms) and the ultimate suppliers of capital (primarily household sector).

financial leverage The use of debt financing to complement equity financing.

financial system The financial sector's primary function is to mobilize savings from households and to allocate those funds among competing users (firms but also households, municipalities, and governments) on the basis of expected risk-adjusted returns. Thus the financial system provides a conduit through which excess savings are channeled to firms in need of cash or financing.

FinTech Digital delivery of financial products and services through the internet, a mobile phone or other electronic device.

Fisher effect A theory according to which the nominal interest rate is the sum of the real interest rate and the expected inflation rate.

floating exchange rate An exchange rate whose value results from the free interplay between suppliers and demanders of a foreign currency and that is not constrained by central bank intervention to remain within a fixed range.

floating rate notes Bonds that pay interest at an agreed margin above a market reference rate such as LIBOR. The interest rate varies according to the market reference rate and is reset periodically.

foreign bonds Bonds issued by nonresidents in a country's domestic capital market. Such bonds are subject to domestic regulations and are underwritten primarily by banks registered in the country where the issue is made.

foreign direct investment (FDI) Purchase of physical assets, such as plant and equipment, in a foreign country, to be managed and controlled by the parent corporation. FDI is distinguished from foreign portfolio investment.

foreign exchange market The market in which the currencies of different nations are bought and sold (in the form of bank deposits) with respect to each other. Most trading takes place with respect to the U.S. dollar.

foreign exchange reserves U.S. dollars and other convertible currencies held by central banks, which can be used for intervening in their currency markets to defend against a devaluation or depreciation.

foreign exchange risk As a first approximation, foreign exchange risk is defined as the additional variability experienced by a multinational corporation in its worldwide consolidated earnings due to unexpected currency fluctuations. However, this focus on *accounting* values is increasingly challenged by a sounder emphasis on *economic* value, defined as the sum of future *free cash flows* discounted at the firm's cost of capital. Exchange risk should then be redefined as the *variance* component in the firm's overall free cash flow due to exchange rate volatility.

foreign portfolio investment Purchase of foreign stocks and bonds, in contrast to foreign direct investment.

forfaiting A technique for arranging nonrecourse medium-term export financing. A third party, usually a specialized financial institution, guarantees the financing.

forward exchange Foreign currency traded for settlement beyond two working or business days from today at a price agreed upon today.

forward premium/discount The difference between the home currency forward price of one unit of foreign currency minus its spot price. If the difference is positive, the currency is said to be at a *premium*. If the difference is negative, the currency is said to be at a *discount*.

franchising A form of licensing whereby the franchisor grants to the franchisee a business system and other property rights such as brand names — rather than technology as in the case of licensing — in exchange for the periodic payment of royalties. In international franchising, the franchisee is a foreign firm.

free alongside (FAS) An international trade term in which the seller's quoted price for goods includes all costs of delivery of the goods alongside a vessel at the port of embarkation.

free cash flows Operating cash flows minus capital expenditures and change in working capital available over a period of time to the firm's owners.

front office A bank's front office is made up of traders who actually buy or sell currencies and their many derivatives to generate profits for the bank.

functional currency In the context of translating financial statements, a functional currency is the primary currency of the foreign subsidiary's economic environment or the currency in which cash inflows and outflows tend to be denominated. Specifically, when there is a high degree of interdependence between a given foreign subsidiary and its U.S. parent firm and relatively low managerial autonomy of the former vis-à-vis the latter, the subsidiary's *functional* currency is deemed to be the U.S. dollar rather than the local currency. In such cases its balance sheet would be restated in U.S. dollars using the *monetary/nonmonetary* translation rule with translation losses and gains flowing through the income statement.

futures contract A forward contract that is standardized in terms of size and delivery date. Futures contracts are traded on futures exchanges and are therefore highly liquid. They are also devoid of counterparty risk because of margining requirements.

gamma The ratio of a change in the option's delta to a small change in the price of the asset on which the option is written. The second partial derivative of the option price with respect to the price of the underlying asset.

generally accepted accounting principles (GAAP) Approved accounting principles for U.S. firms, defined by the Financial Accounting Standards Board (FASB).

global registered shares Similar to ordinary shares, global registered shares have the added benefit of being tradable on equity exchanges around the world in a variety of currencies.

gold standard A monetary system in which national currencies are defined in terms of their gold content, and payment imbalances between countries are settled in gold.

greenfield investment An initial or de novo investment by a multinational corporation in a new foreign subsidiary with no predecessor operation in that location. This is in contrast to a new subsidiary created by the acquisition of an already existing operation.

hedging The use of derivatives such as forwards, swaps, or options to reduce the firm's exposure to risk arising from its underlying business transactions and therefore to lower the volatility of its value.

horizontal merger Two firms in the same sector pooling their resources to become one entity.

household sector The sector of the economy composed of individuals and families.

hyperinflation countries Countries with a very high rate of inflation. Under U.S. FASB 52, these are defined as countries where the cumulative three-year inflation rate amounts to 100 percent or more.

ijara In Islamic finance, the principle of *ijara* is virtually identical to conventional leasing and can hence be referred to as a debt-like instrument. The bank leases an asset to a third party in exchange for a specified rent. The amounts of payments are known in advance, and the asset remains the property of the lessor. Although initially directed primarily at businesses, *ijara* is increasingly used in retail finance, primarily for home mortgages, cars, and household needs. In recent years, leasing contracts have also been commonly used for big-ticket items such as aircraft or ships and have become essential building blocks in project finance.

implicit interest rate The forward premium or discount expressed as a percentage. The absolute difference between forward and spot exchange rates is divided by the spot exchange rate.

implied volatility The future price volatility of a currency currently expected by the market and based on the current price of a particular option contract.

initial margin A requirement to deposit a portion of the initial investment when trading in a futures market.

initial public offering (IPO) When a firm sells equity to the public for the first time.

interest rate arbitrage The comparison of interest rates between domestic and foreign currency–denominated securities of the same risk class. For example, AAA-rated dollar-denominated 30-day U.S. Treasury notes would be compared with AAA-rated euro-denominated German 30-day treasury notes.

interest rate parity An equilibrium condition under which a borrower (or lender) is indifferent between borrowing (or lending) in the domestic currency or in the foreign currency, taking into account the need to convert currency through the spot market, with exchange risk covered by a reverse transaction through the forward market. A restatement of the interest parity condition yields the forward exchange rate as a function of the spot rate and the interest rates on the two currencies.

interest rate swap A contractual obligation entered into by two parties to deliver a fixed sum of money against a variable sum of money at periodic intervals. Typically, it involves an exchange of payments on fixed- and floating-rate debt. If the sums involved are in different currencies, the swap is simultaneously an interest rate swap and a currency swap.

interest subsidy Also known as concessionary financing, an interest subsidy creates value for the borrowing firm when it can raise financing below market interest rates.

internal rate of return (IRR) The discount rate that makes the net present value of a project's cash inflows and cash outflows equal to zero.

international Fisher effect States that the difference in interest rates between two countries reflects the difference in their expected inflation rates.

international licensing Contractual arrangement whereby a domestic firm — the *licensor* — makes available its intangible assets such as patents, technological know-how, trade secrets, or trademarks to a foreign company — the *licensee* — in return for the payment of royalties.

International Monetary Fund (IMF) Organization founded at Bretton Woods in July 1944 and located in Washington, D.C., whose primary function is to oversee exchange arrangements and lending foreign currency reserves to members experiencing temporary difficulties.

international parity conditions Purchasing power parity, covered interest rate parity, uncovered interest rate parity, and the Fisher effect are collectively referred to as international parity conditions. Should they hold conjointly, real – not nominal – interest rates would be equal across different countries.

in-the-money A term used to refer to a call option whose strike price is below, or to a put option whose strike is above, the current price of the asset on which the option is written.

investment grade bonds Highly rated bonds (BBB and above) that can be purchased by pension funds and other institutional investors.

joint venture A business venture that is owned by two or more entities, often from different countries.

Law of One Price (LOP) This law states that any traded good or security should sell for the same price (when expressed in the same currency) regardless of the country where it is sold. If not, arbitrageurs will promptly correct the price discrepancy by buying where it is cheaper and selling where it is more expensive until the price differential is obliterated.

leading and lagging Accelerating (leading) or delaying (lagging) payment between affiliated subsidiaries of a multinational corporation to minimize the impact of exchange rate devaluations (or revaluations).

lessee The user of the asset that is leased.

lessor The owner of the asset that is leased.

letter of credit (L/C) Documentary letters of credit allow the exporter to shift its credit risk exposure from an unknown foreign buyer to a better-known foreign bank that issues the letter of credit. Confirmed letters of credit by the exporter's bank further insulate the exporter from its credit and country risk exposure to the foreign bank since a confirmed letter of credit is a claim against its domestic bank.

levered beta The beta of a stock incorporating financial risk due to leverage (i.e., when the firm is indebted). Also known as market beta. *See also* equity beta.

licensing fees Periodic payments made by a licensee to a licensor for use by the former of the latter's technology, patent, or copyrights. Licensing fees or royalties are set as a small percentage — generally 2 to 5 percent — of the sales volume generated by the licensee using the licensor's technology. *See also* international licensing.

line of credit A nonbinding arrangement in which a bank lends a firm a stated maximum amount of money over a fixed but renewable period of time, usually one year. In general, no fee is charged but a compensating balance is required.

listing The formal process required in order to have the price of a bond, stock, or other security regularly quoted on a stock exchange. Eurobonds are usually listed so that they can be purchased by those institutional investors that are constrained to invest in listed securities.

London Interbank Offered Rate (LIBOR) The rate at which prime banks in London will lend currencies in the interbank market to other prime banks. LIBOR is often used as a basis for pricing Eurodollar and other Eurocurrency loans.

long A term used to describe a position that involves an excess of foreign currency purchases over sales, an excess of foreign currency assets over liabilities, or an excess of purchases of a particular futures contract over sales of the same contract.

Maastricht Treaty Treaty signed in 1992 among the 12 European Union countries that established a charter and timetable for the introduction of a single European currency, to be called the euro.

maintenance margin The minimum amount of money and/or securities a futures exchange requires in a customer's account for each futures contract subsequent to deposit of the initial margin. If equity drops below the maintenance level, funds must be added to the account to bring the equity up to the initial level.

margin The amount of money and/or securities that must be posted as a security bond to ensure performance on a contract. In the futures market, both short and long positions post margin. This ensures that the side with a daily cash-flow loss will be able to meet its payment obligation, thereby eliminating counterparty risk. *See also* initial margin and maintenance margin.

margin call A call for additional deposit from the futures exchange when the margin account has dropped below a preset level *See* initial margin.

market-based forecasts Forecasts that are as simple as taking today's spot or forward rates to be forecasts of future spot rates; they are provided by the foreign exchange market free of charge. Such forecasts are anchored in the theory that foreign exchange markets do indeed constitute efficient markets in an *informational* sense. Thus, if clearly established, the efficient market hypothesis would possibly invalidate the usefulness of building elaborate forecasting models and therefore the relevance of model-based forecasts.

market beta The beta of a stock when the firm is indebted. Same as levered beta. *See also* equity beta.

market capitalization Market value of a firm's equity. Equal to its quoted price per share multiplied by the total number of shares the company has issued. Also referred to as market cap.

market seekers Manufacturers exploiting a competitive advantage based on proprietary products, manufacturing methods, and marketing policies and favoring foreign direct investment as a mode of foreign market entry over exporting or licensing.

market-to-book ratio An accounting ratio defined as share price divided by book value of equity per share. Often used to value firms. *See* valuation by comparables.

mark to market The revaluation of a futures contract or a security to reflect the most recently available market price.

maxi-devaluation (maxi) A large, unscheduled devaluation of a currency that normally follows a mini-devaluation schedule. Often resorted to by countries experiencing hyperinflation.

monetary/nonmonetary translation Method embodied in FASB Statement No. 8 (1976–1981) that required all monetary gains and losses (as opposed to real/physical ones) to be translated at the current/closing rate. Resulting gains and losses flowed through the parent's income statement and were directly added to or subtracted from its earnings per share (EPS).

money market Market in which firms raise short-term funds and in which money market instruments such as commercial paper are issued and traded.

money market funds Financial intermediaries that pool the savings of households to invest in the money market.

monitoring costs Costs resulting from lenders placing restrictions on the use of the funds they lend to companies. These costs are borne by shareholders.

multiple exchange rates A form of controlled exchange rates that imposes different exchange rates to discourage certain types of imports deemed nonessential, whereby central banks are effectively making such imports more expensive.

nationalization Confiscation of a firm's assets by a government without compensation.

nepotism The practice of showing favor to relatives over other qualified persons in conferring such benefits as the awarding of contracts, granting of special prices, or promotions to various ranks.

net cash flow from financing activities The net cash flow from the firm's financing activities during an accounting period.

net cash flow from investing activities The net cash flow from the firm's investing activities during an accounting period.

net operating cash flow (NOCF) The net cash flow originating from the firm's operating activities during the period under consideration (cash inflows from operations minus cash outflows from operations).

netting The mutual offsetting of payments due between two or more business entities.

nominal exchange rate The actual foreign exchange quotation, in contrast to real exchange rate, which is adjusted for changes in purchasing power.

nominal interest rate The quoted interest rate that a borrower will actually pay, including a premium for the rate of inflation.

nonrecourse loan in project finance In financing a project, the loan is secured by the project's assets and future cash flows — not by the balance sheets of the project sponsors who happen to be the equity owners. It allows firms to contribute sizable amounts of equity to mammoth projects without being liable in case of default by the project.

nontariff barriers Trade restrictive practices other than custom tariffs, such as import quotas, voluntary restrictions, local procurement requirements, and special health regulations.

North American Free Trade Agreement (NAFTA) A treaty allowing free trade and investment among Canada, the United States, and Mexico.

open interest The total number of futures contracts for a particular currency or asset that have not been liquidated by an offsetting trade or that have not been fulfilled by delivery.

open position A net long or short foreign currency or futures position whose value will change with a change in the foreign exchange rate or futures prices.

operating exposure *See* economic exposure.

optimal capital structure The debt-to-equity ratio that maximizes the market value of the firm's assets.

optimum currency area A group of (generally) contiguous countries that find it beneficial to adopt a single currency common to all member countries of the currency zone. An optimum currency area meets several conditions: (1) freedom of movements for labor and capital, (2) flexibility of wages and prices, and (3) means to deal with asymmetric shock impacting a region or country in the currency area. The eurozone aspires to become one day an optimum currency area.

Organization of Petroleum Exporting Countries (OPEC) Cartel of most major countries producing crude oil, formed for the purpose of allocating and controlling production quotas so as to influence the price of crude oil in world markets.

Overseas Private Investment Corporation (OPIC) A U.S. government-owned insurance company that insures U.S. corporations against various political risks.

over-the-counter (OTC) markets Markets that do not require companies to meet the listing requirements of organized exchanges. Currencies, commodities, and securities are traded through dealers connected by a network of telephones, computers, and the Internet.

overvaluation A currency is said to be overvalued when its official value far exceeds its fair value, generally derived from purchasing power parity calculations. For example, if the Argentine peso (ARS) is officially valued at ARS 6 = US$1 when its PPP value stands at ARS 8 = US$1, the peso would be deemed overvalued by (8 – 6)/6 = 33%.

owners' equity The difference, at a particular date, between what a firm's shareholders collectively own, called assets, and what they owe, called liabilities. Same as net asset value, net worth, shareholders' equity, and shareholders' funds.

parity grid The system of fixed bilateral par values in the European Monetary System. The central banks of both countries whose currencies were involved in a bilateral exchange rate were supposed to intervene in the foreign exchange market to maintain market rates within a range defined by an upper and a lower band around the par value.

payback period rule Rule whereby the project is accepted if its payback period is shorter than a given cutoff period, or rejected if its payback period is longer than the cutoff period.

pegged yet adjustable exchange rates *See* stabilized exchange rates.

political risk The risk that the cash flows from a project may be affected by changes in local regulations governing foreign investments. Same as country risk.

price-to-earnings (P/E) ratio An accounting ratio widely used to value a firm, defined as the share price divided by the firm's earnings per share. Same as earnings multiple. *See* valuation by comparables.

private placement The sale of a security issue to a small set of qualified institutional buyers.

project finance Generally, the long-term financing of stand-alone, single-purpose, capital-intensive, large-scale infrastructural and industrial projects whose debt servicing and principal repayment are solely secured by the project's future cash flows (rather than the equity sponsors' balance sheets).

purchasing power parity (PPP) A theory according to which exchange rate changes between two countries over the longer term reflect the inflation rate differential (relative purchasing power) between the same countries.

put-call parity This powerful arbitrage relationship binds the options market to the forward exchange market. For example, a 90-day forward sale contract can always be replicated by simultaneously selling a 90-day call and buying a 90-day European put option at the same strike price $E(90)$. The price of such a synthetic forward contract created by combining options can be readily compared to the prevailing rate in the forward market; any discrepancy between these two rates will set in motion arbitrage forces buying the cheaper forward contract to be sold at the higher rate until both rates reach parity. This fundamental equivalence between the option and forward markets drives the constant arbitrage activity between the two markets and is known as the put-call forward exchange parity.

put option A contract giving the purchaser the right, but not the obligation, to sell a particular asset such as a foreign currency at a stated strike price on or before a stated date.

qualified institutional buyer An entity (except a bank or a savings and loan) that owns and invests on a discretionary basis a minimum of $100 million in securities of nonaffiliates.

rating A letter grade given to a bond by a rating agency (such as Moody's or Standard & Poor's) signifying the amount of credit risk on the bond.

real interest rate The market interest rate as commonly quoted (nominal interest rate) minus the rate of inflation of the price level.

real option analysis The application of option theory to capital budgeting decisions.

reference rate The rate of interest used in a standardized quotation, loan agreement, or financial derivative valuation. Such benchmark rates include LIBOR or prime interest rates.

registered bond Corporate or governmental debt in bond form in which the owner's name appears on the bond and in the issuer's records, and interest payments are made to the owner. Also known as a nominal bond.

reinvoicing centers Special-purpose administrative units established by multinational corporations, often domiciled in low-tax jurisdictions, which channel intracorporate trade (cross-border shipments of parts, components, subassemblies, and finished products among sister subsidiaries) to facilitate the netting of all foreign currency transaction exposures held by the multinational's various foreign branches or subsidiaries.

return on equity (ROE) Earnings after tax (EAT) divided by owners' equity. A measure of the firm's profitability to shareholders.

revolving credit A line of bank credit that may be used or not used at the borrower's discretion. Interest is paid on the amount of credit actually in use, while a commitment fee is paid on the unused portion.

rights offering Offering of a firm's common stocks exclusively to its existing stockholders.

risk-free rate The rate of return of a risk-free asset, usually government securities. *See* capital asset pricing model (CAPM).

risk premium The difference between the expected return on a security and the risk-free rate. *See* capital asset pricing model (CAPM).

risk-sharing agreement A contractual arrangement in which the buyer and seller agree to share or split currency movement impacts on payments between them.

samurai bonds Yen-denominated foreign bonds issued in Tokyo by non-Japanese-domiciled firms.

Sarbanes-Oxley Act An act passed in 2002 to regulate corporate governance in the United States.

SEC Rule 144A Rule that permits qualified institutional buyers to trade privately placed securities without requiring Securities and Exchange Commission (SEC) registration.

securitization Consumer financing was traditionally intermediated by commercial banks, thrifts, savings and loans, or finance companies. A consumer seeking medium- to long-term financing for purchasing a home or an automobile would apply for a mortgage or an automobile loan; if approved, the lender would fund the loan by using savings deposits or by securing financing of its own directly from the capital market. The consumer loan would stay on the financial intermediary's balance sheet for its entire life. Securitization unbundled such traditional financial intermediation. By repackaging illiquid consumer loans into liquid and tradable securities, securitization is a more elaborate form of disintermediation that typically results in a lower cost of consumer finance.

selling, general, and administrative expenses (SG&A) Expenses incurred by the firm that relate to the sale of its products and the running of its operations during the accounting period.

sensitivity analysis Analysis of how changes in an input variable affect the value of the output (dependent) variable. In the context of project evaluation, sensitivity analysis would focus on how a change in a key input variable such as quantity sold, price per unit sold, or currency values would impact the project's payback period, IRR, or NPV.

Sharpe ratio A common metric for evaluating a portfolio's risk-adjusted performance. The Sharpe ratio is defined as the portfolio excess return – portfolio return r_p minus risk-free rate r_f divided by its standard deviation σ_p.

Smithsonian Agreement A revision to the Bretton Woods system that was signed at the Smithsonian Institution in Washington, D.C., in December 1971. It called for a new set of par values, widened bands for allowable exchange rate fluctuations to plus or minus 2.25 percent around par, and an increase in the official value of gold to $38 per ounce.

sovereign (country) ceiling The best credit rating that a firm can get for the purpose of international financing regardless of its own financial health.

sovereign (country) risk premium The yield spread between a given country long-term dollar-denominated sovereign bond yield and US treasuries' yield of same maturity.

sovereign risk *See* country risk.

special drawing right (SDR) An artificial reserve asset created and held on the books of the International Monetary Fund (IMF). At the time of first issue on January 1, 1970, the SDR was defined as having a value equal to one ounce of gold. The SDR is now defined as an artificial currency unit (basket of currencies) in terms of the U.S. dollar, euro, Japanese yen, and British pound. It is redefined every five years. As of 2010 its composition was SDR 1 = US$0.6660 plus €0.4230 plus ¥11.20 plus £0.1110.

speculator An individual or firm that attempts to anticipate price movements and to profit from them by taking appropriate long or short positions on market-traded assets.

spread The difference between the buying and selling rates of a currency or a bond, or the difference between borrowing and lending rates on currency deposits.

stabilized exchange rates An exchange rates regime whereby there is a foreign exchange market where buyers and sellers interact, thereby establishing a clearing rate for the currency market. Stabilized exchange rates have to fall within a prescribed publicly declared narrow band of fluctuations around the official par value. Otherwise the central bank steps in to bring back the rate within the allowable tunnel by intervening in the currency market. *See also* central bank intervention.

straddle Simultaneous purchase of one put option and one call option at the same exercise price and maturity. This strategy is especially attractive when one anticipates high exchange rate volatility but is hard-pressed to forecast the direction of the future spot exchange rate.

straight bond A bond with fixed coupon payments and without any option features (such as provisions for conversion into equity, other bonds, or other currencies).

straight-line depreciation method A widely used depreciation method whereby the firm's tangible fixed assets are depreciated by an equal amount each year.

strike price The price at which an option buyer may purchase (if a call option) or sell (if a put option) the asset such as a foreign currency upon which the option is written.

Subpart F income Passive foreign-source income (interest, royalties, or insurance earned by a foreign subsidiary), which is immediately taxable when accrued rather than when repatriated to the home country. Taxation of foreign-source income under the worldwide tax regime is mitigated by the deferral rule whereby *active* foreign-source income is taxed only when dividends (or other form of earnings) are repatriated. Subpart F passive income is an important exception to this deferral rule.

subsidiary A foreign operation incorporated in the host country and owned 50 percent or more by a parent corporation. Foreign operations that are not incorporated are called branches.

sukuk Shariah-compliant financial certificates that are very similar to bonds in Western financial markets. Since interest payments are not permissible, the *sukuk* issuer sells the certificates to an investor group, which then rents the *sukuk* back to the issuer for a predetermined rental fee. The issuer also makes a contractual promise to buy back the bonds at a future date at par value.

sunk costs Money already spent in capital investment projects that cannot be recovered irrespective of future decisions.

syndicated loan A large loan made by a group of banks to a large (often multinational) firm or government. Syndicated loans allow the participating banks to maintain diversification by not lending too much to a single borrower.

synthetic forward contract Also referred to as a no-profit forward contract, a synthetic contract is the result of bundling a spot exchange contract with lending and borrowing in the respective money markets.

systematic risk Risk that remains despite the risk-reduction property of diversification. It is measured with the beta coefficient and is the same as market risk and nondiversifiable or undiversifiable risk. *See* capital asset pricing model (CAPM).

tax deferral Foreign subsidiaries of multinational corporations pay host-country corporate income taxes, but many home/parent countries, including the United States, defer claiming additional taxes on that foreign source income until it is remitted to the parent firm.

tax haven A country with either no or very low tax rates and a lax regulatory infrastructure that uses its tax laws to attract foreign investment or international financial dealings.

tax treaties A network of bilateral treaties that provide a means of reducing double taxation.

technical forecasting Technique that seeks to unearth stable trends from time series of past exchange rates with the presumption that these trends tend to repeat themselves, thereby allowing the forecaster to predict future currency prices or, more precisely, to provide buy/sell signals.

terminal value The value of a firm or a project associated with net cash flows extending beyond a forecasting period; it is hard to estimate with much precision.

term structure The level of interest rates on debt instruments of a particular type viewed as a function of term to maturity. The interest rate level may rise or fall with increasing maturity.

territorial tax regime A country with a national territorial tax regime taxes all income generated within its own borders but no more. France, Germany, and the Netherlands apply a variant of the national tax regime.

time draft A draft that allows a delay in payment. It is presented to the drawee, who accepts it by writing a notice of acceptance on its face. Once accepted, the time draft becomes a promise to pay by the accepting party.

transaction exposure A precise measure (rooted in accounting data) of a firm's outstanding cash inflows or cash outflows that are denominated in a foreign currency and are time differed. Foreign currency-denominated accounts receivable (A/Rs) or accounts payable (A/Ps) are examples of such exposures.

transfer prices The prices at which goods or services are exchanged/sold between two independent parties such as nonaffiliated firms. When the transaction is carried out between the subsidiaries of the same parent multinational, there is discretion for manipulating the actual price up (overinvoicing) or down (underinvoicing) and therefore shifting income out of high-tax countries.

translation exposure The impact of exchange rate fluctuations on the parent firm's consolidated financial statements. Translation exposure is defined as the net balance (assets minus liabilities) of foreign currency-denominated accounts (carried on the subsidiary's balance sheet) that are restated in dollar terms on the basis of the current exchange rate prevailing at time of consolidation.

Treasury bills U.S. government debt instruments that are auctioned by the Federal Reserve and that have a maturity of 3, 6, or 12 months. The bills are sold at a discount from their par or face value, and repay the face value at maturity.

trust/trustee A third party (usually a financial institution) that makes sure the issuer of a bond meets all the conditions and provisions reported in the bond's indenture.

unbiased predictor A theory rooted in the efficient market hypothesis whereby future spot prices are deemed equal to today's forward rates of matching maturities.

undiversifiable risk *See* systematic risk.

unilateral transfers Items in the current account of the balance of payments that correspond to gifts to or from foreigners such as bilateral aid, humanitarian assistance, or expatriate earning remittances.

unlevered asset value The estimated value of assets, assuming they are financed only with equity capital. *See* adjusted present value (APV).

unlevered beta Also known as asset beta, it refers to the beta of a firm assuming that it is all-equity financed.

unsystematic risk Risk that can be eliminated through portfolio diversification. Same as diversifiable risk or company-specific risk.

valuation by comparable A valuation method that uses financial data of firms similar/comparable to the business or firm to be valued in order to estimate the market value of its equity. For example, the estimated equity value of a firm is equal to its earnings after tax (EAT) multiplied by the earnings multiple (or P/E ratio) of the comparable firm.

vertical merger For example, the integration of a car manufacturer with its major supplier or its major distributor.

volatility Unpredictable fluctuations in the market price of an asset. It is usually approximated by the standard deviation of past exchange rate fluctuations. This approximation, in turn, assumes that exchange rates are well enough behaved to follow a normal probability distribution.

weighted average cost of capital (WACC) The weighted average of the after-tax cost of debt and cost of equity. The minimum rate of return a project must generate in order to meet the return expectations of its suppliers of capital (lenders and shareholders).

withholding tax A tax deducted at source, such as a deduction prior to the payment of coupon interest or dividends. Often levied by central banks on cross-border dividends remittance or royalty payments.

working capital requirement (WCR) The difference between operating assets (trade receivables, inventories, and prepaid expense) and operating liabilities (trade payables and accrued expenses). WCR measures the firm's net investment in its operating cycle.

World Bank Formerly known as the International Bank for Reconstruction and Development, it was established as part of the Bretton Woods accord (1944) alongside the IMF. Initially it was charged with providing post-World War II reconstruction loans to devastated countries; later it morphed into a development lender that also provides technical assistance to borrowing nations. The World Bank functions very much like a private-sector bank, funding loans from paid-in capital from member nations, from borrowing from capital markets, and from whatever earnings it generates.

worldwide tax regime Countries like the United States and Japan tax their corporate citizens on their worldwide income — not just on their domestic income — *but only when profits are repatriated*. Such countries have an extraterritorial reach (beyond domestic borders) in defining what to tax.

Yankee bond A dollar-denominated bond issued in New York by a foreign firm.

yield to maturity The rate of interest on a bond when calculated as the rate of interest that, if applied uniformly to future time periods, sets the discounted value of future bond coupon and principal payments equal to the current market price of the bond.

zero-coupon bond A bond that pays no interest but that is redeemed at its face value at maturity. Such bonds are sold at a discount from their face value, and the return to the bond depends solely on the relationship between the purchase price and the face value.

zero-premium option An option whose purchase is financed by the premium of another option. The limitation of the forward contract is that while it gives hedgers 100 percent protection against an adverse movement in the future exchange rate, it also eliminates any opportunity for gain from a subsequent favorable movement in the exchange rate; such a potential missed gain is generally referred to as an opportunity cost. Currency options, in contrast, allow full participation in this upside potential at a substantial upfront cash-flow cost that discourages many would-be users. A *forward range agreement* and a *forward participation agreement* are products based on the idea of combining writing an option whose premium finances the purchase of a zero-premium option so as to create, when superimposed on the underlying naked exposure, the desired risk profile. Thus, partial participation in any upside potential is bundled with downside protection at no cost.

Index

www.ingramcontent.com/pod-product-compliance
Lightning Source LLC
LaVergne TN
LVHW060009210926
848481LV00013B/3678
* 9 7 8 9 8 1 9 8 0 6 9 2 8 *